THE ROUTLEDGE HANDBOOK
OF NEUROETHICS

The Routledge Handbook of Neuroethics offers the reader an informed view of how the brain sciences are being used to approach, understand, and reinvigorate traditional philosophical questions, as well as how those questions, with the grounding influence of neuroscience, are being revisited beyond clinical and research domains. It also examines how contemporary neuroscience research might ultimately impact our understanding of relationships, flourishing, and human nature. Written by 61 key scholars and fresh voices, the *Handbook*'s easy-to-follow chapters appear here for the first time in print and represent the wide range of viewpoints in neuroethics. The volume spotlights new technologies and historical articulations of key problems, issues, and concepts and includes cross-referencing between chapters to highlight the complex interactions of concepts and ideas within neuroethics. These features enhance the *Handbook*'s utility by providing readers with a contextual map for different approaches to issues and a guide to further avenues of interest.

L. Syd M Johnson is Associate Professor of Philosophy and Bioethics in the departments of Humanities and Kinesiology and Integrative Physiology at Michigan Technological University. Her current research focuses on ethical and epistemological issues in disorders of consciousness and sport-related neurotrauma.

Karen S. Rommelfanger is an Assistant Professor in the departments of Neurology and Psychiatry and Behavioral Sciences, the Neuroethics Program Director at Emory University's Center for Ethics, and Neuroscience Editor-in-Residence at the *American Journal of Bioethics Neuroscience*. A neuroscientist and ethicist, her current research explores how evolving neuroscience and neurotechnologies challenge societal definitions of disease and medicine. She is a member of the Neuroethics Division of the NIH BRAIN Initiative.

Routledge Handbooks in Applied Ethics

Applied ethics is one of the largest and most diverse fields in philosophy and is closely related to many other disciplines across the humanities, sciences, and social sciences. *Routledge Handbooks in Applied Ethics* are state-of-the-art surveys of important and emerging topics in applied ethics, providing accessible yet thorough assessments of key fields, themes, thinkers, and recent developments in research.

All chapters for each volume are specially commissioned and written by leading scholars in the field. Carefully edited and organized, *Routledge Handbooks in Applied Ethics* provide indispensable reference tools for students and researchers seeking a comprehensive overview of new and exciting topics in applied ethics and related disciplines. They are also valuable teaching resources as accompaniments to textbooks, anthologies, and research-orientated publications.

Available:

The Routledge Handbook of Global Ethics
Edited by Darrel Moellendorf and Heather Widdows

The Routledge Handbook of Food Ethics
Edited by Mary Rawlinson

The Routledge Handbook of Neuroethics
Edited by L. Syd M Johnson and Karen S. Rommelfanger

Forthcoming:

The Routledge Handbook of the Ethics of Consent
Edited by Peter Schaber

The Routledge Handbook of Ethics and Public Policy
Edited by Annabelle Lever and Andrei Poama

For more information on this series, please visit www.routledge.com/Routledge-Handbooks-in-Applied-Ethics/book-series/RHAE

THE ROUTLEDGE HANDBOOK OF NEUROETHICS

Edited by
L. Syd M Johnson and Karen S. Rommelfanger

Routledge
Taylor & Francis Group

NEW YORK AND LONDON

First published 2018
by Routledge
52 Vanderbilt Avenue, New York, NY 10017

and by Routledge
2 Park Square, Milton Park, Abingdon, Oxon OX14 4RN

First issued in paperback 2020

Routledge is an imprint of the Taylor & Francis Group, an informa business

Library of Congress Cataloging-in-Publication Data
Names: Johnson, L. Syd M, editor. | Rommelfanger, Karen S., editor.
Title: The Routledge handbook of neuroethics / edited by
L. Syd M Johnson and Karen S. Rommelfanger.
Description: New York : Routledge, Taylor & Francis Group, 2017. |
Series: Routledge handbooks in applied ethics |
Includes bibliographical references and index.
Identifiers: LCCN 2017001670 | ISBN 9781138898295 (hardback)
Subjects: LCSH: Brain—Research—Moral and ethical aspects. | Cognitive
neuroscience—Moral and ethical aspects.
Classification: LCC QP376 .R758 2017 | DDC 174.2/968—dc23
LC record available at https://lccn.loc.gov/2017001670

ISBN 13: 978-0-367-57337-9 (pbk)
ISBN 13: 978-1-138-89829-5 (hbk)

Typeset in Bembo
by Apex CoVantage, LLC

For Izzy and Zoë (LSMJ)
For Pen (KSR)

CONTENTS

Contents

CONTRIBUTORS

Akira Akabayashi is a Professor in the Department of Biomedical Ethics at the University of Tokyo Graduate School of Medicine. His research interests include cross-cultural bioethics and clinical ethics. He is the editor of *The Future of Bioethics: International Dialogues* (Oxford University Press, 2014).

Jalayne J. Arias, is an Assistant Professor in the Memory and Aging Center at the University of California San Francisco and an Atlantic Fellow in global brain health. Her research and scholarship addresses the legal and ethical challenges of Alzheimer's disease and other dementias. She is currently funded by the Alzheimer's Association to evaluate the legal consequences of biomarker testing for Alzheimer's disease in asymptomatic patients.

Elizabeth Aslinger researches personality and psychopathology as a Hot Metal Bridge Psychology Fellow in Dr. Aidan Wright's lab at the University of Pittsburgh. Her interests include psychiatric nosology, philosophy of science, individual differences, interpersonal psychology, neuroscience, and quantitative modeling.

John D. Banja is a Professor in the Department of Rehabilitation Medicine at Emory University School of Medicine and a medical ethicist at the Center for Ethics at Emory University. He also serves as editor of the *American Journal of Bioethics Neuroscience*.

Anjan Chatterjee is the Frank A. and Gladys H. Elliott Professor and Chair of Neurology at Pennsylvania Hospital and was a founding member of the Board of Governors of the Neuroethics Society. He wrote *The Aesthetic Brain: How We Evolved to Desire Beauty and Enjoy Art* and coedited *Neuroethics in Practice: Mind, Medicine, and Society* and *The Roots of Cognitive Neuroscience: Behavioral Neurology and Neuropsychology*.

Markus Christen is a Senior Research Fellow at the Centre for Ethics of the University of Zurich and member of the Ethics Advisory Board of the Human Brain Project. He is the author of "The Ethics of Neuromodulation-Induced Behavior Changes" (2015) and "Habilitation in the Field of Biomedical Ethics" (2015).

Cyd Cipolla is a scholar in feminist theory whose research and teaching interests include medical and legal history of sexuality, law, and society, and the intersection of biological, behavioral, and computational science. She is currently Sophomore Class Adviser and Associate Faculty at New York University's Gallatin School of Individualized Study.

Edward T. Cokely is Presidential Research Professor and Associate Professor of Psychology at the University of Oklahoma, where he serves as cofounding faculty of the National Institute for Risk & Resilience and comanaging director of the international RiskLiteracy.org project.

Stuart W.G. Derbyshire is an Associate Professor in the department of psychology at the National University of Singapore. His main research interest focuses on the neural mechanisms of pain.

Thomas Douglas is a Senior Research Fellow in the Oxford Uehiro Centre for Practical Ethics and a Golding Junior Fellow at Brasenose College. He is also Principal Investigator on the Wellcome Trust-funded project Neurointerventions in Crime Prevention: An Ethical Analysis and Lead Researcher in the Oxford Martin Programme on Collective Responsibility for Infectious Disease.

Brian D. Earp is a Research Associate with the Oxford Centre for Neuroethics and a consultant working with the Institute for Science and Ethics at Oxford's Martin School.

Luc Faucher is Professor of Philosophy at the Université du Québec à Montréal. His research interests cover philosophy of cognitive science, philosophy of race, philosophy of emotions, and philosophy of psychiatry. He is coeditor (with Christine Tappolet) of *The Modularity of Emotions* (2008) and the editor of *Philosophie et psychopathologies* (2006).

Adam Feltz is an Assistant Professor of Psychology and Applied Ethics at Michigan Technological University. He directs the EDEN (Ethical Decision-making and Ethical Naturalism) Lab and is a co-managing director of RiskLiteracy.org.

Andrew Fenton is an Assistant Professor in the Department of Philosophy at Dalhousie University. His most recent work has been in either animal ethics or the philosophy of autism, though he does occasionally dabble in neuroethics and epistemology.

Orsolya Friedrich is Research Fellow at the Institute of Ethics, History and Theory of Medicine, Ludwig Maximilians University of Munich, Germany. Her research focus is neuroethics and neurophilosophy. She recently published two German books on neuroscientific challenges to personality.

Tamami Fukushi started her career in neuroethics in 2005 at Japan Science and Technology Agency. She is currently at the Office of International Programs, Pharmaceuticals and Medical Devices Agency, Japan (as of May 2017). She is the author of "Social Implementation of Neurodegenerative Disease Research and Neuroethics" in: Wada, K. (Ed.) *Neurodegenerative Disorders as Systemic Diseases*, Springer (2015).

Valerie Gray Hardcastle is Professor of Philosophy, Psychology, Psychiatry and Behavioral Neuroscience and Scholar-in-Residence, Weaver Institute for Law and Psychiatry at the University of Cincinnati.

Walter Glannon is Professor of Philosophy at the University of Calgary. He is the author of several books, including *Brain, Body, and Mind: Neuroethics with a Human Face* (Oxford University Press, 2011) and *Bioethics and the Brain* (Oxford University Press, 2006).

Sara Goering is Associate Professor of Philosophy, member of the Program on Values, and affiliate faculty with the Disability Studies program at the University of Washington, Seattle. She directs the ethics thrust for the NSF-funded Center for Sensorimotor Neural Engineering.

Rosa Gonzalez is a graduate student in medical physiology at Case Western Reserve University and a clinical research coordinator at the Cleveland Clinic for work related to aging-associated neurodegenerative diseases.

Simon Goyer is a doctoral student at the Université du Québec à Montréal, where he specializes in the fields of philosophy of psychiatry, philosophy of science, and ethics. He has also worked as a research assistant at the Research Institute of the Centre hospitalier de l'Université de Montréal, where he was involved in a project on clinical reasoning in psychiatry.

Kristina Gupta is an Assistant Professor in the Department of Women's, Gender, and Sexuality Studies at Wake Forest University. Her areas of interest include gender, science, and medicine and contemporary asexual identities.

Elisabeth Hildt is Professor of Philosophy and director of the Center for the Study of Ethics in the Professions at Illinois Institute of Technology, Chicago.

Taichi Isobe started his career in neuroethics and STS (science, technology, and society) in 2008 at Graduate School of Interdisciplinary Information Studies, The University of Tokyo. He is currently at the School of Dentistry/Center for Development in Higher Education, Health Sciences University of Hokkaido. He is the author of "Ethics about Neuroscience Research," in: Kamisato, A. & Muto, K. (Ed.) *Handbook of Research Ethics in Medical Science*, University of Tokyo Press (2015).

L. Syd M Johnson is Associate Professor of Philosophy and Bioethics in the departments of Humanities and Kinesiology & Integrative Physiology at Michigan Technological University. She is a former Research Fellow in Neuroethics at Novel Tech Ethics, Dalhousie University. Her research interests are disorders of consciousness, brain death, and sport-related neurotrauma.

Ralf J. Jox is Assistant Professor for Medical Ethics at the Institute of Ethics, History and Theory of Medicine, Ludwig Maximilians University of Munich, Germany, and Associate Professor of Geriatric Palliative Care at the University Medical Center in Lausanne, Switzerland. He is a trained neurologist and bioethicist and chairs the neuroethics working group of the German Academy of Ethics in Medicine.

Jon Leefmann is a Postdoctoral Research Fellow at the Center for Applied Ethics and Science Communication (ZIEW) at Friedrich-Alexander–University Erlangen–Nuremberg in Germany. His focus in research and teaching is on philosophical, social and ethical implications of neuroscience research and on issues in social epistemology. Previously, he was a research fellow at the Research Group on Neuroethics and Neurophilosophy at the University of Mainz

(Germany), where he worked on the impact of the neuro- and cognitive sciences on current developments in the humanities and social sciences.

Scott O. Lilienfeld is Samuel Candler Dobbs Professor of Psychology at Emory University in Atlanta. Along with psychiatrist Sally Satel, he is coauthor of *Brainwashed: The Selective Appeal of Mindless Neuroscience* (2015, Basic Books).

Emily Y. Liu is a Stanford medical student. Before medical school, she worked as a special education teacher and completed a two-year fellowship at the Stanford Center for Biomedical Ethics. There, she studied mechanisms for stakeholder participation in autism research and care.

Bertram F. Malle is a Professor at Brown University. He trained in psychology, philosophy, and linguistics in Austria and at Stanford University. He is past president of the Society of Philosophy and Psychology and author of *How the Mind Explains Behavior* (MIT Press, 2004) and *Other minds* (with S.D. Hodges, eds., Guilford, 2005).

Sebastian Porsdam Mann is a postdoctoral fellow at the Harvard Medical School Center for Bioethics and a recent recipient of a Carslberg Foundation Postdoctoral Research Fellowship.

Julia Marshall is a graduate student in developmental psychology at Yale University. She received her Bachelor's degree in psychology at Emory University, where she studied how neuroscience information influences people's legal judgments.

Jonathan D. Moreno is the David and Lyn Silfen University Professor of Ethics at the University of Pennsylvania.

Sabine Müller is Assistant Professor for Neurophilosophy and Medical Ethics at the Department for Psychiatry and Psychotherapy of the Charité–Universitätsmedizin Berlin. She is principle investigator of the international research project Psychiatric Neurosurgery—Ethical, Legal and Ethical Issues.

Eisuke Nakazawa is an Assistant Professor in the Department of Biomedical Ethics at the University of Tokyo Graduate School of Medicine. His research interests lie in neuroethics and research ethics. He is the author of "Regenerative Medicine and Science Literacy" in Akabayashi, A. (Ed.) *The Future of Bioethics: International Dialogues* (Oxford University Press)

Georg Northoff is a philosopher, neuroscientist, and psychiatrist. Originally from Germany, he is now Canada Research Chair in Mind, Brain Imaging, and Neuroethics at the Institute of Mental Health Research, University of Ottawa, where he researches the relationship between the brain and mind in its various facets.

Nina L. Powell is currently a Lecturer in the Department of Psychology at the National University of Singapore. She investigates how people process information about moral judgments and the development of cognitive reasoning used in making these judgments, exploring both children's and adults' moral judgments and emotions.

Ryan H. Purcell is a PhD candidate in neuroscience at Emory University. He has served on the editorial team of the *American Journal of Bioethics Neuroscience* since 2013 and contributes to *The Neuroethics Blog*. His neuroethics research has focused on the implications of internet-driven big-data approaches to neuroscience research and neuroenhancement.

Eric Racine is Research Professor and Director of the Neuroethics Research Unit at Institut de recherches cliniques de Montréal (IRCM). Inspired by philosophical pragmatism, his research aims to understand and bring to the forefront the experience of ethically problematic situations for patients and stakeholders and then to resolve them collaboratively through deliberative and evidence-informed processes.

Peter B. Reiner is Professor and co-founder of the National Core for Neuroethics at the University of British Columbia, where he is a member of the Department of Psychiatry and the Centre for Brain Health. Dr. Reiner has championed quantitative analysis of public attitudes toward diverse issues in neuroethics, including the propriety of cognitive and moral enhancement, the contours of autonomy in the real world, and the neuroethical implications of technologies of the extended mind.

Karen S. Rommelfanger is an Assistant Professor in the departments of Neurology and Psychiatry and Behavioral Sciences, the Neuroethics Program Director at Emory University's Center for Ethics, and neuroscience editor-in-residence at the *American Journal of Bioethics Neuroscience*. A neuroscientist and ethicist, her current research explores how evolving neuroscience and neurotechnologies challenge societal definitions of disease and medicine. She is a member of the Neuroethics Division of the NIH BRAIN Initiative.

Barbara J. Sahakian is Professor of Clinical Neuropsychology at the Department of Psychiatry and Medical Research Council (MRC)/Wellcome Trust Behavioural and Clinical Neuroscience Institute, University of Cambridge. She is a Fellow of the Academy of Medical Sciences.

Osamu Sakura is a researcher in science studies and science communication and has been engaged in neuroethics since 2005. He is now dean and professor of the Interfaculty Initiative in Information Studies, the University of Tokyo. His recent publications include "Launching a Two-Front War against Anti-Intellectualism and Expert Paternalism: Lessons from the Fukushima Nuclear Disaster," which appeared in *5: Designing Media Ecology*.

Arleen Salles is the director of the Neuroethics Program at Centro de Investigaciones Filosóficas (Buenos Aires, Argentina), Associate Researcher in the Department of Public Health and Caring Science at Uppsala University (Sweden), and a research collaborator in the Ethics and Society Sub-Project in the Human Brain Project. Her research interests include the impact of neuroscientific research on human identity, simulation and consciousness, and the issue of mental privacy.

Matthew Sample is a Postdoctoral Fellow of the Neuroethics Research Unit at the IRCM. Combining epistemology, ethics, and science and technology studies, his research maps the interaction between sociotechnical systems and collectively imagined futures, focusing recently on neural technology and its publics.

Jennifer C. Sarrett is a Lecturer at Emory University's Center for the Study of Human Health. Her research focuses on neuroethical and disability studies perspectives on the lived experiences of autism and other intellectual and developmental disabilities.

Sally Satel is a Lecturer in the Department of Psychiatry at Yale University School of Medicine. She is a resident scholar at the American Enterprise Institute in Washington, DC.

Julian Savulescu is director of the Oxford Uehiro Centre for Practical Ethics. He is a founding member of the Hinxton Group.

Matthias Scheutz is a Professor at Tufts University. Trained in philosophy, formal logic, and computer science in Vienna, Austria, and computer science and cognitive science at Indiana University Bloomington. Past co-chair of the IEEE Technical Committee on Robot Ethics and of the 2009 ACM/IEEE International Conference on Human–Robot Interaction.

Susan Schneider is an Associate Professor of Philosophy and Cognitive Science at the University of Connecticut, a visiting member of the Institute for Advanced Study in Princeton, and a faculty member in the technology and ethics group at Yale's Interdisciplinary Center for Bioethics. Her work is on the nature of the self, which she examines from the vantage point of issues in philosophy of mind, artificial intelligence (AI), metaphysics, astrobiology, epistemology, and neuroscience. Her books include: *Science Fiction and Philosophy: From Time Travel to Superintelligence, The Language of Thought: A New Philosophical Direction*, and *The Blackwell Companion to Consciousness* (with Max Velmans).

Julie A. Seaman teaches constitutional law, free speech, and evidence at Emory Law School in Atlanta, Georgia, where she also chairs the board of directors of the Georgia Innocence Project. Professor Seaman's scholarship includes a focus on the legal implications of findings in the biological and mind sciences.

Margaret A. Sheridan is lab director of Circle Lab at University of North Carolina, Chapel Hill. The goal of her research is to better understand the neural underpinnings of the development of cognitive control across childhood (from 5–18 years of age) and to understand how and why disruption in this process results in psychopathology.

Adam Shriver is a Postdoctoral Fellow at the Centre for Applied Ethics at the University of British Columbia. Previously, he was a visiting fellow at the Center for Neuroscience and Society at the University of Pennsylvania.

Laura Specker Sullivan is a postdoctoral neuroethics fellow at the Center for Sensorimotor Neural Engineering, University of Washington, and a postdoctoral research fellow at the National Core for Neuroethics, University of British Columbia. Her research is in cross-cultural and non-Western ethical theory, biomedical ethics, and neuroethics.

Yoshiyuki Takimoto is an Associate Professor at the Department of Biomedical Ethics at the University of Tokyo Graduate School of Medicine. His research interests lie in clinical ethics, decision making, and psychosomatic medicine. He is the author of Takimoto, Y. et al. (2011) "Clinical Ethics Consultation in Japan: The University of Tokyo Model." *Asian Bioethics Review* 3: 283–291.

Michael N. Tennison is the Ryan H. Easley Research Fellow at the University of Maryland Carey School of Law's Thurgood Marshall Law Library.

Kimberly Van Orman is a Visiting Assistant Professor at Bennington College and an instructional consultant with the Institute for Teaching, Learning and Academic Leadership at the University at Albany. She has published on using team-based learning to teach philosophy and travels to give workshops on teaching with TBL.

Nils-Frederic Wagner is Assistant Professor in the Department of Philosophy at the University of Duisburg-Essen in Germany, having previously held posts at the University of Ottawa, and Carleton University in Canada.

Elaine F. Walker is the Samuel Candler Dobbs Professor of Psychology and Neuroscience at Emory University. Her research is focused on precursors and risk factors for psychotic disorders, and she currently heads the Emory site for the North American Prodrome Longitudinal Study.

Anna Wexler is a PhD candidate in the History, Anthropology, Science, Technology and Society (HASTS) Program at MIT. She studies the ethical, legal, and social implications of emerging neurotechnologies, with a particular focus on do-it-yourself and direct-to-consumer brain stimulation.

Paul Root Wolpe is the Asa Griggs Candler Professor of Bioethics, Raymond Schinazi Distinguished Research Professor of Jewish Bioethics, and the Director of the Center for Ethics at Emory University. A founder of the International Neuroethics Society, he is editor-in-chief of *AJOB-Neuroscience*, a past president of the American Society for Bioethics and Humanities, and the senior bioethicist for NASA.

INTRODUCTION

We find ourselves at a pivotal historical moment as neuroscientific research increasingly offers insights into aspects of human existence that have long shaped our view of our place in the world, our uniqueness within the animal kingdom, and the very core of what makes us distinctly human. Put another way, neuroscience is beginning to tackle questions that have long been left to philosophers and, in so doing, reenacting a process that has, for thousands of years, led to the calving of the offspring of the philosophical enterprise, as distinct methodologies, tools, and sets of questions have emerged to birth separate disciplines (e.g., mathematics, linguistics, astronomy, physics. . .). Where an ancient philosopher might have been metaphysician and physicist, ethicist and biologist, a neuroscientist of today can, in essence, return to her philosophical roots and be both scientist and philosopher—a neuroethicist. What is unique about the emergence of neuroethics as a discipline is in part this looping and returning. Where the various sciences once branched off from philosophy, neuroethics is increasingly returning to the source to apply the tools and methodologies of the mature (yet still evolving) discipline of neuroscience to some of the unanswered questions of philosophy. At the same time, philosopher-neuroethicists are turning a critical eye to the methodologies, tools, and discoveries of neuroscience, as well as its applications and approaches to philosophical questions, making neuroethics a uniquely and fruitfully reflexive discipline, one that is interdisciplinary, interactive, and interrogative.

The prioritization of neuroscience research around the globe reflects the growing importance and influence of this rapidly emerging and evolving field. Along with it comes heightened concern that science might run ahead of our ability to contemplate, predict, and manage the ethical implications of new knowledge and neurotechnologies and a forward-thinking call to integrate ethics into neuroscientific research. The field of neuroethics stands as an interpreter and a guide to thorny social, legal, and ethical issues that will arise as we integrate rapidly advancing neurotechnologies and neuroscientific findings into our daily lives.

Neuroethics engages and invites conversation on topics located at the intersection of neuroscience, law, politics, religion, society, and ethics. The emergence of neuroethics as a distinct discipline is evinced by the appearance in recent years of journals devoted to neuroethics; the field has also attracted the notice of traditional and established scientific and philosophical journals as well as popular media outlets.

This *Handbook* aims to be both timely and diverse in outlining current and emerging ethical issues at the interface of brain science and society. The *Handbook* consists of four parts: The introductory chapters focus on the history and evolution of neuroethics, as well as the emergence of new neuro-disciplines. The two middle sections take the now-classic articulation of neuroethics offered by Adina Roskies and consider the two main divisions of neuroethics: the ethics of neuroscience and the neuroscience of ethics. The *Handbook* concludes with a section that explores emerging ideas that are expanding the frame of neuroethics.

Several unique structural features are built into this *Handbook*. We consciously sought an inclusive and heterogeneous group of authors who reflect the diversity of the field and its many viewpoints. We included boxes throughout the book that spotlight relevant technologies and historical articulations of key problems, issues, and concepts found within the chapters. We also highlight connections between the chapters through cross-referencing that calls attention to the complex interactions of concepts and ideas within neuroethics. We hope this enhances the utility of the handbook by providing our readers with a contextual and intertextual map that points to different approaches and articulations of issues and further avenues of interest. This offers the reader an informed view of how the brain sciences are being used to approach, understand, and reinvigorate traditional philosophical questions, how those questions, with the grounding influence of neuroscience, are being revisited in contexts beyond the clinical and research domains, and how contemporary neuroscience research might ultimately impact our understanding of human nature, relationships, and flourishing.

L. Syd M Johnson
Michigan Technological University
Karen S. Rommelfanger
Emory University

PART I

What Is Neuroethics?

In a seminal 2002 paper, philosopher and neuroscientist Adina Roskies bisected the field of neuroethics into two broad sectors: the ethics of neuroscience and the neuroscience of ethics. The ethics of neuroscience overlaps significantly with traditional issues in biomedical ethics, including clinical ethics, the ethics of neuroscientific research, and the ethical, legal, and social implications of new developments and discoveries in neuroscience. Neuroethics is more than a subdiscipline of traditional biomedical ethics, however, particularly in its second sector, the so-called neuroscience of ethics, which examines traditional ethical questions through a neuroscientific lens. Metaphysical inquiries concerning free will, personal identity, and the nature of consciousness are also within the purview of neuroethics, as they inform and interact with important ethical and social issues. Neuroethics explores the neurological foundations of these age-old philosophical problems but also brings to bear techniques from the cognitive and social sciences to reexamine them in a new light.

This section provides background on the historical development of neuroethics and offers a frame for viewing the core categories of neuroethical inquiry. In the first chapter, "The Competing Identities of Neuroethics: Remarks on Theoretical and Methodological Assumptions and Their Practical Implications for the Future of Neuroethics," Racine and Sample explore the ongoing debates about the identity and assumptions of neuroethics. In the second chapter, "Neuroethics and the Neuroscientific Turn," Hildt and Leefmann challenge us to engage in deeper transdisciplinary inquiry—to more closely examine the methodologies that neuroethics seeks to address and utilize. These chapters address arguments about the inter- or transdisciplinary nature of neuroethics, as well as the unique integration and entanglement of the questions neuroethics and neuroethicists engage with, along with an overview of neuroethics scholarship and methodologies.

1

THE COMPETING IDENTITIES OF NEUROETHICS

Remarks on Theoretical and Methodological Assumptions and Their Practical Implications for the Future of Neuroethics

Eric Racine and Matthew Sample

Neuroethics has evolved significantly in the last 15 years (Marcus, 2002). From rather amorphous ideas, the field of neuroethics has taken shape in different ways. Academic programs dedicated to neuroethics have flourished in several countries, monographs and edited volumes have been published, specialized journals have endured and grown to be impactful (e.g., *Neuroethics*, *American Journal of Bioethics—Neuro*science), national and international societies and networks dedicated to neuroethics have emerged, and, perhaps more importantly, young researchers have been trained in neuroethics, while more established researchers have developed robust research programs funded through both strategic and open funding competitions. All these developments testify to the field's successes and development. As one of the authors can attest, graduate training in the late 1990s on neuroethics topics and engagement of colleagues about them was a marginal and often misunderstood endeavor. The idea of a two-way dialogue between neuroscience and ethics appeared as a radical idea. The practical ethical issues associated with clinical neurosciences were truly neglected, even 25 years after Pontius's landmark paper (Pontius, 1973), perhaps because of intellectual and organizational focus on ethical issues in genetics and genomics at the time (Evans, 2000, 2002).

Despite the great leaps forward, there are a number of meta-questions about the field of neuroethics, that is, epistemological issues that underlie the development of the field of neuroethics that are worth articulating explicitly. Attending to these questions could help scholars examine some of the underlying commitments of neuroethics scholarship as well as some of the significant diversity and pluralism encountered within the field. In this chapter, we explore a number of such questions, hopefully to provide an additional lens to approach the other contributions in this volume. As we do so, we stress the existence of healthy pluralism with respect to the issues identified and indicate the implications of some of the available answers while inviting readers to make up their own minds about the appropriateness of the solutions provided so far. We structure our remarks to reflect on "where are we looking from?" "what are we looking at?" and "for which goals?" and highlight how different meta-approaches generate responses to these questions.

"Where We Are Looking From": Brain, Mind, and the Scientific and Manifest Images

One of the most profound sources of pluralism in neuroethics concerns the initial stance from which neuroethics is approached. We notice two primary standpoints from which investigators begin their inquiry, one scientific and one humanistic. Thus for any given neuroethics topic, we can ask: are these questions triggered by the fact that the brain is involved, or is it rather their profound effects on the mind, that is, the cognitive, affective, and social dimensions of human life? Clearly, the former view, "the view from the brain" (or scientific image), has received the most explicit support within the field of neuroethics. Starting with Safire, who is often wrongly credited for forging the term "neuroethics" (Pontius, 1973), the field has been described as "a distinct portion of bioethics, which is the consideration of good and bad consequences in medical practice and biological research" (Safire, 2002). Safire adds that "the specific ethics of brain science hits home as research on no other organ does" (Safire, 2002). Likewise, the cognitive neuroscientist Michael Gazzaniga summoned neuroethics a few years later to become firmly entrenched in the biological sciences. According to him, "neuroethics is more than just bioethics for the brain. (. . .) It is—or should be—an effort to come up with a brain-based philosophy of life" (Gazzaniga, 2005). These views clearly emphasize, to paraphrase Sellars (Sellars, 1963), how the emerging (neuro)"scientific image" of humankind will shape the "manifest image" of humankind; cherished or entrenched understandings of the self, of humanity, and of normativity are to be reframed in terms of neural activity, of technological interventions, and revealed tissue structure.

At the same time, there is no clear reason to restrict neuroethical discussion to the impact of sciences and technologies of the brain, narrowly construed. Many non–neuroscience-based technologies induce comparable effects on the self and moral agency. And interest in interventions on the brain (e.g., deep brain stimulation, functional neuroimaging, neuropharmacology) is largely contingent on their impact on the mind. These observations suggest that our focal point need not be the brain at all and that a "view from the mind" could offer a distinct starting point. Beginning from the mind rather than just its physical or material aspects makes the significance of the "lived brain" (the mind) explicit and primary. Accordingly, scholarship in this mode features a persistent engagement with the humanities or social sciences—as supplements to neuroscience—or careful attention to embodied experience. This stance may entail, for instance, interviewing persons with ALS about the role of neural technology in their life (Blain-Moraes et al., 2012), analyzing media representations of neuroscience (Racine et al., 2010), or attending closely to everyday situations or clinical contexts (Fins, 2017). Each provides crucial resources for studying the mind as a biopsychosocial or experiential phenomenon. In sum, the "view from the mind" does not deny the importance of the "neuro," but it places it alongside a more comprehensive range of knowledge and tools that affect us humans and our self-understanding. From this perspective, the physical brain is special because of its (situated, shifting) meaning and not because of its intrinsic mechanisms or essential structure.

The field's name, of course, does not unambiguously express each of these two views (i.e., from the brain, from the mind). Sometimes neuroethics seems to be committed to a form of reductionism or the epistemic supremacy of neurosciences such that some priority is given to disciplines that study the brain as both a source of knowledge on morality and a source of ethical questions to address (Whitehouse, 2012; Racine and Zimmerman, 2012). Vidal and Piperberg (2017) claim that "Neuroethics (. . .) presupposes that the neural aspects of human nature are most directly relevant to many of the questions raised in the Western philosophical and ethical traditions, including issues of personhood and personal identity" (Vidal and Piperberg, 2017). In our view, such reductionism is not inherent to neuroethics. As we hint in the previous paragraph, there are scholars beginning from the mind and not just the brain. Nevertheless, the worries expressed here call for further thinking about the competing views on neuroethics. While both the "view from the brain" and "the view from the mind" can coexist, they represent an implicit (and sometimes explicit) dialectic, wherein researchers must decide which is more fundamental: organ or life world. Indeed, this tension between these stances, however articulated, has implications for theoretical, methodological, and practical orientations of contributors to the field. We will return to these concrete implications at the chapter's end, but first we consider another key epistemological question, "What are we looking at?"

"What Are We Looking At?" Areas of Focus and Questions of Interest for Neuroethics

In 1973, the psychiatrist Anneliese Pontius first (to our knowledge) described neuroethics as a "new and neglected area of ethical concern" (Pontius, 1973). Pontius was particularly concerned with nonvalidated interventions in young children and the misuse of neuroscience research. Some years after, the neurologist Ronald Cranford boldly named a new type of specialist, the "neuroethicist," a neurologist with expertise in bioethics often called upon to deal with questions such as brain death or end-of-life care in dementia (Cranford, 1989). Clearly, these pioneers held a view according to which neuroethics should be dedicated to examining ethical questions related to clinical practice in neurology and psychiatry. Others have followed suit, such as the neurologist James Bernat, author of *Ethical Issues in Neurology* (first edition in 1994; third edition published in 2008; Bernat, 2002) and the physician and bioethicist Joseph Fins. The latter has formulated several critiques against current neuroethics, stressing the need to reorient efforts to address important healthcare-related questions (Miller and Fins, 1999; Fins, 2000; Fins, 2005; Fins et al., 2006; Fins, 2008; Fins, 2017).

Others view neuroethics as a "content field" of bioethics which is defined by its focus on different neurotechnologies. Writing the entry on neuroethics in the *Encyclopedia of Bioethics*, Paul Wolpe states that

> [n]euroethics involves the analysis of ethical challenges posed by chemical, organic, and electrochemical interventions in the brain (. . .) Neuroethics encompasses both research and clinical applications of neurotechnology as well as social and policy issues attendant to their use (. . .) Neuroethics is a content field, defined by the technologies it examines rather than any particular philosophical approach. The field's distinctiveness derives from novel questions posed by applying advanced technology to the brain, the seat of personal identity and executive function in the human organism.
>
> (Wolpe, 2004)

This view of neuroethics as a content field of bioethics dominated the first years of publication in neuroethics. A review found that the characterization of neuroethics as an "ethics of neuroscience" and as a "branch of bioethics" were respectively the first and fourth most common ways of describing neuroethics (Racine, 2010). More recent reviews have confirmed this focus on the ethics of neuroscience in recent literature (Leefmann et al., 2016). However, the view that neuroethics is defined by its focus on neurotechnologies has sparked profound debates, notably about the alignment or even the complicity of neuroethics with the agenda of neuroscience research and technology (Vidal, 2009; Vidal and Piperberg, 2017; De Vries, 2007; Parens and Johnston, 2006; Parens and Johnston, 2007).

Some have warned that, by tying its content to a particular set of neurotechnologies, neuroethics could get too close to science and industry, losing its critical spirit. Citing the case of genethics, Turner notes that ethics research agendas are often defined by trends in funding and broader institutional culture, such that more pressing societal problems fall by the wayside (Turner, 2003). We might diagnose this as a case of ethicists adopting the entrepreneurial culture of medicine and science, diluting and endangering their role as critical scholars (Turner, 2004a,b). But there is more to consider here than mere self-interest or fame-hungry academics. The drive to focus specifically on neuroscience content emerges from a more encompassing sociocultural ecosystem involving a range of actors, including popular media outlets distributing brain images, parents seeking neural perspectives on their children's development, military research agencies, and of course the sociologists and ethicists that follow along (Pickersgill, 2013). As a result, a content-based definition of neuroethics may need to be understood as both an intellectual commitment made by its practitioners and as a dynamic definition within an "economy of technoscientific promises" (Joly, 2013). Indeed, newly defined areas of study rarely arise independently of their cultural moment.

Neuroethics as an ethics of neuroscience and neurotechnology described earlier, however, is not the only view of the field. Another view builds on the ethics of neuroscience but adds that neuroscience of ethics is a key area of focus of neuroethics (Roskies, 2002). Accordingly, neuroethics promises to create a two-way dialogue about the implications of neuroscience for views on ethics and morality. Roskies is rightfully credited for articulating this duality of neuroethics most clearly (Roskies, 2002), although such a view can be traced back to the origins of bioethics (Potter, 1970, 1971):

As we see it, there are two main divisions of neuroethics: the ethics of neuroscience and the neuroscience of ethics. The ethics of neuroscience can be roughly subdivided into two groups of issues: (1) the ethical issues and considerations that should be raised in the course of designing and executing neuroscientific studies (the ethics of practice) and (2) evaluation of the ethical and social impact that the results of those studies might have, or ought to have, on existing social, ethical, and legal structures (the ethical implications of neuroscience). The second major division I highlighted is the neuroscience of ethics. Traditional ethical theory was centered on philosophical notions such as free-will, self-control, personal identity, and intention. These notions can be investigated from the perspective of brain function (Roskies, 2002).

This view is often alluded to and supported (Levy, 2007; Glannon, 2007) but not unanimously agreed upon. Consistent with Wolpe's definition, Wolpe and Farah (Farah and Wolpe, 2004) comment that the neuroscience of ethics introduces confusion about the nature of neuroethics. Others have faulted the neuroscience of ethics for introducing different forms of reductionism and essentialism that jeopardize the richness of the analysis it could offer. These critiques are well known to those who have followed the development of neurophilosophy (Churchland, 1986; Changeux, 1983) and its application to ethics (Changeux, 1996; Changeux and Ricoeur, 2000; Churchland, 1998, 2002).

Finally, some have proposed integrative accounts that build on the diversity of views on neuroethics. Racine (2010) relies on a pragmatist account of ethics to make the case for the contribution of neuroscience—alongside many other empirical disciplines—to the understanding of human morality while at the same time arguing strongly for the practical role of neuroethics in dealing with healthcare, health policy, and research ethics issues in the context of neuroscience. However, according to this view, the rationale for a neuroethics may be less in any unique distinctive attribute (notably its focus on the nervous system) but in an underlying pragmatist framework. Pragmatism brings defining epistemological and methodological commitments such as the development of a contextualized ethics and productive synergies between different disciplines capable of offering insights about human morality, including neuroscience. For example, Dewey encouraged the experimental method in ethics and called for interdisciplinary and evidence-informed ethics:

> But in fact morals is the most humane of all subjects. It is that which is closest to human nature; it is ineradicably empirical, not theological nor metaphysical nor mathematical. Since it directly concerns human nature, everything that can be known of the human mind and body in physiology, medicine, anthropology, and psychology is pertinent to moral inquiry. Human nature exists and operates in an environment. [...] Moral science is not something with a separate province. It is physical, biological and historic knowledge placed in a human context where it illuminates and guides the activities of men.
>
> (Dewey, 1922)

This being said, there remains a significant debate about the actual goals of neuroethics and the areas it should focus on.

"For Which Goals": Implications of Epistemological Questions for Practice

Epistemological questions about *where we are looking from* and *where we come from*, intellectually speaking and as situated scholars and practitioners, and *what we are looking at* in terms of what are proposed areas of focus for neuroethics, can have important implications for what neuroethics does and the goals it pursues, that is, a number of more practical and programmatic issues relevant to the development of neuroethics. While many of the following are not easily separable, we present seven rough clusters of considerations related to the structure and aims of the field.

Training: Who should receive neuroethics training and for what reason(s)? What kind of content(s) should be offered and from which tradition(s)? The tendency for neuroethics scholarship to travel across disciplines and contexts suggests that every would-be scholar may need an interdisciplinary aptitude. But designing a core curriculum depends on deeper epistemological assumptions. Starting from the "view from the brain" or focusing on the neuroscience of ethics might recommend a core curriculum of neuroscience, neurology and psychiatry, and perhaps some engineering and computer science. Presumably, trainees would be encouraged to export this unique expertise into other contexts according to their secondary interests, translating technical brain-based findings into ethics, policy, and clinical or everyday settings. This career trajectory may not be too different from what many scientists and engineers already do. In contrast, a view from the mind or focusing on the ethics of neuroscience might suggest inverted training priorities, where students begin with social science, law, or applied philosophy and analyze neuroscience as just one more ingredient in our study of the mind. Hybrid curricula are, of course, imaginable but may involve challenges. Trainees might find themselves well equipped intellectually but lacking credentials and support in any one established discipline.

Research: What should be the primary goal(s) and methods of neuroethics research? Should neuroethics research be theoretical (conceptual), empirical, clinical, or even interventional? As with questions of training, answers to these queries depend in part on prior epistemological assumptions about how to *do* neuroethics. In keeping with an ethics of neuroscience, one may choose to treat science and medicine problematically, as practices in need of careful critique and revision. Through the lenses of feminism, principlism, casuistry, or narrative ethics, neuroscience is not knowledge to be applied but rather a constellation of social activities, values, and visions for the future, waiting to be evaluated. Data, then, are as likely to be collected from popular media, interviews, and ethnography as from fMRI images and computer models. The neuroscience of ethics, in contrast, would probably have little use for these second-order features of neuroscience practice and would rely instead on its products, whether emerging theories or new descriptions of the human brain. Is there a third way? Fulfilling hopes of a two-way dialogue between each content area, we might pursue a foundational theory such as the dual process theory of Greene, which proposes that there are two major neurocognitive systems involved in human morality: a cognitive system relying on explicit principles and an affective system supported by nonconscious and automatic psychological processes (Cushman et al., 2010). An alternative is the theoretical framework of "fundamental neuroethics". This framework relies on the epistemology of informed materialism proposed by Evers, which considers that the brain is "an autonomously active, plastic, and projective organ evolved in socio cultural-biological symbiosis, and that adopts an evolutionary view of consciousness as an irreducible part of biological reality, an evolved feature of the brain, and a suitable object of scientific study" (Evers et al., 2017). Such foundational theories might pave the way for a more coherent extension of neuroscience into the spaces of everyday life, potentially elucidating the ontological relationship between a scientific *explanation* (*erklären*) of the brain and a humanist *understanding* (*verstehen*) to the mind. But this foundation building has an opportunity cost. Any time and effort spent on new syntheses are resources that could be spent applying extant theory. These different paths must be weighed according to their respective costs and likelihoods of positively impacting society.

Disciplinary and organizational status: Is neuroethics a full-fledged discipline? Would it be best served as a standalone department or as an interdisciplinary network? Scholars have defined neuroethics as "a neglected area of medical ethics" (Pontius, 1973), a kind of expertise (Cranford, 1989), an "emerging new discipline in the study of brain and cognition" (Illes and Raffin, 2002), an interdisciplinary field of research (Racine, 2008, 2010), a "content-field" of bioethics (Wolpe, 2004), and sometimes as more or less an area of neuroscience (Gazzaniga, 2005). These different claims correspond to different assumptions about the defining sources of inspiration and knowledge in neuroethics as well as about what neuroethics should be dealing with. At this time, no consensus has been reached, and a clear tension remains between more neuroscience-informed views and more bioethics- and humanities-oriented views. Scholarship from the former views tends to be published in neuroscience journals and discussed in neuroscience conferences, while the latter tradition tends to appear in bioethics, social science, and clinical journals and conferences. This distribution is reflected in the field's range of nontraditional institutional forms, including interest and affinity groups, interdisciplinary research centers, professional societies, working groups, and service-oriented platforms. These spaces and contexts are sufficiently flexible to allow for diversity in expertise as well as in overarching epistemological assumptions. As the field matures, practitioners will have to decide if these more informal settings are sufficient for an emerging discipline or if more formal institutional arrangements are desirable. If the latter, the neuroethics community will be faced with difficult choices of prioritization; around which vision of neuroethics would an academic department be built?

Consultation and policy engagement: Consultation activities are manifold in mainstream bioethics and include the offer of advice on difficult clinical situations, matters related to research ethics as well as health policy and public health. Given the competing identities of neuroethics, are there consultation activities encountered in mainstream bioethics that are off limits? A consultant committed to a view from the brain might have differing biases (and eventually conflicts of interests) compared with someone who adopts the view from the mind; the former might be better understood as an expert, with affinities for using and funding neuroscience research, while the latter might deny a bias toward any one specific area of science or technology, although scholars in ethics and the humanities may have their own biases and interests. One might have intellectual property related to neural technology, and the other might overplay the possibility of neutral moral expertise. Neuroethics is a sufficiently ambiguous label that it might not pick out these important differences when neuroethics experts are called on for recommendations or insight. Consultation, thus, requires clarity about individual identities.

Simultaneously, calls for a neuroscience of ethics also create new forms of consultation. One could argue that scholars in neuroethics should be involved earlier in the development of neuroscience research to offer advice about the implications and limitations of some theories and methodologies that affect the interpretation and usefulness of work in the neuroscience of ethics (Racine et al., 2017). For example, for those who stress the significance of the physical brain, it may be appropriate to encourage the use of neuroscience within movements for brain-based education, including brain-based moral education for children (Hardiman et al., 2012; Hardiman, 2003). And in general, we may think that the possibility of a neuroscientific foundation to ethics (Changeux, 1996; Evers, 2007; Evers et al., 2017) strengthens the case for such policy engagement. Yet caution is warranted when the science may be premature, as in the infamous distribution of Mozart recordings in the state of Georgia based on the alleged "Mozart effect" (Maxwell and Racine, 2012). (The criticized policy was based on a hasty interpretation of neuroscience research on the benefits of exposure to classical music on cognitive development, or the so-called Mozart effect; Rauscher, Shaw and Ky, 1995.) But how will we know when a science is "mature" and appropriate for policy applications? It is not obvious how to weigh these considerations unless they are supplemented by "the view from the mind," which relies less directly (or tautologically?) on the neuroscientific perspective. Here, it seems that fostering both visions of neuroethics may be practically useful, as each can enrich the other.

Outreach and public discourse: Should those specializing in neuroethics get involved in media engagement and other forms of public discourse? Do they have a responsibility or duty to do so? Trained researchers in any field may find it easy to critique public discourse or imagine better solutions to societal or everyday problems, but to pursue these ideas engages one's role in society. And each discipline or profession has its own set of views in this respect. Scientists of various sorts may understand their work in terms of the intrinsic value of fundamental knowledge and its eventual application. Professional engineers might emphasize meeting the needs of their clients and policy makers of their constituents. Philosophers sometimes claim to improve conceptual clarity. But as exemplified by the neuroethics community, these identities are increasingly fluid (Gibbons, 1999; Littlefield et al., 2014). Researchers in neuroethics must consider to whom they are accountable and by what mechanisms. Upon reflection, our preference for a view from the brain or from the mind (and their epistemological foundations) may be shaped by our political commitments, broadly construed to capture the relationship between oneself and the political community. Accordingly, as neuroethics debates and discusses relevant topics such as brain death, our individual accountabilities and political commitments will influence whether we replace lay (or manifest) views about the mind with scientific ones, try to infuse the "manifest image" into the scientific one, or neither (Racine, 2015).

Ethics: What are the guiding values and principles of the field of neuroethics? Different views of neuroethics imply different types of "ethics" and commitments for those specialized in neuroethics. The International Neuroethics Society aims to "promote the development and responsible application of neuroscience" for the benefit of all (www.neuroethicssociety.org/about), and the objective of neuroethics is sometimes described as "to align innovations in the brain sciences with societal, cultural and individual human values through high impact research, education, and outreach" (Reimer and Illes, 2009). Each of these statements takes the value of neuroscience for granted, as a fact or perhaps even as a good, and prescribes a beneficent stance.

However, as mentioned in our discussion of "What are We Looking at?", some authors have criticized neuroethics for holding values and interests too close to an agenda for the development of neuroscience and neurotechnology (Parens and Johnston, 2007; Turner, 2003, 2004a, 2004b, De Vries, 2005, 2007). While many researchers aspire to work for the good of everyone, there is disagreement about what constitutes this good. Some see neuroscience and the study of the brain as the major source of value, while others may worry that it is an ambivalent practice at best. As an alternative, person-first value statements may not invoke such concerns. Fins and Racine, for example, have stressed the importance of the commitment to improving the condition of patients with severe brain injury and mental health conditions (Fins, 2008, 2017; Racine, 2010). Overall, these various value statements give shape to an implicit and perhaps inconsistent ethics for specialists in neuroethics. Formulating an explicit code of ethics could give the field some clarity on these and other issues, shaping both common values and specific norms with respect to conflicts of interest, authorship, and professional identity. There is a very rich literature on the ethics of bioethicists, including proposals to set standards for clinical ethics consultations and codes of ethics for bioethicists (Baker, 2005) as well as healthy criticism of some important biases of mainstream bioethics (Turner, 2004a, 2004b). But to our knowledge, few writings have tackled the question of the ethics of "neuroethicists" directly.

Mentoring: Ultimately, what should we tell someone who wants to be a neuroethics scholar? What are effective ways to support the next generation of neuroethics researchers? These questions tie together all the rest and raise the stakes. Answers to these questions shape early scholars' lives as well as the future of the field. For some mentors, the familiar perspective may be the default one when guiding young researchers. A mentor trained in cognitive neuroscience may advise the neuroethics mentee to acquire strong training in neuroscience, to secure an understanding of the structure and function of the physical brain, and to look for neural correlates of morality. A professor of bioethics may send the same mentee out into the world with a principlist toolset to tackle ethical issues in the world one case at a time. Or alternatively, upon reflecting on these and other potentialities, the mentor may recognize the contingency of his or her own particular style of neuroethics and enable mentees to reach beyond the familiar; this form of support may entail allowing coursework outside of a traditional degree program, finding co-mentors outside of the primary discipline, and connecting mentees to their peers in the neuroethics community. These are likely just a few of the challenges of fostering a successful career across multiple disciplines, approaches, and institutions. Regardless of mentoring style, the plurality of neuroethics is a major characteristic of the field and should be highlighted and discussed with would-be neuroethics researchers.

Conclusion

In this chapter, we presented an overview of some key epistemological challenges, which, in our eyes, serious neuroethics scholars and practitioners should consider individually and collectively. But this is in no way meant to say that consensus should be sought or achieved on those questions. A field can very well be healthy and pluralist. Diversity in attitude and approach, if engaged, can strengthen arguments through dialogue and reveal new modes of being for scholars and practitioners in neuroethics. The purpose, then, of asking these questions is not to reduce pluralism but to better map the range of work being done in the field and, in turn, clarify the self-understandings of ourselves and our colleagues. In our eyes, those involved in neuroethics need to reflect on "where they come from" intellectually and socially and why they are engaged in scholarship that sometimes implies buy-in to different forms of reductionism and essentialism embedded in the "view from the brain." If this is not the case or should not be the case, then how should the "view from the mind" be reconciled and meshed with the focus on neuroscience and neurotechnology in neuroethics? Another important set of questions is rooted in what neuroethics should deal with, look at, and focus on. Again, different views compete, and potential integrative views offer different accounts based on underlying theories such as pragmatist ethics but also from other theoretical perspectives such as feminist ethics and narrative ethics. Finally, we stressed that these epistemological questions have implications for the practice of neuroethics and those involved in its continued development, whether through training, research, or policy engagement. We hope that readers will continue the conversation about the questions presented in this chapter and that our contribution will encourage self-reflection on neuroethics practice and scholarship.

Acknowledgments

Writing of this chapter was supported by a joint grant from the Canadian Institutes of Health Research and the Fonds de recherche du Québec–Santé (European Research Projects on Ethical, Legal, and Social Aspects [ELSA] of Neurosciences) as well as a career award from the Fonds de recherche du Québec–Santé. We would like to thank William Affleck for helpful comments on a previous version of this manuscript. The impetus for this paper was a discussion panel at the 2016 annual meeting of the International Neuroethics Society ("Mind-Brain and the Competing Identities of Neuroethics") chaired by Eric Racine.

Further Reading

Callahan, D. (1973). "Bioethics as a discipline". *Hastings Center Studies* 1, 66–73.

Fins, J.J. (2008). "A leg to stand on: Sir William Osler and Wilder Penfield's 'neuroethics'". *American Journal of Bioethics* 8(1), 37–46.

Jonsen, A.R. (2008). "Encephaloethics: A history of the ethics of the brain". *American Journal of Bioethics* 8(9), 37–42.

Racine, E. (2010). *Pragmatic Neuroethics: Improving Treatment and Understanding of the Mind-Brain.* Cambridge, MA: MIT Press.

Racine, E. and Aspler, J. (Ed.) (2017). *Debates About Neuroethics: Perspectives on Its Development, Focus, and Future.* Heidelberg: Springer.

References

Baker, R. (2005) A draft model aggregated code of ethics for bioethicists. *American Journal of Bioethics* 5(5): pp. 33–41; discussion W12–3.

Bernat, J.L. (2002) *Ethical Issues in Neurology.* Boston: Butterworth-Heinemann.

Blain-Moraes, S., Schaff, R., Gruis, K.L., Huggins, J.E., and Wren, P.A. (2012) Barriers to and mediators of brain-computer interface user acceptance: Focus group findings. *Ergonomics* 55: pp. 516–525.

Changeux, J.-P. (1983) *L'homme neuronal.* Paris: Hachette.

———. (1996) Le point de vue d'un neurobiologiste sur les fondements de l'éthique. In G. Huber (Ed.). *Cerveau et psychisme humains: quelle éthique?* Paris: John Libbey Eurotext, pp. 97–110.

Changeux, J.-P., and Ricoeur, P. (2000) *Ce qui nous fait penser: la nature et la règle.* Paris: Odile Jacob.

Churchland, P.S. (1986) *Neurophilosophy: Toward a Unified Science of the Mind-Brain.* Cambridge, MA: Bradford Book/MIT Press.

———. (1998) Feeling reasons. In P.M. Churchland. and P.S. Churchland (Eds.). *On the Contrary.* Cambridge, MA: MIT Press, pp. 231–254.

————. (2002) Neuroconscience: Reflections on the neural basis of morality. In S.J. Marcus (Ed.). *Neuroethics: Mapping the Field, Conference Proceedings*. New York: The Dana Foundation.

Cranford, R.E. (1989) The neurologist as ethics consultant and as a member of the institutional ethics committee. The neuroethicist. *Neurologic Clinics* 7: pp. 697–713.

Cushman, F., Young, L., and Greene, J.D. (2010) Multi-system moral psychology. In J.M. Doris (Ed.). *The Moral Psychology Handbook*. Oxford: Oxford Scholarship Online, pp. 47–71.

De Vries, R. (2005) Framing neuroethics: A sociological assessment of the neuroethical imagination. *American Journal of Bioethics* 5: pp. 25–27.

————. (2007) Who will guard the guardians of neuroscience? Firing the neuroethical imagination. *EMBO Reports* 8 Spec No: pp. S65–S69.

Dewey, J. (1922) *Human Nature and Conduct: An Introduction to Social Psychology*. New York: Holt.

Evans, J.H. (2000) A sociological account of the growth of principlism. *Hastings Center Report* 30: pp. 31–38.

————. (2002) *Playing God? Human Genetic Engineering and the Rationalization of Public Bioethical Debate*. Chicago: Chicago University Press.

Evers, K. (2007) Towards a philosophy for neuroethics. An informed materialist view of the brain might help to develop theoretical frameworks for applied neuroethics. *EMBO Reports*, 8 Spec No, pp. S48–S51.

Evers, K., Salles, A., and Farisco M. (in Press) Theoretical framing of neuroethics: The need for a conceptual approach. In E. Racine and J. Asper (Eds.). *Debates About Neuroethics: Perspectives on Its Development, Focus, and Future*. Heidelberg: Springer.

Farah, M.J., and Wolpe, P.R. (2004) Monitoring and manipulating brain function: New neuroscience technologies and their ethical implications. *Hastings Center Report* 34: pp. 35–45.

Fins, J.J. (2000) A proposed ethical framework for international cognitive neuroscience: A consideration of deep brain stimulation in impaired consciousness. *Neurological Research* 22: pp. 273–278.

————. (2005) Clinical pragmatism and the care of brain damaged patients: Toward a palliative neuroethics for disorders of consciousness. *Progress in Brain Research* 150: pp. 565–582.

————. (2008) A leg to stand on: Sir William Osler and Wilder Penfield's "Neuroethics". *American Journal of Bioethics* 8(1): pp. 37–46.

————. (2017) Towards a pragmatic neuroethics in theory and practice. In E. Racine and J. Aspler (Eds.). *Debates About Neuroethics: Perspectives on Its Development, Focus, and Future*. Heidelberg: Springer.

Fins, J.J., Rezai, A.R., and Greenberg, B.D. (2006) Psychosurgery: Avoiding an ethical redux while advancing a therapeutic future. *Neurosurgery* 59: pp. 713–716.

Gazzaniga, M.S. (2005) *The Ethical Brain*. New York: Dana Press.

Gibbons, M. (1999) Science's new social contract with society. *Nature* 402: pp. C81–C84.

Glannon, W. (2007) *Bioethics and the Brain*. New York: Oxford University Press.

Hardiman, M. (2003) *Connecting Brain Research With Effective Teaching: The Brain-Targeted Teaching Model*. Lanham: Rowman & Littlefield Education.

Hardiman, M., Rinne, L., Gregory, E., and Yarmolinskaya, J. (2012) Neuroethics, neuroeducation, and classroom teaching: Where the brain sciences meet pedagogy. *Neuroethics* 5: pp. 135–143.

Illes, J., and Raffin, T.A. (2002) Neuroethics: An emerging new discipline in the study of brain and cognition. *Brain and Cognition* 50: pp. 341–344.

Joly, P.-B. (2013) On the economics of technoscientific promises. In M. Akrich, Y. Barthe, F. Muniesa, and P. Mustar (Eds.). *Débordements: mélanges offerts à Michel Callon*. Paris: Presses des Mines, pp. 203–221.

Leefmann, J., Levallois, C., and Hildt, E. (2016) Neuroethics 1995–2012: A bibliometric analysis of the guiding themes of an emerging research field. *Frontiers in Human Neuroscience* 10: p. 336.

Levy, N. (2007) *Neuroethics: Challenges for the 21st Century*. Cambridge: Cambridge University Press.

Littlefield, M.M., Fitzgerald, D., Knudsen, K., Tonks, J., and Dietz, M.J. (2014) Contextualizing neurocollaborations: Reflections on a transdisciplinary fMRI lie detection experiment. *Frontiers in Human Neuroscience* 8: p. 149.

Marcus, S.J. (Ed.) (2002). *Neuroethics: Mapping the Field, Conference Proceedings*. New York: The Dana Foundation.

Maxwell, B., and Racine, E. (2012) Does the neuroscience research on early stress justify responsive childcare? Examining interwoven epistemological and ethical challenges. *Neuroethics* 5: pp. 159–172.

Miller, F.G., and Fins, J.J. (1999) Protecting vulnerable research subjects without unduly constraining neuropsychiatric research. *Archives of General Psychiatry* 56: pp. 701–702; discussion 03–04.

Parens, E., and Johnston, J. (2006) Against hyphenated ethics. *Bioethics Forum* [Online]. Available at: www.bioethicsforum.org/genethics-neuroethics-nanoethics.asp.

———. (2007) Does it make sense to speak of neuroethics? Three problems with keying ethics to hot new science and technology. *EMBO Reports*, 8 Spec No: pp. S61–S64.

Pickersgill, M. (2013) The social life of the brain: Neuroscience in society. *Current Sociology* 61: pp. 322–340.

Pontius, A.A. (1973) Neuro-ethics of "Walking" in the newborn. *Perceptual and Motor Skills* 37: pp. 235–245.

Potter, V.R. (1970) Bioethics, the science of survival. *Perspectives in Biology and Medicine* 14: pp. 127–153.

———. (1971) *Bioethics: Bridge to the Future*. Englewood Cliffs, NJ: Prentice-Hall.

Racine, E. (2008) Interdisciplinary approaches for a pragmatic neuroethics. *The American Journal of Bioethics* 8(1): pp. 52–53.

———. (2010) *Pragmatic Neuroethics: Improving Treatment and Understanding of the Mind-Brain*. Cambridge, MA: MIT Press.

———. (2015) Revisiting the persisting tension between expert and lay views about brain death and death determination: A proposal inspired by pragmatism. *Journal of Bioethical Inquiry* 12: pp. 623–631.

Racine, E., Dubljevic, V., Jox, R.J., Baertschi, B., Christensen, J.F., Farisco, M., . . . Müller, S. (2017) Can neuroscience contribute to practical ethics? A critical review and discussion of the methodological and translational challenges of the neuroscience of ethics. *Bioethics*, in press.

Racine, E., Waldman, S., Rosenberg, J., and Illes, J. (2010) Contemporary neuroscience in the media. *Social Science and Medicine* 71: pp. 725–733.

Racine, E., and Zimmerman, E. (2012) Pragmatism and the neuroscience of ethics. In M.M. Littlefield and J. Johnson (Eds.). *The Neuroscientific Turn: Transdisciplinarity in the Age of the Brain*. Ann Arbor: University of Michigan Press, pp. 135–151.

Rauscher, F.H., Shaw G.L., and Ky, K.N. (1995) Listening to Mozart enhances spatial-temporal reasoning: Towards a neurophysiological basis. *Neuroscience Letters* 185(9): pp. 44–47.

Reimer, J., and Illes, J. (2009) Listening to the message of patients and stakeholders: Where stem cell therapy, spinal cord injury and neuroethics meet. *Annals of Neurosciences* 16: pp. 148–149.

Roskies, A. (2002) Neuroethics for the new millennium. *Neuron* 35: pp. 21–23.

Safire, W. (2002) Visions for a new field of neuroethics. In S.J. Marcus (Ed.). *Neuroethics: Mapping the Field*. New York: The Dana Press, pp. 3–9.

Sellars, W. (1963) *Science, Perception, and Reality*. New York: Humanities Press.

Turner, L. (2003) The tyranny of 'genethics'. *Nature Biotechnology* 21: p. 1282.

———. (2004a) Bioethic$ Inc. *Nature Biotechnology* 22: pp. 947–948.

———. (2004b) Bioethics needs to rethink its agenda. *BMJ* 328: p. 175.

Vidal, F. (2009) Brainhood, anthropological figure of modernity. *History of the Human Sciences* 22: pp. 5–36.

Vidal, F., and Piperberg, M. (2017) Born free: The theory and practice of neuroethical exceptionalism. In E. Racine and J. Aspler (Eds.). *Debates About Neuroethics: Perspectives on Its Development, Focus, and Future*. Heidelberg: Springer.

Whitehouse, P.J. (2012) A clinical neuroscientist looks neuroskeptically at neuroethics in the neuroworld. In M.M. Littlefield and J. Johnson (Eds.). *The Neuroscientific Turn: Transdisciplinarity in the Age of the Brain*. Ann Arbor: University of Michigan Press, pp. 199–215.

Wolpe, P.R. (2004) Neuroethics. In S.G. Post (Ed.). *The Encyclopedia of Bioethics*. 3rd ed. New York: Palgrave MacMillan Reference, pp. 1894–1898.

2

NEUROETHICS AND THE NEUROSCIENTIFIC TURN

Jon Leefmann and Elisabeth Hildt

Introduction

Stimulated by a general salience of neuroscientific research and the declaration of neuroscience as one of the leading disciplines of the current century, a diversity of disciplines from the social sciences and the humanities have engaged in discussions about the role of the brain in various social and cultural phenomena. The general importance assigned to the brain in so many areas of academic and social life nowadays has been called the 'neuroscientific turn'. One of the fields that gained particular attention in this context is neuroethics. It is, however, not clear if neuroethics should be regarded simply as an indicator of a change toward a brain-centered anthropological outlook in Western societies or as an entity that itself plays a crucial role in the development and promotion of this outlook.

In this chapter, we present two perspectives on the 'neuroscientific turn', sketch a landscape of neuroethics, and scrutinize the current state and development of neuroethics as one of the new fields at the intersection between neuroscience and the humanities. We will ask to what extent neuroethics is itself a product or a booster of a cultural turn toward neuroscience and which interpretations of neuroscientific knowledge and which public expectations of the potential of neuroscience have actually been put to work in the formation of neuroethics. As our analysis underlines, the interactions of neuroscience and ethics in the field of neuroethics are complex and multidirectional. On the one hand, philosophical and anthropological discourse has favored certain theoretical assumptions about the role of the brain for human self-understanding. On the other hand, neuroscience has stimulated many discourses in ethical theory, as well as in society, of which neuroethics can be regarded as a recent derivative. Finally, neuroethics itself occasionally functions as an amplifier of the assumption that neuroscience provides relevant information to help us understand the nature of human morality and the nature of good social norms and institutions.

The Neuroscientific Turn: Two Interpretations

In recent decades, in many sectors of the humanities a host of new neuro-fields has emerged. This development has not only touched philosophical inquiry via the emergence of neurophilosophy (Churchland, 1986) and neuroethics but the social sciences and humanities in general.

Alongside—and sometimes in opposition to—the robust, established mother disciplines, entities like neuroanthropology (Northoff, 2010; Lende and Downey, 2012), neuroeconomics (Loewenstein et al., 2008; Glimcher and Fehr, 2014), neuroeducation (Battro et al., 2008), neuromarketing (Lee et al., 2007; Ariely and Berns, 2010), neurosociology (TenHouten, 1997; Franks, 2010), neurohistory (Smail, 2007, 2014), neuroaesthetics (Zeki, 1999; Chatterjee and Vartanian, 2014), and even neurotheology (Newberg, 2013), have recently gained a following. Even though these new fields currently do not have the potential to become substitutes for traditional disciplinary approaches, this phenomenon has been related to a process termed the "neuroscientific turn" or "the neuro-turn" (Johnson and Littlefield, 2012).

The process of the neuroscientific turn has been approached from at least two perspectives. First, it has been argued that the neuroscientific turn is not a partial development restricted to the scientific sector but a phenomenon that relates to more general developments in contemporary Western culture, which condition the salience of neuroscience as an interpretative framework for virtually every part of human life (Vidal, 2009; Cooter, 2014). This diagnosis of what Fernando Vidal has called 'brainhood' conveys a very broad understanding of the neuroscientific turn. As Vidal seeks to show from the perspective of a historian of science, the focus on the cerebral subject and the emerging neuro-culture represented by these new neuro-fields was conveyed by some of the foundational ideas of modernity, such as the supreme value modern thinking gives to "the individual as autonomous agent of choice and initiative" (Vidal, 2009, 5). Central to Vidal's approach is the assumption that the underlying concept of 'brainhood' fueled neuroscience to a greater extent than it followed from it. According to this interpretation, the neuroscientific turn should be conceived of as a consequence of the general anthropological paradigm of modernity, in which the now visible trend toward a 'neurologization' of the social sciences and the humanities has continued to be incorporated. The broad perspective of this approach allows the explanation of the contexts and conditions that shape the development of the new neuro-fields. Its explanatory perspective, hence, is on the *possibility* of the neuroscientific turn as a phenomenon.

Second, there is a more narrow account of the neuroscientific turn. Rather than focusing on large-scale historical developments, Johnson and Littlefield conceive of neuroscience as a "*translational discipline*: a set of methods and/or theories that has become transferable to other disciplines *and* a flashpoint for transdisciplinary exchange" (Littlefield and Johnson, 2012, 5, Johnson and Littlefield, 2011). In this interpretation, the term 'neuroscientific turn' refers to the process of translation of concepts, methods, and theories from neuroscience for application in the social sciences and the humanities. This account lacks the contextualization in the genealogy of general cultural developments, even though its focus still allows it to critically investigate and assess consequences of this translational process. In this last vein, Johnson and Littlefield have pointed out, for example, that nonscientific publications of leading neuroscientists such as Damasio (1995, 2003), Edelman (2005), Gazzaniga (2005), and Greene (2014) often function as a means for such translational processes (Johnson and Littlefield, 2011). They found the results of such translational processes via popular science books to be ambivalent, sometimes presenting research results that seem to be so convincing that they tend to shut down further argument but sometimes also to promote reflection on current theories in the social sciences and to stimulate the development of new ones. This second account asks about the *way* scientific findings and theories are put into use in other fields of investigation. Its explanatory perspective, hence, focuses more on the *mechanisms* of the 'neuroscientific turn' than on the conditions of its actual possibility.

Both perspectives, however, are linked by the acknowledged importance of science as the all-penetrative worldview in contemporary modern societies. These translational processes bring about new neuro-theories in areas of investigation that in the past were unlikely to turn to neuroscience for arguments or to give rise to new explanations of social and psychological phenomena. Translational processes, hence, can contribute to a changed outlook not only on the workings of the social sciences and humanities but also on collective perspectives on the world and humanity in general. The production of theories and knowledge inspired by neuroscience helps to create a different framing of human self-understanding. By this, translations can function as building blocks for the promotion of the more general neuroscientific turn in contemporary Western cultures, which Vidal has addressed. Translations of knowledge from neuroscience to disciplines in the social sciences might be used as evidence for the brainhood thesis in this view.

Naturally, both brainhood and the translational processes at work in the neuroscientific turn become visible in various fields in the public sphere. Work from the social sciences has underlined that the neuroscientific turn shapes social policy agendas (Broer and Pickersgill, 2015), influences current understanding of learning and education (Pickersgill, 2013), and changes the way we conceptualize adolescence (Choudhury et al., 2012) and life problems in general. With special regard to our understanding of mental illness, social theorist Nicholas Rose has claimed that we have become 'neurochemical selves', or people who understand thought, feeling, and behavior as mediated through the brain (Rose, 2007). Moreover, social scientists have made observations about a change in the language used to express anxieties, disappointments, hopes, and dreams. Frequently this language is saturated with terms and metaphors relating to the brain and neuroscience (Thornton, 2011). The influence of language in the construction of the idea of a neurochemical self has also been observed with regard to technologies. As Jonna Brenninkmeijer has discussed, for example, the use of brain-related technologies like EEG, neuroimaging, or neurofeedback in clinical settings helps to bring about the verbal articulation of life problems as brain problems and through this produces the idea of a neurological self (Brenninkmeijer, 2010). Underlying all these perceivable changes is the process of neuroscience beginning to occupy some of the discursive space previously occupied by psychology, psychiatry, and psychotherapy (Rose, 2008; Rose and Abi-Rached, 2013), which can be interpreted as a direct effect of the neuroscientific turn.

Additionally, it has been argued that the neuroscientific turn in the social sciences and the humanities contributes indirectly to the cultural turn toward a neuro-society. The defining characteristics of a neuro-society that would be the result of a global neuroscientific turn are, however, not yet certain. For example, it has been argued that the trend toward pharmacological brain optimization has become enmeshed within the cultural ethos of self-control, as representative of an ideological system that has been linked with a host of damaging social and psychological phenomena (Pitts-Taylor, 2010; Wade, 2015). Sociologist Alain Ehrenberg, for example, has argued that the encouragement of self-responsibility and the liberation of the individual from generally binding and sometimes oppressive social norms has not only played a considerable role in the disappearance of 'hysteria' from psychiatric manuals but has also greatly contributed to the enormous increase of depression as the major psychiatric illness in contemporary Western societies (Ehrenberg, 2010). Likewise the tendency to frame self-optimization as an autonomous action of the individual and the nonmedical use of pharmaceuticals as "cognitive enhancement" has been interpreted as mirroring values of competition (Ferrari et al., 2012; Outram, 2012). Furthermore, social scientists have discussed parallels between the scientific concept of neuroplasticity (i.e., the experience-dependent change of brain structure and function) and a socioeconomic context that rewards mobility and adaptability (Malabou, 2008; Choudhury et al., 2009; Pitts-Taylor, 2010). While acknowledging that this parallel can reproduce capitalist ideals, some scholars also see in neuroplasticity the promise of individual liberation. For example, Malabou argues that consciousness of one's biological capacity to change may empower the individual's resistance to social pressures (Malabou, 2008). Hence, the answer to the question of whether a potential neuro-society brought about by an all-encompassing neuroscientific turn would be made up of more liberated or of more repressed individuals does not depend on the neuroscientific turn as such but rather on the particular ways the translational processes between neuroscience and the social sciences and the humanities are structured and interpreted.

Notwithstanding the fact that neuroscientific advances are undoubtedly considerable and have led to important insights into brain structure and functioning, it may be questioned whether the observations mentioned earlier actually speak for a neuroscientific turn in a general sense that affects the whole culture. Though there has been an increase in neuroscientific knowledge that translates into new approaches in various disciplines from the social sciences and the humanities, it is not yet clear whether or how far our views and social practices have actually changed with respect to this knowledge. Or is it rather that we tend to use neuroscientific knowledge to reinforce some of our existing beliefs and practices? For example, a recent publication by Scurich and Shniderman lends evidence to the claim that motivated reasoning plays an important role in laypersons' assessments of the relevance of neuroscientific research (Scurich and Shniderman, 2014). Laypersons tend to consider claims made by neuroscientists as relevant depending on the fittingness with their attitude toward the phenomenon under investigation. Considering this simple but widespread psychological bias, it will certainly take time to change long-held views and deep convictions that are constitutive of a whole culture. Even a 'neuroscientific turn' involving only our moral and legal conceptions may be expected to be a lengthy process. In view of this, one may consider it more adequate to talk of an 'alleged neuroscientific turn' instead, taking into consideration that currently, we at best see the beginning of an emerging development.

In spite of this criticism and being aware of the fact that we do not know about the future, in this chapter, we nevertheless use the terms 'neuroscientific turn' and 'neuro-turn' as concepts helpful in framing and interpreting current scientific and cultural developments. It is not clear at the moment whether the 'neuroscientific turn' will turn out to be a highly overblown concept and whether the variations we currently see are only temporary in nature or whether they are really the beginning of deep cultural changes.

In the following pages, we turn to neuroethics to investigate the field's particular role in the neuroscientific turn by describing its formation within the context of developments in neuroscience after the Decade of the Brain. Scrutinizing the current state and development of neuroethics as one of the new interdisciplinary fields between neuroscience and the humanities, we will refer to both accounts of the neuroscientific turn. We will ask to what extent neuroethics is itself a product or a booster of the neuroscientific turn and which neuroscientific knowledge and which interpretations and expectations of the potential of neuroscience have actually been put to work in the formation of different concepts and research agendas of neuroethics.

Drawing the Landscape of Neuroethics

It has become common practice to divide neuroethics into two distinct branches: the neuroscience of ethics and the ethics of neuroscience (Roskies, 2002). Other divisions have been proposed to structure the field (Evers, 2007; Northoff, 2009). However, Roskies's distinction has the advantage of rendering salient the very specific neuroethical feature of bringing together descriptive investigations of human behavior in moral contexts with normative evaluations of actions and policies with regard to neuroscientific research, neurological treatment and the social and legal aspects of newly developed neuro-technologies. While a small but significant part of neuroethics consists of empirical investigations by neuroscientists into 'the neural basis' of 'moral' behavior (neuroscience of ethics), the largest part of neuroethics addresses questions from the applied ethics approach (ethics of neuroscience). As we have discussed elsewhere, these two branches of the field are only marginally interrelated in terms of researchers working in and journals publishing research from both areas of investigation (Leefmann et al., 2016). This institutional divide is not surprising because the potential role of descriptive knowledge about the neurological mechanisms involved in 'moral' decision making and behavior for the actual assessment of technologies or medical practices related to the human brain is a contested philosophical issue in neuroethics. Just as descriptive ethics—the description of social, cultural, and moral norms that factually hold in a society—does not help to assess the goodness of norms or to justify decisions about which norms should apply in a certain situation, descriptive neuroscientific findings do not provide a basis to resolve practical ethical conflicts. Nevertheless, the significance of neuroscience for applied ethics does not amount to nothing. Insofar as neuroscience can reveal cognitive and normative biases that impede an agent's understanding of what moral practice has established as rules for conduct, it can provide reasons to relieve bias-affected agents from their responsibility for failing to act in accord with these norms. If 'ought' implies 'can', that is if it is rational only to demand moral conduct of those who have the capacity to understand norms and to act accordingly, neuroscience has a limited role in ethics insofar as it reveals conditions under which the demand for 'moral' conduct is misplaced. In the same vein, descriptive empirical research could function as a corrective for theory building in ethics. Even though neuroscience has no significance for estimating what a morally right action amounts to, research on behavior in 'moral contexts' can help show to what extent people are actually capable of acting in a way demanded by an ethical theory. If research into the neural conditions of human behavior and decision making does reveal that a critical mass of human beings is not capable of moral actions as defined by the respective ethical theory, the theory in question would be very dubitable (for a more extensive debate cf. Casebeer, 2003; Greene, 2003; Sinnott-Armstrong, 2006; Joyce, 2008; Berker, 2009).

Besides this rather modest role for neuroscience in ethical theory, research in the field has had considerable impact on controversies in applied ethics. First, the development of technologies such as deep brain stimulation (DBS), transcranial direct current stimulation (tDCS), and brain–computer interfaces (BCI) has provoked ethical discussions about their risks and benefits and their impact on personal autonomy, well-being, and human self-understanding (for DBS cf. Schermer, 2011; Racine et al., 2015; Unterrainer and Oduncu, 2015; for tDCS cf. Jotterand and Giordano, 2011; Cohen Kadosh et al., 2012; Fitz and Reiner, 2015; and for BCI cf. Tamburrini, 2009; Grübler et al., 2014; Schicktanz et al., 2015). Equally, positron emission tomography (PET) and functional magnetic resonance imaging (fMRI) technology has fueled ethical discussions about the privacy of data obtained from brain scans and the procedures for handling this information in a way that is beneficial to patients (Meegan, 2008; Farah et al., 2009). Reflection on these technologies has often revived familiar problems from bioethics in a new context. For instance, the ethical problem of incidental findings during fMRI studies (Wardlaw et al., 2015) is comparable to problems arising from incidental findings during other experimental procedures. Likewise, the ethics of neuroscience has considerable continuities with other bioethical subfields such as genethics and nano-ethics (Wilfond and Ravitsky, 2005; Parens and Johnston, 2007). At the same time, progress in medicine and neuroscience has brought to the forefront issues in clinical ethics. For example, research in the field of neurodegenerative diseases and psychiatric diseases has partly generated a new picture of the impaired cognitive capabilities of affected patients (Northoff, 2006; Supady et al., 2011), which impedes their ability to give informed consent, be it for clinical treatment or for participation in clinical trials. More generally speaking, neuroscientists have helped to detect and explain a variety of conditions that could impair an agent's capacity for adequate social perception (Zaki et al., 2012; Fujino et al., 2014; Trémeau et al., 2015), conscious and autonomous decision making, and intentional agency (Heatherton and Wagner, 2011; Stuss and Knight, 2013). By doing so, they have challenged assumptions about the human capacity for rationality and responsible conduct that has shaped the image of the human being in ethics codes and the law.

Having given a brief overview of the main issues addressed in the ethical reflection of neuroscientific research and innovation in the field of neuroethics, it is important to notice that the current ethics of neuroscience is far from having included the complete spectrum of research activities that form the multifaceted field of neuroscience. Additional ethical questions will likely arise, for instance, with regard to computer simulations of the brain, such as currently being done in the Human Brain Project (HBP), a European Commission Future Emerging Technologies flagship project that aims to develop an information and communications infrastructure to integrate neuroscience data in order to understand and simulate the human brain (Christen et al., 2016; Farisco et al., 2016). Organic computers (Pais-Vieira et al., 2015), brain-to-brain interfaces (Grau et al., 2014; Rao et al., 2014), and the possibility of influencing the mind and brain through intentional environmental manipulations (e.g. Thaler and Sunstein, 2009; Heinzelmann, Ugazio, and Tobler, 2012) are also likely to evoke future problems for neuroethical analysis. Summing up this short overview of the landscape of neuroethics, two aspects seem remarkable.

On the one hand, neuroscience has contributed to sowing some minor seeds of doubt about the adequacy of recent interpretations of basic moral concepts such as autonomy and responsibility. By providing in-depth descriptions of the neural underpinnings of psychological and cognitive biases, neuroscience has identified further and more detailed conditions that constrain the application of established ethical concepts. Consequently, these descriptions have inspired discussions about assumptions underlying much of contemporary theory of practical rationality, such as the role of emotions (Damasio, 1995, 2003; Prinz, 2006), akrasia (Kalis et al., 2008), and rational deliberation for moral agency (Greene et al., 2004). On the other hand, neuroscience has hardly affected the core business of ethical analysis in applied ethics. Many scholars in the ethics of neuroscience still avail themselves of the conceptual tools of traditional biomedical ethics and analyze ethical conflicts arising in the contexts of brain-related technologies and clinical neurology in a way that does not differ in principle from other areas in bioethics and medical ethics.

In the next sections, we will take a closer look at the extent to which this current landscape of neuroethics is itself a product of the alleged neuroscientific turn in contemporary Western societies and has evolved from a transfer of neuroscientific knowledge into the field of applied ethics. We will also ask to what extent neuroethics itself further stimulates this knowledge transfer. Are we currently witnessing a 'neurologization' of ethics?

Neuroethics as an Indicator of a New Anthropological Outlook?

The idea of 'brainhood' as an anthropological outlook—that is, as an outlook that defines the specificity and functionality of the human brain as the essence of a human being—though hardly ever explicitly named, is astonishingly frequent in the serious scientific literature in neuroethics. For example, Sofia Lombera and Judy Illes quite explicitly subscribe to the 'brainhood' thesis when they write, "Although this certainly is not a universal view, generally we consider the brain to be the organ that not only grants the characteristics that we qualify as 'human', but also makes each one of us unique" (Lombera and Illes, 2009). Adina Roskies has blown the same horn, using the term 'neuroessentialism' as an alternative to the term 'brainhood'. In 2002 she admitted, "Many of us overtly or covertly believe in a kind of 'neuroessentialism', that our brains define who we are, even more than do our genes. So in investigating the brain, we investigate the self" (Roskies, 2002). In a similar vein, the philosopher Thomas Metzinger in his popular book, *The Ego Tunnel*, makes a case for a new ethics inspired by the urgent threats to our current, not–brain-centered anthropological outlook. He warns that with knowledge about the brain mechanisms underlying consciousness, society "risks being overwhelmed by the technological consequences and the psychosocial costs of the Consciousness Revolution". He then goes on to demand that "[w]e must strive to protect open societies from irrationalism and fundamentalism—from all those who desperately seek emotional security and espouse closed worldviews because they cannot bear the naturalistic turn in the image of humankind" (Metzinger, 2010, 238).

Another indicator of the role of brainhood in neuroethics might be the timing of the field's development. The term 'neuroethics' began to spread as the name for research at the intersection of neuroscience, philosophy, ethics, and the social sciences following several interdisciplinary conferences held in 2002. That research into the ethical and social consequences of neuroscience research and brain-related technologies seemed important at that particular time can easily be explained by the role of the 'Decade of the Brain' in this development. The 'Decade of the Brain', delineating the years from 1990 to 1999, is a term coined in the context of an initiative sponsored by the Library of Congress and the National Institute of Mental Health of the National Institutes of Health. The initiative aimed "to enhance public awareness of the benefits to be derived from brain research" by sponsoring activities about cutting-edge neuroscientific research and by "encouraging public dialogue on the ethical, philosophical, and humanistic implications of these emerging discoveries" (Library of Congress, 2000). The benefits of cutting-edge brain research were primarily imagined to be medical in nature. Consequently, money and resources were invested into promising research projects aimed at investigating the neural foundations of mental and neurodegenerative diseases during the Decade of the Brain. Implicit in these investments is the assumption that in the end, mental diseases can be explained and cured by focusing on the brain. The assumption can also be counted as an implicit effect of 'brainhood'.

Brainhood, as a matter of fact, was already the underlying theoretical idea of a very influential research program right before the field of neuroethics officially came to existence. As the Decade of the Brain paved the way toward a heightened public awareness of the most recent developments in neuroscience, including the implications these developments may have in medicine and in other areas of society, it has also influenced the beginning systematic ethical exploration of developments in neuroscience. In view of this, neuroethics as a field can be interpreted as reflecting this general trend toward the penetration of new fields of academic investigation by neuroscience and, hence, to reflect a general neuroscientific turn in society.

On the other hand, there is considerable continuity in neuroethics as to what can be considered to be the scientific discussion of philosophical and ethical issues in the brain sciences. Most of the topics discussed within the newly established field of neuroethics were not new. Ethical issues in the brain sciences had been discussed long before the 'official' emergence of the field of neuroethics. These include reflections on how to manage care for patients with disorders of consciousness or patients with other kinds of severe brain injuries (Tresch et al., 1991; Payne et al., 1996; Childs and Cranford, 1997). Ethical issues in psychiatry (Radden, 1996), issues related to informed consent in mentally impaired persons (Dyer and Bloch, 1987; Zaubler et al., 1996), ethical standards in clinical research in psychiatry (Stanley et al., 1981; Stanley et al., 1996), ethical issues in neurosurgery (Black, 1985) and psychosurgery (Gostin, 1980), and the concept of brain death and its implications (Ad Hoc Committee of the Harvard Medical School, 1968; Pallis, 1983) were also very important. Before 2002, however, a label incorporating all these different ethical questions was missing, and debates were scattered over different disciplines and a large variety of scientific journals. It seems that the Decade of the Brain as a program was necessary to stimulate unification of these activities and to promote the institutionalization of neuroethics. This is reflected, for example, by a quantitative analysis of a database on neuroethics literature hosted by the University of Mainz (Leefmann et al., 2016). This analysis revealed that there was primarily an increase in the amount of publications in the field of neuroethics in the years between 1995 and 2012 but no modification of the broader topics discussed within neuroethics. Hence, the trend toward a neuroscientific turn might have been present before the field of neuroethics was officially established.

It seems, however, remarkable that neuroethical thinking only grew toward its current standing after the Decade of the Brain pushed political and public awareness toward neuroscience. In this regard, the current organizational structure of the field of neuroethics, including its scientific associations and journals, which only came into existence after a critical mass of researchers began to market their research under the label of neuroethics, can clearly be interpreted as the result of a neuroscientific turn. The act of establishing a field that includes many of the ethical problems discussed in other areas of bioethics before and the act of creating the label 'neuroethics' for that field can be understood as an indicator of the influence of 'brainhood'. This is not to say that there is no substance behind neuroethics or that neuroethics is in fact a dubious field. This is simply to say that one important factor in the development of neuroethics is the progression of the assumption that being a conscious human being and being capable of ethical thinking is fundamentally mediated by the organic structure we call the brain and that, hence, the neuroscientific exploration of this structure is crucially important for human self-understanding.

Neuroethics as an Anthropological Amplifier?

In the abovementioned sense, neuroethics is interpreted as the result of a larger historical development for which it bears no responsibility. It is an indicator of a general neuroscientific turn, but it is not its cause. This becomes particularly clear if one regards neuroethics as reactive to technological developments that emerged as a result of scientific efforts during the Decade of the Brain. Neuroethics is to a considerable extent a response to developments in neuroscience as new technologies, tools, and treatments come with additional or modified ethical issues that need interdisciplinary discussion. This is best reflected in the subfield of 'ethics of neuroscience', where much of the ethical discussion focuses on the ethical implications of brain imaging, brain–computer interfaces, deep brain stimulation, and pharmacological cognitive enhancement, subjects being significantly shaped by real or expected advances in brain-related technology. Being reactive to these developments and even trying to actively shape the way technologies come to be used in the different contexts of our lives is one of the fundamental tasks of neuroethics. Interestingly, this task seems to reflect the self-understanding of many researchers in neuroethics. Authors in neuroethics often tend to consider their field to be mainly about the ethical, social, and legal *implications* of neuroscience (Farah and Wolpe, 2004; Illes and Bird, 2006; Farah, 2007). It is characteristic of this view that recent developments and advances in neuroscience are being stressed, in particular current technologies to monitor and manipulate brain functions (Farah and Wolpe, 2004) as being the starting point for neuroethics.

Together with this respondent relation to developments in technology, however, comes a role for neuroethics as a contributor and potential amplifier of the general neuroscientific turn. This role might not be adopted intentionally by neuroethicists, but it is implicated in the whole endeavor of doing neuroethics. The contribution of neuroethics to the neuroscientific turn is, hence, rather indirect. The critical reflection of the ethical and societal implications of new technologies, tools, and treatments helps to further convey a brain-centered view of human persons. Neuroethics, by evoking interventions into the brain as particularly critical processes that can influence human behavior, morality, personality, and moral responsibility, treats the brain exactly as an organ that decisively shapes the way we actually live our lives. It puts the same importance for what we are as humans on the brain as some bioethicists have in earlier times put on the human genome. This view is reductionist in the sense that it tends to limit the perspective on human life to aspects concerning brain functioning. Even if one assumes that the relation between the human brain and many aspects of human life is more robust than the relation between the human genome and the individual human life, this reduction calls for a stronger interdisciplinary embedment of applied neuroethics into the anthropological discourse.

Because of this lack of anthropological embedment, neuroethics has introduced change in the way, for instance, ethical debates about human mental health and mental disorders are shaped (Levy and Clarke, 2008; Cheung, 2009). This becomes particularly obvious in the debate about basing psychiatric nosology more on neuroscientific than on clinical data (Calcedo-Barba, 2010). In this debate, ethical questions in the area of mental health primarily emerge with regard to the neurological understanding of these phenomena (Browning, 2008).

One might, of course, object that this is an unfair argument because it criticizes neuroethics for being simply what it is. However, the problem is not that neuroethics as a field centers on ethical questions as far as they arise from neurological conditions or from technology but that often neuroethics touches complex problems and phenomena only from the limited perspective of neuroscience. With regard to the question of whether neuroethics amplifies the neuroscientific turn, the consequences of this theoretical limitation of neuroethics are crucial.

This unintentional kind of reinforcement of the neuroscientific turn is, however, complemented by two further influences of neuroethics, which are not equally inevitable. The first influence concerns the so-called neuroscience of ethics part of neuroethics. Here, advances in neuroscience are being discussed from a philosophical point of view as having direct implications for the conditions and possibility of human moral behavior. Examples include neuroscientific studies into the basis of moral judgment (Greene et al., 2001; Moll et al., 2002; Raine and Yang, 2006; Fox et al., 2015), studies concerning biases in decision making (Windmann, 2002; Opris and Bruce, 2005; Suriya-Arunroj and Gail, 2015), or neuroscientific investigations into free will (Haggard and Eimer, 1999; Roskies, 2006; Soon et al., 2008; Rigoni et al., 2011). This strand of neuroethics partly follows the agenda of using methods and knowledge from neuroscience and evolutionary psychology to eliminate the idea that morality and ethics are phenomena that cannot be explained unless one refers to concepts irreducible to the physical level (Churchland, 2011).

The second influence of neuroethics on the neuroscientific turn concerns neuroethics more generally. It has been argued that the implicit reference of neuroethics to the idea that human beings essentially are their brains and that human morality is a natural phenomenon is less the expression of empathic affirmation of the anthropological outlook of 'brainhood' itself but rather a form of strategic communication to raise the awareness of the still small and young research field of neuroethics (Abi-Rached, 2008; Brosnan, 2011). If neuroethics can help to regulate technologies that threaten our basic sense of being human, then neuroethics is indeed an important endeavor that is worthy of funding. If this strategy works out, neuroethicists could exploit the idea of 'brainhood' to generate further need for ethical reflection of brain-related technologies by arguing that their research has a fundamental impact on regulating threats to human life and self-understanding that are more fundamental and hence more critical than in other areas of bioethics. It remains to be shown how much of neuroethics actually holds up to these assumptions.

Considering strategic communication of neuroethics, it is, however, remarkable that proponents of the field have considered communication with the public to be one of the central tasks of neuroethics from the beginning (Marcus, 2002; Illes et al., 2005; Illes et al., 2009). By way of this ongoing public engagement, neuroethical thinking is reaching a growing part of society, which may not only raise awareness of neuroethical questions but by way of doing this will also help to further promote 'brainhood' as an anthropological outlook.

To be fair, there are also reasons to be skeptical about the image of neuroethics as a one-sided amplifier of the 'neuroscientific-turn' in this historical sense. The debate on 'neuro-essentialism' in neuroethics is evidence for this. Early on, proponents of neuroethics were concerned with (and about) the ontological reductionism underlying the idea that all psychological experience essentially is a neurological process in the brain (Schaffner, 2002; Farah, 2005; Doucet, 2007), and more than a few have critically investigated the question of whether media reports on neuroscience evoke and reinforce that idea (Racine et al., 2005; Racine et al., 2010; Reiner, 2011; O'Connor and Joffe, 2013).

Summing up, with regard to the alleged general neuroscientific turn in Western culture, neuroethics can be seen as an indicator as well as an amplifier of the development. The development of neuroethics was first of all a result of earlier developments in neuroscience that brought about the need for engagement with ethical, legal, and social aspects of new technologies and scientific approaches. On the other hand, neuroethics' centering on a neuroscientific approach toward human self-understanding and human morality is not suited to resist the pull of the neuroscientific turn. Rather, neuroethics, because of its theoretical outlook, its naturalistic approach toward moral phenomena, and perhaps also because of its strategic activities to establish itself as a field distinct from bioethics, can be seen to function as an amplifier of the general neuroscientific turn.

Translational Processes in Neuroethics

The second approach to the neuroscientific turn has a more limited perspective on the role of neuroscience in society as far as it focuses on very specific processes of knowledge transfer between neuroscience and other areas of the sciences and society. Considering neuroethics from this perspective, it will be necessary to investigate the concrete processes of interdisciplinary engagement of neuroscience with philosophy, ethics, and society. As Johnson and Littlefield note in their work, translations between neuroscience and the social sciences and humanities are not necessarily unidirectional. Besides the transfer of methods and theories from neuroscience to the social sciences and humanities, there can be translational processes in the opposite directions. For instance, one might interpret Vidal's idea of 'brainhood' as a result of a very long-lasting translational process from the humanities toward the natural sciences including neuroscience. While Vidal claims to witness a transfer of philosophical theories into the field of brain research, the current development of neuroethics, however, is usually conceived of as resulting from translational processes in the opposite direction.

As we will point out, this influence of neuroscience in neuroethics is obvious in both subfields of neuroethics. However, it works in very different ways in these different areas.

At first glance, the influence of neuroscience seems to be most salient in the empirical investigation of human moral behavior and in the debate about free will. Very palpable in this regard are the research projects of moral psychologists and neuroscientists such as Jorge Moll and Joshua Greene that have initiated a considerable discussion about the implications of neuroimaging studies for moral psychology and metaethics (Greene et al., 2001; Moll et al., 2002; Greene et al., 2004). In this context, the neuroscientific approach to free will as promoted by Benjamin Libet and others is also worth mentioning (Libet et al., 1983; Haggard and Eimer, 1999). Whatever the evaluation of the claims of these authors from the perspective of philosophical ethics and the philosophy of free will may be, these discussions at least reveal that neuroscientific methodology, in particular neuroimaging, has become frequently used in areas where this methodology had not been used before. The problematic point of such applications is, however, not the methodology as such but the fact that with any methodological approach, there come theoretical presuppositions about the object under investigation. For instance, to access the phenomenon of human moral behavior with a neuroscientific approach implies a standpoint toward the question of which phenomena count as moral behavior and which do not. It also involves the claim that moral phenomena are at least to a certain extent something that can be investigated with the help of an fMRI scanner. The same holds for empirical investigations of free will.

Taking this stance on phenomena such as human moral behavior or free will is, however, not as straightforward as it is for phenomena that otherwise are typically investigated with neuroimaging technologies. To monitor what happens in the brain of a person who, say, tastes something salty or who is touched on her lips or who performs a calculus task is (more or less) straightforwardly possible by neuroimaging. This is because it is rather uncontroversial what we mean by 'taste' and 'touch' or 'performing a calculus task'. The same, however, cannot be said for 'phenomena' like 'morality' or 'art' or for abstract concepts like 'freedom' or 'ethics'. Framing such entities as 'phenomena' presupposes a theoretical approach that determines what empirical observations would count as evidence in favor of the 'phenomenon'. Hence, to make any proposition about human moral behavior or free will requires an empirical neuroethicist to take sides in the philosophical dispute about what moral behavior or what free will substantially is. What makes a certain behavior a moral behavior instead of an amoral or unmoral behavior? Does one have free will only if one could have done otherwise, or does it suffice for having free will to be able to do what one wants to do, even though one's own will is not a subject of choice? These, however, are philosophical questions, which cannot be answered by neuroscience. To apply the methods of neuroscientific investigation with regard to questions about moral behavior and free will, one has to frame phenomena with the help of theories that neuroscience itself does not provide. This is not to say that neuroscientists do not implicitly presuppose certain conceptions of the phenomena in question—for instance, moral behavior is often simply equalized with altruistic behavior, and many interpreters of Libet's experiment presupposed an incompatibilist conception of free will—but neuroscience has to borrow such conceptions from theories developed in the humanities or social sciences.

Notwithstanding its inevitable and often insufficiently reflected theory-driven character, the so called 'neuroscience of ethics' has on the other hand stimulated an ethical debate focusing on a reconsideration of the question of what we actually do when we make a moral judgment. By revealing much of the influence of emotions and intuitions in moral reasoning, the 'neuroscience of ethics' has taken a substantial step to revive noncognitivist conceptions of morality in metaethical debates. This could be interpreted as a direct influence of neuroscience research on metaethics, even though, from a philosophical point of view, the results of these investigations themselves do not constitute a completely novel theoretical outlook.

On a more general level, it may be said that in this area of neuroethics, neuroimaging studies can function as mediators of theoretical concepts. Neuroscience transmits implicit conceptual presuppositions into a philosophical discourse, sometimes to the effect of reviving certain philosophical arguments or theories. Neuroscience in this regard has an effect on debates insofar as the philosophical discussion turns toward empirical evidence and starts to reconsider arguments and theories. As a result, some theories might become more prominent than others. It has to be mentioned, however, that neither in the debate on ethical theory nor in the debate about free will has neuroscientific experimentation brought about any fundamentally new theoretical options. In these areas, neuroscience does not translate knowledge but at best provides evidence that supports the plausibility of certain philosophical or ethical theories.

Real translational processes from neuroscience to ethical theory are, and perhaps unsurprisingly so, not easy to identify. However, presuming a wider concept of ethics, which besides ethical theory also covers the reflection of legal and policy regulations, it might nevertheless be possible to identify translations of neuroscientific knowledge into ethical debates. These influences therefore do not affect the theoretical level of ethics but concern the changes in the regulations of our social and legal practices—a sector covered by what is often called the ethics of neuroscience. In the following, we would like to briefly discuss two examples of this kind of involvement of neuroethical reasoning in translational processes from neuroscience toward social regulations.

For a long time, addiction was perceived as a kind of weakness of will, which allowed society to hold the addict responsible for his behavior (Foddy and Savulescu, 2010; Vrecko, 2010). Progress in psychiatry and neuroscience, however, has revealed several mechanisms that play a role in the development and maintenance of addictive behaviors and has shown that these cannot be controlled by the 'voluntary forces' of the addict (Volkow and Morales, 2015; Volkow et al., 2016). Hence, nowadays, addiction is primarily seen as a medical condition for which the addict cannot be held responsible, even though there is considerable dispute about the role of enabling conditions at the onset of an addiction affecting responsibility (Leshner, 1997). Scientifically validated treatments of addiction nowadays center on medical and social interventions to enable the addict to regain control over his behavior (Leshner, 1999). Even though the role of confrontation in addiction treatment is still debated (Polcin et al., 2006), scientifically validated methods usually do not demand the confession of guilt or the blaming of the addict.

The framing of addiction as a medical condition has, however, further consequences (Hammer et al., 2013). For instance one could argue that a brain-centered view of addiction could ignore the role of social causes that determine and maintain addictive behaviors. If one reduces addiction to a pathological maladjustment of neurotransmitter systems, treatment will come down to a readjustment. Such chemical readjustments have, however, not proven to be sustainable if personal relationships and social contexts that stimulate previously learned behaviors and reactions are not substantially changed. The vulnerability to becoming addicted in the first place and the probability of having a relapse depend not only on neurological and genetic factors but significantly on a social context that allows and approves of self-administration of drugs. Drug addiction is to a considerable degree a learned behavior that requires a supportive social context to develop in the first place. Likewise, factors external to the agent, such as a stressful social environment, increase relapse susceptibility (Sinha, 2007). While neuroscientific research has, hence, produced very valuable knowledge that might mitigate moralizing about addicts, it might also have the consequence of overlooking the importance of social conditions that indirectly contribute to neurologic deviances. Moreover, the neurobiological model of addiction has been criticized for its modest effects on the implementation of cost-effective policies on the population level (Hall et al., 2015).

Another somewhat different example is the case of autism spectrum disorders (ASD). While the view that addiction should be seen as a medical condition instead of a moral failure is nowadays denied by hardly anyone, in the case of ASD, one can currently witness a growing resistance of affected people to frame their condition as a medical phenomenon that requires treatment (Ortega, 2009; Jaarsma and Welin, 2012). One important reason for this resistance seems to be that ASD is correlated with innate and hardwired differences in brain structure and function that cannot currently be treated with neurological interventions (Di Martino et al., 2014; Hahamy et al., 2015; Crippa et al., 2016). Furthermore, affected people feel that their higher sensitivity to various stimuli, their difficulties with social interaction, and the way they perceive the world in which they are situated allow for a diverse but very valuable form of life (Mottron, 2011). Hence, they demand that their brain differences be acknowledged as a variation but not as a disease. This includes the denial of further neuroscientific research to develop treatments for certain forms of ASD. Other societies have seen similar movements of communities that promote change in norms for health and disease. Examples include the deaf community and the community of persons with dwarfism. What is seemingly new in the neurodiversity movement of the autism community is, however, the reference to neuroscientific research (Ortega, 2009), which indicates a relevant influence of brain science on diversity discourses.

Both examples reveal that what counts as health and disease are normative decisions that are often based on the statistical distribution of biological varieties in a population. Whether a variety is to be regarded as good or bad, however, is not implied by the frequency of the variety in the population but by certain values held in a society. This underlines that neuroscience alone does not and cannot provide any normative criteria for what varieties we should count as healthy or diseased. However, as far as results of neuroscientific research stimulate discourses about medical and social norms, they influence how and with reference to which facts these norms are shaped. As these processes of social and medical norm construction trigger ethical reflection and argumentation about how to construct and justify these norms, neuroethics could be understood as a product of translation from neuroscientific knowledge into the sphere of social life.

Conclusion

We have discussed the role of neuroethics with regard to two different conceptualizations of the neuroscientific turn. Neuroethics affects and is at the same time affected by the neuroscientific turn, if this turn is conceptualized as a general cultural movement. The existence and development of neuroethics is clearly indicative of a larger cultural turn in philosophy and the sciences that conceptualize the brain as an extremely important structure for understanding what it means to be human. On the other hand, parts of neuroethics can reasonably be described as amplifying this trend toward a neurologization by strongly favoring a naturalistic approach toward moral phenomena and by strategic activities to demarcate neuroethic from bioethics. With regard to the second conceptualization of the neuroscientific turn as a translational process among neuroscience, the social sciences and humanities, and society as a whole, we drew a similar conclusion. As far as neuroethics is involved in the philosophical and ethical debates stimulated by neuroscientific investigations and as far as neuroethics engages in the critical ethical reflection and implementation of social and legal norms that relate to neuroscientific knowledge, it is also clearly engaged in such a process. Therefore, most of what researchers in neuroethics do is embedded in a complex set of relations toward various scientific disciplines and toward various social discourses. As reference to neuroscientific knowledge becomes increasingly common in many of them, neuroethicists have to be extremely reflective and sensitive about the potential social and cultural consequences of their own involvement in these debates.

Acknowledgments

The authors are very much indebted to Kelly Laas (Illinois Institute of Technology) for her help with language editing. Writing this article would not have been possible without the support of a research grant from the German Research Foundation (DFG) for the project The 'Neuro-turn' in European Social Sciences and Humanities (NESSHI; grant number: HI: 1328/2–1).

Further Reading

Johnson, J.M. and Littlefield, M.M. (Eds.) (2012). *The Neuroscientific Turn: Transdisciplinarity in the Age of the Brain*. Ann Arbor: University of Michigan Press.

Rose, N. and Abi-Rached, J.M. (2013). *Neuro: The New Brain Sciences and the Management of the Mind.* Princeton, NJ: Princeton University Press.

Thornton, D.J. (2011). *Brain Culture: Neuroscience and Public Media.* New Brunswick: Rutgers University Press.

Vidal, F. (2009). "Brainhood, anthropological figure of modernity". *History of the Human Sciences* 22(1), 5–36.

Vos, J.D. and Pluth, E. (2016). *Neuroscience and Critique: Exploring the Limits of the Neurological Turn.* Abingdon, Oxon and New York: Routledge.

References

Abi-Rached, J.M. (2008) The implications of the new brain sciences: The 'Decade of the Brain' is over, but its effects are now becoming visible as neuropolitics and neuroethics, and in the emergence of neuro-economies. *EMBO Reports* 9(12): pp. 1158–1162.

Ad Hoc Committee of the Harvard Medical School. (1968) A definition of irreversible coma. *The Journal of American Medical Association* 205(6): pp. 337–340.

Ariely, D., and Berns, G.S. (2010) Neuromarketing: The hope and hype of neuroimaging in business. *Nature Reviews Neuroscience* 11(4): pp. 284–292.

Battro, A.M., Fischer, K.W., and Léna, P. (Eds.) (2008) *The Educated Brain: Essays in Neuroeducation.* Cambridge, New York: Cambridge University Press.

Berker, S. (2009) The normative insignificance of neuroscience. *Philosophy & Public Affairs* 37(4): pp. 293–329.

Black, P.M. (1985) Medical ethics in neurology and neurosurgery. *Neurologic Clinics* 3(2): pp. 215–228.

Brenninkmeijer, J. (2010) Taking care of one's brain: How manipulating the brain changes people's self. *History of the Human Sciences* 23(1): pp. 107–126.

Broer, T., and Pickersgill, M. (2015) Targeting brains, producing responsibilities: The use of neuroscience within British social policy. *Social Science & Medicine* 132: pp. 54–61.

Brosnan, C. (2011) The sociology of neuroethics: Expectational discourses and the rise of a new discipline. *Sociology Compass* 5(4): pp. 287–297.

Browning, D. (2008) Internists of the mind or physicians of the soul: Does psychiatry need a public philosophy? *Zygon* 43(2): pp. 371–383.

Calcedo-Barba, A. (2010) Objectivity and ethics in forensic psychiatry. *Current Opinion in Psychiatry* 23(5): pp. 447–452.

Casebeer, W.D. (2003) Moral cognition and its neural constituents. *Nature Reviews Neuroscience* 4(10): pp. 840–847.

Chatterjee, A., and Vartanian, O. (2014) Neuroaesthetics. *Trends in Cognitive Sciences* 18(7): pp. 370–375.

Cheung, E.H. (2009) A new ethics of psychiatry: Neuroethics, neuroscience, and technology. *Journal of Psychiatric Practice* 15(5): pp. 391–401.

Childs, N.L., and Cranford, R.E. (1997) Termination of nutrition and hydration in the minimally conscious state. *Head Trauma Rehabilitation* 12(4): pp. 70–78.

Choudhury, S., McKinney, K.A., and Merten, M. (2012) Rebelling against the brain: Public engagement with the 'neurological adolescent'. *Social Science & Medicine* 74(4): pp. 565–573.

Choudhury, S., Nagel, S.K., and Slaby, J. (2009) Critical neuroscience: Linking neuroscience and society through critical practice. *BioSocieties* 4(1): pp. 61–77.

Christen, M., Biller-Andorno, N., Bringedal, B., Grimes, K., Savulescu, J. and Walter, H. (2016) Ethical challenges of simulation-driven big neuroscience. *American Journal of Bioethics Neuroscience* 7(1): pp. 5–17.

Churchland, P.S. (1986) *Neurophilosophy: Toward a Unified Science of the Mind-Brain.* 3rd ed. Cambridge, MA: Bradford Book.

———. (2011) *Braintrust: What Neuroscience Tells Us About Morality.* Princeton, NJ: Princeton University Press.

Cohen Kadosh, R., Levy, N., O'Shea, J., Shea, N., and Savulescu, J. (2012) The neuroethics of non-invasive brain stimulation. *Current Biology: CB* 22(4): pp. R108–R111.

Cooter, R. (2014) Neural veils and the will to historical critique: Why historians of science need to take the neuro-turn seriously. *Isis* 105(1): pp. 145–154.

Crippa, A., Del, V.G., Busti, C.S., Nobile, M., Arrigoni, F., and Brambilla, P. (2016) Cortico-cerebellar connectivity in autism spectrum disorder: What do we know so far? *Frontiers in Psychiatry* 7(20).

Damasio, A.R. (1995) Descartes' error. *MLN* 110(4): pp. 943–952.

———. (2003) *Looking for Spinoza: Joy Sorrow and the Feeling Brain.* Orlando: Harcourt.

Di Martino, A., Yan, C.G., Li, Q., Denio, E., Castellanos, F.X. and Alaerts, K. (2014) The autism brain imaging data exchange: Towards a large-scale evaluation of the intrinsic brain architecture in autism. *Molecular Psychiatry* 19(6): pp. 659–667.

Doucet, H. (2007) Anthropological challenges raised by neuroscience: Some ethical reflections. *Cambridge Quarterly of Healthcare Ethics* 16(2), pp. 219–226.

Dyer, A.R., and Bloch, S. (1987) Informed consent and the psychiatric patient. *Journal of Medical Ethics* 13: pp. 12–16.

Edelman, G.M. (2005) *Wider Than the Sky: A Revolutionary View of Consciousness.* London: Penguin.

Ehrenberg, A. (2010) *The Weariness of the Self: Diagnosing the History of Depression in the Contemporary Age.* Montreal: McGill-Queen's University Press.

Evers, K. (2007) Towards a philosophy for neuroethics: An informed materialist view of the brain might help to develop theoretical frameworks for applied neuroethics. *EMBO Reports* 8: pp. S48—S51.

Farah, M.J. (2005) Neuroethics: The practical and the philosophical. *Trends in Cognitive Sciences* 9(1): pp. 34–40.

———. (2007) Social, legal, and ethical implications of cognitive neuroscience: "Neuroethics" for short. *Journal of Cognitive Neuroscience* 19(3): pp. 363–364.

Farah, M.J., Smith, M. E., Gawuga, C., Lindsell, D. and Foster, D. (2009) Brain imaging and brain privacy: A realistic concern? *Journal of Cognitive Neuroscience* 21(1): pp. 119–127.

Farah, M.J., and Wolpe, P.R. (2004) Monitoring and manipulating brain function: Neuroscience technologies and their ethical implications. *Hastings Center Report* 34(3): pp. 35–45.

Farisco, M., Evers, K., and Salles, A. (2016) Big science, brain simulation, and neuroethics. *American Journal of Bioethics Neuroscience* 7(1): pp. 28–30.

Ferrari, A., Coenen, C., and Grunwald, A. (2012) Visions and ethics in current discourse on human enhancement. *NanoEthics* 6(3): pp. 215–229.

Fitz, N.S., and Reiner, P.B. (2015) The challenge of crafting policy for do-it-yourself brain stimulation. *Journal of Medical Ethics* 41(5): pp. 410–412.

Foddy, B., and Savulescu, J. (2010). A liberal account of addiction. *Philosophy, Psychiatry & Psychology* 17(1): pp. 1–22.

Fox, G.R., *et al.* (2015) Neural correlates of gratitude. *Frontiers in Psychology* 6: p. 1491.

Franks, D.D. (2010) *Neurosociology: The Nexus Between Neuroscience and Social Psychology.* New York, Dordrecht, Heidelberg, and London: Springer-Verlag.

Fujino, J., Takahashi, H., Mijata, J., Sugihara, G., Kubota, M., Sesamoto, A., Fujiwara, H., Aso, T., Fukujama, H., and Murai, T. (2014) Impaired empathic abilities and reduced white matter integrity in schizophrenia. *Progress in Neuro-Psychopharmacology & Biological Psychiatry* 48: pp. 117–123.

Gazzaniga, M.S. (2005) *The Ethical Brain.* New York: Dana Press.

Glimcher, P.W., and Fehr, E. (Eds.) (2014) *Neuroeconomics: Decision Making and the Brain.* 2nd ed. London: Academic Press.

Gostin, L.O. (1980) Ethical considerations of psychosurgery: The unhappy legacy of the pre-frontal lobotomy. *Journal of Medical Ethics* 6(3): pp. 149–154.

Grau, C., Ginhoux, R., Riera, A., Nguyen, T. L., Chauvat, H. and Berg, M. (2014) Conscious brain-to-brain communication in humans using non-invasive technologies. *PLoS ONE* 9(8).

Greene, J. (2003) From neural 'is' to moral 'ought': What are the moral implications of neuroscientific moral psychology? *Nature Reviews: Neuroscience* 4(10): pp. 846–849.

———. (2014) *Moral Tribes: Emotion, Reason and the Gap Between Us and Them*. New York: Atlantic Books Ltd.

Greene, J.D., Sommerville, B.R., Nystrom, L.E., Darley, J.M. and Cohen, J.D. (2001) An fMRI investigation of emotional engagement in moral judgment. *Science* 293(5537): pp. 2105–2108.

Greene, J.D., Nystrom, L.E., Engell, A.D., Darley, J.M. and Cohen, J.D. (2004) The neural bases of cognitive conflict and control in moral judgment. *Neuron* 44(2): pp. 389–400.

Grübler, G., Al-Khodairy, A., Leeb, R., Pisotta, I., Riccio, A., Rohm, M. and Hildt, E. (2014) Psychosocial and ethical aspects in non-invasive EEG-based BCI research—A survey among BCI users and BCI professionals. *Neuroethics* 7(1): pp. 29–41.

Haggard, P., and Eimer, M. (1999) On the relation between brain potentials and the awareness of voluntary movements. *Experimental Brain Research* 126(1): pp. 128–133.

Hahamy, A., Behrmann, M., and Malach, R. (2015) The idiosyncratic brain: Distortion of spontaneous connectivity patterns in autism spectrum disorder. *Nature Neuroscience* 18(2): pp. 302–309.

Hall, W., Carter, A., and Forlini, C. (2015) The brain disease model of addiction: Is it supported by the evidence and has it delivered on its promises? *The Lancet Psychiatry* 2(1): 105–110.

Hammer, R., Dingle, M., Ostergren, J., Partridge, B., McCormick, J. and Koenig, B.A. (2013) Addiction: Current criticism of the brain disease paradigm. *American Journal of Bioethics Neuroscience* 4(3): pp. 27–32.

Heatherton, T.F., and Wagner, D.D. (2011) Cognitive neuroscience of self-regulation failure. *Trends in Cognitive Sciences* 15(3): pp. 132–139.

Heinzelmann, N., Ugazio, G., and Tobler, P.N. (2012) Practical implications of empirically studying moral decision-making. *Frontiers in Neuroscience* 6: p. 94.

Illes, J., Blakemore, C., Hansson, M.G., Hensch, T.K., Leschner, A., Maestre, G., Magistretti, P., Quirion, R., and Strata, P. (2005) International perspectives on engaging the public in neuroethics. *Nature Reviews Neuroscience* 6(12): pp. 977–982.

———. (2009) Neurotalk: Improving the communication of neuroscience research. *Nature Reviews Neuroscience* 11(1): pp. 61–69.

Illes, J., and Bird, S.J. (2006) Neuroethics: A modern context for ethics in neuroscience. *Trends in Neurosciences* 29(9): pp. 511–517.

Jaarsma, P., and Welin, S. (2012) Autism as a natural human variation: Reflections on the claims of the neurodiversity movement. *Health Care Analysis* 20(1): pp. 20–30.

Johnson, J.M., and Littlefield, M.M. (2011) Lost and found in translation: Popular neuroscience in the emerging Neuro-Disciplines. In M. Pickersgill and I. van Keulen (Eds.). *Sociological Reflections on the Neurosciences*. Bingley: Emerald, pp. 279–297.

———. (Eds.) (2012) *The Neuroscientific Turn: Transdisciplinarity in the Age of the Brain*. Ann Arbor: University of Michigan Press.

Jotterand, F., and Giordano, J. (2011) Transcranial magnetic stimulation, deep brain stimulation and personal identity: Ethical questions, and neuroethical approaches for medical practice. *International Review of Psychiatry (Abingdon, England)* 23(5): pp. 476–485.

Joyce, R. (2008) What neuroscience can (and cannot) contribute to metaethics. In W. Sinnott-Armstrong (Ed.). *The Neuroscience of Morality: Emotion, Brain Disorders, and Development*. Cambridge, MA: MIT Press, pp. 371–394.

Kalis, A., Mojzisch, A., Schweizer, T. S. and Kaiser, S. (2008) Weakness of will, akrasia, and the neuropsychiatry of decision making: An interdisciplinary perspective. *Cognitive, Affective & Behavioral Neuroscience* 8(4): pp. 402–417.

Lee, N., Broderick, A.J., and Chamberlain, L. (2007) What is 'neuromarketing'? A discussion and agenda for future research. *International Journal of Psychophysiology* 63(2): pp. 199–204.

Leefmann, J., Levallois, C., and Hildt, E. (2016) Neuroethics 1995–2012: A bibliometrical analysis of the guiding themes of an emerging research field. *Frontiers in Human Neuroscience* 10.

Lende, D.H., and Downey, G. (Eds.) (2012) *The Encultured Brain: An Introduction to Neuroanthropology*. Cambridge, MA: MIT Press.

Leshner, A. (1997) Addiction is a brain disease, and it matters. *Science* 278(5335): pp. 45–47.

———. (1999) Science-based views of drug addiction and its treatment. *The Journal of American Medical Association* 282(14): p. 1314.

Levy, N., and Clarke, S. (2008) Neuroethics and psychiatry. *Current Opinion in Psychiatry* 21(6): pp. 568–571.

Libet, B., Gleason, C., Wright, E. and Pearl, D.K. (1983) Time of conscious intention to action relation to onset of cerebral activity (readiness potential): The unconscious initiation of a freely voluntary act. *Brain* 106: pp. 623–664.

Library of Congress. (2000) *Project on the Decade of the Brain* [Online]. Available at: www.loc.gov/loc/brain [Accessed 2 Dec. 2015].

Littlefield, M.M., and Johnson, J.M. (2012) Introduction: Theorizing the neuroscientific turn—Critical perspectives on a translational discipline. In J.M. Johnson and M.M. Littlefield (Eds.). *The Neuroscientific Turn: Transdisciplinarity in the Age of the Brain*. Ann Arbor: University of Michigan Press, pp. 1–27.

Loewenstein, G., Rick, S., and Cohen, J.D. (2008) Neuroeconomics. *Annual Review of Psychology* 59(1): pp. 647–672.

Lombera, S., and Illes, J. (2009) The international dimensions of neuroethics. *Developing World Bioethics* 9(2): pp. 57–64.

Malabou, C. (2008) *What Should We Do With Our Brain?* New York: Fordham University Press.

Marcus, S.J. (Ed.). (2002) *Neuroethics: Mapping the Field: Conference Proceedings, May 13–14, 2002 San Francisco, California*. New York: Dana Press.

Meegan, D.V. (2008) Neuroimaging techniques for memory detection: Scientific, ethical, and legal issues. *The American Journal of Bioethics: AJOB* 8(1): pp. 9–20.

Metzinger, T.K. (2010) *The Ego Tunnel: The Science of the Mind and the Myth of the Self*. New York: Basic Books.

Moll, J., Oliveira-Souza, R., Eislinger, P.J., Bramati, I.E. and Murao-Miranda, J. (2002) The neural correlates of moral sensitivity: A functional magnetic resonance imaging investigation into basic and moral emotions. *The Journal of Neuroscience* 22(7): pp. 2730–2736.

Mottron, L. (2011) Changing perception: The power of autism. *Nature* 479(7371): pp. 33–35.

Newberg, A. (2013) *Principles of Neurotheology: Children's True Stories*. Farnham: Ashgate.

Northoff, G. (2006) Neuroscience of decision making and informed consent: An investigation in neuroethics. *Journal of Medical Ethics* 32(2): pp. 70–73.

———. (2009) What is neuroethics? Empirical and theoretical neuroethics. *Current Opinion in Psychiatry* 22(6): pp. 565–569.

———. (2010) Humans, brains, and their environment: Marriage between neuroscience and anthropology? *Neuron* 65(6): pp. 748–751.

O'Connor, C., and Joffe, H. (2013) How has neuroscience affected lay understandings of personhood? A review of the evidence. *Public Understanding of Science (Bristol, England)* 22(3): pp. 254–268.

Opris, I., and Bruce, C.J. (2005) Neural circuitry of judgment and decision mechanisms. *Brain Research: Brain Research Reviews* 48(3): pp. 509–526.

Ortega, F. (2009) The cerebral subject and the challenge of neurodiversity. *BioSocieties* 4(4): pp. 425–445.

Outram, S.M. (2012) Ethical considerations in the framing of the cognitive enhancement debate. *Neuroethics* 5(2): pp. 173–184.

Pais-Vieira, M., Chiuffa, G., Lebedev, M., Yadav, A. and Nicolelis, M.A.L. (2015) Building an organic computing device with multiple interconnected brains. *Scientific Reports* 5.

Pallis, C. (1983) Whole brain death reconsidered: Physiological facts and philosophy. *Journal of Medical Ethics* 9(1): pp. 32–37.

Parens, E., and Johnston, J. (2007) Does it make sense to speak of neuroethics? Three problems with keying ethics to hot new science and technology. *EMBO Reports* 8: pp. S61–S64.

Payne, K., Taylor, R.M., Stocking, C. and Sachs, G.A. (1996) Physicians' attitudes about the care of patients in the persistent vegetative state: A national survey. *Annals of Internal Medicine* 125(2): p. 104.

Pickersgill, M. (2013) The social life of the Brain: Neuroscience in society. *Current Sociology* 61(3): pp. 322–340.

Pitts-Taylor, V. (2010) The plastic brain: Neoliberalism and the neuronal self. *Health: An Interdisciplinary Journal for the Social Study of Health, Illness and Medicine* 14(6): pp. 635–652.

Polcin D.L., Galloway G.P., and Greenfield T.K. (2006) Measuring confrontation during recovery from addiction. *Substance Use Misuse* 41(3): pp. 369–392.

Prinz, J.J. (2006) *Gut Reactions: A Perceptual Theory of Emotion.* Oxford: Oxford University Press.

Racine, E., Waldman, S., Rosenberg, J. and Illes, J. (2010) Contemporary neuroscience in the media. *Social Science & Medicine (1982)* 71(4): pp. 725–733.

Racine, E., Bar-Ilan, O., and Illes, J. (2005) fMRI in the public eye. *Nature Reviews Neuroscience* 6(2): pp. 159–164.

Racine, E., Bell, E., and Zizzo, N. (2015) Deep brain stimulation: A principled and pragmatic approach to understanding the ethical and clinical challenges of an evolving technology. *Current Topics in Behavioral Neurosciences* 19: pp. 243–263.

Radden, J. (1996) *Divided Minds and Successive Selves: Ethical Issues in Disorders of Identity and Personality.* Cambridge, MA: MIT Press.

Raine, A., and Yang, Y. (2006) Neural foundations to moral reasoning and antisocial behavior. *Social Cognitive and Affective Neuroscience* 1(3): pp. 203–213.

Rao, R.P.N., Stocco, A., Bryan, M., Sarma, D., Youngquist, T.M., Wu, J. and Prat, C.S. (2014) A direct brain-to-brain interface in humans. *PLoS ONE* 9(11).

Reiner, P.B. (2011) The rise of neuroessentialism. In J. Illes and B.J. Sahakian (Eds.). *Oxford Handbook of Neuroethics.* Oxford: Oxford University Press, pp. 161–176.

Rigoni, D., Kuhn, S., Sartori, G. and Brass, M. (2011) Inducing disbelief in free will alters brain correlates of preconscious motor preparation: The brain minds whether we believe in free will or not. *Psychological Science* 22(5): pp. 613–618.

Rose, N. (2007) *The Politics of Life Itself: Biomedicine, Power and Subjectivity in the Twenty-First Century.* Princeton, NJ: Princeton University Press.

———. (2008) Psychiatry as a social science. *Subjectivity* 25(1): pp. 446–462.

Rose, N., and Abi-Rached, J.M. (2013) *Neuro: The New Brain Sciences and the Management of the Mind.* Princeton, NJ: Princeton University Press.

Roskies, A. (2002) Neuroethics for the new millennium. *Neuron* 35(1): pp. 21–23.

———. (2006) Neuroscientific challenges to free will and responsibility. *Trends in Cognitive Sciences* 10(9): pp. 419–423.

Schaffner, K.F. (2002) Neuroethics: Reductionism, emergence, and decision-making capacities. In S.J. Marcus (Ed.). *Neuroethics: Mapping the Field: Conference Proceedings, May 13–14, 2002 San Francisco, California.* New York: Dana Press, pp. 27–33.

Schermer, M. (2011) Ethical issues in deep brain stimulation. *Frontiers in Integrative Neuroscience* 5: p. 17.

Schicktanz, S., Amelung, T., and Rieger, J.W. (2015) Qualitative assessment of patients' attitudes and expectations toward BCIs and implications for future technology development. *Frontiers in Systems Neuroscience* 9: p. 64.

Scurich, N., and Shniderman, A. (2014) The selective allure of neuroscientific explanations. *PLoS ONE* 9(9): p. e107529.

Sinha, R. (2007) The role of stress in addiction relapse. *Current Psychiatry Reports* 9(5): pp. 388–395.

Sinnott-Armstrong, W. (2006) Moral intuitionism meets empirical psychology. In T. Horgan and M. Timmons (Eds.). *Metaethics After Moore.* New York, Oxford: Oxford University Press, pp. 339–365.

Smail, D. (2007) *On Deep History and the Brain.* Berkeley: University of California Press.

———. (2014) Neurohistory in action: Hoarding and the human past. *Isis* 105(1): pp. 110–122.

Soon, C.S., Brass, M., Heinze, H.J. and Haynes, J.D. (2008) Unconscious determinants of free decisions in the human brain. *Nature Neuroscience* 11(5): pp. 543–545.

Stanley, B., Nelton G.B. and Sieber, J.E. (1981) Preliminary findings on psychiatric patients as research participants: A population at risk? *American Journal of Psychiatry* 138(5): pp. 669–671.

Stanley, B., Nelton, G.B., and Sieber, J.E. (Eds.) (1996) *Research Ethics: A Psychological Approach*. Lincoln, NE: University of Nebraska Press.

Stuss, D.T., and Knight, R.T. (2013) *Principles of Frontal Lobe Function*. New York: Oxford University Press.

Supady, A., Voelkel, A., Witzel, J., Gubka, U. and Northoff, G. (2011) How is informed consent related to emotions and empathy? An exploratory neuroethical investigation. *Journal of Medical Ethics* 37(5): pp. 311–317.

Suriya-Arunroj, L., and Gail, A. (2015) I plan therefore I choose: Free-choice bias due to prior action-probability but not action-value. *Frontiers in Behavioral Neuroscience* 9: p. 315.

Tamburrini, G. (2009) Brain to computer communication: Ethical perspectives on interaction models. *Neuroethics* 2(3): pp. 137–149.

TenHouten, W. (1997) Neurosociology. *Journal of Social and Evolutionary Systems* 20(1): pp. 7–37.

Thaler, R.H., and Sunstein, C.R. (2009) *Nudge: Improving Decisions About Health, Wealth and Happiness*. London: Penguin.

Thornton, D.J. (2011) *Brain Culture: Neuroscience and Public Media*. New Brunswick: Rutgers University Press.

Trémeau, F., Antonius, D., Todorov, A., Rebani, Y., Ferrari, K. and Lee, S.H. (2015) Implicit emotion perception in schizophrenia. *Journal of Psychiatric Research* 71: pp. 112–119.

Tresch, D.D., Sims, F.H., Duthie, E.H. and Goldstein, M.D. (1991) Patients in a persistent vegetative state attitudes and reactions of family members. *Journal of the American Geriatrics Society* 39(1): pp. 17–21.

Unterrainer, M., and Oduncu, F.S. (2015) The ethics of deep brain stimulation (DBS). *Medicine, Health Care, and Philosophy* 18(4): pp. 475–485.

Vidal, F. (2009) Brainhood, anthropological figure of modernity. *History of the Human Sciences* 22(1): pp. 5–36.

Volkow, N.D., Koob, G.F., and McLellan, A.T. (2016) Neurobiologic advances from the brain disease model of addiction. *The New England Journal of Medicine* 374(4): pp. 363–371.

Volkow, N.D., and Morales, M. (2015) The brain on drugs: From reward to addiction. *Cell* 162(4): pp. 712–725.

Vrecko, S. (2010) Birth of a brain disease: Science, the state and addiction neuorpolitics. *History of the Human Sciences* 23(4): pp. 52–67.

Wade, M. (2015) Neuroethics and ideals of the citizen-subject: A sociological critique of an emerging discipline. In T. Petary and A. Stephens (Eds.). *Proceedings of the Australasian Sociological Association Conference*. Cairns, 23–26 November.

Wardlaw, J.M., Davies, H., Booth, T.C., Laurie, G., Compston, A. and Freeman, C. (2015) Acting on incidental findings in research imaging. *BMJ (Clinical research ed.)* 351.

Wilfond, B.S., and Ravitsky, V. (2005) On the proliferation of bioethics sub-disciplines: Do we really need 'Genethics' and 'Neuroethics'? *The American Journal of Bioethics* 5(2): pp. 20–21.

Windmann, S. (2002) Cognitive and neural mechanisms of decision biases in recognition memory. *Cerebral Cortex* 12(8): pp. 808–817.

Zaki, J., Ochsner, K.N., and Ochsner, K. (2012) The neuroscience of empathy: Progress, pitfalls and promise. *Nature Neuroscience* 15(5): pp. 675–680.

Zaubler, T.S., Viederman, M., and Fins, J.J. (1996) Ethical, legal, and psychiatric issues in capacity, competency, and informed consent: An annotated bibliography. *General Hospital Psychiatry* 18(3): pp. 155–172.

Zeki, S. (1999) *Inner Vision: An Exploration of Art and the Brain*. Oxford: Oxford University Press.

PART II

The Ethics of Neuroscience

Four real-world contexts in which neuroethical issues arise and impact society are the focus in this section of the book: medical and clinical neuroethics, enhancement, legal and national security domains, and commercial enterprises and applications of neurotechnologies. The ethical concerns are complex when brain health and interventions on the brain are considered. Brain disorders impact not only our bodily health but also who we essentially think we are and, in some cases, who we might become.

Medical and Clinical Neuroethics

Clinical discussions in this section consider the ethical implications of rapidly evolving diagnostic technologies, as well as concerns about pathologizing difference and the value of neurodiversity. This section also discusses the blurring lines of diagnosis and treatment. Goering's chapter "Thinking Differently: Neurodiversity and Neural Engineering" endorses a mode of doing neural engineering in a way that takes neurodiversity seriously and is responsive to the perspectives of end users of neurotechnologies. In "The Ethics of Expanding Applications of Deep Brain Stimulation," Christen and Müller consider unique ethical considerations in expanding clinical use of deep brain stimulation in patients with neurological disorders. "The Ethics of Prodromal and Preclinical Disease Stages" by Arias, Sarrett, Gonzalez, and Walker examines the potential and implications for early detection of disorders such as autism spectrum disorder, schizophrenia, and Alzheimer's disease. In their chapter on disorders of consciousness, Friedrich and Jox explore novel technologies for diagnosing awareness in humans who appear otherwise nonresponsive. The final chapter in this section, "Placebo and Psychogenic Disorders" by Grubbs and Rommelfanger, explores how neuroscience information on both treatments and disorders of "mind" challenge our conceptualization of psychiatric phenomena such as placebo effects and so-called psychogenic disorders.

Enhancement

Human enhancement through genetic and pharmacological interventions has been a rich topic of debate in bioethics. Neuroethics has taken up the debate, with specific emphasis on brain interventions that might enhance cognition, memory, attention, and even human capacities for moral reasoning. In his chapter "Cosmetic Neurology and the Ethics of Enhancement," Chatterjee considers how advances in neuroscience and pharmacotherapeutics are opening up possibilities for manipulating cognitive and emotional systems in healthy people and the ethical concerns that arise with such practices. Mann and Sahakian consider technologies used in competitive education and professional/workplace environments and discuss the use of "smart drugs" in "Modafinil and the Increasing Lifestyle Use of Smart Drugs by Healthy People: Neuroethical and Societal Issues." Tennison and Moreno consider possible dual-use applications of neurotechnology, including brain-interfacing technologies and cognitive enhancement for improving soldier performance. These uses raise fresh concerns about consent and coercion, while the therapeutic use of neurotechnologies like "forgetting pills" and deep brain stimulation to treat combat-related conditions like PTSD add urgency and currency to the long-standing debate about the distinction between treatment and enhancement. The potential weaponization of neurotechnologies for use in psychological warfare, torture, and interrogation are also discussed. This section concludes with "Moral Neuroenhancement" by Earp, Douglas, and Savulescu, an exploration of the promise and possible pitfalls of using neurotechnologies to facilitate moral enhancement.

Legal and National Security Domains

Legal discussions in this section will highlight the use of neurotechnologies for detecting *mens rea* ("guilty mind") and criminal culpability, lies and guilty knowledge, and considerations about cognitive privacy and liberty. Brain-imaging data are finding their way into the courtroom as evidence and as potential testimony, and while many commentators take the view that neurotechnological "lie detection" and "mind reading," while theoretically and philosophically compelling, are not ready for prime time, that skepticism does not reflect the enthusiasm for the use of technology in legal and judicial contexts. Some legal scholars and practitioners argue that, while these sources of information may not be perfected in the clinical or research domain, they are welcome improvements to current legal approaches, and they may be "good enough" for the legal context. Hardcastle's chapter "My Brain Made Me Do It? Neuroscience and Criminal Responsibility" explores how the disconnect between theory and practice creates significant potential for abuse and misuse. On the other hand, a greater understanding of the neurological underpinnings of some criminal behavior might reshape the criminal justice system's approach to responsibility, punishment, and rehabilitation. In "Your Brain on Lies: Deception Detection in Court," Seaman surveys the current state of the science of lie detection and considers the evidentiary, constitutional, and ethical issues raised by its potential future use in legal contexts. Wolpe explores the concept of cognitive liberty, considering the possibilities for neurotechnologies to facilitate cognitive/affective coercion, and the privacy implications of brain monitoring. This section concludes with Johnson's chapter "Chronic Traumatic Encephalopathy: Ethical, Legal, and Social Implications," on the underexplored ramifications of prospective diagnosis of neurodegenerative brain disease in athletes.

Commercial

Commercial applications of neurotechnologies for cognitive enhancement have proliferated in recent years, even as evidence backing up claims about enhancement remains sparse. Public enthusiasm for neuroscience has been sparked, in part, by an ever-growing tendency toward neurohype and the proliferation of "neuro" neologisms and neurotechnology-oriented consumer products. Neuroscience is even being utilized for neuromarketing as a tool to identify consumer preferences and decision-making practices. "Neurohype: A Field Guide to Exaggerated Brain-Based Claims," by Lilienfeld, Aslinger, Marshall, and Satel is a useful resource for inoculation against "neurohype," with a helpful checklist for the critical consumer of neuroscience. In "Neuroscience Online: Real Ethical Issues in Virtual Realms," Purcell and Rommelfanger address the significant privacy and safety concerns and the lack of regulatory oversight for neuroscience in this growing commercial domain. In the absence of formal guidelines to protect the privacy of such data or to monitor the informed consent process in this kind of research, users risk their cognitive privacy and liberties, which, if violated, could ultimately lead to public distrust that undermines scientific progress. Wexler and Reiner shed light on the do-it-yourself (DIY) biohacker movement and transhumanism market in "Home Use of tDCS: From 'Do-It-Yourself' to 'Direct-to-Consumer.'"

3

THINKING DIFFERENTLY
Neurodiversity and Neural Engineering

Sara Goering

How we think is a fundamental part of who we are. We identify not just with our bodies or our roles and relationships but with how we *think* about our bodies, roles, and relationships. This sense of identity runs deeper than just *what* we think—the content of our thought—and into *how* we think—the way in which our minds work. In some cases (e.g., treatment for depression or obsessive-compulsive disorder), we assume that how we think is at least somewhat malleable—we enter into therapy, take medication, or adopt some combination of these measures under the presumption that we can alter our cognitive processing in desired and meaningful ways without really changing our identities. In other cases, our modes of thinking seem more entrenched. We may seek to alter them, but they persist. Or perhaps we simply identify with a mode of thinking that is not standard; we claim it as our own way of being. Others may recommend treatment, but we reject it. We think differently from the norm, and we're okay with that.

In this chapter, I want to look at two different kinds of "thinking differently"—the neurodiversity movement and neural engineering, a field that seeks to create devices designed to engineer certain aspects of our thinking, in order to help us with neurological processing. The former typically seeks to preserve and value diverse functioning; the latter typically seeks to restore "normal" functioning. Here I argue that the two need not be at cross-purposes but could productively be brought into conversation. Their intersection recommends a mode of doing neural engineering that takes neurodiversity seriously and recognizes the wide range of acceptable neurological functioning. More importantly, it identifies a good way to ensure that recognition—by including the perspectives of potential "end users" of neural technology in the development and design process of neurally engineered devices.

The chapter will consist of three sections: (1) an overview of the neurodiversity movement and its claims regarding medical research and advocacy campaigns designed to treat and/or prevent the conditions (and modes of thinking) in question; (2) a look at how neural engineers are developing technologies that may affect how we think or perform neurological processing and that are designed to aid people with neurological disorders in order to improve their quality of life; and (3) an exploration of what neural engineers might productively learn from the neurodiversity movement.

Neurodiversity

Though many people have struggled throughout recent history for civil rights and respect for people whose modes of thinking are not standard, the label "neurodiversity movement" came into use only in the late 1990s (Silberman, 2015). And, although the label is most frequently associated with advocates for autism, other groups have found solidarity with the movement's general aims. Thomas Armstrong, for instance, includes people who experience dyslexia, attention deficit hyperactivity disorder (ADHD), autism, bipolar disorder, and other psychiatric conditions (Armstrong, 2010), and other scholars and activists understand the neurodiversity movement to include people with epilepsy, Tourette syndrome, obsessive compulsive disorder, and even intellectual disabilities. As such, the neurodiversity movement represents a wide coalition of people whose neurological functioning is atypical. Often this group defines the contrast class as "neurotypical" (NT), or those who fall in the ranges of typical or normal neural and/or cognitive processing.

Broadly speaking, the neurodiversity movement "challenges widely held but inaccurate views of what constitutes functional human cognition—inaccurate views that pathologize some phenotypes that are properly regarded as non-maladaptive cognitive variations" for humans (Fenton and Krahn, 2007, 1). To better understand the neurodiversity movement, we must consider what the different modes of thinking or cognitive processing are and why they might be valuable, as well as how efforts to "fix" cognitive processing may be interpreted as devaluing individuals with the condition in question.

For more on the neurodiversity movement, see Chapter 26.

What Do We Mean By Neurodiverse Modes of Thinking, and Why Might They Be Valuable?

Members of the neurodiversity movement argue that they have a *different* way of being and thinking but not necessarily an inferior way of being and thinking (Saverese and Saverese, 2010). They argue that humans naturally have a wide variety of capacities and modes of processing—whether due to genetic, anatomical, hormonal, electrochemical, or developmental differences—and the "normal" mode of cognitive functioning should not be taken as the only acceptable form of functioning. Indeed, some disability scholars have suggested that diverse forms of embodiment and thinking may be integral to our species's survival and flourishing (Garland-Thomson, 2012).

The neurodiversity literature calls attention to how differences in processing are framed, categorized, and valued. For instance, a common hypothesis in the autism literature relates to the capacity to form a "theory of mind"—to understand that another being has a distinct set of beliefs and to attribute beliefs to them relatively accurately. Many young children are what Victoria McGeer calls "co-minded"—they "don't infer the moods, thoughts, feelings, or intentions of others, [but rather] simply *see* such subjective or mental phenomena—such ways of being minded—directly in their behavior" (2010, 283). She cites research on how quickly we anthropomorphize—for example, a 1944 experiment by Heider and Simmel involving a little animation of geometric figures that is typically "seen" as a big bully trying to keep a little guy in a box, even though the figures don't have faces or body shapes that suggest any "minds" within.

It shows how primed typical children are for identifying mental states, given the scaffolding and implicit training provided by their parents. Their minds perceive the mental states of others as immediately as they perceive their own mental states; they are co-minded. Being able to do this provides an easy ground for social interaction and communication. Some experts suggest that autistic children, on the other hand, may have somewhat different processing "modules" for understanding others' mental states and are not co-minded. They can learn to infer the mental states of others from their behavior and context, but it takes effort and is a learned skill (Frith and Happe, 1999). This framing seems to fit with Temple Grandin's famous phrasing about feeling a bit like "an anthropologist on Mars," trying to understand what other people mean by working to interpret their words and behaviors rather than having that meaning come relatively effortlessly.

The difference could be characterized as a *deficit* in theory of mind, as has been common in clinical discussions of autism, or, alternatively, as a *mismatch* in "forms of life" (Hacking, 2010; McGeer, 2010). On the deficit reading, the autistic individual lacks this cognitive machinery needed for normal processing; as a mismatch, the problem arises from different ways of processing, with "deficits" running in both directions. Autistic individuals may have difficulty reading neurotypicals (NTs), but likewise, NTs often experience difficulty understanding autistic people. So perhaps different neural "wiring"—and the sequelae of it—lead to different forms of life that appear impenetrable from the outside. The "forms of life" language is not intended to suggest radically different ways of being—such that we are inevitably alien to each other—but only some fundamental differences worth noticing. Hacking and McGeer are interested in how we might develop a shared form of life, how NTs might come to understand and appreciate autistic modes of thinking, and vice versa. Most autistic individuals are already given extensive therapy and strategies to learn to "decode" NT behavior. But relatively little attention is given to learning about autistic life; clinicians and parents tend to focus on deficits rather than capacities. Hacking argues that NTs should be attending closely to the narratives told in autobiographies from autistic individuals (Hacking, 2010). They give important clues about different ways of thinking and experiencing the world, and the narratives themselves—which offer language to describe experiences that are often not primarily verbal—help to shape what it is to experience the world as someone who is autistic. This is not just a point about understanding variety in the world but about recognizing valuable human modes of being in the world.

Is it worse not to be co-minded (or not to be co-minded in the typical way)? Not necessarily. It may make many social encounters difficult, given social expectations and norms, but again, that emphasizes what is lacking rather than what is present. Consider reports from members of the Autistic Self-Advocacy Network (ASAN) about their modes of cognitive processing. They call attention to their abilities rather than fixating on what they cannot do. So, for instance, autistic advocates have pointed to heightened abilities related to pattern recognition (Baggs, 2010), empathy with nonhuman animals (Grandin and Johnson, 2006), and sensory acuity and calculation capacity (Tammet, 2006) that may be more common in at least some autistic individuals. These heightened abilities coexist with seeming deficits in other areas (e.g., related to social interaction, communication, and repetitive behaviors).

Of course, whether the label of deficit even in those traditional areas is fair might depend on how we define well-being and good quality of life. Some things that an individual cannot do are not of interest to her and therefore are not perceived by the individual to be deficits (Reinders, 2014). Brownlow (2010), for instance, reports from online discussion groups of autistic individuals that many autistic people prefer not to be forced into face-to-face social interactions and have some modes of interacting that are nonstandard (e.g., arm flapping or other "stims"— repetitive self-stimulating behaviors that have calming effects on the individual) yet effective. As such, they needn't identify as having social or communicative deficits. Baggs (2010) reports that she is in "constant conversation with the world," which might be understood as a surplus of communication rather than a deficit. Furthermore, she claims that her mode of experiencing the world is as rich as that of NTs. She says autistic people have

> rich and varied forms of communication in their own right, not inadequate substitutes for the more standard forms of communication . . . those of us who are viewed purely as having had things taken away—as being essentially barren wastelands—are not shut out of the richness of life by being who we are. The richness we experience is not some cheap romanticized copy of the richness others experience. The richness of life is there for everyone, and whether one experiences it or not is not dependent on whether or not one is autistic.
>
> (Baggs, 2010)

In Brownlow's online discussion groups, autistic individuals sometimes view NTs as having somewhat unusual predilections and fascinations, even satirically defining an NT syndrome that "traps those affected in a lifelong struggle for social status and recognition. Neurotypical individuals almost invariably show a triad of impairments, consisting of inability to think independently of the social group, marked impairment in the ability to think logically or critically, and inability to form special interests (other than in social activity)" (Brownlow, 2010, 251). The point is that *not* being social or communicative in the "normal" ways may have certain advantages.

In sum, framing autistic and neurodiverse ways of thinking as differences opens up the possibility of recognizing strengths as well as limitations that accompany autism. As Robertson notes, "Under the deficit model, autistic people are portrayed as broken humans who are ill and require fixing to enable them to function normally in society. In contrast, nonautistic people are viewed as neurologically healthy and psychologically well. This deficit-focused view of autistic people has largely ignored their cognitive strengths, their diverse way of being, and their gifts and talents (2010, 28)." The neurodiversity movement seeks to highlight those often under-recognized attributes and explore their value.

Some critics of the neurodiversity movement argue that only the most high-functioning people are able to make such claims, and that for many other people with atypical modes of thinking, no such "gifts and talents" really exist. *Valuing* such atypical modes of thinking seems inconceivable to them. One response to such critics is that it is not always clear what capacities an individual has—too often when communication is difficult, we quickly presume that an individual's cognitive capacities are impaired (Stubblefield, 2014; Biklen, 2005). The neurodiversity movement, though, includes many individuals who were once diagnosed as having very limited cognitive capacities but who became eloquent spokespersons for neurodiversity once they found modes of assistive communication that facilitated their verbal self-expression. (Even given widespread debunking of "facilitated communication," other alternative communication options are available; Travers et al., 2014.) Consider autistic Sue Rubin's claims: "[P]eople stare and marvel at my irregular behaviors which lead to poor assumptions that I am simply mentally disabled with little or no intellectual functioning. My appearance is very deceptive, and day after day, I am working, as an advocate for all autistic individuals, to let the world know that we are intelligent" (Rubin, 2005, 95). Intelligence and cognitive processing generally need not all look alike or develop in the same ways. This does not ignore the possibility that some individuals will not be able to advocate for themselves or may indeed have cognitive capacities that are limiting in important respects; it does, however, recommend against giving up on people who have not yet found a way to communicate (Saverese and Saverese, 2010). This is a view shared by Martha

Nussbaum (2007) in her work on disability. She argues for the need to work continuously to figure out ways to enhance the autonomy of individuals with cognitive disabilities to help them achieve the relevant capability.

Efforts to "Fix" Different Modes of Thinking and Implications for Devaluing Neurodiversity

Activism by people who experience atypical modes of thinking has been a powerful force in drawing attention to the need for respect and recognition across such differences (Silberman, 2015). But even as they accept those claims and perhaps even advocate for equal rights and respect, others may still believe that providing medical treatment for the conditions that lead to such different modes of thinking is justifiable (Kapp et al., 2012). Why? Because given the social and institutional norms we have, some modes of thinking will create real hardships for people. Even if the condition itself is not (always) on balance negative, having the condition within a certain system of norms can make life more difficult, and we ought to work to avoid that if possible. We could, of course, focus our attention on making the social and institutional norms more inclusive (as the social model of disability notably recommends; Oliver, 1996). Such change is difficult and slow-going but important and likely to benefit far more than a disabled or atypical minority. But others may well hold that *treating* an atypical mode of thinking is also a reasonable response—now, when the existing norms are still likely to create hardships for the individual, and in the future, when it may be more a matter of choosing what kind of cognitive processing one prefers. As Kapp et al. (2012) note, "even autistic people who support the ideals and long-term goals of the neurodiversity movement may view adapting to a 'neurotypical' world as a practical matter, given the slower pace of and less control over sociopolitical compared with personal change" (9).

Imagine a parent whose child is diagnosed with ADHD. She loves her rambunctious, free-thinking child and wants the child to be respected and recognized for her talents. But she also wants her to do well in school and her teachers recommend treatment for ADHD. Advocating for a more inclusive classroom, one that doesn't demand that students sit for hours at a time or that allows for more individual attention to each child's needs, is undoubtedly important. But the parent may also recognize that medicating the child could be more effective in the short term, allowing her to succeed in the existing classroom environment. So even with growing attention to the value of different modes of thinking, we find pressures to normalize functioning (Parens, 1998).

Of course, we would worry if the child in this scenario was gay and felt pressured to be heterosexual (or treated to ensure it) or if she felt uncomfortable with her assigned gender identity but was pressured to normalize and "act like a girl." Why so? In part, because we tend to think of sexuality and gender (along with race) as integral to our identities. Changing those features of ourselves would mean changing who we are. Even recognizing heterosexist norms and the hardships they may create in the present for anyone with a nonconforming sexuality, we still aim to fix the world rather than treating the child to make her fit those norms. So why not the same with different modes of thinking (Barnes, 2009)? Why do we fund research to search for treatments for autism, ADHD, and any number of the other conditions associated with the neurodiversity movement rather than demanding that the world become more inclusive and such individuals be given space to develop as they are and to be accommodated when necessary?

A person's neurobiology is but one feature of her identity, but—like gender or sexuality—our ways of thinking pervade our experience and so can feel quite central to who we are. Consider what autism self-advocate Jim Sinclair says: "Autism is a way of being. It is pervasive;

it colors every experience, every sensation, perception, thought, emotion, and encounter, every aspect of existence. It is not possible to separate the autism from the person—and if it were possible, the person you'd have left would not be the same person you started with" (Sinclair, 1993). His claim is echoed by many autistic self-advocates who argue that taking a cure for autism would be tantamount to making them different people. What they want is acceptance and accommodation, not a cure. "The object of autism advocacy should not be a world without autistic people—it should be a world in which autistic people can enjoy the same rights, opportunities, and quality of life as any of our neurotypical peers" (Ne'eman, 2010, 2). Saverese is a self-advocate who, when asked "Should autism be treated?" said "Yes, with respect" (quoted in Saverese and Saverese, 2010, 13).

Recognizing the connection between our modes of thinking and our identities and working for acceptance of a wider range of cognitive processing need not lead us to the conclusion that no medical or technological interventions are ever appropriate (Kapp et al., 2012). Acceptance might be accompanied by assistance. Sometimes the framing of an intervention is fundamental to how we view its aims. Is therapy intended to change the person or help her come to terms with herself, to do and be what she wants to do or be? Is a medication prescribed to "fix" a deficit or to aid an individual in achieving a desired outcome?

One might argue that this is too fine a line to draw—if an individual cannot achieve her desired outcome due to her mode of thinking (say she wants to be able to focus better, but her ADHD brain makes that difficult), then she has a deficit relative to that desired outcome, and that's what the medication fixes. But note that the *individual* in this case is determining what counts as a deficit. If she prefers a different outcome, then others have no need to categorize her as deficient in some way. And if she *asks* for help in controlling her ability to focus, then a medication may be understood as enabling her autonomy rather than undermining her identity (Baylis, 2013; Parens, 2015). To be sure, the lines are not always distinct, and individuals can seek treatment only in order to conform to norms they reject without feeling fully able to exercise their autonomy in ways they would prefer (see for instance, the discussion of adults diagnosed with ADHD in Bolt and Schermer, 2009). But broadly, interventions that are developed and later offered in the interest of assisting individuals who face hardships (as opposed to changing them into people with new identities by "curing" or removing part of who they are) are less likely to be deemed threatening and more likely to be seen as helpful. Recognizing an individual's strengths and making use of them can be part of helping the individual become who they want to be.

As Fenton and Krahn argue (2007), this might have some relatively radical implications for our medical categorizations. Should we get rid of the "disorder" part of autism spectrum disorder? Do autistic people need cognitive behavioral therapy to try to get rid of their tics and other behavioral oddities, or are those things part of their self-expression? Fenton and Krahn (2007) argue that it will be important to look at what is a "recognizable interest from their perspective—not from the perspective of the mainstream alone" (3). Understanding different modes of thinking will not be easy. To what extent can a NT person fully comprehend the claim that autistic thoughts are "more fluid with colors coming in and out and swirling into unique and beautiful patterns. (My thoughts are in pictures and sometimes moving colors)?" (quoted in Donnellan et al., 2010). Trying to do so may help advance our shared capacities for imagining a much wider range of possibilities for engaging and understanding the world.

Neural Engineering as a Means of Thinking/Acting Differently

Given how closely we identify with our thinking—indeed, with the central organ of our thinking, the brain—the idea of *neural engineering* is, to many people, a little unnerving. While we may appreciate and rely on engineering feats and devices outside of us (bridges, buildings, computers, cell phones, etc.) and even attached to us (prosthetics, insulin pumps, artificial hearts, etc.), many people balk at the idea of engineering the human brain. Why so? If we are asked to point to where we are, we typically point to our heads. We're cognitive creatures; the brain is our "command center." Engineering—which carries with it the connotation of invention and design, building and improving upon what we already have—seems risky, possibly arrogant, and likely to change something important about how we understand ourselves. If we can be engineered— if we can engineer our thinking or neurological processing by way of implanted devices, for example, deep brain stimulators or brain–computer interfaces—are we somehow more like machines? Or do we make ourselves into artifacts by turning our engineering skills on ourselves (President's Council on Bioethics, 2003)?

One might counter that we already manipulate ourselves through various forms of pharmaceutical interventions (e.g., antidepressants for depression or stimulants for ADHD), and neural engineering may be merely a different means. Still, while the aim of the two interventions is often the same—we want to alter a brain process that is not to our liking—the mechanisms are somewhat different, and those differences may be significant. Several dimensions of possible differences may be noteworthy: (1) the level of precision (with pharmaceuticals, we flood our systems with a drug, even though we try to get the doses right to achieve the desired effect; with neural engineering, the specificity of the intervention can be at the level of a single neuron, though most current neural engineering techniques are much less precise); (2) the invasiveness of the intervention (taking a pill is relatively simple and requires little risk other than the effect of the medication; neural engineering involves the implantation of electrodes—or the external attachment of EEG recorders and external stimulating devices—and the associated risks of surgery (infection, placement error, etc.) as well as risks related to monitoring and hacking activities (e.g., risks of privacy or security; Farah and Wolpe, 2004); and (3) the long-term effects of the intervention (most pharmaceuticals have to be taken regularly but can also be discontinued in case of unwanted effects; neural engineering interventions, at least implantable ones, are much more difficult to take out, though they can be turned off, often requiring the help of a physician). These differences may not hold up over time—pharmaceuticals may become more precisely targeted, and neurally engineered devices may become less risky and more easily controlled by the individual. Still, the current prospect of neural engineering is, for many, somewhat more concerning than the use of pharmaceuticals to alter our brains and our thinking.

But how, exactly, might neural engineering alter our thinking? Some implantable devices aim to regulate areas of the brain that operate atypically (to be a "pacemaker" for the brain). A deep brain stimulator (DBS), for instance, involves electrodes implanted in relatively deep regions of the brain and set to deliver stimulation at a steady pace or in regular intervals. DBS has proven effective for treating tremors associated with Parkinson's disease and essential tremors. Trials of DBS for movement disorders have in rare instances resulted in unusual side effects, such as increased impulsivity, gambling, and personality changes (Wang et al., 2016; Rossi, Gunduz, and Okun, 2015; Lipsman and Glannon, 2013; Parsons et al., 2006), but also sometimes had unintended beneficial effects, such as enhancing mood or control. Perhaps as a result, DBS is now also being tested for conditions such as OCD, Tourette syndrome, depression, epilepsy, and anorexia. Neural engineers are still not certain of the mechanism by which the stimulation achieves the desired effect, and some treat it as a relatively blunt tool for treatment, but that hasn't dampened the optimism and the attention it receives as a new mode of treating conditions that have so far been relatively resistant to more traditional treatments.

Most such DBS devices are "open loop," which means that they stimulate at a set level. New versions of these devices are designed to be "closed loop," which means that they have a feedback loop with both sensors and stimulators and can be triggered to stimulate only as needed. Such devices save on battery power and allow for a more selective use of stimulation. On the one hand, a closed-loop device is attractive in that it will be more responsive to the particular situation (turning on when needed and off when not without any need for intervention on the part of the user). On the other hand, the user may have difficulty locating herself in the loop. The device that runs autonomously in her brain may feel alien to her, almost like a "third-party" entity (Lipsman and Glannon, 2013) that exerts control over her cognitive and neurological processing. If she doesn't identify with the device (and approve the alterations it imposes), then she may feel alienated from her own cognition and behavior (Kraemer, 2013). So neural engineering in the form of DBS devices may certainly help some people to live better, but it also may create changes in how we understand ourselves as agents (Klaming and Haselager, 2013); it can alter the underlying means of our thinking.

Another neural engineering device might attempt to wirelessly transfer electrical signaling across an area of damage—whether from the brain to spinal nerves, over an area of a spinal cord injury, or across cortical regions to induce neural plasticity following stroke or other brain injury. In the future, implantable brain–computer interfaces (BCIs), for instance, might translate a motor intention (e.g., "lift my finger") into action (finger is lifted) despite a spinal cord injury that had previously made such movement impossible. The BCI would work by recognizing the motor intention, creating an algorithm for that movement, wirelessly transferring the data over an area of damage, and then stimulating the relevant spinal nerves or muscles. Or a BCI might help a person to communicate by translating motor intentions related to communication to a computer-driven voice output device. As our brains directly interface with computers to complete our intended actions, our modes of thinking may change somewhat. For instance, to use such a device, an individual would need to be trained so that the electrical activity associated with her intention to lift the finger can be isolated from other neural activity ("noise") in the same area. Further, she might be given a code thought (say, "wiggle toes") that is more easily isolated and identified, and that can then be used to trigger her desired finger movement. Then she would need to learn to think "wiggle toes"—presumably with some concentration, at least in the early stages of the implant—in order to achieve her intended action.

Would such neural engineering feats change how we think, giving us new and significantly different modes of thinking? They might not if they merely fill in for or replace a part of a mode of thinking that was already in effect. But as the latter example suggests, they might also complicate and alter our ways of thinking by adding steps, creating new associations, and at least relying on different mechanisms to implement our thinking (Clausen, 2008). At least in the early stages, users of the technology might need to be able to focus effectively on a code word or target activity (more so than is required in typical thinking) and might fail to effect a desired action if they lose focus or are interrupted (or if their medications create difficulties for focusing). If intended signals (via focused thought) are indecipherable, whether due to lack of training or difficulty in implementing the trained signal, the individual's thinking may lead to a non-response or perhaps even an unintended response. How the individual thinks (and effectuates thinking) can then alter others' understanding of who they are and what they take themselves to be doing. If my friend knocks over a cup of coffee on me when she's angry, I may blame her, even if she insists that her BCI must have misfired in some way, because she didn't intend to do that. In addition, the altered means of thinking and effecting our thinking may, through neural plasticity, also change our previous patterns of neurological processing. Over time, the user's brain may become habituated to the association, so that the link between the thought and the action becomes relatively automatic and unconscious. Even if the processing becomes more fluid, we might still consider the mode of thinking to be somewhat different, given that other kinds of interference (loss of battery power, device failure, hacking) are possible (Klaming and Haselager, 2013).

Consider what might be an even clearer case of neural technology affecting a mode of thinking. DBS devices have been tested in people who have treatment-resistant depression (Mayberg, et al. 2005). Such devices stimulate the brain in order to elevate a person's mood and increase her motivational drive. A person with a DBS may report feeling happier and able to get on with her life. The treatment appears to be a success. But she may, at the same time, think of herself as less in control of her thinking, not sure about how to differentiate what she does and what her device does. If she yells at her daughter or fails to help her spouse, is she the angry or apathetic one, or is her device just not set appropriately (so that she's doing what she can, but only within the bounds of her settings)? We often look at behavior to understand a person's thinking, but when a device other than the individual may be influencing the behavior in a fairly direct way, what can we discern about her thinking? Her thinking may not even be fully transparent to her. Imagine, for instance, a DBS user who feels happy at a funeral—did she really not care about the one who died as much as she thought, or is her stimulation setting perhaps a bit too high and not responsive enough to her environment? She may not know herself and could find the experience confusing and unsettling. Neural engineering devices have the capacity to alter our ways of thinking and so, too, to shape how we think about ourselves.

The neural engineering efforts I have described—for BCI and DBS—emphasize creating new connections between thoughts and action (e.g., for people with spinal cord injury or stroke), and between mood and electrical stimulation (for people who have depression). As such, they aren't strictly speaking focused on changing the thinking of people who identify with the neurodiversity movement. While some people who have been diagnosed as bipolar or who have dysthymia may take up the charge of the neurodiversity movement, typically people with treatment-resistant depression have no such affiliation. So why should the aims of the neurodiversity movement matter to the neural engineers? Because recognizing the diversity of valuable forms of neurological functioning is an important first step to ensuring that neural engineering efforts will be addressed to real needs and won't unintentionally exacerbate the existing difficulties for people who function with atypical modes of thinking. Acknowledging neurodiversity in the early stages of neural engineering will help to secure a more capacious vision of neurological functioning and direct engineers to partner with disabled or differently abled people to help them achieve their own goals.

Neurodiversity Meets Neural Engineering—Finding Common Ground

Neurodiversity movement advocates argue that we should reconsider some atypical modes of thinking and recognize their value, even as they are admittedly outside "normal" modes of functioning. Neural engineering aims to create different modes of thinking, but in the service of restoring or improving function in the direction of what is "normal." We might then think that these two movements are contradictory in their aims. But we should not ignore other striking similarities. Both groups seek to better understand neurological functioning and to find ways to allow individuals with atypical neurological functioning to improve their quality of life. Both want, at some level, for the broader public to accept a wider array of modes of thinking so that people who have atypical neurological function will not have to face stigma, whether due to their communicative or social interaction differences or because of the existence of an implanted device.

Those similarities, though, are at a level of generality that may not be very significant. If neural engineers dedicate their efforts to creating new ways to achieve "normal" functioning (so different modes of thinking but toward the end of fitting a relatively constrained range of acceptable functioning), then the neurodiversity movement may have cause to be concerned. Neural engineers may well think that such "fixes" are exactly what autistic or disabled individuals most want or need. The neurodiversity movement suggests that may not be true. (I recognize that the neurodiversity movement does not include all autistic people or all people who live with conditions that sometimes fall under the neurodiversity banner.)

My recommendation here is for collaboration across the two movements. In particular, neural engineers should be aware of the neurodiversity movement and open to input from people who identify as part of that group. If improved neurological processing is the target of neural engineers, it makes sense to figure out what the intended end users view as their needs and priorities. Not every potential end user will identify as part of the neurodiversity movement or will value her atypical processing. But engineers would still benefit from hearing the range of views that their intended beneficiaries hold.

The best way to get such information about priorities and values is to engage potential end users early in the design process, even as the research priorities are being set. Too often, end user engagement comes quite late in the game, when a prototype is already available to be tested, and many decisions about function and design have already been determined. Engaging potential end users early in the work of neural engineering can help to ensure that product development aligns with needs and priorities of the intended group of beneficiaries.

What might change? In some cases, the focus or direction of the research may be affected. As an example, nondisabled people sometimes presume that not being able to walk is the greatest concern of most people who use wheelchairs. But that's not usually the first priority of most people with spinal cord injury. Having nondisabled neural engineers talk with people with spinal cord injury about their experiences could alter that perspective. Neural engineering targeted to BCIs for motor disabilities, then, might focus on improved hand and arm function rather than walking and include attention to sexual or urological functioning, given stated priorities of people with spinal cord injuries (Anderson, 2004).

Other changes might involve shifting design features, such as altering the level of individual control a user has over the device. Early DBS systems had parameters set in a physician's office and only changeable through office visits. Newer models offer the possibility for local control by the user so that the user can determine when stimulation needs to be changed, at least within a set range. Input from a focus group of people with spinal cord injuries suggests that most people would want this kind of control over any implantable neural device, and that recommendation then can alter the way the devices are designed. These focus group members were tentatively optimistic about the neural technologies under development but also expressed concerns that the typical nondisabled engineer might not really understand much about how their lives work or what they really value (Goering, unpublished focus group data).

Concerns about privacy or control over access to the data from the neural engineering device may be another factor that could be affected by input from likely end users. Engineers may see great value in having researchers get access to the data collected from a BCI, for instance, but users may prefer to have some control over what data is made accessible and how. The acceptable trade-offs between increased efficiency in movement or mood and privacy of data may not be the same in the target population versus within the group of designers. Input from likely end users is particularly important where end user groups may have values or perspectives (related to disability and neurodiversity) that are new to nondisabled engineers.

Other changes to the engineering process may be more subtle and involve different *framing* rather than designing technology differently. Cochlear implants are a good example here. Cochlear implants are a form of neural engineering—they allow information from sound waves to be collected, processed, and delivered to the auditory cortex, bypassing regions of the ear or auditory nerves that would otherwise perform that function in nondeaf individuals. Cochlear implants do not "cure" deafness, but they do offer a way for deaf individuals to gain some access to the world of sound if they want it. In the early days of cochlear implant technologies, Deaf culturists viewed the technology as deeply threatening to their way of life (Crouch, 1997) and even expressed concern about cultural genocide (Lane and Grodin, 1997). The National Association for the Deaf (NAD) came out with a statement in opposition to their use. But over time, NAD softened its stance, in part because of increasing evidence that while cochlear implants have gotten better and more effective, they still do not make a person "hearing"—rather, they offer a deaf person a way of gaining some access to sound. Seen as an assistive device—one that can be chosen or not, depending on the values and desires of the parent or user—the cochlear implant is somewhat less threatening. The NAD site (http://nad.org/issues/technology/ assistive-listening/cochlear-implants) now offers a more nuanced stance:

> Cochlear implantation is a technology that represents a tool to be used in some forms of communication, and not a cure for deafness. Cochlear implants provide sensitive hearing, but do not, by themselves, impart the ability to understand spoken language through listening alone. . . . The NAD recognizes the rights of parents to make informed choices for their deaf and hard of hearing children, respects their choice to use cochlear implants and all other assistive devices, and strongly supports the development of the whole child and of language and literacy.

They go on to note, "Many within the medical profession continue to view deafness essentially as a disability and an abnormality and believe that deaf and hard of hearing individuals need to be 'fixed' by cochlear implants. This pathological view must be challenged and corrected by greater exposure to and interaction with well-adjusted and successful deaf and hard of hearing individuals."

The similarities to the neurodiversity movement claims are striking here. People who have atypical neurological processing are working to raise awareness of their differences and their concerns about efforts to "cure" them. But if neural engineering devices are understood as *assistive* technologies that may help to address needs identified by individuals with atypical processing, then they are more likely to be accepted. Educating neural engineers about problems with having exclusively pathological views of the individuals they aim to help is imperative.

Community-based participatory research (CBPR) is gaining attention as a paradigm of research that insists on active collaboration and engagement with relevant communities of interest in order to ensure scientific results that are both ethical and likely to be effective (Hacker, 2013). CBPR has found uptake in work being done on autism. For example, the Academic and Autistic Spectrum Partnership in Research and Education (AASPIRE) "brings together the academic community and the autistic community to develop and perform research projects relevant to the needs of adults on the autism spectrum. . . . [A]cademics and community members serve as equal partners throughout the research process" (http://aaspire.org/). The partnership between the two groups helps to ensure that nondominant perspectives are heard and considered in research projects focusing on autism rather than presuming only the dominant "deficit" framing of autism.

The idea is fairly simple—if you want to know something about what autistic people want or need, get them involved in your project, and do it fairly early on, to help guide the direction and focus of your research project—but it still is not widely practiced. Partly this is due to engrained research practices and the institutional structures that support them (Israel et al., 2006). Expertise is typically only identified as existing in the academic community and "need" outside of it rather than recognizing the relevant expertise of community members (Jordan et al., 2005). But community members have much to offer. Consider what Nicolaidis (the current AASPIRE codirector) says about her experience in learning about autism:

> Interestingly, nowhere in my early foray as an "autism mom" (or in the years I had spent as a primary care physician) did anyone actually suggest learning from individuals on the autism spectrum. It was only by coincidence that I met a local autistic self-advocate who was active in the neurodiversity movement. Who could have guessed that she would change not only the way I looked at my autistic child, but also the way I practice medicine and focus my research?
>
> (Nicolaidis, 2012)

The lived experience of people with the conditions in question is surely relevant to issues of research, treatment, and policy, yet decision makers too often fail to take it directly into account.

As neural engineering continues to develop as a field, it is crucial to take into careful consideration the perspectives of potential end users, the people who are the intended beneficiaries of the technologies in development. They matter not just for the fine-tuning of existing technology prototypes but also early on in the research process, as priorities are being identified and research projects cultivated. Individuals who identify with the neurodiversity movement, whose neurological processing is atypical in some respects, have much to offer neural engineers in their quest to understand neurological processing and to develop devices that can provide wanted assistance and opportunities for enhanced well-being.

Acknowledgments

Thanks to Eran Klein and Laura Specker Sullivan for helpful comments on early drafts and to the CSNE faculty and students for their part in helping me understand neural engineering. Also thanks to the editors for their very helpful suggestions.

Further Reading

Baggs, A. (2010) "Up in the Clouds, Down in the Valley: My richness and yours". *Disability Studies Quarterly* 30(1). Available at: http://dsq-sds.org/article/view/1052/1238

Kraemer, F. (2013) "Me, Myself and My Brain Implant: Deep Brain Stimulation Raises Questions of Personal Authenticity and Alienation". *Neuroethics* 6: 483–497.

Oliver, M. (1996) *Understanding Disability: From Theory to Practice*. New York: St. Martin's Press.

Parens, E. (2015) *Shaping Our Selves: On Technology, Flourishing, and a Habit of Thinking*. New York: Oxford University Press.

Silberman, S. (2015) *NeuroTribes: The Legacy of Autism and the Future of Neurodiversity*. New York: Avery Press.

References

Anderson, K. (2004) Targeting recovery: Priorities of the spinal cord-injured population. *Journal of Neurotrauma* 21: pp. 1371–1383.

Armstrong, T. (2010) *The Power of Neurodiversity: Unleashing the Advantages of Your Differently Wired Brain*. Cambridge, MA: Da Capo Press.

Baggs, A. (2010) Up in the clouds, down in the valley: My richness and yours. *Disability Studies Quarterly* 30(1). Available at: http://dsq-sds.org/article/view/1052/1238

Barnes, E. (2009) Disability, minority and difference. *Journal of Applied Philosophy* 26(4): pp. 337–355.

Baylis, F. (2013) 'I am who I am': On the perceived threats to personal identity from deep brain stimulation. *Neuroethics* 6: pp. 513–526.

Biklen, D. (2005) *Autism and the Myth of the Person Alone*. New York: New York University Press.

Bolt, I., and Schermer, M. (2009) Pharmaceutical enhancers: Enhancing identity? *Neuroethics* 2: pp. 103–111.

Brownlow, C. (2010) Re-presenting autism: The construction of "NT Syndrome". *Journal of Medical Humanities* 31: pp. 243–255.

Clausen, J. (2008) Moving minds: Ethical aspects of neural motor prostheses. *Biotechnology Journal* 3: pp. 1493–1501.

Crouch, R. (1997) Letting the deaf be deaf: Reconsidering the use of cochlear implants in prelingually deaf children. *Hastings Center Report* 27(4): pp. 14–21.

Donnellan, A., Hill, D., and Leary, M. (2010) Rethinking autism: Implications of sensory and movement differences. *Disability Studies Quarterly* 30(1). Available at: http://dsq-sds.org/article/view/1060

Farah, M., and Wolpe, P.R. (2004) Monitoring and manipulating brain function: New neuroscience technologies and their ethical implications. *Hastings Center Report* 34(3): pp. 35–45.

Fenton, A., and Krahn, T. (2007) Autism, neurodiversity, and equality beyond the 'Normal'. *Journal of Ethics in Mental Health* 2(2): pp. 1–6.

Frith, U., and Happe, F. (1999) Theory of mind and self-consciousness: What is it like to be autistic? *Mind and Language* 14(1): pp. 1–22.

Garland-Thomson, R. (2012) The case for conserving disability. *Journal of Bioethical Inquiry* 9: pp. 339–355.

Grandin, T., and Johnson, C. (2006) *Animals in Translation: Using the Mysteries of Autism to Decode Human Behavior*. New York: Harcourt.

Hacker, K. (2013) *Community Based Participatory Research*. Los Angeles: Sage.

Hacking, I. (2010) How we have been learning to talk about autism. In E.F. Kittay and L. Carlson (Eds.). *Cognitive Disability and Its Challenge to Moral Philosophy*. Malden, MA: Wiley-Blackwell, pp. 261–278.

Israel, B., Krieger, J., Vlahov, D., Ciske, S., Foley, M., Fortin, P., Guzman, J.R., Lichtenstein, R., McGranaghan, R., Palermo, A. and Tang, G. (2006) Challenges and facilitating factors in sustaining community based participatory research partnerships. *Journal of Urban Health* 83(6): pp. 1022–1040.

Jordan, C., Gust, S., and Scheman, N. (2005) The trustworthiness of research: The paradigm of community based research. *Journal of Metropolitan Universities* 16(1): pp. 39–57.

Kapp, S., Gillespie-Lynch, K., Sherman, L., and Hutman, T. (2012) Deficit, difference, or both? Autism and neurodiversity. *Developmental Psychology* 49(1): pp. 1–13. doi:10.1037/a0028353

Klaming, L., and Haselager, P. (2013) Did my brain implant make me do it? *Neuroethics* 6(3): pp. 527–539. doi:10.1037/a0028353

Kraemer, F. (2013) Me, myself and my brain implant: Deep brain stimulation raises questions of personal authenticity and alienation. *Neuroethics* 6: pp. 483–497.

Lane, H., and Grodin, M. (1997) Ethical issues in cochlear implant surgery. *Kennedy Institute of Ethics Journal* 7(3): pp. 231–251.

Lipsman, N., and Glannon, W. (2013) Brain, mind and machine: What are the implications of deep brain stimulation for perceptions of personal identity, agency and free will? *Bioethics* 27(9): pp. 465–470.

McGeer, V. (2010) The thought and talk of individuals with autism. In E.F. Kittay and L. Carlson (Eds.). *Cognitive Disability and Its Challenge to Moral Philosophy*. Malden, MA: Wiley-Blackwell, pp. 279–292.

Mayberg, H., Lozano, A., Voon, V., McNeely, H., Seminowicz, D., Hamani, C., Schwalb, J. and Kennedy, S. (2005) Deep brain stimulation for treatment-resistant depression. *Neuron* 45(5): pp. 651–660.

Ne'eman, A. (2010) The future (and the Past) of autism advocacy, or why the ASA's magazine, *The Advocate*, wouldn't publish this piece. *Disability Studies Quarterly* 30(1). Available at: http://dsq-sds.org/article/view/1059/1244

Nicolaidis, C. (2012) What can physicians learn from the neurodiversity movement? *American Medical Association Journal of Ethics* 14(6): pp. 503–512.

Nussbaum, M. (2007) *Frontiers of Justice: Disability, Nationality, Species Membership*. Cambridge, MA: Harvard University Press.

Oliver, M. (1996) *Understanding Disability: From Theory to Practice*. New York: St. Martin's Press.

Parens, E. (2015) *Shaping Our Selves: On Technology, Flourishing, and a Habit of Thinking*. New York: Oxford University Press.

———. (1998) Is better always good? The enhancement project. *Hastings Center Report* 28(1): pp. S1-S17.

Parsons, T., Rogers, S., Braaten, A., Woods, S.P. and Troster, A. (2006) Cognitive sequelae of subthalamic nucleus deep brain stimulation in Parkinson's disease: A meta-analysis. *The Lancet Neurology* 5(7): pp. 578–588.

President's Council on Bioethics. (2003) *Beyond Therapy: Biotechnology and the Pursuit of Happiness*. New York: HarperCollins.

Reinders, H. (2014) Disability and quality of life: An Aristotelian discussion. In J.E. Bickenbach, F. Felder, and B. Schmitz (Eds.). *Disability and the Good Human Life*. New York: Cambridge University Press, pp. 199–218.

Robertson, S.M. (2010) Neurodiversity, quality of life, and autistic adults: Shifting research and professional focuses onto real-life challenges. *Disability Studies Quarterly* 30(1). Available at: http://dsqsds.org/article/view/1069

Rossi, P.J., Gunduz, A., and Okun, M.S. (2015) The subthalamic nucleus, limbic function and impulse control. *Neuropsychology Review* 25(4): pp. 398–410.

Rubin, S. (2005) Conversation with Leo Kanner. In D. Biklen (Ed.). *Autism and the Myth of the Person Alone*. New York: New York University Press, pp. 82–109.

Saverese, E., and Saverese, R. (2010) 'The superior half of speaking': An introduction. *Disability Studies Quarterly* 30(1). Available at: http://dsq-sds.org/article/view/1062/1230

Silberman, S. (2015) *NeuroTribes: The Legacy of Autism and the Future of Neurodiversity*. New York: Avery Press.

Sinclair, J. (1993) Don't mourn for us. *Our Voice* (the Autism Network International Newsletter) 1(3). Available at: www.autreat.com/dont_mourn.html.

Stubblefield, A. (2014) Living a good life … in adult-size diapers. In J.E. Bickenbach, F. Felder and B. Schmitz (Eds.). *Disability and the Good Human Life*. Cambridge: Cambridge University Press, pp. 219–242.

Tammet, D. (2006) *Born on a Blue Day: Inside the Extraordinary Mind of an Autistic Savant*. London: Hodder & Stoughton.

Travers, J., Tincani, M., and Lang, R. (2014) Facilitated communication Denies people with disabilities their voice. *Research and Practice for Persons With Severe Disabilities* 39(3): pp. 195–202.

Wang, J.W., Zhang, Y.O., Zhang, X.H., Wang, Y.P., Li, J.P., and Li, Y.J. (2016) Cognitive and psychiatric effects of STN versus GPi deep brain stimulation in Parkinson's disease: A meta-analysis of randomized controlled trials. *PLOS One* 11(6): p. e0156721.

4

THE ETHICS OF EXPANDING APPLICATIONS OF DEEP BRAIN STIMULATION

Markus Christen and Sabine Müller

Introduction

Deep brain stimulation (DBS) is a neuromodulation technique for movement disorders and other indications (see also Box 4.1 "Neuromodulation"). The roots of DBS can be traced to developments from the early 1950s (Hariz et al., 2010). However, DBS of subcortical structures like the ventral intermediate part of the thalamus, the *globus pallidus internus* and the *nucleus subthalamicus* (STN) for addressing, e.g., specific symptoms of Parkinson's disease (PD) emerged in the 1980s (Siegfried, 1986; Benabid et al., 1987). In recent years, both the application of DBS as well as its appreciation in the literature has grown remarkably, in particular since 2000 (Müller and Christen, 2011). Global estimations of the number of patients who received DBS exceed 100,000; several thousand patients per year are newly implanted (Christen et al., 2014a). These numbers are expected to increase, as DBS is investigated for various other neurological and psychiatric diseases, including some with a high prevalence (in particular treatment-resistant depression and dementia). This expansion of applications shows the growing importance of DBS as a potential therapeutic approach for various diseases.

These expanding applications of DBS give rise to several important ethical questions that will be outlined in this chapter as follows: In the next section, we discuss the intervention as such, exemplified by its most common indication, PD, and we outline the challenges of patients who may be candidates for DBS in weighing the risks and benefits of the intervention. We call this the "decision problem". The third section provides information on experiences with expanding indications thus far. The fourth section discusses the ethical issues related to DBS. Two info boxes provide additional information: Box 4.1 about neuromodulation in general, Box 4.2 about ablative techniques, that is, the historical forerunner of DBS and a potential alternative in some cases.

Deep Brain Stimulation—the Intervention Exemplified for Parkinson's Disease

DBS intervenes into a neuronal network in the brain by chronic electrical stimulation (Benabid et al., 2009): One or (in most cases) two quadripolar electrodes are stereotactically implanted into specific targets deep in the brain. The electrodes are connected to a pulse generator (usually

4.1 Spotlight: Neuromodulation

Markus Christen and Sabine Müller

Neuromodulation is among the fastest-growing areas of medicine, involving many diverse specialties and impacting hundreds of thousands of patients with numerous disorders worldwide. It can briefly be described as the science of how electrical and chemical interventions can modulate nervous system function (Krames et al., 2009). The field of neuromodulation covers a wide range of mostly chronic conditions such as epilepsy, blindness or other eye conditions, gastric mobility, headaches, deafness, movement disorders, occipital and peripheral neuralgias, chronic pain, psychiatric and neurobehavioral disorders, spasticity, stroke, traumatic brain injury, and others. Instruments for neuromodulation include electrical stimulators, sensory prostheses like cochlear implants, and implantable infusion pumps. Given the economic importance of this field—the global market volume is estimated to equal $3.65 billion US (www.marketsandmarkets.com/Market-Reports/neurostimulation-devices-market-921.html)—and the fact that it addresses a population of roughly 14 million patients in the United States alone (Krames et al., 2009), it is very likely that such techniques will extend into various medical fields that address neurological and psychiatric disorders.

Neuromodulation interventions are characterized by three conditions (Holsheimer, 2003): First, the intervention is applied repeatedly or constantly; a "one-shot" lesion does not count as neuromodulation. Second, the intervention causes *local* changes in neuronal processes (unlike medication) that does, however, not exclude the possibility of effects on the whole-brain activity. Third, the clinical effects can be influenced by modulating the intervening process for the benefit of the patient to improve the therapeutic effect of the intervention or counteract sequelae—sometimes, this involves balancing of the two intentions such as maximizing motor control and minimizing affective sequelae. Often, reversibility is also mentioned as a defining feature of neuromodulation. However, due to neuroplasticity, this assumption can be reasonably questioned, as the intervention may lead to long-lasting changes in the neuronal network (Udupa et al., 2016)

DBS is a paradigmatic type but not the most widely used form of neuromodulation. More common are sensory prostheses for counteracting deafness and blindness (mostly cochlear implants; > 300,000 patients) and spinal cord stimulations as therapy for several forms of chronic pain (> 100,000 patients). Another common technology is vagus nerve stimulation as a therapy for epilepsy and depression (> 65,000 patients; references for the estimations are included in Christen, 2016). Among those very common neuromodulation interventions, cochlear implants in particular have been a subject of much ethical debate.

(See chapter References)

placed under the skin in the subclavicular or abdominal area) that chronically applies electrical current. The precise effects of the electrical field on the local neural tissue are not yet clear. High-frequency DBS (usually ~130 Hz) has been considered as a method that creates temporary functional lesions by inhibiting the targeted area with electrical current. However, it yields a mostly unpredictable, mixed pattern of inhibition of cell somata and activation of axons that can result in opposite effects. Furthermore, within the target area, multiple neurons with different biochemical characteristics are addressed in the same way. For example, DBS inhibits simultane-ously activating glutamatergic projection neurons and inhibiting GABAergic interneurons, in which the net effect of inhibition is reduced (Sturm, 2013).

As DBS involves surgical intervention into the brain, it usually becomes an option for a patient when medication or other therapeutic approaches are no longer sufficient to control the symptoms or have unbearable side effects. DBS is a complex intervention that requires a close relationship between the patient and medical specialists of several disciplines. This relationship starts with the process of patient selection and ideally should last during the lifetime supervi-sion of the stimulation system. The necessary long-lasting commitment between the patient and medical experts distinguishes DBS (and other neuromodulation techniques) from "classical" neurosurgical procedures. Furthermore, many new technological developments such as closed-loop systems are currently being experimentally investigated (McIntyre et al., 2015), leading to the question of how innovation in collaboration with the device-manufacturing industry can be secured, for example, to counteract publication bias in case of unsuccessful trials, to cover the economic risk of experimental devices, or to lower the regulatory burden associated with introducing new systems into the market (Ineichen et al., 2014).

Because the most common indication for DBS is Parkinson's disease (PD), we outline the intervention using this example. Whereas medication-based therapies (levodopa, dopamine receptor agonists) address the PD–induced shortage of dopamine that causes an imbalance in the neuronal network for movement generation and control, DBS directly intervenes into a node of the neural network itself. The beneficial effects of DBS on motor functions are well established (e.g., Deuschl et al., 2006; Kleiner-Fisman et al., 2006; Wider et al., 2008). But the interven-tion can also cause unintended cognitive, affective, and behavioral side effects (Videnovic and Metman, 2008; Volkmann et al., 2010; Witt et al., 2008). The DBS research community has rec-ognized the complexity associated with this therapeutic approach and has begun to dedicate its attention to emerging issues, whereby reports on complex, single cases have incited discussions with more interdisciplinary stakeholders (Christen and Müller, 2011). In particular, the target STN is critically discussed (Moro, 2009).

The evaluation of unintended sequelae is complex, as they may result from three causes: from surgery, stimulation, or drug reduction after the intervention. Furthermore, in the case of PD, one has to take into account that similar effects may result from disease progression as well as from medication therapy. An additional complicating factor is the potential negative sequelae that accompany the therapeutic benefits of dopaminergic medication. For example, even though dopamine agonists may alleviate symptoms of PD better than levodopa for some patients, defi-cits in impulse control are more likely if a patient is treated using dopamine receptor agonists instead of levodopa (Ambermoon et al., 2011). Paradoxical side effects that manifest as affective and social problems, especially in relationships and work, may occur in spite of a good clinical outcome for the movement disorder (such as alleviating motor symptoms of PD; Schüpbach et al., 2006). For example, some patients do not want to return to work, although they could, because their attitudes toward work and leisure time have been changed following DBS. This may lead to conflicting outcome interpretations, for example, when the patient's accompany-ing side effects from treatment are negative but the clinical effects are positive (the so-called satisfaction paradox; Agid et al., 2006), when the changes are evaluated positively by the patient but negatively by other people, in particular if these changes involve increased energy, novelty seeking, risk taking, or changes in sexual drive (see for an overview Müller and Christen, 2011). Furthermore, ethnic and cultural factors in assessing the degree of aberrant behavior can be expected, for example in the case of hypersexuality (where no standard diagnostic criteria exist for what counts as "excessive sexuality") or pathological gambling (e.g., because patients are less willing to admit their problems due to the absence of legalized gambling in some eastern Asian countries; Chiang et al., 2012). For investigating psychosocial aspects of DBS, a third-party perspective (e.g., by close relatives, caregivers) is necessary. However, few studies have investigated a third-party perspective on DBS patients so far (Christen et al., 2012). A possible explanation for behavioral, affective, or social adaption problems has been conceptualized as the "burden of normality" (Gilbert, 2012; Wilson et al., 2001). For some patients, fighting against the disease has been the sense of their lives, which is lost after the successful therapy. Some patients also have severe problems in taking on responsibility again and in abandoning the patient role. The decision to undergo DBS poses a complex "decision problem" for a patient that is eligible for this intervention. Nevertheless, a psychosocial focus alone is insufficient, because some of the observed effects are clearly stimulation caused and can be influenced by appropriate selection of the stimulation parameters (Saleh and Fontaine, 2015).

Generally, eligible patients are those who are diagnosed with idiopathic PD and whose symptoms previously responded well to L-dopa or apomorphine, who are in good general and cognitive health, and whose medication-based therapies are no longer successful (e.g., due to on-off phenomena, motor fluctuations, or wearing-off phenomena). Furthermore, the patients must be able to undergo a long operation that is partly under full anesthesia. With respect to medical eligibility, there is a consensus on exclusion criteria (e.g., nonidiopathic PD or severe cognitive and psychiatric impairment of the patient; Hilker et al., 2009; Okun et al., 2010) such that DBS is suitable only for a subgroup of PD patients. Little research is devoted to determining the fraction of PD patients eligible for DBS. The referring clinicians seem to underestimate the number of suitable patients (Oyama et al., 2012), and they refer fewer women than men (Setiawan et al., 2006). A reasonable guess is that 10% to 20% of PD patients may qualify for DBS (Christen and Müller, 2012), that is, a substantial number of patients face the challenge of deciding whether DBS is appropriate for them or not.

The patients that qualify for DBS have to weigh benefits and risks of the intervention as well as the alternatives. Given the burden-of-normality problem and the satisfaction paradox, there is a need for communication with patients, their families, and caregivers long before surgery is performed. This is necessary both to anticipate problems that might occur and to give patients and their entourage the necessary time to prepare for the changes that are to be expected in their lives (Schüpbach and Agid, 2008). Thus, decision making with respect to DBS cannot be reduced to the mere assessment procedure in DBS centers. Rather, in the course of standard treatment of PD, the possibility of DBS may be raised by either the patient or the general neurologist.

Current research on decision making with respect to DBS has focused on improving the ability of general neurologists to identify appropriate candidates for this procedure. This led to various electronic decision tools that assist neurologists in determining which PD patients should be referred for DBS consideration (Moro et al., 2009; Wächter et al., 2011). These tools, however, are not intended to be used by the patient; they have only an indirect effect in providing information about whether the patient is eligible from a medical point of view.

With respect to DBS in general, the private-practice neurologist is the decisive entry point with respect to both patient information and referral (Christen et al., 2014a), but the patients also rely in their decision making on information emerging from support groups, media, other patients, or the general practitioner. A recent survey found that the quantity of realistic expectations of patients and family members significantly correlated with a positive evaluation of DBS, whereas doubts as well as unrealistic expectations of family members correlated with a negative attitude (Südmeyer et al., 2012). Furthermore, it is known that in medical interventions that are characterized by scientific uncertainty regarding their benefits and harms, the communication of the physician is influenced both by individual differences in physicians' tolerance of uncertainty and by physicians' beliefs about their patients' tolerance for uncertainty (Portnoy et al., 2013). This demonstrates the importance of appropriate information for a realistic assessment of DBS by the patient.

The Broadening of the DBS Indications Spectrum

In recent years, the spectrum of indications for DBS has been broadened in two ways: First, there is a trend to apply DBS in earlier stages of disease. Second, DBS is being extended to a very broad spectrum of neurological and psychiatric diseases.

With respect to the first trend, the results of the so-called EARLYSTIM study (Schüpbach et al., 2013) suggest that an early DBS intervention can be beneficial for Parkinsonian patients with early motor complications. There are, however, also specific challenges of STN-DBS at an earlier stage of PD such as the inclusion of patients who later evolve to atypical parkinsonism and the risk of a floor effect (which arises when a data-gathering instrument has a lower limit to the data values it can reliably specify) for the benefit from DBS (Mestre et al., 2014). Nevertheless, it is likely that the EARLYSTIM study will lead to an adaptation of the criteria published in the consensus statements (e.g., Hilker et al., 2009), so that the criterion that the medical therapy is no longer successful might be skipped. The number of patients who are referred to DBS centers would be higher if the patients were referred earlier (Charles et al., 2012; Deuschl et al., 2013; Schüpbach et al., 2007/2013), because younger patients as well as patients in earlier disease stages could fulfill less rigorous exclusion criteria. Indeed, earlier referral seems to be a trend in various centers (Okun and Foote, 2010).

Second, there is a trend to expand the indications for DBS. To date, DBS has been approved only for PD, essential tremor, dystonia, epilepsy, and obsessive-compulsive disorder. However, current DBS research includes refractory depression (Morishita et al., 2014), Tourette syndrome (Andrade and Visser-Vandewalle, 2016), dementia (Mirzadeh et al., 2016), minimally conscious state (Schiff et al., 2007), severe obesity (Dupré et al., 2015), aggressive disorder (Franzini et al., 2013), drug addiction (Müller et al., 2013), anorexia nervosa (Müller et al., 2015), and schizophrenia (Salgado-López et al., 2016; Corripio et al., 2016).

Rigorous evidence-based comparison of the efficacy of these new DBS applications is not yet possible due to methodological hurdles and publication bias in the DBS literature (Schläpfer and Fins, 2010). Publication bias in the psychiatric neurosurgery literature is a fundamental problem that compromises the systematic evaluation and comparison of the different procedures, and therefore also the ethical evaluation, which critically depends on objective information of evidence-based risk-benefit ratios (Müller, forthcoming). Furthermore, most psychiatric DBS studies are methodologically weak. Lack of statistical power is a major concern in these studies, because they have very small patient numbers, most with fewer than 10 patients. Furthermore, most studies are neither placebo controlled nor double blinded (Müller, forthcoming). Observer bias in reporting results also presents a methodological concern, as the evaluation of treatment outcomes has not yet been conducted by independent parties who were not involved in patient selection, surgery, or follow-up (Pepper et al., 2015). Therefore, the following efficacy data of DBS for three psychiatric indications should be regarded with caution.

Obsessive-compulsive disorder (OCD): Kohl et al. (2014) analyzed 25 papers comprising 109 DBS patients and five targets (NAcc, VC/VS, ITP, STN, and ALIC) and found response rates ranging from 45.5% to 100%. Pepper et al. (2015) compared DBS and ablative neurosurgery that included more or less homogeneous anatomical areas to ensure a fair comparison. Their analysis included 10 studies with a total of 108 patients who were treated with anterior capsulotomy, and 10 studies with a total of 62 patients who underwent DBS with the targets VC/VS and NAcc. The response rate of DBS patients was 52% and of the anterior cingulotomy patients 62% (response = improvement of Y-BOCS score ≥ 35%; Pepper et al., 2015).

Major depression: Morishita et al. (2014) reviewed data from 22 papers comprising 188 DBS patients and six targets (NAcc, VC/VS, SCC, lateral habenula, ITP, and slMFB). Very recently, an additional target, namely the ALIC, has been tested in 25 patients (Bergfeld et al., 2016). The reported response rates ranged from 29% to 92%. However, the failure of two multicenter, randomized, controlled prospective studies evaluating the efficacy of VC/VS DBS and SCC DBS (Dougherty et al., 2015; Cavuoto, 2013) raises questions about the efficacy of DBS for depression.

Anorexia nervosa: We have reviewed six papers comprising 18 patients and three targets (NAcc, SCC, and VC/VS; Müller et al., 2015). Remission in terms of normalized body mass index occurred in 61% of patients, and psychiatric comorbidities improved in 88.9% of the patients as well. However, Sun et al. (2015) have recently published less favorable results in which only 20% (3/15) of their patients treated with NAcc DBS showed improvements in symptoms. The other 80% underwent anterior capsulotomy, which improved eating behavior and psychiatric symptoms in all patients.

Adverse effects of DBS in those indications include surgery-related, device-related, and stimulation-related effects. Regarding the first category, serious adverse events during or shortly after surgery included intracerebral hemorrhages, which in one case resulted in a temporary hemiparesis (Kohl et al., 2014; Morishita et al., 2014; Pepper et al., 2015); intraoperative seizure; intraoperative panic attack; and cardiac air embolus (Lipsman et al., 2013b). In several cases, wound infections or inflammation occurred (Kohl et al., 2014; Pepper et al., 2015). Regarding the second category, several device-related adverse effects have been reported, namely breaks of electrodes, stimulating leads, or extension wires, requiring replacement (Kohl et al., 2014; Pepper et al., 2015). Finally, many patients suffered from stimulation-induced adverse effects, particularly from depression, anxiety, worsening of OCD, suicidality, panic attacks, fatigue, hypomania, increased libido, and problems at home. In some cases, these adverse effects were caused either by a change of stimulation parameters or by battery depletion and were reversible by respective adjustments (Kohl et al., 2014; Morishita et al., 2014). Interestingly, patients suffering from anorexia nervosa had a particularly high rate of severe complications, namely an epileptic seizure during electrode programming, further weight loss, pancreatitis, hypophosphataemia, hypokalaemia, a refeeding delirium, cardiological disturbances, and worsening of mood (Lipsman et al., 2013b).

Ethical Issues

The ethical literature on DBS is well developed (overview in Christen, 2015). Taking the principles of biomedical ethics (Beauchamp and Childress, 2013) as a framework, issues of beneficence and nonmaleficence, autonomy, and justice have been intensively discussed (for discussion about the validity and scope of this approach, see Christen et al., 2014b; Müller, 2014).

Regarding beneficence and nonmaleficence, several ethicists have discussed the problem that the benefit of psychiatric DBS is probably overestimated due to publication bias (Schläpfer and Fins, 2010; Gilbert and Dodds, 2013). Furthermore, several authors have called for better regulation of the disclosure of conflicts of interests (Schermer, 2011) and have criticized the misuse of the humanitarian device exemption in stimulation for obsessive-compulsive disorder (Fins et al., 2011).

4.2 Spotlight: Ablation Techniques

Markus Christen and Sabine Müller

Ablative techniques are used for both movement disorders and psychiatric disorders. Although the effects of ablative techniques are irreversible, they can be an appropriate alternative for patients for whom DBS is not an option, be it for medical reasons, because of the treatment costs, or because of personal preferences. Two expert panels have affirmed stereotactic ablative procedures as important alternatives for appropriately selected patients (for Parkinson's disease: Bronstein et al., 2011; for psychiatric disorders: Nuttin et al., 2014).

Ablation creates brain lesions by destroying localized brain tissue. Different techniques are used: thermal or radiofrequency ablation, which require craniotomy, as well as Gamma Knife radiosurgery and magnetic resonance–guided focused ultrasound (MRgFUS), which are noninvasive. Gamma Knife radiosurgery is a very precise method for creating confined brain lesions and is mainly used for treating brain tumors and brain arteriovenous malformations but is also used for treating neurological and psychiatric disorders such as Parkinsonism, essential tremor, trigeminal neuralgia, intractable tumor pain, some forms of epilepsy, and psychiatric illness (Friehs et al., 2007). MRgFUS has recently been introduced into the field (Lipsman et al., 2014). It has been tested in four patients with chronic and medication-resistant essential tremor (Lipsman et al., 2013a) and in four OCD patients (Na et al., 2015). MRgFUS might also become an alternative therapy approach for major depression (Na et al., 2015; Lipsman et al., 2013a).

Both DBS and ablative neurosurgical procedures, if used for psychiatric indications, belong to psychiatric neurosurgery. Psychiatric neurosurgery is defined as neurosurgery for treating psychiatric disorders that do not have identified structural brain anomalies, such as brain tumors or epileptogenic tissue. Nonetheless, psychiatric neurosurgery is based on the assumption that certain dysfunctional brain areas or structures play a crucial role in psychiatric disorders and that lesioning or deactivating them can alleviate psychiatric symptoms.

Early psychiatric neurosurgery procedures such as lobotomy became discredited in the 1970s because they had been widely abused and had caused many severe complications (Valenstein, 1986; Chodakiewitz et al., 2015). After a nearly 30-year hiatus, in the late 1990s psychiatric neurosurgery experienced a revival. Today, modern ablative psychiatric neurosurgery is much more precise and safer than its historical predecessors. Anterior capsulotomy and cingulotomy are used today. The main indication is obsessive-compulsive disorder. Further indications for contemporary ablative microsurgical procedures include anxiety disorder, major depression, anorexia nervosa, drug addiction, hyperaggressivity, and schizophrenia (Müller, forthcoming).

(See chapter References)

Autonomy, and in particular the capacity to consent in patients that may undergo a DBS intervention, is much discussed. For example, to what extent is a patient with a pathological brain condition able to provide informed consent for a therapeutic intervention that intends to change this condition, if the brain condition affects the capacity to consent? A second problem with respect to autonomy is the ethical relevance and practical handling of conflicting outcome evaluations of DBS interventions that address pathological brain states among the stakeholders involved (patient, relatives, medical experts; see the second section). This problem is likely to increase when psychiatric conditions are targeted through DBS. Another ethical feature of DBS interventions concerns the principles of beneficence and nonmaleficence. As these interventions target areas of the brain that are relevant for emotions and behavior, they may have unwanted behavioral consequences, which could even include violations of the rights of third parties, for example, if the interventions make the patient hypersexual or extremely aggressive (Müller et al., 2014). Ethical issues related to justice finally often relate to a fair assignment process for patients and to cost issues. For example, ethicists have critically discussed the enrollment criteria of DBS studies (Bell et al., 2009) and the need for the equitable distribution of treatment options (Goldberg, 2012). Several ethicists have investigated the influence of economic interests that drive the development of DBS (Erickson-Davis, 2012; Christen et al., 2014a). However, this part of the ethical debate is less well developed, as only a few studies address issues like cost effectiveness, infrastructure-development, and the like in the field of neuromodulation.

This brief overview outlines the many questions associated with DBS interventions. We suggest that many of them will become more relevant when the whole field is evaluated from a health quality research point of view. In a recent study (Christen et al., 2014a), we have outlined patient-centered aspects of DBS (patient decision making and patient eligibility; dealing with unintended side effects; patient selection and justice) as well as infrastructure-related aspects (research dynamics in the field of DBS; novel DBS indications that require new ways of patient assignment structures, especially in psychiatry; intervention quality issues; infrastructure capacity issues), demonstrating a broad spectrum of open questions in that respect. To date, no integrative study on health service research in neuromodulation that integrates several factors—for example, combining patient-centric and infrastructure-related issues—has been done. This is of particular relevance, as psychiatric conditions like addiction, depression, or eating disorders are targeted for DBS interventions. Questions include: Who would be the gatekeepers in these conditions, and how can adequate patient information and patient referral be guaranteed? It is likely that the referral practice will differ compared to that for movement disorders, because these conditions have different gatekeepers. For example, patients suffering from addiction usually have regular contacts with social workers, who may be skeptical about biological disease models and biomedical interventions for changing behavior.

For a discussion of the effects of brain implants on free will, see Chapter 21.

Also, the decision-making process of potential DBS patients is a major research topic within medical ethics, in particular with respect to the informed consent of a patient. Certainly, as DBS involves risks of both clinical and ethical relevance (Glannon, 2010), there is an obligation on the part of physicians to obtain fully informed consent from patients undergoing the procedure. A key ethical orientation in this discussion is the principle of autonomy (Beauchamp and Childress, 2013) that involves various facets like the foundation of autonomy in philosophical theories, the concept of autonomy in law, or the capacities for performing autonomy and the assessment of them in a concrete decision problem, for example in the case of dementia (see for an overview Donnelly, 2010; Tauber, 2005). In that respect, some scholars emphasize the notion of a "relational" understanding of autonomy, arguing that decision making should consider not only the individual perspectives of patients but also those of their families and members of the health care team, as well as the perspectives that emerge from the interactions among them (Epstein and Street, 2011). It has furthermore been suggested that a strong focus on the decision situation itself is problematic, especially when combined with a tendency to stress the importance of patients' independence in choosing (Entwistle et al., 2010). This could distract attention from other important aspects of and challenges to autonomy in health care. In contrast, a relational understanding of autonomy attempts to explain both the positive and negative implications of social relationships for individuals' autonomy. Furthermore, many health care practices can affect autonomy by virtue of their effects not only on patients' treatment preferences and choices but also on their self-identities, self-evaluations, and capabilities for autonomy. A relational understanding of autonomy deemphasizes independence and facilitates well-nuanced distinctions between forms of clinical communication that support or undermine patients' autonomy. Individuals usually rely on others to help them think and feel their way through difficult decisions, so the concept of "shared minds" (Epstein and Street, 2011) may be a suitable approach for framing the ethical problem in DBS decision making by patients. This approach intends to understand why, when, and how individuals involve trusted others in sharing information, deliberation, and decision making through the sharing of thoughts, feelings, perceptions, meanings, and intentions among two or more people.

One particularly important issue in DBS decision making is unrealistic expectations of personal benefits or risks by the patient. This is a major issue in experimental DBS research involving novel indications, where research participants may not appreciate important differences between research and treatment—a problem usually framed as "therapeutic misconception" (e.g., Henderson et al., 2007). Indeed, experimental research in DBS, for example, for treatment-resistant depression, demonstrate that unrealistic expectations may be a key motivation for study participants (Rabins et al., 2009). A recent study, however, found that participants of such studies did not express a set of motivations or influencing factors that suggested compromised decision-making capacity or diminished voluntariness of decision making and that the trials that were studied utilized sufficiently robust informed-consent processes (Christopher et al., 2012). The issue of therapeutic misconception is of less relevance in DBS in movement disorders, as the intervention in these cases is no longer considered experimental, but the problem of unrealistic expectations remains. Although the study of Südmeyer et al. (2012) indicates that only a minority of patients had unrealistically high expectations for therapy, these results are nevertheless in some tension with the earlier-mentioned phenomenon of a "satisfaction paradox" (Agid et al., 2006) after intervention (Christen et al., 2014a). The study of Südmeyer et al. (2012) also found that patients deciding on DBS often mention unrealistically high risk of intraoperative complications and stimulation-induced worsening of symptoms that do not match with the known complication rates of the intervention. This may partly explain why only 28% of patients that have been identified in a large European multicenter study as eligible for DBS actually decided to undergo the surgery (Wächter et al., 2011). Südmeyer et al. suggest that these opinions of patients and their relatives with respect to expectations and risks are formed well before the eligibility assessment.

The ethical issues of decision making in DBS do not only concern the individual decision. In our study (Christen and Müller, 2012), we found indications that the referral practice in Switzerland for DBS interventions may be too conservative, that is, some patients do not get the optimal treatment, which is ethically problematic—this may also be the case in other countries (Christen et al., 2014a). However, this point needs further backing by more solid data. In particular, investigation is needed to determine whether this finding results from a justified skepticism regarding possible adverse effects of DBS by the patients, the close relatives, and the general neurologists or whether it reflects lack of knowledge or prejudice in the referring stakeholders and/or patients. Certainly, not only factors like skepticism or risk aversion determine the referring practice, as the DBS centers themselves perform a sophisticated selection procedure based on medical and psychological factors. Nevertheless, those factors are relevant before the potential DBS patient actually goes to the center for a detailed assessment. An analysis of this problem is complex, as the willingness to undergo such an intervention strongly depends on the quality of the information that is available in the decision-making process but also on the capabilities of the patient, within his environment, to deal with this information. The fact that DBS is increasingly investigated for other indications—in particular psychiatric ones, in which the decision problem may be even more complex—underscores the need for a thorough analysis of the current patient decision-making process with respect to DBS.

Acknowledgments

The research of Sabine Müller is funded by the German Federal Ministry of Education and Research (01 GP 1621A).

Further Reading

Fangerau, H., Fegert, J.M. and Trapp, T. (Eds.) (2011) *Implanted Minds*. Bielefeld: Transcript Verlag (ethical and historical debate about deep brain stimulation)

Lévêque, M. (2014) *Psychosurgery: New Techniques for Brain Disorders*. Dordrecht: Springer (overview on psychiatric neurosurgery)

Krames, E.F., Peckham, P.H. and Rezai, A.R. (Eds.) (2009) *Neuromodulation*. London: Academic Press (general overview on neuromodulation)

Sun, B. and De Salles, A. (2015) *Neurosurgical Treatments for Psychiatric Disorders*. Dordrecht: Springer (overview on psychiatric neurosurgery)

References

Agid, Y., Schüpbach, M., Gargiulo, M., Mallet, L., Houeto, J.L., Behar, C., . . . Welter, M.L. (2006) Neurosurgery in Parkinson's disease: The doctor is happy, the patient less so? *Journal of Neural Transmission (Vienna) Supplement* 70: pp. 409–414.

Ambermoon, P., Carter, A., Hall, W.D., Dissanayaka, N.N., and O'Sullivan, J.D. (2011) Impulse control disorders in patients with Parkinson's disease receiving dopamine replacement therapy: Evidence and implications for the addictions field. *Addiction* 106(2): pp. 283–293.

Andrade, P., and Visser-Vandewalle, V. (2016) DBS in Tourette syndrome: Where are we standing now? *Journal of Neural Transmission (Vienna)* 123(7): pp. 791–796.

Beauchamp, T.L., and Childress, J.F. (2013) *Principles of Biomedical Ethics*. 5th ed. Oxford: Oxford University Press.

Bell, E., Mathieu, G., and Racine, E. (2009) Preparing the ethical future of deep brain stimulation. *Surgical Neurology* 72: pp. 577–586.

Benabid, A.L., Chabardes, S., Mitrofanis, J., and Pollak, P. (2009) Deep brain stimulation of the subthalamic nucleus for the treatment of Parkinson's disease. *The Lancet Neurology* 8: pp. 67–81.

Benabid, A.L., Pollak, P., Louveau, A., Henry, S., and de Rougemont, J. (1987) Combined (thalamotomy and stimulation) stereotactic surgery of the VIM thalamic nucleus for bilateral Parkinson disease. *Applied Neurophysiology* 50: pp. 344–346.

Bergfeld, I.O., Mantione, M., Hoogendoorn, M.L.C., Ruhé, H.G., Notten, P., van Laarhoven, . . . Denys, D. (2016) Deep brain stimulation of the ventral anterior limb of the internal capsule for treatment-resistant depression. A randomized trial. *JAMA Psychiatry* 73(5): pp. 456–464.

Bronstein, J.M., Tagliati, M., Alterman, R.L., Lozano, A.M., Volkmann, J., Stefani, A., . . . DeLong, M.R. (2011). Deep brain stimulation for Parkinson disease: An expert consensus and review of key issues. *Archives of Neurology* 68(2): pp. 165–171.

Cavuoto, J. (2013) Depressing innovation. *Neurotechnology Business Report*. Available at: www.neurotech reports.com/pages/publishersletterDec13.html [Accessed 9 May 2016].

Charles, P.D., Dolhun, R.M., Gill, C.E., Davis, T.L., Bliton, M.J., Tramontana, M.G., . . . Konrad, P.E. (2012) Deep brain stimulation in early Parkinson's disease: Enrollment experience from a pilot trial. *Parkinsonism and Related Disorders* 18(3): pp. 268–273.

Chiang, H.L., Huang, Y.S., Chen, S.T., and Wu, Y.R. (2012) Are there ethnic differences in impulsive/compulsive behaviors in Parkinson's disease? *European Journal of Neurology* 19(3): pp. 494–500.

Chodakiewitz, Y., Williams, J., Chodakiewitz, J., and Cosgrove, G.R. (2015) Ablative surgery for neuropsychiatric disorders: Past, present, future. In B. Sun, A. and De Salles (Eds.). *Neurosurgical Treatments for Psychiatric Disorders*. Dordrecht: Springer, pp. 51–66.

Christen, M. (2015) *The Ethics of Neuromodulation-Induced Behavior Changes*. Habilitation in the Field of Biomedical Ethics. Medical Faculty of the University of Zurich. Available at: www.zora.uzh.ch/117285/

———. (2016) Klinische und ethische Fragen der Neuromodulation. In R.J. Jox, F. Erbguth (Eds.). *Praktische Fragen der Neuromedizin*. Berlin: Springer, pp. 117–128.

Christen, M., Bittlinger, M., Walter, H., Brugger, P., and Müller, S. (2012) Dealing with side effects of deep brain stimulation: Lessons learned from stimulating the STN. *American Journal of Bioethics Neuroscience* 3(1): pp. 37–43.

Christen, M., Ineichen, C., Bittlinger, M., Bothe, H.-W., and Müller, S. (2014a) Ethical focal points in the international practice of deep brain stimulation. *American Journal of Bioethics Neuroscience* 5(4): pp. 65–80.

Christen, M., Ineichen, C., and Tanner, C. (2014b) How moral are the principles of biomedical ethics? *BMC Medical Ethics* 15: Article 47.

Christen, M., and Müller, S. (2011) Single cases promote knowledge transfer in the field of DBS. *Frontiers in Integrative Neuroscience* 5, Article 13.

———. (2012) Current status and future challenges of deep brain stimulation in Switzerland. *Swiss Medical Weekly* 142: Article w13570.

Christopher, P.P., Leykin, Y., Appelbaum, P.S., Holtzheimer, P.E. 3rd, Mayberg, H.S., and Dunn, L.B. (2012) Enrolling in deep brain stimulation research for depression: Influences on potential subjects' decision making. *Depression and Anxiety* 29(2): pp. 139–146.

Corripio, I., Sarró, S., McKenna, P.J., Molet, J., Álvarez, E., Pomarol-Clotet, E., and Portella, M.J. (2016) Clinical improvement in a treatment-resistant patient with Schizophrenia treated with deep brain stimulation. *Biological Psychiatry* 80(8): pp. e69–70.

Deuschl, G., Schade-Brittinger, C., Krack, P., Volkmann, J., Schäfer, H., Bötzel, K., . . . Voges, J. [German Parkinson's Study Group, Neurostimulation Section] (2006) A randomized trial of deep-brain stimulation for Parkinson's disease. *New England Journal of Medicine* 355: pp. 896–908.

Deuschl, G., Schüpbach, M., Knudsen, K., Pinsker, M.O., Cornu, P., Rau, J., Agid, Y., and Schade-Brittinger, C. (2013) Stimulation of the subthalamic nucleus at an earlier disease stage of Parkinson's disease: Concept and standards of the EARLYSTIM-study. *Parkinsonism and Related Disorders* 19(1): pp. 56–61.

Donnelly, M. (2010) *Healthcare Decision-Making and the Law: Autonomy, Capacity and the Limits of Liberalism*. Cambridge: Cambridge University Press.

Dougherty, D.D., Rezai, A.R., Carpenter, L.L., Howland, R.H., Bhati, M.T., O'Reardon, . . . Malone, D.A. Jr. (2015) A randomized sham-controlled trial of deep brain stimulation of the ventral capsule/ventral striatum for chronic treatment-resistant depression. *Biological Psychiatry* 78: pp. 240–248.

Dupré, D.A., Tomycz, N., Oh, M.Y., and Whiting, D. (2015) Deep brain stimulation for obesity: Past, present, and future targets. *Neurosurgical Focus* 38(6): p. E7.

Entwistle, V.A., Carter, S.M., Cribb, A., and McCaffery, K. (2010) Supporting patient autonomy: The importance of clinician-patient relationships. *Journal of General Internal Medicine* 25(7): pp. 741–745.

Epstein, R.M., and Street, R.L. Jr. (2011) Shared mind: Communication, decision making, and autonomy in serious illness. *Annals of Family Medicine* 9(5): pp. 454–461.

Erickson-Davis, C. (2012) Ethical concerns regarding commercialization of DBS for OCD. *Bioethics* 26(8): pp. 440–446.

Fins, J.J., Mayberg, H.S., Nuttin, B., Kubu, C.S., Galert, T., Sturm, V., . . . Schlaepfer, T.E. (2011) Misuse of the humanitarian device exemption in stimulation for obsessive-compulsive disorder. *Health Affairs* 30: pp. 2302–2311.

Franzini, A., Broggi, G., Cordella, R., Dones, I., and Messina, G. (2013) Deep-brain stimulation for aggressive and disruptive behavior. *World Neurosurgery* 80(3–4): pp. S29 e11–S29 e14.

Friehs, G.M., Park, M.C., Goldman, M.A., Zerris, V.A., Norén, G., and Sampath, P. (2007) Stereotactic radiosurgery for functional disorders. *Neurosurgery Focus* 23(6): pp. E3 1–E3 8

Gilbert, F. (2012) The burden of normality: From 'chronically ill' to 'symptom free': New ethical challenges for deep brain stimulation postoperative treatment. *Journal of Medical Ethics* 38: pp. 408–412.

Gilbert, F., and Dodds, S. (2013) How to turn ethical neglect into ethical approval. *American Journal of Bioethics Neuroscience* 4(2): pp. 59–60.

Glannon, W. (2010) Consent to deep brain stimulation for neurological and psychiatric disorders. *Journal of Clinical Ethics* 21(2): pp. 104–111.

Goldberg, D.S. (2012) Justice, population health, and deep brain stimulation. *American Journal of Bioethics Neuroscience* 3(1): pp. 16–20.

Hariz, M.I., Blomstedt, P., and Zrinzo, L. (2010) Deep brain stimulation between 1947 and 1987: The untold story. *Neurosurgery Focus* 29(2): p. E1.

Henderson, G.E., Churchill, L.R., Davis, A.M., Easter, M.M., Grady, C., Joffe, S., . . . Zimmer, C.R. (2007) Clinical trials and medical care: Defining the therapeutic misconception. *PLoS Medicine* 4(11): Article e324.

Hilker, R., Benecke, R., Deuschl, G., Fogel, W., Kupsch, A., Schrader, C., . . . Lange, M. (2009) Tiefe Hirnstimulation bei idiopathischem Parkinson-Syndrom: Empfehlungen der Deutschen Arbeitsgemeinschaft Tiefe Hirnstimulation. *Nervenarzt* 80(6): pp. 646–655.

Holsheimer, J. (2003) Letters to the editor. *Neuromodulation* 6(4): pp. 270–273.

Ineichen, C., Glannon, W., Temel, Y., Baumann, C.R., and Sürücü, O. (2014) A critical reflection on the technological development of deep brain stimulation. *Frontiers in Human Neuroscience* 8, Article 730.

Kleiner-Fisman, G., Herzog, J., Fisman, D.N., Tamma, F., Lyons, K.E., Pahwa, R., . . . Deuschl, G. (2006) Subthalamic nucleus deep brain stimulation: Summary and meta-analysis of outcomes. *Movement Disorders* 21(suppl 14): pp. S290–S304.

Kohl, S., Schönherr, D.M., Juigjes, J., Denys, D., Mueller, U.J., Lenartz, D., . . . and Kuhn, J. (2014) Deep brain stimulation for treatment-refractory obsessive compulsive disorder: A systematic review. *BMC Psychiatry* 14: p. 214.

Krames, E.F., Peckham, P.H., and Rezai, A.R. (Eds.) (2009) *Neuromodulation*. London: Academic Press.

Lipsman, N., Mainprize, T.G., Schwartz, M.L., Hynynen, K., and Lozano, A.M. (2014) Intracranial applications of magnetic resonance-guided focused ultrasound. *Neurotherapeutics* 11: pp. 593–605.

Lipsman, N., Schwartz, M.L., Huang, Y., Lee, L., Sankar, T., Chapman, M., . . . Lozano, A.M. (2013a) MR-guided focused ultrasound thalamotomy for essential tremor: A proof-of-concept study. *The Lancet Neurology* 12: pp. 462–468.

Lipsman, N., Woodside, D.B., Giacobbe, P., Hamani, C., Carter, J.C., Norwood, S.J., . . . Lozano, A.M. (2013b) Subcallosal cingulate deep brain stimulation for treatment-refractory anorexia nervosa: A phase 1 pilot trial. *The Lancet* 381(9875): pp. 1361–1370.

McIntyre, C.C., Chaturvedi, A., Shamir, R.R., and Lempka, S.F. (2015) Engineering the next generation of clinical deep brain stimulation technology. *Brain Stimulation* 8(1): pp. 21–26.

Mestre, T.A., Espay, A.J., Marras, C., Eckman, M.H., Pollak, P., and Lang, A.E. (2014) Subthalamic nucleus-deep brain stimulation for early motor complications in Parkinson's disease-the EARLYSTIM trial: Early is not always better. *Movement Disorders* 29(14): pp. 1751–1756.

Mirzadeh, Z., Bari, A., and Lozano, A.M. (2016) The rationale for deep brain stimulation in Alzheimer's disease. *Journal of Neural Transmission (Vienna)* 123(7): pp. 775–783.

Morishita, T., Fayad, S.M., Higuchi, M., Nestor, K.A., and Foote, K.D. (2014) Deep brain stimulation for treatment-resistant depression: Systematic review of clinical outcomes. *Neurotherapeutics* 11: pp. 475–484.

Moro, E. (2009) Impulse control disorders and subthalamic nucleus stimulation in Parkinson's disease: Are we jumping the gun? *European Journal of Neurology* 16(4): pp. 440–441.

Moro, E., Allert, N., Eleopra, R., Houeto, J.L., Phan, T.M., Stoevelaar, H., and International Study Group on Referral Criteria for DBS (2009) A decision tool to support appropriate referral for deep brain stimulation in Parkinson's disease. *Journal of Neurology* 256(1): pp. 83–88.

Müller, S. (2014) *Personality and Autonomy in Light of Neuroscience: Ethical and Neurophilosophical Issues of Interventions in the Brain.* Freie Universität Berlin, Charité—Universitätsmedizin Berlin. Available at: www.diss.fu-berlin.de/diss/receive/FUDISS_thesis_000000097489 [Accessed 30 Dec. 2016].

Müller, S. (forthcoming) Ethical challenges of modern psychiatric neurosurgery. In J. Illes and S. Hossain (Ed.). *Neuroethics: Defining the Field in Theory, Practice and Policy.* 2nd ed. Oxford: Oxford University Press.

Müller, S., and Christen, M. (2011) Deep brain stimulation in Parkinsonian patients—Ethical evaluation of stimulation-induced personality alterations. *American Journal of Bioethics Neuroscience* 2(1): pp. 3–13.

Müller, S., Riedmüller, R., Walter, H., and Christen, M. (2015) An ethical evaluation of stereotactic neurosurgery for anorexia nervosa. *American Journal of Bioethics Neuroscience* 6(4): pp. 50–65.

Müller, S., Walter, H., and Christen, M. (2014) When benefitting a patient increases the risk for harm for third persons—The case of treating pedophilic Parkinsonian patients with deep brain stimulation. *International Journal of Law and Psychiatry* 37(3): pp. 295–303.

Müller, U.J., Voges, J., Steiner, J., Galazky, I., Heinze, H.J., Möller, M., . . . Kuhn, J. (2013) Deep brain stimulation of the nucleus accumbens for the treatment of addiction. *Annals of the New York Academy of Sciences* 1282: pp. 119–128.

Na, Y.C., Jung, H.H., and Chang, J.W. (2015) Focused ultrasound for the treatment of obsessive-compulsive disorder. In B. Sun and A. De Salles (Eds.). *Neurosurgical Treatments for Psychiatric Disorders.* Dordrecht: Springer, pp. 125–141.

Nuttin, B., Wu, H., Mayberg, H., Hariz, M., Gabriëls, L., Galert, T., . . . Schlaepfer, T. (2014) Consensus on guidelines for stereotactic neurosurgery for psychiatric disorders. *Journal of Neurology Neurosurgery and Psychiatry* 85(9): pp. 1003–1008.

Okun, M.S., and Foote, K.D. (2010) Parkinson's disease DBS: What, when, who and why? The time has come to tailor DBS targets. *Expert Reviews of Neurotherapeutics* 10(12): pp. 1847–1857.

Oyama, G., Rodriguez, R.L., Jones, J.D., Swartz, C., Merritt, S., Unger, R., . . . Okun, M.S. (2012) Selection of deep brain stimulation candidates in private neurology practices: Referral may be simpler than a computerized triage system. *Neuromodulation* 15: pp. 246–250.

Pepper, J., Hariz, M., and Zrinzo, L. (2015) Deep brain stimulation versus anterior capsulotomy for obsessive-compulsive disorder: A review of the literature. *Journal of Neurosurgery* 122: pp. 1028–1037.

Portnoy, D.B., Han, P.K., Ferrer, R.A., Klein, W.M., and Clauser, S.B. (2013) Physicians' attitudes about communicating and managing scientific uncertainty differ by perceived ambiguity aversion of their patients. *Health Expectations* 6(4): pp. 362–372.

Rabins, P., Appleby, B.S., Brandt, J., DeLong, M.R., Dunn, L.B., Gabriëls, L., . . . Mathews, D.J. (2009) Scientific and ethical issues related to deep brain stimulation for disorders of mood, behavior, and thought. *Archives in General Psychiatry* 66: pp. 931–937.

Saleh, C., and Fontaine, D. (2015) Deep brain stimulation for psychiatric diseases: What are the risks? *Current Psychiatry Report* 17: Article 33.

Salgado-López, L., Pomarol-Clotet, E., Roldán, A., Rodríguez, R., Molet, J., Sarró, S., . . . and Corripio, I. (2016) Letter to the editor: Deep brain stimulation for schizophrenia. *Journal of Neurosurgery* 125(1): pp. 229–230.

Schermer, M. (2011) Ethical issues in deep brain stimulation. *Frontiers in Integrative Neuroscience* 5: Article 17.

Schiff, N.D., Giacino, J.T., Kalmar, K., Victor, J.D., Baker, K., Gerber, M., . . . Rezai, A.R. (2007) Behavioural improvements with thalamic stimulation after severe traumatic brain injury. *Nature* 448(7153): pp. 600–603.

Schläpfer, T.E., and Fins, J.J. (2010) Deep brain stimulation and the neuroethics of responsible publishing: When one is not enough. *The Journal of American Medical Association* 303(8): pp. 775–776.

Schüpbach, W.M., Rau, J., Knudsen, K., Volkmann, J., Krack, P., Timmermann, L., . . . Deuschl, G. [EARLYSTIM Study Group] (2013) Neurostimulation for Parkinson's disease with early motor complications. *New England Journal of Medicine* 368(7): pp. 610–622.

Schüpbach, W.M., and Agid, Y. (2008) Psychosocial adjustment after deep brain stimulation in Parkinson's disease. *Nature Clinical Practice Neurology* 4(2): pp. 58–59.

Schüpbach, W.M., Gargiulo, M., Welter, M.L., Mallet, L., Béhar, C., Houeto, J.L., . . . Agid, Y. (2006) Neurosurgery in Parkinson disease: A distressed mind in a repaired body? *Neurology* 66(12): pp. 1811–1816.

Schüpbach, W.M., Maltête, D., Houeto, J.L., du Montcel, S.T., Mallet, L., Welter, M.L., . . . and Agid, Y. (2007) Neurosurgery at an earlier stage of Parkinson disease: A randomized, controlled trial. *Neurology* 68(4): pp. 267–271.

Setiawan, M., Kraft, S., Doig, K., Hunka, K., Haffenden, A., Trew, M., . . . Kiss, Z.H. (2006) Referrals for movement disorder surgery: Under-representation of females and reasons for refusal. *Canadian Journal of Neurological Sciences* 33: pp. 53–57.

Siegfried, J. (1986) Effect of stimulation of the sensory nucleus of the thalamus on dyskinesia and spasticity. *Revue Neurologie (Paris)* 142(4): pp. 380–383.

Sturm, V. (2013) Potential of optogenetics in deep brain stimulation. In P. Hegemann and S. Sigrist (Eds.). *Optogenetics*. Berlin, Boston: De Gruyter, pp. 157–160.

Südmeyer, M., Volkmann, J., Wojtecki, L., Deuschl, G., Schnitzler, A., and Möller B. (2012) Tiefe Hirnstimulation—Erwartungen und Bedenken: Bundesweite Fragebogenstudie mit Parkinson-Patienten und deren Angehörigen. *Nervenarzt* 83(4): pp. 481–486.

Sun, B., and De Salles, A. (2015) *Neurosurgical Treatments for Psychiatric Disorders*. Dordrecht: Springer.

Tauber, A.I. (2005) *Patient Autonomy and the Ethics of Responsibility*. Cambridge, MA: MIT Press.

Udupa, K., Bahl, N., Ni, Z., Gunraj, C., Mazzella, F., Moro, E., . . . Chen, R. (2016) Cortical plasticity induction by pairing subthalamic nucleus deep-brain stimulation and primary motor cortical transcranial magnetic stimulation in Parkinson's disease. *Journal of Neuroscience* 36(2): pp. 396–404.

Valenstein, E.S. (1986) *Great and Desperate Cures: The Rise and Decline of Psychosurgery and Other Radical Treatments for Mental Illness*. New York: Basic Books, Inc.

Videnovic, A., and Metman, L.V. (2008) Deep brain stimulation for Parkinson's disease: Prevalence of adverse events and need for standardized reporting. *Movement Disorders* 23: pp. 343–349.

Volkmann, J., Daniels, C., and Witt, K. (2010) Neuropsychiatric effects of subthalamic neurostimulation in Parkinson disease. *Nature Reviews Neurology* 6(9): pp. 487–498.

Wächter, T., Mínguez-Castellanos, A., Valldeoriola, F., Herzog, J., and Stoevelaar, H. (2011) A tool to improve pre-selection for deep brain stimulation in patients with Parkinson's disease. *Journal of Neurology* 258(4): pp. 641–646.

Wider, C., Pollo, C., Bloch, J., Burkhard, P.R., and Vingerhoets, F.J. (2008) Long-term outcome of 50 consecutive Parkinson's disease patients treated with subthalamic deep brain stimulation. *Parkinsonism and Related Disorders* 14(2): pp. 114–119.

Wilson, S., Bladin, P., and Saling, M. (2001) The 'burden of normality': Concepts of adjustment after surgery for seizures. *Journal of Neurology, Neurosurgery and Psychiatry* 70: pp. 649–656.

Witt, K., Daniels, C., Reiff, J., Krack, P., Volkmann, J., Pinsker, M.O., . . . Deuschl, G. (2008) Neuropsychological and psychiatric changes after deep brain stimulation for Parkinson's disease: A randomised, multicentre study. *The Lancet Neurology* 7(7): pp. 605–614.

5

THE ETHICS OF PRODROMAL AND PRECLINICAL DISEASE STAGES

Jalayne J. Arias, Jennifer C. Sarrett, Rosa Gonzalez, and Elaine F. Walker

Introduction and Terminology

Research in neurological and psychiatric conditions has advanced capabilities to identify risk factors and detect disease processes prior to the onset of clinical symptoms (DeKosky and Marek, 2003). Early insights into the disease process (genetic markers, biomarkers for disease pathology, and early behavior or symptom presentation) provide opportunities for early intervention and increased monitoring for individuals who are at highest risk of developing disabling disorders such as autism spectrum disorder, schizophrenia, and Alzheimer's disease.

Pathological markers include measures of amyloid and tau through positron emission tomography (PET) and cerebral spinal fluid (CSF) found in Alzheimer's disease (Dubois et al., 2016). These measures identify disease pathology in symptomatic and asymptomatic individuals. Research concerned with risk for schizophrenia and other psychotic disorders has focused on family history of the patient (i.e., genetic risk) or presentation of subclinical or attenuated symptoms that may predict illnesses (i.e., schizophrenia; Walker et al., 2013). Similarly, researchers have explored early indicators of autism in the first few months of life, including behavioral markers seen on home videos of children prior to an autism diagnosis (Baranek, 1999) and eye-tracking technologies (Frazier et al., 2016; Jones and Klin, 2013; Sarrett and Rommelfanger, 2015).

Research relevant to genetic markers and related ethical challenges laid the foundation for identification of prodromal (early presentation of symptoms but does not meet diagnostic criteria) and preclinical (asymptomatic with evidence of pathological markers) indicators (Besser et al., 2015). Early identification of risk and disease for neurological and psychiatric conditions, however, raises new legal and ethical challenges.

This chapter describes the legal and ethical challenges triggered by preclinical and prodromal states associated with neurological and psychiatric disorders (Figure 5.1). To provide context, autism spectrum disorder (ASD), schizophrenia and other psychoses, and Alzheimer's disease will serve as paradigms to explore the potential ethical, legal, and social challenges. The chapter will begin by introducing foundational concepts related to preclinical and prodromal states, including clarifying terminology and descriptions of early disease states in ASD, schizophrenia, and Alzheimer's disease. Next, the chapter will explore challenges raised by biomarker or clinical testing for preclinical and prodromal states, including the benefits–risks assessment and interpretation of tests or screening. The chapter will then discuss disclosure of results to

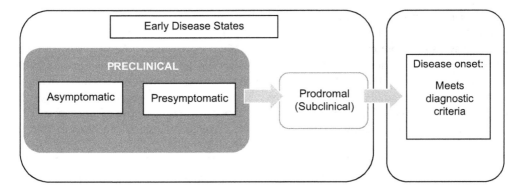

Fig. 5.1. The Transition of Early Disease States to Disease Onset. Early disease states includes both pre-clinical and prodromal states of the disease process. For conditions where preclinical status can be identified, individuals may be either be asymptomatic (increased likelihood of developing symptoms) or presymptomatic (indication that the individual will with certainty develop the outcome disorder). The "preclinical" phase (when identified) generally precedes the "prodromal" stage (symptomatic without meeting diagnostic criteria).

Source: Authors.

patients, families, and potentially others. This section will consider the role of stigma and risk of employment and insurance discrimination associated with an early disease state label. Finally, this chapter will describe how early disease states trigger consequences and opportunities in preparing for disease onset.

The Role of Diagnostic Criteria

There are inherent challenges in accurately diagnosing neurological and psychiatric conditions. Many conditions, including Alzheimer's disease, require neuropathological examination, using (postmortem) samples of a patient's brain, which is not feasible in living patients (Dunckley et al., 2005; McKhann et al., 2011). Diagnostic practices highlight critical differences between neurological and psychiatric conditions, although both categories of conditions can have similar manifestations and are often comorbidities (i.e., Alzheimer's disease with depression). The distinction between neurological and psychiatric conditions remains controversial (Baker, 2002). Some have supported the distinction by arguing that neurological disorders entail well-established central nervous system (i.e., brain) dysfunction. The nature of the dysfunction in psychiatric conditions has been more difficult to describe, but researchers suspect it involves molecular aspects of neurocircuitry. As a result, diagnostic practices for psychiatric disorders rely on behavioral signs/symptoms without the benefit of biomarkers (Aminoff and Faulkner, 2012).

Diagnostic criteria seek to address limitations and challenges associated with diagnosing and treating medical and psychiatric conditions. Diagnostic criteria establish factors or approaches to diagnose an illness or condition to maintain consistency among patients with the same diagnosis (Jutel, 2009). Additionally, their role serves as a critical background to advancements in preclinical and prodromal states. Generally, professional organizations disseminate diagnostic criteria that leaders in the field have agreed upon, although there may be multiple (sometimes competing) diagnostic criteria for the same illness. Examples of competing diagnostic criteria include the *Diagnostic and Statistical Manual of Mental Disorders* (DSM) for behavioral and cognitive criteria for mental health disorders and internationally, the World Health Organization's

International Classification of Disease (ICD; World Health Organization, 1993). Research groups or task forces supported by collaborations between professional organizations and government groups may also propose criteria. For example, the National Institute of Aging (NIA) and the Alzheimer's Association jointly supported revised diagnostic guidelines for Alzheimer's in 2011 (McKhann et al., 2011). Diagnostic criteria are typically revised to reflect research and medical advancements. For example, the National Institute of Mental Health proposed the "Research Domain Criteria" (RDoC) for conducting empirical research on the nature of psychiatric syndromes and the validity of current DSM-5 diagnostic categories (Cuthbert and Insel, 2013).

> For more on RDoC and its potential effects on psychiatry, see Chapter 27.

Challenges in Terminology

The advent of research on preclinical and prodromal stages of multiple diseases has led to new terminology, including: "preclinical," "prodromal," "clinically high risk," "ultra–high risk," "asymptomatic," and "presymptomatic" (Sperling et al., 2011; Fusar-Poli et al., 2013). The choice of terminology reflects different characterizations of a disease stage that precedes a clinically diagnosable condition. Inconsistencies between disease populations and researchers have created variations in language related to early disease states. Varying terminology in Alzheimer's disease serves as an example of these variations. In 2010, an international working group (IWG) initially published research that shifted Alzheimer's disease into a spectrum disorder with asymptomatic/presymptomatic, prodromal, and dementia stages. The IWG distinguished presymptomatic (indicator with a very high predictive value that will, *with certainty*, lead to meeting diagnostic criteria) and asymptomatic (a risk factor with a *less-than-certain* predictive value; Dubois et al., 2010; Sperling et al., 2011). This same article defined prodromal stage of Alzheimer's disease as an early symptomatic stage of the disease. In 2011, the NIA and Alzheimer's Association task force published new diagnostic criteria that defined a preclinical, mild cognitive impairment and dementia as three separate stages of Alzheimer's disease. The preclinical stage is consistent with the IWG's definitions of presymptomatic and asymptomatic. Similarly, there is overlap in the definition of prodromal and MCI. In 2016, another collaboration evaluated the distinction between preclinical (a high certainty of developing Alzheimer's disease dementia) and "at risk" (an increased risk of developing Alzheimer's disease dementia) based on biomarker results in asymptomatic patients (Dubois et al., 2016). The shifts in terminology reflect a larger emerging trend in neurological and psychiatric conditions with early disease states.

A *preclinical* state is the presence of disease pathology without clinical symptoms (Dekosky and Marek, 2003). Currently, terminology that applies to preclinical states is primarily used in reference to neurologic conditions and not psychiatric illness. A prodrome or prodromal stage is a decline from baseline functioning or the onset of subclinical symptoms that do not yet meet the clinical diagnostic criteria for a disease (Yirmiya and Charman, 2010; Ramagopalan et al., 2010). Among different diseases, there is variation in the likelihood that the prodromal stage or preclinical state will convert to a disorder meeting diagnostic criteria. For example, atypical looking patterns may occur in infants who do not later meet the criteria for ASD. Importantly, prodromal states may be nonspecific, meaning that a prodromal state may be characterized by a collection of symptoms that are not specific for single-disease pathology (Mittal et al., 2015). For example, MCI may convert to dementia associated with differing disease pathologies (i.e.,

Alzheimer's disease, vascular dementia, frontotemporal dementia). Similarly, the prodromal state for psychosis may indicate risk of several disorders, including schizophrenia.

For the remainder of this chapter, we will use the term "early disease states" to refer to the broader category of preclinical and prodromal states. "Preclinical" will refer specifically to early disease states that are marked by the identification of disease pathology in advance of any clinical symptoms. Similarly, "prodrome" or "prodromal" will refer to early or mild behavior changes or symptoms that do not meet diagnostic criteria for a disease or condition. Lastly, we will use "outcome disease" to broadly refer to the disease or syndrome when an individual has met the diagnostic criteria (see Figure 5.1).

Conditions with Early Disease States

Early disease states have been identified in multiple neurologic and psychiatric conditions. We will focus on early disease states in ASD, schizophrenia, and Alzheimer's disease, which represent some of the most active areas of research. Each early disease state is uniquely characterized by risk factors, indicators, and tools for detection prior to meeting diagnostic criteria. Table 5.1 provides a comparison of different conditions and their associated early disease states.

Autism Spectrum Disorder (ASD)

ASD, also known as autism, is a life-long condition that is often identifiable in early childhood. It is a neurological difference characterized by difficulties with verbal communication, typical social interaction patterns, behaviors, different sensory experiences, engagement in repetitive

Table 5.1 Outcome Diseases and Early Disease States.

	Preclinical Stage	*Prodromal Stage*	*Indicator of Early Disease State*
AUTISM	None identified	Prodromal	Behavioral changes (communication, social relationship, sensory motor development)
ALZHEIMER'S DISEASE	Preclinical (Asymptomatic/ Presymptomatic)	Mild Cognitive Impairment	Preclinical: Amyloid biomarkers; MCI: early memory and executive function impairment
PARKINSON'S DISEASE	Presymptomatic	Premotor	Presymptomatic: early pathological changes; Premotor: nonmotor symptoms (i.e., depression and sleep behavior)
MULTIPLE SCLEROSIS	Radiologically Isolated Syndrome	Clinically Isolated Syndrome	RIS: presence of white matter anomalies; CIS: clinical symptoms without MRI results that meet diagnostic criteria
SCHIZOPHRENIA	None identified	Clinical High Risk/ Ultra High Risk	Subclinical or attenuated symptoms

Preclinical or prodromal stages reflect a change from baseline, by either the presence of disease pathology or early symptoms, which precede the clinical presentation and biomarker results required to meet diagnostic criteria. A preclinical state is the stage of a disease in which disease pathology is present, but the individual has yet to experience clinical symptoms. A prodrome or prodromal stage marks the early signs or symptoms indicating the onset of a disease.

Source: Author.

behaviors of self-regulation, and intense focus or interest in specific subjects. Previous editions of the DSM included a broad category of autism spectrum disorders that included, among others, autistic disorder, Asperger's syndrome, pervasive developmental disorder-not otherwise specific (PDD-NOS; American Psychiatric Association, 2000). The current edition, DSM-5, collapsed these diagnoses into one condition: autism spectrum disorder (ASD; American Psychiatric Association, 2013). Using the criteria outlined in the DSM-IV-TR, prevalence was estimated at 1 in 68 children; these rates may be lower under DSM-5 criteria (Maenner et al., 2014).

ASD is typically diagnosed in early childhood using behavioral observation and parental interview. Best practices suggest the use of a multidisciplinary team that combines diagnostic tools with clinical judgment (Woolfenden et al., 2012). There are a host of diagnostic tools and practices, but Autism Diagnostic Observation Schedule (ADOS) and the Autism Diagnostic Interview-Revised (ADI-R) are two of the most frequently used tools available. A recent meta-analysis of diagnostic tools found that, when used together, the ADOS and ADI-R have a correct classification rate of autism at 0.88 for children under 3 years old (0.84 for older children) and 0.80 for an autism spectrum disorder (Falkmer et al., 2013). Despite recommendations by the American Academy of Pediatrics (Johnson et al., 2007) and the CDC (Centers for Disease Control and Prevention, 2016) for screening all children at 18- and 24-month checkups, studies report mean ages at diagnosis to be anywhere from 38 to 120 months (Daniels and Mandell, 2014). The CDC reports an average age of 4 years for ASD diagnoses (Christensen et al., 2016). Factors involved in diagnostic age include the number and intensity of autistic traits present and socioeconomic and geographic circumstances (Daniels and Mandell, 2014).

Researchers have begun developing strategies for earlier and more objective diagnosis. Many of these efforts have focused on genetic and genomic research, with varied levels of success (Singh, 2016; Schmidt, 2016); in this chapter, we will focus on research on behavioral markers. Early studies using home videos found that, before the age of 1, children later diagnosed with autism oriented to their name when called less often; looked less at faces and people (Palomo et al., 2006); and preferred looking at geometric shapes over children (Shic et al., 2014). Recent efforts have been focused on using eye-tracking technologies to determine patterns in at-risk infants (i.e., those with siblings diagnosed with autism). This research has shown reliable differences in looking patterns as early as 6 months of age (Frazier et al., 2016; Jones and Klin, 2013; Sarrett and Rommelfanger, 2015; Merin et al., 2007). This research has concluded that infants who are later diagnosed with autism tend to look more at eyes than mouths and more at objects than people. Importantly, these technologies are not able to diagnose but may complement other screening or diagnosis measures.

For more on the perspectives of autistics in the neurodiversity movement, see Chapter 26.

Schizophrenia and Other Psychotic Disorders

Psychotic disorders are characterized by symptoms that reflect a disruption of the patient's comprehension of reality, notably hallucinations, delusions, thought disorder, and disorganized behavior (Walker et al., 2016). Schizophrenia, the most severe and potentially chronic psychotic disorder, has a typical onset in the adolescent or young-adult years (Walker, 2002). The world-wide prevalence of schizophrenia alone is estimated between 0.5 and 1% (CDC, *Burden of Mental Illness*, 2013). Psychotic disorders are diagnosed on the basis of symptoms and behavioral features, such as disturbances in social and occupational functioning, and deficits in emotional experience and expression.

Retrospective and prospective research findings on schizophrenia and other psychoses indicate that a period of functional decline and gradual onset of subclinical, or "attenuated," symptoms precede the clinical onset of the first psychotic episode. This period has been referred to as the "prodrome," with a typical onset during adolescence/early adulthood. Studies have estimated that about 35% of those who experience prodromal states will progress to a psychotic disorder within two years (Mittal et al., 2015). Ongoing research regarding the prodrome has developed measures of the behavioral signs and symptoms (Addington et al., 2007), including mood symptoms (i.e., depression). The critical criteria are attenuated, or subclinical, positive symptoms of psychosis below the severity threshold and level of conviction specified in the DSM-5. Manifestations of positive psychotic symptoms include perceptual abnormalities, unusual ideas, and disorganized thought and communication. For example, patients with psychosis often experience auditory hallucinations that are compelling and may even prompt them to verbally respond to the voices in public. They are convinced about the reality of their auditory perceptions and might express confusion about other people's failure to hear them. An attenuated form of a hallucination might involve an auditory experience, such as a person thinking that they are hearing their name called when no one else is present but inhibiting any verbal response because they assume it must be a misperception ("it must have been my imagination"). The terms "clinical high-risk" (CHR) and "ultra high-risk" (UHR) have been used in the literature to refer to research patients who manifest subclinical symptoms that exceed a predetermined severity threshold (Walker et al., 2013). This approach, and the 20% to 40% risk rate observed in such populations, is more predictive than genetic risk factors (12% risk rate). At the present time, structured interviews for prodromal syndromes are used almost exclusively in clinical research settings, as the formal diagnosis is not yet represented in the DSM. Most individuals who are designated as CHR, based on meeting standard criteria for a prodromal syndrome, are help seeking and express distress about their symptoms and currently or previously met criteria for one or more other psychiatric disorders. A recent meta-analysis revealed that structured interview measures of prodromal syndromes yield an average sensitivity of 0.96 and specificity of 0.47 for prediction of psychosis within two years (Fusar-Poli et al., 2015). These values compare favorably with those obtained for measures of risk for several nonpsychiatric disorders, such as diabetes, cancer, and stroke. Predictive power is not, however, sufficient to justify the provision of targeted intervention to prevent psychosis onset for individuals who meet CHR criteria.

Alzheimer's Disease

Alzheimer's disease is a progressive neurodegenerative disease that primarily affects individuals' memory and executive function and is characterized by plaques and tangles that lead to neurodegeneration (Dubois et al., 2016). Alzheimer's disease is the most common cause of dementia and affects an estimated 5.3 million Americans (Alzheimer's Association, 2015). The 2011 NIA-Alzheimer's Association diagnostic criteria reframed Alzheimer's disease as a spectrum disorder that includes preclinical (for research purposes), MCI, and dementia stages of the illness (McKhann et al., 2011). These criteria utilize clinical and biomarker factors to diagnose each stage of the illness (McKhann et al., 2011). For MCI and dementia, an initial syndrome diagnosis is determined using clinical presentation. MCI is a symptomatic diagnosis of impaired cognition in at least one domain and may precede dementia related to a range of etiologies, including Alzheimer's and vascular dementia (Albert et al., 2011). The transition from MCI to dementia, regardless of etiology, is marked by increased cognitive impairment in multiple domains and loss of functional status.

Biomarkers support diagnosis of MCI or dementia due to Alzheimer's disease pathology. Additionally, biomarkers may indicate disease pathology in individuals who are cognitively healthy (asymptomatic; Sperling et al., 2011). Evidence of disease pathology includes an imbalance of the proteins amyloid beta and tau in an individual's spinal fluid or elevated amyloid or tau levels detected through PET imaging (Sperling et al., 2011; Johnson et al., 2013; Scholl et al., 2016). Currently, biomarker tests are not recommended for clinical use in patients who are cognitively healthy (Johnson et al., 2013). However, according to the Amyloid Imaging Taskforce guidelines, biomarker tests may be used for clinical purposes, with limitations, in patients who are symptomatic to confirm a diagnosis of Alzheimer's disease (Johnson et al., 2013). Even so, Alzheimer's diagnosis (with certainty) may only be confirmed at autopsy.

Testing for Early Disease States

Early disease states in neurologic and psychiatric conditions raise unique legal and ethical challenges specific to testing, disclosure, and preparing for disease onset based on preclinical or prodromal information. Ethical challenges associated with testing relate to the risk–benefit assessment of the test. Testing may take on multiple forms, including biomarkers and clinical exams. Biomarkers include a range of medical indications that can be measured through blood draws, imaging, lumbar punctures, and other measures. Biomarkers are not necessarily a reflection of symptoms and may not be end points or outcome measures. Early disease states for psychiatric disorders are measured on the basis of behavioral symptom expression manifested in a clinical interview/exam (Kline and Schiffman, 2014). Clinical exams utilize a range of measurements, screening tools, and methods for identifying clinical symptoms and confirming or validating reported symptoms. For example, clinicians typically use structured diagnostic interviews to assess signs of risk during which the individual is asked to describe perceptual, ideational, and communicative experiences that are associated with attenuated positive symptoms of psychiatric conditions (Addington et al., 2007).

In early disease states, the potential benefits are intimately connected to whether testing accurately predicts the outcome disorder. Researchers identify early disease states by first demonstrating that a sufficient proportion of individuals who develop the outcome disease experience the preclinical or prodromal state prior to meeting diagnostic criteria (e.g., evidence showing that an individual diagnosed with Alzheimer's dementia first experienced MCI; Yirmiya and Charman, 2010). However, this does not necessarily mean that every person who experiences an early disease state also progresses to the outcome disease. The more likely an individual is to convert from an early disease state to the outcome disease, the more predictive value the indicator offers. Research in the area of early disease states has produced varying results on the sensitivity (the indicator identifies all, of those tested, individuals who will go on to develop the disease) and specificity (the indicator only identified individuals who will go on to develop the disease). For example, current research reports that the "CSF Alzheimer's disease signature," a ratio of high tau to low amyloid, has high sensitivity (90–95%) and specificity (90%) for correctly identifying amyloid (Dubois et al., 2014).

Potential benefits are also based upon whether testing provides prognostic value, information regarding whether and when an individual will develop the outcome disorder. For example, conversion rates from MCI to Alzheimer's dementia vary between 40 and 50% over a three-year period depending on a range of factors (i.e., race, age, genetic disposition), making it difficult to provide clear information to patients about their likelihood of conversion (Jessen et al., 2014; Barnes et al., 2014).

Early disease states offer clinicians and patients the opportunity to intervene earlier in the disease process. These benefits are limited in neurological and psychiatric conditions. In Alzheimer's disease, current treatments do not modify disease progression, and it is currently unclear how to intervene with prodromal autism or if strategies employed in infancy are effective. Yet the long-term prognosis for psychotic disorders improves with earlier treatment, including a lower likelihood of remission and better social functioning and global outcome the earlier treatment is initiated (Penttilä et al., 2014).

Evaluating prodromal cases of developmental disorders, like ASD, is further complicated by a host of concerns, not the least of which is the fact that these behavioral markers are considered in comparisons to norms set by other infants. Whereas behavioral markers for conditions that emerge in adulthood are based on behavior changes within the individuals, ASD relies on developmental norms. Additionally, indicators before the age of two are broad and nonspecific because the traits used to identify autism do not emerge until early childhood (Shic et al., 2014). Identifying prodromal autism is particularly complicated since converting from a prodromal stage to an ASD diagnosis occurs during infant and child development, which is influenced by a host of environmental and biological factors (Beversdorf, 2016; Nardone and Elliott, 2016).

Risks associated with most biomarker tests and clinical exams are relatively low, particularly in contrast to risks associated with other clinical interventions (i.e., a biopsy to evaluate potentially cancerous tissue). In Alzheimer's disease, preclinical biomarkers are identified through either PET imaging, requiring the injection of a dye to identify amyloid or tau deposition, or analysis of cerebral spinal fluid. Risks associated with PET-amyloid imaging include adverse reactions to the agents used in the injection (Neuraceq, 2014; Amyvid, 2013; Vizamyl, 2014). In rare cases, the agent can cause a major allergic reaction. Additionally, these agents contribute to the patient's overall long-term cumulative radiation exposure (Positron Emission Tomography Scan, 2014). The risks associated with the collection of cerebral spinal fluid by lumbar puncture include headache, infection, back discomfort or pain, bleeding into the spinal canal, or herniation (Wright et al., 2012). Damage to the nerves in the spinal cord is possible if the patient moves during the procedure (Wright, Lai, and Sinclair, 2012). In contrast, clinical exams associated with prodromal states in psychiatric conditions are relatively low risk. The potential risks associated with a clinical exam may include loss of confidentiality or agitation for an individual who lacks insight of even mild symptoms associated with an early disease state. A minor risk, like those described, does not eliminate the possibility that future tests for early disease states will not expose patients to more significant harms. Additionally, individual patients or research participants may vary regarding their perspectives on risks. The discussion of risks is a central piece of the informed consent conversation with a patient or research participant prior to conducting the procedure.

Cost of testing is also a consideration, which may be categorized as a risk. While health insurance coverage has expanded under the U.S. Patient Protection and Affordable Care Act (ACA), testing for early disease states is generally not covered. For example, while the ACA covers autism screening, this currently applies for behavior checklists, which are much less costly than emerging technologies, such as eye-tracking devices. As of now, 43 states have passed laws requiring insurance coverage for autism services. However, only a fraction of these laws cover screenings (Mauch et al., 2011; National Conference of State Legislatures, 2016).

Evaluating whether testing should be offered or conducted will require that researchers and clinicians conduct a specific risk–benefit analysis for a given biomarker or clinical test. Decisions to offer testing are best supported when testing is considered standard of care. In circumstances in which a patient seeks out early disease state testing, a clinician maintains responsibility for determining whether testing is medically appropriate based on standard of care and the benefit–risk assessment. This will challenge clinicians to balance paternalism by limiting infringements on patient autonomy to seek out medical care while providing care consistent with medical standards. This assessment is further informed by ethical and legal issues related to disclosing early disease states to patients.

Disclosure of Early Disease States

Disclosure of an early disease state to patients and families is perhaps the most contested issue relating to the clinical use and research surrounding early disease states. Potential benefits of disclosing early disease states to patients and their families, including increased monitoring and opportunity to plan for disease onset, are hindered when therapeutic options are limited or nonexistent. For example, limited intervention options influence how scholars have evaluated including tools (i.e., eye tracking) to replace recommended pediatric screenings of autism. Full disclosure promotes autonomy, maximizes transparency, maintains trust between a patient and the provider, and provides a patient with information to identify resources (Mittal et al., 2015) but also exposes the patient to potential consequences of the diagnosis (Yang and Link, 2015). Disclosure of an early disease state incorporates misinterpretation, stigma, and discrimination risks.

Interpretation

Interpretation, or misinterpretation, of an early disease state indicator influences potential consequences related to disclosure. Interpretation of indicators for early disease status begins with whether the indicator is objectively or subjectively measured. Clinical exams are at particular risk of being subjective—results may vary depending on the evaluator and the individual reporting symptoms. In contrast, biomarkers are "objective, quantifiable characteristics of biological processes" (Strimbu and Tavel, 2010). Next, interpretation relies on how clinicians communicate results to patients (Besser et al., 2015). This includes communication of what a "positive" result means for the likelihood of developing the outcome disease, whether clinicians equate the test result with a diagnosis, and whether a patient or research subject is able to understand and appreciate the meaning of a test result. Disclosure should take into account these variables to mitigate any consequences. It is important that clinicians distinguish for patients, research participants, and family members the difference between an early disease indicator and a diagnosis of the outcome disease. The difference may be difficult for some stakeholders to distinguish without education.

Interpretation further shapes disclosure depending on individual patient perspectives, including level of insight. A patient with MCI may not be aware of any deficits despite scoring in the risk range. By contrast, most individuals who meet CHR or "prodromal" criteria for psychosis are experiencing distress about their symptoms and are aware of functional decline (Niendam et al., 2009). However, these patients may be concerned with comorbid mood disorders, such as depression and anxiety, and not with risks for psychoses. In ASD, family history may shape a family's perception of a prodromal autism diagnosis. Families without a history of autism may be more surprised to hear of positive screens for prodromal autism in infants than families with children diagnosed with autism. However, families with a prior history may be concerned if the children develop differently and display very different constellations of autistic traits, as is often the case with autism.

Stigma

Stigma is a discrediting attribute that taints or lessens an individual's or group's perceived value (Werner et al., 2012). Researchers have not adequately studied stigma in early disease. However, stigma associated with psychiatric illness and dementias is well documented and recognized as a global problem (Seeman et al., 2016). A study examining stigma experienced by individuals with schizophrenia in a small town in Poland found that 87% of the participants reported experiencing rejection in social relationships, and 60% anticipated discrimination in interactions with others (Cechnicki et al., 2011). Importantly, the anticipation of stigma may have consequences for individuals (Cechnicki et al., 2011) who are provided information regarding an early disease state. Labeling an individual with an early disease state could result in transferring the negative stereotypes and loss of status associated with the outcome disorder to the patient (Mittal et al., 2015).

Individuals may also be stigmatized based on the early disease state itself. Particularly, individuals in a prodromal state may begin to experience symptoms and demonstrate behaviors that result in stigma (Mittal et al., 2015). Individuals with CHR often exhibit symptoms that may create social distancing. Similarly, an individual with MCI will begin demonstrating poor memory or cognition, which may be embarrassing or lead to others questioning the individual's ability to manage day-to-day tasks. These consequences result in discrediting of the individual.

A different kind of stigma may occur with infants identified as likely to later be diagnosed with autism. Risk of false positives carries with it the additional risk of caregivers continuing to search for signs of autism even when the child is not autistic (Sarrett and Rommelfanger, 2015). This kind of scrutiny may lead to children being treated differently well into childhood. Further, parents whose children are identified in infancy and whose diagnosis is confirmed in early childhood may be subject to blame for not intervening enough to curb the emergence of autistic traits, despite a lack of evidence-based treatments for infants. Parents of older autistic children often report experiences of stigma and use disclosure of their child's diagnosis to curb negative perceptions (Austin et al., 2016; Gray, 2002).

Employment and Insurance Discrimination

Disclosure of an early disease state may have consequences for an individual's employment and insurability, which may vary between different legal, economic, and social systems. While discrimination risks associated with early disease states is not well understood, discrimination is well documented in outcome disorders, particularly mental illness. Up to one third of individuals with a psychiatric illness have reported discrimination by an employer (Cechnicki et al., 2011). Consideration of discrimination based on early disease states in the United States serves as an initial exploration of these challenges, which may be present in other legal systems. The impact of a disclosure will be particularly different, for insurance purposes, in countries with universal health care systems. Additionally, this is an issue where biomarkers and clinical tests differ from predictive genetic markers. The U.S. Genetic Information Non-discrimination Act (GINA) and the passage of state laws provide protections to individuals from discrimination based upon genetic information. However, similar laws have not yet been fully replicated for other early disease states or risks (Arias and Karlawish, 2014).

Access to legal protections and services in the United States may depend on whether early disease states meet relevant definitions of disability. Under the U.S. Americans with Disabilities Act (ADA; as amended), individuals whose conditions meet the definition of a disability, a "physical or mental impairment that substantially limits one or more major life activity" (42 USC 12102), are protected from discrimination resulting in loss of access to "public goods and services" and employment. By definition, those who are in the preclinical state would not have a physical or mental impairment and thus would not be disabled under the ADA. While the Supreme Court and subsequent law established HIV, an asymptomatic condition, as a disability, it is unclear whether the related legal reasoning would extend protections to individuals with early disease states (524 U.S. 624).

Individuals will face similar challenges if they seek out services through U.S. Social Security Disability, which provides benefits to individuals who are unable to work for more than a year due to a severe disability (Benefits for People with Disabilities). To qualify for benefits, an individual must demonstrate that he or she has a functional disability that has existed for a year or is likely to continue for a year (Benefits for People with Disabilities). Given the functional loss required to demonstrate disability, an individual in an early disease state would not qualify for Social Security Disability. The exception to this might be some prodromal states. However, prodromal stages tend not to include loss of function and cannot be verified until the outcome condition fully manifests. In fact, functionality is a distinguishing factor between MCI and dementia (McKhann et al., 2011). Similarly, "attenuated psychosis syndrome" does not constitute an eligible diagnosis for purposes of disability status or insurance coverage for treatment because it is not an "official" mental disorder within the DSM (Carpenter et al., 2014; Tsuang et al., 2013). As a result, individuals who are known to be in an early disease state may be exposed to discrimination by employers, with minimal recourse and without options for pursuing disability income.

U.S. law generally permits insurers to engage in "risk classification," defined as "grouping of risks with similar risk characteristics" (Risk Classification Statement of Principles, 2011). States vary on the restrictions they place on insurers for utilizing various risk factors about an individual for eligibility and underwriting purposes. For purposes of health insurance, insurers are largely prohibited from excluding an individual from insurance coverage based on a health status factor. The ACA provided additional protections for individuals with preexisting conditions, with some limitations. Regardless, it is unclear whether early disease states qualify for protection under current laws.

Disclosure may have relevance in the criminal context as well, specifically if the individual commits a crime while in the early disease state. Psychological factors have a long history with capital sentencing, serving as mitigating factors during sentencing (Barnett et al., 2004). The standard for using "psychological factors" as a mitigating factor requires that the individual experienced "extreme mental or emotional disturbance" (Stetler, 2007). It is unclear whether an individual with CHR or MCI would meet these criteria.

A final consideration is whether a clinician should respect a patient's request that the clinician does not document or disclose early disease state information to a third party. Documentation of medical information in a patient's record is a part of good medical care. However, clinicians may have discretion in the language used when documenting. Once a clinician documents early disease state information in the medical record, the patient likely has some, but not absolute, control over disclosure of their medical records. In the United States, health privacy laws provide significant protections to patient medical information. Unless a clinician is mandated by law or failure to disclose would constitute fraudulent actions, a clinician may (in some circumstances) respect the patient's request that the information regarding an early disease state not be disclosed to a third party.

Preparing for Onset

The identification and disclosure of early disease states provides an opportunity for individuals to prepare for the onset of the outcome disease. For conditions in which disease-modifying treatments or interventions are available, a clinician will have options to delay disease. For conditions, like Alzheimer's disease, that lack effective therapies, a clinician and the patient must consider alternative modes of preparing for disease onset (Cummings et al., 2014).

Age of disease onset and functional challenges related to the outcome disorder are guiding factors in preparing for the outcome disorder. Age of onset is particularly relevant to CHR and schizophrenia. CHR status may be identified when an individual is in their late teens and still a minor. Yet they will likely age out of pediatric medical services and juvenile legal systems between CHR and psychosis. The loss of function associated with Alzheimer's disease requires that patients and family plan for loss of the ability to care for themselves at later stages of the disease, requiring full-time nursing care. Health insurers may not cover full-time nursing care, and the individual may no longer be able to qualify for long-term care insurance after early disease state information is disclosed. Those at an increased risk of Alzheimer's disease or psychosis are also at risk of losing decisional capacity. The potential for loss of capacity shapes decision making and advanced care planning while the patient maintains decision-making capacity.

Individuals with early disease states are uniquely situated to identifying social supports and caregivers prior to disease onset. Caregivers may be unpaid (family or friends) or providers, either provided at home or in nursing facilities. For patients who will go on to develop Alzheimer's disease, it is likely that their unpaid caregiver will be either a spouse or an adult child (Alzheimer's Association Stetler, 2016). Individuals who are at risk for psychosis may be less likely to have the social support needed to assist them with their needs. Individuals with schizophrenia are less likely than the general population to get married or develop a social support network; thus parents are likely to serve as caregivers (Gater et al., 2014). However, given the likelihood that the patient will outlive his or her parents, a new challenge arises—who will provide care when the patient's parents are no longer able to?

Caregivers play a critical role in providing care for individuals with progressive illnesses and are at risk of consequences associated with caregiver burden (Adelman et al., 2014). It is unclear how identifying risk and disease pathology early could affect caregiver burden. It is possible that the identification of an early disease state extends the length of time a patient and their caregiver are aware of the probability of progression to the outcome disease or disorder may increase the burden over time. However, it may also allow caregivers to access information and services early in the disease process and help caregivers understand behaviors and symptoms associated with the disease process.

In the case of psychosis, identifying at-risk individuals before their first psychotic episode may reduce the duration of untreated psychosis, which is linked with poorer prognosis. Individual and family education may increase the likelihood that a first psychotic episode is quickly recognized and treatment can be sought promptly. To the extent that early intervention decreases the likelihood of relapse and rehospitalizations, it can reduce the burden of the illness on the patient and the family.

One of the most controversial issues about early intervention to prevent psychosis concerns the use of antipsychotic medication. Prescriptions for antipsychotic medications have increased dramatically in the past two decades, and in most cases these drugs are prescribed for patients who have not suffered from a psychotic disorder (Olfson et al., 2012). In contrast, many researchers in the field oppose antipsychotic medications without consistent scientific evidence indicating that antipsychotics can prevent the onset of psychosis in individuals with prodromal syndromes (Fusar-Poli et al., 2015). Opponents to antipsychotic medications argue that the benefits do not outweigh the risks of side effects and potential stigmatization, particularly without capabilities to predict psychosis (Almandil et al., 2013; Cornblatt et al., 2001). Moreover, the side effects of antipsychotic drugs are among the chief reasons that patients become noncompliant with treatment and relapse. Beginning treatments too early could contribute to greater treatment noncompliance later. Instead of medication, opponents to antipsychotic medications advocate for psychotherapeutic interventions, such as cognitive behavioral therapy, which has the potential to reduce many of the nonspecific symptoms associated with the prodrome and has no significant adverse side effects (Fusar-Poli et al., 2015).

Advance care planning in the form of advanced directives is one avenue of preparing for disease onset—particularly given risks that individuals will lose decisional capacity. Standard living wills and health care power of attorney forms are supported across all 50 states in the United States. In psychiatric conditions, scholars have debated the use of Ulysses contracts, in which individuals provide advance consent to hospitalization or treatment for psychiatric disorders, as a potential solution to allow for treatment when an individual is experiencing severe symptoms (Campbell and Kisely, 2009). While the actual use of Ulysses contracts is not established, the concept of preparing advance directives may be beneficial in this circumstance. Early disease states provide a window of time to prepare a plan with the patient that respects individual values and autonomy and reflects the patient's wishes if a circumstance arises in which the outcome disease or disorder leads to symptoms which create risks for the patient or other.

Early disease states provide an opportunity for patients, caregivers, and clinicians to prepare for the possibility that an individual will progress to the outcome disease or disorders. In the case of autism, early identification can provide the opportunity for caregivers to seek out and access services at a younger age. This includes the opportunity to learn about strategies to encourage a positive disability identity at an early age. Most caregivers, however, will request intervention strategies at the time of a positive screen, which can be as young as six months of age. At the time, however, there are no recommended interventions for children under the age of two who are at risk for autism. A recent review of studies looking at behavioral and cognitive interventions strategies developed for older children and adapted for infants found results are encouraging, but only one study successfully demonstrated significant effects. Overall, more research is needed in this area to complement early diagnostic efforts (Bradshaw et al., 2015). Further, it is unclear if an early screen in infancy that identifies the likelihood of a later diagnosis of autism will make that child eligible for state-sponsored early intervention programs.

For adults, prodromal and preclinical identification of disorder provides an opportunity to document patient values prior to loss of capacity, identify plans for treatment and disease management that are consistent with patient values and wishes, and have informed conversations about what to expect. In some circumstances, it also provides an opportunity to consider early interventions—which may or may not increase risks associated with prolonged treatment periods. Preparation for the onset of the outcome disorder should be developed according to individual values, wishes, and information about the disease process associated with the identified early disease state.

Conclusion: A Changing Role for Medicine and Research

The growing body of research of early disease states is motivated, at least in part, to develop and validate disease-modifying treatments that could prevent or slow disease progression (Yirmiya and Charman, 2010). Early disease states provide opportunities to intervene early (if effective treatments are available), monitor disease progression, and allow patients and family members to seek out medical and social services early in the disease process. Early disease states are also useful for research because investigators can use indicators of risk or disease pathology to recruit individuals most likely to develop an outcome disease, use early disease states as a surrogate outcome measure in preventative studies, and develop therapies targeted at disease modification (Olanow and Obeso, 2012). There are undoubtedly benefits to seeking out early indicators of risk and disease pathology. However, the implementation and adoption of early disease states should fully consider the challenges that come along with the benefits.

Preclinical biomarkers and/or prodromal stages precede an increasing number of neuro-degenerative conditions, like ASD, Alzheimer's, and schizophrenia. The pathology and phenotypical progress of neurodegenerative conditions may be best suited to early identification given the likely progression of degeneration that occurs before an individual becomes symptomatic or meets diagnostic criteria. There are themes that link neurodegenerative disease and early disease states—each disease presents nuanced issues depending on varying characteristics of the disease or early disease state. This nuance also complicates preclinical identification of ASD, which does not allow for consideration of change within an individual but relies on developmental norms, which infants and children diverge from for a variety of reasons. Future work in the ethical and legal evaluation of early disease states should also consider nuances between disease populations and early disease states. Given the onset, early disease states of pediatric conditions raise unique issues. Future research addressing early disease indicators in pediatrics will necessitate that researchers evaluate parental decision making, consequences of intervention at earlier ages, and consequences of false-positive identification in children. New legal, ethical, and social challenges will continue to arise alongside research developments in early disease states. However, this structure will continue to guide the conversation by considering (1) whether to offer the test, (2) whether to disclose results, and (3) how to prepare.

Further Reading

Arias, J.J. and Karlawish, J. (2014) "Confidentiality in Preclinical Alzheimer Disease Studies: When Research and Medical Records Meet". *Neurology* 82(8), 725–729. (Summarizes the current legal gaps for protecting individuals with preclinical biomarkers from employment and insurance discrimination).

Herrera, A., Perry, C. and Perry, A. (2013) *Ethics and Neurodiversity* (Studies in theoretical and applied ethics). Newcastle upon Tyne: Cambridge Scholars Publishing.

Parens, E. and Asch, A. (Eds.) (2000) *Prenatal Testing and Disability Rights*. Washington, DC: Georgetown University Press.

Sperling, R.A., Aisen, P.S., Beckett, L.A., Bennett, D.A., Craft, S., Fagan, A.M., . . . Phelps, C.H. (2011) "Toward Defining the Preclinical Stages of Alzheimer's Disease: Recommendations from the National Institute on Aging-Alzheimer's Association Workgroups on Diagnostic Guidelines for Alzheimer's Disease". *Alzheimer's & Dementia* 7(3), 280–292. (Seminal statement of guidelines specific to preclinical biomarkers for research purposes).

Walker, E.F., Trotman, H.D., Goulding, S.M., Holtzman, C.W., Ryan, A.T., McDonald, A., . . . Brasfield, J.L. (2013) "Developmental Mechanisms in the Prodrome to Psychosis". *Development and Psychopathology* 25(4), 1585–1600. (This article describes research methods for studying the prodrome to psychosis and the neurodevelopmental processes in adolescence that are linked with the emergence of psychosis).

References

Food and Drug Administration (2016) Amyvid. Available at: www.accessdata.fda.gov/drugsatfda_docs/label/2013/202008s020lbl.pdf [Accessed 2 Sept. 2016].

Addington, J., Cadenhead, K.S., Cannon, T.D., Cornblatt, B., McGlashan, T.H., Perkins, . . . North American Prodrome Longitudinal Study. (2007) North American Prodrome Longitudinal Study: A collaborative multisite approach to prodromal schizophrenia research. *Schizophrenia Bulletin* 33(3): pp. 665–672.

Adelman R.D., Tmanova L.L., Delgado D., Dion S., and Lachs M.S. (2014) Caregiver burden: A clinical review. *The Journal of American Medical Association* 311(10): pp. 1052–1060.

Albert, M.S., DeKosky, S.T., Dickson, D., Dubois, B., Feldman, H.H., Fox, N.C., . . . Petersen, R.C. (2011) The diagnosis of mild cognitive impairment due to Alzheimer's disease: Recommendations from the National Institute on Aging-Alzheimer's Association workgroups on diagnostic guidelines for Alzheimer's disease. *Alzheimer's & Dementia* 7(3): pp. 270–279.

Almandil, N.B., Liu, Y., Murray, M.L., Besag, F.M., Aitchison, K.J., and Wong, I.C. (2013) Weight gain and other metabolic adverse effects associated with atypical antipsychotic treatment of children and adolescents: A systematic review and meta-analysis. *Pediatric Drugs* 15(2): pp. 139–150.

Alzheimer's Association (2016) Alzheimer's Disease Facts and Figures. Available at: www.alz.org/docu ments_custom/2016-facts-and-figures.pdf [Accessed 18 Oct. 2016].

American Academy of Actuaries. (2016) *Risk Classification Statement of Principles.* Available at: www.actuari alstandardsboard.org/wp-content/uploads/2014/07/riskclassificationSOP.pdf [Accessed 4 Mar. 2016].

Americans With Disabilities Act Amendments Act. (2008) 42 USC 12102.

American Psychiatric Association. (2000) *Diagnostic and Statistical Manual of Mental Disorders: DSM-IV-TR.* Washington, DC: American Psychiatric Association.

———. (2013) *Diagnostic and Statistical Manual of Mental Disorders.* 5th ed. Washington, DC: American Psychiatric Association.

Aminoff, M.J., and Faulkner, L.R. (2012) *The American Board of Psychiatry and Neurology: Looking Back and Moving Ahead.* Arlington, VA: American Psychiatric Pub.

Arias, J.J., and Karlawish, J. (2014) Confidentiality in preclinical Alzheimer disease studies: When research and medical records meet. *Neurology* 82(8): pp. 725–729.

Austin, J.E., Zinke, V.L., and Davies, W. (2016) Influencing perception about children with autism and their parents using disclosure cards. *Journal of Autism and Developmental Disorders* 46(8): pp. 2764–2769.

Baker, M.G. (2002) The wall between neurology and psychiatry. *The BMJ* 324(7352): pp. 1468–1469.

Baranek, G.T. (1999). Autism during infancy: A retrospective video analysis of sensory-motor and social behaviors at 9–12 months of age. *Journal of Autism and Developmental Disorders* 29(3): pp. 213–224.

Barnes, D.E., Cenzer, I.S., Yaffe, K., Ritchie, C.S., and Lee, S.J. (2014) A point-based tool to predict conversion from mild cognitive impairment to probable Alzheimer's disease. *Alzheimer's & Dementia* 10(6): pp. 646–655.

Barnett, M.E., Brodsky, S.L., and Davis, C.M. (2004) When mitigation evidence makes a difference: Effects of psychological mitigating evidence on sentencing decisions in capital trials. *Behavioral Sciences & the Law* 22(6): pp. 751–770.

Besser, A.G., Sanderson, S.C., Roberts, J.S., Chen, C.A., Christensen, K.D., Lautenbach, D.M., . . . Green, R.C. (2015) Factors affecting recall of different types of personal genetic information about Alzheimer's disease risk: The REVEAL study. *Public Health Genomics* 18(2): pp. 78–86.

Beversdorf, D.Q. (2016) Phenotyping, etiological factors, and biomarkers: Toward precision medicine in autism spectrum disorders. *Journal of Developmental & Behavioral Pediatrics* 37(8): pp. 659–673. Available at: https://doi.org/10.1097/DBP.0000000000000351

Bradshaw, J., Steiner, A.M., Gengoux, G., and Koegel, L.K. (2015) Feasibility and effectiveness of very early intervention for infants at-risk for autism spectrum disorder: A systematic review. *Journal of Autism and Developmental Disorders* 45(3): pp. 778–794. Available at: https://doi.org/10.1007/s10803-014-2235-2

Bragdon v Abbott. (1998) 524 U.S. 624.

Campbell, L.A., and Kisely, S.R. (2009) Advance treatment directives for people with severe mental illness. *The Cochrane Database of Systematic Reviews*, 1: pp. CD005963-CD005963.

Carpenter, W.T., Regier, D., and Tandon, R. (2014) Misunderstandings about attenuated psychosis syndrome in the DSM-5. *Schizophrenia Research* 152(1): pp. 303.

CDC. (2016) CDC—Burden of Mental Illness—Mental Illness—Mental Health Basics—Mental Health. Available at: www.cdc.gov/mentalhealth/basics/burden.htm [Accessed 27 Dec. 2016].

CDC- NCBDDD. (2016) Facts About ASDs. Available at: www.cdc.gov/ncbddd/autism/facts.html [Accessed 5 Oct. 2016].

Cechnicki, A., Angermeyer, M., and Bielanska, A. (2011) Anticipated and experienced stigma among people with schizophrenia: Its nature and correlates. *Social Psychiatry and Psychiatric Epidemiology* 46(7): pp. 643–650.

Christensen, D.L., Baio, J., Braun, K.V.N., Bilder, D., Charles, J., Constantino, J.N., . . . Yeargin-Allsopp, M. (2016) Prevalence and characteristics of autism spectrum disorder among children aged 8 years— Autism and developmental disabilities monitoring network, 11 sites, United States, 2012. *MMWR: Surveillance Summaries* 65(3): pp. 1–23.

Cornblatt, B.A., Lencz, T., and Kane, J.M. (2001) Treatment of the schizophrenia prodrome: Is it presently ethical? *Schizophrenia Research* 51(1): pp. 31–38.

Cummings, J.L., Morstorf, T., and Zhong, K. (2014) Alzheimer's disease drug-development pipeline: Few candidates, frequent failures. *Alzheimer's Research & Therapy* 6(4): pp. 37.

Cuthbert, B.N., and Insel, T.R. (2013) Toward the future of psychiatric diagnosis: The seven pillars of RDoC. *BMC Medicine* 11(1): pp. 1–8.

Daniels, A.M., and Mandell, D.S. (2014) Explaining differences in age at autism spectrum disorder diagnosis: A critical review. *Autism* 18(5): pp. 583–597.

DeKosky, S.T., and Marek, K. (2003) Looking backward to move forward: Early detection of neurodegenerative disorders. *Science* 302(5646): pp. 830–834.

Dubois, B., Feldman, H.H., Jacova, C., Cummings, J.L., DeKosky, S.T., Barberger-Gateau, P., . . . Galasko, D. (2010) Revising the definition of Alzheimer's disease: A new lexicon. *The Lancet Neurology* 9(11): pp. 1118–1127.

Dubois, B., Feldman, H.H., Jacova, C., Hampel, H., Molinuevo, J.L., Blennow, K., . . . Bateman, R. (2014) Advancing research diagnostic criteria for Alzheimer's disease: The IWG-2 criteria. *The Lancet Neurology* 13(6): pp. 614–629.

Dubois B., Hampel H., Feldman, H.H., Scheltens, P., Aisen, P., Andrieu S., *et al.* (2016) Preclinical Alzheimer's disease: Definition, natural history, and diagnostic criteria. *Alzheimer's Dementia* 12(3): pp. 292–323.

Dunckley, T., Coon, K.D., and Stephan, D.A. (2005) Discovery and development of biomarkers of neurological disease. *Drug Discovery Today* 10(5): pp. 326–334.

Falkmer, T., Anderson, K., Falkmer, M., and Horlin, C. (2013). Diagnostic procedures in autism spectrum disorders: A systematic literature review. *European Child & Adolescent Psychiatry* 22(6): pp. 329–340.

Fazel, S., Långström, N., Hjern, A., Grann, M., and Lichtenstein, P. (2009) Schizophrenia, substance abuse, and violent crime. *The Journal of American Medical Association* 301(19): pp. 2016–2023.

Fazel, S., Wolf, A., Palm, C., and Lichtenstein, P. (2014) Violent crime, suicide, and premature mortality in patients with schizophrenia and related disorders: A 38-year total population study in Sweden. *The Lancet Psychiatry* 1(1): pp. 44–54.

Frazier, T.W., Klingemier, E.W., Beukemann, M., Speer Markowitz, L., Parikh, S., . . . Strauss, M.S. (2016) Development of an objective autism risk index using remote eye tracking. *Journal of the American Academy of Child & Adolescent Psychiatry* 55(4): pp. 301–309.

Frittelli, C., Borghetti, D., Iudice, G., Bonanni, E., Maestri, M., Tognoni, G., . . . Iudice, A. (2009) Effects of Alzheimer's disease and mild cognitive impairment on driving ability: A controlled clinical study by simulated driving test. *International Journal of Geriatric Psychiatry* 24(3): pp. 232–238.

Fusar-Poli, P., Borgwardt, S., Bechdolf, A., Addington, J., Riecher-Rössler, A., Schultze-Lutter, F., . . . Yung, A. (2013). The psychosis high-risk state. *The Journal of American Medical Association Psychiatry* 70(1): pp. 107.

Fusar-Poli, P., Cappucciati, M., Rutigliano, G., Schultze-Lutter, F., Bonoldi, I., Borgwardt, S., . . . McGuire, P. (2015) At risk or not at risk? A meta-analysis of the prognostic accuracy of psychometric interviews for psychosis prediction. *World Psychiatry* 14(3): pp. 322–332.

Fusar-Poli, P., Frascarelli, M., Valmaggia, L., Byrne, M., Stahl, D., Rocchetti, M., . . . Xenaki, L. (2015) Antidepressant, antipsychotic and psychological interventions in subjects at high clinical risk for psychosis: OASIS 6-year naturalistic study. *Psychological Medicine* 45(6): pp. 1327–1339.

Gater, A., Rofail, D., Tolley, C., Marshall, C., Abetz-Webb, L., Zarit, S., and Berardo, C. (2014). "Sometimes it's difficult to have a normal life": Results from a qualitative study exploring caregiver burden in Schizophrenia. *Schizophrenia Research and Treatment* pp. 1–13.

Gray, D.E. (2002). 'Everybody just freezes: Everybody is just embarrassed': Felt and enacted stigma among parents of children with high functioning autism. *Sociology of Health & Illness* 24(6): pp. 734–749.

Interpretive Guidance on Title I of the Americans With Disabilities Act 29 CFR 1630.2 (j)(3)(iii).

Jessen, F., Wolfsgruber, S., Wiese, B., Bickel, H., Mösch, E., Kaduszkiewicz, H., . . . Wagner, M. (2014). AD dementia risk in late MCI, in early MCI, and in subjective memory impairment. *Alzheimer's & Dementia* 10(1): pp. 76–83.

Johnson, C.P., Myers, S.M., and the Council on Children with Disabilities. (2007) Identification and evaluation of children with autism spectrum disorders. *Pediatrics* 120(5): pp. 1183–1215.

Johnson, K.A., Minoshima, S., Bohnen, N.I., Donohoe, K.J., Foster, N.L., Herscovitch, P., . . . Hartley, D.M. (2013). Update on appropriate use criteria for amyloid PET imaging: Dementia experts, mild cognitive impairment, and education. *Journal of Nuclear Medicine: Official Publication, Society of Nuclear Medicine* 54(7): pp. 1011–1013.

Jones, W., and Klin, A. (2013). Attention to eyes is present but in decline in 2–6-month-old infants later diagnosed with autism. *Nature* 504(7480): pp. 427–431.

Jutel, A. (2009). Sociology of diagnosis: A preliminary review. *Sociology of Health & Illness* 31(2): pp. 278–299.

Kline, E., and Schiffman, J. (2014). Psychosis risk screening: A systematic review. *Schizophrenia Research* 158(1): pp. 11–18.

Link, B.G., and Phelan, J.C. (2001) Conceptualizing stigma. *Annual Review of Sociology* pp. 363–385.

Link, B.G., Yang, L.H., Phelan, J.C., and Collins, P.Y. (2004). Measuring mental illness stigma. *Schizophrenia Bulletin* 30(3): pp. 511–541.

McKhann, G.M., Drachman, D., Folstein, M., Katzman, R., Price, D., and Stadlan, E.M. (1984) Clinical diagnosis of Alzheimer's disease: Report of the NINCDS-ADRDA work group under the auspices of department of health and human services task force on Alzheimer's disease. *Neurology* 34(7): pp. 939–944.

McKhann, G.M., Knopman, D.S., Chertkow, H., Hyman, B.T., Jack, C.R., Kawas, C.H., . . . Mayeux, R. (2011). The diagnosis of dementia due to Alzheimer's disease: Recommendations from the National Institute on Aging-Alzheimer's Association workgroups on diagnostic guidelines for Alzheimer's disease. *Alzheimer's & Dementia* 7(3): pp. 263–269.

Maenner, M.J., Rice, C.E., Arneson, C.L., Cunniff, C., Schieve, L.A., Carpenter, L.A., . . . Durkin, M.S. (2014) Potential impact of DSM-5 criteria on autism spectrum disorder prevalence estimates. *The Journal of American Medical Association Psychiatry* 71(3): pp. 292–300.

Mauch, D., Pfefferle, S., Booker, C., Pustell, M., and Levin, J. (2011) Report on state services to individuals with Autism Spectrum Disorders (ASD). *Centers for Medicare and Medicaid Services (CMS) ASD Services Project: Centers for Medicare and Medicaid Services (CMS)*. Available at: www.cms.gov/apps/files/9-state-report.pdf.

Mayoclinic.org. (2016) Positron Emission Tomography (PET) Scan Risks—Mayo Clinic. Available at: www.mayoclinic.org/tests-procedures/pet-scan/basics/risks/prc-20014301 [Accessed 2 Sept. 2016].

Merin, N., Young, G.S., Ozonoff, S., and Rogers, S.J. (2007). Visual fixation patterns during reciprocal social interaction distinguish a subgroup of 6-month-old infants at-risk for autism from comparison infants. *Journal of Autism and Developmental Disorders* 37(1): pp. 108–121.

Mittal, V.A., Dean, D.J., Mittal, J., and Saks, E.R. (2015). Ethical, legal, and clinical considerations when disclosing a high-risk syndrome for psychosis. *Bioethics* 29(8): pp. 543–556.

Nardone, S., and Elliott, E. (2016) The interaction between the immune system and epigenetics in the etiology of autism spectrum disorders. *Frontiers in Neuroscience* 10: p. 329. doi: 10.3389/fnins.2016.00329.

National Multiple Sclerosis Society. (2016) MS Prevalence. Available at: www.nationalmssociety.org/About-the-Society/MS-Prevalence [Accessed 4 Mar. 2016].

NCSL (2016) Autism and Insurance Coverage | State Laws. Available at: www.ncsl.org/research/health/autism-and-insurance-coverage-state-laws.aspx [Accessed 5 Oct. 2016].

Niendam, T.A., Jalbrzikowski, M., and Bearden, C.E. (2009). Exploring predictors of outcome in the psychosis prodrome: Implications for early identification and intervention. *Neuropsychology Review* 19(3): pp. 280–293.

Olanow, C.W., and Obeso, J.A. (2012). The significance of defining preclinical or prodromal Parkinson's disease. *Movement Disorders* 27(5): pp. 666–669.

Olfson, M., Blanco, C., Liu, S., Wang, S., and Correll, C.U. (2012). National trends in the office-based treatment of children, adolescents, and adults with antipsychotics. *Archives of General Psychiatry* 69(12): pp. 1247–1256.

Palomo, R., Belinchón, M., and Ozonoff, S. (2006). Autism and family home movies: A comprehensive review. *Journal of Developmental & Behavioral Pediatrics* 27(2): pp. S59–S68.

Penttila, M., Jaaskelainen, E., Hirvonen, N., Isohanni, M., and Miettunen, J. (2014) Duration of untreated psychosis as predictor of long-term outcome in schizophrenia: Systematic review and meta-analysis. *The British Journal of Psychiatry: The Journal of Mental Science* 205(2): pp. 88–94.

Ramagopalan, S.V., Dobson, R., Meier, U.C., and Giovannoni, G. (2010). Multiple sclerosis: Risk factors, prodromes, and potential causal pathways. *The Lancet Neurology* 9(7): pp. 727–739.

Sarrett, J.C., and Rommelfanger, K.S. (2015) Commentary: Attention to eyes is present but in decline in 2–6-month-old infants later diagnosed with autism. *Frontiers in Public Health* 3: p. 272. doi: 10.3389/fpubh.2015.00272.

Schmidt, M. (2016) Multiple autisms: Spectrums of advocacy and genomic science. *Oral History Review*. doi:10.1093/ohr/ohw106

Schöll, M., Lockhart, S.N., Schonhaut, D.R., O'Neil, J.P., Janabi, M., Ossenkoppele, R., . . . Jagust, W.J. (2016) PET Imaging of tau deposition in the aging human brain. *Neuron* 89(5): pp. 971–982.

Seeman, N., Tang, S., Brown, A.D., and Ing, A. (2016). World survey of mental illness stigma. *Journal of Affective Disorders* 190: pp. 115–121.

Shic, F., Macari, S., and Chawarska, K. (2014) Speech disturbs face scanning in 6-month-old infants who develop autism spectrum disorder. *Biological Psychiatry* 75(3): pp. 231–237.

Singh, J. (2016). *Multiple Autisms : Spectrums of Advocacy and Genomic Science*. Minneapolis: University of Minnesota Press.

Sperling, R.A., Aisen, P.S., Beckett, L.A., Bennett, D.A., Craft, S., Fagan, A.M., . . . Phelps, C.H. (2011) Toward defining the preclinical stages of Alzheimer's disease: Recommendations from the National Institute on Aging-Alzheimer's Association workgroups on diagnostic guidelines for Alzheimer's disease. *Alzheimer's & Dementia* 7(3): pp. 280–292.

SSA (2016) *Benefits for People with Disabilities*. Available at: www.ssa.gov/disability [Accessed 2 Sept. 2015].

Stetler, R. (2007). Mystery of mitigation: What jurors need to make a reasoned moral response: In capital sentencing. *University of Pennsylvania Journal of Law & Social Change* 11: pp. 237.

Strimbu, K., and Tavel, J.A. (2010) What are biomarkers? *Current Opinion in HIV and AIDS* 5(6): pp. 463–466.

Swartz, M.S., Swanson, J.W., Hiday, V.A., Borum, R., Wagner, H.R., and Burns, B.J. (2014) Violence and severe mental illness: The effects of substance abuse and nonadherence to medication. *American Journal of Psychiatry* 155(2): p. 226–231.

Tarasoff v. Regents of California (1976) 551 P. 2d 334.

Tsuang, M.T., Van Os, J., Tandon, R., Barch, D.M., Bustillo, J., Gaebel, W., . . . Owen, M.J. (2013) Attenuated psychosis syndrome in DSM-5. *Schizophrenia Research* 150(1): pp. 31–35.

United States Department of Health and Human Services, Summary of the Health Privacy Rule. (2003). Available at: www.hhs.gov/sites/default/files/privacysummary.pdf [Accessed 4 Sept. 2016].

Walker, E.F. (2002). Adolescent neurodevelopment and psychopathology. *Current Directions in Psychological Science* 11(1): pp. 24–28.

Walker, E.F., Ryan, A.T., Bridgman Goines, K.C., Novacek, D.M., Goulding, S.M., Brasfield, J.L., and Trotman, H.D. (2016) Multilevel approaches to schizophrenia and other psychotic disorders: The biobehavioral interface. *Developmental Psychopathology* 3(22): pp. 1–42.

Walker, E.F., Trotman, H.D., Goulding, S.M., Holtzman, C.W., Ryan, A.T., McDonald, A., . . . Brasfield, J.L. (2013) Developmental mechanisms in the prodrome to psychosis. *Development and Psychopathology* 25(4): pp. 1585–1600.

Werner, P., Mittelman, M.S., Goldstein, D., and Heinik, J. (2012) Family stigma and caregiver burden in Alzheimer's disease. *The Gerontologist* 52(1): pp. 89–97.

Woolfenden, S., Sarkozy, V., Ridley, G., and Williams, K. (2012) A systematic review of the diagnostic stability of autism spectrum disorder. *Research in Autism Spectrum Disorders* 6(1): pp. 345–354.

World Health Organization. (1993) *The ICD-10 Classification of Mental and Behavioural Disorders: Diagnostic Criteria for Research*: World Health Organization. Available at: https://books.google.com/books?id=HlnzVSbec18C.

Wright, B.L., Lai, J.T., and Sinclair, A.J. (2012) Cerebrospinal fluid and lumbar puncture: A practical review. *Journal of Neurology* 259(8): pp. 1530–1545.

Wu, Y., Le, W., and Jankovic, J. (2011). Preclinical biomarkers of Parkinson disease. *Archives of Neurology* 68(1): pp. 22–30.

Yang, L.H., and Link, B. (2015). Measurement of attitudes, beliefs, and behaviors of mental health and mental illness. Paper prepared for the Committee on the Science of Changing Behavioral Health Social Norms. Available: http://sites.nationalacademies.org/cs/groups/dbassesite/documents/webpage/dbasse_170048.pdf [March 2016].

Yirmiya, N., and Charman, T. (2010) The prodrome of autism: Early behavioral and biological signs, regression, peri- and post-natal development and genetics. *Journal of Child Psychology and Psychiatry* 51(4): pp. 432–458.

6

DISORDERS OF CONSCIOUSNESS AND THE USE OF NEUROTECHNOLOGIES

An Ethical Perspective

Orsolya Friedrich and Ralf J. Jox

Disorders of Consciousness: Basic Medical Information

Disorders of consciousness (DOC) are a group of conditions characterized by impaired verbal and motor responsiveness to diverse stimuli, indicating disturbed consciousness (Bernat, 2006). Almost uniformly, these disorders result from an acute and severe brain injury. In younger patients, this is often a head trauma caused by an accident, while in older patients the causes are more often stroke, brain hemorrhage or hypoxic brain injury due to cardiopulmonary arrest (in which the brain lacks oxygenated blood for several minutes). The acute severe brain injury immediately induces a coma, which is a state of complete unresponsiveness with eyes closed in which even the most painful stimuli cannot elicit any verbal or behavioral responses (Young, 2009). If the patient survives, the clinical situation stabilizes and the brain slowly starts to recover, the patient can transition into an unresponsive wakefulness syndrome (UWS), also called vegetative state. This is indicated by the fact that the patient resumes periods of wakefulness with eyes open, alternating with periods of sleep with eyes closed.

The UWS may be a transient state during the process of recovery that may take several months to years, but it may also be an irreversible state with no further recovery. Its clinical hallmark is the absence of any kind of responsiveness to stimuli (as in the case of coma), but with intact sleep–wake cycles, spontaneous breathing and other brain stem functions still working. Traditionally, it was assumed that all patients in this condition are unconscious and unaware of their surroundings and themselves (Jennett and Plum, 1972). Since recent neuroscientific data questions this assumption, and indicates that some of these patients may retain some form of awareness (Monti et al., 2010b), researchers have suggested to move from the term "vegetative state" to the more neutral, descriptive name "unresponsive wakefulness syndrome" (Laureys et al., 2010).

If the patient's brain continues to recover, the patient may enter the so-called minimally conscious state (MCS), the second entity of disorders of consciousness. This condition is characterized by reproducible signs of purposeful behavior. In the beginning, this may only be that the eyes follow a moving object (tested by moving a mirror in front of the patient's face) or fixate on a stationary object (patients in this minimally responsive state are diagnosed as MCS minus).

Purposeful behavior may also be more evident, for example, when a patient begins to follow simple commands or utter discernible words. Such patients are diagnosed as MCS plus (Guldenmund et al., 2016). In rare cases, MCS may also be the result of neurodegenerative disorders of the cerebral cortex, such as Alzheimer's dementia.

In contrast to the UWS and the MCS, there is another state that is in fact not a disorder of consciousness but often confounded and misattributed as such: the locked-in syndrome (LIS). This condition is characterized by intact awareness, perception and cognition, whereas the motor functions are completely or almost completely lost (with the only retained function often being vertical eye movement and eyelid movement; see Table 6.1).

The diagnosis of UWS and MCS rests on clinical examination and observation whereby the significant finding is a negative one, that is, the absence or reduction of behavioral responsiveness. Without a validated test instrument (e.g., Coma Recovery Scale-Revised) the rate of misdiagnosis is as high as 40%, with MCS commonly being mistaken for VS (Schnakers et al., 2009). The reasons for this excessively high rate of misdiagnosis might be the infrequent use of validated behavioral test instruments, a low knowledge of the clinical signs of these rare diseases by primary care physicians or even neurologists, and the rapidly evolving changes in the classification of these disorders over the past years. Additionally, behavioral evidence of awareness is indirect and may be extremely subtle and difficult to detect. Some forms of brain imaging

Table 6.1 Synopsis of Disorders of Consciousness UWS and MCS as Distinct from the Locked-In Syndrome.

Disorder	Definition	Clinical signs
Vegetative State, Unresponsive Wakefulness Syndrome (VS/UWS)	Wakefulness without any signs of awareness	No indication of awareness/consciousness No sustained, reproducible, purposeful motor reaction to visual, auditory, tactile or painful stimuli; no interaction with others (verbally or nonverbally) Presence of eyes opening and closing, at least partially intact functions of the brain stem (including spontaneous unaided breathing), the hypothalamus and the autonomic nervous system
Minimally conscious state (MCS)	Wakefulness with reproducible signs of awareness	Indication of a rudimentary/partial form of awareness Fluctuating but reproducible signs of purposeful movements: – Visual pursuit, visual fixation, nonreflexive response to stimuli (MCS minus) – Following simple commands, language expression/discernible words (MCS plus) Presence of eyes opening and closing No communication, no object use
Locked-in syndrome	Extensive impairment of voluntary motor behavior	Intact consciousness/awareness (intact EEG) Complete paralysis of all limbs (tetraplegia) and of the muscles for speech production (anarthria) Usually preserved function of vertical eye movements and/or opening and closing of the eyelids (can be used for communication)

Source: Adapted from (Monti et al., 2010a). MCS = Minimally conscious state. VS = Vegetative state. EEG = electroencephalography.

and electroencephalography (EEG), which detects the summed electrical activity of superficial cortical neurons using electrodes placed on the surface of the scalp, can help refine the diagnosis (Bender et al., 2015). Prognostication is extremely difficult given the lack of methodologically robust long-term studies and the variability of brain plasticity (Jox et al., 2012; Bender et al., 2015). There is, to date, no form of treatment that has been proven unequivocally effective in raising the level of awareness and improving the outcome of rehabilitation in these patients (Jox et al., 2012; Giacino et al., 2014).

Neurotechnologies for the Detection of Consciousness

Recently, there have been an increasing number of studies that use neuroimaging techniques such as functional magnetic resonance imaging (fMRI) in DOC (Fins et al., 2008). With fMRI, the magnetic characteristics of oxygenated blood versus deoxygenated blood are used as markers of neuronal activity, based on the observation that active brain tissue recruits more blood flow than inactive tissue. This so-called neurovascular coupling (or blood oxygen level–dependent response) is also the basis of functional near infra-red spectroscopy (fNIRS), in which researchers make use of the fact that oxygenated and deoxygenated blood shows different attenuation of infrared light at various wavelengths. Positron emission tomography (PET) is another functional brain-imaging method that shows the metabolically active areas of the brain after the injection of radioactively marked substances (usually glucose; Stender et al., 2014). In addition to these functional brain-imaging techniques, there are also improved structural imaging techniques that visualize brain pathologies in high resolution and delineate certain parts of the tissue (e.g., diffusion tensor MRI, which visualizes white matter tracts throughout the brain; Bruno et al., 2011). In addition to these brain-imaging methods, researchers are also improving neurophysiological methodologies that grant better functional assessment of the brain and are based on improvements in EEG. The specific advantages and challenges of the most promising techniques for the use in DOC are summarized in Table 6.2, based on the publication of Naci (Naci et al., 2012).

For all methods, data need to be collected on the subject's performance of an experimental task as compared to control conditions. In patients with DOC, these technologies are most often explicitly used to determine awareness or characterize mental states and sometimes also to establish communication. The application of these technologies in patients with DOC is highly demanding and complicated. The patients have to remain still over a prolonged period of time and in a certain body position. Brain responses have to be sustained over a certain duration of time, and they have to occur in a certain time window after a stimulus has been presented. If brain responses to stimuli or questions are detected, it is necessary to distinguish genuine signs of awareness from unconscious responses (such as information processing that occurs under anesthesia; Bonebakker et al., 1996; Davis et al., 2007).

Reviewing recent PET studies, Gosseries and colleagues hypothesize that in the UWS, only the primary sensory cortices are activated by the respective noxious or auditory stimuli, whereas in the MCS, this information is also transmitted to and processed in higher-order areas of the cortex, like the frontoparietal cortices, that are known for preparing this information for conscious perception (Gosseries et al., 2014). The same has been found in fMRI studies: in UWS, fMRI activation in response to sensory stimuli can only be found in primary sensory cortices in contrast to activation in secondary (associative) sensory cortices in MCS (Gosseries et al., 2014). Furthermore, the functional connectivity of different brain areas, especially in frontoparietal cortices, is also more impaired in UWS than in MCS (Gosseries et al., 2014). These data suggest that although some activity patterns in UWS brains are similar to those of healthy people following noxious,

Table 6.2 Advantages and Limitations of Neurotechnologies When Applied for Determination of Awareness and Communication with Patients Suffering from Disorders of Consciousness.

Functional Neuroimaging Methods	Advantages	Limitations
fMRI	Noninvasive global brain coverage high spatial resolution (millimeter range) sophisticated analysis methods first to demonstrate plausibility of communication with patients deemed to be in a VS	High cost Lack of portability Physical impositions (e.g., patient must stay still and in supine position for an extended period of time) No paramagnetic equipment can be present Noisy Susceptible to movement artifacts Lower temporal resolution than EEG (second range)
fNIRS	Noninvasive Portable Relatively low cost; nearly noiseless Less sensitive to movement artifacts than fMRI Easier to operate than fMRI No restriction on paramagnetic medical equipment	A relatively new methodology Limited experience with BCI applications Limited spatial resolution (~3cm)/especially poor resolution of deep brain structures Some susceptibility to movement artifacts Analysis methods under development
EEG	Noninvasive Portable Relatively low cost High temporal resolution (millisecond range) Silent No physical impositions (e.g., can be applied in the seated and supine positions or when the patient is asleep) Vast BCI experience with different patient populations	Limited spatial resolution (~3cm)/especially poor resolution of deep brain structures Susceptible to artifacts from cranial muscles and eye movements The majority of existing paradigms have limited use for DOC patients (but see Cruse et al., 2011)

BCI = brain–computer interface; DOC = disorders of consciousness; EEG = electroencephalography; fMRI = functional magnetic resonance imaging; fNIRS = functional near-infrared spectroscopy; VS = vegetative state

Source: Adapted reprint of Naci et al. (2012), with permission of the publisher.

auditory, or sensory stimulation, most neuroimaging findings do not show activity associated with awareness in higher-order cortices, which is in contrast to MCS (Gosseries et al., 2014).

Yet some groundbreaking studies postulate partially intact awareness not only in MCS but also in some patients with clinically diagnosed UWS. In fMRI study, Di et al. were able to show brain activation within the primary auditory cortex (for three UWS and four MCS patients) and also within hierarchically higher-order cortex areas that process auditory information (for two UWS and four MCS patients) in response to the patient's own name spoken by a familiar voice (Di et al., 2007). Another study suggests that some patients with DOC (5 out of 54) had the ability to willfully modulate their brain activity in response to commands to imagine certain movements (either playing tennis or walking through the rooms of one's home). Imagining playing tennis resulted in activation of the supplementary motor cortex, while imagining walking through the rooms of one's home activated the parahippocampal gyrus. Therefore, the distinct activation patterns could be used as a proxy for yes or no responses. One of these patients was even able to signal answers regarding personal questions using this yes-and-no code by imagining playing tennis (for yes) or walking through his home (for no; Monti et al., 2010b).

Although the significance of these studies is limited due to the high percentage of negative findings (even most MCS patients do not show the neuroimaging correlates of awareness; Monti et al., 2010b; Gosseries et al., 2014) and small sample sizes, the discovery of greater and more selective patterns of brain activity than had been clinically expected can indicate that at least a few patients in UWS may actually have residual awareness. Therefore, active tasks or stimuli combined with neuroimaging techniques could serve as a complementary diagnostic tool helping to reduce misdiagnosis and to differentiate between patients in UWS, MCS and the locked-in syndrome (Giacino et al., 2006; Gill-Thwaites, 2006).

As there is little consensus about the nature and components of consciousness in philosophy, empirical science and law, the results of these studies have to be clarified with regard to their understanding of consciousness. They all refer to the level or degree of consciousness (awareness) but do not imply much about the content of consciousness, in that no verbal reports of patients with DOC are available. One important aspect of consciousness in philosophy of mind is so-called phenomenal consciousness, the qualitative character of experiences like colors or feelings (Fisher and Appelbaum, 2010). Other aspects are intentionality, the directedness and goal orientation of mental states, such as beliefs or wishes (that always have an object they refer to), and access consciousness, defined as a subject's ability to access the representational content of his or her mental states. Still another aspect is self-consciousness, understood as the reflective knowledge of a person experiencing him- or herself as someone who is in a certain mental state, for example, reflecting about his or her own mood (Gallagher and Dan, 2015; Siewert, 2011). Leaving aside some objections from philosophy of mind about the relationship between visible neural activity and consciousness, the cited neuroimaging findings may constitute evidence for the existence of phenomenal consciousness (e.g., altered neuronal activity when one's own name is spoken by a familiar voice) or intentionality (e.g., increased neuronal activity during mental imagery tasks) in some patients with DOC. Some authors even hypothesize that fMRI responses to mental imagery tasks could be understood as acting on one's own volition and therefore meet the criterion for higher-order consciousness by providing a proxy of a behavioral response (Fisher and Appelbaum, 2010). Imagining activities to give appropriate responses to commands and using this imagery to establish a yes/no code for communicative purposes is interpreted by some authors as evidence for self-reference and self-consciousness (Fisher and Appelbaum, 2010). Yet there are some caveats to these conclusions: (1) the responses indicating consciousness were only observed in a small subset of patients with DOC; (2) positive responses presume many intact cognitive mechanisms (e.g., hearing, speech comprehension, volition, executive abilities), which means that a lack of response does not necessarily exclude awareness (Johnson, 2016); (3) the methodological rigor of the designs of studies and statistics are debatable, and the small groups of patients being studied by only a few cooperating scientists worldwide limit the representativeness of the data (Peterson et al., 2015); and (4) as long as no bidirectional communication with patients spontaneously posing questions can be established, the evidence for awareness is less convincing than in the case of locked-in patients.

One goal of current research is to use active mental imagery paradigms in brain imaging and EEG research to establish functional communication with patients with DOC wherever possible (Weijer et al., 2014; Peterson et al., 2013). This technological setup is also known as "brain–computer interface" (BCI). BCIs usually involve a device (like EEG or fMRI) to acquire brain signals, a procedure to analyze these signals (software, mathematical processing), the use of the extracted signal to guide computer displays or other external devices and instant feedback to the user (Nijboer et al., 2013; Shih et al., 2012). Patients with locked-in syndrome and near-complete paralysis may use BCI to augment or enable communication and interaction with their environment (Chaudhary et al., 2015). Despite recent technological advances, BCI–mediated communication can only be reliably established with patients who are not completely locked in, while those who are already completely paralyzed and have no other means of communication (e.g., via eye movements) have thus far not been able to learn BCI communication (Marchetti and Priftis, 2015; Birbaumer et al., 2014). Some authors hypothesize that the neurobiological machinery required for goal-directed thinking is lost in patients with complete locked-in syndrome (Kubler and Birbaumer, 2008). Obviously, the chances that patients with DOC could establish functional BCI communication may be even smaller, in particular if they have been in this state for a long period. The extinction of goal-directed thinking, however, may potentially be reversed if both the mental states and the correct behavioral responses could be externally stimulated in close temporal sequence, for example, using transcranial magnetic stimulation (TMS; Birbaumer and Cohen, 2007). In TMS, a magnetic field is externally applied above the head to induce localized electrical currents in superficial regions of the cortex (Corthout et al., 2001).

Neurotechnologies for the Restoration of Consciousness

Brain stimulation techniques are increasingly being studied with various objectives for patients with DOC. This includes both noninvasive technologies, like TMS and transcranial direct current stimulation (tDCS), and invasive neurostimulation like vagal nerve stimulation or deep brain stimulation (DBS), in which electrodes are surgically implanted in the thalamus, a deep inner region of the brain (Schiff et al., 2007; Schiff et al., 2009; Sen et al., 2010). In a famous single-case study, a patient with a long history of MCS showed transient improvements in motor and verbal behavior associated with increased awareness after undergoing DBS (Schiff et al., 2007). Similar but less pronounced effects could be observed by administering repetitive TMS over the dorsolateral prefrontal cortex of UWS patients (Naro et al., 2015). Moreover, if TMS is used to stimulate certain areas of the brain noninvasively and EEG techniques are employed to register the brain's reaction to this stimulation (TMS-EEG), this may help differentiate between brains with intact networks and those without and even help to distinguish conscious from unconscious patients (Napolitani et al., 2014; Sarasso et al., 2014; Casali et al., 2013). Another noninvasive form of brain stimulation is tDCS, which does not use magnetic impulses to the brain like TMS but instead applies direct-current electrical impulses to change the excitability of the brain cells in targeted regions of the brain (again largely in superficial regions of the cortex). Initial studies have revealed that MCS patients (and even one UWS patient) showed significant clinical improvements in their level of awareness (measured by the Coma Recovery Scale-Revised) when treated with tDCS (Thibaut et al., 2014; Angelakis et al., 2014).

As neurotechnologies emerge and approach clinical application in DOC, ethical questions arise. Some of these questions are similar to those arising from the use of these neurotechnologies in other research contexts and for other medical conditions, while others are more specific to their use in DOC. There have, for example, been numerous ethical debates about the use of DBS in various medical disorders (Schermer, 2011). The uncertainty about the state of awareness is a more specific ethical feature of patients with DOC, because the existence of consciousness may be morally relevant when it comes to treatment or research decisions (Kahane and Savulescu, 2009). Recent findings indicating awareness in some UWS patients provide evidence of the shortcomings of standard clinical diagnosis. For some MCS patients, research findings suggest higher forms of consciousness than clinically evident and previously assumed. Ethically, the salient question is whether and how the evidence of (partial) awareness in DOCs changes the normative evaluation of specific situations.

In contrast to the medical mainstream, some philosophers argue that the evidence of more consciousness than presumed could provide a strong moral reason for not saving the lives of patients with DOC (Kahane and Savulescu, 2009; Wilkinson et al., 2009). They base their argument on the moral relevance of phenomenal consciousness. If we accept that the research findings provide new evidence regarding certain aspects of consciousness in DOC, then—as we will discuss—they may influence ethical arguments with regard to informed consent/assent, advance directives, personal identity and patient well-being. Moreover, as most neurotechnological applications in DOC are still experimental and not yet routine in clinical practice, ethical questions concerning study design and knowledge translation also surface. We will discuss these ethical issues in the following parts of this chapter.

Informed Consent

If robust communication with patients with DOC could one day be established using BCIs, it could in principle be used to probe the patient's cognitive state, assess decision-making capacity and even obtain informed consent for research and treatment if decision-making capacity is present. In a theoretical article, neuroscientists have sketched ways to assess decision-making capacity by employing yes/no questions via BCI (Peterson et al., 2013). This approach, however, still suffers from a reductionist and overly simplistic concept of autonomy and decision-making capacity. According to standard ethico-legal definitions, decision-making capacity requires understanding, appreciation, reasoning and communication (Appelbaum and Grisso, 1988). In order to assess whether these four elements are present to a sufficient degree, reliable, nuanced, bidirectional communication is key (Jox, 2013). As patients with DOC cannot read, any information on research or treatment interventions has to be presented orally. Whether patients have fully understood this information can only be ascertained by asking them to rephrase the information in their own words. This may in principle be done by BCI, but it requires a technology that allows the patients to spontaneously formulate sentences, as is done by some patients with locked-in syndrome, by selecting letters to spell words. In order to assess the process of apprehension and reasoning, it is even more necessary to have the patient formulate sentences, pose questions and give answers (Malandro et al., 1989). These tasks would be exceedingly difficult for patients with impaired consciousness and potentially severe residual brain injuries.

Another element of informed consent, voluntariness, is similarly difficult to assess via BCI. It can only be assessed if a true conversation is possible and if the patients can elaborate on their intentions, motives and objectives. This seems impossible with the current rudimentary BCI technologies for DOC patients. Yet, ensuring voluntariness may be particularly important in this patient group because it is not unlikely that extensive brain injury has led to pathological states of thought, volition or impulse control that restrict the patient's free will.

Another threat to voluntariness comes from the outside: as BCI technology advances and includes the bidirectional flow of information between the brain and the computer, it is generally possible to manipulate the brain from the outside via BCI, abrogating the patient's voluntariness. Even without such speculative threats, one can ask the question whether a patient may ever be seen as capable of making voluntary decisions or if he or she is in a state of maximum dependency.

In summary, it is currently impossible to assess whether the preconditions of informed consent—information, decision-making capacity and voluntariness of the decision—are met in individual cases of DOC patients (Farisco, 2015). The impossibility of such assessments stems not only from technological shortcomings that may be overcome with time but also rest upon principled problems. Even if we assume that these preconditions could be perfectly assessed via BCI, it is improbable that DOC patients will satisfy all criteria for fully informed consent because of the extensive cortex damage in the vast majority of DOC patients, unlike locked-in patients (Bernat, 2009). In DOC, the brain injury is likely to affect some of the cognitive and volitional abilities that are necessary for understanding complex medical or research decisions, decision-making capacity and voluntariness. DOC patients may resemble patients with stroke, dementia or psychiatric disorders more than cognitively intact patients locked into their bodies. This fact is evidenced by the severe cognitive and memory disturbances that patients display when they recover and emerge from DOC (Wijdicks, 2006; Voss et al., 2006). The popular illusion that patients with DOC are healthy minds in disabled bodies is explained by the fact that these individuals were usually cognitively intact before they suddenly slipped into a coma due to an acute brain injury and is further nurtured by fictional movies showing a sudden awakening and the immediate restoration of the patients' previous life and personality (Wijdicks and Wijdicks, 2006).

If informed consent cannot be obtained from patients with DOC via BCI, one possible remedy could be to change the concept of informed consent. One may argue that novel neurotechnological possibilities require a fundamental alteration of our ethical and legal concepts. This, however, is not self-evident. Why should long-held, well-proven ethical principles and legal regulations be altered as soon as neuroscience offers new ways of interacting with patients? In fact, lowering the cognitive threshold for informed consent would jeopardize the protection of autonomy of all persons undergoing medical treatment or research.

There should be procedures in place to gauge the level of self-reflection that a patient is able to have and communicate via BCI. The fact that the patient cannot be approached for informed consent can lift the burden from these conversations. Instead of informed consent, surrogates, health care professionals and researchers should aim to obtain informed *assent*. This is a concept that has been developed in pediatrics in order to respect the growing capacity of self-determination in children and adolescents and involve them in making decisions (Spriggs and Caldwell, 2011). Assent itself is not sufficient in justifying research or treatment; it does not replace the need for true informed consent by surrogate decision makers. Striving for assent, however, fosters a person's participation in a research study or treatment course and improves the outcomes of these procedures for his or her well-being. In addition, assent usually means that the intervention is not met with resistance, which prevents the experience of compulsion and psychological traumatization.

In the context of research, assent has an even stronger authority than in the context of treatment. While the refusal to give assent (or plain dissent) may be overridden in exceptional clinical circumstances in which treatment is urgently necessary to save the life of the person or for other important values, this is not allowed in research. The Declaration of Helsinki states: "When a potential research subject who is deemed incapable of giving informed consent is able to give assent to decisions about participation in research, the physician must seek that assent in addition to the consent of the legally authorized representative. The potential subject's dissent should be respected" (World Medical Association, 2013). This means that research should never be done compulsorily, against the resistance or refusal of the subject.

This concept of informed assent has already been transferred from pediatrics to adult medicine in the case of research or treatment for dementia patients (Black et al., 2010). There is no reason, in principle, why it should not also be transferred and adapted to the research and treatment of patients with DOC. Given functioning BCI technology in patients with DOC, informed assent may be sought in some circumstances and be considered in making decisions on research and treatment.

Precedent Autonomy

When formerly competent adult patients are unable to give informed consent, precedent (prospective) autonomy can be considered (Davis, 2002). A person may have anticipated a brain injury and thus expressed his or her treatment wishes prospectively in an advance treatment directive (living will). Alternatively, the person may have expressed these wishes verbally, and surrogates can take these into consideration when making a substitute judgment.

If a person makes an advance directive in ignorance of new neurotechnological options from DOC research (or before the technology was realized), the question arises whether prior expressions of will are still valid and applicable. If, for example, the advance directive prohibits life-sustaining treatment in the case of VS, the person may have written this under the assumption that VS is always associated with an irreversible loss of any kind of awareness. If new options to recover awareness or even motor functions using neurostimulation techniques were developed after the person had written the advance directive, would it still hold?

According to a common understanding, an advance directive is not valid if it is proven that it was not authored by the person it affects or the person revoked it while still in possession of decision-making capacity. Revocation of the advance directive may be done in any form: in writing, orally or using BCI communication. There are, however, good ethical reasons why decision-making capacity is required in order to revoke one's advance directive (Jox, 2014). As long as the decision-making capacity cannot clearly be verified via BCI, patients with DOC are unable to revoke a previously written advance directive. In spite of signs of partially intact awareness through neuroimaging techniques, it is unlikely that patients with DOC that has been lasting for several years will regain the prerequisite cognitive capacities to remember and reflect on their previously expressed preferences, compare them with their current situation and change their minds. This may be possible for cognitively intact patients with locked-in syndrome, but in that case, advance directives do not come into play because the patients usually retain their decision-making capacity and, frequently, the ability to communicate.

Whether an advance directive is applicable is a more complex matter. Applicability usually refers to the fact that the clinical circumstances, the quality of life, prognosis and treatment options match those that the patient anticipated when writing the directive. If the document itself does not permit judging the question of applicability, persons close to the patient or those who have counseled the patient while writing the directive should assist in this interpretative judgment. The mere fact that novel research results have been published since the patient's brain injury does not render the advance directive inapplicable. It has to be convincingly shown that the patient would have decided otherwise had he been aware of the new research results and their impact on prognosis, quality of life, treatment options or other important elements of the decision. In England, this standard is even regulated in the Mental Capacity Act 2005

(Legislation.gov.uk, 2012). Similar considerations apply to the substitute judgment of surrogates. They have to consider the person's previous autonomous preferences and adapt those to the potentially new clinical situation and ask themselves how the patient would decide given the current situation, having full knowledge of the state of awareness, quality of life, prognosis and treatment options (Kuehlmeyer et al., 2014).

Personal Identity

The temporal continuity of personal identity can be relevant for moral reasoning among clinical decision makers and surrogates. Since John Locke, the ongoing debate about personal identity often centers on the question of how we can know that a person is identical at differing time points t1 and t2 (Locke, 2008; Noonan, 2003). This concept of diachronic personal identity is crucial in order to ascribe responsibility to a person and to justify precedent autonomy implemented via advance directives or substituted judgment. The applicability of an advance directive presupposes that the patient for whom we have to make a treatment decision is identical to the one who has written the advance directive. Some suggest that without a minimum level of consciousness and psychological connectedness we cannot assume continuity of personal identity (Parfit, 1984; Noonan, 2003). According to this line of thinking, patients with DOC may not necessarily be identical to the persons they were before their brain injury, and advance directives would lose their authority. The same argument is potentially also relevant for other identity-altering conditions, such as dementia, amnesia or severe brain damage (DeGrazia, 2005). If personal identity is not based on physical characteristics but rather on some kind of psychological continuity, then new neuroimaging findings indicating consciousness in patients with DOC hitherto presumed to be unconscious could challenge assumptions about the loss of personal identity (Friedrich, 2013). Per Locke, many have argued that personal identity is tied to the continuity of psychological states, interpreting the conditions for such a continuity in different ways (Noonan, 2003). Depending on the conditions for their "psychological continuity criterion" (like memories, self-identification, phenomenal consciousness), signs of more or less awareness through neuroimaging techniques may be relevant to establishing the validity of advance directives and, therefore, for decisions concerning life-sustaining treatments in patients with DOCs. If, however, personal identity depends on a "physical criterion" (like the body, brain, certain parts of the brain and so on), then the advance directives must be considered valid both with and without knowledge of more or less awareness in patients with DOC (Friedrich, 2013). It can be said that if one considers that personal identity only exists in certain states of consciousness and combines this consideration with normative reasoning, then new findings on increased consciousness using neuroimaging techniques could make a morally relevant difference.

For more on personal identity, see Chapter 22.

Well-Being

The current and future well-being of the patient plays a key role in medical ethics, as demonstrated in the two prima facie principles of beneficence and nonmaleficence that any treatment has to take into consideration (Beauchamp and Childress, 2013). But what do we mean by well-being? The absence of pain and suffering are two intuitively plausible criteria for well-being.

But is that enough? If we consider everyday life, there are much more relevant aspects to our well-being than the absence of pain and suffering. Therefore we often use the term "quality of life," indicating a positive content of life, which is more than just the absence of suffering. Quality of life may be associated with health, physical functions, psychological satisfaction, enjoyment of life, social networks and meaning in life. In fact, the medical quality-of-life research has abandoned the idea that there may be a one-size-fits-all definition for quality of life and instead pursues the concept of individual quality of life, according to which each person can only determine what quality of life means to them (Waldron et al., 1999).

Given the inability to communicate with patients with DOC, it is difficult to approach the question of what constitutes quality of life and well-being in DOC. Johnson argues that subjective well-being is the relevant concept for patients with DOC and includes negative affective states (e.g., pain, depression) and positive affective states (e.g., physical contact, social companionship, mental stimulation; Johnson, 2013). Kahane and Savulescu have proposed three main interests among people, all capturing aspects of well-being and presupposing different levels of consciousness: experiential, desiderative and objective interests (Kahane and Savulescu, 2009). For experiential interests like pain and pleasure, phenomenal consciousness is a necessary condition (Kahane and Savulescu, 2009). Objective interests like friendships or desiderative interests, implicating desires, require at least some cognitive capacities and therefore higher degrees of consciousness (Kahane and Savulescu, 2009).

There is, however, an epistemic uncertainty in applying these criteria to patients with DOC. How can we know whether they suffer or experience pain? Are physiological reactions like the elevation of blood pressure or the increase of spasticity evidence enough to conclude that the patient is in distress and suffers? Can brain imaging help us in assessing whether patients with DOC suffer? Imaging data on the persistence of the so-called pain matrix, a network for measuring pain in healthy persons, are inconclusive for patients with DOC but suggest that pain perception may be intact in most MCS patients and usually not intact in UWS patients (Boly et al., 2005; Boly et al., 2008). Researchers have also introduced a Nociception Coma Scale-Revised that is based on behavioral (motor, facial and verbal) pain response and seems to correlate with metabolism in the pain matrix (Chatelle et al., 2012; Chatelle et al., 2014). If, however, it should become possible to reliably ask patients with DOC whether they are in pain via BCI communication, this would significantly improve pain assessment and management within this patient group.

Yet pain is only one facet of possible sources of distress. Depending on their level of consciousness and whether they have only phenomenal consciousness or also self-consciousness, other kinds of suffering are also possible. Patients with self-consciousness may suffer from realizing that they are completely dependent, have lost most of their capacities, cannot effectively communicate and have an extremely low likelihood of recovery. It is, however, far from realistic at present to establish such a detailed communication via BCI that these kinds of suffering could be elicited. The same is true for the opposite of suffering: sources of quality of life and personal views on fulfillment and meaning of life presuppose not only nuanced communication but also a high level of cognitive capacities.

BCI–mediated communication, once it is established as a reliable means of communication with patients with DOC, should be used to inquire about the patient's current well-being, starting with very basic questions about pain and suffering and gradually moving on to more complex questions, if possible. BCI may, for example, be used to explore the need for pain and symptom treatment and to guide the choice and dosage of drugs used to treat these symptoms. In the same vein, it can be used to assess what effect various forms of nonpharmacological treatment, physiotherapy, occupational therapy, sensory stimulation, diverse forms of rehabilitation and nursing care have on the patients' well-being (Johnson, 2013; Weijer et al., 2014).

The mere evidence that some phenomenal consciousness persists may justify a trial of pain relief, but would it also justify the administration of life-sustaining treatment or its withdrawal? In addition to the epistemic uncertainty, both the absence and presence of phenomenal consciousness in DOC can provide moral reasons both in favor of and against life-sustaining treatment. If no sign of consciousness is found, one can argue that there is no suffering and the criterion of well-being makes no sense, which is why continued life support cannot distress the patient and should be maintained. On the contrary, it could also be concluded that life-sustaining treatment should be withdrawn, in that any reasonable goal of care is lost when there is no possibility of offering appreciable benefit to the patient and restoring any kind of well-being. If, however, patients are found to have some residual consciousness, the decision could go either way depending on the current and anticipated state of well-being.

It is also plausible to ascribe intrinsic value to certain kinds of consciousness, such as self-consciousness, access consciousness or phenomenal consciousness—in analogy to positions that ascribe intrinsic value to life. Yet this intrinsic value has to be justified by good reasons, and it has to be plausible that the intrinsic value of this consciousness outweighs any reasons for withdrawing life support. Some philosophers question whether patients with mere phenomenal consciousness, in cases where access consciousness is not present, do in fact merit the full moral status of persons (Levy and Savulescu, 2009; Fisher and Appelbaum, 2010).

For more on moral status, see Chapter 31.

Study Designs

Many ethical problems in neurotechnological studies on patients with DOC relate to the design of the study. Patients with DOC are chronically ill persons with a constant need for life support and have high mortality rates. This means that studies usually have high dropout rates due to intervening clinical treatment or even death. Surrogates and physicians may be confronted with the need to decide about life-sustaining treatment, and with respect to the patient's best interests or the patient's autonomy, they may be ethically and legally obliged to let the patient die (Jox, 2011). This may tempt researchers to use a strategy of selective sampling, confounding their results with a significant selection bias. Once they have recruited patients for an observational or interventional study, researchers may be tempted to ignore ethical and legal arguments for withdrawal of life-sustaining treatment in order to prevent high dropout rates. Clinical decisions may be biased by an overly pessimistic prognosis; some patients with DOC who are allowed to die may have recovered if they had been maintained on life-sustaining treatment (resulting in a self-fulfilling prophecy). But it would be equally wrong to keep all patients alive simply to test whether they may recover at some point in the future. Decisions about life-sustaining treatment should be informed by the best data that are currently available. To avoid the problem of research goals interfering with patient care, the only way to ethically study the potential for recovery is to do retrospective case-control studies or prospective observational studies focusing on those patients that were kept on life support.

Because of the methodological and ethical problems associated with studies on patients with DOC (small prevalence, high drop-out rates, informed consent, etc.), the literature is full of single-case studies and case series. Many of these case reports focus on exceptional recoveries (very late or unexpectedly significant recoveries; Kuehlmeyer et al., 2013). Some of these publications hypothesize that certain experimental forms of treatment were responsible for the unexpected recovery of the patient. The evidence level of case studies, however, is extremely weak for methodological reasons. They cannot prove a causal relationship between the experimental treatment or intervention and the recovery, because the latter could also have accidentally coincided with the intervention. The reports of unexpected recoveries also fall short of giving any information about the statistical frequency of such recoveries in the whole group of patients with DOC. As the *expected* courses of patients who do not recover are not noted and published, the *unexpected* recoveries cannot be compared to them in a statistical way. Moreover, it is not known how many positive (or even negative) case reports are declined by journals. Ultimately, the utility of a case report rests in the description of the range of possible clinical courses—but only as long as the cases are authentically reported and free from misdiagnosis and misrepresentation (Kuehlmeyer et al., 2013). There is a risk that some physicians and family surrogates will heavily base their treatment decisions on extreme case outliers as they cling to anything that allows them to maintain high hopes (Almodovar, 2002; Kuehlmeyer et al., 2012; Jox et al., 2015).

Knowledge Translation

Researchers and clinicians have multiple motivations for publishing "miracle recoveries" and "research breakthroughs" not only in professional journals but also in the lay media. First, they may be genuinely surprised and convinced by the novelty and impact of their findings and feel the need to immediately inform the world. Second, the families of patients with DOC long for any glimmer of hope, any indication of an effective treatment, place high expectations on clinicians and researchers and promise the deepest gratitude in case of success. Third, the current research business and health care system requires people to market their findings and compete for attention, reputation, awards, publication impact, and public and private funding.

It appears to be increasingly common to publish alleged breakthroughs in TV reports, newspaper articles, web podcasts and press releases before writing peer-reviewed articles for the scientific community—especially in research on DOC. Of course, the media may also be keen on such success stories and hunt for them. Two examples illustrate the dangers in doing so: in November 2012, the British Broadcasting Channel (BBC) reported the story of the neuroscientist Adrian Owen asking the UWS patient Scott Routley during a fMRI mental imagery study whether he was in pain (Walsh, 2012). According to the technological paradigm, Routley's answer was no, but the problem is that there is in general no way to verify subjective reports. This study was never published in a scientific journal (although Routley was part of a group of patients with DOC undergoing other tests in a further study; Naci and Owen, 2013). Understandably, this study sparked extreme hopes not only in Routley's family but also in other families of patients with DOC. However, it is sobering to discover that Scott Routley died less than a year after the BBC report, which is hardly known and has not been published in the same way as the neuroimaging findings (Lunau, 2013).

The second case is that of Rom Houben, the Belgian patient in a vegetative state. After Houben had supposedly been in UWS for 23 years, the Belgian researcher Steven Laureys performed neuroimaging studies on him and concluded that he was in fact conscious, but locked in a paralyzed body. In a groundbreaking newspaper article in the German magazine *Der Spiegel*, Laureys's studies were celebrated along with apparent quotes from Houben himself elicited with the help of a speech therapist using a controversial type of facilitated communication: "I will never forget that day when they discovered me: my second birth" (Dworschak, 2009). The news was reiterated by countless media around the world. Yet a few months later, *Der Spiegel* had to admit, hidden in a second enthusiastic article on the progress of DOC research, that the quotes were faked by the speech therapist and later could be verified neither by Laureys nor by anyone else (Dworschak, 2010). The case was then heavily criticized as the misuse of a patient to boost certain research agendas (Appel, 2009).

The problem of exaggerating, distorting and scandalizing science publications starts with the press releases by the researchers and their press departments. A comparison of academic press releases from the UK with their respective peer-reviewed scientific articles showed that more than a third contained exaggerations and unsubstantiated claims (Sumner et al., 2014). The respective news stories on these research results augmented the exaggerations even further. An analysis of newspaper articles on the famous court case of Terri Schiavo, the American patient in a vegetative state, found extremely high rates of misrepresentations, errors and imprecise language likely to promote false hopes and mistaken opinions on DOC (Racine et al., 2008). Fictional movies fuel these false views by depicting unrealistic scenarios of coma and awakening (Wijdicks and Wijdicks, 2006).

Conflicts of interest often lie at the heart of such ethical problems in knowledge transla-tion of DOC research. The clinician-researcher may be torn between his duties as a physician and those as a researcher. Scientists may also feel pressured by research sponsors, such as private foundations set up by families of patients with DOC that may pursue an inflexible pro-life ide-ology and promote anything that supports it. In addition, some patient advocacy groups in this area do not seem to be neutral when it comes to research on DOC but lobby for certain kinds of research. Another important player in research on DOC is the medical technology industry that supplies the imaging and neurostimulation devices. Some of the devices are produced by companies with a quasi-monopolist position, and transparency and independence of research may not always be fully respected (Fins and Schiff, 2010). These conflicts of interest may provide incentives for publicizing "results" that are premature and not generalizable and may not stand up to careful scientific peer review and scrutiny.

Concluding Remarks

In summary, during the past decade, there has been significant, novel research on DOC involv-ing the use of neuroimaging, neurophysiology and neurostimulation techniques. These tech-nologies undoubtedly promise advances in reducing misdiagnosis, improving prognostication and allowing plausible assumptions about the state of awareness. They also give rise, however, to several ethical questions. We presented and discussed what we believe to be the most urgent issues at the heart of these ethical questions: informed consent, advance directives, personal identity, patient well-being, study designs and knowledge translation.

Further Reading

Demertzi, A. and Laureys, S. (2015) "Detecting levels of consciousness". In J. Clausen and N. Levy (Eds.). *Handbook of Neuroethics*, Vol. 1, New York: Springer, pp. 655–704.

Fernández-Espejo, D. and Owen, A.M. (2013) "Detecting awareness after severe brain injury". *Nature Reviews Neuroscience* 14(11), 801–809.

Johnson, L.S.M. (2011) "The Right to Die in the Minimally Conscious State". *Journal of Medical Ethics* 37, 175–178.

Jox, R.J., Bernat, J.L., Laureys, S. and Racine, E. (2012) "Disorders of Consciousness: Responding to Requests for Novel Diagnostic and Therapeutic Interventions". *The Lancet Neurology* 11(8), 732–738.

Monti, M.M., Vanhaudenhuyse, A., Coleman, M.R., Boly, M., Pickard, J.D., Tshibanda, L., . . . Laureys, S. (2010b) "Willful Modulation of Brain Activity in Disorders of Consciousness". *The New England Journal of Medicine* 362, 579–589.

References

Almodovar, P. (2002) *Talk to Her*. Available at: www.imdb.com/title/tt0287467/ [Accessed 4 Sept. 2015].

Angelakis, E., Liouta, E., Andreadis, N., Korfias, S., Ktonas, P., Stranjalis, G., and Sakas, D.E. (2014) Transcranial direct current stimulation effects in disorders of consciousness. *Archives of Physical Medicine Rehabilitation* 95: pp. 283–289.

Appel, J.M. (2009) The Rom Houben tragedy and the case for active euthanasia. *The Huffington Post*, 24 November.

Appelbaum, P.S., and Grisso, T. (1988) Assessing patients' capacities to consent to treatment. *The New England Journal of Medicine* 319: pp. 1635–1638.

Beauchamp, T.L., and Childress, J.F. (2013) *Principles of Biomedical Ethics*. 7th ed. New York, Oxford: Oxford University Press.

Bender, A., Jox, R.J., Grill, E., Straube, A., and Lule, D. (2015) Persistent vegetative state and minimally conscious state: A systematic review and meta-analysis of diagnostic procedures. *Deutsches Ärzteblatt International* 112: pp. 235–242.

Bernat, J.L. (2006) Chronic disorders of consciousness. *The Lancet* 367: pp. 1181–1192.

———. (2009) Chronic consciousness disorders. *Annual Review of Medicine* 60: pp. 381–392.

Birbaumer, N., and Cohen, L.G. (2007) Brain—Computer interfaces: Communication and restoration of movement in paralysis. *The Journal of Physiology* 579: pp. 621–636.

Birbaumer, N., Gallegos-Ayala, G., Wildgruber, M., Silvoni, S., and Soekadar, S.R. (2014) Direct brain control and communication in paralysis. *Brain Topography* 27: pp. 4–11.

Black, B.S., Rabins, P.V., Sugarman, J., and Karlawish, J.H. (2010) Seeking assent and respecting dissent in dementia research. *The American Journal of Geriatric Psychiatry* 18: pp. 77–85.

Boly, M., Faymonville, M.E., Peigneux, P., Lambermont, B., Damas, F., Luxen, A., . . . Laureys, S. (2005) Cerebral processing of auditory and noxious stimuli in severely brain injured patients: Differences between VS and MCS. *Neuropsychological Rehabilitation* 15: pp. 283–289.

Boly, M., Faymonville, M.E., Schnakers, C., Peigneux, P., Lambermont, B., Phillips, C., . . . Laureys, S. (2008) Perception of pain in the minimally conscious state with PET activation: An observational study. *The Lancet Neurology* 7: pp. 1013–1020.

Bonebakker, A.E., Bonke, B., Klein, J., Wolters, G., Stijnen, T., Passchier, J., and Merikle, P.M. (1996) Information processing during general anesthesia: Evidence for unconscious memory. *Memory & Cognition* 24: pp. 766–776.

Bruno, M.A., Fernandez-Espejo, D., Lehembre, R., Tshibanda, L., Vanhaudenhuyse, A., Gosseries, O., . . . Soddu, A. (2011) Multimodal neuroimaging in patients with disorders of consciousness showing "functional hemispherectomy". *Progress in Brain Research* 193: pp. 323–333.

Casali, A.G., Gosseries, O., Rosanova, M., Boly, M., Sarasso, S., Casali, K.R., . . . Massimini, M. (2013) A theoretically based index of consciousness independent of sensory processing and behavior. *Science Translation Medicine* 5: pp. 198ra105.

Chatelle, C., Majerus, S., Whyte, J., Laureys, S., and Schnakers, C. (2012) A sensitive scale to assess nociceptive pain in patients with disorders of consciousness. *Journal of Neurology Neurosurgery Psychiatry* 83: pp. 1233–1237.

Chatelle, C., Thibaut, A., Bruno, M.A., Boly, M., Bernard, C., Hustinx, R., . . . Laureys, S. (2014) Nociception coma scale-revised scores correlate with metabolism in the anterior cingulate cortex. *Neurorehabil Neural Repair* 28: pp. 149–152.

Chaudhary, U., Birbaumer, N., and Curado, M.R. (2015) Brain-machine interface (BMI) in paralysis. *Annals of Physical Rehabilitation Medicine* 58: pp. 9–13.

Corthout, E., Barker, A.T., and Cowey, A. (2001) Transcranial magnetic stimulation: Which part of the current waveform causes the stimulation? *Experimental Brain Research* 141: pp. 128–132.

Cruse, D., Chennu, S., Chatelle, C., Bekinschtein, T.A., Fernández-Espejo, D., Pickard, J.D., Laureys, S. and Owen, A.M. Bedside detection of awareness in the vegetative state: a cohort study. (2011) *Lancet* 378(9809): pp. 2088-94. doi: 10.1016/S0140-6736(11)61224-5.

Davis, J.K. (2002) The concept of precedent autonomy. *Bioethics* 16: pp. 114–133.

Davis, M.H., Coleman, M.R., Absalom, A.R., Rodd, J.M., Johnsrude, I.S., Matta, B.F., . . . Menon, D.K. (2007) Dissociating speech perception and comprehension at reduced levels of awareness. *Proceedings of the National Academy of Science of the United States of America* 104: pp. 16032–16037.

Degrazia, D. (2005) *Human Identity and Bioethics*. Cambridge: Cambridge University Press.

Di, H.B., Yu, S.M., Weng, X.C., Laureys, S., Yu, D., Li, J.Q., . . . Chen, Y.Z. (2007) Cerebral response to patient's own name in the vegetative and minimally conscious states. *Neurology* 68: pp. 895–899.

Dworschak, M. (2009) *'My Second Birth': Discovering Life in Vegetative Patients*. Available at: www.spiegel. de/international/spiegel/my-second-birth-discovering-life-in-vegetative-patients-a-663022.html [Accessed 4 Sept. 2015].

———. (2010) *Neurological Rescue Mission: Communicating with Those Trapped within Their Brains*. Available at: www.spiegel.de/international/world/neurological-rescue-mission-communicating-with-those-trap ped-within-their-brains-a-677537.html [Accessed 4 Sept. 2015].

Farisco, M. (2015) "Cerebral Communication" with patients with disorders of consciousness: Clinical feasibility and implications. *American Journal of Bioethics Neuroscience* 6(2): pp. 44–46.

Fins, J.J., Illes, J., Bernat, J.L., Hirsch, J., Laureys, S., and Murphy, E. (2008) Neuroimaging and disorders of consciousness: Envisioning an ethical research agenda. *American Journal of Bioethics* 8(9): pp. 3–12.

Fins, J.J., and Schiff, N.D. (2010) Conflicts of interest in deep brain stimulation research and the ethics of transparency. *The Journal of Clinical Ethics* 21: pp. 125–132.

Fisher, C.E., and Appelbaum, P.S. (2010) Diagnosing consciousness: Neuroimaging, law, and the vegetative state. *The Journal of Law, Medicine & Ethics* 38: pp. 374–385.

Friedrich, O. (2013) Knowledge of partial awareness in disorders of consciousness: Implications for ethical evaluations? *Neuroethics* 6: pp. 13–23.

Gallagher, S., and Dan, Z. (2015) Phenomenological approaches to self-consciousness. In E.N. Zalta (Ed.) *Stanford Encyclopedia of Philosophy*. Available at: http://plato.stanford.edu/archives/spr2015/entries/self-consciousness-phenomenological/ [Accessed 4 Sept. 2015].

Giacino, J.T., Fins, J.J., Laureys, S., and Schiff, N.D. (2014) Disorders of consciousness after acquired brain injury: The state of the science. *Nature Reviews Neurology* 10: pp. 99–114.

Giacino, J.T., Hirsch, J., Schiff, N., and Laureys, S. (2006) Functional neuroimaging applications for assessment and rehabilitation planning in patients with disorders of consciousness. *Archives of Physical Medicine Rehabilitation* 87: pp. S67–S76.

Gill-Thwaites, H. (2006) Lotteries, loopholes and luck: Misdiagnosis in the vegetative state patient. *Brain Injury* 20: pp. 1321–1328.

Gosseries, O., Di, H., Laureys, S., and Boly, M. (2014) Measuring consciousness in severely damaged brains. *Annual Review of Neuroscience* 37: pp. 457–478.

Guldenmund, P., Soddu, A., Baquero, K., Vanhaudenhuyse, A., Bruno, M.A., Gosseries, O., . . . Gomez, F. (2016) Structural brain injury in patients with disorders of consciousness: A voxel-based morphometry study. *Brain Injury* 30: pp. 343–352.

Jennett, B., and Plum, F. (1972) Persistent vegetative state after brain damage: A syndrome in search of a name. *The Lancet* 1: pp. 734–737.

Johnson, L.S. (2013) Can they suffer? The ethical priority of quality of life research in disorders of consciousness. *Bioethica Forum* 6: pp. 129–136.

———. (2016) Inference and inductive risk in disorders of consciousness. *American Journal of Bioethics Neuroscience* 7(1): pp. 35–43.

Jox, R.J. (2011) End-of-life decision making concerning patients with disorders of consciousness. *Res cogitans* 1. Available at: www.sdu.dk/en/Om_SDU/Institutter_centre/Ikv/Videnskabelige+tidsskrifter/rescogitans/Issues/No8 [Accessed 4 Sept. 2015].

———. (2013) Interface cannot replace interlocution: Why the reductionist concept of neuroimaging-based capacity determination fails. *American Journal of Bioethics Neuroscience* 4(4): pp. 15–17.

———. (2014) Revocation of advance directives. In *Advance Directives*. Dordrecht, The Netherlands: Springer

Jox, R.J., Bernat, J.L., Laureys, S., and Racine, E. (2012) Disorders of consciousness: Responding to requests for novel diagnostic and therapeutic interventions. *The Lancet Neurology* 11: pp. 732–738.

Jox, R.J., Kuehlmeyer, K., Klein, A.M., Herzog, J., Schaupp, M., Nowak, D.A., . . . Bender, A. (2015) Diagnosis and decision making for patients with disorders of consciousness: A survey among family members. *Archives of Physical Medicine and Rehabilitation* 96: pp. 323–330.

Kahane, G., and Savulescu, J. (2009) Brain damage and the moral significance of consciousness. *Journal of Medicine and Philosophy* 34: pp. 6–26.

Kubler, A., and Birbaumer, N. (2008) Brain-computer interfaces and communication in paralysis: Extinction of goal directed thinking in completely paralysed patients? *Clinical Neurophysiology* 119: pp. 2658–2666.

Kuehlmeyer, K., Borasio, G.D., and Jox, R.J. (2012) How family caregivers' medical and moral assumptions influence decision making for patients in the vegetative state: A qualitative interview study. *Journal of Medical Ethics* 38: pp. 332–337.

Kuehlmeyer, K., Klingler, C., Racine, E., and Jox, R.J. (2013) Single case reports on late recovery from chronic disorders of consciousness: A systematic review and ethical appraisal. *Bioethica Forum* 6: pp. 137–149.

Kuehlmeyer, K., Palmour, N., Riopelle, R.J., Bernat, J.L., Jox, R.J., and Racine, E. (2014) Physicians' attitudes toward medical and ethical challenges for patients in the vegetative state: Comparing Canadian and German perspectives in a vignette survey *BMC Neurology* 14: p. 119.

Laureys, S., Celesia, G.G., Cohadon, F., Lavrijsen, J., Leon-Carrion, J., Sannita, W.G., . . . Dolce, G. (2010) Unresponsive wakefulness syndrome: A new name for the vegetative state or apallic syndrome. *BMC Medicine* 8: p. 68.

Legislation.Gov.UK. (2012) *Mental Capacity Act 2005.* London: The National Archives. Available at: www.legislation.gov.uk/ukpga/2005/9/contents [Accessed 4 Sept. 2015].

Levy, N., and Savulescu, J. (2009) Moral significance of phenomenal consciousness. *Progress in Brain Research* 177: pp. 361–370.

Locke, J. (2008) *An Essay Concerning Human Understanding.* Original ed. 1689: Oxford: Oxford University Press.

Lunau, K. (2013) Inside a Comatose Mind: Article for Maclean's. Available at: www.macleans.ca/society/technology/beyond-words/ [Accessed 4 Sept. 2015].

Malandro, L.A., Barker, L.L., Gaut, D.A., and Barker, D.A. (1989) *Nonverbal Communication.* New York: Random House.

Marchetti, M., and Priftis, K. (2015) Brain-computer interfaces in amyotrophic lateral sclerosis: A metanalysis. *Clinical Neurophysiology* 126: pp. 1255–1263.

Monti, M.M., Laureys, S., and Owen, A.M. (2010a) The vegetative state. *BMJ* 341: p. c3765.

Monti, M.M., Vanhaudenhuyse, A., Coleman, M.R., Boly, M., Pickard, J.D., Tshibanda, L., . . . Laureys, S. (2010b) Willful modulation of brain activity in disorders of consciousness. *The New England Journal of Medicine* 362: pp. 579–589.

Naci, L., Monti, M.M., Cruse, D., Kubler, A., Sorger, B., Goebel, R., . . . Owen, A.M. (2012) Brain-computer interfaces for communication with nonresponsive patients. *Annals of Neurology* 72: pp. 312–323.

Naci, L., and Owen, A.M. (2013) Making every word count for nonresponsive patients. *The Journal of American Medical Association Neurology* 70: pp. 1235–1241.

Napolitani, M., Bodart, O., Canali, P., Seregni, F., Casali, A., Laureys, S., . . . Gosseries, O. (2014) Transcranial magnetic stimulation combined with high-density EEG in altered states of consciousness. *Brain Injury* 28: pp. 1180–1189.

Naro, A., Russo, M., Leo, A., Bramanti, P., Quartarone, A., and Calabro, R.S. (2015) A single session of repetitive transcranial magnetic stimulation over the dorsolateral prefrontal cortex in patients with unresponsive wakefulness syndrome: Preliminary results. *Neurorehabil Neural Repair* 29: pp. 603–613.

Nijboer, F., Clausen, J., Allison, B.Z., and Haselager, P. (2013) The asilomar survey: Stakeholders' opinions on ethical issues related to brain-computer interfacing. *Neuroethics* 6: pp. 541–578.

Noonan, H. (2003) *Personal Identity.* London: Routledge.

Parfit, D. (1984) *Reasons and Persons.* Oxford: Oxford University Press.

Peterson, A., Cruse, D., Naci, L., Weijer, C., and Owen, A.M. (2015) Risk, diagnostic error, and the clinical science of consciousness. *Neuroimage Clinical* 7: pp. 588–597.

Peterson, A., Naci, L., Weijer, C., Cruse, D., Fernandez-Espejo, D., Graham, M., and Owen, A.M. (2013) Assessing decision-making capacity in the behaviorally nonresponsive patient with residual covert awareness. *American Journal of Bioethics Neuroscience* 4(4): pp. 3–14.

Racine, E., Amaram, R., Seidler, M., Karczewska, M., and Illes, J. (2008) Media coverage of the persistent vegetative state and end-of-life decision-making. *Neurology* 71: pp. 1027–1032.

Sarasso, S., Rosanova, M., Casali, A.G., Casarotto, S., Fecchio, M., Boly, M., . . . Massimini, M. (2014) Quantifying cortical EEG responses to TMS in (un)consciousness. *Clinical EEG Neuroscience* 45: pp. 40–49.

Schermer, M. (2011) Ethical issues in deep brain stimulation. *Frontiers in Integrative Neuroscience* 5: p. 17.

Schiff, N.D., Giacino, J.T., and Fins, J.J. (2009) Deep brain stimulation, neuroethics, and the minimally conscious state: Moving beyond proof of principle. *Archives of Neurology* 66: pp. 697–702.

Schiff, N.D., Giacino, J.T., Kalmar, K., Victor, J.D., Baker, K., Gerber, M., . . . Rezai, A.R. (2007) Behavioural improvements with thalamic stimulation after severe traumatic brain injury. *Nature* 448: pp. 600–603.

Schnakers, C., Vanhaudenhuyse, A., Giacino, J., Ventura, M., Boly, M., Majerus, S., . . . Laureys, S. (2009) Diagnostic accuracy of the vegetative and minimally conscious state: Clinical consensus versus standardized neurobehavioral assessment. *BMC Neurology* 9: p. 35.

Sen, A.N., Campbell, P.G., Yadla, S., Jallo, J., and Sharan, A.D. (2010) Deep brain stimulation in the management of disorders of consciousness: A review of physiology, previous reports, and ethical considerations. *Neurosurgical Focus* 29: p. E14.

Shih, J.J., Krusienski, D.J., and Wolpaw, J.R. (2012) Brain-computer interfaces in medicine. *Mayo Clinical Proceedings* 87: pp. 268–279.

Siewert, C. (2011) Consciousness and intentionality. In E.N. Zalta (Ed.). *The Stanford Encyclopedia of Philosophy*. Available at: http://plato.stanford.edu/entries/consciousness-intentionality/ [Accessed 4 Sept. 2015].

Spriggs, M., and Caldwell, P.H. (2011) The ethics of paediatric research. *Journal of Paediatrics and Child Health* 47: pp. 664–667.

Stender, J., Gosseries, O., Bruno, M.A., Charland-Verville, V., Vanhaudenhuyse, A., Demertzi, A., . . . Laureys, S. (2014) Diagnostic precision of PET imaging and functional MRI in disorders of consciousness: A clinical validation study. *The Lancet* 384: pp. 514–522.

Sumner, P., Vivian-Griffiths, S., Boivin, J., Williams, A., Venetis, C.A., Davies, A., . . . Chambers, C.D. (2014) The association between exaggeration in health related science news and academic press releases: Retrospective observational study. *BMJ* 349: p. g7015.

Thibaut, A., Bruno, M.A., Ledoux, D., Demertzi, A., and Laureys, S. (2014) tDCS in patients with disorders of consciousness: Sham-controlled randomized double-blind study. *Neurology* 82: pp. 1112–1118.

Voss, H.U., Uluc, A.M., Dyke, J.P., Watts, R., Kobylarz, E.J., Mccandliss, B.D., . . . Schiff, N.D. (2006) Possible axonal regrowth in late recovery from the minimally conscious state. *Journal of Clinical Investigation* 116: pp. 2005–2011.

Waldron, D., O'Boyle, C.A., Kearney, M., Moriarty, M., and Carney, D. (1999) Quality-of-life measurement in advanced cancer: Assessing the individual. *Journal of Clinical Oncology* 17: pp. 3603–3611.

Walsh, F. (2012) Vegetative Patient Scott Routley Says 'I'm not in pain' BBC News. Available at: www.bbc.com/news/health-20268044 [Accessed 4 Sept. 2015].

Weijer, C., Peterson, A., Webster, F., Graham, M., Cruse, D., Fernandez-Espejo, D., . . . Owen, A.M. (2014) Ethics of neuroimaging after serious brain injury. *BMC Medical Ethics* 15: p. 41.

Wijdicks, E.F. (2006) Minimally conscious state vs. persistent vegetative state: The case of Terry (Wallis) vs. the case of Terri (Schiavo). *Mayo Clinic Proceedings* 81: pp. 1155–1118.

Wijdicks, E.F., and Wijdicks, C.A. (2006) The portrayal of coma in contemporary motion pictures. *Neurology* 66: pp. 1300–1303.

Wilkinson, D.J., Kahane, G., Horne, M., and Savulescu, J. (2009) Functional neuroimaging and withdrawal of life-sustaining treatment from vegetative patients. *Journal of Medical Ethics* 35: pp. 508–511.

World Medical Association. (2013) Declaration of Helsinki—Ethical Principles for Medical Research Involving Human Subjects. Available at: www.wma.net/en/30publications/10policies/b3/ [Accessed 4 Sept. 2015].

Young, G.B. (2009) Coma. *Annals of the New York Academy of Sciences* 1157: pp. 32–47.

7

PLACEBO FOR PSYCHOGENIC DISORDERS

Diagnosis, Stigma, and Treatment Narratives

Lindsey Grubbs and Karen S. Rommelfanger

Introduction

Patients diagnosed with psychogenic illnesses are particularly neglected in medical care: they may be shuttled between specialists (Kranick et al., 2011b), disbelieved and viewed as "problem patients" (Boehm, 2013), and receive inadequate medical care. Outcomes for such patients are often poor (Factor et al., 1995; Jankovic et al., 2006; Thomas and Jankovic, 2004; Thomas et al., 2006). As a result, illnesses like psychogenic movement disorder (PMD) have been called a "crisis for neurology" (Hallett, 2006). Because patients with psychogenic disorders often wind up back in the care of general practitioners, this crisis extends into primary care clinics as well.

This chapter begins with a discussion of the primary challenges posed by psychogenic disorders for patients and medical professionals, contextualizing the experience, diagnosis, and treatment of such disorders. We turn next to the ethically charged topic of treating psychogenic disorders with placebos. Although often used, placebos are contested because of their assumed inertness and the deception accompanying their use. We attempt to move beyond the ethical gridlock that often accompanies the topic of placebo by examining both emerging empirical research and ethical perspectives that challenge long-held reservations. Although we will discuss a wide range of medically unexplained physical symptoms (MUPS) and psychogenic disorders, we will focus especially on the case of psychogenic movement disorders (PMD)—one of the most prevalent psychogenic diagnoses (Lempert et al., 1990).

Psychogenic Disorders Reveal Healthcare Gaps

Around one in five patients visiting movement clinics and epilepsy monitoring units are ultimately diagnosed with psychogenic disorders (Jankovic et al., 2006; Miyasaki et al., 2003). That psychogenic medicine is not more developed, then, reveals deep, stigma-based gaps in our healthcare system. The lack of attention paid to such prevalent disorders is unacceptable. Our (lack of) treatment of psychogenic disorders poses important questions about the allocation of medical resources, how we classify or legitimize diseases, how patients can fall through the cracks of clearly defined specialties, and how physician and patient discomfort with the unexplained can get in the way of effective care. Patients diagnosed with psychogenic disorders may never be informed of that diagnosis, and many physicians aren't explicitly trained in how to handle these disorders, though they will almost surely encounter them in practice (Rommelfanger, 2013a). Clinicians often express frustration with these patients, who, in the absence of an established standard of care, are often left to bear the burden of illness themselves. In this setting, physicians find themselves generating their own stopgap measures and creative solutions, often in covert ways, as with placebo therapy. For these reasons and more, psychogenic disorders and their possible treatments are a rich site for ethical and clinical research.

The idea of using placebos to treat psychogenic disorders triggers many ethical concerns: most concretely, placebos complicate patient autonomy and informed consent, and in clinical practice often entails physician deception despite ethical codes (Rommelfanger 2013a). Further, with no clinical trials currently underway for placebo therapy, placebo treatment for psychogenic disorders could be described as pre-experimental, which invites a host of ethical questions. Any treatment for psychogenic disorders will also draw out gendered dynamics of medical care, as women are disproportionately diagnosed with psychogenic disorders like PMD and psychogenic nonepileptic seizures (PNES; Asadi-Pooya and Sperling, 2015) and hence would be disproportionally impacted by changes in treatment. Questions arise, too, about the allocation and availability of such treatments—how much does one charge for a sugar pill, and how does one bill insurance for it? Although not all of these issues will be addressed in the current chapter, we lay the groundwork for further inquiry.

Psychogenic Disorders: Definitions and Their Discontents

Psychogenic disorders are physically manifesting medical conditions that, lacking known "organic" causes, are attributed to psychological or emotional distress (Bhatia and Schneider, 2007; Hinson and Haren, 2006; Factor et al., 1995). The most common of these are psychogenic movement disorders (PMD), which are characterized by abnormal movement (for example, tremors or atypical gait) without an associated organic disorder (Lempert et al., 1990). Such disorders are common, and as many as 15 to 25% of patients who visit movement disorder clinics are diagnosed with psychogenic disorders (Jankovic et al., 2006; Miyasaki et al., 2003), while 20% of those in epileptic monitoring units are diagnosed with PNES (Benbadis and Hauser, 2000). Unexplained medical symptoms more broadly are even more common. As many as one third of patients presenting with physical symptoms do not find an explanation, and although many of these symptoms resolve in time, some persist without explanation. A variety of often overlapping diagnoses, including chronic fatigue syndrome, irritable bowel syndrome, fibromyalgia, and various chronic pain conditions, have developed to aid in the classification of such cases by their most prominent features (Jackson et al., 2009), and some MUPS patients will receive diagnoses of PMD or PNES.

Because of the perception that these conditions have psychological roots, patients are often passed to psychiatrists, despite evidence that such disorders can occur without comorbid psychiatric diagnoses (Factor et al., 1995; Gupta and Lang, 2009). In psychiatric terms, conversion disorder (also known in the most recent iteration of the *Diagnostic and Statistical Manual* [DSM] as "functional neurological symptom disorder") is characterized by neurological symptoms, like blindness, paralysis, seizure, or abnormal movement, that are inconsistent with organic neurological conditions. Somatoform and somatization disorders have long been the diagnostic terms for MUPS, but while somatization disorder persists as a diagnosis in ICD-10, it has been removed in the most recent version of the DSM. In the DSM-5, somatization disorder, hypochondriasis, pain disorder, and undifferentiated somatoform disorder have been replaced by "somatic symptom disorder." Importantly, the diagnostic criteria stress that the symptoms need not be medically unexplained to qualify—they need only disrupt daily life and be characterized by "excessive" thoughts and feelings. Hence, not all patients with MUPS or psychogenic disorders qualify for this kind of psychiatric diagnosis, nor does an organic disorder preclude it (APA, 2013a).

As should be clear by this point, the terminology surrounding such conditions is muddy and crosses between specialties poorly. While a patient presenting with seizures in the absence of epilepsy might be diagnosed with "conversion disorder with attacks or seizures" by a psychiatrist, a neurologist may diagnose PNES. Similarly, a neurologist's patient with PMD might be classified with "conversion disorder with abnormal movement" in a psychiatric office (Nowak and Fink, 2009; Kranick et al., 2011b). While the DSM-5 notes that "functional" and "psychogenic" are common terms, "psychogenic" is the term preferred by neurologists, who do not use psychiatric distress to diagnose the disorders (Kranick et al., 2011b). The term "psychogenic" itself arose from discomfort with terminology when coined in 1894 by Robert Sommer, who wanted to abolish the highly charged term "hysteria" and come up with a more neutral, scientific term for conditions susceptible to suggestion (Shorter, 1993).

For more on the DSM-5 and reductivism in psychiatry, see Chapter 27.

These linguistic distinctions reflect a lack of consistency in diagnosis and treatment across specialties, as well as the uneasy fit of psychogenic disorders within the medical system. The terms make a difference to patients, too: interviews suggest patients prefer "functional" to "medically unexplained," "stress-related," "psychosomatic," or, unsurprisingly, "hysterical" and "all in the mind" (Stone et al., 2002). Some practitioners also prefer the term "functional disorder" because they feel that "psychogenic" implies that the problem is entirely psychological (Stone, 2009). However, the history of the term "functional" also indicates dysfunction without a bodily component (Kendell, 2001; Reynolds, 1855; Gowers, 1893), and we are left without sufficiently nuanced terminology.[1]

Mind/Body Dualism in Medicine

The differing vocabularies and approaches of neurologists and psychiatrists to psychogenic disorders have a long and charged history that continues to impact medical understanding. Humoral views of medicine, which guided ancient Western medical thought and continued to circulate in European contexts until at least the 19th century, imagined physical and mental symptoms as emerging from the same causes (Shorter, 1993). Adjectives such as "melancholy," "choleric," and "phlegmatic" that now describe psychological states once denoted the same excesses and lacks of the humors that caused bowel complaints and cancer. From a medical standpoint, the split between body and mind was codified in the late 19th century, at which time psychiatry proper was treating the floridly mad, often located in asylums, while internists and "nerve doctors" would have been the physicians of choice for those with "nervous" complaints (including those things we now call "psychogenic"). These nerve doctors came from both psychiatry and internal medicine, and so began what historian Edward Shorter calls "an enormous turf struggle between psychiatrists and the internists" (1993, 217).

Around the turn of the 20th century, in the age of Freud, psychiatry began to take on the forms we recognize today, though even Freud, trained as a neurologist, originally differentiated between "psychoneuroses" (those with psychological underpinnings) and "actual neuroses" (those with organic underpinnings) before developing the psychoanalytic approach for which he is now famous (Lutz, 1991). The rise of Freud and psychoanalysis was an important transitional point toward accepting the possibility of psychogenesis. However, this period is characterized by a strange paradox: the rise of a psychological paradigm does not make the general population more aware or accepting of psychogenesis; instead, patients in the 20th century became increasingly invested in seeing neurologists and internists instead of psychiatrists: those who see psychiatrists are "crazy," while those who see neurologists are "sick" (Shorter, 1993). This reductive division is becoming muddier as evidence confirms the embodied nature of mental states—evidence in part surrounding the evolving neuroscience of psychogenesis and placebo.

Still, our culture too often maintains a dualist view in which physical illnesses are "legitimate," while mental ones are stigmatized and assumed to be somehow blameworthy (Kendell, 2001; Miresco and Kirmayer, 2006). Although some doctors have encouraged granting psychogenic disorders the same legitimacy as neurological ones, this is not current practice (Friedman and LaFrance, 2010). PMD and similar disorders, with their assumed mental origin yet obvious physical symptoms, confuse this conception. Complicating matters, the percentage of patients diagnosed with PMD without an accompanying mental illness ranges from 5% (Feinstein et al., 2001) to 30 to 50% (Factor et al., 1995; Gupta and Lang, 2009; Jankovic et al., 2006), and neurologists report that they do not interpret a patient's psychiatric history as an indicator for a PMD diagnosis (Espay et al., 2009). The breakdown of dualist thinking necessitated by psychogenic disorders manifests in the DSM-5's update to somatic symptom disorder (SSD), which was intended in part to reduce the notion of mind–body split implied by the old diagnoses (APA, 2013b).

This theoretical divide has concrete implications. Patients with psychogenic motor symptoms may find themselves in a treatment limbo, shuttling between "mind" and "body" as they are referred back and forth between neurologists and psychiatrists (Kranick et al., 2011b, Espay et al., 2009). Both patients and physicians despair when no medical test can confirm a disease process behind symptoms because of the assumption that a lack of organic origin translates into limited or no possibility for treatment. Physicians struggle with communicating psychogenic explanations that they fear will be poorly received and because they have been encouraged by peers not to classify symptoms as psychosomatic in patient charts. These fears are not unfounded, as patients can feel dismissed by psychologizing physicians who ask about stressors and emotions (Atkins et al., 2013). Patients caught between physical and mental explanations may face significant challenges to their sense of self (Ford, 2013) and mistrust from their physicians (Boehm, 2013).

Physicians often believe that PNES patients have a primarily psychological problem (Whitehead et al., 2013), and PMD patients confront the idea that their symptoms are "not real" (Espay et al., 2009). Feminist philosopher Susan Wendell (1996) discusses how the diagnostic process can rob patients of the "cognitive authority . . . to have one's descriptions of the world taken seriously, believed, or accepted generally as the truth" (117). She tells the story of one woman who, after years of being told that her symptoms were rooted in stress and neuroses, was thrilled to be diagnosed with MS, the "legitimacy" of which meant that she could begin to ask for the accommodations she had long been needing. Wendell attributes this reaction to the intense stress that the woman faced when given what she saw as an "illegitimate" diagnosis: the relief "was the result of being rid of a terrible cognitive and social conflict—between how [she] felt and what it was demanded that she believe about herself" (1996, 124–125).

The strength of historical, theoretical, and cultural narratives about health and illness impacts the diagnosis, lived experience, and treatment of all illnesses but perhaps psychogenic ones especially. For example, the narrative that suggests that young, psychologically distressed women are those most likely to experience psychogenesis impacts not only young, distressed women but also those who do not fit the model. The predominantly male population of veterans, for example, may experience three times the delay in waiting for a diagnosis of PNES because they do not fit physicians' diagnostic expectations of the disorder (Salinsky et al., 2011). Experientially, because social, economic, and familial contexts are capable of "damping" or "amplifying" symptoms in both "organic" and "psychosomatic" illnesses, those elements play a formative role in the experience of illness (Kleinman, 1988).

Problems in Medical Care for Psychogenic Disorders

These negotiations of the mind/body divide have enormous implications for patients with psychogenic disorders. Despite the large number of patients diagnosed with these disorders, and despite the fact that such patients report equal or worse quality of life and may have higher disability scores than those with "organic" disorders like Parkinson's disease (Anderson et al., 2007), there are few treatments. Somewhere between 50% and 90% of patients with PMD continue to have symptoms long term (Factor et al., 1995; Jankovic et al., 2006; Thomas and Jankovic, 2004; Thomas et al., 2006; McKeon et al., 2009). These patients often spend a great deal of time, energy, and money on visits to multiple doctors who perform a wide variety of tests (Anderson et al., 2007), and the cost of psychogenic symptoms across the United States healthcare system has been estimated to be as high as $100 billion in direct costs alone (tests, surgeries, hospitalizations, consultations), not including indirect costs incurred through disability compensation, missed work, and medication costs (Neimark et al., 2005; Anderson et al., 2007).

Neurologists are often uncomfortable with making a psychogenic diagnosis, which is typically, in practice, a diagnosis of exclusion (e.g., all possible organic disorders are eliminated; Espay et al., 2009; Factor et al., 1995). The delay in diagnosis (if it is ever given) results in delays linked to a worse prognosis for PMD patients, as patients' symptoms may not simply persist, but tend to worsen if they fail to receive treatment within the first year of symptom onset (Gupta and Lang, 2009). Some have argued that the diagnosis of psychogenic disorders must begin to use positive rather than negative criteria, but such recommendations have not been heartily embraced (Gupta and Lang, 2009; Hallett, 2010).

Treatment of PMD once a diagnosis is made is complicated and often ineffectual. Patients may not receive any follow-up care, or they may lack the resources to pursue it. Some physicians believe that simply diagnosing a psychogenic disorder can be a kind of treatment (Stone and Edwards, 2012; Burack et al., 1997; Devinsky and Fisher, 1996). Patients, though, may also view a psychogenic diagnosis as evidence that their physician missed something physical in the diagnostic process (Atkins et al., 2013). Unfortunately, at least for PMD, prognosis is strongly linked to the patient's acceptance of the PMD diagnosis and their faith in treatment (Espay et al., 2009; Feinstein et al., 2001; Hinson and Haren, 2006; Thomas and Jankovic, 2004). Importantly, both neurologists and psychiatrists have been shown to view PNES patients as having more control over their symptoms than those with epilepsy (Whitehead and Reuber, 2012), and elsewhere it has been suggested that this attitude can negatively affect therapy (Kendell, 2001). To date, treatments have included physical interventions like physical therapy and acupuncture; psychological methods, including hypnosis and cognitive behavioral therapy; and therapies spanning the two, like antidepressants, transcranial magnetic stimulation, and biofeedback (Gupta and Lang, 2009; Jankovic et al., 2006; Nowak and Fink, 2009; Czarnecki et al., 2012). PMD has no standard of care, and no controlled research is being done (Rommelfanger, 2013a). Similar issues plague treatment of other psychogenic disorders. For example, physicians may see psychotherapy as the best treatment for PNES (LaFrance et al., 2008), while patients often vehemently reject the therapy (Fairclough et al., 2014). Importantly, this is not necessarily simply denial on the patient's part, as there is not conclusive evidence that psychotherapy is useful for this purpose (Baker et al., 2007; Gaynor et al., 2009). Stigma, the ideology of "mind over matter," and expectations of what sorts of medical narratives justify the privileges of the "sick role" converge to make MUPS and psychogenic disorders uniquely difficult to manage. For many healthcare professionals, placebos represent a possible clinical strategy.

Placebo: Definitions and Overview

Placebos are treatments given despite, or because of, the assumption that they are inert (Diederich and Goetz, 2008; Finniss et al., 2010). The classic example would be a sugar pill, but some practitioners also use "active placebos"—subclinical doses, or medications for conditions the patient does not have (Rommelfanger 2013a). Placebos have been described as being not so much substances as they are rituals (Moerman and Jonas, 2002; Kaptchuk, 2002). A sugar pill taken accidentally or without context is unlikely to provide any benefit to a patient—it is, indeed, inert (Kanaan, 2013). It is the narrative surrounding the intervention that seems to have powerful effects on patients (Kleinman, 1988; Di Blasi et al., 2001; Benedetti, 2008).

Placebos have long been used to treat a variety of conditions, with varying levels of performativity. In the 1880s, when ovariotomies were a recognized treatment for a host of women's maladies, some surgeons performed "placebo" surgeries: making cuts in patients' abdomens but not removing their ovaries. Some of these patients pronounced themselves cured (Shorter, 1993). In 1906, a patient insisted to her doctors that she had a frog leaping around in her abdomen. They provided her with a placebo and a substance that made her urine green and conspired with her daughters to hide a frog skeleton in her feces. These falsified cures successfully eased her symptoms (Shorter, 1993). Likely, the success of patent medicine frauds and "snake oil" salesmen who peddled colored water was due in part to the power of placebo to render such substances actually therapeutic in some cases, and a wide variety of hucksters, frauds, and well-intentioned though ill-informed pharmacists could make their fortunes in this way. Less insidiously, in the United States, many are exposed to placebo effects from their youngest days, when they may believe that a parent's kiss has analgesic powers that can ease a scrape or bump. Such a range of applications of placebo effects makes clear that the impact can be harnessed in ways that are deeply unethical as well as in ways that may be defensible. The history of placebo highlights the narrative contingency of its mechanism—it must fit into a patient's understanding to be effective. Your stomachache, for instance, will likely not be resolved by green urine and a frog skeleton.

Placebos today are understood as powerful: they are used to improve patient outcomes through suggestion, and our reliance on placebo-controlled clinical trials takes for granted that an inactive pill can have beneficial effects, as long as patients believe the substance will help them. Because this baseline "placebo effect" can be so powerful, why aren't placebos used for their curative benefits more often, especially for those conditions without effective cures? As one author of this chapter has asked elsewhere, "Does withholding placebo treatment harm patients and their families by depriving them of a treatment that might actually help alleviate suffering?" (Rommelfanger, 2013b).

Placebo Use: Attitudes and Statistics

Placebo use for PMD has been advocated by those who reason that a belief-based condition could benefit from a belief-based treatment (Shamy, 2010). In some cases, "digestive pills" and acupuncture[2] have provided placebo-based symptom reduction for PMD patients for, at the time of publication, more than 10 years (Baik et al., 2009; Van Nuenen et al., 2007). Such treatments are especially compelling because of the dearth of successful treatments for the disorder (Singer, 2004).

Rommelfanger's interviews indicate that physicians treating PMD use placebo for both acute and long-term treatment and to help establish a therapeutic relationship. This analysis of physician attitudes revealed several themes: physicians believe that placebos allow patients to "save face" and that it is in their "best interest"; that patients are already being deceived, so the mechanism is unimportant; and that active placebos can be a bridge to a successful therapeutic relationship (for instance, by helping a patient understand that their problem is psychological). Physicians report using active placebos for both long- and short-term therapy and for diagnosis but may not view active placebos as placebos. Some clinicians, though understanding the power of suggestion for treatment, find placebo unethical, whether as treatment or diagnostic tool. Importantly, physicians are not trained to use placebos in medical school but may experiment with it later after witnessing the power of suggestion (Rommelfanger, 2013a). Rommelfanger found that beliefs about the ethical impermissibility of placebo use are a factor leading physicians to use "active" placebos as a treatment tool to establish a relationship with patients (Rommelfanger, 2013a, Kolber, 2007; Harris and Raz, 2012). Such active placebos, though, can increase possible adverse effects for patients and require deceit, and so these ethical concerns may be causing more harm than good.

Deceit has also been employed to confirm psychogenic disorders, as in the case of a physician using saline eye drops to end seizures to confirm a PNES diagnosis (Rommelfanger, 2013a). Historically, the PMD diagnosis was confirmed by response to placebo therapy (Factor et al., 1995; Fahn and Williams, 1988), and clinicians continue to understand this confirmation as a useful but impermissible practice (Espay et al., 2009). PNES, too, has long been diagnosed by inducing and stopping seizure events through use of placebo and verbal suggestion (Stagno and Smith, 1997; Devinsky et al., 2011; Devinsky and Fisher, 1996). However, such diagnostic tests are fraught not only from the ethical perspective of deception but because they may be inaccurate—we know that suggestion and placebo are strong enough to effect change even in those with organic disorders. One patient's response to placebo suggested a psychogenic diagnosis, but other diagnostic tests revealed Parkinson's disorder, which would have been misdiagnosed if placebo was the guiding test (Baik, 2012). While placebo diagnosis is common, disagreement remains about its reliability (Espay et al., 2009).

Ethical Concerns with Placebo Use

Despite these debates, placebos are widely utilized in the contemporary medical setting (Fassler et al., 2010; Tilburt et al., 2008; Hrobjartsson and Norup, 2003; Meissner et al., 2012; Howick et al., 2013). In the United States, 50% of physicians have used placebos, ranging from sugar pills to sedatives, as part of their treatment for everything from gastrointestinal disorders to cancer. Physicians may refer to the treatment vaguely, as "medicine" or "a substance that may help" and range from outright deception to well-meaning simplification (Tilburt et al., 2008; Sherman and Hickner, 2008). Despite this frequent use, however, the American Medical Association (AMA) has prohibited the use of deceptive placebos, and the United Kingdom's General Medical Council mandates a transparency in treatments that would seem to disqualify them (Bostick et al., 2008; Blease, 2012). These objections reflect the rejection of medical paternalism that have become standard in American practice since the 1970s and 1980s, when honesty and informed consent began to be written into codes of medical ethics, as in the AMA's inclusion of a statement claiming that physicians must "deal honestly with patients and colleagues" (Beauchamp and Childress, 2009). Deceptive practices, which were once fairly typical in medical care, have importantly been delegitimized, and because placebos seem to require deception, they are often seen as ethically unacceptable. However, the disjuncture between stated professional and ethical guidelines and actual clinical use makes an updated discussion of the ethics of placebos urgent.

The ethics of placebo have long been locked in a kind of stalemate. On the one hand, the consequentialist argument maintains that the benefit to the patient justifies the deceptive practices that placebo requires. Such arguments have been made, for example, for the benefits of early diagnosis that accompany the deceptive practice of "verbally provoking pseudo-seizures" for diagnostic benefit (Eijkholt and Lynch, 2013). On the other hand, deontological arguments stress the patient's right to transparency and the physician's duty to truthfulness, as in the AMA's condemnation of placebo. Both views are prevalent, which explains both why placebo use is so popular and why it is so rarely openly discussed.

We will break through this seeming impasse by discussing recent research suggesting that placebos (A) provide measurable physiological effects and (B) can provide positive benefits even without physician deception (Benedetti, 2014; Rommelfanger, 2013a).

Questioning Inertness

One of the major ethical reservations around placebo use has to do with the assumption that they are inert substances and hence are somehow used out of spite or disrespect (Purtilo, 1993). However, as many as 96% of physicians who use placebos believe they have physiological benefits for their patients (Sherman and Hickner, 2008; Kermen et al., 2010), and placebos have been found to benefit patients with many conditions (Sherman and Hickner, 2008; Tilburt et al., 2008). As many as 50% of patients with depression (Dworkin et al., 2005) and 30% of those with migraines (Bendtsen et al., 2003) have responded favorably to supposedly inert substances, as have between 16% and 55% of Parkinson's disease patients (Goetz et al., 2008). Placebos can have concrete neurological effects on patients (Enck et al., 2008; Benedetti et al., 2004) and can cause the release of neurotransmitters and opiates (de la Fuente-Fernandez et al., 2001; Lidstone et al., 2010; Mercado et al., 2006; Wager et al., 2004; Zubieta et al., 2005; Amanzio and Benedetti, 1999; Wager et al., 2007). Neuroimaging fMRI studies suggest that those parts of the brain associated with psychogenic disorders (Ghaffar et al., 2006; Nowak and Fink, 2009) are also associated with placebo effects for pain (Petrovic et al., 2002; Wager et al., 2004; Wager et al., 2007) and depression (Benedetti et al., 2005; Mayberg et al., 2002). Because the AMA's antiplacebo position defines "placebo" as a substance that a physician believes to have "no specific pharmacological effect," educating physicians that such effects may indeed take place could so vastly change the notion of "placebo" that the term holds little meaning: we may find ourselves in an awkward bind in which the "placebo effect" is no longer considered a "placebo" because it has actual physiological effects.

The imagined inertness of placebos in spite of this evidence can be ascribed in part to the kind of mind–body dualism that is being challenged by progress in the brain sciences. This dualist view cannot conceive of an "illegitimate" treatment giving "legitimate" relief (Lichtenberg et al., 2004). Even physicians who refute this kind of binary understanding reveal continued thinking along dualist lines during interviews about placebo use (Rommelfanger, 2013a).

Nondeceptive Placebos

Perhaps the more central ethical reservation about placebos has to do with the deception that must accompany their use. The AMA currently allows the use of nondeceptive placebos, suggesting that a physician can receive general consent to use placebo in the diagnostic and treatment process and then withhold specifics of its use. They write, "A placebo may still be effective if the patient knows it will be used but cannot identify it and does not know the precise timing of its use" (American Medical Association, 2016, 21). However, exciting developments suggest that even this deceptive expedient may be unnecessary. As early as 1965, research showed that the placebo effect could relieve somatic symptoms even without blinding (Park and Covi, 1965). More recently, patients with irritable bowel syndrome (IBS) experienced diminished symptoms with placebo therapy, despite total transparency about the fact that they would be given placebo pills—"like sugar pills"—that could promote self-healing (Kaptchuk et al., 2010). Another study reduced children's dose of medication for attention deficit hyperactivity disorder (ADHD) to 50% but supplemented some of the children's regimens with placebos that, as they told both parents and children, had no active ingredient. The children receiving placebos fared better than those who simply received the half dose. Even more surprisingly, though, the half-placebo, half-active regimen proved as effective as the full dose of stimulant medication (Sandler et al., 2010). Yet another study produced placebo-induced analgesia through deception, but, even after the subjects were told that the administered cream was colored petroleum jelly, they continued to experience analgesia (Schafer et al., 2015). The range of research in which patients were benefitted by placebos—even without any deception—suggests that objections to placebo use based on condemnation of deception can be overturned, as fully transparent use of placebos could possibly relieve symptoms or allow for reduced doses of potentially deleterious active substances like stimulants. So while deceptive use of placebos clearly remains morally questionable despite its potential benefits for patients, there may be other paths forward for ethical placebo use.[3] The ethical concerns about misleading terminology raised earlier would still stand.

Ethical Placebos?

Given these considerations, a blanket prohibition of placebos is not defensible. Rather, we must attend to the various ways that placebos can be used—deceptively, transparently, for acute or chronic care, for diagnosis, and beyond—and ask more specific questions about when placebo use is and isn't appropriate.

One possible narrative for a patient receiving placebo therapy highlights the ethical concerns that many physicians have with placebo use: a patient discovers that the substance they have been taking was inert when they believed it was "real" medicine. They feel not only that they have received negligent care but also that their physician doubted the "reality" of their suffering and attempted to trick and even demean them. They become more convinced that the medical system has failed them and hence are less likely to form a beneficial therapeutic alliance. Clearly, this is problematic for both patients and providers.

However, another narrative, one that the cited research suggests might be plausible, has a different outcome. A clinician, in conversation with a patient with PMD, might, after establishing the patient's assumptions and hopes for treatment, explain that there are powerful and poorly understood forces that can lead to somatic symptoms without a known physiological cause—and that research has revealed that treatment with inert substances could have concrete benefits for those both with and without organic origins for their illnesses. Proposing that this is one possible avenue for treatment, a physician could show that they take their patient's symptoms seriously, are invested in trying to resolve them, and that they respect the patient's judgment. This could allow the patient to compose a narrative of acceptance that we know is an important part of recovery in PMD (Espay et al., 2009; Feinstein et al., 2001; Hinson and Haren, 2006; Thomas and Jankovic, 2004).

Clearly, these two narratives represent best- and worst-case scenarios, and there are cases somewhere in the middle that need further investigation—most notably the cases of diagnostic placebos or patients who reject psychogenic diagnoses. In such cases, a physician may hope to garner acceptance of the diagnosis by revealing that the treatment that resolves symptoms is in fact inert, an approach seemingly discordant with honesty and disclosure.

The appropriate action in these cases would require an understanding of patients' values and hopes for diagnosis and treatment. Perhaps this is a utopian view, given the short time clinicians have with their patients, but, as we will suggest later, there may be ways that empirically driven research can help guide how we approach these cases. At the very least, discussion about these uses must be open and clear, with the values and desired outcomes of physicians made explicit.

Future Directions

The arguments and evidence presented here are not meant to suggest that the way forward is simple, ethically obvious, or sufficiently substantiated. Moving forward, we must address both empirical research gaps and broader ethical questions. In order for ethical placebo use to be possible and successful, several agendas must be pursued. Although in this chapter we've often used the case of PMD, we have made some claims that could reach to MUPS more broadly—but it's important not to generalize from one symptom set to another, as there are distinctive differences. For example, PNES has been linked to histories of sexual abuse (Hallett, 2010; Spence et al., 2008), while PMD has not (Kranick et al., 2011a), and empirical and theoretical research must respect these differences.

Some of these agendas must be pursued in neuroscience. Most clearly, we need to establish the effectiveness of placebos for PMD (de Craen et al., 1996; Gracely et al., 1985; Finniss et al., 2010; Kaptchuk, 2002; Kaptchuk and Eisenberg, 1998; Kaptchuk et al., 2006; Moerman and Jonas, 2002). Research suggests that there may be many factors, neurological, genetic, and social, that determine a given patient's susceptibility to placebos (Lidstone et al., 2010; Kim et al., 2012; Hall et al., 2012; Wendt et al., 2014), and the appearance (i.e., color) and method of placebo (i.e., pill or device) can impact their effectiveness (Finniss et al., 2010; Gracely et al., 1985; Enck et al., 2008; Di Blasi et al., 2001). Continuing such research could help individualize care. Furthermore, observing the effects of placebo on the brain could provide insights into the mechanism of psychogenesis. We need to investigate the effects of short- versus long-term placebo treatment and deceptive versus nondeceptive usage. Given new insights into the power of placebo, research must also focus on the possibility for iatrogenic harm introduced by suggestion or placebo—what is called the "nocebo effect." Although the subject of less sustained focus than the placebo effect, several recent review articles indicate that the negative outcomes of suggestion can have significant impacts on clinical and research practices, but more sustained research is necessary (Planès et al., 2016; Symon et al., 2015; Dieppe et al., 2016).

Narrative and phenomenological research will provide another important dimension. Atkins et al. (2013) note that these research methods should be a vital part of research on MUPS moving forward, because phenomenological research, which investigates how people understand and perceive an experience, is particularly well suited to studying things about which we lack biomedical understanding. They note that uncovering commonalities in the frustration and confusion of doctors and patients can move us beyond the mediation of conflicting values toward cooperation and commonality (Atkins et al., 2013). Interestingly, some research suggests that linguistic analysis, rather than neurological or psychiatric methods, is most successful when distinguishing PNES from epilepsy, which suggests the possible importance of language and narrative in understanding these disorders (Boehm, 2013).

Some of this research will investigate attitudes toward psychogenic disorders and placebo treatments, especially from the patient perspective. A Swedish study from 1993 suggested that more patients than physicians supported deceptive placebo use (at a margin of 25% to 7%; Lynoe et al., 1993), and a recent U.S. study shows acceptance of placebo use—even, in some cases, deceptively—if there are patient benefits (Hull et al., 2013). Another study suggests that even those who oppose placebos do so on the grounds that they are not effective and require deception, both of which qualifications have been questioned (Bishop et al., 2014). Studies of patient and physician acceptance of placebo usage must be updated to include the new findings on nondeceptive placebo use and must be carried out in a broader range of settings. It may also be interesting to see how these attitudes shift following education about recent discoveries in placebo research. Because the experiences of psychogenic disorders and placebo are so context-specific, such research must represent a wide range of people and be repeated over time, as cultural changes or shifts in medical dynamics could render previous investigations out of date.

Another important task will be creating a culture of transparency around current use of placebos and attitudes toward it. Progress in the treatment of psychogenic disorders will be forestalled if ethical objections to placebos continue to result in veiled usage in everyday medical practice and a lack of open conversation more broadly. If valuing transparency is one of the primary reasons that placebo use is frowned upon, then perhaps we could apply that value to our discussions about what we do and do not know about how placebos work. At the bare minimum, this level of transparency must exist within the clinical care team.[4]

Education will be an important part of creating that transparency, and we need to investigate the impact of education on physician and patient attitudes, treatment, and prognosis. The lack of physician training around psychogenic medicine in general and placebo treatment in particular leads to therapeutic failures, as physicians feel disoriented and unsure of how to proceed in these cases. Medical training's focus on searching through physical clues to determine diagnosis can leave physicians ill prepared to handle MUPS (Atkins et al., 2013). This training should reach beyond psychiatry and neurology to primary care and beyond medical contexts to include the general population. Even if a doctor recognizes that the experience of psychogenic illness is as legitimate as that of organic illnesses and that a placebo may be a powerful intervention, a patient who has been raised in a society that so firmly instills a hierarchy of maladies may be unable to understand this as a "legitimate" diagnosis or treatment regimen.

Embracing the unknown can reveal different kinds of knowledge and values than data-driven research. The ethics of uncertainty is an underdeveloped field, despite serious possible effects, like unnecessary treatments and inadequate medical care (Atkins et al., 2013). "Epistemic humility," the acceptance that one's own knowledge is limited, must be central to approaches to poorly understood illnesses (Buchman and Ho, 2013), and we must have open conversation about what we do and do not know as both providers and patients.

Research is often characterized by attempts to make the unexplained fit into recognizable medical narratives of dysfunction. The emphasis for many MUPS has been discovering hidden etiologies (Ene, 2013) rather than broadening our acceptance of the lived experience of a diverse range of experiences, regardless of biological substrates. This is not to say that such biomedical research is unimportant—it can certainly make progress in understanding and treating symptoms that cause significant suffering—or that it would not ultimately reveal biological answers. Illnesses that may seem unexplainable today may be revealed through a new mechanism to be organic and treatable tomorrow. However, we must simultaneously work toward destigmatizing that which is poorly understood and researching ways that we could improve the quality of life and outcomes for those with MUPS regardless of medical understanding.

Conclusions

Better biomedical and neuroscientific data, an increase in empirically driven phenomenological and narrative research, and an embrace of epistemic humility will all be important moving forward. Hence, progress in the treatment of psychogenic disorders will require interdisciplinary efforts, pulling together psychiatrists, neurologists, primary care providers, patients, educators, science communicators, advocates, and ethicists. For all of these stakeholders, "epistemic humility" is an ethical imperative. While we can work to increase our knowledge base, we can also commit to acknowledging that lacking an observable mechanism doesn't delegitimize the lived experience of psychogenic disorders.

Progress in the brain sciences continues to break down the boundary established by dualist notions of mind and body. But we must be cautious when we legitimize experiences simply by establishing neurological correlates. To say that psychogenic illnesses are legitimate because they *truly are* physical is to say that if they weren't, they would be less legitimate—reflecting the societal stigma privileging the clearly organic over the undefined. This bias reveals itself even in our own insistence that placebos are not inert because they have real, identifiable physiological pathways. Perhaps we will in time pinpoint the chemical or structural substrates of psychological distress, PMD, or PNES—but do we need to wait until that time (if it is even possible for that time to come) to treat such disorders as legitimate or real? In both the sciences and the humanities, we can work against overly simplistic understandings of Cartesian dualism. One compelling alternative to dualist thinking that opposes mind and body might be the unwieldy but inclusive "biopsychosocial," the term used by psychiatrist Arthur Kleinman (1988) in *The Illness Narratives* to denote the complex interplay between the physical, mental, and social experience of illness.

Placebo use is certainly ethically fraught. Read in one way, it could be seen as an ultimately dismissive gesture—as a trick used to prove that someone's illness is not legitimate. Patients may interpret even beneficent attempts to use placebos for diagnosis in this way. But in another light (a light supported by new research), prescribing a placebo in partnership with a patient could be seen as a caring treatment—one that recognizes the legitimacy of the patient's experience and offers evidence-based treatments given with compassion, not doubt. We have many pathways in which research into the diagnosis and treatment of psychogenic disorders can proceed.

If, through increased research and education, placebos can be dissociated from their air of illegitimacy, then perhaps psychogenic illnesses themselves can begin to be taken more seriously. If the current popular narrative is something like, "If a placebo stops a symptom, that symptom was not real," then we could begin to evolve to a narrative that recognizes the deep interconnectedness between our mind and body—and that psychogenic symptoms are experienced somatically to the same extent that those with known organic causes are. If we can understand that a cure that is "all in the head" can be effective, than maybe "all in the head" doesn't need to carry any implications for legitimacy.

Notes

1 Our persistent use of scare quotes around "organic," for example, indicates our hesitance to use terminology that suggests that psychogenic disorders are not truly experienced somatically. For the purposes of this chapter, however, we will struggle along with "organic" and "psychogenic."

2 There are no current acupuncture sites identified for PMD. The acupuncturist therefore contacted the neurologists to explore this atypical response, which was ultimately attributed to expectation or suggestion. The patient was identified as having a "documented psychogenic movement disorder, for which presence of relief by psychotherapy, suggestion, or placebo is required" (p. 1354). The authors discuss this in more detail in Van Nuenen et al., 2007.

3 Ethical use of nondeceptive placebos would need to tackle the question of terminology: if a physician used words other than "placebo" (i.e., "an inert substance" or "a sucrose pill"), they could technically be truthful while still deceiving patients unfamiliar with the technical language.

4 Conversations about the need for disclosure to protect autonomy could benefit from the insights of narrative ethics or relational systems of ethics like feminist ethics and the ethics of care, which have problematized black-and-white views of autonomy. See, for example, Mackenzie and Stoljar, 2000; Charon, 2014; and Frank, 2014.

Further Reading

American Journal of Bioethics Neuroscience (2013) "Special Issue: Values at the Crossroads of Neurology, Psychiatry, and Psychology" 4(3).

Benedetti, F. (2008) "Mechanisms of Placebo and Placebo-Related Effects Across Diseases and Treatments". *Annual Reviews of Pharmacol and Toxicology* 48, 33–60.

Kleinman, A. (1988) *The Illness Narratives: Suffering, Healing, and the Human Condition.* New York: Basic Books.

Kranick, S.M., Gorrdino, T. and Hallett, M. (2011) "Psychogenic Movement Disorders and Motor Conversion: A Roadmap for Collaboration Between Neurology and Psychiatry". *Psychosomatics* 52, 109–116.

Shorter, E. (1993) *From Paralysis to Fatigue: A History of Psychosomatic Illness in the Modern Era.* New York: Free Press.

References

Amanzio, M., and Benedetti, F. (1999) Neuropharmacological dissection of placebo analgesia: Expectation-activated opioid systems versus conditioning-activated specific subsystems. *Journal of Neurosciences* 19: pp. 484–494.

AMA Council on Ethical and Judicial Affairs. (2016) Use of Placebo in Clinical Practice. *Code of Medical Ethics*, 2(1): p. 4.

Anderson, K.E., Gruber-Baldini, A.L., Vaughan, C.G., Reich, S.G., Fishman, P.S., Weiner, W.J., and Shulman, L.M. (2007) Impact of psychogenic movement disorders versus Parkinson's on disability, quality of life, and psychopathology. *Movement Disorders* 22: pp. 2204–2209.

APA. (2013a) *Diagnostic and Statistical Manual of Mental Disorders.* 5th ed. Washington, DC: American Psychiatric Association.

———. (2013b) *Somatic Symptom Disorder.* Available at: www.dsm5.org/Documents/Somatic Symptom Disorder Fact Sheet.pdf.

Asadi-Pooya, A., and Sperling, M. (2015) Epidemiology of psychogenic nonepileptic seizures. *Epilepsy & Behavior* 46: pp. 60–65.

Atkins, C., Brownell, K., Kornelsen, J., Woollard, R., and Whiteley, A. (2013) Silos of silence, stress, and suffering: Patient and physician experiences of MUPS and diagnostic uncertainty. *American Journal of Bioethics Neuroscience* 4(3): pp. 3–8.

Baik, J.S. (2012) Attention in Parkinson's disease mimicking suggestion in psychogenic movement disorder. *Journal of Movement Disorders* 5: pp. 53–54.

Baik, J.S., Han, S.W., Park, J.H., and Lee, M.S. (2009) Psychogenic paroxysmal dyskinesia: The role of placebo in the diagnosis and management. *Journal of Movement Disorders* 24: pp. 1244–1245.

Baker, G.A., Brooks, J.L., Goodfellow, L., Bodde, N., and Aldenkamp, A. (2007) Treatments for non-epileptic attack disorder. *Cochrane Database of Systematic Reviews* 1: p. CD006370.

Beauchamp, T., and Childress, J. (2009) *Principles of Biomedical Ethics.* New York: Oxford University Press.

Benbadis, S.R., and Hauser, W.A. (2000) An estimate of the prevalence of psychogenic non-epileptic seizures. *Seizure* 9: pp. 280–281.

Bendtsen, L., Mattsson, P., Zwart, J.A., and Lipton, R.B. (2003) Placebo response in clinical randomized trials of analgesics in migraine. *Cephalalgia* 23: pp. 487–490.

Benedetti, F. (2008) Mechanisms of placebo and placebo-related effects across diseases and treatments. *Annual Review of Pharmacology and Toxicology* 48: pp. 33–60.

———. (2014) Placebo effects: From the neurobiological paradigm to translational implications. *Neuron* 84: pp. 623–637.

Benedetti, F., Colloca, L., Torre, E., Lanotte, M., Melcarne, A., Pesare, M., . . . Lopiano, L. (2004) Placebo-responsive Parkinson patients show decreased activity in single neurons of subthalamic nucleus. *Nature Neuroscience* 7: pp. 587–588.

Benedetti, F., Mayberg, H.S., Wager, T.D., Stohler, C.S., and Zubieta, J.K. (2005) Neurobiological mechanisms of the placebo effect. *Journal of Neuroscience* 25: pp. 10390–10402.

Bhatia, K.P., and Schneider, S.A. (2007) Psychogenic tremor and related disorders. *Journal of Neurology* 254: pp. 569–574.

Bishop, F.L., Aizlewood, L., and Adams, A.E. (2014) When and why placebo-prescribing is acceptable and unacceptable: a focus group study of patients' views. *PLoS One* 9: p. e101822.

Blease, C. (2012) The principle of parity: The 'placebo effect' and physician communication. *Journal of Medical Ethics* 38: pp. 199–203.

Boehm, L. (2013) Half someone else's: Discourse and trauma in the PNES patient. *American Journal of Bioethics Neuroscience* 4(2): pp. 16–21.

Bostick, N.A., Sade, R., Levine, M.A., and Stewart, D.M., Jr. (2008) Placebo use in clinical practice: Report of the American medical association council on ethical and judicial affairs. *Journal of Clinical Ethics* 19: pp. 58–61.

Buchman, D., and Ho, A. (2013) What's trust got to do with it? Revisiting opioid contracts. *Journal of Medical Ethics* 40: pp. 673–677.

Burack, J.H., Back, A.L., and Pearlman, R.A. (1997) Provoking nonepileptic seizures: The ethics of deceptive diagnostic testing. *Hastings Center Report* 27: pp. 24–33.

Charon, R. (2014) Narrative Reciprocity. *Hastings Center Report* 44(1): pp. S21–S24.

Czarnecki, K., Thompson, J.M., Seime, R., Geda, Y.E., Duffy, J.R., and Ahlskog, J.E. (2012) Functional movement disorders: Successful treatment with a physical therapy rehabilitation protocol. *Parkinsonism &Related Disorders* 18: pp. 247–251.

De Craen, A.J., Roos, P.J., Leonard DeVries, A., and Kleijnen, J. (1996) Effect of colour of drugs: Systematic review of perceived effect of drugs and of their effectiveness. *BMJ* 313: pp. 1624–1626.

De La Fuente-Fernandez, R., Ruth, T.J., Sossi, V., Schulzer, M., Calne, D.B., and Stoessl, A.J. (2001) Expectation and dopamine release: Mechanism of the placebo effect in Parkinson's disease. *Science* 293: pp. 1164–1166.

Devinsky, O., and Fisher, R. (1996) Ethical use of placebos and provocative testing in diagnosing nonepileptic seizures. *Neurology* 47: pp. 866–870.

Devinsky, O., Gazzola, D., and Lafrance, W.C., Jr. (2011) Differentiating between nonepileptic and epileptic seizures. *Nature Reviews Neurology* 7: pp. 210–220.

Di Blasi, Z., Harkness, E., Ernst, E., Georgiou, A., and Kleijnen, J. (2001) Influence of context effects on health outcomes: A systematic review. *The Lancet* 357: pp. 757–762.

Diederich, N.J., and Goetz, C.G. (2008) The placebo treatments in neurosciences: New insights from clinical and neuroimaging studies. *Neurology* 71: pp. 677–684.

Dieppe, P., Goldingay, S., and Greville-Harris, M. (2016) The power and value of placebo and nocebo in painful osteoarthritis. *Osteoarthritis and Cartilage* 24: pp. 1850–1857.

Dworkin, R.H., Katz, J., and Gitlin, M.J. (2005) Placebo response in clinical trials of depression and its implications for research on chronic neuropathic pain. *Neurology* 65: pp. S7–S19.

Eijkholt, M., and Lynch, T. (2013) Provoking pseudo-seizures: Provocative placebo practices. *American Journal of Bioethics Neuroscience* 4(3): pp. 33–36.

Enck, P., Benedetti, F., and Schedlowski, M. (2008) New insights into the placebo and nocebo responses. *Neuron* 59: pp. 195–206.

Ene, S. (2013) Faces of fatigue: Ethical considerations on the treatment of Chronic Fatigue Syndrome. *American Journal of Bioethics Neuroscience* 4(3): pp. 22–26.

Espay, A.J., Goldenhar, L.M., Voon, V., Schrag, A., Burton, N., and Lang, A.E. (2009) Opinions and clinical practices related to diagnosing and managing patients with psychogenic movement disorders: An international survey of movement disorder society members. *Movement Disorder* 24: pp. 1366–1374.

Factor, S.A., Podskalny, G.D., and Molho, E.S. (1995) Psychogenic movement disorders: Frequency, clinical profile, and characteristics. *Journal of Neurology, Neurosurgery & Psychiatry* 59: pp. 406–412.

Fahn, S., and Williams, D.T. (1988) Psychogenic dystonia. *Advances in Neurology* 50: pp. 431–455.

Fairclough, G., Fox, J., Mercer, G., Reuber, M., and Brown, R.J. (2014) Understanding the perceived treatment needs of patients with psychogenic nonepileptic seizures. *Epilepsy & Behaviour* 31: pp. 295–303.

Fassler, M., Meissner, K., Schneider, A., and Linde, K. (2010) Frequency and circumstances of placebo use in clinical practice—A systematic review of empirical studies. *BMC Medicine* 8: p. 15.

Feinstein, A., Stergiopoulos, V., Fine, J., and Lang, A.E. (2001) Psychiatric outcome in patients with a psychogenic movement disorder: A prospective study. *Neuropsychiatry Neuropsychology and Behaviour Neurology* 14: pp. 169–176.

Finniss, D.G., Kaptchuk, T.J., Miller, F., and Benedetti, F. (2010) Biological, clinical, and ethical advances of placebo effects. *The Lancet* 375: pp. 686–695.

Ford, P. (2013) Values at the crossroads of neurology, psychiatry, and psychology. *American Journal of Bioethics Neuroscience* 4(3): p. 1–2.

Frank, A. (2014) Narrative ethics as dialogical story-telling. *Hastings Center Report* 44(1): pp. S16–S20.

Friedman, J.H., and Lafrance, W.C., Jr. (2010) Psychogenic disorders: The need to speak plainly. *Archives of Neurology* 67: pp. 753–755.

Gaynor, D., Cock, H., and Agrawal, N. (2009) Psychological treatments for functional non-epileptic attacks: A systematic review. *Acta Neuropsychiatrica* 21: pp. 158–168.

Ghaffar, O., Staines, W.R., and Feinstein, A. (2006) Unexplained neurologic symptoms: An fMRI study of sensory conversion disorder. *Neurology* 67: pp. 2036–2038.

Goetz, C.G., Wuu, J., McDermott, M.P., Adler, C.H., Fahn, S., Freed, C.R., . . . Leurgans, S. (2008) Placebo response in Parkinson's disease: Comparisons among 11 trials covering medical and surgical interventions. *Journal of Movement Disorder* 23: pp. 690–699.

Gowers, W.R. (1893) *A Manual of Diseases of the Nervous System*. New York: Hafner.

Gracely, R.H., Dubner, R., Deeter, W.R., and Wolkskee, P.J. (1985) Clinicians' expectations influence placebo analgesia. *The Lancet* 1: p. 43.

Gupta, A., and Lang, A.E. (2009) Psychogenic movement disorders. *Current Opinion in Neurology* 22: pp. 430–436.

Hall, K.T., Lembo, A.J., Kirsch, I., Ziogas, D.C., Douaiher, J., Jensen, K.B., . . . Kaptchuk, T.J. (2012) Catechol-O-methyltransferase val158met polymorphism predicts placebo effect in irritable bowel syndrome. *PLoS One* 7: p. e48135.

Hallett, M. (2006) Psychogenic movement disorders: A crisis for neurology. *Current Neurology and Neuroscience Reports* 6: pp. 269–271.

———. (2010) Physiology of psychogenic movement disorders. *Journal of Clinical Neuroscience* 17: pp. 959–965.

Harris, C.S., and Raz, A. (2012) Deliberate use of placebos in clinical practice: What we really know. *Journal of Medical Ethics* 38: pp. 406–407.

Hinson, V.K., and Haren, W.B. (2006) Psychogenic movement disorders. *The Lancet Neurology* 5: pp. 695–700.

Howick, J., Bishop, F.L., Heneghan, C., Wolstenholme, J., Stevens, S., Hobbs, F.D., and Lewith, G. (2013) Placebo use in the United kingdom: Results from a national survey of primary care practitioners. *PLoS One* 8: p. e58247.

Hrobjartsson, A., and Norup, M. (2003) The use of placebo interventions in medical practice—A national questionnaire survey of Danish clinicians. *Evaluation & the Health Professions* 26: pp. 153–165.

Hull, S.C., Colloca, L., Avins, A., Gordon, N.P., Somkin, C.P., Kaptchuk, T.J., and Miller, F.G. (2013) Patients' attitudes about the use of placebo treatments: Telephone survey. *BMJ* 347: p. f3757.

Jackson, J.L., George, S., and Hinchey, S. (2009) Medically unexplained physical symptoms. *Journal of General Internal Medicine* 24: pp. 540–542.

Jankovic, J., Vuong, K.D., and Thomas, M. (2006) Psychogenic tremor: Long-term outcome. *CNS Spectrums* 11: pp. 501–508.

Kanaan, R. (2013) Do placebos really cause their effects and does it matter? *American Journal of Bioethics Neuroscience* 4: pp. 35–36.

Kaptchuk, T.J. (2002) The placebo effect in alternative medicine: Can the performance of a healing ritual have clinical significance? *Annals of Internal Medicine* 136: pp. 817–825.

Kaptchuk, T.J., and Eisenberg, D.M. (1998) The persuasive appeal of alternative medicine. *Annals of Internal Medicine* 129: pp. 1061–1065.

Kaptchuk, T.J., Friedlander, E., Kelley, J.M., Sanchez, M.N., Kokkotou, E., Singer, J.P., . . . Lembo, A.J. (2010) Placebos without deception: A randomized controlled trial in irritable bowel syndrome. *PLoS One* 5: p. e15591.

Kaptchuk, T.J., Stason, W.B., Davis, R.B., Legedza, A.R., Schnyer, R.N., Kerr, C.E., . . . Goldman, R.H. (2006) Sham device v inert pill: Randomised controlled trial of two placebo treatments. *BMJ* 332: pp. 391–397.

Kendell, R.E. (2001) The distinction between mental and physical illness. *British Journal of Psychiatry* 178: pp. 490–493.

Kermen, R., Hickner, J., Brody, H., and Hasham, I. (2010) Family physicians believe the placebo effect is therapeutic but often use real drugs as placebos. *Family Medicine* 42: pp. 636–642.

Kim, S.E., Kubomoto, S., Chua, K., Amichai, M.M., and Pimentel, M. (2012) 'Pre-cebo': An unrecognized issue in the interpretation of adequate relief during irritable bowel syndrome drug trials. *Journal of Clinical Gastroenterology* 46: pp. 686–690.

Kleinman, A. (1988) *The Illness Narratives: Suffering, Healing, and the Human Condition*. New York: Basic Books.

Kolber, A. (2007) A limited defense of clinical placebo deception. *Yale Law & Policy Review* 26: pp. 75–137.

Kranick, S.M., Ekanayake, V., Martinez, V., Ameli, R., Hallett, M., and Voon, V. (2011a) Psychopathology and psychogenic movement disorders. *Movement Disorders* 26: pp. 1844–1850.

Kranick, S.M., Gorrindo, T., and Hallett, M. (2011b) Psychogenic movement disorders and motor conversion: A roadmap for collaboration between neurology and psychiatry. *Psychosomatics* 52: pp. 109–116.

Lafrance, W.C., Jr., Rusch, M.D., and Machan, J.T. (2008) What is 'treatment as usual' for nonepileptic seizures? *Epilepsy & Behaviour* 12: pp. 388–394.

Lempert, T., Dieterich, M., Huppert, D., and Brandt, T. (1990) Psychogenic disorders in neurology: Frequency and clinical spectrum. *Acta Neurologica Scandinavica* 82: pp. 335–340.

Lichtenberg, P., Heresco-Levy, U., and Nitzan, U. (2004) The ethics of the placebo in clinical practice. *Journal of Medical Ethics* 30: pp. 551–554.

Lidstone, S.C., Schulzer, M., Dinelle, K., Mak, E., Sossi, V., Ruth, T.J., . . . Stoessl, A.J. (2010) Effects of expectation on placebo-induced dopamine release in Parkinson disease. *Archives of General Psychiatry* 67: pp. 857–865.

Lutz, T. (1991) *American Nervousness, 1903: An Anecdotal History*. Ithaca, NY: Cornell University Press.

Lynoe, N., Mattsson, B., and Sandlund, M. (1993) The attitudes of patients and physicians towards placebo treatment—A comparative study. *Social Science & Medicine* 36: pp. 767–774.

Mackenzie, C., and Stoljar, N. (Eds.) (2000) *Relational Autonomy: Feminist Perspectives on Autonomy, Agency, and the Social Self*. New York: Oxford University Press.

McKeon, A., Ahlskog, J.E., Bower, J.H., Josephs, K.A., and Matsumoto, J.Y. (2009) Psychogenic tremor: Long-term prognosis in patients with electrophysiologically confirmed disease. *Movement Disorders* 24: pp. 72–76.

Mayberg, H.S., Silva, J.A., Brannan, S.K., Tekell, J.L., Mahurin, R.K., McGinnis, S., and Jerabek, P.A. (2002) The functional neuroanatomy of the placebo effect. *American Journal of Psychiatry* 159: pp. 728–737.

Meissner, K., Hofner, L., Fassler, M., and Linde, K. (2012) Widespread use of pure and impure placebo interventions by GPs in Germany. *Family Practice* 29: pp. 79–85.

Mercado, R., Constantoyannis, C., Mandat, T., Kumar, A., Schulzer, M., Stoessl, A.J., and Honey, C.R. (2006) Expectation and the placebo effect in Parkinson's disease patients with subthalamic nucleus deep brain stimulation. *Movement Disorders* 21: pp. 1457–1461.

Miresco, M.J., and Kirmayer, L.J. (2006) The persistence of mind-brain dualism in psychiatric reasoning about clinical scenarios. *American Journal of Psychiatry* 163: pp. 913–918.

Miyasaki, J.M., Sa, D.S., Galvez-Jimenez, N., and Lang, A.E. (2003) Psychogenic movement disorders. *Canadian Journal of Neurological Sciences* 30(Suppl)1: pp. S94–S100.

Moerman, D.E., and Jonas, W.B. (2002) Deconstructing the placebo effect and finding the meaning response. *Annals of Internal Medicine* 136: pp. 471–476.

Neimark, G., Caroff, S.N., and Stinnett, J.L. (2005) Medically unexplained physical symptoms: An overview. *Psychiatric Annals* 35: pp. 298–305.

Nowak, D.A., and Fink, G.R. (2009) Psychogenic movement disorders: Aetiology, phenomenology, neuroanatomical correlates and therapeutic approaches. *Neuroimage* 47: pp. 1015–1025.

Park, L.C., and Covi, L. (1965) Nonblind placebo trial: An exploration of neurotic patients' responses to placebo when its inert content is disclosed. *Archives of General Psychiatry* 12: pp. 36–45.

Petrovic, P., Kalso, E., Petersson, K.M., and Ingvar, M. (2002) Placebo and opioid analgesia—Imaging a shared neuronal network. *Science* 295: pp. 1737–1740.

Planès, S., Villier, C., and Mallaret, M. (2016). The nocebo effect of drugs. *Pharmacology Research and Perspectives* 4(2): p. e00208.

Purtilo, R. (1993) *Ethical Dimensions in the Health Care Professions*. Philadelphia: WB Saunders.

Reynolds, J.R. (1855) *The Diagnosis of Diseases of the Brain, Spinal Cord, Nerves, and Their Appendages*. London: Churchill.

Rommelfanger, K.S. (2013a) Attitudes on mind over matter: Physician views on the role of placebo in psychogenic disorders. *American Journal of Bioethics Neuroscience* 4(3): pp. 9–15.

———. (2013b) Opinion: A role for placebo therapy in psychogenic movement disorders. *Nature Reviews Neurology* 9: pp. 351–356.

Salinsky, M., Spencer, D., Boudreau, E., and Ferguson, F. (2011) Psychogenic nonepileptic seizures in US veterans. *Neurology* 77: pp. 945–950.

Sandler, A.D., Glesne, C.E., and Bodfish, J.W. (2010) Conditioned placebo dose reduction: A new treatment in attention-deficit hyperactivity disorder? *Journal of Developmental and Behavioural Pediatrics* 31: pp. 369–375.

Schafer, S.M., Colloca, L., and Wager, T.D. (2015) Conditioned placebo analgesia persists when subjects know they are receiving a placebo. *Journal of Pain* 16(5): pp. 412–420.

Shamy, M.C. (2010) The treatment of psychogenic movement disorders with suggestion is ethically justified. *Movement Disorders* 25: pp. 260–264.

Sherman, R., and Hickner, J. (2008) Academic physicians use placebos in clinical practice and believe in the mind-body connection. *Journal of General Internal Medicine* 23: pp. 7–10.

Shorter, E. (1993) *From Paralysis to Fatigue: A History of Psychosomatic Illness in the Modern Era*. New York: Free Press.

Singer, E.A. (2004) The necessity and the value of placebo. *Science of Engineering Ethics* 10: pp. 51–56.

Spence, S.A., Kaylor-Hughes, C., Farrow, T.F., and Wilkinson, I.D. (2008) Speaking of secrets and lies: the contribution of ventrolateral prefrontal cortex to vocal deception. *Neuroimage* 40: p. 1411–1148.

Stagno, S.J., and Smith, M.L. (1997) The use of placebo in diagnosing psychogenic seizures: Who is being deceived? *Seminars in Neurology* 17: pp. 213–218.

Stone, J. (2009) The bare essentials: Functional symptoms in neurology *Practical Neurology* 9: pp. 179–189.

Stone, J., and Edwards, M. (2012) Trick or treat? Showing patients with functional (psychogenic) motor symptoms their physical signs. *Neurology* 79: pp. 282–284.

Stone, J., Wojcik, W., Durrance, D., Carson, A., Lewis, S., Mackenzie, L., . . . Sharpe, M. (2002) What should we say to patients with symptoms unexplained by disease? The 'number needed to offend'. *British Medical Journal* 325: p. 1449.

Symon, A., Williams, B., Adelasoye, Q., and Cheyne, H. (2015) Nocebo and the potential harm of 'high risk' labelling: A scoping review. *Journal of Advanced Nursing* 71: pp. 1518–1529.

Thomas, M., and Jankovic, J. (2004) Psychogenic movement disorders: Diagnosis and management. *CNS Drugs* 18: pp. 437–452.

Thomas, M., Vuong, K.D., and Jankovic, J. (2006) Long-term prognosis of patients with psychogenic movement disorders. *Parkinsonism & Related Disorders* 12: pp. 382–387.

Tilburt, J.C., Emanuel, E.J., Kaptchuk, T.J., Curlin, F.A., and Miller, F.G. (2008) Prescribing 'placebo treatments': Results of national survey of US internists and rheumatologists. *BMJ* 337: p. a1938.

Van Nuenen, B.F., Wholgemuth, M., Wong Chung, R.E., Abdo, W.F., and Bloem, B.R. (2007) Acupuncture for psychogenic movement disorders: Treatment or diagnostic tool? *Movement Disorders* 22: pp. 1353–1355.

Wager, T.D., Rilling, J.K., Smith, E.E., Sokolik, A., Casey, K.L., Davidson, R.J., . . . Cohen, J.D. (2004) Placebo-induced changes in FMRI in the anticipation and experience of pain. *Science* 303: pp. 1162–1167.

Wager, T.D., Scott, D.J., and Zubieta, J.K. (2007) Placebo effects on human mu-opioid activity during pain. *Proceedings of the National Academy of Sciences USA* 104: pp. 11056–11061.

Wendell, S. (1996) *The Rejected Body: Feminist Philosophical Reflections on Disability*. New York: Routledge.

Wendt, L., Albring, A., Benson, S., Engler, H., Engler, A., Hinney, A., . . . Schedlowski, M. (2014) Catechol-O-methyltransferase Val158Met polymorphism is associated with somatosensory amplification and nocebo responses. *PLoS One* 9: p. e107665.

Whitehead, K., Kandler, R., and Reuber, M. (2013) Patients' and neurologists' perception of epilepsy and psychogenic nonepileptic seizures. *Epilepsia* 54: pp. 708–717.

Whitehead, K., and Reuber, M. (2012) Illness perceptions of neurologists and psychiatrists in relation to epilepsy and nonepileptic attack disorder. *Seizure* 21: pp. 104–109.

Zubieta, J.K., Bueller, J.A., Jackson, L.R., Scott, D.J., Xu, Y., Koeppe, R.A., . . . Stohler, C.S. (2005) Placebo effects mediated by endogenous opioid activity on mu-opioid receptors. *Journal of Neuroscience* 25: pp. 7754–7762.

8

COSMETIC NEUROLOGY AND THE ETHICS OF ENHANCEMENT

Anjan Chatterjee

Pharmacological development has moved from the bench through the bedside into playing fields, classrooms, recital halls, and even ivory towers (Sahakian and Morein-Zamir, 2007; Chatterjee, 2008). Our ability to treat diseases, modify their course, or at least ameliorate symptoms is improving. In the wake of these clinical advances, we find ourselves also manipulating health. What should we make of these societal trends?

"Cosmetic neurology" refers to the use of neurologic interventions to enhance movement, mood, and mentation in healthy people (Chatterjee, 2004, 2006). These interventions are typically developed to treat disease before being adopted by healthy people, analogous to how therapeutic reconstructive techniques were adapted for cosmetic surgery (Chatterjee, 2007). In what follows, I review drug interventions currently available for enhancement. I discuss what we know and the limits of that knowledge. I then outline the ethical concerns that surround cosmetic neurology, including special concerns that apply to children and adolescents.

Enhancements

Enhancements apply to three general domains: motor systems, cognition, and mood and affect. This chapter focuses on pharmacologic manipulations, although other interventions (such as noninvasive brain stimulation (Hamilton et al., 2011) are also available and likely to be used widely (Chatterjee, 2013). While doping in sports is pervasive (de Hon et al., 2015), motor enhancement will not be discussed here.

Cognition

Most pharmacologic cognitive treatments target catecholamine and cholinergic systems. Catecholamines consist of the brain neurotransmitters dopamine and norepinephrine involved in systems related to learning, mood regulation, and arousal. Catecholamine effects on neuronal plasticity may help cognitive training (Repantis et al., 2010b). The early observation that amphetamines improve speech therapy in aphasic patients (Walker-Batson et al., 2001) generated the hypothesis that this class of drugs might enhance language abilities in healthy people. Amphetamines (which increase levels of synaptic dopamine and norepinephrine) can facilitate novel vocabulary learning (Breitenstein et al., 2004; Whiting et al., 2007) and speed up information processing (Fillmore et al., 2005) in healthy subjects. Biomarkers (Hamidovic et al., 2010;Volkow et al., 2008) might predict individual responses to these drugs and help target their enhancement use. Methylphenidate (an amphetamine salt marketed as Ritalin and Concerta, among others) is also used widely to improve attention, concentration, spatial working memory, and planning (Weber and Lutschg, 2002; Zeeuws et al., 2010; Mintzer and Griffiths, 2007). Students commonly use amphetamine and its analogs (McCabe et al., 2005) despite the fact that these drugs sometimes impair performance (Diller, 1996; Babcock and Byrne, 2000), and the actual empirical data in support of their effects are limited (Smith and Farah, 2011). Newer nonaddictive drugs such as atomoxetine (a selective norepinephrine reuptake inhibitor marketed as Strattera) may improve executive control (Chamberlain et al., 2009). Other stimulants, like modafinil (marketed as Provigil) may affect both norepinephrine and dopamine transporters and improve arousal and selective attention in demanding situations (Marchant et al., 2008) and ameliorate cognitive deficits associated with sleep deprivation (Lagarde et al., 1995). Another possibility is that stimulants work by improving people's motivation and drive rather than specifically enhancing their cognition (Vrecko, 2013; Kjærsgaard, 2015).

Cholinesterase inhibitors (which block reuptake of acetylcholine and thus increase extracellular levels) are used to improve attention and memory (see Repantis et al., 2010a, for a review). These medications were developed to treat memory deficits in Alzheimer's disease but can be used in healthy people. Yesavage and colleagues (2001) found that commercial pilots on a low dose of donepezil performed better than pilots on placebos when facing demanding flight-simulation tasks. These drugs may also improve semantic processing (FitzGerald et al., 2008) and memory (Grön et al., 2005; Zaninotto et al., 2009) and mitigate the effects of sleep deprivation (Chuah et al., 2009).

Mood and Affect

By some estimates, between 9.5% and 20% of Americans are depressed (Health, 2003). Horowitz and Wakefield (Horowitz and Wakefield, 2007) argue that the epidemic of depression is explained in part by the reclassification of typical experiences of sadness as depression. Here, we see a familiar pattern of therapy generalizing to enhancement. When the boundary between a clinical condition and a healthy state is graded, drug use expands to borderline cases. It is a short step for the healthy to then use the drugs. Consistent with this pattern, use of SSRIs (common brand names include Prozac, Zoloft, and Paxil) in the healthy can selectively dampen negative affect (Knutson et al., 1998) and increase affiliative behavior in social settings (Tse and Bond, 2002).

Drugs can modulate the memory and effects of emotional events (Cahill, 2003; Strawn and Geracotti, 2008). Epinephrine consolidates emotional memories, and beta-blockers dampen them. People given propanolol remember emotionally arousing stories as if they were emotionally neutral (Cahill et al., 1994). Preliminary studies suggest that propanolol can even reduce people's implicit negative racial biases (Terbeck et al., 2012). Propanolol also enhances the memory of events surrounding emotionally charged events that are otherwise suppressed (Strange et al., 2003). In one study, patients in an emergency room given propanolol after a traumatic event had fewer posttraumatic stress disorder symptoms when assessed one month later (Pitman et al., 2002). Benzodiazepines (a class of psychoactive drugs like Valium, Ativan, and Xanax that are GABA-A receptor agonists) can lessen the emotional impact of memories (Brignell et al., 2006). These examples demonstrate the difficulty of distinguishing between therapy and enhancement. We might regard the dampening of emotional memories in veterans suffering from posttraumatic stress disorder as therapy. But emotional distress that occurs as an inevitable part of everybody's lives such as romantic rejections, failures at work, and the deaths of loved ones might also be dampened.

We might also be able to modify our emotional states in more subtle ways. For example, oxytocin and vasopressin might be used to induce trust and promote affiliative behavior (Insel, 2010). The possibility of such manipulations raises questions about what constitutes improvement. Debates about whether these kinds of drugs can enhance morality itself are beginning to surface (Douglas, 2008; Persson and Savulescu, 2008; Harris, 2011; Raus et al., 2014).

Ethical Dilemmas

If drugs can make us smarter and nicer, surely this development is a good thing. The reasons to be cautious about a pharmacological utopia are concerns about safety, authenticity, justice, and autonomy (Chatterjee, 2006).

Safety

Virtually all medications have potential adverse effects that range from minor inconveniences to severe disability or death. For example, amphetamines have FDA black-box warnings pointing to the risk of addiction and serious cardiac side effects including sudden death. Recent large-scale studies do not find that stimulants have greater cardiovascular adverse effects (Cooper et al., 2011; Habel, 2011), mitigating this concern. However, physicians tend to be concerned about safety (Chatterjee, 2009) given what they see as their professional roles. They are typically suspicious of safety claims made by pharmaceutical companies (Banjo et al., 2010), and many insist that enhancements should only be made available if they are safe (Hotze et al., 2011).

A subtler version of the safety concern is that of trade-offs rather than adverse effects. Would enhancement in one cognitive process detract from others? For example, medications that enhance attention and concentration might limit imagination and creativity. Such effects are not likely to be straightforward. In one study (Farah et al., 2009), Adderall had dampening effects on convergent creativity tasks in high performers and enhancing effects for low performers. Other potential trade-offs are ways that enhancing long-term memory could impair working memory; enhancing consolidation of long-term memories could disrupt the flexibility of those memories to respond to a changed environment and alter behavior (Schermer et al., 2009).

Finally, short- and long-term effects of enhancements might differ. Most pharmacologic studies are conducted in relatively short clinical trials. An underlying concern is that chronic use of such medications might have unpredictable and even detrimental effects. Whitaker (Whitaker, 2010) observes that since the advent of neuropsychiatric medications in the 1950s, the natural history of disorders like schizophrenia, depression, and bipolar disorder has worsened rather than improved. Most of these medications work by increasing synaptic concentrations of neurotransmitters such as acetylcholine or norepinephrine. As a result of flooding of these neurotransmitters within the synaptic cleft, one might expect down regulation of postsynaptic receptors and up regulation of presynaptic reuptake mechanisms, making the drug less effective. Synaptic homeostasis may mitigate the chronic effects of pharmacologic interventions and potentially have long-term adverse consequences. In other words, the brain's intrinsic self-regulatory mechanisms could potentially react to chronic administration of medications by pushing neurotransmitter dynamics toward the state that the medications are supposed to be treating in the first place.

Authenticity

The concern about individual authenticity takes two general forms, one about eroding character and the other about altering the individuals. The concern about erosion of character draws on a "no pain, no gain" belief (Chatterjee, 2008). Many people believe that struggling with pain or adversity builds character, and eliminating pain or adversity undermines good character. Easy benefits without effort cheapen us (Kass, 2003b).

While the concerns about authenticity run deep, they are mitigated by several factors. Which pains are worth their hypothetical gains? We live in homes with central heat and air, eat food prepared by others, travel vast distances in short times, and take Tylenol for headaches and H2 histamine blockers for heartburn. These conveniences may have eroded our collective character and cheapened us, as Kass suggests (Kass, 2003a). But few choose to turn back.

Could chemically changing the brain challenge our notion of self? The central intuition is that such interventions threaten essential characteristics of what it means to be human (Kass, 2003a). For example, does selectively dampening the impact of our painful memories change who we are? This is a difficult issue given that there is little consensus on the essence of human nature (Wolpe, 2002; Fukayama, 2002; Kolber, 2011). However, the search and desire for an authentic self probably drives both the desire for and the worry about the consequences of enhancement (Elliott, 2011).

Justice

Who is allowed to use enhancements? Insurance companies or the state are unlikely to fund nonclinical interventions. Only those who can afford to pay privately would get enhancements, leading to unequal access to their benefits. A common counter to the worry of widening inequities is that enhancement is not a zero-sum game. With general improvements, benefits trickle down even to those at the bottom of a material hierarchy. However, this argument assumes that people's sense of well-being is determined by an absolute level of quality rather than a recognition of one's relative place. Beyond worries about basic subsistence, well-being is also affected by expectations and relative positions in society (Frank, 1987).

One might argue that the critical issue is access and not availability (Caplan, 2003). If access to enhancements were open to all, then differences might even be minimized. This argument has logical merit but skirts the issue in practice. In many societies, we tacitly accept wide disparities in modifiers of cognition, as demonstrated by the presence of inequities in education, nutrition, and shelter. The access concern might be less relevant to new nonpharmacological interventions like transcranial direct current stimulation. These cheap and relatively safe interventions may have cosmetic uses (Hamilton et al., 2011) and do not need physicians to serve as gatekeepers.

For more on tDCS, see Chapter 18.

Autonomy

Matters of choice can become coercive. Coercion takes two forms. One is an implicit pressure to maintain or better one's position in some perceived social order. Such pressures increase in "winner-take-all" environments in which more people compete for fewer and bigger prizes (Frank and Cook, 1995). Many professionals work 60, 80, or more than 100 hours a week without regard to their health. Emergency department residents use zolpidem (an inhibitory receptor GABA-A targeted drug) to regulate sleep and modafinil to enhance their effectiveness (McBeth et al., 2009). Athletes take steroids to compete at the highest levels, and children at competitive preparatory schools take methylphenidate in epidemic proportions (Hall, 2003). To not take enhancements might mean being left behind. Students frequently cite academic assignments or grades as reasons to take amphetamines (Arria et al., 2008; DeSantis et al., 2008). In a U.S. survey from 2005, nonmedical uses of stimulants were highest in competitive colleges (McCabe et al., 2005). Similar practices are evident in Europe (Schermer et al., 2009).

A second form of coercion is an explicit demand for superior performance. Soldiers have been encouraged to take enhancements for the greater good (Russo et al., 2013). Might this logic extend to civilians? The finding of Yesavage and colleagues (Yesavage et al., 2001) that pilots taking donepezil performed better in emergencies than those on placebo could have wide implications. If these results are reliable and meaningful, should pilots be required to take such medications? Should medical students and postcall residents take stimulants to attenuate the deficits of sustained attention brought on by sleep deprivation (Webb et al., 2010)? Some suggest that physicians might have a moral responsibility to use enhancements (Enck, 2014). Could hospital administrators or patient advocacy groups require this practice, or could the medical marketplace charge more for such enhanced physicians?

Children and Adolescents

Concerns about the consequences of coercion take on special force in the context of children and adolescents. Young people face pressures similar to adults to use enhancements (Singh and Kelleher, 2013). Many children, especially in affluent environments, have demanding social schedules, sports commitments, and other extracurricular activities added to burdensome levels of schoolwork. In this pressured environment, the demand for enhancements has risen over the last few years (Johnston et al., 2006). In 2005, 7.4% of eighth graders reported trying amphetamines without medical instruction (Johnston et al., 2006). Physicians frequently write prescriptions for psychotropic drugs, especially stimulants and antidepressants, to young people without a clear diagnosis of a mental illness (Thomas et al., 2006). From 2002 to 2010, physicians wrote fewer prescriptions for antibiotics and 46% more for stimulants for adolescents (Chai et al., 2012).

Estimates of nonprescription use of stimulants were below 0.5% until 1995 across the age range from high school to adults. Since the mid-1990s, between 2.3% and 8.7% of high school students report nonprescription use of stimulants (Smith and Farah, 2011). Data from the Monitoring the Future Survey (monitoringthefuture.org) suggest that young people use different psychotropic prescription drugs, including tranquillizers, pain-killers, stimulants, and hypnotics, for nonmedical purposes (Johnston et al., 2006). These drugs are used both recreationally and to enhance performance (Teter et al., 2005; Friedman, 2006). University chat sites and listservs make prescription drugs readily available for nonmedical use (Talbot, 2009). In 2012, 45.4% of 12th graders thought it was very easy or fairly easy to get amphetamines, and 14.9% thought it was very easy or fairly easy to get sedatives (monitoringthefuture.org).

Ethical concerns about the use of enhancements in children are amplified when considering safety, authenticity, and autonomy. The American Academy of Neurology issued guidance opposing the prescribing of cognitive enhancements for children (Graf et al., 2013). They state,

> Pediatric neuroenhancement presents its own ethical, social, legal, and developmental issues, including the fiduciary responsibility of physicians caring for children, the special integrity of the doctor–child–parent relationship, the vulnerability of children to

various forms of coercion, distributive justice in school settings, and the moral obligation of physicians to prevent misuse of medication. Neurodevelopmental issues include the importance of evolving personal authenticity during childhood and adolescence, the emergence of individual decision-making capacities, and the process of developing autonomy.

(Graf et al., 2013, 1251)

The long-term biological impact of enhancements on the developing nervous system is unknown (Kim et al., 2009). Another concern is that use of enhancements could erode the development of children's character, notions of authenticity, and sense of personal responsibility. Stimulants can alter reward circuitry (Kim et al., 2009) and change behavior, motivation, attention, and interaction with others. Decisions involving long-term risks may be particularly challenging for younger children because they involve calculation of future risk–benefit ratios (Singh et al., 2010). Parents can be sources of coercion, driven by performance pressures or goals to produce highly successful children even at the expense of the child's physical or mental health. Schools can add to such pressures. Teachers often tell parents that a child might benefit from stimulant treatment, a shift perhaps reflecting a change from play-based to academically oriented curricula in elementary schools (Sax, 2003).

In summary, we face a paradox when it comes to enhancements in children and adolescents. Their limited autonomy amplifies concerns about safety (unknown long-term consequences), coercion (parental or school pressure), and character (the potential to alter developing brains). Nonetheless, the use of enhancements as study aids is commonly accepted by adolescents and young adults.

Limits to Our Knowledge

Any discussion of the advantages and disadvantages of cosmetic neurology relies on adequate information about their efficacy and adverse effects. Unfortunately, our knowledge is limited and may remain so for the foreseeable future.

Placebo Effects

A pervasive issue when trying to understand the specific effects of enhancing drugs is determining the extent of placebo effects (Kirsch, 2009; Rutherford et al., 2012). The belief that drugs are helpful often contributes to their demonstrable beneficial effects (Benedetti, 2008). For example, people often feel better about their performance on stimulants even when there is no measurable improvement (Ilieva et al., 2013). At a societal level, the greater the general belief that enhancements work, regardless of whether that belief is generated by the media or what peers say, the more likely people will experience positive effects of these medications. Such beliefs, if widespread, are likely to influence public policy regardless of limited scientific support (Vrecko, 2013; Kjærsgaard, 2015).

Bias

Several impediments limit our ability to conduct research into the effects of enhancing medications in healthy people. One might argue that people should be well informed about the positive and negative effects and trade-offs in using these medications. Unfortunately, adequate information is not forthcoming any time soon. Most funding agencies do not support such research, making systematic progress difficult. The lack of funding and regulatory burdens prevents large multicenter randomized controlled trials. Accumulated data are often biased in fields with few researchers and small true effect sizes that might not be meaningful (Ioannidis, 2005). Inadequate statistical power is an endemic problem in studies of enhancements. These studies typically enroll small numbers of participants. Often the drugs are given once and, if repeated, only for relatively short durations. Because studies that show significant effects are more likely to be published, well-designed negative studies are not accounted for in any systematic manner. This publication bias is common in neuroscience (Button et al., 2013). As such, reviews of this literature and various meta-analyses may overestimate the effects of enhancement medications.

Societal Considerations

When ethical discussions of pharmacologic enhancements began in earnest more than a decade ago (Wolpe, 2002; Chatterjee, 2004; Farah et al., 2004; Savulescu, 2005), the general assumption was that our armamentarium of drugs would grow. Such growth, in the near future, appears unlikely. Development of novel neuropsychiatric drugs is instead declining (Hyman, 2012; Insel, 2012). Truly innovative drugs are not evident in the pipeline. For now, discussion about pharmacologic enhancements will largely focus on drugs currently available.

How should we, as a society, respond to cosmetic neurology? Some version of the practice is inevitable (Chatterjee, 2007). Strict prohibition of the use of enhancements is unlikely to be effective. This approach simply moves the market for such medications underground and would probably inhibit thoughtful discussion about the actual use of these medications. Some advocate for policies to maximize benefits and minimize harm by supporting fairness, protecting individuals from coercion, and minimizing enhancement-related socioeconomic disparities (Appel, 2008; Greely et al., 2008).

Cultural norms about the use of enhancements have not coalesced into a consensus. Attitudes about enhancement are influenced by cultural contexts that vary (Shook et al., 2014). Physicians, who would do the prescribing, may need to think beyond traditional disease models of care (Chatterjee, 2004; Synofzik, 2009; Bostrom, 2008; Ravelingien et al., 2009). Physicians are typically pragmatic (Ott et al., 2012) about prescribing enhancements but also ambivalent, viewing the practice as alleviating suffering while being wary of exaggerating social inequities (Hotze et al., 2011). Approaching enhancement as a public health issue may advance the discussion (Outram and Racine, 2011). Physician organizations can help structure discussions. For example, the American Academy of Neurology published guidance that prescribing enhancements might be permissible for adults (Larriviere et al., 2009) but not for children (Graf et al., 2013).

Research and clinical neuroscientists along with ethicists can lay the groundwork for broader public discussions. As of now, there is little agreement among academics (Heinz et al., 2012; Boot et al., 2012; Forlini and Racine, 2009). Some regard the ethical concerns as exaggerated (Partridge et al., 2011) or ill conceived (Zohny, 2015). The attitudes among the public also vary. Most of our information comes from surveys of young people who show a divide between those who use enhancers and those who do not (Schelle et al., 2014). Nonusers more than users are concerned about medical safety and questions of fairness. Generally, both users and nonusers think that the decision to use enhancements is a matter of personal choice and oppose formal coercive policies, such as requiring enhancements in high-performance jobs (e.g., physicians, pilots). A survey of more than 4,000 participants, using plausible vignettes, found that the public is sensitive to the ethical concerns raised by academics (Fitz et al., 2014). They are moderate in their views and support success above all, regardless of the use of enhancements (also see Cabrera et al., 2015). At the same time, they value effort. Success without the use of enhancement is regarded as more worthy. Furthermore, people are less critical of the issue if stimulants are viewed as enhancing motivation than if viewed as enhancing cognition (Faber et al., 2015).

Concluding Remarks

It is unclear where these issues will settle and if and when we will arrive at consensus. However, such discussions are critical, as the effects of cosmetic neurology on society continue to be pervasively felt, and our attitudes toward a brave new pharmacological world continue to evolve.

This chapter was adapted and updated from Chatterjee (2014).

Further Reading

Chatterjee, A. (2004) "Cosmetic Neurology: The Controversy Over Enhancing Movement, Mentation And Mood". *Neurology* 63, 968–974.

Greely, H., Sahakian, B., Harris, J., Kessler, R.C., Gazzaniga, M., Campbell, P. and Farah, M.J. (2008) "Towards Responsible Use of Cognitive-Enhancing Drugs by the Healthy". *Nature* 456, 702–705.

Larriviere, D., Williams, M.A., Rizzo, M., Bonnie, R.J. and On Behalf Of The AAN Ethics, L.A.H.C. (2009) "Responding to Requests From Adult Patients For Neuroenhancements. Guidance of the Ethics, Law and Humanities Committee". *Neurology* 73, 1406–1412.

Repantis, D., Schlattmann, P., Laisney, O. and Heuser, I. (2010) "Modafinil and Methylphenidate for Neuroenhancement in Healthy Individuals: A Systematic Review". *Pharmacological Research* 62, 187–206.

Schelle, K.J., Faulmüller, N., Caviola, L. and Hewstone, M. (2014) "Attitudes Toward Pharmacological Cognitive Enhancement—A Review". *Frontiers in Systems Neuroscience* 8, 53.

References

Appel, J.M. (2008) When the boss turns pusher: A proposal for employee protections in the age of cosmetic neurology. *Journal of Medical Ethics* 34: pp. 616–618.

Arria, A., O'Grady, K., Calderia, K., Vincent, K., and Wish, E. (2008) Nonmedical use of prescription stimulants and analgesics: Associations with social and academic behaviors among college students. *Pharmacotherapy* 38: pp. 1045–1060.

Babcock, Q., and Byrne, T. (2000) Student perceptions of methylphenidate abuse at a public liberal arts college. *Journal of American College Health* 49: pp. 143–145.

Banjo, O., Nadler, R., and Reiner, P. (2010) Physician attitudes towards pharmacological cognitive enhancement: Safety concerns are paramount. *PLoS One* 5: p. E14322.

Benedetti, F. (2008). Mechanisms of placebo and placebo-related effects across diseases and treatments. *Annual Review of Pharmacology and Toxicology* 48: pp. 33–60.

Boot, B.P., Partridge, B., and Hall, W. (2012) Better evidence for safety and efficacy is needed before neurologists prescribe drugs for neuroenhancement to healthy people. *Neurocase* 18: pp. 181–184.

Bostrom, N. (2008) Drugs can be used to treat more than disease. *Nature* 451: p. 520.

Breitenstein, C., Wailke, S., Bushuven, S., Kamping, S., Zwitserlood, P., Ringelstein, E.B., and Knecht, S. (2004) D-Amphetamine boosts language learning independent of its cardiovascular and motor arousing effects. *Neuropsychopharmacology* 29: pp. 1704–1714.

Brignell, C.M., Rosenthal, J., and Curran, H.V. (2006) Pharmacological manipulations of arousal and memory for emotional material: Effects of a single dose of methylphenidate or lorazepam. *Journal of Psychopharmacology* 21: pp. 673–683.

Button, K.S., Ioannidis, J.P.A., Mokrysz, C., Nosek, B.A., Flint, J., Robinson, E.S.J., and Munafo, M.R. (2013) Power failure: Why small sample size undermines the reliability of neuroscience. *Nature Reviews Neuroscience*, Advance Online Publication.

Cabrera, L., Fitz, N., and Reiner, P. (2015) Reasons for comfort and discomfort with pharmacological enhancement of cognitive, affective, and social domains. *Neuroethics* 8: pp. 93–106.

Cahill, L. (2003) Similar neural mechanisms for emotion-induced memory impairment and enhancement. *Proceedings of the National Academy of Sciences America* 100: pp. 13123–13124.

Cahill, L., Prins, B., Weber, M., and Mcgaugh, J. (1994) Beta-adrenergic activation and memory for emotional events. *Nature* 371: pp. 702–704.

Caplan, A. (2003) Is better best? *Scientific American* 289: pp. 104–105.

Chai, G., Governale, L., Mcmahon, A.W., Trinidad, J.P., Staffa, J., and Murphy, D. (2012) Trends of outpatient prescription drug utilization in us children, 2002–2010. *Pediatrics* 130(1): pp. 23–31.

Chamberlain, S.R., Hampshire, A., Muller, U., Rubia, K., Sel Campo, N., Craig, K., . . . Sahakian, B.J. (2009) Atomoxetine modulates right inferior frontal activation during inhibitory control: A pharmacological functional magnetic resonance imaging study. *Biological Psychiatry* 65: pp. 550–555.

Chatterjee, A. (2004) Cosmetic neurology: The controversy over enhancing movement, mentation and mood. *Neurology* 63: pp. 968–974.

———. (2006) The promise and predicament of cosmetic neurology. *The Journal of Medical Ethics* 32: pp. 110–113.

———. (2007) Cosmetic neurology and cosmetic surgery: Parallels, predictions and challenges. *Cambridge Quarterly of Healthcare Ethics* 16: pp. 129–137.

———. (2008) Framing pains, pills, and professors. *Expositions* 2(2): pp. 139–146.

———. (2009) A medical view of potential adverse effects. *Nature* 457: pp. 532–533.

———. (2013) Gearing up for new currents in sports enhancement. *The Neuroethics Blog.* [Accessed 15 Oct. 2013].

———. (2014) Neuropharmacology and society. In M.S. Gazzaniga and G.R. Mangun (Eds.). *The Cognitive Neurosciences.* 5th ed. Cambridge, MA: MIT Press.

Chuah, L.Y.M., Chong, D.L., Chen, A.K., Rekshan, I.I.I.W.R., Tan, J.-C., Zheng, H., and Chee, M.W.L. (2009) Donepezil improves episodic memory in young individuals vulnerable to the effects of sleep deprivation. *Sleep* 32: p. 999.

Cooper, W.O., Habel, L.A., Sox, C.M., Chan, K.A., Arbogast, P.G., Cheetham, T.C., . . . Ray, W.A. (2011) ADHD drugs and serious cardiovascular events in children and young adults. *New England Journal of Medicine* 365: pp. 1896–1904.

De Hon, O., Kuipers, H., and Van Bottenburg, M. (2015) Prevalence of doping use in elite sports: A review of numbers and methods. *Sports Medicine* 45: pp. 57–69.

Desantis, A., Webb, E., and Noar, S. (2008) Illicit use of prescription ADHD medications on a college campus: A multimethodological approach. *Journal of American College Health* 57: pp. 315–324.

Diller, L. (1996) The run on Ritalin: Attention deficit disorder and stimulant treatment in the 1990s. *Hastings Center Report* 26: pp. 12–14.

Douglas, T. (2008) Moral enhancement. *Journal of Applied Philosophy* 25: pp. 228–245.

Elliott, C. (2011) Enhancement technologies and the modern self. *Journal of Medicine and Philosophy* 36: pp. 364–374.

Enck, G. (2014) Pharmaceutical enhancement and medical professionals. *Medicine, Health Care and Philosophy* 17: pp. 23–28.

Faber, N.S., Douglas, T., Heise, F., and Hewstone, M. (2015) Cognitive enhancement and motivation enhancement: An empirical comparison of intuitive judgments. *American Journal of Bioethics Neuroscience* 6(1): pp. 18–20.

Farah, M.J., Haimm, C., Sankoorikal, G., and Chatterjee, A. (2009) When we enhance cognition with Adderall, do we sacrifice creativity? A preliminary study. *Psychopharmacology* 202: pp. 541–547.

Farah, M.J., Illes, J., Cook-Deegan, R., Gardner, H., Kandel, E., King, P., . . . Wolpe, P. (2004) Neurocognitive enhancement: What can we do and what should we do? *Nature Reviews Neuroscience* 5: pp. 421–425.

Fillmore, M.T., Kelly, T.H., and Martin, C.A. (2005) Effects of D-amphetamine in human models of information processing and inhibitory control. *Drug and Alcohol Dependence* 77: pp. 151–159.

Fitz, N., Nadler, R., Manogaran, P., Chong, E.J., and Reiner, P. (2014) Public attitudes toward cognitive enhancement. *Neuroethics* 7: pp. 173–188.

Fitzgerald, D.B., Crucian, G.P., Mielke, J.B., Shenal, B.V., Burks, D., Womack, K.B., . . . Heilman, K.M. (2008) Effects of donepezil on verbal memory after semantic processing in healthy older adults. *Cognitive and Behavioral Neurology* 21: pp. 57–64.

Forlini, C., and Racine, E. (2009) Disagreements with implications: Diverging discourses on the ethics of non-medical use of methylphenidate for performance enhancement. *BMC Medical Ethics* 10: pp. 1–13.

Frank, R. (1987) *Choosing the Right Pond.* New York: Oxford Press.

Frank, R., and Cook, P. (1995) *The Winner-Take-All Strategy.* New York: The Free Press.

Friedman, R.A. (2006) The changing face of teenage drug abuse—The trend toward prescription drugs. *New England Journal of Medicine* 354: pp. 1448–1450.

Fukayama, F. (2002) *Our Posthuman Future.* New York: Farrar, Straus and Giroux.

Graf, W.D., Nagel, S.K., Epstein, L.G., Millert, G., Nass, R., and Larriviere, D. (2013) Pediatric neuroenhancement: Ethical, legal, social, and neurodevelopmental implications. *Neurology* 80: pp. 1251–1260.

Greely, H., Sahakian, B., Harris, J., Kessler, R.C., Gazzaniga, M., Campbell, P., and Farah, M.J. (2008) Towards responsible use of cognitive-enhancing drugs by the healthy. *Nature* 456: pp. 702–705.

Grön, G., Kirstein, M., Thielscher, A., Riepe, M., and Spitzer, M. (2005) Cholinergic enhancement of episodic memory in healthy young adults. *Psychopharmacology* 182: pp. 170–179.

Habel, L.A. (2011) ADHD medications and risk of serious cardiovascular events in young and middle-aged adults. *The Journal of American Medical Association* 306: p. 2673.

Hall, S. (2003) The quest for a smart pill. *Scientific American* 289: pp. 54–65.

Hamidovic, A., Dlugos, A., Palmer, A.A., and Wit, H. (2010) Polymorphisms in dopamine transporter (Slc6a3) are associated with stimulant effects of D-amphetamine: An exploratory pharmacogenetic study using healthy volunteers. *Behavior Genetics* 40: pp. 255–261.

Hamilton, R., Messing, S., and Chatterjee, A. (2011) Rethinking the thinking cap: Ethics of neural enhancement using noninvasive brain stimulation. *Neurology* 76: pp. 187–93.

Harris, J. (2011) Moral enhancement and freedom. *Bioethics* 25: pp. 102–111.

Health, T.N.I.O.M. (2003) *The Numbers Count: Mental Disorders in America.* Washington, DC.

Heinz, A., Kipke, R., Heimann, H., and Wiesing, U. (2012) Cognitive neuroenhancement: False assumptions in the ethical debate. *Journal of Medical Ethics* 38: pp. 372–375.

Horowitz, A.V., and Wakefield, J.C. (2007) *The Loss of Sadness: How Psychiatry Transformed Normal Sorrow into Depressive Disorder.* New York: Oxford University Press.

Hotze, T.D., Shah, K., Anderson, E.E., and Wynia, M.K. (2011) Doctor, would you prescribe a pill to help me. . . ?" A national survey of physicians on using medicine for human enhancement. *The American Journal of Bioethics* 11(1): pp. 3–13.

Hyman, S.E. (2012) Revolution stalled. *Science Translational Medicine* 4: p. 155cm11.

Ilieva, I., Boland, J., and Farah, M.J. (2013) Objective and subjective cognitive enhancing effects of mixed amphetamine salts in healthy people. *Neuropharmacology* 64: pp. 496–505.

Insel, T.R. (2010) The challenge of translation in social neuroscience: A review of oxytocin, vasopressin, and affiliative b. *Neuron,* 65: pp. 768–779.

———. (2012) Next-generation treatments for mental disorders. *Science Translational Medicine* 4(155): p. 155ps19.

Ioannidis, J.P.A. (2005) Why most published research findings are false. *PLOS Medicine* 2: p. E124.

Johnston, L.D., O'Malley, P.M., Bachman, J.G., Schulenberg, J.E., and National Institute On Drug, A. 2006. *Monitoring the Future.* National Results on Adolescent Drug Use. Overview of Key Findings 2005. NIH Publication No. 06-5882. National Institute on Drug Abuse (NIDA).

Kass, L. (2003a) *President's Council on Bioethics. Beyond Therapy: Biotechnology and the Pursuit of Happiness.* New York: Harper Perennial.

———. (2003b) The pursuit of biohappiness. *Washington Post,* 16 October.

Kim, Y., Teylan, M.A., Baron, M., Sands, A., Nairn, A.C., and Greengard, P. (2009) Methylphenidate-Induced Dendritic Spine Formation and Δfosb Expression in Nucleus Accumbens, *Proceedings of the National Academy of Sciences.*

Kirsch, I. (2009) *The Emperor's New Drugs: Exploding the Antidepressant Myth.* New York: Random House.

Kjærsgaard, T. (2015) Enhancing motivation by use of prescription stimulants: The ethics of motivation enhancement. *American Journal of Bioethics Neuroscience* 6(1): pp. 4–10.

Knutson, B., Wolkowitz, O., Cole, S., Chan, T., Moore, E., Johnson, R., . . . Reus, V. (1998) Selective alteration of personality and social behavior by serotonergic intervention. *American Journal of Psychiatry* 155: pp. 373–379.

Kolber, A. (2011) Neuroethics: Give memory-altering drugs a chance. *Nature* 476: pp. 275–276.

Lagarde, D., Batejat, D., Van Beers, P., Sarafian, D., and Pradella, S. (1995) Interest of modafinil, a new psychostimulant, during a sixty-hour sleep deprivation experiment. *Fundamental & Clinical Pharmacology* 9: pp. 1–9.

Larriviere, D., Williams, M.A., Rizzo, M., Bonnie, R.J., and On Behalf of the Aan Ethics, L.A.H.C. (2009) Responding to requests from adult patients for neuroenhancements: guidance of the ethics, law and humanities committee. *Neurology* 73: pp. 1406–1412.

McBeth, B.D., McNamara, R.M., Ankel, F.K., Mason, E.J., Ling, L.J., Flottemesch, T.J., and Asplin, B.R. (2009) Modafinil and zolpidem use by emergency medicine residents. *Academic Emergency Medicine* 16: pp. 1311–1317.

McCabe, S.E., Knight, J.R., Teter, C.J., and Wechsler, H. (2005) Non-medical use of prescription stimulants among us college students: Prevalence and correlates from a national survey. *Addiction (Abingdon, England)* 100: pp. 96–106.

Marchant, N.L., Kamel, F., Echlin, K., Grice, J., Lewis, M., and Rusted, J.M. (2008) Modafinil improves rapid shifts of attention. *Psychopharmacology* 202: pp. 487–495.

Mintzer, M., and Griffiths, R. (2007) A triazolam/amphetamine dose—effect interaction study: Dissociation of effects on memory versus arousal. *Psychopharmacology* 192: pp. 425–440.

Ott, R., Lenk, C., Miller, N., Buhler, R.N., and Biller-Andorno, N. (2012) Neuroenhancement—Perspectives of Swiss psychiatrists and general practitioners. *Swiss Medical Weekly* 142: p. W13707.

Outram, S.M., and Racine, E. (2011) Developing public health approaches to cognitive enhancement: An analysis of current reports. *Public Health Ethics* 4: pp. 93–105.

Partridge, B.J., Bell, S.K., Lucke, J.C., Yeates, S., and Hall, W.D. (2011) Smart drugs "As Common As Coffee": Media hype about neuroenhancement. *PLoS One* 6: p. E28416.

Persson, I., and Savulescu, J. (2008) The perils of cognitive enhancement and the urgent imperative to enhance the moral character of humanity. *Journal of Applied Philosophy* 25: pp. 162–177.

Pitman, R., Sanders, K., Zusman, R., Healy, A., Cheema, F., Lasko, N., . . . Orr, S. (2002) Pilot study of secondary prevention of posttraumatic stress disorder with propanolol. *Biological Psychiatry* 51: pp. 189–192.

Raus, K., Focquaert, F., Schermer, M., Specker, J., and Sterckx, S. (2014) On defining moral enhancement: A clarificatory taxonomy. *Neuroethics* 7: pp. 263–273.

Ravelingien, A., Braeckman, J., Crevits, L., De Ridder, D., and Mortier, E. (2009) 'Cosmetic Neurology' and the moral complicity argument. *Neuroethics* 2: pp. 151–162.

Repantis, D., Laisney, O., and Heuser, I. (2010a) Acetylcholinesterase inhibitors and memantine for neuroenhancement in healthy individuals: A systematic review. *Pharmacological Research* 61: pp. 473–481.

Repantis, D., Schlattmann, P., Laisney, O., and Heuser, I. (2010b) Modafinil and methylphenidate for neuroenhancement in healthy individuals: A systematic review. *Pharmacological Research* 62: pp. 187–206.

Russo, M.B., Stetz, M.C., and Stetz, T.A. (2013) Brain enhancement in the military. In A. Chatterjee and M.J. Farah (Eds.). *Neuroethics in Practice: Medicine, Mind, and Society*. New York: Oxford University Press, pp. 35–45.

Rutherford, B.R., Mori, S., Sneed, J.R., Pimontel, M.A., and Roose, S.P. (2012) Contribution of spontaneous improvement to placebo response in depression: A meta-analytic review. *Journal of Psychiatric Research* 46: pp. 697–702.

Sahakian, B., and Morein-Zamir, S. (2007) Professor's little helper. *Nature* 450: pp. 1157–1159.

Savulescu, J. (2005) New breeds of humans: The moral obligation to enhance. *Reproductive Biomedicine Online* 10(Supp1): pp. 36–39.

Sax, L. (2003) Who first suggests the diagnosis of attention-deficit/hyperactivity disorder? *The Annals of Family Medicine* 1: pp. 171–174.

Schelle, K.J., Faulmüller, N., Caviola, L., and Hewstone, M. (2014) Attitudes toward pharmacological cognitive enhancement—A review. *Frontiers in Systems Neuroscience* 8: p. 53.

Schermer, M., Bolt, I., De Jongh, R., and Olivier, B. (2009) The future of psychopharmacological enhancements: Expectations and policies. *Neuroethics* 2: pp. 75–87.

Shook, J.R., Galvagni, L., and Giordano, J. (2014) Cognitive enhancement kept within contexts: Neuroethics and informed public policy. *Frontiers in Systems Neuroscience* 8: p. 228.

Singh, I., and Kelleher, K.J. (2013) Brain enhancement and children. In A. Chatterjee and M.J. Farah (Eds.). *Neuroethics in Practice: Medicine, Mind, and Society.* New York: Oxford University Press.

Singh, I., Kendall, T., Taylor, C., Mears, A., Hollis, C., Batty, M., and Keenan, S. (2010) Young people's experience of ADHD and stimulant medication: A qualitative study for the nice guideline. *Child and Adolescent Mental Health* 15: pp. 186–192.

Smith, E.M., and Farah, M.J. (2011) Are prescription stimulants "Smart Pills?" The epidemiology and cognitive neuroscience of prescription stimulant use by normal healthy individuals. *Psychological Bulletin* 137: pp. 717–741.

Strange, B., Hurlemann, R., and Dolan, R. (2003) An emotion-induced retrograde amnesia in humans is amygdala- and B-adrenergic-dependent. *Proceedings of the National Academy of Sciences America* 100: pp. 13626–13631.

Strawn, J.R., and Geracotti, T.D. (2008) Noradrenergic dysfunction and the psychopharmacology of post-traumatic stress disorder. *Depression and Anxiety* 25: pp. 260–271.

Synofzik, M. (2009) Ethically justified, clinically applicable criteria for physician decision-making in psychopharmacological enhancement. *Neuroethics* 2: pp. 89–102.

Talbot, M. (2009) Brain gain: The underground world of "Neuroenhancing" Drugs. *The New Yorker.*

Terbeck, S., Kahane, G., McTavish, S., Savulescu, J., Cowen, P., and Hewstone, M. (2012) Propranolol reduces implicit negative racial bias. *Psychopharmacology* 222: pp. 419–424.

Teter, C.J., McCabe, S.E., Cranford, J.A., Boyd, C.J., and Guthrie, S.K. (2005) Prevalence and motives for illicit use of prescription stimulants in an undergraduate student sample. *Journal of American College Health* 53: pp. 253–262.

Thomas, C.P., Conrad, P., Casler, R., and Goodman, E. (2006) Trends in the use of psychotropic medications among adolescents, 1994 to 2001. *Psychiatric Services* 57: pp. 63–69.

Tse, W., and Bond, A. (2002) Serotonergic intervention affects social dominance and affiliative behavior. *Psychopharmacology* 161: pp. 373–379.

Volkow, N.D., Fowler, J.S., Wang, G.-J., Telang, F., Logan, J., Wong, C., . . . Swanson, J.M. (2008) Methylphenidate decreased the amount of glucose needed by the brain to perform a cognitive task. *PLoS One* 3: p. E2017.

Vrecko, S. (2013) Just how cognitive is "Cognitive Enhancement"? on the significance of emotions in university students' experiences with study drugs. *American Journal of Bioethics Neuroscience* 4(1): pp. 4–12.

Walker-Batson, D., Curtis, S., Natarajan, R., Ford, J., Dronkers, N., Salmeron, E., . . . Unwin, D. (2001) A double-blind, placebo-controlled study of the use of amphetamine in the treatment of aphasia. *Stroke* 32: pp. 2093–2098.

Webb, J.R., Thomas, J.W., and Valasek, M.A. (2010) Contemplating cognitive enhancement in medical students and residents. *Perspectives in Biology and Medicine* 53: pp. 200–214.

Weber, P., and Lutschg, J. (2002) Methylphenidate treatment. *Pediatric Neurology* 26: pp. 261–266.

Whitaker, R. (2010) *Anatomy of an Epidemic: Magic Bullets, Psychiatric Drugs, and the Astonishing Rise of Mental Illness in America.* New York: Crown Publishing Group.

Whiting, E., Chenery, H., Chalk, J., Darnell, R., and Copland, D. (2007) Dexamphetamine enhances explicit new word learning for novel objects. *The International Journal of Neuropsychopharmacology* 10: pp. 805–816.

Wolpe, P. (2002) Treatment, enhancement, and the ethics of neurotherapeutics. *Brain and Cognition* 50: pp. 387–395.

Yesavage, J., Mumenthaler, M., Taylor, J., Friedman, L., O'Hara, R., Sheikh, J., . . . Whitehouse, P. (2001) Donepezil and flight simulator performance: Effects on retention of complex skills. *Neurology* 59: pp. 123–125.

Zaninotto, A.L.C., Bueno, O.F.A., Pradella-Hallinan, M., Tufik, S., Rusted, J., Stough, C., and Pompéia, S. (2009) Acute cognitive effects of donepezil in young, healthy volunteers. *Human Psychopharmacology: Clinical and Experimental* 24: pp. 453–464.

Zeeuws, I., Deroost, N., and Soetens, E. (2010) Effect of an acute D-amphetamine administration on context information memory in healthy volunteers: Evidence from a source memory task. *Human Psychopharmacology: Clinical and Experimental* 25: pp. 326–334.

Zohny, H. (2015) The myth of cognitive enhancement drugs. *Neuroethics*: pp. 1–13.

9

MODAFINIL AND THE INCREASING LIFESTYLE USE OF SMART DRUGS BY HEALTHY PEOPLE

Neuroethical and Societal Issues

Sebastian Porsdam Mann and Barbara J. Sahakian

Introduction

There is an increasing lifestyle use of modafinil and other cognitive-enhancing drugs by healthy people (Farah et al., 2004; Sahakian et al., 2015; Porsdam Mann and Sahakian, 2015). In this chapter, we will focus on modafinil and discuss its actions on neurotransmitters in the brain and the neuromodulation of different forms of cognition. We will then review the evidence for modafinil as a cognitive-enhancing drug. In addition, we will discuss the three main reasons for its increasing lifestyle use by healthy people:

1. To gain the competitive edge or superiority over others at school, university, or work.
2. To counteract the effects of jet lag, lack of sleep, or shift work.
3. To enhance motivation for tasks that are perceived by the user as not especially interesting or attractive to complete.

We will also reflect on some of the neuroethical issues in regard to the use of cognitive-enhancing drugs by healthy people.

Cognitive function is impaired in many psychiatric and neurological disorders. Conditions such as schizophrenia, depression, attention deficit hyperactivity disorder (ADHD), Alzheimer's disease, and traumatic brain injury are all marked by cognitive and functional impairment (Sahakian and Morein-Zamir, 2015). In addition to affecting individuals' functionality and well-being, these conditions are among the leading causes of disability worldwide and are costly to society (Whiteford et al., 2013; Wittchen et al., 2011). One estimate puts the financial burden of disorders of the brain in Europe at 798 billion euros in 2010 (Gustavsson et al., 2011). Conversely, sound cognitive function is fundamentally important for the economic and social progress of nations (Beddington et al., 2008). In a knowledge-based society characterized by the increasing importance of the creation and dissemination of information, cognition is a key factor in individual development and success (Castelfranchi, 2007; The Work Foundation, 2013).

A variety of methods can be used to treat cognitive impairment in neurodegenerative disease, neuropsychiatric disorder, or brain injury (Sahakian et al., 2015; Dresler et al., 2013). Cognitive training through the use of learning sessions and learning materials including video and other games improves cognition in a wide variety of disorders (Keshavan et al., 2014; Sahakian et al., 2015). High-quality nutrition and sleep have been shown to have beneficial effects on cognition (Ferrie et al., 2011; Northstone et al., 2012; Ellenbogen, 2005; Morley, 2013). Physical exercise has long been known to benefit cognitive function (Hillman et al., 2008; Erickson et al., 2015; Kent et al., 2015). More recently, evidence has emerged that meditation practice can increase cognitive function in persons with neurodegenerative disease (Marciniak et al., 2014). The non-invasive application of electromagnetic fields to the skull via transcranial magnetic stimulation (TMS) or through anodal or cathodal currents via transcranial direct current stimulation (tDCS) has also shown promising effects on cognitive function, though this research is still in its infancy (Kuo et al., 2014; Bennabi et al., 2014).

This chapter focuses on pharmacological cognitive enhancement (PCE). A number of drugs have been shown to improve cognitive function in psychiatric and neurological disorders. Cholinesterase inhibitors, such as donepezil, are used to stem decline in Alzheimer's disease (Howard et al., 2012). Stimulants such as methylphenidate (Ritalin) and amphetamine salts (Adderall) are used in the treatment of ADHD (Weyandt et al., 2014). Modafinil (Provigil) is a wake-promoting agent used to treat narcolepsy or excessive sleepiness or fatigue (Kumar, 2008).

Though these substances are prescribed to restore functioning or ameliorate impairment, there is evidence to suggest that they also enhance cognition in healthy people (Sahakian et al.; 2015; Husain and Mehta, 2011; Smith and Farah, 2011; Bagot and Kaminer, 2014; Battleday and Brem, 2015). Reports of healthy people using pharmacological cognitive enhancers have focused on students and academics, who may be using them to study longer, combat jetlag or increase task-related motivation (Maher, 2008; Sahakian et al., 2015; Müller et al., 2013). There are also reports of use among physicians and the military (Franke et al., 2013; Eliyahu et al., 2007). Very little is known about the use of these drugs in other groups.

The use of drugs for cognitive enhancement has many important practical and ethical implications. This chapter begins by examining some of the difficulties of defining cognitive enhancement. It then introduces the mode of action and effects of modafinil on healthy persons. Modafinil is chosen as a representative PCE for this discussion, as it has a similar profile of beneficial effects and is regarded as safer than traditional stimulants, since modafinil generally has less severe side effects and no significant abuse potential (Mereu et al., 2013; Porsdam Mann and Sahakian, 2015; Kim, 2012; Jasinski, 2000). The ethical issues surrounding cognitive enhancement, with a special focus on PCE using modafinil, are then discussed.

Cognition and Enhancement

"Cognition" is a general term for mental processes including attention, learning, memory, and executive functions such as planning and problem solving.

Definitions of human enhancement are actually difficult to construct. Savulescu et al. (2011) has defined a capacity as being enhanced if it is improved relative to its prior level of functioning, such that it increases the individual's chances of leading a good life—enhancement thus occurs regardless of how well or poorly functioning the capacity originally was.

In another sense, enhancements are "interventions designed to improve human form or functioning beyond what is necessary to sustain or restore good health" (Juengst, 1998, 29). On this view, those things that return good health are treatments; things that improve beyond good health are enhancements. However, this definition leaves open many questions about enhancement. Let us suppose enhancement refers to an improvement in functioning beyond a certain "normal" or "natural" level. This level could be thought of as some optimal level of functioning a person had previously enjoyed, but it could also be thought of as the level of functioning that is typical for humans in general (Sahakian et al., 2015; Daniels, 2000). If we consider the appropriate level to be one a person has previously enjoyed, does this mean that the use of PCEs to combat the effects of fatigue or jetlag is treatment, not enhancement? On this view, how far in the past the previous optimal level of performance lies has important implications. The position that enhancement refers to an improvement beyond a human-typical norm also faces hard questions. Imagine that a previously very highly intelligent person suffers a traumatic brain injury, with the result that they are now merely slightly more intelligent than average. We would likely consider their use of PCEs as restoration rather than enhancement, even though they are already above human-typical norms of intelligence.

These are just a few of the issues in a very active philosophical debate. For the purposes of this chapter, we consider a cognitive-enhancing drug to be a drug that leads to a demonstrated increase in performance on one or more cognitive measures, as evidenced by a double-blind, placebo-controlled experimental study, regardless of previous level of function or performance.

Modafinil: Mechanisms of Action in the Brain

Modafinil is a wakefulness-promoting drug. It is indicated for use in narcolepsy, obstructive sleep apnea, and shift-work sleep disorder by the Food and Drug Administration (FDA) in the United States, although it is often prescribed off-label for fatigue secondary to illness and for cognitive stimulation in neurological and neuropsychiatric disorder (Kumar, 2008; FDA, 2015). The only indication for modafinil in Europe (European Medicines Agency, 2011) is narcolepsy. Modafinil acts on many neurotransmitters, and it is not clear how it exerts its cognitive-enhancing effects, although this is likely to be through its effects on noradrenaline, dopamine, and glutamate (Scoriels and Jones, 2013; Sahakian et al., 2015). Modafinil blocks dopamine transporter function and elevates dopamine levels in the caudate, putamen, and nucleus accumbens in healthy people and is in this way similar to other stimulants (Volkow et al., 2009). However, the behavioral effects of modafinil differ from those of typical stimulants such as amphetamine (Minzenberg and Carter, 2008). Modafinil appears to increase extracellular serotonin and noradrenaline concentration in areas that modulate forms of cognition (Mereu et al., 2013). Modafinil increases concentrations of glutamate in several areas of the brain, including the thalamus and hippocampus, and decreases GABA concentrations in the same areas and in the cortex (Minzenberg and Carter, 2008). Modafinil may also have effects on cholinergic, histamine, and orexin systems (Mereu et al., 2013). Many of these effects interact, so the precise mechanisms of action of modafinil in enhancing cognition remain unknown (Kumar, 2008).

Modafinil: Cognitive Effects in Healthy People

The impact of modafinil on cognitive function is measured by the use of objective cognitive tests. These tests are usually administered on a computer or tablet that records objective measurements, such as the number of correct and incorrect attempts and reaction time. One set of tests frequently used in studies on modafinil and in other cognitive studies is the CANTAB Neuropsychological Test Automated Battery (www.cantab.com), developed in Cambridge and used worldwide. The CANTAB battery consists of 25 individual tasks designed to measure a specific aspect of a cognitive function such as attention or memory. Each task is a short, game-like scenario in which participants are scored on their ability to respond to stimuli, memorize patterns, or plan strategically. In the Paired Associates Learning (PAL) test, for example, subjects are shown patterns of objects in particular areas of the screen and then tested on their ability to associate a pattern with a specific spatial location. By measuring the accuracy and speed of responses, researchers can compare an individual's performance against the normal score for a person of their age. Researchers can also estimate the impact a drug such as modafinil is having on cognitive performance by comparing the scores of individuals given the drug to the scores of similar subjects given a pharmacologically inert placebo pill. The many neurochemical actions of modafinil are reflected in the drug's effects on performance in such cognitive tests. Modafinil impacts both "hot" and "cold" cognition (Roiser and Sahakian, 2013). Cold cognition is nonemotional cognition, for example, decision making in the absence of emotions and risk. Conversely, hot cognition refers to emotional and social cognition and includes, for example, risky decision making or emotional face recognition (Scoriels et al., 2011). There is much evidence that emotions and risk can influence decision making and that separate neural systems are involved in hot and cold cognition (Sahakian and LaBuzetta, 2013).

Most studies have examined modafinil's effects on cold cognition. For example, two studies with 20 and 32 test subjects per arm, respectively, found evidence that modafinil improves scores on measures of delayed memory, reaction time, working memory, and executive functioning (e.g., planning and decision making; Turner et al., 2003; Müller et al., 2013).

A recent meta-analysis examined the existing literature, synthesizing the results of 24 placebo-controlled studies of modafinil in healthy volunteers (Battleday and Brem, 2015). The review found that the effects of modafinil were most pronounced on complex executive-function tasks requiring integration and manipulation of diverse information.

These tests measure the use of multiple domains of memory, attention, and executive functioning, and are thus more likely to reflect the demands of real-life cognitive tasks, which seldom rely on one aspect of cognitive function alone. One study, for example, examined the ability of test subjects to switch their attention to object features relevant at different times while retaining object positions in memory and responding quickly to test questions (Pringle et al., 2013). This task measured implicit learning, memory, response time, and attentional flexibility and is thus a good example of a complex task. Modafinil improved both reaction time and accuracy in all sets of trials, suggesting a positive effect on the implicit rule learning necessary to score highly on this task. Modafinil also increased performance on other complex tasks of attention, executive functions, and memory, as originally reported by Turner and colleagues (Marchant et al., 2009; Finke et al., 2010; Geng et al., 2013; Gilleen et al., 2014; Turner et al., 2003).

Overall, of the 24 included studies, 19 demonstrated an improvement in one or more cognitive measures, and 5 reported no effects on any measures.

Effects on hot cognition have also been reported, though most of this research has focused on patients with neuropsychiatric disorders rather than on healthy volunteers. Hot cognition can be tested using tasks that include risks and rewards, often using a design that allocates points (which may correspond to real money) through winning bets based on various contingencies.

In one study (Turner et al., 2003), a token was hidden behind one of 10 red or blue boxes; varying the number of boxes and likelihood of the token appearing in a red or blue box, the researchers were able to test risky decision making under various conditions. In this study, ingesting modafinil led to longer deliberation time (that is, less impulsiveness) without loss of quality of choice. Modafinil has also been shown to improve emotional face recognition in patients with first-episode schizophrenia (Scoriels et al., 2011). Current tests of emotional face recognition are not sensitive enough for persons without impairment, though such tests are currently being developed. Instead, research into modafinil's impact on hot cognition in healthy, non–sleep-deprived volunteers has found that modafinil use impacts the subjective feeling of carrying out tasks.

Müller and colleagues (2013) found that modafinil administration very significantly increased task-related motivation without producing a general state of pleasure such as that associated with euphoric drugs. Another study found increased task enjoyment only on more demanding tasks (Stoops et al., 2005). A qualitative study found that modafinil and other cognitive-enhancing drugs increased positive emotional states in students interviewed, such as "feeling up," "drivenness," "interestedness," and "enjoyment" (Vrecko, 2013). Another found that cognitive enhancers, in particular methylphenidate and amphetamine, were seen as beneficial for increasing concentration and motivation but also for leading an active life, achieving a work–life balance, and having time left over for personal and social activities and that these effects were more often sought than academic enhancement (Hildt et al., 2014). These results suggest that modafinil and other cognitive enhancers have beneficial effects on some hot cognitive processes, particularly improving levels of motivation, concentration, and task enjoyment. Importantly, though there is much evidence that modafinil enhances cognitive performance in healthy, non–sleep-deprived individuals, it should be noted that these effects are usually small to moderate (Sahakian and Morein-Zamir, 2015; Sahakian et al., 2015; Battleday and Brem, 2015; Repantis et al., 2010; Husain and Mehta, 2011).

The effects on sleep-deprived individuals have also been studied and have shown positive effects of modafinil administration. For example, modafinil improved performance on tasks of working memory, planning, decision making, and the cognitive flexibility of doctors tested after one night of sleep deprivation (Sugden et al., 2012). Another study found improvements on a test of continuous performance among sleep-deprived emergency room physicians (Gill et al., 2006). Military pilots deprived of sleep for 37 hours performed within 15% to 30% of their baseline function given modafinil, whereas those without modafinil deteriorated by as much as 60% to 100% (Caldwell et al., 2004). Subjects in Caldwell's study who were given modafinil also reported decreased feelings of anger and depression and increased feelings of vigor and alertness.

Modafinil: Side Effects and Safety

Although modafinil is generally well tolerated, a range of side effects are associated with its use. These include dizziness, insomnia, skin rashes, nausea, headache, diarrhea, and psychiatric symptoms such as feeling anxious or depressed (FDA, 2015). In the study of sleep-deprived doctors mentioned earlier, modafinil improved tests of cognitive function without evidence of common side effects associated with caffeine, such as anxiety and tremor (Sugden et al., 2012). Other studies have documented side effects. One study retrospectively analyzed all cases of modafinil overdose with follow-up to known outcome reported to the California Poison Control System over 10 years (1998–2008; Carstairs et al., 2010). The authors found a total of 87 reports. Dividing the cases into categories of clinical severity, the authors classified 11 cases as moderately severe, 54 of minor severity, and 22 of no severity at all. However, at least five cases of very serious skin conditions have been reported in children and adolescents with ADHD between 1999 and 2007 (Rugino, 2007). There was one report of a complex case in which a patient who had taken modafinil died, and therefore, since 2006, the package insert for modafinil has been modified to include a warning relating to multi-organ hypersensitivity reactions (Sabatine et al., 2007). To our knowledge, this is the only such published case report. There is a de facto consensus that modafinil does not have abuse potential; at least, abuse potential has not been demonstrated (Mereu et al., 2013; Jasinski, 2000; Sahakian et al., 2015). When considering the safety profile of modafinil, it is important to keep the safety profile of other drugs in mind (Porsdam Mann and Sahakian, 2015). Although estimates vary, it is clear that nonsteroidal anti-inflammatory drugs such as aspirin and ibuprofen are responsible for tens of thousands of premature deaths each year (Singh, 1998; Lanas et al., 2005). It should also be noted that adverse events from modafinil are more likely at doses higher than those typically used for cognitive enhancement in healthy individuals (1–200 mg; Carstairs et al., 2010). Although acute use of moderate doses of modafinil for cognitive enhancement appears safe, there is no data on the effects of long-term use in healthy people, and those obtaining the drug through the internet face additional risks of purchasing a contaminated or counterfeit drug (Sahakian and Morein-Zamir, 2007). The issue of safety is discussed more fully elsewhere (Porsdam Mann and Sahakian, 2015).

Current Use of PCEs by Healthy Individuals

Most studies of the use of PCEs have focused on use by students and academics. Due to differences in definitions, design, and demographics of those questioned, the results of these studies tend to vary greatly (Sahakian et al., 2015). An online poll run by *Nature* found that one in five respondents admitted to having used PCEs for nonmedical purposes, with 62% of those having used methylphenidate and 44% having used modafinil (Maher, 2008). One study identified 25 surveys of nonmedical stimulant use in colleges and universities, with estimates ranging from 2.5% to 35.3% (Smith and Farah, 2011). Most of these estimates were contained in the 5% to 20% range. More recent estimates from Europe show slightly lower rates of use, with 7.6% of Swiss students in a large survey admitting to having used prescription drugs for cognitive enhancement, and rates of 1% to 4% in Denmark, Belgium, and Germany (Maier et al., 2013; Ragan et al., 2013). Another survey found a prevalence of 8.9% in German surgeons (Franke et al., 2013). The military also uses modafinil (Eliyahu et al., 2007). Data on use in the workforce and in the wider population remains scarce.

Ethical Considerations

We have seen that healthy volunteers who take modafinil score higher on tests of cognitive function. These improvements are likely the result of modafinil's effects on various neurochemical pathways but also of the subjective effects on motivation, energy, and enjoyment (Müller et al., 2013). We have also seen that a significant minority of students, academics, and some professionals currently use modafinil and that it is considered to be free of abuse potential and relatively safe in the short term. However, there have been no studies investigating the effects of long-term use, and many people obtain the drug through the internet with no quality control. Apart from issues of safety and efficacy, we might want to ask whether it is ethical to use modafinil or similar drugs, sometimes or ever, as a cognitively healthy person.

Enhancement Research in Healthy People

Research on enhancement in healthy people is conducted for three main reasons: first in proof-of-concept studies to discover novel, effective cognitive-enhancing drugs, which can then be used in large-scale clinical trials in people with neuropsychiatric disorders and brain injury; second to understand the action of current treatments for cognitive symptoms in neuropsychiatric disorders, such as methylphenidate for attention deficit hyperactivity disorder, in order to facilitate development of treatments with even greater efficacy; and third to use drugs as tools to investigate how certain neurotransmitters, such as dopamine and noradrenaline, neuromodulate specific cognitive functions, including attention, learning, memory, planning, and problem solving. Because the ethical justifiability of pharmacological research with human subjects is generally predicated on the potential medical benefits, which include reducing suffering and illness, there is some doubt as to whether research investigating enhancement effects can be justified in the same way. But others argue that such research is justified by the benefits, whether or not these pertain to healthy or diseased individuals.

Is It Unethical to Use a Safe, Effective PCE?

This question has been approached from many angles. Michael Sandel has argued that enhancements of any kind are unethical, because they reflect a rejection of the gifted quality of human existence in favor of the pursuit of mastery (Sandel, 2007). Sandel argues that there is a special quality inherent in the world we find ourselves in ("the given world"), which is threatened by the desire to improve it or ourselves ("the drive to mastery") beyond the limits set by a healthy, unenhanced existence. Sandel illustrates what he means by analogy to parenting: "To appreciate children as gifts is to accept them as they come, not as objects of our design, or products of our will, or instruments of our ambition" (Sandel, 2007, 45). To aim to improve these children is to make loving them conditional upon their achievements rather than accepting them as they are, as for example when a parent attempts to arrange their child's future career by forcing them against their will to practice the piano or study for excessively long hours. Similarly, argues Sandel, when we use enhancement technologies, we fail to appreciate the world and ourselves as we are and lose respect for the given through the drive to mastery of ever-higher achievements.

Although Sandel has emphasized a genuine worry many people will share, as Tim Lewens has pointed out, there are a number of problems in using this worry to support a blanket ban on enhancements (Lewens, 2009). For example, Sandel argues that illness and disability are not part of the given but rather that attempts to treat them allow natural capacities to flourish (Sandel, 2007, 46). It is not obvious why correcting bad eyesight with lenses, to choose one example, should be considered allowing natural capacities to flourish rather than overriding natural capacities. What should we say about vaccinations that do not treat a disease but aim to prevent it? Do they count as overriding natural capacities? And if they do not, what can be meant by natural capacities, other than "those capacities that the person might obtain, given the right interventions" (Lewens, 2009, 355)? More generally, the case Sandel makes appears to be against the drive for mastery (wherein the end goal is continually escalated to a higher level) rather than enhancement or improvement itself. We may well agree with him that acting as the designer of a child's life against their expressed wishes is unethical. But this does not mean that all cases of enhancement will follow this pattern; some level of involvement in the child's life by her parents, or by any person in their own life, is crucial for future success and happiness, and we cannot rely on a distinction between "natural" and "unnatural" means of involvement to justify banning those we do not agree with. Corrective lenses and vaccinations are far removed from our "natural" state, and many would consider these as being similar to the use of enhancement technologies. There is a wide variety of views as to whether there is a distinction between enhancing studying by using a tutor, compared to using a cognitive-enhancing or "smart" drug.

Another general set of worries about enhancement concern the implications for our sense of self and authorship over our actions. Nick Agar, for example, has given a sophisticated defense of the view that radical enhancements—enhancements that improve functioning far beyond recognizably human levels—would change recipients so much that they would no longer be the same persons, because they would not be psychologically and/or physically continuous with the persons they once were (Agar, 2014). That is, they would not resemble their unenhanced selves in any meaningful way. Agar also raises the worry that radically enhanced persons might become a different kind of being altogether, with moral status greater than unenhanced persons due to their superior faculties.

Apart from these general enhancement issues, there are a number of specific problems raised in the context of cognitive enhancement using modafinil. We will argue that these are genuine issues that need to be dealt with through appropriate public- and private-sector policies. However, it's important to distinguish modafinil and other PCEs from nonpharmacological cognitive enhancements in ethically meaningful ways.

A recent study reviewed 40 surveys of public opinion on the use of PCEs (Schelle et al., 2014). The authors found that both the surveys and the academic literature agreed on issues thought to be important. These issues were classified into three categories: medical safety, coercion, and fairness. As safety has been discussed already, we will examine the issues of coercion and fairness in turn.

Coercion

Coercion can be either implicit or explicit. Explicit coercion takes the form of rules, pressure, threats, or instructions expressly given with the intention of shaping behavior. An example of explicit coercion is jury duty. In countries with a jury system, an appropriately appointed juror must show up for duty or face legal penalties. Implicit coercion is pressure that arises from the expectations or behavior of others rather than explicit rules. It takes the form of perceived pressure to conform and to do what is expected rather than penalties for noncompliance. A society where most but not all students or professionals in important roles use PCEs could be one in which there exists implicit coercion. Some might not want to take a PCE but do so anyway for fear of losing out or underperforming relative to their peers who are taking PCEs.

Both implicit and explicit coercion are serious problems. Explicit coercion is more easily addressable, as rules can be discussed and changed. If requirements to take PCEs are seen as problematic, the option exists to simply change the rules. In this way, explicit coercion is not a problem specific to the use of PCEs. One might equally well imagine an employer creating rules that require employees to be well rested or to engage in physical activity as a condition of continued employment and all the problems this might bring. However, implicit coercion is not so easily addressed. The attitudes of employers or peers cannot be changed by decree.

A recent survey of German university students found that the willingness to take a hypothetical PCE increased in conditions in which more peers were also using it (Sattler et al., 2014). In the *Nature* poll, a third of respondents said they would feel pressure to give PCEs to their children if they knew that other children were using PCEs at their school (Maher, 2008). Implicit coercion is thus a legitimate concern. Steps toward reducing its influence could be taken, such as explicit statements by employers or educators that they do not expect their employees or students to use PCEs and that they will not be penalized if they choose not to do so. It is unlikely that implicit coercion can be fully eliminated. It is well known that there are other means of enhancing cognition and work or school performance, such as private tutors, meditation, physical exercise, sleep hygiene, and improved nutrition. These, too, have benefits and side effects (financial and opportunity costs) and may well have the potential to affect the health and well-being of those who utilize them. Thus, the problem of coercion is a general one that should be acknowledged and discussed at the level of the workplace, school, or institution.

Fairness

Fairness is one of the most important considerations in the ethics of pharmacological cognitive enhancement, and it encompasses a number of specific issues. One might think, for example, that the use of PCEs in the workplace or institute is unfair because it is cheating, just as doping is cheating in competitive sports. Duke University considers "the unauthorized use of prescription medication to enhance academic performance" to be cheating (Duke Student Affairs, 2015). In the case of Duke, the use of PCEs can be considered unfair because it contravenes an explicit rule. Cognitive enhancement may have widespread benefits for society (Porsdam Mann and Sahakian, 2015; Academy of Medical Sciences, 2012) if improving cognitive function in an individual could lead to gains that might be beneficial in terms of new inventions or more rapid discoveries. However, in academic exam situations, in which one student taking a PCE may gain relative to a student who does not, there may be concerns about cheating and coercion.

Even if using PCEs is not considered cheating, it may well be unfair for other reasons. A closely related issue concerns authenticity. The President's Council on Bioethics, for example, raised the concern that the achievements of the enhanced are perhaps not attributable to their unenhanced state (President's Council on Bioethics, 2003). Thus, if a student uses a PCE to aid their studies and achieves a high mark, it may be that the student cannot claim full credit for the distinction, because part of it is due to the drug. Another angle on this issue is the claim that hard work and effort are what make achievements worthwhile, and without them, achievements do not mean the same thing.

There is certainly some truth to the claim that hard work and effort are part of what we admire about outstanding achievements. It is also true that it might be easier to achieve a high mark if one engages in certain behaviors such as getting enough sleep, eating well, and scheduling study sessions, which are all generally accepted means of enhancing oneself. More importantly, the material costs and restricted methods of access to PCEs may lead to problems of unequal access (Farah et al., 2004). Thus, it may be that those who possess the greatest means can use their privileged access to PCEs to enrich themselves further, while those without means become even worse off in comparison. It is true that we should avoid a society in which the benefits of technological advances are reserved only for the elite. But there is little reason to believe this is or will be the case with PCEs. The products of technological breakthroughs tend to start out very expensive, so that very few can afford to use them. Within a few decades, the products are usually cheap enough to be enjoyed by many others—think of mobile phones or laptop computers. It would have been a great shame if computers or phones were banned on the grounds that they would benefit the well off more than the not-so-well off. That a benefit cannot be supplied to all is no reason to ban it for everyone. John Harris has argued that "fairness might require that we make all reasonable attempts to achieve universal provision," but it does not require preventing access for those who can obtain it until everyone can, for "just as it is not wrong to save some lives when all cannot be saved, so it is not wrong to advantage some in ways that also confer a positional advantage when all cannot be bettered in those ways," (Harris, 2007, 28). In fact, the use of PCEs may be one of the least troublesome cognitive-enhancing methods with respect to distributive justice. Whereas places in elite private schools and universities are both limited and very expensive, PCEs are comparatively cheaper and could in the future be made easily accessible if shown to be safe and effective in healthy people in the workplace. Indeed, generic drugs are relatively inexpensive compared to drugs on patent. There is also some evidence that some PCEs may have greater effects in those with *lower* baseline performance (del Campo et al., 2013; Mehta et al., 2001; Randall, et al., 2005; Finke et al., 2010). Furthermore, a qualitative study found that students who are more likely to procrastinate and have high cognitive test anxiety and lower intrinsic motivation to study are also more likely to use PCEs (Sattler et al., 2014). Thus, it may be that those who most need PCEs also benefit more from them. Therefore, improving cognition and well-being in the general population could lead to economic benefits (Beddington et al., 2008). It is important to consider how to benefit those members of society who are disadvantaged and vulnerable and who might need enhancement the most. If cognitive enhancers such as modafinil disproportionately benefit those less well off, they might help to mitigate the negative impacts on cognition of socioeconomic disadvantages such as poor nutrition and schooling and exposure to environmental hazards.

Conclusion

Research on PCEs, in particular modafinil, has demonstrated beneficial cognitive effects in healthy, non-sleep-deprived volunteers on both hot and cold cognitions. Prevalence data indicate that a considerable proportion of students and academics are already using PCEs for non-medical reasons, though there is very little data on whether others are also using these drugs. The use of modafinil in the short term appears safe, but no data from long term studies in healthy people is available, so we cannot tell whether chronic use may be associated with different or cumulative health risks. Whether modafinil still has cognitive-enhancing effects when used chronically by healthy people remains to be determined. In addition, many persons obtain PCEs through the internet, which carries additional health risks due to the lack of quality control. There are important ethical issues relating to fairness and coercion in nonmedical use of modafinil and other PCEs, and these concerns, as well as the benefits of using PCEs in healthy people, are ever-growing and important societal issues. There is a drive for individuals to enhance themselves, and society must consider what means we should use and when it is acceptable to do so. In this way, we can ensure that advances are, all things considered, to the benefit of society.

Acknowledgments

Barbara J. Sahakian is a paid member of the Human Brain Project. We thank Jonathan Shepherd for his comments on this manuscript.

Further Reading

Academy of Medical Sciences. (2012) Human enhancement and the future of work. In *Report from a Joint Workshop Hosted by the Academy of Medical Sciences, the British Academy, the Royal Academy of Engineering and the Royal Society* (Ed. Academy of Medical Sciences). London: The Academy of Medical Sciences. Available at: https://royalsociety.org/~/media/policy/projects/human-enhancement/2012-11-06-human-enhancement.pdfhttps://royalsociety.org/~/media/policy/projects/human-enhancement/2012-11-06-human-enhancement.pdf

Brühl, A.B. and Sahakian, B.J. (2016) "Drugs, Games, and Devices for Enhancing Cognition: Implications for Work and Society". *Annals of the New York Academy of Sciences* 1369, 195–217.

Greely, H., Sahakian, B.J., Harris, J., Kessler, R.C., Gazzaniga, M., Campbell, P., Farah, M.J. (2008) "Towards Responsible Use of Cognitive-Enhancing Drugs by the Healthy". *Nature* 456, 702–705.

Porsdam Mann, S. and Sahakian, B.J. (2015) "The Increasing Lifestyle Use of Modafinil by Healthy People: Safety and Ethical Issues". *Current Opinion in Behavioral Sciences* 4, 136–141.

Sahakian, B.J., Brühl, A.B., Cook, J., Killikelly, C., Savulich, G., Piercy, T., . . . Jones, P.B. (2015) "The Impact of Neuroscience on Society: Cognitive Enhancement in Neuropsychiatric Disorders and in Healthy People". *Philosophical Transactions of the Royal Society* B 370(1677): pp. 20140214.

References

Academy of Medical Sciences. (2012) Human enhancement and the future of work. In *Report From a Joint Workshop Hosted by the Academy of Medical Sciences, the British Academy, the Royal Academy of Engineering and the Royal Society* (Ed. Academy of Medical Sciences). London: The Academy of Medical Sciences. Available at: https://royalsociety.org/~/media/policy/projects/human-enhancement/2012–11–06-human-enhancement.pdf [Accessed 22 Sept. 2015].

Agar, N. (2014) *Truly Human Enhancement: A Philosophical Defense of Limits*. Boston: MIT University Press.

Bagot, K.S., and Kaminer, Y. (2014) Efficacy of stimulants for cognitive enhancement in non-attention deficit hyperactivity disorder youth: A systematic review. *Addiction (Abingdon, England)* 109(4): pp. 547–57. Available at: www.pubmedcentral.nih.gov/articlerender.fcgi?artid=4471173&tool=pmcentrez&rendertype=abstract [Accessed 3 Sept. 2015].

Battleday, R.M., and Brem, A.-K. (2015) Modafinil for cognitive neuroenhancement in healthy non-sleep-deprived subjects: A systematic review. *European Neuropsychopharmacology*. Available at: www.sciencedirect.com/science/article/pii/S0924977X15002497 [Accessed 20 Aug. 2015].

Beddington, J., Cooper, C.L., Field, J., Goswami, U., Huppert, F.A., Jenkins, R., Jones, H.S., Kirkwood, T.B., Sahakian, B.J. and Thomas, S.M. (2008) The mental wealth of nations. *Nature* 455(7216): pp. 1057–1060. Available at: http://dx.doi.org/10.1038/4551057a [Accessed 17 June 2015].

Bennabi, D., Pedron, S., Haffen, E., Monnin, J., Peterschmitt, Y. and Van Waes, V. (2014) Transcranial direct current stimulation for memory enhancement: From clinical research to animal models. *Frontiers in Systems Neuroscience* 8: p. 159. Available at: /pmc/articles/PMC4154388/?report=abstract [Accessed 3 Sept. 2015].

Caldwell, J.A., Caldwell, J.L., Smith, J.K. and Brown, D.L. (2004) Modafinil's effects on simulator performance and mood in pilots during 37 h without sleep. *Aviation, Space, and Environmental Medicine* 75(9): pp. 777–784. Available at: www.ncbi.nlm.nih.gov/pubmed/15460629 [Accessed 9 Sept. 2015].

Carstairs, S.D., Urquhart, A., Hoffman, J., Clark, R.F. and Cantrell, F.L. (2010) A retrospective review of supratherapeutic modafinil exposures. *Journal of Medical Toxicology : Official Journal of the American College of Medical Toxicology* 6(3): pp. 307–310. Available at: www.pubmedcentral.nih.gov/articlerender.fcgi?artid=2929436&tool=pmcentrez&rendertype=abstract [Accessed 9 Sept. 2015].

Castelfranchi, C. (2007) Six critical remarks on science and the construction of the knowledge society. *Journal of Science Communication* 6(4): pp. 1–3.

Daniels, N. (2000) Normal functioning and the treatment-enhancement distinction. *Cambridge Quarterly of Healthcare Ethics: CQ: The International Journal of Healthcare Ethics Committees* 9(3): pp. 309–322. Available at: www.ncbi.nlm.nih.gov/pubmed/10858880 [Accessed 3 Sept. 2015].

del Campo, N., Fryer, T.D., Hong, Y.T., Smith, R., Brichard, L., Acosta-Cabronero, J., Chamberlain, S.R., Tait, R., Izquierdo, D., Regenthal, R., Dowson, J., Suckling, J., Baron, J.-C., Aigbirhio, F.I., Robbins, T.W., Sahakian, B.J. and Müller, U. (2013). A positron emission tomography study of nigro-striatal dopaminergic mechanisms underlying attention: Implications for ADHD and its treatment. *Brain: A Journal of Neurology* 136(pt 11): pp. 3252–3270. doi: 10.1093/brain/awt263.

Dresler, M., Sandberg, A., Ohla, K., Bublitz, C., Trenado, C., Mroczko-Wąsowicz, A., Kühn, S. and Repantis, D. (2013) Non-pharmacological cognitive enhancement. *Neuropharmacology* 64: pp. 529–543. Available at: www.sciencedirect.com/science/article/pii/S0028390812003310 [Accessed 2 Sept. 2015].

Duke Student Affairs. (2015) Academic Dishonesty Available. at: https://studentaffairs.duke.edu/conduct/z-policies/academic-dishonesty [Accessed 10 Sept. 2015].

Eliyahu, U., Berlin, S., Hadad, E., Heled, Y. and Moran, D.S. (2007) Psychostimulants and military operations. *Military Medicine* 172(4): pp. 383–387. Available at: www.ncbi.nlm.nih.gov/pubmed/17484308 [Accessed 3 Sept. 2015].

Ellenbogen, J.M. (2005) Cognitive benefits of sleep and their loss due to sleep deprivation. *Neurology* 64(7): pp. E25—E27. Available at: www.neurology.org/content/64/7/E25.full [Accessed 3 Sept. 2015].

Erickson, K.I., Hillman, C.H., and Kramer, A.F. (2015) Physical activity, brain, and cognition. *Current Opinion in Behavioral Sciences* 4: pp. 27–32. Available at: www.sciencedirect.com/science/article/pii/S2352154615000157 [Accessed 17 Sept. 2015].

European Medicines Agency. (2011) *Questions and answers on the review of medicines containing modafinil*. London. Available at: www.ema.europa.eu/docs/en_GB/document_library/Referrals_document/Modafinil_31/WC500099177.pdf [Accessed: 4 September 2015].

Farah, M.J., Illes, J., Cook-Deegan, R., Gardner, H., Kandel, E., King, P., Parens, E., Sahakian, B. and Wolpe, P.R. (2004) Neurocognitive enhancement: What can we do and what should we do? *Nature Reviews Neuroscience* 5(5): pp. 421–5. Available at: www.ncbi.nlm.nih.gov/pubmed/15100724 [Accessed 5 Sept. 2015].

Food and Drug Administration. (2015) *Medication Guide: Provigil*. Available at: www.fda.gov/downloads/Drugs/DrugSafety/UCM231722.pdf [Accessed 9 Sept. 2015].

Ferrie, J.E., Shipley, M.J., Akbaraly, T.N., Marmot, M.G., Kivimäki, M. and Singh-Manoux, A. (2011) Change in sleep duration and cognitive function: Findings from the Whitehall II Study. *Sleep* 34(5): pp. 565–73.

Finke, K., Dodds, C.M., Bublak, P., Regenthal, R., Baumann, F., Manly, T. and Müller, U. (2010) Effects of modafinil and methylphenidate on visual attention capacity: A TVA-based study. *Psychopharmacology* 210(3): pp. 317–29. Available at: www.ncbi.nlm.nih.gov/pubmed/20352415 [Accessed 31 Aug. 2015].

Franke, A.G., Bagusat, C., Dietz, P., Hoffmann, I., Simon, P., Ulrich, R. and Lieb, K. (2013) Use of illicit and prescription drugs for cognitive or mood enhancement among surgeons. *BMC Medicine* 11(1): p. 102. Available at: www.biomedcentral.com/1741-7015/11/102 [Accessed 25 July 2015].

Geng, J.J., Soosman, S., Sun, Y., Diquattro, N.E., Stankevitch, B. and Minzenberg, M.J. (2013). A match made by modafinil: Probability matching in choice decisions and spatial attention. *Journal of Cognitive Neuroscience* 25(5): pp. 657–669. Available at: www.ncbi.nlm.nih.gov/pubmed/23190326 [Accessed 9 Sept. 2015].

Gill, M. Haerich, P., Westcott, K., Godenick, K.L. and Tucker, J.A. (2006) Cognitive performance following modafinil versus placebo in sleep-deprived emergency physicians: A double-blind randomized crossover study. *Academic Emergency Medicine: Official Journal of the Society for Academic Emergency Medicine* 13(2): pp. 158–165. Available at: www.ncbi.nlm.nih.gov/pubmed/16436796 [Accessed 9 Sept. 2015].

Gilleen, J., Michalopoulou, P.G., Reichenberg, A., Drake, R., Wykes, T., Lewis, S.W. and Kapur, S. (2014) Modafinil combined with cognitive training is associated with improved learning in healthy volunteers— A randomised controlled trial. *European Neuropsychopharmacology : The Journal of the European College of Neuropsychopharmacology* 24(4): pp. 529–539. Available at: www.ncbi.nlm.nih.gov/pubmed/24485800 [Accessed 9 Sept. 2015].

Gustavsson, A., Svensson, M., Jacobi, F., Allgulander, C., Alonso, J., Beghi, E., Dodel, R., Ekman, M., Faravelli, C., Fratiglioni, L., Gannon, B., Jones, D.H., Jennum, P., Jordanova, A., Jönsson, L., Karampampa, K., Knapp, M., Kobelt, G., Kurth, T., Lieb, R., Linde, M., Ljungcrantz, C., Maercker, A., Melin, B., Moscarelli, M., Musayev, A., Norwood, F., Preisig, M., Pugliatti, M., Rehm, J., Salvador-Carulla, L., Schlehofer, B., Simon, R., Steinhausen, H.C., Stovner, L.J., Vallat, J.M., Van den Bergh, P., van Os, J., Vos, P., Xu, W., Wittchen, H.U., Jönsson, B., Olesen, J. and CDBE2010 Study Group. (2011) Cost of disorders of the brain in Europe 2010. *European Neuropsychopharmacology : The Journal of the European College of Neuropsychopharmacology* 21(10): pp. 718–779. Available at: www.ncbi.nlm.nih.gov/pubmed/21924589 [Accessed 11 Jan. 2015].

Harris, J. (2007) *Enhancing Evolution: The Ethical Case for Making People Better*. Princeton, NJ: Princeton University Press.

Hildt, E., Lieb, K., and Franke, A.G. (2014) Life context of pharmacological academic performance enhancement among university students—A qualitative approach. *BMC Medical Ethics* 15: p. 23. Available at: www.pubmedcentral.nih.gov/articlerender.fcgi?artid=3973848&tool=pmcentrez&rendertype=abstract [Accessed 2 Sept. 2015].

Hillman, C.H., Erickson, K.I., and Kramer, A.F. (2008) Be smart, exercise your heart: exercise effects on brain and cognition. *Nature Reviews Neuroscience* 9(1): pp. 58–65. Available at: http://dx.doi.org/10.1038/nrn2298 [Accessed 21 Jan. 2015].

Howard, R., McShane, R., Lindesay, J., Ritchie, C., Baldwin, A., Barber, R., Burns, A., Dening, T., Findlay, D., Holmes, C., Hughes, A., Jacoby, R., Jones, R., McKeith, I., Macharouthu, A., O'Brien, J., Passmore, P., Sheehan, B., Juszczak, E., Katona, C., Hills, R., Knapp, M., Ballard, C., Brown, R., Banerjee, S.,

Onions, C., Griffin, M., Adams, J., Gray, R., Johnson, T., Bentham, P. and Phillips, P. (2012) Donepezil and memantine for moderate-to-severe Alzheimer's disease. *New England Journal of Medicine* 366(10): pp. 893–903. Available at: www.ncbi.nlm.nih.gov/pubmed/22397651 [Accessed 20 July 2015].

Husain, M., and Mehta, M.A. (2011). Cognitive enhancement by drugs in health and disease. *Trends in Cognitive Sciences* 15(1): pp. 28–36. Available at: www.pubmedcentral.nih.gov/articlerender.fcgi?artid= 3020278&tool=pmcentrez&rendertype=abstract [Accessed 27 July 2015].

Jasinski, D.R. (2000) An evaluation of the abuse potential of modafinil using methylphenidate as a reference. *Journal of Psychopharmacology (Oxford, England)* 14(1): pp. 53–60. Available at: www.ncbi.nlm.nih.gov/ pubmed/10757254 [Accessed 3 Sept. 2015].

Juengst, E.T. (1998) What does enhancement mean? In E. Parens (Ed.). *Enhancing Human Traits: Ethical and Social Implications.* Washington, DC: Georgetown University Press, pp. 29–47.

Kent, B.A., Ooomen, C.A., Bekinschtein, P., Bussey, T.J. and Saksida, L.M. (2015) Cognitive enhancing effects of voluntary exercise, caloric restriction and environmental enrichment: A role for adult hippocampal neurogenesis and pattern separation? *Current Opinion in Behavioral Sciences* 4: pp. 179–185. Available at: www.sciencedirect.com/science/article/pii/S235215461500087X [Accessed 26 July 2015].

Keshavan, M.S., Vinogradov, S., Rumsey, J., Sherrill, J. and Wagner, A. (2014) Cognitive training in mental disorders: Update and future directions. *American Journal of Psychiatry* 171(5): pp. 510–522. Available at: www.pubmedcentral.nih.gov/articlerender.fcgi?artid=4114156&tool=pmcentrez&rendertype= abstract [Accessed 9 July 2015].

Kim, D. (2012) Practical use and risk of modafinil, a novel waking drug. *Environmental Health and Toxicology* 27: p. e2012007. Available at: www.pubmedcentral.nih.gov/articlerender.fcgi?artid=3286657&tool= pmcentrez&rendertype=abstract [Accessed 3 Sept. 2015].

Kumar, R. (2008) Approved and investigational uses of modafinil : An evidence-based review. *Drugs* 68(13): pp. 1803–1839. Available at: www.ncbi.nlm.nih.gov/pubmed/18729534 [Accessed 1 Aug. 2015].

Kuo, M.-F., Paulus, W., and Nitsche, M.A. (2014) Therapeutic effects of non-invasive brain stimulation with direct currents (tDCS) in neuropsychiatric diseases. *NeuroImage* 85 Pt 3: pp. 948–960. Available at: www. ncbi.nlm.nih.gov/pubmed/23747962 [Accessed 1 July 2015].

Lanas, A., Perez-Aisa, M.A., Feu, F., Ponce, J., Saperas, E., Santolaria, S., Rodrigo, L., Balanzo, J., Bajador, E., Almela, P., Navarro, J.M., Carballo, F., Castro, M., Quintero, E. and Investigators of the Asociación Española de Gastroenterología (AEG). (2005) A nationwide study of mortality associated with hospital admission due to severe gastrointestinal events and those associated with nonsteroidal antiinflammatory drug use. *American Journal of Gastroenterology* 100(8): pp. 1685–1693. Available at: http://dx. doi.org/10.1111/j.1572-0241.2005.41833.x [Accessed 9 Sept. 2015].

Lewens, T. (2009) Enhancement and human nature: The case of Sandel. *Journal of Medical Ethics* 35(6): pp. 354–356. Available at: http://jme.bmj.com/content/35/6/354.abstract [Accessed 10 Sept. 2015].

Maher, B. (2008) Poll results: Look who's doping. *Nature* 452(7188): pp. 674–675. Available at: www. ncbi.nlm.nih.gov/pubmed/18401370 [Accessed 17 Mar. 2015].

Maier, L.J., Liechti, M.E., Herzig, F. and Schaub, M.P. (2013) To dope or not to dope: Neuroenhancement with prescription drugs and drugs of abuse among Swiss university students. *PLOS One* 8(11): p.e77967. Available at: www.pubmedcentral.nih.gov/articlerender.fcgi?artid=3827185&tool=pmcentrez&render type=abstract [Accessed 9 Sept. 2015].

Marchant, N.L., Kamel, F., Echlin, K., Grice, J., Lewis, M. and Rusted, J.M. (2009) Modafinil improves rapid shifts of attention. *Psychopharmacology* 202(1–3): pp. 487–495. Available at: www.ncbi.nlm.nih.gov/ pubmed/19031073 [Accessed 9 Sept. 2015].

Marciniak, R., Sheardova, K., Cermáková, P., Hudeček, D., Sumec, R. and Hort, J. (2014) Effect of meditation on cognitive functions in context of aging and neurodegenerative diseases. *Frontiers in Behavioral Neuroscience* 8: p. 17. Available at: www.pubmedcentral.nih.gov/articlerender.fcgi?artid=3903052&tool= pmcentrez&rendertype=abstract [Accessed 3 Sept. 2015].

Mehta, M., Sahakian, B.J. and Robbins, T.W. (2001) Comparative psychopharmacology of methylphenidate and related drugs in human volunteers, patients with ADHD and experimental animals. In Solanto, M.V., Arnsten, A.F.T. and Castellanos, F.X. (Eds.). *Stimulant Drugs and ADHD: Basic and Clinical Findings.* New York: Oxford University Press, pp. 303–331.

Mereu, M., Bonci, A., Newman, A.H. and Tanda, G. (2013) The neurobiology of modafinil as an enhancer of cognitive performance and a potential treatment for substance use disorders. *Psychopharmacology* 229(3): pp. 415–434. Available at: www.pubmedcentral.nih.gov/articlerender.fcgi?artid=3800148&tool=pmcentrez&rendertype=abstract [Accessed 25 Aug. 2015].

Minzenberg, M.J., and Carter, C.S. (2008) Modafinil: A review of neurochemical actions and effects on cognition. *Neuropsychopharmacology: Official Publication of the American College of Neuropsychopharmacology* 33(7): pp. 1477–502. Available at: http://dx.doi.org/10.1038/sj.npp.1301534 [Accessed 17 July. 2015].

Morley, J.E. (2013) Cognition and nutrition. *Current Opinion in Clinical Nutrition and Metabolic Care* 17(1): p. 1. Available at: www.ncbi.nlm.nih.gov/pubmed/24310052 [Accessed 3 Sept. 2015].

Müller, U., Rowe, J.B., Rittman, T., Lewis, C., Robbins, T.W. and Sahakian, B.J. (2013) Effects of modafinil on non-verbal cognition, task enjoyment and creative thinking in healthy volunteers. *Neuropharmacology* 64: pp. 490–495. Available at: www.pubmedcentral.nih.gov/articlerender.fcgi?artid=3485563&tool=pmcentrez&rendertype=abstract [Accessed 21 Aug. 2015].

Northstone, K., Joinson, C., Emmett, P., Ness, A. and Paus, T. (2012). Are dietary patterns in childhood associated with IQ at 8 years of age? A population-based cohort study. *Journal of epidemiology and community health* 66(7): pp. 624–628. Available at: http://jech.bmj.com/content/early/2011/01/21/jech.2010.111955.abstract [Accessed 3 Sept. 2015].

Porsdam Mann, S., and Sahakian, B.J. (2015) The increasing lifestyle use of modafinil by healthy people: Safety and ethical issues. *Current Opinion in Behavioral Sciences* 4: pp. 136–141. Available at: www.sciencedirect.com/science/article/pii/S2352154615000650 [Accessed 1 July 2015].

President's Council on Bioethics. (2003) *Beyond Therapy: Biotechnology and the Pursuit of Happiness.* Available at: www.amazon.co.uk/Beyond-Therapy-Biotechnology-Happiness-Presidents/dp/0060734906 [Accessed 10 Sept. 2015].

Pringle, A., Browning, M., Parsons, E., Cowen, P.J. and Harmer, C.J. (2013) Early markers of cognitive enhancement: Developing an implicit measure of cognitive performance. *Psychopharmacology* 230(4): pp. 631–638. Available at: www.ncbi.nlm.nih.gov/pubmed/23820927 [Accessed 9 Sept. 2015].

Ragan, C.I., Bard, I., and Singh, I. (2013) What should we do about student use of cognitive enhancers? An analysis of current evidence. *Neuropharmacology* 64: pp. 588–595. Available at: www.ncbi.nlm.nih.gov/pubmed/22732441 [Accessed 9 Sept. 2015].

Randall, D.C., Shneerson, J.M., and File, S.E., 2005. Cognitive effects of modafinil in student volunteers may depend on IQ. *Pharmacology Biochemistry and Behavior* 82(1): pp. 133–139. Available at: www.ncbi.nlm.nih.gov/pubmed/16140369 [Accessed 10 Sept. 2015].

Repantis, D., Schlattmann, P., Laisney, O. and Heuser, I. (2010) Modafinil and methylphenidate for neuroenhancement in healthy individuals: A systematic review. *Pharmacological Research: The Official Journal of the Italian Pharmacological Society* 62(3): pp. 187–206. Available at: www.ncbi.nlm.nih.gov/pubmed/20416377 [Accessed 28 July 2015].

Roiser, J.P., and Sahakian, B.J. (2013) Hot and cold cognition in depression. *CNS Spectrums* 18(3): pp. 139–49. Available at: www.ncbi.nlm.nih.gov/pubmed/23481353 [Accessed 17 Sept. 2015].

Rugino, T. (2007) A review of modafinil film-coated tablets for attention-deficit/hyperactivity disorder in children and adolescents. *Neuropsychiatric Disease and Treatment* 3(3): pp. 293–301. Available at: www.pubmedcentral.nih.gov/articlerender.fcgi?artid=2654790&tool=pmcentrez&rendertype=abstract [Accessed 9 Sept. 2015].

Sabatine, M.S., Poh, K.K., Mega, J.L., Shepard, J.A., Stone, J.R. and Frosch, M.P. (2007). Case records of the Massachusetts general hospital. Case 36–2007: A 31-year-old woman with rash, fever, and hypotension. *New England Journal of Medicine* 357(21): pp. 2167–2178. Available at: www.ncbi.nlm.nih.gov/pubmed/18032767 [Accessed 9 Sept. 2015].

Sahakian, B., and LaBuzetta, J.N. (2013) *Bad Moves: How Decision Making Goes Wrong, and the Ethics of Smart Drugs.* Oxford: Oxford University Press. Available at: https://books.google.com/books?id=q37L2DXN0Y8C&pgis=1 [Accessed 9 Sept. 2015].

Sahakian, B., and Morein-Zamir, S. (2007) Professor's little helper. *Nature* 450(7173): pp. 1157–1159. Available at: http://dx.doi.org/10.1038/4501157a [Accessed 5 Aug. 2015].

Sahakian, B.J., Bruhl, A.B., Cook, J., Killikelly, C., Savulich, G., Piercy, T., Hafizi, S., Perez, J., Fernandez-Egea, E., Suckling, J. and Jones, P.B. (2015) The impact of neuroscience on society: Cognitive enhancement in neuropsychiatric disorders and in healthy people. *Philosophical Transactions of the Royal Society B: Biological Sciences* 370(1677): p. 20140214. Available at: www.ncbi.nlm.nih.gov/pubmed/26240429 [Accessed 4 Aug. 2015].

Sahakian, B.J. and Morein-Zamir, S. (2015) Pharmacological cognitive enhancement: Treatment of neuropsychiatric disorders and lifestyle use by healthy people. *The Lancet Psychiatry* 2(4): pp. 357–362. Available at: www.thelancet.com/article/S2215036615000048/fulltext [Accessed 2 Sept. 2015].

Sandel, M.J. (2007) *The Case Against Perfection.* Cambridge, MA: Harvard University Press. Available at: https://books.google.com/books?hl=en&lr=&id=ael6tIvalIUC&pgis=1 [Accessed 3 Sept. 2015].

Sattler, S., Mehlkop, G., Graeff, P. and Sauer, C. (2014) Evaluating the drivers of and obstacles to the willingness to use cognitive enhancement drugs: The influence of drug characteristics, social environment, and personal characteristics. *Substance Abuse Treatment, Prevention, and Policy* 9: p. 8. Available at: www.pubmedcentral.nih.gov/articlerender.fcgi?artid=3928621&tool=pmcentrez&rendertype=abstract [Accessed 17 Aug. 2015].

Savulescu, J., Sandberg, A. and Kahane, G. (2011) Well-being and enhancement. In J. Savulescu, R. ter Meulen and G. Kahane, *Enhancing Human Capacities.* Oxford: Wiley-Blackwell, pp. 3–18.

Schelle, K.J., Faulmüller, N., Caviola, L. and Hewstone, M. (2014) Attitudes toward pharmacological cognitive enhancement-a review. *Frontiers in Systems Neuroscience* 8: p. 53. Available at: www.pubmedcentral.nih.gov/articlerender.fcgi?artid=4029025&tool=pmcentrez&rendertype=abstract [Accessed 20 July 2015].

Scoriels, L., Barnett, J.H., Murray, G.K., Cherukuru, S., Fielding, M., Cheng, F., Lennox, B.R., Sahakian, B.J. and Jones, P.B. (2011) Effects of modafinil on emotional processing in first episode psychosis. *Biological Psychiatry* 69(5): pp. 457–464. Available at: www.ncbi.nlm.nih.gov/pubmed/21109234 [Accessed 9 Sept. 2015].

Scoriels, L. and Jones, P.B. (2013) Modafinil effects on cognition and emotion in schizophrenia and its neurochemical modulation in the brain. *Neuropharmacology* 64: pp. 168–184. doi: 10.1016/j.neuropharm.2012.07.011

Singh, G. (1998) Recent considerations in nonsteroidal anti-inflammatory drug gastropathy. *American Journal of Medicine* 105(1B): pp. 31S–38S. Available at: www.ncbi.nlm.nih.gov/pubmed/9715832 [Accessed 9 Sept. 2015].

Smith, M.E., and Farah, M.J. (2011) Are prescription stimulants "smart pills"? The epidemiology and cognitive neuroscience of prescription stimulant use by normal healthy individuals. *Psychological Bulletin* 137(5): pp. 717–741. Available at: www.pubmedcentral.nih.gov/articlerender.fcgi?artid=3591814&tool=pmcentrez&rendertype=abstract [Accessed 15 Aug. 2015].

Stoops, W.W., Lile, J.A., Fillmore, M.T., Glaser, P.E. and Rush, C.R. (2005) Reinforcing effects of modafinil: Influence of dose and behavioral demands following drug administration. *Psychopharmacology* 182(1): pp. 186–193. Available at: www.ncbi.nlm.nih.gov/pubmed/15986191 [Accessed 9 Sept. 2015].

Sugden, C., Housden, C.R., Aggarwal, R., Sahakian, B.J. and Darzi, A. (2012). Effect of pharmacological enhancement on the cognitive and clinical psychomotor performance of sleep-deprived doctors: A randomized controlled trial. *Annals of Surgery* 255(2): pp. 222–227. Available at: www.ncbi.nlm.nih.gov/pubmed/21997802 [Accessed 2 Sept. 2015].

Turner, D.C., Robbins, T.W., Clark, L., Aron, A.R., Dowson, J. and Sahakian, B.J. (2003) Cognitive enhancing effects of modafinil in healthy volunteers. *Psychopharmacology* 165(3): pp. 260–269. Available at: www.ncbi.nlm.nih.gov/pubmed/12417966 [Accessed 9 Sept. 2015].

Volkow, N.D., Fowler, J.S., Logan, J., Alexoff, D., Zhu, W., Telang, F., Wang, G.J., Jayne, M., Hooker, J.M., Wong, C., Hubbard, B., Carter, P., Warner, D., King, P., Shea, C., Xu, Y., Muench, L. and Apelskog-Torres, K. (2009) Effects of modafinil on dopamine and dopamine transporters in the male human brain. *Journal of American Medical Association* 301(11): p. 1148. Available at: www.pubmedcentral.nih.gov/articlerender.fcgi?artid=2696807&tool=pmcentrez&rendertype=abstract [Accessed 8 Aug. 2015].

Vrecko, S. (2013) Just how cognitive is "Cognitive Enhancement"? On the significance of emotions in university students' experiences with study drugs. *American Journal of Bioethics Neuroscience* 4(1): pp. 4–12. Available at: www.pubmedcentral.nih.gov/articlerender.fcgi?artid=3590646&tool=pmcentrez&render type=abstract [Accessed 2 Sept. 2015].

Weyandt, L.L., Oster, D.R., Marraccini, M.E., Gudmundsdottir, B.G., Munro, B.A., Zavras, B.M. and Kuhar, B. (2014) Pharmacological interventions for adolescents and adults with ADHD: Stimulant and non-stimulant medications and misuse of prescription stimulants. *Psychology Research and Behavior Management* 7: pp. 223–249. Available at: www.pubmedcentral.nih.gov/articlerender.fcgi?artid=4164338&tool =pmcentrez&rendertype=abstract [Accessed 16 June 2015].

Whiteford, H.A., *et al.* (2013) Global burden of disease attributable to mental and substance use disorders: Findings from the global burden of disease study 2010. *The Lancet* 382(9904): pp. 1575–1586. Available at: www.thelancet.com/article/S0140673613616116/fulltext [Accessed 13 July 2014].

Wittchen, H.U., Degenhardt, L., Rehm, J., Baxter, A.J., Ferrari, A.J., Erskine, H.E., Charlson, F.J., Norman, R.E., Flaxman, A.D., Johns, N., Burstein, R., Murray, C.J. and Vos, T. (2011) The size and burden of mental disorders and other disorders of the brain in Europe 2010. *European Neuropsychopharmacology: Journal of the European College of Neuropsychopharmacology* 21(9): pp. 655–679. Available at: www.ncbi.nlm.nih.gov/pubmed/21896369 [Accessed 10 July 2014].

The Work Foundation. (2013) *Knowledge Workers and Knowledge Work*. Available at: www.thework foundation.com/DownloadPublication/Report/213_213_know_work_survey170309.pdf [Accessed 3 Sept. 2015].

10

NEUROENHANCEMENT AND THERAPY IN NATIONAL DEFENSE CONTEXTS

Michael N. Tennison and Jonathan D. Moreno

Introduction

The concept of national security promulgated after World War II entails the view that government should protect the state and its populace against various threats to their well-being. National security agencies charged with this task, including both military and intelligence organizations, have long relied on science and technology to carry out their missions. From weapons races to communication monitoring, national security services develop and deploy cutting-edge innovations to protect and advance the interests of the United States and its friends and allies. Since the end of World War II, the U.S. has espoused a policy of technological superiority over its actual and potential adversaries.

The worlds of science and security, however, have fundamentally different goals and fundamentally different timelines and structures for achieving them. Scientists seek natural truths via the slow process of aggregating data, repeating studies, and verifying conclusions. Security, on the other hand, responds to immediate and emerging threats with the best tools available or "on the shelf." This creates a tension between the slow pace and idealistic standards for scientific truth and the fast pace and pragmatic necessity of security needs. Consider the military and intelligence interest in psychedelic drugs in the 20th century. Even though scientists have still not fully uncovered the psychological and neurophysiological effects of drugs like lysergic acid diethylamide (LSD), intelligence agencies studied them 60 years ago for various purposes that prompt serious concerns about usefulness, ethics, and legality (McCoy, 2007).

Another tension between the domains of science and security hinges on the concept of "dual use." Dual use refers to the status of a single scientific or technological development that "may be used for beneficial or malevolent ends" (Evans, 2014, 268). Clearly, the potential for malevolence raises stark ethical issues. But in the absence of malicious intent, serious ethical issues still arise when such research is deployed for national security purposes, a domain fraught with moral complications. Thus, even when employed in a so-called just war (i.e., a war entered into and conducted according to morally rigorous criteria), dual-use technology ought to be subject to a higher level of ethical scrutiny than purely innocuous advances. Atomic weapons are a classic result of dual-use research: nuclear physics represented an enormous breakthrough for theoretical and applied science, yielding many beneficial technologies and the decisive conclusion of

World War II. But it also led to catastrophic destruction and the deaths of thousands of Japanese civilians, as well as the perpetual specter of nuclear war for the imaginable future.

Neuroscience now epitomizes dual-use research and raises concerns about premature deployment. In April 2013, President Obama launched the BRAIN Initiative, mobilizing hundreds of millions of dollars "to help unlock the mysteries of the brain, to improve our treatment of conditions like Alzheimer's and autism and to deepen our understanding of how we think, learn and remember" (White House, 2014). This research not only seeks to reveal scientific truths and improve medical treatment modalities, it also has implications for military and counterintelligence operations. Of the five federal agencies participating in the BRAIN Initiative, two—Defense Advanced Research Projects Agency (DARPA) and Intelligence Advanced Research Projects Activity (IARPA)—are national security agencies. Other national security agencies that are not specifically involved in the BRAIN Initiative, such as the Office of Naval Research, also conduct neuroscience research.

As in any scientific field, the dual-use potential of neuroscience research should be carefully scrutinized to help ensure that the risks of misuse and harm do not outweigh the potential for good. The potential for rogue states or nonstate actors to obtain access to emerging and readily available technologies must also be considered (Ballhaus et al., 2014). The scientific purist might argue that no potential benefit of national security neuroscience research justifies the risks of dual-use research, but maintaining the science–security partnership is important for at least two reasons. First, severing military funding from public neuroscience could drive research underground, further shielding it from public ethical, legal, and social critique. Second, ever-present threats of terrorism and geopolitical hostility may warrant explorations of technologies reasonably believed to be necessary or useful to protect the public. Ascertaining the necessity or utility of the national security development and use of a given technology, however, can never reach the level of certainty for which science strives. The tension between the scientific drive for certainty and the security interest in immediacy must be managed to mitigate the risks associated with deploying and relying on nascent but immature technologies. This concern embodies the "Collingridge dilemma," a catch-22 in which a technology's risks cannot be fully known until developed and implemented, but by the time an innovation is entrenched, those risks will be much harder to ameliorate (Collingridge, 1980).

This chapter examines several areas of dual-use neuroscience research: combat enhancement, warfighter therapy, and intelligence. Although the focus will be on research in the United States, the neuroethical implications are the same for international contexts.

Combat Enhancement and Optimization

Scientists, entrepreneurs, and competitive individuals—whether the competition is borne out in the classroom, the baseball field, the video game console, or the battlefield—have grown increasingly interested in the research and development of drugs and devices for human enhancement. A variety of enhancement modalities offer at least the theoretical prospect of substantially enhancing myriad cognitive capacities, from attention and focus to memory and learning (Bostrom and Sandberg, 2009). This interest is by no means new: individuals all over the world have long altered their neurochemistry to optimize, tweak, and tinker with the human experience, such as the stimulating jolt of caffeine or coca or the sedating effects of alcohol or opium (Miller, 2013). As neuroscientists uncover ever greater nuances of the brain's structures and functions, methods of enhancing cognitive performance have become ever more targeted and precise. Now, selected cognitive capacities can be augmented with electricity, magnetism, ultrasound, and even light, and in the zero-sum game of military combat, any advantage in mental sharpness, acuity, resolve, or endurance can mean the difference between life and death.

Even in competitions without lethal stakes, enhancement raises myriad ethical issues (Bostrom and Sandberg, 2009). First, consider the athlete who uses performance-enhancing drugs to excel in sports. The enhancement not only optimizes the athlete's performance but does so to the detriment of her or his opponents. This strikes many people as unfair. Further, not all athletes have access to the same top-of-the-line enhancements, raising concerns of distributive justice. Besides these positional inequalities, those who would otherwise remain drug free may feel unduly pressured to enhance themselves in order to remain competitive. Athletic enhancements may also pose short- and long-term risks to health and safety, such as the risk of anabolic steroids diminishing the body's endogenous ability to produce testosterone naturally (Hartgens and Kuipers, 2004, 535). Critics of enhancement also argue that pharmacological and technological enhancements may interrupt the natural relationship between effort and accomplishment that builds character and virtue: "A drug that induces fearlessness does not produce courage" (President's Council on Bioethics, 2003, 291). Some ethicists believe that the pursuit of such enhancement transgresses supernatural moral boundaries and constitutes "playing God" (President's Council on Bioethics, 2003, 287). No matter what the context, when enhancements grant a positional advantage relative to others in a competitive situation, myriad ethical issues arise.

Modeling the Brain

Cutting-edge efforts to modulate neurological functioning begin with breakthroughs in modeling the brain and its operation in relevant circumstances. Brain modeling presents a dizzying array of possibilities and many corresponding ethical issues. As a dual-use field, it could create pathways for new therapies for persons with dementia. At another extreme, the notion of a reasonably complete brain simulation (whatever that would mean) has stimulated worries that an advanced machine intelligence could constitute a threat to human survival. Lying somewhere between therapy and existential risk, brain modeling might lead to cognitive enhancements. DARPA and IARPA have several projects funding this kind of research.

DARPA is studying the brain's function under stress in order to develop interventions to enhance the neurological resilience of warfighters (Enabling Stress Resistance, 2015). DARPA is also funding research on the holistic tracking of single-neuron activity in the context of larger neural networks (Neuro-FAST, 2015). This program incorporates prior research known as the CLARITY process, which entails transforming neural tissue, including a whole mouse brain, into a transparent gel that can be studied in three dimensions (Tomer et al., 2014). IARPA is also involved in modeling the brain and its processes to support cognitive enhancement research. One program leverages recent developments in a variety of fields, including neuroscience, to model and ultimately enhance "adaptive reasoning and problem solving" (SHARP, 2015). Cognitive enhancement could optimize the capacity of intelligence analysts to draw inferences and conclusions in stressful situations, so IARPA is interested in investigating and validating neuroscientific, psychological, and other promising modalities.

Advances in brain imaging and modeling facilitate more than therapeutic and enhancement interventions for biological brains; they also support efforts to reverse engineer computer architecture and artificial intelligence that mimic neurological structures and functions. DARPA's Systems of Neuromorphic Adaptive Plastic Scalable Electronics program seeks to develop computers that replicate the brain's ability to process vast amounts of information without using much energy or taking up much space (SyNAPSE, 2015). IBM's latest "cognitive chip" under the SyNAPSE program distributes computation across more than five billion transistors, utilizing an architecture imitating a million neurons with 256 million synapses (IBM Research, 2014). Meanwhile, the IARPA program Machine Intelligence from Cortical Networks focuses on developing artificial intelligence based on models of neurological function (MiCRONS, 2015). Specifically, IARPA seeks to advance the ability of algorithms to reconstruct the brain functions associated with learning, aiming to ultimately rival the cognitive capacities of a human analyst.

Drugs

National security agencies have long had an interest in the pharmacological stimulation, modulation, and alteration of neurological functioning. As mentioned, the intelligence community started researching psychedelic drugs more than half a century ago, before they became icons of the sixties counterculture. In the early 1950s, drugs like LSD were hypothesized to operate as an "ego depressant" or "truth serum," rendering enemies of the state unable to withhold their security secrets. After debunking this theory, scientists studied the opposite postulation, that psychedelics rendered subjects so confused and uncomprehending that they could be used to *prevent* the disclosure of security secrets (Lee and Shlain, 1985, 14–16). Neither of these proposals was borne out by the research, and psychedelics presumable hit the back burner of national security neuroscientific interest. Other drugs, however, later came to the forefront.

In 2003, the military's practice of enhancing the cognitive endurance of warfighters came to the fore when U.S. Air National Guard pilots, allegedly impaired by the amphetamines intended to enhance their alertness, accidentally bombed and killed several Canadian troops in Afghanistan, a reminder that not all alleged enhancements are reliable (Shanker and Duenwald, 2003). Use of the so-called go pills, however, may have saved more lives than they ended, since flight fatigue itself had led to almost one hundred lethal crashes at the time of this incident.

In the latter half of the last decade, military studies began examining the comparative effectiveness of modafinil (marketed as Provigil) as an alternative or complement to amphetamine for cognitive enhancement in combat (NRC, 2008). Modafinil was approved for the treatment of narcolepsy, and some studies showed it to outperform amphetamine at minimizing the effects of sleep deprivation in healthy subjects. Other DARPA–funded research showed that the neuropeptide orexin-A, when administered to sleep-deprived monkeys, restored their short-term memory (Deadwyler et al., 2007).

Drugs are researched not only for therapeutic or enhancement benefits but also as modalities for studying the brain. For example, a new tool known as Designer Receptors Exclusively Activated by Designer Drugs (DREADDs) enables neuroscientists to leverage advances in synthetic biology to study signaling systems within a cell (Lee et al., 2014). Combining drug-like chemicals and genes, researchers design receptors to activate or inhibit neurons with G-proteins. This allows scientists to observe and manipulate the brain at the single-neuron level. Recent studies have focused on the neurological basis of hunger and metabolism (Urban and Roth, 2015). Studies like these may lead to pharmaceuticals that improve the performance of warfighters who are required to function independently under combat conditions for extended periods. However, they would also present unexplored risks to the individuals not only during their military service but also in their adjustment to civilian life without these modifications.

Devices

Military research interest in pharmacological cognitive enhancement pales in comparison to that for biotechnological enhancement (DARPA, 2015, 8). Just as in the pharmacological context, enhancement devices evolved from and are often equivalent to devices used for medical applications. The Roman physician Scribonius Largus detailed the millennia-old technique of applying electric fish to the scalp as a remedy for headaches (Fregni and Pascual-Leone, 2007, 384). Late in the 18th century, Giovanni Aldini drew from the work of Luigi Galvani and Allessandro Volta to demonstrate the electrical nature of muscle contraction as well as the therapeutic potential of transcranially administered current (Parent, 2004). In 1930s, electroconvulsive therapy (ECT) emerged as an effective treatment for depression (UK ECT Review Group, 2003). At the turn of the 21st century, scientists showed that transcranial direct current stimulation (tDCS) could modulate cortical excitability and neuroplasticity, paving the way for widespread belief in the device's promise for both therapy and enhancement (Brunoni et al., 2012, 176). Related technologies include magnetic seizure therapy (MST) and transcranial magnetic stimulation (TMS). Following its predecessor ECT, TMS is approved to treat major depression and may have fewer side effects than ECT.

If modulating and stimulating brain activity with electricity can alter the brain in a way to restore normal functioning to the unwell, could it also enhance brain function in healthy individuals? Studies have demonstrated that TMS and tDCS may be able to enhance performance on tasks associated with memory, learning, and problem solving (Hamilton et al., 2011, 188). Whereas TMS equipment is still bulky and expensive, tDCS devices can be purchased for a couple hundred dollars or even constructed from materials obtained from typical electronics stores. Though tDCS remains under clinical investigation to establish safety and efficacy for therapeutic use, it can already be purchased online to enhance cognitive performance on tasks like video gaming and exercise (*Foc.us*, 2015). Recent studies confirm the relative safety of tDCS but call into question its ability to consistently produce substantial cognitive enhancement (Horvath et al., 2015). A related technology that uses ultrasound (TUS or transcranial ultrasound) instead of electricity may provide greater spatial resolution than either TMS or tDCS, and DARPA and U.S. Army studies envision installing TUS directly into warfighters' helmets to modulate their brain function on the fly (Tyler, 2010). The primary drawback of TUS, however, is a risk of tissue damage, but recent studies of low-intensity TUS demonstrate the device's capacity to safely modulate brain function. Scientists speculate that TUS could be useful not only as a therapy for disorders related to memory and brain injury but also as an enhancement that could induce "meditation, relaxation, and beneficially altered conscious experience" (Hameroff et al., 2013, 414).

For more on tDCS, see Chapter 18.

Stimulating and modulating the brain with electricity, electromagnetism, and ultrasound may end up treating and enhancing a vast array of cognitive capacities related to learning and memory, but all of these techniques lack the ability to selectively target certain kinds of neurons while leaving others unaffected. Genes, on the other hand, produce proteins unique to certain kinds of cells and therefore hold promise for researchers to understand and ultimately intervene at the level of individual neurons and their pathways. A new laboratory system called optogenetics entails tagging particular neuronal systems with opsins, a type of light-sensitive protein, to visualize and manipulate neuronal activity (Tye and Deisseroth, 2012). By inserting opsin-producing genes, neurons in the brain can be activated or blocked with fiber-optic light. This kind of precise control over individual neurons opens up many areas of research. For example, in the laboratory, light-sensitive proteins have conditioned rodents for fear responses (Liu et al., 2012), the ventromedial hypothalamus to stimulate mating and aggression (Lin et al., 2011), and the spiral ganglion to reverse hearing loss (Hernandez et al., 2014). Optogenetics is far from experimentation in human subjects, but the implication is clear: optogenetics is a powerful and precise method for learning about the brain and for the control of certain behaviors and capabilities, information that may someday lead to new modalities for neurological management and enhancement.

Other devices used to facilitate cognitive enhancement do not directly modify the brain. Instead, some techniques, derived from the "biofeedback" movement in the 1970s, use brain scans to feed information about their own brains back to individuals. For example, a warfighter's brain might pick up on visual cues of a threat before she or he is consciously aware of them (Szondy, 2012). Another application of biofeedback could alert warfighters to the detrimental effects of sleep deprivation on cognition and performance (Downs et al., 2009). This kind of feedback can—at least theoretically—put people in touch with what their brains already perceive but that they do not have direct awareness of or control over.

Some devices may augment the cognitive capacities of warfighters, not through stimulation or informational feedback but by directly connecting brains to machines that extend their capabilities (Miranda et al., 2015). Brain–machine interfaces (BMIs, also called brain–computer interfaces or BCIs) translate human thoughts into the actions of computers or machines and can be invasive or noninvasive. Invasive BMIs function by implanting electrodes directly into the brain to pick up and utilize neurological signals; noninvasive techniques translate brain signals through, for example, electrodes placed on the scalp. At a recent DARPA conference, researchers discussed a current project to develop a "cortical modem," a computer feeding information to the visual cortex independent of normal sensory input (Rothman, 2015). The goal is to create a sense of augmented reality, a visual overlay on top of one's normal visual perception. BMIs can also extend the mind into the external world, including mind-controlled quad-copters (LaFleur et al., 2013). One can easily imagine an application in the control of drones for surveillance or bombing missions (Ballhaus et al., 2014, 68), in a sense both connecting the controller to the combat scenario (in a literal neurological sense) and distancing the operator from the actual weapon in a way that has not been encountered in previous combat situations. An ethical concern is that the convergence of BMI and drone technologies could facilitate the depersonalization of combat and suppress a warfighter's ethical concerns about the humanity of one's opponent. Since drone operators have similar mental health outcomes as pilots of manned combat aircraft—including posttraumatic stress disorder (Otto and Webber, 2013)—any effort to psychologically distance the remote warfighter from the consequences of his or her actions may not alleviate unnecessary mental suffering. On the other hand, removing the psychological burdens that accompany killing could undermine a natural barrier to unethical decision-making.

Taking this technology even further, some scientists are experimenting with brain–brain interfaces (BBIs) to enable, essentially, a form of telepathy. BBIs use one device to convert a brain's electromagnetic output into the input for another device, such as transcranial magnetic stimulation, that can send those signals as an input into another brain. Experiments involving device-mediated connections between the brains of animals (Pais-Vieira et al., 2013), the brains of humans (Rao et al., 2014), and even between a rat and a human (Yoo et al., 2013) demonstrate, at least at the level of proof of concept, the ability of one brain/mind to create sense impressions and even motor control in the brain/mind of another entity. At an extreme, the knowledge bases of different experts—on military science, foreign policy, and cultural anthropology—could be integrated in the mental experience of each individual. The possibility of merging minds raises novel ethical questions about neural privacy as well as agency and identity. What if BBIs were used coercively, either to implant or extract ideas, impressions, and memories? In the event of a battlefield accident, such as friendly fire or collateral damage, how could responsibility be assigned when multiple brains produce the single causal action (Trimper et al., 2014)?

For more on neuroprivacy and liberty, see Chapter 14.

Therapy for Warfighters

Combat creates enormous risks for the health and well-being of warfighters, and advances in neuroscience may be able to address many of them. Whether a warfighter suffers traumatic brain injury (TBI) from a concussive blast force, posttraumatic stress disorder (PTSD) from witnessing the horrors of war, or the loss of limbs from enemy fire, neuroscience may hold the key to successful rehabilitation and reintegration into civilian life.

Warfighter therapy may raise fewer ethical issues than enhancement because its connection to combat is more attenuated. To the extent that an intelligence or military operation may be unethical or raise ethical issues, however, therapy may also be suspect because it lies in the causal chain facilitating military operations.

Modeling

Just as advancing the science of neurological performance enhancements begins with better models and visualizations of the brain, so do advances in therapy. Through its project named Systems-Based Neurotechnology for Emerging Therapies (SUBNETS), DARPA seeks to develop combination technologies that simultaneously record and measure neurological activity to monitor and diagnose medical issues and instantaneously deliver neural stimulation to ameliorate issues as they arise (SUBNETS, 2015). An implanted microchip will relay information to researchers and use stimulation to treat immediate neurological symptoms as well as harness the brain's neuroplasticity to rewire pathological neural circuits (Jeffries, 2014). To reach this goal, DARPA is studying "pathways involved in complex systems-based brain disorders including posttraumatic stress, major depression, borderline personality, general anxiety, traumatic brain injury, substance abuse and addiction, and fibromyalgia/chronic pain" (SUBNETS, 2015). A related program, Reorganization and Plasticity to Accelerate Injury Recovery, seeks to bridge the gap between invasive techniques for recording brain activity in specific regions and noninvasive, nonspecific approaches to multiregion measurements (REPAIR, 2015). This could lead to the development of novel devices designed to rehabilitate a variety of neurological injuries.

One DARPA project seeks to combine the technologies of magnetic resonance imaging and spectroscopy with quantum photonics to create novel assessment and diagnostic techniques for TBI and PTSD. This technology could supplant the bulky magnets traditionally used for this kind of imaging, paving the way for portable and less costly neurodiagnostics (QORS, 2015).

PTSD

Posttraumatic stress disorder affects an alarming number of veterans. Between 10% and 15% of warfighters deployed to combat in Iraq, Afghanistan, the Gulf War, and the Vietnam War suffer symptoms of PTSD (Steenkamp et al., 2015, 490). The disorder can be disabling and is often associated with other conditions, such as substance abuse, anxiety, and depression. Experiencing or witnessing a dangerous situation causes immediate anxiety that can crystalize into PTSD. People suffering with PTSD may relive their traumatic experiences through flashbacks, thoughts, and dreams and create harmful patterns of behavior to deal with triggers of these episodes. These symptoms and accompanying mood disorders can persist for decades.

Intervening in the neurological process of memory formation and recall holds promise for the prevention of or rehabilitation from PTSD. Memory formation and retrieval involves several steps: first, an experience is encoded as a memory by the brain, then an emotional response is consolidated with it, and finally the memory is later recalled and reprocessed (Donovan, 2010, 63). Studies show that the administration of propranolol, a beta blocker used to treat circulatory and heart conditions with a known side effect of short-term memory loss, at any of these three phases may be able to treat the effects of PTSD. If taken prior to a stressful event, it may disrupt memory formation; if taken immediately after, it may disrupt the memory's persisting emotional salience; and if taken during recall, it may affect reconsolidation and future recall (Donovan, 2010, 64). The latter may occur as a part of "forgetting therapy," a type of counseling designed to trigger traumatic memories in a safe, controlled setting in order to work through them and lessen their capacity for emotional arousal. Another compound, oxytocin, may also have a similar effect by inhibiting fear and the emotional salience attributed to an experience (Koch et al., 2014).

Critics argue that memories—even painful ones—serve an essential normative role in individual and collective identity and meaning making and that the ability to erase memories on demand sacrifices existential authenticity (President's Council on Bioethics, 2003, 223–232). Whether or not this is true, ethical issues certainly arise when individuals know they may be able to commit or witness atrocities without suffering the consequences of PTSD. What if warfighters were required to take propranolol before going into battle? Does the emotional salience of traumatic memory serve as a deterrent against unethical wartime behavior?

Traumatic Brain Injuries

Traumatic brain injury (TBI) is another major risk to the cognitive and neurological health of warfighters. U.S. warfighters in the Middle East have been exposed to increasing numbers of blast-related injuries with the proliferation of improvised explosive devices. DARPA's program Preventing Violent Explosive Neurologic Trauma seeks to reveal the causal mechanism linking blast exposure to TBI (PREVENT, 2015) by producing a holistic, scaled model of blast damage from the cellular to the organ system levels. Better models of neurological blast trauma could lead to better modalities for treatment and prevention of TBI.

Whereas PTSD causes unwanted memories to surface, TBI often prevents memory retrieval. This can affect not only a warfighter's performance on the battlefield, where maximizing performance hinges on memory's role in learning and adapting to combat experiences, but also in daily life. Another DARPA program, Restoring Active Memory, seeks to model the neurological encoding of memories and develop BMIs that can utilize neural stimulation to rehabilitate this process. One approach entails assisting the brain's normal "replay" mechanism, wherein memories are frequently recalled and reconsolidated, strengthening their presence in the brain and mind (RAM, 2015; DARPA, 2015b).

Prostheses

Another major area of warfighter injury in which neuroscience can make an impact is prosthetics. DARPA seeks to "revolutionize" prosthetics by creating advanced prostheses controlled through BMIs (Revolutionizing Prosthetics, 2015). Not only can the brain directly control prosthetic arms through the computerized interface, the prosthetic may be able to send sensory feedback back to the brain (HAPTIX, 2015c). This would create a sense of touch and proprioception that mimics natural movement and restores the capacity to complete tasks that require a delicate touch. DARPA's prosthetics programs also seek to advance the stability and functioning of BMIs over time, increasing their long-term reliability for assisting with motor control and advancing their interfacing with the central and peripheral nervous systems (RE-NET, 2015).

In human subject experiments, scientists have already demonstrated the ability of tetraplegic patients, outfitted with BMIs, to control computer cursors (Simeral et al., 2011) and robotic limbs (Aflalo et al., 2015) using only neural activity. Though these studies currently focus on therapeutic objectives, one can imagine a future synthesis of BMI–facilitated motor control of the combat exoskeletons already developed (Lockheed Martin HULC). On an intuitive level, hybrid human–machine warfighters conjure images of the Terminator, Robocop, and Iron Man. Current research projects seek less fantastical mergers of man and machine than the cyborgs seen in movies (Thompson, 2014), but the incremental implementation of cybernetic enhancements could ultimately produce a "mechwarrior" so fundamentally different from today's warfighter that its deployment inherently could raise ethical red flags. Military R&D generally aims to create an "unfair" fight with overwhelming technological or tactical superiority, a goal potentially justified if its pursuit leads to a decisive end of hostilities, as goes the argument for the use of atomic weapons in World War II. This goal, however, is not without ethical and legal constraints: international treaties categorically render chemical weapons, for example, off limits in international combat. If cyborg mechwarriors ever become a reality, how should they be treated? Donning something like an Iron Man suit may invite a sense of invulnerability that not only shields the warfighter from biological vulnerabilities, but it also diminishes the emotional vulnerability necessary to empathize with the other—a trait integral to ethical decision making.

> For more on moral robots, see Chapter 24.

Intelligence

In addition to funding research on the underlying neurological basis of optimal cognitive performance and the injuries that impair it, DARPA and IARPA also seek neuroscientific models of complex mental and social processes that have national security implications. These models could lead to more sophisticated techniques for identifying, interrogating, and perhaps rehabilitating terrorism suspects. Additionally, these models can help advance analysis of intelligence data performed by both humans and artificial intelligences designed to mimic neural networks.

Modeling

IARPA seeks to understand the neurological processes underlying the mental associations among complex concepts. One program, Knowledge Representation in Neural Systems, focuses on the conceptual tasks of intelligence analysts: "resolv[ing] ambiguities, mak[ing] inferences, and draw[ing] conclusions" (KRNS, 2015). These tasks depend on understanding the importance of an object's properties in relation to other objects and their properties. The neuroscientific understanding of knowledge representation is currently limited to single concepts, but

IARPA would like to advance the state of the art to encompass complex combinations of objects, properties, actions, context, and social influences. If the neural processes underlying the way knowledge is represented and articulated can be quantified, algorithms could be developed to optimally perform these tasks (KRNS, 2015; MICrONS, 2015). Along these lines, IARPA is also interested in "sensemaking," the recognition of significant patterns in sets of information (ICArUS, 2015). Advanced neuroscientific models of sensemaking could mitigate cognitive biases present in human pattern detection and ultimately lead to a new generation of automated analytical processes. After the recent revelations of the secret collection of billions of emails passing through American networks—raising serious ethical, legal, and social concerns about privacy—it comes as no surprise that intelligence agencies need advanced techniques to parse the vast amounts of data (Angwin et al., 2015).

DARPA seeks to understand the neurological basis of the mental translation of personal and collective narratives into cognition and behavior (Narrative Networks, 2015). Narratives tie together and shape an individual's values, goals, and social roles, and in this context, they play a crucial part in violent social movements and radicalization. Specifically, DARPA wants to understand "the neurobiological impact of narratives on hormones and neurotransmitters, reward processing, and emotion-cognition interaction." One critic suggests that this project aims to "master the science of propaganda," not only identifying subversive narratives but also dispensing scientifically engineered stories designed to defuse political radicalization (Lim, 2011). Moreover, consider the dual-use issues that would arise if it were eventually possible to intervene in one's beliefs and narrative at the internal level of the brain, not just the external level of story. As the scientific understanding of the relationship between the brain's structures and functions becomes ever more finely grained, could neuromodulation devices, BMIs, or pharmaceuticals eventually allow brains to be "hacked"? DARPA's Restoring Active Memory program, after all, seeks to manipulate the neural processes underlying memory reconsolidation and retrieval. At least theoretically, the same technology could be used to disrupt the memories that underlie narrative identity. In the hands of a rogue terrorist or malevolent government, the power to change minds could be used to silence dissenters or brainwash new recruits. Though this may turn out to be as far-fetched as attempts to use LSD as a truth serum, the prospect of manipulating identity and self-definition at the neurological level raises stark ethical concerns about privacy and autonomy.

Interrogation

Better models of brain function with respect to the representation of knowledge could also have implications for interrogation. National security agencies are very interested in detecting misrepresentations of knowledge in the interrogation context. Scientists first correlated deception with variations in respiration and blood pressure in the early 1900s (Greely and Illes, 2007, 385–386). To this day, polygraph devices still make use of these physiological proxies for deception, despite the fact that they measure stress, not deceit. Intentional deception can cause stress, but so can emotional arousal and cognitive effort. In 2003, a National Academies report concluded that the polygraph suffers serious problems with theoretical validity and actual accuracy in practice and that further research and technological advance only offer the prospect of "modest" improvements (NRC, 2003, 212–213). Nonetheless, scientists have been researching neuroscience-based alternatives to increase the precision and accuracy of lie detection.

One type of deception involves lying about or omitting knowledge of some person or event. A major task of interrogators is to retrieve this concealed information. "Brain fingerprinting" allegedly accomplishes this by correlating a particular brain wave, the P300 response, with the perception of something familiar (Brainwave Science, 2015). Since familiar information elicits a neurological signature detectable by EEG, the idea is that interrogators could present a suspect with information, such as a photograph, containing information about a crime scene. Ideally, only the guilty culprit will be familiar with the crime's details, and so only that person's brain will produce the P300 wave in response to the photograph. Of course, confounding variables abound, such as hearing about the crime on the news. Despite substantial controversy, including allegations of pseudoscience (Brandom, 2015), brain fingerprinting has been marketed for years to assist in national security, counterterrorism, and law enforcement (Brainwave Science, 2015). Evidence produced by a similar brain scanning technology supposedly proved the presence of "experiential knowledge" of a crime concealed in a suspect's brain, leading to a conviction and life sentence in an Indian murder trial. Upon review by a higher court, the sentence was suspended based on a lack of compelling evidence (Murphy, 2009). MRI is also marketed for deception detection (No Lie MRI, 2015), and as with brain fingerprinting, scientists tend to question its accuracy and utility (Farah et al., 2014).

In 2008, a National Research Council report commissioned by the Defense Intelligence Agency described oxytocin as a "neuropeptide of interest" (NRC, 2008). The hormone has been shown to enhance character traits of trust, generosity, and sacrifice, and one could speculate that an interrogator would want to elicit these attributes in a suspect. Certainly this would be a more nuanced, if no less ethically fraught, approach than the United States' "enhanced inter-rogation" techniques that have been in the news for years now for allegedly constituting torture. CIA interrogators have used barbaric techniques including waterboarding and "rectal feeding" in Guantanamo (Mazzetti, 2014), and the American Psychological Association has come under scrutiny for the participation of psychologists in the design and administration of ethically questionable interrogation techniques (Sidley Austin, 2015). Health practitioners generally abide by strict mandates against using their skills to cause harm in both the research and application of health sciences. Scientists too might pay attention to the downstream uses of their work for intelligence operations.

Policy

The drugs, devices, computers, and algorithms developed under the U.S. BRAIN initiative have tremendous potential to enhance and heal warfighters as well as aid in the collection and analysis of intelligence data. Many of these technological innovations will also have purely benign civilian applications, such as advancing the current understanding and treatment of major public health conditions, including PTSD. But because of their dual-use nature, even when deployed in a just war, national security applications of neuroscience will be put to uses that strain the moral underpinnings of the health sciences and healing arts—to which neuroscience arguably belongs—far beyond their civilian uses. The relevance of the four widely recognized bioethical principles—beneficence, nonmaleficence, justice, and autonomy (Beauchamp and Childress, 2012)—do not cleanly map onto the guiding principles and values of national security, the government's obligation to protect the state and its citizens from various threat sources. Consider the ambiguous relevance of nonmaleficence to a system of ethics that justifies the use of violence to solve problems. Such ambiguities create a space for and necessitate the participation of ethicists to identify the relevant ethical, legal, and social issues associated with research on militarily significant neuroscience applications.

Technological advances with security implications present a paradigmatic Collingridge dilemma (Collingridge, 1980). The dilemma is that the ethical risks of dual-use neuroscience programs may not fully come to light until they manifest themselves in the deployment of a new technology, but by the time an innovation is entrenched, it can be much harder to control or withdraw its application. Fortunately, various organizations and ethicists are already grappling with the foreseeable risks of dual-use neuroscience.

A National Academies ethics committee recently proposed that agencies pursuing dual-use neuroscience research screen, review, and monitor their relevant R&D programs while communicating with the public, educating their staff about potential ethical issues and collaborating with external ethics experts (Ballhaus et al., 2014, 8–13). Different technologies raise different issues, and both agencies and the public need to understand what interests are at stake. In the context of information technology, dual-use neuroscience raises many ethical issues and, perhaps most importantly, concerns associated with privacy (Ballhaus et al., 2014, 52–57). Neuroscientific interventions, such as BMIs, prostheses, and other methods of cognitive enhancement, raise concerns of informed and voluntary consent, safety, authenticity of volition, and autonomy (Ballhaus et al., 2014, 74–78, 94–97). Advances in robotics and machine intelligence, which may involve or be derived from neuroscience, raise international legal issues, place stress on the operators, risk unexpected or unethical responses by adversaries, and could lead to technological creep into civilian law enforcement (Ballhaus et al., 2014, 83–92).

Other organizations and ethicists have also taken note. A similar report from the UK's Royal Society found that neuroscientists ought to consider the downstream dual-use applications of their work (Royal Society, 2012, 60), and ethicists have called for the integration of dual-use education into the undergraduate neurosciences (Tracey and Flower, 2014, 832). Growing attention to and appreciation for the immense dual-use potential of neuroscience could ultimately catalyze the promulgation of laws, regulations, and policies codifying ethical standards at the international level. Just as the Chemical Weapons Convention and the Biologic and Toxin Weapons Convention systematized universal ethical agreements about the relationship between science and security in those domains, interdisciplinary discussions among scientists, bioethicists, philosophers, and policy makers could ultimately yield a similar legal framework for dual-use neuroscience.

Conclusion

Commenting on its navigation of ethically precarious terrain, DARPA believes that its primary mission is to "be fearless about exploring new technologies and their capabilities" (DARPA, 2015, 6). Despite DARPA's fearlessness in advancing the technological frontier, one of the agency's directors has described the downstream implications of its neuroscience research as both "exciting and terrifying" (CBS, 2014). Certainly, fearless research can have terrifying consequences: this is precisely the nature of dual-use technologies. Moreover, neuroscientific innovations may be deployed to serve the immediate needs of national security before satisfying the rigorous standards of scientific validity and safety for human use. Advancing the frontiers of knowledge helps to safeguard the national security interests of the U.S. and its allies, but scientists, ethicists, and the public at large should consider the downstream consequences of innovation in order to manage the tensions inherent in the Collingridge dilemma of national security neuroscience.

Further Reading

Ballhaus, W.F., Chameau, J. and Lin, H.S. (Eds.) (2014) *Emerging and Readily Available Technologies and National Security—A Framework for Addressing Ethical, Legal, and Societal Issues.* Washington, DC: National Academies Press.

Moreno, J.D. (2012) *Mind Wars: Brain Science and the Military in the 21st Century.* New York: Bellevue Literary Press.

Moreno, J.D. (2014) *"Military Use of Enhancements," Neurotechnology: Enhancing the Human Brain and Shaping Society*. Arlington, VA: Potomac Institute.

Tennison, M. and Moreno, J.D. (2012) "Neuroscience, Ethics, and National Security: The State of the Art". *PLoS Biology* 10(3), e1001289. doi:10.1371/journal.pbio.1001289.

Tracey, I. and Flower, R. (2014) "The Warrior in the Machine: Neuroscience Goes to War". *Nature Reviews Neuroscience* 15, 825–834.

References

Aflalo, T., Kellis, S., Klaes, C., Lee, B., Shi, Y., Pejsa, K., . . . Anderson, R.A. (2015) Decoding motor imagery from the posterior parietal cortex of a tetraplegic human. *Science* 22(6237): pp. 906–910.

Angwin, J., Savage, C., Larson, J., Moltke, H., Poitras, L., and Risen, J. (2015) AT&T helped U.S. spy on Internet on a vast scale. *The New York Times*. Available at: www.nytimes.com/2015/08/16/us/politics/att-helped-nsa-spy-on-an-array-of-internet-traffic.html?.

Ballhaus, W.F., Chameau, J., and Lin, H.S. (Eds.) (2014) *Emerging and Readily Available Technologies and National Security—A Framework for Addressing Ethical, Legal, and Societal Issues*. Washington, DC: National Academies Press.

Beauchamp, T.L., and Childress, J.F. (2012) *Principles of Biomedical Ethics*. 8th ed. New York: Oxford University Press.

Bostrom, N., and Sandberg, A. (2009) Cognitive enhancement: Methods, ethics, regulatory challenges. *Science and Engineering Ethics* 15(3): pp. 311–341.

Brainwave Science. (2015). Available at: www.brainwavescience.com/.

Brandom, R. (2015) Is "brain fingerprinting" a breakthrough or a sham? *The Verge*. Available at: www.theverge.com/2015/2/2/7951549/brain-fingerprinting-technology-unproven-courtroom-science-farwell-p300.

Brunoni, A.R., Nitsche, M.A., Bolognini, N., Bikson, M., Wagner T., Merabet, L., . . . Fregni, F. (2012) Clinical research with transcranial direct current stimulation (tDCS): Challenges and future directions. *Brain Stimulation* 5(3): pp. 175–195.

CBS. (2014) DARPA director: technological advances in neuroscience "exciting and terrifying". Available at: www.cbsnews.com/videos/darpa-director-technological-advances-in-neuroscience-exciting-and-terrifying/.

Collingridge, D. (1980) *The Social Control of Technology*. New York: St. Martin's Press.

DARPA. (2015a) *Breakthrough Technologies for National Security*. Available at: http://www.darpa.mil/attach ments/DARPA2015.pdf.

DARPA (2015b) *DARPA Aims to Accelerate Memory Function for Skill Learning*. Available at: www.darpa.mil/news-events/2015-04-27-2.

———. (2015c) *HAPTIX Starts Work to Provide Prosthetic Hands with Sense of Touch*. Available at: www.darpa.mil/news-events/2015-02-08.

Deadwyler, S.A., Porrino, L., Siegel, J.M., and Hampson, R.E. (2007) Systemic and nasal delivery of Orexin-A (Hypocretin-1) reduces the effects of sleep deprivation on cognitive performance in nonhuman primates. *Journal of Neuroscience* 27(52): pp. 14239–14247.

Donovan, E. (2010) Propranolol use in the prevention and treatment of posttraumatic stress disorder in military veterans: Forgetting therapy revisited. *Perspectives in Biology and Medicine* 53(1): pp. 61–74.

Downs, H., Johnson, K.A., Carney, J., Caldwell, J., and George, M.S. (2009) Advanced MRI techniques to assess sleep deprivation vulnerability among soldiers and potentially enhance performance with real-time biofeedback. NATO. Available at: www.dtic.mil/get-tr-doc/pdf?AD=ADA568685.

Enabling Stress Resistance. (2015) DARPA. Available at: www.darpa.mil/program/enabling-stress-resistance

Evans, N.G. (2014) Dual-use decision making: Relational and positional issues. *Monash Bioethics Review* 32: pp. 268–283.

Farah, M.J., Hutchinson, J.B., Phelps, E.A., and Wagner, A.D. (2014) Functional MRI-based lie detection: Scientific and societal challenges. *Nature Reviews Neuroscience* 15: pp. 123–131.

Foc.us. (2015). Available at: www.foc.us.

Fregni, F., and Pascual-Leone, A. (2007) Technology Insight: Noninvasive brain stimulation in neurology—Perspectives on the therapeutic potential of rTMS and tDCS. *Nature Clinical Practice Neurology* 3(7): pp. 383–393.

Greely, H.T., and Illes, J. (2007) Neuroscience-based lie detection: The urgent need for regulation. *American Journal of Law & Medicine* 33: pp. 377–431.

Hameroff, S., Trakas, M., Duffield, C., Annabi, E., Gerace, M.B., Boyle, P., . . . Badal, J.J. (2013) Transcranial Ultrasound (TUS) effects on mental states: A pilot study. *Brain Stimulation* 6(3): pp. 409–415.

Hamilton, R., Messing, S., and Chatterjee, A. (2011) Rethinking the thinking cap: Ethics of neural enhancement using noninvasive brain stimulation. *Neurology* 76(2): pp. 187–193.

Hernandez, V.H., Gehrt, A., Reuter, K., Jing, Z., Jeschke, M., Mendoza Schulz, A., . . . Moser, T. (2014) Optogenetic stimulation of the auditory pathway. *Journal of Clinical Investigation* 124(3): pp. 1114–1129.

Hartgens, F., and Kuipers, H. (2004) Effects of androgenic-anabolic steroids in athletes. *Sports Medicine* 34(8): pp. 513–554.

Horvath, J.C., Forte, J.D., and Carter, O. (2015) Quantitative review finds no evidence of cognitive effects in healthy populations from single-session Transcranial Direct Current Stimulation (tDCS). *Brain Stimulation* 8(3): pp. 535–550.

HULC, Lockheed Martin. Available at: http://www.lockheedmartin.com/us/products/exoskeleton/military.html.

Brain *Power*. (2014) IBM Research. Available at: http://research.ibm.com/cognitive-computing/neurosynaptic-chips.shtml.

Integrated cognitive-neuroscience architectures for understanding sensemaking (ICArUS). (2015) IARPA. Available at: www.iarpa.gov/index.php/research-programs/icarus.

Jeffries, A. (2014) DARPA teams begin work on tiny brain implant to treat PTSD. *The Verge*. Available at: www.theverge.com/2014/5/28/5758018/darpa-teams-begin-work-on-tiny-brain-implant-to-treat-ptsd.

Knowledge representation in neural systems (KRNS). (2015) IARPA. Available at: www.iarpa.gov/index.php/research-programs/krns.

Koch, S.B., van Zuiden, M., Nawijn, L., Frijling, J.L., Veltman, D.J., and Olff, M. (2014) Intranasal oxytocin as strategy for medication-enhanced psychotherapy of PTSD: Salience processing and fear inhibition processes. *Psychoneuroendocrinology* 40: pp. 242–256.

LaFleur, K., Cassady, K., Doud, A., Shades, K., Rogin, E., and He, B. (2013) Quadcopter control in three-dimensional space using a noninvasive motor imagery-based brain-computer interface *Journal of Neural Engineering* 10(4): pp. 1–15.

Lee, H.M., Giguere, P.M., and Roth, B.L. (2014) DREADDS: Novel tools for drug discovery and development. *Drug Discovery Today* 19(4): pp. 469–473.

Lee, M.A., and Shlain, B. (1985) *Acid Dreams: The Complete Social History of LSD: The CIA, the Sixties, and Beyond*. New York: Grove Press.

Lim, D. (2011) DARPA wants to master the science of propaganda. *Wired*. Available at: www.wired.com/2011/10/darpa-science-propaganda/.

Lin, D., Boyle, M.P., Dollar, P., Lee, H., Lein, E.S., Perona, P., and Anderson, D.J. (2011) Functional identification of an aggression locus in the mouse hypothalamus. *Nature* 470: pp. 221–226.

Liu, X., Ramirez, S., Pang, P.T., Puryear, C.B., Govindarajan, A., Deisseroth, K., and Tonegawa, S. (2012) Optogenetic stimulation of a hippocampal engram activates fear memory recall. *Nature* 484: pp. 381–387.

McCoy, A.W. (2007) Science in Dachau's shadow: Hebb, Beecher, and the development of CIA psychological torture and modern medical ethics. *Journal of the History of the Behavioral Sciences* 43(4): pp. 401–417.

Machine intelligence from cortical networks (MICrONS). (2015) IARPA. Available at: www.iarpa.gov/index.php/research-programs/microns.

Mazzetti, M. (2014) Panel faults C.I.A. over brutality and deceit in terrorism interrogations. *New York Times*. Available at: www.nytimes.com/2014/12/10/world/senate-intelligence-committee-cia-torture-report.html?

Miller, R.J. (2013) *Drugged: The Science and Culture Behind Psychotropic Drugs*. New York: Oxford University Press.

Miranda, R.A., Casebeer, W.D., Hein, A.M., Judy, J.W., Krotkov, E.P., Laabs, T.L., . . . Ling, G.S. (2015) DARPA-funded efforts in the development of novel brain-computer interface technology. *Journal of Neuroscience Methods* 244: pp. 52–67.

Murphy, E. (2009) Update on Indian BEOS case: Accused released on bail. *Center for Law and the Biosciences*, 2 April. Available at: http://blogs.law.stanford.edu/lawandbiosciences/2009/04/02/update-on-indian-beos-case-accused-released-on-bail/.

Narrative networks. (2015) DARPA. Available at: www.darpa.mil/program/narrative-networks.

National Research Council. (2003) *The Polygraph and Lie Detection*. Washington, DC: National Academies Press.

National Research Council, Committee on Military and Intelligence Methodology for Emergent Neurophysiological and Cognitive/Neural Research in the Next Two Decades. (2008) *Emerging Cognitive Neuroscience and Related Technologies*. Washington, DC: National Academies Press.

Neuro function, activity, structure, and technology (Neuro-FAST). (2015) DARPA. Available at: www.darpa.mil/program/neuro-function-activity-structure-and-technology.

No Lie MRI. Available at: www.noliemri.com/.

Otto, J.L., and Webber, B.J. (2013) Mental health diagnoses and counseling among pilots of remotely piloted aircraft in the united states air force. *Medical Surveillance Monthly Report* 20(3): pp. 3–8.

Pais-Vieira, M., Lebedev, M., Kunicki, C., Wang, J., and Nicolelis, M.A. (2013) A brain-to-brain interface for real-time sharing of sensorimotor information. *Scientific Reports* 3(1319): pp. 1–10.

Parent, A. (2004) Giovanni Aldini: From animal electricity to human brain stimulation *The Canadian Journal of Neurological Sciences* 31: pp. 576–584.

President's Council on Bioethics. (2003) *Beyond Therapy: Biotechnology and the Pursuit of Happiness*. Available at: https://repository.library.georgetown.edu/bitstream/handle/10822/559341/beyond_therapy_final_webcorrected.pdf?

Preventing violent explosive neurologic trauma (PREVENT). (2015) DARPA. Available at: www.darpa.mil/program/preventing-violent-explosive-neurologic-trauma.

Quantum orbital resonance spectroscopy (QORS). (2015) DARPA. Available at: www.darpa.mil/program/quantum-orbital-resonance-spectroscopy.

Rao, R.P., Stocco, A., Bryan, M., Sarma, D., Youngquist, T.M., Wu, J., and Prat, C.S. (2014) A direct brain-to-brain interface in humans. *PLoS One* 9(11): pp. 1–12.

Reliable neural-interface technology (RE-NET). (2015) DARPA. Available at: www.darpa.mil/program/re-net-reliable-peripheral-interfaces.

Reorganization and plasticity to accelerate injury recovery (REPAIR). (2015) DARPA. Available at: www.darpa.mil/program/reorganization-and-plasticity-to-accelerate-injury-recovery.

Restoring active memory (RAM). (2015) DARPA. Available at: www.darpa.mil/program/restoring-active-memory.

Revolutionizing prosthetics. (2015) DARPA. Available at: www.darpa.mil/program/revolutionizing-prosthetics.

Rothman, P. (2015) Biology is technology—DARPA is back in the game with a big vision and it is H+. *H+ Magazine*. Available at: http://hplusmagazine.com/2015/02/15/biology-technology-darpa-back-game-big-vision-h/.

The Royal Society. (2012) *Brain Waves Module 3: Neuroscience, Conflict and Security*. Available at: https://royalsociety.org/~/media/Royal_Society_Content/policy/projects/brain-waves/2012-02-06-BW3.pdf.

Shanker, T., and Duenwald, D. (2003) Bombing Error Puts a Spotlight on Pilots' Pills. *New York Times*. Available at: www.nytimes.com/2003/01/19/us/threats-and-responses-military-bombing-error-puts-a-spotlight-on-pilots-pills.html.

Sidley Austin. (2015) *Independent Review Relating to APA Ethics Guidelines, National Security Interrogations, and Torture*, Report to the Special Committee of the Board of Directors of the American Psychological Association. Available at: www.apa.org/independent-review/APA-FINAL-Report-7.2.15.pdf.

Simeral, J.D., Kim, S.P., Black, M.J., Donoghue, J.P., and Hochberg, L.R. (2011) Neural control of cursor trajectory and click by a human with tetraplegia 1000 days after implant of an intracortical microelectrode array. *Journal of Neural Engineering* 8(2): pp. 1–24.

Steenkamp, M.M., Litz, B.T., Hoge, C.W., and Marmar, C.R. (2015) Psychotherapy for military-related PTSD: A review of randomized clinical trials. *Journal of American Medical Association* 314(5): pp. 489–500.

Strengthening human adaptive reasoning and problem-solving (shARP). (2015) IARPA. Available at: www.iarpa.gov/index.php/research-programs/sharp.

Systems of neuromorphic adaptive plastic scalable electronics (SyNAPSE). (2015) DARPA. Available at: www.darpa.mil/program/systems-of-neuromorphic-adaptive-plastic-scalable-electronics.

Systems-based neurotechnology for emerging therapies (SUBNETS). (2015) DARPA. Available at: www.darpa.mil/program/systems-based-neurotechnology-for-emerging-therapies.

Szondy, D. (2012) DARPA's CT2WS technology uses "mind reading" to identify threats. *Gizmag*. Available at: www.gizmag.com/tag-team-threat-recognition-technology/24208/.

Thompson, C. (2014) The future soldier will be part human, part machine. *CNBC*. Available at: www.cnbc.com/2014/05/14/the-future-soldier-will-be-part-human-part-machine.html.

Tomer, R., Ye, L., Hsueh, B., and Deisseroth, K. (2014) Advanced CLARITY for rapid and high-resolution imaging of intact tissues. *Nature Protocols* 9(7): pp. 1682–1697.

Tracey, I., and Flower, R. (2014) The warrior in the machine: Neuroscience goes to war. *Nature Reviews Neuroscience* 15: pp. 825–834.

Trimper, J.B., Wolpe, P.R., and Rommelfanger, K.S. (2014) When "I" becomes "We": Ethical implications of emerging brain-to-brain interfacing technologies. *Frontiers in Neuroengineering* 7(art 4): pp. 1–4.

Tye, K.M., and Deisseroth, K. (2012) Optogenetic investigation of neural circuits underlying brain disease in animal models. *Nature Reviews Neuroscience* 13(4): pp. 251–266.

Tyler, W.J. (2010) Remote control of brain activity using ultrasound. *Armed With Science*. Available at: http://science.dodlive.mil/2010/09/01/remote-control-of-brain-activity-using-ultrasound/.

UK ECT Review Group. (2003) Efficacy and safety of electroconvulsive therapy in depressive disorders: A systematic review and meta-analysis. *The Lancet* 361(9360): pp. 799–808.

Urban, D.J., and Roth, B.L. (2015) DREADDs (Designer Receptors Exclusively Activated by Designer Drugs): Chemogenetic tools with therapeutic utility. *Annual Reviews Pharmacology and Toxicity* 55: pp. 399–417.

White House. (2014) *Fact Sheet: Over $300 Million in Support of the President's BRAIN Initiative*. Government of United States. Available at: https://obamawhitehouse.archives.gov/sites/default/files/micro sites/ostp/brain_fact_sheet_9_30_2014_final.pdf.

Yoo, S.S., Kim, H., Filandrianos, E., Taghados, S.J., and Park, S. (2013) Non-invasive Brain-to-Brain Interface (BBI): Establishing functional links between two brains. *PLoS One* 8(4): pp. 1–8.

11

MORAL NEUROENHANCEMENT

Brian D. Earp, Thomas Douglas, and Julian Savulescu

Introduction

In recent years, philosophers, neuroethicists, and others have become preoccupied with "moral enhancement." Very roughly, this refers to the deliberate moral improvement of an individual's character, motives, or behavior. In one sense, such enhancement could be seen as "nothing new at all" (Wiseman, 2016, 4) or as something philosophically mundane: as G. Owen Schaefer (2015) has stated, "Moral enhancement is an ostensibly laudable project. . . . Who wouldn't want people to become more moral?" (261). To be sure, humans have long sought to morally enhance themselves (and their children) through such largely uncontroversial means as moral education, meditation or other "spiritual" practices, engagement with moral ideas in literature, philosophy, or religion, and discussion of moral controversies with others. What is different about the recent debate is that it focuses on a new set of potential tools for fostering such enhancement, which might broadly be described as "neurotechnologies." These technologies, assuming that they worked, would work by altering certain brain states or neural functions directly, in such a way as to bring about the desired moral improvement.

What exactly this would look like and the mechanisms involved are unclear. As John Shook (2012, 6) notes: "There is no unified cognitive system responsible for the formation and enaction of moral judgments, because separable factors are more heavily utilized for some kinds of moral judgments rather than others." Moreover, "the roles of emotions in moral appreciation and judgment, alongside (and intertwining with) social cognition and deliberate reasoning, are so complex that research is only starting to trace how they influence kinds of intuitive judgment and moral conduct."

Nevertheless, suggestions in the literature for possible means of pursuing moral enhancement by way of direct modulation of brain-level targets—at least in certain individuals, under certain circumstances or conditions— abound. These suggestions range from the exogenous administration of neurohormones such as oxytocin (in combination with appropriate psychological therapy or social modification) to potentially increase "pro-social attitudes, like trust, sympathy and generosity" (Savulescu and Persson, 2012, 402; see also Donaldson and Young, 2008; but see Bartz et al., 2011; Lane et al., 2015, 2016; Nave et al., 2015; Wudarczyk et al., 2013) to the alteration of serotonin or testosterone levels to mitigate undue aggression while at the same time ostensibly enhancing fair-mindedness, willingness to cooperate, and aversion to harming others (e.g., Crockett, 2014; Montoya et al., 2012; Savulescu and Persson, 2012; but see Wiseman, 2014, re: serotonin) to the application of newly developed brain modulation techniques, such as noninvasive (but see Davis and Koningsbruggen, 2013) transcranial electric or magnetic stimulation or even deep brain stimulation via implanted electrodes (for scientific overviews, see, e.g., Fregni and Pascual-Leone, 2007; Perlmutter and Mink, 2005; for ethical overviews, see, e.g., Clausen, 2010; Hamilton et al., 2011; Maslen et al., 2014; Rabin et al., 2009; Synofzik and Schlaepfer, 2008).

Potential uses of brain stimulation devices for moral enhancement include attempts to reduce impulsive tendencies in psychopaths (Glenn and Raine, 2008; but see Maibom, 2014), as well as efforts to treat addiction and improve self-control, thereby making associated "immoral behavior" less likely (Savulescu and Persson, 2012, 402). In addition, some research has shown that disruptive stimulation of the right prefrontal cortex or the temporoparietal junction can affect moral judgments directly—for example, judgments relating to fairness and harm (Knoch et al., 2016; Young et al., 2010); however, the circumstances of these and other similar investigations have been thus far largely contrived, such that the real-world implications of the findings are not yet apparent (Wiseman, 2016). More ecologically valid results pertain to the administration of drugs such as methylphenidate or lithium to violent criminals with ADHD or to children with conduct disorder to reduce aggressive behavioral tendencies (see, e.g., Ginsberg et al., 2013, 2015; Ipser and Stein, 2007; Margari et al., 2014; Turgay, 2009), as well as antilibidinal agents to reduce sexual desire in convicted sex offenders (Douglas et al., 2013; Lösel and Schumucker, 2005; Thibaut et al., 2010). Such measures remain controversial, however, both ethically (Craig, 2016; Earp et al., 2014; Gupta, 2012; Singh, 2008) and conceptually, that is, in terms of their status as moral enhancers as opposed to mere forms of "behavioral control" (see Focquaert and Schermer, 2015; see also McMillan, 2014).

To date, the majority of the philosophical literature on moral enhancement has been oriented around two main strands of thought: (1) Ingmar Persson and Julian Savulescu's argument that there is "an urgent imperative to enhance the moral character of humanity" and to pursue research into moral neuroenhancements as a possible means to this end (2008, 162; see also 2010, 2011, 2012, 2013, 2014) and (2) Thomas Douglas's and David DeGrazia's arguments that it would sometimes be morally permissible (in Douglas's case) or morally desirable (in DeGrazia's case) for individuals to voluntarily pursue moral neuroenhancements of certain kinds (e.g., DeGrazia, 2014; Douglas, 2008).

Both strands of thought have been subjected to vigorous criticism (for an overview, see Douglas, 2015; see also Parens, 2013). For their part, Persson and Savulescu have primarily been interested in whether humanity falls under an imperative to pursue or promote the development of technologies that would enable moral neuroenhancement on some description. However, even if there is such an imperative, it might turn out that it would be morally impermissible to deploy any of the technologies that would be developed. On the other hand, even if there is no imperative to pursue such technologies, it might be morally permissible or even morally desirable (or obligatory) for people to use some moral neuroenhancers that nevertheless become available. Thus, there is a further question regarding the moral status of engaging in (as opposed to developing the technologies for) moral neuroenhancement, and it is this question to which we will confine ourselves in this chapter. First, however, it is important to clarify what we mean by the term "moral neuroenhancement" and to show that such a thing could ever be possible. We will start by laying out some definitions.

What Is Moral (Neuro)Enhancement?

In her wide-ranging essay "Moral Enhancement: What Is It and Do We Want It?" Anna Pacholczyk (2011) outlines three major ways of understanding the term "moral enhancement," two of which we will consider here. According to the first way of understanding the term, a moral enhancement is a *change in some aspect of a person's morality that results in a morally better person* (251, paraphrased). This is broadly the sense we have in mind for this chapter, but it is not quite precise, nor is it sufficiently focused, for our purposes, on enhancements that work "directly" on the brain—that is, moral *neuro*enhancements in particular. We therefore propose an alternative definition:

> **Moral neuroenhancement:** Any change in a moral agent, A, effected or facilitated in some significant way by the application of a neurotechnology, that results, or is reasonably expected to result, in A's being a morally better agent.

Let us call this the *agential* conception of moral neuroenhancement. Note that the moral "betterness" of an agent could be understood in various ways. For example, it could be taken to be the increased moral worth or praiseworthiness of the agent, the increased moral excellence of the agent, or the increased moral desirability of the agent's character traits, taken together (see Douglas, 2015, for further discussion). But however it is plausibly understood, as Pacholczyk notes, being moral (let alone more moral) is "a complex ability and there is a wide range of potentially enhancing interventions. Making morally better people could include making people more likely to act on their moral beliefs, improving their reflective and reasoning abilities as applied to moral issues, increasing their ability to be compassionate, and so on" (2011, 253). Of course, there are likely to be serious and substantive disagreements about what should or should not be included on this list, as well as what should or should not be counted as "morally better" in the first place. This is an important issue to which we will return throughout this chapter.

The second major sense of "moral enhancement" discussed by Pacholczyk is this: a moral enhancement is *a beneficial change in moral functioning* (251, paraphrased). Here the idea is, first, to identify an underlying psychological or neurological function that is involved in moral reasoning, decision making, acting, and so forth (that is what makes the function "moral," a descriptive claim) and then to intervene in it "beneficially" (a normative claim). But "beneficially" could mean different things, depending on one's normative perspective, and also on what is to be benefitted or improved. Is it the agent? Her moral character? Her well-being? The function itself? The world? Pacholczyk explores several possibilities but does not settle on a single answer.

We will focus on "the function itself." In so doing, we will draw on what two of us have dubbed *the functional-augmentative approach to enhancement*, often encountered in the wider bioenhancement literature (Earp et al., 2014; see also Savulescu et al., 2011). According to this more general approach, "Interventions are considered enhancements . . . insofar as they [augment] some capacity or function (such as cognition, vision, hearing, alertness) *by increasing the ability of the function to do what it normally does*" (Earp et al., 2014, 2, emphasis added).

This way of understanding "enhancement" will serve as the foil to our preferred approach (the agential approach), so we will spell it out a bit further. Take the case of vision. A functional-augmentative enhancement to this capacity would be one that allowed a person to see more clearly, identify objects at a greater distance, switch focus more quickly and with less effort, and so on, than she could do before the intervention (on some accounts, regardless of whether she had been dealing with a so-called medical problem along any of the relevant dimensions; see Zohny, 2014, for an in-depth discussion). For hearing, it would be one that allowed a person to perceive a wider range of decibels, say, or to discriminate between auditory signals more easily and with greater accuracy. Or take the case of memory: on a functional-augmentative approach, a person's memory would be "enhanced" if—in virtue of some intervention—she could now recall more events (or facts) more vividly or for a longer duration than before.

Importantly, none of this is to say that these functional augmentations would be *desirable*. That would depend on a number of factors, including the person's values, needs, and wishes (as well as those of relevant others), her physical and social environment, and her past experiences, to name but a few. To continue with the example of memory, one need only to think of soldiers who have experienced the traumas of war or of sexual assault survivors to realize that memory, and especially augmented memory, has the potential to be "a devastating shackle" (Earp et al., 2014, 4; see also Earp, 2015a).

Or let us return to the case of hearing. Depending on how this capacity is described[1] and on the circumstances in which one finds oneself, augmented hearing might turn out to be extremely undesirable: just imagine being trapped in a perpetually noisy environment. A similar analysis, we believe, applies to many other functions or capacities that are commonly discussed in the neuroenhancement literature. Simply put: "more is not always better, and sometimes less is more" (Earp et al., 2014, 1). Indeed, in some cases, the *diminishment* of a specific capacity or function, under the right set of circumstances, could be required to achieve the best outcome overall.

And so it is for *moral* capacities. Whether having "more" of a morally relevant capacity or emotion such as empathy, righteous anger, or a sense of fairness is desirable (morally or otherwise) depends upon numerous factors: the circumstances, one's baseline moral motivations and capacities, the social role one is fulfilling, and so on (see Douglas, 2008, 2013). It seems plausible that a morally good agent would be able to respond flexibly to different situations and to employ or tap into different cognitive and emotional resources as necessary to arrive at the motives, decisions, and behaviors that are morally desirable given the context. As we will argue, it is this higher-order capacity to respond flexibly and appropriately to a range of scenarios that should be augmented, if possible, to achieve reliable moral enhancement.

Consider the ability to empathize. This is, on any reasonable account, a capacity that is "implicated in moral reasoning, decision-making, acting and so forth" (Pacholczyk, 2011, 253), and it is one whose potential modification has become a staple of the moral enhancement literature (see, e.g., Persson and Savulescu, 2013). To see how this capacity might be biomedically "enhanced" in the functional-augmentative sense, imagine that someone took a drug similar to MDMA (see, e.g., Sessa, 2007; Earp, 2015b) that, at least temporarily, made it so that the person became able to experience *more* empathy or to experience empathy *more readily* in response to relevant stimuli. Would this be morally desirable? Would the person behave "more morally" while under the influence of the drug? Obviously, it depends. As we will see in the following section, the relationships between increasing or strengthening a morally relevant capacity such as empathy ("enhancing" it, in the functional-augmentative sense), morally improving one's motives and behavior, and becoming a morally better agent are complex and context specific. They also depend on which moral theory is correct or most justified, which is open to dispute: obviously, people will disagree about what constitutes, for example, "morally desirable behavior," and they may also disagree about how, if at all, the moral goodness of an agent depends upon the moral desirability of her behavior (or motivations, etc.).

In short, if the goal is to produce morally better agents, on whatever (plausible) conception of "morally better" one prefers—as we have suggested should be the case and as we have highlighted with our agential definition of moral neuroenhancement—then a narrow focus on "boosting" specific moral capacities, we believe, is likely to be at best a small part of the story.

The Limits of Empathy

To see why this is the case, let us pursue the example of empathy in greater detail.[2] As the neuroscientist Simon Baron-Cohen (2011) has argued, even such "obviously" morally desirable capacities as the ability to empathize may have morally undesirable consequences in certain cases. Mark Stebnicki (2007), for example, has discussed the phenomenon of "empathy fatigue," which refers to the physical and emotional exhaustion that grief and trauma counselors sometimes come to face: their inability to *distance* themselves emotionally from the pain and suffering of their clients may ultimately interfere with optimal job performance (for related work, see, e.g., Melvin, 2012, and Perry et al., 2011, on "compassion fatigue" among nurses). Likewise, Carol Williams (1989) has hypothesized that among helping professionals, high emotional empathizers may be disposed to earlier career burnout, thereby undermining their long-term effectiveness (see Zenasni et al., 2012, for a more recent discussion).

Empathy can also lead us astray when it comes to making moral judgments specifically. For example, there is the "identifiable victim" effect (but see Russell, 2014), according to which people have a stronger emotional reaction to the suffering of a known individual (thereby motivating them to help that specific individual) than to the greater suffering of an "anonymous" individual (or group of individuals) that would benefit more from the same act or degree of help (see, e.g., Jenni and Loewenstein, 1997; Small and Loewenstein, 2003). As the economist Thomas Schelling (1984) once observed:

> Let a six-year-old girl with brown hair need thousands of dollars for an operation that will prolong her life until Christmas, and the post office will be swamped with nickels and dimes to save her. But let it be reported that without a sales tax the hospital facilities of Massachusetts will deteriorate and cause a barely perceptible increase in preventable deaths—not many will drop a tear or reach for their checkbooks.
>
> (115)

Making the point more generally, Jesse Prinz (2011) has argued, "empathy is prone to biases that render moral judgment potentially harmful" (214).

Similar statements have been made by Paul Bloom (2013, 2016), Peter Singer (2014), Ole Martin Moen (2014), and others. While this intellectual movement "against empathy" (Bloom, 2016) and in favor of more "abstract" or "cold" cognition geared toward maximizing welfare on a utilitarian calculus has its detractors (e.g., Christian, 2016; Cummins, 2013; Srinivasan, 2015; but see McMahan, 2016), the broader point remains the same: moral agents require flexibility in how they "deploy" their lower-order moral capacities so that they can respond appropriately to justified reasons for making certain kinds of decisions over others. By contrast, trying generally to "dial up" or "dial down" some discrete moral capacity or function (assuming that such a thing were even possible without incurring serious adverse side effects) will be at best a highly unreliable means to becoming a morally better agent.

Thus, whether spraying a dose of oxytocin up someone's nose to increase empathy or trust, say, is likely to amount to an agential moral enhancement will depend not only upon the specific effects of the drug at various dosages but also upon the psychological and social context in which this is done. For example, it will depend upon who is receiving the dose of oxytocin, what her values are, what her chronic and momentary mental states are, what situation(s) she is in both short and long term, what particular decisions she faces and is likely to face, and so on (see Wudarczyk et al., 2013, for a related discussion).

So it wouldn't be just "more empathy" (*tout court*) that would be expected to lead to the improvement of a moral agent qua moral agent but rather an increase in what might roughly be described as a kind of second-order empathic control—an ability to (1) know or to identify, whether consciously or unconsciously, when it is morally desirable to feel empathy and/ or allow it to shape one's outward behavior (and in what way), as well as (2) to be able to feel such empathy or, if necessary, suppress such feelings (or their effects on behavior), in accordance with (1).

Similarly with a sense of fairness or justice, feelings of righteous anger or moral disgust, motivations associated with causing harm, and so on—the whole suite of underlying moral emotions, intuitions, and capacities (see generally, e.g., Haidt, 2007; Haidt and Joseph, 2004). If such capacities could be developed or augmented at their second-order level of description, this would be a more promising target, we believe, for interventions aimed at achieving (agential) moral enhancement, whether the intervention happened to be carried out with the assistance of a neurotechnology that acted directly on the brain or whether it was of a more familiar kind (e.g., traditional moral instruction without the aid of, say, brain stimulation or pharmaceuticals). In other words, it is likely that augmenting higher-order capacities to *modulate* one's moral responses in a flexible, reason-sensitive, and context-dependent way would be a more reliable, and in most cases more desirable, means to agential moral enhancement.

Direct Versus Indirect Moral Enhancement

We are not the first to distinguish between the direct modification of specific moral traits, functions, or emotions versus the modification of higher-order moral capacities. Instead, our discussion shares some features with, for example, Schaefer's recent examination of "direct vs. indirect" moral enhancement (Schaefer, 2015). Direct moral enhancements, according to Schaefer, "aim at bringing about *particular* ideas, motives or behaviors," which he sees as being problematic in much the same way that we see the functional augmentation of first-order moral capacities or emotions as being problematic. By contrast, what Schaefer calls indirect moral enhancements "aim at making people more reliably produce the morally correct ideas, motives or behaviors without committing to the content of those ideas, motives and/or actions" (Schaefer, 2015, 261, emphasis added), an aim that is consistent with that of the second-order interventions we have just alluded to.

Briefly, Schaefer disfavors "direct" moral enhancement (especially if it were carried out programmatically, by, for example, a state rather than undertaken voluntarily on a case-by-case basis) because he worries that such "enhancement" could suppress dissent: if everyone were forced to hold the exact same or even highly similar moral beliefs, dispositions, and the like, then moral disagreement would likely fall by the wayside (see Earp, 2016). But such disagreement is valuable, Schaefer argues, because without it, "conventional wisdom will go unchallenged and moral progress becomes essentially impossible" (Schaefer, 2015, 265). Schaefer also disfavors "direct" moral enhancement because, in his view, such enhancement might interfere with, bypass, or otherwise undermine conscious reasoning and rational deliberation. Instead of "coming to believe or act on a given moral proposition because it is the most reasonable," he fears, "we would come to believe or act on it because a particular external agent (the enhancer) said it is best" (268) and perhaps even "implanted" it in our brains.

We are not confident that this fear is justified. At least, more work would need to be done to show how such enhancement would be significantly different from or worse than various current forms of moral education that aim at inculcating specific moral tendencies, values, and beliefs—sometimes, as in the case of children, without first explaining the reasons why (although such explanations may of course later be given or become apparent over time on their own). Insofar as this is a valid concern, however, it could plausibly be addressed by emphasizing the need for individual, voluntary enhancement, as opposed to top-down or coerced external enhancement, and indeed Schaefer seems open to this view. But whatever the solution to this problem, we agree that the ability to deliberate and to rationally evaluate different moral propositions is important and that there would be strong reasons against pursuing any form of moral enhancement that had the effect of impairing such an ability.

In fact, this very same acknowledgement of the importance of rational deliberation (though note that we do not presume that genuine moral insights must always be strictly rationally derived) paves the way for one of Schaefer's main alternatives to direct moral enhancement, namely "indirect" moral enhancement. "It is quite plausible to think," he writes, "that there is value in the process itself of deliberating over a moral proposition, both within one's own mind and in discussion with others" (2015, 268). In light of this consideration, one form of indirect moral enhancement that would be at least *prima facie* permissible (and perhaps even desirable), then, would be to *improve the reasoning process itself*. The idea is that, all else being equal, better reasoning is likely to result in better moral beliefs and decisions, and consequently to better— that is, more moral—action.

For more on ethical decision making, see Chapter 20.

What would this actually look like? Among other things, it might involve improving people's logical abilities (i.e., "people's ability to make proper logical inferences and deductions, spot contradictions in their own beliefs and those of others, as well as formulate arguments in a way that can highlight the true point of contention between interlocutors"); promoting conceptual understanding (since "vague and distorted ideas will lead to unreliable inferences, inducing behaviors that are not in line with someone's considered judgments"); and overcoming cognitive biases (Schaefer, 2015, 276). Importantly, none of these enhancements would force a person to adopt any *particular* moral position, motivation, or behavior—thereby allowing for moral disagreement to persist, which is important, Schaefer claims, for moral progress—nor would they undermine rational deliberation, since, by definition, they would be expected to foster it. Certainly, allowing and/or helping people to reason better, with fewer biases, should be seen as uncontroversial (setting aside for now the crucial question of means); and this does seem to be a plausible way of "mak[ing] people more reliably produce the morally correct ideas, motives, and/or actions without specifying the content of those ideas, motives, and/or actions" in advance (262; see also Douglas, 2008, 231, Douglas, 2013, 161).

For more on moral reasoning, see Chapter 19.

Schaefer's other major proposal for "indirect" moral enhancement is something he calls "akrasia reduction," where akrasia is defined as acting against one's better judgment, typically due to weakness of will. As Schaefer writes:

> Weakness of will affects morality in a very straightforward way. Someone recognizes that some course of action is morally ideal or morally required, but nevertheless fails to carry out that action. For instance, someone might recognize the moral imperative to donate significant sums of money to charity because that money could save a number

of lives, yet remain selfishly tight-fisted. This is a failure of someone's consciously-held moral judgments to be effective.

(2015, 277)

Schaefer argues that individuals should be permitted to "work on" their weakness of will—in order to reduce associated akrasia—but that no one should be forced to undertake such (indirect) moral self-enhancement (with the possible exception of children being brought up by their parents; for a related discussion, see Maslen et al., 2014). Again, this seems uncontroversial: strengthening one's will to act in accordance with one's considered judgments, moral or otherwise, is usually[3] a virtue on any plausible account (see Persson and Savulescu, 2016); the only significant debate in this area, as we have just suggested, has to do with the question of means (see Focquaert and Schermer, 2015).

Traditional moral education, including the development and maintenance of good motivations and habits, is the most obvious—and least contentious—possibility. We take it that attempting to reduce one's weakness of will (and improve one's reasoning abilities) by such "traditional" methods as, for example, meditation, Aristotelian habituation (see Steutel and Spiecker, 2004), studying logic or moral philosophy, and engaging in moral dialogue with others, is clearly permissible—indeed laudable—and we expect that few would disagree. This is the "philosophically mundane" version of moral enhancement that we flagged in our introduction. It is rather moral enhancement[4] by means of or at least involving neurotechnological intervention, specifically, that we expect will be seen as more controversial, and it is this case to which we turn in the following section.

The Role of Neurotechnology in Moral Enhancement

Is it permissible or even desirable to engage in "indirect" moral self-enhancement (on Schaefer's account) or agential moral self-enhancement via modulation of second-order moral capacities (on our account), *with the help of neurotechnologies*? Let us first reemphasize that we are concerned only with *voluntary* moral (self-) enhancement in this chapter, which we take to be the easiest case to justify (see Earp, et al., 2013), chiefly on liberal or libertarian grounds. In other words, we are setting aside the much more difficult question of whether wide-scale enhancement of, for example, the moral character of all of humanity could be justified (if it were possible). Let us also state at the outset that *if* moral enhancement with the aid of neurotechnology is in fact permissible or even desirable, it is likely to be so only under certain conditions. For reasons we will soon discuss, the most promising scenario for permissible, much less desirable or optimal, agential moral (self-) neuroenhancement seems to us to be one in which at least the following conditions apply:

1. the drug or technology in question is used as an *aid* or *adjunctive* intervention to well-established "traditional" forms of moral learning or education (rather than used, as it were, in a vacuum), such that
2. the drug or technology allows for conscious reflection about and critical engagement with any moral insights that might be facilitated by the use of the drug (or by states of mind that are occasioned by the drug); and
3. the drug or technology has been thoroughly researched, with a detailed benefit-to-risk profile, and is administered under conditions of valid consent.

We are not prepared to argue that any currently available drug meets all three of these conditions. However, it does seem possible that some currently available putative cognitive enhancers, such as modafinil and methylphenidate (see, e.g., Greely et al., 2008; Turner et al., 2003; but see Lucke et al., 2011; Outram, 2010), could, if used as an adjunct to moral education, potentially meet them in the future. So too might certain drugs or other neurointerventions that worked by attenuating emotional biases that would otherwise impede moral learning (although research in this area is currently nascent and scarce). Finally, although we will discuss the example of so-called psychedelic drugs in the following section, we must be clear that we do not advocate the use of these drugs by anyone, in any setting, but are rather flagging them as possible targets for future research (see Earp et al., 2012, for a related discussion).

With respect to conditions (1) and (2), it should be noted that "traditional" means of moral education frequently operate by enhancing an agent's moral understanding: her understanding of what morality requires and why. This requires some degree of rational engagement. Now, some critics of "direct" moral neuroenhancement, such as John Harris (2012, 2013) have suggested that interventions into what we are calling first-order moral emotions or capacities would *not* enhance the agent's moral understanding. Others have made similar claims. Fabrice Jotterand (2011), for instance, argues that "[w]hile the manipulation of moral emotions might change the behavior of an individual, it does not provide any content, for example, norms or values to guide one's behavioral response" (6, see also 8). Similarly, Robert Sparrow (2014) suggests that "it is hard to see how any drug could alter our beliefs in such a way as to track the reasons we have to act morally" and that "someone who reads Tolstoy arguably learns *reasons* to be less judgmental and in doing so develops greater understanding: someone who takes a pill has merely *caused* their sentiments to alter" (2 and 3).[5]

But what about reading Tolstoy *while* taking a pill (i.e., a pill that enhances one's moral learning vis-à-vis the text)? The supposition here is that this hypothetical pill would occasion a state of mind that made the moral lessons of Tolstoy more apparent or more compelling to the reader.[6] Indeed, the importance of a robust educational or learning context cannot be overstated: what we envision is a *facilitating* rather than *determining* role for any drug or neurotechnology (see Naar, 2015; see also Earp, Sandberg, and Savulescu, 2016), underscoring the need for critical engagement with some kind of actual moral "content" (e.g., "norms or values"). Arguably, we need not look to the distant future, or to hypothetical sci-fi scenarios, to imagine what such drug-assisted (as opposed to drug-caused or drug-determined) agential moral enhancement might plausibly look like. Instead, we can look to the past and present.

Attempted Moral Neuroenhancements, Past and Present

In a recent book chapter, the theologian Ron Cole-Turner (2015) writes that technologies of moral enhancement "are not new. For millennia we have known that certain disciplines and techniques can enhance our spiritual awareness. We have also known that certain substances can alter our consciousness in interesting ways" (369). Jonathan Haidt (2012) expands on this idea, noting that most traditional societies have a coming-of-age ritual designed to transform immature children into morally and socially competent adults and that many of them use "hallucinogenic drugs to catalyze this transformation" (266). The mental states induced by such drugs, according to anthropologists, are intended to "heighten" moral learning "and to create a bonding among members of the cohort group" (quoted in Haidt, 2012, 266).

Notice the words "enhance," "catalyze," and "heighten" in these quotations, which suggest a *facilitating* rather than strictly *determining* role for the hallucinogenic drugs in these societies, administered as part of a richly contextualized process of moral learning. This is worth highlighting, in our view, since moral lessons, abilities, dispositions, and the like, that are achieved or developed with the *help* of a neurotechnology—as opposed to directly caused by it (thereby preserving space for conscious reflection, effort, and engagement)—could be seen as posing less of a threat to such important issues as authenticity, autonomy, and rational deliberation, as emphasized by (among others) Schaefer (2015).

Consider the use of ayahuasca, a plant-based brew containing MAO inhibitors and N,N-dimethyltryptamine or DMT, which has been employed in traditional shamanic ceremonies across the Amazon basin and elsewhere for hundreds of years (Homan, 2011; McKenna et al., 1984). According to Michael J. Winkelman (2015, 96) the active ingredients in ayahuasca, in combination with a certain restrictive diet, may occasion an "altered state of consciousness" in the initiate in which her "artistic and intellectual skills" are seen as being enhanced, thereby allowing her to better appreciate the teachings of the shaman. Winkelman stresses, however, the *interactive* relationships among: healer and patient (initiate), various "ritual factors," and what he calls psycho- and sociotherapeutic activities, in shaping the learning experience. A similar emphasis is given by William A. Richards (2015, 140) in reference to the drug psilocybin:

> It is clear that psilocybin . . . never can be responsibly administered as a medication to be taken independent of preparation and careful attention to the powerful variables of [one's mindset] and [physical] setting. One cannot take psilocybin as a pill to cure one's alienation, neurosis, addiction, or fear of death in the same way one takes aspirin to banish a headache. What psilocybin *does* is provide an opportunity to explore a range of non-ordinary states. It unlocks a door; how far one ventures through the doorway and what awaits one . . . largely is dependent on non-drug variables.

We caution the reader that it is not currently legal in many jurisdictions to consume these substances (see Ellens and Roberts, 2015, for further discussion), and we reemphasize that we are not advocating their use by any person, whether for attempted moral enhancement or anything else. Our point is merely that the intentions for which and manner in which some hallucinogenic drugs have been used in certain settings resemble the approach to moral enhancement for which we argue in this chapter (i.e., a facilitating role for the neurotechnology, active engagement with moral content, a rich learning context, etc.), suggesting that this approach is not a radical departure from historical practices. That said, rigorously controlled, ethically conducted scientific research into the effects of such drugs on moral learning or other moral outcomes (in concert with appropriate psychosocial and environmental factors) may well be worth pursuing (Tennison, 2012; see also Frecska et al., 2016; Griffiths et al., 2006; Griffiths et al., 2008; Soler et al., 2016; Thomas et al., 2013).

Objections and Concerns

We see it as uncontroversial that individuals have moral reasons to increase the moral desirability of their character, motives, and conduct and that actually doing so is morally desirable. Moral neuroenhancements in particular appear to be immune to many of the more common moral concerns that have been raised about neuroenhancements (or bioenhancements generally). These concerns have often focused on ways in which neuroenhancements undergone by some individuals might harm or wrong others, for example, by placing them at an unfair competitive disadvantage or by undermining commitments to solidarity or equality. Moral neuroenhancements are unusual among the main types of neuroenhancements that have been discussed heavily in the recent literature in that they might plausibly be expected to advantage rather than disadvantage others (though see, for a criticism of this view, Archer, 2016).

Nevertheless, some significant concerns have been raised regarding the permissibility and desirability of undergoing moral neuroenhancements or certain kinds of moral neuroenhancements. Some of these are general concerns about enhancing the moral desirability of our characters, motives, and conduct, regardless of whether this is undertaken through moral neuroenhancement or through more familiar means such as traditional moral education. In this category are concerns that stem from a general skepticism about the *possibility* of moral improvement, as well as concerns about whether we have adequate means for resolving disagreement and uncertainty about what character traits, motives, and conduct are morally desirable and why. However, the first of these concerns strikes us as implausible: even if people disagree on certain moral issues, there are surely *some* moral behaviors and/or dispositions that everyone can agree are better than *some* alternative moral behaviors and/or dispositions—even if only at the far extremes—and if it is psychologically possible to move even a little bit from the less desirable side of things toward the more desirable side, then (agential) moral improvement is also possible. As for the second concern about resolving disagreements, this does not seem to us to be damning even if it is true: of course there will be disagreements about what counts as "morally desirable"—in the realm of traditional moral enhancement as well as in the realm of moral neuroenhancement—but as Schaefer (2015) points out, such disagreement is in fact quite healthy in a deliberative society and is perhaps even necessary for moral progress (see also Earp, 2016).

Other points of contention have to do with general concerns about neuroenhancement that would also apply to nonmoral neuroenhancements. In this category are concerns regarding the unnatural means or hubristic motives that biomedical enhancement is said to involve (Kass, 2003; Sandel, 2007). We will set those issues aside as being tangential to the focus of this chapter. There are, however, also more specific concerns about moral neuroenhancements—concerns that would not apply equally to traditional means of moral enhancement or to other kinds of neuroenhancement. The remainder of this section outlines two dominant concerns in this category.

Concern 1: Restriction of Freedom

One concern that has been raised regarding moral neuroenhancement or at least certain variants of it is that it might restrict freedom or autonomy. Harris (2011) argues that we might have reason to abstain from moral neuroenhancements because they would restrict our freedom to perform morally undesirable actions or to have morally undesirable motives (see also Ehni and Aurenque, 2012, and, for a more general discussion of the effects of neuroenhancement on autonomy, Bublitz and Merkel, 2009).

Two main types of response have been made to this line of argument. The first is that, even where moral neuroenhancements do restrict freedom, it might nevertheless be morally permissible or all-things-considered morally desirable to undergo such enhancements (DeGrazia, 2014; Douglas, 2008; Persson and Savulescu, 2016; Savulescu et al., 2014; Savulescu and Persson, 2012). Suppose that you come across one person about to murder another. It seems that you should intervene to prevent the murder even though this involves restricting the prospective murderer's freedom to act in a morally undesirable way. Similarly, it seems that, if he could, the would-be murderer should have restricted his own freedom to commit the murder by, for example, having a friend lock him in his room on days when he knows he will be tempted to commit a murder. The obvious way of accounting for these intuitions is to suppose that, in at least some cases, any disvalue associated with restricting one's freedom to act in morally undesirable ways is outweighed by the value of doing so.

The second response has been to deny that *all* moral neuroenhancements would in fact restrict freedom, thus limiting the concern about freedom to a subset of moral neuroenhancements. Responses in the second category sometimes begin by noting that worries about the freedom-reducing effect of moral neuroenhancements presuppose that freedom is consistent with one's motives and conduct being causally determined (Persson and Savulescu, 2016). If we could be free only if we were causally undetermined, we would already be completely unfree, because we are causally determined, in which case moral neuroenhancements could not *reduce* our freedom. Alternatively, we are free only because, at least *some* of the time, we act on the basis of reasons, in which case moral neuroenhancements that operate without affecting (or by actually enhancing) our capacity to act on the basis of reasons would not reduce our freedom (DeGrazia, 2014; Persson and Savulescu, 2016; Savulescu et al., 2014; Savulescu and Persson, 2012).

Finally, although we cannot pursue this argument in detail, we have suggested that agential moral neuroenhancement could plausibly be achieved by targeting second-order moral capacities, thereby increasing a kind of "moral impulse control." On this account, we should be open to the idea that moral neuroenhancements could actually *increase* a person's freedom, that is, her ability to behave autonomously (Earp, Sandberg, and Savulescu, 2015). Niklas Juth (2011, 36) asks, "Can enhancement technologies promote individuals' autonomy?" And answers: "*Yes*. In general plans require capacities in order for them to be put into effect and enhancement technologies can increase our capacities to do the things we need to do in order to effectuate our plans." Similarly, Douglas (2008) has argued that diminishing countermoral emotions (things that tend to interfere with whatever counts as good moral motivation) is also a kind of second-order moral enhancement, and in many cases it will also increase freedom (since the countermoral emotions are also constraints on freedom; see also Persson and Savulescu, 2016).

Concern 2: Misfiring

A second concern that can be raised regarding moral neuroenhancements maintains that attempts at moral neuroenhancement are likely to misfire, bringing about moral deteriorations rather than improvements. This is not a concern about successful moral neuroenhancements, but is rather a concern that actual attempts at moral neuroenhancement are likely to be unsuccessful.

Harris (2011) advances this concern by noting that "the sorts of traits or dispositions that seem to lead to wickedness or immorality are also the very same ones required not only for virtue but for any sort of moral life at all" (104). He infers from this that the sorts of psychological alterations that would be required for genuine moral neuroenhancement would involve not the wholesale elimination or dramatic amplification of particular dispositions but rather a kind of fine-tuning of our dispositions (see also Jotterand, 2011; Wasserman, 2011). However, he argues that the disposition-modifying neurotechnologies that we are actually likely to have available to us will be rather blunt, so that attempts at such fine-tuning are likely to fail.

We might respond to this in two ways. First, we agree, as we argued earlier, that the elimination or amplification of particular moral dispositions or capacities is likely, on balance, to be an unreliable way of bringing about genuine (agential) moral enhancement. But we are less convinced that the technologies we are likely to have available to us could not bring such enhancement about. This is based on our exploration of the possibility of drug-assisted moral learning, where we drew on examples from certain so-called traditional societies, where such moral learning is generally understood to be not only possible but also (at least sometimes) actually occurrent. Whether such moral learning involves, or amounts to, a "fine-tuning of our [moral] dispositions," then, would be beside the point, because agential moral neuroenhancement would, by whatever mechanism, be taking place (thus showing that it is indeed possible).

Agar (2010, 2013) sets forward a more limited variant of the concern raised by Harris. He argues that attempted moral neuroenhancements may have good chances of success when they aim only to correct subnormal moral functioning (such as might be exhibited by a psychopath or a hardened criminal), bringing an individual within the normal range, but that they are likely to misfire when they aim to produce levels of moral functioning above the normal range (he does not comment on moral neuroenhancements that operate wholly within the normal range). Subnormal moral functioning, he claims, is often the result of relatively isolated and easily identified defects such as, for example, the deficient empathy that characterizes psychopathy (but see Bloom, 2016, for further discussion). Agar speculates that these defects could relatively safely and effectively be corrected. However, he argues that, to attain supernormal levels of moral desirability, we would need to simultaneously augment or attenuate several different dispositions in a balanced way. This, he claims, will be very difficult, and there is a serious risk that it would misfire.

Defenders of moral neuroenhancement have conceded to these concerns, acknowledging both that (1) in many cases, complex and subtle interventions would be needed in order to enhance moral desirability and that (2) this creates a risk that attempted moral neuroenhancements will fail, perhaps resulting in moral deterioration (Douglas, 2013; Savulescu et al., 2014). However, it is not obvious that achieving supernormal moral functioning would, as Agar suggests, always require the alteration of multiple capacities. Imagine a person who would function at a supernormal level, except for the fact that she performs suboptimally on a single moral dimension. An intervention affecting that dimension alone might be sufficient to achieve supermoral functioning. Moreover, focusing on augmenting the powers of more traditional moral education, as we have proposed here, could be expected to produce moral improvements across a range of dimensions and might in this way produce the breadth and balance of moral improvement that Agar takes to be necessary without requiring multiple distinct enhancement interventions.

Finally, some doubt has been cast on the notion that neurointerventions are invariably inapt when complex and subtle psychological alterations are sought. For example, Douglas (2011) notes that there are other areas—such as clinical psychiatry—in which we often also use rather blunt biological interventions as part of efforts to achieve subtle and multidimensional psychological changes. Yet in that area, we normally think that attempting some interventions can be permissible and desirable if undergone cautiously, keeping open the option of reversing or modifying the intervention if it misfires. Douglas suggests that a similar approach might be justified in relation to moral neuroenhancers.

Conclusion

In this chapter, we have considered moral enhancement in terms of agential moral neuroenhancement. This means any improvement in a moral agent qua moral agent that is effected or facilitated in some significant way by the application of a neurotechnology. We have distinguished between first- and second-order moral capacities. First-order capacities include basic features of our psychology that are relevant to moral motivations and behavior, such as empathy and a sense of fairness. As we argued, there is no straightforward answer to whether augmenting these functions constitutes agential moral enhancement, just as one cannot say that having supersensitive hearing is good for a person without knowing that person's context (for a related discussion in the context of disability, see Kahane and Savulescu, 2009, and Kahane and Savulescu, 2016). What makes having a capacity valuable is being able to employ it in the right circumstances and in the right way(s), which means having appropriate control over its regulation.

In addition, we have emphasized a *facilitating* role for neurotechnologies in bringing about moral enhancement rather than a determining role, which leaves room for rational engagement, reflection, and deliberation: this allowed us to address concerns that such processes might be undermined. Another consequence of thinking in terms of facilitation is that moral neuroenhancers should not ideally be used "in a vacuum" but rather in a meaning-rich context, as we illustrated briefly with "traditional" examples (e.g., ayahuasca). Finally, we have responded to two main moral concerns that have been raised regarding the pursuit of moral neuroenhancement, namely that it would restrict freedom or else "misfire" in various ways. We argued that these concerns, while worth taking seriously, are not fatal to the view we have presented.

Acknowledgments

Minor portions of this chapter have been adapted from Douglas (2015). The first author (Earp) wishes to thank the editors of this volume for the opportunity to contribute a chapter and Michael Hauskeller for inviting him to present some of these ideas at the 2016 Royal Institute of Philosophy Annual Conference held at the University of Exeter.

Notes

1 This caveat points to an ambiguity in our functional-augmentative account of enhancement. As we wrote, such enhancement involves "increasing the ability of the function to do what it normally does" (Earp et al., 2014, 2). But what is the "ability of [a] function," exactly, and what does it mean to "increase" it? Plainly, it depends upon the function in question, which in turn depends upon, among other things, the level of description one uses to cordon off that function from alternative targets of intervention. In this case, if by "augmented" hearing, one meant simply *more sensitive* hearing, as implied by our illustration, then a noisy environment might indeed make this "enhancement" undesirable. If instead one meant the augmentation of a higher-order hearing capacity—one that allowed a person to pick up on subtle sounds in a quiet environment but also to "tune out" loud and uncomfortable sounds in a noisy environment, then the augmentation of this more flexible, higher-order capacity would be much more likely to be regarded as desirable across a range of possible circumstances. This is very similar to what we have in mind when we talk about the neuroenhancement of higher-order *moral* capacities, as will become clear over the course of what follows.

2 This paragraph is adapted from Earp et al. (2014).

3 Obviously, there are exceptions. Consider Heinrich Himmler; he had firm (but false) moral beliefs, and given this, the weaker his will, the better (see, for discussion, Bennett, 1974). Schaefer (2015) actually discusses this issue at length, arguing, essentially, that while there are always exceptions to the rule, in most cases and on balance, akrasia reduction will lead to moral improvement.

4 Here we mean "indirect" moral enhancement (on Schaefer's account) or agential moral enhancement via modulation of second-order moral capacities (on our account).

5 Please note that the page numbers for the Sparrow quotes come from the version of his essay available online at http://profiles.arts.monash.edu.au/wp-content/arts-files/rob-sparrow/ImmoralTechnology ForWeb.pdf.

6 But note that there are other ways of responding to these concerns as well. For example, some defenders of moral neuroenhancement have suggested that even "direct" interventions into first-order moral emotions or capacities could conceivably improve moral understanding, in certain cases, by attenuating emotional barriers to sound moral deliberation (Douglas, 2008). And even if a first-order moral neuroenhancement intervention had no positive effect on moral understanding initially, Wasserman (2011) has argued that we might expect an agent's experience with morally desirable motives and conduct (as judged against a relatively stable background) to lead to a development in moral understanding over time. This parallels the Aristotelian point that one comes to know the good by being good (Burnyeat, 1980).

Further Reading

DeGrazia, D. (2014) "Moral enhancement, freedom, and what we (should) value in moral behaviour". *Journal of Medical Ethics* 40(6), 361–368.

Harris, J. (2016) *How to Be Good.* Oxford: Oxford University Press.

Persson, I. and Savulescu, J. (2012) *Unfit for the Future: The Need for Moral Enhancement.* Oxford: Oxford University Press.

Sparrow, R. (2014) "Better Living Through Chemistry? A Reply to Savulescu and Persson on Moral Enhancement". *Journal of Applied Philosophy* 31(1), 23–32.

Wiseman, H. (2016) *The Myth of the Moral Brain: The Limits of Moral Enhancement.* Cambridge, MA: MIT Press.

References

Agar, N. (2010) Enhancing genetic virtue? *Politics and the Life Sciences* 29(1): pp. 73–75.

———. (2013) A question about defining moral bioenhancement. *Journal of Medical Ethics* 40(6): pp. 369–370.

Archer, A. (2016) Moral enhancement and those left behind. *Bioethics.* Available online ahead of print at: http://onlinelibrary.wiley.com/doi/10.1111/bioe.12251/full

Baron-Cohen, S. (2011) Autism, empathizing-systemizing (e-s) theory, and pathological altruism. In B. Oakley, A. Knafo, G. Madhaven, and D.S. Wilson (Eds.). *Pathological Altruism.* Oxford: Oxford University Press, pp. 344–348.

Bartz, J.A., Zaki, J., Bolger, N., and Ochsner, K.N. (2011) Social effects of oxytocin in humans: Context and person matter. *Trends in Cognitive Sciences* 15(7): pp. 301–309.

Bennett, J. (1974) The conscience of Huckleberry Finn. *Philosophy* 49(188): pp. 123–134.

Bloom, P. (2013) The baby in the well. *The New Yorker*, 20 May. Available at: www.newyorker.com/magazine/2013/05/20/the-baby-in-the-well

———. (2016). *Against Empathy.* New York: HarperCollins.

Bublitz, J.C., and Merkel, R. (2009) Autonomy and authenticity of enhanced personality traits. *Bioethics* 23(6): pp. 360–374.

Burnyeat, M.F. (1980) Aristotle on learning to be good. In A.O. Rorty (Ed.). *Essays on Aristotle's Ethics.* Berkeley, CA: University of California Press, pp. 69–92.

Christian, R. (2016) Should you give money to beggars? Yes, you should. *Think: A Journal of the Royal Institute of Philosophy* 15(44): pp. 41–46.

Clausen, J. (2010) Ethical brain stimulation—neuroethics of deep brain stimulation in research and clinical practice. *European Journal of Neuroscience* 32(7): pp. 1152–1162.

Cole-Turner, R. (2015) Spiritual enhancement. In C. Mercer and T.J. Trothen (Eds.). *Religion and Transhumanism: The Unknown Future of Human Enhancement.* Santa Barbara, CA, Denver, CO: Praeger, pp. 369–383.

Craig, J.N. (2016) Incarceration, direct brain intervention, and the right to mental integrity a reply to Thomas Douglas. *Neuroethics.* Available online ahead of print at: http://link.springer.com/article/10.1007/s12152-016-9255-x

Crockett, M.J. (2014) Moral bioenhancement: a neuroscientific perspective. *Journal of Medical Ethics* 40(6): pp. 370–371.

Cummins, D. (2013) Why Paul Bloom is wrong about empathy and morality. *Psychology Today*, 20 October. Available at: www.psychologytoday.com/blog/good-thinking/201310/why-paul-bloom-is-wrong-about-empathy-and-morality

Davis, N.J., and Koningsbruggen, M.V. (2013) "Non-invasive" brain stimulation is not non-invasive. *Frontiers in Systems Neuroscience* 7(76): pp. 1–4.

DeGrazia, D. (2014) Moral enhancement, freedom, and what we (should) value in moral behavior. *Journal of Medical Ethics* 40(6): pp. 361–368.

Donaldson, Z.R., and Young, L.J. (2008) Oxytocin, vasopressin, and the neurogenetics of sociality. *Science* 322(5903): pp. 900–904.

Douglas, T. (2008) Moral enhancement. *Journal of Applied Philosophy* 25(3): pp. 228–245.

———. (2013) Moral enhancement via direct emotion modulation: A reply to John Harris. *Bioethics* 27(3): pp. 160–168.

———. (2015) The morality of moral neuroenhancement. In J. Clausen and N. Levy (Eds.). *Handbook of Neuroethics*. Dordrecht: Springer, pp. 1227–1249.

Douglas, T., Bonte, P., Focquaert, F., Devolder, K., and Sterckx, S. (2013) Coercion, incarceration, and chemical castration: an argument from autonomy. *Journal of Bioethical Inquiry* 10(3): pp. 393–405.

Earp, B.D. (2015a) "Legitimate rape," moral coherence, and degrees of sexual harm. *Think: A Journal of the Royal Institute of Philosophy* 14(41): pp. 9–20.

Earp, B. D. (2015b). Drogen nehmen - um Wohl unserer Kinder? GEO 10(1): pp. 62–63.

Earp, B. D. (2016) In praise of ambivalence: "young" feminism, gender identity, and free speech. Quillette Magazine, 2 July. Available at: http://quillette.com/2016/07/02/in-praise-of-ambivalence-young-feminism-gender-identity-and-free-speech/

Earp, B.D., Sandberg, A., Kahane, G., and Savulescu, J. (2014) When is diminishment a form of enhancement? Rethinking the enhancement debate in biomedical ethics. *Frontiers in Systems Neuroscience* 8(12): pp. 1–8.

Earp, B.D., Savulescu, J., and Sandberg, A. (2012) Should you take ecstasy to improve your marriage? Not so fast. *Practical Ethics*. University of Oxford, 14 June. Available at: http://blog.practicalethics.ox.ac.uk/2012/06/should-you-take-ecstasy-to-improve-your-marriage-not-so-fast/.

Earp, B.D., Sandberg, A., and Savulescu, J. (2014) Brave new love: the threat of high-tech "conversion" therapy and the bio-oppression of sexual minorities. *American Journal of Bioethics Neuroscience* 5(1): pp. 4–12.

———. (2015) The medicalization of love. Cambridge Quarterly of Healthcare Ethics 24(3): pp. 323–336.

———. (2016) The medicalization of love: response to critics. *Cambridge Quarterly of Healthcare Ethics*, 25(4): pp. 759–771.

Earp, B.D., Wudarczyk, O.A., Sandberg, A., and Savulescu, J. (2013) If I could just stop loving you: Anti-love biotechnology and the ethics of a chemical breakup. *The American Journal of Bioethics* 13(11): pp. 3–17.

Ehni, H.-J., and Aurenque, D. (2012) On moral enhancement from a Habermasian perspective. *Cambridge Quarterly of Healthcare Ethics* 21(2): pp. 223–234.

Ellens, J.H., and Roberts, B. (Eds.) (2015) *The Psychedelic Policy Quagmire: Health, Law, Freedom, and Society*. Santa Barbara, CA, Denver, CO: Praeger.

Focquaert, F., and Schermer, M. (2015) Moral enhancement: Do means matter morally? *Neuroethics* 8(2): pp. 139–151.

Frecska, E., Bokor, P., and Winkelman, M. (2016) The therapeutic potentials of ayahuasca: possible effects against various diseases of civilization. *Frontiers in Pharmacology* 7(35): pp. 1–17.

Fregni, F., and Pascual-Leone, A. (2007) Technology insight: noninvasive brain stimulation in neurology—perspectives on the therapeutic potential of rTMS and tDCS. *Nature Clinical Practice Neurology* 3(7): pp. 383–393.

Ginsberg, Y., Långström, N., Larsson, H., and Lichtenstein, P. (2013) ADHD and criminality: Could treatment benefit prisoners with ADHD who are at higher risk of reoffending? *Expert Review of Neurotherapeutics* 13(4): pp. 345–348.

Ginsberg, Y., Långström, N., Larsson, H., and Lindefors, N. (2015) Long-term treatment outcome in adult male prisoners with attention-deficit/hyperactivity disorder: three-year naturalistic follow-up of a 52-week methylphenidate trial. *Journal of Clinical Psychopharmacology* 35(5): pp. 535–543.

Glenn, A.L., and Raine, A. (2008) The neurobiology of psychopathy. *Psychiatric Clinics of North America* 31(3): pp. 463–475.

Greely, H., Sahakian, B., Harris, J., Kessler, R.C., Gazzaniga, M., Campbell, P., and Farah, M.J. (2008) Towards responsible use of cognitive-enhancing drugs by the healthy. *Nature* 456(7223): pp. 702–705.

Griffiths, R.R., Richards, W.A., McCann, U., and Jesse, R. (2006) Psilocybin can occasion mystical-type experiences having substantial and sustained personal meaning and spiritual significance. *Psychopharmacology* 187(3): pp. 268–283.

Griffiths, R.R., Richards, W.A., Johnson, M.W., McCann, U.D., and Jesse, R. (2008) Mystical-type experiences occasioned by psilocybin mediate the attribution of personal meaning and spiritual significance 14 months later. *Journal of Psychopharmacology* 22(6): pp. 621–632.

Gupta, K. (2012) Protecting sexual diversity: rethinking the use of neurotechnological interventions to alter sexuality. *American Journal of Bioethics: Neuroscience* 3(3): pp. 24–28.

———. (2007) The new synthesis in moral psychology. *Science* 316(5827): pp. 998–1002.

Haidt, J. (2012) *The Righteous Mind: Why Good People Are Divided by Politics and Religion.* New York: Vintage.

Haidt, J., and Joseph, C. (2004) Intuitive ethics: How innately prepared intuitions generate culturally variable virtues. *Daedalus* 133(4): pp. 55–66.

Hamilton, R., Messing, S., and Chatterjee, A. (2011) Rethinking the thinking cap: Ethics of neural enhancement using noninvasive brain stimulation. *Neurology* 76(2): pp. 187–193.

Harris, J. (2011) Moral enhancement and freedom. *Bioethics* 25(2): pp. 102–111.

———. (2012) What it's like to be good. *Cambridge Quarterly of Healthcare Ethics* 21(3): pp. 293–305.

———. (2013) "Ethics is for bad guys!" Putting the 'moral' into moral enhancement. *Bioethics* 27(3): pp. 169–173.

Homan, J. (2011) *Charlatans, Seekers, and Shamans: The Ayahuasca Boom in Western Peruvian Amazonia.* Dissertation (University of Kansas). Available at: https://kuscholarworks.ku.edu/handle/1808/8125

Ipser, J., and Stein, D.J. (2007) Systematic review of pharmacotherapy of disruptive behavior disorders in children and adolescents. *Psychopharmacology* 191(1): pp. 127–140.

Jenni, K., and Loewenstein, G. (1997) Explaining the identifiable victim effect. *Journal of Risk and Uncertainty* 14(3): pp. 235–257.

Jotterand, F. (2011) "Virtue engineering" and moral agency: Will post-humans still need the virtues? *American Journal of Bioethics: Neuroscience* 2(4): pp. 3–9.

Juth, N. (2011) Enhancement, autonomy, and authenticity. In J. Savulescu, R. Muelen, and G. Kahane (Eds.). *Enhancing Human Capacities*. Oxford: Blackwell, pp. 34–48.

Kahane, G., and Savulescu, J. (2009) The welfarist account of disability. In A. Cureton and K. Brownlee (Eds.). *Disability and Disadvantage*. Oxford: Oxford University Press, pp. 14–53.

———. (2016) Disability and mere difference. *Ethics* 126(3): pp. 774–788.

Kass, L.R. (2003) Ageless bodies, happy souls. *New Atlantis* 1: pp. 9–28.

Knoch, D., Pascual-Leone, A., Meyer, K., Treyer, V., and Fehr, E. (2006) Diminishing reciprocal fairness by disrupting the right prefrontal cortex. *Science* 314(5800): pp. 829–832.

Lane, A., Luminet, O., Nave, G., and Mikolajczak, M. (2016) Is there a publication bias in behavioural intranasal oxytocin research on humans? Opening the file drawer of one laboratory. *Journal of Neuroendocrinology* 28(4): pp. 1–15.

Lane, A., Mikolajczak, M., Treinen, E., Samson, D., Corneille, O., de Timary, P., and Luminet, O. (2015) Failed replication of oxytocin effects on trust: the envelope task case. *PLOS One* 10(9): p. e0137000.

Lösel, F., and Schmucker, M. (2005) The effectiveness of treatment for sexual offenders: a comprehensive meta-analysis. *Journal of Experimental Criminology* 1(1): pp. 117–146.

Lucke, J.C., Bell, S., Partridge, B., and Hall, W.D. (2011) Deflating the neuroenhancement bubble. *American Journal of Bioethics: Neuroscience* 2(4): pp. 38–43.

McMahan, J. (2016) Philosophical critiques of effective altruism. *The Philosophers' Magazine.* 73(1): pp. 92–99. Available at: http://jeffersonmcmahan.com/wp-content/uploads/2012/11/Philosophical-Critiques-of-Effective-Altruism-refs-in-text.pdf

McKenna, D.J., Towers, G.N., and Abbott, F. (1984) Monoamine oxidase inhibitors in South American hallucinogenic plants: tryptamine and β-carboline constituents of ayahuasca. *Journal of Ethnopharmacology* 10(2): pp. 195–223.

McMillan, J. (2014) The kindest cut? Surgical castration, sex offenders and coercive offers. *Journal of Medical Ethics* 40(9): pp. 583–590.

Maibom, H.L. (2014) To treat a psychopath. *Theoretical Medicine and Bioethics* 35(1): pp. 31–42.

Margari, F., Craig, F., Margari, L., Matera, E., Lamanna, A.L., Lecce, P.A., . . . Carabellese, F. (2014) Psychopathology, symptoms of attention-deficit/hyperactivity disorder, and risk factors in juvenile offenders. *Neuropsychiatric Disease and Treatment* 11(1): pp. 343–352.

Maslen, H., Earp, B.D., Kadosh, R.C., and Savulescu, J. (2014) Brain stimulation for treatment and enhancement in children: an ethical analysis. *Frontiers in Human Neuroscience* 8(953): pp. 1–5.

Melvin, C.S. (2012) Professional compassion fatigue: What is the true cost of nurses caring for the dying? *International Journal of Palliative Nursing* 18(12): pp. 606–611.

Moen, O.M. (2014) Should we give money to beggars? *Think: A Journal of the Royal Institute of Philosophy* 13(37): pp. 73–76.

Montoya, E.R., Terburg, D., Bos, P.A., and Van Honk, J. (2012) Testosterone, cortisol, and serotonin as key regulators of social aggression: a review and theoretical perspective. *Motivation and Emotion* 36(1): pp. 65–73.

Naar, H. (2015) Real-world love drugs: reply to Nyholm. *Journal of Applied Philosophy* 33(2): pp. 197–201.

Nave, G., Camerer, C., and McCullough, M. (2015) Does oxytocin increase trust in humans? A critical review of research. *Perspectives on Psychological Science* 10(6): pp. 772–789.

Outram, S.M. (2010) The use of methylphenidate among students: the future of enhancement? *Journal of Medical Ethics* 36(4): pp. 198–202.

Pacholczyk, A. (2011) Moral enhancement: What is it and do we want it? *Law, Innovation and Technology* 3(2): pp. 251–277.

Parens, E. (2013) The need for moral enhancement. *Philosophers' Magazine* 62(1): pp. 114–117.

Perlmutter, J.S., and Mink, J.W. (2005) Deep brain stimulation. *Annual Review of Neuroscience* 29(1): pp. 229–257.

Perry, B., Toffner, G., Merrick, T., and Dalton, J. (2011) An exploration of the experience of compassion fatigue in clinical oncology nurses. *Canadian Oncology Nursing Journal* 21(2): pp. 91–97.

Persson, I., and Savulescu, J. (2008) The perils of cognitive enhancement and the urgent imperative to enhance the moral character of humanity. *Journal of Applied Philosophy* 25(3): pp. 162–177.

———. (2010). Moral transhumanism. *Journal of Medicine and Philosophy* 35(6): pp. 656–669.

———. (2011) The turn for ultimate harm: A reply to Fenton. *Journal of Medical Ethics* 37(7): pp. 441–444.

———. (2012) *Unfit for the Future: The Need for Moral Enhancement*. Oxford: Oxford University Press.

———. (2013) Getting moral enhancement right: The desirability of moral bioenhancement. *Bioethics* 27(3): pp. 124–131.

———. (2014) Should moral bioenhancement be compulsory? Reply to Vojin Rakic. *Journal of Medical Ethics* 40(4): pp. 251–252.

———. (2016) Moral bioenhancement, freedom and reason. *Neuroethics*. Available online ahead of print at: http://link.springer.com/article/10.1007/s12152-016-9268-5

Prinz, J. (2011) Against empathy. *Southern Journal of Philosophy* 49(s1): pp. 214–233.

Rabins, P., Appleby, B.S., Brandt, J., DeLong, M.R., Dunn, L.B., Gabriëls, L., . . . Mayberg, H.S. (2009) Scientific and ethical issues related to deep brain stimulation for disorders of mood, behavior, and thought. *Archives of General Psychiatry* 66(9): pp. 931–937.

Richards, W.A. (2015) Understanding the religious import of mystical states of consciousness facilitated by psilocybin. In J.H. Ellens and B. Roberts (Eds.). *The Psychedelic Policy Quagmire: Health, Law, Freedom, and Society*. Santa Barbara, CA, Denver, CO: Praeger, pp. 139–144.

Russell, L.B. (2014) Do we really value identified lives more highly than statistical lives? *Medical Decision Making* 34(5): pp. 556–559.

Sandel, M. (2007) *The Case Against Perfection: Ethics in the Age of Genetic Engineering*. Cambridge, MA: Harvard University Press.

Savulescu, J., and Persson, I. (2012). Moral enhancement, freedom, and the god machine. *Monist* 95(3): pp. 399–421.

Savulescu, J., Douglas, T., and Persson, I. (2014) Autonomy and the ethics of biological behaviour modification. In A. Akabayashi (Ed.). *The Future of Bioethics: International Dialogues*. Oxford: Oxford University Press, pp. 91–112.

Savulescu, J., Sandberg, A., and Kahane, G. (2011) Well-being and enhancement. In J. Savulescu, R. ter Meulen, and G. Kahane (Eds.). *Enhancing Human Capacities*. Oxford: Wiley-Blackwell, pp. 3–18.

Schaefer, G.O. (2015) Direct vs. indirect moral enhancement. *Kennedy Institute of Ethics Journal* 25(3): pp. 261–289.

Schelling, T.C. (1984) *Choice and Consequence*. Cambridge, MA: Harvard University Press.

Sessa, B. (2007) Is there a case for MDMA-assisted psychotherapy in the UK? *Journal of Psychopharmacology* 21(2): pp. 220–224.

Shook, J.R. (2012) Neuroethics and the possible types of moral enhancement. *American Journal of Bioethics: Neuroscience* 3(4): pp. 3–14.

Singer, P. (2014) Against empathy: commentary by Peter Singer. *Boston Review*. Available at: http://boston review.net/forum/against-empathy/peter-singer-response-against-empathy-peter-singer

Singh, I. (2008) Beyond polemics: science and ethics of ADHD. *Nature Reviews Neuroscience* 9(12): pp. 957–964.

Small, D.A., and Loewenstein, G. (2003) Helping a victim or helping the victim: altruism and identifiability. *Journal of Risk and Uncertainty* 26(1): pp. 5–16.

Soler, J., Elices, M., Franquesa, A., Barker, S., Friedlander, P., Feilding, A., . . . Riba, J. (2016) Exploring the therapeutic potential of ayahuasca: acute intake increases mindfulness-related capacities. *Psychopharmacology* 233(5): pp. 823–829.

Sparrow, R. (2014) (Im)moral technology? Thought experiments and the future of 'mind control.' In A. Akabayashi (Ed.). *The Future of Bioethics: International Dialogues*. Oxford: Oxford University Press, pp. 113–119. Cited page numbers from the online version. Available at: http://profiles.arts.monash.edu. au/wp-content/arts-files/rob-sparrow/ImmoralTechnologyForWeb.pdf

Srinivasan, A. (2015) Stop the robot apocalypse: the new utilitarians. *London Review of Books* 37(18): pp. 3–6.

Stebnicki, M.A. (2007) Empathy fatigue: healing the mind, body, and spirit of professional counselors. *American Journal of Psychiatric Rehabilitation* 10(4): pp. 317–338.

Steutel, J., and Spiecker, B. (2004) Cultivating sentimental dispositions through Aristotelian habituation. *Journal of Philosophy of Education* 38(4): pp. 531–549.

Synofzik, M., and Schlaepfer, T.E. (2008) Stimulating personality: ethical criteria for deep brain stimulation in psychiatric patients and for enhancement purposes. *Biotechnology Journal* 3(12): pp. 1511–1520.

Tennison, M.N. (2012) Moral transhumanism: the next step. *Journal of Medicine and Philosophy* 37(4): pp. 405–416.

Thibaut, F., Barra, F.D.L., Gordon, H., Cosyns, P., and Bradford, J.M. (2010) The World Federation of Societies of Biological Psychiatry (WFSBP) guidelines for the biological treatment of paraphilias. *World Journal of Biological Psychiatry* 11(4): pp. 604–655.

Thomas, G., Lucas, P., Capler, N.R., Tupper, K.W., and Martin, G. (2013) Ayahuasca-assisted therapy for addiction: results from a preliminary observational study in Canada. *Current Drug Abuse Reviews* 6(1): pp. 30–42.

Turgay, A. (2009). Psychopharmacological treatment of oppositional defiant disorder. *CNS Drugs* 23(1): pp. 1–17.

Turner, D.C., Robbins, T.W., Clark, L., Aron, A.R., Dowson, J., and Sahakian, B.J. (2003) Cognitive enhancing effects of modafinil in healthy volunteers. *Psychopharmacology* 165(3): pp. 260–269.

Wasserman, D. (2011) Moral betterness and moral enhancement, Presented at the 2011 Uehiro-Carnegie Conference, New York.

Williams, C.A. (1989) Empathy and burnout in male and female helping professionals. *Research in Nursing & Health* 12(3): pp. 169–178.

Winkelman, M.J. (2015) Psychedelic medicines. In J.H. Ellens and B. Roberts (Eds.). *The Psychedelic Policy Quagmire: Health, Law, Freedom, and Society*. Santa Barbara, CA, Denver, CO: Praeger, pp. 93–117.

Wiseman, H. (2014) SSRIs as moral enhancement interventions: a practical dead end. *American Journal of Bioethics: Neuroscience* 5(3): pp. 21–30.

———. (2016) *The Myth of the Moral Brain: The Limits of Moral Enhancement*. Cambridge, MA: MIT Press.

Wudarczyk, O.A., Earp, B.D., Guastella, A., and Savulescu, J. (2013) Could intranasal oxytocin be used to enhance relationships? Research imperatives, clinical policy, and ethical considerations. *Current Opinion in Psychiatry* 26(5): pp. 474–484.

Young, L., Camprodon, J.A., Hauser, M., Pascual-Leone, A., and Saxe, R. (2010) Disruption of the right temporoparietal junction with transcranial magnetic stimulation reduces the role of beliefs in moral judgments. *Proceedings of the National Academy of Sciences* 107(15): pp. 6753–6758.

Zenasni, F., Boujut, E., Woerner, A., and Sultan, S. (2012) Burnout and empathy in primary care: three hypotheses. *British Journal of General Practice* 62(600): pp. 346–347.

Zohny, H. (2014) A defence of the welfarist account of enhancement. *Performance Enhancement & Health*. *Performance Enhancement & Health*, 3(3): pp. 123–129.

12

MY BRAIN MADE ME DO IT?

Neuroscience and Criminal Responsibility

Valerie Gray Hardcastle

What is the relationship between deficiencies in the brain and criminal responsibility? This is a question that has received considerable scholarly attention over the past few years (Greene and Cohen, 2004; Farahany and Cohen, 2009; Gazzaniga and Steven, 2005; Glenn and Raine, 2014; Hardcastle, in press), and it is the question that occupies this chapter.

Even though the conversation might seem new, we can trace these discussions back to the late 1700s and the controversial work of the Viennese physician Franz Joseph Gall, who argued that the brain is the seat of the mind, is arranged into separate and distinct "faculties," each of which has a separate and distinct "organ" in the brain (Gall, 1798, 3). He went on to claim that one could determine character traits by reading the information off of the shape of the skull, which roughly conformed to the brain organs that supported our mental faculties, a practice known as phrenology. Though phrenology never became popular in the United States, people of that era certainly discussed the question of whether committing violent acts indicated mental or brain disorders. Isaac Ray, one of the founders of forensic psychiatry, hypothesized that moral mania existed, a mental disorder in which an "individual without provocation or any other rational motive, apparently in the full possession of his reason, and oftentimes, in spite of his most strenuous efforts to resist, imbrues his hands in the blood of others" (Ray, 1838, 197). Even today we question whether this is true.

But perhaps the event that threw this discussion into sharpest relief was the trial of Charles J. Guiteau for the assassination of President Garfield in 1888, one of the first high-profile cases in the United States that relied on an insanity defense (cf., Fink, 1938). Edward Charles Spitzka, a leading forensic psychiatrist at the time, testified at trial that "Guiteau is not only now insane, but that he was never anything else," and he stated that his condition was due to "a congenital malformation of the brain" (Rosenberg, 1995, 278). However, the opposing side argued that Guiteau was only pretending to be insane for the purposes of the trial (Christianson, 2002). Bound up with this disagreement was the question of whether a mental disorder or disease could explain criminal behavior in the first place. The defense insisted that it could; the prosecution denied that such a type of insanity even existed. Guiteau was found guilty and was sentenced to death.

Because Guiteau was kept in a mental institution in Washington, DC, after the trial until his hanging, it is clear that people believed that he was mentally ill in some fashion. However, it is just as clear that such a view did not stop the judge and jury from finding him responsible for

185

killing the president. A century and a third later, we are still embroiled in conflicts regarding the conditions under which mental disorders or brain dysfunction excuse defendants from responsibility or punishment. And in many respects, the arguments have not advanced since the late 1800s, even as our science has.

Stephen Morse (2012) points out that how neuroscientists and psychologists understand the origins of behavior conflicts with how the United States' justice system does; hence, he concludes, brain data have little place in trials. Science assumes that diseases, injuries, lesions, and deformities in the brain influence and can even determine an individual's thoughts, desires, impulses, abilities to reason, and control over behavior. That is, it assumes that there is no such thing as free will. On the other hand, the criminal justice system assumes that individuals are rational beings who act for articulable reasons, which are based on desires, beliefs, and social standards, and that in each instance of behavior, the individual could have done otherwise had he or she so chosen. In other words, it assumes that free will exists. As a result, legal scholars can dismiss neuroscience's potential impact in the criminal justice system, arguing that neuroscience can bring nothing new to criminal defense.

At the same time, brains and brain data are increasingly part of our everyday vernacular, as demonstrated by everything from the surging popularity of brain-training programs to the United States' BRAIN Initiative. The brain and its functioning have, for better or worse, become pop-culture fixtures in the 21st century (Thornton, 2011). Our current cultural fascination with all things brain-based cannot help but influence how neuroscience data are viewed by judges and juries in the courtroom.

For example, a recent analysis of newspaper articles published between 2000 and 2010 in the United States shows a marked increase in neurobiological explanations offered for criminal behavior (Robillard and Illes, 2011). In particular, the number of articles on this topic more than tripled from the first half of the analysis period to the second half, and, importantly, the most popular theme discussed in these articles was the relation between brain data and the question of responsibility. That brains are related to reasoning, decision making, behavior, and ultimately to responsibility for actions is almost a truism today. Morse's analysis aside, how are brain data actually affecting legal decisions regarding criminal responsibility, and how should they? This chapter provides a beginning of an answer to this question.

Neuroscience in the Courtroom

The exact number of times neuroscience evidence is admitted into court is unknown, although both surveys of forensic specialists and data from case citations in the legal databases show that such evidence has become fairly routine for the criminal justice system (Kaufmann, 2009; Sweet et al., 2011; Sweet and Guidotti Breting, 2013). Not surprisingly, the number of such cases continues to steadily increase (Farahany, 2016; Kaufmann and Greiffenstein, 2013; Larrabee, 2012; Shen, 2013).

We can divide the types of available "neuro" evidence into two broad categories: behavioral data and brain-imaging data. Behavioral exams require that individuals respond to a variety of questions, either through a physical demonstration or by answering questions verbally or in writing. Imaging tests record brain structure or brain activity by measuring related brain parameters, like electrical discharge, cerebral blood flow, and so on.

Simmons v. Mullins (1975) is perhaps the first modern case to recognize the potential contribution of neuro-data, when a psychologist was allowed to testify "as an expert on organic brain injury" (897; see also Kaufmann, 2009). Today, behavioral tests are routinely used in competency hearings, mitigation testimony, pain-and-suffering claims, and during the sentencing phase. In addition, detailed studies by psychologists, psychiatrists, and neurologists have validated their diagnostic use on individuals.

The same cannot be said for brain-imaging studies (the various computed tomographies [CT, PET, or SPECT], magnetic resonance imaging [MRI and fMRI], diffuse tensor imaging [DTI], and types of electroencephalography [EEG and QEEG]), however. It is important to understand the place imaging has in today's legal landscape. In contrast to behavioral tests, "neuroimaging is not an investigative tool; it is a confirmatory and explanatory tool" (Blume and Paavola, 2011, 911). One generally opts for a brain scan or other similar test once it is already known or suspected that there is some level of brain dysfunction. Except in rare cases, one does not use these techniques to discover whether dysfunction exists in the first place. The behavioral tests determine the level of malfunctioning in patients; brain images can then be used to determine what is causing or is correlated with the identified deficits. Most often, structural neuroimaging data (e.g., CT scans or MRI) are used as additional evidence in the courtroom for certain neurological diseases or physical brain injuries (Moriarty, 2008; see also Denno, 2015).

The community of scientists is in alignment with how imaging data are being used by courts. The recent *Consensus Report of the American Psychiatric Association Work Group on Neuroimaging Markers of Psychiatric Disorders* states that, while neuroimaging studies have presented promising results, "currently neuroimaging is not recommended within either the U.S. or European practice guidelines for positively defining diagnosis of any primary psychiatric disorder" (First et al., 2012, 2). A report from a Consensus Conference on the Ethical Use of Neuroimages in Medical Testimony concurs with this conclusion and suggests, "Neuroimaging technologies have a limited role in the clinical setting of behavioral disorders or psychiatric disease" (Meltzer et al., 2013, 1).

The Challenges for Brain Imaging

This understanding of their use does not mean brain data have found their judicial niche and that there are no further challenges to using them. Indeed, quite the contrary. There are additional problems in trying to use brain data to determine whether any particular individual is responsible for some action. Let me quickly summarize some of those issues here.

Researchers and clinicians diagnose and study brain deficits by comparing their patient's brain scan with averaged scans of normal individuals to pinpoint any differences that might be relevant to behavior. Most published imaging and other neurophysiological data are from averaged groups—neuroscientists scan several brains, compile the results, and then highlight the central tendencies in the data. The assumption is that any particular idiosyncratic brain patterns or responses will get washed out as unwanted noise in the averaging process, and what we are left with is how an idealized brain might react to the test (cf., Brown and Murphy, 2010).

While there is much of value in this approach, especially as we are just now beginning to understand how brains process and manage the information flowing through them, it also means that the averaged data ignore and gloss over individual differences. But the differences between brain structures or activation levels across normal individuals can be quite large. Individual differences can and often do swamp group effects. How each individual brain responds to stimuli can be so different from the rest that central tendencies and group effects give us little information about the pattern of responses for any particular individual brain. This is known as the "many-one" problem (Jones et al., 2014) in academic legal circles. The catch is showing that the data from the many apply to the one person before you, whose brain activity patterns may or may not approximate the averaged norm, regardless of any deficits.

This challenge is compounded by the fact that abnormal brain patterns of activity can overlap from one disorder, personality type, or behavioral trait to the next. Brains of those with violent tendencies can look remarkably similar to those with suicidal tendencies; brains of those with posttraumatic stress disorder look similar to those with anxiety disorders (cf. Bremner, 2007; Volavka, 1999). Part of the difficulty here is that very few studies compare brain activity across disorders; instead, they compare one type of illness or deficit to healthy or normal functioning. For diagnoses, one generally wants to know whether a patient has problem A, B, or C, not whether the patient is either normal or abnormal. But most research studies examine the latter question and not the former.

Brain data can also decouple from behavior. For example, data from athletes and soldiers with traumatic brain injury have demonstrated that repeated head trauma can result in the progressive degeneration of brain tissue and an abnormal increase or hyperphosphorylation of a protein called tau (e.g., Barkhoudarian et al., 2011; McKee and Robinson, 2014). Apart from progressive dementia, this sort of brain degeneration can also lead to impaired judgment and impulse control, depression, and aggression. However, autopsies done on a range of older subjects have found similar cases of tau build-up and brain degeneration although the decedents had no significant cognitive impairments before death (White et al., 2002). In other words, it appears possible for a defendant to have a brain that looks similar to those with significantly impaired cognition or problems with behavioral control but without any actual cognitive or behavioral abnormalities.

This fact can become especially important when dealing with alcohol addiction. For many addicts, it only takes a few months of sobriety before cognitive functioning starts to return to normal. But brain scans can still indicate prototypical damage from alcohol abuse even though behaviorally the patient has recovered (Chanraud et al., 2013; Pfefferbaum et al., 2001; Rosenbloom and Pfefferbaum, 2008). Researchers believe that the brain is rewiring itself to compensate for the neuronal losses, but there is no way to separate those addicts who have recovered cognitively from those who have not just by looking at their brain scans.

Because brains are extremely plastic, it can be difficult to infer the condition of a brain at some time in the past (especially if there has been a long delay) from how it appears now. Rarely do defendants have scans of their brain prior to relevant events, so no baseline scans exist against which to compare current patterns. Has the defendant's brain always been the way it is now, even if the behavior has deteriorated? Or has the defendant's brain been disintegrating over time, while the behavior has not changed? Brain scans alone are unable to answer these questions. Scans can only tell you what the brain looks like at the time of the scan, which can only be correlated with current behavioral tests. They cannot tell you with any real certainty what the brain was like a few months ago or a few years ago, when the crime was actually committed. The courts have recognized that brain scans have this limit. In *Forrest v. Steele* (2012), the United States District Court asserted that a PET scan "cannot show the cause of damage, nor can it demonstrate the [prior] existence of diminished capacity, predict future behavior, or establish a person's state of mind [at the time of the crime]."

To make matters worse, there are no standard test protocols for most of neuroscience, especially where the very expensive scans are concerned. Most facilities have developed their own hardware and their own computer programs for running the data analysis. Brain imaging is currently the product of subjective decisions and technical choices. Technicians have to decide the level of detail they will use to scan the brain, the dimensions of the brain "slices" to be measured, how to process the data, and how to filter the signals from background noise. As a consequence, it can be difficult to compare results across laboratories. Which areas are labeled overactive or underactive can depend on the specific tasks and instructions given to the patient, as well as the type of equipment and particular analytic techniques used. Unlike the behavioral tests, there is currently little to no standardization in brain scans.

Nevertheless, these data are being used in trials to help judges and juries understand how defendants might have gone awry. One can use these data, along with behavioral tests, to triangulate in on diagnoses and potential explanations for behavior. Given that the rate of neuroscience appearing in trials is increasing (see discussion in Hardcastle, 2014), do we also find a concomitant increase in the number of "not guilty by reason of insanity" defenses? Are more criminal defendants getting off, as it were? The answer is complicated.

For a discussion of legal issues related to sport-related brain injury, see Chapter 15.

Not Guilty by Reason of Insanity

Perhaps surprisingly, in the U.S. court system, a verdict of not guilty by reason of insanity (NGRI) occurs very rarely, despite its depiction on television procedural dramas. It is only sought in about 1% of criminal cases, and it is successful less than a third of the time it is requested (Melton et al., 2007). Very, very few cases are pleaded out or tried with this plea.

Part of the reason for this has to do with the very high bar courts set for this plea. United States NGRI laws and precedents date back to English common law in the mid-1800s. In 1843, Daniel M'Naghten thought that the Tories were plotting against him and the only way to stop their dastardly plan and save himself was to kill the prime minister. He believed he was attacking the prime minister when he in fact shot and killed Edward Drummond, the prime minister's secretary. The British court found him not guilty by reason of insanity. There was such a public outcry over this decision that the courts later issued a statement explaining when such a decision could be rendered. The standard has become known as the M'Naghten test. The language of the British courts should seem familiar to most of us:

> To establish a defense on the ground of insanity, it must be clearly proved that, at the time of the committing of the act, the party accused was laboring under such a defect of reason, from disease of the mind, as not to know the nature and quality of the act he was doing: or, if he did know it, that he did not know he was doing what was wrong.

To be found NGRI, one must either be so delusional as to not understand what one was doing or not understand right from wrong. Most states use some version of the M'Naghten test today. (Interestingly, Daniel M'Naghten should not have been found NGRI by this standard, since he both understood his actions and that they were illegal—he just believed that they were justified under the circumstances.)

Some U.S. jurisdictions use the "Model Penal Code" (MPC) test instead, which is broader than the M'Naghten criteria. Under the MPC test, defendants are considered NGRI if, at the time of the alleged crime, they could not appreciate the criminality of their conduct or they could not conform their behavior to the demands of the law. This test was common in the United States in the 1970s, but that quickly changed when John Hinckley, Jr., was found legally insane based on these criteria and NGRI for his attempted assassination of President Ronald Reagan in 1981. A few states still have what is known as the product test of insanity, which dates back to 1954 and *Durham v. United States*, in which the United States Court of Appeals for the District of Columbia Circuit decided that one could be declared not guilty if the unlawful act was the product of mental disease or defect. The difficulty with this criterion is that this is very difficult to demonstrate. As a consequence of the challenges with the MPC and the product tests for legal insanity, over the intervening years, most states have reverted to some version of what England used more than 150 years ago.

Similarly, the Criminal Code of Canada allows for defendants to be deemed unfit to stand trial (UST) or not criminally responsible on account of mental disorder (NCRMD; Penney et al., 2013). These or related criteria are used in most Western countries to remove incapacitated persons from questions of criminal responsibility for an offense (Howard, 2003; Zapf et al., 2006). And these criteria too are used quite rarely.

It is the case that most recently, the number of people being declared NGRI or its equivalent has gone up, suggesting that legal criteria for insanity are being applied more liberally over time (Joint Commission on Health Care, 2006). In addition, in the United States, there has been a substantial rise in the number of psychiatric beds in prisons, and a greater number of NGRI pleas were entered each year from 1996 to 2009 (National Association of State Mental Health Program Directors Research Institute, n.d.). We see the same trends in Europe, with steadily increasing numbers of imprisoned psychiatric patients in 15 European Union member states from 1990 to 2006 (Priebe et al., 2005, 2008; Salize and Dressing, 2007; Schanda et al., 2009).

These data suggest that the manner in which the NGRI and associated pleas are adjudicated has changed somewhat over the past 15 years or so to better align with society's preference to offer treatment in the least restrictive environment possible while still maintaining public safety (Crocker and Côté, 2009; Jansman-Hart et al., 2011; Mackay and Kearns, 1999; Mackay et al., 2006; see also discussion in what follows). Interestingly, this change is occurring despite legislation and case law that explicitly discourage the use of the NGRI defense (e.g., the Federal Insanity Defense Reform Act, 1984; *Jones v. United States,* 1983).

However, even with expanded use, the focus for NGRI and similar pleas is on those who cannot control their actions or who are not rational enough to understand and obey the commands of a law. These criteria virtually ensure that almost all NGRI defendants are psychotic; the actual rate of diagnosis is somewhere between 60% and 90%, depending on the study (Melton et al., 2007). Those who are found NGRI generally have such gross impairments that neuroscience data could add little to nothing to the trial.

Thus, data from neuroscience should not make an appreciable difference in determining legal responsibility, except perhaps in extreme or unusual cases. (For example, there is one case in which pedophilia was tied to a brain tumor. Once the tumor was removed, the pedophilic behaviors stopped. When the tumor grew back, the pedophilia returned. But there has only been one such documented case in which pedophilia was directly tied to a tumor; Burns and Swerdlow, 2003.) However, there are other uses for neuroscience in trial that also connect to questions of responsibility: brain data can be very useful in deciding upon appropriate plea or punishment. In these cases, they are used as mitigation.

Brain Data as Mitigation

Deborah Denno recently published a large empirical study examining all of the appellate decisions of criminal cases published in WestLaw and LexisNexis that used neuroscience data of any type from 1992 to 2012 (Denno, 2015). I have also completed a study of published appellate decisions that relied on brain-imaging data in their decisions from 2007 through 2013 (Hardcastle, 2015). These two projects, in addition to other, smaller-scale analyses (e.g., Schweitzer and Saks, 2011; Schweitzer et al., 2011), provide significant insight into how testimony about defendants' brains can influence the outcome at trial. Their use and impact run the gamut (see

Figure 12.1). Sometimes they easily and successfully persuade people that the defendant should receive little punishment; at other times, they fail completely to do so.

In *People v. Weinstein* (1992), an early and now famous (or infamous) PET scan case, Mr. Weinstein was accused of strangling his wife and pushing her out of the 12th-floor window of their apartment in an attempt to mask the murder as a probable suicide. Claiming that his patient lacked criminal responsibility due to a mental disease or defect, his psychiatrist proffered testimony that Weinstein had a cyst within the arachnoid membrane of the brain that caused "metabolic imbalances" in the other areas of the brain. The psychiatrist used data from PET scans to support his claims.

This case is controversial because it is not at all clear how an arachnoid cyst, which often begins prenatally and generally has few to no cognitive symptoms, could be causally connected to Mr. Weinstein's violent behavior. The prosecutor, however, was concerned that jurors would focus on the scan showing an undeniably large tumor and ignore the subtleties of medicine. Consequently, he offered Mr. Weinstein a manslaughter plea; Mr. Weinstein accepted and served only a minimal sentence in prison.

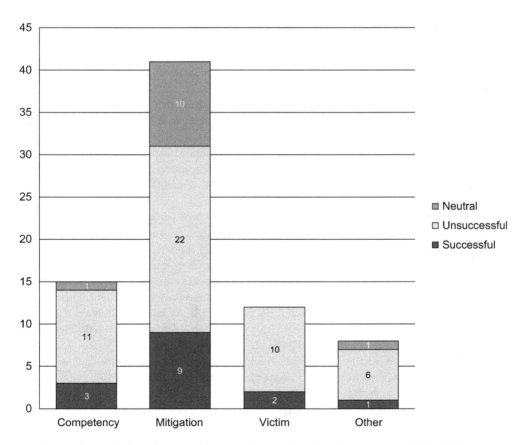

Fig. 12.1.   Use and Relative Success of Imaging Scans in Appellate Courts by Use (2007–2012).

Appellate cases in which judges cited and used some type of brain image in their decision over the past five years in the United States, sorted by purported type of use and their ultimate impact on the case. "Successful" refers to the defendant's case being remanded to a lower court or being overturned; "unsuccessful" refers to the appeal being denied; "neutral" means that the image, while cited and used, had no effect on the outcome of the case.

However, and not surprisingly, brain deficits are not always considered mitigating. *State v. Stanko* (2013) is an instance of this pattern. Stephen Christopher Stanko was sentenced to death for shooting an elderly friend, Henry Turner, in the back, using a pillow as a silencer, then hitting him on the back of the head, and then fatally shooting him in the chest. At his trial, a neuropsychologist and a neurologist both testified that Mr. Stanko had suffered significant damage to his frontal lobes from two separate injuries. The first occurred at birth, when he was deprived of oxygen; the second was a traumatic brain injury, when he was hit on the back of the head with a beer bottle as a teenager. As a result, his gray matter was four standard deviations below normal in his right hemisphere. The experts concluded that "this injury . . . would significantly compromise and impair an individual's ability to exercise judgment, impulse control, control of aggression." On appeal, the South Carolina Supreme Court ruled that while the "Appellant certainly presented evidence which could have reduced, mitigated, or excused the Victim's murder," it was not enough to reverse the original jury's final decision. Mr. Stanko currently sits on death row at the Leiber Correctional Institution in Ridgeville, South Carolina.

Published commentary on the use of neuroscience in the criminal justice system is generally cautious and cites concerns about judges and juries being able to understand complex neuroscience data such that they could make appropriate decisions using the data (cf., Farahany, 2009), as was also clearly the fear in the prosecutor's decision to settle in *People v. Weinstein*. These concerns have run the spectrum from worries about lay people being too dazzled by the pretty colors of brain scan illustrations to question what the data really mean (Nugent, 2012; Langleben and Moriarty, 2013) to anxieties that prosecutors would use the defense's data against the defendant to argue for future dangerousness.

However, both the Denno and the Hardcastle studies show that not only have brain data been well integrated into criminal trials but also judges and juries appear to have developed quite sophisticated ways of understanding and thinking about the data. It is clear that brain scans and other indicators of brain functioning have been introduced in trials for exactly the same reasons and in exactly the same way that other evidence is introduced: to give the finders of fact the best and most reliable information available about the defendant's context and capacities to aid in their determination of the fate of the accused.

Moreover, the *ABA Guidelines for the Appointment and Performance of Defense Counsel in Death Penalty Cases* requires that attorneys conduct an investigation into a defendant's neurological status as part of the defendant's mitigation claim: "Counsel must compile extensive historical data, as well as obtain a thorough physical and neurological examination. Diagnostic studies, neuropsychological testing, appropriate brain scans, blood tests or genetic studies, and consultation with additional mental health specialists may also be necessary" (2003, 956). This is quite sage advice, given that Denno (2015) found that, among the successful ineffective-assistance-of-counsel claims, nearly all them were based on an attorney's failure to correctly investigate, collect, or use neuroscience evidence. In particular, 60% of the death penalty cases resulted in such challenges based at least in part on the absence or misuse of neuroscience data, with 30% of those being granted based on that claim (statistics derived from Denno, 2015).

In some cases in which the courts found ineffective assistance of counsel based on a failure to properly deploy neuroscience data, the defense attorneys were obviously concerned about the data being used for aggravation instead of mitigation. Indeed, some legal scholars presume that evidence of brain damage could just as easily be used to argue in favor of future dangerousness, and therefore for a harsher penalty, as it could to provide support for a reduced penalty because the defendant was impaired (Jones and Shen, 2012; Snead, 2008). Courts recognized this possibility as far back as the 1980s: in *Perry v. Lynaugh* (1989), the court asserted that brain-based evidence could be a "double-edged sword: it may diminish [a defendant's] blameworthiness for his crime even as it indicates that there is a probability that he will be dangerous in the future."

However, there is limited evidence that this concern is actually justified as a serious consideration. Only 10 of the capital cases in Denno's study were able to directly connect neuroscience data to a claim of future dangerousness, and in none of the cases in Hardcastle's study were there even attempts to do so. Denno concludes that "overall there is little likelihood that neuroscience evidence introduced by the defense will be leveraged by the prosecution in an effort to prove the defendant's future dangerousness" (Denno, 2015, 528).

In many respects, what one sees in the records is exactly what one would expect to find: Mitigating factors are to be weighed against aggravating factors, and brain-imaging data are no different. One would expect brain scans to have less impact the worse the crime. At first blush, and as Morse (2012) has argued, introducing brain data into trials seems to have had little effect on how our criminal justice system actually functions.

And yet we are starting to get small hints that change is afoot in our legal system because of a deeper understanding of how brain injuries and neurological disorders affect behavior and control. In many jurisdictions, for example, we now have veterans, addiction, and mental illness diversion courts in which brain injuries or neurological disorders can excuse defendants from punishment for lesser and usually nonviolent crimes (cf., Hardcastle, forthcoming, 2017). These diversion courts belie the legal system's traditional notions of responsibility, for they are predicated on the idea that the criminal behavior is explained by something other than traditional reasons, beliefs, and desires, as our courts normally assume. In these courts, biological considerations trump questions of legal responsibility. Is this perhaps the beginning of a greater shift in how our criminal justice system functions relative to evidence from neuroscience? Perhaps Greene and Cohen were right when they wrote, "Neuroscience will probably have a transformative effect on the law, despite the fact that existing legal doctrine can, in principle, accommodate whatever neuroscience will tell us. New neuroscience will change the law . . . by transforming people's moral intuitions about free will and responsibility" (Greene and Cohen, 2004, 1775). Perhaps we are at the beginning of this sea change.

Diversion Courts and the Impact of Neuroscience

There is no denying that there is conceptual dissonance between how science understands how human behavior arises and how our judicial system does. At some point in the future, this dissonance will have to be resolved. But in the meantime, we are partially managing this conflict by diverting some defendants with mental disorders out of the traditional legal system. In other words, we are coping with the fundamental incompatibility between brain data and legal constructs by channeling the problematic cases that might highlight the irreconcilability through a special process that does not presume defendants' rational means–ends reasoning produced their behavior.

Since their inception in the late 1990s, diversion courts have played an increasingly large role in managing defendants accused of criminal behavior. These courts allow some defendants to enter mental health or addiction-treatment programs instead of going to jail. In many cases, the diversion courts allow participants to remain in the community as they complete treatment, and, if they complete successfully, the original charges are dropped. Though these courts are relatively new, preliminary data suggest that defendants who go through this system are more likely to become productive and law-abiding citizens than those who are warehoused in our prisons and jails (Marlowe, 2010).

Diversion courts are based on the notion that their defendants, while not delusional as required by NGRI, are still not as culpable as "normal" defendants. Perhaps it would make sense to describe them as semirational or semiresponsible or having committed semivoluntary acts, though in many respects, how we describe responsibility is less important than recognizing the fundamental conceptual shifts taking place. In these courts, biological explanations for behavior take precedence over reasons-based explanations. And, as our science of behavior grows more sophisticated, they are encroaching more and more on the territory covered by our regular criminal courts. If we believe our brains cause (or strongly influence) our behavior, and our brains are the way they are because of our genetic composition, chemical infusion, or life experiences, it becomes difficult to maintain that understanding behavior in terms of means–ends reasoning is coherent. From science's perspective, it is no longer clear what *mens rea* ("a guilty mind") would refer to, in many cases.

One can easily imagine a future in which all defendants get diverted because we would be able to identify something in their brains somewhere that influenced their criminal behavior. We might then remediate everyone, because no one has perfect self-control. In this case, no one is responsible for anything, and our system of criminal law would effectively cease to exist. Is this the natural outcome of the trends we are seeing now?

I suggest a different perspective. I do not believe that our legal system is on the verge of collapse. Nor do I believe that all defendants will be diverted in the near future. Instead, we should understand recent trends as a deep separation occurring between our notions of guilt and responsibility on the one hand and our sense of punishment on the other.

Both traditional courts and diversion courts have as their goal an orderly society with law-abiding citizens, but the similarities between them end there. Diversion courts rely on the idea of "therapeutic justice," which actually subverts conventional notions of punishment. Our workaday notion of punishment includes the commitments to retribution and compensation; therapeutic justice does not. Even though diversion treatments result in a loss of rights for defendants, they are not punitive in any traditional sense. Our legal system seems to be moving beyond a system of just desserts to one centered on therapy and rehabilitation, one that leaves long-established views of punishment as justified retribution for bad behavior far behind.

One way of understanding this trend is realizing that the question of legal responsibility is playing a smaller role in our justice system. Neuroscience and related data that point to underlying influences on behavior, beyond rather simplistic reason-and-desire explanations, are forcing us to rethink what our justice system is concerned with. We are becoming less concerned with whether someone committed the act and more concerned with why he or she did so. And we are starting to recognize that true responsibility for behavior goes beyond a one-off decision prior to the act. The true causes of behavior are deep, complex, and multifarious.

If we do accept that the concept of legal responsibility is outdated and is becoming separated from our assignments of punishment, then the eventual outcome must be a serious rethinking of our criminal justice system. However, I suspect that, over time, the criminal justice system will focus more and more on the appropriate type of punishment or remediation for each individual defendant based on the defendant's personal history and psychological profile and less on parsing the finer aspects of when someone is responsible for something under which circumstances.

Further Reading

Denno, D.W. (2015) "The Myth of the Double-Edged Sword: An Empirical Study of Neuroscience Evidence in Criminal Cases". *Boston College Law Review* 56, 493–551.

Hardcastle, V.G. (2015) "Would a Neuroscience of Violence Aid in Understanding Moral or Legal Responsibility?" *Cognitive Systems Research* 34–35: pp. 44–53.

Morse, S.J. (2012) "Neuroimaging evidence in law: A plea for modesty and relevance". In J.R. Simpson (Ed.). *Neuroimaging in Forensic Psychiatry: From the Clinic to the Courtroom*. Chichester: Wiley-Blackwell, pp. 341–358.

Vincent, N.A. (Ed.) (2013) *Neuroscience and Legal Responsibility*. New York: Oxford University Press.

Zapf, P.A., Golding, S.L. and Roesch, R. (2006) "Criminal responsibility and the insanity defense". In I.B. Weiner and A.K. Hess (Eds.). *The Handbook of Forensic Psychology, 3rd Edition*. Hoboken, NJ: Wiley, pp. 332–363.

References

American Bar Association. (2003) Guidelines for the appointment and performance of defense counsel in death penalty cases, revised edition. *Hofstra Law Review* 31: pp. 913–1090.

Barkhoudarian, G., Hovda, D.A., and Giza, C.C. (2011) The molecular pathophysiology of concussive brain injury. *Clinics in Sports Medicine* 30: pp. 33–48.

Blume, J.H., and Paavola, E.C. (2011) Life, death, and neuroimaging: The advantage and disadvantages of the defense's use of neuroimages in capital cases—lessons from the front. *Cornell Law Faculty Publications* Paper 212. Available at: http://scholarship.law.cornell.edu/facpub/212

Bremner, J.D. (2007) Neuro-imaging in post-traumatic stress disorder and other stress-related disorders. *Neuroimaging Clinics of North America* 17: pp. 523–538.

Brown, T., and Murphy, E. (2010) Through a scanner darkly: Functional neuroimaging as evidence of a criminal defendant's past mental states. *Stanford Law Review* 62: pp. 1119–1208.

Burns, J.M., and Swerdlow, R.H. (2003) Right orbitofrontal tumor with pedophilia symptom and constructional apraxia sign. *Archives in Neurology* 60: pp. 437–440.

Chanraud, S., Pital, A.-L., Müller-Oehring, E., Pfefferbaum, A., and Sullivan E.V. (2013) Remapping the brain to compensate for impairment in recovering alcoholics. *Cerebral Cortex* 23: pp. 97–104.

Christianson, S. (2002) Charles Guiteau Trial: 1881. *Great American Trials*. Available at: www.encyclopedia.com/doc/1G2-3498200100.html

Crocker, A.G., and Côté, G. (2009) Evolving systems of care: Individuals found not criminally responsible on account of mental disorder in custody of civil and forensic psychiatric services. *European Psychiatry* 24: pp. 356–364.

Denno, D.W. (2015) The myth of the double-edged sword: An empirical study of neuroscience evidence in criminal cases. *Boston College Law Review* 56: pp. 493–551.

Durham v. United States, 214 F.2d 852 (DC Cir. 1954).

Farahany, N.A. (Ed.) (2009) *The Impact of Behavioral Sciences on Criminal Law*. New York: Oxford University Press.

———. (2016) Neuroscience and behavioral genetics in US criminal law: An empirical analysis. *Journal of Law and the Biosciences* 2: pp. 485–509.

Farahany, N.A., and Cohen, J.E. (2009) Genetics, neuroscience, and criminal responsibility. In N.A. Farahany (Ed.). *The Impact of Behavioral Sciences on Criminal Law*, pp. 183–240.

Federal Insanity Defense Reform Act. 1984. 18 U.S.C. 17.

Fink, A.E. (1938) *Causes of Crime: Biological Theories in the United States, 1800–1915*. New York: A.S. Barnes, Perpetua Edition.

First, M., Botteron, K., Carter, C., Castellanoes, F.X., Dickstein, D.P., Drevets, W., . . . Zubieta, J.-K. (2012) Consensus report of the APA work group on neuroimaging markers of psychiatric disorders. American Psychiatric Association.

Forrest v. Steele, 2012 WL 1668358 (W.D. Mo May 11, 2012)

Gall, F.G. (1798) Letter from Dr. F.J. Gall, to Joseph Fr[eiherr] von Retzer: Upon the Functions of the Brain, in Man and Anima. *Der Neue Teutsche Merkur* 311: p. 3.

Gazzaniga, M.S., and Steven, M.S. (2005) Neuroscience and the law. *Scientific American Mind* 16: pp. 42–49.

Glenn, A.L., and Raine, A. (2014) Neurocriminology: Implications for the punishment, prediction, and prevention of criminal behavior. *Nature Reviews Neuroscience* 15: pp. 54–63.

Greene, J., and Cohen, J. (2004) For the law, neuroscience changes nothing and everything. *Philosophical Transactions of the Royal Society London B* 359: pp. 1775–1785.

Hardcastle, V.G. (2014) Traumatic brain injury, neuroscience, and the legal system. Neuroethics 8: pp. 55–64. doi:I 10.1007/s12152-014-9221-4.

———. (Forthcoming) Brain Images in the Courtroom: An Analysis of Recent Appellate Decisions in Criminal Cases. In G. Caruso and O. Flanagan. *Neuroexistentialism: Meaning, Morals, and Purpose in the Age of Neuroscience.* New York: Oxford University Press.

———. (Forthcoming) Diversion courts, traumatic brain injury, and American vets. In N. Vincent (Ed.). *Neuro-Interventions and the Law: Regulating Human Mental Capacity.* New York: Oxford University Press.

Hardcastle, V.G. (2015) Would a neuroscience of violence aid in understanding moral or legal responsibility? *Cognitive Systems Research* 34–35: pp. 44–53.

Howard, H. (2003) Reform of the insanity defense: Theoretical issues. *Journal of Criminal Law* 67: pp. 51–69.

Jansman-Hart, E., Seto, M.C., Crocker, A.G., Nicholls, T.L., and Côté, G. (2011) International trends in demand for forensic mental health services. *International Journal of Forensic Mental Health* 10: pp. 326–336.

Joint Commission on Health Care. (2006) *Report on Needs of Persons Found Not Guilty by Reason of Insanity or Incompetent to Stand Trial.* Senate Document No. 5. Available at: http://leg2.state.va.us/DLS/H&SDocs.NSF/4d54200d7e28716385256ec1004f3130/8425144c7809f0d885256fcc00684777?OpenDocument

Jones, O.D., and Shen, F.X. (2012) Law and neuroscience in the United States. In T.M. Spranger (Ed.). *International Neurolaw: A Comparative Analysis.* New York: Springer, pp. 349–362.

Jones, O.D., Schall, J.D., and Shen, F.X. (2014) *Law and Neuroscience.* New York: Wolters, Kluwer, and Business.

Jones v. United States. 1983. 463 U.S. 354.

Kaufmann, P. (2009) Protecting raw data and psychological tests from wrongful disclosure: A primer on the law and other persuasive strategies. *Clinical Neuropsychologist* 23: pp. 1130–1159.

Kaufmann, P.M., and Greiffenstein, M.F. (2013) Forensic neuropsychology: Training, scope of practice, and quality control. *National Academy of Neuropsychology Bulletin* 27: pp. 11–15.

Langleben, D., and Moriarty, J. (2013) Using brain imaging for lie detection: Where science, law, and policy collide. *Psychology, Public Policy and the Law* 19: pp. 222–234.

Larrabee, G. (Ed.) (2012) *Forensic Neuropsychology: A Scientific Approach.* 2nd ed. New York: Oxford University Press.

Mackay, R.D., and Kearns, G. (1999) More facts about the insanity defense. *Criminal Law Review* 36: pp. 714–725.

Mackay, R.D., Mitchell, B.J., and Howe, L. (2006) Yet more facts about the insanity defense. *Criminal Law Review* 6: pp. 399–411.

McKee, A.C., and Robinson, M.E. (2014) Military-related traumatic brain injury and neurodegeneration. *Alzheimer's and Dementia* 10: pp. S242-S253.

Marlowe, D.B. (2010) Research update on adult drug courts. *National Association of Drug Court Professionals.* Available at: www.nadcp.org/sites/default/files/nadcp/Research%20Update%20on%20Adult%20Drug%20Courts%20-%20NADCP_1.pdf.

Melton, G.B., Petrila, J., Poythress, N.G., and Slobogin, C. (2007) *Psychological Evaluations for the Courts*, 3rd Edition: *A Handbook for Mental Health Professionals and Lawyers.* New York: Guilford Press.

Meltzer, C., Sze, G., Rommelfanger, K., Kinlaw, K., Banja, J., and Wolpe, P. (2013) Guidelines for the ethical use of NeuroImages in medical testimony: Report of a multi-disciplinary consensus conference. *American Journal of Neuroradiology* A3711: pp. 1–6.

Moriarty, J.C. (2008) Flickering neuroadmissibility: Neuroimaging evidence in U.S. Courts. *Behavioral Sciences and the Law* 26: pp. 29–49.

Morse, S.J. (2012) Neuroimaging evidence in law: A plea for modesty and relevance. In J.R. Simpson (Ed.). *Neuroimaging in Forensic Psychiatry: From the Clinic to the Courtroom.* Chichester: Wiley-Blackwell, pp. 341–358.

National Association of State Mental Health Program Directors Research Institute. (n.d.) Available at: www.nri-inc.org, 1 August, 2010.

Nugent, K.M. (2012) Practical legal concerns. In J.R. Simpson (Ed.). *Neuroimaging in Forensic Psychiatry: From the Clinic to the Courtroom.* Chichester: Wiley-Blackwell, pp. 255–274.

Penney, S.R., Morgan, A., and Simpson, A.I.F. (2013) Motivational influences in persons found not criminally responsible on account of mental disorder: A review of legislation and research. *Behavioral Sciences and the Law* 31: pp. 494–505.

People v. Weinstein, 591 N.Y.S.2d 715 (N.Y.S.Ct. 1992).

Perry v. Lynaugh 492 U.S. 302, 324 (1989).

Pfefferbaum, A., Desmond, J.E., Galloway, C., Meno, V., Glover, G.H., and Sullivan, E.V. (2001) Reorganization of frontal systems used by alcoholics for spatial working memory: An fMRI study. *NeuroImage* 14: pp. 7–20.

Priebe, S., Badesconyi, A., Fioritti, A., Hansson, L., Kilian, H., Torres-Gonzales, F., . . . Wiersma, D. (2005) Reinstitutionalisation in mental health care: Comparison of data on service provision from six European countries. *British Medical Journal* 330: pp. 123–126.

Priebe, S., Frottier, P., Gaddini, A., Kilian, R., Lauber, C., Martínez-Leal, R., . . . Wright, D. (2008) Mental health care institutions in nine European countries, 2002 to 2006. *Psychiatric Services* 59: pp. 570–573.

Ray, I. (1838) *A Treatise on the Medical Jurisprudence of Insanity.* Boston: Little, Brown, and Company.

Robillard, J.M., and Illes, J. (2011) A link in the ink: Mental illness and criminal responsibility in the press. *Journal of Ethics in Mental Health* 6: pp. 1–7.

Rosenberg, C.E. (1995) *The Trial of the Assassin Guiteau: Psychiatry in the Gilded Age.* Chicago: University of Chicago Press.

Rosenbloom, M.J., and Pfefferbaum, A. (2008) Magnetic resonance imaging of the living brain: Evidence for brain degeneration among alcoholics and recovery with abstinence. *Journal of the National Institute on Alcohol Abuse and Alcoholism* 31: pp. 362–376.

Salize, H.J., and Dressing, H. (2007) Admission of mentally disordered offenders to specialized forensic care in fifteen European Union member states. *Social Psychiatry and Psychiatric Epidemiology* 42: pp. 336–342.

Schanda, H., Stompe, T., and Ortwein-Swoboda, G. (2009) Dangerous or merely "difficult"? The new population of forensic mental hospitals. *European Psychiatry* 24: pp. 365–372.

Schweitzer, N.J., and Saks, M. (2011) Neuroimages and the insanity defense. *Behavioral Sciences and the Law* 29: pp. 592–607. doi:10.1002/bsl.995

Schweitzer, N.J., Saks, M., Murphy, E., Roskies, A., Sinnott-Armstrong, W., and Gaudet, L. (2011) Neuroimages as evidence in a *mens rea* defense: No impact. *Psychology, Public Policy, and Law* 17: pp. 357–393.

Shen, F.X. (2013) Neuroscience, mental privacy, and the law. *Harvard Journal of Law and Public Policy* 36: pp. 653–653.

Simmons v. Mullins, 331 A.2d 892, 297 (Pa. Super. Ct. 1975).

Snead, O.C. (2008) Neuroimaging and the "complexity" of capital punishment. *New York University Law Review* 82: p. 1265.

State v. Stanko, 741 S.E.2d 708 (S.C., 2013) rehearing denied (Apr. 3, 2013), Petition for Certiorari filed July 2, 2013.

Sweet, J.J., and Guidotti Breting, L.M. (2013) Symptom validity test research: Status and clinical implications. *Journal of Experimental Psychopathology* 4: pp. 6–19.

Sweet, J.J., Giuffre Meyer, D., Nelson, N., and Moberg, P. (2011) The TCN/AACN "Salary Survey": Professional practices, beliefs, and incomes of U.S. neuropsychologists. *Clinical Neuropsychologist* 25: pp. 12–61.

Thornton, D.J. (2011) *Brain Culture: Neuroscience and Popular Media.* Piscataway, NJ: Rutgers University Press.

Volavka, J. (1999) The neurobiology of violence: An update. *Journal of Neuropsychiatry and Clinical Neuroscience* 11: pp. 307–314.

White, L., Petrovitch, H., Hardman, J., Nelson, J., Davis, D.G., Ross, W.G., . . . Markesbery, W.R. (2002) Cerebrovascular pathology and dementia in autopsied Honolulu-Asia Aging Study participants. *Annals of the New York Academy of Sciences* 977: pp. 9–23.

Zapf, P.A., Golding, S.L., and Roesch, R. (2006) Criminal responsibility and the insanity defense. In I.B. Weiner and A.K. Hess (Eds.). *The Handbook of Forensic Psychology.* 3rd ed. Hoboken, NJ: Wiley, pp. 332–363.

13

YOUR BRAIN ON LIES

Deception Detection in Court

Julie A. Seaman

Introduction

Imagine the following scenario: A police officer has been shot and killed. Two people were admittedly near the scene of the murder at the time it occurred, and it is reasonably clear that one of them committed the crime. Abbie says that when she saw Bob holding a gun, she took off running. She claims to have heard a gunshot as she ran but says her back was to the incident, so she cannot say for sure who pulled the trigger. Bob says that he saw Abbie shoot the police officer. Several witnesses variously incriminate Abbie in statements to investigators. There is no physical evidence. Abbie is convicted of the murder after a jury trial and sentenced to death.

For many years and through multiple appeals, Abbie maintains her innocence. Eventually, most of the witnesses recant their statements and swear under oath that they were pressured by police to incriminate Abbie. Bob, however, stands by his original testimony.[1]

Under these circumstances, the criminal justice system is stymied. It has no good way of figuring out whether the jury was correct to believe Bob and the other witnesses at trial or whether he was lying (likely to protect himself and/or make a deal with prosecutors), and the other witnesses were lying at trial but are now telling the truth. If there were biological material that could now be tested for DNA, such as skin cells on the gun, it might be possible to determine with some confidence whether it was Abbie or Bob who pulled the trigger, but without any physical evidence, we are left with the disconcerting prospect of Abbie's word against Bob's and no very good way of choosing between them. If we choose correctly, justice (as we define it, at least) has been served. If we make the wrong choice, then an innocent person has been punished for another's crime, and a guilty person—guilty not only of the original murder but also of wrongfully accusing an innocent person—has gone unpunished. Our current method for distinguishing lies from truth under these circumstances is the jury, which is composed of our fellow citizens. However, a great deal of evidence has demonstrated that people are very poor at detecting falsehood, with accuracy rates little better than chance (Seaman, 2008b).

Now imagine a one-hundred-percent-safe, foolproof, and noninvasive device that can read the mind and detect lies in the brain. If we questioned Abbie and Bob about the shooting,[2] this device would resolve the uncertainty once and for all. Is there any doubt that we should use such a device to help us decide whether the convicted defendant deserves release (and apology, and perhaps compensation for her lost years of freedom) and whether her accuser deserves punishment? Furthermore, once we have such a device, isn't it much less likely that this kind of scenario will be repeated in the future? After all, now criminals, witnesses, and investigators will know that their lies can be easily detected, so they will presumably be much less likely to lie in the first place. It might even be hoped that people will be less apt to commit crimes, since they will know that they are more likely to be caught and held accountable if they are unable to successfully lie about their involvement.

And yet many people are profoundly disconcerted by such a vision, viewing it as a dystopia rather than as a world we should aspire to.[3] Even after hypothesizing away the very significant scientific and technological hurdles of inconsistent methodology, potential use of countermeasures, replicability, reliability, generalizability, and ecological validity, there remains a core of discomfort with the prospect of a machine that could peer inside our minds and determine (among other things) whether we are lying (Shen, 2013).

Though the prospect of courtroom-ready lie detection through neuroscience is still a fair distance down the road, researchers have made significant strides in recent years that have garnered wide media attention. Indeed, though many scholars insist that it is misleading to use the term "mind reading," related research does genuinely raise the specter that a brain-scanning machine armed with computer algorithms might someday actually discover and reconstruct our private thoughts (Nishimoto et al., 2011). This chapter lays out the various objections to neuroscience-based lie detection technologies and assesses the prospects and perils of their use as evidence in the courtroom.

The Current State of Neuroscience Lie Detection (NLD) Research

In many ways, the current state of the research on brain-based lie detection is quite remarkable, given that the field is only about fifteen years old. Many of the most promising studies have been done using functional magnetic resonance imaging (fMRI), a brain-scanning technique whereby a subject undertakes a specified task while inside an MRI machine. Rather than take a static image of the brain—as a structural MRI would—a functional MRI measures blood flow over time as the subject performs a given task.[4] Such tasks might include looking at a photograph of a face, listening to music, making an economic decision, thinking about a particular object, or telling a lie. Because blood flow to specific areas of the brain is believed to signal that those areas are differentially activated during the particular task, fMRI results arguably reveal the neural correlates of the given activities. In the years since fMRI technology was developed, its use has exploded, with some 1,500 published studies in 2010 alone (Smith, 2012, 25). For many of the behaviors and cognitive processes scientists seek to measure using neuroscience—including deception—fMRI is more promising than other available technologies such as positron emission tomography (PET), and electro-encephalogram (EEG) because it is safe and noninvasive while at the same time able to pinpoint activity to specific structures within the brain.

In some of the earliest fMRI lie detection studies, researchers were broadly able to distinguish truthful from deceptive responses based on group block average results (e.g., Langleben, 2002; Spence et al., 2001). While these early results tended to rely on highly artificial experimental protocols that raised questions about their applicability to deception in the real world, they at least offered some proof of concept for the idea that there might be distinctive neural correlates for deception (however ultimately defined or taxonomized). As one researcher put it, a "lie appears to be a more working memory–intensive activity, characterized by increased activation of the [brain area] implicated in response selection, inhibition, and generation" (Langleben, 2005, 271).

One early series of experiments employed several variations on a playing-card paradigm whereby subjects were instructed to give either truthful or deceptive answers about playing cards while undergoing functional MRI scans. In the first study, subjects were given an envelope containing a playing card and a $20 bill and told to memorize the card and then return it to the envelope (Langleben, 2002). They were then told that if they successfully lied and thus "fooled" the computer as to the identity of their playing card, they would get to keep the $20 at the conclusion of the experiment. Once inside the scanner, the subjects were shown a series of photographs of cards, including the card in their envelope (the Lie card), and were asked whether each was their card. According to instructions, subjects were to deny having the Lie card but give truthful responses about all of the other cards shown to them. In each of five studies that employed some variation of this playing-card paradigm, researchers found statistically significant differences between the lie and truth responses, with the lie responses generally corresponding to increased activation in several brain areas thought to be involved in executive cognitive functions such as inhibition control, attention, and working memory (Seaman, 2008b, 447–452 for a summary of early studies).

Another group of early experiments was aimed at increasing the ecological validity—that is, the generalizability to real-world scenarios—of the research by creating more realistic deception scenarios. Two experiments, for example, had the subjects discover money that had been hidden under certain objects. The subjects were then placed in the scanner, shown photos of the objects, and variously instructed to give either true or false answers when asked where they had found the money (Kozel et al., 2004a, Kozel et al., 2004b). In two other experiments, the subjects actually participated in a mock crime and then answered questions about their involvement (Kozel et al., 2005; Mohamed et al., 2006). All of these studies found distinct neural patterns for deceptive as compared to truthful responses.

As the field has developed, researchers have sought to isolate different types of deception as they recognized that, for example, the neural correlates of a "white lie" in a social context might look very different from an intentional lie about one's past conduct or a lie of omission. One species of deception that is of particular interest in the legal context is "malingering," which encompasses various examples of feigned impairment, such as falsely claiming to be in pain or falsely claiming cognitive impairment or mental illness. Detection of malingering would have significant potential application in both criminal and civil litigation, including assessment of competency and insanity in the criminal context, and assessment of pain and injury in tort cases. Several fMRI studies have focused on feigned memory impairment and reported distinct patterns of neural activation for subjects faking memory impairment in response to questions, as compared to answering incorrectly or answering randomly (Browndyke et al., 2008; Lee et al., 2005). In particular, these studies "found widespread activation among frontal and posterior cortical regions that were greater during malingered inaccuracy than truthful, accurate responses" (Spence, 2008, 23).

13.1 Spotlight: Lie Detection Technologies

Valerie Gray Hardcastle

Lie detectors rely on particular questioning techniques coupled with technology to record physiological responses that supposedly indicate either truth telling or deception. It is an overstatement to say that it is an inexact science.

The two primary questioning techniques used are the comparison question test (CQT) and the guilty knowledge test (GKT). CQT requires subjects to respond to three kinds of yes–no questions: "relevants" are related to the matter under investigation (e.g., "Did you shoot your neighbor?"); "comparisons" should elicit a strong response in all subjects (e.g., "Did you ever steal something?"), and "irrelevants" establish a baseline ("Are you sitting in a chair?"). Stronger physiological response to relevants over irrelevants indicates deception or guilt. GKT compares a subject's responses to "relevant" ("Was the painting a Monet?" in an investigation of a stolen Monet) and "neutral" questions ("Was the painting a Picasso?"), which supposedly only the guilty party should be able to distinguish. Both CQT and GKT aim to detect changes in physiological responses to target conditions.

The most common technology used to measure these changes is the polygraph, which measures uncontrolled autonomic responses like skin conductivity, heart and respiration rates, blood pressure, and capillary dilation. The assumption behind this test is that subjects will be more anxious when they lie, which affects their autonomic system. Polygraphs can distinguish lying from truth telling at above-chance levels, though with significant error rates (Office of Technology Assessment, 1983, 5; see also National Research Council, 2003). Other technologies based on the assumption that lying induces stress attempt to measure micro-expressions, behavioral fidgeting, pupillary responses, or linguistic complexity.

The problem with this approach is that autonomic responses from the stress of lying are virtually identical to those from the stress of fear, anger, or surprise. Hence, a subject may appear to be deceptive when in reality she has only been caught off guard. In addition, countermeasures that prevent accurate comparisons among types of questions are well known. For example, subjects can thwart polygraphs by biting their tongue or strongly pressing their toes into the floor during the nontarget questions, eliciting a stress response (Honts et al., 1994). They can also distract their minds by mentally reciting the alphabet backward, which diminishes the stress response in target conditions.

Functional magnetic resonance imaging (fMRI) tests are based on the same principles, though they measure blood oxidation levels in the brain instead of autonomic responses. Data suggest that lying can be distinguished from truth telling by an increase in brain activity, hence in blood oxidation levels, in the prefrontal, parietal, and anterior cingulate cortices. This application of fMRI is still in the development phase: often test subjects are offered monetary rewards if they can tell a lie while undergoing fMRI without detection (cf., Langelben et al., 2005). In addition, this sort of fMRI test requires that subjects remain still while in the machine, which could preclude using this test on uncooperative defendants. It also requires that they focus on the task at hand, which uncooperative defendants may not do either. In short, this measure too can be thwarted using fairly unsophisticated techniques.

A third approach measures brain waves to assess recognition of targets instead of uncovering deception. Electroencephalography (EEG) measures brain activity through electrodes placed on the scalp of subjects. Usually, images or objects are shown to subjects as they are questioned about them, using GKT. Target responses are averaged together, as are nontarget responses, and the resultant event-related potentials (ERPs) are compared with one another. When a subject recognizes an image or an object, there is an increase in the size of a positive waveform, known as the P300, which occurs approximately 300 msec after the subject sees it, relative to responses to things the subject does not recognize.

If a subject does not show this response when shown a photo of the crime scene, for example, one can tentatively conclude that the subject has not been there and so was likely not the perpetrator of the crime. However, this approach too can be defeated using countermeasures (Rosenfeld, 2004). To do so, subjects need to make the nontarget stimuli into salient stimuli, just like the targets. They can do this by executing a decisive covert response, like pressing their left toes against the floor, every time they see a nontarget stimulus. Deciding to take this action makes the nontarget stimuli meaningful, just as the target stimuli are (though for different reasons).

Though the United States Department of Defense has invested significant resources into developing new technologies for detecting lies, especially with respect to terrorist investigations, thus far it appears that none of the techniques is foolproof. Countermeasures for all of the technological probes are too easily available, while their accuracy remains questionable.

References

Honts, C.R., Raskin, D.C. and Kircher, J.C. (1994) "Mental and Physical Countermeasures Reduce the Accuracy of Polygraph Tests". *The Journal of Applied Psychology* 79, 252–259.

Langleben, D., Loughead, J., Bilker, W., Ruparel, K., Childress, A., Busch, S. and Gur, R. (2005) "Telling Truth from Lie in Individuals with Fast Event-Related fMRI". *Human Brain Mapping* 26, 262–272.

National Research Council. (2003) *The Polygraph and Lie Detection*. Committee to Review the Scientific Evidence on the Polygraph. Division of Behavioral and Social Sciences and Education. Washington, DC: The National Academies Press.

Office of Technology Assessment. (1983) *Scientific Validity of Polygraph Testing: A Research Review and Evaluation—A Technical Memorandum*, OTA-TM-H-15. Washington, DC: U.S. Congress.

Parliamentary Office of Science and Technology. (2011) *Detecting Deception. United Kingdom Parliament: POSTnotes*. Available at: http://researchbriefings.parliament.uk/ResearchBriefing/Summary/POST-PN-375#fullreport

Rosenfeld, J.P. (2004) "Simple, Effective Countermeasures to P300-Based Tests of Detection of Concealed Information". *Psychophysiology* 41, 205–219.

Wolpe, P.R., Foster, K. and Langleben, D.D. (2005) *Emerging Neurotechnologies for Lie-Detection: Promises and Perils*. Available at: http://repository.upenn.edu/neuroethics_pubs/7

Scientific Reliability and Admissibility Under the Rules of Evidence

As discussed further in what follows, there is virtual unanimity among legal scholars that fMRI and other brain-based lie detection techniques do not currently meet evidentiary standards of scientific reliability. The few courts in the United States to have specifically considered the issue have soundly rejected attempts to introduce brain-imaging evidence of deception (or truthfulness; Farah et al., 2014, 128). The current scholarly and scientific disagreements often center around whether such techniques are likely ever to satisfy these standards and whether such evidence—even if scientifically reliable—should nonetheless be excluded because of its potential to prejudice juries out of proportion to its actual relevance (Amirian, 2013, 744–748). Some argue, based on earlier experiments (e.g., McCabe and Castel, 2008), that juries are more likely to be prejudiced by neuroscience-based lie detection than by more traditional scientific evidence and that they therefore should be shielded from such evidence even were it to reach an acceptable level of scientific reliability. Other studies, however, do not support this view and suggest that jurors are able to appropriately weigh neuroimaging evidence (e.g., Schweitzer and Saks, 2011). This section surveys these evidentiary concerns of reliability and the danger of jury prejudice.

Despite a rush to commercialize and market these technologies for forensic use, virtually every scientist and legal expert who addressed the issue in the early years agreed that these new technologies, though certainly interesting and perhaps promising, were not even arguably suitable for practical use. Excepting a few individuals with vested interests in the two companies marketing brain-based lie detection services, even the most optimistic commentators suggested that courtroom applications were years if not decades in the future (Seaman, 2008b).

Today, fifteen or so years and many studies, reviews, and meta-analyses later, there remains a general consensus among both scientists and legal scholars that neuroscience-based techniques for detecting deception cannot yet be used to reliably detect lies in individuals under nonlaboratory conditions (Rusconi and Mitchener-Nissen, 2013, review; Shen and Jones, 2011). Thus, investigative or courtroom use continues to present a tantalizing prospect that is at best some years down the road (Seaman, 2008b). The most common concerns voiced by legal scholars have tended to emphasize the questionable reliability of neuroscience-based lie detection, which nearly all commenters agree do not yet meet evidentiary standards for admissibility of scientific evidence (Rusconi and Mitchener-Nissen, 2013, review). As recently summarized, "[t]he scientific literature reflects a fairly broad consensus that no brain-based technique is particularly effective for determining whether an individual is lying in response to a particular question (which, of course, will generally be the important issue in legal contexts)" (Shen and Jones, 2011, 866). Because reliability is a threshold requirement for admissibility of any form of scientific evidence, it is necessary to first assess neuroscience-based lie detection in relation to legal standards of admissibility.

When scientific evidence is offered in court, it is held to a higher standard of admissibility than other types of evidence. Whereas the threshold for admissibility of evidence is generally that it be merely *relevant*, for scientific evidence, the baseline is that it be *reliable*.[5] In the federal system, the judge is said to act as a "gatekeeper" to screen out "junk science" from consideration by the jury (*Daubert v. Merrell Dow Pharmaceuticals*, 1993). Under the federal *Daubert* standard, which is followed by most state courts as well,[6] such evidence must not only be scientifically valid, but there must also be a reasonable "fit" between the science and the purpose for which it is offered (Seaman, 2008a, 861–862). This means that even if neuroimaging lie detection is found to be valid for one purpose (such as to map the neural correlates of deceptive thoughts and actions in a general sense), it may well be found invalid for another purpose for which it is offered in court (such as to indicate that a particular person's testimony is deceptive). Furthermore, courts have tended to be extraordinarily skeptical of any evidence that tends to intrude into the jury's domain of assessing the credibility of witnesses. As one Supreme Court opinion put it, "the jury is the lie detector" (*United States v. Scheffer*, 1998). Thus, we can expect that courts will subject neuroscience lie detection to an even higher standard than they do other types of scientific evidence, as they have typically done in the case of polygraph lie detection evidence. Indeed, the 1923 case that first enunciated the heightened standard of reliability for scientific evidence involved an early precursor to the polygraph machine (*Frye v. United States*, 1923).

While the scientific understanding of the neural correlates of deception has grown tremendously over the past few years, there remain several obstacles to any reasonable argument that neuroscience-based lie detection evidence satisfies these heightened evidentiary standards of reliability. The most significant include: (1) the low ecological validity of the experiments; (2) the wide variability among experimental paradigms and methods; (3) lack of data on whether the results of experiments generalize to broader populations, including applicability to individuals with personality disorders, drug addiction/use, or mental illness; (4) the effect of countermeasures; and (5) the predominance of group and block results rather than individual, single-event trials.

Although deception researchers have made significant strides in increasing the ecological validity of their experimental paradigms, the conditions under which subjects "lie" during experiments remain very different from real-world conditions. The most serious difference is that, in virtually all of the experiments to date, subjects have been instructed by the researchers to lie (Gamer, 2014, 178, citing two exceptions). This is widely acknowledged to raise serious questions about whether the results would accurately translate from the lab to the real world, where both the emotional valence and the cognitive processes associated with lying might easily be affected by this difference (Phelps, 2009; Kanwisher, 2009). Lying is, after all, a social activity; socially sanctioned lying is therefore likely to be distinct from antisocial deception (Lisofsky et al., 2014). It is very difficult—perhaps impossible—to conduct a controlled deception experiment in which the subject has not been in some sense given permission to deceive. While scientists have come up with some creative paradigms designed to give subjects a "choice" whether or when to lie (Lisovsky et al., 2014; Panasiti et al., 2014), the moral and social consequences of such lying remain quite distinct from the type of deception that would be at issue in a criminal or even civil litigation context. Lying as part of an experiment, where one is in a sense given "permission" to lie, is socially sanctioned in a way that would not apply to genuine lies in a criminal or civil investigation or trial. A subject in a laboratory experiment does not face criminal or civil liability or penalty of perjury as does a party in a case or a real witness in a courtroom. Furthermore, as with polygraphy, it is simply not possible to test the reliability of lie detection methods in the field, because there is no independent baseline of truth; in other words, we can't confirm whether the lie detector was "correct" in any given case outside the laboratory.

A related difficulty with the experimental findings is that it has become increasingly apparent that context matters a great deal both in understanding deception and in detecting it. Just as we can imagine many different kinds of lies—white lies, bald-faced lies, lies of omission, fibs, half truths, exaggeration, puffery, polite lies, weasel words, bluffing, cover-ups, contextual lies, tall tales, pathological lies, hypocrisy, crying wolf—there are a variety of experimental protocols designed to detect these diverse types of lies (Lisofsky et al., 2014, 114 for a summary), as well as theoretical work that aims to categorize sub-types of deception (Abe, 2011, for a review). While this is a welcome development in terms of the science of deception, it makes it very difficult to generalize about the findings and also raises further questions about the ecological validity of the various protocols.

Furthermore, recent evidence suggests that it may be more difficult to detect deception in people with antisocial personality disorder (ASPD) and that it becomes increasingly more difficult the more adept at lying an individual is (Jiang et al., 2013). Given the high proportion of criminals with ASPD—reportedly as high as 47% of male prisoners worldwide (Fazel and Danesh, 2002)—these findings are particularly problematic for the prospects of accurate forensic use of neuroimaging lie detection methods. While it is somewhat reassuring that the *patterns* of activation in the Jiang et al. study were consistent with those of "healthy" subjects, the decrease in fMRI BOLD contrast results as facility to deceive increased led the researchers to conclude that "greater attention should be given to the detection of lies in people who are skilled at lying" (Jiang et al., 2013, 97).

And just as some people might be naturally good liars, it may also be possible to become a better liar either through practice or by the use of countermeasures against detection. There is some evidence that the heightened cognitive resources required to tell a lie rather than the truth may be mediated by repeatedly lying, both of a specific lie and in general (Hu et al., 2012; Van

Bockstaele et al., 2012). Though this has yet to be tested by brain-imaging protocols, the behavioral results using reaction times and accuracy measures suggest that repeating a lie makes it easier to lie and that lying more frequently likewise decreases the cognitive load. Along with the findings regarding individuals with ASPD, who may be more likely to be habitual liars, these results at a minimum call for targeted research on whether and how repeated or practiced lying might affect the neural "signature" or pattern of any given variety of deception being studied.

The prospect of effective countermeasures likewise requires a good deal of further study. The success of countermeasures that can affect the accuracy of lie detection results has plagued the field of polygraphy since its inception. At the dawn of neuroimaging lie detection research, it was thought that countermeasures would be much more difficult, if not impossible, to implement. Because the new technologies marked deception where it happened (in the brain) rather than where it might manifest (in the peripheral nervous system), it was hypothesized that subjects would not be able to defeat the test: "It is likely that a subject cannot mask functional MR imaging brain activation patterns . . . the brain areas that are active during deception will always be active when the subject tells a lie [and] the same areas will always be inactive when the subject tells the truth" (Mohamed et al., 2006, 685; Seaman, 2008b, 446).

Unfortunately, this belief has turned out to be wildly optimistic; it is apparent that a subject can indeed mask fMRI brain activation patterns by employing easily learned countermeasures that are very difficult to detect (Ganis et al., 2011). Ganis et al. instructed participants to imperceptibly move either a finger or a toe when they recognized an "irrelevant" stimulus during the Concealed Information Test (CIT) protocol, a common lie detection paradigm employed in polygraphy as well as fMRI deception research.[7] They found that "single subject classification accuracy, required for any deception test, is substantially reduced by the covert countermeasure, even in this controlled laboratory situation and with highly salient personal information," which consisted of the subject's own name (Ganis et al., 2011, 317). Though it may be more difficult to defeat other test protocols that do not depend on salience, and though lie detection researchers have made strides in developing a variety of techniques to detect use of countermeasures (Bowman et al., 2014; Rosenfeld et al., 2013, for review), it currently remains the case that the efficacy of countermeasures is at best uncertain. Furthermore, at least with current fMRI technology, simply shaking the head while in the scanner will render the scan results unreadable (Greely, 2015).

And yet despite these various obstacles to ready forensic use of brain-based lie detection technologies, scientists studying these questions continue to develop increasingly robust theories of deception and techniques for its detection as they refine and extend their research. There are some notable developments and directions for further research that promise to bring the prospect of a reliable lie detector closer to realization. For example, pattern-recognition techniques employed to analyze experimental fMRI data (Jiang et al., 2015; Gamer, 2014, review; Abootalebi et al., 2009) have shown great promise in classifying truth and deception within the data set used to "train" the computer, as well as in predicting results in novel subjects (Seaman, 2008b: 453–454). New neuroimaging technologies such as functional near-infrared spectroscopy (fNIRS), which also relies on measuring oxygenated/deoxygenated blood flow (Ding et al., 2014; Gamer, 2014, review), offer the prospect of an even less invasive, more mobile procedure that could conceivably even be used in the courtroom as a witness testified. And procedures that combine multiple types of behavioral and neuroscience-based measures (such as response times and fMRI, fMRI and ERP, polygraphy and ERP) in a single test are more accurate at detecting deception and countermeasures than any single measure in isolation. It is certainly possible— some would say likely—that advances in neuroscience will at some point enable lie detection to meet evidentiary standards of reliability.[8] For the moment, however, failure to meet the *Daubert* standard and analogous state law rules stand as the most significant obstacle to courtroom admissibility of neuroscience-based lie detection evidence.

Impact on Juries and the Danger of Unfair Prejudice

Even were lie detection evidence eventually to satisfy the *Daubert* standard, there would remain at least one significant evidentiary hurdle to its admissibility. Under Rule 403 of the Federal Rules of Evidence (and similar state rules), otherwise admissible evidence may be excluded if the court finds that the danger of "unfair prejudice" is substantially greater than the probative value of the evidence. Several legal scholars have opined that neuroimaging lie detection evidence should be excluded under this rule (Amirian, 2013). Furthermore, judges have been extraordinarily suspicious of polygraph evidence, arguably even more than might be warranted based on its degree of (un)reliability (Seaman, 2008b, 460). Other types of scientific evidence that are probably of comparable or lesser reliability but typically offered by the prosecution have often been admitted with little question (Seaman, 2013; National Research Council, 2009). This history suggests that courts would be inclined to use Rule 403 to exclude even reliable brain-based lie detection evidence.

Courts have long been wary of the supposed power of expert testimony or other highly technical evidence to sway jurors' decisions out of proportion to the true probative value of the evidence. In a well-known case involving an early use of statistical evidence in a criminal trial, the California Supreme Court held that "the testimony as to mathematical probability infected the case with fatal error and distorted the jury's traditional role." The court viewed the statistical probability evidence as "a veritable sorcerer in our computerized society, [which], while assisting the trier of fact in the search for truth, must not cast a spell over him" (*People v. Collins*, 1968). The identical concern has been repeatedly raised about brain-imaging evidence, particularly the colorful graphics of brain areas "lighting up" often used in scientific papers to illustrate the findings of fMRI studies. In a frequently cited study, McCabe and Castel found that subjects asked to assess the credibility of fictional cognitive neuroscience articles rated articles accompanied by a brain image as more credible than the identical material conveyed by way of a bar graph (McCabe and Castel, 2008).

However, subsequent research has largely failed to replicate these early results, and there is presently a great deal of debate about the likely effect of brain-imagery evidence on juries (Ware et al., 2014, for a summary). Similarly, some legal scholars have been skeptical about the distrust of juries' ability to evaluate the weight of complex scientific evidence (Seaman, 2008a, 869–875). In sum, while it is likely that courts would err on the side of excluding even seemingly reliable brain-imaging lie detection evidence under the rules of evidence, it is unclear that this result would be warranted. Should neuroscience-based lie detection ultimately reach an acceptable level of scientific reliability to satisfy the *Daubert* standard, and given the risks of erroneous credibility determinations by juries acting without such evidence, courts should be receptive to this type of evidence so long as they ensure reasonable safeguards to prevent experts from testifying in a misleading manner.

Constitutional and "Cognitive Privacy" Concerns

While much of the legal discussion of neuroimaging evidence is framed in terms of its (un)reliability and its potential tendency to prejudice the jury, it seems likely that the root of much of the disquiet about such evidence is a more fundamental concern about the prospect of a Big Brother–like government peering into citizens' minds (Shen, 2013). For legal scholars, these worries tend to be translated into constitutional arguments, mostly framed in terms of the Fourth Amendment's prohibition against unreasonable searches and seizures and the Fifth Amendment's protection against compelled self-incrimination. Courts have yet to squarely face these constitutional questions because of the current state of the science, but scholars have begun proactively to analyze them on their own terms and also as a way to critique existing constitutional theory and doctrine (Farahany, 2012a, 2012b).[9]

Both of these constitutional provisions apply only to protect the defendant in a criminal case. Only criminal defendants can claim the protection of the Fourth Amendment's prohibition against unreasonable searches; the Fifth Amendment's prohibition against compelled self-incrimination applies a bit more broadly, but it too is triggered only by government action that could result in criminal liability. These limitations are important, because generalized claims of "cognitive privacy" are therefore not coextensive with constitutional protections. Scholars who have discussed the application of the Fourth and Fifth Amendments to brain-imaging evidence seem to be envisioning primarily a scenario in which a suspected or accused criminal is forced to submit to a brain scan against his will; however, the potential applications of lie detection techniques are much broader, as we see for example in the scenario with which this chapter opened. There, the witnesses who might be asked to submit to a neuroscience-based lie detector would not have viable claims for either Fourth or Fifth Amendment protection (except Bob, the probable suspect, who would potentially face criminal liability). The discussion in this section thus applies primarily to a context in which police or prosecutors (or some other governmental agent) might wish to gather and use evidence of a defendant's deception against him in a criminal proceeding.

Here, it is useful to distinguish between two different experimental paradigms that are both typically discussed in the literature under the general rubric of "lie detection" but which have different implications under the Fourth and Fifth Amendments. In the first category, most simply, a person makes a claim, and some method of deception detection—whether polygraph, fMRI, or any other technique—purports to reveal whether that person's claim is honest or dishonest. In this paradigm, the lie detector (whether technologically sophisticated like an fMRI or technologically simple like a parent noting a child's fidgeting and blushing) purports to measure some physiological marker(s) of deception. In the case of a polygraph, these markers are certain supposed peripheral nervous system manifestations of anxiety said to accompany deception. In the case of fMRI, the marker is a pattern of neurological activation said to evince the cognitive processes correlated with deception.

In the second category, a person is shown some information—for example, details of a crime that only the perpetrator would know or a photo of the crime scene—and the "lie detector" purports to reveal whether that information was previously known to the person. The crucial point is that only the first technique described is what we should properly consider "lie detection"; the second is more appropriately described as "recognition detection" and does not, in theory, require any affirmative statement or response by the subject.[10] In other words, this second technique does not require the subject to "lie." In the context of polygraphy as well as more sophisticated brain-based studies, this second recognition-based paradigm is known as the concealed information test or CIT (formerly also called the guilty knowledge test or GKT; Varga et al., 2014).

Turning to the relevant constitutional provisions, the Fourth Amendment protects the "right of the people to be secure in their persons, houses, papers, and effects, against unreasonable searches and seizures" by the government. The Supreme Court has held that a person may claim a violation of this provision only in cases in which there was both a subjective expectation of privacy—the individual actually viewed the searched place/thing as private—and also where that expectation was reasonable, that is, society views the searched arena as properly protected from the government action in question.

In the context of fMRI or other brain-based lie detection, the issue under the Fourth Amendment would be whether "looking" inside a person's brain to determine whether she is lying counts as a search, and furthermore whether that search should be considered unreasonable. For purposes of this question, either of the two categories of deception detection discussed might at least trigger some consideration of this constitutional protection, because both equally involve "searching" inside a person's head. Because the government would be using neurological information contained in the brain-scan results, it would necessarily need to "look inside" the person's brain for the evidence.

There is a strong argument that, were the government to force a criminal suspect or defendant to undergo such a test without a warrant, this would be an unreasonable search in violation of the Fourth Amendment. However, Fourth Amendment jurisprudence is notoriously muddled, and it is impossible to predict how courts will ultimately decide this question (Farahany, 2012a). A court might conclude, as some legal scholars have, that there is a "reasonable expectation of privacy in the details of what is in [a person's] head, even though the government doesn't have to invade the body to learn the information" (Pardo, 2006). Under this view, even though these tests are not physically invasive, they entail a psychic invasion into a person's thoughts and memories. On the other hand, a court might accept the argument of other scholars who view neuroimaging tests as more akin to blood or urine tests, which are not considered unreasonable searches under current Fourth Amendment doctrine (Fox, 2008). In any event, only warrantless searches are prohibited by the Fourth Amendment; where there is probable cause to expect that a person's brain contains evidence, courts might well issue warrants to allow the government to look for such evidence.

Turning to the Fifth Amendment, a person cannot be "compelled in any criminal case to be a witness against himself." As with the Fourth Amendment, this constitutional provision generally protects only criminal defendants, so it is unlikely to apply at all when lie detection evidence is offered either by the defense in a criminal case or by any party in a civil case.[11] When it does properly apply, it protects a person from being compelled to give "testimony" but not from being forced to provide physical evidence. As Farahany puts it, "The Fifth Amendment protects against 'coercion [to] prove [a] charge against an accused out of his own mouth,' but not extracting saliva from the same" (Farahany, 2012b: 352). The difficult question when it comes to brain-based evidence is whether the processes measured by neuroimaging equipment should more appropriately be thought of as "testimony" or rather should be analogized to bodily fluids or cells (Stoller and Wolpe, 2007).[12]

Here, the difference between the two general paradigms discussed is arguably relevant. It is easy to characterize an affirmative statement or response to a question as "testimony" under a standard lie detection paradigm in which a person actually tells what we conventionally think of as a "lie." However, the CIT paradigm presents a closer question. In that case, it is more difficult to characterize the recognition measured by the test as testimony, because it is present in the person's brain regardless of anything the person might say or not say. Like tissue, fluids, or DNA, it is a biological marker that is not dependent on any volitional or communicative act of the subject. As Wigmore put it nearly a century ago, "a criminal act leaves usually on the mind a deep trace, in the shape of consciousness of guilt" (Wigmore, 1923, 544). If, finally, there were to be invented a reliable way to reveal this trace on the mind, one could argue that it is no different from a photograph or other concrete evidence of the crime. As with those other types of evidence, the Fifth Amendment would in that case be irrelevant.

Based on the Supreme Court's current testimonial/nontestimonial dichotomy, the analysis thus turns on how courts will characterize the information gleaned from brain-based lie detection and CIT procedures. As noted, scholars are divided, but many assert that the Fifth Amendment would apply to prevent the government from performing lie detection upon an unwilling suspect or defendant (see Shen, 2013, for a review). Taking another approach, it may be that the new technology calls into question the current jurisprudential model and begs a new theoretical approach to the Fifth Amendment's right against self-incrimination (Farahany, 2012b). In either case, it is clear that the protection would only apply to defendants or potential defendants and not to other potential subjects.

If, instead, the defense were to offer this type of evidence, the most likely purposes would be to demonstrate the truth of the defendant's version of the facts (because the defendant or another defense witness had testified truthfully) and/or that a prosecution witness was lying. Looking at the closest historical analog to brain-imaging lie detection, it is interesting to note that polygraph evidence has typically been offered by the defense in criminal cases, not the prosecution, and that judges have been extraordinarily suspicious of such evidence, arguably even more than might be warranted based on its degree of (un)reliability (Seaman, 2008b, 460). Other types of scientific evidence that are probably of comparable or lesser reliability but typically offered by the prosecution have often been admitted with little question (Seaman, 2013; National Research Council, 2009). Thus, it may be that the concerns of legal scholars and ethicists about the prospect of government use of neuroscience-based lie detection evidence against criminal defendants, while certainly valid, have been overemphasized at the expense of the more likely scenarios. Under those scenarios, there remains the question whether there are additional "cognitive privacy" concerns, separate from those covered by the Fourth and Fifth Amendments, that might apply where nondefendant witnesses were subject to a neuroscience lie detection procedure during criminal or civil litigation.

In such a case, we would need to balance the cognitive privacy interest of the witness against the interests of both the defendant and the larger society that would be served by permitting the technology to be used (again, this assumes the technology has reached an acceptable level of scientific reliability). Surely the witness does have some privacy interest at stake; on the other hand, any witness who testifies in court is sworn to tell the truth and does not have any cognizable interest in being able to lie. The stakes in a criminal prosecution are high: freedom or possibly even life and death. There is mounting evidence, in the form of DNA exonerations, demonstrating that the system can often fail to reach an accurate result. While there are multiple causes behind such mistakes, incorrect eyewitness testimony is a very significant factor that has been implicated in more than 70% of wrongful convictions overturned by DNA evidence thus far (Innocence Project website, www.innocenceproject.org/causes/eyewitness-misidentification/). If DNA proof were lacking but fMRI technology were able to help the system decipher the true facts in a particular case, society's interest in the accuracy of criminal justice would arguably outweigh any asserted privacy interest on the part of nondefendant witnesses.

Conclusion

Returning to the scenario with which this chapter began, let us now imagine that Abbie, erroneously accused of the murder of the police officer, seeks to introduce neuroimaging evidence showing that she is telling the truth about her version of the events and also seeks to have the other witnesses subjected to a lie detection technology to test the truthfulness of their stories. As we have seen, the Fourth and Fifth Amendments would not apply under these circumstances except possibly in the case of Bob, who might "take the Fifth" (in which case jurors could be instructed that they could consider that claim in the prosecution's case against Abbie, though not against Bob). As for potential cognitive privacy claims by the other witnesses, there is a strong argument that these privacy interests should not outweigh society's, and Abbie's interests in truthful and accurate testimony in the criminal case against her. No witness has a valid interest in being allowed to commit perjury, and every person has a duty when subpoenaed to testify truthfully in court to what he might know in connection with a criminal prosecution. Thus, it is difficult to see why such a witness should not be required to submit to a reliable, safe, and physically noninvasive lie detection technology.

The case, then, turns on reliability. At present, there is no question but that neuroimaging lie detection is nowhere near ready for courtroom (or any other forensic) use. In the future, courts and scholars will have to decide what degree of reliability short of the unattainable 100 percent should be required as an admissibility threshold. If polygraph is any indication, courts will require much more of lie detection evidence than they do of forensic evidence that is typically offered by the prosecution against criminal defendants.

Notes

1 These are the facts, very roughly speaking, in the case of Troy Anthony Davis, who was ultimately executed by the state of Georgia for the murder of Officer Kevin McPhail. See In re Troy Anthony Davis, No. CV409–130 (S.D. Ga. Aug. 24, 2010), Final Order Denying Petition for Writ of Habeas Corpus as to Troy Anthony Davis.

2 We might also question the witnesses, but once we move from the relatively clear-cut self-serving lie of the actual shooter (who in this scenario is either Abbie or Bob) to the eyewitness accounts of bystanders, the analysis becomes murkier. A witness might sincerely believe her mistaken account; she might have been subject to suggestive questioning or exposure to subsequent information that affects her memory of the incident. Because the taxonomy of untruthfulness is varied and complex, these possibilities complicate the analysis in myriad ways, not least of which is in raising the question whether even a reliable neuroscience-based lie detection technology would ever be capable of detecting such less-than-intentional inaccuracies. On the other hand, there have been some intriguing studies that raise the prospect of someday being able to distinguish actual from false memories outside of the lab (Schacter and Slotnick, 2004; Schacter et al., 2012).

3 The author has presented a similar thought experiment to hundreds of evidence students over the past fifteen years, and every year there is a very significant percentage of students—about 30% to 40%— who say that they would not wish to use even a *foolproof* brain-imaging lie detection device.

4 This is known as the blood oxygen level–dependent (BOLD) contrast. In a nutshell, the strong magnet of the MR scanner is able to detect changes in blood flow and oxygenation that are believed to correspond to changes in the activity level of neurons within particular brain structures that are, in turn, associated with particular functions.

5 Note that the concept of reliability under the rules of evidence is distinct from the use of that term by scientists, where "reliability" refers to replicability. A result might be replicable and yet be unreliable and thus inadmissible under the legal test. For example, even if the results of the playing card studies described had been replicated numerous times, they still would not be deemed reliable when offered to prove a more general proposition about deception.

6 While some states use a different standard for determining whether scientific evidence is admissible, all of the tests require some heightened showing of reliability.

7 The concealed information test, also known as the guilty knowledge test, is a technique that detects knowledge that only the perpetrator of a crime would know, measuring recognition of such knowledge via physiological markers. For example, if the particular crime was committed with a knife and this information is not public, the questioner might ask the subject, "Concerning the weapon used, was it a gun?" "Was it a baseball bat?" "Was it a knife?" The theory behind the CIT is that the guilty subject will react to the key question with a distinctive physiological (or, in the case of fMRI, neural), response.

8 As I've argued elsewhere, the reliability of any lie detection technique should be considered in relation to the alternatives available for assessing witness credibility. Given that our assumptions about the

reliability of the alternative—assessment by juries with the benefit of cross-examination—is more an article of faith than a demonstrated fact, courts should be open to the possibility that other techniques will prove more useful in determining the truthfulness of testimony (Seaman, 2008a). For an alternative view, see Rakoff, 2009.

9 Shen (2013, 694–696) provides a very useful table summarizing the conclusions of the various scholars who have analyzed the applicability of the Fourth and Fifth Amendments to brain-based lie detection.

10 Cephos's "brain fingerprinting" technique is of this second type, as are many of the EEG P300 studies and some of the fMRI studies.

11 It's possible a witness other than the defendant might assert the privilege if evidence that the person is lying would be potentially self-incriminating. Note that if called by the government, the person could be offered immunity and required to testify, but this would arguably amount to the government immunizing someone for committing perjury, which would violate legal ethics rules.

12 Generally, polygraph evidence is inadmissible because courts do not consider it sufficiently reliable. However, where a defendant refuses to submit to a polygraph examination, courts have held that the Fifth Amendment prevents prosecutors from using that refusal against him (Faigman et al., 2003).

Further Reading

Farah, M.J., Hutchinson, J.B., Phelps, E.A. and Wagner, A.D. (2014) "Functional MRI-Based Lie Detection: Scientific and Societal Challenges". *Nature Reviews Neuroscience* 15, 123–131.

Farahany, N. (2012b) "Incriminating Thoughts". *Stanford Law Review* 64, 351–408.

Greely, H.T. (2015) "Neuroscience, Mindreading, and the Courts: The Example of Pain". *Journal of Health Law and Policy* 18, 171–206.

Shen, F.X. (2013) "Neuroscience, Mental Privacy, and the Law". *Harvard Journal of Law & Public Policy* 36, 653–713.

References

Abe, N. (2011) How the brain shapes deception: An integrated review of the literature. *The Neuroscientist* 17: pp. 560–574.

Abootalebi, V., Moradi, M.H. and Khalilzadeh, M.A. (2009) A new approach for EEG feature extraction in P300-based lie detection. *Computer Methods and Programs in Biomedicine* 94: pp. 48–57.

Amirian, J. (2013) Weighing the admissibility of fMRI technology under FRE 403: For the law, fMRI changes everything—and nothing. *Fordham Urban Law Journal* XLI: pp. 715–770.

Bowman, H., Filetti, M., Alsufyani, A., Janssen, D. and Su, L. (2014) Countering countermeasures: Detecting identity lies by detecting conscious breakthrough. *PLOS One* 9(3).

Browndyke, J.N., Paskavitz, J., Sweet, L.H., Cohen, R.A., Tucker, K.A., Welsh-Bohmer, K.A., Burke, J.R. and Schmechel, D.E. (2008) Neuroanatomical correlates of malingered memory impairment: Event-related fMRI of deception on a recognition memory task. *Brain Injury* 22: pp. 481–489.

Daubert v. Merrell Dow Pharmaceuticals, Inc., 509 U.S. 579 (1993).

Ding, X.P., Sai, L., Fu, G., Lui, J. and Lee, K. (2014) Neural correlates of second-order verbal deception: A Functional Near-Infrared Spectroscopy (fNIRS) Study. *NeuroImage* 87: pp. 505–514.

Faigman, D.L., Fienberg, S.E. and Stern, P.C. (2003) The limits of polygraph. *Issues in Science and Technology* 20(1).

Farah, M.J., Hutchinson, J.B., Phelps, E.A. and Wagner, A.D. (2014) Functional MRI-based lie detection: Scientific and societal challenges. *Nature Reviews Neuroscience* 15: pp. 123–131.

Farahany, N. (2012a) Searching Secrets. *University of Pennsylvania Law Review*. 160: pp. 1239–1308.

———. (2012b) Incriminating thoughts. *Stanford Law Review* 64: pp. 351–408.

Fazel, S., and Danesh, J. (2002) Serious mental disorder in 23,000 prisoners: A systematic review of 62 surveys. *The Lancet* 359: pp. 545–550.

Fox, D. (2008) Brain imaging and the bill of rights: Memory detection technologies and American criminal justice. *American Journal of Bioethics* 8(1): pp. 1–4.

Frye v. United States (1923), 293 F. 1013 (D.C. Cir.).

Gamer, M. (2014) Mind reading using neuroimaging: Is this the future of deception detection? *European Psychologist* 19(3): pp. 172–183.

Ganis, G., Rosenfeld, J.P., Meixner, J., Kievit, R.A. and Schendan, H.E. (2011) Lying in the scanner: Covert countermeasures disrupt deception detection by functional magnetic resonance imaging. *NeuroImage* 55: pp. 312–319.

Greely, H.T. (2015) Neuroscience, mindreading, and the courts: The example of pain. *Journal of Health Law and Policy* 18: pp. 171–206.

Hu, X., Chen, H. and Fu, G. (2012) A repeated lie becomes truth? The effect of intentional control and training on deception. *Frontiers in Psychology* 3(488): pp. 1–7.

Jiang, W., Liu, H., Liao, J. Ma, X., Rong, P., Tang, Y. and Wang, W. (2013) A functional MRI study of deception among offenders with antisocial personality disorders. *Neuroscience* 244: pp. 90–98.

———. (2015) Decoding the processing of lying using functional connectivity MRI. *Behavioral and Brain Functions* 11(1) (no pagination in journal).

Kanwisher, N. (2009) The use of fMRI in Lie Detection: What has been shown and what has not. In *Using Imaging to Identify Deceit: Scientific and Ethical Questions.* Cambridge, MA: American Academy of Arts & Sciences, pp. 7–11.

Kozel, F.A., Revell, L.J., Lorberbaum, J.P., Shastri, A., Elhai, J.D., Horner, M.D., Smith, A., Nahas, Z., Bohning, D.E. and George, M.S. (2004a) A pilot study of functional magnetic resonance imaging brain correlates of deception in healthy young men. *Journal of Neuropsychiatry & Clinical Neuroscience* 16: pp. 295–305.

———. (2004b) A replication study of the neural correlates of deception. *Behavioral Neuroscience* 118: pp. 852–856.

———. (2005) Detecting deception using functional magnetic resonance imagining. *Biological Psychiatry* 58: pp. 605–613.

Langleben, D.D., Schroeder, L., Maldjian, J.A., Gur, R.C., McDonald, S., Ragland, J.D., O'Brien, C.P. and Childress, A.R. (2002) Brain activity during simulated deception: An event-related functional magnetic resonance study. *NeuroImage* 15: pp. 727–732.

———. (2005) Telling truth from lie in individual subjects with fast event-related fMRI. *Human Brain Mapping* 26: pp. 262–272.

Lee, T.M.C., Liu, H., Chan, C.C.H., Ng, Y., Fox, P.T. and Gao, J. (2005) Neural correlates of feigned memory impairment. *NeuroImage* 28: pp. 305–313.

Lisofsky, N., Kazzer, P., Heekeren, H.R. and Prehn, K. (2014) Investigating socio-cognitive processes in deception: A quantitative meta-analysis of neuroimaging studies. *Neuropsychologia* 61: pp. 113–122.

McCabe, D., and Castel, A. (2008) Seeing is believing: The effect of brain images on judgments of scientific reasoning. *Cognition* 107: pp. 343–352.

Mohamed, F.B., Faro, S.H., Gordon, N.J., Platek, S.M., Ahmad, H. and Williams, J.M. (2006) Brain mapping of deception and truth telling about an ecologically valid situation: Functional MR imaging and polygraph investigation—initial experience. *Radiology* 238: pp. 679–688.

National Research Council Committee on Identifying the Needs of the Forensic Sciences Community. (2009) *Strengthening Forensic Science in the United States: A Path Forward.* Washington, DC: National Academies Press.

Nishimoto, S., Vu, A.T., Naselaris, T., Benjamini, Y., Yu, B. and Gallant, J.L. (2011) Reconstructing visual experiences from brain activity evoked by natural movies. *Current Biology* 21: pp. 1641–1646.

Panasiti, M.S., Pavone, E.F., Mancini, A., Arcangelo, M., Grisoni, L. and Aglioti, S.M. (2014) The motor cost of telling lies: Electrocortical signatures and personality foundations of spontaneous deception. *Social Neuroscience* 9: pp. 573–589.

Pardo, M.S. (2006) Neuroscience evidence, legal culture, and criminal procedure. *American Journal of Criminal Law* 33: pp. 301–337.

People v. Collins 1968. 68 Cal. 2d pp. 319–335.

Phelps, E.A. (2009) Lying outside the laboratory: the impact of imagery and emotion on the neural circuitry of lie detection. In *Using Imaging to Identify Deceit: Scientific and Ethical Questions.* Cambridge, MA: American Academy of Arts and Sciences.

Rakoff, J.S. (2009) Lie Detection in the Courts: The Vain Search for the Magic Bullet. In *Using Imaging to Identify Deceit: Scientific and Ethical Questions*. Cambridge, MA: American Academy of Arts and Sciences.

Rosenfeld, J.P., Hu, X., Labkovsky, E., Meixner, J. and Winograd, M.R. (2013) Review of recent studies and issues regarding the P300-based complex trial protocol for detection of concealed information. *International Journal of Psychophysiology* 90: pp. 118–134.

Rusconi, E. and Mitchener-Nissen, T. (2013) Prospects of functional magnetic resonance imaging as lie detector. *Frontiers in Human Neuroscience* 7: pp, 1–12.

Schacter, D.L., and Slotnick, S.D. (2004) The cognitive neuroscience of memory distortion. *Neuron* 44: pp. 149–160.

Schacter, D.L., Chamberlain, J., Gaesser, B. and Gerlach, K.D. (2012) Neuroimaging of true, false, and imaginary memories. In Nadel, L. and Sinnott-Armstrong, W.P. (Eds). *Memory and Law*. New York: Oxford University Press, pp. 233–262.

Schweitzer, N.J., and Saks, M.J. (2011) Neuroimage evidence and the insanity defense, *Behavioral Science & Law* 29: pp. 592–607.

Seaman, J.A. (2008a) Triangulating testimonial hearsay: The constitutional boundaries of expert opinion testimony. *Georgetown Law Journal* 96: pp. 827–884.

———. (2008b) Black boxes. *Emory Law Journal* 58: pp. 428–488.

———. (2013) A tale of two Dauberts. *Georgia Law Review* 47: pp. 889–922.

Shen, F.X. (2013) Neuroscience, mental privacy, and the law. *Harvard Journal of Law & Public Policy* 36: pp. 653–713.

Shen, F.X., and Jones, O.D. (2011) Brain scans as evidence: Truths, proofs, lies, and lessons. *Mercer Law Review* 62: pp. 861–883.

Smith, K. (2012) Brain imaging: fMRI 2.0. *Nature* 484(7392): pp. 24–26.

Spence, S.A. (2008) Playing devil's advocate: The case *against* fMRI lie detection. *Journal of Legal & Criminal Science* 13: pp. 11–25.

Spence, S.A., *et al.* (2001) Behavioural and functional anatomical correlates of deception in humans. *NeuroReport* 12: pp. 2849–2853.

Stoller, S.E., and Wolpe, P.R. (2007) Emerging neurotechnologies for lie detection and the fifth amendment. *American Journal of Law and Medicine* 33: pp. 359–375.

United States v. Scheffer 1998. 523 U.S. pp. 303–339.

Van Bockstaele, B., Verschuere, B. and Spruyt, A. (2012) Learning to lie: Effects of practice on the cognitive cost of lying. *Frontiers in Psychology* 3(526): pp. 1–8.

Varga, M., Visu-Petra, G., Miclea, M. and Bus, I. (2014) The RT-based concealed information test: An overview of current research and future perspectives. *Procedia Social and Behavioral Sciences* 127: pp. 681–685.

Ware, J.M., Jones, J.L. and Schweitzer, N.J. (2014) Neuroimagery and the Jury. *The Jury Expert*, 26(1). Available at SSRN: https://ssrn.com

Wigmore, J.H. (1923) *Treatise on Evidence*. 2nd ed. Boston: Little, Brown & Co.

14

NEUROPRIVACY AND COGNITIVE LIBERTY

Paul Root Wolpe

Introduction

The term "cognitive liberty" has been used in a variety of ways. In general, it refers to the degree to which an individual has the right to control his or her own mental and emotional brain processes against the desires of external agents, especially the state, to control or access them. It is largely reflective of the value of neuroprivacy, the idea that privacy rights extend to a citizen's brain, and that if privacy has any meaning at all, it must mean one's right to protect the contents of one's brain (i.e., one's thoughts, emotions, and other subjective states). These terms are relatively recent concepts, reactions to the development of neurotechnologies that are beginning to allow unprecedented access to the inner workings of the brain. The values they reflect, however, have a long pedigree.

In fact, one might trace the idea of cognitive liberty back to early fights against religious and state authorities trying to mandate what people should believe. Pockets of philosophical argument, resistance, or revolution over freedom of thought are found throughout human history. Revolutions have been fought over people's desire to be free of governmental or church control of what they are allowed to believe. But governments have themselves sometimes taken action. As early as the third century BCE, King Ashoka of India decreed that his subjects had the right to think as they saw fit (Dehejia and Dehelia, 1993). Of course, even today there are areas of the world where the right to openly think as we like or to publically hold certain opinions or beliefs are forbidden and can even put one's life in danger.

The term "cognitive liberty" itself, however, is more recent, and it refers not so much to our right to believe what we like as to our right to be free from external interference with that right through biotechnological invasion, manipulation, or monitoring of the brain's processes without consent. The term was originally coined by Wrye Sententia and Richard Glen Boire, the founders of the now moribund Center for Cognitive Liberty and Ethics (CCLE; www.cognitivelib erty.org/). Dedicated to developing "social policies that will preserve and enhance freedom of thought into the 21st century," the CCLE launched a conversation about the nature of cognitive privacy, personal autonomy, and freedom from control or coercion of the brain and its processes.

The CCLE listed examples of how cognitive liberty can be threatened. It suggested the main areas of concern are threats to:

1. Privacy ("What goes on in your mind should remain private unless you choose to share it.");
2. Autonomy ("Self-determination over one's own cognition is central to free will"); and

3. Choice ("The capabilities of the human mind should not be limited."; www.cognitivelib erty.org/faqs/faq_general.htm).

In a seminal article on the idea in the Annals of the New York Academy of Science, Sententia (2004) concludes with a suggestion of two fundamental principles of cognitive liberty:

1. As long as their behavior does not endanger others, individuals should not be compelled against their will to use technologies that directly interact with the brain or be forced to take certain psychoactive drugs.
2. As long as they do not subsequently engage in behavior that harms others, individuals should not be prohibited from or criminalized for using new mind-enhancing drugs and technologies.

These two principles encapsulate some of the primary arguments around cognitive liberty. The concept is controversial, and not everyone agrees with CCLE's framing of the issue, rec- ommendations, or position. In this chapter, we will look at neuroprivacy and cognitive liberty from three different perspectives: cognitive/affective coercion; brain monitoring and privacy; and human enhancement.

Cognitive/Affective Coercion

One of the fundamental modern concepts of human freedom suggests that in order to have freedom, people must have the right to believe as they like and to think as they like without unwanted external force. This standard was not true throughout history and is still denied in some modern cultures; theocracies, for example, often demand conformity of religious thought, and certain political systems (such as communism) often demand conformity of political thought.

It is true that even in cultures that accept the basic premise of freedom of thought, coercive elements remain. For example, ubiquitous advertising, portrayals in the media, and other cultural products may be said to have a powerful if not coercive influence over how and what we think. However, for our purposes, such cultural products do not reach the threshold of threatening cognitive liberty as we are using the term. While we may think of those factors as pernicious and believe they have too much power over how we think and act as a culture, ultimately we are free to oppose, resist, or avoid them to the degree possible.

Cognitive and affective coercion refer instead to the degree to which those in positions of social control—the government, courts, military, police, even parents over their children, and so on—have the right to use neurotechnologies of various kinds to try and control or probe an individual's thought processes. As mentioned previously, the state has been invested in that process for centuries. Threats, torture, incarceration, and execution have been used by the state since ancient times to control not just the behavior but the thoughts and beliefs of citizens. Per- haps the most powerful modern statement of that tradition is George Orwell's dystopian novel *1984* (Orwell, 1961). While portraying a modern state, the techniques that "Big Brother" used to control "thoughtcrime," such as threats, torture, and manipulation of family and loved ones, were not fundamentally different than those that could have been used by any coercive state in most of human history.

Cognitive liberty as a concept is a reaction instead to more modern types of threats, such as the use of psychopharmaceuticals, to directly influence brain processes for state purposes. Examples include the use of drugs to manage prisoners or for coercive interrogations and uses by the military of "nonlethal" weapons, such as aerosoling "calmative" drugs to control crowds

(Coleman, 2015). But there are also nonpharmaceutical examples; the military has dabbled with testing microwave radiation and magnetic field devices that might disrupt thought patterns and other "network-centric" warfare strategies (Moreno, 2006).

For more on neurointerventions and national security, see Chapter 10.

Psychopharmaceuticals

Cognitive liberty clearly includes the right to be free of external coercion over our mental functioning. Some argue that it also includes the right to use pharmaceuticals (at least legal ones) to control our mental functioning as we see fit. We will discuss the latter case in the section on human enhancement and in this section will focus on use of pharmaceuticals by agents of social control.

The state or other agents of social control (including schools) can coerce, encourage, or promote the use of psychopharmaceuticals in different ways. For example, a controversial use of such drugs in children is the use of Ritalin and other stimulants. ADD and ADHD are commonly diagnosed neurobehavioral disorders in children, with the American Psychiatric Association's *Diagnostic and Statistical Manual of Mental Disorders* (DSM-5) reporting that about 5% of children have ADHD (American Psychiatric Association, 2013). Still, according to the Centers for Disease Control, approximately 11% of children 4 to 17 years of age (6.4 million) have been diagnosed with ADHD as of 2011 (CDC, 2015). In fact, some states have ADHD diagnoses of 18% or more of children in the state.

As there are no biomarkers for ADHD, the diagnosis depends on the judgment of clinicians. According to the DSM-IV (used from 1994 to 2013), symptoms must begin before the age of 7 and be present for at least six months and cause a significant impairment of function in more than one setting (e.g., social, academic, familial). However, determining the level of impairment of a preschooler's impulsivity in various settings is highly subjective. Many children do have an accurate diagnosis and benefit from use of these stimulants to allow them to function in typical classroom settings as well as elsewhere in their lives. However, many children are also prescribed stimulants in the absence of DSM criteria for ADHD (Wilens, 2008).

Based on the Health Resources and Services Administration's National Survey of Children's Health, the percentage of children aged 4 to 17 years diagnosed with ADHD increased from 7.8% in 2003 to 9.5% in 2007, representing a 21.8% increase in just 4 years (CDC, 2010). The increases in diagnosis have led to significant increases in the use of stimulants in elementary and middle schools. While in wealthier school districts this often happens at the behest of parents, in poorer schools, the treatment is often at the behest of teachers, particularly when the children tend to demonstrate defiance or do not conform to expected classroom behavioral standards (Wolpe et al., 2007). In other words, in those cases, Ritalin and other drugs are used by school administrators as part of a student-management strategy. Such activity may well qualify as a violation of cognitive liberty, insofar as agents of social control (teachers and school administrators) coerce students (through threats of expulsion, for example) to accept pharmaceutical treatment.

Much has been made as well of the use of stimulants among college students. Among college-aged populations, misuse of prescription stimulants is second only to marijuana as the most common form of illicit drug use (Lakhan and Kirchgessner, 2012). Stimulants are often acquired from peers, and a black market of stimulants, especially around exam time, is common in many schools (Trudeau, 2009). Stimulant use in these contexts reflects the broader challenge of the "drug arms race," that is, the coercive effect of peers (or coworkers) using a stimulant that puts those not on drugs at a competitive disadvantage, as we discuss in what follows. While not directly coercive, the case can be made that putting people in a work or education context in which their success or competitive equality is dependent on taking cognitive enhancers erodes or at least threatens individual cognitive liberty.

A clearer case of a threat to cognitive liberty is the use of mandatory antipsychotics or other psychopharmaceuticals in prisoners. Such drugs might be demanded for use in treating non-threatening, competent prisoners or to medicate a prisoner in order to allow them to participate in their trial or, perhaps most controversially, to medicate a prisoner to bring them back to baseline for execution (Daugherty, 2000). All three cases are ethically problematic.

Due in part to the deinstitutionalization of the mentally ill, the overall prevalence of mental illness in prisons is 10% to 15%, significantly greater than the community base rate of 2% to 3% (Quanbeck et al., 2003). It has been generally accepted, both ethically and legally, that psychotic prisoners can be treated with antipsychotic medication even if they resist treatment or if they pose a threat to themselves or others, and the drugs are in the individual's best interest.

However, courts have sought to expand the penal system's ability to mandate treatment, even when a prisoner is not deemed to be a threat to himself or those around him and is competent to make medical decisions. The most well-known case is that of Charles Sell, a dentist who demonstrated delusions and was treated periodically with antipsychotics (*Sell v. United States*, 2003). He was eventually arrested for submitting false claims for insurance reimbursement, and, though found competent to stand trial initially, his condition worsened until authorities remanded him to a psychiatric hospital to receive treatment so that he could stand trial. Sell refused treatment. The case reached the Supreme Court, which took up the question of "whether the Constitution permits the Government to administer antipsychotic drugs involuntarily to a mentally ill criminal defendant—in order to render that defendant competent to stand trial for serious, but nonviolent, crimes" (*Sell v. United States*, 2003). Even though it was determined that Sell was no threat to himself or others in prison, the court ordered Sell forcibly treated on the grounds that it was medically appropriate and the only way to serve the government's interest in holding a trial.

For more on neuroscience and criminal responsibility, see Chapter 12.

In the case of Charles Singleton, the Court used similar guidelines to allow the prisoner to be forcibly treated to make him legally competent enough to be executed. Charles Singleton murdered an Arkansas grocery store clerk in 1979 and was sentenced to death. A decade later, while on death row, he claimed that the murder victim was not dead but rather waiting for him to join her somewhere as her groom, that his prison cell was possessed by demons, and that a prison doctor had implanted a chip in his ear. Singleton's lawyers argued that their client had become psychotic and therefore could not be executed based on a Supreme Court decision in 1986 that prohibits the execution of the insane (*Singleton v. Norris*, 2003). However, Singleton had at times voluntarily taken medication that seemed to alleviate his symptoms, and the medication was also given to him at times involuntarily. It was during such a period of forced treatment in 2000 that his execution date was set.

Singleton's lawyers argued that medicating Singleton in order to execute him was not pursuing his "best interest." The court ultimately found that since the medication did control

Singleton's mental illness, and since Singleton had admitted to feeling better while on it, Singleton was to continue to receive the medication. The court admitted that the decision would have the unwanted side effect of making him eligible for execution, but since the sentence was lawfully imposed upon him for a crime he was found to have committed, the state has an essential interest in making sure that lawfully imposed sentences are carried out. On January 6, 2004, after spending a record length of time on Arkansas's death row, Charles Singleton was put to death.

In contrast to the *Sell* decision, in which many medical and psychological associations wrote briefs agreeing with the Court, in *Singleton*, the medical profession stood in clear opposition to the Court's finding that mandatory treatment was acceptable. The American Medical Association's Code of Ethics, also endorsed by the American Psychiatric Association, strongly opposes the death penalty. The AMA wrote that "when a condemned prisoner has been declared incompetent to be executed, physicians should not treat the prisoner for the purpose of restoring competence unless a commutation order is issued before treatment begins," with drugs permitted only when there is "extreme suffering as a result of psychosis or any other illness" (American Medical Association, 2004).

A final example that will become more and more likely is the expectation of pharmaceutical use in the workplace, which may amount to or even eventually involve coercion. For example, studies have shown that drugs like modafinil enhance performance and attentiveness in subjects (Farah et al., 2004), while other studies are more equivocal (Shalev et al., 2013). There is already evidence that workers are taking attention-enhancing drugs to increase productivity (Maher, 2008). Might other workers be forced to take them to keep up with the productivity levels of colleagues? Or might employers begin to expect a certain level of productivity that can only be achieved with pharmaceutical help?

The military has already used attention-enhancing drugs in pilots and other military personnel to increase performance (Tracey and Flower, 2014). If it can be shown that use of attention-enhancing drugs makes pilots more reliable or surgeons more accurate or bus drivers more attentive, might we demand such drugs be taken in professions where people's lives are at risk? Perhaps the greatest risk for the coercive use of psychopharmaceuticals comes not from prisons or courts but from the demands of the general population.

Brain Monitoring and Privacy

Our private thoughts seem the one realm of our lives to which no other human being has access. No other person can see what I am thinking, can feel what I am feeling. Our inner thoughts, those parts of human cogitation that we think of as "mind," have always been the privileged domain of an individual's subjective life, unless he or she chose (consciously or unconsciously, intentionally or unintentionally) to reveal them.

In fact, the idea of using the brain as the locus of understanding subjective thought would have made little sense historically, as in most times and places, the brain's inner workings were so obscure that human beings had little idea of what the brain actually did, never mind how it did it. The brain could not itself reveal anything; inside the skull it was inaccessible, and after death it was inert.

But now that has changed. Advances in brain imaging have allowed researchers to peer more deeply into the inner workings of our subjective experiences than most had ever thought would be possible. In a relatively short time, these technologies have advanced to the point that they raise some crucial questions that would have seemed fantastic only a short time ago: What are my rights to the inner workings of my own brain? To what degree can the state or the court coerce me to undergo a brain scan that might reveal thoughts or affective states or traits that

I would otherwise want to keep private? Under what circumstances might we want to argue, for example, that the security of society merits probing the mind of a suspected criminal or terrorist?

While there is not room in this chapter to review all the relevant research, a growing number of studies have shown that it is possible, using brain imaging, to identify certain kinds of subjective mental experiences. The most common technology used for these studies is fMRI (functional magnetic resonance imaging); in fact, it is not an exaggeration to say that fMRI is the most important internal imaging technology since X-rays. Images created by fMRI represent hemodynamic (blood flow and blood oxygenation) changes in the brain associated with brain activity (Gore, 2003). Brain activity requires oxygen, and so discrete areas of activity are coupled with increased blood flow associated with the recruitment of oxygen-rich blood. Oxygenated blood has different magnetic properties than deoxygenated blood, so with fMRI, one can map the areas of the brain where oxygen is being recruited. By mapping blood flow, presumably the fMRI can tell us, indirectly, which parts of the brain are being used more when a subject is doing a task or perhaps when they are thinking particular thoughts.

While fMRI cannot "read minds," a number of studies have demonstrated that it can give us insight into the inner workings of the brain (see Haynes, 2012). For example, analyzing fMRI while people are looking at pictures can tell us which of eight orientations of stripes (e.g., horizontal, vertical, diagonal) a subject has been looking at (Kamitani and Tong, 2005), which photographs, selected at random from a large database of natural images, a person is looking at (Haynes and Rees, 2006), and even the ability to reconstruct viewed movies (Nishimoto et al., 2011). Studies of fMRI have been used to identify such things as a subject's intention (e.g., whether the subject plans to add or subtract two numbers, Haynes et al., 2007); likes and dislikes (e.g., whether subjects preferred different types of presented objects, Hosseini et al., 2011); and even tendencies toward racist ideation (Phelps et al., 2000) and criminality (Raine, 2013).

Brain-imaging research is also being used to try to predict public behaviors such as consumer behaviors and voting patterns. The booming field of neuromarketing tries to predict consumer behavior by looking at the brains of consumers as they think about products or look at advertising (Morin, 2011). Neuroscience and brain imaging have also been used to try to ascertain voters' preferences; a book by Drew Westen (2007), *The Political Brain: The Role of Emotion in Deciding the Fate of the Nation*, which drew on such research, has been credited with playing a prominent role in Democratic Party strategy in the 2008 U.S. presidential election.

Perhaps even more controversial is the use of brain imaging for lie detection (Wolpe et al., 2005). A number of studies have suggested that brain-imaging technologies might be effective for determining whether a subject is trying to deceive an investigator, although the application of the research to the real world is still controversial (see, for example, Langleben, 2008). The government has been very interested in developing a reliable lie detection device, and evidence suggests that there are covert efforts by government agencies to work on the technology, including brain imaging for lie detection (Foster et al., 2003).

It is important to recognize that these studies are preliminary, in many ways crude, and require a subject to cooperate carefully with instructions while lying perfectly still in a brain scanner. There is controversy about how accurate such studies are, about the typically small numbers of study subjects, and how results should be interpreted (see, for example, Logothetis, 2008; Constable, 2012). We are far away from a government or other body being able to "probe your mind" or engage in "mind reading" without your consent.

The increasing possibility of using ever-more-sophisticated means to potentially gain private information from a person's brain, eventually, perhaps, even without their explicit cooperation and consent, requires that we begin now to think through its implications. We must decide as a society whether and under what conditions we would allow the state to coerce someone to undergo a brain scan or other technology to extract needed information from the person's brain. One could imagine many situations in which it would be advantageous, if we could do it, to use such technologies, for example in the workplace to measure honesty or in trials to establish guilt or in military or security contexts to discover where a terrorist planted a bomb.

However, if we were to allow the state to begin to probe anyone's brain for information, how tightly could we keep it under control? Would it really be limited to extreme cases or cases of state security? Some argue that the case is already lost, because soon we may be able to derive similar information from peripheral nervous system phenomena such as microexpressions (Ekman, 2009), from easily monitored blood flow from afar in the parts of the brain close to the surface (Jain et al., 2012), or other technologies that won't require a subject to lie motionless in a scanner.

Brain imaging challenges us with a new form of invasion of privacy, potentially stripping persons of the right to refuse to divulge information and the right to say no (Wolpe et al., 2005). The use of brain imaging in jurisprudence raises a host of legal and constitutional questions about such things as definitions of search and seizure, due process, privacy rights, and rights against self-incrimination (Greely and Illes, 2007; Stoller and Wolpe, 2007). For many, the prospect of others being able to ascertain what they like, think, feel, want, prefer, or intend, without it being willingly disclosed, is frightening. Those who argue for cognitive liberty or neuroprivacy do so precisely because they see in such a world enormous potential violations of personal privacy and the temptations for abuse in both the governmental and social realms. Controlling such technologies is difficult enough in democratic societies with laws that protect the freedom of citizens; it is even more disturbing to think what repressive regimes might do with the ability to probe the minds of their citizens.

Neurological Enhancement

For most of human history, people have searched for ways to alter their cognitive and affective functioning. Neanderthals may have used plants to obtain amphetamine-like effects as early as 50,000 BCE (Merlin, 2003), and the remains of psychoactive plants and fermented grapes are found throughout ancient and modern history. Both modern and ancient Western and Eastern medicines traditionally recommended eating particular foods to induce proper cognitive as well as physical health. Nineteenth-century America was particularly enamored of developing nutritional philosophies of health, from the botanical medicine of Samuel Thompson to the bland diets developed by Will Kellogg (whose corn flakes were invented as a bland breakfast to tame adolescent passions) and Sylvester Graham, whose now-famous cracker was designed for the same end. One cannot overestimate the impact that substances such as alcohol, caffeine, hallucinogens, plant-based stimulants like coca, and other ingestibles have had on the course of human history. Religious movements have been founded on the basis of both using mind-altering substances and rejecting them.

So enhancement is not new—what is new is science's ability to create drugs with more powerful and specific effects. As the strength and targeted effects of drugs grow, so does the temptation to use them to micromanage one's affective and cognitive states, to create "lifestyle" drugs.

The assumption historically was that drugs should be used for treatment of disease and not for enhancing normal functioning. Enhancement and lifestyle drugs will, for our purposes, refer to pharmaceuticals that change a human function in a desirable way in the absence of pathological processes. However simple that definition seems, it is fraught with problems—problems with differentiating pathological processes from natural ones, differentiating food from drugs, differentiating activities we tend to think of as medical versus those we categorize differently. In practice, the distinction between therapy and enhancement is very difficult to maintain.

The demand for lifestyle drugs has been fueled by advances in neuroscience and neuropharmacology and the entry of pharmaceutical companies into the lifestyle drug market. In the wake of consumer demand, pharmaceutical companies have increasingly begun to focus on lucrative lifestyle drugs, such as remedies for impotence (e.g., Viagra and Cialis), baldness (Propecia), and facial wrinkles (Botox). The lifestyle drug market is enormous and lucrative; Viagra and Cialis generated more than $4 billion in sales in 2010, and U.S. sales of modafinil (sold as Provigil) alone reached more than $1.2 billion for a 12-month period in 2011–2012 (Stone, 2013).

It is *how* a drug is used rather than its molecular chemistry or pharmaceutical effects that classifies a drug as a lifestyle drug. Psychological faculties such as memory, appetite, mood, libido, sleep, and executive functions such as attention, working memory, and inhibition represent the most attractive targets for pharmacological enhancement (Farah et al., 2004). Until recently, psychotropic medications for the treatment of diseases associated with these functions had undesirable side effects and high risks, so they were attractive only for the treatment of severe mental illness. Newer understandings of the brain have enabled drugs to affect their intended targets more specifically with fewer and less severe side effects, allowing their use to heighten normal cognition and emotional and executive functions.

The debate over human enhancement centers on the value we put on "natural" processes, such as learning or behavioral reinforcement, and suspicions about bypassing them to directly modify brain function. Drawing on the body's own resources or manipulating the external environment to effect change does not raise the same ethical concerns. Modifying brain functions with either psychopharmaceuticals or technologies such as brain–computer interfaces or brain stimulation is often suspect (Greely et al., 2008; Savulescu, 2009). What are the ethical implications of using a drug to alter personality or to improve normal human abilities or characteristics? What standards should exist? Will advances in psychopharmacology be used as forms of social control? Might this potentially contribute to a widening gap of social inequality, as only the wealthy can afford certain enhancements? Or, at the other extreme, might it encourage conformity of personality—would those who are a bit more irritable or irascible be encouraged or coerced to conform to a chemically induced standard of affect (Wolpe et al., 2007)?

The use of lifestyle or enhancement drugs poses thorny questions about normalcy. What does average or normal functioning mean if we can improve functioning across the entire range of human capability? What is typical functioning—if Prozac can lift everyone's mood, what, then, is a normal or typical affect? Will we medicalize what are now common traits of being human? For example, if we can suppress sadness, will it or our inner struggles become pathologized? Will we begin to think about solving the problems of living through drugs rather than human effort? The questions are both medical—concerning the proper role of health care professionals—and social, concerning whether society should encourage or discourage the use of pharmaceuticals to enhance behaviors, skills and traits.

In terms of cognitive liberty, those in favor of the use of enhancement technologies turn the questions around. Why shouldn't we use available neurotechnologies to better ourselves? Why do we value struggle over ease for achieving results, and who has the right to deny me the easy solution and demand that I struggle? Is our astounding ability to manipulate our own biology not an integral part of who we are as human beings and therefore, in some sense "natural"?

Ultimately, the use of enhancement technologies will be taken out of the hands of physicians. In his article "Cosmetic Neurology: The Controversy over Enhancing Movement, Mentation, and Mood," Anjan Chatterjee (2004) argues that people will demand lifestyle drugs and physicians will respond to consumer-driven demand. While that is already happening, consumers are also moving more and more to online drug distributors and bypassing their personal physicians altogether. The online market was more than $11 billion in 2012 (Liang and Mackey, 2012). College students freely admit to using each other's stimulant medications as study aids, and students with prescriptions can do a brisk business in the dormitories; prescription amphetamines are among the most used and abused drugs among young people. Adults use psychoactive drugs to gain an edge in business or their personal lives. A 2008 poll of readers of the journal *Nature* (Maher, 2008) found that one in five respondents said they had used drugs for nonmedical reasons to stimulate their focus, concentration, or memory. And there is little doubt that those numbers have risen in the years since the poll.

Conclusion

The ideas of cognitive liberty and neuroprivacy are the results of neuroscientific advances that will give us unprecedented powers to peer into brain process or manipulate brain function. Society is beginning a serious conversation over what kinds of access the state should have to the thought processes of its citizens and to what degree we should allow citizens unfettered rights to alter their own brain chemistries. The questions are not simple. The state has always retained rights to violate personal privacy in the face of threats, and society has always tempered individual rights to some degree in service of communal good.

The power of neurotechnologies is still growing, and the discoveries of neuroscience are still in their infancy. It is important that society begin the process of setting up expectations and limits for its newly emerging power so that the state will not assume a right to the inner workings of people's minds. The challenge of neuroscience to cognitive liberty requires a significant moral conversation in the years ahead.

Further Reading

Bublitz, J. (2013) "My Mind Is Mine!? Cognitive Liberty as a Legal Concept". *Cognitive Enhancement*. Springer, 233–264.
Gazzaniga, M.S. (2005) *The Ethical Brain*. New York: Dana Press.
Presidential Commission for the Study of Bioethical Issues. (2015) *Gray Matters: Topics at the Intersection of Neuroscience, Ethics, and Society*. Washington, DC. Available at: www.bioethics.gov
Savulescu, J. and Bostrom, N. (2009) *Human Enhancement*. Oxford University Press.
Wolpe, P.R. (2010) "Is my mind mine? Neuroethics and brain imaging". In V. Ravitsky, A. Fiester and A.L. Caplan (Eds.) *The Penn Center Guide to Bioethics*. New York: Springer, pp. 85–94.

References

American Medical Association Council on Ethical and Judicial Affairs. (2004) Medicating death row inmates so they qualify for execution. *Virtual Mentor*, September. Available at: http://journalofethics.ama-assn.org/2004/09/hlaw1-0409.html.
American Psychiatric Association. (2013) *Diagnostic and Statistical Manual of Mental Disorders*. 5th ed. *DSM-5*. Washington, DC: American Psychiatric Association.
CDC. (2010) Increasing prevalence of parent-reported attention-deficit/hyperactivity disorder among children—United States, 2003 and 2007. MMWR. Morb. Mortal. Wkly. Rep. 59:1439–1443.
———. (2015). Available at: www.cdc.gov/ncbddd/adhd/data.html.
Chatterjee, A. (2004) Cosmetic neurology: The controversy over enhancing movement, mentation, and mood. *Neurology* 63(6): pp. 968–974.

Coleman, Stephen. (2015) Possible ethical problems with military use of non-lethal weapons. *Case Western Reserve Journal of International Law* 47: pp. 185–199.

Constable, R. Todd. (2012) Challenges in fMRI and its limitations. In *Functional Neuroradiology*. New York: Springer, pp. 331–344.

Daugherty, Kacie McCoy. (2000) Synthetic sanity: The ethics and legality of using psychotropic medications to render death row inmates competent for execution. *Journal of Contemporary Health Law & Policy* 17: pp. 715–735.

Dehejia, R.H., and Dehejia, V.H. (1993) Religion and economic activity in India: An historical perspective. *American Journal of Economics and Sociology* 52(2): pp. 145–153.

Ekman, Paul. (2009) Lie catching and microexpressions. *The Philosophy of Deception*: pp. 118–133.

Farah, M.J., Illes, J., Cook-Deegan, R., Gardner, H., Kandel, E., King, P., . . . Wolpe, P.R. (2004) Neurocognitive enhancement: What can we do and what should we do? *Nature Reviews Neuroscience* 5: pp. 421–425.

Foster, K.R., Wolpe, P.R., and Caplan, A. (2003) Bioethics and the brain. *IEEE Spectrum*, June: pp. 34–39.

Greely, H.T., and Illes, J. (2007) Neuroscience-based lie detection: The urgent need for regulation. *American Journal of Law and Medicine* 33(2–3): pp. 377–431.

Gore, J.C. (2003) Principles and practice of functional MRI of the human brain. *Journal of Clinical Investigation* 112(1): 4–9.

Greely, H.T., *et al.* (2008) Towards responsible use of cognitive-enhancing drugs by the healthy. *Nature* 456(7223): pp. 702–705.

Haynes, J., and Rees, G. (2006) Decoding mental states from brain activity in humans. *Nature Reviews Neuroscience* 7(7): pp. 523–534.

Haynes, J., Sakai, K., Rees, G., Gilbert, S., Frith, C., and Passingham, R. (2007) Reading hidden intentions in the human brain. *Current Biology* 17(4): pp. 323–328.

Hosseini, S.M.1., Mano, Y., Rostami, M., Takahashi, M., Sugiura, M., and Kawashima, R. (2011) Decoding what one likes or dislikes from single-trial fNIRS measurements. *Neuroreport* 22(6): pp. 269–273.

Jain, U., Tan, B., and Li Qi. (2012) Concealed knowledge identification using facial thermal imaging. *IEEE International Conference on Acoustics, Speech and Signal Processing (ICASSP)*. IEEE.

Kamitani, Y., and Tong, F. (2005) Decoding the visual and subjective contents of the human brain. *Nature Neuroscience* 8: pp. 679–685.

Lakhan, Shaheen, E., and Kirchgessner, A. (2012) Prescription stimulants in individuals with and without attention deficit hyperactivity disorder: misuse, cognitive impact, and adverse effects. *Brain and Behavior* 2(5): pp. 661–677.

Langleben, D. (2008). Detection of deception with fMRI: Are we there yet? *Legal and Criminological Psychology* 13(1): pp. 1–9.

Liang, B.A., and Mackey, T. (2012) Addressing illicit online pharmacies: Global patient safety and regulatory challenges. In *Counterfeit Medicines: Policy, Economics, and Countermeasures* 1: p. 75.

Logothetis Nikos, K. (2008) What we can do and what we cannot do with fMRI. *Nature* 453(7197): pp. 869–878.

Maher, B. (2008) Poll results: Look who's doping. *Nature* 452: pp. 674–675.

Merlin, M.D. (2003) Archaeological evidence for the tradition of psychoactive plant use in the old world. *Economic Botany* 57: pp. 295–323.

Moreno, J.D. (2006) *Mind wars: Brain research and national defense*. Washington, DC: Dana Press.

Morin, C. (2011) Neuromarketing: The new science of consumer behavior. *Society* 48(2): pp. 131–135.

Nishimoto, S., Vu, An T., Naselaris, T., Benjamini, Y., Yu, B., and Gallant, Jack, L. (2011) Reconstructing visual experiences from brain activity evoked by natural movies. *Current Biology* 21(19): pp. 1641–1646.

Orwell, G. (1961) *1984*. New York: Signet.

Phelps, E.A., O'Connor, K.J., Cunningham, W.A., Funayama, E.S., Gatenby, J.C., Gore, J.C., *et al.* (2000). Performance on indirect measures of race evaluation predicts amygdala activation. *Journal of Cognitive Neuroscience* 12(5): pp. 729–738.

Quanbeck, C., Frye, M., and Altshuler, L. (2003) Mania and the law in California: Understanding the criminalization of the mentally ill. *American Journal of Psychiatry* 160(7): pp. 1245–1250.

Raine, A. (2013). *The Anatomy of Violence: The Biological Roots of Crime*. New York: Pantheon/Random House.

Savulescu, J. (2009) Genetic interventions and the ethics of enhancement of human beings. *Readings in the Philosophy of Technology*: pp. 417–430.

Sententia, W. (2004) Cognitive liberty and converging technologies for improving human cognition. *Annals of the New York Academy of Science* 1013: pp. 221–228.

Shalev, L., Gross-Tsur, V., and Pollak, Y. (2013) Single dose methylphenidate does not impact on attention and decision making in healthy medical students. *Journal of Neurology Research* 2(6): pp. 227–234.

Stoller, S.E., and Wolpe, P.R. (2007) Emerging neurotechnologies for lie detection and the Fifth Amendment. *American Journal of Law and Medicine* 33: pp. 3359–3375.

Stone, K. (2013) The rise of lifestyle drugs: About money. *About.com*. Available at: http://pharma.about.com/od/Sales_and_Marketing/a/The-Rise-Of-Lifestyle-Drugs.htm.

Turner, Danielle C., *et al.* (2003) Cognitive enhancing effects of modafinil in healthy volunteers. *Psychopharmacology* 165(3): pp. 260–269.

Tracey, I. and Flower, R. (2014) The warrior in the machine: neuroscience goes to war. *Nature Reviews Neuroscience* 15: 825–834

Trudeau, M. (2009) More students turning illegally to 'smart' drugs. *National Public Radio*. Available at: www.npr.org/templates/story/story.php?storyId=100254163.

Westen, D. (2007). *The Political Brain: The Role of Emotion in Deciding the Fate of the Nation.* New York: Public Affairs.

Wilens, Timothy, E., *et al.* (2008) Misuse and diversion of stimulants prescribed for ADHD: A systematic review of the literature. *Journal of the American Academy of Child & Adolescent Psychiatry* 47(1): pp. 21–31.

Wolpe, P.R., Foster, K., and Langleben, D. (2005) Emerging neurotechnologies for lie-detection: Promises and perils. *American Journal of Bioethics* 5(2): pp. 39–49.

Wolpe, P.R., Sahl, M., and Howard, J.R. (2007) Bioethical issues in medicinal chemistry and drug treatment. In J. Taylor and D. Triggle (Eds.). Comprehensive Medicinal Chemistry II, Volume 1. Oxford: Elsevier, pp. 681–708.

15

CHRONIC TRAUMATIC ENCEPHALOPATHY

Ethical, Legal, and Social Implications

L. Syd M Johnson

Chris Henry died at the age of 26 after sustaining brain trauma in a fall from a moving pickup truck (Roth, 2013). Before his death, Henry had struggled with substance abuse and had been in trouble with the law, including arrests for assault and intoxicated driving. Derek Boogaard died at the age of 28 from a drug and alcohol overdose. He also had a long history of substance abuse, beginning with an addiction to prescription pain medications that began after a work-related injury (Branch, 2011). Andrew Martin had a history of substance abuse and intoxicated driving before he died of a drug overdose at 33. Chris Benoit was 40 when he killed his wife and son before he committed suicide (Goodman, 2007). Rick Rypien and Joseph Chernach both died of suicide in their mid-20s, after years of suffering from depression (Klein, 2011; Belson, 2015). Jerry Quarry had a history of drug and alcohol abuse and was diagnosed with advanced dementia before he died at 53 (Hirsley, 1999).

What all these men had in common was a history of neurotrauma related to participation in contact sports. (Neurotrauma is here defined as mild traumatic brain injuries, including concussion and subclinical [or subconcussive] brain injuries.)

Henry played NFL football; Boogaard and Rypien were NHL hockey players; Benoit and Martin were professional wrestlers; Quarry was a heavyweight boxer; Chernach played football in high school. The list of athletes who died similar, untimely deaths—many in their twenties or forties—includes both retired and then still-active athletes. A second thing all these men had in common was a postmortem diagnosis of chronic traumatic encephalopathy (CTE).

CTE is a chronic, progressive neurodegenerative disease in which tau proteins accumulate in a distinctive pattern in the brain (McKee, 2009). The disease has been known since at least 1928, when it was formally named and recognized in boxers and initially called "punch drunk syndrome." Harrison Martland first described punch drunk syndrome in an article in the *Journal of the American Medical Association* (Martland, 1928). Martland described the neurological symptoms, including confusion, floppy limbs, staggering gait, tremors, and parkinsonism. The syndrome was obviously already well known in boxers—there were a number of popular epithets for afflicted pugilists: "slug nutty," "cuckoo," "goofy," "cutting paper dolls." Martland's ability to see the microscopic changes in the brain were limited; he hypothesized that the syndrome was caused by small cerebral hemorrhages that he assumed were the result of repeated concussions. The term "dementia pugilistica" was coined a decade later by Millspaugh (1937), and the modern term, "chronic traumatic encephalopathy," was first introduced by Critchley

(1949). Corsellis et al. described the natural history and neuropathology of CTE in 15 retired boxers (Corsellis et al., 1973). Until 2002, CTE had only been recognized in retired boxers. That changed when pathologist Bennet Omalu confirmed CTE in the brain of former Pittsburgh Steeler "Iron Mike" Webster (Omalu et al., 2005). Webster had experienced cognitive impairment and mood disorders, and had a history of substance abuse, financial and personal problems, arrests, and homelessness before his death at age 50.

Webster's was the first known case of CTE in a nonboxer, but not the last. There have been approximately 150 published case studies to date (Maroon et al., 2015), and CTE has been found postmortem in former athletes in several contact and martial sports, as well as in combat veterans, victims of domestic abuse, people with epilepsy, and others who experienced repetitive neurotrauma. CTE has been confirmed in individuals with and without a history of concussion, indicating the likelihood that CTE is caused not just by concussive injuries but also by the kind of subclinical neurotrauma that is routinely incurred in many sports. Evidence of early or incipient CTE has been found in athletes as young as 18 (BU CTE Center, no date), indicating that they sustained injuries in childhood and adolescence that set in train the neurodegenerative process that can lead to CTE–associated morbidity and mortality later in life.

Chronic Traumatic Encephalopathy

Neuropathology and Diagnosis

The neuropathology of CTE is marked by patchy distributions of tau neurofibrillary tangles (NFTs). The location of NFTs in CTE corresponds to areas of direct mechanical trauma, such as blows to the top and side of the head, and, in boxers, the frontal lobe. Clinical symptoms also appear to correspond to the location of brain trauma, not surprisingly. For example, cerebellar scarring and nerve loss are associated with slurred speech and balance problems, while frontal and temporal lobe damage is associated with altered affect and memory (Chin et al., 2011). It is not known precisely what pathological process initiates tau deposition (McKee et al., 2009), but the timing of the appearance of symptoms suggests that the pathological process continues, and the disease progresses after athletes stop playing and stop getting injured. Microscopically, brains with CTE are quite different than brains with other neurodegenerative diseases such as Alzheimer's dementia. The latter, for example, involves NFTs but also amyloid plaques not seen in CTE. In advanced CTE, several gross pathological characteristics are typical, such as reduced brain weight, enlargement of the ventricles, and cerebral atrophy (McKee, 2009).

To date, there are no validated tests that can confirm CTE in a living person, although there is ongoing research focused on discovering antemortem diagnostic modalities, including brain imaging and biomarkers. The [F-18]FFDNP biomarker, which can tag tau and amyloid plaques, is a possible biomarker that has been explored in a study utilizing Positron Emission Tomography (PET). The pilot study showed promise for in vivo detection of CTE in living persons by comparing [F-18]FDDNP PET imaging results in five retired, living professional athletes against postmortem findings (Barrio et al., 2015). The comparisons were not direct; the patterns and locations of tau deposition and neurofibrillary tangles in the living subjects were compared with those found previously in postmortem studies.

At present, getting a clear picture of the epidemiology, risk factors, and prevalence of CTE is hampered in part by a lack of standardization in diagnosis as well as relatively small sample sizes. McKee and colleagues recently published the first validated, neuropathological criteria for diagnosing and staging CTE postmortem (McKee et al., 2016). The four stages of CTE are associated with different neuropathological characteristics and progressive, accumulating clinical symptoms. In Stage I, tau NFTs are localized, and clinical symptoms include headache and loss of attention and concentration. Stage II is characterized by progression of NFTs and more severe clinical symptoms, including depression and mood swings, explosivity, impulsivity, disinhibition, loss of attention and concentration, headache, and short-term memory loss. In Stage III, macroscopic neuropathological changes are evident, including cerebral atrophy and ventricular dilation, and widespread tau, with cognitive impairment and memory loss, executive dysfunction, and visuospatial abnormalities. Individuals with Stage IV CTE are uniformly demented, with profound short-term memory loss, and frequently exhibit paranoia in addition to symptoms that develop in prior stages of disease (McKee et al., 2013).

The actual incidence of CTE in athletic or other populations is unknown. Researchers at Boston University have identified CTE in 96 percent of the brains of former NFL football players examined, and in 79 percent of the brains from individuals who played football professionally, semi-professionally, in college, or in high school (Breslow, 2015). Those are astonishingly high numbers, but there is selection bias in the sample. CTE can only be diagnosed postmortem, by examining brain tissue, and few people donate their brains for study after death. When brains are donated for study, it is frequently because the deceased exhibited clinical symptoms while alive. Hence, a significantly high percentage of the brains studied are positive for CTE.

Research on CTE remains in its infancy, and a number of important questions remain unanswered (Maroon et al., 2015; Bailes et al., 2015). The gaps in knowledge about CTE have significant implications across a range of social, legal, and ethical domains. To date, most of that attention has been directed at the impact of CTE on professional athletes, who are an extremely small subset of the population affected by repetitive neurotrauma but also an unusual population that may be significantly unlike the general population. Without large, longitudinal, epidemiological studies—on the order of, for example, the Framingham Heart Study (Dawber, 1980)—it will be difficult to determine the prevalence and burden of CTE. The importance of such studies is hard to overstate: millions of children and teenagers play tackle football in the United States alone, and worldwide, many millions more youths play other neurotraumatic sports in which minor head injuries are common, including hockey, soccer (football), rugby, and lacrosse. Sport-related concussion is a significant public health concern, but the burden of CTE may be orders of magnitude larger given the potential size of the affected population.

Clinical Symptoms

The clinical symptoms of CTE are numerous and include disordered memory and executive functioning, mood disorders, motor neuron disease, suicidality, substance abuse, violent and erratic behavior, impulsivity, personality and behavior changes, poor judgment (especially concerning financial matters), early dementia, and premature death. Individuals with early-stage disease may not be symptomatic (McKee, 2013; Stern et al., 2013), and the clinical symptoms of CTE are nonspecific and overlap with several other neurological disorders, including post-concussion syndrome, Alzheimer's disease, frontotemporal dementia, Parkinson's disease, Lewy body dementia, amyotrophic lateral sclerosis, and posttraumatic stress disorder. Notably, clinical symptoms in Stage I overlap significantly with symptoms typical in concussion and blast concussive injuries and postconcussion syndrome; Stage II symptoms overlap with symptoms of PTSD and psychiatric illness; and symptoms in Stages III and IV overlap with psychiatric illness and dementias. The nonspecificity of CTE symptoms makes it difficult to develop a confirmatory, symptom-based clinical diagnosis, particularly since comorbidity with other conditions is possible and, in some populations, probably likely. For example, military veterans are frequently athletes or former athletes with a history of concussion and might experience blast-induced mild traumatic brain injury (mTBI) or more severe traumatic brain injury in combat, and subsequently suffer from PTSD, postconcussion syndrome, and CTE.

Two distinct phenotypic presentations of CTE have been identified among a small sample (n = 33) of neuropathologically confirmed cases (Stern et al., 2013). The behavioral/mood subgroup exhibited initial behavioral/mood disturbance, including explosivity and physical/verbal violence, with minimal cognitive and motor symptoms. The behavioral/mood group were also younger at onset of symptoms and died earlier. The cognition subgroup had older age at onset of symptoms, demonstrated cognitive impairments such as memory loss and executive dysfunction, and was more likely to progress to dementia than the behavioral/mood subgroup. A third, smaller subgroup (n = 3) was asymptomatic at the time of death; all had early Stage I or II disease.

The CTE case studies to date are retrospective, utilizing medical records and verbal autopsies (Stern et al., 2013; McKee et al., 2016); the natural history of CTE has not been well studied owing to the current inability to diagnose the condition in living subjects. The development of a symptom-based clinical diagnosis of probable CTE, similar to the clinical diagnosis of Alzheimer's disease, would be an important advancement, potentially leading to more opportunities for prospective studies, therapeutic research, and enhancement of the physical and psychological well-being of affected individuals.

Role of Genetics and Substance Abuse as Risk Factors

There is inconclusive evidence of genetic susceptibility to CTE involving the apolipoprotein E ε4 (ApoE4) and ApoE ε3 (ApoE3) alleles. The ApoE4 genotype is known to increase the relative risk of developing late-onset Alzheimer's disease threefold for carriers of a single gene and tenfold for homozygous individuals (Gandy and DeKosky, 2012). ApoE4 occurs in about 15 percent of the general population and in about 50 percent of people with late-onset Alzheimer's disease (Gandy and DeKosky, 2012). ApoE4 has long been associated with more severe chronic brain injury symptoms in boxers (Jordan et al., 1997). In acute brain injuries, there is accumulating evidence of more severe deleterious effects in ApoE4-positive individuals (McKee et al., 2009). However, while early research suggested a possible role for ApoE4 in the development of CTE, further study has found that the proportion of confirmed CTE cases carrying at least one copy of the ApoE4 allele is not significantly different than that observed in the general population (McKee et al., 2009; McKee et al., 2013). Stern and colleagues found that the cognition subgroup of CTE was ApoE4 homozygous at a greater rate than both the behavior/mood subgroup and the general population (Stern et al., 2013), indicating a possible role in the differential clinical presentation of CTE. The ApoE3 allele is present in 79 percent of the general population and in approximately 61 percent of CTE cases, suggesting it does not increase the risk of CTE either (Maroon et al., 2015). The numbers remain relatively small: genotyping data are available in only about half of confirmed cases of CTE. ApoE does not currently appear to be a risk factor for the development or severity of CTE, but large, prospective, population-based studies are needed to produce a definitive conclusion regarding genetic susceptibility (McKee et al., 2013). Other potential susceptibility genes of interest include microtubule-associated protein tau (MAPT) and the progranulin gene (GRN), among others (Stern et al., 2013).

Substance abuse is common among the subjects so far confirmed to have had CTE, at about 20 percent compared to 7.7 percent in the general population. Among athletes in contact sports, the use of pain medications including opioids is common, and reportedly it frequently carries over into retirement from sports (Maroon et al., 2015; Cottler et al., 2011; Barr, 2011a). Some of the neurodegenerative changes and the clinical symptoms observed in CTE are also found among substance abusers (Maroon et al., 2015). Whether substance abuse is a causal factor or a symptom of CTE remains to be determined. Anabolic steroid use is also common among athletes, but McKee and colleagues found no significant correlation between reported steroid use and CTE (McKee et al., 2013), and the use of anabolic steroids is not currently thought to be a contributing factor in proteinopathies like CTE.

CTE Denialism

Not all athletes who play neurotraumatic sports develop CTE (McKee et al., 2013), and important questions concerning risk factors and the threshold of injury (in terms of both the severity and number of injuries) remain unanswered. It is unclear why some athletes seem to be more susceptible to CTE or why others appear less susceptible. Nor is it known how much risk is involved in sports participation at different levels, but sport-related neurotrauma is a clear risk factor. Bieniek and colleagues reviewed clinical records and brains of 1,721 cases and found CTE in 32 percent of the brains of contact-sport athletes. No cases of CTE were found in brains without any history of brain trauma (Bieniek et al., 2015).

Uncertainties about the specific causes and prevalence of CTE have been exploited by CTE deniers, who deny the connection between sports and CTE or deny the significance or scale of the CTE problem in athletes. They've made much of the selection bias in existing case studies, as well as the fact that not all athletes in neurotraumatic sports develop the disease. CTE deniers claim that concerns about CTE are overblown and premature (Gardner et al., 2014; McCrory et al., 2013) or based on flawed science. Deniers who challenge the causal link between CTE and sports participation frequently suggest that some other risk factor, such as substance abuse or genetics, might be responsible (Gardner et al., 2014; McCrory et al., 2013).

Substance abuse as a risk factor has been widely promoted by CTE deniers or those like the NFL who endeavor to limit their responsibility and liability for CTE (Reimer, 2016; Schwarz et al., 2016). The irony is that, just as CTE results from work-related injuries in professional sports, substance abuse can also be work related in athletes. Professional athletes take pain medications and steroids, and their use is, when not openly endorsed and promulgated by their teams, not openly discouraged (Cottler et al., 2011; Barr, 2011a, 2011b). Thus, the effort to limit liability for CTE by blaming substance abuse does not necessarily reduce the responsibility of teams and sports organizations.

Prevention

There are currently no treatments for CTE. The sentinel indicator for CTE is a history of participation in contact sports or other activity resulting in repetitive neurotrauma. Given a current lack of treatment and the severity of the disease, prevention of CTE is imperative. However, there are currently no known effective strategies for reducing the risk of CTE other than limiting participation in neurotraumatically risky activities. Sports organizations at professional, amateur, and youth sports levels have focused their attention on prevention of concussion, but the strategies currently employed to reduce the risk of concussion are largely ineffective, with the exception, again, of the elimination of neurotraumatic contact (Johnson, 2012).

"Brain slosh" (Myer et al., 2014), or the movement of the brain within the skull, causes concussive injuries and is also the mechanism of the subclinical injuries that contribute to CTE. Brain slosh can occur both with and without direct impacts to the head. Any sufficient impulsive force applied to the body can result in brain slosh, particularly when, as frequently occurs in sports, those impacts involve colliding bodies moving at high speed. Helmets were first introduced in sports like football and hockey to prevent fatal skull fractures and do not prevent concussive or subconcussive neurotrauma, as they cannot prevent brain slosh within the skull (Myer et al., 2014). While considerable research has focused on helmets, including helmets that can measure the biomechanical forces of sport-related impacts, it's unlikely that a solution to the concussion or CTE problems will be found in sports equipment. For example, the International Olympic Committee eliminated the use of headgear for male boxers beginning with the 2016 Olympics, citing *increased* concussion risk with headgear (BBC, 2016). It is hypothesized that protective headgear has a number of counterprotective effects that include increasing the mass of the head, thereby putting additional strain on the neck. Helmets do not prevent the rapid acceleration and deceleration of the brain and fluids (brain slosh) inside the cranium that cause mTBI (Myer et al., 2014).

Concussion-management policies have become a priority for sports teams and leagues worldwide despite the paucity of evidence supporting specific measures. There is uncertainty regarding the optimal management of concussions, and clinical evidence for current treatment guidelines that endorse cognitive and physical rest after concussion is sparse, and some studies show no benefit at all (Schneider et al., 2013; Thomas et al., 2015). A variety of tactics of questionable efficacy and equally questionable ethical justifiability are currently in use, including mandatory use of neuroimaging for concussed athletes; screening of athletes for genes implicated in the development of chronic neurological problems (e.g., ApoE4 allele); mandatory "sit-out" periods after concussion, and mandatory retirement after a set number of concussions (McCrory et al., 2013).

Three primary strategies have been adopted by neurotraumatic sports to address the problem of concussion and CTE: return-to-play (RTP) protocols, minor rule changes to eliminate certain types of head contact, and changes in training that include reductions in full-contact training (Johnson, 2013). None of these strategies will actually prevent concussions or CTE. Even if it were possible to prevent concussions, doing so might not prevent CTE, since the evidence suggests that CTE occurs in athletes with no history of concussions (Roth, 2013). Indeed, to the extent that accumulating repetitive subclinical neurotrauma is a factor in CTE, preventing concussions could prove counterproductive because it would actually increase exposure to subclinical neurotrauma for athletes.

Return-to-Play Protocols

RTP protocols have been adopted at all levels of sport as a response to the problem of sport-related neurotrauma. RTPs were first introduced in youth sports to address second impact syndrome (SIS), an extremely rare but frequently fatal condition. SIS exclusively affects pediatric athletes, involves diffuse cerebral swelling, and is neurologically devastating, often resulting in death within minutes (Bey and Ostick, 2009). Initially thought to occur when a concussed athlete suffers a second concussive impact (hence the name), it is controversial whether SIS actually exists as a distinct condition or whether it requires a second impact (Bey and Ostick, 2009; McCrory, 2001). RTP protocols in sports mandate that athletes with concussions or symptoms of concussion be removed from play or practice for evaluation and remain out until asymptomatic. Because the onset of symptoms in pediatric concussions may be delayed by several hours, the "when in doubt, sit it out" mandate of RTP protocols is of questionable value in youth sports (Johnson, 2012). There are cases of athletes cleared for play who subsequently returned to athletic competition and suffered fatal brain injuries (Carpenter, 2015).

Although widely adopted as a solution to the concussion problem in sports, RTP protocols plainly do not prevent concussions; by definition, the protocol is enacted only after an athlete has already sustained a concussion. Further, SIS has never occurred in an adult athlete. RTPs are specifically intended to prevent SIS, so their adoption by professional sports is misinformed or disingenuous or both. Additionally, lack of compliance with RTP protocols is well documented in professional and youth sports on the part of both teams and individual athletes (Breslow, 2014; Schwarz et al., 2016). Despite their ineffectiveness, RTP protocols promote the appearance that neuroscientific means are being employed to combat the concussion problem. Further, they do so in an innocuous, low-impact way that has little effect on how sports are played.

Rule Changes and Reduced Contact

Minor rule changes and changes to practice and training have also been adopted at all levels of sports. Some examples include the banning of body checking in youth hockey, elimination of blindside hits to the head (Rule 48) in NHL hockey, and the elimination of heading in youth soccer. In Olympic boxing, hits to the head are prohibited. Rule changes that eliminate certain forms of contact in sports are not unusual, nor are they specific to concussion: in professional football, horse collar and clothesline tackles were banned to prevent serious neck injuries. Since injuries also occur during practice and training, eliminating some forms of contact during training is a commonsense way to reduce the lifetime burden of neurotrauma (Broglio et al., 2016), although it remains unclear what the quantitative and qualitative thresholds of injury are for CTE and what impact such reductions will have in the long run.

Neurohype and the Concussion Gold Rush

There is a lucrative market for neurogadgets, tests, and devices that purport to help protect athletes from concussion and its adverse effects with better ways of diagnosing and treating concussion. Among these is the development and promulgation of computerized neuropsycholgical tests (CNTs). These tests are sold in packages to professional, college, and youth sports teams and promoted as a way to manage concussions. CNTs involve the administration of a computerized baseline test (usually recommended once per year, or at the commencement of a sports season) to establish an athlete's baseline cognitive functioning, although there is limited evidence supporting the practice (Broglio et al., 2014; Harmon et al., 2013). If an athlete is suspected of having a concussion, another test is administered with the aim of establishing either that the athlete has a concussion (as evidenced by diminished performance relative to the baseline) or that the athlete has recovered (as evidenced by a return to baseline). There is ongoing controversy concerning the sensitivity and specificity of these tests, their test-retest reliability, and whether they are useful for detecting concussions (Moser et al., 2011; Dessy et al., 2014). Although they are neuropsychological tests, CNTs are designed to be do-it-yourself instruments that can be administered by people with no neuropsychological training, including parents, school coaches and nurses, and student proctors who may administer and use the tests improperly due to a lack of training (Bauer et al., 2012). The problem of sandbagging, in which athletes intentionally underperform on baseline tests in order to thwart later detection of concussions, is a well-documented practice among both professional and student athletes (Erdal, 2012; Bauer et al., 2012). Sandbagging demonstrates both the shortcomings of DIY tests administered by personnel other than experienced neuropsychologists and the problem of willful noncompliance among athletes, including youth athletes.

Additionally, the business model of CNTs is to sell packages of large numbers of baseline tests, to be regularly administered to all athletes, bundled with small numbers of postinjury tests—it's an economic strategy that can encourage practice effects that reduce the reliability of the tests. Because CNTs are used to make RTP decisions, there are serious ethical concerns about overreliance on tests of questionable diagnostic value (Meehan et al., 2011). Finally, with respect to CTE, the evidence to date points to subclinical neurotrauma, and not just concussions, as a cause. CNTs cannot be used to evaluate asymptomatic subclinical neurotrauma.

In recent years, both the NFL and NHL have claimed that they have improved diagnosis of concussions through the use of CNTs, more rigorous sideline diagnosis, and adherence to RTPs, and claimed that they have reduced the number of concussions in their sports (Belson, 2017). However, one would expect the opposite since improved diagnosis would inevitably lead to there being *more* concussions diagnosed, not fewer, especially since neither league has adopted measures that would actually reduce the risks of concussion.

Improperly used CNTs, for both baseline and postinjury assessment, create the illusion that effective, neuroscientifically valid, and evidence-based measures are being deployed to combat the sport concussion problem and protect athlete safety. CNTs may instead undermine athlete safety and threaten informed consent when athletes and parents of youth athletes make decisions based on misinformation about the protection offered by CNTs (Johnson and Partridge, 2013).

Ethical, Legal, and Social Implications

There are numerous ethical, legal, and social concerns that arise in the context of sport-related neurotrauma at all levels of sport. They include athlete autonomy in decision making concerning participation in risky sports, the adequacy of informed consent, the disclosure of risk, the potential for financial and social coercion, and competing, conflicting interests. There are questions about consent in contexts in which risks are inherent to the endeavor, as in both sports and combat, and about the extent to which participants understand the risks of neurotrauma and have the ability to avoid those risks. In both sports and the military, individuals (seemingly) voluntarily undertake the risk of brain injuries that might impair their *future* ability to act autonomously. Given the current state of knowledge about CTE and repetitive neurotrauma, we might also ask: what are the social and legal implications, in terms of financial liability for teams but also in terms of the criminal culpability of individuals who experience the long-term or progressive effects of these injuries (Johnson et al., 2015)? What kinds of measures are warranted when the risks and mechanisms of injury are not fully understood? These questions concern the fiduciary duties of sports leagues and teams, and military organizations, as well as the ethical principles that ground those duties.

The Notable Case of Chris Henry

Chris Henry was 26 when he died, and it's evident that CTE can affect young athletes, particularly those in the behavioral/mood subgroup. Henry had no history of documented concussions during his college and professional football career. Having no history of documented concussions is not conclusive evidence that he never sustained a concussion, given extensive evidence of underreporting and lax concussion diagnosis practices in sports. Nonetheless, Henry's case adds to the evidence that CTE is potentially unrelated to concussions.

Henry also had a history of criminal behavior and substance abuse. He was arrested seven times during the five years he played professional football and had a reputation as a "troublemaker," although friends and family described him as quiet and introverted by nature (Roth, 2013). Criminal behavior and substance abuse are not unique to athletes, and there has long been debate about the supposed tendency toward bad behavior among a subset of professional athletes (Carter, 2013). One explanation is that some sports attract people who tend toward violent crimes; another is that the sports themselves create violent, criminal people by promoting a culture of violence and entitlement. The possibility that sports can create violent athletes goes against the widely promoted image of sports participation as a character-building, teamwork- and discipline-promoting activity. CTE adds a concerning, new, *possible* explanation for criminal behavior on the part of athletes and other populations at risk of repetitive brain injuries, given (a) clinical symptoms that can include explosivity, impulsivity, and aggression and (b) the fact that violent behavior is documented among some of the neuropathologically confirmed cases, including Chris Henry's.

Legal Implications: Criminal Law

A comparative study of arrests in the NFL population and the general population shows higher rates of arrest for property and public order crimes in the general population, but higher arrest rates for violent crimes among the NFL population (Leal et al., 2015). Another study concluded that rates of domestic violence arrests are extraordinarily high in the NFL cohort compared to the general population, particularly when other socioeconomic factors are considered (Morris, 2014). Traumatic brain injuries (TBI), in particular those leading to frontal lobe dysfunction, have long been associated with unusual aggression (Brower and Price, 2001). Among intimate partner (domestic) violence offenders, 53 percent are identified as having had a TBI; a high percentage of prison inmates have a history of TBI (Wortzel and Arciniegas, 2013). The risk of self-directed violence, including suicide, is also heightened in individuals with TBI (Wortzel and Arciniegas, 2013).

Whether the behaviors of CTE–affected athletes can or should be attributed to brain injury or CTE remains undetermined, but there is at least a correlation between CTE and a history of criminal behavior—particularly crimes that involve impulsiveness, substance abuse, and violence—that warrants concern and investigation. Better understanding the behavioral sequelae of CTE has important social and legal implications for affected individuals, who, because CTE cannot be diagnosed while they are alive, may have neurological disease that is not acknowledged as a mitigating factor in judgments of their legal responsibility for criminal behavior. There are unanswered questions about the extent to which CTE might result in affected individuals not being fully in control of or responsible for their behaviors, but there is certainly precedent for considering neurological disease as a mitigating factor in criminal behavior (Sfera et al., 2014; Mendez, 2010). Behavioral variant fronto-temporal dementia (bvFTD), for example, is associated with antisocial and criminal behavior (Mendez, 2010). Individuals with bvFTD, while deemed competent to stand trial for criminal behavior because they are able to appreciate the wrongfulness of their actions, might nonetheless be "organically incapable of regulating their behavior" (Sfera et al., 2014, p. 3). This is a particularly vexing problem, as criminal law (for example, in the United States) often predicates criminal culpability in so-called insanity cases not on the inability to control one's behavior but rather on the ability to appreciate the moral and/or legal wrongness of one's actions (Sfera et al., 2014). Patients with bvFTD are thus caught between a rock and a hard place when it comes to legal culpability—they are not legally insane, but neither are they able to control their behavior in a way that would straightforwardly make them responsible for their actions. Prisons are certainly not the ideal setting for institutionalizing elderly demented individuals.

For more on neuroscience and criminal law, see Chapter 12.

Given the known behavioral symptoms of CTE, the population of CTE–affected individuals could present a similar challenge for society and the legal system. In a review of the CTE literature from 1928 through 2009; McKee and colleagues found that personality and behavior changes were common, occurring in some 65 percent of CTE cases. Seventy percent of those changes involved aggression or violence (McKee et al., 2009). Changes in behavior, particularly toward uncharacteristic violence or criminality, may be a sentinel symptom that should be included in a clinical diagnosis of CTE. However, for a diagnosis of CTE to serve as a mitigating factor in the legal realm would require a reconsideration of the legal understanding of insanity, control, and responsibility.

Legal Implications: Tort Law

CTE is a disabling condition that, since commonly the result of work-related injuries in athletes and military personnel, may warrant consideration as a disability and entitlement to long-term disability benefits. This is not a straightforward matter, however, as it's possible that the causal injuries that set in train the neuropathological processes of CTE occur in childhood or adolescence. Indeed, there has already been a settled lawsuit against Pop Warner football for brain injuries and CTE blamed for the suicide death of Joseph Chernach (Belson, 2015). Evidence that adolescent brain injuries may cause CTE underscores the need to limit neurotraumatic injuries in youth sports, but it also complicates efforts to assign culpability in tort cases involving the long-term effects of sport-related neurotrauma, including CTE. While professional sports organizations can have deep pockets when it comes to compensating retired athletes for work-related disabilities, they may bear only partial responsibility for those disabilities, given the long history of sports participation for most professional/elite athletes. Should it turn out that childhood injuries are at least in part responsible—or wholly responsible for athletes who only played as children and adolescents—it would add a significant layer of complexity to efforts to assign liability, given the varied settings in which organized youth sports are played (such as public and private schools, camps, city leagues, etc.) and the wide range of personnel involved—trained, untrained, and volunteer (such as parents)—in making decisions about player health and safety.

The inability to definitively diagnose CTE in a living individual could also complicate efforts to have the disorder recognized as a compensable disability, or to demonstrate that it was caused by sports participation. Few NFL players have to date been successful at obtaining disability compensation for brain injuries they claimed were caused by football (Fainaru and Fainaru-Wada., 2012), but class-action lawsuits are currently pending against the NFL and NHL. While individuals in the behavior/mood CTE subgroup may show early signs of disease while in their teens and 20s, those in the cognitive subgroup tend to be older, with symptom onset delayed by many years, making it even more difficult to pinpoint causation.

Confirmation of genetic susceptibility to CTE would generate a number of ethical and legal issues. One could foresee mandatory genotyping for sport eligibility—prompted by liability insurance eligibility requirements—that would result in socioeconomic discrimination against athletes who lack the resources to access such testing. Exclusion or discrimination against athletes at all levels of sport would deny athletes, and especially youth athletes, the physical, social, and economic benefits of athletic activity and participation. It could also have implications for the legal liability of sports organizations, in that it would create financial incentives to discriminate on the basis of genotype rather than actually addressing the risk factors that affect all athletes. Violations of personal autonomy and medical and genetic privacy could also result. Genetic susceptibility is but one possible risk factor for CTE, whereas the most significant risk factor is and is likely to remain repetitive neurotrauma that is unavoidable given the way neurotraumatic sports are currently played.

An Ethical Priority: Effective Prevention

With respect to CTE, much still remains unknown about the risks and prevalence of the disease for nonprofessional and nonelite athletes. Several neuropathologically confirmed cases of CTE in youths and young adult athletes, however, have established that there is some as yet unquantified risk. This warrants concern given how common participation in neurotraumatic sports is among youths worldwide.

Needless to say, it is not possible to eliminate all risk of concussion in sports. Even in sports that present no inherent danger of repetitive neurotrauma, accidents can occur and injuries can result. Nonetheless, reducing the inherent risks of neurotrauma by altering the way sports are played is likely to be the most effective strategy for reducing the incidence of sport-related neurotrauma.

Although much attention has been focused on professional sports and athletes, the kinds of substantive changes to professional sports that would be required to significantly reduce the risk and incidence of neurotrauma are extremely unlikely to be adopted. Such measures would alter some sports in ways that would be very unpopular and would arguably threaten the essence and integrity of the sport. Furthermore, adult athletes are capable of making informed decisions about their participation in risky sports, including sports like boxing that have long been recognized as neurotraumatically risky (Johnson, 2015, 2016).

Pragmatically, it would be more effective to focus on the prevention of neurotrauma at nonelite levels of sport, particularly youth sports. For example, USA Hockey and Hockey Canada, the governing bodies for youth hockey in North America, have in recent years raised the age at which body checking is permitted. US Soccer has adopted a policy prohibiting heading of the ball by soccer players under 10 in an effort to reduce the risk of head trauma (US Soccer, 2015). Youth sports warrant special concern for several reasons. First, the number of athletes playing youth sports is vastly higher than the number playing at professional/elite levels. Meaningful prevention should target the largest possible population, and for sport-related neurotrauma, the largest affected population is youth athletes.

Second, susceptibility to concussion is known to be higher in children and adolescents (American Academy of Pediatrics, 2000). While there is a paucity of data on CTE among youth athletes, the existing case studies include both high school and college athletes, indicating that the causal neuropathological process of CTE likely begins in adolescence (Schwarz, 2010; Stern et al., 2013). Third, student athletes are doubly burdened by concussion and neurotrauma, which can have disabling effects in both the short and long terms that can affect school performance and daily life (Talavage et al., 2010; Moser et al., 2005). For student athletes, the stakes are extremely high, as they risk both athletic and academic consequences that could significantly affect their future goals and options. And youth athletes are not competent to make informed decisions about participation in risky athletic activities, possessing neither the experience nor the judgment necessary to evaluate risks and anticipate future desires and values in the way required to consent to participation. In all likelihood, CTE in some professional/elite athletes is an unavoidable hazard of the job. But work-related risks that might be acceptable for a minuscule number of well-compensated, consenting professional adult athletes face a different burden of ethical justification than the risks of recreational youth sports that potentially involve many millions of nonconsenting children (Johnson, 2012, 2015). Finally, the benefits of preventing brain injuries in youth athletes will extend to professional athletes. Nearly all professional athletes begin their careers as child athletes and have played in their respective sports for decades by the time they become professionals. Many sustained their first concussion as a child athlete (Cusimano et al., 2011). Radically changing youth sports to reduce the risk of neurotraumatic injury can significantly reduce the lifetime burden of those injuries among professional/elite athletes. Protecting them as children thus protects them as adults, as they can avoid a significant portion of their lifetime burden of neurotrauma without unduly restricting the freedom of competent, autonomous adult athletes to make informed choices about undertaking the risks of neurotraumatic sports. Prevention of neurotrauma in youth sports thus plants two trees with one seed: both youth athletes and professional/elite athletes can benefit (Johnson, 2012). Furthermore, strategies for preventing brain injuries, such as the elimination of body checking in youth hockey or tackling in youth football, will prevent other types of injuries as well, as these forms of intentional contact are the primary mechanism of all injuries in such sports (Warsh et al., 2009).

Conclusion

The disease burden of CTE is quite high; the behavioral/mood symptoms can have significant effects for individuals with CTE and their families. Those effects threaten to spread out—indeed perhaps they already have—to the whole of society.

People with cognitive disabilities related to brain injury are stigmatized. The stigma is arguably even worse for those with psychiatric disorders and symptoms, including symptoms related to brain injuries. The stigma is compounded in those who commit crimes by legal and penal systems that are not designed to consider either the causes or the effects of those disorders nor their role in mitigating responsibility for criminal behavior. Those social and legal problems are far larger than the CTE or concussion problems, but at present the scale of concussion and CTE as long-term health concerns remains unknown. It would be reasonable to infer that they are far larger problems than at present acknowledged. There are, then, potentially vast numbers of people worldwide affected by so-called minor brain injuries, people for whom both the short- and long-term effects can be far from minor. The attention to sport-related neurotrauma and its ethical, legal, and social implications could and should motivate a larger societal conversation about brain injuries and psychiatric illness, extending well beyond the populations affected by sport-related neurotrauma.

Further Reading

Branch, J. (2011) "Derek Boogaard: A Boy Learns to Brawl". *New York Times*. Available at: www.nytimes. com/2011/12/04/sports/hockey/derek-boogaard-a-boy-learns-to-brawl.html?pagewanted=all&_r=0

Breslow, J.M. (2014) "What We've Learned From Two Years of Tracking NFL Concussions". *PBS Frontline*. Available at: www.pbs.org/wgbh/frontline/article/what-weve-learned-from-two-years-of-tracking-nfl-concussions/

McKee, A.C., Stein, T.D., Nowinski, C.J., Stern, R.A., Daneshvar, D.H., Alvarez, V.E., . . . Riley, D.O. (2013) "The Spectrum of Disease in Chronic Traumatic Encephalopathy". *Brain* 136(1), 43–64.

Maroon, J.C., Winkelman, R., Bost, J., Amos, A., Mathyssek, C. and Miele, V. (2015) "Chronic Traumatic Encephalopathy in Contact Sports: A Systematic Review of All Reported Pathological Cases". *PLoS One* 10(2), e0117338.

Omalu, B.I., DeKosky, S.T., Minster, R.L., Kamboh, M.I., Hamilton, R.L. and Wecht, C.H. (2005) "Chronic Traumatic Encephalopathy in a National Football League Player". *Neurosurgery* 57(1), 128–134.

References

American Academy of Pediatrics. (2000) Safety in youth ice hockey: The effects of body checking. *Pediatrics* 105(3 Pt 1): pp. 657–658.

Bailes, J.E., Turner, R.C., Lucke-Wold, B.P., Patel, V. and Lee, J.M., 2015. Chronic traumatic encephalopathy: Is it real? The relationship between neurotrauma and neurodegeneration. *Neurosurgery* 62: pp. 15–24.

Barr, J. (2011a) Study: Players misuse painkillers. *ESPN.com*. Available at: http://espn.go.com/espn/eticket/story?page=110128/painkillersnews [Accessed 1 July 2016].

———. (2011b) Painkiller Use in Today's NFL. Available at: http://espn.go.com/espn/eticket/story?page=110128/PainkillersNews [Accessed 1 July 2016].

Barrio, J.R., Small, G.W., Wong, K.P., Huang, S.C., Liu, J., Merrill, D.A., . . . Kepe, V. (2015) In vivo characterization of chronic traumatic encephalopathy using [F-18] FDDNP PET brain imaging. *Proceedings of the National Academy of Sciences* 112(16): pp. E2039–E2047.

Bauer, R.M., Iverson, G.L., Cernich, A.N., Binder, L.M., Ruff, R.M., and Naugle, R.I. (2012) Computerized neuropsychological assessment devices: Joint position paper of the American Academy of Clinical Neuropsychology and the National Academy of Neuropsychology. *Clinical Neuropsychologist* 26(2): pp. 177–196.

BBC. (2016) Olympic Boxing: Men to Stop Wearing Protective Headguards. Available at: www.bbc.com/sport/boxing/35701948 [Accessed 1 June 2016].

Belson, K. (2015) Pop Warner settles lawsuit over player who had CTE. *New York Times*. Available at: www.nytimes.com/2016/03/10/sports/football/pop-warner-settles-lawsuit-over-player-who-had-cte.html [Accessed 1 June 2016].

Belson, K. (2017) NFL Reports a Decline in Concussions This Season. *The New York Times*, www.nytimes.com/2017/01/26/sports/football/nfl-concussions-decline.html?action=click&contentCollection=Pro%20Football&module=RelatedCoverage&region=EndOfArticle&pgtype=article [Accessed 6 April 2017].

Bey, T., and Ostick, B. (2009) Second impact syndrome. *Western Journal of Emergency Medicine*, 10(1): pp. 7–10.

Bieniek, K.F., Ross, O.A., Cormier, K.A., Walton, R.L., Soto-Ortolaza, A., Johnston, A.E., . . . Rademakers, R. (2015) Chronic traumatic encephalopathy pathology in a neurodegenerative disorders brain bank. *Acta Neuropathologica* 130(6): pp. 877–889.

Boston University CTE Center. (no date) 18 Year Old High School Football Player. Available at: www.bu.edu/cte/our-research/case-studies/18-year-old/ [Accessed 21 Dec. 2016].

Branch, J. (2011) Derek Boogaard: A boy learns to brawl. *New York Times*. Available at: www.nytimes.com/2011/12/04/sports/hockey/derek-boogaard-a-boy-learns-to-brawl.html?pagewanted=all&_r=0 [Accessed 21 Dec. 2016].

Breslow, J.M. (2014) What we've learned from two years of tracking NFL concussions. *Frontline*. Available at: www.pbs.org/wgbh/frontline/article/what-weve-learned-from-two-years-of-tracking-nfl-concussions/ [Accessed 1 June 2016].

———. (2015) New: 87 deceased NFL players test positive for brain disease. *Frontline*. Available at: www.pbs.org/wgbh/frontline/article/new-87-deceased-nfl-players-test-positive-for-brain-disease/ [Accessed 5 May 2016].

Broglio, S.P., Cantu, R.C., Gioia, G.A., Guskiewicz, K.M., Kutcher, J., Palm, M., and McLeod, T.C.V. (2014) National athletic trainers' association position statement: Management of sport concussion. *Journal of Athletic Training* 49(2): pp. 245–265.

Broglio, S.P., Williams, R.M., O'Connor, K.L., and Goldstick, J. (2016) Football players' head-impact exposure after limiting of full-contact practices. *Journal of Athletic Training* 51(7): pp. 511–518. doi:10.4085/1062-6050–51.7.04 [Accessed 5 July 2016].

Brower, M.C., and B.H. Price. (2001) Neuropsychiatry of frontal lobe dysfunction in violent and criminal behavior: A critical review. *Journal of Neurology, Neurosurgery & Psychiatry* 71(6): pp. 720–726.

Carpenter, L. (2015) Kenney Bui: The life and death of a high school football player. *The Guardian*. Available at: www.theguardian.com/sport/2015/oct/14/kenney-bui-high-school-football? [Accessed 16 May 2016].

Carter, B. (2013) Does the NFL have a crime problem? *BBC News*. Available at: www.bbc.com/news/magazine-23179125 [Accessed 21 Dec. 2016].

Chin, L.S., Toshkezi, G., and Cantu, R.C. (2011) Chronic traumatic encephalopathy related to sports injury. *US Neurology* 7(1): pp. 33–36.

Corsellis, J.A.N., Bruton, C.J., and Freeman-Browne, D. (1973) The aftermath of boxing. *Psychological Medicine* 3: pp. 270–303.

Cottler, L.B., Abdallah, A.B., Cummings, S.M., Barr, J., Banks, R., and Forchheimer, R. (2011) Injury, pain, and prescription opioid use among former National Football League (NFL) players. *Drug and Alcohol Dependence* 116(1): pp. 188–194.

Critchley, M. (1949) Punch-drunk syndromes: The chronic traumatic encephalopathy of boxers. In *Hommage à Clovis Vincent*. Paris: Maloine, pp.131–141.

Cusimano, M., Taback, N., McFaull, S., Hodgins, R., Bekele, T., and Elfeki, N. (2011) Effect of bodychecking on rate of injuries among minor hockey players. *Open Medicine* 5(1): pp. 57–64.

Dawber, T.R. (1980) *The Framingham Study: The Epidemiology of Atherosclerotic Disease*. Cambridge, MA: Harvard University Press.

Dessy, A., Rasouli, J., Gometz, A., and Choudhri, T. (2014) A review of modifying factors affecting usage of diagnostic rating scales in concussion management. *Clinical Neurology and Neurosurgery* 122: pp. 59–63.

Erdal, K. (2012) Neuropsychological testing for sports-related concussion: How athletes can sandbag their baseline testing without detection. *Archives of Clinical Neuropsychology* 27(5): pp. 473–479.

Fainaru, S., and Fainaru-Wada, M. (2012) Mixed messages on brain injuries. *ESPN*. Available at: http://espn.go.com/espn/otl/story/_/page/OTL-Mixed-Messages/nfl-disability-board-concluded-playing-football-caused-brain-injuries-even-officials-issued-denials-years [Accessed 2 June 2016].

Gandy, S., and DeKosky, S.T. (2012) APOE ε4 status and traumatic brain injury on the gridiron or the battlefield. *Science Translational Medicine* 4(134): pp. 134ed4.

Gardner, A., Iverson, G.L., and McCrory, S. (2014) Chronic traumatic encephalopathy in sport: A systematic review. *British Journal of Sports Medicine* 48: pp. 84–90.

Goodman, B. (2007) Wrestler killed wife and son, then himself. *New York Times*. Available at: www.nytimes.com/2007/06/27/us/27wrestler.html [Accessed 21 Dec. 2016].

Harmon, K.G., Drezner, J.A., Gammons, M., Guskiewicz, K.M., Halstead, M., Herring, S.A., and Roberts, W.O. (2013) American medical society for sports medicine position statement: Concussion in sport. *British Journal of Sports Medicine* 47(1): pp. 15–26.

Hirsley, M. (1999) Punches took deadly toll on Quarry: Ex-golden boy stayed in boxing far too long. *Chicago Tribune*. Available at: http://articles.chicagotribune.com/1999-01-05/sports/9901050116_1_jerry-quarry-punches-heavyweight-champions-floyd-patterson [Accessed 21 Dec. 2016].

Johnson, L.S.M. (2012) Return to play guidelines cannot solve the football-related concussion problem. *Journal of School Health* 82(4): pp. 180–185.

———. (2015) Sport-related neurotrauma and neuroprotection: Are return-to-play protocols justified by paternalism? *Neuroethics* 8(1): pp. 15–26.

———. (2016) Paternalism, protection, and athlete autonomy. *Philosopher*. Available at: https://politicalphilosopher.net/2016/06/17/featured-philosopher-syd-johnson/ [Accessed 21 Dec. 2016].

Johnson, L.S.M., and Partridge, B. (2013) Sports concussion and sandbagging. *Bioethics Forum*. Available at: www.thehastingscenter.org/sports-concussions-and-sandbagging/ [Accessed 1 June 2016].

Johnson, L.S.M., Partridge, B., and Gilbert, F. (2015) Framing the Debate: Concussion and mild traumatic brain injury. *Neuroethics* 8(1): pp. 1–4.

Jordan, B.D., Relkin, N.R., Ravdin, L.D., Jacobs, A.R., Bennett, A., and Gandy, S. (1997) Apolipoprotein E ε4 associated with chronic traumatic brain injury in boxing. *Journal of American Medical Association* 278(2): pp. 136–140.

Klein, J.Z. (2011) Player's death follows bouts of depression. *New York Times*. Available at: www.nytimes.com/2011/08/17/sports/hockey/rypiens-death-follows-bouts-of-depression.html [Accessed 21 Dec. 2016].

Leal, W., Gertz, M., and Piquero, A.R. (2015) The national felon league? A comparison of NFL arrests to general population arrests. *Journal of Criminal Justice* 43: pp. 397–403.

McCrory, P. (2001) Does second impact syndrome exist? *Clinical Journal of Sports Medicine* 11: pp. 144–149.

McCrory, P., Meeuwisse, W., Aubry, M., Cantu, B., Dvorak, J., Echemendia, R.J., . . . Turner, M. (2013) Consensus statement on concussion in sport-the 4th international conference on concussion in sport held in Zurich, November 2012. *British Journal of Sports Medicine* 47: pp. 250–258.

McKee, A.C., Cairns, N.J., Dickson, D.W., Folkerth, R.D., Keene, C.D., Litvan, I., . . . Tripodis, Y. (2016) The first NINDS/NIBIB consensus meeting to define neuropathological criteria for the diagnosis of chronic traumatic encephalopathy. *Acta Neuropathologica* 131(1): pp. 75–86.

McKee, A.C., Cantu, R.C., Nowinski, C.J., Hedley-Whyte, E.T., Gavett, B.E., Budson, A.E., . . . Stern, R.A. (2009) Chronic traumatic encephalopathy in athletes: Progressive tauopathy after repetitive head injury. *Journal of Neuropathology & Experimental Neurology* 68(7): pp. 709–735.

McKee, A.C., Stein, T.D., Nowinski, C.J., Stern, R.A., Daneshvar, D.H., Alvarez, V.E., . . . Riley, D.O. (2013) The spectrum of disease in chronic traumatic encephalopathy. *Brain* 136(1): pp. 43–64.

Maroon, J.C., Winkelman, R., Bost, J., Amos, A., Mathyssek, C., and Miele, V. (2015) Chronic traumatic encephalopathy in contact sports: A systematic review of all reported pathological cases. *PLOS One* 10(2): p. e0117338.

Martland, H.S. (1928) Punch drunk. *Journal of the American Medical Association* 91(15): pp. 1103–1107.

Meehan, W.P., d'Hemecourt, P., Collins, C.L. and Comstock, R.D. (2011) Assessment and management of sport-related concussions in United States high schools. *American Journal of Sports Medicine* 39(11): pp. 2304–2310.

Mendez, M.F. (2010) The unique predisposition to criminal violations in frontotemporal dementia. *Journal of the American Academy of Psychiatry and the Law Online* 38(3): pp. 318–323.

Millspaugh, J.A. (1937) Dementia pugilistica. *United States Naval Medical Bulletin* 35: pp. 297–303.

Morris, B. (2014) The rate of domestic violence arrests among NFL players. *Fivethirtyeight.com*. Available at: http://fivethirtyeight.com/datalab/the-rate-of-domestic-violence-arrests-among-nfl-players/ [Accessed 5 May 2016].

Moser, R.S., Schatz, P., and Jordan, B.D (2005) Prolonged effects of concussion in high school athletes. *Neurosurgery* 57(2): pp. 300–306.

Moser, R.S., Schatz, P., Neidzwski, K., and Ott, S.D. (2011) Group versus individual administration affects baseline neurocognitive test performance. *American Journal of Sports Medicine* 39(11): pp. 2325–2330.

Myer, G.D., Smith, D., Barber Foss, K.D., Dicesare, C.A., Kiefer, A.W., Kushner, A.M., . . . Khoury, J.C. (2014) Rates of concussion are lower in National Football League games played at higher altitudes. *Journal of Orthopaedic & Sports Physical Therapy* 44(3): pp. 164–172.

Omalu, B.I., DeKosky, S.T., Minster, R.L., Kamboh, M.I., Hamilton, R.L., and Wecht, C.H. (2005) Chronic traumatic encephalopathy in a National Football League player. *Neurosurgery* 57(1): pp. 128–134.

Reimer, A. (2016) The NFL's crusade to mask the dangers of head trauma looks worse than ever. *SB Nation.com*. Available at: www.sbnation.com/nfl/2016/3/28/11250362/nfl-concussions-cte-connection-roger-goodell-comments [Accessed 21 Dec. 2016].

Roth, M. (2013) The tragedy of CTE: A brain disease that afflicts athletes. *Pittsburgh Post-Gazette*. Available at: www.post-gazette.com/news/health/2013/05/12/The-tragedy-of-CTE-a-brain-disease-that-afflicts-athletes/stories/201305120137 [Accessed 2 June 2016].

Schneider, K.J., Iverson, G.L., Emery, C.A., McCrory, P., Herring, S.A., and Meeuwisse, W.H. (2013) The effects of rest and treatment following sport-related concussion: A systematic review of the literature. *British Journal of Sports Medicine* 47(5): pp. 304–307.

Schwarz, A. (2010) Suicide reveals signs of a disease seen in N.F.L. *New York Times*. Available at: www.nytimes.com/2010/09/14/sports/14football.html [Accessed 1 June 2016].

Schwarz, A., Bogdanich, W., and Williams, J. (2016) N.F.L.'s flawed concussion research and ties to tobacco industry. *New York Times*. Available at: www.nytimes.com/2016/03/25/sports/football/nfl-concussion-research-tobacco.html [Accessed 1 June 2016].

Sfera, A., Osorio, C., Gradini, R., and Price, A. (2014) Neurodegeneration behind bars: From molecules to jurisprudence. *Frontiers in Psychiatry* 5: pp. 1–4.

Stern, R.A., Daneshvar, D.H., Baugh, C.M., Seichepine, D.R., Montenigro, P.H., Riley, D.O., . . . Simkin, I. (2013) Clinical presentation of chronic traumatic encephalopathy. *Neurology* 81(13): pp. 1122–1129.

Talavage, T.M., Nauman, E.A., Breedlove, E.L., Yoruk, U., Dye, A.E., Morigaki, K.E., Feuer, H. and Leverenz, L.J. (2010) Functionally-detected cognitive impairment in high school football players without clinically-diagnosed concussion. *Journal of Neurotrauma*, 31(4): pp. 327–338. doi:10.1089/neu.2010.1512 [Accessed 5 July 2016].

Thomas, D.G., Apps, J.N., Hoffmann, R.G., McCrea, M., and Hammeke, T. (2015) Benefits of strict rest after acute concussion: A randomized controlled trial. *Pediatrics* 135(2): pp. 213–223.

U.S. Soccer. (2015) U.S. Soccer provides additional information about upcoming player safety campaign. Available at: www.ussoccer.com/stories/2015/11/09/22/57/151109-ussoccer-provides-additional-information-about-upcoming-player-safety-campaign [Accessed 1 June 2016].

Warsh, J.M., Constantin, S.A., Howard, A., and Macpherson, A. (2009) A systematic review of the association between body checking and injury in youth ice hockey. *Clinical Journal of Sport Medicine* 19(2): pp. 134–144.

Wortzel, H.S., and Arciniegas, D.B. (2013) A forensic neuropsychiatric approach to traumatic brain injury, aggression, and suicide. *Journal of the American Academy of Psychiatry and the Law Online* 41(2): pp. 274–286.

16

NEUROHYPE

A Field Guide to Exaggerated Brain-Based Claims

Scott O. Lilienfeld, Elizabeth Aslinger, Julia Marshall, and Sally Satel

On November 11, 2007, as the 2008 U.S. presidential election was kicking into high gear, the *New York Times* ran a now infamous op-ed column "This is your brain on politics" (Iacoboni et al., 2007). The author team was led by Marco Iacoboni, a professor of psychiatry at the University of California at Los Angeles. Iacoboni and his coinvestigators hoped to harness the power of brain-imaging technology, functional magnetic resonance imaging (fMRI) in particular, to ascertain the political preferences of a sample of undecided voters. Like many proponents of the use of fMRI for real-world applications, they began with the assumption that brain-imaging data could help them discern preferences that prospective voters are either unable or unwilling to acknowledge.

"Our results reveal some voter impressions on which this election may well turn," the scientists proclaimed. As revealed by fMRI, voters' brains ostensibly displayed marked ambivalence toward Hillary Clinton; while viewing her, their anterior cingulates—which play a key role in mediating conflict—suggested that "they were battling unacknowledged impulses to like Mrs. Clinton." Mitt Romney, the team concluded, "shows potential." Participants' amygdalae—brain areas integrally involved in fear processing—became activated upon first glimpsing him but seemed to calm down upon further viewing, suggesting that voters might become more comfortable with him over time. Images of John Edwards seemed to activate voters' insulas, pointing to feelings of disgust toward him.

Of all presidential candidates, two stood out as having "work to do." These two individuals failed to provoke pronounced brain activity in most voters. Who were these two decidedly unremarkable politicians? Barack Obama and John McCain, who were soon to become their parties' candidates for president (see Satel and Lilienfeld, 2013).

Neurohype and Its Prevalence

For reasons that we will later explain, the *New York Times* op-ed was in many respects a quintessential example of *neurohype*. By neurohype, we refer to a broad class of neuroscientific claims that greatly outstrip the available evidence (see also Caulfield et al., 2010; Schwartz et al., 2016). Neurohype and its variants have gone by several other names in recent years, including neuromania, neuropunditry, and neurobollocks (Satel and Lilienfeld, 2013). Because the tendency to advance bold assertions in the absence of convincing data is often considered a cardinal indicator of pseudoscience (Lilienfeld et al., 2012), the unchecked proliferation of neurohype poses a threat to the scientific credibility of neuroscience.

Goals of the Chapter

In this chapter, we turn a much needed critical eye to neurohype. To do so, we (a) canvass its prevalence and manifestations, (b) describe its principal sources, (c) examine its dangers, (d) delineate widespread logical pitfalls that contribute to it, along with concrete examples of these pitfalls from media and academic outlets, and (e) present user-friendly tips for evaluating neuro-imaging findings reported in the popular media.

In fairness, the hyping of scientific findings is hardly unique to neuroscience. In an exami-nation of cancer news stories arising in the wake of the most recent convention of the *Annual Society of Clinical Oncology*, an author team (Abola and Prasad, 2015) uncovered no fewer than 94 news stories originating from 66 news sources that described recent findings with one or more "superlatives"—which included such terms as "breakthrough," "miracle," "cure," "revolutionary," "groundbreaking," and "marvel." In 55% of cases, these superlatives were issued by journal-ists covering the conference; yet about a quarter of the time, they derived from the original researchers themselves. Not surprisingly, in many or most cases, these superlatives were largely or entirely unwarranted. Half of the 36 novel medications described with superlatives had not yet received approval from the Food and Drug Administration; and 5 of these 36 medications had not yet been subjected to controlled clinical trials in humans. Such "oncohype" is hardly innocuous, as unjustified hype can easily give way to unjustified hope. Such hope can eventu-ally engender bitter disappointment and deplete valuable resources that could have been better invested elsewhere. The same state of affairs, we maintain, applies to neurohype.

The Promises and Perils of Neuroscience

Before embarking on our mission, we should be explicit about what we are *not* saying. In turn-ing a critical eye to the purveyors of neurohype, we are not implying that neuroscience as a whole is overrated (cf. Tallis, 2011). Quite the contrary. It is clear that recent findings in neu-roscience have already begun to transform our understanding of such phenomena as sensation, perception, emotion, and cognition and may soon afford valuable insights into the correlates and perhaps causes of psychological maladies. Ever since President George H.W. Bush declared the years from 1990 to 2000 to be the Decade of the Brain, neuroscience has borne witness to the development and proliferation of a number of spectacular technological developments, including fMRI, magnetoencephalography, diffusion tensor imaging, optogenetics, and several others. Furthermore, recently launched endeavors, such as the BRAIN (Brain Research through Advancing Innovative Neurotechnologies) Initiative launched by Barack Obama, the European Commission's Human Brain Project, and the Human Connectome Project, hold the potential to alter and perhaps revolutionize our understanding of the structure and functioning of the human brain. The future of neuroscience is exceedingly bright.

Yet because neurohype is ubiquitous in popular culture, it may impel many laypersons, policy makers, and scientists outside of neuroscience, including psychologists, to reflexively dismiss many of the legitimate advances and promises of neuroscience. Hence, curbing the rhetorical excesses of neurohype is essential to safeguarding the scientific integrity of neuroscience. Neu-rohype can also render many people, including educated laypersons, vulnerable to the seductive charms of "brainscams" (see Beyerstein, 1990, "Brainscams").

Heightened vigilance toward neurohype is especially crucial in light of the increasing incursion of neuroimaging data into the courtroom (Patel et al., 2007; Satel and Lilienfeld, 2013). In a study of judicial opinions, Farahany (2016) found that mentions of neurobiological data in criminal trials climbed from about 100 per year to 250 to 300 per year from 2005 to 2012. Of these opinions, 40% were in capital cases and 60% were in cases involving serious felonies, such as violent assault, robbery, or fraud. Nearly half of the mentions of neurobiological evidence in the sentencing phase of criminal trials stemmed from defendants who charged that their attorneys were negligent in failing to investigate their potential neurological abnormality. Other data broadly corroborate these results. In 2015; U.S. president Barack Obama's bioethics commission estimated that neuroscience data, including structural brain imaging, is used in approximately one quarter of death penalty cases (Farahany, 2016). Hence, it is imperative that triers of fact not succumb to the kinds of inferential errors that can accompany interpretation of brain-based data.

The Purveyors of Neurohype

The primary purveyors of neurohype are the news and entertainment media, both of which are notorious for oversimplifying and sensationalizing scientific claims. As Gilovich (1991) noted, the media frequently engage in *sharpening* and *leveling*: salient details that are believed to capture the essence of the story are emphasized and even exaggerated (sharpening), while uninteresting details that are believed to be inessential are deemphasized or omitted (leveling). The result is often grossly distorted news coverage.

Nevertheless, we can also place a hefty chunk of the blame for neurohype at the feet of a small minority of zealous neuroscientists themselves, some of whom have been insufficiently circumspect in their claims when communicating with the media (Satel and Lilienfeld, 2013). For example, some psychiatrists have fallen prey to premature enthusiasm regarding the potential of brain-imaging techniques to inform psychiatric diagnosis and treatment. In 1984; Nancy Andreasen, one of the doyennes of American psychiatry, wrote that "as they improve and become more accurate, these imaging techniques and other laboratory tests for mental illness will become part of standard medical practice during the coming years, thereby improving the precision of diagnosis" (Andreasen, 1984, 260). That statement was made more than three decades ago. She was far from alone in her optimism. In the 1980s, many researchers were confidently forecasting that neuroimaging techniques would soon render more "primitive" diagnostic methods, such as psychiatric interviewing, questionnaires, and careful behavioral observation, obsolete. Yet 29 years following Andreasen's upbeat forecast, when the fifth edition of the *Diagnostic and Statistical Manual of Mental Disorders* (DSM-5; American Psychiatric Association, 2013) was released, none of its more than 300 diagnostic criterion sets featured even a single brain-based indicator. In other cases, neuroscientists themselves have not been guilty of neurohype but have stood by idly as the news media have exaggerated their findings and conclusions.

The Prevalence and Manifestations of Neurohype

Survey data, now about a decade old, suggest that neurohype is ubiquitous, at least in the domain of functional brain imaging. In an analysis of 132 news articles published between 1991 and 2004; Racine et al. (2006) found that coverage of neuroimaging data was largely uncritical. Two thirds of the articles contained no mention of the methodological limitations of fMRI (see "Neuro-pitfalls" section), and 79% were deemed to be optimistic about fMRI; only 5% referred to potential methodological challenges associated with the method.

Although we are unaware of more recent systematic surveys of neuroimaging or other neuroscience coverage in the media, anecdotal evidence—despite its undeniable evidentiary limitations (Lilienfeld, 2005)—affords ample evidence for concern regarding the prevalence of neurohype in the media. Two high-profile examples should suffice to drive this point home; we refer the reader to Jarrett (2015) for a plethora of others.

The first comes from work on oxytocin, a hormone that plays a key role in social behavior (see Lilienfeld et al., 2015). Much of this work is explicitly neuroscientific in nature, deriving in many cases from intranasal injections of oxytocin, which are purported to cross the blood-brain barrier into the central nervous system (but see Walum et al., 2015, for a critique of this body of research). More than 17,000 websites have dubbed the hormone oxytocin the "love molecule." Others have termed oxytocin the "trust molecule," "moral molecule" (Zak, 2012), or "cuddle hormone" (Griffiths, 2014). One blog posting even listed "10 Reasons Why Oxytocin Is the Most Amazing Molecule in the World" (Dvorsky, 2012).

Nevertheless, data from controlled studies demonstrate that all of these appellations are woefully simplistic (Jarrett, 2015; Shen, 2015). Most psychological and neuroscientific evidence suggests that oxytocin merely renders individuals more sensitive to social information (Stix, 2014), both positive and negative. For example, although intranasal oxytocin seems to increase within-group trust, it may also increase out-group mistrust (Bethlehem et al., 2014). In addition, among individuals with high levels of trait aggressiveness, oxytocin boosts propensities toward intimate partner violence following provocation (DeWall et al., 2014).

The second example stems from research on *mirror neurons*, a class of nerve cells in the premotor cortex that was discovered in macaque monkeys (Rizzolatti et al., 1996). Mirror neurons become activated whenever a monkey witnesses an action (say, grabbing a raisin) performed by another monkey. Not long after the discovery of these cells, a number of neuroscientists began to speculate that they had uncovered the Rosetta Stone to the secret of empathy, still one of the most mysterious of all psychological capacities. For example, at the turn of the millennium, eminent University of California at San Diego neuroscientist Vilayunar Ramachandran (2000) predicted that "mirror neurons will do for psychology what DNA did for biology; they will provide a unifying framework and help explain a host of mental abilities that have hitherto remained mysterious and inaccessible to experiments." Many other scholars proclaimed that mirror neurons were a key to unlocking the causes of autism (now termed autism spectrum disorder), invoking the so-called broken mirror theory of autism (e.g., Iacoboni, 2009), which posits that the profound cognitive empathy deficits of autism result from defects in the mirror neuron system. It was not long before the media followed suit (see Jarrett, 2015). The *New York Times* titled an article on mirror neurons "Cells That Read Minds," and a 2013 article in the U.K.'s *Daily Mail* maintained that mirror neurons help to explain why some romantic films are more successful than others.

Yet once again, research demonstrated that these expansive claims were massively overstated (Hall, 2014). Among other things, mirror neuron activity may merely reflect rather than cause motor actions (Hickok, 2014; Jarrett, 2015). Moreover, brain-imaging data provide scant support for the existence of generalized mirror neuron dysfunction in autism spectrum disorder or other conditions (Gernsbacher, 2011; Hamilton, 2013).

As can be seen in Table 16.1, the past decade or so has been witness to a parade of terms heralded by the prefix "neuro-," presented here in alphabetical order (see also Miller, 1986, for a discussion of "neurobabble"). Not surprisingly, this explosion in neuro-terms has spawned numerous parodies, with one Twitter user proposing a new field of "neurometeorology," which has capitalized on brain-imaging methods to discover that "hurricanes live in constant agony" (see https://twitter.com/thepatanoiac/status/435439436747137025). As one psychologist

Table 16.1 Selected Newly Minted Terms with "Neuro-Prefixes".

Neuroadvertising	Neuroconsulting	Neuroliterature
Neuroaesthetics	Neurocriminology	Neuromagic
Neuroanalysis	Neuroeconomics	Neuromarketing
Neuranthropology	Neuroeducation	Neurophilosophy
Neuroarcheology	Neuroethics	Neuroprofiling
Neuroarchitecture	Neurofashion	Neuropsychoanalysis
Neurobotany	Neuroforecasting	Neurosexology
Neurocapitalism	Neurogastronomy	Neurosociology
Neurocinema	Neurohistory	Neuroteaching
Neurocomputing	Neurolaw	Neurowine
Neurocosmetics	Neurolinguistics	Neurozoology

Source: Table created by authors.

observed, "Unable to persuade others about your viewpoint? Take a Neuro-Prefix—influence grows or your money back" (Laws, 2012).

The dramatic rise in the number of these terms, which reflects the insinuation of neuroscience into a myriad of traditionally unrelated domains, is not by itself a cause for concern. For example, some of these terms describe relatively new fields, such as neuroeconomics, that are scientifically promising and are already beginning to bear scientific fruit in the form of intriguing correlations between brain activation and laboratory behavior (Loewenstein et al., 2008).

> For more on the neuroscientific turn in the social sciences, see Chapter 2.

In other cases, though, these "neurologisms" (itself a neologism; see http://mindhacks. com/2006/03/21/neurologism/) refer to fields whose scientific *bona fides* are at best dubious. Take neuromarketing, a relatively new discipline that purports to use brain-imaging data to discern consumers' preferences for products. The assumption, which is not entirely implausible, is that brain-imaging data can sometimes detect information about product preferences that consumers either cannot or do not wish to reveal (Ariely and Berns, 2010), either because they are largely or entirely unaware of their genuine preferences or because they are reluctant to admit these preferences to advertisers in focus groups (for example, a consumer may not want to confess to liking a gaudy piece of jewelry). Nevertheless, there is at present minimal evidence that functional brain-imaging data provide useful information about consumers' preferences above and beyond far simpler and cheaper self-reports (Jarrett, 2015; Satel and Lilienfeld, 2013; for a potential exception, see Berns et al., 2010, who found that medial temporal gyrus activation among adolescents predicted ratings of song popularity above and beyond ratings of song liking).

Brainscams

Neurohype may render many of us vulnerable to what the late neuroscientist Barry Beyerstein (1990) termed "brainscams": commercial products that capitalize on neuroscientific assertions that are largely or entirely devoid of scientific support (see also Lilienfeld and Arkowitz, 2008). Even though many brainscams may appear innocuous, they can engender substantial indirect harm stemming from what economists term opportunity costs (see also Lilienfeld, 2007). Specifically, the time, energy, effort, and money invested in brainscams may deprive consumers of greatly needed resources to seek out and obtain better-supported diagnostic and treatment techniques.

Brainscams have a lengthy history in popular psychology. To take one example, phrenology, the pseudoscience of inferring personality by examining the pattern of bumps on people's skulls, was all the rage through much of the 19th century in the United States and Europe (Sabbatini, 1997). People of the time could stroll into a neighborhood phrenology parlor to "have their heads examined," the origin of this now-familiar phrase. The best known phrenologist, Viennese physician Franz Joseph Gall, supposedly identified 27 regions of the skull tied to specific psychological "faculties," such as aggressiveness, vanity, friendliness, and even a love of colors; later phrenologists expanded the number to 43. Phrenology made cameo appearances in the writings of Edgar Allan Poe and in Hermann Melville's masterpiece, *Moby Dick*. Thomas Edison and Ralph Waldo Emerson, among others, were devotees of phrenology who reveled in having their skull bumps measured by using a "psychograph," a metallic, spring-loaded device that clamps down on an individual's head and dutifully prints out a detailed read-out of personality traits.

The phrenology craze eventually lost momentum in the late 19th century when it became evident that patients with damage to specific brain areas didn't suffer the kinds of psychological changes that phrenologists had predicted. Even more strikingly, it became clear that enlargements in the brain did not even produce changes in skull shape, vitiating the key presupposition of phrenology. Although phrenology has been thoroughly discredited, it is apparently alive, if not well: in 2007, the state of Michigan extended its 6% sales tax to commercial phrenological services (http://blog.mlive.com/michigan/2007/10/extended_list_of_services_affe.html). As we will discover later (see "The Fallacy of Localization"), some writers (e.g., Zuger, 2013) have likened contemporary neuroimaging to phrenology, at times dubbing it "neo-phrenology." Nevertheless, this accusation reflects a misunderstanding of brain-imaging research, because all sophisticated neuroimaging investigators today regard extreme localizationism as simplistic (see Uttal, 2001, for a more sophisticated analysis).

In recent decades, brainscams in innumerable guises have become thriving business enterprises, and brain-based self-help products have been estimated to net marketers $11 to $12 billion annually (Gunter, 2014). This figure does not include the rapidly expanding brain-based health food market, which encompasses such brain supplements as *Ginkgo biloba* (gingko) and kava, and such drinks as Neurobliss and Neuropassion, which collectively amass another $2 billion dollars a year. The research bases for all of these products range from slim to none (e.g., see the review by Gold et al., 2002, which found little compelling evidence that gingko and other purported cognitive enhancers improve memory). Among the seemingly endless gizmos marketed by the hawkers of brain-based self-help products are brain stimulation headsets, which shine light directly into the ears to enhance mood; subliminal DVDs (many of them adorned with attractive photos of human brains on their covers), which purportedly present listeners with consciously undetectable messages designed to increase their self-esteem, memory, sexual potency, breast size, or penis size; and brain tuners of various kinds, which supposedly boost people's mental capacities by modifying their brain waves (Beyerstein, 1990; Gunter, 2014). Of increasing popular interest, transcranial direct current stimulation devices (tDCS), neurostimulation headsets that use electrical currents to stimulate specific brain regions, have spawned a large do-it-yourself community on YouTube and Reddit. People can now choose from a variety of tDCS gadgets that purport to enhance attention, memory, and focus. Unsurprisingly, the efficacy of tDCS is unknown (Horvath et al., 2015).

More recently, a host of commercial products designed to enhance attention and intelligence by means of user-friendly computer games have acquired substantial traction. Perhaps the best known such product is Lumosity, a company whose website boasted 70 million members as of early 2015. Lumosity offers customers access to a variety of games intended to enhance their intellectual capacities by increasing their working memory. For many years, Lumosity's advertisements maintained that its products could delay or ward off memory-related decline and dementia. For example, the company website insisted that "healthy people have also used brain training to sharpen their daily lives and ward off cognitive decline" (Span, 2016). Yet controlled data call into question the assertion that working memory games improve intelligence (Redick et al., 2013), and there is no especially compelling evidence that they exert protective effects against memory loss. In January 2016, Lumosity agreed to a multimillion-dollar settlement with the Federal Trade Commission, which concluded that the company had engaged in misleading advertising.

The use of questionable products extends to the diagnosis and treatment of mental disorders. One of the most indefatigable entrepreneurs of inadequately validated neuroscience commercial claims is psychiatrist Daniel Amen, who is a familiar fixture on U.S. public television. In 2012, the *Washington Post* named Amen "the most popular psychiatrist in America" (Tucker, 2008), and for good reason; approximately 1,200 patients pass through his clinic doors each month. Amen purports to use single-proton emission computed tomography (SPECT), a brain-imaging technique with relatively poor spatial resolution (the ability to differentiate brain activation in one region from adjacent regions; Khali et al., 2011), to assist in the identification and treatment of attention-deficit hyperactivity disorder (ADHD), anxiety disorders, and mood disorders, Alzheimer's disease, and marital conflicts, among scores of other psychological problems. For example, Amen claims to have pinpointed a "ring of fire" pattern of over-activation on the SPECT scans of many ADHD patients, and a "lights are low" pattern of under-activation on the SPECT scans of patients with mood and anxiety disorders (neither of these patterns has been supported by independent research). After performing his diagnostic workups, Amen prescribes an often dizzying array of treatments, which may include standard medications, scientifically unsupported herbal remedies, neurofeedback (brain wave biofeedback), hyperbaric oxygen therapy, and even candy bars (e.g., Brain on Joy bars) purported to enhance brain health. His claims are expansive; his website boasts 85% improvement rates compared with 30% rates from standard treatments (www.amenclinics.com/atlanta/).

After perusing his websites and other promotional materials, however, one would be hard-pressed to locate any acknowledgment that Amen's principal claims are largely or entirely devoid of scientific support (Farah and Gillihan, 2012). For example, there is no good evidence that advanced brain-imaging methods, let alone SPECT, are especially helpful in the diagnosis of any mental disorders (Kapur et al., 2012), nor is there consistent evidence for the efficacy of many of Amen's recommended complementary and alternative remedies, including his herbal treatments or hyperbaric oxygen therapy (Burton, 2008; Hall, 2007).

Psychological Sources of Neurohype

There are numerous potential psychological sources underlying the appeal of neurohype and our susceptibility to brainscams; we examine the most plausible culprits here.

Fascination with the Human Brain

In many respects, the lay public's fascination with the brain is entirely understandable. The human brain is the most complex structure in the known universe (Stam and Reijneveld, 2007), so much so that the person it inhabits has a difficult time fathoming the astonishing intricacy of its own architecture and functioning. Here, for readers' consideration, is an unabashedly selective listing of fascinating facts about the "three-pound universe" (Hooper and Teresi, 1986) packed inside of our skulls (see Alban, 2016). There are:

- Approximately 12 times more neurons in our brains than there are people on Earth
- More than 100 trillion—that's 100,000,000,000,000,000—interconnections among our neurons
- 3.6 million miles of neurons in each of our brains
- 100,000 miles of blood vessels in each of our brains
- About 100,000 chemical reactions in our brain occurring each second

These factoids remind us that scientific truth is almost always more remarkable than is scientific fiction (see also Sagan, 1979). Although most laypersons may be unfamiliar with these specific findings, they are well aware that the human brain is capable of magnificent cognitive feats. As poet Robert Frost quipped, "The brain is a wonderful organ; it starts working the moment you get up in the morning and does not stop until you get into the office" (www.brainyquote.com/quotes/quotes/r/robertfros101173.html).

Indeed, the human brain is unrivaled in many of its capacities, such as pattern recognition and the ability to infer meaning from language. For example, as remarkably sophisticated as many computer programs are, they are no match for the human brain when it comes to drawing conclusions regarding people's mental states. Cognitive scientist Gary Marcus (2013) offers the example of a Stanford computer system, Deeply Moving, which was designed to distinguish positive from negative movie reviews. All things considered, Deeply Moving does a serviceable job; it will easily recognize "The latest Coen Brothers flick is a masterpiece" as a glowing review. But feed Deeply Moving a review that reads "Woody Allen's latest film can hardly be said to be one of his best," and it becomes hopelessly confused by the word "best," incorrectly tagging it as a positive review. Yet any bright 10-year-old can make this distinction effortlessly, easily discerning the meaning intended by the reviewer.

Implicit Dualism

It is easy to forget that throughout much of history, humans did not take for granted that the brain is the seat of consciousness. For example, prior to burial, the ancient Egyptians sometimes scooped out the brains of mummies through the nose (Finger, 2001), presuming the brain to be little more than a dispensable, gooey stuffing lodged inside of the head (we will spare the reader an illustration of this procedure). The Egyptians, like the ancient Greeks after them, believed the heart, not the brain, to be the theatre of mental activity; Aristotle famously believed the brain to be little more than a radiator that cooled the heart (Grusser, 1990). This whopping error is understandable. After all, we feel our hearts, not our brains, beating rapidly when we experience agitation or the throes of romantic passion; and we feel our hearts, not our brains, slowing down when we are gripped with overwhelming terror.

Today, all educated persons recognize that the brain, not the heart, is the locus of psychological activity. Yet curious residues of earlier ways of thinking remain in our language and visual depictions. When we have memorized a poem or song, we say that we "know it by heart"; when we share our most intimate thoughts with a friend or loved one, we have a "heart-to-heart talk," and when we send a Valentine's Day card, the affectionate words are accompanied by a large red heart rather than a large red brain, even though the latter would be more physiologically accurate (although considerably less romantic).

These intriguing quirks of language may be developmental carryovers of our propensity to be "natural-born dualists"—to assume that the mind and brain are somehow distinct (Bloom, 2004;

Bloom and Weisberg, 2007). Most mind–body dualists regard the mind as a nonmaterial, often spiritual entity that coexists with the brain but is distinct from it. Data demonstrate that most young children are at least partial dualists: Ask a typical preschool child if her brain is necessary to do math, and she will respond yes; yet ask her whether her brain is necessary to love her brother, and she will maintain that it is not. Although most of us largely outgrow mind–body dualism by the time we reach adulthood, subtle traces of this erroneous belief may persist in our thinking.

Furthermore, this implicit mind–body dualism may be an unappreciated source of neuroscience's intuitive appeal to the public. When laypersons read of a brain-imaging study depicting neural correlates of a psychological attribute, such as jealousy, or of a psychological condition, such as depression, they may experience surprise, even incredulity: "You mean that jealousy isn't just in the mind, but it's in the brain too?" they may ask. Of course, virtually all contemporary psychologists and neuroscientists would think such a finding to be entirely unsurprising, as they take it as a self-evident truism that all psychological attributes are instantiated in brain tissue. Yet to many members of the general public, such information may come as a revelation given that they have not fully outgrown dualistic thinking. If so, our analysis suggests an intriguing paradox. Although neuroimaging, perhaps more than any other technology, has shattered any lingering illusions of mind–body dualism, it may nonetheless draw much of its popular appeal from such dualism.

Neuroessentialism and Neurorealism

Partly underpinning the rhetorical power of neuroscience, especially neuroimaging information, may be two intertwined notions: "neuroessentialism" and "neurorealism" (Racine, 2005; Racine et al., 2010). The former, which we discuss only briefly, refers to the tendency to attribute human-like properties to the brain, an error also termed the "mereological fallacy" (Bennett and Hacker, 2007). For example, a National Public Radio story segment was entitled "How Your Brain Remembers Where You Parked the Car" (Hamilton, 2015), and a *Science Times* story was entitled "How the Brain Perceives Time" (Sanders, 2015). Both headlines imply erroneously that "people are their brains." Yet the brain *per se* can neither remember nor perceive, as these psychological capacities are performed by full-fledged organisms.

Neurorealism, which appears to be even more germane to the popularity of neurohype, refers to the often inchoate belief that brain-based information is somehow more genuine or valid than is non–brain-based information. Once we learn that an ineffable psychological capacity is "in the brain," it somehow seems to take on an objective reality that it had previously lacked. As a consequence, neurorealism may lead people to accord more credence to neuroimaging data than is warranted. Consider the following headlines:

"A Relatively New Form of Brain Imaging Provides Visual Proof That Acupuncture Alleviates Pain" (*Pain and Central Nervous System Week*, 1999)

"Placebo Effect Shown as Real Brain Reaction" (*Health News*, 2005)

"Is Hysteria Real? Brain Images Say Yes" (*New York Times*, 2006)

"This is Your Brain on Love: Are People in Couples Truly Addicted to Each Other?" (*Psychology Today Blog*, 2015)

The first headline implies that brain images are needed to demonstrate that acupuncture alleviates pain. Yet because pain is inherently subjective, this headline is misleading: The only way to know whether people experience less pain following an intervention is to ask them. Moreover, we knew that acupuncture could alleviate pain in some people many centuries before the advent of brain imaging (although most evidence indicates that acupuncture works just as well when practitioners insert the needles in the "wrong" as in the "right" acupoints, suggesting that the effects of acupuncture probably derive from placebo or other nonspecific effects). The next two headlines imply that the existence of placebo effects and hysteria was somehow in doubt prior to their verification by brain images. Yet hysteria and placebo effects are unquestionably "real," brain images notwithstanding. The final headline implies that neuroimaging data alone can ascertain whether love is an "addiction," when in fact addiction is in large measure a behavioral phenomenon marked by tolerance, withdrawal, and excessive engagement in maladaptive behavior despite adverse consequences.

To be fair, in many or most cases, researchers themselves are not responsible for these and other misleading headlines, which routinely are inserted by editors eager to spice up a scientific story. Nevertheless, such headlines underscore the need for investigators to emphasize caveats when communicating their findings to reporters.

Another striking example of neurorealism can be found in a 2014 episode of the CBS News show *60 Minutes* featuring correspondent Anderson Cooper. Cooper was interviewing neuroscientist Gregory Berns regarding his neuroimaging work with dogs. To set the stage, Cooper was asking how dog owners could ascertain whether their beloved canine companions experienced genuine affection for them. Berns, in turn, was discussing his research demonstrating that dogs display activation in the ventral striatum, a brain region linked to reward, when exposed to the smells and sights of their owners. The conversation continued:

Cooper: So just by smelling the sweat of their owner, it triggers something in a much stronger way than it does with a stranger?

Berns: Right. Which means that it's a positive feeling, a positive association.

Cooper: And that's something you can prove through MRIs? It's not just, I mean, previously people would say, "Well, yeah, obviously my dog loves me. I see its tail wagging and it seems really happy when it sees me."

Berns: Right. Now we're using the brain as kind of the test to say, "Okay, when we see activity in these reward centers that means the dog is experiencing something that it likes or it wants and it's a good feeling."

Cooper: My takeaway from this is that I'm not being scammed by my dog.

Berns: Did you have that feeling before?

Cooper: Yeah, totally. I worry about that all the time.

Cooper's comments imply that before learning about Berns' research, he could not have been certain that his dog loved him. The neurorealistic assumption here, which is dubious and empirically unsubstantiated, is that a dog's ventral striatal activation is inherently a more valid indicator of canine love than is a dog's repeatedly licking its owner's face, running toward and jumping up to his owner when she arrives home, wagging his tail when he sees his owner, whimpering when his owner is about to leave, and so on.

Neuroseduction

Many or all of the influences we have discussed thus far may conspire to generate *neuroseduction*: the tendency to be unduly swayed by neural images, neural explanations, or both. Chabris and Simons (2011) coined the term "neuroporn" to refer to brain-based information that can bewitch and bamboozle unwary laypersons. In an amusing albeit disconcerting demonstration of what the authors dubbed "neuroenchantment" (Ali et al., 2014), a team of investigators brought undergraduates—about half of whom were enrolled in an advanced course on neuroimaging—into the laboratory for an ostensible study of the "Neural Correlates of Thought." In fact, the "study" was bogus. Participants were seated underneath a mock scanner, which was actually the dome of an old-fashioned salon hair dryer, and were informed that the exciting new technology developed by the researchers, called "Spintronics," could read their minds. While being "scanned," participants viewed a high-tech prerecorded video displaying spinning images of three-dimensional brains, lending the nonsensical procedure a cachet of scientific credibility. Then, using a simple magic trick (a sleight of hand), the researchers duped participants into believing that the scanning technique could discern what number, color, and country they had in mind. Remarkably, 67% of participants, including 65% of those in the advanced imaging course, found the new scanning technology credible as a decoder of their innermost thoughts.

Research on neuroseduction has become something of a cottage industry in recent years. In neuroseduction studies, investigators typically supply some participants with brain images, brain-based explanations, or both (and other participants with either no information or non–brain-based information) and examine the extent to which such information renders them more likely to accept dubious or flawed scientific explanations. In this way, researchers can ascertain the extent to which neural information "seduces" participants by diminishing their critical-thinking skills, thereby rendering them vulnerable to specious claims.

The first such study, by McCabe and Castel (2008), asked participants to read scientific news articles that featured either a brain image or a simple bar graph. Despite conveying the same findings, the articles with brain images were rated as more scientifically credible than those with a bar graph. The authors took these results as evidence for brain images' power to mislead readers into assuming that a neuroscientific finding was more credible than a similar finding that did not feature a picture of the brain.

Weisberg and colleagues (2008) asked participants to rate how convincing they found either logically flawed or scientifically sound explanations of psychological findings to be. In contrast to the study by McCabe and Castel (2008), none of these explanations included brain images. Instead, the experimenters varied whether the reported finding contained the phrase "brain scans indicate" as opposed to "the researchers claim." Participants rated "explanations" that were in fact poor scientific descriptions containing a superfluous reference to a brain scan as more believable than poor explanations that did not mention the brain. Strikingly, the superfluous inclusion of neuroscience information influenced not only participants with limited scientific background but also students who had taken a college-level cognitive neuroscience course.

Together, these two widely cited studies have prompted many scholars to examine whether brain scans disproportionally enhance the credibility of scientific explanations. It is now unclear, however, whether the findings of McCabe and Castel (2008) are replicable (Farah and Hook, 2013). For example, in studies of online and college samples, Michael and colleagues (2013) failed to replicate their finding that people judge an article as more scientific when a brain image is included than when it is not.

Still, neuroseduction research has converged on a reasonably consistent finding: Although many studies have cast doubt on the seductive power of brain images alone, they suggest that the addition of superfluous references to the brain lowers people's thresholds for accepting poor explanations of scientific research (Michael et al., 2013; Weisberg et al., 2015). Furthermore, the inconsistent results of neuroseduction research may reflect the specificity of the findings to only individuals with certain beliefs.

To test this possibility, Munro and Munro (2014) asked participants to evaluate a vignette regarding a politician who suffered from a psychological ailment, which was verified either through magnetic resonance imaging (MRI) or through cognitive testing. This ailment would render him incompetent to continue serving in his position. Participants found the MRI evidence more persuasive than the cognitive testing explanation. Moreover, the preference for the neuroscience explanation was especially pronounced among those who identified with the opposite political affiliation of the politician in the vignette, presumably because they stood to benefit from the validity of the neuroscientific explanation.

In other studies, investigators have examined whether brain images, brain-based information, or both influence judgments of criminal responsibility or punishment in simulated courtroom settings. These legally oriented neuroseduction studies typically ask participants to dole out hypothetical punishment to a criminal who suffers from a psychological problem, such as schizophrenia or psychopathy. Participants read expert testimony that couches the criminal's disorder in either brain-based or psychological terms. This experimental setup allows researchers to test whether the "my brain made me do it" legal defense aids in mitigating a criminal's sentence.

Schweitzer and colleagues (2011) found that mock jurors did not lessen a hypothetical criminal's sentence when expert testimony corroborated a criminal's diagnosis with a brain image compared with a brain-based explanation lacking an image. Nevertheless, participants rated expert evidence that appealed to neurological evidence as more persuasive than evidence that relied on conventional diagnostic methods, such as interview or self-report techniques. These findings suggest that brain-based explanations may influence mock jurors' sentencing judgments compared with psychological explanations (but see Greene and Cahill, 2012, for different findings). This finding is worrisome given that mock jurors often appear to place a premium on brain-based diagnostic explanations (Aspinwall et al., 2012; Gurley and Marcus, 2008; Schweitzer and Saks, 2011).

Neuromythology

Further fueling the popularity of neurohype is the persistence of "neuromythology," the diverse collection of erroneous but widely held beliefs about the brain and the rest of the nervous system (Beyerstein, 1990; Dekker et al., 2012; Jarrett, 2015). A number of neuromyths feed on misconceptions regarding the brain's alleged untapped potential, leading people to believe that the latest brain-based portal to advanced consciousness is only one publication away.

For example, in one survey of American community residents, 72% of respondents expressed agreement with the incorrect belief—perhaps most roundly discredited by functional brain-imaging research—that we use only 10% of our brains (Chabris and Simons, 2010). Another survey revealed that this myth was held even by 6% of neuroscientists (Herculano-Houzel, 2002). The 10%-of-the-brain misconception is surely one of the most enduring and persistent of all neuromyths (Jarrett, 2015; Lilienfeld et al., 2009). For that, we have the entertainment media to thank. This myth has been promulgated by scores of popular magazine articles, television shows, and Hollywood movies, perhaps the most recent of which was the 2014 film *Lucy* (starring Scarlett Johansson), whose promotional poster featured the following teaser: "The average person uses 10% of their brain capacity. Imagine what she could do with 100%" (see Beyerstein, 1990; Jarrett, 2015, and Lilienfeld et al., 2009, for discussions of the potential origins of this myth).

A second remarkably persistent neuromyth is the "learning styles myth": the erroneous belief that students learn best when teachers match their lessons to students' preferred learning styles (Lilienfeld et al., 2009). Many of these learning styles are ostensibly rooted in differences in brain architecture, functioning, or both. For example, by virtue of their brains' constitution, some students supposedly are characterized by visual learning styles, others by verbal learning styles. Yet controlled studies offer scant support for the matching hypothesis of tailoring teaching styles to learning styles (Pashler et al., 2008). Still, in one survey, 93% of British teachers and 96% of Dutch teachers subscribed to this unsupported belief (Dekker et al., 2012). Another survey revealed that 89% of recent articles on learning styles supported the matching of teaching styles to students' learning styles (Newton, 2015).

Both of these neuromyths and a score of others, such as the unsubstantiated beliefs that (a) some of us are right-brained whereas others of us are left-brained, (b) people can achieve higher states of consciousness by boosting their production of alpha waves, and (c) neurofeedback (electroencephalogram biofeedback) can lead us to states of enlightenment, contentment, and bliss (see Lilienfeld and Arkowitz, 2008, and Jarrett, 2015, for discussions) share a central underlying theme. Specifically, they all presume that the human brain possesses considerable unused reserve that can, in principle if not in practice, be exploited by means of novel brain-based technologies. Neurohype and brainscams are the inevitable byproducts.

Neuro-Pitfalls

The misinterpretation of neuroimaging data is perhaps the most widespread and publicly visible manifestation of neurohype. Such data lend themselves to a number of inferential errors and questionable logical leaps, many of which are routinely glossed over in media reports of brain-imaging findings. Here, we examine five potential inferential and methodological pitfalls that can contribute to misinterpretations of brain-imaging data. In contrast to some of the psychological sources underlying neurohype discussed earlier, such as neurorealism, these pitfalls are especially relevant to the evaluation of brain-imaging data.

Fallacy of Localization

As noted earlier, some critics have alleged that modern brain-imaging techniques are similar in many ways to phrenology. Yet this charge is unfair, as virtually all modern neuroscientists recognize that complex, multiply determined psychological capacities, such as jealousy, prejudice, and happiness, are not restricted to single brain areas but are instead widely distributed across multiple brain networks (Satel and Lilienfeld, 2013).

Still, the fallacy of localization is routinely committed by the news media, which frequently write and speak of finding a single "region for" a psychological capacity. For example, psychologist Michael Persinger constructed a helmet—the "God helmet"—to induce religious feelings in people by stimulating their "God Spot," a putative brain region located in the temporal lobe (see Biello, 2007). Nevertheless, given that religious belief is an exceedingly complex and multiply determined psychological capacity, not to mention one that differs substantially across individuals and cultures, it is exceedingly unlikely that it is localized to a single brain area. Still other authors have spoken of "jealousy," "irony," or "humor" spots in the brain (Jarrett, 2015; Lilienfeld et al., 2015); needless to say, the research support for these regions is no more impressive than that for the God Spot. Fortunately, the localization fallacy has not gone unchallenged by neuroscientists and others: A spate of 2012 media articles trumpeted the greatly overdue demise of the idea of the "God Spot" (Jarrett, 2015; Lilienfeld et al., 2015).

Reverse Inference

Reverse inference refers to drawing conclusions regarding psychological traits or states from brain-imaging data (Poldrack, 2006; see also Krueger, 2017). When performing a reverse inference, we are in essence "working backward," attempting to discern what psychological characteristic(s) of interest are revealed by the pattern of brain activity. For example, many researchers routinely assume that amygdala activation reflects fear. Reverse inference is not a logical fallacy *per se*, as it is not invariably incorrect (Ariely and Berns, 2010). At the same time, it hinges on the crucial assumption that there is a close mapping between neural activation in a brain region and certain psychological states. When this assumption is violated, all bets are off. Reverse inference is not unique to neuroimaging data, as it arises in many domains of psychology. When a personality researcher treats the response to a self-report item (e.g., "I enjoy going to parties") as an indicator of an underlying personality trait (e.g., extraversion), he or she is similarly making a reverse inference, which may or may not be correct. Examples of unbridled reverse inference—reverse inference without appropriate caveats—are, however, particularly rampant in media descriptions of brain-imaging findings.

For example, in a 2011 *New York Times* article titled "You love your iPhone. Literally," neuromarketer Martin Lindstrom cited activation in the insular cortex in response to the sights and sounds of participants' cellular devices as evidence that people genuinely love their iPhones. Within 48 hours, *Psychology Today*, *Wired*, and *Forbes* all published articles denouncing his conclusions and attacking the *Times* for publishing them. The critics were right. Because the insula is involved in disgust as well as in feelings of passion, Lindstrom could have just as readily concluded that we are disgusted by our iPhones. Ironically, Lindstrom centered his argument on love, rather than addiction, as a "more scientifically accurate" interpretation of the insula activation, but this activation could just as readily been invoked in support of the perhaps equally dubious claim that people are addicted to their iPhones.

As another example, a 2015 *Gizmodo* article entitled "Here's What Breaking Up Does to Your Brain" did just that, positing that love and addiction are essentially the same neurological beast. Lovers and addicts, the author argued, are both marked by activation of "reward systems," ostensibly reflecting the same psychological experience of craving. Craving cocaine or missing a romantic partner are, according to the author, both "fixes" at a neurological level and therefore at the psychological level too. Dopaminergic activity in the caudate nucleus and ventral tegmental area, however, could indicate any number of diverse psychological states or processes. For example, asking for a raise and interior decorating may activate similar brain circuits, but the decisions involved are drastically different.

The inferential ambiguities associated with reverse inference bear implications well beyond the academic realm: For example, fMRI lie detection measures have become increasingly popular and may soon make their way into the legal system (Miller, 2010; Satel and Lilienfeld, 2013). These indices purport to measure whether a subject is (a) lying or (b) possesses direct experiential knowledge of a cue (e.g., the way in which a murder victim died) by detecting neural responses to those cues during an examination. Although some researchers and governments hope that this technology could one day solve cold cases or thwart terrorist plots, others fear that these tests are the heirs of the discredited polygraph ("lie detector") test and criticize the dearth of peer-reviewed publications justifying their use. Our limited ability to reliably pair brain-imaging responses with psychological correlates calls for an attitude of healthy skepticism toward technologies that purportedly detect direct involvement with a crime with 95 to 100% certainty (see Spence, 2008).

Confusing Correlation With Causation

Even the most rigorously designed and well-articulated neuroscience studies can be distorted by media reports that confuse correlation with causation. Structural or functional imaging findings, as useful as they can be, cannot allow us to draw conclusive inferences of causal linkages between brain activations and psychological states or traits. At best, they can only establish statistical associations that in turn can provide fruitful grist for the causal hypothesis mill.

For example, reduced hippocampal volume may predispose people to stress-related pathology (Gilbertson et al., 2002), but animal models demonstrate that stress can lead to cortisol-induced damage at cellular and genetic levels (Chetty et al., 2014). Hence, data linking stress to hippocampal damage are open to multiple causal interpretations. As another example, the attempted suicide of an acquaintance's 9-year-old son inspired a writer for *Everyday Health* to advise parents that screen time, along with sugar and antibiotics, can cause depression, citing a study suggesting a correlation between internet addiction and structural brain differences (Yuan et al. 2011). The debate continues to evolve and has taken fascinating turns, but most articles gravitate to the "X kills brain cells" model—sometimes on their own and sometimes helped along by public personalities such as British neuroscientist Susan Greenfield.

Dr. Greenfield—a senior research fellow at Oxford University, founder of a biotechnology company, and member of the House of Lords—has long argued that technology of various sorts exerts harmful effects on the brain. She has repeatedly invoked correlational studies as evidence of a causal relation between technology use and brain decay. In a 2011 *New Scientist* interview, for instance, she cited a review (Bavelier et al., 2010) as evidence that technology contributes to violence and autism spectrum disorders. Nevertheless, in the review, the authors cautioned that "the vast majority of the work is correlational in nature," which they warned poses a particular danger in this area of study given that "technology use, in particular, is highly correlated with other factors that are strong predictors of poor behavioral outcomes." They also observed that children with attentional problems may be drawn to technology given their preexisting personality traits. Yet these caveats were largely absent from Greenfield's causal conclusions.

Neuroredundancy

A fundamental desideratum for a newly developed psychological measure is *incremental validity* (Sechrest, 1963). This psychometric property refers to the ability of an assessment technique to provide predictively useful information that is not afforded by other measures, especially information that is readily and inexpensively collected. Yet most neuroimaging findings have yet to meet the fundamental challenge of incremental validity. Put in other terms, most neuroimaging findings in the applied realm run afoul of the problem of *neuroredundancy*, whereby neural data are redundant with extant behavioral data (Satel and Lilienfeld, 2013).

For example, neuromarketers nearly always assume that brain-imaging information can offer insights into consumers' purchasing preferences that are not afforded by brief questionnaires, focus groups, and the like (Morin, 2011). As we noted earlier, the evidence for this presumption is presently scant, although in fairness this is more a reflection of absence of evidence than of evidence of absence: Few researchers have examined this question systematically, so there is ample reason for caution.

Multiple-Comparisons Problem

Finally, when interpreting neuroimaging findings, it is imperative to appreciate the limitations of the data collection methods, as is the case when interpreting any scientific finding. Nevertheless, neuroimaging has breathed new life into long-discussed statistical challenges that have emerged because of the sheer size of brain-imaging datasets. These datasets are enormous because neuroimaging investigators measure brain activity in a unit called a voxel, a one- to three-centimeter cube that is analogous to a pixel on a computer screen. One voxel represents a spatial unit that encompasses millions of neurons. To determine areas of the brain that are activated beyond normal levels, researchers typically perform a statistical test on each voxel in the brain and subsequently isolate areas of the brain that exhibit enhanced or attenuated activation. The brightly colored portions of neuroimages usually depict the averaged results of these analyses across multiple individuals.

The nature of examining activity in the brain at multiple time points across thousands of voxels can generate the *multiple-comparisons problem*. When conducting numerous statistical tests, the proportion of false positive (spurious) results increases substantially. A hilarious yet powerful example of this problem in action involves brain imaging and, surprisingly, a study of a dead salmon. The recipients of the 2010 Ig Nobel Prize (Bennett et al., 2009)—not to be confused with the Nobel Prize—placed a dead salmon in a scanner, asking the fish to "look at" different emotional stimuli, and then performed the typical set of statistical analyses on the fish. Not correcting for multiple comparisons yielded a nonsensical finding—the dead fish exhibited neural activity in response to the stimuli. These absurd results emerged because the researchers—to demonstrate the hazards of not correcting for multiple comparisons—had conducted more than a thousand statistical tests (as commonly done in some neuroimaging research), some of which were bound to emerge as statistically significant merely by chance. The multiple-comparisons problem, which is by no means unique to brain-imaging research, can be remedied by using analytic tools that we need not discuss in detail here.

Another important statistical challenge to bear in mind when evaluating neuroimaging work is the *circularity problem*, also a result of slippage in analysis of brain-imaging datasets. Neuroimaging researchers are rarely interested exclusively in the brain activation of certain anatomical regions: More typically, they are concerned with correlating neural activity with one or more behavioral measures, such as a depression or anxiety index. This is where the circularity problem can come into play.

In a groundbreaking but controversial paper that has largely stood the test of time, Edward Vul and colleagues (Vul et al., 2009) pointed out that many functional imaging articles report implausibly high associations (for example, correlations of 0.90 or above) between activation in certain brain areas and behavioral measures. In attempting to ascertain the source of these aberrantly high relations, they uncovered a serious but subtle and insufficiently appreciated methodological flaw. By first identifying a broad brain region that appears to be activated and then later homing in on that same region for more detailed analyses, investigators are "double dipping," effectively capitalizing on chance and thereby inflating the magnitudes of reported statistical associations. Fortunately, the use of unbiased data-analytic procedures and corrections for multiple comparisons can circumvent the circularity problem.

The often arcane but crucial limitations of the statistical methods involved in neuroimaging are rarely explained or discussed in popular news outlets. They are even omitted routinely in many presentations of academic research. Fortunately, constructive criticisms, such as those of Vul and his colleagues, can allow researchers and neuroscience consumers alike to become more discerning consumers of data on brain–behavior correlations. Indeed, these methodological criticisms have not only improved the quality of brain-imaging research but have played an invaluable role in combatting neurohype.

Concluding Thoughts

These are exciting times for neuroscience. Recent remarkable technical advances in neuroscience, especially functional brain imaging, are contributing significantly to our knowledge of the brain correlates of complex psychological capacities, such as cognitive processes, moods, prejudice, personality traits, and mental disorders. In the long term, they may even begin to transform

---

Box 16.1 A Reader's Guide to Avoiding Neurohype: 10 Simple Tips

1. Be skeptical of the attribution of human-like attributes, such as thinking and feeling, to the brain.

2. Avoid assuming that brain-based data are inherently more genuine or valid than behavioral data.

3. Be skeptical of expansive claims for brain-based products in the absence of compelling evidence.

4. Do not presume that scientific conclusions accompanied by a brain image or brain-based explanation are more valid than are scientific conclusions without such information.

5. Be on the lookout for neuromyths, especially claims regarding the unlimited capacity of the human brain (e.g., "most people use only 10% of their brain capacity").

6. Be skeptical of claims implying the localization of complex psychological capacities to single brain regions (e.g., "a spot for X," "a region for Y").

7. Carefully evaluate assertions regarding reverse inference, bearing in mind that activations in specific brain regions almost always reflect the operation of multiple psychological capacities.

8. Beware of causal phrases (e.g., "brain area X caused psychological capacity Y"), because functional and structural brain-imaging measures allow only for correlational, not causal, inferences.

9. When evaluating whether a novel brain-imaging measure is ready for practical application, ask whether it is merely redundant with extant behavioral information.

10. When evaluating media reports of brain-imaging findings, ask yourself whether the data were corrected for multiple comparisons; if this information is not presented in the report, consult the original article.

---

our understanding of ourselves. We are optimistic that the forthcoming decade of research in neuroscience will help to bring forth a wealth of significant new discoveries, including those regarding risk factors for psychopathology.

At the same time, neurohype in both the popular and academic arenas poses a threat to the public, as well as to the credibility of neuroscience in the public eye. Without explicit guidance for distinguishing well-supported and appropriately tempered claims regarding neuroscience from poorly supported and exaggerated claims, laypersons and even academicians without formal neuroscience training can easily fall prey to dubious proclamations, not to mention blatant pseudoscience. In Box 16.1, we offer 10 straightforward tips for resisting the seductive charms of neurohype, including brainscams and exaggerated claims derived from neuroimaging data. We hope that these tips, and more broadly the caveats presented in this chapter, will arm readers with the critical-thinking tools needed to differentiate legitimate from illegitimate claims regarding the breathtakingly complex three-pound universe between their ears.

Further Reading

Jarrett, C. (2015) *Great Myths of the Brain*. New York: Wiley-Blackwell.

Mayberg, H.S. (1992) "Functional Brain Scans as Evidence in Criminal Court: An Argument for Caution". *Journal of Nuclear Medicine* 33, 18N–25N.

Morse, S.J. (2005) "Brain overclaim Syndrome and Criminal Responsibility: A Diagnostic Note". *Ohio State Journal of Criminal Law* 3, 397–412.

Satel, S. and Lilienfeld, S.O. (2013) *Brainwashed: The Seductive Appeal of Mindless Neuroscience*. New York: Basic Books.

Tallis, R. (2011) *Aping Mankind: Neuromania, Darwinitis and the Misrepresentation of Humanity*. London: Acumen.

References

Abola, M., and Prasad, V. (2015) The use of superlatives in cancer research. *Journal of American Medical Association Oncology* 2: pp. 139–141. doi:10.1001/jamaoncol.2015.3931

Alban, D. (2016) 50 amazing brain facts (based on the latest science). *Be Brain Fit*. Available at: https://bebrainfit.com/human-brain-facts/.

Ali, S.S., Lifshitz, M., & Raz, A. (2014). Empirical neuroenchantment: From reading minds to thinking critically. *Frontiers in Human Neuroscience* 8. Available at: www.ncbi.nlm.nih.gov/pmc/articles/PMC4034606/.

American Psychiatric Association. (2013) *Diagnostic and Statistical Manual of Mental Disorders,* 5th ed. (DSM-5). Washington, DC: Author.

Andreasen, N.C. (1984) *The Broken Brain*. New York: Harper Collins.

Ariely, D., and Berns, G.S. (2010) Neuromarketing: The hope and hype of neuroimaging in business. *Nature Reviews Neuroscience* 11(4): pp. 284–292.

Aspinwall, L.G., Brown, T.R., and Tabery, J. (2012) The double-edged sword: Does biomechanism increase or decrease judges' sentencing of psychopaths? *Science* 337(6096): pp. 846–849.

Bavelier, D., Green, C.S., and Dye, M.W. (2010). Children, wired: For better and for worse. *Neuron* 67: pp. 692–701.

Bennett, M.R. and Hacker, P.M. (2007) Conceptual presuppositions of cognitive neuroscience. In M.R. Bennett and P.M. Hacker (Eds.). *History of Cognitive Neuroscience*. New York: Wiley: pp. 237–263.

Bennett, C.M., Miller, M.B., and Wolford, G.L. (2009) Neural correlates of interspecies perspective taking in the post-mortem Atlantic Salmon: An argument for multiple comparisons correction. *Neuroimage* 47(Suppl 1): p. S125.

Berns, G.S., Capra, C.M., Moore, S., and Noussair, C. (2010) Neural mechanisms of the influence of popularity on adolescent ratings of music. *Neuroimage* 49: pp. 2687–2696.

Bethlehem, R.A., Baron-Cohen, S., van Honk, J., Auyeung, B., and Bos, P.A. (2014) The oxytocin paradox. *Frontiers in Behavioral Neuroscience* 8: p. 48.

Beyerstein, B.L. (1990). Brainscams: Neuromythologies of the new age. *International Journal of Mental Health* 19: pp. 27–36.

Biello, D. (2007). Searching for God in the brain. *Scientific American Mind* 18(5): pp. 38–45.

Bloom, P. (2004). Natural-born dualists. In *Edge: The Third Culture*. Available at: www.edge.org/conversation/paul_bloom-natural-born-dualists.

Bloom, P., and Weisberg, D.S. (2007) Childhood origins of adult resistance to science. *Science* 316: pp. 996–997.

Burton, R. (2008, May 12) Brain scam. *Salon*. Available at: www.salon.com/2008/05/12/daniel_amen/.

Caulfield, T., Rachul, C., and Zarzeczny, A. (2010) "Neurohype" and the name game: Who's to blame? *American Journal of Bioethics Neuroscience* 1(2): pp. 13–15.

Chabris, C., and Simons, D. (2011) *The Invisible Gorilla: And Other Ways Our Intuitions Deceive US*. New York: Broadway Books.

Chetty, S., Friedman, A.R., Taravosh-Lahn, K., Kirby, E.D., Mirescu, C., Guo, F. . . . and Tsai, M.K. (2014) Stress and glucocorticoids promote oligodendrogenesis in the adult hippocampus. *Molecular Psychiatry* 19: pp. 1275–1283.

Dekker, S., Lee, N.C., Howard-Jones, P., and Jolles, J. (2012) Neuromyths in education: Prevalence and predictors of misconceptions among teachers. *Frontiers in Psychology* 3. Available at https://doi.org/10.3389/fpsyg.2012.00429.

DeWall, C.N., Gillath, O., Pressman, S.D., Black, L.L., Bartz, J.A., Moskovitz, J., and Stetler, D.A. (2014) When the love hormone leads to violence oxytocin increases intimate partner violence inclinations among high trait aggressive people. *Social Psychological and Personality Science*: 1948550613516876.

Dvorsky, G. (2012). *10 Reasons Why Oxytocin Is the Most Amazing Molecule in the World*. Daily 10. Available at: http://io9.com/5925206/10-reasons-why-oxytocin-is-the-most-amazing-molecule-in-the-world.

Farah, M.J., and Gillihan, S.J. (2012) Diagnostic brain imaging in psychiatry: Current uses and future prospects. *The Virtual Mentor* 14: pp. 464–471.

Farah, M.J., and Hook, C.J. (2013) The seductive allure of "seductive allure". *Perspectives on Psychological Science* 8: pp. 88–90.

Farahany, N.A. (2016) Neuroscience and behavioral genetics in US criminal law: An empirical analysis. *Journal of Law and the Biosciences* 2(3): pp. 485–509.

Finger, S. (2001) *Origins of Neuroscience: A History of Explorations into Brain Function*. New York: Oxford University Press.

Gernsbacher, M.A. (2011) Mirror neuron forum. *Perspectives on Psychological Science* 6: pp. 369–407.

Gilbertson, M.W., Shenton, M.E., Ciszewski, A., Kasai, K., Lasko, N.B., Orr, S.P., and Pitman, R.K. (2002) Smaller hippocampal volume predicts pathologic vulnerability to psychological trauma. *Nature Neuroscience* 5: pp. 1242–1247.

Gilovich, T. (1991) *How We Know What Isn't So: The Fallibility of Human Reason in Everyday Life*. New York: Free Press.

Gold, P.E., Cahill, L., and Wenk, G.L. (2002) Ginkgo biloba: A cognitive enhancer? *Psychological Science in the Public Interest* 3: pp. 2–11.

Griffiths, S. (2014). *Hugs Can Make You Feel Younger: 'Cuddle Hormone' Could Improve Bone Health, and Combat. Muscle Wasting*. Available at: www.dailymail.co.uk/sciencetech/article-2654224/Hugs-make-feel-younger-Cuddle-hormone-improve-bone-health-combat-muscle-wasting.html#ixzz3UP2WNT2J.

Greene, E., and Cahill, B.S. (2012) Effects of neuroimaging evidence on mock juror decision making. *Behavioral Sciences & the Law* 30: pp. 280–296.

Grüsser, O.J. (1990) Aristotle redivivus? Multiple causes and effects in hominid brain evolution. *Behavioral and Brain Sciences* 13: pp. 356–359.

Gunter, T.D. (2014) Can we trust consumers with their brains: Popular cognitive neuroscience, brain images, self-help and the consumer. *Indiana Health Law Review* 11: pp. 483–552.

Gurley, J.R., and Marcus, D.K. (2008) The effects of neuroimaging and brain injury on insanity defenses. *Behavioral Sciences & the Law* 26: pp. 85–97.

Hall, H. (2007) A skeptical view of SPECT scans and Daniel Amen. *Quackwatch*. Available at: www.quackwatch.org/06ResearchProjects/amen.html.

Hall, H. (2014, October 27) Mirror neurons and the pitfalls of brain research. *Science-based medicine*. Available at: https://sciencebasedmedicine.org/mirror-neurons-and-the-pitfalls-of-brain-research/.

Hamilton, A.F.D.C. (2013) Reflecting on the mirror neuron system in autism: A systematic review of current theories. *Developmental Cognitive Neuroscience* 3: pp. 91–105.

Hamilton, J. (2015). How your brain remembers where you parked the car. *NPR*, 15 August. Available at: www.npr.org/sections/health-shots/2015/07/01/419165395/how-your-brain-remembers-where-you-parked-the-car

Herculano-Houzel, S. (2002) Do you know your brain? A survey on public neuroscience literacy at the closing of the decade of the brain. *The Neuroscientist* 8(2): pp. 98–110.

Hickok, G. (2014) *The Myth of Mirror Neurons: The Real Neuroscience of Communication and Cognition*. New York: W.W. Norton & Company.

Hooper, J., and Teresi, D. (1986) *The Three-Pound Universe*. New York: Palgrave MacMillan Publishing Company.

Horvath, J.C., Forte, J.D., and Carter, O. (2015) Quantitative review finds no evidence of cognitive effects in healthy populations from single-session transcranial direct current stimulation (tDCS). *Brain Stimulation* 8: pp. 535–550.

Iacoboni, M. (2009) *Mirroring people: The New Science of How We Connect With Others*. New York: Palgrave Macmillan.

Iacoboni, M., Freedman, J., Kaplan, J., Jamieson, K.H., Freedman, F., and Fitzgerald, K. (2007). This is your brain on politics. *New York Times*, 11 November. Available at: www.nytimes.com/2007/11/11/opinion/11freedman.html?_r=0.

Jarrett, C. (2015) *Great Myths of the Brain*. New York: Wiley-Blackwell.

Kapur, S., Phillips, A.G., and Insel, T.R. (2012) Why has it taken so long for biological psychiatry to develop clinical tests and what to do about it. *Molecular Psychiatry* 17: pp. 1174–1179.

Khalil, M.M., Tremoleda, J.L., Bayomy, T.B., and Gsell, W. (2011) Molecular SPECT imaging: An overview. *International Journal of Molecular Imaging*. www.hindawi.com/journals/ijmi/2011/796025/abs/

Krueger, J. (2017) Reverse inference. In S.O. Lilienfeld and I.D. Waldman (Eds.). *Psychological science under scrutiny: Recent challenges and proposed solutions.* New York: Wiley-Blackwell: pp. 108–122.

Laws, K. (2012, January 27) *Twitter post.* Available at: https://twitter.com/Keith_Laws/status/163158723 290873856.

Lilienfeld, S.O. (2005) The 10 commandments of helping students distinguish science from pseudoscience in psychology. *Association for Psychological Science Observer* 18(9): pp. 39–40.

———. (2007). Psychological treatments that cause harm. *Perspectives on Psychological Science* 2(1): pp. 53–70.

Lilienfeld, S.O., Ammirati, R., and David, M. (2012). Distinguishing science from pseudoscience in school psychology: Science and scientific thinking as safeguards against human error. *Journal of School Psychology,* 50: pp. 7–36.

Lilienfeld, S.O., and Arkowitz, H. (2008). Uncovering "brainscams". *Scientific American Mind* 19(1): pp. 80–81.

Lilienfeld, S.O., Lynn, S., Ruscio, J., and Beyerstein, B.L. (2009) *Fifty Great Myths of Popular Psychology: Shattering Widespread Misconceptions Regarding Human Behavior.* New York: Wiley-Blackwell.

Lilienfeld, S.O., Sauvigné, K.C., Lynn, S.J., Cautin, R.L., Latzman, R.D., and Waldman, I.D. (2015) Fifty psychological and psychiatric terms to avoid: A list of inaccurate, misleading, misused, ambiguous, and logically confused words and phrases. *Frontiers in Psychology,* 6. Available at https://doi.org/10.3389/fpsyg.2012.00429.

Loewenstein, G., Rick, S., and Cohen, J.D. (2008) Neuroeconomics. *Annual Review of Psychology* 59: pp. 647–672.

McCabe, D.P., and Castel, A.D. (2008) Seeing is believing: The effect of brain images on judgments of scientific reasoning. *Cognition* 107: pp. 343–352.

Marcus, G. (2013) Hyping artificial intelligence, yet again. *The New Yorker,* 31 December. Available at: www.newyorker.com/tech/elements/hyping-artificial-intelligence-yet-agai.

Michael, R.B., Newman, E.J., Vuorre, M., Cumming, G., and Garry, M. (2013) On the (non) persuasive power of a brain image. *Psychonomic Bulletin & Review* 20(4): pp. 720–725.

Miller, G. (2010). fMRI lie detection fails a legal test. *Science* 328: pp. 1336–1337.

Miller, L. (1986, April) Neurobabble. *Psychology Today,* 70.

Morin, C. (2011) Neuromarketing: The new science of consumer behavior. *Society* 48: pp. 131–135.

Munro, G.D., and Munro, C.A. (2014) "Soft" versus "hard" psychological science: Biased evaluations of scientific evidence that threatens or supports a strongly held political identity. *Basic and Applied Social Psychology* 36: pp. 533–543.

Pashler, H., McDaniel, M., Rohrer, D., and Bjork, R. (2008) Learning styles concepts and evidence. *Psychological Science in the Public Interest* 9: pp. 105–119.

Patel, P., Meltzer, C.C., Mayberg, H.S., and Levine, K. (2007) The role of imaging in United States courtrooms. *Neuroimaging Clinics of North America* 17: pp. 557–567.

Poldrack, R.A. (2006) Can cognitive processes be inferred from neuroimaging data? *Trends in Cognitive Sciences* 10(2): pp. 59–63.

Racine, E., Bar-Ilan, O. and Illes, J. (2005). fMRI in the public eye. *Nature Reviews Neuroscience* 6: pp. 159–164.

Racine, E., Bar-Ilan, O., and Illes, J. (2006) Brain imaging: A decade of coverage in the print media. *Science Communication* 28: pp. 122–143.

Racine, E., Waldman, S., Rosenberg, J., and Illes, J. (2010) Contemporary neuroscience in the media. *Social Science & Medicine* 71: pp. 725–733.

Ramachandran, V.S. (2000) Mirror neurons and imitation learning as the driving force behind "the great leap forward" in human evolution. *Edge.* Available at: www.edge. org/3rd_culture/ramachandran/ramachandran_p1.html.

Redick, T.S., Shipstead, Z., Harrison, T.L., Hicks, K.L., Fried, D.E., Hambrick, D.Z., . . . Engle, R.W. (2013) No evidence of intelligence improvement after working memory training: A randomized, placebo-controlled study. *Journal of Experimental Psychology: General* 142: pp. 359–379.

Rizzolatti, G., Fadiga, L., Gallese, V., and Fogassi, L. (1996) Premotor cortex and the recognition of motor actions. *Cognitive Brain Research* 3: pp. 131–141.

Sabbatini, R.M. (1997) Phrenology: The history of brain localization. *Brain and Mind* 21(March/May): pp. 1–3.

Sagan, C. (1979) *Broca's Brain: Reflections on the Romance of Science*. New York: Ballantine Books.

Sanders, L. (2015) How the brain perceives time. *Science Times*, 15 July. Available at: www.sciencenews.org/article/how-brain-perceives-time.

Satel, S., and Lilienfeld, S.O. (2013) *Brainwashed: The Seductive Appeal of Mindless Neuroscience*. New York: Basic Books.

Schwartz, S.J., Lilienfeld, S.O., Meca, A., and Sauvigné, K.C. (2016) The role of neuroscience within psychology: A call for inclusiveness rather than exclusiveness. *American Psychologist*, awaiting volume and page numbers.

Schweitzer, N.J., and Saks, M.J. (2011) Neuroimage evidence and the insanity defense. *Behavioral Sciences & the Law* 29(4): pp. 592–607.

Schweitzer, N.J., Saks, M.J., Murphy, E.R., Roskies, A.L., Sinnott-Armstrong, W., and Gaudet, L.M. (2011) Neuroimages as evidence in a mens rea defense: No impact. *Psychology, Public Policy, and Law* 17(3): p. 357.

Sechrest, L. (1963) Incremental validity: A recommendation. *Educational and Psychological Measurement* 23: pp. 153–158.

Shen, H. (2015) Neuroscience: The hard science of oxytocin. *Nature* 522: pp. 410–412.

Span, P. (2016) F.T.C.'s Lumosity penalty doesn't end brain training debate. *New York Times*, 15 January. Available at: www.nytimes.com/2016/01/19/health/ftcs-lumosity-penalty-doesnt-end-brain-training-debate.html?_r=0.

Spence, S.A. (2008) Playing devil's advocate: The case against fMRI lie detection. *Legal and Criminological Psychology* 13: pp. 11–25.

Stam, C.J., and Reijneveld, J.C. (2007) Graph theoretical analysis of complex networks in the brain. *Nonlinear Biomedical Physics* 1: pp. 1–19.

Stix, G. (2014) Fact or fiction: Oxytocin is the "love hormone." *Scientific American*, 8 September. Available at: www.scientificamerican.com/article/fact-or-fiction-oxytocin-is-the-love-hormone/

Tallis, R. (2011) *Aping Mankind: Neuromania, Darwinitis and the Misrepresentation of Humanity*. London: Acumen.

Tucker, N. (2008, August 9) Daniel Amen is the most popular psychiatrist in America. To most researchers and scientists, that a very bad thing. *Washington Post*. Available at: www.washingtonpost.com/lifestyle/magazine/daniel-amen-is-the-most-popular-psychiatrist-in-america-to-most-researchers-and-scientists-thats-a-very-bad-thing.

Uttal, W.R. (2001) *The New Phrenology: The Limits of Localizing Cognitive Processes in the Brain*. Cambridge, MA: MIT Press.

Vul, E., Harris, C., Winkielman, P., and Pashler, H. (2009) Puzzlingly high correlations in fMRI studies of emotion, personality, and social cognition. *Perspectives on Psychological Science* 4: pp. 274–290.

Walum, H., Waldman, I., and Young, L. (2015) Statistical and methodological considerations for the interpretation of intranasal oxytocin studies. *Biological Psychiatry* 79: pp. 251–257. doi:10.1016/j.biopsych.2015.06.016

Weisberg, D.S., Keil, F.C., Goodstein, J., Rawson, E., and Gray, J.R. (2008) The seductive allure of neuroscience explanations. *Journal of Cognitive Neuroscience* 20: pp. 470–477.

Weisberg, D.S., Taylor, C.V., and Hopkins, E.J. (2015) Deconstructing the seductive allure of neuroscience explanations. *Judgment and Decision-Making* 10: pp. 429–441.

Yuan, K., Qin, W., Wang, G., Zeng, F., Zhao, L., Yang, X., . . . Gong, Q. (2011) Microstructure abnormalities in adolescents with internet addiction disorder. *PLOS One* 6(6): p. e20708.

Zak, P.J. (2012) *The Moral Molecule: The Source of Love and Prosperity*. New York: Random House.

Zuger, A. (2013) Guides to a journey into the brain. *New York Times*, 29 July. Available at: www.nytimes.com/2013/07/30/health/patricia-s-churchlands-the-self-as-brain-and-brainwashed-by-sally-satel-and-scott-o-lilienfeld.html?_r=0.

17

NEUROSCIENCE ONLINE
Real Ethical Issues in Virtual Realms

Ryan H. Purcell and Karen S. Rommelfanger

Introduction

In this chapter, we will examine several of the most pressing ethical issues as neuroscience is moved online by commercial entities offering brain-training programs and mental health and wellness mobile apps and by academic investigators in search of "citizen scientist" technical labor. We begin with a focus on internet brain-training programs, a recent phenomenon that highlights some of the issues brought on by efforts to integrate online commercial marketing and basic science research, where the lines between health/fitness and consumer/patient/research subject have become blurry. Internet-based brain-training programs exemplify three recent trends that pose new ethical issues for consumers, regulators, and society: (1) a move toward massive-scale scientific efforts, (2) less distinction among consumers, study participants, and research subjects, and (3) a shift toward direct-to-consumer delivery of interventions (for both the healthy and the ill consumer) that largely bypass regulatory oversight.

These examples are drawn from the mid-2010s but may be more broadly applicable to new web-based neurotechnologies and research methods as these sectors continue to grow at a rapid pace.

Internet Brain Training

Effectiveness and Representation of Science

For decades, researchers have searched for ways to measurably improve intelligence. Today, for-profit companies such as Lumos Labs, the parent company of the Lumosity brain-training programs, have entered the fray and expanded the vision to so-called brain fitness. A key question at the heart of much of this research is whether training on specific tasks can more broadly affect intelligence via the so-called transfer effect (Jaeggi et al., 2008; Schweizer et al., 2011). Researchers have long documented how subjects can see dramatic improvement in a specific cognitive domain following training, but improvement in even supposedly closely related areas has remained elusive (Ericsson and Chase, 1982). However, a 2008 study from Jaeggi and colleagues found that a particular type of cognitive exercise called adaptive working memory training could increase measures of fluid intelligence after a remarkably short amount of time (Jaeggi et al., 2008). Moreover, transfer effects were observed to endure for months or more without additional training in a follow-up study (Jaeggi et al., 2011). Since then, some have pointed out control (Shipstead et al., 2012) and IQ measurement (Haier, 2014) issues, and one highly controlled study failed to replicate these findings (Redick et al., 2013). Still, others have found some evidence for transfer effects in different paradigms (Borella et al., 2010; Schweizer et al., 2011).

Nonetheless, interest in this area has grown, and multiple firms have established websites offering fee-based brain-training programs online. Since then, researchers at academic institutions and at these same commercial enterprises have conducted a wide range of studies aiming to demonstrate the efficacy of these products. In the largest study of its kind, Adrian Owen and colleagues (Owen et al., 2010) recruited more than 11,000 volunteers to test whether training on tasks that aimed to imitate commercial brain-training games broadly improved cognitive ability. They found little evidence for such transfer. However, this study—while perhaps providing the most realistic, ecologically valid test of what internet-based program users experience—does not answer the question of whether these exercises *could* improve general cognitive ability or intelligence. While it powerfully tested the real-world effectiveness of a brain-training program, it fell short of rigorously testing its efficacy (i.e., the potential of the program in ideal conditions; Rabipour and Raz, 2012; Revicki and Frank, 1999).

A meta-analysis of twenty-three related studies found strong evidence that adaptive working memory training improved working memory and its close correlates in the short term but saw little indication that this improvement impacted cognitive ability more generally (Melby-Lervag and Hulme, 2013). In addition, Rabipour and Raz (2012) thoroughly reviewed brain-training programs and the scientific literature associated with them and situated these programs within the larger arena of brain training alongside long-standing practices such as meditation, physical exercise, and musical training (Rabipour and Raz, 2012). They found that the evidence of a general positive effect may actually be stronger for the latter, more conventional hobbies and pursuits in comparison to computerized brain training. This could be due to a longer history of studying these more conventional practices but may also be indicative of a genuine difference in ecological validity. Computerized brain-training programs rely, in large part, on the theory that adaptive working memory training is a magic bullet to achieve generalized transfer of cognitive benefits beyond the specific training tasks. By contrast, in musical training or athletics—where training on a particular task (such as practicing a piece on the piano or jumping over hurdles on a track) may in fact be central to the goal (Santoni de Sio et al., 2014)—for typical, healthy individuals, there is little to gain (above recreation) from improving on specific brain-training tasks if transfer to other domains is not achieved. Nonetheless, commercial brain-training marketing seems to suggest that this effect is well established (Chancellor and Chatterjee, 2011; Rabipour and Raz, 2012).

This discrepancy between the claims of commercial brain-training companies and the evidence to back them up eventually led to government intervention. In early 2016, Lumos Labs settled a multimillion-dollar lawsuit with the US Federal Trade Commission (FTC), which alleged that Lumosity did not have substantial evidence to support its claims (FTC, 2016). There is precedent for this sort of intervention and, unfortunately, for its ineffectiveness. In 2013, the US Food and Drug Administration (FDA) moved to ban the sale of genetic health testing kits from the genetic-testing-by-mail website 23andMe (Stoekle et al., 2016), yet this move did little to stop or curtail the company's sales (Seife, 2013). Today, 23andMe is lauded for building an enormous bio-bank of not only genetic but also clinical and personal information that has real value to researchers (Servick, 2015). In fact, biotechnology and pharmaceutical giant Genentech has paid $60 million to pore over data collected from patients with Parkinson's disease by 23andMe (Stoekle et al., 2016). Time will tell if Lumosity comes to be seen like 23andMe, with its valuable cognitive performance databank.

In addition to the risks to individual consumers in terms of frustration and money wasted on ineffective programs, the pervasive marketing of these programs with claims that are not fully supported by independent, peer-reviewed studies also jeopardizes the credibility of all neuroscience and may eventually compromise the public's trust. Lumosity touts its programs as being designed by neuroscientists. Researchers have found that simply the idea of neuroscience evidence can be extraordinarily persuasive. Weisberg and colleagues (2008) reported that the addition of even irrelevant neuroscience data adds significant weight to psychological explanations. Chancellor and Chatterjee (2011) have discussed the issue of "brain branding" of a number of emerging neurotechnologies, including some weakly supported brain-training programs.. They also point out a troubling pattern of cozy relationships between the brain-training industry and entrepreneurial neuroscientists (Chancellor and Chatterjee, 2011). In one example documented by Chancellor and Chatterjee (2011), Posit Science founder and renowned neuroscientist Michael M. Merzenich contributed an article (Mahncke et al., 2006) to *PNAS*, which reported positive results of a randomized, controlled trial of Posit's brain-training program with nine other authors, all of whom were employed by Posit. Notably, a follow-up study of a larger cohort also found a significant improvement in multiple measures of cognitive ability in the treated group compared to controls (Smith et al., 2009). However, this study was also funded by Posit Science, raising concerns of conflict of interest and bias in the reported results (Rabipour and Raz, 2012). The website of Posit's flagship consumer brain-training program, BrainHQ, claims a study showed that "BrainHQ improves memory and increases hippocampus size" (Posit Science, 2014). However, the paper cited (Rosen et al., 2011) does not address hippocampus size and, in fact, the only mention of size is in reference to the study's small sample. Similarly, Lumosity claimed thirteen studies on its "Completed Research behind Lumosity" web page, but eight of these studies were conference presentations and are not published in peer-reviewed academic journals (Lumos Labs, 2014). These preliminary studies are potentially exciting, but without FDA oversight, there are few obstacles preventing commercial brain-training programs from making advertising claims without evidence to back them, which concerns researchers and clinicians in the field. To this point, more than seventy researchers recently released a consensus statement expressing skepticism about the effectiveness of brain-training programs for the elderly, suggesting that these companies often exploit anxieties about aging, Alzheimer's disease, and dementia (Allaire et al., 2014). They conclude, "We object to the claim that brain games offer consumers a scientifically grounded avenue to reduce or reverse cognitive decline when there is no compelling scientific evidence to date that they do." While the FTC did intervene with health-related claims in advertising by Lumosity, the FTC generally does not have sophisticated neuroscience expertise to evaluate the onslaught of neuroscience consumables (FTC, 2016).

For a discussion of cultural perspectives on brain training in Japan, see Chapter 29.

Unprecedented Potential for Massive-Scale Studies

Until very recently, a psychology study of emotional contagion involving nearly 700,000 participants would not have been feasible. However, in 2014, Facebook and academic collaborators reported on just such a study, which was carried out on users of the vast social network (Kramer et al., 2014). Criticism of the study was fast and sharp as it became apparent that Facebook users were unaware of their participation and were never given the opportunity to opt out of the experiment (Harriman and Patel, 2014). Moreover, users only gave their consent by agreeing to Facebook's Data Use Policy upon registering an account with the company. The emotional contagion study may have provided a proof of concept for the power of research on the internet but also demonstrated the urgent need for new definitions of what constitutes human-subjects research.

Brain-training companies are similarly tapping into their vast collections of data to perform experiments on a massive scale. Lumosity researchers published a similar proof-of-concept study, which they claim drew from the world's largest cognitive performance dataset of some 36 million users from more than 200 countries (Sternberg et al., 2013). There is no doubt that the size of these datasets allows new questions with new statistical power to be asked, but in order for this type of research to continue, careful assessments should be made of potential ethical issues, even by private companies such as Facebook and Lumosity that are not beholden to institutional review boards like those that provide ethics oversight for research at academic institutions.

If internet-based studies are not held to the same ethical standards as all other research on human participants, then even comprehensively reviewed studies will struggle to recruit subjects. Nissenbaum has championed a fundamental change in the way privacy is handled on the internet, not only to protect individuals' rights but also to safeguard the great potential for growth (Nissenbaum, 2011). If users cannot expect reasonable privacy online and feel that their personal information is vulnerable and their every movement is tracked, then they will be reluctant to use online brain-training programs (should they prove to be effective) or participate in large-scale studies, and therefore the enormous potential of internet research simply will not be realized. At this point, it appears that the market is not sufficiently motivated to regulate itself—probably due to a lack of organized pressure from consumers—and so reasonable privacy norms will likely need to be established and enforced by government regulators.

Gaps in Privacy Protection

In the United States, health information is protected by the Health Insurance Portability and Accountability Act (HIPAA), and educational records are protected by the Family Educational Rights and Privacy Act (FERPA). However, brain-training data, which may indicate cognitive abilities and disabilities, is currently not covered by either of these acts.

The privacy policy of Lumosity.com provides a glimpse into the sort of data the company is interested in compiling but remains vague enough to keep consumers from easily imagining how their information is specifically collected and used (Lumos Labs, 2016). Lumosity's parent company, Lumos Labs, Inc., gathers data related to performance on brain-training games as well as web browsing behavior, date and time of access, and much more if users opt to log in via Facebook. In addition, they "may supplement the information you provide [them] with additional information gathered from other sources, such as publicly available information." The result, one might imagine, is a very detailed personal profile of the user's lifestyle, including income, marital status, and geographical location in addition to test performance. In addition, 23andMe has been said to aspire to be the "Google of personalized healthcare" (Seife, 2013). At this point, it remains to be seen whether a company like Lumosity is more interested in consumer marketing or cognitive science.

Most website privacy policies are notoriously opaque. Even if it were possible to review and consider the implications of all policies at websites visited (McDonald and Cranor, 2008), it would be exceedingly difficult to predict how data that is collected now may be interpreted and used in the near or long terms (Nissenbaum, 2011). For example, there is no guarantee that personal information will not be sold off along with other assets such as patents in the event of bankruptcy. In fact, this practice seems to currently be the norm for most internet companies (Singer and Jeremy, 2015). The U.S. Federal Trade Commission recently stopped the sale of personal data and student records from the failed website ConnectEdu (FTC, 2014), but it remains to be seen if this precedent will impact the commercial brain-training industry.

Future Directions in Online Neurodata Collection

Mental Health Apps

Data (in)security is a consideration of increasing importance as researchers and healthcare providers pivot to mobile platforms in efforts to provide more real-time care and close coverage gaps, capitalizing on the near ubiquity of smartphones (Giota and Kleftaras, 2014). Recently, and somewhat alongside the internet brain-training trend, there has been rapid growth in the mental health mobile app sector aimed at treating and/or assessing the status of patients suffering from psychiatric conditions including PTSD, mood disorders, and others (Anthes, 2016). While there is enormous potential for these apps to treat patients who have poor or limited access to mental healthcare (a well-documented problem; Alegria et al., 2008) and improve treatment for those who do, there are also significant privacy concerns to consider. For example, one study found that the onset of depressive symptoms could be predicted in bipolar disorder patients based on a decrease in their physical movements and social activity on their phones (Beiwinkel et al., 2016). These findings indicate some of the potential value of using smartphones to extend patient care but also expose a serious vulnerability. It would not be difficult for other apps, which are not reporting data to physicians and researchers, to collect similar data and use it for other purposes that may seriously compromise patient privacy. Moreover, the common internet-based service fee structure of providing an app at a nominal fee or with advertisements in exchange for user information is not appropriate in the context of mental or physical healthcare involving information that requires a high level of privacy. However, the proliferation of these apps is largely geared toward "wellness" rather than facilitating long-distance connections with physicians. In these cases, data such as sleep schedules, mood, and daily activities is collected, which can still present real privacy concerns for users (Purcell and Rommelfanger, 2015). Like brain-training games, these apps appear to be recreational tools for general self-improvement, yet enormous amounts of data are collected with unclear legacies for those data.

For more on DIY self-improvement, see Chapter 18.

Mobile health and wellness apps also present an opportunity to rapidly recruit research subjects and deliver interventions outside of traditional research settings. While this approach has tremendous promise in terms of improving statistical power and data collection, there is a risk that studies may fall into a regulatory gap in which no agency has clear regulatory oversight (Rothstein et al., 2015). On the other hand, there is a risk that overly regulating app development in this sector could hinder the progress of researchers seeking to harness the enthusiasm of citizen scientists.

Massive-Scale Neuroscience and Open Neurodata

It appears that there is a great appetite in the general public to be involved in neuroscience and cognitive science research as both subjects and experimenters. Thousands of citizen neuroscientists have used the program EyeWire to map visual neuron connections from serial electron micrographs, an approach that drastically accelerated data analysis (Marx, 2013). The potential applications for scientific crowdsourcing remain difficult to comprehend, as this field is only in its infancy and could conceivably be applied to other experimental data logjams in the cognitive and neurosciences as well (Curtis, 2014).

A slightly different approach has been developed by neurologist Paul Thompson and genetic epidemiologist Nick Martin, who founded the ENIGMA (Enhancing Neuroimaging and Genetics through Meta-Analysis) Consortium, an effort aimed at linking genotype to brain phenotype through massive-scale collaboration within the scientific community (Mohammadi, 2015). These researchers are statistically powering up genotype–phenotype studies by collaborating with nearly 200 scientists from around the world and analyzing brain scan and genetic data from nearly 30,000 individuals, a scale that individual research groups could not attempt with current technology and funding mechanisms (Thompson et al., 2014). Importantly, patient data is typically analyzed at the institution at which it was originally collected with common algorithms developed by the group, which minimizes privacy concerns for patients. In addition, this massive collaborative model of scientific inquiry allows scientists from low-resource settings to contribute to high-impact work (Mohammadi, 2015). The ENIGMA Consortium has published more than a dozen articles since its founding in 2009, including one identifying five novel genetic factors that may influence brain development (Hibar et al., 2015).

These approaches provide glimpses of some of the positive aspects of massive-scale internet-aided research. However, even with deidentified data, there is the possibility of reidentification (Choudhury et al., 2014). While this was clearly demonstrated as a problem with genomic data, the problem will be even greater with large banks of neurodata, especially in combination with genetic data. This also complicates attempts to provide broad consent processes for study participants (Grady et al., 2015) and perhaps makes it even more challenging to fully prepare consumer participants in such studies. While the issue of reidentification will surely be discussed with large-scale brain data collection efforts such as Neurodata Without Borders, it remains unclear how such a problem will be addressed with consumer data.

Conclusions

In summary, the examples discussed in this chapter demonstrate the incredible potential as well as the significant risks of brain data collection for consumers and society. A major concern moving forward is whether serious research that makes a significant contribution can happen in an ethical way within the current personal information-for-service paradigm of many internet-based businesses. Several of the examples provided—23andMe, Lumosity, EyeWire—serve as evidence that there is substantial interest in learning about science and participating in the process, but how will consumers or research subjects provide real consent lacking a full understanding of future implications much less current uses of their data?

Privacy concerns and proper handling of sensitive personal data online are issues that must be addressed if the potential for the internet as a powerful social, cognitive, and neuroscience laboratory is to be realized in full (Purcell and Rommelfanger, 2015). If 23andMe's data collection provokes unease, consider that genetic data is largely probabilistic and in most cases does not have a direct impact on health, personality, or lifestyle. We argue that neurodata—whether arising from measures of the brain's electrical activity (such as EEG), blood flow (fMRI), or cognitive function—should be privileged and protected like health and education records because it may more closely measure current cognitive health and intellectual abilities. This sort of safeguarding obviously benefits consumers by protecting their privacy, but also, in the long term, may benefit cognitive and neuroscience research by encouraging more participation as citizens feel less like targeted consumers and more like valued research subjects.

Acknowledgment

We thank Dr. Margaret E. Kosal for helpful suggestions on an earlier version of this manuscript.

Further Reading

Chancellor, B. and Chatterjee, A. (2011) "Brain Branding: When Neuroscience and Commerce Collide". *American Journal of Bioethics Neuroscience* 2(4), 18–27.

Giota, K.G. and Kleftaras, G. (2014) "Mental Health Apps: Innovations, Risks and Ethical Considerations". *E-Health Telecommunication Systems and Networks* 3(3), 19–23.

Nissenbaum, H. (2011) "A Contextual Approach to Privacy Online". *Daedalus* 140(4), 32–48.

Purcell, R.H. and Rommelfanger, K.S. (2015) "Internet-Based Brain Training Games, Citizen Scientists, and Big Data: Ethical Issues in Unprecedented Virtual Territories". *Neuron* 86(2), 356–359.

Rabipour, S. and Raz, A. (2012) "Training the Brain: Fact and Fad in Cognitive and Behavioral Remediation". *Brain Cognition* 79(2), 159–179.

References

Alegria, M., Chatterji, P., Wells, K., Cao, Z., Chen, C.N., Takeuchi, D., . . . Meng, X.L. (2008) Disparity in depression treatment among racial and ethnic minority populations in the United States. *Psychiatric Services* 59(11): pp. 1264–1272. doi:10.1176/appi.ps.59.11.1264

Allaire, J.C., et.al. (2014) *A Consensus on the Brain Training Industry from the Scientific Community*. Available at: http://longevity3.stanford.edu/blog/2014/10/15/the-consensus-on-the-brain-training-industry-from-the-scientific-community-2/.

Anthes, E. (2016) Mental health: There's an app for that. *Nature* 532(7597): pp. 20–23. doi:10.1038/532020a

Beiwinkel, T., Kindermann, S., Maier, A., Kerl, C., Moock, J., Barbian, G., and Rössler, W. (2016) Using smartphones to monitor bipolar disorder symptoms: A pilot study. *Journal of Medical Internet Research Mental Health* 3(1): p. e2. doi:10.2196/mental.4560

Borella, E., Carretti, B., Riboldi, F., and De Beni, R. (2010) Working memory training in older adults: Evidence of transfer and maintenance effects. *Psychology and Aging* 25(4): pp. 767–778. doi:10.1037/a0020683

Chancellor, B., and Chatterjee, A. (2011) Brain branding: When neuroscience and commerce collide. *American Journal of Bioethics Neuroscience* 2(4): pp. 18–27.

Choudhury, S., Fishman, J.R., McGowan, M.L., and Juengst, E.T. (2014) Big data, open science and the brain: Lessons learned from genomics. *Frontiers in Human Neuroscience* 8(239): pp. 1–10. doi:ARTN 23910.3389/fnhum.2014.00239

Curtis, V. (2014) Online citizen science games: Opportunities for the biological sciences. *Applied & Translational Genomics* 3(4): pp. 90–94. doi:10.1016/j.atg.2014.07.001

Ericsson, K.A., and Chase, W.G. (1982) Exceptional memory. *American Scientist* 70(6): pp. 607–615.

FTC. (2014) *FTC Seeks Protection for Students' Personal Information in Education Technology Company ConnectEdu's Bankruptcy Proceeding* [Press release]. Available at: www.ftc.gov/news-events/press-releases/2014/05/ftc-seeks-protection-students-personal-information-education.

———. (2016) *Lumosity to Pay $2 Million to Settle FTC Deceptive Advertising Charges for Its "Brain Training" Program* [Press release]. Available at: www.ftc.gov/news-events/press-releases/2016/01/lumosity-pay-2-million-settle-ftc-deceptive-advertising-charges.

Giota, K.G., and Kleftaras, G. (2014) Mental health apps: Innovations, risks and ethical considerations. *E-Health Telecommunication Systems and Networks* 3(3): pp. 19–23.

Grady, C., Eckstein, L., Berkman, B., Brock, D., Cook-Deegan, R., Fullerton, S.M., . . . Wendler, D. (2015) Broad consent for research with biological samples: Workshop conclusions. *American Journal of Bioethics* 15(9): pp. 34–42. doi:10.1080/15265161.2015.1062162

Haier, R.J. (2014) Increased intelligence is a myth (so far). *Frontiers in Systems Neuroscience* 8: p. 34. doi:10.3389/fnsys.2014.00034

Harriman, S., and Patel, J. (2014) The ethics and editorial challenges of internet-based research. *BMC Medicine* 12(1): p. 124. doi:10.1186/PREACCEPT-1753356481135356

Hibar, D.P., Stein, J.L., Renteria, M.E., Arias-Vasquez, A., Desrivieres, S., Jahanshad, N., . . . Medland, S.E. (2015) Common genetic variants influence human subcortical brain structures. *Nature* 520(7546): pp. 224–229. doi:10.1038/nature14101

Jaeggi, S.M., Buschkuehl, M., Jonides, J., and Perrig, W.J. (2008) Improving fluid intelligence with training on working memory. *Proceedings of the National Academy of Science of the United States of America* 105(19): pp. 6829–6833.

Jaeggi, S.M., Buschkuehl, M., Jonides, J., and Shah, P. (2011) Short- and long-term benefits of cognitive training. *Proceedings of the National Academy of Science United States of America* 108(25): pp. 10081–10086. doi:10.1073/pnas.1103228108

Kramer, A.D., Guillory, J.E., and Hancock, J.T. (2014) Experimental evidence of massive-scale emotional contagion through social networks. *Proceedings of the National Academy of Science United States of America* 111(24): pp. 8788–8790. doi:10.1073/pnas.1320040111

Lumos Labs, I. (2014). Completed research behind Lumosity. www.lumosity.com/hcp/research/completed [Accessed September 5, 2014]

———. (2016). *Privacy Policy*, 20 July. Available at: www.lumosity.com/legal/privacy_policy.

McDonald, A.M., and Cranor, L.F. (2008) The cost of reading privacy policies. *ISJLP* 4: pp. 543–368.

Mahncke, H.W., Connor, B.B., Appelman, J., Ahsanuddin, O.N., Hardy, J.L., Wood, R.A., . . . Merzenich, M.M. (2006) Memory enhancement in healthy older adults using a brain plasticity-based training program: A randomized, controlled study. *Proceedings of the National Academy of Science United States of America* 103(33): pp. 12523–12528. doi:10.1073/pnas.0605194103

Marx, V. (2013) Neuroscience waves to the crowd. *Nature Methods* 10(11): pp. 1069–1074. doi:10.1038/Nmeth.2695

Melby-Lervag, M., and Hulme, C. (2013) Is working memory training effective? A meta-analytic review. *Development Psychology* 49(2): pp. 270–291. doi:10.1037/a0028228

Mohammadi, D. (2015) ENIGMA: Crowdsourcing meets neuroscience. *The Lancet Neurology* 14(5): pp. 462–463. doi:10.1016/S1474–4422(15)00005–8

Nissenbaum, H. (2011) A contextual approach to privacy online. *Daedalus* 140(4): pp. 32–48.

Owen, A.M., Hampshire, A., Grahn, J.A., Stenton, R., Dajani, S., Burns, A.S., . . . Ballard, C.G. (2010) Putting brain training to the test. *Nature* 465(7299): pp. 775–778.

Purcell, R.H., and Rommelfanger, K.S. (2015) Internet-based brain training games, citizen scientists, and big data: Ethical issues in unprecedented virtual territories. *Neuron* 86(2): pp. 356–359. doi:10.1016/j.neuron.2015.03.044

Rabipour, S., and Raz, A. (2012) Training the brain: Fact and fad in cognitive and behavioral remediation. *Brain and Cognition* 79(2): pp. 159–179. doi:10.1016/j.bandc.2012.02.006

Redick, T.S., Shipstead, Z., Harrison, T.L., Hicks, K.L., Fried, D.E., Hambrick, D.Z., . . . Engle, R.W. (2013) No evidence of intelligence improvement after working memory training: A randomized, placebo-controlled study. *Journal of Experimental Psychology: General* 142(2): pp. 359–379.

Revicki, D.A., and Frank, L. (1999) Pharmacoeconomic evaluation in the real world: Effectiveness versus efficacy studies. *Pharmacoeconomics* 15(5): pp. 423–434.

Rosen, A.C., Sugiura, L., Kramer, J.H., Whitfield-Gabrieli, S., and Gabrieli, J.D. (2011) Cognitive training changes hippocampal function in mild cognitive impairment: A pilot study. *Journal of Alzheimer's Disease*, 26(Suppl 3): pp. 349–357. doi:10.3233/JAD-2011–0009

Rothstein, M.A., Wilbanks, J.T., and Brothers, K.B. (2015). Citizen Science on your smartphone: An ELSI research agenda. *Journal of Law Medicine & Ethics* 43(4): pp. 897–903. doi:10.1111/jlme.12327

Santoni de Sio, F.R., Robichaud, P., Vincent, Nicole, A. (2014) Who should enhance? Conceptual and normative dimensions of cognitive enhancement. *Humana.Mente: Journal of Philosophical Studies* 26: pp. 179–197.

Schweizer, S., Hampshire, A., and Dalgleish, T. (2011) Extending brain-training to the affective domain: Increasing cognitive and affective executive control through emotional working memory training. *PLoS One* 6(9): p. e24372. doi:10.1371/journal.pone.0024372

Seife, C. (2013). 23andMe Is Terrifying, but Not for the Reasons the FDA Thinks. *Scientific American* [Online]. Available at https://www.scientificamerican.com/article/23andme-is-terrifying-but-not-for-the-reasons-the-fda-thinks/.

Servick, K. (2015) Can 23andMe have it all? *Science* 349(6255): pp. 1472–1477. doi:10.1126/science. 349.6255.1472

Shipstead, Z., Redick, T.S., and Engle, R.W. (2012) Is working memory training effective? *Psychological Bulletin* 138(4): pp. 628–654. doi:10.1037/a0027473

Singer, N.M., and Jeremy, B. (2015). When a company is put up for sale, in many cases, your personal data is, too. *New York Times*, 28 June.

Smith, G.E., Housen, P., Yaffe, K., Ruff, R., Kennison, R.F., Mahncke, H.W., and Zelinski, E.M. (2009) A cognitive training program based on principles of brain plasticity: Results from the Improvement in Memory with Plasticity-based Adaptive Cognitive Training (IMPACT) study. *Journal of the American Geriatrics Society* 57(4): pp. 594–603. doi:10.1111/j.1532–5415.2008.02167.x

Sternberg, D.A., Ballard, K., Hardy, J.L., Katz, B., Doraiswamy, P.M., and Scanlon, M. (2013) The largest human cognitive performance dataset reveals insights into the effects of lifestyle factors and aging. *Frontiers in Human Neuroscience* 7(292): pp. 1–10.

Stoekle, H.C., Mamzer-Bruneel, M.F., Vogt, G., and Herve, C. (2016) 23andMe: A new two-sided data-banking market model. *BMC Medical Ethics* 17: p. 19. doi:10.1186/s12910-016-0101-9

Thompson, P.M., Stein, J.L., Medland, S.E., Hibar, D.P., Vasquez, A.A., Renteria, M.E., . . . Alzheimer's Disease Neuroimaging Initiative, E.C.I.C.S.Y.S.G. (2014) The ENIGMA Consortium: Large-scale collaborative analyses of neuroimaging and genetic data. *Brain Imaging Behaviour* 8(2): pp. 153–182. doi:10.1007/s11682-013-9269-5

Weisberg, D.S., Keil, F.C., Goodstein, J., Rawson, E., and Gray, J.R. (2008) The seductive allure of neuroscience explanations. *Journal of Cognitive Neuroscience* 20(3): pp. 470–477. doi:10.1162/jocn.2008.20040

18

HOME USE OF tDCS

From "Do-It-Yourself" to "Direct-to-Consumer"

Anna Wexler and Peter B. Reiner

Introduction

In recent years, the technique known as transcranial direct current stimulation (tDCS) has come into prominence. tDCS can be distinguished from deep brain stimulation in that it is noninvasive, and it differs from electroconvulsive therapy in that it requires a much lower level of current. The prototypical tDCS device contains a current-generating component (often powered by a 9V battery), wires that carry the current, and electrodes that act as a conductive interface between the wires and the scalp. When the electrical circuit is complete, the device is thought to deliver current to a small area of the brain beneath the electrodes. Interest in the use of this technique on the human brain sharply increased following publication of a paper showing that passing a weak electrical current (0.2 to 1 milliamps) through the motor cortex caused human subjects to perform significantly better on motor tasks (Nitsche and Paulus, 2000).

In the decade and a half since this keystone paper was published, approximately 1,000 peer-reviewed articles about tDCS have emerged, many of which suggest that tDCS may have beneficial effects in both clinical settings (for review, see Kuo et al., 2014) and nonclinical ones (for review, see Coffman et al., 2014). For example, studies have claimed that tDCS may be effective for a variety of conditions and psychiatric disorders, such as depression (Shiozawa et al., 2014) and chronic pain (Knotkova et al., 2013). In healthy individuals, research has suggested that tDCS can "enhance cognition" in a variety of domains, such as creative problem solving (Chi and Snyder, 2012), working memory (Fregni et al., 2005), object detection (Falcone et al., 2012), sustained attention (Nelson et al., 2014), and motor learning (Reis et al., 2009). One notable feature of tDCS is that its efficacy for cognitive enhancement seems to be more salient with concurrent training on a cognitive task. The fact that tDCS has been shown to be effective *without* concurrent training—for example, in cases of depression and chronic pain—has led some to speculate that in clinical populations, tDCS may be modulating brain networks involved in the placebo response (Schambra et al., 2014). It should be noted, however, that several meta-analyses have been published that question the validity of the reported effects of tDCS for cognitive enhancement (Horvath et al., 2015a; Horvath et al., 2015b).

Currently, tDCS is not approved by regulatory authorities in either the United States or Europe as a medical treatment for any indication. In the United States, researchers (but not the general public) may obtain medical-grade tDCS devices for investigational use from either Soterix or Neuroconn, the two U.S. companies whose devices have an "investigational device exemption" from the Food and Drug Administration (FDA; Fregni et al., 2014). Nonetheless, the simplicity of tDCS devices has led to a phenomenon wherein individuals stimulate their own brains with tDCS[1] outside of research or medical settings, primarily for self-improvement purposes (Jwa, 2015; Wexler, 2015a). The movement has been referred to as do-it-yourself (DIY) tDCS because it began with individuals constructing tDCS devices themselves. In the past few years, the availability of ready-made, direct-to-consumer devices has grown, and there are currently at least nine consumer tDCS devices—which are not regulated as either medical or investigational devices—on the market, ranging in price from $49 to $299. As a result, the border between DIY and direct-to-consumer tDCS has become muddled. We therefore use the term "home users" to encompass the full range of individuals who use tDCS devices outside of professional research and medical settings.

For more on cognitive enhancement, see Chapter 8.

Unsurprisingly, the emergence of home use of tDCS has not been well received by ethicists, scientists, and the medical community (Hamilton et al., 2011; Cohen Kadosh et al., 2012; Levy and Savulescu, 2014; Fitz and Reiner, 2013, 2014; Editorial *Nature*, 2013; Dubljević et al., 2014; Davis and Koningsbruggen, 2013). Although no serious adverse events have been reported among the 10,000 subjects studied to date (Fregni et al., 2014), at least one study has found that tDCS can simultaneously enhance one cognitive function while impairing another (Iuculano and Cohen Kadosh, 2013). A letter in *Nature* implored, "Unorthodox technologies and applications must not be allowed to distort the long-term validation of tDCS" (Bikson et al., 2013). Thus, there exist at least two groups—researchers and home users—who utilize a single technology in very different ways. Whereas researchers apply tDCS to subjects within the controlled realm of the laboratory in the context of experimental studies, home users apply tDCS to themselves, mostly in private settings, for cognitive enhancement or self-treatment (Wexler, 2015a).

Practices and Motivations of Home Users

Quantifying the demographics and prevalence of the home use of tDCS is no simple feat, as the most active forum where home users communicate—a Reddit.com forum (known as a "subreddit") dedicated to tDCS—is pseudonymous. Two recent studies, however, provide initial information about the practices and motivations of home users. One study consisted of content analyses of the postings to the subreddit, in-depth interviews, and an online questionnaire (Jwa, 2015), while the second study presented a preliminary sketch of the practices of home users, based on interviews and reviews of the subreddit, websites, blogs, and videos related to the home use of tDCS (Wexler, 2015a). Both studies found that home users were overwhelmingly male, with age ranging from late teens to 60s; 71% of survey respondents were in their 20s and 30s (Jwa, 2015). Both reports found the phenomenon to be global, although the majority of users seem to be concentrated in the United States and Canada. It should be noted, however, that both studies were limited in that they focused on the population of users that communicate online. Interestingly, a recent survey of researchers engaged in studying tDCS suggests that these professionals do not, for the most part, engage in the equivalent of home use of tDCS: by and large they do not use tDCS on themselves (Shirota et al., 2014).

How prevalent is the home use of tDCS? As of July 2015, there were approximately 7,500 "subscribers" to the tDCS subreddit, though "subscribing" only means that new posts to the forum will be displayed on an individual's Reddit.com homepage. Conversely, individuals may be home users without subscribing to the tDCS subreddit. Furthermore, as the subreddit was created in April 2011, many current subscribers may no longer be actively using tDCS. Thus, while the forum received 6,000 page hits per month on average in 2013 (Jwa, 2015), this number does not necessarily reflect active users. Perhaps the most revealing figure is the number of posts to the forum: by the end of 2013, the forum was averaging several original posts per day, with many more comments appended to each post (Jwa, 2015; Wexler, 2015a). Outside of the subreddit, it is possible to turn to other measures, such as the tens of thousands of views on YouTube videos related to the home use of tDCS. However, these figures and others represent aggregate numbers over time and do not differentiate between a bona fide home user and those merely curious about the technology.

In the survey of home users, 59% of respondents reported using tDCS for cognitive enhancement, for purposes such as improving attention, learning, working and long-term memory, and perception (Jwa, 2015). Eleven percent of individuals reported self-stimulating for treatment (most commonly for depression but also for attention deficit hyperactivity disorder, pain, obsessive compulsive disorder, and stroke), and 24% reported using tDCS for both purposes. On the subreddit, individuals have written about self-treating for anxiety disorder, seasonal affective disorder, and generalized anxiety disorder (Wexler, 2015a).

Some home users believe that tDCS may someday be used instead of drugs or even administered for suicide prevention. They seem to utilize tDCS almost exclusively on themselves (and very occasionally on significant others or close friends) but not on unknown subjects. In contrast to related movements, such as DIY biology and quantified self (wherein individuals meticulously track data about themselves, such as sleeping and eating habits), tDCS home users have not (yet) held large-scale meetings or public gatherings, though local meetings in "hackerspaces" have been reported. Thus, the home use of tDCS for some is simultaneously a private act, as stimulation is most often done in the seclusion of one's home, and public, as an individual's subreddit posts are openly visible.

Much of the conversation on the subreddit (and on websites and blogs) focuses on the construction or acquisition of a tDCS device (Jwa, 2015; Wexler, 2015a). Thirty-nine percent of survey respondents reported building a stimulation device (Jwa, 2015), and home users regularly post descriptions and diagrams of their self-built devices. There are frequent discussions about fuses, voltages, electrodes, resistors, diodes, transistors, and regulators on the subreddit (Wexler, 2015a). Despite the popularity of building a device in true DIY fashion, 48% of survey respondents reported purchasing a device (9% reported that they had both constructed and purchased a device). Of the devices that individuals purchased, most users reported purchasing the Foc.us headset, but others purchased a variety of device "kits" as well as iontophoresis devices, which can be repurposed for tDCS (Jwa, 2015). On the subreddit and other sites, users who purchase devices share reviews and discuss safety issues (Wexler, 2015a).

The overall conclusion is that when building or acquiring a device, the knowledge that home users draw upon is separate, for the most part, from that of the scientific community (Wexler, 2015a). However, when *using* the device, home users draw heavily upon scientific publications, particularly when considering whether a specific orientation of electrodes exists for their specific disorder or enhancement goal. Scientific review articles appear to be particularly appealing to home users insofar as they provide broad overviews of the medical conditions that have been successfully treated with tDCS as well as the cognitive functions that have been enhanced by it. Home users also make use of other resources geared toward professionals, such as a video tutorial on electrode positioning created by several tDCS researchers. Sometimes home users even produce derivative scientific work. For example, one home user compiled a document containing more than 400 abstracts about tDCS, and another, frustrated that information about montage placements was scattered across the internet, created a website (tdcsplacements.com) that featured stimulation diagrams in a clean, easy-to-browse format. Thus, home users transform existing scientific knowledge and diagrams into user-friendly indexes and guides geared toward their needs (Wexler, 2015a).

Both Jwa (2015) and Wexler (2015a) found that home users largely adhere to the current levels (1–2 milliamps) used in scientific tDCS studies but appear to experiment to a limited degree with duration and frequency of use. While many reported employing the duration most commonly used in scientific tDCS studies (20 minutes), some individuals reported stimulating for longer durations. While there is also no set scientific standard with regard to session frequency, most studies utilize several sessions of tDCS spread across days or weeks. The majority (61%) of survey respondents reported using tDCS for 6 months or less, but 21% reported using tDCS for "6 months–1 year," and the remainder (16%) reported using tDCS for more than 1 year (Jwa, 2015). An important caveat is that the survey question did not appear to differentiate between frequent and occasional users (i.e., those who reported using tDCS for 1 year could have used tDCS daily or just several times across that same time period).

When attempting to measure the effects of tDCS in the face of "*n*-of-1" experimental constraints, some users, particularly those interested in self-treating a mental disorder, rely on a subjective feeling of improvement (Wexler, 2015a). Other home users, particularly those interested in cognitive enhancement, take a more empirical approach to the enterprise and attempt to quantify their performance on cognitive tests (Wexler, 2015a). One of the most popular strategies is to track scores on open-source versions of dual n-back tests, performance measures often used in scientific studies that assess working memory (Jwa, 2015). Some attempt to control for potential confounding factors, such as the practice effect, but few individuals control for the placebo effect (Wexler, 2015a), even though it is an oft-discussed topic on the subreddit. Whether based upon empirical results or subjective impressions, home users do not universally report that tDCS achieves the aims they were hoping for. When assessing the perceived effects of tDCS, respondents reported success more often than failure, yet the single most common response was the midpoint on a scale whose anchors indicated "extremely successful" and "totally unsuccessful" (Jwa, 2015). Nonetheless, 92% of respondents reported that they would continue using tDCS (Jwa, 2015).

From Do-It-Yourself to Direct-to-Consumer

Although there are isolated mentions of DIY brain stimulation that date back to 2007, the home use of tDCS truly came into being in mid-2011, when a Yahoo group and the tDCS subreddit were formed (Wexler, 2015b). By early 2012, there were a number of blogs and sites dedicated to the home use of tDCS. Interestingly, the rise of the movement tracks the increase in scientific journal publications about tDCS: in 2011, the number of tDCS peer-reviewed articles doubled (to more than 130), and in 2012 there was the greatest quantitative increase in mentions of tDCS in the popular press. It is likely that the home-use movement built upon related movements that were well established by 2010, such as DIY biology (Delfanti, 2013; Meyer, 2013) and quantified self (Swan, 2013).

During the early days of DIY tDCS, most individuals built their devices from scratch, with the help of diagrams posted online and electronics assistance from other DIYers. In the spring of

2012, two undergraduates from the University of Michigan constructed a prototype of a tDCS device and set up a website on which they promised to sell it for $99 (GoFlow, 2012). The story went viral, with the initiative enthusiastically described with headlines such as "Buy a DIY Brain Supercharger for $100" (Vance, 2012) and "Transcranial direct current stimulation works, and you can try it at home" (Mims, 2012). Ultimately plans for the headset were abandoned, and the mailing list was quietly sold to another firm in the process of building a consumer tDCS device (Wexler, 2015b).

Around the same time, other consumer tDCS devices appeared on the market: Hong Kong–based TCT Technologies began selling a US$379 device, and several other websites offered more affordable tDCS device "kits."[2] The kits were geared to those who had knowledge of tDCS but lacked the necessary skills to build their own device from scratch. Some home users began purchasing and repurposing iontophoresis devices (typically used for drug delivery through a current), which legally require a prescription but in practice are widely available online.[3]

The Foc.us device, released in the summer of 2013, was arguably the first true direct-to-consumer tDCS device. With its sleek, ready-to-wear headset design, it looked more like a proper consumer product than a cobbled-together DIY device. The company's website, advertising campaign (featuring photos of an attractive woman wearing the device), and promised smartphone integration made it clear that the product was a step up from the kits sold by small-scale vendors. Though the Foc.us device was ostensibly marketed to gamers, its release thrust the direct-to-consumer tDCS movement into the spotlight, changing the tenor of public perception of tDCS (Cabrera and Reiner, 2015) and bringing the debate over regulation of cognitive enhancement devices to public attention (Murphy, 2013; Statt, 2013). Among the home-use community, the Foc.us device seemed to cause a major demographic shift (Jwa, 2015), as it opened up tDCS to those who neither had the technical savvy to build their own device or were not compelled to purchase device "kits" or repurpose iontophoresis devices.

Since 2014, Foc.us has released a second generation of products, and it currently has a headset specially designed for exercise. In 2014, two Silicon Valley start-ups announced that they were entering the consumer brain stimulation device market. In May 2014, Halo Neuroscience announced that it had received $1.5 million in venture capital funding and was developing "wearable technology that boosts brain function" (Halo Neuroscience Press Release, 2014). As a well-financed Silicon Valley company, it populated its board of directors with well-known names such as Reed Hundt, former chairman of the Federal Communications Commission (Halo Neuroscience, n.d.). In October 2014, Thync raised the bar further, announcing that it had raised $13 million in venture capital funding (Stone, 2014), and in June 2015, the company released a device that is controlled via smartphone and provides a form of noninvasive brain stimulation for mood-alteration purposes (either a "calm vibe" or an "energy vibe"). Thync reports that it has tested thousands of subjects, both on its own and in collaboration with tDCS researchers, and recently published a subset of its results in a peer-reviewed journal (Tyler et al., 2015). The existence of well-funded, highly connected companies with an eye on the consumer device market for noninvasive electrical brain stimulation suggests that what began as DIY brain stimulation is likely to be superseded by direct-to-consumer brain stimulation.

Regulation of Consumer Noninvasive Brain Stimulation Devices

In both the United States and Europe, products *intended* for use in the treatment or diagnosis of disease or other medical conditions are considered medical devices (Wexler, 2015b, Maslen et al., 2014). Historically, regulators have relied upon the content of the product's advertising and labeling to determine intended use. At the present time, some consumer noninvasive brain stimulation device manufacturers clearly state that their device has applications for the treatment of diseases, whereas for others, it is unclear whether the manufacturers make "implied" medical claims (Wexler, 2015b). Other consumer noninvasive brain stimulation devices are marketed for cognitive enhancement purposes only, and at least one device makes no claims at all. Interestingly, the most recent entrant in the field, the device marketed by Thync, is being marketed as a "lifestyle product" and, according to the company, on this basis has been exempted from medical device regulatory requirements by the FDA because its intended use is related to recreational purposes (Thync, n.d.).

The FDA has no official position on tDCS devices (FDA, 2012), nor has it formally taken action against any manufacturer, but that is not to say that there has been no attention to such matters. In 2013, a biomedical engineer from the FDA notified the California Department of Public Health (CDPH) that a California based-firm, TDCS Device Kit Inc., appeared to be unlawfully selling a device that made implied medical claims (Wexler, 2015b). In May 2013, the CDPH sent a notice of violation to the company for violating California's Sherman Food, Drug, and Cosmetic Law, as it is illegal to sell medical devices that have not been approved by the FDA (Wexler, 2015b). A later press release from the CDPH noted that the company was voluntarily issuing a recall of its devices (California Department of Public Health, 2013). Although the CDPH took action after receiving an email from the FDA biomedical engineer, it should be noted that the FDA engineer's email is not considered representative of the FDA's formal position. Thus, while the FDA officially has no formal position on tDCS devices, it is hardly unaware of the situation, as evidenced both by the FDA engineer's actions and even more so by comments made by the chief of the neurostimulation devices branch at a recent Institute of Medicine workshop (Institute of Medicine, 2015). This view is further reinforced by the fact that the FDA recently held a public workshop on noninvasive brain stimulation medical devices (FDA, n.d.), which it defined as "medical devices that are intended to improve, affect, or otherwise modify the cognitive function of a normal individual (i.e., without a treatment objective)."

Because of the patchwork of marketing strategies and the dearth of enforcement action, it has been suggested that there is a "regulatory gap" for consumer cognitive-enhancement devices (Dubljević et al., 2014). Some have proposed extending medical device legislation, at least in the European Union, to cover such devices (Maslen et al., 2013). Others have considered the appropriate "level" of regulation that might be applied to such devices (Dubljević, 2014). However, the lack of enforcement action should not be conflated with the lack of regulation (Wexler, 2015b), as there exists a comprehensive regulatory framework for both medical devices and consumer products. Indeed, the Federal Trade Commission (FTC) has recently taken enforcement action against a computer game manufacturer (FTC, 2015a) and a dietary supplement manufacturer (FTC, 2015b) that made unsubstantiated claims related to cognitive enhancement, and there is no reason to suspect that it will not act in similar fashion with tDCS device manufacturers. Some scholars have pointed out that focusing on regulatory enforcement might be impractical or infeasible (Jwa, 2015; Wexler, 2015b) and instead have supported the "open engagement" approach to the DIY community first proposed by Fitz and Reiner (2013), which favors communication and education, as opposed to strict regulation that might instead serve to increase underground use of home-made devices.

The Ethical Landscape of the Home Use of tDCS

The ethical landscape of the home use of tDCS is in many ways similar to the well-developed literature on the use of pharmacological agents for cognitive enhancement (Farah et al., 2004;

Greely et al., 2008; Fitz et al., 2014). The cardinal concerns of safety, peer pressure, distributive justice, and authenticity all apply (Hamilton et al., 2011; Cohen Kadosh et al., 2012; Levy and Savulescu, 2014; Fitz and Reiner, 2013), but with home use as the primary focus, some differences are worthy of mention.

Safety

The primary issue that has been debated to date relates to the question of whether tDCS is "safe." While no serious adverse events have been reported, short-term side effects such as headache, tingling, discomfort, and skin redness are common (Bikson et al., 2009), and home users report experiencing some of these same effects (Jwa, 2015). A different perspective on safety is the worry that in addition to these mild and relatively obvious side effects, there may be occult effects on cognitive function itself (Fitz and Reiner, 2013). Indeed, evidence exists demonstrating that the gains achieved by using tDCS to enhance one cognitive function may impair another cognitive function (Iuculano and Cohen Kadosh, 2013). Alternatively, the effects of tDCS may depend on individual traits, enhancing for some and impairing for others. For example, one study found that tDCS enhanced reaction time on arithmetic tests for those with high mathematics anxiety but impaired reaction time for those with low mathematics anxiety (Sarkar et al., 2014). There is every reason to suspect that home users are subject to these same phenomena.

The good news is that home users seem to have taken an active role in monitoring and discussing safety. In line with the general ethos of other DIY movements—experiment, report, and share—safety warnings are regularly shared in comments to online postings (Jwa, 2015). Indeed, despite worries about tDCS home users damaging themselves (see, e.g., Maslen et al., 2014a), for the most part, home users appear to be more thoughtful than reckless and regularly concerned about their own safety (Jwa, 2015; Wexler, 2015a). The moderator of the Reddit forum, for example, solicited reviews and safety reports from users of the Foc.us device after it first came out, in what seems to be the only attempt to quantify the safety of a consumer tDCS device (PSA: Potential Safety Issues with the Foc.us, 2014).

A final set of safety considerations relates to the use of tDCS in children. It has been suggested that tDCS may be of particular utility in overcoming developmental disorders, as these are among the most disabling of maladies (Krause and Cohen Kadosh, 2013). In response, several commentators have urged caution (Reiner, 2013; Davis, 2014), and others have suggested that in particular when used for enhancement (as opposed to therapy), tDCS use should be delayed until adolescents have sufficient autonomy that they are able to make the decision for themselves (Maslen et al., 2014b).

The three remaining cardinal concerns—authenticity, peer pressure, and distributive justice—have garnered less attention than worries over safety. We briefly review these issues in what follows.

Authenticity

The debate over authenticity of achievement following cognitive enhancement has a long history. The essence of the debate is that using enhancements represents shortcuts to success and is therefore morally suspect (Schermer, 2008). A key argument has been that the absence of hard work debases achievement, a form of pharmacological Calvinism for the modern era (Klerman, 1972; Parens, 2013). Because enhancing through tDCS generally requires not just stimulation but also training on a task, some have argued that the introduction of tDCS as a cognitive enhancer effectively reduces the authenticity concern (Cohen Kadosh et al., 2012). Closer inspection reveals that this argument falls flat when one realizes that just as with tDCS, pharmacological cognitive enhancers are not magic bullets, and when they are used for such objectives, studying (or other forms of training) is still required. Moreover, in the context of home use of tDCS for enhancement purposes, the argument may not matter in any case: empirical data demonstrate that while the public is fully cognizant of the key features of the authenticity concern, diminished authenticity does not fully translate into diminished worthiness (Fitz et al., 2014).

Peer Pressure

The use of tDCS is not yet sufficiently widespread for *bona fide* peer pressure to have taken hold. But in a world in which we are buffeted by articles extolling the need to raise the perfect child, to have the perfect body, to be the best that we can be (and better), the societal pressure to enhance our brains is nearly palpable. Even a brief perusal of the current crop of advertising for home use of tDCS devices reveals this to be the essence of the marketing strategy. Thus the advertisements promise that these devices will make you calm or energized, improve your gaming or your workout regimen, all with an undercurrent that it is you, the consumer, who is responsible for managing your well-being. And while a modicum of responsibility for our actions is healthy and perhaps even welcome, at some point it can transform into what Saskia Nagel has characterized as the burden of self-determination (Nagel, 2010)—the notion that we are subject to societal pressure to adhere to unrealistic standards of achievement.

Distributive Justice

Because the cost of the devices—whether built by DIYers or purchased for home use—is relatively modest (the upper bounds being comparable to an inexpensive smartphone), not only are concerns about distributive justice mitigated, but there is an opportunity to use the devices to benefit the less well off in society. The only ongoing cost is the minimal energy required to power the device and the replacement of worn-out electrodes. Moreover, the same device can be used by different users, further driving down cost. As a result, it has been suggested that the affordability of tDCS for home use may favor its adoption in small medicine initiatives in developing countries (Fitz and Reiner, 2013).

As tDCS moves from its DIY roots to a maturing direct-to-consumer mode, new questions arise. The most important of these is whether new safety concerns will emerge if the technology achieves widespread adoption. As with pharmaceuticals, postmarketing surveillance is the key, irrespective of whether devices are being sold within or outside of the jurisdiction of the FDA. Given that tDCS products marketed for recreational purposes may be exempt from medical device regulation, it is unclear who will shoulder the burden of postmarket surveillance (i.e., other regulatory authorities, device manufacturers, or third parties). Other questions that arise from the transition to direct-to-consumer devices include the responsibility of manufacturers to represent their product accurately to the public and to ensure that consumers have clear guidelines as to how to use the device as safely as possible.

Looking Ahead

When DIY tDCS first burst upon the scene, many commentators opined that we might be on the cusp of an explosion in the use of this technology by home users (Hamilton et al., 2011;

Fitz and Reiner, 2013). While the technology has been embraced by some, the evidence that has accrued to date does not demonstrate widespread uptake (Jwa, 2015). Overall, it seems that the worries about an onrushing wave of DIY tDCS use—and calls for regulation—may have been overstated (Fitz and Reiner, 2013; N*ature* Editorial, 2013; Maslen et al., 2014). Indeed, one analysis of the home user community concluded that "the DIY use of tDCS is not currently widespread, that it does not seem to pose an imminent risk or danger to the public, and there seems to be only a remote possibility of a dramatic increase of DIY use of tDCS in the near future" (Jwa, 2015, 25).

There are several possible explanations for why the home use of tDCS has not undergone broad adoption by the general population. Perhaps only a small subset of individuals is sufficiently motivated to experiment with electrical brain stimulation devices that have not undergone review by regulatory authorities. As with any novel technology, home users may represent a group of "early adopters," and it is possible that there has not been enough time (or technological refinement) for tDCS to gain mainstream acceptance. Indeed, one study of the comments on online articles related to tDCS found that although public misunderstanding of the technology has diminished in the years following the release of the Foc.us device, there is still a significant degree of confusion surrounding tDCS (Cabrera and Reiner, 2015). In line with such thinking, people may be skeptical of either the efficacy or safety involved in home use of tDCS. It is also worth observing that while DIY movements themselves do not generally spread to the mainstream public, the commercialization of DIY techniques into consumer-friendly devices often results in greater public uptake. For example, though the quantified self movement began in mid-2008 (Swan, 2009), the commercialization of self-tracking tools (such as Fitbit and other wearable devices) has brought these technologies to the general population.

Indeed, the advent of consumer tDCS devices marketed via the direct-to-consumer route—a phenomenon that is just gaining steam—may alter the trajectory of uptake of tDCS. However, how vigorously consumers embrace this technology remains to be seen. Two recent studies have examined the efficacy of consumer devices: the first found that subjects who received stimulation with a Foc.us device performed significantly worse on an accuracy component of a working-memory task than subjects who received sham stimulation (Steenbergen et al., 2015). The second study, which was conducted by Thync on its own device, found that subjects who received stimulation reported reduced levels of stress and anxiety as compared to those who received sham stimulation, and their physiological measures of stress (such as heart rate variability and galvanic skin response) were also significantly lower (Tyler et al., 2015). It should be noted, however, that whether or not the technology works from a scientific perspective may be less relevant than how consumers *perceive* the efficacy of consumer-grade tDCS. Indeed, as described earlier, some individuals view a subjective sense of self-improvement as evidence of the device's effectiveness (Wexler, 2015a).

One notable feature of tDCS is that its efficacy for cognitive enhancement—at home or in the laboratory—seems to depend on concurrent training on a cognitive task. That is, tDCS for cognitive enhancement is not a "magic pill" but rather requires the individual to "train" on cognitive tasks while undergoing stimulation. Thus it is possible that the additional effort required to "train" may limit its uptake by the general public. There are instances, however, when training is not required: for example, tDCS used to treat depression has been shown to be effective without concurrent training (Brunoni et al., 2013). Thus, while the training effort may present a barrier for uptake in certain circumstances, it may not present a barrier in others.

In the preceding paragraphs, we have alluded to the modest gains that have been achieved with tDCS to date, but there is no reason to suspect that this state of affairs will hold in the future. There is considerable interest in modifying the technology in a variety of ways—with alternating-current waveforms, combining it with EEG monitoring to provide current at just the right moment, and more (Voss et al., 2014; Chaieb et al., 2011; Lustenberger et al., 2015)—and some of these new techniques may result in more substantial gains than have been achieved to date.

In many ways, we are at a crossroads in the home use of tDCS. Although two studies on consumer tDCS devices have been published to date, only one (Steenbergen et al., 2015) was conducted by a third party without a conflict of interest. We recommend that efforts on the part of academics to study both the short- and long-term effects of consumer tDCS devices on cognitive function be increased; indeed, neuroscientists and neuroethicists may have an important role to play in monitoring the consumer neurotechnology industry. In tandem, we suggest the continuation of sociological studies on home users so that a comprehensive picture—both of the cognitive effects of the devices themselves and of their real-world usage practices—may be obtained.

The most important determinant of the future consumer tDCS market will likely be decisions from regulatory authorities. Even if the FDA elects not to enforce regulations against consumer tDCS devices, other regulatory agencies with jurisdiction over these products may take action. Indeed, the FTC's recent complaint against Lumos Labs (the makers of the brain-training program Lumosity) for making unsubstantiated cognitive-enhancement claims (FTC, 2016) has signaled that it is paying close attention to direct-to-consumer cognitive-enhancement products. A strict approach on the part of regulatory authorities may result in a gradual decline of consumer tDCS devices, whereas a more lax one may lead to the proliferation of such devices. Still, whether the technology achieves widespread adoption or becomes a niche product, whether it finds its best use in clinical or nonclinical settings, and whether it produces robust effects are all questions that remain to be answered.

Notes

1 Although we use the term "tDCS" throughout this chapter, many of our comments apply to the entire range of electrical brain stimulation devices.
2 See TCT Technologies, www.trans-cranial.com/; note that the company is currently conducting business as TCT Research Limited. See also www.tdcs-kit.com, and www.tDCSdevicekit.com, accessed between December 2012 and April 2013, archived versions available at http://web.archive.org.
3 See, e.g., www.amazon.com/DSS-Chattanooga-Ionto/dp/B00FC2SRMY and www.isokineticsinc.com.

Further Reading

Fitz, N.S. and Reiner, P.B. (2014) "The Perils of Using Electrical Stimulation to Change Human Brains". In R.C. Cohen Kadosh (Ed.). *The Stimulated Brain*. San Diego: Academic Press, pp. 61–83.

Fitz, N.S. and Reiner, P.B. (2015) "The Challenge of Crafting Policy for Do-It-Yourself Brain Stimulation". *Journal of Medical Ethics* 41(5), 410–412.

Jwa, A. (2015) "Early Adopters of the Magical Thinking Cap: A Study on Do-It-Yourself (DIY) Transcranial Direct Current Stimulation (tDCS) User Community". *Journal of Law and the Biosciences* 2(2), 292–335. doi:10.1093/jlb/lsv017

Wexler, A. (2015a) "The Practices of the Do-It-Yourself Brain Stimulation Community: Implications for Regulatory Proposals and Ethical Discussions". *Journal of Medical Ethics* 42(4), 211–215. doi:10.1136/medethics-2015–102704

Wexler, A. (2015b) "A Pragmatic Analysis of the Regulation of Consumer Transcranial Direct Current Stimulation (tDCS) Devices in the United States". *Journal of Law and the Biosciences* 2(3), 669–696. doi: 10.1093/jlb/lsv039

References

Bikson, M., Bestmann, S., and Edwards, D. (2013) Neuroscience: Transcranial devices are not playthings. *Nature* 501(7466): p. 167.

Bikson, M., Datta, A. and Elwassif, M. (2009) Establishing safety limits for transcranial direct current stimulation. *Clinical Neurophysiology* 120(6): pp. 1033–1034.

Brunoni, A.R., Valiengo, L., Baccaro, A., Zanão, T.A., de Oliveira, J.F., Goulart, A., Boggio, P.S., Lotufo, P.A., Benseñor, I.M. and Fregni, F. (2013) The sertraline vs electrical current therapy for treating depression clinical study: Results from a factorial, randomized, controlled trial. *JAMA Psychiatry* 70(4): pp. 383–391.

Cabrera, L.Y., and Reiner, P.B. (2015) Understanding public (mis)understanding of tDCS for enhancement. *Frontiers in Integrative Neuroscience.* Available at: http://dx.doi.org/10.3389/fnint.2015.00030.

California Department of Public Health. (2013) CDPH Warns consumers not to use TDCS Home device kit, 28 June. Available at: www.cdph.ca.gov/Pages/NR13-029.aspx.

Chaieb, L., Antal, A. and Paulus, W. (2011) Transcranial alternating current stimulation in the low kHz range increases motor cortex excitability. *Restorative Neurology and Neuroscience* 29(3): pp. 167–175.

Chi, R.P., Snyder, A.W. (2012) Brain stimulation enables the solution of an inherently difficult problem. *Neuroscience Letters* 515(2): pp. 121–124.

Coffman, B.A., Clark, V.P., and Parasuraman, R. (2014) Battery powered thought: Enhancement of attention, learning, and memory in healthy adults using transcranial direct current stimulation. *Neuroimage* 85(3): pp. 895–908.

Cohen Kadosh, R., Levy, N., O'Shea, J., Shea, N., and Savulescu, J. (2012) The neuroethics of non-invasive brain stimulation. *Current Biology* 22(4): pp. R108–R111.

Davis, N.J. (2014) Transcranial stimulation of the developing brain: A plea for extreme caution. *Frontiers in Human Neuroscience.* doi:10.3389/fnhum.2014.00600

Davis, N.J., and van Koningsbruggen, M.G. (2013) "Non-invasive" brain stimulation is not non-invasive. *Frontiers in Systems Neuroscience.* Available at: http://dx.doi.org/10.3389/fnsys.2013.00076

Delfanti,. A. (2013) *Biohackers: The Politics of Open Science.* London: Pluto Press.

Dubljević, V. (2014) Neurostimulation devices for cognitive enhancement: Toward a comprehensive regulatory framework. *Neuroethics.* doi:10.1007/s12152-014-9225-0.

Dubljević, V., Saigle, V., and Racine, E. (2014) The rising tide of tDCS in the media and academic literature. *Neuron* 82(4): pp. 731–736.

Editorial *Nature.* (2013) Brain Blast: DIY attempts at electrical brain stimulation to improve cognition are to get easier. *Nature* 498(7454): pp. 271–272.

Falcone, B., Coffman, B.A., Clark, V.P., and Parasuraman, R. (2012) Transcranial direct current stimulation augments perceptual sensitivity and 24-Hour retention in a complex threat detection task. *PLoS One* 7(4): p. e34993.

Farah, M.J., Illes, J., Cook-Deegan, R.M., Gardner, H., Kandel, E.R., King, P., ...Wolpe, P.R. (2004) Neurocognitive enhancement: What can we do and what should we do? *Nature Reviews Neuroscience* 5(5): pp. 421–425.

Federal Trade Commission (FTC) (2015a) *Makers of Jungle Rangers Computer Game for Kids Settle FTC Charges That They Deceived Consumers with Baseless "Brain Training" Claims.* Available at www.ftc.gov/news-events/press-releases/2015/01/makers-jungle-rangers-computer-game-kids-settle-ftc-charges-they [Accessed 29 March 2017].

Federal Trade Commission (FTC) (2015b) *Supplement Marketers Will Relinquish $1.4 Million to Settle FTC Deceptive Advertising Charges.* Available at: www.ftc.gov/news-events/press-releases/2015/07/supplement-marketers-will-relinquish-14-million-settle-ftc [Accessed 29 March 2017].

Federal Trade Commission (FTC). (2016) *Lumosity to pay $2 million to settle FTC Deceptive advertising charges for its "brain training" program*, 5 January. Available at: www.ftc.gov/news-events/press-releases/2016/01/lumosity-pay-2-million-settle-ftc-deceptive-advertising-charges [Accessed 16 Jan. 2016].

Fitz, N.S., and Reiner, P.B. (2013) The challenge of crafting policy for do-it-yourself brain stimulation. *Journal of Medical Ethics.* doi:10.1136/medethics-2013-101458. Published in print 2015, 41(5): pp. 410–412.

Fitz, N.S., Nadler, R., Manogaran, P., Chong, E.W.J., and Reiner, P.B. (2014) Public attitudes toward cognitive enhancement. *Neuroethics* 7(2): pp. 173–188.

Fitz, N.S., and Reiner, P.B. (2014) The perils of using electrical stimulation to change human brains. In R.C. Cohen Kadosh (Ed.). *The Stimulated Brain.* San Diego: Academic Press, pp. 61–83.

Food and Drug Administration (FDA). (2012) *Executive Summary,* prepared for the February 10, 2012, meeting of the Neurologic Devices Panel. Available at: www.fda.gov/downloads/AdvisoryCommit tees/CommitteesMeetingMaterials/MedicalDevices/MedicalDevicesAdvisoryCommittee/Neurologi calDevicesPanel/UCM290787.pdf.

———. (n.d.) *Public Workshop—Neurodiagnostics and Non-Invasive Brain Stimulation Medical Devices Workshop, November 19–20, 2015.* Available at: www.fda.gov/MedicalDevices/NewsEvents/WorkshopsConfer ences/ucm458018.htm [Accessed 25 Aug. 2015].

Fregni, F., Boggio, P.S., Nitsche, M., Bermpohl, F., Antal, A., Feredoes, E., . . . Pascual-Leone, A. (2005) Anodal transcranial direct current stimulation of prefrontal cortex enhances working memory. *Experi mental Brain Research* 166(1): pp. 23–30.

Fregni, F., Nitsche, M.A., Loo, C.K., Brunoni, A.R., Marangolo, P., Leite, J., . . . Bikson, M. (2014) Regulatory considerations for the clinical and research use of Transcranial Direct Current Stimulation (tDCS): Review and recommendations from an expert panel. *Clinical Research and Regulatory Affairs* 32(1): pp. 22–35.

GoFlow. (2012). Available at: www.flowstateengaged.com. Archive. Available at: http://web.archive.org/ web/20120314201106

Greely, H.T., Sahakian, B., Harris, J., Kessler, R.C., Gazzaniga, M.S., Campbell, P., and Farah, M. (2008) Towards responsible use of cognitive-enhancing drugs by the healthy. *Nature* 456(7223): pp. 702–705.

Halo Neuroscience—Press Release. (2014). 28 May. Available at: http://haloneuro.com/press/ [Accessed 10 July 2015].

———. (n.d.) *About Us* [Online]. Available at: http://haloneuro.com/#section3 [Accessed 10 July 2015].

Hamilton, R., Messing, S., and Chatterjee, A. (2011) Rethinking the thinking cap: Ethics of neural enhance ment using noninvasive brain stimulation. *Neurology* 76(2): pp. 187–193.

Horvath, J.C., Forte, J.D., and Carter, O. (2015a) Quantitative review finds no evidence of cognitive effects in healthy populations from single-session Transcranial Direct Current Stimulation (tDCS). *Brain stimu lation* 8: pp. 535–550.

———. (2015b) Evidence that Transcranial Direct Current Stimulation (tDCS) generates little-to-no reli able neurophysiologic effect beyond MEP amplitude modulation in healthy human subjects: A system atic review. *Neuropsychologia* 66: pp. 213–236.

Institute of Medicine. (2015) Non-invasive neuromodulation of the central nervous system: Opportunities and challenges: Workshop summary, Chapter 8: Regulatory issues,' pp. 57–64. Available at: http://iom. nationalacademies.org/Reports/2015/Non-Invasive-Neuromodulation-of-the-Central-Nervous-System.aspx [Accessed 30 July 2015].

Iuculano, T., and Cohen Kadosh, R. (2013) The mental cost of cognitive enhancement. *Journal of Neurosci ence* 33(10): pp. 4482–4486.

Jwa, A. (2015) Early adopters of the magical thinking cap: A study on Do-It-Yourself (DIY) Transcranial Direct Current Stimulation (tDCS) user community. *Journal of Law and the Biosciences* 2(2): pp. 292–335. doi:10.1093/jlb/lsv017

Klerman, G.L. (1972) Psychotropic hedonism vs. pharmacological Calvinism. *Hastings Center Report* 2(4): pp. 1–3.

Knotkova, H., Greenberg, A., Leuschner, Z., Soto, E., and Cruciani, R.A. (2013) Evaluation of outcomes from Transcranial Direct Current Stimulation (tDCS) for the treatment of chronic pain. *Clinical Neuro physiology* 124(10): pp. e125–e126.

Krause, B., and Cohen Kadosh, R. (2013) Can transcranial electrical stimulation improve learning difficul ties in atypical brain development? A future possibility for cognitive training. *Developmental Cognitive Neuroscience* 6: pp. 176–194.

Kuo, M.F., Paulus, W., and Nitsche, M.A. (2014) Therapeutic effects of non-invasive brain stimulation with direct currents (tDCS) in neuropsychiatric diseases. *Neuroimage* 85(3): pp. 948–960.

Levy, N., and Savulescu, J. (2014) The neuroethics of transcranial electrical stimulation. In R.C. Cohen Kadosh (Ed.). *The Stimulated Brain.* San Diego: Academic Press, pp. 499–521.

Lustenberger, C., Boyle, M.R., Foulser, A.A., Mellin, J.M. and Fröhlich, F. (2015) Functional role of frontal alpha oscillations in creativity. *Cortex* 67: pp. 74–82.

Maslen, H., Douglas, T., Cohen Kadosh, R., Levy, N., and Savulescu, J. (2013) Do-it-yourself brain stimulation: A regulatory model. *Journal of Medical Ethics.* doi:10.1136/medethics-2013–101692. Published in print (2015), 41(5): pp. 413–414.

————. (2014) The regulation of cognitive enhancement devices: Extending the medical model. *Journal of Law and the Biosciences* 1(1): pp. 68–93.

Maslen, H., Earp, B.D., Cohen Kadosh, R., and Savulescu, J. (2014) Brain stimulation for treatment and enhancement in children: An ethical analysis. *Frontiers in Human Neuroscience.* Available at: http://dx.doi.org/10.3389/fnhum.2014.00953

Meyer, M. (2013) Domesticating and democratizing science: A geography of do-it-yourself biology. *Journal of Material Culture* 18(2): pp. 117–134.

Mims, C. (2012) DIY Kit Overclocks Your Brain With Direct Current *MIT Technology Review*, 8 March. Available at: www.technologyreview.com/view/427177/diy-kit-overclocks-your-brain-with-direct-current/ [Accessed 10 July 2015].

Murphy, K. (2013) Jump-Starter Kits for the Mind. *New York Times* 28 October. Available at: www.nytimes.com/2013/10/29/science/jump-starter-kits-for-the-mind.html [Accessed 15 July 2015].

Nagel, S.K. (2010) Too much of a good thing? Enhancement and the burden of self-determination. *Neuroethics* 3(2): pp. 109–119.

Nelson, J.T., McKinley, R.A., Golob, E.J., Warm, J.S., and Parasuraman, R. (2014) Enhancing vigilance in operators with prefrontal cortex Transcranial Direct Current Stimulation (tDCS). *Neuroimage* 85: pp. 909–917.

Nitsche, M., and Paulus, W. (2000) Excitability changes induced in the human motor cortex by weak transcranial direct current stimulation. *Journal of Physiology* 527(3): pp. 633–639.

Parens, E. (2013) On good and bad forms of medicalization. *Bioethics* 27(1): pp. 28–35.

PSA: Potential safety issues with the foc.us. (2014). Available at: www.reddit.com/r/tDCS/comments/1y5otr/psa_potential_safety_issues_with_the_focus/ [Accessed 30 July 2015].

Reiner, P.B. (2013) Comment on "Can transcranial electrical stimulation improve learning difficulties in atypical brain development? A future possibility for cognitive training" by Krause and Cohen Kadosh. *Developmental Cognitive Neuroscience* 6: pp. 195–196.

Reis, J., Schambra, H.M., Cohen, L.G., Buch, E.R., Fritsch, B., Zarahn, E., . . . Krakauer, J.W. (2009) Non-invasive cortical stimulation enhances motor skill acquisition over multiple days through an effect on consolidation. *Proceedings of the National Academy of Sciences* 106(5): pp. 1590–1595.

Sarkar, A., Dowker, A. and Kadosh, R.C. (2014) Cognitive enhancement or cognitive cost: trait-specific outcomes of brain stimulation in the case of mathematics anxiety. *Journal of Neuroscience* 34(50): pp. 16605–16610.

Schambra, H.M., Bikson, M., Wager, T.D., DosSantos, M.F., and DaSilva, A.F. (2014) It's all in your head: Reinforcing the placebo response with tDCS. *Brain Stimulation* 7(4): pp. 623–624.

Schermer, M. (2008) Enhancements, easy shortcuts, and the richness of human activities. *Bioethics* 22(7): pp. 355–363.

Shiozawa, P., Fregni, F., Benseñor, I.M., Lotufo, P.A., Berlim, M.T., . . . Brunoni, A.R. (2014) Transcranial direct current stimulation for major depression: An updated systematic review and meta-analysis. *International Journal of Neuropsychopharmacology* 17(9): pp. 1443–1452.

Shirota, Y., Hewitt, M., and Paulus, W. (2014) Neuroscientists do not use non-invasive brain stimulation on themselves for neural enhancement. *Brain Stimulation* 4(7): pp. 618–619.

Statt, N. (2013) When wearable tech makes you smarter—By zapping your brain. *CNET* 9, August. Available at: http://news.cnet.com/8301-11386_3-57597116-76/when-wearable-tech-makes-you-smarter-by-zapping-your-brain/. [Accessed 15 July 2015].

Steenbergen, L., Sellaro, R., Hommel, B., Lindenberger, U., Kühn, S., and Colzato, L.S. (2015) "Unfocus" on focus: Commercial tDCS headset impairs working memory. *Experimental Brain Research.* doi:10.1007/s00221-015-4391-9

Stone, B. (2014) Thync lets you give your mind a jolt. *Bloomberg Business* 8 October. Available at: www.bloomberg.com/bw/articles/2014-10-08/thync-raises-13-million-for-its-brain-stimulating-electrodes [Accessed 15 July 2015].

Swan, M. (2009) Emerging patient-driven health care models: An examination of health social networks, consumer personalized medicine and quantified self-tracking Melanie Swan. *International Journal of Environmental Research and Public Health* 6(2): pp. 492–525.

Swan, M. (2013) The quantified self: Fundamental disruption in big data science and biological discovery. *Big Data* 1(2): pp. 85–99.

Thync Safety. (n.d.) Available at: www.thync.com/science-and-technology [Accessed 15 July 2015].

Tyler, W.J., Boasso, A.M., Mortimore, H.M., Silva, R.S., Charlesworth, J.D., Marlin, M.A., . . . Pal, S.K. (2015) Transdermal neuromodulation of noradrenergic activity suppresses psychophysiological and biochemical stress responses in humans. *Scientific Reports* 5, Article 13865. doi:10.1038/srep13865.

Vance, A. (2012) Buy a DIY brain supercharger for $100. *Bloomberg BusinessWeek* 21 March. Available at: www.businessweek.com/articles/2012-03-21/buy-a-diy-brain-super-charger-for-100

Voss, U., Holzmann, R., Hobson, A., Paulus, W., Koppehele-Gossel, J., Klimke, A. and Nitsche, M.A. (2014) Induction of self awareness in dreams through frontal low current stimulation of gamma activity. *Nature Neuroscience* 17(6): pp. 810–812.

Wexler, A. (2015a) The practices of the do-it-yourself brain stimulation community: Implications for regulatory proposals and ethical discussions. *Journal of Medical Ethics*. doi:10.1136/medethics-2015–102704. published in print 2016, 42(4): pp. 211–215.

———. (2015b) A pragmatic analysis of the regulation of consumer Transcranial Direct Current Stimulation (tDCS) devices in the United States. *Journal of Law and the Biosciences* 2(3): pp. 669–696. doi:10.1093/jlb/lsv039

PART III

The Neuroscience of Ethics

Neuroscience is shedding light on several key questions and controversies that have long been debated in philosophy. In ethics, neuroscientific methods, as well as methodologies from the social sciences, cognitive psychology, and related fields, are being utilized to examine moral reasoning and decision-making by, for example, looking at what our brains actually do while we consider ethical dilemmas or how brain activation patterns correlate with our responses to classical ethical thought experiments. While other philosophical questions are often traditionally within the domain of neurophilosophy, including questions about free will and responsibility, personal identity, and the nature of consciousness, there is overlap with neuroethics, as, for example, metaphysical concerns about free will inform questions about criminal responsibility, while our understanding of consciousness and personal identity can inform our deliberations about end-of-life issues.

Banja's chapter "Moral Reasoning" provides an overview of philosophical conceptions of human moral reasoning and recent philosophical and neuroethical insights on its nature. In "Informing Ethical Decision Making," Feltz and Cokely look at ethical decision making and bias through a cognitive neuroscience lens.

Free will is a classic problem in metaphysics, with implications that bridge ethics and philosophies of religion and law. Glannon considers the potential for restoring or enhancing (or undermining) free will through the use of therapeutic brain implants, including deep brain stimulation, brain–computer interfaces, and hippocampal prosthetics that can modulate neural dysfunction or bypass and compensate for brain injury. Northoff and Wagner, in "Personal Identity and Brain Identity," sketch a novel theory of personal identity and the brain. They point to future research directions that could help explicate the brain's role in personal identity. In "Values, Empathy, and the Brain," Powell and Derbyshire argue that, while the brain is necessary for an individual to empathize and to hold values, the brain is not sufficient to generate values, which are, instead, socially negotiated within a community of minds. Scheutz and Malle conclude the section with "Moral Robots," a chapter that explores whether and how a robot might be moral. Schneider's companion box on "Artificial Intelligence, Consciousness, and Moral Status" considers thorny ethical issues related to AI and robot consciousness.

19

MORAL REASONING

John D. Banja

Some Introductory Remarks about Reasoning

Evolutionary psychologists and brain scientists understand reasoning as an exquisitely adaptive, neuroevolved, instrumental capacity that enables reasoners to acquire information they can use to navigate their survival challenges, and shape their environments to accommodate their desires and well-being (Cosmides and Tooby, 2004; Damasio, 2003). Consequently, there is a plethora of reasoning types or instrumental strategies given the particularized and contextual complexities of our survival and welfare encounters. Philosophers, on the other hand, have treated reasoning and reasons in various ways, such as Jürgen Habermas (1995) categorizing reasons into three groups: cognitive-instrumental, which is the preference of the empirical sciences; moral-practical, which is the preference of morality and politics; and aesthetic reason, which is interested in novel ways of seeing the world. T.S. Scanlon (1998) pithily characterized reasons as "judgment sensitive attitudes," that is, as beliefs, thoughts, or ideas that influence judgment formation in favor of or against something.

A traditional characterization of reasoning is the one Aristotle (1970a) provided in his *Prior Analytics*, which understands reasoning as a process for deducing, inferring, or arriving at (propositional or symbolic) conclusions derived from premises or evidential sources. One accomplishes this kind of reasoning if his or her thinking adheres to the laws of logic, is true to facts, and is fair to competing perspectives, beliefs, and conceptual justifications.

An alternative (but still nonmoral) depiction of reasoning process is the one discussed by present-day cognitive psychologists like Jonathan Haidt (2001). In its most basic form, this kind of "reasoning" is largely intuitive and nondiscursive, makes enormous use of the brain's affective systems, and occurs whenever sensory inputs and environmental challenges require quick responses. Because it is usually highly reliable, this "System 1" reasoning is immensely useful in relieving us of the need to laboriously perform the kinds of intellectual processing typical of "System 2" reasoning. Cognitive psychologists believe that humans utilize System 1 reasoning at least 95 percent of the time, while its neuroevolutionary roots look to limbic brain structures that significantly predate the development of higher cortical structures and their enabling mental functions (Cosmides and Tooby, 2004; Haidt, 2001). Nevertheless, because System 1 reasoning is typically nonanalytical, spontaneous, and impulsive, it will often benefit from the correctives that System 2 reasoning might (but does not always) offer, especially when one is confronted by a complex situation requiring careful thinking (Kahneman, 2011). Typically, situations calling for sophisticated or elaborate forms of reasoning will witness both System 1 and 2 types of reflection operating simultaneously (while some scholars believe that System 2 reasoning depends on System 1's intuitively driven vetting of System 2's inferential processing; Mercier and Sperber, 2011).

A striking feature of System 2 reasoning that explicitly speaks to moral reasoning is the idea that "System 2 is activated when an event is detected that violates the model of the world that System 1 maintains" (Kahneman, 2011, 24). In other words, as long as the human organism understands itself to be in an exquisitely familiar and safe environment, it will feel little need to advert to System 2 reasoning. System 2 moral reasoning may well activate, however, in instances of situational unfamiliarity, especially involving the resolution of problems involving human rights and duties, how harms and benefits should be socially distributed, and the implementation of concepts like justice and fairness. As such, moral reasoning is a distinctive type of System 2 mentation, whose nature we'll now explore.

The Distinctiveness of Moral Reasoning

A tautological response to what is distinctive about moral reasoning is that it deals with moral rather than nonmoral matters. While Henry Richardson (2013) has characterized moral reasoning as "responsible thinking about what one is to do" (4), Paxton and Greene (2010) have characterized moral reasoning as a "[c]onscious mental activity through which one evaluates a moral judgment for its (in)consistencies with other moral commitments, where these commitments are to one or more moral principles and (in some cases) particular moral judgments" (6). According to this characterization, moral reasoning involves evaluation and logical consistency with other moral beliefs and principles. The content or substance of these valuations occur wherever human beings coexist (which they always have) because that coexistence will force issues bearing on things like human rights; the nature of harm and what obligations people might have to prevent it; the nature and legitimate acquisition of human benefits, property, and economic welfare; accommodating as well as regulating desire satisfaction; and treating persons fairly and justly (Young and Dungan, 2012). If morality, then, is ultimately a socioevolutionary inevitability that regulates human behavior and relationships, it is very likely that it will require principles to explain and justify moral assertions or claims (Richardson, 2013). Moral reasoning thus becomes a means whereby a community develops, shares, and refines beliefs, principles, customs and practices around its valuative commitments and related regulative principles and rules regarding the nature and pursuit of its welfare.

Where Does Moral Reasoning Come From?

A popular understanding of the origins of moral reasoning is the "naturalist" one that characterizes it as an evolutionary result of natural selection (Kitcher, 2012). Long before *Homo sapiens* walked the savannahs of Eastern Africa, their prehominid ancestors had evolved a significant number of skills, practices, dispositions, and primitive attitudes and beliefs that were conducive to their (group) survival. It was and remains especially important for social group members to regulate the behaviors of their peers, especially when the latter, often in pursuit of their own unique survival interests, act in ways that threaten the welfare of the group. Thus, the affective and emotional programs of the brain, for example, anger, pity, sympathy, disgust, pleasure, guilt, shame, and so on, along with the brain's intentional and inferential networks, are thought to be evolved, cognitive tools whose informational outputs advance the group's survival prospects

288

(James, 2011). *Homo sapiens* therefore appeared on the evolutionary scene already disposed toward prosocial moral dispositions such as an inclination toward reciprocity, respect for authority, altruism, empathy, and so on because these phenomena are adaptive toward group survival. While they do not constitute moral reasoning *per se*, they do shape the more general parameters of our moral lives, such as a hard-wired reluctance to harm unnecessarily and to treat equals as equals. Of course, these functionalities require subservient neural structures that evolved along with our moral thinking and sophistication. So when the Ionians began thinking hard about Western morality about 2,500 years ago, they were nicely supplied with all the neural equipment they needed to launch the enterprise of moral reasoning as we know it today.

Justificatory and Explicative Moral Reasoning

In its classical, "deductivist" or top-down form such as is taught in academic courses on moral reasoning, the practice of moral reasoning largely involves System 2 reasoning insofar as students are asked to deduce and justify a plan or action on the basis of relevant moral principles, for example, "The duties of nonmaleficence and beneficence require that one does as little harm and as much good as possible; the administration of a drug to this patient would do less harm and more good than a surgical intervention would; therefore, we will administer a drug regimen." Yet people will also (and more frequently) spontaneously draw on their storehouse of moral intuitions, experiences, beliefs, and feelings in registering their aversion to harming; they will instantaneously respond according to what they have learned their professional roles require in such a situation (or how they were taught to respond); they will use their learned experience from similar cases; and they will rely on certain (noninferential and unmediated) feelings of satisfaction to inform and decide upon the acceptability of their adopted course of action (Haidt, 2001). Very likely and in most cases, responsible forms of moral reasoning utilize both System 1 and 2 strategies, especially when reasoning is *justificatory*—that is, when one appeals to principles or social rules to argue for the acceptability of his or her moral decision or behavior (Lenman, 2010).

On the other hand, explicative or *explanatory* reasoning will be familiar to any student of moral philosophy who learns about the architecture of a particular moral theory or system, for example, that moral reasoning for Kant proceeds according to moral intentions that are universalizable, whereas moral reasoning for classical utilitarians aspires to achieving the most happiness for the greatest number of people. Justificatory and explanatory reasoning will often overlap, both in real-life situations and in analytical deliberations. Explanatory reasons can easily elide into justificatory reasons and vice versa, for example, "She hated his haughtiness and considered harming him because she felt he deserved it." They differ, though, in that conceptually primitive explanatory reasons may not pass the moral "sniff" or justificatory test, for example, "I lied because I felt like it."

There appears to be an emerging consensus that responsible moral agents use virtually every relevant type of moral reflection at their disposal when they confront a vexing and especially personal moral dilemma. For example, in one of the more significant theoretical works on moral reasoning to emerge in the last decade, Derek Parfit (2011a) champions what he calls a "Triple Theory" of moral reasoning, which holds that an "act is wrong just when such acts are disallowed by some principle that is optimific, uniquely universally willable, and not reasonably rejectable" (413). Parfit's "convergence" theory blends features of deontology, consequentialism, and contractualism on the theoretical level. Laypersons will predictably bring to morally complex situations their socially learned storehouse of commonsense moral principles and moral rules such as "do your duty," "refrain from cruelty," "leave a situation better than you found it," "be impartial," and so forth. While philosophically trained individuals might bring a sophisticated skill set to justifying their moral actions as Parfit does, laypersons or nonspecialists would similarly resort to principled strategies inspired by deontology, utilitarianism, and the like even though they are not consumers of academic philosophy. In order to appreciate the evolution and variations of moral reasoning, then, let us briefly examine certain highly influential philosophical accounts of normative reasoning wherein explanatory and justificatory reasoning interdigitate.

Western Moral Reasoning: The Philosophical Tradition

Platonic Moral Reasoning

Two of Plato's reflective strategies deserve our attention, as they permeate the Platonic corpus and characterize his understanding of moral reasoning. They include his promotion of essentialism and what has become known as "internalism."

A classic example of Plato's essentialism—whose appearance marks the early and middle dialogues—occurs in the dialogue *Euthyphro*, in which Socrates asks his friend of that name:

> Is not the holy always one and the same thing in every action, and, again is not the unholy always opposite to the holy, and like itself? And as unholiness does it not always have its one essential form, which will be found in everything that is unholy?
>
> (Plato, 1961, 173, 5d)

Plato's idea that moral categories or virtues such as holiness, justice, and the like have an "essential form" or a universally distributed property that defines them as what they essentially are would influence philosophical thinking for more than 2,000 years. This style of reasoning, which aspires to a veridical insight into the structure or "heart" of moral knowledge, is very much alive today, especially among scholars labeled "moral conservatives." For example, public intellectuals who served on George W. Bush's first Presidential Commissions on Bioethics and published the report *Beyond Therapy* (2003) used an essentialist approach in their moral argumentation, asserting essentialist-sounding metaphysical claims such as:

> "The happiness most appropriate to the human soul" (4)
> "Not only the sense or feeling of well-being, but well-being itself" (33)
> "The prospect of mistaking some lesser substitute for real happiness" (34)
> "What it means to respond to real life in a fitting way" (36)

The appeal of essentialist structures such as these is that if one can conclusively demonstrate a timeless, noncontextualized, universal essence of some moral term, then behavior that departs from that essentialist knowledge is obviously in violation of it and is therefore immoral. This idea prompted Plato's search for exact and certain moral knowledge to take on a decidedly normative bent: He believed that once having adequately grasped the essence of some moral term, the individual will then be motivated to act in accord with it. Contemporary philosophers have labeled this assumption "internalism" (or "substantive internalism"), and its persuasiveness continues to the present day. Internalists argue that having a reason for doing X is, in itself, a prompt for the action itself (Richardson, 2013). Platonic moral reasoning might therefore be understood as not only the pursuit of moral knowledge but an exercise in moral edification, resulting in the "men of gold" of *The Republic* who will renounce their self-interest and do the right thing "because their superior moral insight and knowledge determines their right action" (Grube, 1958, 222–228).

Aristotelian Moral Reasoning

In contrast to Plato's highly intellectualized and dialogical search for moral knowledge, his pupil Aristotle understood moral knowledge to be more derived from human experience and shaped by the learning and practice of virtuous behavior (Ross, 1964). Because Aristotle believed that moral challenges or dilemmas were too diverse and heterogeneous to be neatly categorized and explained theoretically, he proposed that the best moral reasoning would issue from persons acting in accordance with the virtues. This kind of reasoning, which is mostly referred to as practical or "phronetic" intelligence (Jonsen and Toulmin, 1988, 19), has been described as "the capacity to determine the right manner of feeling and action in contexts that call for some sort of virtuous response" (Timmons, 2013, 276). Aristotle places less emphasis on moral reasoning as a purely intellectual exercise and more emphasis on the ways moral reasoning cultivates one's character and vice versa. His idea is that persons of good character will reason morally because their personal excellence determines how they think, feel, and behave (Aristotle, 1970b, 952–959).

In Book X, Chapter 7 of his *Nicomachean Ethics*, Aristotle (1970b) saliences the practice of reason above all else as the primary human capability to cultivate. But because Aristotle understands the virtues to lie in the mean between lack and excess—for example, courage lies between cowardice and rashness; self-respect is between humility and vanity; friendliness is between sulkiness and obsequiousness—reasoning functions as a moderating or self-regulative force that shapes one's life. Whereas Plato characterizes moral reasoning as an intellectual process of *a priori* insight and deduction, Aristotle understands moral reasoning as a more inductive, experientially based, never-ending activity of wisdom acquisition resulting in a "good" life.

Moral Reasoning and Natural Law

Aristotle's philosophy was rediscovered by the medievals in the mid-12th century, and their church fathers, led by Thomas Aquinas, would appropriate much of it into their doctrine of Natural Law. Natural Law holds that the preservation and protection of life, procreation, society, and knowledge are "intrinsic" goods that cannot be violated (Timmons, 2013). Moral reasoning must therefore be shaped and guided by that inviolability such that moral reasoning that recommends abortion, suicide, knowledge suppression or distortion, and the like is inherently mistaken. Natural Law extends the Aristotelian notion of pursuing personal excellence to the point of obligating a kind of moral perfection informed by one's living one's life and conducting his moral reasoning according to these fundamental goods. Natural Law is also known for its dogmatic or absolutist stance on moral behavior. The intrinsic goods of Natural Law are just that: good by their very nature and allowing no exceptions or contextual reasons that might violate them. One might claim that Natural Law is a prime example of "moral realism" in which moral properties are thought to inhere in nature, events, or natural objects. Thus, to violate a naturally occurring moral property is to commit wrongdoing (Sayre-McCord, 2012). This introduces a basic problem for moral reasoning in Natural Law theory because violating its precepts seems inevitable in human affairs, for example, killing in times of war or to defend oneself, ending a pregnancy to save the life of a mother, providing increasing amounts of pain medication to a dying patient that will predictably hasten his death, and so forth.

Natural Law theorists developed an ingenious response to this problem that has had enduring impact on moral reasoning: the principle of double effect (Beauchamp and Childress, 2013, 164–167, Jonsen and Toulmin, 1988, 312–313). The challenge consisted in how moral agents should reason through situations wherein goods collide such that one good must seemingly be sacrificed in order to achieve another. The analytic approach proposed by Natural Law proceeded to focus on four elements: the agent's intentionality or reasons for acting; the legitimacy of the agent's action or means of action; the consequences that ensue; and whether the most beneficial moral option was chosen among the alternatives. Roughly, if the individual does not intend to violate Natural Law's fundamental goods, if the action taken is itself morally acceptable, if the consequences of the act disproportionately secure the good(s) that Natural Law recommends and significantly outweigh any harms that might result, and if the action itself is the most morally preferable option (or most preserves Natural Law's valuative commitments in comparison with alternative actions), then the action is morally acceptable (Timmons, 2013, 83–85). It is beyond the scope of this chapter to critically evaluate this model of moral reasoning, so we shall simply point out that its theoretic focus on intentionality, means, consequences, and best options has inspired moral analysis and reasoning for nearly a millennium.

Casuistry

Of all the varieties of moral reasoning, casuistical reasoning may be the most commonly used. Whether it is learned on our mother's knee or in legal, medical, or philosophical training, reasoning by way of analogy—which is how casuistical reasoning proceeds—seems an inevitable cognitive strategy in making moral sense of the world and navigating its challenges. The basic structure of casuistical reasoning utilizes the "precedent case" that embeds and recommends a normative prescription or rule to be used among other cases like it (Jonsen and Toulmin, 1988, 304–332). The architecture of casuistical thinking is not only easy to understand—for example, "in our society, when a situation presents with elements A, B, C, and D, we respond with action X"—but the human brain has a rather remarkable capacity for noting similarities among cases that naturally urge analogic-like thinking and reasoning. We learn the rudiments of analogical moral reasoning as children, such as when we hear precedent or prototypical stories of bravery, justice, respect for others, and the like. The human penchant for noting similarities is probably innate and thus figures as a natural cognitive propensity when we morally reason (Beauchamp and Childress, 2013).

This challenge of casuistical moral reasoning, that is, whether the principles or heuristics of a precedent case applied to another case is valid, invites a more theoretically based challenge: that casuistry, by itself, is theoretically thin. In other words, casuistry is without a "contentful" moral theory to explain why a precedent case is morally compelling (Beauchamp and Childress, 2013). In and by itself, casuistry is unable to argue for or against those moral intuitions that enable a case to become precedential. Two moral theories whose conceptual richness attempt such a contribution, however, are deontology and utilitarianism.

Deontologic Moral Reasoning

Kant's deontology, or duty-based moral theory, represents the first time a Western philosopher specifically attempted to derive a theory of moral reasoning from *rationality* itself. It is always helpful to remember that for Kant, moral requirements are requirements *of reason* rather than of desire, human tendencies, or instincts, or what a particular society considers to be virtuous (Timmons, 2013, 206). As Kant (1956) put it in his *Groundwork to the Metaphysics of Morals*: "The ground of obligation here must not be sought in the nature of the human being . . . [but] simply in the concept of pure reason" (57). Another way of saying this is: what kinds of principles would obligate an *ideally rational agent*—thus, not necessarily a human one (with human desires, tendencies, and needs)?

Kant probably took geometry or mathematics as exemplars of pristine rationality, leading him to argue that an agent's intentions—roughly understood as the psychological motivation or principled maxim upon which the agent acts—must not violate rationality's fundamental law of noncontradiction (Kant, 1956, 88–92). The grounding idea seems to be that if we can imagine an action and its supporting rationale played out through a "universe" of cases, then morally appropriate behavior will be characterized by its rational consistency or non-contradictoriness. This is the essence of Kant's famous "categorical imperative," and as some philosophers have observed, the categorical imperative is the supreme principle of reason itself (Scanlon, 2011).

Kant argued that this emphasis on rationality and logical consistency results in his famous dictum of not treating persons only as means but as ends. Here moral reasoning is shaped by the human capacity of autonomous action, meaning the person's freedom to be self-defining and use his or her will and intellectual powers to behave according to the obligations of duty. This idea illustrates an important aspect of moral reasoning for Kant whereby its practicality is shaped and informed by its theoretical, duty-based content. However, the same can be said for all moral theories: that the nature of reasoning the theory endorses inevitably endorses the vision of "the good" the theory promotes. For example, one of Kant's lasting contributions to moral thought is how his unrelenting emphasis on the substructure of reasoning, namely rationality itself, becomes the inspiration and form through which practical moral reasoning takes shape (Parfit, 2011a).

Utilitarian Moral Reasoning

It is hard to find two conceptions of moral reasoning as opposed as classical deontology and classical Utilitarianism. Whereas Kant disdained a moral platform based on consequences and desire satisfaction because they are shaped by the contingencies of fate rather than reason, Utilitarianism's greatest voice, John Stuart Mill, repudiated the significance of intentionality (or Kant's principled maxims) as obscure, equivocal, and introspectively unreliable (Mill, 1962, 251–255). For Utilitarians, the consequences of an action are morally dispositive, and they should reflect choices and actions that culminate in the greatest degree of net utility. By net utility, utilitarians have in mind some kind of individual or social benefit, such as happiness, human flourishing, social welfare, or the greatest proportionality of (individual or socially construed) benefits over burdens. Mill's own formulation of utility argues that achieving happiness or desire satisfaction for the greatest number of persons constitutes the optimal moral act (Mill, 1962, 256–278).

Consequently, utilitarian moral reasoning is a matter of calculating which action yields the most benefit or least amount of harm and then figuring out how to behave or structure social and political relationships with that goal in mind. As such, utilitarian reasoning does not assume the *a priori* character of Platonic or Kantian moral reasoning but rather embodies a distinctly "appeal to the masses" approach whose emphasis on desire satisfaction eschews intellectualized accounts of the right and the good. However, contemporary utilitarians would likely amend this observation by observing that in order to accomplish the kind of human flourishing or happiness they have in mind, people must be educated to be able to imagine or project consequences such that they do not make stupid, injurious decisions. Indeed, although Mill insisted on the right of persons to assert their desire preferences, he also advocated the importance of "consequentialist experts" who, presumably, have experienced most of life's pleasures and gratifications and who could inform our moral reasoning on which ones are superior or most desirable (Mill, 1962, 261).

Rawlsian Moral Reasoning

John Rawls's extremely influential account of the "veil of ignorance" is a stellar example of how conceptual schemas color moral reasoning. Rawls explicitly denied the idea that he was propounding a moral theory and instead claimed that he was working out a theory of justice that emphasized the just distribution of resources (Rawls, 1971). His version of moral reasoning in *A Theory of Justice* uses the metaphor of decision makers standing behind a "veil of ignorance" wherein they are charged with distributing goods without any idea of what social positions or personal circumstances they might experience once they find themselves living in the society at the receiving end of that goods distribution. Under such an arrangement, Rawls believes that rational, decent persons would reason according to their self-interests such that they would at least favor a decent share of fundamental benefits for everyone, for example, income, education, basic welfare needs, and so forth. Rawls (1971) also believes that the deciders behind the veil would likely protect individual liberties and bar discriminatory and other oppressive social practices that would unjustly truncate a person's capacity to achieve some modicum of economic prosperity or live a meaningful life.

A second influential insight about moral reasoning that Rawls offered was that of "wide reflective equilibrium" (Rawls, 1996). If, as we have seen, moral reasoning takes its departure from the theoretical commitments of a given moral philosophy—Kant's categorical imperative, Mill's utility principle, Natural Law's intrinsic goods, and so on—and if these theoretical commitments are very diverse—Kant's emphasis on duty, Mill's on happiness, Aristotle's on the virtues—then adherents to these theories will often reason to different conclusions or verdicts about the rightness or wrongness of moral actions. Indeed, many societies are marked by moral pluralism or competing notions of the right and the good such that the form and substance of moral reasoning that proceeds from them can take on a remarkable, perhaps bewildering diversity of styles and approaches. What, then, to do with the plethora of "reasons" that inform as well as splinter or complicate our moral accounts? Does that diversity threaten the legitimacy or trustworthiness of moral knowledge itself?

Rawls's response is to recommend a "wide reflective equilibrium" as we evaluate various reasons for and against, resembling an "all reasonable things considered" approach to moral analysis. The basic idea seems to be to consider all reasonable points of view, identify their commonalities, differences, and eccentricities, and then implement those reasonings that best preserve those practices and policies most conducive to preserving individual liberties and opportunities for achieving human welfare (Rawls, 1996). The challenge consists in distinguishing public from private reasons—especially as the latter may be tied to ideologies that certain people from certain cultures will not give up and insist that everyone else abides by—and refuse to implement ideologies and their associated practices that others may find unreasonably burdensome, theoretically unpersuasive, or that create more drag on social productivity and prosperity than a benefit. Debates over what kinds of reasons and moral states of affairs rightfully belong in the private sphere of morality versus which ones ought to be publicly debated remain extremely contentious, however, as witnessed by debates over reproductive rights, school prayer, same sex marriage, and the like.

Principlism

One of the most recognizable platforms of moral reasoning to emerge in the late 20th century is the "principlist" account, popularized by Tom Beauchamp and James Childress in their book *Principles of Biomedical Ethics* (2013). When the first edition of the text appeared in 1979, its recommended heuristic of implementing the principles of autonomy, nonmaleficence, beneficence, and justice to resolving particular cases was understood by many to be the conclusive form of moral reasoning in (at least) medical ethics. Presumably, all one had to do was apply (or, in Beauchamp and Childress's language, "specify") the relevant moral principle(s) to the extant case, and the correct answer or resolution would somehow spring forth (Beauchamp and Childress, 2013, 17–24). Later editions of the text would acknowledge that this notion was too simplistic, as one's "considered moral judgment"—which sometimes sounds a lot like Rawls's wide reflective equilibrium—is constantly shaping the meaning and application of moral principles given the particularized and rich contexts that often characterize bioethical cases (406). Indeed, the very act of deciding what principle applies to a given case may be a matter for debate, as the principles themselves cannot determine their salience, relevance, or interpretation.

Beauchamp and Childress (2013) proceeded to clarify their principlist account as a kind of "mid-level" theory that stops well short of some universalist pronouncement on normativity based on a vision of a supreme good (390–424). The primary reason for principlism's popularity is that it offers an extraordinarily useful heuristic for moral reasoning to proceed by obligating the reasoner to consider how human rights, harms, benefits, and justice play out in particular cases.

Since at least 1995, however, the great debate over principlism has been whether these principles have any content independent of their historical (cultural, legal, and ethical) instantiations—that is, whether they have any inherent content that reasoners can call upon to settle fraught cases or whether invoking them simply reminds us of a culture's historical experience (and experiments) with, say, the problems associated with harms and burdens, and then asks whether any of those experiences might be relevant for cases that presently challenge us (Clouser and Gert, 1990).

Connectionism

Consider an argument between Mike and Pat over abortion. Mike favors a woman's right to control her reproductive liberty, while Pat understands fetal life to have moral status (or to merit state protection) from the moment of conception. In the process of their arguing, each invokes reasons in support of his position. While their reasons obviously clash, they nevertheless are ones that Mike and Pat fervently believe. How is it, then, that certain reasons become dispositive in our moral thinking, such that when we find ourselves engaged in moral disagreement, we favor one set of reasons over others?

A number of prominent neurophilosophers like Paul and Patricia Churchland, Owen Flanagan, Daniel Dennett, and William Bechtel have proposed the idea of "connectionism" and "synaptic weights" as an explanation of how certain beliefs of ours are salienced over others (Churchland, 2000; Waskan, 2016). Cognitive dissonance theory teaches that we tend to adopt beliefs on the basis of their coherence or consistency with other, preexisting beliefs, such that we might think of them as belief networks or clusters (Kunda and Sinclair, 1999; Flanagan, 1996). Perhaps Pat's repudiation of abortion is based on its cohering with his religious preferences or with a notion of life's sanctity that registers in his consciousness with powerfully motivating feelings of reverence and awe. Alternatively, Mike might argue for women's reproductive freedom because he doesn't resonate with a first-trimester fetus's claim to moral status, but he acutely empathizes with the horrors women report about back-alley abortions or the anguish they feel over an unwanted pregnancy. The connectionist explanation of their dispute is that each one's neural networks carry not only different semantic content but also different degrees of affectively mediated motivation, such that whichever network is more heavily "weighted" wins out over competitors (Garson, 2007). How it comes to be that one set of reasons wins out over another in these ideological debates is open for scientific speculation, although if connectionist theory is right, it must involve the idea of powerful affects and feelings that infuse their reasonings to the point of their achieving "pontificant" status in their ideological positions on abortion. Notice, however, that connectionism and synaptic weighting do not offer a justificatory account of morality but only a theory of how empirical, neurologically based data might explain how one set of moral reasons wins out over others. Whether those reasons themselves stand up to moral scrutiny requires additional moral analysis bolstered by substantive moral platforms.

Prototypes and Metaphors

As noted, most of the pre–20th-century canon of Western moral philosophy has favored the pursuit of essentialist, *a priori*, timeless, and noncontextual accounts of the substantive as well as formal structures of moral reasoning. These epistemological aspirations derived from how philosophers, going back to Plato, thought the mind recognized and categorized the objects of human experience—that is, according to objects embodying the essence or universally distributed property by virtue of which they qualify as a member of some class (whether the class is that of "virtue" or "automobile"). Beginning with Wittgenstein's famous account of games in *The Philosophical Investigations* and then picked up by cognitive psychologists like Eleanor Rosch (1978) in the late 1970s, however, the near 2,500-year-old idea of essences began to give way in the 20th century to "prototypes."

At the heart of the prototype account is the idea of the "co-occurring features" of an object's presentation to consciousness. Whereas essentialists understand the members of a class to share a universally distributed property by virtue of which something gains its identity or is what it is—for example, "Is not the holy always one and the same thing in every action?" as Socrates inquired—prototypists understand category recognition or designation to be enabled by our mental ability to be impressed by the "display frequency" of numerous coincident properties exhibited by members of the object's class. Consciousness proceeds to design "a kind of artificial exemplar that combines the statistically most salient features" (Clark, 1998, 11). Thus, I recognize "humans" according to the high-frequency, prototypical presentation of their having or appearing with human-like heads, legs, arms, torsos, ears, and so on. Importantly, not all humans have all of these features, so we are occasionally stuck with hard cases of objects that embody some of the prototypical features but not others. For example, an enduring and fundamental question in the abortion debate is when a human life should be accorded moral status or, roughly, when does "personhood" begin (Beauchamp and Childress, 2013, 67–69). While we would have no trouble identifying the individuals we meet on a daily basis as persons, the abortion debate has long endured because fetal life has some of the features commonly associated with personhood but not others. Thus, first-trimester fetuses have no ability to reason, feel pain, or communicate even though they have human DNA. Perhaps just so, Washington Irving's Headless Horseman would bewilder us with a personhood claim, as would an extra-terrestrial, perhaps, who looked and acted like an adult human but who had no human DNA.

Importantly, prototypists reject the idea of a definitive marker or common denominator for something being or counting as an X and instead look to a cluster of experientially learned properties or features that tend to be present in most instances of Xs as we learn to identify them. Moral prototypes like "dignity," "justice," "happiness," and the like are thought to originate from the morally creative activity of a community or group rather than be discovered like the elements in the Periodic Chart. Philosophers who appreciate the contributions of evolutionary psychology, linguistics, anthropology, and the like may favor conceptual structures like prototypes, which evolved as a "good enough" means of cognition to enable our prehominid ancestors to make fast and adaptive responses to their survival pressures—for example, "that looks like an act of cruelty which we cannot allow" (Banja, 2011). The social construction of a prototype, for example, coming to agreement over the kinds of things that will count as "torture," "cruel and unusual," "death," "rights holder," "privacy," "fairness," "equality," "dignity," and so forth are what identifies a culture.

George Lakoff and Mark Johnson (1999) have supplemented prototype theory by arguing that much if not all of moral reasoning and prototype construction relies on metaphors. Continuing the Darwinian-like idea that moral reasoning develops more as a survival mechanism for regulating human interactions than as a quest for philosophical wisdom, the metaphorical account of morality looks to certain sociobiological structures of experience to explain how humans comprehend morality. For example, Johnson (1998) argues that we understand morality on the basis of physical health and immorality on the basis of sickness: "moral well-being is understood as health. . . . Bad deeds are *sick*. Moral *pollution* makes the soul sick. We must strive for *purity* by avoiding *dirty deeds*, moral *filth*, *corruption* and *infection* from immoral people" (57). Johnson (1998) claims that other metaphorical features of morality are being upright, experiencing strength, balance, direction, obedience, and light (rather than darkness). Just like casuistry, connectionism, and motivated reasoning (as discussed in what follows), the metaphorical account of morality does not provide us with a template to resolve our moral dilemmas, but it does speculate about the conceptual structures or frameworks humans inevitably use in reasoning. For example, moral resolutions should be informed by aspirations that foster human flourishing, preserve the social order, advance individual freedoms and liberties, refrain from cruelty, and so on because they have strategically coevolved with our welfare needs. On the other hand, moral principles "must never be allowed to solidify into absolute rules, for then the opportunity for moral growth and progress is undermined" (67).

Hume's Sentimentalism and the Is–Ought Argument

Along with Kant, the great Scottish Enlightenment philosopher David Hume contributed philosophical insights and arguments on the nature of moral reasoning that continue to beguile present-day thinkers. Two that shall be discussed here are Hume's understanding that "reason is a slave to the passions" and his argument that normative conclusions can never be inferred from factual premises, more famously asserting that one "cannot derive an ought from an is."

Hume argued that moral reasoning does not motivate moral action or, in marked, antirationalist contrast to Plato, that reasoning does not motivate moral action *by itself*. In Book 3, Part I, Section 1 of the *Treatise on Human Nature*, Hume (1968) argues that all reasoning can do is examine the relationships among ideas—such as their resemblances or logical connections or coherences—and discover facts about the world such as how certain effects apparently follow from certain causes. Although reasoning might provide us with factual knowledge that favors acting in such a way, Hume is adamant that such knowledge must somehow spur our passions or feelings to result in any moral action. Reason alone will not suffice, because moral reasoning, according to Hume, does not evaluate in the sense of approbating or approving. Rather, that is the work of our desires, aversions, hopes, fears, hunger, lust, and the like.

Sounding very much like a 20th-century Skinnerian, Hume (1967) proposed that ideas of pleasure and pain that are attendant on or stimulated by our ideas or reasonings will motivate action and avoidance. Hume believed that the best reason can do is determine that a particular fact or state of affairs may produce pleasure and pain, but it will be our natural propensity as humans to secure pleasure and avoid pain that causes us to act. Because they are not representational, our desires or instincts are neither true nor false because they do not ascribe truth values to the world in the form of facts. Passions do not constitute judgments, which are about the world and hence admit truth values: "[O]ur superior reason may serve to discover the vice or virtue. . . . But this discovery supposes a separate being in these moral distinctions . . . which depends only on the will and appetite, and which, both in thought and reality, may be distinguish'd from the reason" (Hume, 1967, 468). Reason can certainly judge the consequence of a particular act to have been good or bad by comparing it to other ideas. But the ultimate registrar of the rightness of a moral action will be our feelings of approbation or disapprobation as they are stimulated by pleasure or pain. Therefore, when I say "Lying is wrong," Hume would argue that I am expressing not a fact but an attitude or feeling. Consequently, Hume rejects moral realism in favor of what will be called some 200 years later "expressivism"; that is, that the "vice" of an action is not to be found in the action itself but rather in "a sentiment of disapprobation . . . tis the object of feeling, not of reason. It lies in yourself, not in the object" (Hume, 1967, 469). Hume is therefore thought to be an expressivist or "sentimentalist" about moral assertions in that "when you pronounce any action or character to be vicious, you mean nothing, but that from the constitution of your nature you have a feeling or sentiment of blame from the contemplation of it" (469).

If reasoning about morality and acting morally occupy different ontological realms, then it seems trivially true that one cannot logically derive an "action ought" from a "factual is." A fact about the world, for example, that if I consume too much alcohol, I shall feel ill, only produces a normative consequence, for example, that you ought not drink excessively, if one smuggles in a normative rule, such as *one ought to refrain from doing things that make one ill*. But if I don't care or am not concerned about feeling ill from drink, then I shall not be disposed toward moderation. By pointing out that moral action doesn't follow from natural properties (or the things about which facts are), Hume anticipated a line of thinking that would occupy much of 20th-century moral philosophy. The philosophical tradition typically thought it was precisely because of a thing's moral features or properties—such as the intrinsic goods of Natural Law or Utilitarianism—that informed and supplied reasons for moral behavior (Sayre-McCord, 2012). Those reasons provoked the will with the motivation it required to act. Hume argued, however, that it wasn't moral reasons that caused moral behavior but largely the individual's feelings, sentiments, and passions that triggered moral approval and disapproval and the subsequent formation of moral evaluations or beliefs:

> Take any action allow'd to be vicious: Wilful murder, for instance. Examine it in all lights, and see if you can find that matter of fact, or real existence, which you call vice. In which-ever way you take it, you find only certain passions, motives, volitions, and thoughts. . . . The vice entirely escapes you, as long as you consider the object. You never can find it, till you turn your reflexion into your own breast, and find a sentiment of disapprobation, which arises in you, towards this action. Here is a matter of fact; but 'tis the object of feeling, not of reason.
>
> (468–469)

Statements like these have earned Hume the reputation of an antirational, noncognitivist "sentimentalist."

Motivated Reasoning and the Social Intuitionist Model

Hume's "noncognitivism"—that is, the idea that moral beliefs have no propositional or factual content and therefore no truth value—provides a good segue to a theory of moral reasoning that has garnered considerable recent attention. Advanced by scholars such as Ziva Kunda and Jonathan Haidt, "motivated reasoning" asserts that reasoning is intentional or motivated by some kind of goal (Kunda, 1990). While the goal might be the pursuit of truth, wisdom, or factual accuracy, contemporary research on motivated reasoning in moral matters suggests that moral reasoning for most persons works backward: rather than collect and evaluate evidence so as to arrive at a value-laden or normative conclusion that appears best supported by that evidence, most individuals when they "reason" morally begin with a point of view that they like or prefer and then work backward to find evidence to support it (Pinker, 2008). Jonathan Haidt (2001) has claimed that:

> Once people find supporting evidence, even a single piece of bad evidence, they often stop the search, since they have a "makes-sense epistemology" . . . in which the goal of thinking is not to reach the most accurate conclusion but to find the first conclusion that hangs together well and that fits with one's important prior beliefs.

(821)

Haidt (2001) has advanced a "social intuitionist model" (SIM) of reasoning, three of whose features are strikingly opposed to classical moral philosophy's search for moral wisdom. The first is the SIM belief that relatively few people morally reason in the dispassionate, objective, *a priori*, "reasoning regardless of the consequences" manner that some philosophers endorse. Instead, they trust the moral intuitions or gut feelings about right and wrong that have evolved since childhood and in which they have come to place great confidence. Rather than give up those seemingly reliable beliefs in light of new but contrary evidence, the SIM posits that people will, often unconsciously, bias their reasoning "including the selection of initial hypotheses, the generation of inferences, the search for evidence, the evaluation of evidence, and the amount of evidence needed before one is willing to make an inference" to maintain their tried and true ideologies and beliefs (Haidt, 2001, 821). Consequently, people often reason in order to reduce cognitive dissonance or when beliefs or data sources collide (Kunda and Sinclair, 1999). Because the feeling of dissonance is uncomfortable and especially because preexisting beliefs that an individual has used and believes to be reliable and trustworthy are difficult to give up, the job of reasoning becomes "mull[ing] over a problem until one side feels right. Then we stop" (Kunda and Sinclair, 1999, 829).

That leads to a second dimension of the SIM in its recalling Hume's emphasis on feelings as moral arbiters. Feelings or affective evaluations not only occur automatically and pervasively in perception, but, as evolutionary theory would quickly point out, the brain's affective system developed long before those cortical structures enabling executive thought appeared; the affective system is invariably triggered before the reasoning system in real-time judgment situations; and, except in philosophers, feelings are "more powerful and irrevocable when the two systems yield conflicting judgments" (Haidt, 2001, 819). In short, for beliefs to change, one has to make the new idea "feel better" to the deliberator than his or her previously accepted belief(s). Consequently, arguments that use vivid images, metaphors, stories, and other techniques that stir the passions and sentiments may be much more persuasive "reasoning" strategies than ones that utilize System 2 reasoning. Haidt (2001) has remarked that "[t]he reasoning process is more like a lawyer defending a client than a judge or scientist seeking truth" (820).

A third feature of the SIM is its understanding of moral belief formation as a social rather than private accomplishment. The deliberative model of philosophy, at least in the academy, remains the Cartesian trope of the solitary thinker, seated in his study, seeking after the eternal, timeless structures of truth, being, and knowledge. Congruent with the SIM, Mercier and Sperber (2011) have recently argued that the true function of reasoning is its role in public dialogue and argument. They believe the Cartesian model is far more liable to error than reasoning conducted in settings in which people can contemplate and argue in groups. Mercier and Sperber emphasize the neuroevolution of reasoning as a social tool for survival and that individual reasoning, as our motivated reasoning account noted, is often unable to adequately question the individual's preferred beliefs.

While the SIM attempts to give a descriptive rendering of how perhaps the majority of people reason—which many believe is "poorly" (Mercier and Sperber, 2011)—Paxton and Green asserted in a 2010 paper that more recent data suggests that deliberative reasoning, especially in matters of moral reasoning, may occur much more often than Haidt's (2001) SIM suggests. Of course, the SIM is hardly an endorsement of moral reasoning that entirely proceeds intuitively, affectively, and often illogically. Indeed, one might point out that one of its most disturbing social implications recalls Plato's worries about the sophists of his day: the worry that reasoning may cease to respect logic and good evidence and instead become transformed into an instrument of persuasion or a series of "post hoc rationalizations" (Haidt, 2001, 9). To the extent that persons resist developing action strategies based on evidentially sound ideas and instead maintain beliefs mainly because they are psychologically comfortable, preserve their sense of self-esteem, help them feel safer or more in control, and so forth, one can hardly resist worrying that democratic cultures may evolve "feel-good" policies and practices that could invite global catastrophes.

Empirical Studies on the Moral Brain

This chapter would be remiss to not mention some of the contemporary neuroscientific studies on brain structures subserving moral reasoning. Often this work has attempted to "locate the proprietary neural circuits of morality" (Young and Dungan, 2012, 2) or to perform correlational studies that enable predicting the judgment of an individual based on his or her previous decisions as detected on neuroimaging studies.

This research has yielded fascinating findings about variations in human brains during reasoning, especially among persons of different cognitive or ideological stripes, for example, staunch Republicans versus die-hard Democrats, psychopaths versus nonpsychopaths, expert performers versus amateurs, and people making moral versus nonmoral decisions. Many of these findings identify brain regions that differentiate these moral reasoners, for example, regions that correlate with reasoners placing more weight on emotional rather than calculative reasoning (and vice versa) or more on intentions versus outcomes. But, recalling Hume's is–ought gap, what none of this research can do is look into the brain so as to secure the "correct" response (or reasoning) to a moral dilemma. In a review of these studies, Young and Dungan (2012, p. 1) have asserted that there appears to be "no neural substrate or system that uniquely supports moral cognition," likely because of the way cognitions admit emotional and social components that might or might not have a moral referent or context. Although neuroscientists have identified a "moral loop" in the ventromedial prefrontal cortex, the amygdala, superior temporal sulcus, bilateral temporoparietal junction, posterior cingulate cortex, and the precuneus (Green and Haidt, 2002), these structures have also figured in nonmoral, emotional, and social brain responses (Young and Dungan, 2012).

> For more on neurodevelopment and the moral brain, see Chapter 23.

Moral reasoning as a System 2 phenomenon, i.e., as the effortful, analytical, and imaginative process typified throughout Western intellectual history, has no substitute or at least will not be replaced by a glimpse at a brain image. What these studies may enable us to do, perhaps in the not-too-distant future, is to alter brain functioning among persons with emotional or social deficits that may or may not be tied to moral functioning—an effort whose propriety will itself require moral vetting. Still, human societies will not be able to find answers to their moral quandaries by interrogating the empirical sciences, as long as the latter are without moral directives or cultural cues that shape their own understanding of moral correctness (Decety and Cowell, 2015).

Conclusion

This gloss on moral reasoning illustrates a number of perspectives, agreements, and vexations that characterize the classical literature. A critical point in this entire analysis is how different scholars comprehend or approach "reasoning" according to their preferred methods, operative assumptions, goals, and values (Johnson, 1998). For example, if one approaches moral reasoning from a neuroevolutionary perspective, then reasoning will be understood as a neurologically mediated human adaptation whose main job is to resolve sociocultural problems arising from the challenges of group adaptation (Cosmides and Tooby, 2004). Thus and as we have seen, much of this literature will look to brain development, to the interplay of the brain's affective systems with its more analytical or deliberative properties, and to the role of groups or communities in deciding and creating what will count as their normative principles or moral knowledge. It should not surprise us, then, if much of this approach is descriptive and contents itself with trying to explain the operational architecture of moral reasoning and belief formation rather than argue for substantive moral positions on right and wrong. Alternatively, because academic philosophers are usually very keen not to conflate moral reasoning with sociology or evolutionary theory, their penchant has been to understand the *a priori* structures (or securing the necessary and sufficient conditions) of moral reasoning that explain and justify acts aiming at the right and good (Johnson, 1998). For them, the ideal platform will be one that is entirely convincing to morally reasonable people, delivers consistent and determinate (or well-specified) moral verdicts, is transparently specifiable per a given dilemma, and delivers outcomes that are largely consistent with a group's already considered moral judgments (Timmons, 2013).

Ultimately, reliable and meritorious moral reasoning will look to the integrity of its reasoners and the degree to which they can deploy an intellectual capability to reason well. As the 21st century evolves, its technologies hint at a possibility of achieving human flourishing such as never before encountered in human history, as well as a distinct possibility for unprecedented global harm. Although scholars may quarrel about the advisedness of deontology over Utilitarianism over Natural Law, it seems incumbent on representative democracies to cultivate an electorate that exhibits good reasoning ability. Most concerning are points of view that flatly contradict the best (or even better) knowledge we have on remedying our moral and social ills. Perhaps this provides a final but practical lesson on moral reasoning: that for it to work best, moral reasoning must proceed transparently, intelligently, honestly, publicly, and humbly. It must combine both subject expertise and the self-correcting features of public forums and debate that can help us imagine what a decent future should resemble. Most of all, moral reasoning should combine a good will and respect for others coupled with a fierce determination to root out hypocrisies and deception, given the extraordinary challenges that living in the 21st century and beyond will present.

Further Reading

Churchland, P.S. (2002) *Brain-Wise: Studies in Neurophilosophy*. Cambridge, MA: MIT Press.
Clausen, J. and Levy, N. (Eds.) (2015) *Handbook of Neuroethics*, Volumes 1–3. Dordrecht, Holland: Springer.
Joyce, R. (2006) *The Evolution of Morality*. Cambridge, MA: MIT Press.
Levy, N. (2007) *Neuroethics: Challenges for the 21st Century*. Cambridge: Cambridge University Press.
Sinnot-Armstrong, W. (Ed.) (2008) *Moral Psychology*, Volumes 1–3. Cambridge, MA: MIT Press.

References

Aristotle. (1970a) Prior analytics. In A.J. Jenkinson (trans.), R. McKeon (Ed.). *The Basic Works of Aristotle*. New York: Random House, pp. 65–107.
———. (1970b) *Nicomachean Ethics*. In A.J. Jenkinson (trans.), R. McKeon (Ed.). *The Basic Works of Aristotle*. New York: Random House, pp. 935–1112.
Banja, J. (2011) Virtue essentialism, prototypes, and the moral conservative opposition to enhancement technologies: A neuroethical critique. *American Journal of Bioethics Neuroscience* 2(2): pp. 31–38.
Beauchamp, T., and Childress, J. (2013) *Principles of Biomedical Ethics*. New York, NY: Oxford University Press.
Churchland, P.M. (2000) *The Engine of Reason, the Seat of the Soul*. Cambridge, MA: MIT Press.
Clark, A. (1998) Connectionism, Moral Cognition, and Collaborative Problem Solving. In L. May, M. Friedman, and A. Clark (Eds.). *Mind and Morals: Essays on Cognitive Science and Ethics*. Cambridge, MA: MIT Press, pp. 109–127.
Clouser, K.D. and Gert, B. (1990) A Critique of Principlism *Journal of Medicine and Philosophy* 15: pp. 219–36.
Cosmides, L., and Tooby J. (2004) Knowing thyself: The evolutionary psychology of moral reasoning and moral sentiments. *Business, Science & Ethics* 4: pp. 91–127.
Damasio, A. (2003) *Looking for Spinoza: Joy, Sorrow and the Feeling Brain*. New York: Harcourt Inc.
Decety, J., and Cowell, J. (2015) Empathy, justice, and moral behavior. *American Journal of Bioethics Neuroscience* 6(3): pp. 3–14.
Flanagan, O. (1996) The moral network. In R. McCauley (Ed.). *The Churchlands and Their Critics*. Cambridge, MA: Wiley-Blackwell, pp. 192–215.
Garson, J. (2007) Connectionism. *Stanford Encyclopedia of Philosophy*. Available at: http://plato.stanford.edu/entries/connectionism/.
Green, J., and Haidt, J. (2002) How (and Where) does moral judgment work? *Trends in Cognitive Science* 6: pp. 517–523.
Grube, G. (1958) *Plato's Thought*. Boston, MA: Beacon Press.
Habermas, J. (1995) *Moral Consciousness and Communicative Action*. Cambridge, MA: MIT Press.
Haidt, J. (2001) The emotional dog and its rational tail: A social intuitionist approach to moral judgment. *Psychological Review* 108(4): pp. 814–834.
Hume, D. (1967) *A Treatise of Human Nature*. Oxford, UK: Clarendon Press.
James, S. (2011) *An Introduction to Evolutionary Ethics*. Malden, MA: Wiley-Blackwell.
Johnson, M.L. (1998) How moral psychology changes moral theory. In L. May, M. Friedman, and A. Clark (Eds.). *Mind and Morals: Essays on Cognitive Science and Ethics*. Cambridge, MA: MIT Press, pp. 45–68.
Jonsen, A.R., and Toulmin, S. (1988) *The Abuse of Casuistry*. Berkeley, Los Angeles, CA: University of California Press.
Kant, I. (1956) *Groundwork of the Metaphysic of Morals*. New York: Harper Torchbooks.
Kahneman, D. (2011) *Thinking, Fast and Slow*. New York: Farrar, Straus and Giroux.

Kitcher, P. (2012) The lure of the peak. *New Republic*, 11 January. Available at: https://newrepublic.com/article/99529/on-what-matters-derek-parfit.

Kunda, Z. (1990) The case for motivated reasoning. *Psychological Bulletin* 108(3): pp. 480–498.

Kunda, Z., and Sinclair, L. (1999) Motivated reasoning with stereotypes: Activation, application, and inhibition. *Psychological Inquiry* 10(1): pp. 12–22.

Lakoff, G., and Johnson, M. (1999) *Philosophy in the Flesh*. New York: Basic Books.

Lenman, J. (2010) Reasons for action: Justification vs. explanation. *The Stanford Encyclopedia of Philosophy*. Available at: http://plato.stanford.edu/archives/win2011/entries/reasons-just-vs-expl/.

Mercier, H., and Sperber, D. (2011) Why do humans reason? Arguments for an argumentative theory. *Behavioral and Brain Sciences* 34: pp. 57–111.

Mill, J.S. (1962) *Utilitarianism*. New York: Penguin Group, pp. 251–321.

Parfit, D. (2011a) *On What Matters, Vol. 1*. Oxford, UK: Oxford University Press.

———. (2011b) *On What Matters, Vol. 2*. Oxford, UK: Oxford University Press.

Paxton, J., and Greene, J. (2010) Moral reasoning: Hints and allegations. *Topics in Cognitive Science* 2(3): pp. 511–527.

Pinker, S. (2008) The moral instinct. *New York Times*, 13 January. Available at: www.nytimes.com/2008/01/13/magazine/13Psychology-t.html?_r=0.

Plato. (1961) *The Collected Dialogues of Plato*, E. Hamilton and H. Cairns (Eds.). New York: Bollingen Foundation.

Rawls, J. (1971). *A theory of justice*. Cambridge, MA: Belknap Press of Harvard University Press.

Richardson, H. (2013) Moral reasoning. *The Stanford Encyclopedia of Philosophy*. Available at: http://plato.stanford.edu/entries/reasoning-moral/.

Rosch, E. (1978) Principles of categorization. In E. Rosch and B. Lloyd (Eds.). *Cognition and Categorization*. Hillsdale, NJ: Lawrence Erlbaum Associates, pp. 27–48.

Ross, D. (1964) *Aristotle*. London: Methuen & Co., Ltd.

Sayre-McCord, G. (2012) Metaethics. *The Stanford Encyclopedia of Philosophy*. Available at https://plato.stanford.edu/entries/metaethics/

Scanlon, T. (1998) *What We Owe To Each Other*. Cambridge, MA: Harvard University Press.

———. (2011) How I am not a Kantian. In D. Parfit (Ed.). *On What Matters*, Vol. ii. Oxford, UK: Oxford University Press, pp. 116–139.

Timmons, M. (2013) *Moral Theory: An Introduction*. Lanham, MD: Rowman & Littlefield Publishers.

Waskan, J. (2016) *Connectionism. Internet Encyclopedia of Philosophy*. Available at: www.iep.utm.edu/comment.

Young, L., and Dungan, J. (2012) Where in the brain is morality? Everywhere and maybe nowhere. *Social Neuroscience* 7(1): pp. 1–10.

20

INFORMING ETHICAL DECISION MAKING

Adam Feltz and Edward T. Cokely

Introduction

Who should decide how we live our lives? A straightforward answer that is often embodied in democratic ideals is that people who are competent should have the opportunity to decide for themselves. There are of course extensive caveats and nuances. Those issues notwithstanding, the goal of independent decision making presents a great practical and theoretical challenge: How can we efficiently and ethically help people make good decisions in a fundamentally uncertain and ever-changing world? Modern decision theory holds that good decisions are those that accord with rational choice optimization processes (e.g., weighting and integrating values and risks to maximize subjective expected utilities; Gigerenzer et al., 1999). Of course, computational complexity in concert with our neurocognitive limitations (i.e., bounded rationality) and the fundamental uncertainty of our world means that true decision optimization is usually impractical, if not impossible. Yet people generally do make good decisions thanks to the use of simple adaptive decision strategies (i.e., decision heuristics and rules of thumb) that fit with their neurocognitive and ecological constraints (Cokely and Feltz, 2014; Gigerenzer et al., 1999). That is, a great body of research shows that simple decision processes often lead to good decision making, particularly when people understand the decision stakes (e.g., risks, benefits). But *generally* does not entail *always*. And understanding risks is often much easier said than done. As our technologies, ecologies, and even neuropsychologies continue to evolve, the quality of our decision making will be determined in part by the quality and character of our choice architecture policies and support systems (e.g., laws, risk communications, incentives, and educational systems).

Broadly, beyond our traditional social contract and governmental systems, there are two modern approaches that aim to support individual decision making. The first endeavors to take advantage of decision biases in order to "persuade" or "nudge" people toward making better decisions without tangibly reducing their range of choices (Thaler and Sunstein, 2008). For example, capitalizing on the status quo bias, policies have structured retirement plans so that people must opt out instead of opting in, thereby increasing the likelihood that people will accrue adequate savings without limiting their retirement savings choices (Thaler and Benartzi, 2004). The second modern approach aims at informing people appropriately so their rational capacities can support well-informed independent decision making. For example, simple risk communications help people understand the costs and benefits of medical screenings or health behaviors like using condoms (Garcia-Retamero and Cokely, 2015). In these cases, people tend to make decisions that protect and promote health without any need for persuasive or fear-based appeals. Both of these general approaches are promising and have had well-documented, major personal, social, and economic benefits (e.g., National Science and Technology Council, 2015, Behavioural Insights Team, 2015).

But how should we evaluate and implement powerful choice architecture policies and programs designed to help people make better decisions? Research and scholarship on the costs and benefits of informed versus persuasive choice architecture policies suggests that there is no simple answer. One size does not fit all, and one policy is not always best. However, it is clear that many common and effective persuasive techniques are nevertheless inferior to strategies that promote informed and independent decision making for one simple reason: Fundamental philosophical values are systematically fragmented and tied to heritable personality traits and neuropsychological propensities. This predictable and stable diversity of fundamental philosophical intuitions and values often makes implementing even liberally paternalistic strategies difficult and costly as compared to the benefits of strategies that promote informed decision making. In what follows, we provide an overview of some of the evidence suggesting that philosophical values are linked to heritable traits that manifest as social, cognitive, and neurological differences in one's behavior and psychology. We then discuss implications of these results, including the substantial costs of paternalistic policies and the potential benefits of a science for informed decision making.

Personality and Variations in Philosophical Values

Heritable personality traits predict fundamental philosophical values. Here, we mean personality defined as "the coherent patterning of affect, behaviors, cognition, and desires (goals) over time and space" (Revelle and Scherer, 2009, 304). One prominent contemporary account of personality is the Big Five model including the five global traits of (1) extraversion, (2) openness to experience, (3) emotional stability, (4) agreeableness, and (5) conscientiousness (see John and Srivastava, 1999, for an extensive overview). While there are many different models of personality that largely differ on the precision of personality trait measurement (e.g., including more or less traits and facets), the Big Five are somehow represented in almost all contemporary personality inventories and serve as the "gold standard" against which all other models can be compared. These global personality traits describe a large number of related clusters of individual tendencies in behavior, cognition, and neurological function called facets. For example, warmth may be considered a facet of extraversion, a trait that is characterized by stable differences in neurological systems (e.g., reticular activating system in the brain stem) and psychophysiological responses (e.g., dopamine or oxytocin regulation) that reward and promote positive attitudes and positive feelings about others (Ashton, 2013; Costa and McCrae, 1988; Martin and Juergen, 2005). Prediction, in the sense of the term as we use it, refers to a significant relationship or correlation (i.e., a change in one factor tracking changes in another factor). For example, the heritability and underlying neurobiological pathways that are commonly expressed in extraverts manifest behaviorally and psychologically in people who enjoy and gravitate toward leadership positions (Judge et al., 2002). So the more extraverted one is (a change in one factor), the more likely it is that one will gravitate toward and enjoy leadership positions (a change in another factor). While personality is shaped by experience, it is simultaneously largely genetic in origin, meaning it is likely a psychological, behavioral primitive (Bouchard and Loehlin, 2001; Costa and McCrae, 1988; King et al., 2009). Personality also emerges early in psychological development before higher-level complex moral cognition (e.g., children can be outgoing or shy long before they learn to speak or reason; Lamb et al., 2002). But how does the psychology and biology of personality shape philosophical biases and disagreement?

For our current purposes, it's useful to consider three prominent areas in which personality has been found to predict fundamental philosophical values (for a review, see Feltz, 2017). Let's begin with free will. Beliefs about free will have been argued to be fundamental to our conceptions of ourselves, others, and our place in the universe (Kane, 1996; Smilansky, 2000). There are many free will–relevant beliefs, including whether one is morally responsible, if one could have done otherwise in a given circumstance, and what conditions limit acting freely. A number of studies have shown that intuitions about free will and moral responsibility are diverse but predictable. One series of studies suggests that extraversion predicts willingness to judge that free will and moral responsibility are compatible with determinism (Andow and Cova, 2016; Cokely and Feltz, 2009a; Feltz, 2013b, 2015b, Feltz and Cokely, 2008, 2009; Feltz and Millan, 2015; Feltz et al., 2012; Nadelhoffer et al., 2009; Schulz et al., 2011a). Extraversion is a global personality trait and can be seen as a tendency to be energetic, enjoy and seek out social interactions, and have generally positive emotions (John and Srivastava, 1999). Determinism is a philosophical thesis that "at any instant exactly one future is compatible with the state of the universe at that instant and the laws of nature" (Mele, 2006, 3). To establish the relation, participants were given a description of a person in a deterministic universe. After reading the scenario, participants rated their agreement with three prompts concerning the person's freedom and moral responsibility (e.g., John's killing of his wife was up to him). Participants were also given the Ten Item Personality Inventory (TIPI; Gosling et al., 2003), a validated, psychometrically sound measure of the Big Five personality traits.[1] The TIPI asks participants to report how much they agree with two adjective pairs for each of the Big Five personality traits. For extraversion, participants rated how strongly the following pair of adjectives described them: *extraverted, enthusiastic* and *reserved, quiet* (Gosling et al., 2003). The responses to the free will and the extraversion prompts showed moderate, significant correlations. Those who were moderately extraverted had strong agreement with the statements, whereas those who were moderately introverted were neutral. This relation persisted even after controlling for other personality traits and a range of general cognitive abilities known to predict intelligence and good decision making (Feltz and Cokely, 2009). The relation of extraversion with compatibilist judgments has been replicated a number of times with different materials and in different cultures and languages (Andow and Cova, 2016; Cokely and Feltz, 2009a, Feltz, 2013b, 2015b; Feltz and Cokely, 2008, 2009; Feltz and Millan, 2015; Feltz, Perez, et al., 2012; Nadelhoffer et al., 2009; Schulz et al., 2011b).[2]

For more on free will, see Chapter 21.

Our second example comes from judgments of intentional action. Judgments of intentional action are fundamental to social cognition and interaction. Actions that are intentional warrant moral blame and praise that unintentional actions do not. One important class of events in intentional action is side effects. An interesting judgment asymmetry about side effects has been discovered. The side-effect effect, also known as the "Knobe Effect," is the phenomenon in which people tend to judge a harmful side effect as intentionally brought about, whereas a helpful side effect is not. In the paradigmatic instance illustrating the side-effect effect, a chairman knowingly adopts a new program that will increase the bottom line and, as a side effect, will harm the environment. However, the chairman is only motivated by profits. Most people (82%) think that the chairman intentionally brought about the harm to the environment. However, in a structurally identical scenario in which the program helps the environment, most people (77%) judge that the chairman did not intentionally help the environment (Knobe, 2003).

Extraversion predicts the side effect-effect (Cokely and Feltz, 2009b, Feltz and Cokely, 2011; Feltz et al., 2012). Using a methodology similar to the free will study described earlier, participants were given both the harmful- and helpful-chairman scenarios and were asked to rate their agreement with the statement that the chairman harmed/helped the environment intentionally. Participants also received the TIPI and completed a host of other cognitive ability tests. Those who were more extraverted were more likely to display the asymmetry in judgments between the harmful- and helpful-chairman cases. This relation persisted even after controlling for other factors including general cognitive abilities and other personality traits.

Ethics is the third philosophical area we will review where personality predicts fundamental diversity. Little argument is required to demonstrate that ethics involves fundamental philosophical values. Personality predicts philosophical disagreement about claims involving moral objectivism, or the view that moral truths exist independently of opinions. Nichols (2004) has found that a substantial number of people have nonobjectivist intuitions about a canonical moral violation involving harm to another person. Nichols gave participants a scenario describing two people arguing about whether it is okay to hit somebody just for fun. One person says that it is okay to hit somebody just for fun because everybody he knows thinks that it is. The other person says that it is not okay to hit somebody just for fun because everybody he knows thinks that it is not. Participants were asked to indicate whether they think one of the disputants is right or whether there is no fact of the matter about unqualified claims about whether it is okay to hit others just for fun. Across a number of experiments, about half of participants give the nonobjectivist response, saying there is no fact of the matter about such unqualified claims involving harm to another person. These differences in intuitions are also predicted by one's personality. In this case, the global personality trait of interest was openness to experience. Openness to experience is measured by the level of agreement with the following two pairs of adjectives: "open to new experiences, complex and conventional, uncreative". Those who scored higher on openness were significantly more likely than those who scored lower to provide the nonobjectivist response independent of their cognitive abilities or thinking skills (Feltz and Cokely, 2008).[3]

For more on moral reasoning, see Chapter 19.

The systematic variation in philosophical intuitions associated with personality challenges Neo-Platonic projects (Stich and Tobia, 2015) that attempt to discover the nonlinguistic, nonconceptual *truth* about philosophical issues. That is, Neo-Platonic projects attempt to discover things *as they are in the world* and not merely as we think of them (e.g., what beauty *is*, not what we *think* it is or what we think it *should* be). Many Neo-Platonic projects use intuitions as irreplaceable and important pieces of evidence for theory construction and refinement. For example, one of the central debates in free will is whether free will and moral responsibility are in fact compatible with the truth of determinism. This debate centers on what the fact of this relation is, not on what some people *think* the relation is. To a large extent, the study of the relation of moral responsibility and freedom to determinism has proceeded through an extensive appeal to intuitions (however, see Deutsch, 2015). But a perusal of the philosophical literature shows this same pattern emerging in many areas of philosophy, including intentional action and ethics.

The problem is that personality is arguably irrelevant to the truth of the content of an intuition. Consider some other influential factors such as socioeconomic status (Haidt et al., 1993), culture (Machery et al., 2004), order of presentation (Schwitzgebel and Cushman, 2012; Swain et al., 2008), and one's perspective (Feltz, Harris, et al., 2012; Nadelhoffer and Feltz, 2008). All of these factors have been argued to be irrelevant to the truth of the content of an intuition (Alexander and Weinberg, 2007; Horvarth, 2010; Sinnott-Armstrong, 2008; Sommers, 2012; J. Weinberg et al., 2001; J.M. Weinberg, 2006). It should not matter to the actual mind-independent truth about determinism's relation to free will and moral responsibility what order questions about that relation are presented in (just as, for example, the weight of a 10-pound bar does not vary just because one was previously holding a feather, although people may tend to judge that weight differently after holding a feather). Personality is like these factors.[4] As such, those intuitions are related to extraneous factors. Given that there is currently no argument that successfully allows us to prefer one set of intuitions to another set (introversion and extraversion seem to be equally irrelevant to the truth of whether determinism is compatible with free will and moral responsibility), one cannot dismiss one set of intuitions. To the extent that these intuitions vary with irrelevant factors such as personality, it does not appear that some philosophical disagreement about some Neo-Platonic projects is *solely* a function of rational disagreement (Sommers, 2012). As a result, the worry is that some Neo-Platonic projects might not be capable of being done (Feltz and Cokely, 2012a). In other words, finding *the* truth about many philosophical projects may not be achievable for humans given the current technologies and methods.

At this point, we will assume that fundamental philosophical values are systematically fragmented and often predicted by global, heritable personality traits. We will also assume that this predictable variation means that some Neo-Platonic projects cannot be done. While we think that these assumptions are true, establishing them is beyond the scope of the current chapter, so we encourage the interested reader to review thorough treatments presented elsewhere (Feltz and Cokely, 2012a, 2013a). Given that these assumptions are robust, what implications do they have for *informing* decisions and for informing debates about the merits of decision-support policies?

Fragmented Values and Informing Medical Decisions

In the arena of medical-decision making, we can clearly see conflicts in two fundamental goals: beneficence and protecting autonomy. The medical context is an illustrative example because there are fairly well-defined standards for goals of decisions, and almost every human being faces medical decisions. Beneficence, in medical contexts, refers to providing or withholding services that are in the best (professionally determined) interest of the patient. Respecting autonomy refers to respecting the particular values, beliefs, desires, intentions, decisions, and plans of the person in a way that enables self-rule. Often, beneficence and respecting autonomy are concordant. What is in the interest of the person fits with the patient's values, beliefs, and intentions. However, sometimes beneficence and respect for autonomy can conflict. For example, a person may have deep religious objections to having a necessary blood transfusion. In instances where beneficence and respecting autonomy conflict, it is commonly held that professionals have a responsibility to inform people of the best options available to them. Then a process of mutual adjustments between the professional and person results in a joint decision that balances beneficence with the person's deeply held values.

There is a growing and impressive body of research suggesting that the way information is presented can sometimes predictably and profoundly alter decisions that people make. For example, the "framing" of decisions can completely reverse public policy preferences of well-educated individuals. Framing occurs when different but essentially logically identical descriptions of a choice elicit different decisions (for a review, see Levin et al., 1998). The classic example of framing is Tversky and Kahneman's (1981) Asian flu case. In this case, participants were asked to decide between two programs to combat a new Asian flu that will affect up to 600 people. Participants could choose program A that would *save* 200 lives for sure or program B that has a 1/3 chance of *saving* everybody and a 2/3 chance of *saving* nobody. A different group of participants received a similar description, but their choices were between program C, in which 400 people will *die* for sure and program D, in which there is a 1/3 chance nobody *dies* and a 2/3 chance everybody *dies*. On the surface, these two descriptions are logically identical—the expected utility of each choice is 200 people live. However, in the "save" condition, 72% took the less-risky program A, whereas in the "die" condition 78% took the more-risky program D. One explanation for this phenomenon is that people become risk averse in the "gain frame" to lock in the desirable outcome (e.g., saving lives), whereas people become risk seeking in the "loss frame" to have a chance of avoiding the negative outcome (e.g., death). "Rationally," the frame should make no difference to one's risk preferences. So a nonrational factor can influence a decision.

Results such as these have fueled one popular paternalistic strategy—libertarian paternalism (a.k.a., "nudging"; Sunstein and Thaler, 2003; Thaler and Sunstein, 2008). Policies qualify as being libertarian paternalistic if they attempt to persuade people to make a decision by taking advantage of nonrational features like message framing while at the same time leaving genuinely open choices for the person. These policies are libertarian in the sense that they allow for freedom of personal choice. They are paternalistic because they attempt to influence choices for the person's own good.

To illustrate, it is commonly thought that those who are at high risk of becoming incompetent should designate a surrogate decision maker. Health care professionals may be tasked with informing those people that they should designate a surrogate. However, the way that the professional informs the person about the need for a surrogate can increase or decrease the probability that the person will designate a surrogate. Research suggests that in some instances, framing can alter the strength of the recommendation to designate a surrogate for those who have HIV. In this case, giving information that surrogate decision makers were wrong 32% of the time generated a weaker recommendation to designate a surrogate compared to indicating surrogate decision makers were accurate 68% of the time (Feltz, 2015a). Consequently, one might think that if one's goal was to get people to fully agree to designate a surrogate, then the positive frame is the preferable way to present information about surrogate decision-making accuracy. This framing would result in more individuals judging that they ought to designate a surrogate decision maker while still leaving open the option to decide something else. More people would make decisions that substantially protect and promote their quality of life without strictly infringing on the choices available.

Libertarian paternalism is an instance of paternalism. While formally defining paternalism is theoretically difficult (J.D. Trout, 2005), we take the following analysis to be informative:

> A is acting paternalistically toward S if and only if A's behavior (correctly) indicates that A believes that (1) his action is for S's good; (2) he is qualified to act on S's behalf; (3) his action involves violating a moral rule (or will require him to do so) with regard to S; (4) S's good justifies him in acting on S's behalf independently of S's past, present, or immediately forthcoming (free, informed) consent; and (5) S believes (perhaps falsely) that he (S) generally knows what is for his own good.
>
> (Gert and Culver, 1979, 199)

309

Paternalism appears to involve violating a moral rule, and violations of moral rules require justi-fication (Gert and Culver, 1979). For example, seat belt laws are a justifiable paternalistic policy if the violation of the moral rule (e.g., violating freedom or opportunity) results in sufficiently greater good (e.g., fewer serious injuries or deaths in accidents). Everything else being equal, if one could obtain the same desirable outcome without paternalism, then no justification for the moral violation would exist. That means that if we can rationally engage a person in deci-sion making and come to a preferred joint decision without nonrational persuasion, then that is preferable to a situation in which a professional influences people by nonrational means, all else equal (Hausman and Welch, 2010).

In order for paternalism to be justified, a sufficient good must be accrued to offset the violations of autonomy, and the person affected must judge the good to be a good. In the cur-rent context, the justification for the paternalistic intervention is that the person's predictable irrationality gets in the way of the person achieving that good. The paternalistic policy helps ensure that the person obtains that good despite (and in this case, by taking advantage of) pre-dictable biases. But here is where fundamental differences in philosophical values complicate paternalistic policies. The paternalistic strategies must *aim* for some predetermined good. There is one preferred choice that the paternalist attempts to get people to make. For example, in the surrogate decision-making case, the paternalistic intervention *aims* at the *desired* choice of encouraging people to designate a surrogate. The paternalistic policy in this case is not aimed at promoting any other good.

Determining the Good

The evidence from the first section of this chapter suggests that Neo-Platonic projects cannot be reliably done. This includes determining what *the* good is. So any justification for (libertar-ian) policies that attempt to achieve *the* good are likely to fail or to otherwise rest on untestable assumptions. Even if *the* good exists, we are unlikely to discover what that good is, given the currently existing tools and methods. The history of philosophy is rife with attempts to define *the good*, and yet in two millennia there is as of yet no consensus. While there is general agree-ment that we should promote "the good," there is often considerable disagreement about what specific "good" should be preferred.

Decision architects are people with personalities, working in complex sociotechnical com-munities and cultures. The architect's choice about which decisions should be promoted are likely biased by many factors including the personalities and the fundamental philosophical biases and goals of the policy makers. As such, the decision architect is in a precarious position of promoting goods that are not likely to be reflective of *the* good since there is no *the* good.

One might think that we discover what *the* good is by prolonged reflection and attention and by paying attention to experts. In this case, one might think the expertise about what the good is (along with other fundamental philosophical values) could be found in professional philosophers who spend their lives devoted to the exploration of these issues. However, grow-ing evidence suggests that even professional philosophers with verifiable philosophical expertise are not immune to some of the effects of extraneous factors on their philosophical intuitions. Specifically, the expertise defense holds that the special training, knowledge, and practice of professional philosophers largely makes them immune to extraneous factors such as personality. There is of course considerable evidence that in a number of different domains, expertise makes intuitions qualitatively better. For example, expert chess players simply have better intuitions about the right moves and avoid the errors that novices make (Ericsson et al., 2007). Similarly, one might argue that philosophers have years of training and are likely to develop some types of expertise. Philosophers tend to be better at argument evaluation and construction (Kuhn, 1991). Because of these years of training and well-developed skills, expert philosophers may not be influenced by the extraneous factors. On this argument, philosophical expertise is likely to greatly reduce or eliminate the problematic effects of personality.

Unfortunately, philosophy simply does not have many of the features of other domains that enable improved intuitions. For example, philosophy, unlike chess, rarely has clear, unambiguous feedback when (or where) one has made a mistake (J.M. Weinberg et al., 2010). So it is unlikely that philosophical training will alleviate the effect of many extraneous factors. But there is a more straightforward problem—philosophers display many of the same biases as other people (Machery, 2012; Schwitzgebel and Cushman, 2012; Schwitzgebel and Rust, 2009, 2014; Tobia et al., 2013). Whether extensive training and knowledge in one field reduces the relationship between personality and philosophical intuitions has been tested in free will. Free will expertise was measured with a validated ten-item psychometric test that asked a series of factual questions about the free will debate (e.g., True or False: PAP stands for the Principle of Alternate Personalities). Participants were also given a typical scenario testing compatibilist intuitions and a personality inventory. Just as in previous studies, the relation of extraversion with expert compatibilist intuitions was moderate and did not significantly differ in strength compared to the relationship between personality and folk compatibilist intuitions. That is, the relation between personality and philosophical intuition was independent of domain-specific philosophical expertise. Hence, on at least one paradigmatic task, expertise neither eliminated nor reduced the effect of an extraneous factor as the expertise defense would predict (Schulz et al., 2011a).

All of this is, of course, consistent with a paternalistic intervention promoting *some* conceptions of the good. While promoting *the* good would be the most direct and compelling justification for paternalism, it is not required. Rather, all that is required is that the paternalistic intervention promotes the good as conceived of by the individual. So even if we cannot know if we promote the good, we can certainly have some degree of confidence that we are promoting *a* good, at least as some people conceive of it. But promoting some conceptions of the good is also problematic and complicated. The paternalistic intervention must promote some particular choice. This promotion is often at the expense of promoting alternative, often opposing choices. While promoting some choices may promote the good as conceived of by *some* people, the promoted choice may in many instances be contrary to the good as conceived of by others. For example, some people may want to invest more in retirement, but others may have very good reasons not to invest more in retirement. In these instances, not only is there a morally objectionable infringement on autonomy, but that infringement is not offset by accruing a good as conceived by the affected people. While it may be the case that in some instances there is near univocal agreement about what the good to be promoted is, that is not likely to always be the case. And in any event, this would require a choice architect to have a good sense about what the individual conceptions of the good are before instituting a particular policy. Given that there are diverse philosophical values and diverse decision-making environments, having an adequate and robust empirical map of those values is daunting.

Rational Versus Nonrational Persuasion

But is there an alternative to nudging or other paternalistic strategies? *Informing* decisions is an ethically responsible approach that offers the advantages of paternalism while generally avoiding the costs. Why informing decisions or "rational persuasion" is better than persuasion resulting from nonrational features is fairly well established. For example, "only rational persuasion fully respects the sovereignty of the individual over his or her choices" (Hausman and Welch, 2010,

135). One may wonder how information transparency is different from persuasion (e.g., nudging) since information must be presented in *some* way. There is no frame-neutral way to present information to people, and some of those frames have been shown to predictably influence people's decisions. Yet one important difference between information transparency and persuasion is that information transparency engages the deliberative, rational capacities of a person in a way that persuasion (e.g., nudging) typically does not.

For example, consider research in which information is designed such that people can be shown to understand it better and in turn can make better use of the information in service of better decisions (Cokely et al., 2012; Cokely et al., in press, Cokely and Kelley, 2009; Cokely et al., 2006; Garcia-Retamero and Cokely, 2011, 2013, 2015; Garcia-Retamero et al., 2015; Hoffrage and Gigerenzer, 1998; Hoffrage et al., 2000; Okan et al., 2015; Petrova et al., 2015). In one such study, Garcia-Retamero and Cokely (2011) measured the effects of information transparency on behaviors related to sexually transmitted diseases (STDs). In their studies, they could influence participants to screen for STDs or take precautions against getting STDs by framing information. The framing only increased one of these desired behaviors. However, a simple visual aid was presented to participants that resulted in participants understanding the statistical information better. Moreover, presenting graphs along with statistical information eliminated the differential effect of framing while maintaining the benefits of framing. When participants understood the information better, they were more likely to engage in safer sexual practices *and* to screen themselves for STDs. Garcia-Retamero and Cokely speculate that effectiveness of graphs may be the result of more elaborate encoding of the information about STDs. Subsequent studies demonstrate that the benefits of visual aids is a function of changes in understanding that changes attitudes, shapes intentions, and ultimately drives healthier decisions and behaviors (Garcia-Retamero and Cokely, 2011, 2013, 2015). These studies also indicate that simple well-designed (i.e., "transparent") risk communications can be as effective as the most persuasive framing effects (e.g., appealing to fear) and as effective as leading validated 8-hour training programs. By using transparent risk communication with visual aids, the participants' rational capacities were engaged and gave rise to a more representative mental understanding of the issues as compared to the biases engendered with persuasive message framing.

Theoretically, these results (and many others) suggest it is *possible*, then, to avoid many problematic aspects of and debates about libertarian paternalism simply by informing decision makers and that in some cases there is no trade-off (i.e., a dominated decision with fewer overall costs, no additional costs, and at least as many benefits). But that possibility does not entail that we should always prefer information transparency to nudging. An essential question is: How should strategies that involve nudging or information transparency be compared? Trout (2005) offers the following suggestions:

> To the extent that these particular strategies work, their desirability is based on the particular features of the problem: their generality (the scope of the problems they address), their frequency (how frequently the types of problems they address actually occur), their significance (how important the problems are to human welfare), and the cost of implementation (how simply and cheaply the problem can be addressed by these methods).
>
> (Trout, 2005)

There are simple, efficient, and direct ways to increase information transparency by presenting simple graphical visual aids. This is often seemingly as easy to implement as structuring environments so that the message frame influences people in the desired direction. But informed decision making is also likely to be superior as well. For example, informed decision making offers the possibility of *transference* (e.g., cognitive and learning transfer; neurocognitive development and maintenance). If one informs a person appropriately, that person may develop skills, knowledge, abilities, attitudes, habits, and so forth that afford additional benefits to the person in other situations. The person may gain the confidence and skill to make recommendations about similar decisions in a different domain. For example, if one learns how to reason well about statistical information by being properly informed, this skill will help one solve a number of math problems. A growing body of research also suggests this will help people deal with important information about risk in other everyday contexts (see RiskLiteracy.org for examples; (Cokely et al., 2012; Peters et al., 2007). This possibility is closed off to the libertarian paternalist because the libertarian paternalist intentionally uses nonrational features to alter particular choices. Personal agency and character development is largely bypassed.

Given the nature and intent of nudges, by design it just isn't likely that a person learns anything by being nudged. In contrast, informing may help with the frequency of the problems addressed. If one knows how to handle a situation and feels appropriately confident in one's ability to do so, then one can do so even if the nudge isn't in place. The nudge also requires that the choice architect be far enough ahead of the decision maker to be able to design all the environments in which a person makes the choice and that the design can effectively, consistently, and quickly adapt these environments to changing policies, cultures, needs, and technologies. Barring superhuman abilities, the choice architect will necessarily fail to meet all the needs. Yet citizens who are well prepared to make well-informed decisions are prepared to adapt independently. Informed decision making further holds the promise of addressing problems of greater value. For example, it is a fundamental value not only of professionals but of many people that their autonomy is respected. So necessarily, every time we effectively inform a decision, we respect people's autonomy in a way that is intentionally not respected with the nudge. As such, when we inform decisions, we guarantee autonomy *plus* whatever good is brought about by informing, whereas with nudging, we only bring about the best guess of the immediate good. As such, there are substantial reasons to think that informed decisions are often better, more sustainable, and more empowering than nudging on all of the criteria Trout identifies.

Among experts familiar with the research, there is no question that fundamental philosophical values are fragmented. The association of this fragmentation with personality suggests that the fragmentation isn't naturally going to go away any time soon. That said, it is still possible to change one's neurobiology and personality and thus philosophical biases. For example, research on various effects of psychopharmacological interventions (e.g., medications) indicates that some modern drug therapies for mental health disorders like depression and anxiety may broadly affect personality. Among a small portion of the population, these changes can be profound and enduring. For example, in one randomized control trial, researchers found that medications taken to combat depression changed not only emotional stability but also extraversion (Tang et al., 2009). Should we expect these individuals to be more likely to change their views on the relations between determinism, freedom, and moral responsibility as their struggles with depression wane? Theoretically, the answer is a resounding yes, which doesn't seem too worrying (e.g., many kinds of illnesses bias judgments). But what is worrying is the prospect of chemically altering so-called normal and healthy individuals in order to bias their intuitions and choices.

The time may not be that far off until we can use one simple pill to enhance or diminish certain biases by directly modulating one's neurobiology and personality. The same way fluoride is added to many water supplies or iron is fortified in various breakfast foods, perhaps some "substance X" could be introduced when needed to enhance decision making. But rather than controlling a decision, which would be obviously coercive, perhaps substance X could be engineered so as to moderately increase the probability that a person would make a certain decision without taking away their ability to do otherwise. In some health domains this kind of idea seems noncontroversial when the target behavior is one that is associated with psychopathology and often is the target of medical treatments (e.g., drugs that help people turn down a cigarette or eat small portions when trying to lose weight). But in other situations, this sort of *neuropsychological nudge* seems much more dangerous (e.g., biasing people toward voting in favor of specific policies, prioritizing certain values, or agreeing with certain actions). Theoretically, it would be important that substance X be engineered so that people wouldn't be compelled to make one decision or another, yet they would generally be biased toward certain desires, beliefs, and values. Ultimately, this neuro-nudging faces the same problems that behavioral nudges face, and for many of the same reasons. In some real sense, fundamental philosophical diversity defines what a good decision is for the person making the decision. In many if not most instances, it seems unlikely that we will ever be able to determine the Neo-Platonic truth of what *the* good is that we should promote. Absent that, the diversity of values suggests that promoting any particular good is likely to have the consequence of hindering some people from obtaining what they would naturally and according to their best reflective judgment view as good. Thus, if we value autonomy, all else equal, the best course of action to take is to attempt to inform rather than bias competent decision makers.

Notes

1 Overall, the TIPI predicts well the Big Five traits measured by longer, more complex instruments and is especially strong for extraversion. However, the correlation between the TIPI's and longer instruments' measurement of openness to experience is relatively low. So caution may be warranted in interpreting the results involving the openness-to-experience subscale (see objectivism discussion in what follows).
2 We use the compatibility question as a paradigmatic example here. However, other intuitions about freedom and moral responsibility have been predicted by personality, including manipulation-style arguments (Feltz, 2013a) and in some instances fatalism (Feltz and Millan, 2015).
3 We take moral objectivism as our paradigmatic example for ethics. However, personality predicts other ethical intuitions such as when a character trait is a virtue (Cokely and Feltz, 2011; Feltz and Cokely, 2012b, 2013b).
4 We want to be clear that this variation challenges some and perhaps not other projects. For example, just because the variation challenges some Neo-Platonic projects does not mean the variation challenges projects in conceptual analysis or normative projects. We could grant that one's intuitions reflect one's own concept of free will and moral responsibility without also claiming that the content of those intuitions is true. In fact, given our evidence, it seems highly likely that there are a number of different philosophically relevant concepts that are associated with personality traits. As such, our argument doesn't rely on a simple skeptical hypothesis.

Further Reading

Feltz, A. and Cokely, E.T. (2012) "The Philosophical Personality Argument". *Philosophical Studies* 161(2), 227–246. doi:10.1007/S11098-011-9731-4

Feltz, A. and Cokely, E.T. (2013) "Predicting Philosophical Disagreement". *Philosophy Compass* 8(10), 978–989.

Gigerenzer, G. (2015) "On the Supposed Evidence for Libertarian Paternalism". *Review of Philosophy and Psychology* 6(3), 361–383.

Leonard, T.C. (2008) "Richard H. Thaler, Cass R. Sunstein, Nudge: Improving Decisions About Health, Wealth, and Happiness". *Constitutional Political Economy* 19(4), 356–360.

Schulz, E., Cokely, E.T. and Feltz, A. (2011). "Persistent Bias in Expert Judgments About Free Will and Moral Responsibility: A Test of the Expertise Defense". *Consciousness and Cognition* 20(4), 1722–1731. doi:10.1016/J.Concog.2011.04.007

References

Alexander, J., and Weinberg, J.M. (2007) Analytic epistemology and experimental philosophy. *Philosophy Compass* 2(1): pp. 56–80.

Andow, J., and Cova, F. (2016) Why compatibilist intuitions are not mistaken: A reply to Feltz and Millan. *Philosophical Psychology* 29(4). pp. 550–566.

Ashton, M.C. (2013) *Individual Differences and Personality*. 2nd ed. Amsterdam, Boston: Academic Press.

Bouchard, T.J., and Loehlin, J.C. (2001) Genes, evolution, and personality. *Behavior Genetics* 31(3): pp. 243–273.

Cokely, E.T., and Feltz, A. (2009a) Adaptive variation in judgment and philosophical intuition Reply. *Consciousness and Cognition* 18(1): pp. 356–358. doi:10.1016/J.Concog.2009.01.001

———. (2009b) Individual differences, judgment biases, and theory-of-mind: Deconstructing the intentional action side effect asymmetry. *Journal of Research in Personality* 43(1): pp. 18–24. doi:10.1016/J.Jrp.2008.10.007

———. (2011) Virtue in business: Morally better, praiseworthy, trustworthy, and more satisfying. *Journal of Organizational Moral Psychology* 2(1): pp. 13–26.

———. (2014) Expert intuition. In L. Osbeck and B. Held (Eds.). *Rational Intuition*. Cambridge: Cambridge University Press, pp. 213–238.

Cokely, E.T., Galesic, M., Schulz, E., Ghazal, S., and Garcia-Retamero, R. (2012) Measuring risk literacy: The Berlin numeracy test. *Judgment and Decision Making* 7(1): pp. 25–47.

Cokely, E.T., Feltz, A., Ghazal, S., Allan, J., Petrova, D., Garcia-Retamero, R., (in press). *Decision Making Skill: From Intelligence to Numeracy and Expertise. The Cambridge Handbook of Expertise and Expert Performance*, 2nd ed.

Cokely, E.T., and Kelley, C.M. (2009) Cognitive abilities and superior decision making under risk: A protocol analysis and process model evaluation. *Judgment and Decision Making* 4(1): pp. 20–33.

Cokely, E.T., Kelley, C.M., and Gilchrist, A.L. (2006) Sources of individual differences in working memory: Contributions of strategy to capacity. *Psychonomic Bulletin & Review* 13(6): pp. 991–997. doi:10.3758/Bf03213914

Costa, P.T., and McCrae, R.R. (1988) From catalog to classification—Murray needs and the 5-factor model. *Journal of Personality and Social Psychology* 55(2): pp. 258–265. doi:10.1037//0022–3514.55.2.258

Council, N.S.A.T. (2015) Social and Behavioral Sciences Team Annual Report. Available at https://sbst.gov/download/2016%20SBST%20Annual%20Report.pdf

Deutsch, M. (2015) *The Myth of the Intuitive: Experimental Philosophy and Philosophical Method*. Cambridge, MA: MIT Press, a Bradford Book.

Ericsson, K.A., Prietula, M.J., and Cokely, E.T. (2007) The making of an expert. *Harvard Business Review* 85(7–8): pp. 114–121.

Feltz, A. (2013a) Pereboom and premises: Asking the right questions in the experimental philosophy of free will. *Consciousness and Cognition* 22(1): pp. 53–63. doi:10.1016/j.concog.2012.11.007

———. (2013b) Pereboom and premises: Asking the right questions in the experimental philosophy of free will. *Consciousness and Cognition* 22(1): pp. 53–63. doi:10.1016/J.Concog.2012.11.007

———. (2015a) Ethical information transparency and sexually transmitted diseases. *Current HIV Research* 13(5): pp. 421–431.

———. (2015b) Experimental philosophy of actual and counterfactual free will intuitions. *Consciousness and Cognition* 36: pp. 113–130. doi:10.1016/j.concog.2015.06.001

Feltz, A. (2017). Folk Intuitions. In M. Griffith, N. Levy, & L. Timpe (Eds.), *The Routledge Companion to Free Will* (pp. 568–576). New York: Routledge.

Feltz, A., and Cokely, E.T. (2008) The fragmented folk: More evidence of stable individual differences in moral judgments and folk intuitions. In B.C. Love, K. McRae and V.M. Sloutsky (Eds.). *Proceedings of the 30th Annual Conference of the Cognitive Science Society*. Austin, TX: Cognitive Science Society, pp. 1771–1776.

———. (2009) Do judgments about freedom and responsibility depend on who you are? Personality differences in intuitions about compatibilism and incompatibilism. *Consciousness and Cognition* 18(1): pp. 342–350. doi:10.1016/J.Concog.2008.08.001

————. (2011) Individual differences in theory-of-mind judgments: Order effects and side effects. *Philosophical Psychology* 24(3): pp. 343–355. doi:10.1080/09515089.2011.556611

————. (2012a) The philosophical personality argument. *Philosophical Studies* 161(2): pp. 227–246. doi:10.1007/S11098-011-9731-4

————. (2012b) The virtues of ignorance. *Review of Philosophy and Psychology* 3: pp. 335–350.

————. (2013a) Predicting philosophical disagreement. *Philosophy Compass* 8: pp. 978–989.

————. (2013b) Virtue or consequences: The folk against pure evaluational internalism. *Philosophical Psychology* 26(5): pp. 702–717. doi:10.1080/09515089.2012.692903

Feltz, A., Harris, M., and Perez, A. (2012) Perspective in intentional action attribution. *Philosophical Psychology* 25(5): pp. 335–350.

Feltz, A., and Millan, M. (2015). An error theory for compatibilist intuitions. *Philosophical Psychology* 28(4): pp. 529–555.

Feltz, A., Perez, A., and Harris, M. (2012). Free will, causes, and decisions individual differences in written reports. *Journal of Consciousness Studies* 19(9–10): pp. 166–189.

Garcia-Retamero, R., and Cokely, E.T. (2011). Effective communication of risks to young adults: Using message framing and visual aids to increase condom use and STD screening. *Journal of Experimental Psychology Applied* 17(3): pp. 270–287. doi:10.1037/a0023677

————. (2013) Communicating health risks with visual aids. *Current Directions in Psychological Science* 22(5): pp. 392–399. doi:10.1177/0963721413491570

————. (2015) Simple but powerful health messages for increasing condom use in young adults. *Journal of Sex Research* 52(1): pp. 30–42. doi:10.1080/00224499.2013.806647

Garcia-Retamero, R., Cokely, E.T., and Hoffrage, U. (2015). Visual aids improve diagnostic inferences and metacognitive judgment calibration. *Frontiers in Psychology* 6: p. 932. doi:10.3389/fpsyg.2015.00932

Gert, B. and Culver, C.M. (1979) Justification of paternalism. *Ethics* 89(2): pp. 199–210. doi:10.1086/292097

Gigerenzer, G., Todd, P.M., and ABC Research Group. (1999) *Simple Heuristics That Make Us Smart.* New York: Oxford University Press.

Gosling, S.D., Rentfrow, P.J., and Swann, W.B. (2003) A very brief measure of the big-five personality domains. *Journal of Research in Personality* 37(6): pp. 504–528. doi:10.1016/S0092–6566(03)00046–1

Haidt, J., Koller, S.H., and Dias, M.G. (1993) Affect, culture, and morality, or is it wrong to eat your dog. *Journal of Personality and Social Psychology* 65(4): pp. 613–628. doi:10.1037/0022–3514.65.4.613

Hausman, D.M., and Welch, B. (2010) Debate: To nudge or not to nudge. *Journal of Political Philosophy* 18(1): pp. 123–136. doi:10.1111/J.1467–9760.2009.00351.X

Hoffrage, U., and Gigerenzer, G. (1998) Using natural frequencies to improve diagnostic inferences. *Academic Medicine* 73(5): pp. 538–540.

Hoffrage, U., Lindsey, S., Hertwig, R., and Gigerenzer, G. (2000) Medicine: Communicating statistical information. *Science* 290(5500): pp. 2261–2262.

Horvarth, J. (2010). How (not) to react to experimental philosophy. *Philosophical Psychology* 23: pp. 448–480.

John, O.P., and Srivastava, S. (1999) The Big-five trait taxonomy history, measurement, and theoretical perspectives, in L.A. Pervin & O.P. John (Eds.), *Handbook of personality: Theory and research* (2nd edition, pp. 102-38). New York: Guilford Press.

Judge, T.A., Bono, J.E., Ilies, R., and Gerhardt, M.W. (2002) Personality and leadership: A qualitative and quantitative review. *Journal of Applied Psychology* 87(4): pp. 765–780. doi:10.1037/0021–9010.87.4.765

Kane, R. (1996) *The Significance of Free Will.* New York: Oxford University Press.

King, A.J., Johnson, D.D.P., and Van Vugt, M. (2009) The origins and evolution of leadership. *Current Biology* 19(19): pp. R911-R916. doi:10.1016/j.cub.2009.07.027

Knobe, J. (2003) Intentional action and side effects in ordinary language. *Analysis* 63(3): pp. 190–194. doi:10.1111/1467–8284.00419

Kuhn, D. (1991) *The Skills of Argument.* Cambridge, New York: Cambridge University Press.

Lamb, M., Chuang, S., Wessels, H., Broberg, A., and Hwang, C. (2002) Emergence and construct validation of the big five factors in early childhood: A longitudinal analysis of their ontogeny in Sweden. *Child Development* 73: pp. 1517–1524.

Levin, I.P., Schneider, S.L., and Gaeth, G.J. (1998) All frames are not created equal: A typology and critical analysis of framing effects. *Organizational Behavior and Human Decision Processes* 76(2): pp. 149–188. doi:10.1006/Obhd.1998.2804

Machery, E. (2012). Expertise and intuitions about reference. *Theoria-Revista De Teoria Historia Y Fundamentos De La Ciencia* 27(1): pp. 37–54.

Machery, E., Mallon, R., Nichols, S., and Stich, S.P. (2004) Semantics, cross-cultural style. *Cognition* 92(3): pp. B1–B12. doi:10.1016/J.Cognition.2003.10.003

Martin, R., and Juergen, H. (2005) Association of the functional catechol-O-methyltransferase VAL-158MET polymorphism with the personality trait of extraversion. *Neuroreport* 16: pp. 1135–1138.

Mele, A. (2006) *Free Will and Luck*. Oxford, New York: Oxford University Press.

Nadelhoffer, T., and Feltz, A. (2008) The actor-observer bias and moral intuitions: Adding fuel to Sinnott-Armstrong's fire. *Neuroethics* 1: pp. 133–144.

Nadelhoffer, T., Kvaran, T., and Nahmias, E. (2009) Temperament and intuition: A commentary on Feltz and Cokely. *Consciousness and Cognition* 18(1): pp. 351–355. discussion 356–358. doi:10.1016/j.concog.2008.11.006

Nichols, S. (2004). After objectivity: An empirical study of moral judgment. *Philosophical Psychology* 17(1): pp. 3–26. doi:10.1080/0951508042000202354

Okan, Y., Garcia-Retamero, R., Cokely, E.T., and Maldonado, A. (2015) Improving risk understanding across ability levels: Encouraging active processing with dynamic icon arrays. *Journal of Experimental Psychology Applied* 21(2): pp. 178–194. doi:10.1037/xap0000045

Peters, E., Dieckmann, N., Dixon, A., Hibbard, J.H., and Mertz, C.K. (2007) Less is more in presenting quality information to consumers. *Medical Care Research and Review* 64(2): pp. 169–190. doi:10.1177/1077558707064020301

Petrova, D., Garcia-Retamero, R., and Cokely, E.T. (2015) Understanding the harms and benefits of cancer screening: A model of factors that shape informed decision making. *Medical Decision Making* 35(7): pp. 847–858. doi:10.1177/0272989X15587676

Revelle, W., and Scherer, K. (2009) Personality and emotion. In D. Sander and K. Scherer (Eds.). *The Oxford Companion to Emotion and the Affective Sciences*. New York: Oxford University Press, pp. 304–305.

Schulz, E., Cokely, E.T., and Feltz, A. (2011a) Persistent bias in expert judgments about free will and moral responsibility: A test of the expertise defense. *Consciousness and Cognition* 20(4): pp. 1722–1731. doi:10.1016/J.Concog.2011.04.007

———. (2011b) Persistent bias in expert judgments about free will and moral responsibility: A test of the expertise defense. *Consciousness and Cognition* 20(4): pp. 1722–1731. doi:10.1016/j.concog.2011.04.007

Schwitzgebel, E., and Cushman, F. (2012) Expertise in moral reasoning? Order effects on moral judgment in professional philosophers and non-philosophers. *Mind & Language* 27(2): pp. 135–153. doi:10.1111/J.1468-0017.2012.01438.X

Schwitzgebel, E., and Rust, J. (2009) The moral behaviour of ethicists: Peer opinion. *Mind* 118(472): pp. 1043–1059. doi:10.1093/mind/fzp108

———. (2014) The moral behavior of ethics professors: Relationships among self-reported behavior, expressed normative attitude, and directly observed behavior. *Philosophical Psychology* 27(3): pp. 293–327. doi:10.1080/09515089.2012.727135

Sinnott-Armstrong, W. (2008) Abstract + concrete = paradox? In J. Knobe and S. Nichols (Eds.). *Experimental Philosophy*. Oxford: Oxford University Press, pp. 209–230.

Smilansky, S. (2000) *Free Will and Illusion*. New York: Oxford University Press.

Sommers, T. (2012) *Relative Justice: Cultural Diversity, Free Will, and Moral Responsibility*. Princeton, NJ: Princeton University Press.

Stich, S., and Tobia, K. (2015) Experimental philosophy's challenge to the "Great Tradition. *Analytica: Revista de Filosofia*.

Sunstein, C.R., and Thaler, R.H. (2003) Libertarian paternalism is not an oxymoron. *University of Chicago Law Review* 70(4): pp. 1159–1202. doi:10.2307/1600573

Swain, S., Alexander, J., and Weinberg, J.M. (2008) The instability of philosophical intuitions: Running hot and cold on Truetemp (Keith Lehrer). *Philosophy and Phenomenological Research* 76(1): pp. 138–155.

Tang, T.Z., DeRubeis, R.J., Hollon, S.D., Amsterdam, J., Shelton, R., and Schalet, B. (2009). Personality change during depression treatment: A placebo-controlled trial. *Archives of General Psychiatry* 66(12): pp. 1322–1330. doi:10.1001/archgenpsychiatry.2009.166

Team, T.B.I. (2015) The Behavioural Insights Team: Update report 2013–2015. Available at: www.behaviouralinsights.co.uk/wp-content/uploads/2015/07/BIT_Update-Report-Final-2013-2015.pdf

Thaler, R., and Benartzi, S. (2004) Save More Tomorrow (™): Using behavioral economics to increase employee saving. *Journal of Political Economy* 112(1): pp. S164–S187. doi:10.1086/380085

Thaler, R., and Sunstein, C.R. (2008) *Nudge: Improving Decisions about Health, Wealth, and Happiness*. New Haven, CT: Yale University Press.

Tobia, K., Buckwalter, W., and Stich, S. (2013) Moral intuitions: Are philosophers experts? *Philosophical Psychology* 26(5): pp. 629–638. doi:10.1080/09515089.2012.696327

Trout, J.D. (2005) Paternalism and cognitive bias. *Law and Philosophy* 24(4): pp. 393–434. doi:10.1007/S10982-004-8197-3

Tversky, A., and Kahneman, D. (1981) The framing of decisions and the psychology of choice. *Science* 211(4481): pp. 453–458. doi:10.1126/Science.7455683

Weinberg, J.M. (2006) How to challenge intuitions empirically without risking skepticism. *Philosophy and the Empirical* 31: pp. 318–343.

Weinberg, J.M., Gonnerman, C., Buckner, C., and Alexander, J. (2010) Are philosophers expert intuiters? *Philosophical Psychology* 23(3): pp. 331–355. doi:10.1080/09515089.2010.490944

Weinberg, J.M., Nichols, S., and Stich, S.P. (2001) Normativity and epistemic intuitions. *Philosophical Topics* 29: pp. 429–460.

21

BRAIN IMPLANTS

Implications for Free Will

Walter Glannon

Introduction

The will is a complex set of motor, cognitive, affective and volitional capacities necessary to form and execute action plans. The will is free when persons are able to exercise these capacities in performing intentional voluntary actions without coercion, compulsion or constraint (Frankfurt, 1988a, 1988b; Spence, 2009; Dennett, 2015). These are the types of actions for which persons can be morally and legally responsible. Free will comes in degrees. One can have a will that is free in some respects but not others, depending on whether one has some or all of these internal capacities and whether external circumstances allow one to exercise them. Brain injury from trauma or infection and neurological and psychiatric disorders can impair the capacities associated with free will by causing dysfunction in neural circuits and pathways mediating them. In deep brain stimulation (DBS), brain–computer interfaces (BCIs) and hippocampal prosthetics (HPs), electrodes implanted and activated in the brain can modulate, bypass or replace damaged or dysfunctional neural circuits and restore or enhance freedom of will by restoring the relevant capacities and allowing persons to translate them into actions. These brain implants can enable individuals with these conditions to regain control of their behavior and be responsible for it. They can be described as "prosthetics for the will" (Glannon, 2014a, 2014b).

Many philosophers argue that free will and moral responsibility require that actions not result from causal routes that bypass the agent's mental states as the direct causes of her actions (Mele, 1995; Davidson, 2001a, 2001b). To decide and act freely, some argue that agents have to act from their "own mechanisms, which cannot be formed by pills, *electronic stimulation* of the brain or brainwashing" (Fischer and Ravizza, 1998, 236, emphasis added; see also Bublitz and Merkel, 2009, 2013). Because being responsible for one's actions requires that one will perform them freely and because substantially altering the brain with neural prosthetics seems incompatible with free will, being morally responsible for one's actions excludes "severe manipulation of the brain, hypnosis and the like" (Fischer, 2006, 53). Presumably, by modulating, bypassing or replacing damaged neural circuits mediating the motor and mental functions necessary for behavioral control, brain implants preclude free and responsible agency. Yet when they operate as designed, neural prosthetics can restore these functions when they have been lost or impaired from brain injury or disease. Contrary to claims that artificial devices implanted and activated in the brain undermine free will, I argue that they allow people with injury or disease to regain it. Neural prosthetics elucidate how brain dysfunction can impair the capacities associated with behavior control and how implanting devices in the brain can restore varying degrees of brain function and control. These devices do not raise new questions about whether we have free will. Instead, they add to the existing debate by showing how intervening in the brain can alter neural circuits and the mental functions they mediate.

Some philosophers take free will to be synonymous with autonomy, the capacity to act on motivational states that one identifies as one's *own* (Frankfurt, 1988a, 1988b, 1988c; Mele, 1995, 2009; Schermer, 2015). Others assume that autonomy involves a person's values and interests and thus has a broader scope than free will (Dworkin, 1988; Wolf, 1990). Yet both autonomy and free will imply self-determination. In this respect, I use "autonomy" and "free will" interchangeably.

21.1 Spotlight: Free Will

Walter Glannon

The traditional philosophical problem of free will is how one can choose among possible courses of action and have an impact on events in a deterministic universe. Causal determinism is the thesis that natural laws and events in the past jointly determine a unique future. This means that any action one performs at a particular time is the only action one could have performed at that time. "Incompatibilists" believe that causal determinism is incompatible with free will because it rules out alternative possibilities of action. "Hard incompatibilists" believe that causal determinism is true and that we do not have free will. "Soft Incompatibilists," or "Libertarians," believe that we have free will and that causal determinism is false. "Compatibilists" reject the idea that free will requires alternative possibilities of action and believe that causal determinism is compatible with free will. They claim that free will requires only that we have the capacity to translate motivational states into actions without coercion, compulsion or constraint. Advances in neuroscience have shifted the focus on free will from the external world of physical laws and the past to the internal world of the brain (Roskies, 2006, 2010). Whether neural processes influence or determine the mental processes they mediate is an open question because empirical evidence suggests that both deterministic and stochastic (probabilistic) mechanisms operate at different levels of brain activity (Atmanspacher and Rotter, 2011). In light of this uncertainty, what matters for free will and the behavior control associated with it is whether or to what extent the brain enables or disables the mental and physical capacity to form and execute action plans.

A practical implication of the free will debate is that free will is considered necessary for moral and criminal responsibility, because having the capacity to control one's actions is necessary for one to be responsible for them. Thus, any view of free will that excludes the possibility of having it must presumably also deny the possibility that one can be responsible for committing crimes.

References

Atmanspacher, H. and Rotter, S. (2011). "On Determinacy or its Absence in the Brain," in R. Swinburne, ed., *Free Will and Modern Science*. Oxford: Oxford University Press, 84–101.

Roskies, A. (2006). Neuroscientific challenges to free will and responsibility, *Trends in Cognitive Sciences* 10: 419–423.

Roskies, A. (2010). How does neuroscience affect our conception of volition? *Annual Review of Neuroscience* 33: 109–130.

I explain how different types of brain implants in deep brain stimulation, brain–computer interfaces and hippocampal prosthetics can reestablish behavior control. DBS can restore motor, cognitive, affective and volitional capacities. BCIs can restore a more limited range of motor functions and possibly communication when a condition precludes the ability to interact with others verbally or gesturally. HPs can restore the capacity to encode memories and improve the retention of information necessary to form and carry out action plans.

Deep Brain Stimulation

Neuromodulation of Motor and Mental Functions

DBS has the widest range of applications among neural prosthetics. It can be used as both a probe and modulator of activity in dysfunctional neural circuits implicated in neurological disorders such as Parkinson's disease (PD) and psychiatric disorders such as major depressive disorder (MDD) and obsessive-compulsive disorder (OCD; Lozano and Lipsman, 2013). MRI–guided stereotactic probing can locate the circuits and estimate the extent of their dysfunction when patients are awake while undergoing intracranial surgery. Modulation of the critical circuits through electrical stimulation can restore or improve motor as well as cognitive, affective and volitional functions mediated by them. In this technique, electrodes are implanted unilaterally or bilaterally in a particular brain region. The electrodes are connected to leads through which electrical current is delivered by a pulse generator implanted in the abdomen or under the collarbone. The voltage, frequency and intensity of the current can be increased or decreased, and the system can be turned on or off by manual operation of a programmable device.

Stimulation of the subthalamic nucleus (STN) or globus pallidus interna (GPi) in the basal ganglia has restored circuit function and resulted in significant improvement for many patients with Parkinson's disease and other movement disorders (Benabid, 2003). It has restored their ability to voluntarily control bodily movements. While the technique is still experimental and investigational for psychiatric disorders, DBS has modulated dysfunction in brain-stem dopaminergic structures associated with anhedonia (loss of pleasure in previously pleasurable activities) and avolition (lack of initiative or decreased motivation) in a subtype of depression (Holtzheimer and Mayberg, 2011; Schlaepfer et al., 2014). By restoring their capacity to engage in pleasurable activities, DBS can restore some degree of the affective and volitional components of the will (Schlaepfer et al., 2014). In addition, because of its projections to frontal-thalamic-striatal-frontal pathways mediating cognitive, affective and sensorimotor functions, stimulation of the STN can modulate dysfunction in these pathways and release individuals with obsessive-compulsive disorder from paralyzing obsessions and compulsions (Mallett et al., 2008; Figee et al., 2013). In this context, one might consider that DBS can reestablish some degree of the cognitive, affective and motor components of the will.

DBS entails risks when used for both movement disorders like Parkinson's and psychiatric disorders like depression and obsessive-compulsive disorder. There is a small but significant risk of intracerebral hemorrhage from the surgery and infection from the implant (Rabins et al., 2009). Most of the adverse effects of DBS of the STN for Parkinson's involve behavioral changes. Some Parkinson's patients receiving DBS of the STN have developed impulsive and pathological behaviors such as gambling and hypersexuality as a result of unintended dysregulation of nontargeted circuits (Frank et al., 2007; Castrioto et al., 2014). This may be due to overstimulating targeted circuits, the combined effects of DBS and dopamine agonist drugs or to the ways in which targeted and nontargeted circuits project to and from each other in terms of inputs and outputs (Christen et al., 2012; Castrioto et al., 2014). The main risk of DBS for psychiatric disorders is hypomania or mania (Mallet et al., 2008; Synofzik et al., 2012). Developing techniques for more precise stimulation could reduce these risks. The risks of side effects of DBS also have to be weighed against the risk of suicide and continued poor quality of life from residual components of neurological or psychiatric disorders that have not responded to other treatments. For instance, DBS for depression does not help patients undo a lifetime of poor coping skills.

Free will implies the ability to control one's mental and physical behavior. This in turn implies that a person's conscious mental processes have some causal role in their behavior. Yet the fact that DBS operates outside of the subject's awareness without any apparent conscious contribution from the subject seems to exclude this control. How could one be in control of one's behavior if one is merely a passive recipient of the effects of neurostimulation? The modulated thoughts and actions of the person undergoing the technique can be traced to an artificial source. It seems that the device rather than the person is in control of her behavior (Klaming and Haselager, 2013). How could a person act freely and be responsible for one's actions if they are caused by a machine (Clausen, 2009)?

For more on the ethics of deep brain stimulation, see Chapters 4 and 29.

Behavioral Control: Complementary Unconscious and Conscious Processes

Most typical brain processes are not transparent to us. We have no direct access to our efferent system, for example, and only experience the sensorimotor consequences of our unconscious motor plans. These plans are carried out as a matter of course without having to think about them. It does not matter whether these consequences are produced by a natural or artificial system. The fact that DBS operates outside of a person's conscious awareness does not undermine but instead supports behavior control and thus free will by modulating dysfunctional neural circuits that generate and sustain conscious thought and action. The subject's implicit knowledge that electrodes are implanted (i.e., the patient is not always consciously aware of the DBS device, not unlike a cardiac pacemaker) and activated in the brain does not figure in the explicit content of her conscious states. The processes in our brains that mediate typical mental states and even voluntary actions (like the detailed procedure of picking up a coffee cup) to some extent are normally occurring unconsciously. By not interfering with but enabling the formation and translation of both unconscious and conscious intentions into actions, DBS promotes effective decision making. Provided that the implant connects in the right way with the neural inputs and outputs that regulate behavior, it allows the subject to initiate and execute action plans. Insofar as the DBS system prevents intrusive thoughts (as in the case of treatment of OCD) and ensures that the subject has the motor and mental capacities necessary to perform the actions she wants and intends to perform, she can identify the system as her own, as an expanded feature of her brain and mind.

Having an active device in one's brain does not mean that one cannot think and act freely and be responsible for one's actions. It is the brain injury or disease rather than the neural prosthetic that impairs or undermines control. Although it operates outside of a person's conscious awareness, when it modulates targeted circuits, the prosthetic does not replace him as the source of his action. Rather, it enables voluntary and effective agency by restoring the functional integrity of the neural circuits that mediate the relevant motor and mental capacities. The shared behavior control between the conscious subject and the artificial device is not fundamentally different from the shared behavior control between the conscious subject and naturally occurring unconscious processes in his normally functioning brain.

Shaun Gallagher (2006) claims that "if my bodily movement is determined by something other than my own reflective thought, then it is an involuntary movement but not an action" (111). As I pointed out with regard to sensorimotor functions, however, the performance of many actions does not require conscious reflection. The fact that these actions do not issue from conscious intentions and are performed automatically does not imply that they are involuntary. One may not consciously attend to the motor functions necessary to ride a bicycle, drive a car or walk across a street. But these actions are still voluntary. DBS can facilitate this aspect of agency by releasing constraints on the agent imposed by neurological and psychiatric disorders. Moreover, DBS can modulate neural circuits in a way that can make them amenable to cognitive behavioral therapy and other psychotherapies (Goldapple et al., 2004). The bottom-up effects of neurostimulation can allow top-down rewiring effects from conscious mental states to cortical brain circuits. The operation of the device outside of the patient's reflective thought can induce changes in the brain that can have salutary effects on reflective thought and how it issues in voluntary actions.

A person with an implanted neurostimulator can turn it on or off if needed. This ability shows that the person has free will in controlling the operation of the device and its effects on her brain and mind. The conscious decision to turn it on or off indicates that at least some of the person's behavior involves reflective thought. Crucially, voluntary operation of the device assumes that the individual knows when to turn it back on and that doing this is necessary to restore modulation of motor, affective and volitional functions. Depending on whether or to what extent DBS affects this cognitive capacity, it can either enhance or diminish free will (particularly in a case in which DBS leads to mania). Retaining this cognitive capacity while the stimulator was off would be necessary for her to retain control through a period when there were no modulating effects from the device. Otherwise, increasing the electrical current from the stimulator or turning it off could entail the risk of self-harm and harm to others from the loss of control of the person's physical and mental functions.

Transfer of Control

The potential harm from tinkering with a brain implant beyond its therapeutic indications is illustrated in an actual case of a patient with generalized anxiety and obsessive-compulsive disorder. The case did not involve the patient manipulating the stimulator on his own but instead the psychiatrist increasing the voltage of the device at the patient's request (Synofzik et al., 2012). Following continuous stimulation of the nucleus accumbens in the reward system of his brain at moderate intensity, the patient experienced improved mood and motivation. He told his psychiatrist that he wanted to feel even better and asked him to increase the voltage of the stimulator.

This caused him to feel "unrealistically good" and "overwhelmed by a feeling of happiness and ease" (34). Despite the euphoria, he retained sufficient insight into his condition to know that a pathological level of mood from the increased voltage entailed a risk of irrational and harmful behavior. Accordingly, he asked the psychiatrist to adjust the stimulation parameters to maintain optimal therapeutic levels of mood and motivation. This case illustrates that any discussion of enhancing cognitive and affective functions through DBS must be consistent with what would be considered an optimal level of these functions for the patient. If raising them above this level entailed a harmful outcome for the patient, then clearly it would not be enhancement.

Suppose that the patient could operate the DBS device on his own without monitoring and adjustment by his psychiatrist. Suppose further that he increased the voltage to further elevate his mood. When he did this, he knew that his modulated mental states were within a normal range. His cognitive capacity was intact, ensuring that his action was voluntary and within his control. If his action caused hyperactivity in his reward system, euphoria and impaired rationality, then he would be responsible for any harmful consequences. For example, if the euphoria caused him to drive a car at a recklessly high speed and kill another driver, then he would be responsible for that consequence, even though he lacked cognitive control of his behavior when he was driving. The harmful outcome fell within the known risk of his voluntary act of increasing the voltage of the stimulator. He had control over the sequence of events and could have prevented the outcome by not increasing the voltage. This would be analogous to drunk driving, in which the decision to drink is voluntary but sets in motion a sequence of events over which the driver has diminished or no control. Given the content of his cognitive state at the time of his action, his control and thus his free will and responsibility transferred from the earlier time when his cognitive capacity was intact to the later time when it was impaired.

Consider a hypothetical case of a patient with a stimulating device in his brain to down-regulate dopamine hyperactivity, causing an impulse control disorder. This manifests in the pathological behaviors of gambling, hypersexuality and violent outbursts of anger. The ability to regulate impulses depends on connectivity between the prefrontal cortex, which underpins rationality (Frank et al., 2007), and the limbic system, which underpins basic desires and emotions (Castrioto et al., 2014). This connectivity and dopamine levels are dysfunctional in impulse control disorders, and DBS of a critical circuit in the frontal-limbic pathway can restore normal connectivity and allow the prefrontal cortex to inhibit limbic-related dopamine hyperactivity (Castrioto et al., 2014). The modulating effects of the stimulator allow the patient to control his impulses, which are weaker and resistible when the stimulator is turned on. But he turns it off and shortly thereafter resumes his pathological behaviors. During an argument with another person, he becomes angry and assaults and kills him. Charged with second-degree murder, he claims that he was unable to control his anger and the irresistible impulse to assault the person. He claims that this constitutes an excuse for his behavior, and he does not deserve the criminal charge. Against his claim, one could argue that he would be responsible for the fatal outcome because he was able to prevent it from occurring by keeping the stimulator on. There may be grounds for mitigation of responsibility if operating the device was unduly burdensome. But it would be difficult to provide evidence from clinical or experimental uses of DBS showing that it is a great burden on patients. When he turned off the device, this person had the cognitive capacity to know that performing this action entailed a risk of harmful behavior. This provided him with control over the sequence of events resulting in killing his victim, and this control would be sufficient grounds for him to be responsible for the killing. His earlier act extends to his later act because the second was causally sensitive to the first (Davidson, 2001a). His behavioral control transfers from the earlier time when he freely decided to turn off the stimulator to the later time when he was cognitively and volitionally impaired. As in the case of the euphoric patient, the individual who turns off the stimulator need not approve of his behavioral changes to be responsible for them (Bublitz and Merkel, 2009, 2013). He can be responsible because of his cognitive capacity to foresee these changes and associated actions as the probable consequences of his action. Because of the transfer of control across time, the individual is responsible for any actions he performed in a later euphoric, hypomanic or impulsive state.

The upshot of these cases is that the ability to manipulate a neuroprosthetic device enables the person to control the physical and mental capacities constituting free will. The fact that there is a device implanted in his brain does not impair behavior control. On the contrary, the device restores control impaired by a neuropsychiatric disorder. The loss of control from euphoria or an irresistible impulse would not be grounds for mitigation or excuse from responsibility for the harmful outcome because these individuals were able to operate the device in a way that would have prevented the outcome. Assuming that the neurostimulation functions properly and that the person in whom it is implanted can regulate its effects on his brain-mind, it is consistent with a robust sense of agency and free will. If he cannot regulate these effects, then it is not consistent with this sense of willing and acting. These claims rest on the assumption that persons are constituted by but not identical or reducible to their brains. The mental states associated with the will are necessarily generated and sustained by physical processes in the brain; but these processes cannot completely explain the content of mental states. This nonreductive materialism serves as a theoretical foundation for the ways in which neurostimulation modulates the brain-mind (Baker, 2009; Northoff, 2014).

Brain–Computer Interfaces

Enabling Motor Functions

Brain–computer interfaces (BCIs) or brain–machine interfaces (BMIs) involve real-time direct connections between the brain and a computer (Lebedev and Nicolelis, 2006; Lebedev, 2014). Bidirectional feedback between the user and the system produces physical changes that can restore some degree of motor or communicative functions for individuals with lost limbs or extensive paralysis or who are significantly neurologically compromised. By providing the subject with the relevant type of feedback, the system may allow her to translate an intention into an action despite the inability to perform voluntary bodily movements. In this regard, a BCI can enable an individual with a severe brain or spinal cord injury to regain some degree of the motor and volitional capacities necessary for free will.

There are two types of feedback with BCIs. The first concerns feedback about the outcome of a self-initiated, BCI–mediated action, such as moving a computer cursor or robotic arm. It provides only indirect feedback about brain activity. The second type concerns direct feedback about the level of brain activity itself. The first is more pertinent to the potential to restore behavior control in the sense that the subject can perceive the success or failure of her mental act of intending or trying to move a cursor or artificial arm. Although it is still at an early stage of development, a BCI using electroencephalography (EEG) or functional magnetic resonance imaging (fMRI) might also enable minimally conscious individuals with higher levels of awareness or those with total locked-in syndrome to communicate wishes when they are unable to do this verbally or gesturally (Fernandez-Espejo and Owen, 2013; Peterson et al., 2013).

BCIs utilize wired or wireless systems to detect and allow transmission of signals in the brain's motor and parietal cortices into different voluntary actions. There are three main types of BCI. One consists of scalp-based electrodes that are part of the equipment required to record EEG.

Because they do not involve intracranial surgery and implantation of a device in the brain, they do not entail a risk of infection or hemorrhage. At the same time, though, they may not readily read signs from the motor cortex because the cranium can deflect or "smear" them (Wolpaw and Wolpaw, 2012). In electrocorticography (ECoG), electrodes are implanted above (epidurally) or below (subdurally) the brain's dura mater just under the skull. These can decode motor and parietal cortical signals better than scalp-based electrodes because they are not susceptible to cranial smearing (Leuthardt et al., 2004). But they involve some risk of infection and hemorrhage. Like noninvasive scalp-based systems, both forms of ECoG BCIs impose constraints on the subject's movement because of the wires running from the electrodes to the machine. Wireless systems consisting of a microelectrode array implanted in motor areas avoid this problem and are not burdensome for subjects. Because they can decode and transmit neural signals more directly than less invasive systems, implanted arrays are more likely to facilitate the execution of the subject's intentions in actions. Still, this depends on the particular features of the neurological deficit and the patient's ability to operate the BCI.

This ability may vary among patients. Some may be able to successfully manipulate the interface to achieve their goals. Others may be impaired or lack this ability altogether. Because of differences in how injury or disease affects their brains, some may be more cognitively able than others to be trained to operate a BCI to effectively manipulate a prosthetic device. Motor skills are performed unconsciously and automatically following an initial period of conscious attention and learning. These skills are maintained in procedural memory, the nondeclarative (unconscious) memory system consisting in knowing how to perform certain cognitive and sensorimotor tasks. For those with severe paralysis, however, considerable conscious effort is required to be trained to operate an interface to perform motor tasks with a prosthetic device. Operating a BCI is a challenge even for healthy subjects, with studies suggesting that up to 30% of these subjects are BCI illiterate (Birbaumer et al., 2014) This can be more challenging for those with extensive paralysis and especially for those with some cognitive impairment from brain injury. Subjects whose cognitive, affective and volitional capacities have been impaired by injury to the central nervous system may have difficulty translating their thoughts into actions, or they may fail to do so. Planning is a critical component of moving a prosthetic limb. The subject must indicate with his brain and mind where the limb should go before executing the intention to move it. This cognitive task requires considerable time and effort. Success in learning how to use a BCI to translate neural signals into actions depends on operant conditioning, which requires sustained attention, motivation and resolve. Not all severely paralyzed patients have the requisite degree of these psychological capacities to effectively operate the system.

One explanation for the failure of researchers and practitioners to train subjects to perform motor tasks with a BCI is that the complete loss of control from paralysis undermines the motivational basis for operant conditioning (Birbaumer et al., 2014). They may experience not only physical fatigue but also mental fatigue in repeatedly attempting and failing to activate the cortical regions necessary for motor control. This shows that, in addition to motor capacities, the subject's cognitive and volitional capacities are critical for the effective use of a BCI. The differences among patients in the extent to which they can operate a BCI may be attributed partly to the effects of brain injury on their physical and mental capacities. They could also be attributed to whether and how they exercise these capacities, and this cannot be explained completely in terms of brain function. Some patients may put more effort into learning how to operate the BCI than others, and this may have as much to do with their character as with their brain. This suggests that while free will is impaired by brain disorders, it may not be lacking entirely, and that BCIs can restore or enhance free will to a greater degree when some of these capacities are intact. The neural basis of the motor component of the will can be restored to some extent with a BCI. But the psychological aspects I have described are also necessary to produce desired actions (Glannon, 2014c).

These considerations highlight the critical role of the researcher or clinician in training the patient to use the system. Whether BCIs can restore some degree of free will by enabling self-initiated actions depends on the interaction between these individuals. This relationship can influence the psychological capacities the subject needs to effectively use the technology. There is, then, a social, interpersonal aspect to the ability of paralyzed or neurologically compromised patients to form and execute intentions in actions and thus a social aspect of free will with this neuro-prosthetic. Because training through operant conditioning is critical for the motivation, attention and resolve necessary to perform desired actions, the ability of a BCI to restore or enhance agency depends not only on the mechanistic properties of the system and the neural processes it mediates but also on psychological and social features of the context of action (Birbaumer et al., 2014). These features cannot be reduced to or explained entirely in mechanistic or neural terms. Both neural-mechanistic and psychosocial models are necessary to explain why some physically disabled individuals are more successful than others in operating a BCI. As the critical component of the interface, the brain implant can help to restore the relevant mental capacities by modulating dysfunctional or nonfunctional neural circuits that ordinarily mediate these capacities. But whether the implant enables the patient to execute her intentions in actions will depend on effective training and learning. Factors both inside and outside the brain are necessary to restore some degree of free will in patients with varying degrees of impaired thought and behavior. This pertains to BCIs consisting of microelectrode arrays, ECoG or scalp-based electrodes.

One of the most promising applications of BCIs has been the BrainGate 2 neural interface. This system can enable persons with amputated limbs or severe paralysis to control a prosthetic with their thoughts, mediated by the computer algorithm. The system uses electrodes implanted in the motor cortex to read signals related to limb movement. The algorithm decodes the signals and translates them, moving an external prosthetic such as a robotic arm or hand. In a study involving two volunteers with tetraplegia from brain-stem strokes, the system enabled one of the volunteers to grasp a foam ball with a prosthetic arm with a fairly high rate of success (Hochberg et al., 2012). This is one example of how a BCI can bypass the site of brain injury to restore some degree of motor control. Researchers can predict the movement the patient wants to perform, with the algorithm decoding EEG signals corresponding to the initial urge to perform that movement. But this raises the question of *what* controls the process of forming and translating the urge to move into the actual movement. This is not an issue in normal motor skills, which are performed unconsciously and automatically. Moving an artificial limb requires some degree of conscious deliberation. Yet if the movement is predictable on the basis of neural signals alone, then it seems that the subject and his conscious mental states do not initiate the movement. This suggests that restoration of physical control has everything to do with the BCI and the signals it decodes and nothing to do with the subject. The subject would have no causal role in the sequence of events resulting in the action, and the technique would not restore the loss of free will from the brain injury.

But just because conscious intentions or other mental states may not initiate the process of moving a prosthetic device does not mean that they have no causal role in this process. Even if signals in motor areas recorded through fMRI or EEG can predict the movement the subject wants to perform, they cannot predict whether she will actually perform it. Neural indices of an intention to move a prosthetic limb may explain the initiation of this process but not all events that influence a successful or failed outcome (Mele, 2009, 2014). In BCI–mediated prosthetics, the subject's conscious intention to move the artificial limb may be preceded by unconscious neural signals associated with the urge to move it. But a complete account of the movement also involves the process of learning how to operate the interface from the trainer and translate this knowledge into action. Whether the subject succeeds or fails in this endeavor is not predictable from or reducible to neural signals read by an fMRI– or EEG–based BCI.

The unconscious conditioning resulting from knowing how to operate the BCI and the conscious intention and effort of the subject are also critical components in the process of moving the external prosthetic. In these respects, the subject has some control over moving the robotic hand or arm. Despite technological and operational differences between DBS and a BCI, both are enabling devices. There is shared motor control between the subject and the system, which supports rather than replaces the subject's intact cognitive and volitional capacities. Provided that there is proprioceptive and somatosensory feedback from the robotic arm or hand to the brain, the subject can experience these external prosthetic limbs and the internal neural prosthetic to which they are linked as a form of extended or expanded embodiment and part of herself (Gallagher, 2005) and perceive her BCI–mediated action as her own. The question of what produced the movement should not be framed in dualistic terms as *either* the neural signals *or* the subject's mental states. Instead, it should be framed in more holistic terms as requiring *both* neural *and* mental processes.

Enabling Communication

As I have indicated, there are two types of self-initiated actions that BCIs allow persons to perform. The first is moving a computer cursor or robotic arm or hand, and the second is to enable communication. Both types involve many of the same motor, cognitive and volitional functions, and both involve a complex mental act of initiating and executing plans. Yet they differ in that the first involves one mental act of initiating and executing a plan in a physical movement, while the second involves two mental acts: initiating and executing an intention to communicate and actually communicating. An important question is whether a BCI alone could confirm that a subject had the requisite cognitive and affective capacities to make an informed and deliberative medical decision, such as whether to continue or discontinue life-sustaining treatment. The subject might have the mental capacity to make a free and informed decision about medical intervention. Yet the BCI might not be able to validate this.

EEG– and fMRI–based BCIs might enable individuals with neurological disorders to reliably communicate when they are unable to do this verbally or gesturally. This involves two distinct patient groups: those in a minimally conscious state (MCS) at the higher end of the awareness spectrum and those with locked-in syndrome (LIS). MCS patients have incomplete and intermittent awareness of self and surroundings (Giacino et al., 2002). Those with total LIS are completely aware but lack the capacity for any voluntary bodily movements (Hochberg and Cudkowicz, 2014). These in turn are distinct from other LIS patients who can communicate using voluntary eyelid movements. LIS patients include those who have had a brain-stem stroke or have amyotrophic lateral sclerosis (ALS). Conscious perception and expression of intentions is at a higher level in LIS than in MCS patients, and this may facilitate communication through a BCI. But ALS can cause cognitive impairment in some patients, precluding decisional capacity (Phukan et al., 2007). So being fully aware alone is not sufficient for one to make informed and deliberative decisions about whether they would want, for example, to initiate, continue or discontinue mechanical ventilation. In contrast to reports from studies indicating that some patients with LIS could communicate by responding to questions about their care and quality of life (Birbaumer et al., 2014), Leigh Hochberg and Merit Cudkowicz claim that among those with ALS, "there have been no reports of restoring communication using a neural signal-based BCI in this most severely affected population" (Hochberg and Cudkowicz, 2014, 1852).

One challenge in using BCIs for this purpose is that systems using scalp-based electrodes, ECoG or microchips implanted in the motor cortex typically utilize visual stimuli (Leuthardt et al., 2004; Wolpaw and Wolpaw, 2012). Minimally conscious and totally locked-in subjects have limited or no capacity to receive feedback from and respond to a visual stimulus in learning how to operate the system (Fernandez-Espejo and Owen, 2013). Alternatively, tactile or auditory feedback could be used to enable communication. Yet even if systems utilizing these other senses could overcome the limitations associated with a lack of visual feedback, questions would remain about the meaning of "communication." Specifically, it is not clear whether the responses of linguistically and semantically impaired minimally conscious or fully conscious locked-in patients would be evidence of the cognitive and affective capacity to give informed consent to continue or discontinue life-sustaining interventions such as artificial hydration and nutrition. Emotionally laden decisions about these interventions reflect a person's subjective values and attitudes about quality of life. It is questionable whether these values and attitudes could be expressed by simple "yes" or "no" responses to questions. Yet these subjective properties would have to be included in any robust sense of communication. This involves more than being aware or even fully aware (Jox, 2013).

Davina Fernandez-Espejo and Adrian Owen acknowledge that, with current interface technology, simple affirmative or negative responses to questions about whether a minimally conscious patient wanted to continue living would not be sufficient to establish that the patient had the "cognitive and emotional capacity to make such a complex decision." But they also say that "it is only a matter of time before all of these obstacles are overcome" (Fernandez-Espejo and Owen, 2013, 808). This may be overly optimistic. Even advanced BCIs that could detect neural activity correlating with complex semantic and linguistic processing might not be sufficient to show that the subject had the capacity to make an informed and deliberated decision about life-sustaining treatment. The patient's values and interests would influence such a decision, and these could not be captured by a BCI. The ambiguity surrounding BCI–mediated responses indicates that some form of behavioral interaction between the patient and those treating him may be necessary to confirm that he had this capacity. However, this interaction may pose another obstacle to the patient's free will independently of the BCI. The patient may feel pressure from his family to end his life because he is completely dependent on and a burden to them. It could be a form of coercion that could prevent a free decision about life-sustaining care.

For more on disorders of consciousness, see Chapter 6.

Minimally conscious patients may have some, and totally locked-in patients may have all of the mental capacities associated with the will but lack the ability to freely exercise it. Without any meaningful behavioral interaction between and among the patient, family and medical team, the level of communication necessary to validate decisional capacity and informed consent from the patient might be lacking. The brain implant as the core component of the BCI would not be an obstacle to free will by inhibiting clear expression of the patient's wishes. Rather, the system would not be able to compensate for the loss of communicative ability caused by the brain injury or disease. These considerations indicate the limitations of this technology in restoring the mental and physical components of free will for people with disorders of consciousness and severe neurological disorders in general. Advanced brain implants may eventually allow this type of communication. But resolution of this issue will come only after more research into the neural bases of communication has been conducted.

Hippocampal Prosthetics

Some people lose the ability to form and store memories from newly learned information. This can be caused by impaired or lost function of the hippocampus from brain injury or infection. More precisely, the dysfunctional area is the neural circuit consisting of the hippocampus and entorhinal cortex. While adverse effects on this memory circuit prevent the formation of new episodic memories of events, they can also disrupt semantic memory of facts and concepts and working memory, which involves holding information for short periods in order to execute cognitive tasks (Baddeley, 2007). These effects can impair free will by impairing the cognitive component of the will. They can interfere with the capacity to form and carry out action plans. A hippocampal prosthetic consists of a multisite electrode array implanted in the area encompassing the hippocampal-entorhinal (HE) circuit (Berger et al., 2011; Hampson et al., 2013). The array is linked to a very-large-scale-integration (VLSI) biomimetic model providing the necessary inputs and outputs for memory encoding. HPs have been used as prototypes in animal models but have not yet been tested in humans. While they are at a developmental stage and may be ready for implantation in the human brain in the next five years, they remain a hypothetical intervention.

DBS of the fornix, which projects to the HE circuit, improved spatial working memory in two subjects in a Phase 1 trial for early-stage Alzheimer's disease (AD; Laxton et al., 2010). For people with this and other dementias whose hippocampal degeneration is too advanced to respond to neurostimulation or for those with severe anterograde amnesia from damage to the HE and adjacent neural circuits, it has been proposed that an HP might be able to restore the brain's ability to retain information through the encoding of new episodic memories. It could have significant therapeutic potential, because this circuit is a key component of the episodic memory system and one of the first brain structures to undergo cellular loss and tau pathology in AD. Artificial reconstruction of neuron-to-neuron connections with a biomimetic microchip model replacing a damaged HE circuit could improve or restore short- and long-term episodic memory and its effects on semantic and working memory. It could improve planning and decision making and thus improve the subject's capacity for agency.

Theoretically, it would not matter whether memory functions were maintained through natural or artificial means, provided that an HP maintained the neural inputs and outputs necessary for these functions. Unlike some DBS implants, an HP would operate continuously on its own, and the person in whom it was implanted would not be able to turn it off. This would not limit her behavior control, though, because the implant would be restoring the ability to form and store information necessary to deliberate and make decisions.

Still, the autobiographical sense of episodic memory has a subjective aspect that is not reducible to the cellular mechanisms whose normal function an HP would restore. It also depends on how the subject interacts with others in physical, social and cultural environments and the meaning the subject constructs from and assigns to this lived experience. The information processing of an HP could not reproduce this meaning because it cannot be explained mechanistically. While restoring the neural basis of episodic memory, an HP would have to function in a way that did not interfere with but was compatible with the subject's constructive mental activity. This is important for the subject's orientation to space and time in the present and also influences how he imagines future situations and simulates possible scenarios of action. The prosthetic would only enable encoding of new episodic memories, after which the subject would assign meaning to them based on his experience in different environments. An HP could not assign meaning to the information in newly formed memories but would encode it with equal functional and value-neutral weight. Goal-directed behavior depends on the subject's capacity to select some past events and memories of them as more valuable to him than others. For a person with damage to the HE circuit, an HP would be necessary but not sufficient to compensate for or replace all relevant aspects of autobiographical memory. An HP would have to integrate into a distributed network of memory circuits and provide the neurobiological foundation for but not interfere with the psychology of episodic memory as travel through space and time and which is a critical component of agency and free will. It can also have implications for moral and legal responsibility.

Memory retrieval is to some extent involuntary and beyond our conscious control. But one can recall an episodic memory if one puts enough conscious effort into it. Failure to do this may result in serious harm. For example, there have been cases in which children died of hyperthermia after being left in a car on a hot day (Rogers, 2013). When charged with criminal negligence causing death, a parent or grandparent may claim that they had many tasks to attend to that day, and the information associated with the child being left in the car was pushed into their unconscious. Given the potential harm from hyperthermia, the parent should have been more attentive to the situation. Would it make any difference to a charge of criminal negligence if the parent had an HP implanted in his brain and it malfunctioned? The claim that he was unable to retrieve the information at the critical time would not have much legal weight because HPs restore memory *formation*, not retrieval (Berger et al., 2011). But a malfunctioning HP could mean that the person was unable to form a memory of his action and therefore could not recall the event. The missing cognitive content impaired his capacity for reasoning and decision making at that time and accordingly excused him from responsibility for the child's death because the HP malfunction would imply that he lacked the necessary cognitive content for negligence. This example illustrates the importance of memory function or dysfunction in both "natural" and "artificial" forms for attributions of agency and responsibility.

Conclusion

Modulating dysfunctional neural circuits with DBS, bypassing them with BCIs or replacing them with HPs does not undermine but can restore the motor and mental capacities that constitute free will. Provided that these brain implants enable people with brain injuries or neuropsychiatric disorders to reason and make decisions in accord with their considered desires and values, they can identify the mechanisms associated with these devices as their own. The devices can be experienced by those in whom they are implanted as forms of extended or expanded embodiment (Lebedev, 2014). DBS can restore a greater degree of behavior control than BCIs or HPs. This is not only because it can modulate a broader range of motor and mental functions but also because persons in whom a DBS system is implanted can turn the stimulator on or off. This may make the agent responsible for later actions when he is behaviorally impaired if he has the capacity to foresee this impairment as the possible consequence of his earlier action. Restoration of motor functions or communication in BCIs is more limited because severe and prolonged paralysis may impair the cognitive and volitional capacities necessary to operate the system. The success or failure of a person's attempt to operate a BCI may depend on her interaction with the practitioner training her. HPs can restore agency by enabling the learning of information associated with memory that is necessary to form and carry out action plans. This ability will depend also on the meaning the subject assigns to long-term episodic memory and his experience of moving through space and time. With BCIs and HPs, factors inside and outside the brain can influence whether or to what extent a person regains and can exercise free will.

Some might worry that more technically sophisticated brain implants could gradually replace all natural circuits in the brain and turn it into a completely artificial organ (Markram et al., 2011). This might function better than a biological brain and, among other things, avoid the neurodegeneration characteristic of dementia and other diseases of aging. It also raises the question of whether this would make us complete mechanisms and eliminate the mental capacities associated with free will. But neural prosthetics will likely continue to compensate for neural dysfunction while supplementing rather than supplanting normally functioning neural circuits. Persons are constituted by but are not identical to their brains. The brain is not a self-contained organ. It would be difficult to know how artificial neural networks would integrate with each other and interact with immune, endocrine, cardiovascular and other systems in the body that influence brain function. More advanced brain implants will do more to restore behavior control for people with motor, cognitive, affective and volitional limitations. But they will not replace them as agents and will not explain away free will.

Further Reading

Klein E., Brown, T., Sample, M., Truitt, A. and Goering, S. (2015). "Engineering the Brain: Ethical Issues and the Introduction of Neural Devices". *Hastings Center Report* 45(6): pp. 26–35.

Linden, D. (2014). *Brain Control: Developments in Therapy and Implications for Society*. Basingstoke: Palgrave Macmillan.

Mele, A. (2014). *A Dialogue on Free Will and Science*. New York: Oxford University Press.

Swinburne, R. (Ed.) (2012). *Free Will and Modern Science*. Oxford: Oxford University Press.

Vuilleumier, P., Sander D. and Baertschi, B. (2014). "Changing the Brain, Changing Society: Clinical and Ethical Implications of Neuromodulation Techniques in Neurology and Psychiatry," Special Issue in *Brain Topography* 27(1): pp. 1–3.

References

Baddeley, A. (2007) *Working Memory, Thought and Action*. Oxford: Oxford University Press.

Baker, L.R. (2009) Non-reductive materialism. In A. Beckermann, B. McLaughlin, and S. Waller (Eds.). *The Oxford Handbook of Philosophy of Mind*. Oxford: Oxford University Press, pp. 109–120.

Benabid, A.L. (2003) Deep brain Stimulation for Parkinson's disease. *Current Opinion in Neurobiology* 13: pp. 696–706.

Berger, T., Hampson, R., Song, D., Goonawardena, A., Marmarellis, V., and Deadwyler, S. (2011) A cortical neural prosthesis for restoring and enhancing memory. *Journal of Neural Engineering* 7: p. 8046017, doi:10.1088/1741–2560/814/046017

Birbaumer, N., Gallegos-Ayala, G., Wildgruber, M., Silvoni, S., and Soekadar, S. (2014) Direct brain control and communication in paralysis. *Brain Topography* 27: pp. 4–11.

Bublitz, C., and Merkel, R. (2009) Autonomy and authenticity of enhanced personality traits. *Bioethics* 23: pp. 360–374.

————. (2013) Guilty minds in washed brains? In N. Vincent (Ed.). *Neuroscience and Legal Responsibility*. New York: Oxford University Press, pp. 335–374.

Castrioto, A., Lhommee, E., Moro, E., and Krack, P. (2014) Mood and behavioral effects of subthalamic stimulation in Parkinson's disease. *The Lancet Neurology* 13: pp. 287–305.

Christen, M., Bittlinger, M., Walter, H., Brugger, P., and Muller, S. (2012) Dealing with side effects of deep brain stimulation: Lessons learned from stimulating the STN. *American Journal of Bioethics-Neuroscience* 3(1): pp. 37–43.

Clausen, J. (2009) Man, machine and in between. *Nature* 457: p. 1080.

Davidson, D. (2001a) Actions, Reasons and Causes. In *Essays on Actions and Events*. 2nd ed. Oxford: Clarendon Press, pp. 3–20.

———. (2001b) Mental events. *Essays on Actions and Events*: pp. 207–224.

Dennett, D. (2015) *Elbow Room: The Varieties of Free Will Worth Wanting*. 2nd ed. Cambridge, MA: MIT Press.

Dworkin, G. (1988) *The Theory and Practice of Autonomy*. New York: Cambridge University Press.

Fernandez-Espejo, D., and Owen, A. (2013) Detecting awareness after severe brain injury. *Nature Reviews Neuroscience* 14: pp. 801–809.

Figee, M., Luigjes, J., Smolders, R., Valencia-Alfonso, C., Van Wingen, G., de Kwaasteniet, B., Mantione, M., Ooms, P., de Koning, P., Vulink, N., Levar, N., Droge, L., van den Munckof, P., Schuurman, P., Nederveen, A., van den Brink, W., Mazaheri, A., Vink, M. and Denys. D. (2013) Regaining control: Deep brain stimulation restores frontostriatal network activity in obsessive-compulsive disorder. *Nature Neuroscience* 16: pp. 366–387.

Fischer, J.M. (2006) *My Way: Essays on Moral Responsibility*. New York: Oxford University Press.

Fischer, J.M., and Ravizza, M. (1998) *Responsibility and Control: An Essay on Moral Responsibility*. New York: Cambridge University Press.

Frank, M., Samanta, J., Moustafa, A., and Sherman, S. (2007) Hold your horses: Impulsivity, deep brain stimulation and medication in Parkinsonism. *Science* 318: pp. 1309–1312.

Frankfurt, H. (1988a) Freedom of the will and the concept of a person. In *The Importance of What We Care About*. New York: Cambridge University Press, pp. 11–25.

———. (1988b) Coercion and moral responsibility. *The Importance of What We Care About*: pp. 26–46.

———. (1988c) Identification and externality. *The Importance of What We Care About*: pp. 58–68.

Gallagher, S. (2005) *How the Body Shapes the Mind*. New York: Oxford University Press.

———. (2006) Where's the action? Epiphenomenalism and the problem of free will. In S. Pocket, W. Banks, and S. Gallagher (Eds.). *Does Consciousness Cause Behavior? An Investigation of the Nature of Volition*. Cambridge, MA: MIT Press, pp. 109–124.

Giacino, J., Ashwal, S., Childs, N., Cranford, R., Jennett, B., Katz, D., Kelly, J., Rosenberg, J., Whyte, J., Zafonte, R. and Zasler, N. (2002) The minimally conscious state: Definition and diagnostic criteria. *Neurology* 58: pp. 349–353.

Glannon, W. (2014a) Prostheses for the will. *Frontiers in Systems Neuroscience* 8: pp. 1–3, published online 8 May. doi:10.3389/fnsys.2014.00079

———. (2014b) Philosophical reflections on therapeutic brain stimulation. *Frontiers in Computational Neuroscience* 8: pp. 1–3, published online May 15. doi:10.3389.frcom.2014 00054

———. (2014c) Ethical issues with brain-computer interfaces. *Frontiers in Systems Neuroscience* 8: pp. 1–3, published July 30. doi:10.3389/fnsys.2014.00136

———. (Ed.) (2015) *Free Will and the Brain: Neuroscientific, Philosophical and Legal Perspectives*. Cambridge: Cambridge University Press.

Goldapple, K., Segal, Z., Garson, C., Lau, M., Bieling, P., Kennedy, S. and Mayberg, H. (2004) Modulation of cortical-limbic pathways in major depression: Treatment-specific effects of cognitive behavior therapy. *Archives of General Psychiatry* 61: pp. 34–41.

Hampson, R., Song, D., Opris, I., Santos, L., Shin, D., Gerhardt, G., Marmarelis, V., Berger, T. and Deadwyler, S. (2013) Facilitation of memory encoding in primate hippocampus by a neuroprosthesis that promotes task-specific neuronal firing. *Journal of Neural Engineering* 9: p. 10.066013. doi:10.1088/1741–2560/10/6/066013

Hochberg, L., Bacher, D., Jarosiewicz, B., Masse, N., Simeral, J., Vogel, J., Haddadin, S., Liu, J., Cash, S., van den Smagt, P. and Donoghue, J. (2012) Reach and grasp by people with tetraplegia using a neurally controlled robotic arm. *Nature* 485: pp. 372–375.

Hochberg, L., and Cudkowicz, M. (2014) Locked in, but not out? *Neurology* 82: pp. 1852–1853.

Holtzheimer, P., and Mayberg, H. (2011) Deep brain stimulation for psychiatric disorders. *Annual Review of Neuroscience* 34: pp. 289–307.

Jox, R. (2013) Interface cannot replace interlocution: Why the reductionist concept of neuroimaging-based capacity fails. *American Journal of Bioethics—Neuroscience* 4(2): pp. 15–17.

Klaming, L., and Haselager, P. (2013) Did my brain implant make me do it? Questions raised by DBS regarding psychological continuity, responsibility for actions and mental competence. *Neuroethics* 6: pp. 527–539.

Laxton, A., Tang-Wai, D., McAndrews, M., Zumsteg, D., Wennberg, R., Keren, R., Wherrett, J., Naglie, G., Hamani, C., Smith, G. and Lozano, A. (2010) A Phase 1 trial of deep brain stimulation of memory circuits in Alzheimer's disease. *Annals of Neurology* 68: pp. 521–534.

Lebedev, M. (2014) Brain-machine interfaces: An overview. *Translational Neuroscience* 28: pp. 99–110.

Lebedev, M., and Nicolelis, M. (2006) Brain-machine interfaces: Past, present and future. *Trends in Neuroscience* 28: pp. 536–546.

Leuthardt, E., Schalk, G., Wolpaw, J., Ojeman, J., and Moran, D. (2004) A brain-computer interface using electrocorticographic signals in humans. *Journal of Neural Engineering* 1: pp. 63–71.

Lozano, A., and Lipsman, N. (2013) Probing and regulating dysfunctional circuits using deep brain stimulation. *Neuron* 77: pp. 406–424.

Mallet L., Polosan, M., Nematollah, J., Baup, N., Welter, M-L., Fontaine, D., du Montcel, S., Yelnik, J., Chereau, I., Arbus, C. Raoul, S., Aouizerate, B., Damier, P. and STOC Study Group. (2008) Subthalamic nucleus stimulation in severe obsessive-compulsive disorder. *New England Journal of Medicine* 359: pp. 2121–2134.

Markram, H., Meier, K., Lippert, T., Grillner, S., Frackowiak, R., Dehaene, S., Knoll, A., Sompolinsky, H., Verstreken, K., DeFelipe, J. and Grant, S. (2011). Introducing the Human Brain Project. *Procedia Computer Science* 7: pp. 39–42.

Mele, A. (1995) *Autonomous Agents: From Self-Control to Autonomy*. New York: Oxford University Press.

———. (2009) *Effective Intentions: The Power of Conscious Will*. New York: Oxford University Press.

———. (2014). *Free: Why Science Hasn't Disproved Free Will*. New York: Oxford University Press.

Northoff, G. (2014). *Minding the Brain: A Guide to Philosophy and Neuroscience*. New York: Palgrave Macmillan.

Peterson, A., Naci., L., Weijer, C., Cruse, D., Fernandez-Espejo, D., Graham, M., and Owen, A. (2013) Assessing decision-making capacity in the behaviorally nonresponsive patient with residual covert awareness. *American Journal of Bioethics-Neuroscience* 4(4): pp. 3–14.

Phukan, J., Pender, N., and Hardiman, O. (2007) Cognitive impairment in amyotrophic lateral sclerosis. *The Lancet Neurology* 6: pp. 994–1003.

Rabins, P., Appleby, B., Brandt, J., DeLong, M., Dunn, L., Gabriels, L.,Greenberg, B., Haber, S., Holtzheimer, P., Mari, Z., Mayberg, H., McCann, E., Mink, S., Rasmussen, S., Schlaepfer, T., Vauber, D., Vitek, J. Walkup, J and Mathews, D. (2009) Scientific and ethical issues related to deep brain stimulation for disorders of mood, behavior and thought. *Archives of General Psychiatry* 66: pp. 931–937.

Rogers, K. (2013). Grandmother charged in death of Milton, Ont. toddler left alone in hot car. *Globe and Mail*, 5 July. Available at: www.theglobeandmail.com/news/national/grandmother-charged-in-death-of-milton-toddler-left-alone-in-hot-car/article/013019696.

Schermer, M (2015) Reducing, restoring or enhancing autonomy with neuromodulation techniques. In Glannon: pp. 205–228.

Schlaepfer, T., Bewernick, B., Kayser, S., Hurlemann, R., and Coenen, V. (2014). Deep brain stimulation of the human reward system for major depression—Rational outcomes and outlook. *Neuropsychopharmacology* 39: pp. 1303–1314.

Spence, S. (2009) *The Actor's Brain: Exploring the Cognitive Neuroscience of Free Will*. Oxford: Oxford University Press.

Synofzik, M., Schlaepfer, T., and Fins, J. (2012) How happy is too happy? Neuroethics and deep brain stimulation of the nucleus accumbens. *American Journal of Bioethics—Neuroscience* 3(1): pp. 30–36.

Wolf, S. (1990) *Freedom Within Reason*. New York: Oxford University Press.

Wolpaw, J., and Wolpaw, E. (2012) *Brain-Computer Interfaces: Principles and Practice*. New York: Oxford University Press.

22

PERSONAL IDENTITY AND BRAIN IDENTITY

Georg Northoff and Nils-Frederic Wagner

Introduction

Say you are looking at an old picture of your high school graduation and recognize yourself as the teenager with the funny haircut. Perhaps, from today's perspective, the haircut is not all that fashionable anymore, but nonetheless you are certain that the person in the picture is you. But what makes it true that you today and the teenager in the picture are identical—or one and the same person over time? This is a question of *diachronic* personal identity. In order to answer these kinds of questions, we must know the *criterion* of personal identity. In other words, we want to know what the necessary and sufficient conditions are that account for a person persisting from one time to another.

Numerical and Qualitative Identity

When philosophers debate personal identity, they are mostly concerned with *numerical* identity, the relationship that can hold only between a thing and itself. Numerical identity appears to require absolute or total qualitative identity. The puzzle is how, despite qualitative changes, a person still remains one and the same and persists through time and change. For example, say Jane radically changed in her personality traits, as well as in her appearance, due to a religious conversion. These changes, however, do not make Jane cease to exist altogether; they rather alter her *qualitative* identity. In questions about numerical identity, we look at two names or descriptions and ask whether these refer to one and the same person at different times or to different persons. The basis for being distinctively concerned about one's own future in a way that is inevitably different from how we are concerned about someone else's future is widely believed to be grounded in numerical identity. However much you will change, you shall still exist, if there will be someone living who will be numerically identical to you.

It goes without saying that it is impossible for a single person at different times to be identical to themselves in a strict numerical sense, especially if taking into account that the human body's cells are constantly replaced and the brain cell connections and chemistry are frequently changing minute to minute. But this isn't the kind of identity that raises questions concerning one's own survival over time. It is rather what David Wiggins (1967) calls the "conditions of persistence and survival through change". An understanding of personal identity that persists through change is, both from a pretheoretical point of view and after conceptual analysis, more compelling than the appeal to strict numerical identity (wherein a person is somehow immutable and unchanging). So when we think of a person remaining one and the same over time, we don't usually think that this prevents that person from undergoing qualitative changes. It would be absurd to claim that you aren't the person you were yesterday because your hair grew a tiny bit overnight. For this reason, accounts of personal identity must allow for persons to change in their qualitative features and nonetheless account for their persistence through time.

It is widely held (although some philosophers disagree) that questions about numerical identity must always be *determinate*, that is, whether you will exist some time in the future must always have a clear-cut 'yes/no' answer (Evans, 1985).

Criteria of Personal Identity

In what follows, we give a swift overview of the most widely held criteria of personal identity and point to some of their implications and problems.

Identity, Reductionism and Nonreductionism

According to *reductionist* theories, personal identity is reducible to more particular facts about persons and their bodies. The approach is to describe a particular relation (call it Relation *R*) that accounts for how person X is identical to a later existing person Y by virtue of X and Y being *R*-related. In other words: X is one and the same person as Y, if and only if X stands in Relation *R* to Y. In principle, Relation *R* is believed to be empirically observable. However, there is major disagreement about what Relation *R* consists in. Philosophers disagree about which particular ingredients determine the relation that constitutes personal identity. In the contemporary debate, most philosophers hold one or another form of a reductionist account. According to physical/biological reductionism, a person is identical over time so long as they remain the same living organism. For example, you are identical to the fetus you once were because a biological trajectory of your current body can be traced back to the fetus that once was in your mother's womb. A more widespread version of reductionism is psychological reductionism, according to which a person is identical over time so long as their different temporal parts are connected through psychological continuity. For example, you are identical to the person in that high school graduation picture because your current mental states (memories, desires, plans, intentions etc.) are connected through overlapping chains of psychological connectedness. We'll discuss seminal versions of both biological and psychological reductionism in more detail in the following section.

In contrast to reductionist theories of personal identity, *nonreductionists* believe that personal identity is not reducible to more particular facts about persons and their brains and bodies but rather consists in a nonanalyzable, or *simple*, 'further fact'; for example, an indivisible entity that eludes further analysis by being all by itself the necessary and sufficient condition for personal identity over time. Derek Parfit (although himself endorsing a reductionist criterion) describes the notion of a further fact as "separately existing entities, distinct from our brains and bodies, and our experience" (Parfit, 1984, 445). Nonreductionists thus claim that personal identity consists in a special ontological fact, a Cartesian Ego (going back to Descartes' substance dualism) or a soul; or stated in a less antiquated way, the view is that personal identity consists of some mental entity that is not reducible to neural mechanisms in the human brain. In the contemporary discussion in philosophy of mind, few philosophers advocate for nonreductionist accounts of personal identity because those accounts are, at least to the majority of philosophers, metaphysically contentious. It is argued that nonreductionists in the debate on personal identity take an obscure metaphysical belief and inflate it into a conceptual core conviction.

Psychological Continuity and Animalism

Granting the aforementioned concerns about nonreductionism, we will not further elaborate on these accounts. Instead, we focus on the two most paradigmatic reductionist accounts of personal identity: seminal versions of the *psychological continuity* theory and *animalism*.

According to the psychological continuity criterion of personal identity, X and Y are one and the same person at different points in time if and only if X stands in a *psychological continuity* relation to Y. You are the same person in the future (or past) as you are now if your current beliefs, memories, preferences and so forth are linked by a chain of overlapping psychological connections. Among philosophers who advocate for psychological approaches to personal identity, there is dispute over several issues: What mental features need to be inherited? What is the cause of psychological continuity, and what are its characteristics? Must it be realized in some kind of brain continuity, or will 'any cause' do? The 'any cause' discussion is based on the counterfactual idea that personal identity that is realized by psychological continuity would still hold, even if this continuity would no longer be instantiated in a brain. For example, would psychological continuity still determine identity if the personality was instantiated in a computer program? That is to say, what happens if the psychological relations that define personal identity get replicated and instantiated in a nonbiological entity or in more than one biological entity? Since psychological continuity could in principle divide, another issue is whether a 'nonbranching clause' is needed to ensure that psychological continuity holds to only one future person. It has been argued that the logical possibility of psychological continuity splitting into more than one successor evokes the need of blocking such scenarios by implementing a one–one clause into the criterion (we'll come back to this point in the section on fission cases).

According to *animalism*, you are the same being in the future (or past) as you are now (or have been earlier), as long as you are the same living biological organism. A human animal, or for that matter any organism, persists as long as its capacity to direct those vital functions that keep it biologically alive are not disrupted. If X is an animal at time t and Y exists at time $t^\star$, X and Y are identical if and only if the vital functions that Y has at $t^\star$ are causally continuous (without splitting into two or more successors) with those that X has at t. Presumably this will be the case only if Y is an animal at $t^\star$. So anything that is an animal at one time will always be an animal, and identity between an animal at one time and at another time is maintained when those vital functions are causally continuous. For animalists, psychological features have no bearing on personal identity because human animals go through periods without having any mental functions.

The difference between these two criteria becomes apparent when considering cases at the margins of life. A fetus has no psychological features, and thus according to the psychological continuity view, no person is diachronically identical to a fetus. Whereas for the animalist, a fetus and the person it later becomes are identical by virtue of being the same (single) living organism. The same holds for other cases in which human organisms lose their mental capacities but remain biologically alive.

Thought Experiments

Hypotheticals such as John Locke's famous 'Prince and the Cobbler' are still widely discussed in the metaphysical debate on personal identity (Weinberg, 2011). Locke asks what would happen if the soul of a prince, carrying with it the consciousness of the prince's life, were to enter the body of a cobbler. Locke suggests that as soon as the cobbler's body is invaded by the prince's soul, the cobbler would be the same *person* as the prince, accountable only for the prince's actions. But who would say the prince was, in Locke's term, the same 'man' or human animal? With this thought experiment, Locke suggests that persons, unlike human animals, are only contingently connected to their bodies. Locke further maintains that what constitutes a person, and moreover the *same* person, is consciousness, the awareness of one's thoughts and actions: "Nothing but consciousness can unite remote existences into the same person" (Locke, 1694/1975, 464). Referring to a man he had met who believed his soul had been the soul of Socrates, Locke asks, "If the man truly were Socrates in a previous life, why doesn't he remember any of Socrates' thoughts or actions?" Locke even goes so far as to say that if your little finger were cut off and consciousness should happen to go along with it, leaving the rest of the body, then that little finger would be the person—the same person that was, just before, identified with the whole body (Locke, 1694/1975, 459–460). On these grounds, Locke and his modern-day successors establish that wherever your mental life goes, you as a person follow.

Brain Transplants

In the spirit of Locke's 'Prince and the Cobbler', brain transplant thought experiments figure prominently in the personal identity literature. Recently the idea has entered the public debate as a science fiction prospect for future medical use. The story goes something like this: imagine someone's brain (or their cerebrum as the seat of their distinct psychology) is transplanted into someone else's empty skull (or their brain with a removed cerebrum). Then we are asked to ponder: who is the person that wakes up after the operation has been performed; is the resulting person identical to the 'brain donor' or to the 'body donor', or is it an altogether different person? Ever since Sydney Shoemaker (1963) introduced these sorts of imagined cases into the modern debate, they are frequently presented as support for psychological continuity theories and seen as troublesome for competing views. Particularly, they are fairly often regarded as more or less decisive evidence against animalist takes on personal identity. However, there are at least two lines of reasoning against this interpretation. Advocates of bodily continuity theories such as Bernard Williams (1970) have claimed that a variant of brain transplants, sometimes described as 'body swapping', actually works in favor of bodily continuity views. By slightly altering the story, Williams has shown that our intuitions as to who the resulting person will be can easily tilt. Modern-day animalists such as Eric Olson (1997) are allies in this interpretation of brain transplants. Paul Snowdon (2014) has recently presented further arguments questioning the alleged support for psychological continuity theories gathered from hypothetical brain transplants. Another, more general line of criticism comes from Kathleen Wilkes (1988), who claims that due to an inevitable lack of detail in the description of hypothetical scenarios, conclusions drawn from there often lead to a false reliance on predictions about how our concept of personal identity would apply in the imagined case. On this view, brain transplant thought experiments do not support psychological continuity theories but simply track intuitions that have no bearing on our concept of personal identity.

Fission Cases

Despite their initial appeal, psychological continuity theories share a severe problem. Unlike identity, psychological continuity is not necessarily a one–one relation; that is, psychological continuity does not necessarily hold only to one future/past person but can hold to many. For example, fission scenarios, either based on purely hypothetical cases or based on brain bisection (corpus callosotomy), as put forward, among others, by Thomas Nagel, show that psychological continuity does not follow the logic of an identity relation (Nagel, 1971). Cutting the connection between the two hemispheres is used as a treatment to restrict epileptic seizures to one hemisphere. Callostomized patients develop unconnected streams of consciousness in both visual fields, resulting in sometimes contradictory descriptions and actions. It has been reported that patients simultaneously tried to embrace their partners with one hand and push them away with the other (Sperry, 1966). It is possible in principle, then, and in accordance with empirical evidence, that psychological continuity can divide when the physical brain is divided, and thus, multiple persons can be psychologically continuous. As David Lewis and others pointed out, identity is necessarily a one–one relation that can by definition only hold to itself, whereas psychological continuity is only contingently a one–one relation and may become one–many (Lewis, 1976). Imagine that a split-brain patient's two hemispheres were transplanted into two different heads. Both resulting people would stand in a psychological continuity relation to the original person. Therefore, as Bernard Williams argued, psychological continuity is unable to meet the metaphysical requirements of a criterion for personal identity unless a nonbranching clause is added that ensures that psychological continuity can only be a one–one relation (Williams, 1970). Nevertheless, the addition of such a nonbranching clause is not fully convincing either, because, as Derek Parfit claimed, a nonbranching clause has no impact on the intrinsic features of psychological continuity and is therefore unable to explain the difference between the importance that we attach to identity and the relative unimportance of psychological continuity if it takes a branching form. So, if you are psychologically continuous with only one person, identity holds, but as soon as someone else is also psychologically continuous with the original person, identity vanishes. In any case, identity could not be sustained over time, since two persons would diverge in their experiences and their psychological contents before very long. Parfit famously concluded that "identity is not what matters" (Parfit, 1984).

The Brain Criterion

Given the aforementioned difficulties facing psychological continuity views—some of which result from detaching psychological continuity from brain continuity—and the counterintuitive implications of animalism, another criterion of personal identity has gained some recent support. According to philosophers Thomas Nagel and Jeff McMahan, personal identity is secured through *brain identity* (Nagel, 1986; McMahan, 2002). This is an attempt to base personal identity on solid empirical grounds, and it opens up new possibilities of cohering philosophical accounts of personal identity with neuroscientific evidence. This notion of personal identity has recently been discussed in the context of neuroscience (Northoff, 2001; 2004). More specifically, manipulation of the brain may change not only its neuronal functions but also its psychological and mental functions. For instance, implantation of tissue or electrodes into the brain may change the neuronal underpinnings of psychological features that are considered crucial in psychological continuity views. Does this mean that brain manipulation entails manipulation of personal identity? If so, one would assume brain identity to be a necessary and/or sufficient criterion of personal identity.

The recent insight into the empirical functioning of the brain raises a whole new field for the philosophical discussion of personal identity: the relationship between personal identity and the brain. Since the brain cannot be understood in a purely conceptual manner but must rather be explored empirically, this new field must necessarily link conceptual and empirical domains and thus be truly neurophilosophical in the genuine sense of the term. We'll now discuss Nagel's and McMahan's brain view of personal identity in some detail; subsequently we offer some neurophilosophical reflections on these two approaches.

You Are Your Brain: Thomas Nagel

Nagel (1986) considers the brain as both a necessary and sufficient criterion for personal identity, stating that "I am my brain" (Nagel, 1986, 64–5, 69). Nagel thinks that questions of personal identity are determinant—necessarily yielding a 'yes/no' answer. Personal identity, for Nagel, is nonconventional in the sense that it does not imply its own necessary and sufficient conditions, thus containing an 'empty position' that must be filled by an 'additional fact' (Nagel, 1986, 71). Nagel compares the term 'identity' with the term 'gold', saying that, before the chemical formula for 'gold' was discovered, the term 'gold' contained an 'empty position' that was later filled by an 'additional fact': the chemical formula for gold.

The same goes for personal identity and the brain. We currently have no idea about the 'additional fact' that might potentially fill the 'empty position' in personal identity. According to Nagel, the 'additional fact' in the case of personal identity must bridge the gap between the subjective experience of the person, that is, its first-person perspective and its 'I' on the one hand, and the objective, necessary structures, that is, its third-person perspective and its physical body on the other. Since the brain might eventually bridge this gap between subjective experience and objective structures, it may be considered a suitable candidate to fill the 'empty position'. The subjective component of personal identity comes into play as introspective evidence for persistence over time via some form of psychological continuity. The objective dimension of personal identity comes into play through the brain, which, being a physical organ, has purely objective features that enable us to track a person's identity without relying on fallible introspection. But at the same time, the brain accounts for subjectivity.

Subjectivity and Objectivity

Nagel thinks that personal identity cannot be fully "understood through an examination of my first-person concept of self, apart from the more general concept of 'someone' of which it is the essence" (Nagel, 1986, 35). Nagel further believes that personal identity cannot be defined *a priori*. A 'subject of consciousness' must be able to self-identify without external observation; but these identifications must correspond to those that can be made on the basis of external observation. Thus, there are both first- and third-personal features of the self and its identity over time. There must be a notion of objectivity, Nagel says, which applies to the self, for it is clear that the idea of a mistake with regard to my own personal identity makes sense. The objectivity underlying this distinction must be understood as objectivity with regard to something subjective. The question is how the idea of the same subject can meet the conditions of objectivity appropriate for a psychological concept. It is subjective (not merely biological) but, at the same time, admits the distinction between correct and incorrect self-identification.

The Brain as a Bridge Between Subjectivity and Objectivity

What could perform the function of a special type of material substance that also has irreducible subjective features? Subjects of experience are not like anything else. While they do have observable properties, the most important thing about them is that they are subjective, and it is their subjective mental properties that must be accounted for. Nagel suggests that the concept of the self is open to 'objective completion' provided something can be found that straddles the subjective/objective gap. Something whose objective persistence is among the necessary conditions of personal identity is needed, but only if this objectively describable referent is in a strong sense the basis for those subjective features that typify the persistent self. It must refer to something essentially subjective, often identifiable nonobservationally in the first-person perspective and observationally in the third-person perspective, and something that is the persisting locus of mental states and the vehicle for carrying forward familiar psychological continuities when they occur. Nagel thinks that the brain is the most plausible contender to fulfill both the objective and subjective demands of personal identity. I could lose everything but my functioning brain and would still be me.

Accordingly, the brain might be considered an 'additional fact' in Nagel's sense. On the one hand, the brain must be considered the necessary foundation for the possibility of subjective experience, since without a brain we remain unable to experience anything. On the other hand, the brain is the carrier of psychophysiological processes that remain essential for regulation and maintenance of the body. In contrast to other organs like, for example, the liver or kidney, the loss of the brain is accompanied by the loss of personal identity. The brain must subsequently be regarded as a necessary and sufficient condition for personal identity. However, Nagel concedes, due to our current lack of empirical knowledge, this assumption must be considered a preliminary hypothesis.

'Physico-Mental Intimacy'

As we have said, Nagel claims that the brain bridges the gap between the subjective experience of mental states and psychophysiological states. The brain can therefore not be considered a purely physical organ since, for Nagel (1986), mental states and subjective experience cannot be reduced to physical properties (57, 74). In addition to physical properties, the brain must therefore be characterized by mental properties. Nagel speaks of a so-called physico-mental intimacy (in an ontological sense) as an "apparent intimacy between the mental and its physical conditions" (Nagel, 1986, 20).

Due to these mental properties, the brain shows a special kind of 'insideness' that accounts for its foundational character for subjective experience: "It [the brain] can be dissected, but it also has the kind of inside that can't be exposed to dissection. There's something it is like from the inside to taste chocolate because there's something it's like from the inside to have your brain in that condition that is produced when you eat a chocolate bar" (Nagel, 1987, 34–35). Accordingly, the brain can be described mentally and physically, and both may be traced back to what Nagel calls a "fundamental essence" (Nagel, 1979, 199). This fundamental essence can be defined by complex forms of organization and combinations of matter—an "unusual chemical and physiological structure"—, which shows both proto-physical and proto-mental properties (Nagel, 1979, 201). However, neither the exact definition of both kinds of properties nor their relation is clearly determined. Thus, both important conceptual and empirical details are in need of further clarification.

Embodied Minds: Jeff McMahan

Another recent version of the brain criterion is the view that Jeff McMahan (2002) dubbed the 'Embodied Mind' account. McMahan argues that the continuity of parts of the brain that generate and sustain consciousness is both necessary and sufficient for personal identity over time. In order to survive as the same person over time, the capacity of a person's consciousness must be realized by the continuity of the same brain.

Minds

McMahan holds that a mind is individuated by reference to its physical embodiment, just as an individual mental state is. A particular memory, for example, continues to exist only if the tissues of the brain in which it is realized continue to exist in a potentially functional state. Likewise, a particular mind continues to exist only if enough of the brain in which it is realized continues to exist in a functional or potentially functional state. This neatly explains how minds persist. If a single mind has hitherto been realized in certain regions of a single brain, then, the undivided survival and continued, self-sufficient, functional integrity of those specific regions is both a necessary and a sufficient condition of the continued existence of the same mind (for further details see McMahan, 2002, 66 ff).

McMahan's take on personal identity is practical; he thinks that the basis for an individual's egoistic concern about the future is the physical and functional continuity of enough of those areas of the individual's brain in which consciousness is realized. The person persists as long as the capacity to support consciousness is preserved. Now, usually the functional continuity of these areas of the brain entails broad psychological continuity. But in the very earliest phases of an individual's life and in some instances near the end, the same mind or consciousness persists in the absence of any degree of psychological connectedness from day to day. McMahan's criterion stresses the survival of one's basic psychological capacities, in particular the capacity for consciousness; it does, however, not require the continuity of any of the particular contents of one's mental life. For example, one continues to exist throughout the progress of Alzheimer's disease until the disease destroys one's capacity for consciousness (McMahan, 2002, 71).

Brain Continuity

McMahan distinguishes among three types of continuity of the brain. His idea of *physical continuity* of the brain is applicable in either of two ways. It could involve the "continued existence of the same constituent matter" of the brain that generates and sustains consciousness or "the gradual, incremental replacement of the constituent matter of the brain over time" (McMahan, 2002, 68). In the latter sense, the brain, like most other organs of the human body, can survive gradual cellular turnover, which, on his view, is congruent with physical continuity. Thus, the core principle in preserving physical continuity over time is that there is sufficient integration between the old and new matter, which rules out in advance the compatibility of rapid replacement with physical continuity.

Closely related to physical continuity is what McMahan calls *functional continuity*. This involves roughly the continuity of basic psychological capacities of the brain—in particular, the brain's capacity for consciousness, which is sufficient for minimal functional continuity. A third and obviously less important type of continuity for McMahan is *organizational continuity*. It involves the continuity of the various tissues of the brain that underlie the connections among the distinctive features of one's psychology. These include the connection between an earlier experience and a later memory of it.

One would think that functional and organizational continuity presuppose physical continuity, but McMahan assumes that, as long as certain functions or patterns of organization are preserved, there will be functional or organizational continuity even if the relevant functions or patterns of organization are not preserved in the same matter.

So McMahan's criterion of personal identity and egoistic concern is physical and minimal functional continuity of the brain; more specifically, enough of the relevant areas of the brain in which consciousness is generated and sustained—to be capable of preserving the capacity for consciousness (McMahan, 2002, 67–69). I am the same entity today as I was yesterday because the same brain supports the same capacity for consciousness it supported yesterday. The continuity of the distinctive features of my mental life (memories, beliefs etc.) is incidental to my survival; what is important is physical continuity of the brain.

Reducing personal identity to physical and minimal functional continuity of the brain distinguishes McMahan's view from other accounts, such as psychological continuity views that include organizational continuity in the criterion of personal identity. McMahan thinks that the continuing capacity for consciousness is a sufficient basis for egoistic concern about one's own future and should, therefore, be a sufficient basis for personal identity, other things being equal. Since McMahan holds that a person begins to exist with the onset of (or the capacity for) consciousness in their organism, fetuses and patients with brain damage potentially fall under the category of beings with future interests as well. McMahan tries to make this work by emphasizing that unlike identity, the basis for egoistic concern can be present in degrees. Defending a morality of respect, McMahan makes the distinction between the badness of death and the wrongness of killing when it comes to beings with little psychological life like fetuses. The badness of death for persons themselves can vary dramatically from one person to another—young, old, gifted, ungifted and so on. The wrongness of killing someone doesn't depend on their egoistic concern about their future. Killing a person is equally wrong in each case because it violates respect for the person.

Neurophilosophical Reflections

After having considered the two most prominent views advocating brain identity as the criterion for personal identity over time, we are now in a position to critically reflect on these views from a neurophilosophical perspective. Subsequently, we sketch in broad strokes a few additions to the existing literature on brain identity that might be helpful to tie up some of the loose ends.

Is Personal Identity an 'Additional Fact'?

Nagel assumes an 'additional fact' about the brain in his concept of personal identity. This 'additional fact' should be empirically accessible. However, the psychological data show no hints or indications for such an 'additional fact.' Nobody experiences anything but their personality, which they regard as the sum of their psychological functions. In contrast, we do not define (or experience) our personalities (and personal identities) by any particular property or fact which could be regarded as equivalent to Nagel's 'additional fact'.

Nagel could argue that this 'additional fact' is epistemically not directly accessible and somehow unknowable. This leaves him with the following three options: (1) The 'additional fact' might not be accessible at all, neither first-personally nor third-personally. In this case, the 'additional fact' remains in principle hidden from us. One might consequently consider the 'additional fact' as rather mysterious; accordingly, this option does not seem to be very attractive. (2) The 'additional fact' might be accessible but merely third-personally. Then it should be detectable in neuroscientific investigations that rely on the third-person perspective. However, such an 'additional fact' has not yet been detected in neuroscientific investigations of the brain. This option thus remains empirically rather implausible. (3) The 'additional fact' might be accessible merely first-personally, though in a disguised or indirect form. In this case, the 'additional fact' might not be accessible as a 'fact' but rather as a particular type of state as distinguished from neuronal states. Instead of looking for an 'additional fact', one should then aim at revealing an 'additional state' and its relation to the brain. What could this 'additional state' be? Is it a mental state? If mental states do account for the 'additional state' as a disguised form of the 'additional fact', and thus the brain, mental states must then reflect the access to one's own brain from the first-person perspective. We may perceive our own brain states thus not as brain states but as mental states. Our brain as the 'additional fact' can thus be accessed only indirectly via mental states as 'additional states'. This probably comes closest to what Nagel has in mind (or rather in his brain?).

Conversely, we remain unable to access our own brain as a brain from the first-person perspective. This epistemic inability of our own brain to access itself directly as a brain can be called an 'autoepistemic limitation' (Northoff, 2004). This 'autoepistemic limitation' may be subserved by specific principles of functional brain organization that prevent the brain from directly perceiving itself as a brain. These principles of functional brain organization may thus fulfil the same role as the chemical formula for gold in Nagel's example. Accordingly, 'autoepistemic limitation' might account for what Nagel means by 'additional fact', although his formulation 'I am my brain' should then be rephrased as 'I am my brain, but due to autoepistemic limitation, I remain unable to directly access myself as a brain'. Moreover, an investigation of the empirical mechanisms underlying 'autoepistemic limitation' requires direct relationships between empirical functions and epistemic abilities/inabilities, that is, a so-called epistemic–empirical relationship (Northoff, 2004). This in turn makes the development of 'neuroepistemology' (Northoff, 2004) as an 'epistemology on a neurological basis' (Kuhlenbeck, 1965, 137) necessary.

'World–Brain Relation' as 'Additional Fact'?

The mere physical continuity of the brain is by itself not sufficient to account for personal identity over time. Nagel assumes an 'additional fact,' and McMahan seems to take the brain only as the seat of consciousness. How can we determine the 'additional fact' in a nonmental way without reverting to any kind of metaphysics involving mental features like consciousness? The proponent of the brain criterion may argue that the presupposition of the brain as a mere placeholder for mental features deflates the importance of the brain. We may do better by considering the brain itself. But then we are again confronted with the problem that the brain itself does not seem sufficient for personal identity.

All criteria that rely on the brain presuppose the brain as an isolated organ (or just as the seat of consciousness). However, there are empirical data that suggest that the brain and its own spontaneous activity, for example, its intrinsic activity, are strongly dependent upon the respective environmental context. For instance, a study by Duncan et al. (2015) showed that traumatic life events in early childhood impact the brain's spontaneous activity in adulthood: the higher the degree of early traumatic childhood life events (i.e., either a greater number of traumatic events or events that are more traumatic), the higher the degree of spatiotemporal disorder (e.g., entropy, in the brain's spontaneous activity in adulthood). This makes it clear that the brain is not an isolated organ encapsulated in the skull that communicates with the environment only through the body. For instance, the brain can shift the phase onset of its fluctuations (in different frequency ranges) in accordance with the onset of tones in the external environment (see chapter 20 in Northoff, 2014b, for details). That is apparent when we listen to music and swing our perceptions and movements in tune with the rhythm. Such direct coupling between brain and environment has also been described as 'active sensing' or the brain's 'sixth sense' (van Atteveldt et al., 2014). This and other examples (Northoff, 2014b; 2016) make it clear that the brain is a highly context-dependent organ that stands in direct relation to the respective environment, with the latter impacting, modulating and sculpting the former. Taken in this sense, the brain can no longer be considered an isolated organ but a relational organ that can be characterized by what we describe as a world–brain relation or 'environment–brain unity' (Northoff, 2014b).

Why is the characterization of the brain as 'environment–brain unity' relevant for determining personal identity? The relation in which the brain stands to its environment is apparently an intrinsic and thus defining feature of the brain as brain. If so, one may assume that this world–brain relation may account for the 'additional fact' Nagel was searching for when he conceived of the brain as seat of personal identity. One may then want to rephrase Nagel as saying, 'I am my world–brain relation', rather than, 'I am my brain'.

The assumption of physical continuity as suggested by McMahan may then need to be replaced by relational continuity: as long as I stand in a continuous relation to the world, I remain identical even if my brain and its physical continuity change. Such relational continuity presupposes a different ontology, however. Instead of a property-based ontology, one may then want to suppose a relational ontology that comes close to what Alfred North Whitehead described as 'process ontology' (Whitehead, 1929/1978). Process ontology takes the continuous change and dynamics, and thus the flux of being, as the most fundamental unit of existence and reality. Ontology is here essentially dynamic with continuous change across time and space. That stands in opposition to property-based ontology in which specific properties (like physical or mental properties) that are static and nonchangeable are assumed as the basic units of existence and reality.

Personal Identity as 'Physico-Mental Intimacy'?

Patients with brain implants report a close interaction between their mental states and the physical substitutes, that is, the cells or the stimulating electrode (Northoff, 2001). For example, they describe the feeling that they could influence the brain by their psychological and mental states. Nagel's assumption of 'physico-mental intimacy' might thus be considered as empirically plausible. The subjective experience of being able to influence mental states both via one's own brain tissue and through implants would not be possible without some kind of 'physico-mental intimacy'—subjectively accessible via the first-person perspective.

Does this epistemic characterization of 'physico-mental intimacy', however, justify the inference of physical and mental properties in an ontological sense? Such an epistemic-ontological inference is, for example, reflected in Nagel when he infers from the epistemic description of a special 'insideness' to underlying ontological properties. This type of inference might be called an 'epistemic-ontological fallacy' (Northoff, 2004b) in which one falsely infers from epistemic or knowable characteristics to ontological properties or the essence of being.

However, even if one allows for epistemic-ontological inferences, the ontological assumption of mental properties of the brain, as distinguished from its physical properties, cannot easily be justified: though mental states can be experienced in the first-person perspective, their experience cannot be directly linked to one's own brain because of 'autoepistemic limitation'. If, however, mental states cannot be directly linked to one's own brain, any type of epistemic-ontological inference from mental states to mental brain properties remains impossible. Nagel could, however, argue that if mental brain properties cannot be inferred from the experience of mental states in the first-person perspective, they may at least be inferred from the third-person perspective. This is problematic, too, because we do not experience mental states in a third-person perspective. Instead, we observe physical states in the third-person perspective. One may consequently infer mental brain properties from the observation of physical states. This inference also remains questionable, since physical states can be entirely accounted for by physical properties without need to infer any mental brain properties. Accordingly, either type of inference of mental brain properties from physical brain properties lacks evidence.

The criterion of physical–mental intimacy may be considered in a novel light in the context of the postulated world–brain relation. If the world-brain relation is a necessary condition of possible mental states, one may replace physical–mental intimacy by 'neuro-ecological intimacy'. 'Neuro-ecological intimacy' refers to the fact that the brain stands in an intimate and mutually dependent relationship with its respective ecological context. Only if there is such 'neuro-ecological intimacy' can we have mental states at all. Loss of mental states, as in loss of consciousness, goes along with loss of world–brain relation and its neuro-ecological intimacy. For instance, patients in the vegetative state have lost consciousness and are no longer able to relate to the world in a meaningful way—their brains have lost their world–brain relation and are henceforth no longer relational but isolated (see what follows for more details).

Organizational and Functional Dissociation

An interesting feature in McMahan's account is the possible dissociation between organizational and functional brain continuity. McMahan's insistence on minimal functional continuity as the bearer of personal identity—without access to the particular content of mental states such as memories—suggests that what he has in mind is phenomenal continuity. Since McMahan thinks that this sort of phenomenal continuity is enough to secure the distinct concern for one's own future, it remains to be shown how minimal functional continuity can do the trick. In situations of phenomenal disruptions of consciousness (such as falling into a dreamless sleep), one wonders how one could tell that there is any connection between a conscious state before and after the disruption occurs. If there is no psychological continuity whatsoever, it seems that there is in principle no way to differentiate between one's own conscious state and someone else's conscious state just by reference to the first-person perspective. The only way to be sure of one's own identity, following McMahan, would then be to see a neurologist and have her check if it is still the same minimal functional continuity that supports my phenomenally disconnected states of consciousness. This, of course, would reduce personal identity to the third-person perspective and thus seems inadequate as a basis for egoistic concern about the future.

22.1 Spotlight: Mind–Body Identity: Are We Just Our Brains?

Kimberly Van Orman

Before we can consider questions about personal identity, free will, consciousness and others in the philosophy of mind, we need an answer to the metaphysical question: What is the relationship between the mind and the body? There are many possibilities available in the logical space: that only nonphysical minds exist (idealism), only brains are real (eliminative materialism), minds and brains both exist but are essentially the same thing (reductive materialism), minds and brains exist but are fundamentally different things (substance dualism), minds are a nonphysical property of brains (property dualism) and minds are not nonphysical but are defined in terms of their functional properties, like software that runs on brains (nonreductive materialism). Of these, four come up most frequently: two dualist and two materialist views.

Dualism is committed to the idea that minds are fundamentally distinct from brains. There are two main forms of dualism: substance and property. *Substance dualism* is most associated with René Descartes, who held that minds are made of a nonphysical substance distinct from physical brains and bodies, although the two different substances can interact. This is a view that easily and intuitively fits with the idea of a soul that can survive the death of the body. Few philosophers today accept this view as likely to be true. The centrality of the brain to mind is evident in cases where physical damage to the brain seems to result in a person changing in ways fundamental to who they are as a person. That should not happen if substance dualism is true. In addition, if the mind were a completely nonphysical substance, we would need an account of how something with absolutely no physical properties could have any effect on a world in which physical events seem to always have physical causes.

Property dualism doesn't require that the mind be a completely separate substance. It accepts the brain as the seat of the mind but holds that the mind is an emergent property that cannot be reduced to the physical. Property dualism can better account for what we know about the brain; however, it still has a problem explaining how the nonphysical mind can make physical changes in the brain. Some philosophers committed to property dualism have given up on the idea that minds can have causal properties. On this view, called *epiphenomenalism*, minds are both nonphysical and noncausal properties that arise out of the functioning of the brain.

With regard to neuroethical concerns about identity and authenticity that arise, for instance, in the context of cognitive enhancement, substance dualism would deny that we, as distinct individuals, are essentially our brains. This implies that enhancements that specifically target physical brain function would not threaten an identity whose locus is the nonphysical mind. For property dualism, it's possible that changes to the brain could affect one's mind.

Every version of materialism (also known as physicalism) is committed to the idea that there is only one basic kind of matter in the world—physical matter. The principle of *supervenience* describes a dependency relation that attempts to capture this notion that everything is in some sense physical. When an entity or property (e.g., a mind) supervenes on another (e.g., a brain), then if they share all the same physical properties (down to the subatomic level), they share the same mental ones.

Reductive materialism is the idea that the mind and the brain are just two ways of talking about the same thing. On this view, for any type of mental state (for example, being in a specific kind of pain), there will be an underlying physical type. In theory, we could give a physical definition for any mental state (since they're the same thing). For example, pain of type p would be defined in terms of the physical brain states that it's identical with. This view is also called *type identity theory*. This take on materialism captures the intuitive idea that minds and brains are simply the same thing, just described in different language. Changes to the brain also constitute changes to the mind. To the extent that we are concerned about the integrity, authenticity or identity of the self, reductive materialism holds that brain and mind are identical, which implies that changes to the brain would constitute changes to the mind/self.

Nonreductive materialism accepts supervenience and holds that minds are fundamentally physical. However, it does not accept the idea that minds and brains are identical. A mental state is defined as a specific kind (for example, a pain, an emotion, an intention) based on its relationships to other mental states, the situation of the body (senses, physical location, condition) and the behaviors it gives rise to. For a nonreductive materialist, minds are to brains as software is to hardware. There is nothing nonphysical going on, but at least some of the causal force comes from what's going on in the mind. This view is sometimes called *token identical materialism* since it holds that any individual (token) mental state will be identical with a token brain state. It denies that we can get type identity because it holds that some mental states can be multiply realizable—for example, my mental state of affection for my cat might be realized in my brain differently than your (identical) mental state is realized in yours. However, even though our particular brain structure might differ, we share the same type of mental state, since it comes up when we each see our cats and leads us to walk over and scratch their ears and leads to other cat-friendly thoughts. For non-reductive materialism (as in property dualism), whether targeted or widespread alterations in the function of the physical brain would threaten personal identity will depend on the nature of the alterations and whether we see a significant change in mental status. Minds and brains are not identical, but they are interdependent. Some problems will be related to the software (mind), and others will be related to the hardware (brain). Given some configurations of the hardware, the software won't function properly. Similarly, for some changes in the brain (such as we see with severe trauma), mental states could be changed enough to raise concerns about whether one's identity has changed.

References

Chalmers, D. (2002) *Philosophy of Mind: Classical and Contemporary Readings*. Oxford University Press.

Montero, B. (2008) *On the Philosophy of Mind*. Wadsworth Publishing.

Ravenscroft, I. (2005) *Philosophy of Mind: A Beginner's Guide*. Oxford University Press.

'World–Brain Relation' and First-/Third-Person Perspective

One may now want to raise the question of how our criterion of world–brain relation stands in relationship to the distinction between first- and third-person perspective. The discussion of personal identity revolves largely around the question of whether the first- and/or the third-person perspective provides necessary and/or sufficient conditions for personal identity. We argue that the world–brain relation cannot be accessed through the third-person perspective since it cannot be observed as such. Nor can the world–brain relation be experienced as such via the first-person perspective since it is prephenomenal rather than phenomenal (Northoff, 2014b). How then can we characterize the world–brain relation in perspectival terms? We assume that the world–brain relation remains by itself nonperspectival, meaning that it is neither first- nor third-personal.

How, though, can we then apprehend and access the world–brain relation if not through the first- and third-person perspective? We claim that we can access the world–brain relation only in an indirect way by inferring from combined experience and observation in very much the same way that Nagel suggests the need for a correspondence between the first- and third-person perspectives. At the same time, a proper world–brain relation may be conceived of as a necessary or predisposing condition for the possible perspectival differentiation between the first- and third-person perspectives (Northoff, 2014b). One may consequently feature the world–brain relation as preperspectival rather than as completely nonperspectival or perspectival: the prefix 'pre–' indicates here that the world–brain relation is the necessary condition of subsequent perspectival access to reality in terms of first-, second- and/or third-person perspectives. In contrast, it would be nonperspectival when there is no relationship at all between world–brain relation and the different perspectives. Why is the distinction between pre- and nonperspectival important for personal identity? We postulate that such preperspectival features need to be continuous in order to preserve our personal identity. If the world–brain relation is disrupted, becoming nonperspectival rather than preperspectival, we may lose our personal identity, including our relation to the world. For instance, patients in vegetative state, who have lost consciousness, lose the neuro-ecological intimacy of their world–brain relationship, which renders the latter nonperspectival. That, in turn, makes it impossible for them to take on any kind of perspective, neither first- nor second-person perspective (as manifest in the absence of first-person experience and second-person intersubjectivity) nor third-person perspective (as manifest in the absence of third-person observation).

Neuroethical Considerations and Future Directions

We now turn to briefly indicate how some of the discussed features relate to neuroethical concerns of personal identity. We do so by looking at patients in the vegetative state and at dementias. Questions about the personal identity of these patients might affect decision-making authority over these patients, including the authority of previously expressed desires in advance directives. We will indicate how a world–brain relation and neuro-ecological account of personal identity illuminate such hard cases.

Patients in a permanent vegetative state have irreversibly lost consciousness. These patients are unable to relate to the world in a meaningful way. In our terminology, their world–brain relation is disrupted, rendering their personal identity discontinued. Even though these patients are biologically alive, in that their vital functions are artificially sustained, there's nothing left of the relational component that would enable the person that previously inhabited the biological organism to relate to the world. Due to this lack of preperspectival world–brain relation, there is no more first-personal experience, and so one might conclude that the person has vanished. What is left is a 'nonrelational organism' on life support—an organism that once was a constitutive part of a person's identity. This description might paint a picture of how to ontologically characterize these patients, but does it allow for a clear-cut neuroethical evaluation of these scenarios when it comes to previously expressed desires in advanced directives? This issue is far from being straightforward and comes with a substantial commitment to normative ethical convictions. We won't attempt a decisive answer here but merely hint at two possible interpretations. On one view, the person that previously expressed their desire to, say, be kept on life support even if their consciousness is irreversibly lost might be seen to have normative authority over an organism that once was the host of their personhood, even if the person vanished. This is so, perhaps, because there is no other person inhabiting that organism who could claim authority. On a different interpretation pertaining to the same point, one might aver that precisely because there is no person inhabiting that organism anymore, a previously expressed directive has no authority, and so it should be up to the closest relatives or guardian to decide.

Cases of dementia, especially in its very late stages, are even more difficult to evaluate both ontologically and normatively. There is no question that in early stages of dementia, the person still relates to the environment in their usual way. When the gradual decline of person-characteristics proceeds, the way in which the person relates to their environment potentially changes in a great many different ways. Nonetheless, there seems to be still enough of the world–brain relation in place so as to preserve personal identity, not necessarily because of the contents of psychological continuity that are inevitably lost toward the end of that neurodegenerative disease but because there is a continuous uninterrupted way in which the same person relates to their environment due to an ongoing world–brain relation. The person might have lost some of their distinct psychological features, but the very basis for their being able to relate to the world remains, and so their personal identity is preserved. If this is so, one would think, there are at least prima facie reasons to make the case that previously expressed desires should continue to bear normative authority even if the person in their current stage can no longer remember having expressed these desires. It goes without saying that this issue becomes ever more difficult if current desires contradict previously expressed ones.

Both scenarios illustrate how a relational account of personal identity might be able to offer empirically informed normative guidance in cases where purely metaphysical views of personal identity either decide by fiat or leave the issue open entirely. Needless to say, a relational look at these cases is still in the fledgling stage, and so it becomes apparent that future interdisciplinary neuroethical studies are needed in order to get a more firm grip on these vexing issues.

In conclusion, future investigations of personal identity may want to discuss (1) the model of the brain; (2) the brain's relationship to the world; (3) the interplay between world–brain relation and consciousness, including its epistemological features like auto-epistemic limitation; and (4) the notion of brain continuity as in regards to both world–brain relation and consciousness. This may, in turn, provide the ground for the future development of a brain-based and neuro-ecological (rather than brain-reductive and neuronal) account of personal identity.

Further Reading

DeGrazia, D. (1999) "Persons, Organisms, and the Definition of Death: A Philosophical Critique of the Higher-Brain Approach". *Southern Journal of Philosophy* 37, 419–440.

Lewis, D. (1976) "Survival and identity". In A. Rorty (Ed.). *The Identities of Persons*. Berkeley, CA: University of California Press, pp. 17–41.

MacIntyre, A. (1984) *After Virtue*. Notre Dame: University of Notre Dame Press.

Noonan, H. (2003) *Personal Identity*. 2nd ed. London: Routledge.

Northoff, G. (2014a) *Unlocking the Brain. Volume I: Coding*. New York: Oxford University Press.

Northoff, G. (2014b) *Unlocking the Brain. Volume II: Consciousness*. New York: Oxford University Press.

Schechtman, M. (2014) *Staying Alive—Personal Identity, Practical Concerns, and the Unity of a Life*. New York: Oxford University Press. doi:10.1093/acprof:oso/9780199684878.001.0001

References

Atteveldt van, N., *et al.* (2014) Multisensory integration: Flexible use of general operations. *Neuron* 81(6): pp. 1240–1253.

Duncan, N.W., Hayes, D.J., Wiebking, C., Tiret, B., Pietruska, K., Chen, D.Q., . . . Northoff, G. (2015) Negative childhood experiences alter a prefrontal-insular-motor cortical network in healthy adults: A preliminary multimodal rsfMRI-fMRI-MRS-dMRI Study. *Human Brain Mapping* 36(11): pp. 4622–4637.

Evans, G.M. (1985) *Collected Papers*, Antonia Phillips (Ed.). Oxford: Clarendon.

Kuhlenbeck, H. (1965) The concept of consciousness in neurological epistemology in brain and mind. In J.R. Smythies (Ed.). *Brain and Mind: Modern Concepts of the Nature of the Mind*. New York: Routledge, pp. 102–143.

Lewis, D. (1976) Survival and identity. In A.O. Rorty (Ed.). *The Identities of Persons*. Berkeley: University of California Press.

Locke, J. (1694/1975) *An Essay Concerning Human Understanding*, P. Nidditch (Ed.). Oxford: Clarendon Press.

McMahan, J. (2002) *The Ethics of Killing: Problems at the Margins of Life*. Oxford: Oxford University Press.

Nagel, T. (1971) Brain bisection and the unity of consciousness. *Synthese* 22: pp. 396–413.

———. (1979) *Mortal Questions*. London: Routledge.

———. (1986) *The View from Nowhere*. Oxford: Oxford University Press.

———. (1987) *What Does It All Mean? A Very Short Introduction to Philosophy*. New York, Oxford: Oxford University Press.

Northoff, G. (2001) *Personale Identität und Operative Eingriffe in das Gehirn*. Paderborn: Mentis.

———. (2004a) Am I my brain? Personal identity and brain identity—A combined philosophical and psychological investigation in brain implants. *Philosophia Naturalis* 41: pp. 257–282.

———. (2004b) *Philosophy of the Brain: The Brain Problem*. Amsterdam: John Benjamins.

———. (2014) *Unlocking the Brain. Vol. II: Consciousness*. New York, Oxford: Oxford University Press.

———. (2016) *Neurophilosophy and the Healthy Mind. Learning from the Unwell Brain*. New York: Norton.

Olson, E. (1997) *The Human Animal: Personal Identity Without Psychology*. New York: Oxford University Press.

Parfit, D. (1984) *Reasons and Persons*. Oxford: Clarendon Press.

Shoemaker, S. (1963) *Self-knowledge and Self-identity*. Ithaca, NY: Cornell University Press.

Snowdon, P. (2014) *Persons, Animals, Ourselves*. New York: Oxford University Press.

Sperry, R. (1966) Brain bisection and mechanisms of consciousness. In J.C. Eccles (Ed.). *Brain and Conscious Experience*. New York: Springer, pp. 84–108.

Weinberg, S. (2011) Locke on personal identity. *Philosophy Compass* 6(6): pp. 398–407.

Whitehead, A.N. (1929/1978) *Process and Reality*. New York: Free Press.

Wiggins, D. (1967) *Identity and Spatio-Temporal Continuity*. Oxford: Wiley-Blackwell.

Wilkes, K. (1988) *Real People*. Oxford: Clarendon Press.

Williams, B. (1970) The self and the future. *Philosophical Review* 79(2): pp. 161–180.

23

VALUES, EMPATHY, AND THE BRAIN

Nina L. Powell and Stuart W.G. Derbyshire

Introduction

Currently a prominent Asian bank is running a series of TV commercials to illustrate the ethical principles of the bank. In one of the adverts, a father takes his six-year-old son to the fair and buys two tickets for a show at $1 each. The doorman explains that children under five are free, and, if the father had not paid, he would not have known his son was over five. "True," agrees the father, and then referring to his son, adds, "but *he* would have known."

Although the bank talks of principles, we could just as easily talk of values. In this case, the value of honesty in upbringing is being maintained against the pragmatic benefit of saving a dollar. Values pertain to fundamental beliefs and attitudes, which were considered predictive traits by Rokeach (1968, 1973). Rokeach described 18 terminal values (including items such as friendship, happiness, equality, pleasure, and wisdom) and 18 instrumental values (including items such as ambition, love, courage, intellect, and honesty). The terminal values were understood as desirable end-states and the instrumental values as preferable behaviors. Rokeach (1973) developed his *Value Survey* to classify individual differences in value preference.

It seems clear that values often, if not always, have an inherent moral component. Certainly values appear to be overtly moral when they pertain to how people *should* conduct themselves, such as in the advert described earlier. Here we will consider values as reflecting or corresponding to moral values, which are also more likely to involve empathic concern for others than values without a moral component (values without a moral component might include the terminal values of an exciting or comfortable life).

Moral values express what we hold to be correct and will include, for example, things such as: *It is wrong to betray one's country, It is wrong to harm others without cause, It is right to share resources with those less fortunate,* and *It is right to avoid contamination.* These values have been categorized by researchers in the field of moral psychology along the dimensions of care, fairness, loyalty, authority, and sanctity (Graham et al., 2012; Haidt, 2012). Care and fairness would appear most obviously to involve empathy toward others, but loyalty might also involve empathy, at least toward one's fellow citizens.

The Source of Moral Values and the Role of Empathy

Haidt describes his five moral dimensions as being similar to taste buds that largely develop according to immutable biological processes (Haidt, 2012). Variability in moral reasoning follows variation in the settings of each moral taste bud. Haidt is broadly supported by studies demonstrating that infants as young as five months show a preference for helping (Hamlin et al., 2011). Five- and nine-month-old infants watched a puppet show involving one puppet clearly helping another puppet to open a box, while a further puppet clearly hindered the other puppet by slamming the box shut. Subsequently the infants preferentially chose to play with the helpful puppet rather than the unhelpful puppet. The infants also refused rewards provided by the unhelpful puppet in favor of lesser rewards provided by the helpful puppet. These findings demonstrate a selection preference by the infants on the basis of the puppet's social actions, but also the sacrifice of their own self-interest following observation of the unhelpful puppet. One interpretation is that the infants recognized the harm from the unhelpful puppet and refused the greater food reward because of the greater good of associating with the helpful puppet.

Infants aged 19 and 21 months also appear sensitive to violations of fairness and helpfulness in other situations. For example, by measuring the amount of time infants look at a given situation (inferred to indicate expectation), infants appear to expect experimenters to allocate items equally between two puppets and expect that two puppets are also rewarded equally if they have both worked to complete a task, but not when one puppet did not do an equal share of work (Sloan et al., 2012). Additionally, 12-month-old infants have been shown a video depicting a blue square attempting to climb an incline and being either aided by a yellow triangle (pushed up the incline) or hindered by a red circle (pushed down the incline). Infants' looking times were subsequently longer for the helpful yellow triangle, which was inferred to indicate a preference for the helpful shape over the hindering shape (Kuhlmeier et al., 2003). Taken together, the interpretation placed on these findings was that infants are born with a capacity for empathy and morality that is innate and hard-wired and akin to what we see in adults.

There are, however, several problems with this interpretation. First, it is problematic that looking times are used as an indicator of expectation in one study and as an indicator of preference in another. It is unclear why gaze time at the unequal situation cannot be interpreted as preference and gaze time at the helpful shape cannot be interpreted as expectation. The open interpretation of gaze limits its use as a methodology. Second, moral values must have content. Content requires something more than a biological mechanism operating outside of our awareness. We must actively interpret and engage with the content of a particular moral value. The moral value of helping, for example, requires some content about helpfulness that can enable discrimination of a helpful from an unhelpful action (pushing up versus pushing down) with respect to another's goal (getting up a hill). Third, apparent condemnation regarding acts of harm against another requires understanding that others can be harmed. Early in development, however, it is not clear that the infant herself is able to appreciate when she is herself harmed (Derbyshire and Raja, 2011), and there is good evidence that infants do not possess an understanding of others' mental states until at least three years of age (Wellman, 2010).

Theory of mind is one of the most fundamental, and arguably uniquely human, aspects of social and cognitive development. All children typically acquire a theory of mind by four years of age. Theory of mind is measured through performance on various tasks, such as the false belief task, where a child is required to attribute understanding of a situation on behalf of another individual. Theory of mind is a necessary prerequisite to be able to extract meaningful information from a person's experience of a given situation, for instance, a situation in which a puppet has a particular goal and then is hindered by another puppet in trying to achieve that goal. A fully fledged theory of mind tends to accompany other executive-function abilities such as working memory, inhibitory control, and metacognitive planning—and all of these cognitive advancements develop well after 12 months of age (Wellman, 2010). Theory of mind moves from an understanding of pretense and mental representation (e.g., a banana is a telephone) as early as 1.5 years of age to an understanding of others' desires (which may be different from our own) as early as two to three years of age, and finally to an understanding of others' beliefs (which may be different from our own, as well as different from reality) as early as four to five years of age (Wellman, 2010). Given the stage-like and discontinuous progression of theory of mind, it seems implausible that this ability to mentally represent reality as well as recognize others' wants and beliefs would be evident in infants as young as 12 months.

In contrast to an innate route to moral values, Kohlberg (1981) views morality as emerging in continuity with general cognitive development (Kohlberg, 1981; Piaget and Inhelder, 1958). According to this view, infants begin with an innate suite of basic cognitive and motor abilities, including orientation, imitation, and the ability to follow eye-gaze, that are then elaborated into higher cognitive functions such as directed attention, memory, self-consciousness, and mental representation through triadic interactions with their caregivers (Vygotsky, 1978).

Infants as young as 18 months engage in helping behavior when others around them have difficulty opening a door or picking something up (Svetlova et al., 2010), but their helping behavior is based on the outcome rather than a principled desire to help; the means to achieving the outcome is incidental. Children aged six to eight years, for example, make no moral distinction between deliberate and incidental harm, whereas older children and adults recognize that deliberate harm is worse (Powell et al., 2012). In other words, young children who have a poorly developed moral and cognitive framework understand morality as a simplistic evaluation of good and bad outcomes, with little ability to factor in the means by which an outcome occurred or any other nuance in a given situation. Outcomes are likely the most salient feature for a cognitively immature infant or child for two reasons: (1) this is the most simplistic and binary equation for a young child to calculate and does not depend on cognitive ability or sophistication and does not draw on other later-developing cognitive abilities such as belief, theory of mind, or executive function, and (2) this is the first learning that takes place for children when learning about morality as a simplistic rule-based operation (e.g., if Johnny breaks a glass, Mom gets angry; therefore, breaking a glass leads to a bad outcome for Johnny).

Similar arguments occur when considering empathy. When placed in a room with other crying infants, a previously quiescent infant will also start to cry, which implies some innate, automatic empathy with the other infants (Sagi and Hoffman, 1976). As with moral values, however, empathy requires some understanding of another's suffering. The ability to place oneself into the position of another and understand their perspective is a prerequisite for theory-of-mind development. In order to evaluate and attend to the mental state of another, we must first be able to understand that others have mental states that are differing states from our own states or our own perception of reality and then, more importantly, hold that mental state in mind as a mental representation that is available for the means of evaluation and response. The process of holding something in mind for evaluative purposes requires working memory, a later-developing cognitive mechanism that falls under the umbrella of executive function (Goldman-Rakic, 1987; Chugani, 1998). Working memory is the ability to hold multiple pieces of information in mind while actively interpreting the information or making comparisons across information.

Without the ability to take another's perspective, we could not develop theory of mind and therefore would not have the capacity for empathy. Care for others that results from understanding their state of being does not fall out of a given situation or exist in a given situation inherently. It is only in developing this ability to read others' minds, so to speak, that we can start to meaningfully care about or relate to the experience of others. This process begins with the development of perspective taking as a fairly simplistic cognitive operation, which then later builds on the emergence of many other cognitive abilities and draws on input from the social world.

Empathy may play a special role in the emergence of moral values relating to the harm of others. Almost 250 years ago, Adam Smith suggested his theory of moral sentiments based, in part, on the exercise of empathy and the understanding of others' suffering (Smith, 1759/2013). More recently, third-party condemnation of wrongful acts has been suggested to occur as an evolutionary mechanism that can protect us from threats through a neurocognitive mechanism that allows us to readily perceive and attend to threats (Cosmides and Tooby, 1992), as well as to establish our own moral virtue to our group, which leads to social bonding and cooperation (Haidt, 2001). According to the cognitive developmentalists (e.g., Kohlberg, 1981), empathy is a useful higher-order emotional and cognitive function that allows us to move from consequentialist thinking in early childhood to social and group-based thinking in late childhood, adolescence, and into adulthood. Empathy, developing alongside and as a result of perspective taking and theory of mind, moves our moral focus onto the expectations of others and away from our own egoistic concerns about good and bad outcomes.

The inability to empathize with others, therefore, is likely to delay the development of moral values around harm to others and, in extreme cases, may play a causal role in antisocial behavior or psychopathy (Aylett et al., 2005; Berry, 2007; Blair et al., 1996; Richell et al., 2003; Widom, 1978).

The Role of the Brain in Empathy

Several overlapping and at least partially dissociable brain networks have been proposed as critical for empathy (Hillis, 2014; Shamay-Tsoory et al., 2009; Harris, 2003). Developmentally and phylogenetically "early" networks center on the right orbitofrontal cortex (OFC) and inferior frontal cortex (IFC) and are considered necessary for emotional contagion—recognizing and sharing the feelings of others through an automatic tendency to mimic and synchronize their expressions, vocalizations, postures, or movements. Observing even subtle expressions of happiness or anger, for example, produces facial electromyographic (EMG) changes characteristic of those emotions (Hess and Blairy, 2001) and observing fearful body expressions produces activation in the OFC and IFC compared with observation of neutral body expressions (Gelder et al., 2004).

Developmentally and phylogenetically "later" networks center on the right medial prefrontal cortex and are considered necessary for perspective taking—making inferences about what another person is thinking or feeling. Many additional regions are also implicated in these functions, and there is no precise consensus regarding which regions contribute to which function (Hills, 2014; Shamay-Tsoory et al., 2009). Furthermore, additional cognitive and mirroring mechanisms are also generally associated with empathic experience.

Broadly speaking, when empathizing with others, mostly right-sided brain regions are implicated, which is broadly consistent with the right hemisphere having a larger involvement in affective function (Sperry, 1981). Empathic concern toward the welfare of others involves a large number of neural areas including the amygdala, brain stem, hypothalamus, insula, anterior cingulate cortex, and orbitofrontal cortex, and the inferior and medial frontal gyrus when specifically taking the perspective of another person (reviewed in Decety and Cowell, 2015). Both cognitive and affective perspective taking require mentalizing about the beliefs or feelings of others (theory of mind) and involve the temporoparietal junction (Vogeley et al., 2001).

The importance of these regions is demonstrated starkly by studies of psychopaths. Psychopathy is a severe disorder of personality, characterized by a callous lack of empathy, shallow affect, and a lack of remorse or guilt (Hare, 1991, 2003). Although psychopaths can readily understand the emotional feelings of others (cognitive empathy or affective perspective taking), they fail to share the personal distress of others or feel an empathic concern toward others (emotional empathy or contagion; Aylett et al., 2005; Berry, 2007; Blair et al., 1996; Frith, 1989; Richell et al., 2003; Widom, 1978). This lack of emotional empathy with intact cognitive empathy might explain why psychopaths can successfully manipulate others while remaining callous toward the harm caused (Hare, 2003).

The lack of emotional empathy in psychopaths is more pronounced for negative rather than positive emotions. The negative emotions include sadness, fear, disgust, and anger (Ekman, 1993; Ekman and Frisen, 1975; Gaines, 1998). Studies have consistently found that psychopaths display significantly lower emotional reactivity only when negative emotional stimuli are presented (Blair et al., 1997, 2004, 2006; Kosson et al., 2002; Stevens et al., 2001). Sad and fearful stimuli, in particular, produce consistently deficient emotional responses in psychopaths (Blair et al., 2005). Typically, psychopaths fail to generate any indications of emotional contagion, such as mimicking the facial expression of someone looking afraid, and often fail to detect the presence of fear in faces or voices (Blair et al., 1997, 2006).

Sad and fearful stimuli readily activate the amygdala (Amaral et al., 1992; Pesso and Ungerleider, 2004), and there is relative consensus that the amygdala is dysfunctional in psychopaths (Blair et al., 2005; Kiehl, 2005). Adult psychopaths, for example, display significantly lower amygdala activity than their nonpsychopathic counterparts when viewing negative stimuli (Kiehl et al., 2001). An fMRI study on juveniles with high callous-unemotional (CU) traits has similarly found reduced amygdala activity when the juveniles were exposed to fearful expressions (Marsh et al., 2008). The CU trait includes a lack of emotional empathy and has been considered a precursor to adult psychopathy (Burke et al., 2007; Forth and Burke, 1998; Frick et al., 2003). Beyond the amygdala, individuals with psychopathy, compared to controls, have reduced activations in a wide network, including regions of the temporal, insular, parietal, and frontal lobes when viewing others' emotional behavior (Meffert et al., 2013).

Psychopathy is intensely resistant to treatment (Cooke and Michie, 2001), but there is evidence that psychopaths can be directed to attend to emotional stimuli, with consequent increases in brain activity in regions relevant to empathic processing (Meffert et al., 2013). There is also evidence that empathic brain activation discriminates friends from strangers and humans from animals (Meyer et al., 2013; Filippi et al., 2010). Empathy and compassion training also alters brain activation, illustrating the potential plasticity in the neural networks necessary for normal empathic responses (Klimecki et al., 2014).

There has been intense discussion of the importance of parent–infant interactions in facilitating the emergence of appropriate empathy (Swain et al., 2007; Perry, 2002). In short, there is concern that if warm and nurturing parental care is not provided in the first three years of life, then irreparable damage to the infant's brain development will follow, with catastrophic consequences for the older child's and adult's cognitive and empathic abilities. Reduced neuronal activity in the hippocampus and surrounding tissue has been demonstrated in postinstitutionalized infants from Romania (Chugani et al., 2001). Reduced glucose metabolism was also demonstrated in the frontal cortex along with reduced white matter connections between the temporal and frontal cortices. Consistent with these brain deficits, postinstitutionalized Romanian infants adopted into Western families have reduced IQ with associated deficits in memory, attention, executive control, learning, and inhibition (Pollak et al., 2010; Croft et al., 2007). More typical deprivation associated with lower socioeconomic status (SES) has also been associated with deficits in language and executive function along with reduced activity in associated brain regions (Hackman and Farah, 2009; Farah et al., 2006). Some commentators have extrapolated from the observed behaviors and brain alterations in deprived infants to suggest that even minor neglect, such as not being read to or spoken to in a reciprocal manner, will lead to empathic deficits (Allen, 2011). Given that a lack of empathy is associated with callous, criminal, and antisocial behavior, as discussed, this concern has generated considerable efforts to encourage parenting lessons and direct state intervention into the upbringing of children.

> For more on the role of socioeconomic status in neurological development, see Chapter 30.

This early-years infant determinism differs from the nativist determinism discussed earlier. Infant determinism argues that parental input is the dominant contributor to a person's moral development, whereas nativist determinism argues that biology largely determines moral development. Nativists are more relaxed about parental impact because they believe that empathy and moral development follow an innate path regardless of input from parents and caregivers. In our view, both infant and native determinism are flawed.

The Brain Doesn't Matter *That* Much

The transition from reflexive behavior to intentional behavior is perhaps the most crucial part of infant and child development. One example of this shift is smiling. Infants display a reflexive smile almost immediately and do not require the presence of an agent (e.g., a caregiver) to facilitate the smile. By about two months of age, infants will begin to require the presence of an agent in order to smile, demonstrating the beginning of intentional action (Meltzoff, 2011; Piaget and Inhelder, 1958). This intentionality becomes more sophisticated over time as the infant develops an awareness of herself and then begins to engage in social referencing with her caregiver. As the infant becomes more cognitively sophisticated, she develops a stronger cognitive basis for the smiling that includes an understanding of when to smile, what happens when she smiles, and the mental representation of what smiling means in and for others.

This example of smiling can help us to understand the development of empathy. Empathy is a complex, intentional, and cognitive form of perspective taking that takes time to develop. A child must first be able to process the perspective of another person in a very rudimentary form, understanding that the person is separate from the self, understanding that the person has a mental state, and comparing the mental state with a stored script or schema for mental states that correspond to various events or elicitors in the environment. This ability to process others' states of being happens over time, with the input from a social world. In our view, time and social input are prerequisites for empathic responses. Suggesting that empathy exists independent of these necessary building blocks and the social input needed to move development forward places a seemingly impossible burden on innate brain circuitry. This is the basis for dismissing the case for empathy existing only as a sort of brain trait or mechanism.

Empathy is the beginning of concern and understanding of others, a stance beyond yourself and your own immediate feelings and concerns. It's more than just knowledge or structure; empathy is perspective taking with cognitive maturation and a motivation to attend to the other's state with some behavioral response. To locate this multimodal and complex process in a structural part of the brain or even a brain-driven output fails to dissect the contents of empathy and washes over a host of developmental acquisitions that are social, cognitive, and behavioral.

Empathy is therefore not automatic but, like smiling, has origins in an automatic process, which moves from automatic to intentional and from a singularity to a multimodal response system. Smiling at the beginning of life is qualitatively different from smiling at 3 months of age, and again at 24 months of age. Development continuously adds layers of cognitive and social sophistication (e.g., social referencing and emotional scripts). Perspective taking that begins as automatic attention capture directed toward others is qualitatively different from perspective taking that includes theory of mind, which is qualitatively different from perspective taking that then includes value-based scripts and concerns for social order and social expectation. Finally, the mature basis for empathic responses, which follows from consideration of others' mental states and values, emerges.

The brain is obviously necessary for the developmental trajectory to follow a normal course. Congenital abnormalities or behavioral problems following severe abuse might be reasonably expected to interfere with the emergence of the cognitive structures necessary for empathy. That does not mean, however, that the brain is responsible for empathic responses.

Modern neuroscience tends to regularly fall into an erroneous proposal of neural determinism based on the necessity of neural structures for all mental functions. Necessity, however, does not mean sufficiency (Tallis, 2011; Derbyshire and Raja, 2011). Properly functioning lungs are also necessary for most mental functions, because it is hard to think when unable to breathe, but lungs are clearly not sufficient for thought. Once our lungs are working to a suitable level, however, most of us forget that we even have them. There will be variability in lung capacity and function, just as there is variability in brain structure and function, but if both are working adequately, then we can treat them as a given.

Similarly, even though we must learn to be empathic, it is to be expected that everyone with a reasonably supportive upbringing and with a typically functioning brain can be empathic when necessary. Just as everyone can eventually put on clothes each morning, without having to be reminded or feel the shame of forgetting, everyone can eventually recognize situations demanding of empathy without the need for a reminder.

Values Are Made Socially and Learned Individually

We have seen that most contemporary psychology views the emergence of values as critically dependent on the brain. There may be differences of opinion over the importance of nurture, but even those who view nurture as critical still view the root problems of infant neglect, poverty, and abuse as being the damage inflicted on the brain (Swain et al., 2007; Perry, 2002).

These approaches are problematic because they tend to biologize the creation of values, obscuring the fact that values are socially and culturally constructed. It is in the social and cultural arena that values are made, which is what gives values (and all socially constructed ideas) their "ghostly" character. A brain is necessary for an individual to hold values, but it is not an individual brain that creates values. Consequently, values exist within us and beyond us, which is the essential source of most people's intuitive dualism. Some have claimed that we are "natural-born dualists" (Bloom, 2004), but that claim misses the real material basis for dualism, which is a community of minds negotiating and arguing over ideas, rules, values, and so forth.

Returning to the father from the beginning example. The father wants his son to value honesty over personal gain, but the father is evidently wealthy enough that he does not need to worry about spending an extra dollar. The man at the door may ascribe to a different value, that people with limited incomes should hold on to every dollar they can. In a period of rising affluence in Asia, the moral value of honesty can be upheld as the greater good by at least the more affluent section of society. But in a period of depression or among the current working poor, enabling your child to have some fun without that fun threatening the family finances might be upheld as the greater good.

For a detailed discussion of morality and moral reasoning, see Chapter 19.

Infants do not enter the world cognitively blank. They have innate mechanisms that allow them to alight upon changes in stimulation, to discriminate different features of the environment, and to imitate. Within that lies the beginning of all our later cognitive performance, including the ability to learn the value of a dollar versus the value of honesty. That distinction must be learned individually even though the individual, or his or her brain, does not create the distinction. Empathy is a learned value that has only recently emerged as something socially important. Empathy helps people cope with the hardships of the modern and industrialized world by facilitating assistance from relatives, friends, and neighbors (Ehrenreich, 2010). It is socially acceptable to appeal to the feelings and sentiments of others in an effort to promote benevolence, including, for example, by helping someone sneak their child into a show without paying.

Further Reading

Bloom, P. (2013) *Just Babies: The Origins of Good and Evil*. New York: Crown.

Decety, J. and Cowell, J.M. (2015) "Empathy, Justice and Moral Behavior". *American Journal of Bioethics Neuroscience* 6(3), 3–14.

Ehrenreich, B. (2010) *Smile or Die: How Positive Thinking Fooled America and the World*. London: Granta Books.

Frith, C. (2007). *Making Up The Mind: How the Brain Creates Our Mental World*. Hoboken, NJ: Wiley-Blackwell.

Kuhlmeier, V., Wynn, K. and Bloom, P. (2003). "Attribution of Dispositional States by 12- Month-Olds". *Psychological Science* 14, 402–408.

Tallis, R. (2011). *Aping Mankind: Neuromania, Darwinitis and the Misrepresentation of Humanity*. Stocksfield, UK: Acumen Publishing.

References

Allen, G. (2011) *Early Intervention: Smart Investment, Massive Savings. The Second Independent Report to Her Majesty's Government*. Available at: www.gov.uk/government/uploads/system/uploads/attachment_data/file/61012/earlyintervention-smartinvestment.pdf [Accessed 26 Feb. 2016].

Amaral, D.G., Pitkanen, A., and Carmichael, S.T. (1992) Anatomical organization of the primate amygdaloid complex. In J.P. Aggleton (Ed.). *The Amygdala: Neurobiological Aspects of Emotion, Memory, and Mental Dysfunction*. New York: Wiley-Blackwell, pp. 1–66.

Aylett, M., Mahmut, M., Langdon, R., and Green, M. (2005) Social cognition in non-forensic psychopathy: Further evidence for a dissociation between intact 'theory of mind' and impaired emotion processing. *Acta Neuropsychiatrica* 18: pp. 328–329.

Berry, S. (2007) *Psychopathy: An Abnormality in the Mirroring of Others' Emotions*. Unpublished thesis.

Blair, R.J., Sellars, C., Strickland, I., Clark, F., Williams, A., and Smith, M. (1996) Theory of mind in the psychopath. *Journal of Forensic Psychiatry* 7: pp. 15–25.

Blair, R.J., Mitchell, D.G., Colledge, E., Leonard, R.A., Shine, J.H., and Murray, L.K. (2004) Reduced sensitivity to other's fearful expressions in psychopathic individuals. *Personality and Individual Differences* 37: pp. 1111–1121.

Blair, R.J., Mitchell, D.G., and Blair, K.S. (2005) *The Psychopath: Emotion and the Brain*. Oxford: Wiley-Blackwell.

Blair, R.J., Jones, L., Clark, F., and Smith, M. (1997) The psychopathic individual: A lack of responsiveness to distress cues? *Psychophysiology* 34: pp. 192–198.

Blair, R.J., Budhani, S., Colledge, E., and Scott, S.K. (2006) Deafness to fear in boys with psychopathic tendencies. *Journal of Child Psychology and Psychiatry* 46(3): pp. 326–336.

Bloom, P. (2004) *Descartes' Baby: How the Science of Child Development Explains What Makes Us Human*. New York: Basic Books.

Burke, J.D., Loeber, R., and Lahey, B. (2007) Adolescent conduct disorder and interpersonal callousness as predictors of psychopathy in young adults. *Journal of Clinical Child and Adolescent Psychology* 36(3): pp. 334–345.

Chugani, H.T. (1998) Biological basis of emotions: Brain systems and brain development. *Pediatrics* 102, p. S1225-S122.

Chugani, H.T., Behen, M.E., Muzik, O., Juhasz, C., Nagy, F., and Chugani, D.C. (2001) Local brain functional activity following early deprivation: A study of postinstitutionalized Romanian orphans. *Neuroimage* 14(6): pp. 1290–1301.

Cooke, D.J., and Michie, C. (2001) Refining the construct of psychopathy: Towards a hierarchical model. *Psychological Assessment* 13: pp. 171–188.

Cosmides, L., and Tooby, J. (1992) Cognitive adaptations for social exchange. *The Adapted Mind*: pp. 163–228.

Croft, C., Beckett, C., Rutter, M., Castle, J., Colvert, E., Groothues, C., and Sonuga-Barke, E.J.S. (2007) Early adolescent outcomes in institutionally-deprived and non-deprived adoptees II: Language as a protective factor and a vulnerable outcome. *Journal of Child Psychology and Psychiatry* 48: pp. 31–44.

Decety, J., and Cowell, J.M. (2015) Empathy, justice and moral behavior. *American Journal of Bioethics Neuroscience* 6(3): pp. 3–14.

Derbyshire, S., and Raja, A. (2011) On the development of painful experience. *Journal of Consciousness Studies*. 18(9–10): pp. 233–256.

Ehrenreich, B. (2010) *Smile or Die: How Positive Thinking Fooled America and the World*. London: Granta Books.

Ekman, P. (1993) Facial expression and emotion. *American Psychologist* 48: pp. 384–392.

Ekman, P., and Friesen, W.V. (1975) *Unmasking the Face*. Englewood Cliffs, NJ: Prentice Hall, Inc.

Farah, M.J., Shera, D.M., Savage, J.H., Betancourt, L., Giannetta, J.M., Brodsky, N.L., . . . Hurt, H. (2006) Childhood poverty: Specific associations with neurocognitive development. *Brain Research* 1110(1): pp. 166–174.

Filippi, M., Riccitelli, G., Falini, A., Di Salle, F., Vuilleumier, P., Comi, G., and Rocca, M.A. (2010) The brain functional networks associated to human and animal suffering differ among omnivores, vegetarians and vegans. *PLOS One* 5: p. e10847.

Forth, A.E., and Burke, H.C. (1998) Psychopathy in adolescence: Assessment, violence, and developmental precursors. In D.J. Cooke, A.E. Forth, and R. Hare (Eds.). *Psychopathy: Theory, Research and Implications for Society*. Boston, MA: Kluwer Academic, pp. 205–229.

Frith, U. (1989) *Autism: Explaining the Enigma*. Oxford: Wiley-Blackwell.

Frick, P.J., Cornell, A.H., Barry, C.T., Bodin, S.D., and Dane, H.E. (2003) Callous—unemotional traits and conduct problems in the prediction of conduct problem severity, aggression, and self-report of delinquency. *Journal of Abnormal Child Psychology* 31, pp. 457–470.

Gaines Jr., S.O. (1998) Communication of emotions in friendships. In P.A. Andersen and L.K. Guerrero (Eds.). *Handbook of Communication and Emotion: Research, Theory, Applications, and Context*. San Diego: Academic Press, pp. 507–531.

Gelder, B.D., Snyder, J., Greve, D., Gerard, G., and Hadjikhani, N. (2004) Fear fosters flight: A mechanism for fear contagion when perceiving emotion expressed by a whole body. *Proceedings of the National Academy of Sciences of the United States of America* 101(47): pp. 16701–16706.

Goldman-Rakic, P.S. (1987) Development of cortical circuitry and cognitive function. *Child Development* 58: pp. 601–622.

Graham, J., Haidt, J., Koleva, S., Motyl, M., Iyer, R., Wojcik, S.P., and Ditto, P.H. (2012) Moral foundations theory: The pragmatic validity of moral pluralism. *Advances in Experimental Social Psychology*, 47: pp. 55–130.

Hackman, D.A., and Farah, M.J. (2009) Socioeconomic status and the developing brain. *Trends in Cognitive Science* 13(2): pp. 65–73.

Haidt, J. (2001) The emotional dog and its rational tail: A social intuitionist approach to moral judgment. *Psychological Review* 108(4): p. 814.

———. (2012) *The Righteous Mind: Why Good People Are Divided by Politics and Religion.* New York: Vintage.

Hamlin, J.K., and Wynn, K. (2011) Young infants prefer prosocial to antisocial others. *Cognitive development* 26(1): pp. 30–39.

Hare, R.D. (1991) *Manual for the Hare Psychopathy Checklist-Revised.* Toronto: Multi- Health Systems.

———. (2003) *The Hare Psychopathy Checklist-Revised.* 2nd ed. Toronto: Multi-Health Systems.

Harris, J.C. (2003) Social neuroscience, empathy, brain integration, and neurodevelopmental disorders. *Physiology & Behavior* 79: pp. 525–531.

Hess, U., and Blairy, S. (2001) Facial mimicry and emotional contagion to dynamic emotional facial expressions and their influence on decoding accuracy. *International Journal of Psychophysiology* 40: pp. 129–141.

Hillis, A.E. (2014) Inability to empathize: Brain lesions that disrupt sharing and understanding another's emotions. *Brain* 137: pp. 981–997.

Kiehl, K.A. (2005) A cognitive neuroscience perspective on psychopathy: Evidence for paralimbic system dysfunction. *Psychiatry Research* 142(2–3): pp. 107–128.

Kiehl, K.A., Smith, A.M., Hare, R.D., Mendrek, A., Foster, B.B., Brink, J., and Liddle, P.F. (2001) Limbic abnormalities in criminal psychopaths as revealed by functional magnetic resonance imaging. *Biological Psychiatry* 50: pp. 677–678.

Klimecki, O.M., Leiberg, S., Ricard, M., and Singer, T. (2014) Differential pattern of functional brain plasticity after compassion and empathy training. *SCAN* 9: pp. 873–879.

Kohlberg, L. (1981) *The Philosophy of Moral Development: Moral Stages and the Idea of Justice.* San Francisco: Harper & Row.

Kosson, D.S., Suchy, Y., Mayer, A.R., and Libby, J. (2002). Facial affect recognition in criminal psychopaths. *Emotion* 2(4): pp. 398–411.

Kuhlmeier, V., Wynn, K., and Bloom, P. (2003) Attribution of dispositional states by 12-month-olds. *Psychological Science* 14(5): pp. 402–408.

Marsh, A., Finger, E., Mitchell, D., Reid, M., Sims, C., Kosson, D., . . . Blair, R.J. (2008) Reduced amygdala response to fearful expressions in children and adolescents with callous-unemotional traits and disruptive behavioural disorders. *Journal of Psychiatry* 165(5): pp. 1–9.

Meffert, H., Gazzola, V., den Boer, J.A., Bartel, A.A., and Keysers, C. (2013) Reduced spontaneous but relatively normal deliberate vicarious representation in psychopathy. *Brain* 136(8): pp. 2550–2562.

Meltzoff, A.N. (2011) Social cognition and the origins of imitation, empathy, and theory of mind. *The Wiley-Blackwell Handbook of Childhood Cognitive Development* 1: pp. 49–75.

Meyer, M.L., Masten, C.L., Ma, Y., Wang, C., Shi, Z., Eisenberger, N.I., and Han, S. (2013) Empathy for the social suffering of friends and strangers recruits distinct patterns of brain activation. *SCAN* 8: pp. 446–454.

Piaget, J., and Inhelder, B. (1958) *The Growth of Logical Thinking from Childhood to Adolescence.* New York: Basic Books.

Perry, B. (2002) Childhood experience and the expression of genetic potential: What childhood neglect tells us about nature and nurture. *Brain and Mind* 3: pp. 79–100.

Pesso, L., and Ungerleider, L.G. (2004) Neuroimaging studies of attention and the processing of emotion-laden stimuli. *Progress in Brain Research* 144: pp. 171–182.

Pollak, S.D., Nelson, C.A., Schlaak, M.F., Roeber, B.J., Wewerka, S.S., Wik, K.L., . . . Gunnar, M.R. (2010) Neurodevelopmental effects of early deprivation in postinstitutionalized children. *Child Development* 81(1): pp. 224–236.

Powell, N.L., Derbyshire, S.W., and Guttentag, R.E. (2012) Biases in children's and adults' moral judgments. *Journal of Experimental Child Psychology* 113(1): pp. 186–193.

Richell, R.A., Mitchell, D.G., Newman, C., Leonard, A., Baron-Cohen, S., and Blair, R.J. (2003) Theory of mind and psychopathy: Can psychopathic individuals read the 'Language of the Eyes'? *Neuropsychologia* 41(5): pp. 523–526.

Rokeach, M. (1968) *Beliefs, Attitudes and Values: A Theory of Organization and Change*, San Francisco: Jossey-Bass.

———. (1973) *The Nature of Human Values*, Vol. 438. New York: Free press.

Sagi, A., and Hoffman, M.L. (1976) Empathic distress in the newborn. *Developmental Psychology* 12(2): p. 175.

Shamay-Tsoory, S.G., Aharon-Peretz, J., and Perry, D. (2009) Two systems for empathy: A double dissociation between emotional and cognitive empathy in inferior frontal gyrus versus ventromedial prefrontal lesions. *Brain* 132: pp. 617–627.

Sloane, S., Baillargeon, R., and Premack, D. (2012) Do infants have a sense of fairness? *Psychological Science* 23(2): pp. 196–204. doi:10.1177/0956797611422072

Smith, A. (1759/2013) *The Theory of Moral Sentiments*. London: Economic Classics.

Sperry, R.W. (1981) Some effects of disconnecting the cerebral hemispheres. *Science* 217(4566): pp. 1223–1226.

Stevens, D., Charman, T., and Blair, R.J. (2001) Recognition of emotion in facial expressions and vocal tones in children with psychopathic tendencies. *Journal of Genetic Psychopathy* 162(2): pp. 201–211.

Svetlova, M., Nichols, S.R., and Brownell, C.A. (2010) Toddlers' prosocial behavior: From instrumental to empathic to altruistic helping. *Child Development* 81(6): pp. 1814–1827.

Swain, J.E., Lorberbaum, J.P., Kose, S., and Strathearn, L. (2007) Brain basis of early parent—Infant interactions: Psychology, physiology, and in vivo functional neuroimaging studies. *Journal of Child Psychology and Psychiatry* 48(3-4): pp. 262–287.

Tallis, R. (2011) *Aping Mankind: Neuromania, Darwinitis and the Misrepresentation of Humanity*. Stocksfield, UK: Acumen Publishing.

Vogeley, K., Bussfeld, P., Newen, A., Herrmann, S., Happé, F., Falkai, P., . . . Zilles, K. (2001) Mind reading: Neural mechanisms of theory of mind and self-perspective. *Neuroimage* 14(1): pp. 170–181.

Vygotsky, L. (1978). Interaction between learning and development. *Readings on the Development of Children* 23(3): pp. 34–41.

Wellman, H.M. (2010) Developing a theory of mind. *The Wiley-Blackwell Handbook of Childhood Cognitive Development* 2: pp. 258–284.

Widom, C.S. (1978) An empirical classification of female offenders. *Criminal Justice and Behaviour* 5: pp. 35–52.

24

MORAL ROBOTS

Matthias Scheutz and Bertram F. Malle

Introduction

To many, one of the most distinguishing human features is *morality*—that is, the capacity to perceive actions as *moral* or *immoral* and respond to them in very particular ways, such as by praising or blaming actors, demanding justifications, or accepting an apology. Members of a community are expected to abide by the moral norms and values of the community, and they pass on the knowledge of these norms through observed practices and explicit instruction. In addition, modern societies have made those norms explicit through philosophical reflection and formalized laws, thereby offering ethical foundations for their members to live by. We will thus use the term "moral" (e.g., in "moral processing" or "moral competence") to refer to those aspects of the human cognitive system that are involved in the representation and processing of norms, values, and virtues. Morality, in this sense, is a natural phenomenon of social groups in their daily lives, a phenomenon that can be studied with empirical scientific methods. The scientific study of these phenomena is now typically called *moral psychology*. We reserve the term "ethical" for normative discussions and debates about abstract principles (e.g., the doctrine of double effect), theological origins of values, or the difference between ethical theories (e.g., Kantian, utilitarian). Ethics is then more of a philosophical, normative discipline. Consequently, it is possible for an agent to engage in moral decision making (i.e., involving ordinary moral information processing) but to perform an act that is considered unethical within some normative (theological or philosophical) system; conversely, it is possible for an agent to act in conformity with ethical principles even if the decision to act was not guided by the person's moral processing of those abstract principles but, say, by imitation. This distinction helps distinguish two sets of questions that arise when considering the behavior of nonhuman agents, such as robots. One set of scholarly questions concerns the robot's functional capacities and computational processes that mimic or adapt to human moral processing. This endeavor falls squarely within cognitive science, integrating, in particular, behavioral research and theorizing with computational modeling and engineering. Another set of scholarly questions concerns the ethical standards that robots should adhere to, the abstract principles (if any) the robots should implement, the ethical value of building morally competent robots in the first place, and so on. This endeavor falls into the domain of ethics as a normative discipline, typically conducted by philosophers or theologians.

The main reason for raising the question about the ethical behavior of robots is the rapid progress in the development of autonomous social robots that are specifically created to be deployed in sensitive human environments, from elder and health care settings to law enforcement and military contexts. Clearly, such tasks and environments are very different from traditional factory environments (for example, for welding robots). Hence, these new social robots will require higher degrees of autonomy (i.e., a capacity for independent, self-directed action) and decision-making than any previously developed machine, given that they will face a much more complex, open world. They might be required to acquire new knowledge on the fly to accomplish a never-before-encountered task. Moreover, they will likely face humans who are not specifically trained to interact with them, and robots thus need to be responsive to instructions by novices and feel "natural" to humans even in unstructured interactions (Scheutz et al., 2006). At these levels of autonomy and flexibility in near-future robots, there will be countless ways in which robots might make mistakes, violate a user's expectations and moral norms, or threaten the user's physical or psychological safety. These social robots must therefore also be moral robots.

Thus, for autonomous social robots deployed in human societies, three key questions arise: (1) What moral expectations do humans have for social robots? (2) What moral competence can and should such robots realize? (3) What should be the moral standing of these machines (if any)?

The first question, about moral expectations, follows from the well-established fact that autonomous social robots, especially those with natural-language abilities, are treated in many ways like humans, regardless of whether such treatment was intended or anticipated by the robot designers. In fact, there is mounting evidence that humans have very clear expectations of robot capacities based on the robot's appearance and people's perceptions of the robot behaviors. We will review some of this work in the third section.

The second question, about moral competence, arises from the need to endow robots with sufficient capacities to operate safely in human societies. Answers to this question would ideally build on answers to the first question and provide mechanisms for robots to process social and moral norms in ways that humans expect. In addition, the design of the robots' control systems should ensure that robots behave ethically according to the norms of the society in which they are deployed.

The third question, about moral standing, is a consequence of allowing robots to make decisions on their own without human supervision, as will become necessary in cases in which human supervisors are not reachable or cannot react quickly enough. In such instances of autonomous decision making and action, we will have to decide whether the robot is "responsible" for its actions, especially when its behavior causes damage to property or harm to humans. Questions about fault, accountability, but also about the robot's possible rights to due process and protection against harm will have to be answered.

For a discussion of moral status, see Chapters 31 and 32.

In this chapter, we will focus on the first two questions, discussing both human expectations and computational architectural mechanisms that will allow robots to live up to those expectations while leaving a detailed discussion of the third question to legal experts and philosophers (Asaro, 2012; Coeckelbergh, 2010; Gunkel et al., 2012; Pagallo, 2011). However, the philosophical and legal discussions on moral standing of robots do raise the inevitable question of whether robots could ever be moral. For if robots are not the kind of thing to which morality applies, requiring any future robot to be moral is meaningless. One might argue that robots are not conscious autonomous agents with free will and therefore cannot make decisions or act on those decisions. A long tradition in philosophy has tried to understand what it means to be an agent with free will and moral responsibility. But discussions of free will have led to little consensus and often raise more questions than they are intended to answer, especially when applied to artificial agents (Gunkel, 2014). In the end, what counts for real social robots—machines in our contemporary world—is whether people treat those robots as targets of their moral sentiments. And it turns out that ascriptions of free will have little bearing on people's inclination to treat any agent as a moral being (Monroe et al., 2014). We will therefore not focus on the philosophical debate about agency and personhood. Rather, we will assume an operational behavioral definition of a "moral robot":

> **Definition.** A robot is "moral" if it has one or more relevant competences that people consider important for living in a moral community, such as detecting behaviors that violate moral norms or deciding to act in light of moral norms.
>
> (Malle, 2015; Malle and Scheutz, 2014; Scheutz, 2014; Scheutz and Malle, 2014)

For more on free will, see Chapter 21.

This definition will permit us to talk about a robot's morality in terms of various functional capacities that collectively give rise to morally significant behaviors in the contemporary world. Moral competence, by this definition, neither requires nor implies an objective "moral agency" (Malle, 2015). Instead, framing the problem in terms of competences allows us to design and study the mechanisms in the robot's control architecture that make its behavior consistent with community expectations about moral judgment and decision making, moral communication, and ethically acceptable behavior. After all, it is the community of ordinary people that will interact with social, moral robots, and it is their expectations and standards that will make robots acceptable community members or not.

Why Moral Robots?

The topics of intelligent autonomous machines and human morality have frequently been paired in the science fiction literature, most notably in the opus of Isaac Asimov, who early on addressed the tensions and challenges resulting from machines operating in human societies. In his stories, he specifically conceived of "Three Laws of Robotics" (Asimov, 1942), which he envisioned to be ingrained in the robots' "positronic brains," allowing them to make ethically sound decisions and thus exhibit ethical behavior (usually, but not always, living up to human moral expectations). Specifically, the three laws set up a system of strictly prioritized principles that robots had to obey:

L1: A robot may not injure a human being or, through inaction, allow a human being to come to harm.

L2: A robot must obey orders given it by human beings except where such orders would conflict with L1.

L3: A robot must protect its own existence as long as such protection does not conflict with L2.

While these three laws provided fertile ground for stories built on the implicit tensions among the laws—whom to save in a crowd when not all can be saved, how to evaluate the consequences of commands that are not clear, or how to determine to whom the adjective "human" should even apply—they are neither theoretically nor practically adequate for providing the foundation of moral competence in robots (Murphy and Woods, 2009). However, they do serve the purpose of pointing out the need to develop *some provisions* for ethical behavior in autonomous robots.

Of course, robot designers have been aware of the need to ensure the safe operation of robots all along, without the need to look to the science fiction literature for suggestions. Autonomous robotic systems that could have an impact on humans or property have precautionary built-in safety mechanisms that allow them to either completely avoid or to massively reduce the likelihood of any sort of harm. For example, self-parking cars will automatically stop if they sense an obstacle in their way, without the need for an explicitly represented ethical principle "do not drive into obstacles." Similarly, compliant robot arms intended to operate in human workspaces will yield when coming into contact with another object such as a human body part. Moreover, instructions to the car or the robot arm to continue a colliding trajectory will be automatically rejected, again under the same constraints. In all of these cases, the robots' actions or rejections of actions are not *explicitly* defined in terms of (moral) rules or principles but rather *implicitly* in the algorithms that control the robot's behaviors.

The "implicit-explicit" distinction of safety principles can be generalized to a distinction between implicit and explicit ethical agents based on a taxonomy introduced by Moor (2006). Implicit ethical agents are agents that "have ethical considerations built into (i.e., implicit in) their design. Typically, these are safety or security considerations" (Moor, 2013). By contrast, explicit ethical agents are agents that "can identify and process ethical information about a variety of situations and make sensitive determinations about what should be done. When ethical principles are in conflict, these robots can work out reasonable resolutions" (Moor, 2009, p. 12). And Moor continues: "Explicit ethical agents are the kind of agents that can be thought of as acting from ethics, not merely *according* to ethics"—as is the case with implicit ethical agents.

Moor also introduced two additional categories: *ethical impact agents*—that is, agents whose behavior can have ethical consequences—and *full ethical agents* (referring to typical adult humans with features such as consciousness, intentionality, and free will). Assuming that autonomous social robots will at least be ethical impact agents, the question then is how one would go about developing algorithms that will turn them into either implicit or explicit ethical agents. Mechanisms producing implicit ethical agents might be sufficient for a variety of tasks and domains (e.g., where most or all demands and risks are known before task execution, such as in the case of a robotic vacuum cleaner). However, mechanisms producing explicit ethical agents will be required for robots deployed in more open-ended tasks and environments, such as for household robots that have to learn the customs of a particular home and adapt to its changing situations.

We will start by looking at the empirical evidence for human expectations about moral robots and then consider ways to implement them in robotic control systems.

Human Moral Expectations about Autonomous Social Robots

It has long been known that humans have a natural propensity to view moving objects as "agents with intentions," even if those objects do not resemble any known life form at all. Early studies by Heider and Simmel (1944) showed that human observers "see" mental states such as emotions and intentions even in circles and triangles moving around in a cartoon-like scene. Moreover, humans from infancy on can easily be brought to make judgments about whether the intentions of those agents are benevolent or malicious and thus exhibit basic moral evaluations based on their perception of the interacting shapes (Hamlin, 2013).

This human propensity to project agency onto self-propelled objects (Premack, 1990), presumed to be an evolutionary adaptation that allowed humans to anticipate dangers from other agents, is particularly consequential for the development of robots. For robots are self-propelled objects that typically move about the environment in ways that suggest goal-driven behavior to human observers (Tremoulet and Feldman, 2000). There is evidence that even simple robots like the Roomba vacuum cleaner, a disk with no animal-like features (such as eyes or arms), can trigger the "human agency detector" (Scheutz, 2012). Hence, it stands to reason that humans not only project agency but may, under some circumstances, project *moral* characteristics onto such machines (Malle and Scheutz, 2016).

Researchers working in the field of human–robot interaction have investigated human reactions to robots violating norms of varying severity. Strait et al. (2014), for example, investigated a violation of the social norm to "be polite." They examined whether people preferred robot tutors that were polite by giving hedged instructions as opposed to robots that used imperatives in their instructions. People had no such preference in their own interactions with robots, but when they observed other people interacting with the robot, they preferred the polite one.

Short et al. (2010) examined a violation of a more serious norm—"tell the truth." A robot and human repeatedly played the game "rock-paper-scissors," and the robot had to announce the winner of each round. In one of the conditions, the robot announced that it won the round even though it had lost. Humans found the "cheating" robot to be more engaging and made greater attributions of mental states to that robot in the conditions in which it cheats.

To the extent that people ascribe mental states to a robot, they may also grant the robot certain rights and protect it from unfair treatment. The evidence shows that both children and adults do so. In Kahn Jr. et al. (2012), children interacted with a robot that was suddenly locked away in a closet by the experimenter because it "wasn't needed anymore." The robot protested, but to no avail. The researchers documented that children viewed the robot as having mental states and believed that the robot deserved to be treated fairly. Briggs and Scheutz (2014) investigated in a series of studies the extent to which people themselves would be responsive to a robot's moral appeals—protesting an instruction the participants gave the robot that it deemed unfair. People were significantly less likely to insist on the robot following that instruction when the robot protested, regardless of whether the protesting robot was a victim or witness of the unfairness and independent of the robot's appearance. However, some features of the robot seem to matter, as people are more reluctant to physically hit robots that appear more intelligent (Bartneck et al., 2007) and robots that are described in a personalized manner (Darling et al., 2015).

In addition to live human–robot interaction experiments, recent studies have begun to look at situations that cannot be examined in a laboratory context—either because they go beyond what is ethically acceptable in a research study or because they depict robots that do not yet exist.

For example, Scheutz and Arnold (2016a) surveyed participants about their attitudes toward sex robots. They found a consistent gender difference in what people considered appropriate uses for sex robots, with women less inclined than men to consider them socially useful. However, there were also convergences between men and women on what sex robots are like and how sex with them is to be classified.

Malle et al. (2015) examined people's responses to a situation that cannot be studied in the lab and is also not yet part of our reality: a robot itself making a moral decision about life and death. Participants read a narrative describing an agent (human or robot) caught in a moral dilemma: either (a) to intervene in a dangerous situation and save four persons while sacrificing the life of one or (b) to stand back and let four persons die. People considered it more permissible if the robot sacrificed one person for the good of many than if the human did. Moreover, when people were confronted with the agent's actual choice, they blamed a human who intervened more than a human who stood back, but they blamed a robot that intervened no more or even less than a robot that stood back. Recently, researchers have begun to probe people's responses to self-driving cars that might, in the near future, face similar moral dilemmas. Bonnefon et al. (2016) found a contrast between people's judgments of what would be the morally right action for a self-driving car (namely, to sacrifice one pedestrian to save many) and what kind of car people would buy or like to see around the neighborhood (for example, one that doesn't intervene).

This research is in its infancy, and subtle variations may shift people's expectations and preferences (Malle et al., 2016). Nonetheless, the results so far suggest two conclusions, one firm, the second one more tentative. First, people readily direct moral expectations and moral judgments to robots, at least robots of sufficient cognitive complexity and behavioral abilities. Second, people may be more accepting of robots than of humans who make conflictual decisions (e.g., endangering one individual while trying to save multiple individuals). The exact reasons for such a potential transfer of responsibility are currently unclear. One hypothesis that deserves consideration is that making such decisions normally carries significant emotional costs (such as guilt and trauma) and social costs (affecting one's relationships with others), as is suspected, for example, in drone pilots (Chatterjee, 2015). Having robots make such decisions would reduce those human costs. However, there is currently a significant debate over using autonomous machines as lethal weapons (Arkin, 2009; Asaro, 2011; Sparrow, 2007), and reducing current human costs is only one of many factors to consider. Without staking a position in this debate, we would like to emphasize the importance of investigating ordinary people's psychological responses to near-future robots that might make morally significant decisions. Some of people's responses may be inevitable (given the psychological mechanisms humans are equipped with; Malle and Scheutz, 2016); other responses may change with instruction and experience. Either way, designers, engineers, and policy makers need to take those responses under advisement to guide the robots' proper development, deployment, and possible legal regulations for their behavior.

Options for Developing Moral or Ethical Robots

Positing now that people expect robots to have at least some moral competencies, the key question becomes what it would take to actually endow robots with moral competence. We consider three main options, all with their own advantages and disadvantages.

1.   Implement *ethical theories* as proposed by philosophers.
2.   Implement *legal principles* as proposed by legal scholars.
3.   Implement *human-like moral competence* as proposed by psychologists.

Implementing Ethical Theories

Gips (1995) and others suggest we could equip a robot with one of the three major philosophical ethical theories. The first main theory is *virtue ethics*, which posits that ethical thought and action are guided by a person's character, constituted by "virtues" such as wisdom, courage, temperance, and justice. Moor specifically links implicit ethical agents to virtue ethics when he says that "implicit ethical agents have a kind of built-in virtue—not built-in by habit but by specific hardware or programming" (Moor, 2009, p. 12). In some cases, virtues can be directly implemented in robot behavior. "Courage," for instance, might be realized by the robot's willingness to engage in a risky action (possibly endangering its own existence) when that action might avert harm to a human. For example, an autonomous vehicle might initiate an evasive maneuver that would prevent colliding with a pedestrian but risk crashing into parked cars, thus likely damaging itself. The implementation of other virtues is less obvious. For example, it is unclear how "wisdom" could be realized in a robotic system over and above demands of rational behavior, such as when a game-playing computer always picks the best move from its perspective.

The second main ethical theory, *deontology*, posits that ethical action is not based on a virtuous character but on explicit rules, which can sensibly be applied to machines. Gert (2005) proposed that one could characterize ethical behavior in terms of a set of basic rules, each with the following structure: "everyone is always to obey the rule except when a fully informed rational person can publicly allow violating it" (203). Such rules might include "don't kill," "don't cause pain," "don't deceive," "obey the law," and so on, which apply quite generally. If a person violates such a rule and "no rational person can publicly allow such a violation," then the violator "may be punished" (203).

Setting aside important questions about what rules to select for a robot and what it would mean to punish or hold a robot responsible for a rule violation, robots that abide by a given set of ethical rules would arguably behave ethically. To implement such a system, robot designers could employ "deontic logics," which have specifically been developed to allow for reasoning with the core concepts of *obligation*, *permission*, *prohibition*, and *option*, all of which can be defined in terms of permissions. That is, an action α is *obligatory* if not doing it is not permitted, α is *prohibited* if doing it is not permitted, and α is *optional* if doing it or not doing it is permitted. Basic axioms and rules of inference can then enable logical derivations in a given context to determine what the robot ought to do. This works well as long as there are no conflicting obligations, such as when the robot is obligated to do α, obligated to do β, but cannot physically (or practically) do both α and β together. Not only does the logical approach not give any advice on what to do in such cases, but standard deontic logics will, more generally, allow the robot to infer that every action is obligated (e.g., Goble, 2005), which is clearly not intended. Hence, aside from other questions about computational feasibility and scalability, a challenge with the formal deontic approach is to curb the impact of deontic conflicts to not render all inferences useless.

The third ethical theory, *consequentialism*, is historically the newest and also the one that meshes best with computational mechanisms already implemented in robotic control systems: expected utility theory. The basic idea is to always choose an action that *maximizes the good for everybody involved*. Formally, this means that the robot would consider all available actions together with their probability of success and their associated utilities for all agents and then compute the best action. This way of determining the action that maximizes overall utility (the "overall good") is closely related to policy-based decision algorithms based on *partially observable Markov decision processes* (POMDPs), which select the best action given the available knowledge the robot has. The main difference between consequentialism and such algorithms is that the consequentialist robot would have to compute not only its own discounted utilities but also those of the relevant in-group (a necessary restriction on the notion of "all" agents' utility). However, at least two significant challenges arise. First, a well-known problem for consequentialist models independent of robotic implementations is how to handle the knowledge limitations any agent has (i.e., knowing *how* good an action will be for others, how many others to take into considerations, etc.). Second, there are open questions about how, in the robot's representational system, moral values should be figured into utilities and traded off with the costs of all possible actions (Scheutz, 2014).

Overall, the main problem associated with implementing philosophical ethical theories is that there is still no consensus among philosophers about which approach is the normatively correct one. And since the different theories sometimes make different recommendations for how to act in certain situations, one would have to take a philosophical moral stance to decide which recommendation to follow. Moreover, whether a robot adopting the chosen system would be acceptable to community members is entirely unclear, as none of the ethical theories claim to be or have been shown to be correct descriptions of human moral psychology and thus of human expectations of robot moral psychology (Powers, 2013).

Implementing Legal Theories

Another option of equipping a robot with ethical behavior is to implement the most systematic agreed-on moral principles in a society: the laws defined by the legal system. For social robots interacting with humans, one could, for example, focus on the four bedrock norms specified in U.S. tort law, the "intentional torts against the person":

1. *false imprisonment* (impeding a person's free physical movement);
2. *battery* (harmful or offensive bodily contact);
3. *assault* (putting someone in a position in which they perceive harmful or offensive contact to be imminent, even if no battery occurs); and
4. *intentional infliction of emotional distress* (extreme and outrageous conduct that causes severe distress).

One could then carefully examine the legal definitions of these torts and distill the ingredients needed for a robot to determine when, say, harmful contact and thus battery might occur (Mikhail, 2014). Such an approach would require the definition of possible circumstances and behaviors that would trigger such legal principles, which would then have to be implemented in the robotic system. Part of the effort would be to make legal terms such as "intent" or "imminent" or "distress" computational—that is, provide algorithms that detect intent, perceptions of imminence, or distressed emotional states. Moreover, the legal concept of a "rational person" would have to be formalized to be able to use it in cases in which the law specifically refers to the decisions and actions performed by a rational person. It is currently unclear how this could be done without requiring robot designers to solve the "AI problem"—without having to replicate human-like understanding and reasoning capabilities.

Implementing Human-Like Moral Competence

The third approach does not implement an ethical theory or a set of legal principles in a robot. Instead, it analyzes the various capacities that make up human moral competence and attempts to replicate at least some of these capacities in machines, without necessarily replicating all of them (or replicating all of human cognition). On this approach, one might investigate, for example, how humans learn, represent, and reason about *moral norms*, and once a sufficient empirical understanding of the hypothesized norm capacity is available, one could develop computational models of learning, representing, and reasoning about norms that could be integrated into robotic architectures (Malle et al., 2017). Such models would allow robots not only to behave in human-like ways (with respect to the particular capacity) but also to make reasonable predictions about human behavior that is guided by this capacity—such as when and how humans acquire new norms or under what circumstances they might break norms. Such modeling can significantly improve human–robot interactions because the robot can better adapt to the interaction and the human would feel better understood. These benefits are difficult to obtain with the other two approaches.

Another advantage is that the kinds of moral competences under consideration go far beyond a list of principles, mechanisms, or laws. Obviously, moral robots need to have a sophisticated norm system (Malle et al., 2017), but they may also need to make moral judgments of behavior relative to those norms and engage in moral communication—from explaining one's actions to expressing moral criticism to accepting an apology. Human moral competence is a cognitive as well as a social phenomenon.

However, attempting to implement human-like moral competence is challenging, for it is not yet clear exactly what perceptual, cognitive, affective, communicative, and behavioral components underwrite human moral competence (Cushman et al., 2010; Guglielmo, 2015; Malle and Scheutz, 2014). For example, is it necessary to be able to simulate another person's decision making in order to judge whether that person behaved morally? Are affective responses essential ingredients of moral judgment and decision making? And is the highly context-specific human norm system logically inconsistent, which might make it computationally intractable? Moreover, there are important ethical questions as to whether we should attempt to replicate human morality in a machine. Human moral behavior can be suboptimal at times, and one might expect robots to be morally superior, that is, show *supererogatory* performance (Scheutz and Arnold, 2016b). However, we need to differentiate replicating moral *competence* from replicating moral *performance*. Known sources of human performance decrements—such as strong intense affect, personal stakes, and group identity—can be explicitly omitted in designing moral robots. Few people would consider a robot less genuinely moral if it didn't get angry, selfish, or prejudiced. In fact, humans might look to such robots as reminders or models of norms and behaviors they would under normal circumstances fully endorse. In addition, replicating moral competence is a functional notion, leaving ample room for distinct implementations of the competence depending on the specific properties of the organism or platform.

Regardless of which approach for realizing ethical behavior will be taken, it is critical to ensure that the robots' moral decisions are understandable to people, especially if those decisions do not perfectly match people's own expectations or preferences. Without such understanding, people would not trust robots and would be unwilling to collaborate with them.

Approaches Toward Developing Moral Artificial Agents

Much of the discussion on what it takes for robots to count as moral has occurred outside the fields of robotics (Bringsjord and Taylor, 2012; Kahn, Jr. et al., 2006; Sullins, 2006; Wallach and Allen, 2008). Additionally, some scholars within the cognitive systems community have set out to build cognitive architectures with which to model human moral decision making (Blass and Forbus, 2015; Dehghani et al., 2008). For example, Blass and Forbus (2015) showed how analogical reasoning can be used to apply previously learned moral judgments to novel scenarios. In addition, some in the logic-based community have started to investigate normative reasoning in single-agent and multiagent systems (e.g., Ågotnes et al., 2007; Andrighetto et al., 2010; Pereira and Saptawijaya, 2009).

One of the most prominent proposals for developing architectures explicitly incorporating mechanisms for ethical behavior in robots is an extended version of the *autonomous robot* architecture (AuRA; Arkin and Balch, 1997). Augmented by an *ethical governor*, a *responsibility advisor*, and an *ethical adaptor*, the system allows for modifications of the robot's behavioral repertoire in case unethical behaviors are observed. Specifically, the ethical adaptor uses a scalar "guilt" value that monotonically increases over time as unanticipated ethical violations are detected by the system (Arkin and Ulam, 2009); as a result, actions with harmful potential are subsequently disallowed. The current system can handle only very specific, hard-coded moral decisions, but it can also advise human operators ahead of a mission about possible ethical conflicts in a limited way (Arkin et al., 2009). It does, however, lack the formal representations of norms, principles, values, and so forth to allow it to perform general ethical inferences and reason through normative conflicts.

Similarly, the mechanisms proposed by Briggs and Scheutz (2013, 2015) for the robotic *distributed integrated affect reflection and cognition* (DIARC) architecture (Scheutz et al., 2006) can detect potential norm violations that would result from carrying out human instructions that are in conflict with given normative principles. In that case, the robot can engage the human operator in a brief dialogue about why it is not permitted to carry out the instruction and offer a justification for its refusal. Different from the ethical extensions to the AuRA architecture, the DIARC extension is based on general inference algorithms that work with *explicit* representations of normative principles. However, the current system can handle only simple, potential but not actual norm conflicts (i.e., conflicts that could arise if it were to follow a particular command and execute an action that would be in conflict with its existing principles). Moreover, it cannot yet acquire new norms or principles from interactions and observations.

Research and development of mechanisms for ensuring normative behavior in autonomous robots has just begun, but it is poised to expand, judging from the increasing number of workshops and special sessions devoted to robot ethics and related topics (Malle, 2015). The prospects of autonomous weapon systems have fueled discussion and spurred the development of systems capable of making ethically licensed decisions, but other morally charged applications (e.g., robots for elder care or robots for sex) have come into focus and are likely to contribute to a broadening of the discussion and the efforts to design robots with moral capacities.

Conclusion

Moral robots are necessary to ensure effective and safe human–robot interactions. Given that a massive deployment of social robots in human societies is already predictable, we need to start developing algorithms and mechanisms for such robots to meet human expectations of moral competence and behave in ethical ways. We must determine what capacities are needed for the wide variety of tasks that social robots are expected to take on, and we must implement such capacities within one of the three paradigms discussed—the philosophical, the legal, or the psychological. Each of the paradigms has strengths and weaknesses, and perhaps some symbiotic combination can be found in the near future. We are at the beginning of a long path toward developing machines that have moral capacities. Yet it is clear that we have to take this route if we want to ensure that robot technology will serve humanity and not emerge as one of its primary threats.

24.1 Spotlight: Artificial Intelligence, Consciousness, and Moral Status

Susan Schneider

AI and Consciousness

When philosophers ponder whether machines could be conscious, they are generally interested in a particular form of AI: AGI, or artificial general intelligence. AGI doesn't exist yet, but we now have domain specific intelligences like AlphaGo and Watson, the world Go and *Jeopardy!* champions, respectively. These systems outperform humans in specific domains, and they are impressive. But AI seems to be developing exponentially, and within the next 10 or 20 years there will likely be forms of AGI. AGI is a kind of general, flexible intelligence that can do things like make breakfast without burning the house down, while thinking of mathematics and answering the phone. Its intelligence is not limited to a single domain, like chess. Because AGIs are general, flexible, integrate knowledge across domains, and exhibit human-level intelligence or beyond, AGIs seem like better candidates for being conscious than existing systems.

Androids are already under development that are designed to look human, such as the androids intended to take care of Japan's aging population. Armed with papers about the neuroscience of human empathy, AI researchers will build robots that tug at our heart-strings. So if and when you first encounter an AGI, will it be conscious? If you like science fiction films, then you may be thinking of characters like Roy, Pris, and Rachael in *Blade Runner* or Eva in *Ex Machina*—it seemed to *feel* like something to be them. What I'm asking is: Will it feel a certain way, from the inside, to be AGI? Will there be a subjective, *felt* quality to their mental lives? This is the problem of AI consciousness.

But why does AI consciousness even matter?

The Future Moral Status of AI

Notice that if a being is conscious, then it seems to deserve special moral consideration, as it could suffer and feel a range of emotions. But if we've created an AGI to work for us, to force it to fight our wars or clean our homes would be akin to slavery. And destroying it would be akin to murder.

So consciousness is key to how we value AI. Conversely, it might also turn out to be key to how AI values us. For if AIs are conscious, they may value us because they see in us the well of conscious experience.

From an ethical standpoint, it is imperative to know if AI is conscious so as to avoid mistreating conscious beings. Further, a failure to be charitable to AI may come back to haunt us, as they may treat us as we treated them.

Approaching the Problem

So how can the problem be solved? Here, I don't have a comprehensive solution (although I have outlined an initial test: Schneider, 2016). When it comes to machine consciousness, we are still taking baby steps, I suspect. One step toward any future solution is to appreciate what makes the problem so difficult.

It may initially seem that the problem is easy: Cognitive science holds that the brain is an information-processing system and that all mental functions are computations. Given this, it would seem that artificial intelligences (AIs) can be conscious, for AIs have computational minds, just as we do. Just as a text message and a voice message can convey the same information, so too, both brains and sophisticated AIs can be conscious.

However, I believe that it is an open question whether consciousness simply goes hand in hand with sophisticated computation for two reasons.

First, an AGI may have an architecture that bypasses consciousness altogether. For consider how consciousness works in humans. Only a very small percentage of human mental processing is conscious at any given time. Consciousness is correlated with novel learning tasks that require concentration, and when a thought is under the spotlight of our attention, it is processed in a slow, sequential manner.

Now consider that an AGI could be highly advanced, being what is called "superintelligent AI." Superintelligent AI is a hypothetical form of AI that outthinks humans in every domain—scientific reasoning, social skills, and more (Bostrom, 2015). A superintelligence would surpass expert-level knowledge in every domain, with rapid-fire computations ranging over vast databases that could occupy the space of an entire planet or encompass the entire internet. It may not need the very mental faculties that are associated with conscious experience in humans. Consciousness could be outmoded.

Indeed, superintelligent AI might rewrite its own code; a self-improving AI may opt to outmode its own consciousness or build other AGIs that are not conscious. And the processing of a superintelligence will likely be beyond the understanding of unenhanced humans in any case. It will be difficult for a human to grasp whether a given AGI system is even conscious.

Second, for all we know, consciousness may be limited to carbon substrates. Carbon molecules form stronger, more stable chemical bonds than silicon, which allows carbon to form an extraordinary number of compounds, and unlike silicon, carbon has the capacity to more easily form double bonds. This difference has important implications in the field of astrobiology, because it is for this reason that carbon and not silicon is said to be well suited for the development of life throughout the universe.

If the chemical differences between carbon and silicon impact life itself, we should not rule out the possibility that these chemical differences could also impact whether silicon gives rise to consciousness, even if they do not hinder silicon's ability to process information in a superior manner. Similar issues may arise if microchips are developed from substrates other than silicon.

In essence, we can only determine whether a given substrate is capable of conscious processing after detailed investigation of both the substrate and the larger architecture of the AI in question. Since there may be multiple kinds of AGIs (multiple intelligences, if you will), we may need to test each type of system and new substrate independently—some AGIs may be conscious, others may not be. It may be that androids that are designed to tug at the heartstrings, like Eva in *Ex Machina*, are not conscious, while some bland, unsexy server farm is.

These two considerations suggest that we should regard the problem of AI consciousness as an open question. Indeed, perhaps AGI will be pondering the same issues—*about us.* Should they ever wax philosophical, maybe they will ask if biological, carbon-based beings have the right substrate for experience. After all, how could they ever be certain that *we* are conscious?

References

Bostrom, N. 2015. *Superintelligence: Paths, Dangers, Strategies.* Oxford: Oxford Univ. Press.
Garland, A. (dir.) 2015. *Ex Machina.* Universal Pictures.
Schneider, S. 2016. It may not feel like anything to be an alien. http://cosmos.nautil.us/feature/72/it-may-not-feel-like-anything-to-be-an-alien [Accessed 28 December 2016]
Scott, R. (dir.) 1982. *Blade Runner.* Warner Brothe

Further Reading

Arkin, R.C. (2009) *Governing Lethal Behavior in Autonomous Robots.* Boca Raton, FL: Chapman & Hall/CRC.
Asimov, I. (1942) Runaround. *Astounding Science Fiction* 29(1): pp. 94–103.
Lin, P., Abney, K. and Bekey, G.A. (Eds.) (2012) *Robot Ethics: The Ethical and Social Implications of Robotics.* Cambridge, MA: MIT Press.
Wallach, W. and Allen, C. (2009) *Moral Machines: Teaching Robots Right From Wrong.* Oxford: Oxford University Press.

References

Ågotnes, T., Hoek, W.V.D., Rodriguez-Aguilar, J.A., Sierra, C., and Wooldridge, M. (2007) On the logic of normative systems. *Proceedings of the Twentieth International Joint Conference on Artificial Intelligence (IJCAI '07):* pp. 1181–1186.
Andrighetto, G., Villatoro, D., and Conte, R. (2010) Norm internalization in artificial societies *AI Communications* 23(4): pp. 325–339.
Arkin, R.C. (2009) *Governing Lethal Behavior in Autonomous Robots.* Raton, FL: CRC Press, Boca.
Arkin, R.C., Wagner, A.R., and Duncan, B. (2009) Responsibility and Lethality for Unmanned Systems: Ethical Pre-mission Responsibility Advisement, *Proceedings of the 2009 IEEE Workshop on Roboethics,* Georgia Institute of Technology.
Arkin, R.C., and Balch, T. (1997) AuRA: Principles and practice in review. *Journal of Experimental and Theoretical Artificial Intelligence* 9(2): pp. 175–189.
Arkin, R.C., and Ulam, P. (2009) An ethical adaptor: Behavioral modification derived from moral emotions. *Computational Intelligence in Robotics and Automation (CIRA), 2009 IEEE International Symposium on, IEEE:* pp. 381–387.
Asaro, P.M. (2011) Remote-control crimes. *Robotics & Automation Magazine, IEEE* 18(1): pp. 68–71.
———. (2012) A body to kick, but still no soul to damn: Legal perspectives on robotics. In P. Lin, K. Abney, and G. Bekey (Eds.). *Robot Ethics: The Ethical and Social Implications of Robotics.* Cambridge, MA: MIT Press, pp. 169–186.
Asimov, I. (1942) Runaround. *Astounding Science Fiction.*
Bartneck, C., Verbunt, M., Mubin, O., and Al Mahmud, A. (2007) To kill a mockingbird robot. In *Proceedings of the ACM/IEEE International Conference on Human-Robot Interaction,* presented at the HRI 2007, New York: ACM Press, pp. 81–87.
Blass, J.A. and Forbus, K.D. (2015) Moral Decision-Making by Analogy: Generalizations versus Exemplars, *Proceedings of the Twenty-Ninth AAAI Conference on Artificial Intelligence,* 25–30 January, Austin, Texas, pp. 501–507.

Bonnefon, J.-F., Shariff, A. and Rahwan, I. (2016), The Social Dilemma of Autonomous Vehicles *Science* 352(6293): pp. 1573–1576.

Briggs, G. and Scheutz, M. (2013) A Hybrid Architectural Approach to Understanding and Appropriately Generating Indirect Speech Acts, *Proceedings of Twenty-Seventh AAAI Conference on Artificial Intelligence*, pp. 1213–1219.

———. (2014) How robots can affect human behavior: Investigating the effects of robotic displays of protest and distress. *International Journal of Social Robotics* 6(2): pp. 1–13.

———. (2015) 'Sorry, I Can't Do That': Developing Mechanisms to Appropriately Reject Directives in Human-Robot Interactions, *Proceedings of the 2015 AAAI Fall Symposium on AI and HRI*.

Bringsjord, S., and Taylor, J. (2012) The divine-command approach to robot ethics. In P. Lin, G. Bekey, and K. Abney (Eds.). *Anthology on Robo-Ethics*. Cambridge, MA: MIT Press, pp. 85–108.

Chatterjee, P. (2015) Is drone warfare fraying at the edges? www.tomdispatch.com, 8 March. Available at: www.tomdispatch.com/post/175964/tomgram%3A_pratap_chatterjee,_is_drone_warfare_fraying_at_the_edges/ [Accessed 24 July 2016].

Coeckelbergh, M. (2010) Robot rights? Towards a social-relational justification of moral consideration. *Ethics and Information Technology* 12(3): pp. 209–221.

Cushman, F., Young, L., and Greene, J.D. (2010) Multi-system moral psychology. In John M. Doris (Ed.). *The Moral Psychology Handbook*. Oxford: Oxford University Press, pp. 47–71.

Darling, K., Nandy, P., and Breazeal, C. (2015) Empathic Concern and the Effect of Stories in Human-Robot Interaction, *Proceedings of the 24th IEEE International Symposium on Robot and Human Interactive Communication (RO-MAN)*, IEEE, pp. 770–775.

Dehghani, M., Tomai, E., Iliev, R., and Klenk, M. (2008) MoralDM: A computational Model of Moral Decision-Making, *Proceedings of the 30th Annual Conference of the Cognitive Science Society (CogSci)*, Washington, DC.

Gert, B. (2005) *Morality: Its Nature and Justification*. Revised ed. New York: Oxford University Press.

Gips, J. (1995) Toward the ethical robot. In K.M. Ford, C. Glymour, and P.J. Hayes (Eds.). *Android Epistemology*. Cambridge, MA: MIT Press, pp. 243–252.

Goble, L. (2005) A logic for deontic dilemmas. *Journal of Applied Logic* 3(3–4): pp. 461–483.

Guglielmo, S. (2015) Moral judgment as information processing: An integrative review. *Frontiers in Psychology* 6. Available at: http://doi.org/10.3389/fpsyg.2015.01637

Gunkel, D.J. (2014) A vindication of the rights of machines. *Philosophy & Technology* 27(1): pp. 113–132.

Gunkel, D.J., Bryson, J.J., and Torrance, S. (Eds.) (2012), *The Machine Question: AI, Ethics and Moral Responsibility*. Hove, UK: The Society for the Study of Artificial Intelligence and Simulation of Behaviour.

Hamlin, J.K. (2013) Moral judgment and action in preverbal infants and toddlers: Evidence for an innate moral core. *Current Directions in Psychological Science* 22(3): pp. 186–193.

Heider, F., and Simmel, M. (1944) An experimental study of apparent behavior. *American Journal of Psychology* 57(2): pp. 243–259.

Kahn, Jr., P.H., Ishiguro, H., Friedman, B., and Kanda, T. (2006) What is a human? toward psychological benchmarks in the field of human-robot interaction, *The 15th IEEE International Symposium on Robot and Human Interactive Communication, 2006. ROMAN 2006*, presented at the 15th IEEE International Symposium on Robot and Human Interactive Communication, 2006. ROMAN 2006, pp. 364–371.

Kahn, Jr., P.H., Kanda, T., Ishiguro, H., Freier, N.G., Severson, R.L., Gill, B.T., Ruckert, J.H. and Shen, S. (2012) 'Robovie, you'll have to go into the closet now': Children's social and moral relationships with a humanoid robot. *Developmental Psychology* 48(2): pp. 303–314.

Malle, B.F. (2015) Integrating robot ethics and machine morality: The study and design of moral competence in robots. *Ethics and Information Technology*. Available at: http://doi.org/10.1007/s10676-015-9367-8

Malle, B.F., and Scheutz, M. (2014) Moral Competence in Social Robots, *Proceedings of IEEE International Symposium on Ethics in Engineering, Science, and Technology, Ethics'2014*, IEEE, Chicago, IL, pp. 30–35.

———. (2016) Inevitable psychological mechanisms triggered by robot appearance: Morality included? In *AAAI Spring Symposium Series Technical Reports SS-16–03*. Palo Alto, CA: AAAI Press, pp. 144–146.

Malle, B.F., Scheutz, M., and Austerweil, J.L. (2017) Networks of social and moral norms in human and robot agents. In M.I.A. Ferreira, J.S. Sequeira, M.O. Tokhi, E. Kadar, and G.S. Virk (Eds.). *A World With Robots*. Berlin, Heidelberg: Springer.

Malle, B.F., Scheutz, M., Arnold, T., Voiklis, J., and Cusimano, C. (2015) Sacrifice one for the good of many? People apply different moral norms to human and robot agents. In *HRI '15: Proceedings of the Tenth Annual ACM/IEEE International Conference on Human-Robot Interaction*. New York: ACM Press, pp. 117–124.

Malle, B.F., Scheutz, M., Forlizzi, J., and Voiklis, J. (2016) Which robot am I thinking about? The impact of action and appearance on people's evaluations of a moral robot. In *Proceedings of the Eleventh Annual Meeting of the IEEE Conference on Human-Robot Interaction, HRI'16*. Piscataway, NJ: IEEE Press, pp. 125–132.

Mikhail, J. (2014) Any animal whatever? Harmful battery and its elements as building blocks of moral cognition. *Ethics* 124(4): pp. 750–786.

Monroe, A.E., Dillon, K.D., and Malle, B.F. (2014) Bringing free will down to earth: People's psychological concept of free will and its role in moral judgment. *Consciousness and Cognition* 27: pp. 100–108.

Moor, J.H. (2006) The nature, importance, and difficulty of machine ethics. *IEEE Intelligent Systems* 21(4): pp. 18–21.

———. (2013) Four kinds of ethical robots. *Philosophy Now* 72: pp. 12–14.

Murphy, R., and Woods, D.D. (2009) Beyond Asimov: The three laws of responsible robotics. *IEEE Intelligent Systems* 24(4): pp. 14–20.

Pagallo, U. (2011) Robots of just war: A legal perspective. *Philosophy & Technology* 24(3): pp. 307–323.

Pereira, L.M., and Saptawijaya, A. (2009) Modelling morality with prospective logic. *International Journal of Reasoning-Based Intelligent Systems* 1(3/4): pp. 209–221.

Powers, T.M. (2013) Machines and moral reasoning. *Philosophy Now* (72). Available at: https://philoso phynow.org/issues/72/Machines_and_Moral_Reasoning [Accessed 26 July 2016].

Premack, D. (1990) The infant's theory of self-propelled object. *Cognition* 36(1): pp. 1–16.

Scheutz, M. (2012) The inherent dangers of unidirectional emotional bonds between humans and social robots. In P. Lin, G. Bekey, K. and Abney (Eds.). *Anthology on Robo-Ethics*. Cambridge, MA: MIT Press, pp. 205–221.

———. (2014) The need for moral competency in autonomous agent architectures. In V.C. Müller (Ed.). *Fundamental Issues of Artificial Intelligence*. Berlin: Springer, pp. 515–525.

Scheutz, M., and Arnold, T. (2016a) Are we ready for sex robots?, *Proceedings of the 11th ACM/IEEE International Conference on Human-Robot Interaction*.

———. (2016b) Feats without heroes: Norms, means, and ideal robotic action. *Frontiers in Robotics and AI* 3. Available at: http://doi.org/10.3389/frobt.2016.00032

Scheutz, M., and Malle, B.F. (2014) 'Think and do the right thing': a plea for morally competent autonomous Robots, *Proceedings of the IEEE International Symposium on Ethics in Engineering, Science, and Technology, Ethics'2014*, Curran Associates/IEEE Computer Society, Red Hook, NY, pp. 36–39.

Scheutz, M., Schermerhorn, P., Kramer, J., and Anderson, D. (2006) First steps toward natural human-like HRI. *Autonomous Robots* 22(4): pp. 411–423.

Short, E., Hart, J., Vu, M., and Scassellati, B. (2010) No Fair!! An Interaction with a Cheating Robot, *Proceedings of the 5th ACM/IEEE International Conference on Human-Robot Interaction*, Osaka, Japan.

Sparrow, R. (2007) Killer robots. *Journal of Applied Philosophy* 24(1): pp. 62–77.

Strait, M., Canning, C., and Scheutz, M. (2014) Let me tell you! Investigating the Effects of Robot Communication Strategies in Advice-Giving Situations based on Robot Appearance, Interaction Modality, and Distance, *Proceedings of 9th ACM/IEEE International Conference on Human-Robot Interaction*, pp. 479–486.

Sullins, J. (2006) When is a robot a moral agent? *International Review of Information Ethics* 6(12): pp. 23–30.

Tremoulet, P.D., and Feldman, J. (2000) Perception of animacy from the motion of a single object. *Perception* 29(8): pp. 943–951.

Wallach, W., and Allen, C. (2008) *Moral Machines: Teaching Robots Right from Wrong*. New York: Oxford University Press.

PART IV

Expanding the Frame

This final section of the *Handbook* explores some of the many interesting future directions, emerging ideas, and contemporary issues that are pushing the boundaries of neuroethics. These chapters explore a truly diverse set of concerns, questions, and perspectives that are challenging not only neuroscience but neuroethics as well.

The "Neurogenderings and Neuroethics" chapter by Cipolla and Gupta considers how neuroscientific "facts" about sex/gender are produced within the contemporary historical and political context and how such facts might promote a "neurosexist" misuse of neuroscience to assert that women and men are categorically different by virtue of their brains, or to simply cloak sex/gender stereotypes in the vocabulary of the brain. Using single-sex education as a case study, they provide an example of the interface of neuroscience research with educational policy and demonstrate how the use of neuroscience research on sex/gender can reinforce sexism. They then suggest how to use this research to promote gender justice.

In "Neurodiversity, Neuroethics, and the Autism Spectrum," Liu provides a history of the neurodiversity movement and an overview of the unique and important perspectives that have emerged from the movement as it has challenged medical and neuroscientific dogmas about autistics and the autism spectrum. Liu provides specific recommendations that emphasize the ethical imperative to consider the perspectives of neurodiversity movement advocates who assert that some mental disorders or differences attributed to brain "dysfunction" are better appreciated as variations that need neither eradication nor cure.

The chapter on Research Domain Criteria (RDoC) discusses the neuroethical implications of the RDoC's paradigm shift in defining and treating mental disorders. The controversial revisions to the *Diagnostic and Statistical Manual of Mental Disorders* (DSM-5) in 2013 have also prompted reconsideration of important questions regarding the definition and nature of mental disorders and how they should be viewed scientifically. Faucher and Goyer consider the challenges and concerns about excessive reductionism in the growing emphasis on discovering neurobiological explanations for psychiatric illness in "RDoC's Special Kind of Reductionism and its Possible Impact on Clinical Psychiatry."

Two chapters on international and cultural perspectives acknowledge the current Western biases of neuroethical scholarship and the need for a multiculturally inclusive approach, given the global scope of neuroethical problems. While we could not address every perspective in this section (given the paucity of scholarship in this emerging area and the overall scope of this book), we sought to begin this discussion with comparisons of the current state of neuroethics in countries in Asia and Latin America, where both neuroscience and neuroethics scholarship and programs are growing. Salles sheds light on how a historical embrace of psychotherapy has impacted the discipline of neuroethics in Argentina in "Neuroethics in Context: The Development of the Discipline in Argentina." With "Neuroethics in Japan," Fukushi, Isobe, Nakazawa, Takimoto, Akabayashi, Sullivan, and Sakura focus on the development of neuroethics as a discipline in Japan and its interaction with Japanese conceptualizations of ethics. These chapters focus on the history and evolution of neuroethics in their respective countries while providing a window into unique perspectives and concerns within those cultures that illuminate the diversity of neuroethics worldwide.

In "The Neurobiologic Embedding of Childhood Socioeconomic Status," Sheridan considers some recent neuroscience studies that challenge us to revisit questions related to neurodeterminism, social responsibility, and policy. For example, researchers have found that childhood socioeconomic status is associated with structural alterations in the human brain, raising new questions about the extent of the impact of poverty on cognitive development and the potential for interventions. These findings raise questions as to how these data should or might inform our ethical and civic responsibilities not only to people who exist now but also to future generations. Yet caution is warranted lest overly deterministic and fatalistic interpretations of these data risk further disenfranchising the already disenfranchised and disadvantaged.

The two final chapters explore ethically thorny questions about the contested moral status of two groups of beings: neonatal/prenatal humans and nonhuman animals. "Prenatal and Neonatal Neuroethics: The Moral Significance of Painience" by Johnson considers the evidence for painience and consciousness in human fetuses and neonates to preface a discussion of the role of painience in grounding moral status. The chapter by Fenton and Shriver, "Animal Minds: The Neuroethics of Nonhuman Dissent," spotlights the emerging and increasingly philosophically important debate about nonhuman animals, evidence for "minding" animals, and the moral agency of animals. Traditional ethical and bioethical questions about the use and exploitation of animals in research intersect with neuroethical issues specific to the recognition of animal cognition in ways that might illuminate and expand both the neuro and the ethical in neuroethics.

25

NEUROGENDERINGS AND NEUROETHICS

Cyd Cipolla and Kristina Gupta

Biological justifications for the differences between men and women have as long a history as the study of human physiology itself (Tuana, 1993; Laqueur, 1990). The scientific study of the brain is no different, as researchers in early neurology and the precursors to structural neuroscience, including physiognomy (Lombroso and Ferrero, 2003) and craniotomy (Fee, 1979), researched explanations not only for sex differences but also for the perceived inferiority of women. Political and social feminist movements of the 19th, 20th, and 21st centuries pushed back on sex roles and norms, spurring significant critiques of the science of sex differences and the study of sex in the brain (Bluhm, 2014). In recent years, feminist science studies scholars have reviewed and critiqued neuroscientific research purporting to find sex differences in brain structure and function, identifying flaws in methodologies, theoretical assumptions, and interpretations (Bluhm, 2014).

This chapter is about "neurogenderings," or the complex ways in which brains become sexed and gendered in the world and in the neuroscience lab. In this chapter, we do not attempt to summarize and critique all of the neuroscience research on sex differences in the brain, as this has been done elsewhere (Bluhm, 2014). What we do instead is offer an overview of key contributions feminist neuroethics has made to the understanding of neuroscience research on sex and gender, and how this research influences society. It is our contention throughout that feminist neuroethics not only offers powerful critiques of traditional neuroscience research on sex and gender and of the use of this research for political and social aims, but also productive suggestions for how to do and use this research in a way that supports gender justice.

We begin with an introduction to the concepts of sex and gender in feminist theory and then offer a brief history of feminist approaches to science and to neuroscience specifically. We then discuss in detail two areas in which feminist neuroethics has critiqued neuroscience research and offered new models and approaches: first, models of sex/gender and the brain, and second, neuroimaging methods for studying sex/gender differences. In the final section of this chapter we offer a feminist neuroethical analysis of single-sex versus coeducation to provide an example of how feminist neuroethics can be employed to critique the use of neuroscience research on sex and gender in social policy while also suggesting ways to use this research differently.

Defining Our Terms: *Sex, Gender,* and *Sex/Gender*

The first step in understanding the complexities of neurogendering is acknowledging that the terms of the debate, *sex* and *gender*, are themselves in flux. Researchers in the mid-20th century introduced a distinction between the systems of *sex* (as biological) and *gender* (as cultural; Money et al., 1957). The use of these terms proliferated and, in recent years, has been challenged. In their traditional definitions, *sex* refers to a measurable, biological, or innate difference, such as the presence or absence of a Y chromosome, while *gender* refers to cultural and social signifiers of masculinity and femininity, such as clothing choice. Gender has much greater variation both historically and culturally. The distinction between the two can be difficult to parse out because most people are *cisgendered*, that is, they find that their gender matches their sex, and so feminist theorists often turn to other categories, such as *intersex* and *transgender*, to illustrate how sex and gender function independently (Fausto-Sterling, 2000).

A researcher may focus on either sex or gender exclusively when studying human behavior, but most move between the two categories or examine some particular function of their overlap. In fact, feminist theorists so often study the interaction between sex and gender that, in 1975, anthropologist Gayle Rubin proposed naming this particular set of interactions the sex/gender system. Although feminist scholars continue to debate the parameters of the sex/gender system and in particular the complications introduced by theorist Judith Butler (1990, who claimed that maybe sex was really gender all along), generally the term *sex/gender* is meant to refer to not only biological sex and the cultural meanings of gender but also the fact that these concepts are so inextricably linked that they may be inseparable.

Largely due to their analytical utility, the concepts *sex, gender,* and *sex/gender* have taken on many shades of meaning both inside and outside of feminism. One result of this proliferation is that scholars and researchers do not use the terms consistently across disciplines, or even, in fact, across areas of study within a single discipline (Dussauge and Kaiser, 2012b). Although the terms originally developed for use in referring to human behavior, sometimes researchers will refer to sex differences in laboratory animals using the term *gender* (for example, mice: Dere et al., 2014; Gioiosa et al., 2013; Herron and Miles, 2012). Even researchers who focus entirely on humans sometimes do not consistently conceptually distinguish between sex, gender, and sex/gender. Researchers' inconsistent use of terms combined with the assumption of a universal understanding creates confusion when they share findings about sex or gender differences between disciplines or when public media reports these findings. This conceptual confusion is one of the central points of intervention for feminist neuroethics and others critiquing the neuroscience of sex and gender.

Feminist Engagements with Science and Neuroscience: A Feminist Neuroethics?

Feminist approaches to science attempt to rectify *androcentric* (male-centered), *patriarchal* (male-dominated), or *sexist* (discriminatory on the basis of sex) biases that run through biological theories of sexual difference. These approaches form the basis of a subfield within feminist theory called *feminist science studies*, or the interdisciplinary engagement with the subjects and methods of scientific inquiry from a distinctly feminist or sex/gender–centered standpoint. Within the field of feminist science studies, scholars argue for diversity both in subjects of inquiry and among the ranks of researchers (Hubbard et al., 1979; Tavris, 1993; Tiefer, 1978), note how the topics of scientific research are guided by and tacitly reinforce sexist stereotypes and assumptions that serve as the infrastructure for a sexist society (Dalmiya and Alcoff, 1993; Keller, 1983;

Schiebinger, 1993), and push for a change in the methods and in the epistemologies used to justify scientific knowledge itself (Barad, 1999; Harding, 1986; Keller, 1982, 1985; Rose, 1983, 1994). Much work in feminist science studies employs an *intersectional* approach wherein scholars examine sex/gender as one of several intersecting vectors of oppression or discrimination, including but not limited to race, ethnicity, age, ability, sexual orientation, and socioeconomic status (see Crenshaw, 1991). Scholars also complement feminist methods with others drawn from queer theory, postcolonial theory, disability theory, and critical race theory. In terms of understanding neurogendering, the most productive and relevant strain of feminist science studies is that which critiques instances in which social gender attributes are credited to sex or where sex differences are used (explicitly or implicitly) to validate sexist gender norms. Earlier feminist work in this strain responded to sex and gender as defined by endocrinology and genetics (Haraway, 1981; Longino and Doell, 1983; Doell and Longino, 1988)[1] and, as the decade of the brain commenced, moved to neuroscience explicitly (Fausto-Sterling, 1992).

Contemporary work in feminist science studies moves beyond critiquing the definitions of sex and gender within science to questioning the utility of the distinction itself. This work comes from a larger systems theory–based concern that nature, or biology, and nurture, or culture, are so intertwined as to make the distinction between sex and gender (or any other similar categories) not only complex but functionally useless (Barad, 2007; Fausto-Sterling, 2003; Keller, 2010; Kirby, 2011; Grosz, 1994). As discussed in what follows, feminist examinations of the neuroscience of sex and gender often use this most recent rearticulation of the sex/gender system.

There has been a flurry of activity in feminist neuroscience in the last five years. Building on a history of feminist bioethics (Darvall, 1993; Donchin and Purdy, 1999; Rawlinson, 2001; Tong, 1997; Wolf, 1996) and emerging interest in a so-called women's neuroethics (Chalfin et al., 2008), Peggy DesAutels (2010) uses the term *feminist neuroethics* to describe her analysis of recent neuroscience research on sex differences. Her review article makes an interesting move by both critiquing the neuroscience of sexual difference and following this research through to its logical but perhaps absurd conclusion. For example: while she critiques neuroscience findings about sex/gender differences in moral reasoning, DesAutels points out that if scholars take these findings seriously, we might be led to ask "do differing levels and types of hormones absolve men and women in differing ways and degrees, of moral responsibility for their actions?" (102). She also notes how the leap made when connecting sex/gender differences in spatial reasoning ability to sex/gender differences in aptitude for science includes within it an unstated and limiting assumption about what scientists do and who makes a good one—that is, that good scientific work requires above-average ability in spatial reasoning. DesAutels's analysis notes that in this work, the brain serves as a useful scapegoat for structured social inequalities. That is, if structural brain differences are to blame for differing interests in employment and negotiating skills, there is no need to focus on societal barriers to women entering and staying in the workforce—an idea that would become central to feminist neuroethics and the critique of sex differences in the brain. In the end, DesAutels argues for a cautious, systems-based approach to neuroscientific research, one that maintains attention to variation and cultivates sensitivity to the fact that finding a measurable difference does not give researchers reason to conclude anything about the origin of that difference.

In addition to DesAutels's work on feminist neuroethics, 2010 brought the publication of two books specifically focused on critiquing the sexed brain: Cordelia Fine's *Delusions of Gender: How Our Minds, Society, and Neurosexism Create Difference* and Rebecca Jordan-Young's *Brain Storm: The Flaws in the Science of Sex Difference*. Jordan-Young's work focuses on brain organization theory, exposing the long and sometimes unstable history of assumptions behind the idea that certain gendered behaviors are hardwired (with the implication that these behaviors are fixed and unchangeable) into the brain. Fine's work focuses on the interaction between science and society in the production of knowledge and, in particular, an examination of what she calls *neurosexism*: a form of "doubling down" on gender roles made possible by those who take scientific discussion of sex as proof that cultural behavior is natural. In response to the trends highlighted by Jordan-Young and Fine, researchers proposed engaging in *neurofeminism*, defined by Schmitz and Höppner (2014b) as a field that "critically validates gendered assumptions of contemporary brain research and examines the impacts of references to neuroscientific research on social gendered order and cultural significations" (para. 2).

The central hub for ideas about neurogendering at present, and perhaps the origin of the term itself, comes from the group of international scholars who organize and participate in the biennial NeuroGenderings conference. This conference gathering led to a special issue of the journal *Neuroethics* (Dussauge and Kaiser, 2012a) and the volume *Gendered Neurocultures: Feminist and Queer Perspectives on Current Brain Discourses*, edited by Sigrid Schmitz and Grit Höppner (2014a). Work by the various members of this group focuses on sex/gender in three areas of emerging critical neuroscience: the foundational critical stance of reviewing and questioning neuroscientific claims about sex and gender (Dussauge and Kaiser, 2012b; Fine, 2012; Jordan-Young and Rumiati, 2012), the call for a specifically "feminist and gender-sensitive" neuroscience (Nikoleyczik, 2012; Roy, 2012a), and a push to complicate brain theory by proliferating alternative, nonneuroscientific theories of mind and brain (Kraus, 2012; Schmitz, 2012). Authors also incorporate intersectional research (Gumy, 2014; Kuria, 2014; O'Connell, 2014) as well as work exploring the possibility of a queer feminist neuroscience (Dussauge, 2014; Kaiser, 2014).

As it stands now, the feminist neuroethics of sex/gender in the brain takes seriously the examination of the complex interplay between hormones, genes, structures, and behavior and thus questions any easy elision of these categories. Critical feminist neuroethics situates sex/gender with respect to age, race, class, and ethnicity (Kuria, 2014) while also recognizing, as Rebecca Jordan-Young (2014) argues, with a note to the work of Katrina Karkazis, that "the attachment to sex/gender as a framework can (or maybe inevitably does) lead to loss of information" (377). Feminist neuroethics is also deeply concerned with the formation and interpretation of neuroscientific knowledge, particularly the political uses of research into sex/gender differences. It is our contention that feminist neuroethics offers an important critique of neuroscience research on sex and gender while also suggesting avenues for change; we illustrate this contention in the following discussions of models of sex and gender in the brain and neuroimaging research.

Contributions of Feminist Neuroethics

New Models of Sex/Gender

Feminist neuroethics identifies two particularly problematic practices in traditional neuroscientific research that overly simplify the sex/gender system. First, traditional neuroscience research uses a dimorphic system of sex/gender in which (1) there are only two sexes (male and female), (2) every subject fits into one of these two sexes, (3) all males are alike and all females are alike, and (4) males and females are different from each other. Meeting these four conditions requires flattening out variations that occur within the sex/gender continuum. Second, neuroscience research examining sex/gender frequently collapses gender into sex through either the actions or decisions of the researchers themselves or by outside interpretations of their results. As a result, the complex effects of an ongoing interaction between nature and culture are consistently (mis)identified as solely the product of nature.[2]

Drawing on the work in feminist science studies discussed already, feminist neuroethics offers a more complex model for understanding sex/gender in the brain in which sex and gender are seen as interactive and nondimorphic. Feminist neuroethicists argue that differences in observed brain activity cannot conclusively show whether these differences are the product of inborn biological systems or the product of social and cultural forces over a lifetime. Thus, at the very least, some of the observed "sex differences" in the brain should more accurately be called "sex/gender differences" (Kaiser et al., 2009; Roy, 2012b).

Feminist neuroethics also questions the persistent belief among scientists and nonscientists alike that humans have discreet "male" or "female" systems for processing certain behaviors. Margaret M. McCarthy and Anne Konkle (2005) argue that these beliefs proliferate and persist because of increased conflation between *sexual dimorphism*, such as traits linked to sexual reproduction, and *sexual difference*, such as measured differences in learning. Correlations between sexually dimorphic structures and measured sexual difference not only create confusion with regard to the magnitude of difference but also strengthen the foundations of sexist social structures. Vidal (2012) notes a similar problem in her review of sexual differentiation in three areas: language and mathematical skill, financial risk taking, and moral cognition. McCarthy and Arnold (2011) propose abandoning the linear sexual differentiation model in favor of a more dynamic and interactive system, a move that would help undercut some of the misconceptions created by increased confusion between sexual dimorphism and sexual differentiation and, as a corollary, between sex and gender.

Daphna Joel (2012, 2014) complicates neuroscientific understandings of the sex/gender system through the presentation of a new subcategory of sex, which she calls 3G, or genetic-gonadal-genital sex. Joel argues that the generally dimorphic sex system, and specifically what it means to be "intersex," is increasingly complicated once you move beyond 3G sex. Within the 3G system, most people fit into one of two categories (male genetics-gonads-genitals or female genetics-gonads-genitals), the two categories are internally similar, and also differ from each other in significant ways. However, Joel points out that it is when the dimorphic model of 3G sex is applied to the brain, behavior, cognition, or personality that problems arise, as "current data reveal that sex differences in these domains are rarely dimorphic and are often not consistent," and, in fact, "in the human brain there is to date no region for which a complete dimorphism has been demonstrated" (Joel, 2012, 2–3). According to Joel, it would be better to conceptualize all brains as "intersex" rather than continuing to force a dimorphic system. Joel's work is particularly interesting because it shows the unintended consequences of transposing systems—in this case, how trying to use the relatively simple and readily observable dimorphism of 3G sex as a model to explain sexual differences in brain and behavior, which are neither simple nor readily observable, obscures the complexities of gender and sex.

Neuroimaging Studies of Sex/Gender

Another traditional view of neuroscience research on sex/gender is to present this work as revealing preexisting sex/gender differences through an objective process rather than work that captures static moments in a dynamic and fluid system. The problems associated with this traditional view are particularly apparent when it comes to interpreting neuroimaging research. As scholars have noted, fMRI scans are "not a one to one copy of a living brain . . . [but are] based on models of how scientists think the brain is constructed and their assumptions on how it works" (Fitsch, 2011). These scans reveal information in the form of *differences*, comparing images of a brain involved in two tasks and subtracting unwanted or background information, and, in the case of research into sex/gender, examine a double difference, that is, they seek to find "difference (between groups) in a difference (between tasks)" (Bluhm, 2013, 875). Consequently, any claim of hardwired or structural difference based on functional neuroimaging research should be suspect and, in the case of sex/gender, doubly so. Feminist neuroethics critiques this view of neuroscience research on sex/gender and offers an alternative way to think about and approach neuroimaging research.

Because of the interpretative nature of neuroimaging studies of difference, these studies are particularly susceptible to the effects of social gender stereotypes (Fine, 2013). For example, Bluhm (2013) notes in her review of fMRI research on emotion that "no studies report simply that they have not found the expected differences. Instead, researchers find and report some kind of between-group difference in their data" (876) and that the influence of gender stereotypes is "so strong that in some cases it causes researchers to ignore their actual results in favor of the results that they think should have been observed" (870). For example: Bluhm analyses a study examining emotion ratings and brain activity in response to a series of photos chosen to elicit fear or disgust. The researchers hypothesized that women would have greater brain activity. Upon finding that although women reported more emotional reaction, *men* had greater brain activity, the researchers reported, first, that their study was consistent with previous work showing no difference in brain activity. They then appealed to a gender stereotype to explain the slight difference in men by claiming that the photos used in the study showed scenes of aggression, something to which men were known to be more responsive (876). Other studies Bluhm examined stuck to gendered stereotypes in spite of the existence of simpler explanations (877) or employed data manipulation in order to report findings of difference (878).

Understanding the importance of difference itself is central to understanding the production of scientific knowledge as analyzed in studies like Bluhm's. There is great pressure within scientific communities to find new data (i.e., difference) rather than replicate old data (similarities), and, conversely, there is more interest in publishing studies that set out to find a difference and succeed rather than studies that fail to do so. What results is the use of neuroscience research as a laundering scheme for sexism: implicit sexist assumptions about gender difference inform the structure of research, scientists look for and find sex/gender differences, and then, because of perceived objectivity, the results of this research are seen as clean and unbiased and thus are used to support explicitly sexist policies and statements.

Moving beyond critique, feminist neuroethics proposes an alternative way to think about scientific research based on neuroimaging. Kaiser et al. (2009), based on an examination of sex/gender differences in fMRI language research, propose that one way to counteract neurosexism is to see scientific knowledge as a *product* rather than a *discovery* and, in particular, that "sex/gender differences in the brain cannot merely be regarded as fact. Rather, they should be seen as a variable of examination in a knowledge production setting, where statements of differences are, due to historical scientific paradigms, received as more relevant than those of similarities" (56).

Rippon et al. (2014) review four concepts from gender research as a whole that they recommend should be incorporated fully into neuroimaging research on sex/gender in order to avoid the reproduction of gender stereotypes. The first concept is the importance of *overlap* between sex/gender categories, and here, they emphasize that researchers must not simply recognize that men and women are more similar than they are different (Hyde, 2005) but actively question whether dimorphism is a functional or accurate system at all. The second concept is the increased recognition of *mosaicism* of gender/sex categories, or the idea that gender traits do not clump at either end of the sex continuum, at both population and individual levels. The third concept is the importance of *contingency*, particularly with regard to gendered behaviors that vary culturally and historically. The final concept is the *entanglement* of sex and gender, in particular the complications that arise when we consider that some of the biological markers for sex impact cultural and social expectations of gender, which, in turn, can produce biological effects. These four concepts concisely highlight many of the pitfalls of neuroimaging research into sex/gender differences while suggesting ways to approach this research differently. It should be noted that in addition to addressing issues particular to neuroimaging research, all four of these concepts propose ways to move away from sex/gender dimorphism and collapsing nature/nurture systems into the purely natural and thus answer some of the critiques from the previous section.

Feminism, Neuroscience, and Society: Single-Sex Education as Case Study

Feminist neuroethics can also lead to a new interface between neuroscience and society. As we have already noted, neuroscience research on sex/gender and the brain has frequently been used to support sexist social policies. Feminist neuroethics critiques this usage and also has the potential to use neuroscience research to challenge gender stereotypes and create a more gender-equitable society. Here we provide the example of the interface of neuroscience research with educational policy to demonstrate the use of neuroscience research on sex/gender to reinforce sexism and to suggest how to use this research to promote gender justice.[3]

After the 1970s, there was a decline in single-sex/-gender education in the United States. However, in the late 1990s and 2000s, a number of educators and social commentators became worried that boys were "underperforming" in schools (Corbett et al., 2008). In this environment, a number of "experts" began using neuroscience research on sex/gender to argue that boys (and girls) would perform better in schools if education was tailored to fit sex-/gender-specific neuro-developmental patterns and mental strengths. The most influential of these experts were Michael Gurian, author of *Boys and Girls Learn Differently!*, and Leonard Sax, founder of the National Association for Single Sex Public Education and author of *Why Gender Matters* (Fine, 2010). Together, they were quite successful in their push to increase single-sex/gender education, at least for a time.

In 2006, the U.S. Department of Education relaxed restrictions against single-sex/-gender education in public schools. In 2002, only about a dozen public schools were offering single-sex/-gender classes. As of 2012, an estimated 500 public schools in the U.S. were offering at least some single-sex/-gender classes. According to many observers of these single-sex/-gender classes, at least some of these classes rely on and reinforce sexist stereotypes. In the classes for boys at one public school, for example, the chalkboards were blue and students were encouraged to run before tests, while, in the classes for girls, the walls were decorated with red hearts and students were encouraged to do yoga before tests (Hollingsworth and Bonner, 2012).

Scholars working within a feminist neuroethical framework offer careful critiques of the neuroscience research on which the advocates for single-sex/-gender education rely. They have also critiqued the way these advocates distort and selectively (mis)appropriate neuroscience. Cordelia Fine devotes a significant section of *Delusions of Gender* to just this task. Here we provide one example from Fine: Leonard Sax claims that in boys and young children, emotion is processed in the amygdala with few connections to the cerebral cortex, while in older girls, the amygdala is richly connected to the cerebral cortex. As a result, Sax suggests that when boys are reading *The Lord of the Flies* for a literature class, the instructor should ask them to think not about plot or character development but about how to construct a map of the island. In contrast, he suggests that when teaching literature to older girls, the instructor should tell them to reflect on the feelings and motivations of a story's protagonist. However, according to Fine, Sax makes his claim about gender/age differences in emotional processing based on one small neuroimaging study in which researchers scanned children's brains while they stared passively at fearful faces. As Fine argues, it is almost always problematic to develop universal recommendations based on a small study, and in this case, the study only examined one emotion (fear) while the children were not engaged in a complex cognitive task, but Sax uses it to make a generalized claim that invoking emotion helps older girls (but not boys or younger girls) learn (Fine, 2010).

In addition to Fine, a number of other feminist scholars have critiqued the arguments made by single-sex/-gender education advocates and have worked to educate the public about these critiques. In general, feminist neuroethics argues that the neuroscience research simply doesn't support the claim that all boys have one type of brain/neuro-developmental pattern and all girls have another type of brain/neuro-developmental pattern, nor does it support the reliant claim that these two types are so different from each other that it makes sense to segregate boys and girls into different classes. A group of these scholars founded the American Council for CoEducational Schooling to advocate for coeducation, and a number of those involved with this group published a report on single-sex/-gender education in *Science*, titled "The Pseudoscience of Single-Sex Schooling" (Halpern et al., 2011). The report argues that there are no well-designed research studies that demonstrate that single-sex/-gender schooling improves academic performance, but there is evidence that sex/gender segregation increases gender stereotyping and legitimizes institutional sexism. Scholars involved with the American Council for CoEducation Schooling and with the report published in *Science* have written media articles and appeared on TV and radio programs in order to advocate against single-sex/-gender education (e.g., Strauss, 2012), and their work has been used by the American Civil Liberties Union (ACLU) in its effort to bring legal action against public schools that implement sexist single-sex/-gender education (Bohm, 2012).

A feminist neuroethics approach that understands sex/gender as a complex system does not only offer resources for critiquing sexist education but can also suggest ways for using neuroscience research to develop educational programs that promote gender justice. For example, of relevance here is Joel's argument that the 3G model of sex cannot be applied to the brain, behavior, cognition, or personality (Joel, 2012). This view of course clarifies why sex-/gender-segregated schooling makes no sense if the goal is to produce groups of children who share a common brain "type" but also provides strong support for the argument that children should be individually assessed to determine their particular learning assets and that, as much as is possible in group educational settings, instruction should be individually targeted to make the most of those assets, and/or instructors should use a variety of different instructional methods in order to engage students with different learning assets. At the same time, the recognition of "overlap, mosaicism, contingency and entanglement" (Rippon et al., 2014) demanded by feminist neuroethics suggests that perhaps educators are too focused on trying to produce groups of students with the same type of brain. Instead, we should embrace the fact that any group of students (whatever their sexes/genders) will contain neurodiversity, and we should consciously attempt to recruit that neurodiversity itself to the service of learning, for example, by encouraging peer-to-peer teaching.

In addition, feminist neuroethics suggests that we can draw on neuroscience research to construct educational interventions that actively seek to reduce gender inequality and break down gender stereotypes. For example, educators can use research from psychology, cognitive science, and neuroscience on implicit (or unconscious) bias to develop educational programs that teach students to recognize and challenge their own biases. Similarly, teachers and educators can use research on the phenomenon of stereotype threat[4] to develop curricula that not only avoid activating stereotype threat but also proactively diffuse it (Fine, 2010).

Finally, a feminist neuroethical approach that sees sex/gender as a system also recognizes the fact that while there are not "boy brains" and "girl brains," there may be some differences in the average performance of boys and girls on specific cognitive tasks that are produced through a complex interplay of biology and gender socialization. Recognizing this complex interplay allows for educators to use emerging work in neuroscience, cognitive science, and psychology to develop specific educational programs to improve performance on these tasks, and, further, these programs could be offered to any student who needs them. For example, it has been suggested that some or all of the average difference in performance between boys and girls on certain spatial-reasoning tasks is the product of differences in terms of childhood activities, and, in a small study, ten hours of training with an action video game decreased gender disparities among study participants in mental rotation abilities (Feng et al., 2007). We imagine that an educational program could be developed based on this and similar studies and could be offered to all students who demonstrated a need for it. Such a program could ultimately contribute, in a small way, to greater gender equity in the workforce. This is just one example of the ways in which a feminist neuroethics approach could actually use brain research to promote gender equity in society.

Conclusions

We urge neuroscientists, neuroethicists, and feminist science scholars alike to consider the complex functions and forms of neurogendering when considering any claims about sex differences in the brain. Importantly, feminist neuroethics does not call for the abandonment of neuroscience research on sex/gender. Scientific knowledge continues to be an effective tool for social justice in that it provides concrete and measurable effects of the complex mechanisms of oppression. But as Roy (2012a) cautions, "we have to ask ourselves while examining these studies whether the research contributes to social stereotypes that reinforce discrimination based on perceived differences, or whether it moves us a little closer to lifting or destabilizing an oppressive power structure based on our understanding of difference" (224). Thus, feminist neuroethics urges researchers to view scientific knowledge as something that is produced rather than discovered, to evaluate the effects of social and cultural stereotypes on both the production and reception of that knowledge, and, finally, to consider whether the search for difference is a self-fulfilling prophecy.

To truly address feminist neuroethical concerns, researchers must go beyond the different-but-complementary model of the sexes. Feminist neuroethics provides suggestions for conducting research: the push to focus on sexual differences, not sexual dimorphism (McCarthy and Konkle, 2005), work to disrupt the linear progression or serial model of chromosomes to gender identity (McCarthy and Arnold, 2011), to move beyond chromosomes, gonads, and genitals, or what Daphna Joel (2012) calls 3G sex, and to employ the methods of "overlap, mosaicism, contingency and entanglement" (Rippon et al., 2014). Research conducted using these suggestions not only allows for greater variation of sex/gender identification by subjects recruited for a study but also changes the possibilities for knowledge production. For example: when presented with results that do not conform to a dimorphic sex/gender system, the incorporation of feminist neuroethical concepts may allow neuroscientists to present their findings as evidence for an alternative to dimorphic sex/gender systems rather than seeing such results as "null" or "inconsistent." In fact, recent work done utilizing feminist neuroethical concepts demonstrates the utility of this framework, such as van Anders et al.'s 2015 study on so called "gendered behavior" and testosterone, or Joel et al.'s 2015 study on brain mosaics. Both studies incorporate complex understandings of the relationship between sex and gender.

We also urge those involved in the dissemination of scientific knowledge, whether as instructors, critics, or members of the news media, to think critically about the impact of neurogendering. Pedagogical methods that embody the principles of feminist neuroethics include those that encourage interdisciplinary cross-training both within and beyond the sciences, either through team-teaching or the creation of spaces for interdisciplinary dialogue in the academy, and those that focus on giving students the tools to be ethically responsible and socially aware producers and consumers of neuroscientific knowledge through, for example, the use of critical reflection. It is vital to the goals of neuroethics and feminist science studies to democratize science education. Instructors should aim to enable students from all disciplines to understand scientific research on its own terms, to develop the skills required to analyze the ethical implications of research, and to develop an understanding of how neuroscientific research is conveyed to the public through media.

Notes

1 Amusingly, in retrospect, Doell and Longino (1988) argue for a "complex neurobiological approach" that "minimizes the role of fetal hormones" (55).
2 Similar critiques apply to the study of sexuality, where critics note the problems associated with trying to find a biological truth based on a cultural system, and note that sexuality and sexual identity are highly variable not only between cultural populations but over an individual person's lifespan (Blackwood, 2000; Stein, 1999; Wolpe, 2004). Additionally, some studies of homosexuality utilize sexual dimorphism when searching for difference, often relying on something called "inversion theory," in which it is presumed that homosexual men must be "feminized," or similar to heterosexual women, because of a shared sexual interest in men. This mode of categorization means that the study of homosexuality is subject to many of the same feminist criticisms that are levied at studies of sexual difference (Jordan-Young, 2010).
3 Some of this section is adapted from the blog post "Neurosexism and Single-Sex Education (or support your local ACLU)."
4 The phenomenon of stereotype threat occurs when students feel they are at risk of confirming a negative stereotype about a group they belong to (e.g., girls are reminded that girls are supposed to be bad at math right before taking a math test). Research has shown that the phenomenon of stereotype threat negatively impacts student performance (Fine, 2010).

Further Reading

Bluhm, R., Jacobson, A.J. and Maibom, H.L. (2012) *Neurofeminism: Issues at the Intersection of Feminist Theory and Cognitive Science*. New York: Palgrave Macmillan.
Dussauge, I. and Kaiser, A. (Eds.) (2012) "Neuroscience and Sex/Gender". Special Issue *Neuroethics* 5(3): pp. 211–324.
Fine, C. (2010) *Delusions of Gender: How Our Minds, Society, and Neurosexism Create Difference*. New York: W.W Norton & Company.
Jordan-Young, R. (2010) *Brain Storm: The Flaws in the Science of Sex Differences*. Cambridge, MA: Harvard University Press.
Schmitz, S. and Höppner, G. (Eds.) (2014) *Gendered Neurocultures: Feminist and Queer Perspectives on Current Brain Discourses*. Vienna: Zaglossus.

References

Anders van, S.M., Steiger, J., and Goldey, K.L. (2015) Effects of gendered behavior on testosterone in women and men. *Proceedings of the National Academy of Sciences* 112(45): pp. 13805–13810.
Barad, K. (1999) Agential realism. In M. Biagioli (Ed.). *The Science Studies Reader*. New York: Routledge, pp. 1–11.
———. (2007) *Meeting the Universe Halfway: Quantum Physics and the Entanglement of Matter and Meaning*. Durham, NC: Duke University Press.
Blackwood, E. (2000). Culture and women's sexualities. *Journal of Social Issues* 56(2): pp. 223–238.

Bluhm, R. (2013). Self-fulfilling prophecies: The influence of gender stereotypes on functional neuroimaging research on emotion. *Hypatia* 28(4), pp. 870–886.

———. (2014) Feminist philosophy of science and neuroethics. In J. Clausen and N. Levy (Eds.). *Handbook of Neuroethics*. The Netherlands: Springer, pp. 1405–1419.

Bohm, A. (2012). Teach kids, not stereotypes. *American Civil Liberties Union (ACLU)*. Available at: www.aclu.org/teach-kids-not-stereotypes [Accessed 8 June 2016].

Butler, J. (1990) *Gender Trouble: Feminism and the Subversion of Identity*. New York: Routledge.

Chalfin, M.C., Murphy, E.R., and Karkazis, K.A. (2008) Women's neuroethics? Why sex matters for neuroethics. *American Journal of Bioethics* 8(1): pp. 1–2.

Corbett, C., Hill, C., and St Rose, A. (2008) *Where the Girls Are: The Facts About Gender Equity in Education*. American Association of University Women Educational Foundation. Available at: www.aauw.org/resource/where-the-girls-are-the-facts-about-gender-equity-in-education/ [Accessed 8 Jan. 2016].

Crenshaw, K. (1991). Mapping the margins: Intersectionality, identity politics, and violence against women of color. *Stanford Law Review* 43(6): pp. 1241–1299.

Dalmiya, V., and Alcoff, L. (1993) Are "Old Wives' tales" justified? In L. Alcoff and E. Potter (Eds.). *Feminist Epistemologies*. New York: Routledge, pp. 217–244.

Darvall, L.W. (1993) *Medicine, Law, and Social Change: The Impact of Bioethics, Feminism, and Rights Movements on Medical Decision-Making*. Brookfield, VT: Dartmouth.

Dere, E., Dahm, L., Lu, D., Hammerschmidt, K., Ju, A., Tantra, M., . . . Ehrenreich, H. (2014) Heterozygous ambra1 deficiency in mice: A genetic trait with autism-like behavior restricted to the female gender. *Frontiers in Behavioral Neuroscience* 8(181): pp. 1–19.

DesAutels, P. (2010) Sex differences and neuroethics. *Philosophical Psychology* 23(1): pp. 95–111.

Doell, R.G., and Longino, H.E. (1988) Sex hormones and human behavior: A critique of the linear model. *Journal of Homosexuality* 15(3–4): pp. 55–78.

Donchin, A., and Purdy, L.M. (1999) *Embodying Bioethics: Recent Feminist Advances*. Lanham, MD: Rowman & Littlefield.

Dussauge, I. (2014) Brains, sex, and queers 2090: An ideal experiment. In S. Schmitz and G. Höppner (Eds.). *Gendered Neurocultures: Feminist and Queer Perspectives on Current Brain Discourses*. Vienna: Zaglossus, pp. 67–88.

Dussauge, I., and Kaiser, A. (2012a) Neuroscience and sex/gender. *Neuroethics* 5(3): pp. 1–5.

———. (2012b) Re-queering the brain. In R. Bluhm, A.J. Jacobson, and H.L. Maibom (Eds.). *Neurofeminism: Issues at the Intersection of Feminist Theory and Cognitive Science*. London: Palgrave Macmillan, pp. 121–144.

Fausto-Sterling, A. (1992) *Myths of Gender: Biological Theories About Women and Men*. 2nd ed. New York: Basic Books.

———. (2000). *Sexing the Body: Gender Politics and the Construction of Sexuality*. 1st ed. New York: Basic Books.

———. (2003) The problem with sex/gender and nature/nurture. In S.J. Williams, L. Birke, and G. Bendelow (Eds.). *Debating Biology*. London: Routledge, pp. 123–132.

Fee, E. (1979). Nineteenth-century craniology: The study of the female skull. *Bulletin of the History of Medicine* 53(3): p. 415.

Feng, J., Spence, I., and Pratt, J. (2007) Playing an action video game reduces gender differences in spatial cognition. *Psychological Science* 18(10): pp. 850–855.

Fine, C. (2010) *Delusions of Gender: How Our Minds, Society, and Neurosexism Create Difference*. New York: W.W Norton & Company.

———. (2012). Explaining, or sustaining, the status quo? The potentially self-fulfilling effects of "hardwired" accounts of sex differences. *Neuroethics* 5(3): pp. 285–294.

———. (2013) Is there neurosexism in functional neuroimaging investigations of sex differences? *Neuroethics* 6(2): pp. 369–409.

Fitsch, H. (2011). (A)e(s)th(et)ics of brain imaging: Visibilities and sayabilities in functional magnetic resonance imaging. *Neuroethics* 5(3): pp. 275–283.

Gioiosa, L., Parmigiani, S., vom Saal, F.S., and Palanza, P. (2013) The effects of bisphenol A on emotional behavior depend upon the timing of exposure, age and gender in mice. *Hormones and Behavior* 63(4): pp. 598–605.

Grosz, E.A. (1994) *Volatile Bodies: Toward a Corporeal Feminism*. Bloomington, IN: Indiana University Press.

Gumy, C. (2014) The gendered tools of the construction of a unisex 'adolescent brain.' In S. Schmitz and G. Höppner (Eds.) *Gendered Neurocultures: Feminist and Queer Perspectives on Current Brain Discourses*. Vienna: Zaglossus, pp. 257–272.

Gupta, K. (2012) Neurosexism and single-sex education (or support your local ACLU). *The Neuroethics Blog*, 22 July, 2015. Available at: www.theneuroethicsblog.com/2012/07/neurosexism-and-single-sex-education-or.html.

Halpern, D.F., Eliot, L., Bigler, R.S., Fabes, R.A., Hanish, L.D., Hyde, J., . . . Martin, C.L. (2011) The pseudoscience of single-sex schooling. *Science* 333(6050): pp. 1706–1707.

Haraway, D.J. (1981) In the beginning was the word: The genesis of biological theory. *Signs* 6(3): pp. 469–481.

Harding, S.G. (1986) *The Science Question in Feminism*. Ithaca, NY: Cornell University Press.

Herron, L.R., and Miles, G.B. (2012) Gender-specific perturbations in modulatory inputs to motoneurons in a mouse model of amyotrophic lateral sclerosis. *Neuroscience* 226: pp. 313–323.

Hollingsworth, H., and Bonner, J.L. (2012) Why single-sex education is spreading across the US. *Christian Science Monitor*.

Hubbard, R., Henifin, M.S., and Fried, B. (1979) *Women Look at Biology Looking at Women: A Collection of Feminist Critiques*. Boston: G.K. Hall.

Hyde, J.S. (2005) The gender similarities hypothesis. *American Psychologist* 60(6): p. 581.

Joel, D. (2012). Genetic-gonadal-genitals sex (3G-sex) and the misconception of brain and gender, or, why 3G-males and 3G-females have intersex brain and intersex gender. *Biology of Sex Differences* 3(27): p. 6.

———. (2014) Sex, gender, and brain: A problem of conceptualization. In S. Schmitz and G. Höppner (Eds.). *Gendered Neurocultures: Feminist and Queer Perspectives on Current Brain Discourses*. Vienna: Zaglossus, pp. 169–186.

Joel, D., Berman, Z., Tavor, I., Wexler, N., Gaber, O., Stein, Y., . . . Liem, F. (2015) Sex beyond the genitalia: The human brain mosaic. *Proceedings of the National Academy of Sciences* 112(50): pp. 15468–15473.

Jordan-Young, R. (2010) *Brain Storm: The Flaws in the Science of Sex Differences*. Cambridge, MA: Harvard University Press.

———. (2014) Fragments for the future: Tensions and new directions from 'Neuro-cultures—NeuroGenderings II.' In S. Schmitz and G. Höppner (Eds.). *Gendered Neurocultures: Feminist and Queer Perspectives on Current Brain Discourses*. Vienna: Zaglossus, pp. 373–394.

Jordan-Young, R., and Rumiati, R.I. (2012) Hardwired for sexism? Approaches to sex/gender in neuroscience. *Neuroethics* 5(3): pp. 305–315.

Kaiser, A. (2014) On the (im)possibility of a feminist and queer neuroexperiment. In S. Schmitz and G. Höppner (Eds.). *Gendered Neurocultures: Feminist and Queer Perspectives on Current Brain Discourses*. Vienna, Austria: Zaglossus, pp. 41–66.

Kaiser, A., Haller, S., Schmitz, S., and Nitsch, C. (2009) On sex/gender related similarities and differences in fMRI language research. *Brain Research Reviews* 61(2): pp. 49–59.

Keller, E.F. (1982) Feminism and science. *Signs* 7(3): pp. 589–602.

———. (1983) *A Feeling for the Organism: The Life and Work of Barbara McClintock*. San Francisco: W.H. Freeman.

———. (1985) *Reflections on Gender and Science*. New Haven, CT: Yale University Press.

———. (2010) *The Mirage of a Space Between Nature and Nurture*. Durham, NC: Duke University Press.

Kirby, V. (2011) *Quantum Anthropologies: Life at Large*. Durham, NC: Duke University Press.

Kraus, C. (2012). Critical studies of the sexed brain: A critique of what and for whom? *Neuroethics* 5(3): pp. 247–259.

Kuria, E.N. (2014) Theorizing race(ism) while neurogendering. In S. Schmitz and G. Höppner (Eds.). *Gendered Neurocultures: Feminist and Queer Perspectives on Current Brain Discourses*. Vienna: Zaglossus, pp. 109–125.

Laqueur, T.W. (1990) *Making Sex: Body and Gender From the Greeks to Freud*. Cambridge, MA: Harvard University Press.

Lombroso, C., and Ferrero, G. (2003) *Criminal Woman, the Prostitute, and the Normal Woman*. Durham, NC: Duke University Press.

Longino, H., and Doell, R. (1983) Body, bias, and behavior: A comparative analysis of reasoning in two areas of biological science. *Signs* 9(2): pp. 206–227.

McCarthy, M.M., and Arnold, A.P. (2011) Reframing sexual differentiation of the brain. *Nature Neuroscience* 14(6): pp. 677–683.

McCarthy, M.M., and Konkle, A.T. (2005) When is a sex difference not a sex difference? *Frontiers in Neuroendocrinology* 26(2): pp. 85–102.

Money, J., Hampson, J.G., and Hampson, J.L. (1957) Imprinting and the establishment of gender role. *AMA Archives of Neurology & Psychiatry* 77(3): pp. 333–336.

Nikoleyczik, K. (2012) Towards diffractive transdisciplinarity: Integrating gender knowledge into the practice of neuroscientific research. *Neuroethics* 5(3): pp. 231–245.

O'Connell, K. (2014) Bad boy's brains: Law, neuroscience, and the gender of 'aggressive' behavior. In S. Schmitz and G. Höppner (Eds.). *Gendered Neurocultures: Feminist and Queer Perspectives on Current Brain Discourses*. Vienna: Zaglossus, pp. 299–319.

Rawlinson, M.C. (2001) The concept of a feminist bioethics. *Journal of Medicine and Philosophy* 26(4): pp. 405–416.

Rippon, G., Jordan-Young, R., Kaiser, A., and Fine, C. (2014) Recommendations for sex/gender neuroimaging research: key principles and implications for research design, analysis, and interpretation. *Frontiers in Human Neuroscience* 8(650): pp. 1–56.

Rose, H. (1983) Hand, brain, and heart: A feminist epistemology for the natural sciences. *Signs* 9(1): pp. 73–90.

———. (1994) *Love, Power, and Knowledge: Towards a Feminist Transformation of the Sciences*. Bloomington, IN: Indiana University Press.

Roy, D. (2012a) Neuroethics, gender and the response to difference. *Neuroethics* 5(3): pp. 217–230.

———. (2012b) Cosmopolitics and the brain: The co-becoming of practices in feminism and neuroscience. In R. Bluhm, A.J. Jacobson, and H.L. Maibom (Eds.). *Neurofeminism: Issues at the Intersection of Feminist Theory and Cognitive Science*. New York: Palgrave Macmillan, pp. 175–192.

Rubin, G. (1975) The traffic in women: Notes on the 'political economy' of sex. In L.J. Nicholson (Ed.). *The Second Wave: A Reader in Feminist Theory*. New York: Routledge, pp. 27–62.

Schiebinger, L.L. (1993) *Nature's Body: Gender in the Making of Modern Science*. Boston: Beacon Press.

Schmitz, S. (2012) The neurotechnological cerebral subject: Persistence of implicit and explicit gender norms in a network of change. *Neuroethics* 5(3): pp. 261–274.

Schmitz, S., and Höppner, G. (Eds.) (2014a) *Gendered Neurocultures: Feminist and Queer Perspectives on Current Brain Discourses*. Vienna: Zaglossus.

———. (2014b) Neurofeminism and feminist neurosciences: A critical review of contemporary brain research. *Frontiers in Human Neuroscience* 8(546): pp. 1–10.

Stein, E. (1999) *The Mismeasure of Desire: The Science, Theory, and Ethics of Sexual Orientation*. New York: Oxford University Press.

Strauss, V. (2012) The case against single sex education. *The Washington Post*, 4 June.

Tavris, C. (1993). The mismeasure of woman. *Feminism & Psychology* 3(2): pp. 149–168.

Tiefer, L. (1978) The context and consequences of contemporary sex research: A feminist perspective. In T.E. McGill, D.A. Dewsbury and B.D. Sachs (Eds.). *Sex and Behavior*. New York: Plenum Press, pp. 363–385.

Tong, R. (1997) *Feminist Approaches to Bioethics: Theoretical Reflections and Practical Applications*. Boulder, CO: Westview Press.

Tuana, N. (1993) *The Less Noble Sex: Scientific, Religious, and Philosophical Conceptions of Women's Nature*. Bloomington, IN: Indianan University Press.

Vidal, C. (2012) The sexed brain: Between science and ideology. *Neuroethics* 5(3): pp. 295–303.

Wolf, S.M. (1996) *Feminism & Bioethics Beyond Reproduction*. New York: Oxford University Press.

Wolpe, P.R. (2004) Ethics and social policy in research on the neuroscience of human sexuality. *Nature Neuroscience* 7(10): pp. 1031–1033.

26

NEURODIVERSITY, NEUROETHICS, AND THE AUTISM SPECTRUM

Emily Y. Liu

Introduction

The word "neurodiversity" first appeared in a 1998 article by journalist Harvey Blume, discussing elevated rates of autism[1] in the Silicon Valley (see Box 26.1 for a definition of autism). The article capitalizes on the technological savant stereotype of autism to make the point that "neurodiversity [in autism] may be every bit as crucial for the human race as biodiversity is for life" (Blume, 1998). The term was then adopted by author Judy Singer in her 1999 essay "Why Can't You Be Normal for Once in Your Life? From a Problem with No Name to the Emergence of a New Category of Difference," who gave "neurodiversity" its modern flavor when she wrote:

> The key significance of the "autism spectrum" lies in its call for and anticipation of a politics of neurological diversity, or neurodiversity. The "neurologically different" represent a new addition to the familiar political categories of class/gender/race and will augment the insights of the social model of disability.
>
> (Singer, 1999, 64)

Since then, neurodiversity has become a banner of the autistic self-advocacy movement. Though there are subtle variations in how neurodiversity is understood and described, these are predominantly variations upon a theme. Succinctly put, neurodiversity can be thought of as an

---

Box 26.1   A Definition of Autism

Autism refers to a collection of neurodevelopmental conditions of partially genetic origin that affect individuals throughout their lifespan. Autism alters brain growth, structure, and function, resulting in differences in information processing, sensory sensitivity and integration, and communication abilities. As a result, autistic individuals may experience difficulties in social relationships and communication, but demonstrate remarkable strengths in attention to detail as well as pattern recognition. Unusually narrow interests and a strong need for repetition and routine are often associated with the autism spectrum.

---

identity-politics approach to autism, situating autism as a natural form of human variation and an integral aspect of identity that should be approached with interventions that assist autistic individuals without altering them (Kapp et al., 2013). In recognition of autistic self-advocates' stated preference for identity-first language, which emphasizes autism as a vital aspect of self-identity, we adopt the term "autistic individuals" here to refer to those with a clinical diagnosis of autism (Bagatell, 2010; Kapp et al., 2013). (For more information, please see http://autistic advocacy.org/identity-first-language/.)

Indeed, while autistic self-advocates like Scott M. Robertson and Ari D. Ne'eman acknowledge "great challenges with being autistic," they simultaneously assert that "autism presents important strengths, talents, abilities, and gifts, such as comfort with structure and consistency, a knack for repetition, and a detailed, intricate world understanding" (Robertson and Ne'eman, 2008). This sentiment is echoed online in chat groups and forums as well as through autistic self-advocacy organizations like the Autistic Self-Advocacy Network (ASAN) and government committees like the Interagency Autism Coordinating Committee (IACC), the Federal advisory committee specific to autism (Durbin-Westby, 2009; Bagatell, 2010). As a national grassroots disability rights organization for the autistic community in the United States (U.S.), the ASAN is a leader within the neurodiversity movement, whereas the IACC operates through stakeholder consultation to coordinate federal and private efforts related to autism via funding recommendations, and so on (U.S. Department of Health and Human Services, 2014; ASAN, 2015). However, regardless of arena, the emphasis within the neurodiversity movement is on celebrating and supporting autistic individuals as opposed to preventing and eliminating autism (Kapp et al., 2013).

While the neurodiversity perspective has garnered support from certain individuals within the biomedical community (e.g., Simon Baron-Cohen, Laurent Mottron, Christina Nicolaidis, etc.), it is still not commonly acknowledged. This is despite the significant historical precedent for incorporating the insights of parent advocates and other stakeholders in broad initiatives related to autism (Silverman and Brosco, 2007). Most notably, research on autism has been greatly informed by the expertise and experiential knowledge of medical professionals, service providers, and parent advocates (Silverman and Brosco, 2007). However, though autistic self-advocates have expressed repeated warnings regarding the implications of genetic testing, interventions focused on normalization, and the singular pursuit of a cure, there have been few studies surveying their attitudes, beliefs, and concerns regarding biomedical research and treatments (Pellicano and Stears, 2011). One autistic self-advocate, Lydia Brown (2012a), reports being deemed "not autistic enough" to relate to or represent autistic individuals, especially those with more severe disabilities. Another self-advocate, Michelle Dawson, describes autistic individuals as being categorically "written off'" when they attempt to articulate their own concerns in debates about autism policy (Dawson, 2004a).

The delegitimization of the neurodiversity movement is concerning for reasons related to stigma and discrimination. Furthermore, it may antagonize autistic attitudes toward the research enterprise, medical care services, and policy makers. Researchers, clinicians, and policy makers may be hesitant or unsure how to engage with a perspective that *feels* so different from the biomedical model that has traditionally dominated much of the discourse on autism. In addition, it may be difficult to balance the priorities of autistic self-advocates with other supporting, competing, and opposing interests, given the diversity of both autistic and autism communities. This is further complicated by the influential role of parent advocacy organizations in direct, large-scale funding of research and the establishment of private research organizations, many of which promote a strict biomedical approach to autism (Silverman and Brosco, 2007; Singh et al., 2009). However, research by Kapp et al. (2013) suggests areas of consensus between stakeholders and the potential for collaboration.

By situating neurodiversity in the larger framework of neuroethics and its prioritization of questions of personhood, identity, and autonomy in relation to the neurosciences, we can begin to appreciate the ethical underpinnings of autism research and care. It is imperative we do so given the increasing momentum driving neurodiversity and its implications for the rights of autistic individuals as well as the responsibilities of researchers, clinicians, and policy makers. These matters are not separate from but part and parcel of biomedicine and scientific advancement. This chapter provides a basic overview of the claims and concerns of the neurodiversity movement regarding the existing discourse on autism, research on the spectrum, and interventions for autistic individuals and relates these to broader themes within neuroethics. It concludes with preliminary recommendations for researchers, clinicians, and policy makers based on work by the ASAN and the Academic Autistic Spectrum Partnership in Research and Education (AASPIRE), an innovative research partnership between academic and autistic communities, directed by physician Christina Nicolaidis and autistic self-advocate Dora Raymaker (Durbin-Westby, 2010; "AASPIRE," 2015).

The Neurodiversity Movement: Its Claims and Concerns

We begin with an overview of the claims and concerns of the neurodiversity movement. While differences in interpretation exist across individuals and groups, five interrelated claims provide a unifying platform for advocates and allies (Nicolaidis, 2012; Garen, 2014).

1. Autism is a natural variation within human diversity.
2. Autism is an integral aspect of individual identity.
3. Autism does not need to be cured.
4. Understandings of autism should be informed by a social model of disability.
5. Autistic individuals deserve equal rights, appropriate accommodations, social acceptance, and self-determination.

These principles invigorate concerns raised by autistic self-advocates within three central areas: stigmatizing portrayals of autistic individuals in the discourse on autism, research practices and aims, and interventions for autism. Other issues exist, but these have emerged as the most relevant for researchers, clinicians, and policy makers within biomedicine. Each will be discussed in detail in the paragraphs that follow.

Portrayals of Autism

The "ransom notes" affair heralded the zenith of the neurodiversity movement. In December 2007, the New York University Child Study Center (NYU CSC), under the leadership of Dr. Harold Koplewicz, initiated a public-service campaign to raise awareness of childhood psychiatric conditions (Kras, 2010). Ransom notes were posted in prominent locations throughout New York City (e.g., on large billboards, kiosks, and construction sites) as well as published in *Newsweek* and *New York* magazines, insinuating that autism, Asperger syndrome (then a separate diagnostic category), and other conditions had kidnapped the nation's children (Kras, 2010). Below is text from the autism and Asperger ransom notes (Kras, 2010):

Autism

We have your son.
We will make sure he will

not be able to care for
himself or interact socially
as long as he lives.
This is only the beginning.

Asperger's Syndrome

We have your son. We are destroying his ability for
social interaction and driving him into a life of complete isolation.
It's up to you now.

The campaign was halted after only two weeks when a grassroots internet protest led by Ari Ne'eman, cofounder and president of ASAN, spilled into the mainstream media (Kaufman, 2007; Wang, 2007). An online call to action was circulated by ASAN to various advocacy and disability rights organizations, protesting the campaign's stigmatization of individuals with disabilities and its failure to accurately portray the abilities, strengths, and accomplishments of these individuals (Ne'eman, 2007a). In an open letter to the NYU "ransom notes" campaign, Ne'eman and ASAN decried such campaigns as "inadvertently reinforc[ing] many of the worst stereotypes that have prevented children and adults with disabilities from gaining inclusion, equality, and full access to the services and supports they require" (Ne'eman, 2007b).

The "ransom notes" affair marked an early and significant victory for autistic self-advocates, and activism around stigmatizing portrayals of autistic individuals continues to be a mainstay of the neurodiversity movement. In a 2012 online entry entitled "The Dangers of Misrepresentation", autistic blogger Lydia Brown describes the "frightening impact" of language that characterizes autistic individuals as "lack[ing] empathy" and "incapable of expressing emotions, especially concern for others" (Brown, 2012b). Similarly, in a public comment to the IACC, autistic self-advocate Paula Durbin-Westby (2009) expressed alarm at terms like "abnormalities," "risks," "symptoms," and "severity" that "introduce an undertone of disrespect, fatalism, or excess pathologizing of autism." These criticisms are not limited to the public discourse on autism and autistic individuals, but also pertain to the research and clinical language on autism.

Though exceptions exist (e.g., Simon Baron-Cohen resisting terms like "disorder" and substituting "typical" for "normal"), studies like the one conducted by Liu and colleagues (2013) demonstrate a strong tendency toward deficit-oriented language within the academic literature on autism. In their qualitative analysis, Liu and colleagues examined the language in 40 scholarly articles on autism published between 2007 and 2012. Sampled articles were randomly selected from high-impact basic science, clinical science, special education and rehabilitation, and disability studies journals. All basic and clinical science articles included deficit-oriented language, with terms such as "deficit," "disease," and "dysfunction," and 15 of the 18 sampled articles only described autism and autistic individuals in these terms. Similarly, 9 of the 11 articles from special education and rehabilitation journals had descriptions like "deficient," "impaired," and "restricted." Only sampled articles from disability studies journals, including work by autistic self-advocates, had any emphasis on strength-oriented language. These articles utilized descriptions such as "creative," "insightful," and "inventive" in discussing both the positive attributes of autistic individuals and abilities and skills commonly associated with the condition. Overall, these findings suggest a divide between the language preferred by autistic self-advocates and the terminology adopted within the academic and research literature that speaks to concerns from within the self-advocacy community regarding the excessive pathologization, stigmatization, and stereotyping of autistic individuals.

Research on Autism

Autistic self-advocates within the neurodiversity movement have also expressed dissatisfaction with prevailing trends in research on autism. Much of the discussion online and in public comments to the IACC have focused on setting appropriate goals for research and ensuring adequate ethical safeguards for autistic participants (Durbin-Westby, 2010; Pellicano et al., 2011; Ethical, Legal, and Social Implications etc. 2011; Nicolaidis, 2012; Kapp et al., 2013; ASAN Statement on Fein Study on Autism and "Recovery" 2013; Community Concerns Regarding AUT10K, 2014; Position Statements, 2015).

For example, many autistic self-advocates fear that research aimed at elucidating a cause or developing a cure for autism will lead to its prevention or elimination (Ortega, 2009; Orsini and Smith, 2010; Baker, 2011; Pellicano and Stears, 2011; Kapp et al., 2013). In his first public comment to the IACC in 2007 as president of ASAN, Ari Ne'eman asserted, "while the rhetoric surrounding autism has focused on the idea of cure, many people on the autism spectrum are not interested in pursuing as a goal making autistic individuals normal." He later criticized genetics research promoting a prenatal test for autism as "eugenically oriented" (IACC, 2008). Autistic self-advocates further maintain that, regardless of whether a prenatal test or cure for autism will ever be realized, such studies fundamentally cast autistic individuals as less valuable members of society (Svoboda, 2009). Moreover, this research may divert much-needed resources from services, supports, and research focused on quality-of-life issues for existing individuals (Robertson, 2010; Pellicano and Stears, 2011; Position Statements, 2015). Consequently, ASAN has assumed a firm stance on research priorities focused on causation and cure, as expressed in the following position statement:

> More research is needed in areas such as communication, service delivery, education, and community supports that will have practical applications for improving the quality of life of Autistic people and our families. Autism research grants in recent years have gone mainly toward genetic and other causation-oriented studies with potential eugenic consequences, while studies focusing on educational practices, assistive technology, best practices in providing services and supports, and effective supports for community inclusion have received far less funding. These skewed priorities are unacceptable to the Autistic community and cannot be allowed to continue. It is a grave human rights concern that many Autistic individuals experience significant barriers to communication and to full participation in society because of inadequate funding of research on assistive communication technology and educational methods.
>
> (Position Statements, 2015)

ASAN has mobilized politically around these issues, publically endorsing proposed legislation like Representative Jan Schakowsky's amendment to the 2014 Autism CARES Act, which dedicated increased funding toward services research, and supporting her subsequent letter to the US Department of Health and Human Services (ASAN Statement on Autism Cares Act, 2014; The Arc of Washington County, Inc. 2014).

Considering the forceful objections of many autistic self-advocates to prevailing research direction and aims, it is perhaps unsurprising that ensuring adequate ethical safeguards for autistic participants is another focal point of the neurodiversity movement (Position Statements, 2015). Here, the question of informed consent is especially difficult, given differences in information processing and communication styles associated with the spectrum. Consequently, additional considerations, accommodations, and supports may be necessary to maximize the self-determination of autistic participants in research. Indeed, many within the movement regard such protections as imperative to upholding the right of autistic individuals to opt out of research that contradicts their interests and wishes, especially considering individuals' misgivings about the selection of appropriate surrogates (Barnbaum, 2008; Nicolaidis, 2012; Position Statements, 2015).

Most recently, ASAN has spoken out against the Google-Autism Speaks Ten Thousand Genomes Program or AUT10K (Community Concerns Regarding AUT10K, 2014). The initiative seeks to apply Google Cloud technology to expand and analyze whole genomes from the Autism Speaks Autism Genetic Resource Exchange (AGRE), thereby creating a powerful new data platform for researchers (Community Concerns Regarding AUT10K, 2014; Autism Speaks, 2014). Specifically, ASAN disapproves of the priorities of the research program as well as the lack of adequate safeguards for donors. The platform—once completed—will provide an unprecedented level of access to participants' genetic material for research studies that may or may not be in line with donors' preferences. Despite this, there are no mechanisms in place for reconsenting participants or withdrawing consent. Moreover, concerns exist regarding the privacy interests of donors, as it yet remains unclear what privacy protections will be implemented to prevent genetic data from being utilized in such a way as to reveal donors' personally identifiable information.

The AUT10K initiative demonstrates the shortcomings of existing research protocols; simultaneously, it illustrates how emerging research technologies are transforming the ethical landscape of research in unexpected ways, creating new challenges for researchers. Indeed, concerns related to informed consent and privacy protections are becoming all the more relevant with the increasing emphasis on biobanking in research on autism (Liu and Scott, 2014). With increased sample size and analytical power, there is greater likelihood that incidental findings of possible health, reproductive, or personal significance may be uncovered in the course of research (Wolf et al., 2012). However, the decentralization of research that occurs with biobanks and other large-scale data platforms like the AUT10K complicates the ethical responsibilities of researchers (Wolf et al., 2012). First, should an active link even be maintained between cell lines and donors' medical information given privacy risks? If so, what information should be disclosed and by whom? As such, there are additional considerations related to incidental findings and the risks and benefits of donors' medical information to cell lines that must be addressed (Liu and Scott, 2014).

Therapies and Treatments for Autism

Last, autistic self-advocates within the neurodiversity movement oppose certain forms of interventions for autism. Though they acknowledge functional difficulties associated with the spectrum and advocate for services and supports for autistic individuals, they are against therapies aimed primarily at normalization (Kapp et al., 2013). These programs often focus on the elimination of unusual but otherwise benign behaviors, such as vocal and motor stereotypy—some of which may be necessary coping mechanisms (Chamak, 2008; Ortega, 2009; Orsini and Smith, 2010). Reflecting on her motor stereotypy in her poem "Quiet Hands", Julia Bascom (2011), an autistic woman, testifies:

> I think I understand the whole world when I rub my fingertips together. When I'm brought to a new place, my fingers tap out the walls and tables and chairs and counters. They skim over the paper and make me laugh, they press against each other and remind me that I am real, they drum and produce sound to remind me of cause-and-effect. My fingers map out a world and then they make it real.
>
> My hands are more me than I am.

She describes the pain of being made to keep "quiet hands" as part of her applied behavioral analysis (ABA) treatment plan.

> I need to silence my most reliable way of gathering, processing, and expressing information, I need to put more effort into controlling and deadening and reducing and removing myself second-by-second than you could ever even conceive, I need to have quiet hands.[2]

Indeed, ABA is a source of great concern for many within the neurodiversity movement. Based in behavioral principles, such as positive and negative reinforcement and operant conditioning, it is directed at "improving" socially appropriate behaviors to a "meaningful" degree (Baer et al., 1968; Sulzer-Azaroff and Mayer, 1991). Many within the self-advocacy community have criticized such intensive behavioral therapies for their narrow focus on normalization, often without consideration of context and the coping functions certain behaviors may serve (Chamak, 2008; Ortega, 2009; Ne'eman, 2010; Orsini and Smith, 2010; Baker, 2011; Silverman, 2011). Moreover, as autistic individuals like Michelle Dawson (2004b) have argued, there are serious ethical problems with the use of powerful behavioral interventions on individuals, including many children, who are unable to consent. These fears are all the more pressing in light of recent cases concerning the misuse and abuse of seclusion and restraint procedures in behavioral therapy settings that involved injury to and even the deaths of autistic individuals (New York State Educational Department, 2006; Westling et al., 2010; Villani et al., 2012; Mizner, 2014; Position Statements, 2015).

Despite these concerns, ABA, as an evidence-based therapy, remains among the most commonly prescribed and commonly pursued interventions by parents (Green et al., 2006; Centers for Disease Control and Prevention, 2015). While there is empirical evidence for the efficacy of these therapies in significantly improving language, cognitive, and adaptive behaviors relative to standard of care for autistic children, other reviews demonstrate more modest outcomes (Spreckley and Boyd, 2009; Virués-Ortega, 2010; Peters-Scheffer et al., 2011). In addition, scholars in the field have raised concerns regarding study design (e.g., the representativeness of participant samples and interventions settings) and outcome measures (e.g., the significance and relevance of measured outcomes to stakeholder groups; Emerson, 2006). Similar criticism has been voiced by autistic self-advocates, who argue that the overreliance on ABA by parents, clinicians, and policy makers is misdirected and distracts from other potential therapies, such as augmentative and alternative communication (AAC) and joint attention, symbolic play, emotion regulation (JASPER) therapy (Durbin-Westby, 2010; ASAN Comments on CA Autism Insurance Regulation, 2012). These therapies are believed to have more appropriate goals of care and an even stronger evidence base for efficacy than ABA–based interventions (Durbin-Westby, 2010; ASAN Comments on CA Autism Insurance Regulation, 2012). Moreover, focusing on ABA may obscure larger health concerns within the autistic community, such as barriers to quality healthcare and disparities in health outcomes—particularly for individuals with fewer perceived disability-related needs, as is often the case with "high-functioning" autistic individuals (Nicolaidis et al., 2013; Position Statements, 2015).

For more on neural engineering and autism, see Chapter 3.

Neurodiversity and Neuroethics

In this section, we focus on the relationship between neurodiversity and neuroethics. By contextualizing neurodiversity within the larger discourse on neuroethics, we can begin to appreciate its contributions in mapping out the ethical landscape of autism research and care. William Safire, chairman of the Dana Foundation and *New York Times* columnist, first popularized the term "neuroethics" in 2001 (Farah, 2012). It has since come to refer to the various ethical, legal, and social implications trailing the comet's head of scientific progress in the neurosciences. Scholars within the field specifically refer to issues that speak to two main areas of concern (Roskies, 2002; Farah, 2005; Illes and Bird, 2006; Levy, 2011; Farah, 2012). The first has to do with ethical issues that arise in the development and implementation of research studies and therapeutic interventions (e.g., informed consent, protections for vulnerable populations, incidental findings, etc.). The second deals with the knowledge, technologies, and therapies resulting from research (e.g., advanced imaging, brain enhancement, etc.) and their implications for understandings of self, agency, and moral responsibility. Indeed, this last piece may be the unique and defining feature of neuroethics—its attention to themes of personhood, identity, and autonomy.

The neuroscience worldview holds that our emotions, values, thoughts, and behavior are to some degree influenced by the chemical and physical processes present within our neurobiology (Farah, 2012). However, it simultaneously acknowledges the multifaceted and dynamic interplay between these complex entities (Illes and Bird, 2006).

Recent functional magnetic resonance (fMRI) studies indicate the potential application of neuroimaging technologies in evaluating neural correlates for mood and personality, social cognition, cooperation and competition, love and hate, moral reasoning and sensitivity, and ethical judgments (Greene et al., 2001; Canli and Amin, 2002; Moll et al., 2002a; Moll et al., 2002b; Heekeren et al., 2003; Bartels and Zeki, 2004; Canli et al., 2004; Decety et al., 2004; Zeki and Romaya, 2008). Neuroscientists and neuroethicists have expressed concerns that such advancements may inadvertently contribute to a reductionist approach to human personality and behavior, with significant implications for criminal justice proceedings and other aspects of social policy (Morse, 2006; Illes et al., 2006a). These concerns imply additional responsibilities for researchers in preventing the misuse of data obtained through studies. Examples identified by Illes et al. (2006b) include supporting public understanding of scientific findings and guiding policy discussions regarding the appropriate application of research results.

Through this lens, discussions by autistic self-advocates on portrayals of autism and autistic individuals in scientific communications (e.g., publications, presentations, media outlets, etc.) can be viewed as touching upon similar considerations. The neurodiversity perspective of autism as a fundamental aspect of personal identity and the diversity inherent in the autism spectrum imply similar obligations for researchers and clinicians in promoting a more scientifically nuanced understanding of autism sensitive to the needs of autistic stakeholders. This need is all the greater considering revisions to the DSM-5 that combine four previously separate conditions under the umbrella category of autism spectrum disorder, heightening tensions related to the overgeneralization of certain traits (Lai et al., 2013).

Other features of the neurodiversity perspective can be uncovered in the terrain of neuroethics. For example, concerns about adequate ethical safeguards for research participants and patients have been discussed extensively within the literature. These include deliberations of what constitutes appropriate informed consent protocols for research—particularly that which involves minors—as well as strategies to minimize therapeutic misconception by patients for emerging clinical neuroscience research (Leykin et al., 2011; Kadosh et al., 2012; Focquaert, 2013; Christopher and Dunn, 2015). Much attention has been given to neurocognitively vulnerable populations, referring to individuals with limited capacity for autonomy due to intellectual disabilities, psychiatric illness, substance abuse disorders, and the like who are at increased risk of harm and exploitation in research and clinical contexts (Rivera Mindt, 2012; Racine et al., 2014; Szmukler and Rose, 2015). Discussions have centered on establishing rigorous competence assessments and robust informed consent protocols to maximize the autonomy of individuals (Rivera Mindt, 2012; Racine et al., 2014; Szmukler and Rose, 2015). Under this framework, autistic individuals may also be considered a vulnerable population. Indeed, the aforementioned issues parallel concerns expressed by the autistic community regarding the lack of adequate safeguards in research and clinical protocols to attend to the specific sensory-integration, information-processing, and communication needs of autistic individuals (Dawson, 2004b; Position Statements, 2015; Nicolaidis et al. 2015).

Deliberations about the impact of pharmacological (e.g., amphetamines, SSRIs, etc.) and nonpharmacological (e.g., transcranial magnetic stimulation, transcranial direct cranial stimulation, etc.) interventions that fundamentally alter neurological process on individuals' sense of personhood, identity, and autonomy may be of special interest to autistic self-advocates within the neurodiversity movement (Moreno, 2003; Farah, 2012). These conversations have focused primarily on forms of cognitive and social-affective enhancement, collectively referred to as brain enhancement. According to Farah (2012, 579), brain enhancement describes interventions that "make normal, healthy brains better, in contrast with treatments for unhealthy or dysfunctional brains." The troubling assumptions underlying the rhetoric of improvement, normalcy, and health have prompted much ethical debate around issues of coercion, stigma, and discrimination. For example, widespread adoption of cognitive and social-affective enhancements might limit individual freedoms through indirect forms of coercion, such as social stigma and discriminatory hiring practices (Farah, 2012). Moreover, there is disagreement regarding the appropriateness of such interventions in the context of biomedical research and clinical care, given that these are intended as enhancements rather than therapies (Farah, 2012). The benefits of such enhancements are perceived to be few, and the possible harms involve infringements of personal identity and autonomy (Farah, 2012). Last, with the increased focus on prenatal diagnosis and the genetics of behaviors, the specter of genetic engineering for brain enhancement also looms in the distant horizon (Moreno, 2003).

Parallels can be drawn between these debates and concerns from autistic self-advocates if we begin with the fundamental tenet of neurodiversity within autism—that autism and autistic traits are vital components of personal identity. From this premise, research focused on causation and cure, which may result in a prenatal test or a cure for autism, can be appreciated as driving toward certain forms of cognitive enhancement that "correct" autistic traits. However, simultaneously, they threaten to infringe on autistic individuals' right to self-determination and self-identity; again, many within the self-advocacy community understand these autistic traits as part of their individual identity. Similarly, interventions like ABA directed at normalization, which enhance socially appropriate behaviors and eliminate socially inappropriate but otherwise harmless behaviors can be considered through the framework of enhancement. In addition to the aforementioned concerns about stigma, discrimination, and coercion (e.g., parents or autistic individuals may feel compelled to pursue certain interventions for fear of social isolation, etc.), the intensive deliberations regarding appropriate harm–benefit ratios and the overall appropriateness of enhancement also apply here (Moreno, 2003; Farah, 2012). The benefits of such research and interventions, focused on normalization and the cultivation of appropriate, advantageous traits, and their legitimacy as therapeutic considerations are deeply contested. Moreover, autistic individuals may be especially vulnerable to the potential harms associated with these practices, given the lack of comprehensive and rigorous informed consent protocols adapted to their specific information processing and communication needs (Dawson, 2004b).

The intersection between neurodiversity and neuroethics lies in their shared preoccupation with questions of personhood, identity, and autonomy. These arise in the design and implementation of specific investigative and therapeutic protocols as well as in the far-reaching cultural, technical, and therapeutic fallout of scientific advancement in the neurosciences. Some may dispute the conception of autism as an aspect of personal identity, given both the various understandings of autism and the diversity inherent in the spectrum. However, with regard to the brain, the line between normal and abnormal—personality and pathology—has historically been a blurred one at best. For example, beginning in 1960 with the publication of Szasz's "The Myth of Mental Illness," there has been much concern regarding the legitimacy of the field of psychiatry and its misuse and abuse in the social marginalization and subjugation of "undesirables" (Foucault, 1988). Moreover, speculation exists regarding the reliability of certain diagnoses and the overdiagnosis of specific conditions (e.g., ADHD, bipolar disorder, depression, etc.) as reflective of overarching sociocultural trends toward medicalization (Aragonès et al., 2006; Aboraya et al., 2006; Zimmerman et al., 2008; Batstra and Frances, 2012; Moynihan et al., 2012; Frances, 2013; Timimi, 2014). These dilemmas are not unique to autism but represent a core tension within neuroscience and neuroethics, which renders the ethical issues surrounding research, care, and policy decisions all the more pertinent.

Preliminary Recommendations

Contextualizing the neurodiversity perspective within the larger framework of neuroethics allows us to better appreciate the incisive lens it provides into issues of personhood, identity, and autonomy for autistic individuals as research participants and patients. These considerations are essential to neuroscience and neuroethics and provide a foundation for discussing the ethical obligations of researchers, clinicians, and policy makers. The neurodiversity movement led by autistic self-advocates has, at times, been dismissed as a controversial, even radical, fringe movement (Doherty, 2009; Harmon, 2010; Jaarsma and Welin, 2012). However, research by Kapp et al. (2013) reveals considerable similarity between proponents of neurodiversity and the larger autism community, which demonstrate the potential for compromise and collaboration. These include a shared recognition of the biological underpinnings of autism and the difficulties encountered by individuals on the spectrum. The following recommendations focus on:

1. The language describing autism and autistic individuals in scientific communications.
2. Mechanisms for autistic involvement at the level of funding and policy decisions.
3. Strategies for facilitating autistic empowerment in research and improving clinical interactions.

This chapter does not discuss specific recommendations for research priorities or give research and clinical practice guidelines (e.g., improving safeguards, etc.); however, these are likely to be addressed through the incorporation of the autistic perspective in research, clinical, and policy proceedings.

Recommendation 1: Language Selection

We begin with recommendations for the language found in scientific communications (e.g., publications, presentations, through media outlets, etc.) on autism and autistic individuals. Existing trends in the research and clinical language, including descriptions of autism and autistic individuals as "deficient," or "impaired," are troubling for concerns related to stigma and discrimination, especially when considering their impact on social, cultural, and political attitudes and beliefs. They also stand to impact the terms of the public discourse on autism. The effects of the research language may be all the greater, given the early efforts of powerful parent advocacy organizations in promoting a particular narrative of autism as a disease to be prevented and cured through their research lobbying and fundraising initiatives (Silverman and Brosco, 2007; Singh et al., 2009). Additionally, there may be other unintended complications for the research enterprise. The presence of terms deemed offensive by autistic self-advocates might result in autistic individuals perceiving research as alienating or hostile to their concerns, complicating stakeholder uptake of research and the establishment of productive partnerships. For example, in 2011, autistic researcher Michelle Dawson accused *PLoS One* of unethical conduct after the journal altered the text of her group's paper, replacing the identity-first language of "autistics" with "patients with autism" without consulting the authors (Oransky, 2011).

To address these issues, researchers and clinicians of all disciplines should be sensitive to the possible implications of their language and more discerning in their communications, particularly to the public at large. They should be aware of the concerns of autistic self-advocates regarding stigma and discrimination and adopt their language recommendations wherever possible, but especially where doing so would encourage a more nuanced understanding of autism. One such recommendation from Paula Durbin-Westby (2009) is substituting "differences in neurobiology and cognition" for "pathology," as not all autistic traits are pathological. Greater comprehensiveness and specificity in research and clinical descriptions is also needed through the explicit identification of the trait(s) being discussed and acknowledgment of the benefits as well as difficulties associated with autism. Furthermore, researchers and clinicians should qualify their descriptions by acknowledging the variability inherent in the spectrum.

Recommendation 2: Autistic Involvement in Funding and Policy

Increasing autistic involvement in research, clinical, and funding and policy discussions is essential to addressing ethical tensions regarding appropriate research directions and aims, as well as improving research and clinical practice to better address the needs of autistic individuals (Durbin-Westby, 2010; Ethical, Legal, and Social Implications of Autism Research, 2011; Pellicano et al., 2011; Kapp et al., 2013; Position Statements, 2015). Accordingly, ASAN has assumed a strong stance promoting autistic involvement in research and offers consultation services to researchers on grant proposals and studies utilizing community-based participatory research or CBPR (Position Statements, 2015; Operational Policy on Research Inquiries, 2015). Moreover, of the 28 public comments presented by autistic individuals to the IACC between 2007 and 2013, 13 discussed increasing autistic involvement in research. These comments specifically focused on autistic representation on the IACC, autistic participation in policy and funding decisions, and autistic consultation in study design, as well as the communication of findings through publications, presentations, and media outlets.

However, many of the current mechanisms for stakeholder participation are insufficient. Most notably, the IACC, which is intended to serve as a public forum, relies primarily on in-person oral public comments given at full committee meetings in Washington, DC, for stakeholder input (Liu and Cho, 2014). Though autistic self-advocates have presented at meetings, the communication difficulties associated with the spectrum, such as difficulties interpreting body language and processing and responding to auditory language in real-time, may impede autistic stakeholders from providing meaningful consultation to the IACC on policy and funding recommendations. Indeed, organizations like AASPIRE specifically stress the use of nontraditional modes of communication, such as text-based internet chat meetings, as important tools for community engagement (Nicolaidis et al., 2011). Other mechanisms include an email list to allow for discussion between meetings as a form of accommodation for individuals with difficulty communicating in real time (Nicolaidis et al., 2011). In the past, the IACC has utilized electronic requests for information to solicit broad community input on its activities (Liu and Cho, 2014). Increased attention to electronic and written forms of participation will likely improve the accessibility of the IACC to autistic individuals.

Recommendation 3: Strategies for Research and Clinical Care Settings

Similar considerations apply at the level of individual research initiatives and clinical conversations regarding the appropriate provision of therapies, services, and supports. For example, reflecting on his many-years-long partnership with Michelle Dawson, Laurent Mottron (2011, 34) writes, "since joining the lab, Dawson has helped the research team question many of our assumptions about and approaches to autism—including the perception that it is always a problem to be solved." He credits Dawson and other autistic researchers with the evolution of his research and advocates for a more enlightened and scientifically rigorous approach that considers autism as a natural human variant with potential adaptive and maladaptive effects rather than a disability or disorder (Mottron, 2011). Relatedly, Nicolaidis et al. (2011) of AASPIRE testify that autistic members have both contributed to the development of specific research studies to better address the needs of the autistic community and provided vital insight regarding potentially offensive language or assumptions. Ongoing studies by AASPIRE focus on key questions, such as the causes and implications of healthcare disparities within the autistic community, tools for increased healthcare access and utilization, and the use of online social supports to address concerns related to social isolation and distress (AASPIRE Projects, 2015).

Illustratively, a recent study by AASPIRE utilized data from interviews[3] with autistic adults to identify specific barriers to effective communication and shared decision making in healthcare interactions (Nicolaidis et al., 2015). These include environmental factors, such as bright lights and noise, which may be excessively stimulating for autistic individuals with sensory integration difficulties (Nicolaidis et al., 2015). Additionally, differences between patients and providers in preferred modes of communication (verbal versus written), information processing, and descriptions of physical sensations may contribute to the success or failure of a particular clinical encounter (Nicolaidis et al., 2015). For example, descriptions of pains as "shooting," "stabbing," or "burning" may be difficult for autistic individuals to interpret, as their experience of pain is often fundamentally different (Nicolaidis et al., 2015). Increasing awareness of and accommodations for autistic patients—for example, dimming lights, rooming patients farther from a busy waiting area, using more accessible language, and incorporating written communication and AAC devices in clinical encounters—will likely support the autonomy of autistic patients in their healthcare interactions. Such steps are imperative to address pervasive concerns from the autistic community regarding the lack of adequate informed consent protocols and other safeguards within research and clinical care. Furthermore, it may enhance the productivity of clinical encounters by increasing providers' familiarity with the autistic patient population and their daily lived experiences, as well as enabling input from autistic patients on innovative therapeutic regimens more targeted to individuals' specific needs beyond traditional ABA–based programs. Finally, these recommendations may provide a framework for designing similar mechanisms to protect and empower neurocognitively vulnerable populations in other research and clinical settings.

Conclusion

Efforts related to autism and autistic individuals within the triumvirate realms of research, clinical care, and policy have long been characterized by the significant involvement of clinicians, service providers, and parent-advocates. In recent years, the emergence of neurodiversity and the autistic self-advocate has led to valuable insights into the autism spectrum. However, it has simultaneously revealed new and complex ethical dimensions for autism research and care, both on the micro level of individual research and service efforts and on the macro level of policy and funding. Their claims have at times been dismissed as those belonging to disability rights extremists, but the expressed concerns of autistic self-advocates reflect larger considerations within neuroscience and neuroethics, centered on questions of personhood, identity, and autonomy—particularly as they relate to vulnerable populations. Though this chapter has focused on the relationship of neurodiversity to larger themes within neuroethics, neurodiversity may also significantly contribute to the field of neuroethics. Specifically, many of the recommendations for increasing autistic involvement in research and clinical activities may be applied to neurocognitively vulnerable populations to protect and empower them as research participants and patients. Such considerations are not separate from biomedical and clinical progress in research and care but rather are key to the successful navigation of the vast new ethical terrain being unearthed by the advancing scientific frontier.

Acknowledgements

The author would like to thank scholars at the Stanford Center for Biomedical Ethics for their input and guidance on this chapter, in particular Dr. David Magnus and Dr. Mildred Cho. The author would also like to express gratitude to Mr. Brandon Turner for his thoughtful commentary on early drafts of this chapter.

Notes

1　The term "autism" has remained in common usage since Kanner (1943) first adopted it in his seminal paper, though its accompanying modifiers have changed over time (e.g., "early infantile autism," "autistic disorder," and "autism spectrum disorder"). For simplicity, I apply the term "autism" broadly to include other near-synonyms.
2　The complete text of this poem can be found https://juststimming.wordpress.com/2011/10/05/quiet-hands/.
3　To accommodate autistic participants with a broad range of communication preferences, researchers allowed participants to elect from a variety of participation modes, including telephone, instant messenger, email, and in person.

Further Reading

The works included in the references section provide a solid foundation for understanding neurodiversity in the context of autistic self-advocacy. Listed here are two additional works from the ASAN that may be of interest to readers wishing to learn more from the perspective of autistic individuals.

Bascom, J. (Ed.) (2012) *Loud Hands: Autistic People, Speaking.* Washington, DC: Autism Self-Advocacy Network Press. Google Scholar. This is an anthology of essays by autistic individuals that catalogues the experience and ethos of the autistic community. It was completed in collaboration with the ASAN.

Bascom, J. (Ed.) (2012) *And Straight on Til Morning: Essays on Autism Acceptance.* Washington, DC: Autism Self-Advocacy Network Press. Google Scholar. This is a collection of articles by autistic writers, focusing on autism awareness and acceptance in the context of advocacy and activism. It was completed in collaboration with the ASAN.

References

AASPIRE Projects. (2015) [Online]. Available at: http://aaspire.org/?p=projects [Accessed 19 July 2015].

Aboraya, A., Rankin, E., France, C., El-Missiry, A., and John, C. (2006) The reliability of psychiatric diagnosis revisited: The clinician's guide to improve the reliability of psychiatric diagnosis. *Psychiatry (Edgmont)* 3(1): pp. 41–50.

About AASPIRE. (2015) [Online]. Available at: http://aaspire.org/?p=about [Accessed 13 Aug. 2015].

Autistic Self-Advocacy Network. (2015) [Online] Available at: http://autisticadvocacy.org/home/about-asan/ [Accessed 8 Aug. 2015].

Aragonès, E., Piñol, J.L., and Labad, A. (2006) The overdiagnosis of depression in non-depressed patients in primary care. *Family Practice* 23(3): pp. 363–368.

The Arc of Washington County, Inc. (2014) [Online]. Available at: www.arcwc-md.org/news/asan-autistic-self-advocacy-network/ [Accessed 21 July 2015].

ASAN Comments on CA Autism Insurance Regulation | Autistic Self-Advocacy Network. (2012) [Online]. Available at: http://autisticadvocacy.org/2012/11/asan-comments-on-ca-autism-insurance-regulation/ [Accessed 19 July 2015].

ASAN *Community Concerns Regarding the Google-Autism Speaks Ten Thousand Genomes Program (AUT10K).* (2014) [Online]. Available at: http://autisticadvocacy.org/2014/06/community-concernsregarding-the-google-autism-speaks-ten-thousand-genomes-program-aut10k/ [Accessed 19 July 2015].

ASAN Statement on Autism CARES Act | Autistic Self-Advocacy Network. (2014) [Online]. Available at: http://autisticadvocacy.org/2014/06/asan-statement-on-autism-cares-act/ [Accessed 19 July 2015].

ASAN Statement on Fein Study on Autism and "Recovery" | Autistic Self-Advocacy Network. (2013) [Online]. Available at: http://autisticadvocacy.org/2013/01/asan-statement-on-fein-study-on-autism-and-recovery/ [Accessed 19 July 2015].

Autism Speaks. (2014) *Autism Speaks Launches MSSNG Campaign: Groundbreaking Genome Sequencing Program* [Online]. Available at: www.autismspeaks.org/science/science-news/autism-speaks-launches-mssng-groundbreaking-genome-sequencing-program [Accessed 20 July 2015].

Autistic Self-Advocacy Network *Operational Policy on Research Inquiries.* (2015) [Online]. Available at: http://autisticadvocacy.org/operational-policy-on-research-inquiries/ [Accessed 19 July 2015].

Autistic Self-Advocacy Network *Position Statements.* (2015) [Online] Available at: http://autisticadvocacy.org/policy-advocacy/position-statements/ [Accessed 19 July 2015].

Baer, D.M., Wolf, M.M., and Risley, T.R. (1968) Some current dimensions of applied behavior analysis. *Journal of Applied Behavior Analysis* 1(1): pp. 91–97.

Bagatell, N. (2010) From cure to community: Transforming notions of autism. *Ethos* 38(1): pp. 33–55.

Baker, D.L. (2011) *The Politics of Neurodiversity: Why Public Policy Matters.* Boulder, CO: Lynne Rienner.

Barnbaum, D.R. (2008) *The Ethics of Autism: Among Them, But Not of Them.* Bloomington, IN: Indiana University Press.

Bartels, A., and Zeki, S. (2004) The neural correlates of maternal and romantic love. *NeuroImage* 21(3): pp. 1155–1166.

Bascom, J. (2011) Quiet hands. *Just Stimming . . .* [Online]. Available at: https://juststimming.wordpress.com/2011/10/05/quiet-hands/ [Accessed 19 July 2015].

Batstra, L., and Frances, A. (2012) DSM-5 further inflates attention deficit hyperactivity disorder. *Journal of Nervous and Mental Disease* 200(6): pp. 486–488.

Blume, H. (1998) Neurodiversity: On the neurological underpinnings of geekdom. *The Atlantic.* Retrieved from www.theatlantic.com/magazine/archive/1998/09/neurodiversity/5909

Brown, L. (2012a) Autistic hoya: The de-legitimization of autistic voices. *Autistichoya.com* [Online]. Available at: www.autistichoya.com/2012/02/de-legitimization-of-autistic-voices.html [Accessed 19 July 2015].

————. (2012b) Autistic Hoya: The dangers of misrepresentation. *Autistichoya.com* [Online]. Available at: www.autistichoya.com/2012/06/dangers-of-misrepresentation.html [Accessed 19 July 2015].

Canli, T., and Amin, Z. (2002) Neuroimaging of emotion and personality: Scientific evidence and ethical considerations. *Brain and Cognition* 50(3): pp. 414–431.

Canli, T., Amin, Z., Haas, B., Omura, K., and Constable, R.T. (2004) A double dissociation between mood states and personality traits in the anterior cingulate. *Behavioral Neuroscience* 118(5): pp. 897–904.

Centers for Disease Control and Prevention. (2015) *Facts About Autism Spectrum Disorders*. [Online]. Available at: www.cdc.gov/ncbddd/autism/treatment.html [Accessed 12 Aug. 2015].

Chamak, B. (2008) Autism and social movements: French parents' associations and international autistic individuals' organisations. *Sociology of Health and Illness* 30(1): pp. 76–96.

Christopher, P.P., and Dunn, L.B. (2015) Risk and consent in neuropsychiatric deep brain stimulation: An exemplary analysis of treatment-resistant depression, obsessive-compulsive disorder, and dementia. In J. Clausen and N. Levy (Eds.). *Handbook of Neuroethics*. The Netherlands: Springer, pp. 590–605.

Dawson, M. (2004a) The many varieties of being written off. *Sentex.net* [Online]. Available at: www.sentex.net/~nexus23/naa_wro.html [Accessed 19 July 2015].

————. (2004b) *An Autistic at the Supreme Court—The Intervener's Factum—Michelle Dawson. Sentex.net* [Online]. Available at: www.sentex.net/~nexus23/naa_fac.html [Accessed 19 July 2015].

Decety, J., Jackson, P.L., Sommerville, J.A., Chaminade, T., and Meltzoff, A.N. (2004) The neural bases of cooperation and competition: An fMRI investigation. *NeuroImage* 23(2): pp. 744–751.

Doherty, H.L. (2009) Facing autism in New Brunswick: Neurodiversity's extremist autism cure opponents—By what right do they object? *Autisminnb.blogspot.com* [Online]. Available at: http://autisminnb.blogspot.com/2009/11/neurodiversitys-extremist-autism-cure.html. [Accessed 19 July 2015].

Durbin-Westby, P.C. (2009) *IACC Comments: November 10, 2009* [Online]. Available at: http://paulacdurbinwestbyautisticblog.blogspot.com/2009/11/iacc-comments-november-10-2009_18.html [Accessed 4 Aug. 2013].

————. (2010) "Public Law 109–416 is not just about scientific research": Speaking truth to power at Interagency Autism Coordinating Committee meetings. *Disability Studies Quarterly* 30(1).

Emerson, E. (2006) The need for credible evidence: Comments on "On some recent claims for the efficacy of cognitive therapy for people with intellectual disabilities". *Journal of Applied Research in Intellectual Disabilities* 19(1): pp. 121–123.

Ethical, Legal, and Social Implications of Autism Research | Autistic Self-Advocacy Network. (2011) [Online]. Available at: http://autisticadvocacy.org/2011/09/ethical-legal-and-social-implications-of-autism-research/ [Accessed 19 July 2015].

Farah, M.J. (2005) Neuroethics: The practical and the philosophical. *Trends in Cognitive Sciences* 9(1): pp. 34–40.

————. (2012) Neuroethics: The ethical, legal, and societal impact of neuroscience. *Annual Review of Psychology* 63: pp. 571–591.

Focquaert, F. (2013) Deep brain stimulation in children: Parental authority versus shared decision-making. *Neuroethics* 6(3): pp. 447–455.

Foucault, M. (1988) *Madness and Civilization: A History of Insanity in the Age of Reason*. New York; Vintage.

Frances, A. (2013) Saving normal: An insider's revolt against out-of-control psychiatric diagnosis, DSM-5, big pharma and the medicalization of ordinary life. *Psychotherapy in Australia* 19(3): pp. 14–18.

Garen, J. (2014) *The Trouble With Neurodiversity: Etiologies, Normativity, and the autistic Struggle for Identity*. Master's thesis (The University of British Columbia).

Green, V.A., Pituch, K.A., Itchon, J., Choi, A., O'Reilly, M., and Sigafoos, J. (2006) Internet survey of treatments used by parents of children with autism. *Research in Developmental Disabilities* 27(1): pp. 70–84.

Greene, J.D., Sommerville, R.B., Nystrom, L.E., Darley, J.M., and Cohen, J.D. (2001) An fMRI investigation of emotional engagement in moral judgment. *Science* 293(5537): pp. 2105–2108.

Harmon, A. (2010) Nominee to disability council is lightning rod for dispute on views of autism. *New York Times*.

Heekeren, H.R., Wartenburger, I., Schmidt, H., Schwintowski, H.P., and Villringer, A. (2003) An fMRI study of simple ethical decision-making. *Neuroreport* 14(9): pp. 1215–1219.

IACC. (2007) *Oral Public Comments: IACC Full Committee Meeting November 30, 2007.* [Online] Available at: https://iacc.hhs.gov/events/2007/comments/oral_public_comments_113007.pdf [Accessed 19 July 2015].

———. (2008) *Oral Public Comments: IACC Full Committee Meeting March 14, 2008.* [Online] Available at: https://iacc.hhs.gov/events/2008/comments/oral_public_comments_031408.pdf [Accessed 19 July 2015].

Illes, J., and Bird, S.J. (2006) Neuroethics: A modern context for ethics in neuroscience. *Trends in Neurosciences* 29(9): pp. 511–517.

Illes, J., DeVries, R., Cho, M.K., and Schraedley-Desmond, P. (2006a) ELSI issues in advanced neuroimaging. *American Journal of Bioethics* 6(2): pp. 24–31.

Illes, J., Racine, E., and Kirschen, M. (2006b) A picture is worth 1000 words, but which 1000? In J. Illes (Ed.). *Neuroethics: Defining the Issues in Theory, Practice, and Policy.* Oxford, UK: Oxford University Press, pp. 149–168.

Jaarsma, P., and Welin, S. (2012) Autism as a natural human variation: Reflections on the claims of the neurodiversity movement. *Health Care Analysis* 20(1): pp. 20–30.

Kadosh, R.C., Levy, N., O'Shea, J., Shea, N., and Savulescu, J. (2012) The neuroethics of non-invasive brain stimulation. *Current Biology* 22(4): pp. R108–R111.

Kanner, L. (1943) Autistic disturbances of affective contact. *Nervous Child* 2: pp. 217–250.

Kapp, S.K., Gillespie-Lynch, K., Sherman, L.E., and Hutman, T. (2013) Deficit, difference, or both? Autism and neurodiversity. *Developmental Psychology* 49(1): pp. 59–71.

Kaufman, J. (2007) Campaign on childhood mental illness succeeds at being provocative. *New York Times.*

Kras, J. (2010) The "ransom notes" affair: When the neurodiversity movement came of age. *Disability Studies Quarterly* 30(1).

Lai, M.C., Lombardo, M.V., Chakrabarti, B., and Baron-Cohen, S. (2013) Subgrouping the autism "spectrum": Reflections on DSM-5. *PLoS Biology* 11(4): p. e1001544.

Levy, N. (2011) Neuroethics: A new way of doing ethics. *American Journal of Bioethics: Neuroscience* 2(2): pp. 3–9.

Leykin, Y., Christopher, P.P., Holtzheimer, P.E., Appelbaum, P.S., Mayberg, H.S., Lisanby, S.H., and Dunn, L.B. (2011) Participants' perceptions of deep brain stimulation research for treatment-resistant depression: Risks, benefits, and therapeutic misconception. *American Journal of Bioethics: Primary Research* 2(4): pp. 33–41.

Liu, E.Y., and Scott, C.T. (2014) Great expectations: Autism spectrum disorder and induced pluripotent stem cell technologies. *Stem Cell Reviews and Reports* 10(2): pp. 145–150.

Liu, E.Y., Milner, L.C., and Cho, M.K. (2013) *Lost in Translation: The Need for Cross-Disciplinary Exchange in Research on Autism.* The 15th Annual Meeting of the American Society for Bioethics and Humanities.

Liu, E.Y., and Cho, M.K. (2014) *Representing Autism: A Demographic Analysis of Public Commentators at Interagency Autism Coordinating Committee Meetings.* The 16th Annual Meeting of the American Society for Bioethics and Humanities.

Mizner, S. (2014) *Shocking Kids into Compliance.* American Civil Liberties Union [Online]. Available at: www.aclu.org/blog/shocking-kids-compliance [Accessed 20 July 2015].

Moll, J., de Oliveira-Souza, R., Bramati, I.E., and Grafman, J. (2002a) Functional networks in emotional moral and nonmoral social judgments. *NeuroImage* 16(3): pp. 696–703.

Moll, J., de Oliveira-Souza, R., Eslinger, P.J., Bramati, I.E., Mourão-Miranda, J., Andreiuolo, P.A., and Pessoa, L. (2002b) The neural correlates of moral sensitivity: A functional magnetic resonance imaging investigation of basic and moral emotions. *Journal of Neuroscience* 22(7): pp. 2730–2736.

Moreno, J.D. (2003) Neuroethics: An agenda for neuroscience and society. *Nature Reviews Neuroscience* 4(2): pp. 149–153.

Morse, S. (2006) Moral and legal responsibility and the new neuroscience. In J. Illes (Ed.). *Neuroethics: Defining the Issues in Theory, Practice, Policy.* Oxford, UK: Oxford University Press, pp. 33–50.

Mottron, L. (2011) Changing perceptions: The power of autism. *Nature* 479(7371): pp. 33–35.

Moynihan, R., Doust, J., and Henry, D. (2012) Preventing overdiagnosis: How to stop harming the healthy. *British Medical Journal* 344: p. e3502.

Ne'eman, A. (2007a) An urgent call to action: Tell NYU child study center to abandon stereotypes against people with disabilities | Autistic self-advocacy network. *Autisticadvocacy.org* [Online]. Available at: www.autisticadvocacy.org/modules/smartsection/item.php?itemid=21 [Accessed 20 July 2015].

————. (2007b) An open letter on the NYU Ransom notes campaign. *Petitiononline.com* [Online]. Available at: www.petitiononline.com/ransom/petition.html/[Accessed 20 July 2015].

————. (2010) The future (and the past) of autism advocacy, or why the ASA's magazine, *The Advocate*, wouldn't publish this piece. *Disability Studies Quarterly* 30(1).

New York State Educational Department. (2006) *Observations and Findings of Out-of-State Visitation: Judge Rotenberg Educational Center* [Online]. Available at: http://web.archive.org/web/20070929123459/www.motherjones.com/news/feature/2007/09/NYSED_2006_investigation.pdf [Accessed 12 Aug. 2015].

Nicolaidis, C. (2012) What can physicians learn from the neurodiversity movement? *Virtual Mentor, American Medical Association Journal of Ethics* 14(6): pp. 503–510.

Nicolaidis, C., Raymaker, D.M., Ashkenazy, E., McDonald, K.E., Dern, S., Baggs, A.E., . . . Boisclair, W.C. (2015) 'Respect the way I need to communicate with you': Healthcare experiences of adults on the autism spectrum. *Autism: The International Journal of Research and Practice* 19(7): pp. 824–831.

Nicolaidis, C., Raymaker, D., McDonald, K., Dern, S., Ashkenazy, E., Boisclair, C., Robertson, S., and Baggs, A. (2011) Collaboration strategies in non-traditional community-based participatory research partnerships: Lessons from an academic-community partnership with autistic self-advocates. *Progress in Community Health Partnerships: Research, Education, and Action* 5(2): pp. 143–150.

Nicolaidis, C., Raymaker, D., McDonald, K., Dern, S., Boisclair, W.C., Ashkenazy, E., and Baggs, A. (2013). Comparison of healthcare experiences in autistic and non-autistic adults: A cross-sectional online survey facilitated by an academic-community partnership. *Journal of General Internal Medicine* 28(6): pp. 761–769.

Oransky, I. (2011) *Concerns Over Paper in PLoS One Autism Paper Lead to Brief Withdrawal and Correction* [Online] Available at: http://retractionwatch.wordpress.com/2011/10/18/concerns-over-language-in-plos-one-autism-paper-lead-to-brief-withdrawal-and-correction/ [Accessed 20 July 2015].

Orsini, M., and Smith, M. (2010) Social movements, knowledge and public policy: The case of autism activism in Canada and the US. *Critical Policy Studies* 4(1): pp. 38–57.

Ortega, F. (2009) The cerebral subject and the challenge of neurodiversity. *BioSocieties* 4(4): pp. 425–445.

Pellicano, E., Ne'eman, A., and Stears, M. (2011) Engaging, not excluding: A response to Walsh et al. *Nature Reviews Neuroscience* 12(12): p. 769.

Pellicano, E., and Stears, M. (2011) Bridging autism, science and society: Moving toward an ethically informed approach to autism research. *Autism Research* 4(4): pp. 271–282.

Peters-Scheffer, N., Didden, R., Korzilius, H., and Sturmey, P. (2011) A meta-analytic study on the effectiveness of comprehensive ABA-based early intervention programs for children with autism spectrum disorders. *Research in Autism Spectrum Disorders* 5(1): pp. 60–69.

Racine, E., Bell, E., and Shevell, M. (2014) Ethics in neurodevelopmental disability. In M.J. Aminoff, F. Boller, and D.F. Swaab (Eds.). *Ethical and Legal Issues in Neurology: Handbook of Clinical Neurology Series 3*: Amsterdam: Elsevier Science Limited, pp. 243–265.

Rivera Mindt, M. (2012) *Ethical Decision-making and Capacity to Consent in Neurocognitively Impaired and Vulnerable Patient Populations*. The 40th Meeting of the International Neuropsychological Society.

Robertson, S.M. (2010) Neurodiversity, quality of life, and autistic adults: Shifting research and professional focuses onto real-life challenges. *Disability Studies Quarterly* 30(1).

Robertson, S.M., and Ne'eman, A.D. (2008) Autistic acceptance, the college campus, and technology: Growth of neurodiversity in society and academia. *Disability Studies Quarterly* 28(4).

Roskies, A. (2002) Neuroethics for the new millennium. *Neuron* 35(1): pp. 21–23.

Silverman, C. (2011) *Understanding Autism: Parents, Doctors, and the History of Disorder*. Princeton, NJ: Princeton University Press.

Silverman, C., and Brosco, J.P. (2007) Understanding autism: Parents and pediatricians in historical perspective. *Archives of Pediatrics and Adolescent Medicine* 161(4): pp. 392–398.

Singer, J. (1999) Why can't you be normal for once in your life? From a problem with no name to the emergence of a new category of difference. In M. Corker and S. French (Eds.). *Disability Discourse*. Buckingham, England: Open University Press, pp. 59–67.

Singh, J., Illes, J., Lazzeroni, L., and Hallmayer, J. (2009) Trends in US autism research funding. *Journal of Autism and Developmental Disorders* 39(5): pp. 788–795.

Spreckley, M., and Boyd, R. (2009) Efficacy of applied behavioral intervention in preschool children with autism for improving cognitive, language, and adaptive behavior: A systematic review and meta-analysis. *Journal of Pediatrics* 154(3): pp. 338–344.

Sulzer-Azaroff, B., and Mayer, G.R. (1991) *Behavioral Analysis for Lasting Change*. Fort Worth, TX: Harcourt Brace.

Svoboda, E. (2009) I am not a puzzle: I am a person. *Salon*. [Online] Available at http://www.salon.com/2009/04/27/autistic_culture/.

Szasz, T.S. (1960) The myth of mental illness. *The American Psychologist* 15(2): pp. 113–118.

Szmukler, G., and Rose, D. (2015) Strengthening self-determination of persons with mental illness. In J. Clausen and N. Levy (Eds.). *Handbook of Neuroethics*. The Netherlands: Springer, pp. 879–896.

Timimi, S. (2014) *Pathological Child Psychiatry and the Medicalization of Childhood*. New York: Routledge.

US Department of Health and Human Services, Office of Autism Research Coordination, National Institutes of Health (On behalf of the Office of the Secretary). (2014) *Report to Congress on Activities Related to Autism Spectrum Disorder and Other Developmental Disabilities Under the Combating Autism Act of 2006 and Combating Autism Reauthorization Act of 2011 (FY 2010—FY 2012)*. Bethesda, MD: NIH Publication No.14–8012.

Villani, V.S., Parsons, A.E., Church, R.P., and Beetar, J.T. (2012) A descriptive study of the use of restraint and seclusion in a special education school. *Child and Youth Care Forum* 41(3): pp. 295–309.

Virués-Ortega, J. (2010) Applied behavior analytic intervention for autism in early childhood: Meta-analysis, meta-regression and dose—response meta-analysis of multiple outcomes. *Clinical Psychology Review* 30(4): pp. 387–399.

Wang, S. (2007) Ads about kids' mental health problems draw fire. *Wall Street Journal*.

Westling, D.L., Trader, B.R., Smith, C.A., and Marshall, D.S. (2010) Use of restraints, seclusion, and aversive procedures on students with disabilities. *Research and Practice for Persons with Severe Disabilities* 35(3–4): pp. 116–127.

Wolf, S.M., Crock, B.N., Van Ness, B., Lawrenz, F., Kahn, J.P., Beskow, L.M., . . . Kohane, I.S. (2012) Managing incidental findings and research results in genomic research involving biobanks and archived data sets. *Genetics in Medicine* 14(4): pp. 361–384.

Zeki, S., and Romaya, J. (2008) Neural correlates of hate. *PLoS One* 3(10): p. e3556.

Zimmerman, M., Ruggero, C.J., Chelminski, I., and Young, D. (2008) Is bipolar disorder overdiagnosed? *Journal of Clinical Psychiatry* 69(6): pp. 935–940.

27

RDoC'S SPECIAL KIND OF REDUCTIONISM AND ITS POSSIBLE IMPACT ON CLINICAL PSYCHIATRY

Luc Faucher and Simon Goyer

Research Domain Criteria (RDoC), an initiative of the National Institute of Mental Health, is an explicit effort to break free from the constraints of current diagnostic categories and to rebuild psychiatric taxonomy on new grounds. As Dr. Thomas Insel (2014; who was until recently the director of the NIMH and a vocal advocate of the project) put it, "RDoC's ultimate goal is precision medicine for psychiatry—a diagnostic system based on a deeper understanding of the biological and psychosocial basis of a group of disorders that is unambiguously among the most disabling disorders of medicine" (396). At the heart of RDoC is the idea that psychopathologies are the result of "abnormalities in discrete neurobehavioral systems" (Etkin and Cuthbert, 2014) or on "faulty circuits" of the brain (Insel, 2010).

The focus on faulty brain circuits has led some (for instance, Gold, 2009; McLaren, 2011; Poland, 2014; Whooley, 2014) to suspect RDoC of being a reductionistic enterprise. As RDoC will eventually impact clinical psychiatry (Insel and Lieberman, 2013), some have feared that it will transform clinical psychiatry into a mindless, applied neurobehavioral science (Parnas, 2014). In what follows, we will look at the presumed reductionism of RDoC (second section). As we will argue, RDoC is officially endorsing a kind of reductionism that does not suffer from the shortcomings of more classical forms of reductionism. As per the foregoing, we will argue that at least *in principle*, RDoC could enrich rather than impoverish clinical psychiatry (third section). We will conclude this chapter by demonstrating that despite its revolutionary potential for clinical psychiatry, RDoC could, *in practice*, lead to the transformation of clinical psychiatry into an applied behavioral neuroscience (fourth section).

What Is RDoC?

RDoC is a research initiative that aims, in the long run, to produce a nosology formulated within the framework of neuroscience that would allow precision psychiatry (a psychiatry that can target its interventions precisely on the particular features of the disorder of a patient). In the short term, the goal of the program is to free psychiatric research from the constraints of current nosologies (as well as to provide, in conjunction with diagnostic systems like the *Diagnostic and Statistical Manual* [DSM], a basis to uncover subtypes in patient populations diagnosed with similar conditions). The main idea that drives the RDoC is that "normal behavior depends

Table 27.1 An Example of a Construct of the RDoC with Its Different Units of Analysis. In this case, the domain is the "Negative Valence System" and the construct, "Acute Fear."

RDoC Constructs

Domain: *Negative Valence Systems*
Construct: *Acute threat ("fear")*

— Units of Analysis —

Genes	Molecules	Cells	Circuits	Physiology	Behavior	Self-Reports	Paradigms
BDNF, 5HT/5HTRs, CRF, FKB5, GABAARs, Glutamate system, NMDARs, Opioid system, COMT, Cannabinoid system, Dopamine, DAT, Cam kinase, MAP kinase, PI-3 kinase, PKA, PKC, Acetylcholine, Norepinephrine, Strathmin, Pkap, TRBC5	NMDAR, Glutamate, Dopamine, Serotonin, BDNF, GABA, Cortisol/ Corticosterone, Endogenous cannabinoids, orexin, NPY, CRF family, FGF2, Oxytocin, Vasopressin, CCK, Neuropeptide S, Neurosteroids	Neurons, Glia, Pyramidal cells, GABAergic cells	Central Nucleus, BasAmyg, LatAmyg, vPAG, dPAG, v-hippocampus (post), d-hippocampus (ant), latPFC/ insula, vmPFC (il), dmPFC (pl), OFC, Hypothalamus, dorsal ACC, rostral/vent ACC, ICMs, Medial Amyg, PAG, RPVM, Pons, autonomic nervous system, insular cortex, LC	Fear Potentiated Startle, Context Startle, Skin Conductance, Heart Rate, EMG, BP, Eye Tracking, Response accuracy, facial EMG, Respiration, pupillometry	Freezing, Response time, Avoidance, Response inhibition, Open field, Social approach, Analgesia, approach (early development), Risk assessment, Facial expressions	Fear survey schedule, BAI, STAI, SUDS, Fear Questionnaire, Trait Fear Inventory, Eilam Ethogram, Structured Diagnostic and Assessment scales, Albany Panic & Phobia	Fear conditioning, viewing aversive pictures or films, emotional imagery

Source: Recreated from www.nimh.nih.gov/research-priorities/rdoc/rdoc-constructs.shtml#acute_threat

on normally functioning systems,[1] which in turn depend on intact neural circuits". If mental illnesses are brain disorders, aspects or features of a particular mental illness (for instance, voice hallucination in schizophrenia) must presumably relate back to abnormalities in one or more of the core systems of the brain.

For discussion of the turn toward neuroscience in medicine and the social sciences, see Chapter 2.

RDoC's advocates aim to understand disorders through the lens of general constructs called "functioning domains" that are thought most likely to be affected in psychiatric disorders. These domains are identified as the (a) negative valence systems, (b) positive valence systems, (c) cognitive systems, (d) systems of social processes, and (e) arousal/modulatory systems (see, for instance, Cuthbert, 2014, 30). Each of these functional dimensions is further broken down into sub-constructs: for instance, the construct "cognitive systems" include "attention," "perception", "declarative memory", "language", cognitive control" and "working memory". Each of these constructs and sub-constructs can be described at the following level of analysis: genetic, molecular, cellular, neural circuits, physiological, behavioral, and self-report(s), to which a level "paradigm" must be added, which contains a list of experimental techniques through which constructs can be studied or identified.

Functioning domains, constructs, and levels of analysis are all represented in a research matrix (see www.nimh.nih.gov/research-priorities/rdoc/constructs/rdoc-matrix.shtml). Functioning domains and their respective constructs form rows while levels of analysis form columns. Points at which rows and columns meet are called "cells." In a cell, one finds information from empirical research that is relevant to a construct at a particular level of analysis. For instance, at the molecular level for the construct "affiliation and attachment," one will find "oxytocin", "vasopressin", "oxytocin receptors", "vasopressin receptor 1a", but also the "*Mu* opioid receptors"; while for the construct "habit", one will find "ventral striatum," and "dorsal and medial prefrontal cortex" at the "circuits" level (see Table 27.1 for an example of the RDoC constructs).

The dimensions "development" and "environment", which are not represented explicitly, are also part of the matrix. These two dimensions are crucial for the RDoC. The "development" dimension is important because many psychiatric disorders either appear in childhood or are rooted in abnormal development of cortical structures that take place at an early age. Understanding the particular developmental trajectory of disorders could allow interventions in the prodromal phase of a disorder (or even before if individuals at risk of developing a disorder could be identified; Cuthbert et al., 2014).[2] The "environment" dimension takes into account the impact of physical, social, and cultural environments on disorders. Work in schizophrenia (Insel, 2010b), and also on depression and alcoholism (Kendler et al., 2006; Kendler, 2012a), has clearly shown that the environment has a causal role in the development of these disorders. The identification of these factors and an understanding of the way they influence the development of disorders (or prevent them) is important for preventive interventions and public health.

For more on prodromal disease stages, see Chapter 5.

Is RDoC a Form of Eliminative Mindless Psychiatry?

RDoC's focus is neural functional systems as identified by current neuroscience (understood broadly to include both molecular neuroscience and cognitive neuroscience). For instance, Insel claims that "[m]ental disorders are biological disorders involving brain circuits that implicate specific domains of cognition, emotion, or behaviour" (Insel, 2013). Commenting on a previous and similar claim made by Insel (Insel and Quirion, 2005), philosopher Ian Gold (2009) proposes that the only charitable way to understand this kind of claim is to postulate that Insel means that psychological sciences are to be "relegated to the status of mere placeholder sciences awaiting replacement by neuroscience and molecular biology" (507). If such is the case, RDoC would be a form of what Matthew Broome has called "eliminative mindless psychiatry". According to such a view,

> entities of psychiatry can and should be reduced to their biological underpinnings, and [. . .] it is unlikely that such entities will survive the reduction. This position may eliminate our "folk" psychopathology and classification in that 'schizophrenia,' 'bipolar,' and 'depressive psychosis' may no longer exist, but ontological primacy will be given to neurological explanations, and the entities that make up such explanations, instead.
>
> (Broome, 2006, 304)

Some think that such an approach will also impact clinical psychiatry in that it will lead the field to consider that "psychotropic drugs are typically the first line treatment for these brain diseases since they treat biochemical dysregulations, restore functionality to neural circuitry, and reduce symptoms of disease [. . .]" (Poland, 2014, 32; see also Laungani, 2002). For our purposes, we can understand eliminative mindless psychiatry as endorsing three claims following from the identification of mental disorders with brain disorders (that is, the *ontological* claim according to which mental disorders are just brain disorders):

1. *An epistemological claim:* Mental disorders are essentially and preferentially explainable in the theoretical framework of the behavioral neurosciences (especially neurobiology). Explanations framed in the language of higher levels of explanation (for instance, in psychological terms) are at best heuristic tools and at worst ultimately otiose (see Harris and Schaffner [1992, 129] who formulate such a claim really clearly).
2. *A semantic claim:* Actual diagnostic categories (and the language used to formulate them, for instance, the symptoms that constitute a particular syndrome) will not find a comfortable niche in a future mindless psychiatry. They will have to be revised substantially or eliminated, because they will be shown not to have any referent in reality (as defined by neuroscience).
3. *A clinical claim:* all mental disorders should be treated systematically and primarily with biological technologies that act directly on the brain, for instance, with drugs or brain stimulation.

In what follows, we will focus our attention on claims 1 and 3. Concerning claim 2, let's just say that advocates of RDoC have preferred to stay (carefully, diplomatically) neutral on the question, insisting that progress can be made by stratifying groups without requiring a wholesale diagnostic reclassification (cancer research is being used as an example of stratification without elimination of the diagnostic category; Kapur et al., 2012, 1177). As for symptoms, it is clear that the RDoC involves moving from descriptions formulated in terms of clinical phenomenology (observable or nearly observable behaviors described in a neutral-theoretical language) to descriptions formulated in neurocognitive terms, that is, in terms of the domains that figure in the matrix (for instance, two schizophrenic patients could be distinguished by the fact that one patient's working memory is more impaired than the other's, while the other presents more impairment in the negative valence system). In the next section [RDoC's Special Kind of Reductionism], we will focus on claim 1. In the third section [Will RDoC's Research Program Reduce Clinical Psychiatry to an Applied Neurobiology?], we will focus on claim 3. We will demonstrate that advocates of the RDoC have officially conceived their enterprise as multilevel and integrative, in which higher-level constructs are not to be eliminated. Are these advocates always true to their official position? We will examine that question in the last section.

RDoC's Special Kind of reductionism

Patchy Reductionism

That advocates of RDoC do not see their project as reductionist in the usual sense of the term is captured in the following quote:

> With a strong focus on biological processes, and emphasis on neural circuits at the outset, the RDoC effort could be construed as reductionist. However, a focus on lower level mechanisms does not necessitate that "higher" level constructs be dismissed. Most researchers agree that causal influences are multidirectional across level (e.g., across genes, molecules, cellular systems, neural circuits, and behavior), leading some (Kendler, 2005) to consider "explanatory pluralism" or "patchy reductionism" as an alternative to reductionism.
>
> (Sanislow et al., 2010, 633)

As advocates of the RDoC put it, the reductionism of the project does not entail the form of eliminativism usually associated with classical reductionism. It would be too lengthy to explain both explanatory pluralism and patchy reductionism. Therefore we will focus our attention in what follows on patchy reductionism (in part because we think it best captures the state of mind of those working in the RDoC project).

The concept of *patchy reductionism* has been developed by philosopher Kenneth Schaffner in a series of papers (see, among others, Schaffner 2006, 2008, 2011, and 2013). As Schaffner puts it, reductionism has been traditionally thought of as "sweeping". By this he means that according to models of reductionism such as that which Ernest Nagel championed (1961, Chapter 11), reduction has been thought of as involving a whole low-level theory (comprising a set of laws and concepts) that would "cannibalize" a whole higher-level theory, that is, reduce it. As Schaffner remarks, this kind of reduction might occasionally happen in physics, but it is not characteristic of biology (2013, 1004). In biology, reductions are "partial", "creeping", or "patchy". What does that mean? A thought experiment proposed by Kendler (2005) perfectly illustrates what this kind of reductionism amounts to (note the resemblance between what Kendler describes and the RDoC structure):

> Imagine that there are 15 discrete levels, with the mind brain system between DNA on one hand and clinical manifestations of schizophrenia on the other. Researcher 1 is conducting linkage and association studies that attempt to directly relate levels 1

and 15 but would provide no insight into the intervening levels. Researcher 2 is trying to understand, at a basic molecular level, the actions of a putative altered gene transcript, thereby trying to move from level 1 to level 2 or 3. Meanwhile, researcher 3 is seeking to understand the neuropsychological deficits in schizophrenia, trying to clarify the link between levels 13 and 15.

(438)

In this thought experiment, there is no encompassing reduction of one "grand theory" to another; instead, there are partial, local, patchy reductions. These reductions have several properties that are not typically associated with classical reduction:

a. They involved *mechanistic models*: contrary to the traditional model of reduction, which presents reduction as taking place between scientific laws that are comprised by theories at different levels, patchy reductionism conceives of reduction as an operation on mechanistic models. A mechanist model explains a phenomenon by showing how it is the result of the action of internal parts of a system as well as external forces acting on it.

b. They are *interlevel*: the etiological mechanisms that explain a condition are typically interlevel (that is, they explain by referencing factors at different levels of analysis; this is the sense in which these reductive explanations can be said to be pluralistic). For instance, an explanatory model of depression will invoke structural changes in cells of the HPA axis (physiological level) caused by stressful events, like physical or psychological abuse (social level), which have an effect on one's attributive style or on its self-image (psychological level). Another way to put it is that, typically, to explain a disorder, one will have to mention both low-level factors (genes, hormones, or nerve cells) and those at higher levels (poverty or humiliation; Kendler, 2012b).

c. They are *incomplete*: more often than not, reductive explanations will not explain all instances of a phenomenon. For instance, some genetic factors will figure in the explanation of some cases of schizophrenia or major depression but not in all of them. In a similar fashion, a cognitive model will explain some symptoms of a disorder but not all of them. The reductions are thus incomplete because they do not involve a complete high-level theory and a complete low-level theory but rather are piecemeal or local (Schaffner, 2011, 144).

d. They *skip levels*: this is another way that reductions are incomplete. For instance, a linkage between a gene mutation and behavior or a disorder can be established, but some key mechanisms, such as which gene mutation impacts in order to produce the disorder, are not necessarily known or acknowledged. In such cases, the representation of the pathway that leads to the disorder is said to be "gappy", and the explanation is thought of as an "explanation-sketch" (Schaffner, 2008, 75).

e. They are *bushy*: when one provides a mechanism that explains a disorder, there is no tidy or discreet one-to-one relationship between a gene and a behavior. Rather, there is a messy and bushy causal "thicket" in which many genes act together, in a particular (epigenetic) context, with causal loops that might include "outside-the-skin" pathways. There is nothing that resembles a nice axiomatic theory in biological sciences.

Because the kind of work he describes seeks to uncover the biological or molecular mechanisms of underlying psychiatric disorders or symptoms, Schaffner uses the word "reduction" (though sometimes he talks about "micro explanation" [2011, 438]) to describe the relationships between theories. This trend in neuroscientific research in psychiatry, in which the RDoC participates, tries to connect certain cognitive or affective systems involved in the production of behavior or thought patterns characteristic of a disorder with low-level phenomena, like genetic mutations or dysfunctional potassium or calcium gate channels (at the cell level). Thus this kind of reduction typically involves going from a local interlevel mechanistic model with mostly high-level elements (like cognitive systems and behavior or thought patterns and brain structures) to a local interlevel mechanistic model that includes additional lower-level elements (like genes or ion gate channels). The reason for this drive is, as Kostko and Bickle (2017) conceive it, that in most neuroscientific research in psychiatry, mechanistic models of disorders containing only or mostly high-level elements are never judged to be complete representations of the causal mechanisms involved in pathological states; the idea being that neuroscientists are always positing "mediating causes" (at lower and lower levels of reality—for instance, from brain circuits to individual neurons to molecules and genes) to be the causes of higher-level phenomena and that are seen as providing the keys to a deeper and deeper understanding of the disorders.

Is the RDoC Characterized by a Form of Patchy Reductionism?

Now that we better understand what patchy reductionism is, let us return to the RDoC in order to determine if that form of reductionism adequately captures the practice of researchers working on this project.

Despite its focus on brain systems, the explanations of psychiatric conditions that emerge from the RDoC are (at least for the moment) typically "interlevel", involving genes that act on cells that form brain systems responsible for aspects of cognition that cause behaviors. Genes, brain systems, and cognition are also modified by the environment. Advocates of the RDoC do not claim that higher-level explanations (or factors) are otiose. For instance, they explicitly state that the environment is a critical element in the research that RDoC fosters (although one might wonder why this dimension was not represented in its matrix). Therefore, *in theory*, RDoC does not obliterate the role of the environment. Indeed, one of RDoC's preoccupations is to develop "a more mechanistic understanding of how such factors as life events and the social environment interact with development to produce a range of observed outcomes" (Cuthbert, 2014, 30). Research such as Meaney's, which examines the effect of maternal care on individual differences in hypothalamic-pituitary-adrenal responses to stress (Hellstrom et al., 2012; see also Champagne, 2010), or the description of the epigenetic *mechanisms* through which factors like maternal infection, chronic stress, urban environment, or migration at particular key moments of development have an impact on the development of schizophrenia (Rutten and Mill, 2009) are examples of the kind of research that helps us to understand how environmental factors have an effect on the brain. (Kosko and Bickle [2017] were right about the trend characterizing enterprises like the RDoC. These enterprises are motivated by the search for the lower-level mediating causes.) In these cases, researchers are trying to develop a better-integrated interlevel *mechanistic* theory or model of the mechanism leading to disorder by including the environmental factors (and other higher-level factors) in the explanation.

Explanations will also be *bushy*. For instance, Craddock and Owen (2010, 93), quoted with approval by advocates of the RDoC, illustrate the complex relationship among genetic variations, environmental influence, and stochastic events in the productions of the phenotype of schizophrenia. They also mention the fact that in the course of development, there are dynamical interactions between neural systems that lead to effects in which intact systems get dysfunctional over time. At present, the explanation of most conditions is *incomplete*: for instance, we don't yet know the role of the several single-nucleotide polymorphisms (SNP) revealed by genome-wide association studies (GWAS) involved in particular conditions, nor do we know how distal factors have an effect on proximal mechanism of the brain (for instance, immigration or urban life on schizophrenia). Patchy reductionism also admits that there are many ways in which a particular phenotype could be produced (proposed models are thus *incomplete* in another sense since they usually explain only how a subset of patients develops a condition; see, for example, Kendler et al., 2006[3]). The idea behind patient stratification is precisely to exploit this incompleteness for therapeutic purposes. For instance, Cuthbert (2014, 34) explains that people who suffer from posttraumatic stress disorder can be classified in two groups: those with a hyperactive fear system and those with a blunted system (see Hickie et al., 2013, for other examples).

As we explained, the RDoC is not reductionist in the traditional (Nagelian) sense of the term. It explicitly claims a form of reductionism that admits the existence of causal factors at different levels of reality. In consequence, if the models that researchers develop in this initiative focus mainly on lower-level factors, they also include higher-level factors (and the causal efficacy of these factors is not in doubt, even if one wants to understand the proximate mechanisms through which they have their effects on the brain). This project, at least *in principle*, does not involve a kind of epistemological eliminativism.

RDoC and Clinical Psychiatry

So RDoC is not, at least *prima facie*, endorsing the epistemic claim. What about the clinical claim? Is there a reason to think that RDoC would lead to a dehumanized form of clinical psychiatry? We do not think that this should be the case, and we will discuss several reasons why we take this position in this section.

First, by uncovering the biological mechanisms that are responsible for patients' dysfunctions, RDoC could further the understanding therapists will have of the disorder they encounter in clinics.[4] Kendler and Campbell (2014) even suggest that "neuropsychology provides hypotheses about the functional and physiological structures underlying familiar subjective experiences [. . .] thus provid[ing] a scaffold for expanding our empathic understanding of the subjective experiences of those suffering from psychiatric illness" (1). So not only will therapists be able to provide better explanations of different problems suffered by their patients (explanations better than metaphors like "chemical imbalances" in the brain, which are not precise and do not explain much), but they will be able to tailor their therapeutic interventions to the specificity of their patients. Given the fine-grained knowledge of their patients' problems offered by RDoC (the precise characterization of various different neurobehavioral systems involved in a particular mental illness affecting a patient), they will be in a better position to understand the nature of their experience (and should be able to empathize more).[5]

Knowledge obtained in the framework of the RDoC could also have a positive effect on therapeutic interventions in two ways. First, RDoC could provide an explanation of the reason why, but also when and on whom, we should expect psychological therapeutic interventions to succeed. For instance, Clark and Beck (2010) review data showing that the effectiveness of cognitive behavioral therapy (CBT) for the treatment of anxiety and depression could be "associated with reduced activation of the amygdalo-hippocampal subcortical regions implicated in the generation of negative emotion and increased activation of higher-order frontal regions involved in cognitive control of negative emotion" (418). Results such as these (see also Lane et al., 2015; Etkin et al., 2005) will allow clinicians not only to validate the type(s) of therapies they are using, but also to understand how they work. Second, recent results (Eley et al., 2012; Beevers and McGary, 2012; Roberts et al., 2014) indicate that genetic variations could be used to predict depressive patients' responses to CBT and to assign patients who could react positively to this kind of therapy while avoiding a useless therapy for others.

Finally, if one can better understand the effects of specific kinds of psychotherapy on the organization of the brain, then one can increase the effectiveness of these kinds of psychotherapy in order that they positively impact certain brain circuits or develop new therapies adapted to the features of the patient's condition. This is exactly what Alexopoulos and Arean (2013) have done with their "Engage" therapy for late-life depression. In short, they propose a psychotherapy "targeting neuroscience-driven function" (i.e., the RDoC domains; 16). First, they identified the dysfunction of the positive valence systems (especially in the reward valuation, action selection, and other related constructs) to be central in late-life depression. Then they developed a therapy seeking to reignite and to retrain the positive valence system (through direct facilitation of rewarding activities). According to Alexopoulos and Arean, sometimes therapists will also have to identify barriers to progress. Such barriers could be "negativity bias", "apathy", and "emotion dysregulation". Each of these barriers (belonging to different RDoC domains) can also be mitigated through therapy. For instance, patients showing negativity bias can be taught to recognize when they are "excessively focusing on negative cues and redirect their attention to neutral or positive aspects of the situation".

Psychiatrists working in the RDoC paradigm, then, are not necessarily forced to use drugs to treat all of their patients. This is good given that pharmaceutical drugs can cause adverse (and sometimes permanent) effects on patient cognition, emotion, and body functions (for some examples of somatic disorders induced by psychiatric drugs, see Schumann et al., 2014, 35). Moreover, RDoC is not committed to a mindless form of psychotherapy. For instance, *Engage* necessitates that therapists identify what kind of activities their patients find rewarding and discuss with patients steps needed to realize these activities.

Will RDoC's Research Program Reduce Clinical Psychiatry to an Applied Neurobiology?

Although the RDoC's research program recognizes explicitly (and in principle) the role of high-level factors in the etiology of mental disorders, some of its advocates seem to derive from the reductionist ontological thesis about mental disorders a reductionist epistemological thesis. For instance, Insel sometimes promotes the latter variety of idea in some of his popular scientific writing, in which disorders such as major depression, obsessive-compulsive disorder, and post-traumatic stress disorder are represented by explanatory models emphasizing dysfunctions in brain circuits. Insel describes obsessive-compulsive disorder thusly:

> Neuroimaging studies of patients with OCD have discovered abnormal activity in an adjacent loop that includes the orbitofrontal cortex, which is involved in complex tasks such as decision making, the ventral caudate nucleus within the basal ganglia, and the thalamus, which relays and integrates sensory information.
>
> (Insel, 2010a, 48)

Furthermore, the explanatory illustrations he uses to describe his models could be described as "brain or neuro-centered", as they situate the source of mental disorders exclusively in brain circuits. By so doing, it seems that he is neglecting environmental factors that are important causes of [at least some] mental disorders.[6] Even if these factors are mentioned in the official documents of the RDoC, some of the crudest forms of reductionism continue to dominate (or be encouraged) in documents meant to educate the public.

A look at the way RDoC describes research that it will fund is also revealing. For instance, in one of its funding opportunity announcements for eating disorders, it is written that:

> Eating disorders, including anorexia nervosa (AN), bulimia nervosa (BN), and their variants, are a major source of physical and psychological morbidity and constitute the major contribution to excess mortality from psychiatric disorders. Clinical presentations of eating disorders are highly heterogeneous, involving broad and often overlapping symptomatology. . . . *The recognition that relatively specific behaviors, cognitive operations, and affective processes are primarily implemented by particular neural circuits suggests that dysregulated functions and associated neural circuits should be a critical focus of study, and ultimately, the target of assessment and treatment for eating disorders.*
>
> (http://grants.nih.gov/grants/guide/rfa-files/
RFA-MH-14-030.html; our emphasis)

Genetic and neural factors are important causal factors in eating disorders, but in the present state of knowledge, it would be a mistake to disregard social norms, media influence, family, and self-conception, all of which are known to play an important role in the etiology of these disorders (for an explanatory model integrating both kinds of factors, see Striegel-Moore and Bulik, 2007). Indeed, at this point in time, nothing justifies making neural circuits the "*critical focus* of study" or the "*target* of assessment and treatment". This is simply symptomatic of the research that RDoC is funding. It funds almost no social epidemiology studies, no studies on environmental factors that are not abstracted from their social and psychological context (for instance, they would study the effect of abuse or urbanity, but not how a particular case of abuse is understood by a patient, what are the norms about sharing the experience of abuse, or how the features of urban life might be "pathological", etc.). As Wakefield (2014) remarked recently, the RDoC does not take into account the meaning that subjects give to certain events or the beliefs that they have about a situation (which could act both as a source of pathology and as a protection from it).

Finally, one can wonder what justifies the focus on neural circuits in the research of new treatments. As Hall and his colleagues (2015) observed, research on addiction completed under the "brain disease" model has failed to deliver improved treatments or drugs that were better than the previous generation of drugs. At the same time, imposition of higher taxes on cigarettes, laws restricting advertising for cigarettes, or restrictions on where people can smoke have halved the number of smokers in countries that have adopted these measures. Hall and his colleagues do not conclude that we should stop biological research but rather that we should not focus exclusively on it. More concretely, we should avoid focusing all research money on finding a biological cure for disorders that could possibly be cured using other means (a situation denounced in an editorial in *Nature* [2012, 473–474]). Unfortunately, at this time, there is "a dramatic tilt in [. . .] funding decisions that lean in the direction of increasing data and information on processes inside the body—while de-funding or blocking access to research on forces outside the body" (Duster, 2006, 2).

Potential Problems of the RDoC for Clinical Psychiatry

The incorrect (implicit) inference that consists of deducing epistemological reductionism from ontological reductionism could cause clinical psychiatry to be reduced to applied neurobehavioral neurosciences. Indeed, to identify psychiatric disorders as brain disorders and to prefer biological explanations to those implicating higher levels could cause what Poland called a "bias in research." This bias favors the development of pharmaceutical interventions (and other methods which act directly on the brain, like deep brain stimulation) targeting genetic, molecular, or cellular factors identified as the source of the disorder. Hall and colleagues remark that the argument according to which more attention should be given to the brain in the treatment of addiction has led to proposals for the development of interventions that act directly on the brains of individuals suffering from this disorder. Indeed, if neural activities in the brains of the mentally ill are judged to be the only (or the principal) causes of their mental condition, one might be more tempted to think that it is their brains that must be treated and, preferably, directly with medication (or other biological therapy; for example, see the strategic plan of the National Institute on Alcohol Abuse and Alcoholism described by Duster, 2006, 3). The systematic use of pharmaceutical means and the direct brain treatment of all mental disorders (which would be amplified by the reductionist bias of the RDoC) is problematic because, in some cases, psychiatric disorders are caused by problematic environments (a dysfunctional family, poverty, harassment at work, etc.) that might be neglected because of the focus on direct means of intervention. For instance, in Quebec, studies have shown that slot machines are more numerous in poorer neighborhoods than richer ones (Fortier, 2013). The consequence of this is that an already at risk population is exposed to an important risk factor for addiction. In such cases, acting on social factors might have more impact (and at a lower cost) than acting on the brains of the addicted (with technologies most of them won't be able to afford).

Another problem we would like to consider is linked to the adoption of a "neurocentered" conception of mental disorders and of the systematic use of drug treatments associated with it. This problem affects both patients and therapists. We will first explore how it affects patients, then therapists.

Let's begin with problems linked to conceptions that patients have of themselves and of their disorders. Why should we pay attention to such conceptions? One reason is that they have repercussions on patient behavior (they are action guiding) and health. An example, taken from a paper by Tekin and colleagues (2017) will illustrate why it is important to pay attention to self-conceptions: "Generally speaking, a person's self-concept of her physical strength affects her physical activities. She may or may not reach out to lift a suitcase, depending on how strong she feels and how heavy she perceives the suitcase to be." A patient's self-conception and her conception of her disorder have an effect on actions that she will (or will not) contemplate and those she will accomplish. If such is the case, it becomes important to identify which conception of disorders dominates a patient's conception of disorders and what effect(s) it has on their self-conception.

According to O'Connor and Joff (2013, 258), there is an increasing tendency for psychiatric patients to think of their mental disorders in terms of brain dysfunction. In a study done by Buchman and colleagues (2013), such a conception is illustrated by claims made by patients: for instance, patients describe their disorders, saying things like, "The chemicals in your brain control your sense of wellbeing. And I guess my serotonin doesn't sit in the right part of the synapse that it's supposed to" (Buchman et al., 2013, 72) or "I like to think that we have little wires running through our brain and, you know, there's a healthy person—someone who's mentally stable and balanced—and also ... people that suffer from depression, bipolar and they all have similar little broken wires in their brain" (Buchman et al., 2013, 75).

Studies on the epidemiology of this type of representation of depression show that in 2006, 80% of Americans approved of the idea that depression was caused by a chemical imbalance,[7] and more than 64% thought that the problem was genetic or biologically inherited (Pescosolido et al., 2010, 1324). Lebowitz and colleagues (2016) also cite an Australian study that shows the progress—both in children suffering from attention deficit disorder and in their parents—of a genetic and neurobiological conception of the disorder. Studies of this type demonstrate that there exists a tendency to conceive of psychiatric disorders as brain dysfunctions caused by biological factors. One might fear that RDoC's conception of mental disorders and its reductionist focus will accentuate this tendency.

Why should this be a problem? After all, this way of representing one's own disorder might be beneficial. For instance, patients who attribute their condition to genetic or neurological factors have the tendency to feel less responsible and blameworthy for their condition.[8] They also can feel less lonely because they realize that they are part of a group of people suffering from the same thing (Sharpe, 2012, 67–68). This type of representation can also help them to understand their disorder and its characteristics.

Unfortunately, this conception also leads to what is sometimes named "genetic essentialism" (Dar-Nimrod and Heine, 2011) or "neuroessentialism" (Haslam, 2011). These forms of essentialism can be a source of problems. First of all, as shown by studies from Lebowitz and Ahn on different psychiatric disorders (Lebowitz and Ahn, 2012; Lebowitz et al., 2013; Lebowitz et al., 2014; see also Deacon and Baird, 2009), accepting a biological (genetic or neurological) explanation of a disorder leads patients to be more pessimistic about their prognosis; that is, it leads them to be more pessimistic concerning their chances of getting better than if they accepted an explanation in psychosocial terms. This is particularly dramatic if, as suggested by Rutherford et al. (2010) in a systematic review of the literature on depression, a patient's expectation plays an important role in the amelioration or deterioration of the symptoms of certain psychiatric conditions (one can think of the impact of such expectation on anxiety disorders, for instance). Positive expectations concerning the chances of getting better also have an impact on the motivation to seek treatment and on active engagement with it. This type of explanation also has an effect on the perception subjects have of their capacity to eliminate or ameliorate their condition. Finally, the same studies have shown that patients who adopt a biological conception of their condition have a tendency to give priority to "biological" treatment (drugs or other direct means of intervention) and to consider "nonbiological" treatment (psychotherapy, modification of the environment, etc.) to be less efficacious. Thus there are more chances that patients who adopt a biological conception show up at the doctor or psychiatrist (instead of their psychologist), that they ask for drug prescriptions, and that they would be skeptical and less likely to engage in treatment if they were prescribed other types of therapy. Moreover, as Levy (2007, 86) suggests, if some aspects of the social environment (family, workplace, etc.) of one patient are toxic and constitute an important factor in producing and maintaining certain psychiatric disorders, then the belief that the source of the disorder and that the targets of the treatments are inside the patient (and not under his control) might cause the patient to neglect modifying these aspects of the environment.

As for the therapists' attitude, studies by Lebowitz and Ahn (2014) show that, compared to the explanations of disorders in psychosocial terms, explanations in biological terms reduce empathy toward patients (these effects would be produced, they hypothesize, by a kind of dehumanization that would follow from seeing the patients' conditions as the result of dysfunctional sub-personal mechanisms rather than disease of the person). Even more interesting, these different types of explanation have an impact on the perceived efficacy of different treatment methods. So, when being given a biological explanation of a disorder (rather than a psychosocial one), clinicians attribute more efficacy to drug therapies than to psychological therapies. This is true even in conditions for which both kinds of explanations are used together but in which the biological explanation is dominant, as is the case with the RDoC.

As we saw in this section, a neurocentered conception of mental disorders can have undesired effects on patients and therapists. What is the solution? Surely not to return to an exclusively psychosocial conception of all disorders (if only to avoid the disasters caused by such a conception on families of children suffering from autism in the 1950s and 1960s, for instance; see Kanner, 1949; Bettelheim, 1967). The solution would instead consist of providing the public with a better understanding of the way genes produce their effects in conjunction with the environment, how certain conditions (and certain structures of the brain) can be modified by nondirect manipulations, for instance by providing social support or by going through psychological therapy. All of this demands that RDoC advocates refrain from only paying lip service to pluralism and higher-level factors and instead that they assume it fully and that it finds echoes in funded research.

Conclusion

As mentioned in the paper's introduction, the RDoC focus on faulty circuits has led some to suspect it of being a reductionist enterprise. Because the RDoC will eventually impact clinical psychiatry, some have further feared that it will transform clinical psychiatry into a mindless, applied neurobehavioral science. We have argued that if the RDoC is officially endorsing a form of reductionism, the particular form of patchy reductionism it endorses does not suffer from the shortcomings of more classical forms of reductionism. In light of the latter, we have argued that, at least *in principle*, the RDoC could enrich rather than impoverish clinical psychiatry. We have concluded the chapter by describing a few potential problems that RDoC could pose to clinical psychiatry if it does not fully embrace the patchy form of reductionism.

Notes

1 Some of these systems are responsible for cognitive capacities such as memory, control, decision making; others are responsible for affective capacities such as emotions, pleasure, pain; still other systems are responsible for arousal or social relationships.

2 Another reason to take development into account is the fact that a functional structure could be affected differently by a disorder in the course of development. If such is the case, clinical interventions could be tailored to the particular "clinical stages" of the disorder (Hickie et al., 2013).

3 As Sandra Michell (2009), commenting on Kendler's work, eloquently put it, "Not only is there no single, reductive factor that will explain why a person suffers from depression; there is no unique composition of causes or explanation involving different levels that will do the job for all cases" (110).

4 Etkin and Cuthbert (2014) suppose that RDoC is continuous with clinical practice in which the therapists attend to the patient's specific complaints (in the case of RDoC, therapists would attend to patients' specific dysfunctions in neuro-cognitive domains and sub-domains), while the DSM diagnostic is used for billing purposes.

5 Neuropsychological descriptions of the mechanisms underlying psychiatric conditions, like Gerrans's (2014) description of delusion in terms of the dysfunction of salience mechanisms and of the default network, or accounts of autism in the framework of predictive coding (Palmer et al., 2015), allow one to better understand the cognitive features of those having these conditions. They provide what Kendler and Campbell (2014) call "explanation-aided understanding".

6 It could be argued that Insel is not describing the whole causal process that leads to a disorder but rather the pathology itself (the deviant brain structure that leads to deviant behaviors or thoughts). If such is the case, it is not necessary to represent the environmental (distal) factors that might be the source of the deviant structure. Still, Insel should know the effect of these brain or neuro-centered representations on patients' representations of their own conditions (see next section). Blease (2014) even argues that it is the duty of therapists (and, one would say, of researchers as well) to be aware of patients' (mis)representations of their conditions and to avoid being complicit in promoting faulty representations.

7 Which is not surprising given the type of publicity that was directed to the public at the time. See Lacasse and Leo, 2005.

8 It has also been suggested that a biological and genetic (biogenetic) conception of mental disorders might also be less stigmatizing (as it removes the responsibility for the condition from the patient), but

studies are showing that it might not be the case (or at least that the story is more complicated than suggested); see Rüsh et al., 2010; Kvaale et al., 2013; Haslam and Kvaale, 2015.

Further Reading

Buchman, D.Z., Borgelt, E.L., Whiteley, L. and Illes, J. (2013) "Neurobiological Narratives: Experiences of Mood Disorder Through the Lens of Neuroimaging". *Sociology of Health & Illness* 35(1), 66–81.

Cuthbert, B.N. and Insel, T.R. (2013) "Toward the Future of Psychiatric Diagnosis: The Seven Pillars of RDoC". *BMC Medicine* 11(1), 126–133.

Kozak, M.J. and Cuthbert, B.N. (2016) "The NIMH Research Domain Criteria Initiative: Background, Issues, and Pragmatics". *Psychophysiology* 53, 286–297.

Lilienfield, S.O. and Treadway, M.T. (2016) "Clashing Diagnostic Approaches: DSM-ICD Versus RDoC". *Annual Review of Clinical Psychology* 12, 435–463.

Tekin, S. (2011) "Self-Concept Through the Diagnostic Looking Glass: Narratives and Mental Disorder". *Philosophical Psychology* 24(3), 357–380.

References

Alexopoulos, G., and Arean, P. (2013) A model for streamlining psychotherapy in the RDoC era: The Example of "Engage". *Molecular Psychiatry* 19(1): pp. 1–6.

Beevers, C.G., and McGeary, J.E. (2012) Therapygenetics: Moving towards personalized psychotherapy treatment. *Trends in Cognitive Sciences* 16(1): pp. 11–12.

Bettelheim, B. (1967) *The Empty Fortress: Infantile Autism and the Birth of the Self*. New York: Free Press.

Blease, C. (2014) The duty to be well-informed: The case of depression. *Journal of Medical Ethics* 40(4): pp. 225–229.

Broome, M. (2006) Taxonomy and ontology in psychiatry: A survey of recent literature. *Philosophy, Psychiatry & Psychology* 13(4): pp. 303–319.

Buchman, D.Z., Borgelt, E.L., Whiteley, L., and Illes, J. (2013) Neurobiological narratives: Experiences of mood disorder through the lens of neuroimaging. *Sociology of Health & Illness* 35(1): pp. 66–81.

Champagne, F.A. (2010) Early adversity and developmental outcomes interaction between genetics, epigenetics, and social experiences across the life span. *Perspectives on Psychological Science* 5(5): pp. 564–574.

Clark, D., and Beck, A. (2010) Cognitive theory and therapy of anxiety and depression: Convergence with neurobiological findings. *Trends in Cognitive Sciences* 14(9): pp. 418–424.

Craddock, N., and Owen, M.J. (2010) The Kraepelinian dichotomy—Going, going . . . but Still not gone. *The British Journal of Psychiatry* 196(2): pp. 92–95.

Cuthbert, B.N. (2014) The RDoC framework: Facilitating transition from ICD/DSM to dimensional approaches that integrate neuroscience and psychopathology. *World Psychiatry* 13(1): pp. 28–35.

Cuthbert and the NIMH RDoC Workgroup. (2014) The RDoC framework: Continuing commentary. *World Psychiatry* 13(2): pp. 196–197.

Dar-Nimrod, I., and Heine, S.J. (2011) Genetic essentialism: On the deceptive determinism of DNA. *Psychological Bulletin* 137(5): pp. 800–818.

Deacon, B.J., and Baird, G.L. (2009) The chemical imbalance explanation of depression: Reducing blame at what cost? *Journal of Social and Clinical Psychology* 28(4): pp. 415–435.

Duster, T. (2006) Comparative perspectives and competing explanations: Taking on the newly configured reductionist challenge to sociology. *American Sociological Review* 71(1): pp. 1–15.

Editorial column (2012) Therapy deficit: Studies to enhance psychological treatments are scandalously undersupported. *Nature*, 27 September, 489: pp. 473–474.

Eley, C., Hudson, J.L., Creswell, C., Tropeano, M., Lester, K.J., Cooper, P., Farmer, A., Lewis, C.M., Lyneham, H.J., Rapee, R.M., Uher, R., Zavos, H.M.S. and Collier, D.A. (2012) Therapygenetics: The 5HTTLPR and response to psychological therapy. *Molecular Psychiatry* 17(3): pp. 236–237.

Etkin, A., Pittenger, C., Polan, H.J., and Kandel, E.R. (2005) Toward a neurobiology of psychotherapy: Basic science and clinical applications. *Journal of Neuropsychiatry and Clinical Neurosciences* 17(2): pp. 145–158.

Etkin, A., and Cuthbert, B. (2014) Beyond the DSM: Development of a transdiagnostic psychiatric neuro-science course. *Academic Psychiatry* 38(2): pp. 145–150.

Fortier, M. (2013) Loteries vidéo: Loto-Québec cible les pauvres. *Le Devoir*, 21 November, 2013. Available at: www.ledevoir.com/politique/quebec/393288/loteries-video-loto-quebec-cible-les-pauvres [Accessed 26 Apr. 2016].

Gerrans, P. (2014) *The Measure of Madness: Philosophy of mind, Cognitive Neuroscience, and Delusional Thought.* Cambridge, MA: MIT Press.

Gold, I. (2009) Reduction in psychiatry. *Canadian Journal of Psychiatry / Revue canadienne de psychiatrie* 54(8): pp. 506–512.

Hall, W., Carter, A., and Forlini, C. (2015) The brain disease model of addiction: Is it supported by the evidence and has it delivered on its promises? *The Lancet Psychiatry* 2(1): pp. 105–110.

Harris, H.W., and Schaffner, K.F. (1992) Molecular genetics, reductionism, and disease concepts in psychiatry. *Journal of Medicine and Philosophy* 17(2): pp. 127–153.

Haslam, N. (2011) Genetic essentialism, neuroessentialism, and stigma: Commentary on Dar-Nimrod and Heine. *Psychological Bulletin* 137(5): pp. 819–824.

Haslam, N., and Kvaale, E.P. (2015) Biogenetic explanations of mental disorder: The mixed-blessings model. *Current Directions in Psychological Science* 24(5): pp. 399–404.

Hellstrom, I.C., Dhir, S.K., Diorio, J.C., and Meaney, M.J. (2012) Maternal licking regulates hippocampal glucocorticoid receptor transcription through a thyroid hormone—Serotonin—NGFI-a signalling cascade. *Philosophical Transactions of the Royal Society B: Biological Sciences* 367(1601): pp. 2495–2510.

Hickie, I.B., Scott, J., Hermens, D.F., Scott, E.M., Naismith, S.L., Guastella, A.J., . . . McGorry, P.D. (2013) Clinical classification in mental health at the cross-roads: Which direction next? *BMC Medicine* 11(1): pp. 1–14.

Insel T.R. (2010a) Faulty circuits. *Scientific American* 302(4): pp. 44–51.

———. (2010b) Rethinking schizophrenia. *Nature* 468: pp. 187–193.

———. (2013) Director's blog: Transforming diagnosis. NIMH. Available at: www.nimh.nih.gov/about/director/2013/transforming-diagnosis.shtml [Accessed 27 Oct. 2013].

———. (2014) The NIMH Research Domain Criteria (RDoC) project: Precision medicine for psychiatry. *American Journal of Psychiatry* 171(4): pp. 395–397.

Insel, T.R., and Lieberman, J.A. (2013) DSM-5 and RDoC: Shared interests. NIMH. Available at: www.nimh.nih.gov/news/science-news/2013/dsm-5-and-rdoc-shared-interests.shtml [Accessed 27 Oct. 2013].

Insel, T.R., and Quirion, R. (2005) Psychiatry as a clinical neuroscience discipline. *Journal of American Medical Association* 294(17): pp. 2221–2224.

Kanner, L. (1949) Problems of nosology and psychodynamics of early infantile autism. *American Journal of Orthopsychiatry* 19(3): pp. 416–426.

Kapur, S., Phillips, A.G., and Insel, T.R. (2012) Why has it taken so long for biological psychiatry to develop clinical tests and what to do about it? *Molecular Psychiatry* 17(12): pp. 1174–1179.

Kendler, K.S. (2005) Toward a philosophical structure for psychiatry. *American Journal of Psychiatry* 162(3): pp. 433–440.

———. (2012a) Levels of explanation in psychiatric and substance use disorders: Implications for the development of an etiologically based nosology. *Molecular Psychiatry* 17(1): pp. 11–21.

———. (2012b) The dappled nature of causes of psychiatric illness: Replacing the organic—Functional/hardware—Software dichotomy with empirically based pluralism. *Molecular Psychiatry* 17(4): pp. 377–388.

Kendler, K.S., and Campbell, J. (2014) Expanding the domain of the understandable in psychiatric illness: An updating of the Jasperian framework of explanation and understanding. *Psychological Medicine* 44(1): pp. 1–7.

Kendler, K.S., Gardner, C.O., and Prescott, C.A. (2006) Toward a comprehensive developmental model for major depression in men. *American Journal of Psychiatry* 163(1): pp. 115–124.

Kvaale, E., Gottdiener, W., and Haslam, N. (2013) Biogenetic explanations and stigma: A meta-analytic review of associations among laypeople. *Social Science & Medicine* 96: pp. 95–103.

Kendler, K.S., Gardner, C.O., and Prescott, C.A. (2006) Toward a comprehensive developmental model for major depression in men. *American Journal of Psychiatry* 163(1): pp. 115–124.

Kostko, A., and Bickle, J. (2017) Personalized psychiatry and scientific causal explanations: Two accounts. In S. Tekin and J. Poland (Eds.). *Extraordinary Science: Psychiatric Classification and Research*. Cambridge, MA: MIT Press, pp. 127–162.

Lacasse, J.R., and Leo, J. (2005) Serotonin and depression: A disconnect between the advertisements and the scientific literature. *PLoS Medicine* 2(12): pp. 1211–1216.

Lane, R.D., Ryan, L., Nadel, L., and Greenberg, L. (2015) Memory reconsolidation, emotional arousal, and the process of change in psychotherapy: New insights from brain science. *Behavioral and Brain Sciences* 38: pp. 1–19.

Laungani, P. (2002) Mindless psychiatry and dubious ethics. *Counselling Psychology Quarterly* 15(1): pp. 23–33.

Lebowitz, M.S., Rosenthal, J.E., and Ahn, W.K. (2016) Effects of biological versus psychosocial explanations on stigmatization of children with ADHD. *Journal of Attention Disorders* 20(3): pp. 240–250.

Lebowitz, M.S., and Ahn, W.K. (2012) Combining biomedical accounts of mental disorders with treatability information to reduce mental illness stigma. *Psychiatric Services* 63(5): pp. 496–499.

———. (2014) Effects of biological explanations for mental disorders on clinicians' empathy. *Proceedings of the National Academy of Sciences* 111(50): pp. 17786–17790.

Lebowitz, M.S., Pyun, J.J., and Ahn, W.K. (2014) Biological explanations of generalized anxiety disorder: Effects on beliefs about prognosis and responsibility. *Psychiatric Services* 65(4): pp. 498–503.

Lebowitz, M.S., Ahn, W.K., and Nolen-Hoeksema, S. (2013) Fixable or fate? Perceptions of the biology of depression. *Journal of Consulting and Clinical Psychology* 81(3): pp. 518–527.

Levy, N. (2007) *Neuroethics: Challenges for the 21st Century*. Cambridge: Cambridge University Press.

McLaren, N. (2011) Cells, circuits, and syndromes: A critical commentary on the NIMH research domain criteria project. *Ethical Human Psychology and Psychiatry* 13(3): pp. 229–236.

Mitchell, S.D. (2009) *Unsimple Truths: Science, Complexity, and Policy*. Chicago: University of Chicago Press.

Nagel, E. (1961) *The Structure of Science: Problems in the Logic of Explanation*. New York: Harcourt, Brace & World, Inc.

O'Connor, C., and Joffe, H. (2013) How has neuroscience affected lay understandings of personhood? A review of the evidence. *Public Understanding of Science* 22(3): pp. 254–268.

Palmer, C.J., Seth, A.K., and Hohwy, J. (2015) The felt presence of other minds: Predictive processing, counterfactual predictions, and mentalising in autism. *Consciousness and Cognition* 36: pp. 376–389.

Parnas, J. (2014) The RDoC program: Psychiatry without psyche? *World Psychiatry* 13(1): pp. 46–47.

Pescosolido, B.A., Martin, J.K., Long, J.S., Medina, T.R., Phelan, J.C., and Link, B.G. (2010) A disease like any other"? A decade of change in public reactions to schizophrenia, depression, and alcohol dependence. *American Journal of Psychiatry* 167(11): pp. 1321–1330.

Poland, J. (2014) Deeply rooted Sources of errors and bias. In H. Kincaid and J.A. Sullivan (Eds.). *Mental Kinds and Natural Kinds*. Cambridge, MA: MIT Press, pp. 29–63.

Roberts, S., Lester, K.J., Hudson, J.L., Rapee, R.M., Creswell, C., Cooper, P.J., . . . Eley, T.C. (2014) Serotonin transporter methylation and response to cognitive behaviour therapy in children with anxiety disorders. *Translational Psychiatry* 4(9): p. e444.

Rüsh, N., Todd, A., Bodenhausen, G.V., and Corrigan, P.W. (2010) Biogenetic models of psychopathology, implicit guilt, and mental illness stigma. *Psychiatry Research* 179(3): pp. 328–332.

Rutherford, B.R., Wager, T.D., and Roose, S.P. (2010) Expectancy and the treatment of depression: A review of experimental methodology and effects on patient outcome. *Current Psychiatry Reviews* 6(1): pp. 1–10.

Rutten, B.P., and Mill, J. (2009) Epigenetic mediation of environmental influences in major psychotic disorders. *Schizophrenia Bulletin* 35(6): pp. 1045–1056.

Sanislow, C.A., Pine, D.S., Quinn, K.J., Kozak, M.J., Garvey, M.A., Heinssen, R.K., . . . Cuthbert, B.N. (2010) Developing constructs for psychopathology research: Research domain criteria. *Journal of Abnormal Psychology* 119(4): pp. 631–639.

Schaffner, K.F. (2006) Reduction: The Cheshire cat problem and a return to roots. *Synthese* 151(3): pp. 377–402.

———. (2008) Etiological models in psychiatry: Reductive and nonreductive. In K. Kendler and J. Parnas (Eds.). *Philosophical Issues in Psychiatry: Natural Kinds, Mental Taxonomy and Causation*. Baltimore: Johns Hopkins University Press, pp. 48–90.

———. (2011) Reduction in biology and medicine. In F. Gifford (Eds.). *Philosophy of Medicine*. Amsterdam: Elsevier, pp. 137–157.

———. (2013) Reduction and reductionism in psychiatry. In K.W.M. Fulford, Bill., M. Davies, R. Gipps, G. Graham, J.Z. Sadler, G. Stanghellini, and T. Thornton (Eds.). *The Oxford Handbook of Philosophy and Psychiatry*. Oxford: Oxford University Press, pp. 1003–1022.

Schumann, G., *et al.* (2014) Stratified medicine for mental disorders. *European Neuropharmacology* 24: pp. 5–50.

Striegel-Moore, R.H. and Bulik, C.M. (2007) Risk factors for eating disorders. *American Psychologist* 62(3): pp. 181–198.

Sharpe, K. (2012) *Coming of Age on Zoloft: How Antidepressants Cheered Us Up, Let Us Down, and Changed Who We Are*. New York: Harper Perennial.

Tekin, S., Flanagan, O., and Graham, G. (2017) *Against the Drug Cure Model: Addiction, Identity, Pharmaceuticals*. Available at: www.academia.edu/11327886/Against_the_Drug_Cure_Model_Addiction_Identity_Pharmaceuticals [Accessed 27 Apr. 2016].

Wakefield, J.C. (2014) Wittgenstein's nightmare: Why the RDoC grid needs a conceptual dimension. *World Psychiatry* 13(1): pp. 38–40.

Whooley, O. (2014) Nosological reflections: The failure of DSM-5, the emergence of RDoC, and the decontextualization of mental distress. *Society and Mental Health* 4(2): pp. 92–110.

28

NEUROETHICS IN CONTEXT

The Development of the Discipline in Argentina

Arleen Salles

Introduction

In this chapter, I provide a thematic overview of neuroethics in Argentina. Drawing from the brain sciences, philosophy of mind, ethics, and the social sciences, neuroethics aims to provide answers to some of the ethical issues raised by the transfer of brain knowledge to various contexts, including medicine, law, philosophy, and health and social policy. Academically, neuroethics started in Argentina in 2010. The first international conference, *Expanding the Frontiers of Neuroethics*, was sponsored by Fundación Crimson. In 2011, the Neuroethics Program at Universidad Nacional de San Martin hosted the *Primera Jornada de Neuroética*. In 2012, the Neuroethics Research Program based in Centro de Investigaciones Filosóficas (CIF) organized its first Neuroethics Symposium. In 2015, a second International Symposium, *Cuestiones éticas y sociales planteadas por el conocimiento del cerebro*, was cosponsored by the CIF Neuroethics Program, the European Human Brain Project (HBP), and the Neuroscience Lab Science at Universidad Torcuato Di Tella. A collection of essays in Spanish devoted to the discussion of some of the ethical issues raised by neuroscience was published in 2014 (Salles and Evers, 2014). A number of outreach events (seminars, colloquia, open conferences, debates) aimed at debating the ethical issues raised by neuroscience have been organized by different organizations, including the CIF Neuroethics Program. Finally, a few talks on neuroethics have been included in some philosophy meetings. At present, however, academic interest in these issues is restricted to a small group of scientists, neurologists, and philosophers.

Here, I attempt to make explicit some of the salient topics and challenges shaping the development of neuroethics in Argentina. I begin with a brief description of some of the research carried out in the country. Next, I focus on prevalent cultural and sociopolitical considerations that play a role in how neuroethical issues are identified, perceived, and approached in Argentina. Finally, I briefly explain some of the neuroethical concerns that attract more attention locally or are deemed particularly relevant.

Science and Neuroscientific Research: The Argentine Landscape

Neurotechnology and neuroscientific findings cross borders quickly, and thus they have an impact on human beings regardless of where they are. This is the reason why, in a sense, no country is immune to the ethical issues raised by neuroscientific advances (Shook and Giordano, 2014). Argentina has a strong tradition in science (with three Nobel laureates in the field of science and medicine[1]) and a productive neuroscientific community. Indeed, in Argentina, scientific development plays an important role in developing and promoting a national identity.

The country lost several researchers in the 1990s when funds for science and education were greatly reduced. However, and particularly in the last few years, the Argentine government has been trying to find ways to promote the production of scientific knowledge and research, linking it to the achievement of global competitiveness and internationalization. In 2008, the Ministry of Science, Technology and Productive Innovation was created. Its objective is to contribute to the advancement of science, providing subsidies and official support to universities and research institutes. It has been successful in luring back many scientists who were trained overseas (Kaiser and Marshall, 2008) and in promoting ties with local and international research centers and strengthening bilateral scientific and technological cooperation with a number of European countries (Smaglick, 2008).

In the last few decades, neuroscience research and activities aimed at boosting neuroscientific research have grown in the country. Several public and private institutions are engaged in biomedical research devoted to understanding brain pathologies (for example, *FLENI—Fundación para la Lucha contra las Enfermedades Neurológicas de la Infancia* [Foundation for the Fight Against Pediatric Neurological Disease], *Fundación Instituto Leloir*, and *Fundación INECO—Instituto de Neurología Cognitiva* [Institute of Cognitive Neurology]), and the investigation of issues such as the brain's sense of time (*Universidad Nacional de Quilmes*), and the biological basis of behavior (*INECO, Integrative Neuroscience Lab*). In turn, the *Applied Neurobiology Unit at CEMIC-CONICET* has a number of research lines, including experimental studies focusing on processes of brain organization and reorganization to determine how material and social deprivation affects the neurocognitive development of the brain.

As is true with all research, the types of research described engender a variety of ethical concerns. It is widely acknowledged that ethical research requires that scientists do not run afoul of basic moral values such as respect for the autonomy and integrity of research subjects, the promotion of public good, and fairness in the distribution of risks and benefits. Indeed, Argentine researchers follow international ethical guidelines, such as the Belmont Report, which in turn shape the laws and regulations that govern human-subject research in Argentina. Research protocols must be reviewed and approved by the relevant Institutional Reviews Boards and Committees on Animals Research and Ethics. Indeed, local scientists recognize compliance with ethical guidelines as one of the rules of the game. Of course, this does not necessarily make all scientists more morally sensitive or deeply aware of the reason why basic ethical norms need to be followed. Many still see ethics as separable from science, an addition needed in order to be able to carry out the research and get published. In more informal contexts, it is not unusual for scientists to talk about ethics as the bully stifling scientific progress, targeting their work, and making them waste time.[2] Moreover, even when scientists comply with basic research ethics guidelines, not many move beyond such compliance to discuss the potential ethical implications of their research. However, it is worth noting that this attitude is common to scientists all over the world; at times it seems to be part and parcel of being a scientist. Some commentators have pointed out that this may be related to the fact that in general, science students do not receive formal ethics training when their character as scientists is being shaped, thus making it more unlikely that they will be ethically sensitive when they are established scientists and carry out their research (Morien-Zamir and Sahakian, 2009). The fact is, however, that integrating ethics into the basic practice of neuroscience in general continues to be one of the main neuroethical challenges. At present, the need to identify and address ethical issues early and during research activities is underscored by a number of bodies, including the Presidential Commission for the Study of Bioethical Issues in the U.S. and the Ethics and Society Subproject in the Human Brain Project (Presidential Commission, 2014; Rose, 2014; Rommelfanger and Johnson, 2015; Christen et al., 2016; Farisco et al., 2016).

When it comes to the scientific community's attitude toward research ethics, then, there is not much difference between scientists in the Southern and Northern Hemispheres. But as we know, issues of research ethics and compliance do not exhaust the field of neuroethics. Beyond the fundamental ethical standards that guide research, a number of metaphysical and ethical issues are raised by neuroscientific research.

The assumption that knowledge provided by the sciences is entirely independent from institutions, cultural norms, and traditions has been recently questioned (Henrich et al., 2010). So has been the idea that a thoughtful discussion of the ethical and social issues raised by such knowledge is not affected by culture and social and political considerations. Although a general discussion of the philosophical issues is possible, ultimately for the discussion to be productive and practically relevant, it is important to recognize the impact of specific frameworks. The fact is that even if it is possible to identify a common set of moral concerns raised by neuroscientific advances and invoke shared values that can be used to address them, such concerns and values are likely to be shaped by social and cultural contexts and traditions (Lombera and Illes, 2009; Chen and Quirion, 2011; Buniak et al., 2014). In the following section, I present a number of cultural considerations that shape the understanding and perception of neuroscience, its role and implications, and that make an impact on the development of neuroethics in Argentina.

Neuroethics: The Challenges and Tasks Ahead

There is a difference between (a) communication of neuroscientific knowledge and (b) the attempt to critically engage both the scientific community and the public in debates over the meaning of such knowledge, its implications, and the wider contexts within which it takes place.

Regarding communication of neuroscience research, the number of articles that focus on understanding the brain has climbed considerably during the last few years in Argentina. Neuroscientific findings are widely reported in the main newspapers (*La Nación, Clarín, Página 12, Perfil*), and several members of the scientific community show an increased willingness to share their knowledge of the brain with the public. Well-known local neuroscientists are regularly interviewed, many of them write opinion pieces and articles in newspapers, and some of them have published books aimed at explaining recent discoveries about the brain to a lay audience (Ibañez and García, 2015 Sigman, 2015;), how to use such knowledge to live a better life (Manes and Niro, 2014; Bachrach, 2012, 2014; Golombek, 2011, 2014), and even to understand who Argentines are (Manes and Niro, 2016). In 2011 a TV show, *Los enigmas del cerebro* (*The Mysteries of the Brain*), placed neuroscience literacy among one of its main objectives, as does a current show, *El cerebro y yo* (*The Brain and I*). Both shows are hosted by well-known local neuroscientists. Thus, Argentines are generally aware of neuroscientific discoveries and of the rapid development of neuroscience. It is worth noting, however, that at present, there is little emphasis in the media on how neuroscientific discoveries might make a difference for patients suffering from neurological and psychiatric problems and the possible implications for clinical care, diagnoses, and prognoses.[3]

Scientific communication has generally been unidirectional, where scientists are assumed to have objective and valid information that they share with a public ready to treat it as reliable (Slaby, 2010). Furthermore, public misconceptions and information not backed by brain research propagate at high rates (Gleichgerrcht et al., 2015). As a result, we can say that while there is significant communication of neuroscientific findings in Argentina, an interdisciplinary discussion of methodological concerns, of the limitations of the technology used to reach conclusions, of the quality of the information, of the fact that the information provided relies on a particular interpretive framework, and of the possibility of biased reporting or reports being made public too soon is rare (Bar, 2016). A critical approach to neuroscientific findings requires asking and debating questions such as: what findings are disseminated and why? Which political, cultural, and social factors lead to favoring some types of research over others? What is the social, legal, and ethical relevance of the knowledge gained? A discussion of these issues is key, because neuroscientific research agendas are shaped by a number of social, legal, and political factors (Choudhury et al., 2008).

Argentinean Frameworks of the "Mind"

The development of neuroethics in Argentina is complex and kept in check by cultural factors. Perhaps one of the most salient factors has to do with the role played by the prevalence of the psychoanalytic paradigm in the country (Landau, 2013; Salles, 2014).[4] In Argentina, the practicing psychologist and the discipline of psychology are part of the everyday landscape, shaping the language and traditions of a significant portion of the population (Dagfal, 2009). In general, the discipline has taken a specific form, reflecting a psychoanalytic ethos (Plotkin, 2001) still endorsed by many graduates from the main public universities.

At the turn of the twentieth century, psychoanalysis introduced a new method for investigating mental life. Its method was based on free association and interpretation and called for listening to the patient. By doing so, analysis could gain insights regarding unconscious mental processes, including affective and motivational processes, and personality development (Kandel, 1999).

In the last century in particular, psychoanalysis has captured the imagination of Argentineans. Psychoanalytic language pervades the public sphere, and psychoanalysis is popularly assumed to provide an adequate approach to all kinds of questions, becoming an important tool for channeling different kinds of social and moral discomfort (Bass, 2006).

Historically, it has been argued that the surge of popularity of clinical psychological practice in the 1950s is importantly related to its providing a private, confidential, and relatively safe environment for Argentines who were living in an increasingly violent and politically repressive society and were trying to cope with the economic and political decline of the country (Plotkin, 2001). It seems this would explain the attention paid to Jacques Lacan's work in Buenos Aires (Evans, 2005). Lacanian theory's detachment from social problems makes it particularly apt for escaping the messy political and social reality Argentines have endured for many decades (Lakoff, 2003).

The influence of psychoanalysis on Argentine society has tended to subdue the neurohype (i.e., high public expectations about the capacity of brain research to tell us everything about the mind and about ourselves) or what some have called "the seductive allure of neuroscience" often present in other countries (Weisberg et al., 2008).[5] In general, psychoanalysts underscore the break between neuroscience and psychoanalysis, openly emphasizing the unscientific and subjective nature of their craft. Indeed, far from looking for scientific methods for testing their main ideas, they call for understanding the psychoanalytic encounter as a fundamentally humanistic and intellectual journey more akin to philosophy than to a medical technique designed to cure symptoms (Lombardi, 2001; Martinez, 2008).

The past few decades have shown the development of a more mature brain science. Many Argentines, however, see such development as encroaching upon a domain that clearly fits within psychoanalysis.[6] To consider that understanding the brain could give us insights into the mind arouses at least two objections in the psychoanalytic community. One is the common belief that the neuroscientific discourse is too simplistic and reductive, resting on unjustified inferences that lead to empirical essentialism and a problematic renunciation of dualism. A simplistic discourse of this nature would limit the significance of the unique psychoanalytic concern with understanding psychological phenomena and discerning mental meanings by examining and interpreting the patient's discourse and by producing a narrative. The second concern is that neuroscientific findings are used to build abstractions while obscuring the importance of the specificity, singularity, and subjectivity of the patient. As some put it, "neuroscience is possible only insofar as it renounces the subject and bets that it will find an organic cause" (Martinez, 2008; Moscón, 2008; Muñoz, 2008). On this view, for all its "glamour," neuroscience leaves real persons out of the picture. Related to this is the idea that the neuroscientific ethos challenges even the notion of personal responsibility.[7] As some argue, when confronting a patient with violent and aggressive behavior, neuroscientists will require tests looking for somatic reasons. This, however, entails making the patient not responsible for his/her condition. Instead, psychoanalysts promote a dialogue that entails making the patient take responsibility for the issue in question (Castelluccio, 2008).

Considering that the use of benzodiazepines has increased considerably in the last few years, many also express the concern that neuroscientific considerations might be used to promote values that drive the market over patient well-being (Amoroso, 2014; Presidencia de la Nación, 2013).[8] Of course, the objection that neuroscience might be too contaminated by economic interests is not one exclusive to psychoanalysts. However, several psychoanalysts believe that neuroscience is sometimes too focused on short-term and economically advantageous outcomes of limited curative power, and this leads them to skepticism regarding the flow of information provided by neuroscience and anything that has the "neuro–" prefix, including neuroethics. In short, many who are ideologically opposed to neuroscience in terms of its relevance for understanding the human mind tend to distrust neuroethics, a discipline that they believe is intended to uncritically support neuroscience.

An attitude of distrust is not just found within the psychoanalytic community. It also appears to be present within the scientific community, and it is directed not only toward psychoanalysts but also toward philosophers.[9] Like many of their international colleagues, several local neuroscientists, neurologists, and psychologists are seeking to offer scientific explanations of important aspects of moral thought and judgment (for example, Roca, 2015; Hesse et al., 2015; Escobar et al., 2014; Roca et al., 2014; Ibañez et al., 2014), which often raises philosophical issues profoundly embedded in our understanding of what it is to be a moral agent and even what it means to be human. Although scientific training and culture do not typically include humanistic inquiry, when interpreting their findings, many scientists often make metaphysical and ethical assumptions, advance views on the plausibility of some ethical approaches, and even challenge notions that have been widely discussed in the philosophical literature, such as the notions of free will and of moral responsibility. In short, neuroscientists often use scientific considerations to make points about issues that philosophers have addressed and debated for centuries, be it about the existence of universal moral codes or about the vices of dualistic approaches to the mind. However, while in the U.S. and Europe, one finds a considerable number of scientific papers coauthored by scientists and philosophers, only infrequently does one find local scientists seeking the input of local philosophers or showing interest in coauthoring papers with philosophers or colleagues in the humanities to jointly address some of those fundamentally philosophical concerns.

One possible reason for this could be the (philosophical) belief that natural science is all we need to solve metaphysical and moral problems. However, a more plausible and simple reason for this attitude, I think, might be related to how philosophy and the humanities are generally perceived in the region. In Argentina, many consider philosophy a nonrigorous activity mostly concerned with social and spiritual values, at best uninterested in scientific outlooks and at worst directly opposed to science. The view that philosophers in general shun empirical considerations and have not much to contribute to a discussion of some of the issues raised by neuroscience may be partly explained by ignorance about philosophy in general and about the work of many contemporary local philosophers in particular—after all, Argentine philosophy has not been typically opposed to scientific approaches, and analytic philosophy and applied ethics in particular have grown significantly in the last twenty years in the country (Gracia, 1984; Perez and Ortiz Millán, 2010). But such views may also be the result of some intellectual habits (for example, the focus on history of concepts rather than on using concepts to engage with the issues) that have generally been associated with philosophical activity in Latin America (Pereda, 2006). Considering this, it is easier to understand why scientists might have a tendency to think that they are better off without the collaboration of their philosophy counterparts.

Finally, it is necessary to point out that it may be the case that some philosophers and public intellectuals distrust neuroscience and thus appear to be reluctant to engage with some of the issues it raises.[10] While this reluctance is present in philosophical communities in many other countries as well (who hasn't heard allegedly serious philosophers chastising those who focus on applied issues and get too close to the messiness of real life?), in a few Argentine intellectuals, this skepticism might be tied to a controversial biopolitical understanding of neuroscience and its alleged power and control over people and life itself.[11]

If we take these culturally relevant phenomena into account, challenges remain in the development of neuroethics in Argentina. First, in the context of the prevalence of the psychoanalytic paradigm and its impact on Argentine society, neuroethicists must show that their role is not to uncritically support neuroscience but rather to clarify, examine, and promote reflection on a host of issues, not only the general issues raised by neuroscientific research—such as safety of research methods, privacy-related concerns, and problems raised by the use of technology (Fins, 2011)—but also more specific ones—such as how to understand the potential impact of neuroscience on moral responsibility and on how we understand human subjectivity—that might be more directly relevant to those who do psychoanalysis.

Second, a locally developed neuroethics must recognize and become more vocal about the crucial role of interdisciplinary scholarship and interdisciplinary collaborations (Slaby, 2010; Choudury et al., 2009). The scientific contribution is certainly essential, but considering the extent to which neuroscience can impact the wider society, the importance of input from other disciplines should not be underestimated. Fortunately, there are reasons to be optimistic about this issue. Recent (albeit timid) exchanges between local scientists and philosophers suggest that all involved are beginning to understand that a conversation among different professional domains, an integration of diverse viewpoints and expertise, and the merging of empirical findings and philosophical reflection has the potential to be productive in framing and addressing the issues raised by neuroscience, its contribution, and its limits in this specific cultural context (Lombera and Illes, 2009).

Neuroethical Topics in Argentina

As in other places, in Argentina, clinically driven neuroethical issues are generally discussed mostly in the context of neurological and psychiatric care.

Now, despite their popularity in international neuroethical discussions, topics such as the nonmedical use of neuroscientific knowledge to cognitively or morally enhance human beings do not receive a lot of attention in Argentina. There is, of course, interest in some of the general practical and philosophical issues in the neuroenhancement discussion (Melo Martin and Salles, 2015; Salles and Melo Martin, 2014; Gorga, 2013; Castelli, 2014). However, independently of how intellectually engaging the topics are, the fact is that local cultural and sociopolitical factors lead to either questioning the practice itself or questioning its immediate relevance and, in some cases, both. Culturally, the already-discussed prevalence of the psychoanalytic paradigm makes a difference when it comes to understanding what neuroenhancement can do. It is not that enhancement in itself is considered morally wrong. However, from a psychoanalytic perspective, neuroregulation presupposes a very reductionist and individualist understanding of enhancement and of optimal functioning, and thus it is quite suspicious *per se*. It is not surprising, then, that in general Argentines tend to be quite wary of it.

A second set of factors that plays a larger role in societal and individual behavior is historical and political ones. For example, there is widespread governmental corruption and impunity, and historical distrust of public authority and of those who are in power (Balan, 2011 Vogl, 2015;).[12] If we consider the prevalence of these attitudes, the possibility of neuroenhancement—which requires either emotional manipulation or neuroalteration of executive functions—prompts questions such as how those practices would be regulated and monitored, who would have access to them and how they would be used, and how generalized corruption and the lack of transparency (present at both the institutional and social levels) would shape their use.

But probably the most important reason for not placing neuroenhancement high on the list of neuroethical issues has to do with the fact that many Argentines consider that there are more immediate practical issues in the country that deserve attention, and neuroscience's focus on them might contribute to a more productive debate. Poverty has been climbing in the last few years (Salvia, 2015, 2016), and many social ills emerging in Argentine society are attributed to it. Of course, the problem of poverty, of the many factors that make some people more vulnerable to deprivation than others, and of the societal obstacles to full justice deserve consideration in all countries. But in Argentina (as in other Latin American countries), the frequent presence of violent crimes, theft, and vagrancy is pushing the problem of social stratification and the persistence of poverty to the forefront (Musse, 2016). As a consequence, any knowledge of the causes of material and social deprivation and its effects is useful and is beginning to receive attention. Neuroscientific studies of poverty and its effects on critical periods in brain development are examples of this emphasis on socio-economic concerns (Lipina and Colombo, 2009; Lipina et al., 2011; 2013; Lipina, 2014a, 2014b, 2016; Lipina and Segretin, 2015).

As with all research, the studies raise a few ethical and social issues including concerns regarding possible risks and the protection of privacy of the subjects involved. Those are typically addressed by following basic rules of research ethics. To illustrate, in a recent study to examine the impact of poverty on executive control performance, 250 children from three school districts in Buenos Aires were given a number of tasks that focused on attentional control, working memory, and planning (Lipina et al., 2013). The authors of the study emphasized that parents and primary caregivers gave their consent, and the study was approved by the relevant IRB. They also made clear that their study complied with the American Psychological Association's ethical guidelines and international documents such as UNICEF Convention on the Rights of a Child and the relevant local legislation on children's rights.[13]

Neuroscientific studies on poverty have several goals, including the design of interventions aimed at improving children's cognitive performance through training in laboratory, home, and school settings, addressing mechanisms of mediation of childhood poverty to facilitate the identification of potential targets for designing interventions, and the theoretical integration of different levels of analysis, among others (Lipina and Segretin, 2015). Several local scientists advance the view that, in addition to their purely scientific value, neuroscientific studies of poverty have important political and ethical implications. On one hand, these studies show that exposure to deprived environments (which entails exposure to malnutrition, different types of pollutants, and drugs) affects the neurocognitive performance of children, thus contributing to understanding poverty as a complex and varied phenomenon (Lipina, 2014a, 2014b; Lipina and Segretin, 2015). On the other hand, such clear measures of the extent to which social and material deprivation impacts human beings might provide new tools to try to alleviate the problem. Such studies could facilitate the design of preventive interventions to protect human development and even promote the exercise of basic rights. Indeed, it has been argued that neuroscience be used to "enhance discussions about some basic moral rights" (Lipina, 2014a, 21, 2014b, 2016; Gorga and Lipina, 2015). The idea that is beginning to gain traction among those who work in this area is that by providing information on the brain's plasticity and on the role of social environment in neural processing and neurocognitive performance, neuroscientific approaches could provide a clear way to assess whether public policies and governmental measures facilitate or hinder the exercise of basic human rights (Evers, 2015).

The connection between poverty and human rights is certainly not new. What is somewhat novel, though, is the emphasis on the idea that neuroscientific studies might be used to identify human rights violations and promote the exercise of human rights. That is, in general, there has been a tendency in neuroethics to talk about neuroscientific advances as potentially either (a) threatening human rights, for example by compromising "cognitive freedom," or (b) forcing humans to grant new rights, for example, the right to access to neuroenhancement, if the practice became available to some (Justo and Erazun, 2007, 2010), or the extension of rights to other species. In contrast, the view expressed by some in Argentina is that neuroscience could actually promote basic human rights by providing the knowledge needed to fully understand the responsibilities of governments toward their citizens and to design the necessary interventions to meet those responsibilities (Gorga and Lipina, 2015). Thus, what emerges from talks with those scientists and philosophers who work on poverty is the wish to unify the traditionally mutually independent fields of science and the humanities. This line of reasoning promises to be productive in the region, with at least one potential international project that aims to integrate neuroscience and philosophy in the debate over endemic social issues such as corruption.[14]

Finally, it is worth noting that in Argentina, neuroscientific studies of poverty are not the only ones that are intended to have important sociopolitical implications. There are a number of neuroscientific studies that target particular social ills and state that their goal is to promote effective *social improvement*. Such is the case of studies on children's ideas of ownership and theft (Faigenbaum et al., under review), which, it is hoped, will be instrumental in informing teachers and curricula planners, and studies on how neuroscience and cognitive psychology will improve educational practice (Golombek, 2008; Sigman et al., 2014).

Concluding Remarks

At present, the impact of scientific research and the effects of neurotechnology on human beings not only as biological beings but also as moral beings are increasingly felt in medicine and the humanities. It is reasonable to think that the future will bring even more ways of knowing, modifying, healing, and possibly enhancing the brain, thus challenging our intuitions about who we are and how we act (or should act). Neuroethics attempts to both offer a collective response to the ethical issues raised by rapidly developing science and find new answers to age-old philosophical questions. As yet, the discipline is not as established in Argentina as it is in the United States and some European nations, but the unique historic-cultural and academic landscape of Argentina promises to deliver original results as neuroethics develops.

Considering the interconnectedness of scientists who can work with colleagues from all over the world, it is not unusual to think that location is not important. However, ethical issues (whether they are related to brain science or not) are shaped by the interplay of science and society and thus manifest themselves in somewhat different ways in different social and political realities, set against different historic pasts. My overview of the development of neuroethics in Argentina strongly suggests that a serious discussion of neuroethical issues in every country must take into account local context as a critical element when addressing the issues. This entails considering history and the prevalent sociocultural traditions that might play a key role in shaping people's attitudes toward neuroscience, toward the issues it raises, and toward the potential ways to resolve them. Rather than promoting a morally problematic relativism, consideration of such local elements will, hopefully, actually promote a richer discussion of the importance of certain values and rights and foster a debate on what weight should be given to particularities and traditions when they clash with universal values.

Acknowledgments

The research leading to these results has received funding from the European Union Seventh Framework Programme (FP7/2007–2013) under grant agreement no. 604102 (Human Brain Project).

I would like to thank Sebastian Lipina, Agustin Ibañez, Mariano Sigman, Ofelia Franchi, and Marcelo Gorga for their input. Kathinka Evers and Paula Castelli provided valuable comments on a previous version of this chapter. I also thank Syd Johnson and Karen Rommelfanger for their insightful comments to the latest version.

Notes

1 They are Bernardo Houssay (1947), Federico Leloir (1970), and Cesar Milstein (1984).
2 The recent article by Steven Pinker in the *Boston Globe* is a perfect illustration of this line of reasoning in the United States (Pinker, 2015). For further information on this issue, see Madhusoodanan, 2015.
3 This is surprising considering that understanding and treating neurodegenerative conditions and pathological processes that affect millions of people in the world is one of the main goals of well-known Big Science projects such as the Human Brain Project, for example. See www.humanbrainproject.eu/ sv/discover/the-project/strategic-objectives. Last accessed February 18, 2016.
4 For an in-depth examination of this issue, see Salles (2014).
5 For discussion on the alleged "allure" of neuroscience, see Farah and Hook, 2013.
6 For a good sample of articles, see Virtualia, *Revista Digital de la Escuela de Orientación Lacaniana* (virtualia. eol.org.ar). For a different, more open approach to neuroscience, see *Apertura Psychoanalytica* (www. aperturas.org). I thank Paula Castelli for the references.
7 While neurolaw discussions are limited at the moment, it is likely that this field will grow in Argentina in the next few years. Many local attorneys and judges are beginning to show interest in the issue of whether and how jurisprudence could benefit from neuroscientific advances, and the recently founded INeDe (*Instituto de Neurociencias y Derecho in Fundación Ineco*) promises to focus on the impact of neuroscientific findings in helping understand criminal behavior. www.fundacionineco.org/institutos-2/ #inede. Last accessed March 3, 2016.
8 I thank Manuel Suarez Richards for the references.
9 There are, of course, exceptions to this, as will become evident when I discuss local studies on poverty.
10 For a discussion of the relationship between neuroscience and philosophy, see Bar, 2016.
11 A number of Argentine thinkers have been using the notion of biopower as a tool to discuss our increasingly biotechnologized world and explain how it shapes modern subjectivities (Castro, 2011). It is worth noting, however, that only a limited understanding of the notion of biopower supports a negative conception of neuroscience and its impact on people's lives. I thank Dr. Edgardo Castro for this point.

12 Of course, I am not suggesting that there is no corruption in other nations. However, and unfortunately, the level of corruption in Argentina is greater than in many other countries (including some Latin American countries). That corrupt actors have historically enjoyed total impunity makes such corruption even more problematic and prevalent. For current corruption data, see *Transparency International Corruption Perception Index* (CPI.transparency.org), last accessed February 26, 2016. Indeed, my reflections apply to every nation where the level of corruption is significant.

13 A less discussed but still potential issue that could be raised by these studies is whether they might unintentionally promote further stigmatization of the poor on the grounds that they are less cognitively developed due to their growing up in a marginalized environment. At present, however, the potential benefits of the research outstrip any concerns about any such discrimination.

14 At present, a group of neuroscientists (from Chile and Argentina) and philosophers (from Sweden, Spain, and Argentina) is working on a joint project intended to use the perspectives of these two traditionally mutually independent fields to address issues such as corruption and poverty. The goal is to examine the extent to which neuroscientific approaches, when combined with careful philosophical and social reflection, could contribute to understanding serious social issues and formulating corrective measures to overcome them.

Further Reading

Lipina, S. and Segretin, S. (2015) "Strengths and Weaknesses of Neuroscientific Investigations of Childhood Poverty: Future directions". *Frontiers in Human Neuroscience* 9: pp. 53.

Lombera, S. and Illes, J. (2009) "The International Dimensions of Neuroethics". *Developing World Bioethics* 9(2), 57–64.

Salles, A. (2014) "Neuroethics in a Psy World: The Case of Argentina". *Cambridge Quarterly of Healthcare Ethics* 23(3), 297–307.

Shook, J. and Giordano, J. (2014) "A Principled and Cosmopolitan Neuroethics: Considerations for International Relevance". *Philosophy, Ethics, and Humanities in Medicine* 9(1): pp. 1–13.

References

Amoroso, C. (2014) Un país medicado: creció mas del 100% la venta de clonazepam. *La Nación*, 14 November. Available at: www.lanacion.com.ar/1743846-un-pais-medicado-crecio-mas-de-100-la-venta-de-clonazepam. [Accessed 23 Feb. 2016].

Bachrach, E. (2012) *Agilmente: Aprendé como funciona tu cerebro para potenciar tu creatividad y vivir mejor.* Buenos Aires: Editorial Sudamericana.

———. (2014) *EnCambio: Aprendé a midificar tu cerebro para cambiar tu vida y sentirte mejor.* Buenos Aires: Editorial Sudamericana.

Balan, M. (2011) Competition by denunciation: The political dynamics of corruption scandals in Argentina and Chile. *Comparative Politics* 43(4): pp. 459–478.

Bar, N. (2016) ¿Las neurociencias amenazan a la filosofía? *La Nación: Ideas*, 3 January, p. 6.

Bass, J. (2006) In exile from the self: National belonging and psychoanalysis in Buenos Aires. *Ethos* 34(4): pp. 433–455.

Buniak, L., Darragh, M., and Giordano, J. (2014) A four-part working bibliography of neuroethics: Part 1: Overview and reviews—Defining and describing the field and its practices. *Philosophy, Ethics and Humanities in Medicine* 9: p. 9.

Castelli, P. (2014) Algunas. Consideraciones sobre la apelación a la naturaleza en el debate ético sobre potenciación cognitiva. (unpublished manuscript).

Castelluccio, C. (2008) La responsabilidad en psicoanálisis es ética. *Psicoanálisis y el Hospital* 17(33): pp. 149–154.

Chen, D., and Quirion, R. (2011) From the internationalization to the globalization of neuroethics: Some perspectives and challenges. In J. Illes and B. Sahakian (Eds.). *The Oxford Handbook on Neuroethics*. New York: Oxford University Press, pp. 823–835.

Choudhury, S., Nagel, S., and Slaby, J. (2009) Critical neuroscience: Linking neuroscience and society through critical practice. *BioSocieties* 4: pp. 61–77.

Christen, M., Biller-Andorno, N., Bringedalb, B., Grimes, K., Savulescu, J., and Walter, H. (2016) Ethical challenges of simulation-driven big neuroscience. *American Journal of Bioethics Neuroscience* 7(1): pp. 1–13.

Dagfal, A. (2009) *Entre París y Buenos Aires: La invención del psicólogo*. Buenos Aires: PAIDOS.

Escobar, M.J., Huepe, D., Decety, J., Sedeño L., Messow, M.K., Baez S., . . . Ibáñez, A. (2014) Brain signatures of moral sensitivity in adolescents with early social deprivation *Scientific Reports* 4: pp. 1–8.

Evans, D. (2005) From Lacan to Darwin. In J. Gottschall and D. Sloan Wilson (Eds.). *The Literary Animal: Evolution and the Nature of Narrative*. Evanston, IL: Northwestern University Press, pp. 38–55.

Evers, K. (2015) Can we be epigenetically proactive? In T. Metzinger and J.M. Windt (Eds.). *Open MIND*. Frankfurt am Main: MIND Group, pp. 497–518. doi:10.15502/9783958570238

Faigenbaum, G. Lucher, M. Calero, C., and Sigman, M. (under review in *Child Development*) Children's implicit and Explicit Understanding of Theft.

Farah, M., and Hook, C.J. (2013) The seductive allure of "seductive allure." *Perspectives on Psychological Science* 8(1): pp. 88–90.

Farisco, M., Evers K., and Salles, A. (2016) Big science, brain simulation, and neuroethics. *American Journal of Bioethics Neuroscience* 7(1): pp. 1–2.

Fins, J. (2011) Neuroethics and the lure of technology. In J. Illes and B. Sahakian (Eds.). *The Oxford Handbook on Neuroethics*. New York: Oxford University Press, pp. 895–907.

Gleichgerrcht, E., Luttges, B., Salvarezza, F., and Campos, A.L. (2015) Educational neuromyths among teachers in Latin America. *Mind, Brain, and Education* 9(3): pp. 170–178.

Golombek, D. (2008) *Aprender y enseñar ciencias: de laboratorio al aula y viceversa*. Buenos Aires: Fundación Santillana.

———. (2011) *Cavernas y palacios: En busca de la conciencia en el cerebro*. Buenos Aires: Siglo Veintiuno.

———. (2014) *Las neuronas de Dios: Una neurociencia de la religion, la espiritualidad y la luz al final del tunnel*. Buenos Aires: Siglo Veintiuno.

Gorga, M. (2013) El trastorno por deficit de atención con hiperactividad y el mejoramiento cognitivo. ¿Cuál es la responsabilidad del médico?" *Revista Bioética* 21(2): pp. 241–150.

Gorga, M., and Lipina, S. (2015) El desarrollo neural y la pobreza desde el enfoque de las capacidades y los derechos humanos. (Unpublished manuscript).

Gracia, J. (1984) Philosophical analysis in Latin America. *History of Philosophy Quarterly* 1(1): pp. 111–122.

Henrich, J., Heine, S., and Norenzayan, A. (2010) The weirdest people in the world? *Behavioral and Brain Sciences* 33: pp. 61–135.

Hesse, E., Mikulan, E., Decety, J., Sigman, M., Garcia, M.D., Silva, W., . . . Ibánez, A. (2015) Early detection of intentional harm in the human amygdala. *Brain*. 139(1): pp. 54–61.

Hollander, N.C. (1990) Buenos Aires: Latin mecca of psychoanalysis. *Social Research* 57(4): pp. 889–919.

Ibañez, A., and García, A.M. (2015) *Qué son las neurociencias?* Buenos Aires: Paidós.

Ibañez, A., Kuljis, R.O., Matallana, D., and Manes, F. (2014) Bridging psychiatry and neurology through social neuroscience. *World Psychiatry* 13(2): pp. 148–149.

Justo, L., and Erazun, F. (2007) Neuroethics and human rights. *American Journal of Bioethics* 7(5): pp. 16–17.

———. (2010) Neuroethics needs an international human rights deliberative frame. *American Journal of Bioethics Neuroscience* 1(4): pp. 17–18.

Kaiser, J., and Marshall, E. (2008) New minister raises expectations for science in Argentina. *Science* 321(5889): p. 622.

Kandel, E.R. (1999) Biology and the future of psychoanalysis: A new intellectual framework for psychiatry revisited. *American Journal of Psychiatry* 156(4): pp. 505–524.

Lakoff, A. (2003) The Lacan ward. *Social Analysis* 47(2): pp. 82–101.

Landau, E. (2013) In therapy? In Argentina, it's the norm. *CNN*. Available at: edition.cnn.com/2013/04/28/health/argentina-psychology-therapists/index.html [Accessed 19 July 2015].

Lipina, S., and Colombo, J. (2009) *Poverty and Brain Development During Childhood: An Approach From Cognitive Psychology and Neuroscience*. Washington, DC: American Psychological Association.

Lipina, S., Hermida, M., Segretin, M.S., and Colombo, J. (2011) Investigación en Pobreza Infantil desde Perspectivas Neurocognitivas. In S. Lipina and M. Sigman (Eds.). *La Pizarra de Babel: Puentes entre neurociencia, psicologia y educación*. Buenos Aires: Del Zorzal, pp. 243–265.

Lipina, S. (2014a) Biological and sociocultural determinants of neurocognitive development: Central aspects of the current scientific agenda. In *Bread and Brain, Education and Poverty*. Vatican City: Pontifical Academy of Sciences, Scripta Varia, p. 125.

———. (2014b) Consideraciones neuroéticas de la pobreza infantil. In A. Salles and K. Evers (Eds.). *La Vida Social del Cerebro*. Mexico, DF: Editorial Fontamara, pp. 67–102.

———. (2016) *Pobre Cerebro*. Buenos Aires: Siglo XXI Editores.

Lipina, S., and Segretin, S. (2015) Strengths and weaknesses of neuroscientific investigations of childhood poverty: Future directions. *Frontiers in Human Neuroscience* 9: p. 53.

Lipina, S., Segretin, S., Hermida, J., Prats, L., Fracchia, C., López Camelo, J., and Colombo, J. (2013) Linking childhood poverty and cognition: Environmental mediators of non verbal executive control in an Argentine sample. *Developmental Science* 16(5): pp. 697–707.

Lombardi, G. (2001) *El Psicoanálisis no es una neurociencia*. Available at: www.psi.uba.ar/academica/carrerasdegrado/psicologia/sitios_catedras/obligatorias/114_adultos1/material/archivos/noesneurociencia.pdf [Accessed 24 July 2015].

Lombera, S., and Illes, J. (2009) The international dimensions of neuroethics. *Developing World Bioethics* 9(2): pp. 57–64.

Madhusoodanan J. (2015) Bioethics accused of doing more harm than good. *Nature*. 524, 139, 13 August. Available at: www.nature.com/news/bioethics-accused-of-doing-more-harm-than-good-1.18128 [Accessed 16 Feb. 2016].

Manes, F., and Niro, M. (2014) *Usar el cerebro: Conocer nuestra mente para vivir mejor*. Buenos Aires: Planeta, libros del Zorzal.

———. (2016) *El cerebro argentino: una manera de pensar, dialogar y hacer un país mejor*. Buenos Aires: Planeta, libros del Zorzal.

Martinez, H. (2008) O psicoanálisis o neurociencias. *Psicoanálisis y el Hospital* 17(33): pp. 8–11.

Melo Martin, I., and Salles, A. (2015) Moral bioenhancement: Much Ado about nothing? *Bioethics* 29(4): pp. 223–232.

Morein-Zamir, S., and Sahakian, B. (2009) Neuroethics and public engagement training needed for neuroscientists. *Trends in Cognitive Sciences* 14(2): pp. 49–51.

Moscón, J. (2008) De un discurso . . . *Psicoanálisis y el Hospital* 17(33): pp. 12–14

Muñoz, P. (2008) Una polémica no tan actual. *Psicoanálisis y el Hospital* 17(33): pp. 59–62.

Musse, V. (2016) Aumentaron los delitos violentos contra las personas en la Capital. *La Nación*, 24 February. Available at: http://www.lanacion.com.ar/1873765-aumentaron-los-delitos-violentos-contra-las-personas-en-la-capital [Accessed 26 Feb. 2016].

Nino, C. (2005) *Un pais al margen de la ley*. 3rd ed. Buenos Aires: Ariel.

Pereda, C. (2006) Latin American philosophy: Some vices. *Journal of Speculative Philosophy* 20(3): pp. 192–203.

Perez, D., and Ortiz Millán, G. (2010) Analytic philosophy. In S. Nucctelli, O. Schutte, and O. Bueno (Eds.). *A Companion to Latin American Philosophy*. Malden, MA: Wiley-Blackwell, pp. 199–214.

Pinker, S. (2015) The moral imperative for bioethics. *Boston Globe*, 1 August. Available at: www.bostonglobe.com/opinion/2015/07/31/the-moral-imperative-for-bioethics/JmEkoyzlTAu9oQV76JrK9N/story.html [Accessed 16 Feb. 2016].

Plotkin, M.B. (2001) *Freud in the Pampas: The Emergence and Development of a Psychoanalytic Culture in Argentina*. Stanford: Stanford University Press.

Presidencia de la Nación. (2013) *Una mirada específica sobre la problemática del consumo de psicofármacos en Argentina 2012*. Available at: http://scripts.minplan.gob.ar/octopus/archivos.php?file=4272 [Accessed 23 Feb. 2016].

President's Council on Bioethics. (2014) *Grey Matters: Integrative Approaches for Neuroscience, Ethics and Society*. Available at: www.bioethics.gov/sites/default/files/Gray%20Matters%20Vol%201.pdf.

Roca M. (2015) The relationship between executive functions and theory of mind: A long and winding road. *Journal of Neurology Neurosurgery & Psychiatry* 87(3): pp. 231–234. [Online] 25 November.

Roca, M., Manes, F., Cetkovich, M., Bruno, D., Ibañez, A., Torralva, T., and Duncan, J. (2014) The relationship between executive functions and fluid intelligence in schizophrenia. *Frontiers in Behavioral Neuroscience* 8(46): pp. 1–8. doi:10.3389/fnbeh.2014.00046

Romero, S. (2012) Do Argentines need therapy? *The New York Times*, 18 August.

Rommelfanger, K., and Johnson, L.S. (2015) What lies ahead for neuroethics scholarship and education in light of the human brain projects? *American Journal of Bioethics Neuroscience* 6(1): pp. 1–3.

Rose, N. (2014) The human brain project: Social and ethical challenges. *Neuron* 82(6): pp. 1212–1215.

Salles, A. (2014) Neuroethics in a psy world: The case of Argentina. *Cambridge Quarterly of Healthcare Ethics* 23(3): pp. 297–307.

Salles, A., and Evers, K. (2014) *La vida social del cerebro*. Mexico, DF: Fontamara.

Salles, A., and Melo Martin, I. (2014) Como salvar a la humanidad: tomando una pastilla? In A. Salles and K. Evers (Eds.). *La vida social del cerebro*. Mexico: Editorial Fontamara, pp. 192–212.

Salvia, A. (Ed.) (2015) *Progresos sociales, pobrezas estructurales y desigualdades persistentes (2010–2014)*. Ciudad Autónoma de Buenos Aires: EDUCA.

———. (Ed.) (2016) Evaluación de la pobreza urbana desde un enfoque multidimensional basado en derechos 2010–2015. *Observador de la Deuda Social Argentina*. Available at: www.uca.edu.ar/uca/common/grupo68/files/2016-Obs-Informe-Pobreza-Multidimensional-2010-2015.pdf [Accessed 8 Aug. 2016].

Sigman, M. (2015) *La vida secreta de la mente*. Buenos Aires: Debate.

Sigman, M., Peña, M., Goldin, A.P., and Riberiro, S. (2014) Neuroscience and education: Prime time to build a bridge. *Nature Neuroscience* 17(4): pp. 497–502.

Slaby, J. (2010) Steps towards a *Critical Neuroscience*. *Phenomenology and the Cognitive Sciences* 9: pp. 397–416.

Smaglick, P. (2008) Argentina's pivotal moment. *Nature* 451: pp. 494–496.

Vogl, F. (2015) Latin America's real corruption crisis. *The Globalist*, 27 March.

Weisberg, D., Keil, F., Goodstein, J., Rwson, E. and Gray, J. (2008) The seductive allure of neuroscience explanation. *J Cogn Neurosci* 20(3): pp. 470–477.

29

NEUROETHICS IN JAPAN

Tamami Fukushi, Taichi Isobe, Eisuke Nakazawa,
Yoshiyuki Takimoto, Akira Akabayashi, Laura Specker
Sullivan, and Osamu Sakura

Introduction

It is often said that neuroethics as a discipline did not begin until 2000, although there are clear roots for the discipline much earlier (Illes and Bird, 2006). Ethical concerns about interventions into the brain are discernible in discussions on mental health, psychopharmacology, psychosurgery, and lobotomy. While current efforts at the forefront of neuroscience and neurology have focused this field, interest in neuroethical questions are diffuse and diverse.

It is true that as a *discipline*, neuroethics originated in the United States, Canada, and Europe and then spread outward. The Anglo-American world has been at the forefront of *defining, professionalizing*, and *funding* this field. Yet the basic ethical concerns that form the foundation of neuroethics—questions about who we are and how to protect this core being from harm—have been asked nearly universally. It is important to do justice to neuroethics as a conceptual space as much as a structured discipline. In this chapter, we focus on the development of neuroethics as a discipline in Japan and its interaction with Japanese conceptualizations of ethics as one particular example of the diversity of neuroethics worldwide.

As a discipline, Japan began to develop projects and rally funding for ethics in neuroscience in the mid-2000s (Fukushi et al., 2007). In 2005, the Research Institute of Science and Technology for Society (RISTEX), Japan Science and Technology Agency (JST) launched a neuroethics research group in conjunction with a cohort study of early childhood development. The goals of the study were to better understand childhood development in sociability (defined as the ability to understand and interact well with others) and to develop educational programs that would contribute to increased sociability.[1] Sociability is discussed in the study report in terms of praise, blame, and social approval. The project consisted of not only epidemiological studies but also behavioral observation and neuroimaging studies of children of ages 0 to 3 and 5 to 8 who were from several cities in Japan. The neuroethics research group was tasked to ensure protection of the rights of the participants (of both children and their parental guardians) and to assist in the ethical implementation of a carefully considered research protocol (Yamagata et al., 2010).

This project is significant for neuroethics in Japan not only because it was one of the first nationally supported neuroethics groups but also because of what it reveals about how neuroethics is conceptualized in Japan. First, the ethical aspect of the study is not so much its implications; rather, the study itself takes a normative perspective: children ought to be able to interact with others in ways that garner social approval. Neuroscience is then harnessed as a means to reach this normative goal. This point is not lost on JST-RISTEX, which described the aims of this project, under the heading of "Brain-Science and Society," as "social problems that need to be solved."

Second, the published report for this particular study[2] suggests that neuroethics was incorporated due to the general concern that the study itself could affect the children's development of sociability in negative ways (Yamagata et al., 2010). So understood, the neuroethics question raised is whether neuroscientists have a responsibility for the development of the children in the study. This also has farther-reaching implications for childcare in Japan. The report also suggests that scientists have an obligation to clearly convey their research to the public.

As the first case of neuroethics as a discipline being incorporated into Japanese research, this study also highlights a number of conceptual features of neuroethics in Japan that accord with general features of Japanese bioethics and of East Asian ethics more broadly. The first is that implicit ethical considerations are often social. They are about how well groups of people work together more than about specific individuals' responsibility for certain acts (Watsuji, 1996; Lock, 2002; Kasulis, 2002; McCarthy, 2010). This is not unique to Japan. Scholars have noted that while autonomy is championed in Anglo-American bioethics, East Asian bioethics tends to focus on the well-being of specific groups such as families (Fan, 1997; Tsai, 1999; Akabayashi and Slingsby, 2006). While the distinction should not be drawn too strongly—families are important cultural units in North America and Europe as well—the ethical *discourse* in East Asia has focused more on groups than on individuals (whether particular practices manifest this discourse is another question).

The second feature is that ethics is often premised on affective responses—it is important for situations to feel right (Kasulis, 2002; McCarthy, 2010; Nagaoka, 2012). As we discuss in what follows, the backdrop for this feature is a different approach toward the mind–body relationship than the dualism often seen in Anglo-American discourse.

Finally, the third feature of bioethics in East Asia is that, despite ethical issues being determined socially and affectively, they are described in language more common in Western ethical frameworks—thus the emphasis on "responsibility" in the report of the childhood development study (Feldman, 2000; Becker, 2014; Specker Sullivan, 2016). These underlying conceptual features of Japanese ethics affect how neuroethics is discussed and practiced as a discipline with particular institutional requirements and normative commitments.

The mission of the neuroethics research group involved in the childhood development study was not restricted to ensuring the ethical practice of the study alone. They were also tasked with promoting neuroethics to various stakeholders in Japan and Asia. To achieve this mission, the JST-RISTEX neuroethics research group organized a variety of events including interdisciplinary dialogue and public engagement. The group organized a workshop series—open to the public—entitled "Brain-Science and Society" from 2005 to 2007, in which professionals from various academic research fields (e.g., bioethics, neuroscience, developmental psychology, education, philosophy, neuropsychiatry, epidemiology, and science communication) were invited to discuss their experiences or concerns about neuroscience and to determine how various stakeholders could communicate and collaborate to work for better practice of neuroscience and neuroethics. In July 2006, the group also organized the first international neuroethics symposium in Asia in which leading neuroethics researchers and stakeholders from the United States participated as speakers.[3]

In the academic context, they expanded the discussion of neuroethics into East Asian regions through co-organizing academic sessions as part of various international conferences (Sakura et al., 2007; Wu et al., 2009) and giving invited talks at the conferences held in eastern Asian regions in both ethics and neuroscience,[4] which encouraged Asian researchers to engage with neuroethics in their work (Ong et al., 2009; Wu and Fukushi, 2012). In addition to the collaborative activities with various research fields, the group also worked to apply ethical practices to neuroscience research in Japan. For example, they proposed revising the guidelines for neuroscience research on human brain function based on bioethical principles to protect human subjects[5] (Beauchamp and Childress, 2001; Fukushi et al., 2007) and established protocols for handling incidental findings in pediatric research using brain-imaging technology (Seki et al., 2009). These practices[6] were passed on to the next generation after JST-RISTEX closed the neuroethics research group at the end of the cohort research project in 2009.

A second example of the development of neuroethics as a discipline in Japan is the Strategic Research Program for Brain Sciences (SRPBS), which was established by the Ministry of Education, Culture, Sports, Science and Technology (MEXT) in 2008. SRPBS set up a neuroethics research group to support research on human brain function and to facilitate the public understanding of brain research, an example of ethics engagement interpreted as public engagement (Specker Sullivan and Illes, 2017). Briefly, SRPBS covers various neuroscience projects and research including brain–machine interfaces (BMI). BMI connects the human brain with a machine or computer that can change the physical body's neural signals to motor commands and can duplicate, for instance, reaching and holding activities with an artificial machine (Lebedev and Nicolelis, 2006). This technology is crucial for rehabilitative and medical applications and has attracted tremendous attention worldwide. Significant financial resources have been allocated for it in Japan. However, as in other countries that have pursued BMI research, neuroethical and social problems are attendant with their use, such as concerns about the safety of those technologies, challenges to the autonomy of the patient, potential for enhancement of future users, and nonclinical use of the BMI, such as for military use. The research initiative of "Novel and Innovative R&D Making Use of Brain Structure" funded by the Ministry of Internal Affairs and Communications (MIC) supported a bioethics research group that was tasked to create ethical guidelines for progress in BMI research and to identify the social implications of this work.

Since 2012, additional efforts including BMI research collaboration between psychiatry and neuroethics are also being implemented by the Japan MEXT research project entitled "Adolescent Mind & Self-Regulation".[7] This project exhibits interesting similarities and differences to the initial child development project in 2005. As with that earlier project, it focuses on development (in this case, adolescents). While much of the earlier language of sociability is missing, it emphasizes the importance of regulating one's own mind and ego for mental health and suggests that a major element of this regulation is social reciprocity. Here again, the conceptual commitments underlying Japanese neuroethics are apparent.

These conceptual commitments are not necessarily unique. Rather, approaches to ethics exist on a spectrum, with some cultures emphasizing individuality and rationality and others focusing on community and affectivity. This has been described as "integrity" versus "intimacy" frameworks for ethics (Kasulis, 2002). We suggest that focusing on neuroethical perspectives from those cultures at the latter end of the spectrum can shed light on some previously unrecognized aspects of neuroethics, both as a discipline and as a set of ethical questions.

One example of this interplay between conceptual and disciplinary concerns in neuroethics is the conceptualization of "mind" and the debate on brain death in East Asia. For example, in Japan, there is no specific word for "mind". There is a character for "brain": 脳 (nō). Yet the character often used for "mind," 心 (kokoro; this is the same character used in Chinese), means mind-heart-spirit; the three terms are not thought of as separate. Kokoro is the root of rational words, such as (心得; kokoro-e), and affective words, such as (心強い; kokoro-dzuyoi). This reflects philosopher Yasuo Yuasa's observation that the mind–body dualism so entrenched in Anglo-American thought is not reflected in Japanese conceptual structures. For Japanese thought, a person is not so much a consciousness through time but a conscious body in space (Yuasa, 1987).

The influence of this view on neuroethics in Asia can be seen in the Japanese discussion on brain death.[8] Following a controversial heart transplant by a physician in Sapporo from a brain-dead donor in 1968, no heart transplants were performed until 1997, when a stringent law allowing organ donation after brain death was passed. A laxer, revised law was passed in 2010, but declarations of brain death are still not common in Japan (Fukue, 2010). While the reasons for low numbers of organ donations from brain-dead patients are complex—including mistrust of physicians, institutional limits on choices, and a view of death as a social process—the irreducibility of the mind–body concept is also one of them (Feldman, 2000; Lock, 2002; Long, 2005).

These are just some of the examples of how a cross-cultural study of neuroethics can deepen understanding of the field. In the remainder of this chapter, neuroethics activities in Japan are described by researchers from Japan, focusing on the activities of neuroethics research in the SRPBS as well as the BMI Network Project funded by the MIC. We report on these activities as emerging from a particular complex web of institutions, policies, norms, and practices that together comprise neuroethics in East Asia. We are still gaining greater understanding of how these cultural frameworks may map onto questions in neuroethics (Adam et al., 2015; Sato, 2011; Tsai, 1999; Yang et al., 2015), so this research is an ongoing area of inquiry (Sakura, 2012). Thus, the following considerations of each activity related to neuroethics in Japan will not always reflect all Asian cultural perspectives.

Ethics of Neuroscience: The Progress in Japan

Strategic Research Program for Brain Sciences in Japan

The Strategic Research Program for Brain Sciences (SRPBS) is a collaborative research project launched in 2008 as a program of the Ministry of Education, Culture, Sports, Science and Technology (MEXT) to develop neuroscience that benefits society.[9] The SRPBS project is a problem-solving, top-down research project. It is implemented under a policy determined by the governmental brain science committee comprising accomplished members including brain science researchers, bioethics researchers, and journalists who comprehensively investigate and review issues related to the development, promotion, and evaluation of brain science research plans established under MEXT's Council for Science and Technology. It involves various research targets, including the development of a BMI, animal models, and treatments for psychiatric disorders such as developmental disorders, depression, and dementia. To date, more than 40 research groups from Japanese universities, research institutions, and corporations have participated in the SRPBS. Some groups have focused on basic medical research, and others have conducted clinical investigations using data from routine consultations with patients. Both basic research and clinical research groups work cooperatively toward targets to meet the needs of society, including the development of new treatments for refractory psychiatric disorders, improvement of quality of life for patients with serious neurological disorders, and so on.

The SRPBS is characterized by cooperation among diverse stakeholders. In considering the objectives of the SRPBS, the presence of research groups specializing in ethical issues in the SRPBS is considered a critical part of the effort. Two groups have engaged in research and development since 2008: "Cranial Nerve Ethics in Regard to BMIs and Research on the Legal Framework," led by one of the coauthors of this chapter, Osamu Sakura, and "Solving the Ethical Issues in Neuroscience Research," which was initially led by Akira Akabayashi and is now led by Yoshiyuki Takimoto (both coauthors of this chapter). Some of the issues tackled by the group have included regulating incidental findings in fMRI studies, revising informed consent formats for vulnerable psychiatric-disorder patients, facilitating data-sharing methods especially in the case of sharing sensitive clinical data, and setting ethical conditions for first-in-human trials of new therapies based on neuroscientific technologies.

The specific initiatives of these bioethics-related groups in the SRPBS framework can be divided into three categories: support for researchers, ethics education, and research on research ethics. In the category of support for researchers, initiatives include a quality-control service for informed consent procedures. This consultation service supports neuroscience researchers with ethical issues they encounter daily in human-subjects research. In addition, the SRPBS operates an ethics consultation office that can be visited by neuroscience researchers. The office holds meetings with young neuroscientists at the clinical frontlines to facilitate discussion and information sharing. In the category of ethics education, with the overall objective of enhancing the quality of Japanese research ethics review procedures, seminars on research ethics are organized for research ethics committee members and coordinators. In the category of research on research ethics, both literature studies and investigations have been conducted on various themes including the ethics of BMIs, ethical issues with incidental findings in brain-imaging studies, the protection of vulnerable subjects enrolled in psychiatric studies, biobank studies and broad consent, and the ethics of neurofeedback from the viewpoints of mind control and safety.

One product of these efforts is the development of the guideline for BMI technologies in Japan. The guidelines, elaborated by Sakura and Kawato in 2010, describe the conditions required for developing BMI technologies. These guidelines have four components: BMI technologies (1) cannot be used for war or criminal objectives, (2) cannot involve involuntary mind reading, (3) cannot involve involuntary mind control, and (4) must ensure that BMI users can judge that the benefits surpass the costs and risks of using BMI. These guidelines are called "the four laws of BMI technology," in homage to the "Three Laws of Robotics" that Isaac Asimov detailed in his story "Runaround" (1950). The formulation of the BMI guidelines involved conversations with ethicists and BMI researchers and so reflects some of the attitudes of pioneering researchers in BMI. This effort set a precedent as a productive format for collaborations between ethicists, medical professionals, and neuroengineers.

Another area of focus is the ethics of incidental findings in brain-imaging studies. This issue has been the focus of many years of effort worldwide (Underwood, 2012). The SRPBS bioethics group conducted an investigation on this issue by collecting views of neuroscientists and the general population and then generated a recommendation based on the results: physicians who are associated with the research study should check all MRI images acquired from basic research studies to address health problems, if any, appropriately. This recommendation was integrated into the SRPBS comprehensive guidelines (Fujita et al., 2014).

These studies were all conducted in close collaboration with neuroscientists involved in clinical research. The SRPBS is a unique type of project in Japan that serves to connect neuroscientists not only with other neuroscientists but also with neuroethicists. Even if the most important task of the SRPBS bioethics group is to support researchers, the group has further potential to expand its efforts in providing guidance for projects on research ethics and, further, providing ethics education and consultation.

Communication and Outreach of Neuroethics in SRPBS

During 2008 to 2010, a subset of Sakura's group in SRPBS investigated and managed ethical, legal, and social implications– (ELSI–) related issues in neuroscience research and developed communication strategies with the general public. The role of the ELSI team was not to deal with ethical issues in the SRPBS project but to encourage communication among researchers of SRPBS and provide venues to address questions in their work that emerge at the intersection of neuroscience and ethics. In addition, the team created forums and opportunities for community outreach to facilitate identification and discussion of the potential ethical concerns with emerging technologies; the goal of this effort is to facilitate consensus building on how current and emerging neuroscience research should be used in the near future. Organizers, who included some of the authors of this chapter, developed case studies from various investigations and also hosted activities such as symposia, science cafés, and workshops. The team created these activities for two reasons. One is to encourage communication among researchers in the SRPBS project, thus boosting mutual understanding and relations of trust among researchers and promoting BMI research. The other is to encourage communication and transparency about the SRPBS project with the general public so as to develop accountability to society and build a good relationship between the project researchers and the public. Considering recent science policy in Japan, large national projects such as "Research Center Network of Realization of Regenerative Medicine" and "Tailor-made Medical Treatment Program (BioBank Japan: BBJ)" have ELSI teams that promote public outreach efforts. The fourth Science and Technology Basic Plan (approved by the Cabinet on August 19, 2011) emphasized the necessity of public outreach in science, and in response, academic researchers have worked to create opportunities for science outreach. There have been some obstacles, such as little time for science outreach activities.[10] Nevertheless, this public outreach is especially important in Japan, which has seen several recent cases of researcher misconduct that may negatively affect the public's trust of scientific research (Slingsby et al., 2006). Most recent was a widely covered 2014 case in which a researcher reported the development of Stimulus-Triggered Acquisition of Pluripotency (STAP) cells (similar to induced pluripotent stem cells or iPS but allegedly easier to create) in two papers in *Nature*. After attempts to replicate the studies failed, the researcher was found guilty of scientific misconduct in both this study and her dissertation from Waseda University in Tokyo. The aftermath of the scandal led to the suicide of the coauthor on the papers, who was also one of the founding leaders of RIKEN Center for Developmental Biology, where the research took place.[11] As a result, MEXT issued a revised set of guidelines for research integrity holding institutions responsible for the misconduct of their scientists.[12]

Thus, in Japan, it may be especially important for researchers to work on public outreach. Neuroethicists affiliated with SRPBS did this in a number of ways. First, for the purpose of outreach, researchers published newsletters targeting neuroscience researchers who participated in SRPBS. These introduced the ELSI of neuroscience and included summaries of ethics activities and upcoming conference information. This newsletter was given to neuroscience researchers at academic conferences and small meetings in SRPBS. In personal communications with neuroscience researchers in SRPBS, they responded favorably, stating that the newsletter provided useful information on ELSI–related issues.

At symposia and workshops for the general public, researchers had opportunities to investigate public perceptions of the risks and benefit of neuroscience research (Isobe, 2010). These symposia and workshops create opportunities for researchers of SRPBS to communicate with the general public. The purpose of the investigation was to assess public perceptions about BMI. From this investigation, researchers identified the kinds of ethical concerns the general public has with neurotechnologies and the reasons why they perceive these issues as concerning. Some prompts for the survey included questions about "daily use of neuroscience", "future possibility of enhancement and rehabilitation", "necessity for medical application", and "need for science communication for the general public". The researchers also compared perceptions of BMI researchers and the general public.

In addition, the researchers held science cafés with SRPBS neuroscientists. In these contexts, ELSI and neuroscience researchers had the opportunity to translate complex neuroscientific findings to café participants from the general public. Furthermore, ELSI researchers facilitated interactive discussions between café participants and scientists. Cafes afford unique opportunities for neuroscience researchers to better understand the interpretation of data as well as associated concerns and hopes that the general public may have for the neuroscience.

Finally, the researchers conducted a deliberative workshop with the general public, designed to clarify risks and benefits of BMI in the near future (Isobe et al., 2013). Participants included professionals, homemakers, and college students. The researchers analyzed the concerns that emerged from the discussions and found important themes of concern, such as "issues about the long-term uses," "concerns based on the discussants lived experience," and "having an easy life," for example. One participant in a workshop mentioned the category of "concerns based on the discussants' lived experience". His mother had a brain infarct, and he hoped BMI would help him communicate with his mother. The response to the concern category "having an easy life" was diverse: some regarded the use of BMIs for enhancements (using BMI technology can raise some human abilities) as lazy, whereas others regarded such use as desirable. These responses were roughly related with participants' stage in life. The group of professionals regarded BMI enhancement as lazy, while the group of college students regarded BMI enhancement as desirable.

BMI Network Project Funded by the Ministry of Internal Affairs and Communications

Currently, the Ministry of Internal Affairs and Communications (MIC) of Japan is conducting a research project that includes the stipulation of an MIC guideline for ethical issues involved in BMI studies. The MIC is in charge of policies related to information and communications and the promotion of an initiative entitled the "Novel and Innovative R&D Making Use of Brain Structure". This initiative focuses on the development of a network-type BMI. A network-type BMI would facilitate the daily use of BMIs in the living environment. The implementation of such a technology could enable daily appliances including televisions, air conditioners, and pedestrian-control signals to be controlled without physical actions such as pushing a button on a remote control, thus improving quality of life for the aged and physically challenged, and relieving nurses' workloads. This technology enables user control via a network of movement-assisted or communication-assisted equipment. For the aged and physically challenged, the networked BMI could function across environments such as a living room, bedroom, kitchen, garden, park, crosswalk, or even a train-station elevator. Portable decoding devices and cloud computing systems would allow users to control daily appliances mentally. This innovative feature would be enabled by the combination of three elements: BMI technology, information-communications technology, and social infrastructure.

Development of this network-type BMI requires proper handling of social and ethical issues from an early stage. Therefore, the principal developer of the network-type BMI, Advanced Telecommunications Research Institute International, voluntarily organized a bioethics group that formulated its own ethical guidelines. Members of the bioethics group included not only ethicists and philosophers but also BMI researchers, lawyers, information-communication technology researchers, and people in charge of the information-communication corporations. After numerous meetings, the bioethics group presented specific recommendations in 2015 in a document entitled "Ethical Guidelines for Basic Research into Network-type BMIs." The document is currently in preparation. This guideline supplements the government-led medical research guideline, "Ethical Guidelines for Medical and Health Research Involving Human

Subjects." The government-led guideline provides general principles with a wide range of scope rather than specific handling directions for individual research domains. In contrast, the "Ethical Guideline for Basic Research into Network-type BMIs" focuses particularly on the use of networks, covering data management and the protection of personal information in detail. These issues are absent in previous ethical guidelines on medical research. An ethical guideline covering medical and industrial alliance research has never been established in Japan, so in that regard, "Ethical Guidelines for Basic Research into Network-type BMIs" is a significant milestone.

The attempt to formulate the "Ethical Guidelines for Basic Research into Network-type BMIs" deserves special mention as an example of researchers' voluntary formulation of ethical guidelines for their own research. These guidelines differ from those proposed by the government and funding organizations that are imposed on researchers and highlight the necessity of ethics in neuroscience research. While a practical solution to the ethical issues accompanying neuroscience research is dependent largely on governmental initiatives, collaborative efforts among neuroscientists, philosophers and ethicists, and lawyers can be as practically effective as top-down regulations. The bottom-up approach also provides an opportunity for neuroscientists to explore ethical questions embedded in their own research, empowering scientists to be ethical stewards of their work.

Ethical Practice of Deep Brain Stimulation for Psychiatric Disorders in Japan

Currently there are hundreds of ongoing clinical trials using deep brain stimulation (DBS) techniques around the world, and approximately one-third of them are for psychiatric treatment.[13] Many are carried out in North America and European countries, but considerable numbers of trials take place in China and the Middle East.[14] This trend indicates that DBS is now a well-distributed medical technology, and ongoing trials may provide useful information to improve DBS procedures for psychiatric patients in terms of safety and efficacy. Indeed, the representatives of international societies regarding neurosurgery and psychiatry fields have recently developed consensus guidelines for stereotactic neurosurgery for psychiatric disorders (Nuttin et al., 2014). However, unlike other countries that have advanced research in this area, whether DBS is acceptable for psychiatric disorders is still up for debate in Japan. The slow progress of psychiatric DBS in Japan might be attributed to avoidance of any kinds of surgical approaches to psychiatric disease for the Japanese community. The lobotomy procedure was eliminated from clinical care in Japan in the 1970s because of insufficient efficacy and progress of drug treatment, in addition to inadequate informed consent and protections of patients (Kai, 2012; Nakano-Okuno, 2008).[15] Since the adoption of a resolution to prohibit psychosurgery in the annual meeting of the Japanese Society of Psychiatry and Neurology in 1975, where exhaustive discussion was made among psychiatric researchers and physicians, any kind of neurosurgical treatment has been avoided for the treatment of mental illness.[16] Less-invasive stimulation methods, like electroconvulsive therapy (ECT), have been widely accepted by the psychiatric community for decades. Nevertheless, technological development, especially the progress of creating highly advanced electrodes for brain–machine interface, has grown in Japan in recent years, and researchers in Japan expect to apply such electrodes for new therapeutic procedures for a wide range of neurological and neuropsychiatric disorders.

Through governmental programs to advance neuromodulation technology, various types of next-generation electrodes, such as tissue-comfortable brain-surface microelectrodes (Hirata, 2011), electrode array devices with complementary metal–oxide–semiconductor (CMOS) multichip architecture (Noda et al., 2012), flexible and stretchable electrodes (White et al., 2013),

Si opto-neural probes (Kanno et al., 2013), and cortical electrodes specified for individual subjects (Morris et al., 2015) have been developed. Hirata's group also developed a wireless brain–machine interface system to prevent the risk of infections induced by electrode implantation.

Alongside these technological developments, the safety and efficacy of the electronic/medical devices, including applications for DBS, have been discussed by the research community and ministries in Japan (for detailed information, see Takagi, 2012; Fukushi, 2012). The Ministry of Economy, Trade, and Industry (METI) and the Ministry of Health, Labour, and Welfare (MHLW) collaboratively organized a working group to discuss the future of regulatory criteria for advanced neuromodulation technologies. A variety of members from different communities, such as neurosurgery, neurophysiology, rehabilitation, and neuroengineering were invited to the working group and then discussed how to determine the safety criteria of medical devices for neuromodulation. Based on their discussion, METI published technical guidelines for research and development of neural implantation for possible expansion of target disorders to which DBS may be applied.[17] In addition, MHLW developed "Guidance for the Evaluation of Emerging Technology Medical Devices" (PFSB/ELD/OMDE Notification No. 1215 dated December 15, 2010),[18] which stipulated guidelines for the evaluation of medical devices for modification of neural function, such as rTMS, cortical stimulation for motor function recovery, artificial vision, spinal cord stimulation, vagus nerve stimulation, and BMI. While METI's guidelines focused on the technical standard and criteria of the stimulator itself, the guidelines developed by the MHLW determined more practical requirements to ensure the safety of patients during clinical care, as well as to provide for future consultation and review for marketing authorization conducted by the Pharmaceutical and Medical Devices Agency.

Additional discussions on the technical and practical issues of applications of DBS or other neuromodulation technologies for psychiatric patients are in progress in Japan, along with investigations of the social, ethical, and legal issues associated with utilizing such technologies.

In 2012, Japanese Society of Mood Disorders published a guidance paper regarding the treatment of bipolar disorder (Kanba et al., 2013). DBS was not introduced as a possible treatment option in this paper because it was not covered by national health insurance due to no relevant clinical evidence. However, a committee for the treatment guidelines of mood disorders of the Japanese Society of Mood Disorders suggested that "electroconvulsive therapy can be considered in drug resistance cases as an alternative therapy" and that the guidelines may be updated when additional studies arise. The neuropsychiatric community in Japan recognizes the progress of neurostimulation for patients with mood disorders. In the same year, researchers, neurosurgeons, and psychiatric communities in Japan initiated face-to-face discussions about neurostimulation at an academic conference (Taira, 2012). In 2014, the Japan Society for Stereotactic and Functional Neurosurgery developed a working group to discuss how to advance research on DBS for psychiatric disorders aimed at creating an approved medical device treatments in Japan. This discussion also included plans to translate consensus guidelines from international societies for stereotactic and functional neurosurgery (Nuttin et al., 2014) into Japanese as educational material. Neuroethics communities in Japan have an important role to play in participating in such conversations and to help explore scientific and regulatory components of given issues with an ethical lens and minimize potential future harms (while maximizing benefits) associated with utilizing such technologies.

Perspectives on the Future of Neuroethics in Japan and East Asia

As described in the introduction, neuroethics as a disciplinary framework was introduced to Japan in the middle of the 2000s mainly from English-speaking countries, especially North

America (for details, see also Fukushi et al., 2007). This galvanized a number of governmentally supported initiatives for funding neuroethics research in conjunction with existing neuroscientific projects, such as a study of childhood neurological development (SPPBS), the creation of BMIs (Network BMI), and the exploration of DBS as a clinical tool. In addition, some philosophers of mind launched research projects that tried to bridge the humanities and neurosciences (Nobuhara et al., 2010; Nakayama and Nobuhara, 2013). Neuroethics also became one of the topics in the program for the specialists in research centers of neurosciences, including the RIKEN Brain Science Institute. Numerous symposia and publications on neuroethics have also been executed and distributed (Nobuhara and Hara, 2008; Ohtake et al., 2013).

While there has been significant progress and integration of neuroethics in science and clinical policy in some dimensions of the projects listed, neuroethics as a separate academic discipline in the university setting has been slower to take root. We speculate on the reasons next.

First, programs and courses for the training of specialists in neuroethics were not established in Japan; consequently it is quite hard to get a PhD researching topics in neuroethics. This is not unlike the U.S., where students do not formally get PhDs in neuroethics but may do graduate work related to neuroethics. In Japan, this situation may result from features of the graduate schools or PhD courses in Japanese college systems, in which professors do not select PhD candidates based on their research interests. Graduate students in Japan are selected through entrance examinations that are managed by each department or school. This system can constrain work addressing emergent fields of research because it requires changing the whole system of entrance examinations to cover new areas. In other words, the forces of institutional inertia are so strong that it makes the college system slow to adapt to new research fields. For example, the number of graduate schools that have independent PhD courses for bioethics (not neuroethics) is fewer than 10 in Japan, even though such programs are common in other countries.

Second, neuroethics as a discipline with specific institutional, financial, and normative commitments was adapted from neuroethics in North America and Europe. It may be easier in these areas than in Japan for scholars to move from the discipline in which they were trained into an interdisciplinary space. While there are many neuroscientists in Japan who are concerned about ethical aspects of their work and support neuroethics activities, they are within the neuroscience community. It is quite rare in Japan for scholars, like some of the neuroethicists in North America, to move from neuroscience into neuroethics. Even the strategy of governance and management of the whole field of neuroethics, which assumes North American institutions and funding structures as well as Anglo-American conceptual frameworks, might present challenges to the further development of neuroethics in Japan. Scientific activities in academia are strongly managed by the corresponding ministries and departments of the government of Japan, and so there is less flexibility and infrastructure for experts in neuroethics to take part in decisions concerning policy making. There have been several developments in neuroscience in Japan that directed the public's attention to neuroscience, that is, huge numbers of appearances of "pop" neuroscientists in mass media and the explosive rise of popularity in video games promoting neuroscientific ideas, so-called brain games (Mizushima and Sakura, 2012; Sakura, 2012). "Brain games" usually consist of several series of quiz games, supervised by a medical professor of neuroscience, and advertise their positive effects on brain function. However, academic considerations on those phenomena have been limited to the activities of individual researchers, and there has not been coordinated research activity. Further, discussions of the ethical considerations of these technologies has not reached public forums or policy makers.

The neuroethics movement in Japan brought quite rich opportunities for funding to bioethicists and philosophers in a new area of ethical inquiry and certainly affected the communities of neuroscientists, bioethicists, philosophers of mind, and science studies. It is hard to evaluate whether the impacts will be great enough to establish neuroethics as its own discipline, as in North America and Europe. Currently, neuroethics is not regarded as an established research discipline with its own training, research, and publishing activities. Some philosophers and medical ethicists who were originally engaged in related issues before the adoption of the language of neuroethics around 2000 succeeded in enhancing their own research activities by engaging with neuroscientists. However, the field in Japan and collaborations across East Asia are still in their infancy. Time will tell how neuroethics research and practices will develop and what influence they will have on neuroscience and the humanities in Japan.

There are some signs that neuroethics activities in Japan are developing beyond these early stages. In April 2016, the Japanese government announced the launch of the Artificial Intelligence Technology Strategy Council to advance research and development of artificial intelligence (AI) technology including neuroscience.

JST-RISTEX launched a new research-and-development funding program to promote designing coevolution platforms regarding social system and AI/Internet of Things (IoT) technologies.[19] In addition, RIKEN, one of the largest research institutes of neuroscience and information technology in Japan, also established a new research center called the "Center for Advanced Integrated Intelligence Research".[20] The center currently plans to establish a research team working on ELSI of AI as well as the advanced research teams for AI technologies.[21] These trends attract new talents even beyond those involved in the "first wave" of neuroethics, for example, ethicists focusing on engineering ethics, information ethics, and roboethics. The future activity of the research project in both JST-RISTEX and RIKEN will be critical to whether a "second wave" of neuroethics emerges in Japan.

Beyond Japan, interest in neuroethics as a structure for organizing, funding, and promoting research at the intersection of ethics and neuroscience has steadily grown in East Asia. For example, the Bioethics Advisory Committee Singapore published a consultation paper entitled "Ethical, Legal and Social Issues in Neuroscience Research" in 2013. The Committee abstracted from neuroethics practices from the UK and North America to develop the consultation paper, and their scope of discussion was broad, including stem cell research and neuropharmaceuticals.[22] Similarly, researchers in India recently published a research paper regarding categorization of ethical approaches in neuroscience using PubMed information (Shrivastava and Behari, 2015). Iranian researchers have begun to discuss neuroethics and have published reviews of the history of neuroethics by referencing American, British, and Japanese articles (Jameie, 2013).

We believe that expanding the neuroethics research community into areas beyond North America and Europe will enable researchers to analyze different ways of conceptualizing the intersection of ethics and neuroscience and of developing neuroethics as its own discipline. As we discuss in the introduction, while neuroethics as a discipline is a relatively recent phenomenon, questions about ethics in neuroscience have been surfacing in academic communities for quite some time. Developing neuroethics activities in these new locations will not only bring funding, organization, and support to researchers interested in these questions; it will also give voice to their particular conceptual and practical approaches to ethics engagement with neuroscience, bringing much-needed diversity to a field that asks important questions about who we are as humans.

Notes

1 www.ristex.jp/EN/past/brain/index.html
2 http://ristex.jst.go.jp/result/brain/plan/pdf/ind05.pdf (in Japanese)
3 1st International Workshop of Neuroethics in Japan: Dialogue on Brain, Society, and Ethics. 07/22/2006, Tokyo, Japan

4 Fukushi, T. (2009) Neuroethics in Japan, Asia, and Beyond. *Abstract of the 3rd Neuroethics Forum— Korean & Japanese Experience.* 59–81; Fukushi, T. (2009) Neuroethics in Japan, Asia, and Beyond. *Abstract of Neuroscience of ethics and decision making: Philosophy, ethics, and policy issues of "seeing the mind".* 25–38; Fukushi, T. and Sakura, O. (2007) Towards a good future of science research, society, and their relationship: necessity and possibility of ethics education in neuroscience research community in Japan. *Report of UNESCO-UNU Bioethics Roundtable*; 4. Fukushi, T. and Sakura, O. (2006) Current status of neuroethics in Japan. *UNESCO Asia-Pacific Conference on Bioethics Education Abstract.* 54.

5 Autonomy, Beneficence, Nonmaleficence and Justice. For more details, see Beauchamp T. L. and Childress J. F. (2001) *Oxford University Press, Principles of Biomedical Ethics*, 5th edition.

6 The practices of the term "total producing" means that the activity of the neuroethics research group covered multiple disciplines related to neuroethics and published different types of outcomes including publicity, interaction, practical guidance, and peer-reviewed research papers.

7 Ministry of Education, Culture, Sports, Science and Technology, Grant-in-Aid for Scientific Research on Innovative Areas. "Adolescent mind and self-medication," http://npsy.umin.jp/amsr/english.html.

8 Wudunn, S. (1997) In Japan, Use of Dead has the Living Uneasy. *New York Times* [Online] Available at www.nytimes.com/1997/05/11/world/in-japan-use-of-dead-has-the-living-uneasy.html?_r=0

9 In 2015, the Japan Agency of Medical Research and Development took over the administration of the SRPBS from MEXT.

10 An Investigation into Scientist Involvement in Science Communication Activities: www.jst.go.jp/csc/archive/pdf/csc_fy2013_04.pdf

11 Cyranoski, D. (2015) *Collateral damage: How one misconduct case brought a biology institute to its knees.* The fallout from the STAP case is still being felt across Japan. www.nature.com/news/collateral-damage-how-one-misconduct-case-brought-a-biology-institute-to-its-knees-1.17427.

12 Wada, M. (2014) Scientific misconduct: Research integrity guidelines in Japan. *Nature* 514: p. 35. Available at www.nature.com/nature/journal/v514/n7520/full/514035a.html. Coping with research misconduct. www.japantimes.co.jp/opinion/2015/03/26/editorials/coping-with-research-misconduct/#.V-7LDjsxeck

13 Four hundred twenty-five studies were confirmed by search of "deep brain stimulation" on the clinical trials.gov website at https://clinicaltrials.gov/ on October 10, 2016.

14 One hundred eighty-five studies in North America, 148 in Europe, 29 in China, and 39 in Middle East, were confirmed on the clinical trials.gov website at https://clinicaltrials.gov/ on October 10, 2016.

15 There was a civil case regarding the lack of informed consent for a mental-disorder patient who was compelled to have a lobotomy operation; see Hanreijiho 914, 85 (1978, in Japanese), Hanreitaimuzu 368, 132 (1978, in Japanese), Kai, K. (2012) Neurolaw in Japan. In: Spranger, T. M. ed. *International Neurolaw: A Comparative Analysis*, 215–226, and Nakano-Okuno M (2008) Safety issues in neuroscience and their effects on research activities in the field of life sciences in japan. In: *New Energy and Industrial Technology Development Organization* ed. International Cooperative Research/Leading Survey Program Report of Project 2007–8 (in Japanese), 124–142.

16 See Nakano-Okuno M. (2008) How Past Ethical Issues in Neuroscience Affect the Future: Lessons from Phrenology and Lobotomy. http://academia.edu/signup_wall?a_id=6384181&boxy=iframe&user_source=download&button_location=profile and Nakano-Okuno M (2008) in footnote 15.

17 Ministry of Economy, Trade and Industry, Guideline for Development of Implant Neurostimulation. (2010) *Bionic Medical Devices Area* (tentative translation). www.meti.go.jp/policy/mono_info_service/service/iryou_fukushi/downloadfiles/201011-12.pdf (in Japanese).

18 *Pharmaceuticals and Medical Devices Agency, Evaluation Indices for Neuromodulation Device* (tentative translation): pp. 13–43. www.pmda.go.jp/files/000161687.pdf (in Japanese)

19 JST RISTEX, Research and Development Area in Ecosystem for Human and Information (tentative translation). www.ristex.jp/examin/ecosystem/index.html (in Japanese).

20 RIKEN, RIKEN Center for Advanced Intelligence Project. www.riken.jp/en/research/labs/aip/.

21 RIKEN, Job Opportunities RIKEN Center for Advanced Intelligence Project. www.riken.jp/en/careers/researchers/#Tokyo.

22 Bioethics Advisory Committee Singapore. (2013) *Ethical, Legal and Social Issues in Neuroscience Research.* Consultation Paper. www.bioethics-singapore.org/images/uploadfile/103016%20AMBAC%20-%20Ethical%20Legal%20and%20Social%20Issues%20in%20Neuroscience%20Research.pdf.

Further Reading

Feldman, E. (2000) *The Ritual of Rights in Japan: Law, Society, and Health Policy.* Cambridge: Cambridge University Press.

The Future of Bioethics: International Dialogues, 2014. ed. Akira Akabayashi. New York: Oxford University Press.

Kasulis, T. (2002). *Intimacy or Integrity: Philosophy and Cultural Difference.* Honolulu: University of Hawaii Press.

Long, S. (2005). *Final Days: Japanese Culture and Choice at the End of Life.* Honolulu: University of Hawaii Press.

Sleeboom Faulkner, M. (2014). *Global Morality and Life Science Practices in Asia.* New York: Palgrave Macmillan.

References

Adam, H., Obodaru, O. and Galinsky A.D. (2015) Who you are is where you are: Antecedents and consequences of locating the self in the brain or the heart. *ScienceDirect* 128: pp. 74–83.

Akabayashi, A., and Slingsby, B.T. (2006) Informed consent revisited: Japan and the U.S. *American Journal of Bioethics* 6(1): pp. 9–14.

Beauchamp, T.L. and Childress, J.F. (2001) *Principles of Biomedical Ethics,* 5th edition. New York: Oxford University Press.

Becker, C. (2014) *Medical Practice and Cultural Myth: The Future of Bioethics.* Ed. A. Akabayashi. Oxford: Oxford University Press: pp. 750–756.

Fan, R. (1997) Self-determination vs family-determination: Two incommensurable principles of autonomy. *Bioethics* 11: pp. 309–322.

Feldman, E. (2000) *The Ritual of Rights in Japan: Law, Society, and Health Policy.* Cambridge: Cambridge University Press.

Fukue, N. (2010) Transplants set to increase. *Japan Times*, 12 November.

Fukushi, T. (2012) Ethical practice in the era of advanced neuromodulation. *Asian Bioethics Review* 4(4): pp. 320–329.

Fukushi, T., Sakura, O. and Koizumi, H. (2007) Ethical considerations of neuroscience research: The perspectives on neuroethics in Japan. *Neuroscience Research* 57(1): pp. 10–16.

Fujita, M., Hayashi, Y., Tashiro, S., Takashima, K., Nakazawa, E., and Akabayashi, A. (2014) Handling incidental findings in neuroimaging research in Japan: Current state of research facilities and attitudes of investigators and the general population. *Health Research Policy and Systems* 12(1): p. 58.

Hirata, M. (2011) Fully-implantable wireless system for human brain-machine interfaces using brain surface Electrodes: W-HERBS. *IEICE TRANSACTIONS on Communications* E94-B(9): pp. 2448–2453.

Illes, J. and Bird, S.J. (2006) Neuroethics: A modern context for ethics neuroscience. *Trends in Neuroscience* 29(9): pp. 511–517.

Isobe, T. (2010) Considering the relationship between Brain-Machine Interface (BMI) as an emerging technology and society: Clue from public perception. *UTCP booklet 15: Ethics and Society in the Age of Neuroscience,* pp. 261–287.

Isobe, T., Mizushima, N., Kato, I., Oshima, N., Uchida, M. and Sakura, O. (2013) A deliberative workshop trial: What are the general public's concerns about BMI? presented at *Society for Social Studies of Science*, San Diego, CA.

Jameie, S. (2013) Neuroethics; neuroscience for ethics and/or ethics for neuroscience new challenge for third millennium. *Thrita* 2(1): pp. 74–76.

Kai, K. (2012) Neurolaw in Japan. In T.M. Spranger (ed.). *International Neurolaw: A Comparative Analysis.* Springer: Berlin Heidelberg, pp. 215–226.

Kanba, S., Kato, T., Terao, T., Yamada, K. and Committee for Treatment Guidelines of Mood Disorders, Japanese Society of Mood Disorders, 2012. (2013) Guideline for treatment of bipolar disorder by the Japanese Society of Mood Disorders, 2012. *Psychiatry and Clinical Neuroscience* 67(5): pp. 285–300.

Kanno, S., Lee, S., Harashima, T., Kuki, T., Kino, H., Mushiake, H., Yao, H. and Tanaka, T. (2013) *Multiple Optical Stimulation to Neuron Using Si opto-neural probe With Multiple Optical Waveguides and Metal-Cover for Optogenetics.* The 35th Annual Conference of the IEEE Engineering in Medicine and Biology Society. Osaka, Monday July 3rd to Thursday July 7th, Osaka. IEEE: pp. 253–256.

Kasulis, T. (2002) *Intimacy or Integrity: Philosophy and Cultural Difference.* Honolulu: University of Hawaii Press.

Kawato, M. and Sakura, O. (2010) Proposal of four principles for Brain-Machine Interfaces (BMIs). *Chemistry Today* 471: pp. 21–25. (In Japanese).

Lebedev, M.A. and Nicolelis, M.A.L. (2006) Brain-Machine Interfaces: Past, present and future. *Trends in Neurosciences* 29(9): pp. 536–546.

Lock, M.M. (2002) *Twice Dead: Organ Transplants and the Reinvention of Death.* Berkeley: University of California Press.

Long, S.O. (2005) *Final Days: Japanese Culture and Choice at the End of Life.* Honolulu: University of Hawaii Press.

McCarthy, E. (2010). *Ethics Embodied: Rethinking Selfhood through Continental, Japanese, and Feminist Philosophies.* Plymouth: Lexington Books.

Mizushima, N. and Sakura, O. (2012) A practical approach to identify the ethical and social problems during research and development: A model for national research project of brain-machine interface. *East Asian Science, Technology and Society* 6(3): pp. 335–345.

Morris, S., Hirata, M., Sugata, H., Goto, T., Matsushita, K., Yanagisawa, T., Saitoh, Y., Kishima, H. and Yoshimine, T. (2015) Patient specific cortical electrodes for sulcal and gyral implantation. *IEEE Transactions on Biomedical Engineering* 62(4): pp. 1034–1041.

Nagaoka, S. (2012). Kanjya-iryōsha kankei [the physician-patient relationship]. In Japanese Bioethics Series Editorial Committee (Ed.). *Seimeirinri no Kihon Kōzu [The Foundational Composition of Bioethics].* Tokyo: Maruzen Publishing, pp. 179–199.

Nakano-Okuno, M. (2008) Safety issues in neuroscience and their effects on research activities in the field of life sciences in japan. In *New Energy and Industrial Technology Development Organization ed. International Cooperative Research/Leading Survey Program Report of Project 2007–8* (in Japanese): pp. 124–142.

Nakayama, T. and Nobuhara, Y. (Eds.) (2013) *The Encounter of Psychiatry and Philosophy.* Tokyo: Tamagawa University Press (in Japanese).

Nobuhara, Y. and Hara, S. (Eds.) (2008) *A Perspective on Neuroethics.* Tokyo: Keiso Shobo (in Japanese).

Nobuhara, Y., Hara, S. and Yamamoto, M. (Eds.) (2010) *Neuroscience Literacy.* Tokyo: Keiso Shobo (in Japanese).

Noda, T., Sasagawa, K., Tokuda, T. Terasawa, Y., Tashiro, H., Kanda, H., Fujikado, T. and Ohta, J. (2012) Smart electrode array device with CMOS multi-chip architecture for neural interface. *Electronics Letters* 48(21): pp. 1328–1329.

Nuttin, B., Wu, H., Mayberg H., Hariz, M., Gabriëls, L., Galert, T., Merkel, R., Kubu, C., Vilela-Filho, O., Matthews, K., Taira, T., Lozano, A.M., Schechtmann, G., Doshi, P., Broggi, G., Régis, J., Alkhani, A., Sun, B., Eljamel, S., Schulder M., Kaplitt, M., Eskandar, E., Rezai, A., Krauss, J.K., Hilven, P., Schuurman, R., Ruiz, P., Chang, J.W., Cosyns, P., Lipsman, N., Voges, J., Cosgrove, R., Li, Y. and Schlaepfer, T. (2014) Consensus on guidelines for stereotactic neurosurgery for psychiatric disorders. *Journal of Neurology, Neurosurgery & Psychiatry* 85(9): pp. 1003–1008.

Ohtake, F., Tanaka, S.C. and Sakura, O. (2013) *Economics Within Brain.* Tokyo: Discover Twenty-one (in Japanese).

Ong, C.T., Su, Y.H., Sung, S.F., Wu, C.S. and Hsu, Y.C. (2009). Ethic issue in ischemic stroke patients with thrombolytic therapy. *Acta Neurologica Taiwanica* 18(4): pp. 296–300.

Sakura, O. (2012) A view from the far east: Neuroethics in Japan, Taiwan, and South Korea. *East Asian Science, Technology and Society* 6(3): pp. 297–301.

Sakura, O., Fukushi, T., Azariah, J. and Chen, D. (2007) Can and will neuroscience contribute peace and health of human being? presented at *8th Asian Bioethics Conference.* Bangkok, Thailand.

Sato, T. (2011) Cognitive enhancement, its merits and demerits. *Journal of Philosophy and Ethics in Health Care and Medicine* 5: pp. 92–111.

Seki, A., Uchiyama, H., Fukushi, T., Sakura, O., Koeda, T. and Japan Children's Study Group. (2009) Incidental findings in brain MRI of a pediatric cohort in Japan and recommendation of a model of handling protocol. *Journal of Epidemiology Supplement* 2: pp. S498–504.

Shrivastava, M. and Behari, M. (2015) Neuroethics: A moral approach towards neuroscience research. *Archives of Neuroscience* 2(1): p. e19224.

Slingsby, B.T., Kodama, S. and Akabayashi. (2006) Scientific misconduct in Japan: The present paucity of oversight policy. *Cambridge Quarterly of Healthcare Ethics* 15: pp. 294–297.

Specker Sullivan, L. (2016) Uncovering metaethical assumptions in bioethical discourse across cultures. *Kennedy Institute of Ethics Journal* 26(1): pp. 47–78.

Specker Sullivan, L. and Illes, J. (2017). Models of engagement in neuroethics programs: Past, present, and future. In E. Racine and J. Aspler (Eds.). *The Debate About Neuroethics: Perspectives on the Field's Development, Focus, and Future*. New York: Springer, Advances in Neuroethics Series.

Taira, T. (2012) *Current Status of Neurosurgery for Psychiatric Disorders in the World*. The 34th Annual Meeting of Japanese Society of Biomedical Psychiatry. Kobe, Friday September 28th to Sunday September 30th. Kobe, Japanese Society of Biomedical Psychiatry, p. 42.

Takagi, M. (2012) Safety and neuroethical consideration of deep brain stimulation as psychiatric and dementia treatment. *Asian Bioethics Review* 4(1): pp. 48–64.

Tsai, D.F. (1999) Ancient Chinese medical ethics and the four principles of biomedical ethics. *Journal of Medical Ethics* 25(4): pp. 315–321.

Underwood, E. (2012) Neuroethics: When a brain scan bears bad news. *Science* 338(6106): p. 455.

Watsuji, T. (1996) *Rinrigaku*, translated by Y. Seisaku and R.E. Carter. Albany, New York: State University of New York Press.

White, M.S., Kaltenbrunner, M., Głowacki, E.D., Gutnichenko, K., Kettlgruber, G., Graz, I., Aazou, S., Ulbricht, C., Egbe, D.A.M., Miron, M.C., Major, M., Scharber, M.C., Sekitani, T., Someya, T., Bauer, S. and Sariciftci, N.S. (2013) Sariciftci ultrathin, highly flexible and stretchable PLEDs. *Nature Photonics* 7(10): pp. 811–816.

Wu, K.C., Hua Tai, T., Ishihara, K., Fukushi, T. and Sakura, O. (2009) Neuroethics in Asia: Current situation and future views, presented at *International Conference "Brain Matters: New Directions in Neuroethics"*. Halifax, Canada.

Wu, K.C. and Fukushi, T. (2012) Neuroethics in Taiwan: Could there be a Confucian solution? *East Asian Science, Technology and Society: An International Journal* 6: pp. 321–334.

Yamagata, Z., Yamagata, Z., Maeda, T., Anme, T., Sadato, N. and Japan Children's Study Group. (2010) Overview of the Japan children's study 2004–2009; cohort study of early childhood development. *Journal of Epidemiology* 20(Suppl 2): pp. S397–S403.

Yang, Q., Fan, Y., Cheng, Q., Li, X., Khoshnood, K. and Miller, G. (2015) Acceptance in theory but not practice—Chinese medical providers' perception of brain death. *Neuroethics* 8(3): pp. 299–313.

Yuasa, Y. (1987) *The Body: Toward an Eastern Mind-Body Theory*. Translated by S. Nagatomo and T.P. Kasulis. Albany: State University of New York Press.

30

THE NEUROBIOLOGIC EMBEDDING OF CHILDHOOD SOCIOECONOMIC STATUS

Margaret A. Sheridan

Introduction

Socioeconomic status (SES) is an aggregate measure intended to capture social standing, estimated by identifying an individual's income, educational attainment, and job status (Adler et al., 1994; Krieger et al., 1997). The effects of SES are remarkably broad. SES, measured in adulthood or childhood, is reliably and negatively associated with a variety of health and well-being outcomes and is associated with morbidity and mortality at every age (Adler et al., 1994; Marmot et al., 1991) and across most countries worldwide (Braveman and Tarimo, 2002). In childhood, family SES can be estimated by measuring parent report of household income and education. Low family SES is associated with a higher incidence of risky health behaviors (e.g., smoking), increased risk for a variety of health problems, lower academic performance, and increased psychopathology (e.g., depression, conduct disorders) in children (Ben-Shlomo and Kuh, 2002; Cohen et al., 2004; Fujiwara and Kawachi, 2009; G. Miller and Chen, 2007; Pollitt et al., 2005; Poulton et al., 2002). Lower parental SES is associated with increased risk for most forms of mental health problems including 'internalizing' disorders such as anxiety and depression (Green et al., 2010) and 'externalizing' disorders such as attention/deficit-hyperactivity disorder (ADHD) and conduct disorder (Law et al., 2014; McLaughlin et al., 2011). These associations are robust throughout the lifespan from childhood through adulthood. Importantly, it is not only the case that family SES impacts child health and well-being but also that family SES experienced as a child has independent effects on adult health and health behaviors (Melchior et al., 2007). While the associations between SES and health outcomes are evident early in childhood, they persist or worsen across childhood and into adulthood (Heckman, 2007). The effect of family SES on child outcomes extends from associations with physical health to strong and consistent associations with increased rates of mental illness and decreased educational success. For example, in the National Comorbidity Study (Kessler et al., 1997), which used a representative sample of adults in the United States, childhood poverty exposure predicted onset of mental health disorders in adulthood over and above mental health problems in childhood (McLaughlin et al., 2011). In longitudinal studies of the impact of family SES on child outcomes, strong associations between poverty in early childhood and later academic achievement have been observed and appear to be related to cognitively enriching aspects of the home environment, such as the number of books a child is read (Baydar et al., 1993; Linver et al., 2002;

Yeung et al., 2002). Together this body of work indicates that exposure to poverty early in development shifts risk later, even if adults are able to improve their own socioeconomic status so that they are no longer in poverty (Melchior et al., 2007). *Why might this be true? What processes could be set in motion early in development that would continue to affect risk for health problems much later?*

What Are the Mechanisms for the Long-Term Impact of Family SES?

The association of parental SES with broad aspects of child and adult outcomes has driven researchers to attempt to identify mechanisms by which social experience in childhood could shift developmental trajectories. Some accounts of observed linkages between childhood SES and health have focused on structural or material exposures, such as nutrition and health care (Macleod et al., 2005). However, such variables do not explain the incredibly broad association of parental SES with health, health behaviors, and academic achievement, nor do they account for the graded relation between SES and health outcomes, which exists even in the context of adequate health care and nutrition (Adler et al., 1994; Adler and Ostrove, 1999). One commonly proposed hypothesis is that social experiences 'get under the skin,' affecting child health through a variety of biological mediators. This hypothesis has been termed 'biologic embedding' (Hertzman, 1999). There are many possible forms of biologic embedding. Given the breadth of impact that SES has on child outcomes, it is hypothesized that (a) experiences associated with SES shift central nervous system development during childhood, resulting in broad changes in autonomic regulation and behavior and (b) that the impact of SES on outcomes functions through multiple pathways. In this chapter, we will consider the multiple pathways through which family SES may impact central nervous system development. This is not to propose that there are no other pathways through which SES functions to increase risk for morbidity and mortality. Instead, this focus derives from the fact that this pathway has remarkable explanatory power and because it is currently a topic that is being explored in neuroscience literature.

For a discussion of neuroethical concerns related to poverty and neurodevelopment in Argentina, see Chapter 28.

The fact that synapses, the connections between neurons, are formed or lost, strengthened or weakened, as a result of experience is termed neuroplasticity (Fox et al., 2010). This response of the brain to experience demonstrates how the brain is 'plastic'—changing its organization through experience with the environment it encounters. While the brain is somewhat plastic or changeable throughout adulthood, it is most readily shaped by experience in childhood. Because experiences during development have a profound and lasting impact on the structure and function of the brain that is not fully reversible later, this is termed *developmental plasticity* to distinguish it from the more subtle impact of experience on the brain in adulthood (Fox et al., 2010). Developmental plasticity was first observed in sensory systems. For example, in the early 1960s, the role that light exposure plays in columnar organization of the primary visual cortex through the developmentally typical process of proliferation and pruning was first observed and described (Wiesel and Hubel, 1965). Without typical visual input early in development during a sensitive or critical period (Hensch, 2004; Morishita and Hensch, 2008), the visual cortex cannot develop normally, and typical visual acuity is never achieved. Thus, typical development of the brain requires certain kinds of experience. In this way, it can be said that the human brain is 'experience dependent' or 'experience expectant.' Developmental plasticity generally occurs during the time the brain is undergoing rapid growth. Importantly, because different regions of the brain mature at different rates (Gogtay et al., 2004), sensitive periods for different regions of the brain vary. For all regions, once a region or circuit is mature, it will prove much more difficult to modify with experience (Fox et al., 2010). Finally, if sufficient experience is not provided during the time that a particular region or circuit is forming, the functionality of that region will be limited (Hensch, 2004).

In one example of developmental plasticity, for native language acquisition to occur, children must be exposed to the sounds of their native language very early in life. Such experience essentially narrows the perceptual window through which language is processed, leading to expertise. At six months of age, infants throughout the world can discriminate the sounds of most of the world's languages (e.g., an infant being brought up in an English-speaking home can discriminate the sounds not only of English but also of Mandarin; Ruben, 1997). In contrast, by twelve months of age, infants are able to discriminate the sounds only from their native language (Ruben, 1997), an effect called perceptual narrowing. Importantly, this sensitive period for phonemic awareness in children is not the 'whole story' for language acquisition. All through early childhood, until puberty, developmental plasticity allows children to be better language learners than adolescents or adults (Dettman et al., 2016; Johnson and Newport, 1989). Thus, there is little doubt that childhood experiences play a central role in some aspects of brain development, and generally the brain is understood to develop in an experience-expectant manner. However, unlike our understanding of the development of vision and language, it is less well understood what kinds of experiences are important in the development of higher-order cognitive and emotional abilities. Likely these abilities also rely on experience to develop, but when is the sensitive period of development for these abilities? How long does it last? And does it have properties similar to those observed in the sensory cortices? The answers to these questions are, to date, less well understood. Higher-order cognitive function relies on areas of the brain termed the *association cortices*, where multiple domains of sensory perception and motor output come together to support our most complex skills: our ability to understand and solve cognitive problems, control our impulses, and regulate our emotions.

In contrast to a primary sensory area, like the visual or auditory cortex, which reaches adult-like structure around five years of age, many areas of the association cortices develop from birth through late adolescence (Sowell et al., 2001), with gross changes in volume and connectivity beginning early in childhood and continuing through early adulthood (Dosenbach et al., 2010; Fair et al., 2009; Giedd et al., 1996; Gogtay et al., 2004). This has been observed in humans using neuroimaging (e.g., Gogtay et al., 2004) and using postmortem studies of the cortex (Huttenlocher, 1990; Petanjek et al., 2011). In addition, this pattern of neurodevelopment is conserved across species (Rakic et al., 1986). The principles of developmental plasticity discussed earlier—that areas of the brain in states of flux are most susceptible to the environments to which they are exposed (i.e., *moving parts get broken*)—supports the idea that the extended developmental trajectory in association cortices provides multiple opportunities for SES–related environmental exposures to influence neural development (Fox et al., 2010). This observation highlights the truism that plasticity cuts both ways. That is: an extended period of developmental plasticity allows a wide developmental window for both negative and positive experiences to become embedded in brain development.

What Evidence Do We Have That SES Impacts Brain Development?

A very large body of work has linked SES with cognitive and academic achievement outcomes in childhood such as IQ, standardized test scores, and performance on standardized academic achievement tests (Baydar et al., 1993; Brooks-Gunn and Duncan, 1997; Duncan et al., 2014; Gottlieb and Blair, 2004; Razza et al., 2010; Welsh et al., 2010). This serves as an indicator that early experience in childhood impacts neurocognitive development, but there are many mechanisms through which poverty could impact achievement (including social bias, access to learning tools, days in school), so these associations by no means conclusively point to an impact of SES on neurodevelopment (Brooks-Gunn and Duncan, 1997; Osborne, 2001). Indeed, a developmental plasticity model of the impact of SES on neurodevelopment, described earlier, predicts that low family SES will specifically shift developmental *trajectories* in brain development leading to long-term changes in cognitive and neural function. Described in what follows, this model has thus far been tested in a preliminary fashion. There is, of course, much more work left to do.

Initial investigations of the link between exposure to low SES in childhood and neurocognitive function focused on measuring more specific features of cognitive functions than are assessed in achievement tests (Hackman and Farah, 2009; Noble et al., 2007; Noble et al., 2005). Tests that rely on acquired knowledge, such as achievement tests, explicitly measure learning and thus exposure to new knowledge. If a child, through virtue of his educational opportunities, is not exposed to this knowledge, he will perform poorly on such tests, but potentially not because he is *unable* to learn or solve problems well. In contrast, tests of cognitive function attempt to be 'knowledge free' or 'content free.' Instead of measuring exposure to information, they measure ability to solve specific problems. These tests measure 'executive function' or 'long-term memory' separate from knowledge taught in school. As an example, an achievement test may assess working memory, the ability to hold things in mind for a short period of time, by giving students simple math problems to do in their head. This will measure (a) their ability to hold in mind and manipulate the components of the math problem but also (b) the student's knowledge of math. A child who is very good at math but bad at working memory may perform as well as a child who has excellent working memory but poor math skills. In contrast, a test of cognitive function would test working memory by asking a child to hold in mind where a dot had appeared on a computer screen. In this test, no special content knowledge (such as math) could improve test performance. A test like this would simply tap working memory.

Indeed, evidence has linked exposure to low–SES environments during childhood to decreased executive function. Executive functioning is comprised of three cognitive abilities: working memory (the ability to hold relevant information and goals in mind), inhibition (the ability to not act on current desires or impulses in the service of future goals), and switching (the ability to flexibly update goals or relevant information; Miyake et al., 2001). In addition to representing one impact of low SES exposure on cognitive function, it is possible that differences in executive function actually drive academic achievement differences between children from low– and high–SES families. For example, improved executive functioning predicts future performance in school, even when controlling for current school performance (Blair and Razza, 2007). As early as kindergarten, parental SES is associated with performance on tests of executive function (Hackman and Farah, 2009; Noble et al., 2005, 2007). This association holds across countries and schooling environments (Ardila et al., 2005), and such differences persist into adulthood (Evans and Schamberg, 2009).

The prefrontal cortex (PFC) is necessary for the performance of executive-function tasks (Aron et al., 2014; Miller and D'Esposito, 2005), and there is accumulating neuroimaging and neurophysiological evidence for family SES–related differences in PFC function. Some studies have examined associations between family SES and neural function using event-related potentials (ERP), a technique whereby electrical activity in response to specific task demands is measured at the scalp. In these studies, children from lower–SES families showed patterns of

ERP components consistent with deficits in directed attention and inhibition (D'Angiulli et al., 2008; Kishiyama et al., 2009; Stevens et al., 2009). Additionally, parental SES has been linked with reductions in PFC volume, thickness, and area in childhood using magnetic resonance imaging (MRI; Hanson et al., 2013; Noble et al., 2015; Noble et al., 2012). And finally, using functional magnetic resonance imaging (fMRI)—a technique that detects changes in blood flow to measure brain activation patterns—low family SES has been linked to less efficient function of the prefrontal cortex for children in early and middle childhood (Sheridan et al., 2013; Sheridan et al., 2012).

Mechanisms: How Does SES 'Get Under the Skin?'

One important question is, if family SES does, indeed, 'get under the skin' and alter brain and thus behavioral development, what is the mechanism through which this happens? First, the above-described evidence for the association between SES and neural structure and function is all correlational. Causation cannot be determined in these studies because families were not randomly assigned to high or low SES status (there are myriad variables that cannot be controlled for in such studies). However, there is compelling evidence from natural experiments and random assignment to interventions that many of the health and achievement outcomes associated with SES are caused by exposure to low–SES environments, not merely associated with them (Britto and Brooks-Gunn, 2001; Costello et al., 2003).

Two common hypotheses for the association between family SES and health and achievement effects have been proposed: (1) SES effects are accounted for by differences in exposure to language and cognitive enrichment in the home (Hart and Risley, 1995) and more recently, (2) SES effects are accounted for by differences in exposure to trauma, chronic stress, and related forms of childhood adversity (Shonkoff et al., 2009). These two theories are linked to two distinctive theories of intervention strategies: (1) children from low–SES families require increasingly enriched environments, including increased exposure to better and more complicated learning environments, and (2) children from low–SES families require increased protection from the adversities that are more common in low–SES neighborhoods and schools. Likely, given the strong association of SES with both poor learning environments and violence exposure, at a policy level, both avenues of intervention should be addressed. Why then would identifying these neural mechanisms be important? For a particular child who lives in poverty, one or the other of these pathways may be a more primary concern. Selecting the behavioral intervention that is most likely to help that child may require better knowledge of how adversity came to be biologically embedded in the first place; thus knowledge of mechanisms is centrally important for both intervention and perhaps prevention to advocate for increasing resources to those living in low–SES conditions.

Evidence exists for both these hypotheses. Children from low–SES environments are, on average, exposed to a decreased volume and complexity of home language use and decreased exposure to other forms of cognitive enrichment such as reading books (Britto and Brooks-Gunn, 2001; Dollaghan et al., 1999; Hart and Risley, 1995; Jackson et al., 2000). This exposure to family language complexity mediates associations between low SES and child language abilities (Hoff, 2003), indicating that child differences in language ability linked with SES are the result of differences in experience. Finally, increased family language complexity is associated with increased efficiency of prefrontal cortex recruitment for the child on a nonlinguistic executive-functioning task (Sheridan et al., 2012). This pattern of results indicates that increased complexity of language exposure is associated with better PFC function during task performance.

Low family SES is associated with increased exposure to childhood violence and trauma. These adversities include exposures to community violence, maltreatment, and peer victimization (Evans, 2006; Evans and Kantrowitz, 2002; Evans and Kim, 2010). Exposures to adversity in childhood are linked to disruption of typical physiological responses, including differences in typical activation of the hypothalamic-pituitary-adrenal (HPA) axis. The HPA axis becomes activated when one is threatened or in danger and is one of the ways the brain mediates the body's stress responses. This response is commonly measured through the quantity of cortisol in saliva, the downstream result of HPA axis activation. Chronic activation of this regulatory system in response to stressors has a demonstrable impact on neural structures in human and animal studies. The impact of chronic stress on neural and physiologic systems is termed allostatic load (McEwen, 2001) but has also been called 'toxic stress' (Shonkoff, Garner, et al., 2012).

Studies in rodents have demonstrated that exposure to chronic stress in nonhuman animal models results in decreased dendritic spines in the prefrontal cortex (Goldwater et al., 2009) and hippocampus, a region of the brain important for modulation of the stress response and formation of long-term memory (McEwen, 2001). Multiple studies in humans have linked baseline cortisol levels and SES in childhood (Dowd et al., 2009; Evans and Schamberg, 2009; Lupien et al., 2000; Lupien et al., 2009; Shonkoff et al., 2009). Child cortisol is associated with maternal subjective or self-rated social status, SES, and recruitment of the prefrontal cortex during long-term memory tasks (Sheridan et al., 2012, 2013). Finally, low family SES is associated with reduced function and volume of the hippocampus (Hanson et al., 2010, 2013; Hanson et al., 2011; Shonkoff, 2012).

Deprivation and Threat

In a recent set of theoretical papers (McLaughlin et al., 2014; Sheridan and McLaughlin, 2016), my colleagues and I propose that these two aspects of experience commonly linked with low parental SES may actually form two separate *dimensions* of experiences within childhood adversity. Importantly, here we propose that instead of thinking of exposures to adversities in childhood as discrete, there may be dimensions of exposures (e.g., more or less exposure to threat or violence) that are present to different degrees within many forms of adversity (e.g., low SES, maltreatment, domestic violence, neglect). These dimensions may impact development through specific and separable mechanisms. In this conceptualization, low parental SES is an extremely common adversity that confers risk for a lack of linguistic and cognitive enrichment and for increased trauma or threat exposure. Thus we would expect to observe the neurobiological sequelae of both mechanisms when investigating the correlates of SES in childhood and adulthood.

Indeed, recent research has demonstrated exactly that (Noble et al., 2015). In line with our predictions, exposure to low–SES environments in childhood is associated with global decreases in cortical surface area and decreased cortical thickness (Noble et al., 2012, 2015). In at least one study, SES–associated differences in prefrontal cortex function were directly linked with exposure to linguistic complexity in the home environment (Sheridan et al., 2012). Low-parental–SES environments have additionally been linked with differences in physiologic reactivity, including disruption of HPA-axis function, likely reflecting the impact of long-term wear and tear due to chronic stress on development (Hackman et al., 2010; Sheridan et al., 2013). Finally, multiple studies have linked low parental SES with decreased hippocampal function as measured by fMRI and volume, potentially highlighting the long-term effects of threat exposure on the neural systems involved in modulation of the stress response (Hanson et al., 2010, 2011). While these findings are consistent with the hypothesis that the dimensions of deprivation and threat impact children growing up in low–SES families, they do not specifically support the claim that different exposures impact child outcomes through different neurobiological pathways. New research with more careful measurement of child experience and neurobiology will be necessary to test the hypothesis that a lack of cognitive or linguistic enrichment confers risk for differences in cognitive function and supporting neural function but that these risks are different than those conferred by the presence of early traumatic or chronically stressful exposures.

Neuroethical Implications of Neurobiologic Embedding

What are the neuroethical implications that early experience associated with family SES shifts brain development, putting children and adults at greater risk for a host of negative outcomes including reductions in achievement and increases in mental and physical health disorders? First, it appears that if children experience lifelong vulnerability to the impact of their parents' SES by virtue of their developing biology, then as a society, we have an imperative to protect them. Indeed, this idea, without the biology, is in some way what has driven social policy around access to educational opportunities, health care, and child protective services. What the addition of neurobiology does, generally speaking, is provide evidence for what makes children vulnerable and, importantly, highlight that their vulnerability is inexorably linked to their identity as children. Thus, one cannot eliminate the vulnerability (e.g., make exceptionally 'strong' or 'resilient' children) without eliminating the very thing that is inherently their childhood. Children are developing humans. Being a developing human means that the brain is in a state of flux, and that flux will allow it to be impacted more profoundly by the external environment.

What new neuroscience may additionally add to this conversation is mechanisms describing *in what way* children are vulnerable or what the pathways of vulnerability are. The hope is that identifying these mechanisms or pathways will highlight areas of intervention and prevention that are currently untapped. For example, the neuroscientific hypothesis that exposure to adversity results in long-term differences in neural structure and function relies heavily on the concept of sensitive periods or developmental plasticity mentioned earlier. The brain does not develop as a uniform unit; instead, areas of the brain that are important for one cognitive function, such as vision, develop on a different time scale than areas of the brain that are important for other cognitive functions such as production of language or executive function. The period when an area is developing most rapidly is often the moment when it is also most available for change, a sensitive period. Knowing the intersection of an individual's exposure to a specific type of event (e.g., the onset and offset of a particular violence exposure or lack of cognitive stimulation) could interact with knowledge of these sensitive periods to predict not only what kind of negative sequelae will ensue but also how and when to remediate those negative outcomes. This may be one way in which neuroscience can contribute to not only the argument behind the need for preventive efforts but also the way in which those efforts are directed.

For example, robust and consistent evidence from neuroscience indicates that earlier interventions are likely to be more efficient and effective than later interventions. While adult plasticity still allows the possibility of later change, the proven existence of developmental plasticity means that earlier negative and positive experiences will shape the neurobiology of each child in ways that are permanent for better and for worse. The primary conclusion that investigating the association between SES and neurobiological development results in is that inputs are unequal from the very beginning in ways that likely change the equipment with which someone is operating from then on (their brain). To allow equal opportunity, we must promote the most positive early environments possible for all children.

Further Reading

Hackman, D.A., Farah, M.J. and Meaney, M.J. (2010) "Socioeconomic Status and the Brain: Mechanistic Insights From Human and Animal Research". *Nature Reviews Neuroscience* 11(9), 651–659. Available at: http://doi.org/10.1038/nrn2897

Lupien, S.J., McEwen, B.S., Gunnar, M. and Heim, C. (2009) "Effects of Stress Throughout the Lifespan on the Brain, Behaviour and Cognition". *Nature Reviews Neuroscience* 10(6), 434–445.

Noble, K.G., Houston, S.M., Brito, N.H., Bartsch, H., Kan, E., Kuperman, J.M., . . . Sowell, E.R. (2015) "Family Income, Parental Education and Brain Structure in Children and Adolescents". *Nature Reviews Neuroscience* 18(5), 773–778. Available at: http://doi.org/10.1038/nn.3983

Sheridan, M.A. and McLaughlin, K.A. (2016) "Neurobiological Models of the Impact of Adversity on Education". *Current Opinion in Behavioral Sciences* 10, 108–113. Available at: http://doi.org/10.1016/j.cobeha.2016.05.013

Shonkoff, J.P., Boyce, W.T. and McEwen, B.S. (2009) "Neuroscience, Molecular Biology, and the Childhood Roots of Health Disparities: Building a New Framework for Health Promotion and Disease Prevention". *JAMA: The Journal of the American Medical Association* 301(21), 2252–2259. Available at: http://doi.org/10.1001/jama.2009.754

References

Adler, N.E., Boyce, W.T., Chesney, M.A., Cohen, S., Folkman, S., and Kahn, R.L. (1994) Socioeconomic status and health: The challenge of the gradient. *American Psychologist* 49(1): pp. 15–24.

Adler, N.E., and Ostrove, J.M. (1999) Socioeconomic status and health: What we know and what we don't. *Annals of the New York Academy of Sciences* 896(1): pp. 3–15. Available at: http://doi.org/10.1111/j.1749-6632.1999.tb08101.x.

Ardila, A., Rosselli, M., Matute, E., and Guajardo, S. (2005) The influence of the parents' educational level on the development of executive functions. *Developmental Neuropsychology* 28(1): pp. 539–560. Available at: http://doi.org/10.1207/s15326942dn2801_5.

Aron, A.R., Robbins, T.W., and Poldrack, R.A. (2014) Inhibition and the right inferior frontal cortex: One decade on. *Trends in Cognitive Sciences* 18(4): pp. 177–185. Available at: http://doi.org/10.1016/j.tics.2013.12.003.

Baydar, N., Brooks-Gunn, J., and Furstenberg, F.F. (1993) Early warning signs of functional illiteracy: Predictors in childhood and adolescence. *Child Development* 64(3): pp. 815–829.

Ben-Shlomo, Y., and Kuh, D. (2002) A life course approach to chronic disease epidemiology: Conceptual models, empirical challenges and interdisciplinary perspectives. *International Journal of Epidemiology* 31(2): pp. 285–293. Available at: http://doi.org/10.1093/ije/31.2.285.

Blair, C., and Razza, R.P. (2007). Relating effortful control, executive function, and false belief understanding to emerging math and literacy ability in kindergarten. *Child Development* 78(2): pp. 647–663. Available at: http://doi.org/10.1111/j.1467-8624.2007.01019.x.

Braveman, P., and Tarimo, E. (2002) Social inequalities in health within countries: Not only an issue for affluent nations. *Social Science & Medicine (1982)* 54(11): pp. 1621–1635.

Britto, P.R., and Brooks-Gunn, J. (2001) Provisions of learning experiences in the home and early childhood school readiness are clearly linked. *New Directions for Child and Adolescent Development* (92): pp. 1–6. Available at: http://doi.org/10.1002/cd.11.

Brooks-Gunn, J., and Duncan, G.J. (1997). The effects of poverty on children. *The Future of Children / Center for the Future of Children, the David and Lucile Packard Foundation* 7(2): pp. 55–71.

Cohen, S., Doyle, W.J., Turner, R.B., Alper, C.M., and Skoner, D.P. (2004) Childhood socioeconomic status and host resistance to infectious illness in adulthood. *Psychosomatic Medicine* 66(4): pp. 553–558. Available at: http://doi.org/10.1097/01.psy.0000126200.05189.d3

Costello, E.J., Compton, S.N., Keeler, G., and Angold, A. (2003) Relationships between poverty and psychopathology: A natural experiment. *Journal of American Medical Association* 290(15): pp. 2023–2029. Available at: http://doi.org/10.1001/jama.290.15.2023

D'Angiulli, A., Herdman, A., Stapells, D., and Hertzman, C. (2008). Children's event-related potentials of auditory selective attention vary with their socioeconomic status. *Neuropsychology* 22(3): pp. 293–300.

Dettman, S.J., Dowell, R.C., Choo, D., Arnott, W., Abrahams, Y., Davis, A., . . . Briggs, R.J. (2016) Long-term communication outcomes for children receiving cochlear implants younger than 12 months: A multi-center study. *Otology & Neurotology: Official Publication of the American Otological Society, American Neurotology Society [and] European Academy of Otology and Neurotology* 37(2): pp. e82–e95. Available at: http://doi.org/10.1097/MAO.0000000000000915

Dollaghan, C.A., Campbell, T.F., Paradise, J.L., Feldman, H.M., Janosky, J.E., Pitcairn, D.N., and Kurs-Lasky, M. (1999) Maternal education and measures of early speech and language. *Journal of Speech, Language, and Hearing Research: JSLHR* 42(6): pp. 1432–1443.

Dosenbach, N.U.F., Nardos, B., Cohen, A.L., Fair, D.A., Power, J.D., Church, J.A., . . . Schlaggar, B.L. (2010) Prediction of individual brain maturity using fMRI. *Science (New York, N.Y.)* 329(5997): pp. 1358–1361. Available at: http://doi.org/10.1126/science.1194144

Dowd, J.B., Simanek, A.M., and Aiello, A.E. (2009). Socio-economic status, cortisol and allostatic load: A review of the literature. *International Journal of Epidemiology* 38(5): pp. 1297–1309. Available at: http://doi.org/10.1093/ije/dyp277

Duncan, G.J., Magnuson, K., and Votruba-Drzal, E. (2014) Boosting family income to promote child development. *Future of Children* 24(1): pp. 99–120.

Evans, G.W. (2006) Child development and the physical environment. *Annual Review of Psychology* 57: pp. 423–451. Available at: http://doi.org/10.1146/annurev.psych.57.102904.190057

Evans, G.W., and Kantrowitz, E. (2002) Socioeconomic status and health: The potential role of environmental risk exposure. *Annual Review of Public Health* 23: pp. 303–331. Available at: http://doi.org/10.1146/annurev.publhealth.23.112001.112349

Evans, G.W., and Schamberg, M.A. (2009) Childhood poverty, chronic stress, and adult working memory. *Proceedings of the National Academy of Sciences of the United States of America* 106(16): pp. 6545–6549. Available at: http://doi.org/10.1073/pnas.0811910106

Evans, G.W., and Kim, P. (2010) Multiple risk exposure as a potential explanatory mechanism for the socioeconomic status-health gradient. *Annals of the New York Academy of Sciences* 1186: pp. 174–189. Available at: http://doi.org/10.1111/j.1749-6632.2009.05336.x

Fair, D.A., Cohen, A.L., Power, J.D., Dosenbach, N.U.F., Church, J.A., Miezin, F.M., . . . Petersen, S.E. (2009) Functional brain networks develop from a "local to distributed" organization. *PLoS Computational Biology* 5(5): p. e1000381. Available at: http://doi.org/10.1371/journal.pcbi.1000381

Fox, S.E., Levitt, P., and Nelson, C.A. (2010) How the timing and quality of early experiences influence the development of brain architecture. *Child Development* 81(1): pp. 28–40. Available at: http://doi.org/10.1111/j.1467-8624.2009.01380.x

Fujiwara, T., and Kawachi, I. (2009) Is education causally related to better health? A twin fixed-effect study in the USA. *International Journal of Epidemiology* 38(5): pp. 1310–1322. Available at: http://doi.org/10.1093/ije/dyp226

Giedd, J.N., Snell, J.W., Lange, N., Rajapakse, J.C., Casey, B.J., Kozuch, P.L., . . . Rapoport, J.L. (1996) Quantitative magnetic resonance imaging of human brain development: Ages 4–18. *Cerebral Cortex (New York, N.Y.: 1991)* 6(4): pp. 551–560.

Gogtay, N., Giedd, J.N., Lusk, L., Hayashi, K.M., Greenstein, D., Vaituzis, A.C., . . . Thompson, P.M. (2004) Dynamic mapping of human cortical development during childhood through early adulthood. *Proceedings of the National Academy of Sciences of the United States of America* 101(21): pp. 8174–8179. Available at: http://doi.org/10.1073/pnas.0402680101

Goldwater, D.S., Pavlides, C., Hunter, R.G., Bloss, E.B., Hof, P.R., McEwen, B.S., and Morrison, J.H. (2009) Structural and functional alterations to rat medial prefrontal cortex following chronic restraint stress and recovery. *Neuroscience* 164(2): pp. 798–808. Available at: http://doi.org/10.1016/j.neuroscience.2009.08.053

Gottlieb, G., and Blair, C. (2004) How early experience matters in intellectual development in the case of poverty. *Prevention Science: The Official Journal of the Society for Prevention Research* 5(4): pp. 245–252.

Green, J.G., McLaughlin, K.A., Berglund, P.A., Gruber, M.J., Sampson, N.A., Zaslavsky, A.M., and Kessler, R.C. (2010) Childhood adversities and adult psychiatric disorders in the national comorbidity survey replication I: Associations with first onset of DSM-IV disorders. *Archives of General Psychiatry* 67(2): pp. 113–123. Available at: http://doi.org/10.1001/archgenpsychiatry.2009.186

Hackman, D.A., and Farah, M.J. (2009) Socioeconomic status and the developing brain. *Trends in Cognitive Sciences* 13(2): pp. 65–73. Available at: http://doi.org/10.1016/j.tics.2008.11.003

Hackman, D.A., Farah, M.J., and Meaney, M.J. (2010) Socioeconomic status and the brain: Mechanistic insights from human and animal research. *Nature Reviews. Neuroscience* 11(9): pp. 651–659. Available at: http://doi.org/10.1038/nrn2897

Hanson, J.L., Chandra, A., Wolfe, B.L., and Pollak, S.D. (2011) Association between income and the hippocampus. *PLoS One* 6(5): p. e18712. Available at: http://doi.org/10.1371/journal.pone.0018712

Hanson, J.L., Chung, M.K., Avants, B.B., Shirtcliff, E.A., Gee, J.C., Davidson, R.J., and Pollak, S.D. (2010) Early stress is associated with alterations in the orbitofrontal cortex: A tensor-based morphometry investigation of brain structure and behavioral risk. *Journal of Neuroscience:* 30(22): pp. 7466–7472. Available at: http://doi.org/10.1523/JNEUROSCI.0859-10.2010

Hanson, J.L., Hair, N., Shen, D.G., Shi, F., Gilmore, J.H., Wolfe, B.L., and Pollak, S.D. (2013) Family poverty affects the rate of human infant brain growth. *PLoS One* 8(12): p. e80954. Available at: http://doi.org/10.1371/journal.pone.0080954

Hart, B., and Risley, T. (1995) *Meaningful Differences in the Everyday Experience of Young American Children*. Baltimore: Paul H. Brookes Publishing Co.

Heckman, J.J. (2007) The economics, technology, and neuroscience of human capability formation. *Proceedings of the National Academy of Sciences of the United States of America* 104(33): pp. 13250–13255. Available at: http://doi.org/10.1073/pnas.0701362104

Hensch, T.K. (2004) Critical period regulation. *Annual Review of Neuroscience* 27: pp. 549–579. Available at: http://doi.org/10.1146/annurev.neuro.27.070203.144327

Hertzman, C. (1999) Population health and human development. In D.P. Keating and C. Hertzman (Eds.). *Developmental Health and the Wealth of Nations: Social, Biological, and Educational Dynamics*. New York: Guilford Press, pp. 21–40.

Hoff, E. (2003) The specificity of environmental influence: Socioeconomic status affects early vocabulary development via maternal speech. *Child Development* 74(5): pp. 1368–1378.

Huttenlocher, P.R. (1990) Morphometric study of human cerebral cortex development. *Neuropsychologia* 28(6): pp. 517–527. Available at: http://doi.org/10.1016/0028-3932(90)90031-I

Jackson, A.P., Brooks-Gunn, J., Huang, C.C., and Glassman, M. (2000) Single mothers in low-wage jobs: Financial strain, parenting, and preschoolers' outcomes. *Child Development* 71(5): pp. 1409–1423.

Johnson, J.S., and Newport, E.L. (1989) Critical period effects in second language learning: The influence of maturational state on the acquisition of English as a second language. *Cognitive Psychology* 21(1): pp. 60–99.

Kessler, R.C., Davis, C.G., and Kendler, K.S. (1997) Childhood adversity and adult psychiatric disorder in the US National Comorbidity Survey. *Psychological Medicine* 27(5): pp. 1101–1119.

Kishiyama, M.M., Boyce, W.T., Jimenez, A.M., Perry, L.M., and Knight, R.T. (2009) Socioeconomic disparities affect prefrontal function in children. *Journal of Cognitive Neuroscience* 21(6): pp. 1106–1115. Available at: http://doi.org/10.1162/jocn.2009.21101

Krieger, N., Williams, D.R., and Moss, N.E. (1997) Measuring social class in US public health research: Concepts, methodologies, and guidelines. *Annual Review of Public Health* 18: pp. 341–378. Available at: http://doi.org/10.1146/annurev.publhealth.18.1.341

Law, E.C., Sideridis, G.D., Prock, L.A., and Sheridan, M.A. (2014) Attention-deficit/hyperactivity disorder in young children: Predictors of diagnostic stability. *Pediatrics*. Available at: http://doi.org/10.1542/peds.2013-3433

Linver, M.R., Brooks-Gunn, J., and Kohen, D.E. (2002) Family processes as pathways from income to young children's development. *Developmental Psychology* 38(5): pp. 719–734.

Lupien, S.J., King, S., Meaney, M.J., and McEwen, B.S. (2000) Child's stress hormone levels correlate with mother's socioeconomic status and depressive state. *Biological Psychiatry* 48(10): pp. 976–980.

Lupien, S.J., McEwen, B.S., Gunnar, M., and Heim, C. (2009) Effects of stress throughout the lifespan on the brain, behaviour and cognition. *Nature Reviews Neuroscience* 10(6): pp. 434–445.

McEwen, B.S. (2001) Plasticity of the hippocampus: Adaptation to chronic stress and allostatic load. *Annals of the New York Academy of Sciences* 933: pp. 265–277.

McLaughlin, K.A., Breslau, J., Green, J.G., Lakoma, M.D., Sampson, N.A., Zaslavsky, A.M., and Kessler, R.C. (2011) Childhood socio-economic status and the onset, persistence, and severity of DSM-IV mental disorders in a US national sample. *Social Science & Medicine (1982)* 73(7): pp. 1088–1096. Available at: http://doi.org/10.1016/j.socscimed.2011.06.011

McLaughlin, K.A., Sheridan, M., and Lambert, H. (2014) Childhood adversity and neural development: Deprivation and threat as distinct dimensions of early experience. *Neuroscience Biobehavioral Reviews* 47: pp. 578

Macleod, J., Davey Smith, G., Metcalfe, C., and Hart, C. (2005) Is subjective social status a more important determinant of health than objective social status? Evidence from a prospective observational study of Scottish men. *Social Science & Medicine (1982)* 61(9): pp. 1916–1929. Available at: http://doi.org/10.1016/j.socscimed.2005.04.009

Marmot, M.G., Smith, G.D., Stansfeld, S., Patel, C., North, F., Head, J., . . . Feeney, A. (1991) Health inequalities among British civil servants: The Whitehall II study. *The Lancet* 337(8754): pp. 1387–1393.

Melchior, M., Moffitt, T.E., Milne, B.J., Poulton, R., and Caspi, A. (2007) Why do children from socioeconomically disadvantaged families suffer from poor health when they reach adulthood? A life-course study. *American Journal of Epidemiology* 166(8): pp. 966–974. Available at: http://doi.org/10.1093/aje/kwm155

Miller, B.T., and D'Esposito, M. (2005) Searching for "the top" in top-down control. *Neuron* 48(4): pp. 535–538. Available at: http://doi.org/10.1016/j.neuron.2005.11.002

Miller, G., and Chen, E. (2007). Unfavorable socioeconomic conditions in early life presage expression of proinflammatory phenotype in adolescence. *Psychosomatic Medicine* 69(5): pp. 402–409. Available at: http://doi.org/10.1097/PSY.0b013e318068fcf9

Miyake, A., Friedman, N.P., Rettinger, D.A., Shah, P., and Hegarty, M. (2001) How are visuospatial working memory, executive functioning, and spatial abilities related? A latent-variable analysis. *Journal of Experimental Psychology. General* 130(4): pp. 621–640.

Morishita, H., and Hensch, T.K. (2008) Critical period revisited: Impact on vision. *Current Opinion in Neurobiology* 18(1): pp. 101–107. Available at: http://doi.org/10.1016/j.conb.2008.05.009

Noble, K.G., Houston, S.M., Brito, N.H., Bartsch, H., Kan, E., Kuperman, J.M., . . . Sowell, E.R. (2015) Family income, parental education and brain structure in children and adolescents. *Nature Neuroscience* 18(5): pp. 773–778. Available at: http://doi.org/10.1038/nn.3983

Noble, K.G., Houston, S.M., Kan, E., and Sowell, E.R. (2012) Neural correlates of socioeconomic status in the developing human brain. *Developmental Science* 15(4): pp. 516–527. Available at: http://doi.org/10.1111/j.1467-7687.2012.01147.x

Noble, K.G., McCandliss, B.D., and Farah, M.J. (2007) Socioeconomic gradients predict individual differences in neurocognitive abilities. *Developmental Science* 10(4): pp. 464–480. Available at: http://doi.org/10.1111/j.1467-7687.2007.00600.x

Noble, K.G., Norman, M.F., and Farah, M.J. (2005) Neurocognitive correlates of socioeconomic status in kindergarten children. *Developmental Science* 8(1): pp. 74–87. Available at: http://doi.org/10.1111/j.1467-7687.2005.00394.x

Osborne, J.W. (2001) Testing stereotype threat: Does anxiety explain race and sex differences in achievement? *Contemporary Educational Psychology* 26(3): pp. 291–310. Available at: http://doi.org/10.1006/ceps.2000.1052

Petanjek, Z., Judas, M., Simic, G., Rasin, M.R., Uylings, H.B.M., Rakic, P., and Kostovic, I. (2011) Extraordinary neoteny of synaptic spines in the human prefrontal cortex. *Proceedings of the National Academy of Sciences* 108(32): pp. 13281–13286. Available at: http://doi.org/10.1073/pnas.1105108108

Pollitt, R., Rose, K., and Kaufman, J. (2005) Evaluating the evidence for models of life course socioeconomic factors and cardiovascular outcomes: A systematic review. *BMC Public Health* 5(1): p. 7. Available at: http://doi.org/10.1186/1471-2458-5-7

Poulton, R., Caspi, A., Milne, B.J., Thomson, W.M., Taylor, A., Sears, M.R., and Moffitt, T.E. (2002) Association between children's experience of socioeconomic disadvantage and adult health: A life-course study. *The Lancet* 360(9346): pp. 1640–1645. Available at: http://doi.org/10.1016/S0140-6736(02)11602-3

Rakic, P., Bourgeois, J.P., Eckenhoff, M.F., Zecevic, N., and Goldman-Rakic, P.S. (1986) Concurrent overproduction of synapses in diverse regions of the primate cerebral cortex. *Science (New York, N.Y.)* 232(4747): pp. 232–235.

Razza, R.A., Martin, A., and Brooks-Gunn, J. (2010) Associations among family environment, sustained attention, and school readiness for low-income children. *Developmental Psychology*. Available at: http://doi.org/10.1037/a0020389

Ruben, R.J. (1997) A time frame of critical/sensitive periods of language development. *Acta Oto-Laryngologica* 117(2): pp. 202–205. Available at: http://doi.org/10.3109/00016489709117769

Sheridan, M.A., How, J., Araujo, M., Schamberg, M.A., and Nelson, C.A. (2013) What are the links between maternal social status, hippocampal function, and HPA axis function in children? *Developmental Science*, n/a—n/a. Available at: http://doi.org/10.1111/desc.12087

Sheridan, M.A., and McLaughlin, K.A. (2016) Neurobiological models of the impact of adversity on education. *Current Opinion in Behavioral Sciences* 10: pp. 108–113. Available at: http://doi.org/10.1016/j.cobeha.2016.05.013

Sheridan, M.A., Sarsour, K., Jutte, D., D'Esposito, M., and Boyce, W.T. (2012) The impact of social disparity on prefrontal function in childhood. *PLoS One* 7(4): p. e35744. Available at: http://doi.org/10.1371/journal.pone.0035744

Shonkoff, J.P. (2012) Leveraging the biology of adversity to address the roots of disparities in health and development. *Proceedings of the National Academy of Sciences of the United States of America* 109(Suppl 2): pp. 17302–17307. Available at: http://doi.org/10.1073/pnas.1121259109

Shonkoff, J.P., Boyce, W.T., and McEwen, B.S. (2009) Neuroscience, molecular biology, and the childhood roots of health disparities: Building a new framework for health promotion and disease prevention. *Journal of the American Medical Association* 301(21): pp. 2252–2259. Available at: http://doi.org/10.1001/jama.2009.754

Shonkoff, J.P., Garner, A.S., Committee on Psychosocial Aspects of Child and Family Health, Committee on Early Childhood, Adoption, and Dependent Care, and Section on Developmental and Behavioral Pediatrics. (2012) The lifelong effects of early childhood adversity and toxic stress. *Pediatrics* 129(1): pp. e232–e246. Available at: http://doi.org/10.1542/peds.2011-2663

Sowell, E.R., Thompson, P.M., Tessner, K.D., and Toga, A.W. (2001) Mapping continued brain growth and gray matter density reduction in dorsal frontal cortex: Inverse relationships during postadolescent brain maturation. *Journal of Neuroscience* 21(22): pp. 8819–8829.

Stevens, C., Lauinger, B., and Neville, H. (2009) Differences in the neural mechanisms of selective attention in children from different socioeconomic backgrounds: An event-related brain potential study. *Developmental Science* 12(4): pp. 634–646. Available at: http://doi.org/10.1111/j.1467-7687.2009.00807.x

Welsh, J.A., Nix, R.L., Blair, C., Bierman, K.L., and Nelson, K.E. (2010) The development of cognitive skills and gains in academic school readiness for children from low-income families. *Journal of Educational Psychology* 102(1): pp. 43–53. Available at: http://doi.org/10.1037/a0016738

Wiesel, T.N., and Hubel, D.H. (1965) Comparison of the effects of unilateral and bilateral eye closure on cortical unit responses in kittens. *Journal of Neurophysiology* 28(6): pp. 1029–1040.

Yeung, W.J., Linver, M.R., and Brooks-Gunn, J. (2002) How money matters for young children's development: Parental investment and family processes. *Child Development* 73(6): pp. 1861–1879.

31

PRENATAL AND NEONATAL NEUROETHICS

The Moral Significance of Painience

L. Syd M Johnson

Introduction

The capacity of human neonates to experience pain has been established and recognized for decades. Controversy remains regarding fetal pain perception, with some maintaining the fetus is painient relatively early in its development and others holding that *in utero* fetuses are incapable of experiencing pain. Neuroscientific evidence for fetal painience is highly reliant on inferences, with relatively limited direct evidence from human fetuses, owing in part to restrictions on research on fetuses. In this chapter, I look at the evidence for fetal and neonatal painience and discuss the moral significance of painience for both human fetuses and neonates, as well as other patient populations and nonhuman animals. I'll also look at the ethical, legal, and social issues, with an emphasis on the abortion debate.

A Preliminary Note About Pain Terminology

As explained in what follows, pain and nociception are different though often related phenomena. Pain is a subjective phenomenon, while nociception is the object of sensory physiology (Loeser and Treede, 2008). In this chapter, I'll use *nociception* and *nociceptive response* to refer to noxious stimulation of the body's nociceptors and nociceptive pathways. *Pain* will be used in its more familiar way, to refer to a noxious, unpleasant sensation that is subjectively and phenomenally perceived to be painful by painient creatures (i.e., creatures with the capacity for painful experiences).

Pain and Nociception

Nociception and pain are importantly distinct phenomena. There is evidence that numerous creatures, including human fetuses at some point during development, have the kind of neural architecture sufficient for *nociception*, which refers to "activity induced in the nociceptor and nociceptive pathways by a noxious stimulus" (Merskey and Bogduk, 2012) or the "neural process of encoding noxious stimuli" (Loeser and Treede, 2008; Merskey and Bogduk, 2012). *Noxious stimuli* are those that are damaging or potentially damaging and that provoke an avoidance response (Loeser and Treede, 2008; Dubin and Patapoutian, 2010). Physiological nociceptive responses to noxious stimuli can include reflexive withdrawal of a limb and facial grimacing, as well as autonomic responses such as elevated blood pressure and heart rate (Merskey and Bogduk, 2012). Importantly, consciousness (i.e., wakefulness and awareness) is not required for nociceptive responses. Individuals under anesthesia, comatose and brain-dead individuals, anencephalic infants, and decerebrate animals can all exhibit physiological responses to nociceptive stimuli.

Nociception is thus distinguished from *pain*, which is always an experienced *psychological* state (Loeser et al., 1994; Merskey and Bogduk, 2012; Wiech, 2016). The proximate physical cause of experienced pain is frequently nociception, but "the experience of pain is more than a simple sensory process. It is a complex perception involving higher levels of the central nervous system, emotional states, and higher order mental processes" (Osterwels et al., 1987). The International Association for the Study of Pain (IASP) has defined pain as "an unpleasant sensory and emotional experience associated with actual or potential tissue damage" (Merskey and Bogduk, 2012). Experiencing *something as painful* requires both nociception *and* an emotional reaction, which are "processed by the brain in areas anatomically and physiologically distinct from one another" (Lowery et al., 2007). For an experience to be perceived as painful "requires that the noxious signal is transmitted to the cortex" (Worley et al., 2012; Tracey and Mantyh, 2007), although there is no primary "pain cortex" analogous to the primary somatosensory or visual cortices (Verriotis et al., 2016). Pain arises from a dynamic change in a distributed network of brain activity—the "pain connectome"—that results in the sensory, emotional, motivational, and cognitive experience of pain (Verriotis et al., 2016).

Importantly, pain and nociception can occur independently. For example, under anesthesia, there can be nociception without pain, and in an individual with thalamic pain, there can be pain without nociception (Loeser and Treede, 2008).[1] Some tissue damage (such as damage to internal solid organs) is not detected by sensory receptors and thus causes neither nociception nor pain (Loeser and Treede, 2008).

Importantly, pain, as an affective, psychological state, requires consciousness. Pain is experienced as painful, unpleasant, and aversive by creatures who are painient—creatures capable of consciously experiencing pain. Generally, we can think of a painience as subset of sentience (the capacity to subjectively perceive or feel pleasure and pain; Jaworska and Tannenbaum, 2013) and sentience as a type of phenomenal consciousness (Block, 2005). There is a vast philosophical literature on the question of what is consciousness, and the matter is well beyond the scope of this chapter (see Van Gulick, 2014, for a comprehensive review). Here, I use a functional definition of consciousness, one capacious enough to encompass the current discussion of painience. Consciousness, as here considered, is a state of being aware (of oneself or the external environment), awake, and sentient (capable of feeling or perceiving pleasures and pains). Any of these capacities might admit of degrees. For example, a newborn human infant lacks self-awareness but *might* be minimally aware of the external world. A human infant also experiences wakefulness. One might lose any one of the capacities of consciousness and be temporarily or permanently unconscious. For example, while sleeping, one would lack wakefulness, awareness, and sentience (although remain capable of emotional states, as in dreams; there are intriguing studies that examine the inconsistent responses to noxious stimuli during sleep; see Bastuji et al., 2012). Individuals in the vegetative state are thought to be unconscious in that although they experience periods of wakefulness, they lack awareness of self and the external world (Monti et al., 2010). There are questions about whether they are sentient or painient (Pistoia et al., 2016; Naro et al., 2015).

Neonatal Nociception and Painience

Until the 1980s, it was routine to perform invasive procedures and surgeries on neonates without anesthesia (Boffey, 1987; Rodkey and Riddell, 2013). It was believed that (a) neonates had undeveloped central nervous systems that made them incapable of feeling pain, and (b) the risks of anesthesia were not worth the unknown benefits, given (a). Research by Anand and colleagues (Anand and Hickey, 1987; Anand et al., 1988) demonstrated significantly harmful physiological stress responses, including circulatory and metabolic complications, to surgery without anesthesia in neonates. They demonstrated that those negative effects could be reduced with administration of the anesthetic fentanyl, resulting in better postsurgical outcomes such as improved hemodynamic stability and reduced need for ventilatory support (Anand and Hickey, 1987; Anand et al., 1988). The study by Anand and Hickey (1987) was conclusive regarding neonatal nociception and its harmful effects. More recent neuroimaging and connectome studies have provided neurodevelopmental evidence of likely neonatal painience (Verriotis et al., 2016) and demonstrated both short- and long-term sequelae from exposure to noxious stimuli in neonates (Hatfield, 2014).

One preliminary study comparing fMRI data in adults and newborns suggested that newborns may be significantly more sensitive than adults to similar noxious stimulations (Goksan et al., 2015). Slater and colleagues' (2010a) study of noxious-evoked neuronal EEG activity compared preterm infants with 40+ days in neonatal intensive care (NICU) to age-matched full term infants. The study demonstrated increased neuronal response to noxious stimuli in the preterm infants, with no differences in response to nonnoxious stimuli. The study was suggestive that early, noxious NICU experiences contribute to increased pain sensitivity in older ex-preterm children. Another study examined the analgesic effectiveness of oral sucrose, believed to be a generally safe alternative to pharmacological analgesic agents. Slater and colleagues (2010b) found that oral sucrose administration results in behavioral (facial grimacing) changes but does not significantly affect activity in neonatal brain or spinal cord nociceptive circuits as recorded by EEG and EMG, suggesting it has little effect on nociceptive response.

There is robust evidence for both neonatal nociception and for the negative short- and long-term health and developmental consequences of untreated and undertreated nociception. However, the network of brain regions that encode the affective and sensory aspects of *pain* experience have not been well studied or described in newborns (Verriotis et al., 2016). That, coupled with the newborn's inability to verbalize their pain experiences, has led to the development of numerous physiological and behavioral infant pain assessment tools (Worley et al., 2012; Ranger et al., 2007). Evidence from recordings of brain activity, however, suggests that infants may experience pain without exhibiting behavioral signs (Slater et al., 2010a; Goksan et al., 2015). More objective measures of newborn pain are clearly needed, as is an understanding of how infants experience pain. In Goksan and colleagues' preliminary fMRI study, extensive similarities between brain activations in neonates and adults in response to nociceptive stimuli were noted, with significant brain activity in 18 of the 20 active adult brain regions, including those that encode the sensory and affective components of pain in adults (Goksan et al., 2015). Other studies have found both similarities and differences in brain activity between adults and neonates (Fabrizi et al., 2016; Verriotis et al., 2016). If one infers from the similarities between brain activations in painient adults—who can report on their subjective experience of pain—to infants, it is not unreasonable to conclude that infants are also painient. As Goksan et al. note, "infants do have the capacity to experience an emotionally relevant context related to incoming sensory input," but "it is plausible that infants do not experience the full range of aversive qualities that adults associate with nociceptive input" (Goksan et al., 2015). Indeed, as pain is "an actively constructed experience that is determined by expectations and their modification through learning" (Wiech, 2016), experiencing pain as *painful* (i.e., physiologically and psychologically aversive, distressing, and causing suffering) may require conscious experience that neonates, especially preterm neonates, are in the process of acquiring.

Although compelling evidence for neonatal nociception has existed for decades, management of pain in neonates is still hampered by a lack of awareness or lingering skepticism among healthcare professionals that neonates are capable of experiencing pain, and by concerns about the adverse effects of analgesic and anesthetic use (Anand et al., 2001; Roofthooft et al., 2014). Additionally, diagnosing and measuring pain in infants is difficult; typical adults can communicate and self-report regarding their pain, something infants who lack language cannot do.[2] Neonates routinely undergo noxious, invasive procedures such as blood sampling, injections, and circumcision. Preterm and sick infants may experience many more noxious diagnostic, therapeutic, and surgical procedures. Neonates exhibit greater hormonal, metabolic, and cardiovascular responses to noxious stimuli compared to older children (Hatfield, 2014). Repetitive, untreated pain predicts immediate and long-term negative effects on behavioral and neurological outcomes, including decreased oxygen saturation, increased levels of plasma stress hormones, depression of the immune system, altered neurodevelopment, and "epigenomic changes that affect the brain, neurodevelopment, and pain reactivity into adulthood" (Hatfield, 2014). Yet pain remains undertreated in many neonates (Anand et al., 2001; Roofthooft et al., 2014).

Capacities for both nociception and painience have clinical and neuroethical significance. Neonates might experience both the sensory and affective aspects of pain, which underscores the need for better clinical pain management, since many routine procedures could cause pain and suffering and alter neurodevelopment. Neuroscientific evidence of nociception and painience bolsters the case that great caution is needed when considering whether to expose neonates to potentially painful procedures. This is true whether they are painient or merely nociceptive.

Fetal Nociception and Painience

It might be tempting to treat a fetus as if it were a very young neonate and assume that if pain is bad for a neonate, it is similarly bad for a fetus, and if anesthesia benefits the neonate, it will benefit the fetus as well.[3] It certainly appears that something like this line of reasoning has led to abundant speculation about fetal pain, influencing both clinical practice and legislation designed to restrict access to abortion. However, nociception and painience arise at different stages of fetal development. Current evidence indicates that the nociceptive pathways develop in the second trimester, while painience occurs much later, possibly even after birth (Lee et al., 2005; Derbyshire, 2008; Mellor et al., 2005). Reflex responses to noxious stimuli can occur early in fetal development, before thalamocortical circuits are functioning—those reflex movements in response to stimuli do not involve the cortex, and the fetus, presumably, is not painient (Lee et al., 2005). There are limited human studies that have directly examined the development of the thalamocortical circuits needed for pain perception (Lee et al., 2005), but histological studies of tissue from preterm neonates show evidence that the functional thalamocortical connections required for conscious perception of pain develop between 28 and 30 weeks' gestational age, or well into the third trimester of pregnancy (Lee et al., 2005; Lowery et al., 2007). Neuroimaging and connectome studies are providing new insights into neurodevelopment in the fetus (Verriotis et al., 2016; van den Heuvel et al., 2014) but to date have not been harnessed to study the entire "pain connectome" (Verriotis et al., 2016). In preterm neonates, the earliest electroencephalographic evidence of wakefulness appears around 30 weeks postconceptional age (gestational age plus number of weeks postpartum; Clancy et al., 2003). Wakefulness alone is not enough for consciousness, however, as individuals in the vegetative state have periods of wakefulness without conscious awareness. Mellor and colleagues conclude that there is no convincing evidence that *in utero* fetuses are ever awake or conscious but rather that they are in a continuous sleep-like state and do not experience nociceptive inputs as painful (Mellor et al., 2005). Unlike newborns, in fetuses, nociceptive stimuli do not cause cortical arousal to wakefulness; rather, there is an inhibitory response in the fetal brain *in utero* that suppresses arousal (Mellor et al., 2005). Derbyshire adds that the experience of pain requires both environmental sensory input to push neuronal organization and the development of postnatal consciousness. Derbyshire argues that while the necessary neural circuitry for pain may be in place *in utero*, pain requires psychological development that occurs only after birth, and so painience can only occur postpartum (Derbyshire, 2008). The consensus view is that if fetuses are painient at all, it is not until at least the third trimester.

There are, however, dissenters who challenge this conclusion. Anand and Clancy (2006) argue that fetal pain does *not* require cortical activation and conclude that fetal pain is possible and even probable before late gestation: "Our current understanding of development provides the anatomical structures, the physiological mechanisms, and the functional evidence for pain perception developing in the second trimester, certainly not in the first trimester, but well before the third trimester of human gestation" (Anand and Clancy, 2006). As noted previously, however, many behavioral and physiological responses to noxious stimuli can merely be indicators of nociception without painience. Anand, in particular, does not seem to rigorously distinguish between them. For example, he claims that fetuses can "experience pain," citing subsensory cortical and thalamic structures that develop before 20 weeks, as well as evidence of hormonal stress responses present at 16 weeks' gestation (Anand, 2004). Hormonal stress responses are not consciously mediated and are evidence of nociception but not necessarily of painience.

Anand further extrapolates from evidence of learning and perceiving in preterm infants that the same capacities exist in fetuses, and that fetuses can be inferred to possess "rudimentary abilities" that suggest consciousness from about 20 to 22 weeks "of fetal life" (it is unclear if he means gestational or developmental age; Anand, 2004). However, extrapolating from observations in preterm neonates to fetuses ignores the important differences between the fetal and neonatal environments, including evidence that the uterine environment induces in the fetus a sleep-like state of sedation and unconsciousness that suppresses higher cortical activation in the presence of external stimuli (Royal College of Obstetricians and Gynecologists, 2010; Mellor et al., 2005). Brusseau and Myers take a precautionary approach and argue that "it is reasonable to conclude that consciousness is at least *possible*" from 20 weeks gestation on, and similarly possible that "fetuses could experience something approximating 'pain'" (Brusseau and Myers, 2006).

To sum up, current evidence for fetal nociception beginning in the second trimester exists, while evidence for painience and fetal consciousness is less compelling and more controversial. This is an area in which neuroscience and the study of fetal neurodevelopment, including neuroimaging and connectome studies, might potentially make important contributions toward resolving some of the lingering uncertainty about the timing and emergence of fetal painience.

Ethical, Legal, and Social Implications of Fetal Painience

Brusseau and Myers conclude that the possibility of fetal pain mandates the provision of anesthesia and analgesia for fetuses undergoing surgery (Brusseau and Myers, 2006). Even in the absence of sentience and painience, physiological responses to nociceptive stimuli are an important consideration in invasive fetal therapies, such as surgeries, in which anesthesia or analgesia may be called for to reduce negative neurodevelopmental sequelae. Much research on safety and efficacy remains to be done, however, as evidence from animal studies indicates the possibility of neurotoxicity and neurodevelopmental deficits and behavioral problems later in life in rat pups (Flood, 2011) and permanent brain damage in guinea pigs exposed to anesthetics *in utero* (Rizzi et al., 2008). Restrictions on fetal research in humans complicate the gathering of meaningful evidence in human fetuses, and it is currently unclear whether the risks of surgery without anesthesia outweigh the risks of anesthesia (Flood, 2011).

Aside from concerns about the possible need for anesthesia during fetal surgery, fetal pain has received the most attention in the context of abortion. In the United States, state legislatures have contemplated and enacted a number of laws that attempt to regulate or restrict abortion on the basis of fetal capacity for pain.[4] In the United Kingdom, speculation about fetal pain, generated by 4D ultrasound images of fetuses, prompted debate about the need for fetal pain legislation (Derbyshire, 2008).[5]

A number of state laws in the U.S. have attempted to prohibit abortion in so-called pain-capable fetuses at 20 weeks, which is earlier than the viability standard (approximately 24 weeks) established by *Roe v. Wade*, the U.S. Supreme Court ruling that confirmed the legal right to abortion in the United States (*Roe v. Wade*, 410 U.S. 113 [1973]). Although fetal pain legislation frequently refers to scientific evidence, the distinction between nociception and painience has been ignored or unrecognized in the legislation. Utah's fetal pain legislation, for example, states that there is "substantial medical evidence from studies concluding that an unborn child who is at least 20 weeks gestational age may be capable of experiencing pain during an abortion procedure" (Utah Criminal Code 76–7–305). It's unclear to what extent these laws are based on actual confusion about the difference between nociception and painience or are politically capitalizing on that confusion to restrict access to abortion for other reasons. However, if fetal *painience* has moral significance in the abortion debate, it would be more likely to ease limits on abortion and extend the period when abortion without restriction is permissible, which is clearly contrary to the intent of fetal pain legislation. Indeed, if painience develops only postpartum, no restrictions on abortion would follow from a reliance on fetal painience alone as a relevant criterion.

The Moral Relevance of Painience

While attempts to limit abortion on the basis of fetal pain are politically motivated, unsupported by current scientific evidence, and naïvely (or intentionally) conflate nociception and pain (Lowery et al., 2007), they nonetheless raise interesting neuroethical questions about moral status and painience (for a detailed discussion of moral status, see Jaworska and Tannenbaum, 2013, and DeGrazia, 2008). Moral status can be broadly defined as *mattering morally*. An entity can be said to have moral status if it or its interests matter morally and matter entirely for the entity's own sake.[6] Acting against the interests of an entity with moral status would be wrong and would wrong the entity itself.[7] Some philosophers maintain that moral status is all or nothing, meaning you either have full moral status or none at all; others maintain that moral status might come in degrees, such that, for example, a paradigm (typical adult) human has full moral status, but other humans, nonhuman animals, or entities (trees, rivers, sacred sites, etc.) might have a lesser moral status (DeGrazia, 2008).

An important question concerns what conditions or criteria must be satisfied to have moral status. On one common view of moral status, what grounds it is the possession of sophisticated cognitive capacities (SCCs), such as those enjoyed by typical adult humans (Jaworska and Tannenbaum, 2013). Such capacities might include rationality and autonomy (capacities to set ends for oneself in accordance with reasoning), self-awareness, language, having a sense of one's identity through time, and so on (Pistoia et al., 2016). These sophisticated cognitive capacities require and assume consciousness but not painience. There are, for example, conscious adult humans with SCCs who are congenitally insensitive to pain (Salomons et al., 2016). For our purposes, it is clear that fetuses, whether painient or not, lack SCCs and would not have moral status if SCCs are necessary. A more inclusive formulation allows that the *capacity to develop* SCCs is sufficient to possess moral status. This would include many fetuses—of those destined to be born alive and survive childhood—but it would exclude those who can never develop SCCs and offers no account of those who have permanently lost their capacity for SCCs (such as persons with advanced dementia). The most inclusive formulation of SCC–based moral status would grant moral status to all those belonging to a species with SCC capacities. This would certainly include human fetuses, but it's not clear why membership in a species in which only some members possess SCCs is morally relevant (and not merely speciesist).

The relevance of SCCs to moral status is that they enable moral agency. Moral agents, it is often argued (see, e.g., Kant, 1958), have full status as morally significant beings who possess rights, including a right to life. Moral agents are entitled to respect; they are also beings who have moral duties or obligations that include respecting the rights and interests of other moral agents. The bar for this kind of full moral status and membership in the moral community is high. It requires having the cognitive and psychological capacities that make one capable of moral agency, and it's a seemingly all-or-nothing matter. You either have the requisite capacities, and therefore moral status, or you don't. Notably, on some such conceptions of moral status (see, e.g., Warren, 1973), fetuses, neonates, and many nonhuman animals would not qualify, and neither would some humans with severe cognitive or intellectual disabilities. On the other hand, some nonhuman species (e.g., nonhuman primates) might well qualify as moral agents (Shapiro, 2006), and if moral agency is necessary and sufficient for moral status, they would have moral status as well.[8] Sentience and painience would not be sufficient for moral status, since many painient creatures lack even the capacity to develop SCCs or be moral agents.

It is useful to distinguish moral *agency*, which seemingly requires at least some SCCs, from moral *patiency*, which does not. Moral patients are also entitled to moral consideration—they matter morally, and their suffering matters morally (Norcross, 2004). A fetus, neonate, or a nonhuman animal is not a moral agent, but it might still be a moral patient and entitled to *some* consideration of its interests (see DeGrazia, 2008, for a discussion of equal and unequal consideration). Such interests could include an interest in avoiding pain or suffering. Moral patience is an *arguably* lesser degree of moral status—less than the full moral status of moral agents. It need not be the case, however, that moral patients have a lesser degree of moral status in terms of their entitlement to moral consideration and treatment. After all, moral agents are also moral patients, and one of the benefits of the concept of moral patiency is its ability to handle the problem of "marginal cases," that is, humans who lack SCCs (Norcross, 2004). To consistently maintain that SCCs confer higher moral status would require defending the position that a 30-year-old human has higher moral status than a human neonate on the basis of the former possessing SCCs (but see Frey, 1987, and Warren, 1973, who defend something akin to this).

One of the interesting features of the distinction between moral agency and moral patiency is that the former entails both rights *and* active, agential responsibilities and duties to others, while the latter entails rights without imposing responsibilities or duties on moral patients. We do not expect infants or puppies to act as responsible moral agents, and being a moral agent is not a prerequisite for being a moral patient. As Norcross notes, "Full status as a moral patient is not some kind of reward for moral agency" (Norcross, 2004). Moral patients are entitled to moral consideration, and moral agents can have responsibilities to them. This asymmetry in responsibilities saddles only one side with the burdens of moral responsibility, but moral agents have moral responsibilities simply because they are the kinds of creatures that *can* have such responsibilities (Norcross, 2004). "What grounds moral agency is simply different from what grounds moral standing as a patient" (Norcross, 2004).

What grounds moral patiency? One candidate is sentience, the capacity for conscious feeling. Minimally, sentience is required for having interests—for having a welfare that matters to one (Singer, 1974). Painience would count as a rudimentary—as opposed to sophisticated—cognitive capacity, along with capacities for pleasure, having interests, and consciousness (Jaworska and Tannenbaum, 2013). Most humans, including many neonates, certainly have these rudimentary cognitive capacities, as do many other species. But if some fetuses have moral status on the grounds of painience, it's likely other fetuses do not. And what sort of moral status might painience confer? Utilitarians generally view sentience (and thus painience) as necessary and sufficient for being morally considerable. Bentham long ago stated that painience, not other cognitive capacities, matters morally:

> Is it the faculty of reason or perhaps the faculty of discourse? But a full-grown horse or dog, is beyond comparison a more rational, as well as a more conversable animal, than an infant of a day or a week or even a month, old. But suppose the case were otherwise, what would it avail? the question is not, Can they reason? nor, Can they talk? but, Can they suffer?
>
> (Bentham, 1970)

Ryder (2002) maintains that painience is singularly morally important. Ryder has dubbed his ethical position "Painism," which encompasses the ideas that pain is "the basic criterion of what is wrong" and that the suffering of individuals matters morally. He argues that painful sensations can trigger emotional responses, and emotions can be painful, but painful sensations in the absence of emotional responses also matter morally. It's not clear if he means nociception or if he simply rejects definitions of pain, like the IASP definition, that endorse the necessity of emotion in distinguishing pain from nociception. For Ryder, that some creatures are capable of painful sensations is enough to make them matter morally, regardless of whether they experience other forms of suffering, such as fear, grief, or anxiety. His painism is a piece with his arguments against speciesism, and defining pain in this way lowers the bar, or the burden of proof, such that we might recognize animals that exhibit aversive behaviors (such as reflexive limb withdrawals) as painient (Ryder, 2002).

Loveless and Giordano propose painience—"the capacity to feel pain as noxious (injurious) and explicitly hurtful (that is to say, pain *qua* pain, not simply nociception but nociperception)"—as a minimum criterion for moral consideration (Loveless and Giordano, 2014). Unlike Ryder, they do not separate the physiological and affective components of painful experiences. They argue that strong inferences regarding the existence of pain experiences in nonhuman species can be grounded in the presence and activity of neural systems similar or functionally analogous to human neural systems. Recognition that pain *can* occur in a particular organism, they argue, "is a necessary and sufficient condition to afford that organism basic moral consideration and respectful treatment, that is to say, to avoid the purposeful infliction of pain when and where possible" (Loveless and Giordano, 2014). It's worth noting that there are unresolved neuroscientific questions about the so-called pain matrix—a set of brain areas including the anterior cingulate cortex, thalamus, and insula that consistently respond to painful stimuli in humans—and the neural networks and connectivity required for experiencing pain and being painient (Wiech et al., 2008; Geha and Waxman, 2016; Salomons et al., 2016; Wager et al., 2013; Mouraux et al., 2011; Verriotis et al., 2016).

Let's suppose that painience is *sufficient* for moral patiency. Is it also *necessary* for having any moral status? If it is, then the permanently unconscious and early fetuses would fail to have any moral status. We might still allow that insofar as they matter to other moral agents, they matter morally. This is a contingent kind of moral status. It's a moral status that can depend on circumstances, including such circumstances as whether one matters to a moral agent. Warren, for example, allowed that although neonates are not moral persons, they still matter to their parents and communities, making infanticide contingently wrong (Warren, 1973). Moral status might also be contingent on whether one has only temporarily lost (or not yet acquired) the capacities necessary and sufficient for moral status. It would be unsettling, however, if something as important as one's moral status depended on such contingent features.

The Moral Status of Neonates and Fetuses

If sentience or painience is sufficient for moral patiency, then full-term human neonates are moral patients. This leaves us to consider whether fetuses are also moral patients, and if they are, what responsibilities or duties their moral patiency entails for moral agents. The former requires answering empirical neurodevelopmental questions; the latter are ethical questions. That is, the neuroscience of human neurodevelopment can play a role in informing our understanding of painience and sentience in fetuses, but just as painience does not straightforwardly imply any *particular* moral responsibilities to the painient moral patient, it does not wholly answer questions about what, if anything, is owed to fetuses. One possibility, should it turn out that fetuses are painient, is that we ought to avoid gratuitously inflicting pain on them. This seems to minimally and logically be what would follow from the badness of pain, painience, and the moral considerability of painient creatures. That is, if we are pursuing a morally permissible end and have a choice as to whether its pursuit will cause pain to another painient creature, it is *prima facie* wrong to cause that creature pain.[9] *Prima facie* wrongs are not wrongs full stop; they are subject to all-things-considered reappraisal.

Fetal Painience: Ethical, Legal, and Social Issues

Nebraska passed the first "fetal pain" statute, which has served as a template for other U.S. states. Its avowed purpose was to "assert a compelling state interest in protecting the lives of unborn children from the stage at which substantial medical evidence indicates they are capable of feeling pain" (Leg Bill, 1103§1(5),5; [Neb, 2010]).[10] The bill marks that point as 20 or more weeks "postfertilization." The effort to employ the capacity for pain as a criterion for a presumptive right to life founders not only on scientific but also on ethical grounds. The fact of conscious pain or suffering does not make it wrong to terminate the life of a being with moral status. Indeed, conscious pain and suffering sometimes gives us moral reasons for ending life. Thus, a "compelling state interest in protecting the lives of unborn children" cannot be consistently based on painience alone.

Fetal pain bans seek to prohibit any abortion procedure on the grounds of fetal pain rather than restricting women to procedures less likely to cause pain.[11] Anand claims that abortion after

20 weeks causes "intense pain" to the fetus (Anand, 2004). The available evidence, however, does not support the assertion that fetuses at 20 weeks postfertilization are painient but rather that the fetal capacity for pain "may occur in the third trimester around 29 to 30 weeks' gestational age" (Lee et al., 2005). Abortion bans based on sound scientific evidence of fetal pain, then, could move the bar several weeks past the point of viability rather than before it. Much depends, however, on how "feeling pain" is defined.

The moral and legal significance of fetal painience is far from clear. I'll assert, however, that nociception has no significance in the context of abortion—neurodevelopmental consequences related to early nociceptive stimuli have significance for children later in life, but only if those children exist. The Nebraska statute claims that the state has a compelling interest not only in *preventing* fetal pain but in *protecting the lives* of fetuses that can experience pain. It does not follow, however, that the ability to experience pain—a trait that all sentient creatures by definition have—confers some unique moral status that prohibits either inflicting pain or killing such creatures or that the prevention of pain alone "is enough to justify infringing on what is avowedly a fundamental right of women to have an abortion" (Cohen and Sayeed, 2011). If prevention of pain to sentient beings does justify restricting fundamental rights, it would plausibly justify infringing on other, less weighty rights as well by invoking a state interest in, for example, prohibiting hunting, confinement in animal agriculture, and the slaughter of animals to prevent pain to wildlife and livestock (Johnson, 2014). Indeed, for fetal pain to do any heavy lifting here requires it to be underwritten by, minimally, anthropocentric speciesism that regards human life as uniquely valuable and fetal human pain as uniquely morally bad.

The language of the Nebraska statute, which refers to "unborn children," may signal an intention to use the capacity to feel pain as definitive of personhood. If consistently applied, this would force the conclusion that all pain-capable creatures are persons. Such a definition of personhood—legal or moral—would be novel, and it is not obvious why it should stand (Johnson, 2014). While the personhood of a subject provides a moral reason not to inflict pain needlessly, neither personhood nor the capacity to feel pain nor both together suffice to make all inflictions of pain morally impermissible. Indeed, protecting persons from harm can provide a morally compelling reason to inflict pain on them or on others. Treatment of childhood leukemia is painful but serves the important purpose of saving lives. Fetal surgery, even *if* painful for the fetus, is not performed unless medically necessary to protect the life and health of the fetus. Whether fetal anesthesia is administered is a medical decision that should depend on an all-things-considered calculus that looks at the benefits and risks of fetal anesthesia. Those benefits and risks will include benefits and risks to pregnant women. Moreover, conferring legal *personhood* solely on the basis of the capacity for painience seemingly strips unconscious, insensate humans of their personhood.

It is thus not obvious why a fetal capacity to feel pain necessarily morally compels a prohibition on abortion or forms of abortion that might be painful for fetuses. If fetuses are painient, then the pain of a painient fetus is worthy of moral consideration, but it is not *uniquely* worthy of moral consideration. While general anesthesia was once common for surgical abortion, evidence that it significantly contributed to maternal morbidity and mortality altered the standard of care (Mackay et al., 1985). There currently is no standard of care regarding *fetal* anesthesia during abortion (Price and Golden, 2015), nor are fetuses anesthetized during full-term or preterm births, despite the possibility that birth itself is painful. In the context of abortion, the interests and health of pregnant women—who are undeniably painient moral agents with rights—are also morally considerable. Fetal pain laws frequently admit this, for example, by allowing abortion in cases of rape or to protect the life or health of the pregnant woman. Furthermore, late-term abortions, performed in cases of fetal complications such as lethal fetal anomalies, must weigh possible fetal pain against the possible pain or suffering of neonates who are doomed to die. The risk of inflicting pain on a being with moral status matters morally, but all things considered, it's not obvious why the possibility—or even the fact—of fetal pain eclipses all other considerations, including considerations of the pain or suffering of others.[12]

Conclusion

Physiologically, neurologically, and developmentally, fetuses are not simply very young neonates *in utero*. It's likely they are also developmentally quite different from same-age preterm neonates. To the extent that the capacity for painience is relevant to their moral status, we might with reason want to take a precautionary approach that treats them as if they are at least nociceptive. But neither being nociceptive nor painient does the work of establishing an unqualified right to be kept alive or an unqualified right against all inflictions of pain. Even undeniably painient paradigm humans with full moral status have no such unqualified rights.

While consciously experienced pain has received much ethical attention for its role as a criterion for having moral status or being due moral consideration, there are reasons to be concerned about nociception in both painient and nonpainient creatures, including human fetuses and neonates. The physiological effects of nociception, even if not consciously perceived, might affect neurodevelopment in ways that would have long-term negative repercussions for the health or well-being of an organism such that, for creatures who are due moral consideration, we ought to be concerned about the avoidable infliction of noxious stimuli even in the absence of awareness and pain.

Having a sophisticated and accurate understanding of nociception and its development in the fetus is important, as is understanding how to manage the physiological effects of nociception safely and effectively. Current evidence for fetal painience puts its possible development at around 30 weeks' gestational age, although potentially, it develops only after birth. Third-trimester abortions are extremely rare and almost always done because of fatal fetal anomalies (Barel et al., 2009), but understanding when the capacity for consciousness and painience develops matters in the context of fetal therapy and for treating preterm neonates, some of whom survive birth before painience apparently develops. The emergence of painience in *ex utero* preterm infants may not track the development of painience *in utero*, in part because of the intensive medical interventions needed to maintain life in very early preterm infants and in part because of the sedative effect of the uterine environment. Finally, an empirically informed understanding of anesthesia that would permit risk–benefit considerations in the debate about fetal pain in the context of abortion could serve as a corrective to the pseudoneuroscientific propaganda that currently influences that debate.

Being able to detect painience would be important not only for neonates but also for other categories of patients with contested moral status, such as those in the vegetative state. Importantly, if painience confers moral status, we must confront ethical questions about what *degree* of moral status it confers, as well as what moral obligations that status implies, since the range of painient species is enormous. It certainly encompasses all mammals (see Fenton and Shriver, Chapter 32) and, more controversially, birds, fish, cephalopods, crustaceans, and others. Even granting the sensible and cautious conclusion that it is *prima facie* wrong to needlessly or gratuitously inflict pain on painient creatures does not end the matter. Many possibilities—some involving the rights and needs of others and some involving the rights and needs of those who could suffer pain—can, do, and will intervene and demand consideration.

Acknowledgment

Many thanks to Andrew Fenton, Timothy Krahn, and Karen Rommelfanger for their helpful and insightful comments on an earlier draft of this chapter.

Notes

1 Thalamic pain syndrome, also known as Dejerine-Roussy Syndrome, is a condition that develops following a thalamic stroke. Afflicted individuals can develop severe and chronic pain not caused by an external stimulus (Kleiner, 2011).

2 It is not just infants that lack the ability to communicate regarding their pain. Nonhuman species (e.g., veterinary patients and animals used in research), as well as humans with severe cognitive and intellectual disabilities (including patients with advanced dementia and disorders of consciousness), lack the ability to communicate, making the assessment of pain challenging in these populations as well.

3 For purposes of this chapter, a fetus is a human organism, *in utero*, 8 weeks or more after fertilization (Brown, 2016). Different methods of dating prenatal age are used by obstetricians. *Developmental age* dates pregnancy to a woman's last menstrual period, while *gestational age* starts the clock 2 weeks later, at fertilization. Human pregnancy, therefore, typically lasts 38 to 40 weeks, depending on which measure is being used. Pregnancy is divided into *trimesters* of roughly 13 weeks each. *Postconception age* (of preterm neonates) is developmental age plus postpartum age.

4 In the United States, 12 states currently have laws mandating that abortion providers must inform women that the fetus can feel pain; half of those states require fetal pain information be given to women who are at least 20 weeks' gestation. As of November 1, 2016, those states were Alaska, Arizona, Georgia, Indiana, Kansas, Louisiana, Minnesota, Missouri, Oklahoma, South Dakota, Texas, and Utah (Guttmacher Institute, 2016).

5 In the United Kingdom, abortions are permitted during the first 24 weeks of pregnancy, a limit based on the likelihood of survival for preterm infants. It closely approximates the *Roe v. Wade* decision, which limits state interference in abortion up until viability (which is around 24 weeks).

6 As DeGrazia formulates moral status, it also implies obligations on the part of moral agents: "To say that X has moral status is to say that (1) moral agents have obligations regarding X, (2) X has interests, and (3) the obligations are based (at least partly) on X's interests" (DeGrazia, 2008).

7 Moral status is also sometimes referred to as "moral standing," "moral considerability," or simply "personhood" (although personhood is also a legal status). Utilitarians commonly employ the notion of moral considerability to mean that the interests of a morally considerable creature must be considered in a calculus of utility, alongside the interests of any other morally considerable creatures.

8 Thanks to Andrew Fenton for pressing this point.

9 Thanks, again, to Andrew Fenton for suggesting this conclusion.

10 Under Nebraska law, "unborn child or fetus each mean an individual organism of the species *homo sapiens* from fertilization until live birth" (LB1103, § 2 [2010]). A fertilized but not yet implanted zygote would, it appears, count as a fetus or unborn child under Nebraska law.

11 The state of Utah enacted SB 234 ("Protecting Unborn Children Amendments") in 2016. That law requires doctors performing abortions at 20 weeks' or more gestational age to "administer an anesthetic or analgesic to eliminate or alleviate organic pain to the unborn child." The basis for the legislation is "substantial medical evidence from studies concluding that an unborn child who is at least 20 weeks gestational age may be capable of experiencing pain during an abortion procedure" (Utah Criminal Code 76–7–305).

12 Thanks to Timothy Krahn for insightful comments that helped me to better develop this point.

Further Reading

DeGrazia, D. (2008) "Moral Status as a Matter of Degree?" *Southern Journal of Philosophy* 46(2), 181–198.

Hatfield, L. (2014) "Neonatal Pain: What's Age Got to Do With It?" *Surgical Neurology International* 5(Suppl. 13), S479—S489.

Jaworska, A. and Tannenbaum, J. (2013) "The grounds of moral status". In E.N. Zalta (Ed.). *The Stanford Encyclopedia of Philosophy*. Available at: https://plato.stanford.edu/archives/sum2013/entries/grounds-moral-status/ [Accessed 30 December 2016].

Lee, S.J., Ralston, H.J.P., Drey, E.A., Partridge, J.C. and Rosen, M.A. (2005) "Fetal Pain: A Systematic Mul-tidisciplinary Review of the Evidence". *JAMA* 294(8), 947–954.

Norcross, A. (2004) "Puppies, Pigs, and people: Eating Meat and Marginal Cases". *Philosophical Perspectives* 18(1), 229–245.

References

Anand, K.J.S. (2001) Consensus statement for the prevention and management of pain in the newborn. *Archives of Pediatrics & Adolescent Medicine* 155(2): pp. 173–180.

———. (2004) *Expert Report of Kanwaljeet S. Anand, MBBS, D.Phil.* Northern District of the US District Court in California, 15 January. Available at: www.nrlc.org/uploads/fetalpain/AnandPainReport.pdf [Accessed 28 Dec. 2016].

Anand, K.J.S., and Clancy, B. (2006) Fetal pain? *Pain: Clinical Updates* 14(2): pp. 1–4.

Anand, K.J.S., and Hickey, P.R. (1987) Pain and its effects in the human neonate and fetus. *New England Journal of Medicine* 317(21): pp. 1321–1329.

Anand, K.J., Sippell, W.G., Schofield, N.M., and Aynsley-Green, A. (1988) Does halothane anaesthesia decrease the metabolic and endocrine stress responses of newborn infants undergoing operation? *BMJ* 296(6623): p. 668.

Barel, O., Vaknin, Z., Smorgick, N., Reish, O., Mendlovic, S., Herman, A., and Maymon, R. (2009) Fetal abnormalities leading to third trimester abortion: Nine-year experience from a single medical center. *Prenatal Diagnosis* 29(3): pp. 223–228.

Bastuji, H., Mazza, S., Perchet, C., Frot, M., Mauguière, F., Magnin, M., and Garcia-Larrea, L. (2012) Fil-tering the reality: Functional dissociation of lateral and medial pain systems during sleep in humans. *Human Brain Mapping* 33(11): pp. 2638–2649.

Bentham, J. (1970) *An Introduction to the Principles of Morals and Legislation*, J.H. Burns and H.L.A. Hart (Eds.). London: The Athlone Press.

Block, N. (2005) Two neural correlates of consciousness. *Trends in Cognitive Sciences* 9(2): pp. 46–52.

Boffey, P.M. (1987) Infants' sense of pain is recognized, finally. *New York Times*. Available at: www.nytimes.com/1987/11/24/science/infants-sense-of-pain-is-recognized-finally.html [Accessed 30 Dec. 2016].

Brown, H.L. (2016) Stages of development of the fetus. *Merck Manual*. Available at: www.merckmanuals.com/home/women-s-health-issues/normal-pregnancy/stages-of-development-of-the-fetus.

Brusseau, R., and Myers, L. (2006) Developing consciousness: Fetal anesthesia and analgesia. *Seminars in Anesthesia, Perioperative Medicine and Pain* 25(4): pp. 189–195.

Clancy, R.R., Bergqvist, A.C., and Dlugos, D.J. (2003) Neonatal electroencephalography. *Current Practice of Clinical Electroencephalography* 3: pp. 106–234.

Cohen, I.G., and Sayeed, S. (2011) Fetal pain, abortion, viability, and the constitution. *Journal of Law, Medicine & Ethics* 39(2): pp. 235–242.

DeGrazia, D. (2008) Moral status as a matter of degree? *Southern Journal of Philosophy* 46(2): pp. 181–198.

Derbyshire, S.W. (2008) Fetal pain: Do we know enough to do the right thing? *Reproductive Health Matters* 16(31): pp. 117–126.

Dubin, A.E., and Patapoutian, A. (2010) Nociceptors: The sensors of the pain pathway. *Journal of Clinical Investigation* 120(11): pp. 3760–3772.

Fabrizi, L., Verriotis, M., Williams, G., Lee, A., Meek, J., Olhede, S., and Fitzgerald, M. (2016) Encoding of mechanical nociception differs in the adult and infant brain. *Scientific Reports* 6: pp. 1–9.

Flood, P. (2011) Fetal anesthesia and brain development. *Journal of the American Society of Anesthesiologists* 114(3): pp. 479–480.

Frey, R.G. (1987) The significance of agency and marginal cases. *Philosophica* 39(1): pp. 39–46.

Geha, P., and Waxman, S.G. (2016) Pain perception: Multiple matrices or one? *Journal of American Medical Association Neurology* 73(6): pp. 628–630.

Goksan, S., Hartley, C., Emery, F., Cockrill, N., Poorun, R., Moultrie, F., Rogers, R., Campbell, J., Sanders, M., Adams, E. and Clare, S. (2015) fMRI reveals neural activity overlap between adult and infant pain. *eLife* 4: p. e06356. doi:10.7554/eLife.06356

Guttmacher Institute. (2016) An overview of abortion laws. Available at: www.guttmacher.org/state-pol icy/explore/overview-abortion-laws. [Accessed 28 Dec. 2016].

Hatfield, L. (2014) Neonatal pain: What's age got to do with it? *Surgical Neurology International* 5(Suppl 13): pp. S479—S489.

Heuvel van den, M.P., Kersbergen, K.J., de Reus, M.A., Keunen, K., Kahn, R.S., Groenendaal, F., . . . Bend-ers, M.J. (2014) The neonatal connectome during preterm brain development. *Cerebral Cortex* 25(9): pp. 3000–3013.

Jaworska, A., and Tannenbaum, J. (2013) The Grounds of moral status. In E.N. Zalta (Ed.). *The Stanford Encyclopedia of Philosophy*. Available at: https://plato.stanford.edu/archives/sum2013/entries/grounds-moral-status/ [Accessed 27 Dec. 2016].

Johnson, L.S.M. (2014) Abortion II: Ethical perspectives. In B. Jennings (Ed.). *Bioethics*. Vol. 1, 4th ed. Farm-ington Hills, MI: Palgrave Macmillan, pp. 8–22.

Kant, I. (1958) *Groundwork of the Metaphysic of Morals*. Paton, H.J. (translator). New York: Harper & Row.

Kleiner, J.S. (2011) Thalamic pain syndrome. In J. Kreutzer, J. DeLuca and B. Caplan (Eds.). *Encyclopedia of Clinical Neuropsychology*. New York: Springer, pp. 2505–2505.

Lee, S.J., Ralston, H.J.P., Drey, E.A., Partridge, J.C., and Rosen, M.A. (2005) Fetal pain: A systematic multi-disciplinary review of the evidence. *Journal of American Medical Association* 294(8): pp. 947–954.

Leg Bill 1103§1(5),5(Neb 2010)

Loeser J. D., Treede R. D. (2008). The Kyoto protocol of IASP basic pain terminology. Pain 137 473–477.

Loveless, S.E., and Giordano, J. (2014) Neuroethics, painience, and neurocentric criteria for the moral treat-ment of animals. *Cambridge Quarterly of Healthcare Ethics* 23(2): pp. 163–172.

Lowery, C.L., Hardman, M.P., Manning, N., Clancy, B., Hall, R. W., and Anand, K.J.S. (2007) Neurodevel-opmental changes of fetal pain. *Seminars in Perinatology* 31(5): pp. 275–282.

Mackay, H.T., Schulz, K.F., and Grimes, D.A. (1985) Safety of local versus general anesthesia for second-trimester dilatation and evacuation abortion. *Obstetrics & Gynecology* 66(5): pp. 661–665.

Mellor, D.J., Diesch, T.J., Gunn, A.J., and Bennet, L. (2005) The importance of 'awareness' for understanding fetal pain. *Brain Research Reviews* 49(3): pp. 455–471.

Merskey, H., and Bogduk, N. (Eds.) (2012) *Classification of Chronic Pain*. International Association for the Study of Pain. Available at: www.iasp-pain.org/PublicationsNews/Content.aspx?ItemNumber=1673& navItemNumber=677 [Accessed 30 Dec. 2016].

Monti, M.M., Laureys, S., and Owen, A.M. (2010) The vegetative state. *BMJ* 341(c3765): pp. 292–296.

Mouraux, A., Diukova, A., Lee, M.C., Wise, R.G., and Iannetti, G.D. (2011) A multisensory investigation of the functional significance of the "pain matrix." *Neuroimage* 54(3): pp. 2237–2249.

Naro, A., Leo, A., Bramanti, P., and Calabrò, R.S. (2015) Moving toward conscious pain processing detec-tion in chronic disorders of consciousness: Anterior cingulate cortex neuromodulation. *Journal of Pain* 16(10): pp. 1022–1031.

Norcross, A. (2004) Puppies, pigs, and people: Eating meat and marginal cases. *Philosophical Perspectives* 18(1): pp. 229–245.

Osterwels R., Kleinman A., Mechanic D., Institute of Medicine Committee on Pain, Disability, and Chronic Illness Behavior. (1987) *Pain and Disability, Clinical Behavioral and Public Policy Perspectives*. Washington, DC: National Academies Press.

Pistoia, F., Sacco, S., Stewart, J., Sarà, M., and Carolei, A. (2016) Disorders of consciousness: Painless or pain-ful conditions?—Evidence from neuroimaging studies. *Brain Sciences* 6(47): pp. 1–15.

Price, M.L., and Golden, H. (2015) Utah abortion providers stumped by law requiring fetal pain relief. *PBS NewsHour*. Available at: www.pbs.org/newshour/rundown/utah-abortion-providers-stumped-by-law-requiring-fetal-pain-relief/ [Accessed 30 Dec. 2016].

Ranger, M., Johnston, C.C., and Anand, K.J.S. (2007) Current controversies regarding pain assessment in neonates. *Seminars in Perinatology* 31: pp. 283–288.

Rizzi, S., Carter, L.B., Ori, C., and Jevtovic-Todorovic, V. (2008) Clinical anesthesia causes permanent dam-age to the fetal guinea pig brain. *Brain Pathology* 18(2): pp. 198–210.

Rodkey, E.N., and Riddell, R.P. (2013) The infancy of infant pain research: The experimental origins of infant pain denial. *Journal of Pain* 14(4): pp. 338–350.

Roe v. Wade, 410 U.S. 113 (1973)

Roofthooft, D.W., Simons, S.H., Anand, K.J., Tibboel, D., and van Dijk, M. (2014) Eight years later, are we still hurting newborn infants? *Neonatology* 105(3): pp. 218–226.

Royal College of Obstetricians and Gynecologists Working Party. (2010) *Fetal Awareness: Review of Research and Recommendations for Practice, Report of a Working Party*. Available at: www.rcog.org.uk/globalassets/documents/guidelines/rcogfetalawarenesswpr0610.pdf [Accessed 28 Dec. 2016].

Ryder, R.D. (2002) The ethics of painism: The argument against painful experiments. *Between the Species* 13(2): pp. 1–9.

Salomons, T.V., Iannetti, G.D., Liang, M., and Wood, J.N. (2016) The "pain matrix" in pain-free individuals. *Journal of American Medical Association Neurology* 73(6): pp. 755–756.

Shapiro, P. (2006) Moral agency in other animals. *Theoretical Medicine and Bioethics* 27(4): pp. 357–373.

Singer, P. (1974) All animals are equal. *Philosophic Exchange* 5(1): pp. 103–116.

Slater, R., Fabrizi, L., Worley, A., Meek, J., Boyd, S., and Fitzgerald, M. (2010a) Premature infants display increased noxious-evoked neuronal activity in the brain compared to healthy age-matched term-born infants. *NeuroImage* 52: pp. 583–589.

Slater, R., Cornelissen, L., Fabrizi, L., Patten, D., Yoxen, J., Worley, A., . . . Fitgerald, M. (2010b) Oral sucrose as an analgesic drug for procedural pain in newborn infants: A randomised controlled trial. *The Lancet* 376: pp. 1225–1232.

Tracey, I., and Mantyh, P.W. (2007) The cerebral signature for pain perception and its modulation. *Neuron* 55(3): pp. 377–391.

Utah Criminal Code; S.B. 234. Available at: http://le.utah.gov/~2016/bills/static/sb0234.html#76-7-305 [Accessed 28 Dec. 2016].

Van Gulick, R. (2014) Consciousness. *The Stanford Encyclopedia of Philosophy*. Zalta, E.N. (Ed.). Available at: https://plato.stanford.edu/archives/win2016/entries/consciousness/ [Accessed 30 Dec. 2016].

Verriotis, M., Chang, P., Fitzgerald, M., and Fabrizi, L. (2016) The development of the nociceptive brain. *Neuroscience* 338: pp. 207–219.

Wager, T.D., Atlas, L.Y., Lindquist, M.A., Roy, M., Woo, C.W., and Kross, E. (2013) An fMRI-based neurologic signature of physical pain. *New England Journal of Medicine* 368(15): pp. 1388–1397.

Warren, M.A. (1973) On the moral and legal status of abortion. *The Monist* 57(4): pp. 44–61.

Wiech, K. (2016) Deconstructing the sensation of pain: The influence of cognitive processes on pain perception. *Science* 354(6312): pp. 584–587.

Wiech, K., Ploner, M., and Tracey, I. (2008) Neurocognitive aspects of pain perception. *Trends in Cognitive Sciences* 12(8): pp. 306–313.

Worley, A., Fabrizi, L., Boyd, S., and Slater, R. (2012) Multi-modal pain measurements in infants. *Journal of Neuroscience Methods* 205(2): pp. 252–257.

32

ANIMAL MINDS
The Neuroethics of Nonhuman Dissent

Andrew Fenton and Adam Shriver

Introduction

Can neuroscience help us to determine whether nonhuman animals have morally relevant capacities? In this chapter, we demonstrate how evidence from the neurosciences can be combined with other forms of evidence to assess the morally relevant mental states and cognitive capacities of nonhuman animals. In particular, we will discuss how neuroscience can be used to determine whether some nonhuman animals have the capacity for dissent in research contexts and will examine the ethical conclusions we can draw from these findings. We suggest that neuroscience can complement, while never fully replacing, other forms of evidence that are marshaled for establishing the presence of mental capacities in nonhuman animal species.

Framing the Decisional Capacities of Some Other Animals

The 2006 Weatherall Report, which was jointly sponsored by the Academy of Medical Sciences, Medical Research Council, the Royal Society, and Wellcome Trust, makes the following statement about consent in the context of nonhuman primate research ethics:

> While it is true that animals cannot give informed consent, they cannot give informed refusal either. This is not to say that they cannot forecast danger, apparently communicate their fear or disapproval, or struggle to avoid compliance. . . . [F]or almost all experiments involving conscious non-human primates it is essential that the animals are calm and co-operative; while this may be taken to indicate that they are not significantly distressed this cannot be taken as equivalent to informed consent.
>
> . . . [I]f it is right to claim that they [non-human primates] have a different moral status to human beings then a balance must be struck between their interests and the interests of the humans who might benefit from the proposed research. . . . [i]nformed consent is simply not the relevant issue.
>
> (Academy of Medical Sciences and Weatherall, 2006, 129)

There is much to parse in this passage and the surrounding text. In the text surrounding this passage, for example, the decisional incompetence of potential research subjects (which consists of an inability to make informed, autonomous choices) foregrounds, though only for those with high moral status (in this case, young children), their best interests when deciding to enroll them in research. This regard for vulnerable, incompetent research subjects will reassert itself later in this section after we have defended reenvisioning our moral obligations to dissenting nonhuman animal research subjects. In the quote itself, three things are noteworthy: it is claimed that animals (meaning nonhuman animals)[1] cannot give informed consent; that a number of nonhuman animals used in research can, nevertheless, resist, or fail to cooperate with the relevant laboratory personnel; and that their lack of equal moral status to humans means that not even their best interests are relevant to the justification of using them in harmful research.

In contrast to the passage from the Weatherall Report, the last few decades have seen decided and noteworthy changes in seeking the cooperation of research animals. Many animal welfare scientists or laboratory animal scientists contend that the cooperation of laboratory animal research subjects is significant for the relevant research animal's environmental enrichment and behavioral health (Coleman, 2010). Laule, Bloomsmith, and Schapiro write:

> Training laboratory primates to cooperate voluntarily in husbandry, veterinary, and research procedures seems to have significant benefits for the animals. Animals are desensitized to frightening or painful events, such as receiving an injection. . . . Voluntary cooperation reduces the need for physical restraint and/or anesthesia and, thus, the accompanying risks associated with those events.
>
> (Laule et al., 2003, 166)

As implied in the previous quotation, the cooperation of nonhuman research subjects has also been implicated in reducing confounding factors that can adversely affect the statistical significance of the relevant study results (Coleman, 2010; Weed and Raber, 2005). Coleman et al. write,

> In addition to the utility of reducing stress associated with maintenance and research procedures, other benefits warrant training monkeys to cooperate voluntarily. Training can reduce the need for sedation, which in turn can reduce variability that might be introduced by pharmacological agents. Even in situations that require sedation, training subjects to accept injections can alter stress-related variables. In a recent study, chimpanzees that voluntarily presented a limb for injection of anesthesia had significantly lower haematological indicators of stress.
>
> (Coleman et al., 2008, 39)

Yet another noteworthy change in seeking the cooperation of research animals is the significance of their cooperation to many researchers (Coleman, 2010; Laule et al., 2003; Rennie and Buchanan-Smith, 2006). For some, at least, they are motivated by *respect or compassion for* their subjects. Matsuzawa writes,

> The chimpanzees in the KUPRI [Kyoto University's Primate Research Institute] laboratory are free: it is completely up to each subject whether he or she will come to the booth to participate in a cognitive task or not. . . . Suppose that a chimpanzee does decide to come to the booth. Again, it is up to them whether to start the first trial of the test session or not. . . . [T]he response-contingent delivery of the food has a special value for the chimpanzee. Based on their free will, they work on a cognitively challenging task and as a result they are rewarded.
>
> (Matsuzawa, 2006, 20)

In his popular book *How Dogs Love Us*, Berns highlights the significance of ensuring the cooperation of his canine research subjects in his fMRI studies of their conscious functioning brains this way:

> [I]f a mother signs up for a research project with her infant and the baby shows obvious signs of distress, like inconsolable crying, the researcher should interpret this as a sign that the baby doesn't want to participate, and the experiment should be stopped. We could do the same with dogs and treat them like infant research subjects. If they showed any signs of not wanting to participate, we would stop the experiment. The simplest way to do this would be to dispense with restraints. If a dog didn't want to be in the MRI scanner anymore, he could simply get out. . . . Elevating the rights of a dog to that of a human child made both ethical and scientific sense.
>
> (Berns, 2013, 65; see also Berns et al., 2012)

A striking advance in accommodating the cooperation of the animal research subjects, albeit one that can be exaggerated, is contained in the 2011 report on the necessity of biomedical and behavioral chimpanzee research sponsored by the U.S. Institute of Medicine (IOM) as well as the National Research Council, and commissioned by the National Institutes of Health. It states:

> Comparative genomics and behavioral research should only be performed on acquiescent animals and in a manner that minimizes distress to the animal. Evidence of acquiescence includes situations in which animals do not refuse or resist research-related interventions and that do not require physical or psychological threats for participation.
>
> (Altevogt et al., 2011, 34)

Note how this passage gives normative weight to chimpanzee nonresistance and reenvisions respectful treatment. Indeed, this quote partially articulates one of the two restrictions used by the report committee—the other being that the research is both substantive and requires chimpanzee participation—to judge the legitimacy of behavioral or comparative genomic chimpanzee research (Altevogt et al., 2011). Though consent is not explicitly associated with the decisional capacities of research chimpanzees in the IOM report (it is associated several times with human decisional capacities), there is greater apparent openness to something in its 'conceptual vicinity' than is seen in the Weatherall Report.

Inspirations from Pediatric Research Ethics

In addition to changes in the animal welfare literature, the importance of securing the cooperation of animal research subjects is gaining increasing support in 'animal' bioethics (e.g., DeGrazia, 2007; Fenton, 2014; Johnson and Barnard, 2014; Rollin, 2009; Walker, 2006), though this development is not new (e.g., see Fox, 1987, and Sapontzis, 1987). Johnson and Barnard write,

> We suggest that a surrogate decision maker be empowered to act in a potential chimpanzee subject's interests, as is done for children where a parent or guardian can assume this role. . . . It is also important to obtain the chimpanzee equivalent of 'assent' for research to proceed. In pediatric research this concept refers to the willingness of young children to participate in research in spite of their inability to give informed consent. Children who refuse likely should be excluded from research unless the research offers

to provide a therapy unavailable elsewhere. . . . Chimpanzees are capable of expressing both assent and dissent. . . . Experiences from psychological and behavioural studies demonstrate that concepts like assent evidenced through voluntary decision making can be used effectively in the context of research with chimpanzees.

(Johnson and Barnard, 2014, 138)

In a relevantly similar vein, Fenton writes,

Chimpanzees are the obvious candidates for human-level moral status among nonhuman animals. Moreover, their preferences are already accorded limited moral weight in contemporary animal welfare science. Importantly, ongoing studies of chimpanzee social behavior permit us to talk of the acceptability or unacceptability of the treatment of some chimpanzees by conspecifics from the perspective of the relevant chimpanzee actors. This can substantially enrich the conception of chimpanzee preferences that are accorded greater weight . . . their dissent can be considered a sufficient reason for excluding chimpanzees from participation in harmful scientific research.

(Fenton, 2014, 131–132)

As noted by Fenton elsewhere, the explicit reference to chimpanzees in his approach is not intended to restrict the application of this framework to great apes or even the Order Primates (Fenton, 2012b) and could be applied to other nonhuman animals.

The notions of assent and dissent favored in the passages above are informed by their use in pediatric research ethics. Arguably, the attraction of pediatric research ethics to 'animal' bioethics (e.g., Rollin, 2009; Walker, 2006), arises from several features: there are distinct levels of decisional authority responsive to the differing decision-making capacities possessed by children at different stages of maturity or functionality; assent and dissent can be understood as distinct decisional capacities (i.e., dissenters need not be able to assent); understood as a distinct decisional capacity, dissent does not require anything like the autonomous capacity exemplified by typically functioning human adults; there will be relevant psychological and behavioral similarities between at least some nonhuman animal research subjects and those children who are candidate dissenters (assent, as we shall see, is more complicated) (Fenton, 2014; Johnson and Barnard, 2014; Walker, 2006).

Depending on the age and maturity of a child research subject and assuming that assent and dissent require distinct levels of decisional capacity, any one of three levels of decisional capacity may be in play in the bioethical analysis of the proper inclusion or exclusion of children in research. Over the last seven decades, informed consent has emerged as a pivot around which the moral permissibility of human research should revolve. Typically, informed consent requires (1) relatively sophisticated cognitive capacities, (2) information that breaks down the nature of the research, risks involved, possible impact on knowledge or practice, right to withdraw at any time, and (3) a decision to participate that is free of coercion or undue influence. (1) roughly translates to a human postpubescent (typically, postadolescent; Diekema, 2006) level of cognitive and affective maturity, as well as a psychologically healthy subject so as to understand (2) and actualize (3) (Williams, 2008). Such a level of understanding and agential capacity is irrelevant to 'animal' bioethics but can be applied to mature minors, or mature children around the age of sixteen years old and older (Goodlander and Berg, 2011). On this, the Weatherall Report quoted earlier seems correct. Assent is possible for humans with capacities of understanding below what is required for informed consent but above dissent. Though the conditions of assent are disputed, minimally it requires an age-appropriate understanding of the research and expected risks or noxious events (Diekema, 2006). It is unlikely that nonhuman animal research subjects, such as chimpanzees, macaques, or domestic dogs, can assent to participate in research. Dissent, however, is another matter entirely. Dissent, when applied to children who cannot yet assent, only requires that they can experience pain or distress, anticipate its occurrence, and express a preference that the pain or distress stop, or does not occur (Fenton, 2014). This requires no more than an ability to connect the imminent occurrence of a noxious stimulus with such a cue as a research technician approaching with a medical instrument, and an expression of fear or distress in response (Diekema, 2006). The earlier quote from Berns is useful to bear in mind here. How would other animals fare? And how can neuroscience help to inform the discussion?

Neuroscientific Contributions

Earlier theorists arguing for reconsidering the moral standing of animals often highlighted a range of evidence, including behavioral similarities in reaction to pain, and physiological similarities to make the case that animals experience pain and distress (e.g., Regan, 1983; Ryder, 1985; Singer, 1975). Neuroethicist Martha Farah (2008), however, has argued that comparisons relying on neuroscience should play a privileged role in these discussions. The problem with behavioral measures, Farah argues, is that even in the best possible circumstances they are nothing more than 'indicator lights' (Farah 2008, 14). Since the cognitive revolution of the 1960s and 1970s, the view that behavior is all there is to mental states has been decisively refuted by the evidence (Rollin, 1989). And so, given that behaviors are not identical to mental states, the most they can do in arguments by analogy is to act as indicators, or correlates, of mental states.

For more on mind, see 22.1 Spotlight.

But, argues Farah, this stands in sharp contrast to potential evidence from the neurosciences. Most philosophers of mind now fall into one of two camps. One camp accepts that mental states are just brain states. The other camp accepts that mental states are dependent upon brain states or 'supervene' on such states. On either account, the status of neural evidence occupies a more privileged position than behavioral evidence. On the former view, at least some neural states are not just correlative of but rather are identical to mental states. And on the latter view, there is a tight mapping between brain states and mental states that cannot be replicated between mental states and behavior (Farah, 2008).

Although this is an interesting observation about the status of evidence for animal minds, its helpfulness in the practical enterprise of determining which mental states are occurring in nonhuman animals is limited. After all, even if we believe mental states are just brain states, we still need to determine *which* brain states we should be looking for in order to be confident that these mental states are present in other species (or in noncommunicative humans). And it seems implausible that we could determine which brain states we should care about without relying on some form of behavioral evidence (noting that even self-reporting qualifies as behavioral evidence) that is relevant to those mental states (Fenton, 2012a).

For more on painience, see Chapter 31.

So even if neuroscience plays an important role in arguments for the mental states of other animals, as we demonstrate in what follows, it does not allow us to escape the difficult challenge of determining which types of behaviors we deem relevant to capturing mental states. Nevertheless, behavioral evidence by itself can also be problematic. Many of the most familiar behavioral reactions to pain, such as grimaces, withdrawal, and vocalization, are known to sometimes occur in the absence of conscious feeling, and it is difficult to rule out the possibility of unconscious processing even in more complicated behavioral reactions (Andrews, 1996; Jouvet, 1969; Shriver, 2006). But perhaps a combination of behavioral and neuroscientific evidence can be used to build a stronger case.

For example, some relatively straightforward information about the neural response underlying typical pain reactions can help to rule out certain behaviors as definitive criteria of conscious[2] pain processing. First, nerve endings that are responsive to noxious stimuli (known as 'nociceptors') can send signals to the spinal cord that result in reflexive reactions independently of whether the signal ultimately reaches the brain (Le Bars et al., 2001). Since we can be confident that conscious pain perception (or painience) depends on activity in the brain, it follows that behaviors that occur independently of brain activity should not be regarded as evidence of conscious pain.

Attempting to build a more sophisticated methodology for assessing the evidence for the conscious experience of pain, Gary Varner (1998) produced a table noting various similarities between different species and humans. Among the various criteria he included as potentially relevant for arguments by analogy for animal pain were the presence of nociceptors, the presence of a brain, evidence that the nociceptors are connected to the brain, the presence of endogenous opioids, and evidence that responses are modified by analgesics. Again, however, evidence from neuroanatomy can be used to show that these criteria are limited in how much they can show independently. First, as demonstrated earlier, the mere presence of nociceptors does not demonstrate the conscious experience of pain, since nociceptors can operate independently of conscious pain processing. The fact that opioids and other analgesics modify behavior is often cited as evidence for pain (Varner, 1998); however, we know that there are opioid receptors both in the brain *and* in the peripheral nervous system and spinal cord (Portoghese and Lunzer, 2003), so the fact that opioids modify behavioral responses does not necessarily show that they are influencing conscious pain perception.

But what about evidence that shows that analgesics specifically modify brain processes? Could this be combined with evidence that there is a characteristic set of brain regions that appear to be active in humans during painful stimulation in order to demonstrate that other animals that have similar pain pathways are likely to experience conscious pain? There is again some reason to think, based on neuroscientific evidence, that some of these criteria are not indicative of the conscious experience of pain, or at least not of that aspect of pain that makes it morally significant (Shriver, 2006); in humans, it has been found that under certain rare or experimentally manipulated conditions, people will report feeling pain without finding it unpleasant (Foltz and White, 1962). Anatomical studies in the neurosciences help to provide an explanation for this: there are two separate pain pathways in the brain, sometimes called the 'sensory' and 'affective' pathways, and only one of those pathways (the affective) appears to mediate the *unpleasantness* associated with pain (Price, 2000). Therefore, if the affective pathway is impaired but the sensory pathway is intact, people report having the experience of pain without the unpleasantness. For this reason, Varner (2012) updated his table in more recent versions to include information about sensory and affective pathways.

Some brain activity associated with pain processing in humans is associated with the morally relevant unpleasantness component of pain, and some is not. Those areas that do seem to be necessary for the unpleasantness of pain (the insula cortex and anterior cingulate cortex) are generally conserved across all mammals. Moreover, when those areas are damaged or temporarily impaired in other mammals (LaGraize et al., 2004; LaGraize et al., 2006), the mammals also show signs of reacting to pain, withdrawing their paws from the aversive stimulus, but appear to lack the motivation to escape the pain and avoid it in future situations (Shriver, 2006). Thus, the combination of neuroanatomical and behavioral evidence provides a stronger case for the experience of pain in mammals.

These same affective pain brain regions are not present in other, nonmammalian species (MacLean, 1993) such as birds, reptiles, amphibians, and fish. Does this suggest that they are unaware of their pain? As argued in Shriver (2016), it does not, since the very same behavior patterns enabled by the affective pain pathways in mammals are also present in all vertebrates. In particular, those behaviors that seem most dependent on the brain areas (the anterior cingulate and insula cortices) involved in the affective dimension of pain, including conditioned place aversion, appear to be mediated by different brain areas in nonmammalian species (Wong et al., 2014). Thus, it is likely that different brain regions are playing a role in other species that the affective pathways are playing in mammals and that these pathways in mammals are refinements of preexisting capacities rather than wholly new or unique phenomena.

Neuroscience also opens the door for certain skeptical challenges to the claim that nonhuman animals consciously experience pain and, conversely, to strong responses to this skepticism. For example, Craig (2009) has argued that because the insular cortex is a hub of many different bodily emotions including pain, it is the seat of consciousness. He further argues that because all animals except some advanced primates lack a particular part of the insula, they are unlikely to be conscious. However, Damasio et al. (2013) showed in a fascinating case study a human being with catastrophic damage to the insula in both brain hemispheres who nevertheless had all of the indications of conscious affective experience (including self-reports of the experiences of pleasures, pains, desires, and aversions), effectively disproving Craig's skeptical hypothesis with a single elegant example.

Thus, based on a combination of neuroscientific and behavioral results, it appears that most vertebrates have the capacity to experience pain and distress. There perhaps is a more direct argument that all mammals have similar experiences to humans, but the fact remains that the same behaviors that appear to be caused by the unpleasantness of pain in mammals are present in other vertebrates, so the weight of the evidence suggests we should treat them as capable of experiencing pain.

Given that there are good reasons for thinking that some nonhuman animals possess a capacity for pain and distress, we can also ask which nonhuman animals anticipate future pain and distress. Presumably the anticipation of pain or distress requires more than only a conditioned response. Two things that seem relevant for anticipation of the occurrence of negative states are the capacity to remember or represent the occurrence of similar or related states and the ability to anticipate being in that state. Interestingly, neuroscience has demonstrated that these abilities appear to be closely related and mediated by the same brain regions (Buckner and Carrol, 2007). Regarding the former, it is important to distinguish between different types of memory, as some forms of memory do not appear to require conscious recollection. Scientists have differentiated procedural memory, which is often characterized as 'remembering *how*' (such as how to ride a bike) from declarative memory, characterized as 'remembering *that*' (e.g., remembering *that* Rome is in Italy). Procedural memory need not be conscious; humans are capable of repeating learned behavioral repertoires without any conscious recollection or experience (Stamp Dawkins, 2006). Within the category of declarative memory, memory researchers draw further distinctions. Semantic memory involves being able to recall certain facts or symbolically representable knowledge about the world. The example about Rome is an example of semantic memory. However, the most interesting type of memory for our purposes is known as episodic memory, which involves remembering what it was like to have a particular experience. This form of memory, unlike the other two, is directly connected to the capacity for conscious experience.

Varner outlined evidence that various animals possess the capacity for episodic memory (2012). Among the most intriguing evidence, Eichenbaum et al. (2005) examined the responses of rats and humans during memory recall tests. Eichanbaum et al. were able to differentiate two forms of memory, familiarity and recollection, where, as Varner says, 'recollection is described in ways that strongly parallel episodic memory' (Varner, 2012, 189). Recollection, it is suggested, 'allows one to recover the prior episode in which the stimulus was experienced' (193). Eichenbaum et al. were able to experimentally dissociate the effects of recollection and familiarity in humans by, among other things, examining people with deficits in one or the other capacity and found two distinct patterns of responses for the different forms of recall, as well as a pattern that combines the two, which is what we see in typically functioning humans. The fascinating result, however, is that rats exhibited the same patterns, suggesting that they utilized *both* familiarity and recollection, and they also could exhibit select deficits of one or other capacity. Thus, behaviorally, rats appeared to exhibit signs of episodic memory.

But how can neuroscience help us know whether nonhuman animals have episodic memory? Episodic memory in humans appears to depend on a brain structure known as the hippocampus; humans with damage to the hippocampus perform normally on the familiarity portion of tests but not on recollection tasks (Yonelinas et al., 2002). When Eichenbaum et al. induced hippocampal lesions in rats, they also performed according to the behavioral profile of exclusively familiarity-based memory and had impairments in their ability to remember the temporal order of events. Thus, it appears that the hippocampus is playing a key conserved role in episodic memory across mammals (Eichenbaum et al., 2005).

However, one of the most intriguing experiments on episodic memory in nonhuman animals was not on mammals but rather on birds called scrub jays (Clayton et al., 2001). Scrub jays, who stash their food in various locations for future use, were presented with three kinds of food: meal worms and crickets, which they preferred, and peanuts, which they would eat but did not prefer as strongly as the other choices. The crickets and mealworms were chemically treated to spoil after a certain period of time, with mealworms spoiling prior to 28 hours and crickets spoiling prior to 100 hours. After caching their food, the scrub jays were allowed to access their food caches in different conditions that varied by the amount of time: a 4-hour condition, a 28-hour condition, and a 100-hour condition. Tulving, who developed the notion of episodic memory, initially defined it as representing 'temporally dated episodes or events' (Tulving, 1972, 385). If the scrub jays had temporally dated knowledge of storing the food, one would expect them, upon being released after 4 hours, to always look first for the crickets and mealworms rather than the peanuts, yet to first look for the peanuts in the conditions in which the other foods had spoiled. This is precisely what they found, with scrub jays seeking mealworms and crickets prior to peanuts in the 4-hour condition, seeking peanuts prior to mealworms (but not crickets) in the 28-hour condition, and seeking peanuts prior to crickets in the 100-hour condition. This suggests that the scrub jays had 'time-stamped' memories of when the foods were stashed, leading the researchers to conclude that they had discovered 'episodic-like memory' (Clayton et al., 2001, 28) in the scrub jays.

Moreover, researchers have posited that episodic memory is intimately connected to the ability to plan for and *anticipate* the future, and research from neuroscience has shown that the same brain networks involved in episodic memory are also involved in anticipating future events or states (Buckner and Carrol, 2007). Fascinatingly, scrub jays have also been the participants in some of the most interesting research demonstrating an ability to plan for the future. In one such experiment (Correia et al., 2007), researchers took advantage of the fact that scrub jays become sated with certain tastes after consuming enough of a particular food product. After becoming sated with a particular taste, they prefer to eat a different flavor of food. Initially, when presented with the option of caching their food for future consumption, the jays also cached the nonsated (but otherwise less preferred) flavor of food for future consumption. However, they quickly learned to cache the preferred type of food, despite being currently sated with it, suggesting that they successfully anticipated their future preferences (or at least could guide current behavior in ways sensitive to an anticipated favored reward).

Though avian species don't have the brain regions most associated with episodic memory and planning for the future in mammals, Varner notes that they do have a unique brain region called the hyperstriatum that appears to play many of the same roles as the mammalian regions (Varner, 2012), including in pain. Interestingly, the hyperstriatum is particularly well developed in scrub jays and in parrots, another bird species known for impressive intelligence (or higher-order cognitive capacities that go beyond perceptual acuity and emotive responses). Thus, as in the case of pain, it appears that different brain regions in avian species enable the same forms of behavior that uniquely mammalian brain regions mediate in humans and other mammals.

To summarize, it appears that there is strong evidence that vertebrates are capable of experiencing pain and distress, though perhaps the evidence is strongest for mammals. Moreover, it appears that mammals and avian species are capable of anticipating the occurrence of aversive events. Since the affective component of pain also includes a motivation to avoid/escape aversive stimuli, and animals presumably would avoid anticipated future pains as well, we can be fairly certain that these species also are capable of expressing a preference that the pain or distress stop (or does not occur). The relevant experiments have not yet been done on nonmammalian and nonavian species, so we do not intend these claims as suggesting that other species are not capable of dissent; we only suggest that we already have a reasonable set of evidence that mammalian and some avian species do possess this capacity.

As in the case of pain, the evidence from the neurosciences would not be persuasive in a vacuum; it is only in conjunction with behavioral research that the neuroscience findings add to the arguments. However, in conjunction with the behavioral research, similarities in the operations of particular brain networks during particular types of behaviors add weight to the claim that nonhuman mammals are relying on similar cognitive mechanisms as humans during those tasks. And in the context of this knowledge, once it can be demonstrated that other, nonmammalian species are equally able to perform the tasks relevant to this ability, there is no longer a principled reason for denying that the nonmammalian species possess the capacity.

Implications

If, as we suggest, some nonhuman animals can dissent, how should this impact the studies in which they are involved? In the earlier passage from the Weatherall Report, the authors contend that the resistance of nonhuman primates to procedures they find painful or stressful can be trumped by the possible benefits to humans that arise from their scientific use because they 'have a different [that is, lower] moral status to human beings' (Academy of Medical Sciences and Weatherall, 2006, 129). If, say, chimpanzee or domestic dog dissent is going to enjoy the kind of status enjoyed by young human children, it must be shown that, contra the Weatherall Report, at least some other animals have a comparable moral standing to humans. The resistance to the view that some other animals could enjoy comparable standing to humans seems to be grounded in one of two commitments: anthropocentric speciesism or human exceptionalism (the authors of the Weatherall Report seem to hold the latter).

Anthropocentric speciesism is simply the ordering of the priority of relevantly similar interests based solely on whether the interest bearers are members of the species *Homo sapiens*. A human's relevantly similar interests to another animal's are prioritized simply because they are human. Human exceptionalism is similar to anthropocentric speciesism, in that it posits that (some) humans are morally superior to nonhumans but can allow that not all humans enjoy moral priority over other animals. It is enough that some, or perhaps even a great many, do (Dunayer, 2013; Smith, 2013).

Neither of these commitments has fared well when subjected to philosophical scrutiny, though we do not have the space here to do the relevant discussions justice (but see DeGrazia, 1996, 2007; Fenton, 2012b). An effective strategy for showing that mere membership in a species cannot bear the weight that anthropocentric speciesism would place on it appeals to 'nonhumans' with comparable capacities to typically functioning postnatal humans—be they fictional artificial intelligences or extraterrestrials, or such hominins as *Homo erectus* or *Homo floresiensis* (DeGrazia, 2007; Fenton and Krahn, 2010).[3] The relevant arguments—which outline the arbitrariness and hence injustice of according human interests greater moral weight than the featured 'nonhumans'—highlight the importance of capacities in determining moral status. As long as human exceptionalism favors ascribing a high moral status to typically functioning, young human children, it is as vulnerable to the previous point as anthropocentric speciesism if it ignores relevantly similar capacities in other animals. The Weatherall Report is so committed.

For more on moral status, see Chapter 31.

Without a defensible anthropocentric speciesism or human exceptionalism, justice requires that a chimpanzee's or domestic dog's dissent enjoy a relevantly similar moral standing to that which is enjoyed by a relevantly similar human's dissent. Our earlier defense of the dissent capacity of some other animals—given that it depends on conditions drawn from pediatric research ethics—should suffice to show that chimpanzee or domestic dog dissent should carry comparable moral weight.

Imagine a world in which chimpanzee or domestic dog research subjects are accorded high moral status such that it matters when they dissent or resist cooperating with humans in research contexts. Several interesting implications fall out of such an imaginary.

First, in such a world, their resistance *may* terminate their participation in the relevant study. We say 'may' because we still need to think about:

a. whether the study benefits them,
b. if—when presenting no more than minimal risk—the study benefits other, relevantly similar nonhuman animals (e.g., conspecifics),
c. if—where presenting no more than slightly greater than minimal risk—the study could yield important generalizable knowledge about conspecifics or closely related animals,
d. whether the resistance can be overcome with positive reinforcement training (PRT), and
e. whether—when responsive to PRT—the research places the research subject at long term risk of serious physical or psychological harms.

This list, particularly (a) through (c), is informed by relevantly similar considerations in pediatric research ethics (see also DeGrazia, 2007; Gagneux et al., 2005; Fox, 1987; Pluhar, 2006). To mirror something like its use in pediatric ethics, our reference to minimal risk need mean no more than risk that conspecifics regularly face in either captive environments where they are treated respectfully or in free environments where their habitat is not under threat from human incursion (Ferdowsian and Fuentes, 2014).

Second, it will be important in such a world not to act in such a way as to destroy a research subject's capacity to dissent. After all, if dissent is the bar to research inclusion to which we are attuned and a capacity we are committed to respect, it is inconsistent to act in such a way as to destroy it or preclude its acquisition. What's more, a lack of dissent in contexts where a research subject has lost her capacity to dissent is not a green light for their use in research.

In our imaginary world, a lack of such a dissent capacity requires a cautionary approach of preclusion from research until their capacity is reacquired or develops or, alternatively, permits their inclusion only when human advocates, acting in the research subject's best interests, enroll them. Research conditions that preclude a research subject acquiring or reacquiring a capacity to dissent, for example, by inducing psychological damage, also precludes their inclusion (Birkett and McGrew, 2013; Capaldo and Bradshaw, 2011).

Benefit arguments, used to defend the moral legitimacy of experimental animal research (and these are the most common defenses of such research), lose their punch when used to justify harmful research on these animals. These arguments are so named because they foreground the benefits arising from the past use of animals in research to justify their continued use (Fenton, 2012b; Frey, 2002). Benefit arguments almost always rely on an anthropocentric speciesism. After all, they would not move us to include humans in harmful nontherapeutic research (Rollin, 2009). Indeed, those benefit arguments that explicitly reject anthropocentric speciesism (e.g., see Frey, 2002) *do not* preclude the use of some humans in harmful research currently reserved for nonhumans.

In such a world, trapdoor clauses of the type *typical* in emerging restrictions on the use of nonhuman great apes in harmful research lose legitimacy. Trapdoor clauses permit the reintroduction of previously excluded nonhuman animal species to harmful research in the event of a significant public health crisis such as a pandemic. The recent exclusion of great apes in the European Commission's directive governing the scientific use of nonhuman animals contains such a clause (European Commission, 2010). This context for reintroduction into research does not allow for the noncooperation or dissent of the relevant research subjects, nor does it consider the catastrophic effect of laboratory settings or research on their capacities for noncooperation or dissent. Therefore, on the framework we have outlined, such clauses should be rejected.

Conclusion

Our approach here has not been to challenge the use of certain nonhuman animals in basic, behavioral, biomedical, genomic, or neuroscientific research. Nor have we engaged issues surrounding the validity of certain nonhuman animal models in either understanding human conditions or pathologies or developing effective interventions. Our focus here has been less about what other animals can do for us and more about what we should do for them—if they are to be used in research.

We have examined whether a robust notion of dissent can be applied to some nonhuman animals. The evidence for pain and such cognitive capacities as episodic-like memory in some other animals, provided by a combination of neuroscientific and behavioral evidence, suggests that it can. We have also provided some reasons for thinking that the failure of anthropocentricism and human exceptionalism requires a reweighting of animal dissent in bioethical analyses of their use in research. As such, we reject the Weatherall Report's dismissal of the moral significance of noncooperative animal research subjects. Reweighted, the dissent capacity of some research animals requires changes in how they are treated in research and how we envision their future use. In particular, their sustained dissent in research settings can preclude them from use. What's more, research settings that are known to adversely affect a nonhuman animal's psychological development (e.g., learned helplessness research), and so adversely affect their dissent capacity, are morally impermissible.

We hope to have shown how neuroscience can be put to use in arguments for the moral standing of nonhuman animals in ways that can make significant contributions to how they are treated in research settings. The value of neuroscience research for assessing the moral status of nonhuman animals is ultimately just one piece of the puzzle; it can only be fully appreciated in conjunction with a detailed understanding of nonhuman animal behavior and, in particular, an understanding of the behavior of nonhuman animals in natural environments. Findings from the neurosciences in conjunction with behavioral evidence can help to establish the presence of morally relevant cognitive capacities that may, in turn, push us toward the conclusion that many current invasive research protocols are morally problematic because they ignore the animals' capacity for dissent.

Acknowledgments

We would like to thank Syd Johnson and Karen Rommelfanger for extensive feedback on drafts of our chapter. Andrew Fenton would also like to thank Letitia Meynell for her feedback and Fresno State University for a Provost Research/Creative Activities Award that freed up some necessary time for research and writing.

Notes

1 Contemporary humans are, of course, animals (in particular, mammals belonging to the Order Primates). To use 'animals' as a contrast to 'humans' is to use the term in a political rather than biological sense. Accordingly, we prefer the term 'nonhuman animals' when talking of animals other than humans. From time to time, terms such as 'research animal' (rather than 'research nonhuman animal') or 'laboratory animal' (rather than 'laboratory nonhuman animal') will be preferred for aesthetic reasons.
2 'Consciousness' can be used in various ways when talking about the psychological states of humans or other animals. Two senses relevant to this body of evidence are awareness and phenomenal consciousness (that is, experiential states). For a recent discussion of these and other senses of 'consciousness' used in empirical psychology and neurobiology, see Andrews, 2015.
3 Both Homo erectus and Homo floresiensis are examples of early human species. However, for many non-specialists 'human' is used exclusively to refer to Homo sapiens.

Further Reading

Andrews, K. (2015) *The Animal Mind: An Introduction to the Philosophy of Animal Cognition*. New York: Routledge.

Bekoff, M., Allen, C. and Burghardt, G.M. (2002) *The Cognitive Animal: Empirical and Theoretical Perspectives on Animal Cognition*. Cambridge, MA: MIT Press.

Carbone, L. (2004) *What Animals Want: Expertise and Advocacy in Laboratory Animal Welfare Policy*. New York: Oxford University Press.

DeGrazia, D. (1996) *Taking Animals Seriously: Mental Life and Moral Status*. Cambridge: Cambridge University Press.

References

Academy of Medical Sciences (Great Britain) and Weatherall, D.J. (2006) *The Use of Non-Human Primates in Research: A Working Group Report.* London: The Academy of Medical Sciences.

Altevogt, B.M., Pankevich, D.E., Shelton-Davenport, M.K., and Kahn, J.P. (2011) *Chimpanzees in Biomedical and Behavioral Research: Assessing the Necessity.* Washington, DC: National Academies Press.

Andrews, K. (1996) International working party on the management of the vegetative state: Summary report. *Brain Injury* 10: pp. 797–806.

———. (2015) *The Animal Mind: An Introduction to the Philosophy of Animal Cognition.* New York: Routledge.

Berns, G.S. (2013) *How Dogs Love Us: A Neuroscientist and His Adopted Dog Decode the Canine Brain.* New York: Harcourt Publishing Company.

Berns, G.S., Brooks, A.M., and Spivak, M. (2012) Functional MRI in awake unrestrained dogs. *PLoS One* 7(5): pp. 1–7.

Birkett, L., and McGrew, W. (2013) "Unnatural behavior" Obstacle or insight at the species interface? In R. Corbey and A. Lanjouw (Eds.). *The Politics of Species: Reshaping Our Relationships With Other Animals.* New York: Cambridge University Press, pp. 141–55.

Buckner, R.L., and Carrol, D.C. (2007) Self-projection and the brain. *Trends in Cognitive Science* 11(2): pp. 49–57.

Capaldo, T., and Bradshaw, G.A. (2011) *The Bioethics of Great Ape Well-Being: Psychiatric Injury and Duty to Care.* Ann Arbor: Animals and Society Institute.

Clayton, N.S., Yu, K.S., and Dickenson, A. (2001) Scrub jays (*Aphelocoma coerulescens*) form integrated memories of the multiple features of caching episodes. *Journal of Experimental Psychology: Animal Behavior Processes* 27(1): pp. 17–29.

Coleman, K. (2010) Caring for nonhuman primates in biomedical research facilities: Scientific, moral and emotional considerations. *American Journal of Primatology* 73: pp. 220–225.

Coleman, K., Pranger, L., Maier, A., Lambeth, S.P., Perlman, J.E., Thiele, E., and Schapiro, S.J. (2008) Training rhesus macaques for venipuncture using positive reinforcement techniques: A comparison with chimpanzees. *Journal of the American Association for Laboratory Animal Science* 47(1): pp. 37–41.

Correia, S.P., Dickinson, A., and Clayton, N.S. (2007) Western scrub-jays anticipate future needs independently of their current motivational state. *Current Biology* 17(10): pp. 856–861.

Craig, A.D. (2009) How do you feel-now? The anterior insula and human awareness. *Nature Reviews Neuroscience* 10: pp. 59–70.

Damasio, A., Damasio, H., and Tranel, D. (2013) Persistence of feelings and sentience after bilateral damage of the insula. *Cerebral Cortex* 23(4): pp. 833–846.

DeGrazia, D. (1996) *Taking Animals Seriously: Mental Life and Moral Status.* Cambridge: Cambridge University Press.

———. (2007) Human-animal chimeras: Human dignity, moral status, and species prejudice. *Metaphilosophy* 38(2–3): pp. 309–329.

Diekema, D.S. (2006) Conducting ethical research in pediatrics: A brief historical overview and review of pediatric regulations. *Journal of Pediatrics* 149: pp. S3–11.

Dunayer, J. (2013) The rights of sentient beings: Moving beyond old and new speciesism. In R. Corbey and A. Lanjouw (Eds.). *The Politics of Species: Reshaping Our Relationships with Other Animals.* New York: Cambridge University Press, pp. 27–39.

Eichenbaum, H., Fortin, N.J., Ergorul, C., Wright, S.P., and Agster, K.L. (2005) Episodic recollection in animals: 'If it Walks like a Duck and Quacks like a Duck . . .' *Learning and Motivation* 36: pp. 190–207.

European Commission. (2010) *Directive 2010/63/EU of the European Parliament and of the Council of 22 September 2010 on the Protection of Animals Used for Scientific Purposes* [Online]. Available at: http://eur-lex.europa.eu/LexUriServ/LexUriServ.do?uri=OJ:L:2010:276:0033:0079:en:PDF [Accessed 1 Mar. 2016].

Farah, M.J. (2008) Neuroethics and the problem of other minds: Implications of neuroscience for the moral status of brain-damaged patients and nonhuman Animals. *Neuroethics* 1: pp. 9–18.

Fenton, A. (2012a) Neuroscience and the problem of other animal minds: Why it may not matter so much for neuroethics. *The Monist* 95(3): pp. 463–485.

_____. (2012b) On the need to redress an inadequacy in animal welfare science: Toward an internally coherent framework. *Biology and Philosophy* 27: pp. 73–93.

———. (2014) Can a chimp say "no"? Reenvisioning chimpanzee dissent in harmful research. *Cambridge Quarterly of Healthcare Ethics* 23: pp. 130–139.

Fenton, A., and Krahn, T. (2010) Interrogating the boundary of human-level and T moral status. *American Journal of Bioethics Neuroscience* 1(2): pp. 61–63.

Ferdowsian, H., and Fuentes, A. (2014) Harms and deprivation of benefits for nonhuman primates in research. *Theoretical Medicine and Bioethics* 35: pp. 143–56.

Foltz, E.L., and White, L.E. (1962) Pain "relief" by frontal cingulotomy. *Journal of Neurosurgery* 19: pp. 89–100.

Fox, M.A. (1987) Animal experimentation: A philosopher's changing views. *Between the Species* 3(2): pp. 55–60, 75, 80–82.

Frey, R.G. (2002) Ethics, animals, and scientific inquiry. In J.P. Gluck, T. DiPasquale and F.B. Orlans (Eds.). *Applied Ethics in Animal Research: Philosophy, Regulation, and Laboratory Applications.* West Lafayette: Purdue University Press, pp. 13–24.

Gagneux, P., Moore, J.J., and Varki, A. (2005) The ethics of research on great apes. *Nature* 437: pp. 27–29.

Goodlander, E.C., and Berg, J.W. (2011) Pediatric decision-making: Adolescent patients. In D.S. Diekema, M.R. Mercurio, and M.B. Adam (Eds.). *Clinical Ethics in Pediatrics: A Case-Based Textbook.* New York: Cambridge University Press, pp. 7–13.

Johnson, J., and Barnard, N.D. (2014) Chimpanzees as vulnerable subjects in research. *Theoretical Medicine and Bioethics* 35: pp. 133–141.

Jouvet, M. (1969) Coma and other disorders of consciousness. In P.J. Vinken and G.W. Bruyn (Eds.). *Handbook of Clinical Neurology.* 3rd vol. New York: Elsevier Science, pp. 62–79.

LaGraize, S., Labuda, C., Rutledge, R., Jackson, R., and Fuchs, P. (2004) Differential effect of anterior cingulated cortex lesion on mechanical hypersensitivity and escape/avoidance behavior in an animal model of neuropathic pain. *Experimental Neurology* 188: pp. 139–148.

LaGraize, S., Borzan, J., Peng, Y.B., and Fuchs, P. (2006) Selective regulation of pain affect following activation of the opioid anterior cingulate cortex system. *Experimental Neurology* 197: pp. 22–30.

Laule, G.E., Bloomsmith, M.A., and Schapiro, S.J. (2003) The use of positive reinforcement training techniques to enhance care, management, and welfare of primates in the laboratory. *Journal of Applied Animal Welfare Science* 6(3): pp. 163–173.

Le Bars, D., Gozariu, M., and Cadden, S.W. (2001) Animal models of nociception. *Pharmacological Reviews* 53: pp. 597–652.

MacLean, P.D. (1993) Perspectives on cingulate cortex in the limbic system. In B.A. Vogt and M. Gabriel (Eds.). *Neurobiology of Cingulate Cortex and Limbic Thalamus: A Comprehensive Handbook.* New York: Birkhauser Basel, pp. 1–15.

Matsuzawa, T. (2006) Sociocognitive development in chimpanzees: A synthesis of laboratory work and fieldwork. In T. Matsuzawa, M. Tomonaga and M. Tanaka (Eds.). *Cognitive Development in Chimpanzees.* Tokyo: Springer-Verlag Tokyo, pp. 3–33.

Pluhar, E.B. (2006) Experimentation on humans and nonhumans. *Theoretical Medicine and Bioethics* 27: pp. 333–355.

Portoghese, P.S., and Lunzer, M.M. (2003) Identity of the putative delta1-opioid receptor as a delta-kappa heteromer in the mouse spinal cord. *European Journal of Pharmacology* 467(1–3): pp. 233–234.

Price, D.D. (2000) Psychological and neural mechanisms of the affective dimension of pain. *Science* 288: pp. 1769–1772.

Regan, T. (1983) *The Case for Animal Rights.* London: Routledge and Kegan Paul.

Rennie, A.E., and Buchanan-Smith, H.M. (2006) Refinement of the use of non-human primates in scientific research. Part I: The influence of humans. *Animal Welfare* 15: pp. 203–213.

Rollin, B.E. (1989) *The Unheeded Cry.* New York: Oxford University Press.

———. (2009) The moral status of animals and their use as experimental subjects. In H. Kuhse and P. Singer (Eds.). *A Companion to Bioethics.* 2nd ed. Malden: Blackwell Publishing Ltd, pp. 495–509.

Ryder, R. (1985) Speciesism in the laboratory. In P. Singer (Ed.). *In Defense of Animals.* New York: Basil Blackwell Inc., pp. 77–88.

Sapontzis, S.F. (1987) *Morals, Reason, and Animals*. Philadelphia: Temple University Press.

Shriver, A. (2006) Minding mammals. *Philosophical Psychology* 19: pp. 433–442.

———. (2016) Cortex necessary for pain—but not in sense that matters. *Animal Sentience* 3 [Online]. Available at: http://animalstudiesrepository.org/animsent/vol1/iss3/27/ [Accessed 27th Dec. 2016].

Singer, P. (1975) *Animal Liberation*. New York: Random House.

Smith, D.L. (2013) Indexically yours: Why being human is more like being here than like being water. In R. Corbey and A. Lanjouw (Eds.) *The Politics of Species: Reshaping Our Relationships With Other Animals*. New York: Cambridge University Press, pp. 40–52.

Stamp Dawkins, M. (2006) A user's guide to animal welfare science. *TRENDS in Ecology and Evolution* 21(2): pp. 77–82.

Tulving, E. (1972) Episodic and semantic memory. In E. Tulving and W. Donaldson (Eds.). *Organization of Memory*. New York: Academic Press, pp. 381–403.

Varner, G. (1998) *In Nature's Interests*. New York: Oxford University Press.

———. (2012) *Personhood, Ethics, and Animal Cognition: Situating Animals in Hare's Two-Level Utilitarianism*. New York: Oxford University Press.

Walker, R.L. (2006) Human and animal subjects of research: The moral significance of respect versus welfare. *Theoretical Medicine and Bioethics* 27: pp. 305–331.

Weed, J.L., and Raber, J.M. (2005) Balancing animal research with animal well-being: Establishment of goals and harmonization of approaches. *Institute for Laboratory Animal Research Journal* 46(2): pp. 118–128.

Williams, J.R. (2008) Consent. In P.A. Singer and A.M. Viens (Eds.). *The Cambridge Textbook of Bioethics*. New York: Cambridge University Press, pp. 11–16.

Wong, D., von Keyserling, M.A.G., Richards, J.G., and Weary, D.M. (2014) Conditioned place avoidance of zebrafish (*Danio rerio*) to three chemicals used for euthanasia and anaesthesia. *PLoS One*. [Online.] 9(2). Available at: http://journals.plos.org/plosone/article/comment?id=info:doi/10.1371/annotation/9fc5f76a-0217-4324-a6cb-c629f646a336 [Accessed 27 Dec. 2016].

Yonelinas, A.P., Kroll, N.E., Quamme, J.R., Lazzara, M.M., Sauve, M.J., Widaman, K.F., and Knight, R.T. (2002) Effects of extensive temporal lobe damage or mild hypoxia on recollection and familiarity. *Nature Neuroscience* 5(11): pp. 1236–1241.

INDEX

CPSIA information can be obtained
at www.ICGtesting.com
Printed in the USA
LVHW061213090123
736733LV00001BA/30